AN INTRODUCTION TO

Derivative Securities, Financial Markets, and Risk Management

AN INTRODUCTION TO

Derivative Securities, Financial Markets, and Risk Management

Robert A. Jarrow
CORNELL UNIVERSITY

Arkadev Chatterjea
THE UNIVERSITY OF NORTH CAROLINA AT CHAPEL HILL

W. W. NORTON AND COMPANY
NEW YORK   LONDON

W. W. Norton & Company has been independent since its founding in 1923, when William Warder Norton and Mary D. Herter Norton first published lectures delivered at the People's Institute, the adult education division of New York City's Cooper Union. The firm soon expanded its program beyond the Institute, publishing books by celebrated academics from America and abroad. By midcentury, the two major pillars of Norton's publishing program—trade books and college texts—were firmly established. In the 1950s, the Norton family transferred control of the company to its employees, and today—with a staff of four hundred and a comparable number of trade, college, and professional titles published each year—W. W. Norton & Company stands as the largest and oldest publishing house owned wholly by its employees.

Editor: Jack Repcheck
Project Editor: Amy Weintraub
Electronic Media Editor: Cassie del Pillar
Assistant Editor: Hannah Bachman
Marketing Manager, Economics: John Kresse
Production Manager: Ashley Polikoff
Permissions Manager: Megan Jackson
Text Design: Lissi Sigillo
Art Director: Rubina Yeh
Illustration: Dartmouth Publishing, Inc.
Composition: codeMantra
Manufacturing: Courier

The text of this book is composed in Minion with the display set in Avenir.

Library of Congress Cataloging-in-Publication Data

Jarrow, Robert A.
    An introduction to derivative securities, financial markets, and risk management / Robert A. Jarrow, Arkadev Chatterjea. – First Edition.
        pages cm
    Includes bibliographical references and index.
    ISBN 978-0-393-91307-1 (hbk.)
    1. Derivative securities.   2. Financial institutions.   3. Capital market.   4. Risk management.
I. Chatterjea, Arkadev. II. Title.
    HG6024.A3J3747 2013
    332.64'57–dc23
                                    2012048956

W. W. Norton & Company, Inc., 500 Fifth Avenue, New York, NY 10110-0017
wwnorton.com

W. W. Norton & Company Ltd., Castle House, 75/76 Wells Street, London W1T 3QT
1 2 3 4 5 6 7 8 9 0

Bob: To my wife Gail for her patience and understanding.

*Arka: To my wife Sudeshna for her cheerful and steadfast support,
and to our daughters Rushtri, Tvisha, and Roudra (all younger than the book!),
who also cheerfully and proudly supported my writing.*

About the Authors

Robert A. Jarrow is the Ronald P. and Susan E. Lynch Professor of Investment Management at Cornell University. He is among the most distinguished finance scholars of his generation. Jarrow has done research in nearly all areas of derivatives pricing. He is the co-developer of two widely used pricing models in finance, the Heath–Jarrow–Morton (HJM) model for pricing interest-rate derivatives and the reduced form model for pricing securities with credit risk. He is the author of more than 175 academic publications, five books including *Option Pricing* (with Andrew Rudd, 1983), *Modelling Fixed Income Securities and Interest Rate Options* (1996), and *Derivative Securities* (with Stuart Turnbull, 2000), and several edited volumes.

Arkadev Chatterjea did his Ph.D. at Cornell, where he was a student of Robert Jarrow. He is a Research Fellow at the Center for Excellence in Investment Management at the Kenan-Flagler Business School at the University of North Carolina at Chapel Hill. Earlier, he was a professor of finance at the Indian Institute of Management Calcutta. A winner of research and teaching awards, Chatterjea has taught derivatives at Cornell, CU Boulder, the Helsinki School, Hong Kong UST, IIM Ahmedabad, IIM Calcutta, IU Bloomington, and UNC Chapel Hill. Photo by Mr. Kallol Nath.

Brief Contents

Contents

PART II Forwards and Futures

CHAPTER 12 The Extended Cost-of-Carry Model 277

CHAPTER 13 Futures Hedging 307

PART III Options

PART IV   Interest Rate Derivatives

CHAPTER 22 Interest Rate Swaps 614

CHAPTER 26 Risk Management Models 740

Preface

"History has many cunning passages, contrived corridors," wrote T. S. Eliot in the poem "Gerontion." The history of options and futures can be so described. Derivatives have traded for centuries in small, over-the-counter markets in London, New York, and several cities of continental Europe. In 1688, a sophisticated rice futures market was established in Osaka, Japan, that thrived for 250 years. Modern commodity futures markets began in 1848 with the founding of the Chicago Board of Trade to help protect farmers from commodity price swings. After many placid decades, the calm was again broken with the inauguration of the world's first financial futures market in 1972 at the Chicago Mercantile Exchange and in 1973 with the opening of the Chicago Board Options Exchange. Serendipitously, 1973 also saw the publication of the Nobel Prize–winning Black–Scholes–Merton (BSM) option pricing model, which further spurred market expansion by enabling better pricing and hedging.

Sometimes viewed as harmful and sometimes viewed as beneficial by the financial press and the public, derivatives have nonetheless played a significant role in financial markets across the centuries. Following the 2007 credit crisis, derivatives are most recently playing the role of the harmful security again, and new financial regulations have been proposed to rein them in. Although perhaps well intentioned, these attacks on derivatives are hurled by those unfamiliar with their proper use. Derivative securities, if used properly, reduce risk and facilitate real economic growth in the economy. In today's complex world, modern financial institutions cannot succeed without the use of derivatives for managing the varied risks of their assets and liabilities. An understanding of their proper usage comes through a careful study of derivatives, which brings us to the purpose for writing this book.

This book was written to be the first book read on derivatives and not the last. Our aim has been to design a book that is closely connected to real markets, examines the uses of derivatives but warns against their abuses, and presents only the necessary quantitative material in an easily digestible form—and no more!

Given our purpose, this book differs from all existing derivatives textbooks in several important ways:

- First, it is an introduction. We wanted to create a textbook accessible to MBAs and undergraduates both in terms of the concepts and mathematics. Option pricing is normally thought of as a complex, mathematical, and difficult topic. Our experience is that this topic can be presented simply and intuitively.

- Second, it is about financial markets. We wanted to write an economics, not a quantitative, book on derivatives. Since the first textbooks on option pricing,[1]

---

[1] Jarrow and Rudd (1983) and Cox and Rubinstein (1984).

derivatives textbooks have taken a quantitative approach to the topic and are often encyclopedic in presentation. Little if any effort was spent on the underlying economics. In contrast, an economics perspective relates the market structure to the assumptions underlying the models. An understanding of when to use and when not to use a model based on its assumptions must be included. Our book does this.

- Third, it is a book about risk management. Generally speaking, there are four risks to be managed: (1) market risk, which includes commodity (including equity) price risk, interest rate risk, and foreign currency price risk; (2) credit risk; (3) liquidity risk; and (4) operational risk. We walk you through these different risks, with an emphasis on market risk, and discuss how they can be managed in business as well as in one's personal life.

- Fourth, not only do governments regulate the markets, but many government entities use derivatives to promote the public's welfare. The book often discusses the relevant issues from a regulator's point of view and from a public policy perspective.

- Fifth, another unique feature of this book is an intuitive and accessible presentation of the Heath–Jarrow–Morton (HJM) model, which is the most advanced as well as a widely used derivatives pricing model. To make this model accessible, we first present the classical option pricing theory centering on the BSM model in a user-friendly fashion. Our presentation of the BSM model, however, is done with an eye toward the HJM model, emphasizing those aspects of the BSM model that are needed later. Then, when we study the HJM model, less development is needed. This approach enables us to present the HJM model in a parallel fashion to that of the BSM model, so if you see one, you see them both!

- Sixth, option pricing has a fascinating history, filled with colorful people and events. We share this history with the reader. This history is obtained from century-old books (now, uniquely available via the Internet), recent books, newspaper and magazine articles, websites, and personal experiences.

- Seventh, we have included enrichment material for the advanced reader through the use of inserts and appendixes. Many of these inserts include current research insights not available in existing textbooks.

The organization of this book is purposely designed to facilitate its use in many courses relating to options, futures, derivatives, risk management, investments, fixed income securities, and financial institutions. Three major courses that can be taught from this book are: (1) derivatives, (2) futures and commodities, and (3) fixed income securities and interest rate derivatives. In a sense, there are many books within this one cover.

- **Derivatives.** This is a standard course on basic derivatives that gives an introduction to forwards, futures, options, and swaps but excludes interest rate derivatives for the most part. For this, use chapters 1–20 and most of chapter 22. This would be for first-year MBAs and masters of financial engineering and for upper-level undergraduates in business schools, engineering schools, and economics departments.

- **Futures and commodities.** This is a course on futures and commodities, excluding option pricing. For this, use chapters 1–6 and 8–13. The target audience is as for the prior item.

- **Fixed-income securities and interest rate derivatives.** This would be a models-based approach to teaching this material. Integrating ongoing research developments, Jarrow has been teaching such a course at Cornell University for over twenty years. For this, use chapters 1, 2, 4, 6, 9, and 15–26. This course can be taught to MBAs and more mathematically inclined upper level undergraduates.

- **Case-based courses.** We have also recommended cases at the end of each chapter so that instructors can easily develop a case study–oriented derivatives course.

- **Spreadsheet-based courses.** Unlike other textbooks, we do not provide black boxes in which you input data and get a derivative price! In line with current teaching trends, we have woven spreadsheet applications throughout the text. Our aim is for students to achieve self-sufficiency so that they can generate all the models and graphs in this book via Excel. In addition, spreadsheet software—called Priced!—especially designed for this textbook is available to facilitate learning and to teach the course material.

- **Use in courses in other areas.** Courses in accounting and law can use this as background material.

This book is a "download" of our understandings of markets and derivatives obtained from decades of research, teaching, and consulting. The material has been class tested at the Cornell University, Helsinki School of Economics and Business Administration, Hong Kong University of Science and Technology, the Indian Institutes of Management at Ahmedabad and at Calcutta, Indiana University (Bloomington), University of Colorado at Boulder, and the University of North Carolina at Chapel Hill. We hope that the reader will have a better understanding of derivative securities and risk management models after reading this book. Although we have tried to make this textbook error free, please notify us if you discover any errors.

The Ancillaries

This text is accompanied by a number of important ancillaries, each intended to enhance the learning experience for the student and the teaching experience for the instructor.

For Students and Instructors

Online only on wwnorton.com/studyspace

PRICED! Developed by a Cornell computer science Ph.D. Tibor Jánosi specifically for this text and in collaboration with book authors Robert Jarrow and Arkadev Chatterjea, Priced! is Excel-based software that makes the models real rather than hypothetical.

The software computes prices and hedge ratios for the four key derivative security models contained in the book: (1) the binomial model, (2) the Black–Scholes–Merton (BSM) model, (3) the discrete time Heath–Jarrow–Morton (HJM) model, and (4) the HJM Libor model.

The prices and hedge ratios are represented visually—both graphically and in trees—for easy analysis by students and instructors. For quick recognition and clarity, the software's inputs and outputs are color-coded. Priced! is also completely dynamic; when changes are made to inputs, outputs are updated instantaneously.

This software can be used to illustrate all of the key concepts associated with the derivative models discussed in the course. Instructors can illustrate how a model's prices and hedge ratios change when inputs are changed. Students can even use Priced! and current market prices from the financial press to compute actual prices.

For Students

SOLUTIONS MANUAL Written entirely by the text's authors, Robert Jarrow and Arkadev Chatterjea, the solutions manual provides completely worked solutions for all the problems included with the book. ISBN: 978-0-393-92094-9

For Instructors

POWERPOINTS Created by coauthor Arkadev Chatterjea. The slides include lecture slides and all art from the book. There is also a separate set of PowerPoints created by Robert Jarrow for a fixed income course based on selected chapters in the book. *Downloadable from wwnorton.com/instructors.*

TEST BANK Written by the text's authors, Robert Jarrow and Arkadev Chatterjea.
Downloadable formats available on wwnorton.com/instructors.

- *PDF*
- *Word*
- *ExamView® Assessment Suite*

Acknowledgments

Bob thanks Peter Carr, Dilip Madan, Philip Protter, Siegfried Trautmann, Stuart Turnbull, and Don van Deventer for many conversations about derivatives over the years.

For the many helpful discussions, comments, and material that helped improve this book, Bob and Arka would both like to thank Jeffery Abarbanell, Sobhesh K. Agarwalla, Jiyoun An, Warren B. Bailey, Gregory Besharov, Sommarat Chantarat, Surjamukhi Chatterjea, Soikot Chatterjee, Sudheer Chava, Paul Moon Sub Choi, Steve Choi, Hazem Daouk, Werner Freystätter, Suman Ganguli, Nilanjan Ghosh, Michael A. Goldstein, Jason Harlow, Philip Ho, Michael F. Imhoff, Keon Hee Kim,

Robert C. Klemkosky, Junghan Koo, Hao Li, Banikanta Mishra, Debi P. Mohapatra, Gillian Mulley, B. V. Phani, George Robinson, Ambar Sengupta, Asha Ram Sihag, Yusuke Tateno, and Han Zheng.

We thank our family and friends for supporting us during this long project. In particular, Kaushik Basu, Nathaniel S. Behura, Amitava Bose, Alok Chakrabarti, Jennifer Conrad, Judson Devall, Ram Sewak Dubey, David Easley, Diego Garcia, Robert H. Jennings, Surendra Mansinghka, Robert T. Masson, Indranil Maulik, Tapan Mitra, Peter D. McClelland, Uri M. Possen, Erik Thorbecke, and Daniel J. Wszolek.

We were fortunate to have a number of highly conscientious formal reviewers of the manuscript as it was taking shape. Their astute advice had a major impact on the final version of the manuscript. We cannot thank these reviewers enough: Farid AitSahlia (University of Florida), Gregory W. Brown (The University of North Carolina at Chapel Hill), Michael Ferguson (University of Cincinnati), Stephen Figlewski (New York University), Scott Fung (California State University, East Bay), Richard Rendleman (Dartmouth College), Nejat Seyhun (University of Michigan), Joel Vanden (The Pennsylvania State University), Kelly Welch (The University of Kansas), and Youchang Wu (University of Wisconsin–Madison).

Finally, but certainly not least, special thanks to the editorial staff at Norton who have helped turn our manuscript into the finished book you are now reading: Hannah Bachman, Cassie del Pilar, Jack Repcheck, Nicole Sawa, and Amy Weintraub.

I

Introduction

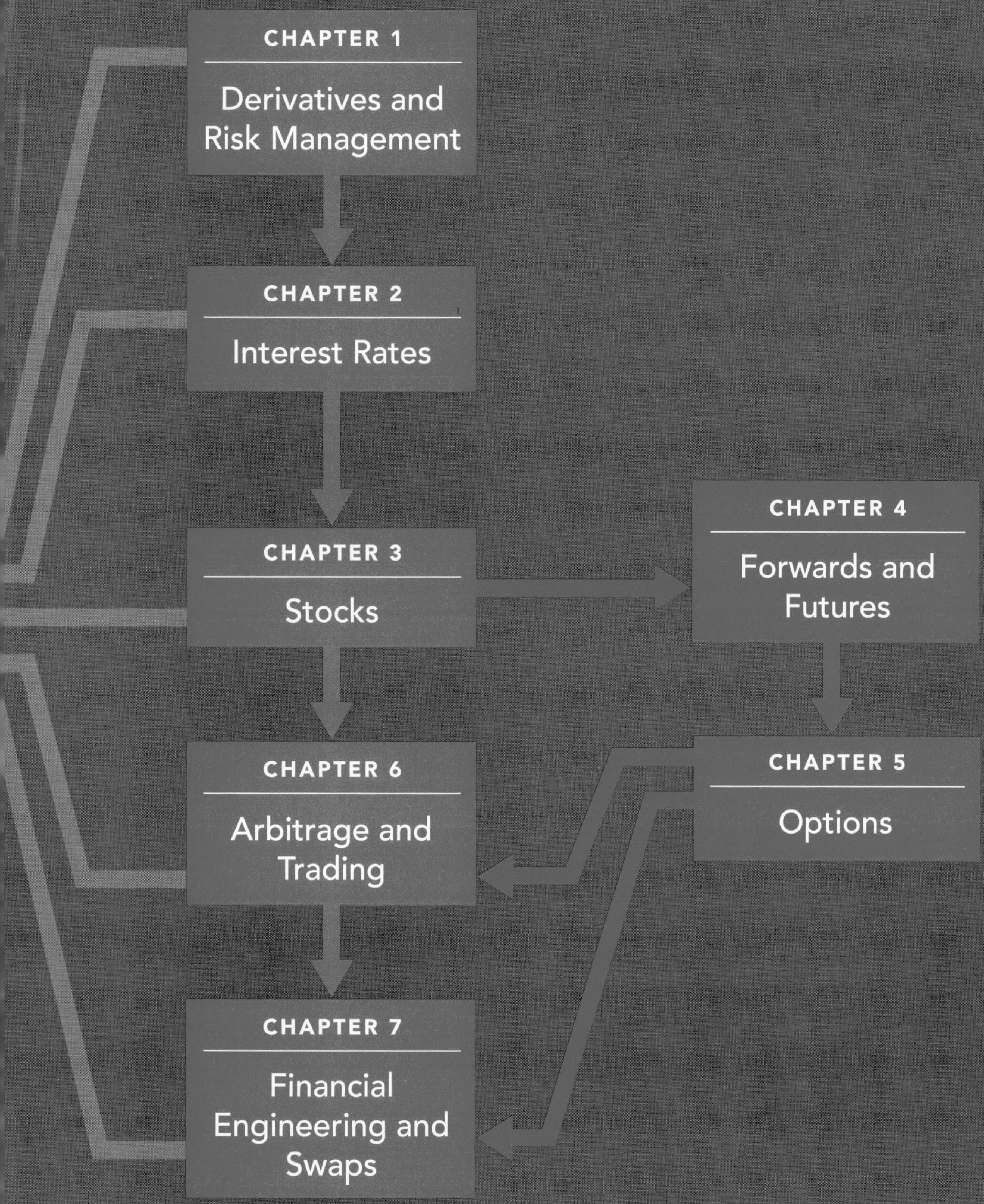

CHAPTER 1

Derivatives and Risk Management

CHAPTER 2

Interest Rates

CHAPTER 3

Stocks

CHAPTER 4

Forwards and Futures

CHAPTER 6

Arbitrage and Trading

CHAPTER 5

Options

CHAPTER 7

Financial Engineering and Swaps

1

Derivatives and Risk Management

1.1 | Introduction

The bursting of the housing price bubble, the credit crisis of 2007, the resulting losses of hundreds of billions of dollars on credit default swaps and credit debt obligations, and the failure of prominent financial institutions have forever changed the way the world views derivatives. Today derivatives are of interest not only to Wall Street but also to Main Street. Credit derivatives are cursed as one of the causes of the Great Recession of 2007–9, a period of decreased economic output and high unemployment.

But what are derivatives? A **derivative security** or a **derivative** is a financial contract that derives its value from an underlying asset's price, such as a stock or a commodity, or even from an underlying financial index like an interest rate. A derivative can both reduce risk, by providing insurance (which, in financial parlance, is referred to as *hedging*), and magnify risk, by speculating on future events. Derivatives provide unique and different ways of investing and managing wealth that ordinary securities do not.

Derivatives have a long and checkered past. In the 1960s, only a handful of individuals studied derivatives. No academic books covered the topic, and no college or university courses were available. Derivatives markets were small, located mostly in the United States and Western Europe. Derivative users included only a limited number of traders in futures markets and on Wall Street. The options market existed as trading between professional traders (called the *over-the-counter* [OTC] *market*) with little activity. In addition, cheating charges often gave the options market disrepute. Derivatives discussion did not add sparkle to cocktail conversations, nor did it generate the allegations and condemnations that it does today. Brash young derivatives traders who drive exotic cars and move millions of dollars with the touch of a computer key didn't exist. Although Einstein had developed the theory of relativity and astronauts had landed on the moon, no one knew how to price an option. That's because in the 1960s, nobody cared, and derivatives were unimportant.

What a difference the following decades have made! Beginning in the early 1970s, derivatives have undergone explosive growth in the types of contracts traded and in their importance to the financial and real economy. Figure 1.1 shows that after 2006, the total notional value of outstanding derivatives contracts exceeded $450 trillion. The markets are now global and measured in trillions of dollars. Hundreds of academics study derivatives, and thousands of articles have been written on the topic of pricing derivatives. Colleges and universities now offer numerous derivatives courses using textbooks written on the subject. Derivatives experts are in great demand. In fact, Wall Street firms hire PhDs in mathematics, engineering, and the natural sciences to understand derivatives—these folks are admirably called "rocket scientists" ("quants" is another name). If you understand derivatives, then you know cool stuff; you are hot and possibly dangerous. Today understanding derivatives is an integral part of the knowledge needed in the risk management of financial institutions.

Markets have changed to accommodate derivatives trading in three related ways: the introduction of new contracts and new exchanges, the consolidation and linking of exchanges, and the introduction of computer technology. Sometimes these changes happened with astounding quickness. For example, when twelve European nations replaced their currencies with the euro in 2002, financial

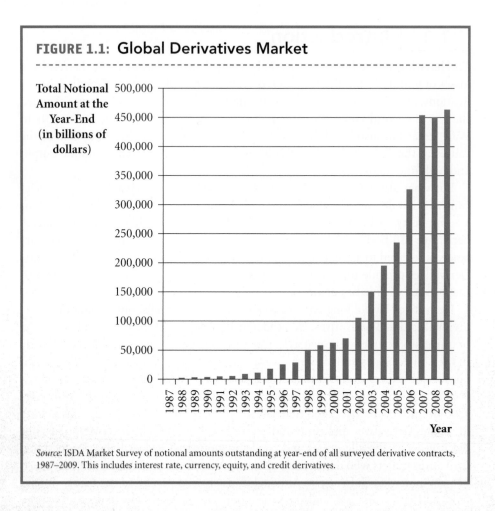

FIGURE 1.1: Global Derivatives Market

Source: ISDA Market Survey of notional amounts outstanding at year-end of all surveyed derivative contracts, 1987–2009. This includes interest rate, currency, equity, and credit derivatives.

markets for euro-denominated interest rate derivatives sprang up almost overnight, and in some cases, they quickly overtook the dollar-denominated market for similar interest rate derivatives.

This chapter tells the fascinating story of this expansion in derivatives trading and the controversy surrounding its growth. An understanding of the meaning of financial risk is essential in fully understanding this story. Hence a discussion of financial *risk* comes next, from the regulator's, the portfolio manager's, and the corporate financial manager's points of view. We explain each of these unique perspectives, using them throughout the book to increase our understanding of the uses and abuses of derivatives. A summary completes the chapter.

1.2 | Financial Innovation

Derivatives are at the core of financial innovation, for better or for worse. They are the innovations to which columnist David Wessel's *Wall Street Journal* article titled "A Source of Our Bubble Trouble," dated January 17, 2008, alludes:

> Modern finance is, truly, as powerful and innovative as modern science. More people own homes—many of them still making their mortgage payments—

because mortgages were turned into securities sold around the globe. More workers enjoy stable jobs because finance shields their employers from the ups and downs of commodity prices. More genius inventors see dreams realized because of venture capital. More consumers get better, cheaper insurance or fatter retirement checks because of Wall Street wizardry.

Expressed at a time when most of the world was in the Great Recession, this view is challenged by those who blame derivatives for the crisis. Indeed, this article goes on to say that "tens of billions of dollars of losses in new-fangled investments [in derivatives and other complex securities] at the largest US financial institutions—and the belated realization that some of those Ph.D.-wielding, computer-enhanced geniuses were overconfident in the extreme—strongly suggests some of the brainpower drawn to Wall Street would have been more productively employed elsewhere in the economy."

But derivatives have been trading in various guises for over two thousand years. They have continued to trade because, when used properly, they enable market participants to reduce risk from their portfolios and to earn financial rewards from trading on special skills and information. Indeed, derivatives help to advance or postpone cash flows (**borrowing and lending**), to accumulate wealth (**saving**), to protect against unfavorable outcomes (**insurance or hedging**), to commit funds to earn a financial return (**investment**), and to accept high risks in the hope of big returns (**speculation or gambling**), which often goes along with magnifying the scale of one's financial returns (**leverage**). Financial markets grow and real economic activity prospers because derivatives make financial markets more efficient. This is a theme to which we return repeatedly throughout the book.

Expanding Derivatives Markets

Many factors have fueled the growth of derivatives markets. These include regulatory reforms, an increase in international commerce, population growth, political changes, the integration of the world's economy, and revolutionary strides in information technology (IT). The interrelated financial markets are now more susceptible to global shocks and financial crises. The financial world has become a mad, bad, and dangerous place—financially speaking! More pronounced business cycles, default by sovereign nations, high-risk leveraged bets by hedge funds, imprudent investment in complicated securities by unsophisticated investors, and fraudulent actions by rogue traders have the potential to shake financial markets to their core. Financial regulators exist to help prevent these catastrophes from happening. And if used properly, derivatives can also help to mitigate their effects on aggregate wealth.

To help achieve this economic stability, the central bank of the United States, the **Federal Reserve System** (often referred to as the **Federal Reserve** or simply the **Fed**), historically used monetary policy tools to keep interest rates stable.[1] In 1979, the Fed also began targeting money supply growth. Despite this oversight, oil

---

[1] Courses in macroeconomics, money and finance, banking, or financial markets and institutions study how central banks fine-tune the economy using the tools of monetary policy: (1) setting the rate at which member banks can borrow from it (called the **discount rate** in the United States), (2) fixing bank **reserve requirements** (which is the percentage of money that a member bank must keep in its vault to support the loans it has made), and (3) buying and selling of government debts/bonds (**open market operations**).

shocks and other supply-side disturbances created double-digit inflation rates in the 1970s and 1980s, which in turn led to double-digit US interest rates that wiggled more than ever before. These highly volatile interest rates created a need for securities to help corporations hedge this risk. Interest rate derivatives arose. The Chicago Board of Trade (CBOT; now part of the CME Group) developed the first interest rate derivative contract, the Ginnie Mae futures, in 1975 and the highly popular Treasury bond futures in 1977.

The foreign exchange market is one of the world's largest financial markets, where billions of dollars change hands daily. From the mid-1940s until the early 1970s, the world economy operated under the **Bretton Woods system** of fixed exchange rates—all the currencies were pegged to the US dollar, and the dollar was pegged to gold at $35 per ounce. This stable monetary system worked well for decades. However, problems arose when gold prices soared. Countries converted their currencies into dollars and bought cheap gold from the United States at the bargain price of $35 per ounce, making huge profits. This was an **arbitrage**, a trade that makes riskless profits with no investment. Consequently, US gold reserves suffered a terrible decline. Because all currencies were tied to the dollar, the United States could not adjust the dollar's exchange rate to fix the problem. Instead, US president Richard Nixon abandoned the Bretton Woods system in 1971.

Currencies now float vis-à-vis one another in a so-called free market, although their values are frequently managed by central banks. Floating exchange rates are more volatile than fixed exchange rates, and to hedge this newly created currency risk, the huge foreign exchange derivatives market was created. In this regard, 1972 saw the opening of the **International Monetary Market**, a division of the Chicago Mercantile Exchange (CME or Merc; now part of the CME Group) to trade foreign currency futures. The world's first exchange-traded financial derivatives contract was born!

Given these regulatory changes and well-functioning interest rate and foreign currency derivatives markets, in the recent past, many economists believed that a new era of greater macroeconomic stability had dawned, dubbed the **Great Moderation**. During the two decades before the new millennium, fluctuations in the growth of real output and inflation had declined, stock market volatility was reduced, and business cycles were tamed. A prominent supporter of this view, Princeton University professor and chairman of the Fed Ben Bernanke provided three explanations for these trends in his February 20, 2004 speech: *structural change* (changes in economic institutions, technology, or other features of the economy), *improved macroeconomic policies*, and *good luck* ("the shocks hitting the economy became smaller and more infrequent").

However, in a surprise to these economists, the tide soon turned. In 2007–9, many nations were mired in the **Great Recession**, with declining economic output and large unemployment. Stock market volatility, as measured by the widely followed VIX Index, shot up from 10 percent to an astonishing 89.53 percent in October 2008.[2] Volatility had returned with a vengeance!

---

[2] See the Chicago Board Options Exchange's website, www.cboe.com/.

Two Economic Motives

Regulatory changes have powerful impacts on markets. In fact, economics Nobel laureate Merton Miller argued in a 1986 article that *regulations and taxes cause financial innovation.* The reason is because derivative securities are often created to circumvent government regulations that prohibit otherwise lucrative transactions. And because most countries tax income from different sources (and uses) at different rates, financial innovations are often designed to save tax dollars as well. *The desire to lower transactions costs also influences financial innovation.* This perspective comes from another Nobel Prize–winning University of Chicago economist, Ronald Coase. Financial institutions often devise derivatives so that brokerage commissions, the difference between a securities dealer's buying and selling prices, are minimized (see Extension 1.1).

This leads us to an (almost) axiomatic truth that will guide us throughout the book: *trading moves to those markets where transaction costs and regulatory constraints are minimized.*

1.3 | Traded Derivative Securities

A **security**, such as a stock or bond, gives its holder ownership rights over some assets and cash flows. It exists as a paper document or an electronic entry record and usually trades in an organized market. You may be familiar with **bonds**, which are debts of the issuer, and **stocks**, which give investors equity in the issuing company. Bonds and stocks require an initial investment. Most bonds pay back a promised amount (**principal** or **par value**) at maturity. Some bonds pay interest (**coupons**) on a regular basis, typically semiannually, while others are **zero-coupon bonds** that pay no interest but are sold at a discount from the principal. The investment in stock is never repaid. Stockholders usually get paid **dividends** on a quarterly basis as compensation for their stock ownership. Stock prices can increase and create **capital gains** for investors, and this profit is realized by selling the stock. Alternatively, stock prices can decrease and create **capital losses**.

Stocks and bonds are often used to create new classes of securities called derivatives, and that's where the variety comes in. As previously noted, a *derivative security* is a financial contract whose value is derived from one or more **underlying** assets or indexes—a stock, a bond, a commodity, a foreign currency, an index, an interest rate, or even another derivative security. Forwards, futures, and options are the basic types of derivatives. These are explained later in the book.

Some common terminology will help us understand the various derivative contracts traded:

1. **Real assets** include land, buildings, machines, and commodities, whereas **financial assets** include stocks, bonds, and currencies—both real and financial assets have tangible values.

2. **Notional variables** include interest rates, inflation rates, and security indexes, which exist as notions rather than as tangible assets.

EXTENSION 1.1:   The Influence of Regulations, Taxes, and Transaction Costs on Financial Innovation

In the old days, *finance* mainly consisted of legal issues, institutional description, and investment rules of thumb. This changed in the middle of the twentieth century, when financial economics sprang to life as an offshoot of economics. In a little over two decades, a new finance based on a rigorous analytics emerged. James Tobin and Harry Markowitz's *portfolio theory* (late 1940s and early 1950s); Franco Modigliani and Merton Miller's *M&M propositions concerning the irrelevance of a firm's capital structure and dividend policy* (late 1950s and early 1960s); William Sharpe, John Lintner, and Jan Mossin's *capital asset pricing model* (mid-1960s); and Fischer Black, Myron Scholes, and Robert Merton's *option pricing model* (early 1970s) established the basic theories. All these works have been celebrated with the Sveriges Riksbank (Bank of Sweden) Prize in Economic Sciences in Memory of Alfred Nobel, popularly known as the Nobel Prize in Economics.[3,4] Other Nobel laureates, including Kenneth Arrow, Ronald Coase, Gerard Debreu, John Hicks, and Paul Samuelson, also contributed to finance. One of the most well known economists of all time, John Maynard Keynes, studied the properties of futures prices, the role of speculators, and stock markets. Two of these Nobel laureates' views concerned financial innovation.

Miller's View: Regulations and Taxes Spur Financial Innovation

What leads to revolutionary change in financial institutions and instruments? University of Chicago professor Merton Miller (1923–2000) argued that a *major cause of financial innovation is regulations and taxes*. Innovative financial securities are often created to avoid government regulations that prohibit otherwise lucrative transactions. And because most countries tax income from different sources (and uses) at different rates, derivative securities can be designed to save tax dollars.

Miller (1986) gives several examples:

- Regulation Q of the United States placed a ceiling on the interest rate that commercial banks could pay on time deposits. Although this wasn't a problem during much of the postwar period, US interest rates rose above this ceiling during the late 1960s and early 1970s. When this occurred, US banks started losing customers. US banks realized, however, that Regulation Q did not apply to dollar-denominated time deposits in their overseas branches, and they soon began offering attractive rates via **Eurodollar** accounts. Interestingly, Regulation Q has long been repealed, but the Eurodollar market still continues to flourish.

- In the late 1960s, the US government imposed a 30 percent withholding tax on interest payments to bonds sold in the United States to overseas investors. Consequently, for non-US citizens, the market for dollar-denominated bonds moved overseas to London and other money centers on the continent. This created the **Eurobond** market that still continues to grow today.

---

[3] Named after the Swedish inventor–industrialist **Alfred Bernhard Nobel** (1833–96). While working in Paris, Nobel came across the highly explosive liquid nitroglycerine. Despite some setbacks, he managed to make it safer by adding a chalklike rock and patented it under the name of "dynamite." Dynamite made him very wealthy, and after his death, he left the bulk of his fortune to fund annual prizes in Physics, Chemistry, Physiology or Medicine, Literature, and Peace. *Source*: "Alfred Nobel—His Life and Work," retrieved from the Nobel Foundation's website, www.nobelprize.org/nobel_prizes/economics/laureates/.

[4] While celebrating its three hundredth anniversary in 1968, the Swedish central bank (Sveriges Riksbank) established the **Sveriges Riksbank Prize in Economic Sciences in Memory of Alfred Nobel**. The prize is awarded and celebrated along with the Nobel Prizes every December in Sweden.

- The British government restricted dollar financing by British firms and sterling financing by non-British firms. **Swaps**, transactions in which counterparties exchange one form of cash flow for another, were developed to circumvent these restrictions.

- It was found in 1981 that US tax laws allowed a linear approximation for computing the implicit interest for long-term deep discount *zero-coupon bonds*. This inflated the present value of the interest deductions so much that a taxable corporation could actually profit by issuing a zero-coupon bond and giving it away! Not surprisingly, US corporations started issuing zero-coupon bonds in large numbers. This supply dwindled after the US Treasury fixed this blunder.

Coase's View: Transaction Costs are a Key Determinant of Economic Activity

In 1937, Ronald Coase, a twenty-seven-year-old faculty member at the London School of Economics, published a simple but profound article titled "The Nature of the Firm." Coase argued that transactions incur costs, which come from "negotiations to be undertaken, contracts have to be drawn up, inspections have to be made, arrangements have to be made to settle disputes, and so on," and firms often appear when they can lower these transaction costs. With respect to financial markets, this logic implies that market participants often trade where they can achieve their objectives at minimum cost. Financial derivatives are often created so that these costs are minimized as well.

The lowering of transaction costs as an economic motivation was especially important during the 1990s and the new millennium. Changes in the economic and political landscape and the IT revolution have made it possible to significantly lower transaction costs, even eliminating age-old professions like brokers and dealers from many trading processes. For example, this motive was a major reason why traders migrated from Treasury securities to Eurodollar markets. Eurodollar markets, being free from Fed regulations and the peculiarities of the Treasury security auction cycle, have fewer market imperfections and lower liquidity costs.

Writing financial contracts on values or cash flows determined by future realizations of real asset prices, financial asset prices, or notional variables creates a derivative security. Early derivatives were created solely from financial and real assets. For example, in the 1960s, agricultural commodity–based futures were the most actively traded derivative contracts in the United States. However, as the economy has evolved, notional variables and derivative securities based on these notional variables have also been created.

Notional variables are often introduced to help summarize the state of the economy. Just open the "Money and Investing" section of the *Wall Street Journal*, and you will be amazed by the variety of indexes out there. You will find not only regular stock price indexes, such as the Dow-Jones and Standard and Poor's, but a whole range of other indexes, including those based on technology stocks, pharmaceuticals stocks, Mexican stocks, utility stocks, bonds, and interest rates. In addition, notional values are often useful for the creation of various derivatives. Perhaps the most famous example of this is a plain vanilla interest rate swap whose underlyings are floating and fixed interest rates.

Diverse Views on Derivatives

It is easy to speculate with derivatives: buy them, take huge one-sided bets, and laugh on the way to the bank or cry on the way to bankruptcy! Imprudent risk taking using derivatives is not uncommon, as illustrated by huge losses at many institutions, including Procter and Gamble (P&G) and Barings Bank. People are uncomfortable with derivatives because they are complex instruments: difficult to understand, highly leveraged, and oftentimes not backed by sufficient collateral. High **leverage** means that small changes in the underlying security's price can cause large swings in the derivative's value.

For these reasons, derivatives attract strong views from both sides of the aisle. The renowned investors Warren Buffett and Peter Lynch dislike derivatives. Lynch (1989) once stated that options and futures on stocks should be outlawed. In his "Chairman's Letter" to the shareholders in Berkshire Hathaway's 2002 annual report, Buffett characterized derivatives as "time bombs, both for the parties that deal in them and the economic system." These concerns were vindicated by the hundreds of billions of dollars of derivatives-related losses suffered by financial institutions during 2007 and 2008, which contributed to the severe economic downturn (see the bio sketch of Buffett in the insert).

By contrast, former Fed chairman Alan Greenspan opined in a speech delivered before the Futures Industry Association in 1999 that derivatives "unbundle" risks by carefully measuring and allocating them "to those investors most able and willing to take it," a phenomenon that has contributed to a more efficient allocation of capital (see the bio sketch of Greenspan in the insert). And in *Merton Miller on Derivatives*, the Nobel laureate (Miller 1997, ix) assessed the impact of the "derivatives revolution" in glowing terms:

> Contrary to the widely held perception, derivatives have made the world a *safer* place, not a more dangerous one. They have made it possible for firms and institutions to deal efficiently and cost effectively with risks and hazards that have plagued them for decades, if not for centuries. True, some firms and some financial institutions have managed to lose substantial sums on derivatives, but some firms and institutions will always find ways to lose money. Good judgment and good luck cannot be taken for granted. For all the horror stories about derivatives, it's still worth emphasizing that the world's banks have blown away vastly more in bad real estate deals than they'll ever lose on their derivatives portfolios.

Interestingly, in 2008, Greenspan admitted in testimony before the US Congress that "he had put too much faith in the self-correcting power of free markets and had failed to anticipate the self-destructive power of wanton mortgage lending" ("Greenspan Concedes Error on Regulation," *New York Times*, October 23, 2008). In relation to Merton Miller's quotation, the losses in this credit crisis were due to both bad real estate loans and poor investments in complex derivatives that none could price and few could understand (see chapter 26 for a detailed analysis of this crisis).

Nobel laureate physicist David Gross provides a nice analogy. He views *knowledge* as expanding outward like a growing sphere and *ignorance* as the surface of that sphere. With respect to derivatives, we have accumulated significant knowledge over the past thirty years, but with respect to the causes of tsunami-like financial crises, there is still much for us to learn.

TABLE 1.A: Bio Sketches of Warren Buffett and Alan Greenspan

Son of a congressman from Omaha, Nebraska, **Warren Buffett** (b. 1930) attended the Wharton School at the University of Pennsylvania, graduated from the University of Nebraska–Lincoln, and got an MS (economics) from Columbia University, where he became a disciple of Benjamin Graham, the famed pioneer of value investing. Buffett filed his first tax return at thirteen, became a millionaire at thirty-two, and topped *Forbes* magazine's list of the world's billionaires in 2008. Famous for his homespun wit, some of his sayings include the following: "It's far better to buy a wonderful company at a fair price than a fair company at a wonderful price," "Our favorite holding period is forever," and "Price is what you pay; value is what you get." A strong critic of derivatives, Buffett nonetheless trades derivatives when he understands the risks involved.

Alan Greenspan (b. 1926) studied clarinet at the famed Juilliard School and joined a traveling orchestra but returned to study at New York University, where he got all his degrees in economics, including a PhD. He founded an influential economic consulting firm and served as the chairman of the US president's Council of Economic Advisors (1974–77) and as chairman of the Federal Reserve Board (1987–2006). Greenspan earned an early reputation for his competent handling of the stock market crash of 1987 and was revered for his understanding of markets. Awarded the highest civilian accolade of the United States, the Presidential Medal of Freedom, Greenspan's steadfast support for free markets and his opposition to greater regulation of derivatives came under criticism during the financial crisis of 2007.

Sources: Quotations are from www.brainyquote.com/quotes/authors/w/warren_buffett.html; Alan Greenspan's biography is from www.alangreenspan.org/.

Applications and Uses of Derivatives

Derivatives trade in **zero net supply markets**, where each buyer has a matching seller. When hedging with a derivative, the other side of the transaction (**counterparty**) may be using it for speculative reasons. Hedging and speculation are often two sides of the same coin, and it is a **zero-sum game** because one trader's gain is the other's loss. Example 1.1 illustrates these concepts.

EXAMPLE 1.1: Hedging and Speculation in a Derivative Transaction

- April is the time when income tax returns are due. It is also the beginning of the corn-growing season, the commodity used in our example.

- Consider Mr. Short, a farmer in the midwestern United States. Short combines land, labor, seeds, fertilizers, and pesticides to produce cheap corn. He hopes to sell his corn harvest in September.

- Expertise in growing corn does not provide a crystal ball for forecasting September corn prices. If Short likes sleeping peacefully at night, he may decide to lock in the selling price for September corn when he plants it in April.

- To see how this is done, let's assume that everyone expects corn to be worth $10.00 per bushel in September. Ms. Long, a trader and speculator, offers to buy Short's corn in September for $9.95 per bushel, which is the **forward price**.

- To remove his risk, Short readily agrees to this forward price. Together they have created a **forward contract**—a promise to trade at a fixed forward price in the future. Although Short expects to lose 5 cents, he is happy to fix the selling price. The forward contract has removed output price uncertainty from his business. Short sees 5 cents as the insurance premium he pays for avoiding unfavorable future outcomes. Having hedged his corn selling price, Short can focus on what he knows best, which is growing corn.

- Ms. Long is also happy—not that she is wild about taking risks, but she is rational and willing to accept some unwanted risk, expecting to earn 5 cents as compensation for this activity. Later in the book, you will see how a speculator may manage her risk by entering into another transaction at a better price but on the other side of the market.

This simple example illustrates a key principle of historical importance—it was precisely to help farmers hedge grain prices that the first modern derivatives exchange, the CBOT, was established in 1848. Even the bitterest critics of derivatives have acknowledged this beneficial role.

Nowadays, the uses of derivatives are many. Consider the following possibilities:

- *Hedging output price risk:* A gold-mining company can fix the selling price of gold by selling gold futures.

- *Hedging input cost:* A sausage maker can hedge input prices by buying pork belly futures.

- *Hedging currency risk:* An American manufacturer buying machines from Germany for which the payment is due in three months can remove price risk from the dollar–euro exchange rates by buying a currency forward contract.

- *Hedging interest rate risk:* A pension fund manager who is worried that her bond portfolio will get clobbered by rising interest rates can use Eurodollar futures (or options on those futures) to protect her portfolio.

- *Protecting a portfolio against a market meltdown:* A money manager whose portfolio has reaped huge gains can protect these gains by buying put options.

- *Avoiding market restrictions:* A trader can avoid short selling restrictions that an exchange might impose by taking a sell position in the options or the futures market.

- *Ruining oneself:* A wretch can gamble away his inheritance with derivatives.

Before you finish this book, you will have a better understanding of the role derivatives play in each of these scenarios, except for the last one. The proclivity to gamble and lose arises from the depths of the human psyche, of which we have no special understanding.

A Quest for Better Models

Great recognition for derivatives came in 1997, when Robert Merton and Myron Scholes won the Nobel Prize in Economics for developing the **Black–Scholes–Merton (BSM) model** for option valuation. A co-originator of the model, Fischer

Black, died earlier and missed receiving the prize, which is not given posthumously. This formula has become a staple of modern option pricing. Although extremely useful—options traders have it programmed into their computers—the BSM model makes a number of restrictive assumptions. These restrictive assumptions limit the application of the model to particular derivatives, those for which interest rate risk is not relevant (the BSM assumptions are discussed in later chapters).

Subsequent researchers have relaxed these restrictive assumptions and developed pricing models suitable for derivatives with interest rate risk. The standard model used on Wall Street for this application is the **Heath–Jarrow–Morton (HJM) model**. The HJM model can be used to price interest rate derivatives, long-lived financial contracts, and credit derivatives. Credit derivatives are among the newest class of derivatives to hit Wall Street. Started in the early 1990s, they now compose a huge market, and they are the subject of intense public debate following the 2007 credit crisis and their role in it.

Introductory texts avoid the HJM model because of its complex mathematics. A unique contribution of our book is a simple intuitive presentation of the HJM model and one of its popular versions, known as the **libor model**. Civilization is replete with examples of today's esoteric notions attaining widespread understanding—what once belonged to specialists soon belongs to the public. This happened to the BSM model. Learning the HJM and libor models will give you an advantage in trading derivatives—it will help you to understand the present and be prepared for the future.

Why develop and study better pricing models? Suppose you trade a variety of securities many times a day. If your models are better, you have an edge over your competitors in determining fair value. Over many transactions, when trading based on fair value—selling above fair value and buying below—your edge will pay off. Investment banking and Wall Street firms have no choice but to use the best models. It's just too important for their survival. Powerful models also help traders manage risk.

1.4 | Defining, Measuring, and Managing Risk

Risk is an elusive concept and hard to define. In finance and business, risk can be defined and measured in many ways, none of them completely universal. Risk often depends on the user's perspective. We begin by looking at risk through a regulator's eyes. Next, we discuss risk from an individual's as well as an institutional trader's viewpoint. Finally, we discuss risk from a corporate management perspective.

1.5 | The Regulator's Classification of Risk

In 1994, the international banking and securities regulators issued guidelines for supervising the booming derivatives market. The Basel Committee on Banking Supervision and the International Organization of Securities Commissions (IOSCO) recommended that for a stable world financial system, the national regulators had to ensure that banks and securities firms have adequate controls over the risks they incur when trading derivatives.[5]

The Basel Committee's Risk Management Guidelines for Derivatives (July 1994, 10–17) identified the following risks in connection with an institution's derivative activities. IOSCO's Technical Committee also issued a similar paper at the time:[6]

- **Credit risk** (including **settlement risk**) is the risk that a counterparty will fail to perform on an obligation.

- **Market risk** is the risk to an institution's financial condition resulting from adverse movements in the level or volatility of market prices. This is the same as **price risk**.

- **Liquidity risk** in derivative activities can be of two types: one related to specific products or markets and the other related to the general funding of the institution's derivative activities. The former is the risk that an institution may not be able to, or cannot easily, unwind or offset a particular position at or near the previous market price because of inadequate market depth or disruptions in the marketplace. Funding liquidity risk is the risk that the institution will be unable to meet its payment obligations on settlement dates or in the event of margin calls (which, we explain later, is equivalent to coming up with more security deposits).

- **Operational risk** (also known as **operations risk**) is the risk that deficiencies in information systems or internal controls will result in unexpected loss. This risk is associated with human error, system failures, and inadequate procedures and controls.

- **Legal risk** is the risk that contracts are not legally enforceable or documented correctly.

Managing market or price risk is the subject of this book. Initially, this topic attracted the sole attention of academics and practitioners alike. It still remains the most important risk for us to understand and to manage. The other risks only appear when normal market activity ceases. Credit risk evaluation is currently a subject of advanced research.[7] As we explain later, exchange-traded derivatives markets are so designed that they are nearly free from credit risk. Liquidity risk is a persistent problem for traders who choose markets in which securities are not easily bought and sold. Chapter 3 discusses what makes markets illiquid. Operational risk is a reality with which one has to live. It is part of running a business, and

---

[5] In 1974, the Group of Ten countries' central-bank governors established the **Basel Committee on Banking Supervision**. The Basel (or Basle) Committee formulates broad supervisory standards and recommends statements of best practice in the expectation that individual authorities will take steps to implement them through detailed arrangements—statutory or otherwise—that are best suited to their own national systems (see "History of the Basel Committee and Its Membership," www.bis.org/bcbs/history.htm). The **International Organization of Securities Commissions**, which originated as an inter-American regional association in 1974, was restructured as IOSCO in 1983. It has evolved into a truly international cooperative body of securities regulators (see www.iosco.org/about/about).

[6] For both reports, see www.bis.org/publ. These definitions are modified only slightly from those contained in the referenced report.

[7] Companies like Moody's and Standard and Poor assess the credit risk of a company or a security by assigning a credit rating. The HJM model provides a way of taking such credit ratings and building them into a pricing model (Jarrow and Turnbull 2000).

appropriate management checks and balances reduce it. Legal risk isn't a problem for exchange-traded contracts; however, it's a genuine problem in OTC markets. We leave this topic for the courts and law schools.

This jargon-laded Basel Committee report also cited the need for appropriate oversight of derivatives trading operations by boards of directors and senior management and the need for comprehensive internal control and audit procedures. It urged national regulators to ensure that firms and banks operate on a basis of prudent risk limits, sound measurement procedures and information systems, continuous risk monitoring, and frequent management reporting. The Basel Committee reports have been extremely influential in terms of their impact on derivatives regulation. We return to the issues again in the last chapter of the book, after mastering the basics of derivatives securities.

1.6 Portfolio Risk Management

Let us examine some issues in connection with portfolio risk management from the perspective of an individual or institutional trader. One of the first pearls of wisdom learned in finance is that *to earn higher expected returns, one has to accept higher risks.* This maxim applies to the risk of a portfolio, called **portfolio risk**, which is measured by the portfolio return's standard deviation.

This portfolio risk, when applied to a single security, can be broken into two parts: (1) **nondiversifiable risk**, which comes from market-wide sources, and (2) **diversifiable risk**, which is unique to the security and can be eliminated via diversification. Pioneering works by Markowitz (1952), Sharpe (1964), Lintner (1965), and Mossin (1966) gave us the capital asset pricing model—the alphas, the betas—ideas and concepts used by market professionals and finance academics.

Modern portfolio theory encourages investors to construct a portfolio in a **top-down** fashion. This involves three steps: (1) do an **asset allocation**, which means deciding how to spread your investment across broad asset classes such as cash, bonds, stocks, and real estate; (2) do **security selection**, which means deciding which securities to hold within each asset class; and (3) periodically revisiting these issues and rebalancing the portfolio accordingly. Portfolio risk management is critical for **investment companies** such as hedge funds and mutual funds. These financial intermediaries receive money from the public, invest them in various financial securities, and pass on the gains and losses to investors after deducting expenses and fees. **Mutual funds** have more restricted investment policies and lower management fees than **hedge funds**. Hedge funds typically make leveraged high-risk bets and are only open to wealthy investors, who may scream and shout if their investments decline but who will not become destitute.

1.7 Corporate Financial Risk Management

Risks That Businesses Face

To understand the risks that businesses face, let's take a look at a typical company's **balance sheet**, a vital accounting tool that gives a snapshot of its financial

TABLE 1.1: Risks That a Business Faces	
Assets	**Liabilities**
Current assets	▪ Accounts payable (interest rate risk, currency risk)
▪ Cash and cash equivalents (interest rate risk)	▪ Financial liabilities (interest rate risk, currency risk)
▪ Accounts receivable (interest rate risk, currency risk)	▪ Pension fund obligations (interest rate risk, market risk)
▪ Inventories (commodity price risk)	
Long-term assets	**Equity**
▪ Financial assets (interest rate risk, market risk, currency risk)	▪ Ownership shares
▪ Property, plant, and equipment (interest rate risk, commodity price risk)	

condition by summarizing its assets, liabilities, and ownership equity on a specific date. An **asset** provides economic benefits to the firm, whereas a **liability** is an obligation that requires payments at some future date. The difference between the two accrues to the owners of the company as **shareholder's equity** (hence the identity *assets equals liabilities plus shareholder's equity*). Depending on whether they are for the short term (one year or less) or for the long haul, assets and liabilities are further classified as current or noncurrent, respectively.[8] Table 1.1 illustrates some risks that affect different parts of a firm's balance sheet.

We see that a typical company faces three kinds of risks: **currency risk**, **interest rate risk**, and **commodity price risk**. These are the three components of market risk.

1. If a big chunk of your business involves imports and exports or if you have overseas operations that send back profits, then exchange rate risk can help or hurt. This is a risk that you must understand and decide whether to hedge using currency derivatives.

2. No less important is interest rate risk. It is hard to find companies like Microsoft, with tens of billions of dollars in cash holdings that can be quickly deployed for value-enhancing investments. Most companies are cash strapped. Interest rate fluctuations therefore affect their cost of funds and influence their investment activities. Interest rate derivatives offer many choices for managing this risk.

3. Unless a financial company, most businesses are exposed to fluctuations in commodity prices. A rise in commodity prices raises the cost of buying inputs that may not always be passed on to customers. For example, if crude oil prices go up,

---

[8] **Current assets** are cash, cash equivalent, or assets held for collection, sale, or consumption within the enterprise's normal operating cycle, or for trading within the next twelve months. All other assets are noncurrent (see IAS 1.57). **Current liabilities** are those to be settled within the enterprise's normal operating cycle or due within twelve months, those held for trading, or those for which the entity does not have an unconditional right to defer payment beyond twelve months. Other liabilities are noncurrent (see IAS 1.60). These definitions appear under the "Statement of Financial Position" in "Summary of IAS 1." IAS refers to "International Accounting Standards" that were developed by the IASC. *Source*: www.iasplus.com/.

so does the price of jet fuel and an airline's fuel costs. Sometimes airlines levy a fuel surcharge, but it is unpopular and often rolled back. Another option is to hedge such risks by using oil-price derivatives.

Nonhedged Risks

Despite the development of many sophisticated derivatives useful for hedging (and speculation), some risks are difficult, if not impossible, to hedge. For example, it is very hard to hedge operational risk. Recall that operational risk is the risk of a loss owing to events such as human error, fraud, or faulty management. Although a bank can buy insurance to protect itself from losses due to fire, no insurance company will insure a bank against the risk that a trader presses the wrong computer button and enters the wrong bond trade. For examples of such operational risk losses, see chapter 26. Other difficult or impossible to hedge risks include losses because of changes in commodity prices for which there is no futures contract trading.

We will now take a bird's-eye view of how a blue chip company uses derivatives for risk management.

Risk Management in a Blue Chip Company

The **SFAS (Statement of Financial Accounting Standards) No. 133**, "Accounting for Derivative Instruments and Hedging Activities," as amended, requires US companies to report all derivative instruments on the balance sheet at fair value and establishes criteria for designation and effectiveness of hedging relationships. Let's take a look at Form 10-K (annual report) filed with the US Securities and Exchange Commission by Procter & Gamble (P&G), a giant company that owns some of the world's best-known consumer product brands.[9]

P&G heavily uses derivatives for risk management. A careful reading of this annual report reveals several interesting characteristics of P&G's risk management activity:

- P&G is exposed to the three categories of risk that we just mentioned.
- P&G consolidates these risks and tries to offset them naturally, which means some risks cancel each other. It then tries to hedge the rest with derivatives.
- P&G does not hold derivatives for trading purposes.
- P&G monitors derivatives positions using techniques such as market value, sensitivity analysis, and value at risk. When data are unavailable, P&G uses reasonable proxies for estimating volatility and correlations of market factors.
- P&G uses interest rate swaps to hedge its underlying debt obligations and enters into certain currency interest rate swaps to hedge the company's foreign net investments.
- P&G manufactures and sells its products in many countries. It mainly uses forwards and options to reduce the risk that the company's financial position will

[9] See www.pg.com/content/pdf/home/PG_2008_AnnualReport.pdf.

be adversely affected by short-term changes in exchange rates (corporate policy limits how much it can hedge).

- P&G uses futures, options, and swaps to manage the price volatility of raw materials.

- P&G designates a security as a hedge of a specific underlying exposure and monitors its effectiveness in an ongoing manner.

- P&G's overall currency and interest rate exposures are such that the company is 95 percent confident that fluctuations in these variables (provided they don't deviate from their historical behavior) would not materially affect its financial statements. P&G expects significant risk neither from commodity hedging activity nor from credit risk exposure.

- P&G grants stock options and restricted stock awards to key managers and directors (employee stock options are valued by using a binomial model that you will learn to implement in Part III of this book).

How does one understand, formulate, and implement hedging and risk management strategies like the ones adopted by P&G? Read on, for that is a major purpose of this book.

1.8 Risk Management Perspectives in This Book

The Basel Committee's risk nomenclature has become the standard way that market participants see, classify, and understand different types of risks in derivatives markets. In this book, we restrict our focus mainly to market or price risk. For this we usually wear four separate hats and look at risk management from the perspectives of an individual trader, a financial institution, a nonfinancial corporation, and a dealer.

In early chapters, we start by examining financial securities and their markets from an *individual trader's standpoint*. This simple and intuitive approach makes it easier to understand the material. It's also historically correct because many markets, including those for stocks, futures, and options, were started by individual traders.

But today's derivatives markets have become playing fields for financial institutions. This is no surprise because as an economy develops, a greater share of its gross domestic product comes from services, of which financial institutions are a major constituent. These institutions generally engage in sophisticated ways of investing. We discuss derivatives and risk management from a *financial institution's viewpoint* because you may eventually be working for one, or at the very least, you are likely to have financial dealings with such institutions on a regular basis. The term **institution** is a catchall phrase that includes commercial and investment banks, insurance companies, pension funds, foundations, and finance companies such as mutual funds and hedge funds. In later chapters, we study swaps and interest rate derivatives, whose markets are the near-exclusive domain of financial (and nonfinancial) institutions.

Nonfinancial companies engage in more real activity than financial companies. Nonfinancials give us food, develop medicines, build homes, manufactures cars, refine crude oil to create gasoline, generate electricity, provide air travel, create household chemicals, and make computers to save and express our ideas. They buy one or more inputs to produce one or more outputs, and different kinds of risk (including exchange rate risk, interest rate risk, and commodity price risk) can seriously affect their businesses. This takes us to *financial engineering*, which applies engineering tools to develop financial contracts to meet the needs of an enterprise. This is our third hat: looking at derivatives from a *nonfinancial company's risk management perspective.*

Sometimes we take a dealer's perspective. A dealer is a financial intermediary who posts prices at which she can buy (wholesale or *bid price*) or sell (retail or *ask price*) securities to her customers. Trying to make a living from the *spread*, or the difference between these two prices, the dealer focuses on *managing books*, which means carefully controlling her inventory of securities to minimize risk. Both an individual trader and a financial institution can play a dealer's role in financial markets.

These four perspectives aren't ironclad, and we flit from one to another as the discussion demands. In the final analysis, this shifting from one category to another isn't bad for the aspiring derivatives expert. In the words of the immortal bard William Shakespeare, from *Hamlet* (if we take the liberty of forgetting about spirits and instead apply this to the mundane), "there are more things in heaven and earth, Horatio, than are dreamt of in your philosophy." So stay awake and study derivatives, develop a sense for risky situations, understand the markets, learn pricing models, and know their limitations.

1.9　Summary

1. Derivatives are financial securities that derive their value from some underlying asset price or index. Derivatives are often introduced to hedge risks caused by increasingly volatile asset prices. For example, during the last three decades of the twentieth century, we have moved away from a regime of fixed exchange rates to a world of floating exchange rates. The market-determined foreign exchange rates increased their volatility, creating the need for foreign currency derivatives.

2. In today's interconnected global economy, risks coming from many different sources can make or break businesses. Derivatives can both magnify risk (leverage and gambling) or reduce risk (hedging). Although gambling with derivatives remains popular in some circles, and derivatives mishaps grab newspaper headlines, most traders prudently use derivatives to remove unwanted risks affecting their businesses.

3. There are many types of risk. Besides market risk, the regulators are concerned about credit risk, liquidity risk, operational risk, and legal risk. Though unglamorous, these risks can eat away profits and jolt the running of smooth-functioning derivatives markets.

4. Derivatives are very useful for managing the risk of a portfolio, which is a collection of securities. Portfolio risk management is important for both individual investors and financial companies such as hedge funds and mutual funds.

5. Many businesses are exposed to exchange rate risk, interest rate risk, and commodity price risk and use derivatives to hedge them. US companies report derivatives usage and exposure on Form 10-K filed annually with the Securities and Exchange Commission. For example, P&G reports that it is exposed to exchange rate risk, interest rate risk, commodity price risk, and credit risk. P&G consolidates risks and attempts to offset them naturally and tries to hedge the remaining risk with derivatives.

6. We look at risk management from several different perspectives: that of an individual trader, a financial institution, a nonfinancial corporation, and a dealer. These perspectives aren't ironclad, and we flit from one to another as the discussion demands.

1.10 | Cases

Hamilton Financial Investments: A Franchise Built on Trust (Harvard Business School Case 198089-PDF-ENG). The case discusses various risks faced by a finance company that manages mutual funds and provides discount brokerage services.

Grosvenor Group Ltd. (Harvard Business School Case 207064-PDF-ENG). The case considers whether a global real estate investment firm should enter into a property derivative transaction to alter its asset allocation and manage its business.

Societe Generale (A and B): The Jerome Kerviel Affair (Harvard Business School Cases 110029 and 110030-PDF-ENG). The case illustrates the importance of internal control systems in a business environment that involves a high degree of risk and complexity in the context of a derivatives trader indulging in massive directional trades that went undetected for over a year.

1.11 | Questions and Problems

1.1. What is a derivative security? Give an example of a derivative and explain why it is a derivative.

1.2. List some major applications of derivatives.

1.3. Evaluate the following statement: "Hedging and speculation go hand in hand in the derivatives market."

1.4. What risks does a business face?

1.5. Explain why financial futures have replaced agricultural futures as the most actively traded contracts.

1.6. Explain why derivatives are zero-sum games.

1.7. Explain why all risks cannot be hedged. Give an example of a risk that cannot be hedged.

1.8. What is a notional variable, and how does it differ from an asset's price?

1.9. Explain how derivatives give traders high leverage.

1.10. Explain the essence of Merton Miller's argument explaining what spurs financial innovation.

1.11. Explain the essence of Ronald Coase's argument explaining what spurs financial innovation.

1.12. Does more volatility in a market lead to more use of financial derivatives? Explain your answer.

1.13. When the international banking regulators defined risk in their 1994 report, what definition of risk did they have in mind? How does this compare with the definition of risk from modern portfolio theory?

1.14. What's the difference between real and financial assets?

1.15. Explain the differences between market risk, credit risk, liquidity risk, and operational risk.

1.16. Briefly present Warren Buffett's and Alan Greenspan's views on derivatives.

1.17. Consider the situation in sunny Southern California in 2005, where house prices have skyrocketed over the last few years and are at an all-time high. Nathan, a software engineer, buys a second home for $1.5 million. Five years back, he bought his first home in the same region for $350,000 and financed it with a thirty-year mortgage. He has paid off $150,000 of the first loan. His first home is currently worth $900,000. Nathan plans to rent out his first home and move into the second. Is Nathan speculating or hedging?

1.18. During the early years of the new millennium, many economists described the past few decades as the period of the Great Moderation. For example,

- an empirical study by economists Olivier Blanchard and John Simon found that "the variability of quarterly growth in real output (as measured by its standard deviation) had declined by half since the mid-1980s, while the variability of quarterly inflation had declined by about two thirds."

- an article titled "Upheavals Show End of Volatility Is Just a Myth" in the *Wall Street Journal*, dated March 19, 2008, observed that an important measure of stock market volatility, "the Chicago Board Options Exchange's volatility index, had plunged about 75% since October 2002, the end of the latest bear market, through early 2007"; the article also noted that "in the past 25 years, the economy has spent only 16 months in recession, compared with more than 60 months for the previous quarter century."

   a. What were the explanations given for the Great Moderation?

   b. Does the experience of the US economy during January 2007 to December 2010 still justify characterizing this as a period of Great Moderation? Report (1) quarterly values for changes in the gross domestic product, (2) quarterly values for changes in the inflation rate, and (3) the volatility VIX Index value during this period to support your answer.

1.19. Drawing on your experience, give examples of two risks that one can easily hedge and two risks that one cannot hedge.

1.20. Download Form 10-K filed by P&G from the company's website or the US Securities and Exchange Commission's website. Answer the following questions based on a study of this report:

a. What are the different kinds of risks to which P&G is exposed?

b. How does P&G manage its risks? Identify and state the use of some derivatives in this regard.

c. Name some techniques that P&G employs for risk management.

d. Does P&G grant employee stock options? If so, briefly discuss this program. What valuation model does the company use for valuing employee stock options?

2

Interest Rates

2.1   Introduction

Gentlemen prefer bonds. Perhaps you are chuckling at our "misquotation" of the famous Marilyn Monroe movie title *Gentlemen Prefer Blondes*. In fact, former US treasury secretary Andrew Mellon made this observation about bonds many decades before the movie.[1] In all likelihood, he said this because bonds are considered safer than stocks. Corporations may miss dividend payments on stocks, but bonds are legally bound to pay promised interest on fixed dates. If the interest payments are not paid, default occurs, and the corporations are vulnerable to lawsuits and bankruptcy. However, at this stage in our presentation, we will assume that all bonds considered have no default (credit) risk. This greatly simplifies the analysis. Consequently, the bonds considered in this chapter are best viewed as US Treasury securities. Credit risk is considered only later in the book (in Chapter 26), after we have mastered default-free securities.

Most bonds make interest payments according to a fixed schedule. Hence bonds are also called **fixed-income securities**. Bonds are useful for moving money from one period to another. Does money retain its value over time? Not really. **Inflation**, the phenomenon of a *rise in the general price level*, chips away money's buying power little by little, year by year. A popular measure of the US inflation rate is the change in the **consumer price index (CPI)**. At each date, the CPI measures the price of a fixed bundle of nearly two hundred goods and services that a typical US resident consumes. Unless you are buying computers and electronic gizmos whose prices have drastically fallen because of technological advances, a hundred dollar bill doesn't quite buy as much as it did ten years ago. To reduce the cost of inflation, money earns interest. Instead of stashing cash under a mattress, one can put it into a savings account and see it grow safely.

What, then, is an interest rate? An **interest rate** is the *rate of return earned on money borrowed or lent*. Ponder and you realize that the cost of borrowing a hundred dollar bill is the interest of perhaps $5 per year that's paid to the lender. Suppose that the inflation rate is 3 percent per year, which is close to the US inflation rate in the new millennium. If the interest rate for risk-free loans is 3.10 percent per year, then borrowing is incredibly cheap, while 30 percent for such loans would be awfully expensive. Interest rates partly compensate the lender for inflation and partly reward her for postponing consumption until a later date.

There are many ways of computing interest rates. Simple, compound, and continuously compounded rates are the three basic kinds. Each interest rate concept has its own use in finance theory as well as in practice. There are interest rates for risky as well as riskless loans. The first interest rates studied in this book are risk-free rates.

How do you find risk-free interest rates? United States Government Treasury securities (the "Treasuries") are considered default-free because of the taxing authority

---

[1] Andrew William Mellon (1855–1937) was an extremely successful businessman—he owned banks, steel plants, and several other industries. He was the US secretary of the treasury under three presidents (1921–32) and introduced "supply-side tax cuts" nearly six decades before President Ronald Reagan popularized the concept. *Source*: Based on biography of Andrew Mellon in the Encyclopedia Britannica Online and on the US Treasury's website, www.ustreas.gov/education/history/secretaries/awmellon.html.

of the mighty federal government. Risk-free interest rates of various maturities can be easily extracted from their prices. We briefly explain how to do this extraction. Then we explain how the US Treasury securities market works, and we describe the bills, notes, bonds, STRIPS, and TIPS that trade in these markets. We conclude the chapter with a discussion of the London Interbank Offered Rate (libor), a key rate used in the global interest rate derivatives market.

We begin by introducing the concept of a rate of return. This, in turn, will lead us to a discussion of the three basic types of interest rates.

2.2 | Rate of Return

In finance, we constantly talk about rates of return computed from prices. Rates of return measure how much an investment has earned. For example, if you buy a security for $50 today and sell it for $52 after six months, then you have earned $2 on your investment. The rate of return earned on your investment over this time period is

$$\frac{52 - 50}{50} = 0.04, \text{ or 4 percent (when multiplied by 100 to express as a percentage)}$$

It is hard to compare rates of return unless we explicitly mention the time interval over which they are computed. We need to know whether we are computing these over six months, or thirty-seven weeks, or ninety-one days. Consequently, it is worthwhile to standardize by computing them over a year. In this case, the **annualized rate of return** is

$$\left(\frac{12}{6}\right) \times 0.04 = 0.08, \text{ or 8 percent per year}$$

A more precise value for the rate of return may be obtained by considering the actual number of days for which the money was invested using 365 days in a year (some computations use 366 days in case of a leap year). Assuming that there were 181 days in this six-month period, we find the (annualized) rate of return as

$$\left(\frac{365}{181}\right) \times 0.04 = 0.0807, \text{ or 8.07 percent per year}$$

The **capital gain**, the difference between the selling (final) and buying (initial) price, is the $2 earned on this investment. But there could be other cash flows at intermediate dates. For example, bonds make coupon payments and stocks pay dividends. If our $50 investment also received $0.50 interest at some intermediate date, then the (annualized) rate of return is

$$\left(\frac{365}{181}\right) \times \left(\frac{52 + 0.50 - 50}{50}\right) = 0.1008, \text{ or 10.08 percent per year}$$

A profit of $2.50 is made on this investment. Expenses like brokerage account fees can cut into your profit. A **profit** occurs when there's an overall gain from an investment or business activity. Businesses define it as total revenue minus total costs and record a profit if this is a positive number and a loss if it's negative. In finance, we define

$$\text{Profit or loss} = (\text{Selling price} + \text{Income}) - (\text{Buying price} + \text{Expenses}) \qquad (2.1)$$

where the selling price is the final price, the buying price is the initial price, and a profit or loss happens if the result is positive or negative, respectively.[2]

We generalize this to develop a formula for computing the annualized rate of return (which is also called arithmetic return).

RESULT 2.1

- -

Annualized Rate of Return

The annualized arithmetic rate of return is

$$\text{Rate of return} = \left(\frac{365}{T}\right)$$

$$\times \left(\frac{\text{Selling price} + \text{Income} - \text{Expenses} - \text{Buying price}}{\text{Buying price}}\right)$$

$$= \left(\frac{365}{T}\right) \times \left(\frac{\text{Profit or loss}}{\text{Buying price}}\right) \qquad (2.2)$$

where T is the time interval, measured by the number of days over which the investment is held, and Income and Expenses denote positive and negative cash flows, respectively, from the investment (Rate of return is often multiplied by 100 and expressed as a percentage).

We need some reasonable conventions regarding rounding and reporting numbers and for measuring time, which we use throughout the book. They are discussed in Extension 2.1.

2.3   Basic Interest Rates: Simple, Compound, and Continuously Compounded

An interest rate is the rate of return *promised* (in case the money is yet to be lent) or *realized* (in case the money has already been lent) on loans. There seem to be a zillion ways of computing interest. Financial institutions like banks and credit card companies have devised clever ways of charging interest that appear less than they really are. That's why many governments came up with a standard yardstick

---

[2] An exception is short selling (see chapter 3), in which selling occurs first and buying second, but the expression retains the positive and negative signs associated with these expressions.

EXTENSION 2.1: Conventions and Rules for Rounding, Reporting Numbers, and Measuring Time

To maintain consistency and to minimize unwanted errors, we follow some rules for rounding, reporting numbers, and calculations. We usually round to four places after the decimal point when reporting results. In all calculations, before reporting the numbers in the text, we retain 16 digits for accuracy. Any differences between reported results based on rounded numbers and calculated results (manipulations of the actual numbers) are due to these rounding errors:

- If the number in the fifth place is more than 5, then add 1 to the fourth digit, e.g., 0.23456 becomes 0.2346.

- If the number in the fifth place is less than 5, then keep it unchanged, e.g., 0.11223 becomes 0.1122.

- If it's exactly 5 and there are numbers after it, then add 1 in the fourth place, e.g., 0.123452 becomes 0.1235.

In some contexts, we need to round to more places after the decimal point. The context will indicate when this is appropriate.

Though we typically report numbers rounded to four places after the decimal point, the final dollar result is usually rounded to two places after the decimal. The dollar sign "$" is usually attached only in the final answer. We sometimes omit dollar signs from the prices when the context is understood.

Different markets follow different time conventions. Treasury bill prices use the actual number of days to maturity under the assumption that there are 360 days in a year. Many banks pay interest compounded daily. Swaps use simple interest applied to a semiannual period, and many formulas use a continuously compounded rate.

Most models measure time in years. If we start computing at time 0 and the security matures at time T, then it has a life of T years. If we start our clock at time t, then the life is $(T - t)$ years. We prefer to use the first convention in our formulas. Time periods are converted by the following conventions:

- If the time period is computed in days, then use the exact number of days and assume 365 days in the year (unless noted otherwise), e.g., 32 days will be $32/365 = 0.0877$ year.

- If the time period is computed in weeks, use fifty-two weeks in the year, e.g., seven weeks will be $7/52 = 0.1346$ year.

- If the time period is computed in months, use twelve months in the year, e.g., five months will be $5/12 = 0.4167$ year.

To summarize, we employ the following rules and conventions.

Rules of Rounding and Conventions of Reporting Numbers and Measuring Time

- Reported numbers are rounded to four places after the decimal point. All calculations are performed using 16 digit numbers, not the rounded numbers. Any differences between reported results based on rounded numbers and calculated results (manipulations of the actual numbers) are due to these rounding errors.

- The final dollar result is rounded to two places after the decimal with the dollar sign attached only in the final answer.

- Time is measured in years. If we start computing from time 0 and the security matures at time T, then it has a life of T years; if the clock starts at time t, then the security has a life of $(T - t)$ years.

to help customers understand interest costs. For example, in the United States, all lenders have to disclose the rate they are charging on loans in terms of an **Annual Percentage Rate (APR)**, a rate that annualizes using a simple interest rate.

There are many different ways of computing interest rates. For a certain quoted rate, the realized interest can vary with (1) the method of compounding, (2) the frequency of compounding (yearly, monthly, daily, or continuously compounded), (3) the number of days in the year (52 weeks; 360 days, or 365, or 366 for a leap year), (4) the number of days of the loan (actual or in increments of months), and (5) other terms and conditions (collect half of the loan now, the other half later; keeping a compensating balance). Rather than bombard you with a list of interest rate conventions for different markets, we focus on the three basic methods: simple, compound, and continuously compounded interest rates. Understanding these concepts will lead to discounting and compounding, which will enable us to transfer cash flows across time.

A **simple interest rate** is used in some sophisticated derivatives like caps and swaps. Money is not compounded under simple interest rates. An annual rate is quoted. When computed over several months, a fraction of the annual rate is used.

Compound interest is when interest is earned on both the original principal and the accrued interest. Banks offer interest on daily balances kept in your account. When compounding interest, divide the annual rate by the number of compounding intervals (daily, weekly, monthly) and multiply these interest components together to compute the loan value at maturity.

Continuous compounding pays interest on a continuous basis. One can view continuous compounding as the limit of compound interest when the number of compounding intervals gets very large and the time between earning interest gets very small! Example 2.1 demonstrates these three methods of interest computation.

EXAMPLE 2.1: Simple, Compound, and Continuously Compounded Interest Rates

Simple Interest Rates

- Suppose you invest $100 today, and 6 percent is the simple interest rate per year.
  - A year from now, it will grow to $106.
  - After six months, it will grow to $100 \times [1 + 0.06 (1/2)] = \$103$.
  - After one day, it will be $100 \times [1 + 0.06(1/365)] = 100.0164 = \$100.02$.
  - After 250 days, it will be $100 \times [1 + 0.06(250/365)] = \$104.11$.

- Summoning the power of algebra, we replace numbers with symbols to develop a formula for money growth under simple interest. Here $L = \$100$ is the **principal**, which is the original amount invested. It is invested at the **rate of interest** $i = 6$ percent per year for T years, where T is measured in years or a fraction of a year. In the preceding expressions, T takes the values 1, 1/2, 1/365, and 250/365, respectively. Consequently, under **simple interest**, L dollars invested at i percent per year becomes after one year $L(1 + i)$ and after T years $L(1 + iT)$. This is illustrated in Figure 2.1. Notice that the simple interest rate is also the rate of return. This is verified by plugging the values in relation (2.2) to get $(365/365)[L(1 + iT) - L]/L = i$ as T is one year.

Compound Interest Rates

■ What about interest earning interest? This leads to the notion of compounding, which involves computing interest on both the principal and the accumulated interest. We split the time period T over which we are investing our money into m intervals. Within each interval, money earns simple interest. At the end of each interval, the principal and accumulated interest become the new principal on which interest is earned.

- If the interest is compounded semiannually, one year from now, $100 will grow to[3]

$$100 \times \left[1 + 0.06\left(\tfrac{1}{2}\right)\right] \times \left[1 + 0.06\left(\tfrac{1}{2}\right)\right]$$
$$= 100 \times \left[1 + 0.06\left(\tfrac{1}{2}\right)\right]^2$$
$$= 106.09$$

- Compounding three times a year, one year from now, it will grow to

$$100 \times \left[1 + 0.06\left(\tfrac{1}{3}\right)\right]^3 = 106.12$$

- What about daily compounding that your local bank offers? With daily compounding, a year from now, the amount invested will grow to

$$100 \times \left[1 + 0.06\left(\tfrac{1}{365}\right)\right] \times \left[1 + 0.06\left(\tfrac{1}{365}\right)\right] \ldots 365 \text{ times}$$
$$= 100 \times \left[1 + 0.06\left(\tfrac{1}{365}\right)\right]^{365}$$
$$= 106.18$$

- Now consider a loan for T years. Continuing with our example of daily compounding, after 250 days (or 250/365 year), $100 will grow to

$$100 \times \left[1 + 0.06\left(\tfrac{1}{365}\right)\right] \times \left[1 + 0.06\left(\tfrac{1}{365}\right)\right] \ldots 250 \text{ times}$$
$$= 100 \times \left[1 + 0.06\left(\tfrac{1}{365}\right)\right]^{250}$$
$$= 104.19$$

- Rewriting the second line of the preceding expression with an eye toward generalization, we get

$$100 \times \left[1 + 0.06\left(\tfrac{1}{365}\right)\right]^{(365)\left(\frac{250}{365}\right)}$$

(The book's appendix gives the rules underlying these manipulations)

■ As before, we replace numbers with symbols to develop a formula for computing compound interest. Let $L = \$100$ be the principal, which is invested at $i = 6$ percent per year for T years; however,

---

[3] The appendix discusses how to write expressions involving exponents (or indexes). It also gives rules for manipulating such expressions. Notice that the APR remains 6 percent, but your investment will earn more than this at year's end. This is captured by the concept of an **effective annual interest rate (EAR)**, which expresses the interest rate realized on a yearly basis. This is given by $(1 + i/m)^m - 1$, where m is the frequency of compounding. Here, because m is 2, the EAR is 0.0609 or 6.09 percent.

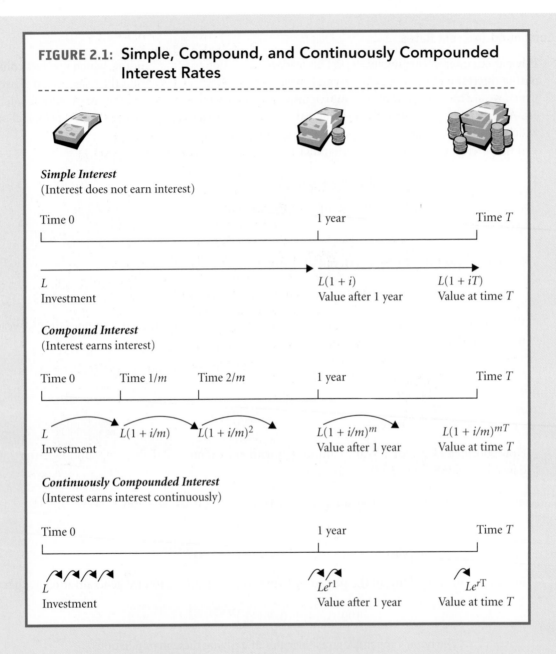

FIGURE 2.1: Simple, Compound, and Continuously Compounded Interest Rates

Simple Interest
(Interest does not earn interest)

Time 0   1 year   Time T

L
Investment

$L(1 + i)$
Value after 1 year

$L(1 + iT)$
Value at time T

Compound Interest
(Interest earns interest)

Time 0   Time $1/m$ Time $2/m$ 1 year   Time T

L
Investment

$L(1 + i/m)$ $L(1 + i/m)^2$

$L(1 + i/m)^m$
Value after 1 year

$L(1 + i/m)^{mT}$
Value at time T

Continuously Compounded Interest
(Interest earns interest continuously)

Time 0   1 year   Time T

L
Investment

Le^{r1}
Value after 1 year

Le^{rT}
Value at time T

the interest is compounded m times every year. In the preceding expressions, m takes the values 1/2, 1/3, and 1/365, respectively. $T = 1$ year, except in the last example where it takes the value (250/365). Consequently, under **compound interest**, L dollars invested for one year becomes $L(1 + i/m)^m$, and when invested for T years, it becomes (which is also shown in Figure 2.1)

$$L(1 + \tfrac{i}{m})^{mT}$$

Continuously Compounded Interest Rates

■ But why stop at 365? Why not compound 1 million times a year? Then the investment grows to $106.1836545 at year's end. Two things are happening here. As the compounding frequency increases, so does earned interest, but it grows at a decreasing rate—the money doesn't grow very fast after a while. For example, compounding 10 million times will only give $106.1836547 at year's end.

■ We can talk about "continuous compounding," where the interest rate r (we now use r instead of i to denote the interest rate) is continuously compounded. This happens when the annual frequency of compounding m becomes larger and larger but the interest rate charged r/m becomes smaller and smaller during each of the compounding intervals. In that case, $1 becomes $1e^r$ at year's end, where the exponential function e is the base of the natural logarithm (mathematically, we define $\log x \equiv \ln(x) = M$ as equivalent to $e^M = x$). It is approximated as 2.7183. Calculators have this as e^x or exp (…), denoting the exponential function.

■ But that was for one year. The dollar investment grows to e^{rT} after T years. To summarize, under **continuous compounding**, L dollars invested at r percent per year for one year becomes Le^r, and when invested for T years, it becomes Le^{rT}. (The appendix shows how this happens, and Figure 2.1 illustrates the result in a diagram.) In our example, this will give at year's end

$$100e^{0.06} = 106.1836547$$

Notice that the APR remains at 6 percent but the effective annual interest rate $= e^r - 1 = 6.1837$ percent.

This is an example of a **continuously compounded return** (or **logarithmic return**). Continuously compounded interest rates are used as an input in the Black–Scholes–Merton model. Our example suggests that continuous compounding (which gives $106.18 at year's end) is a much better approximation to daily compounding (which also gives $106.18) than is simple interest (which only gives $106).

We collect these three interest computation methods as Result 2.2.

RESULT 2.2

- -

Simple, Compound, and Continuously Compounded Interest Rates

Simple Interest

A principal of L dollars when invested for T years becomes

$$L(1 + iT) \tag{2.3a}$$

where i percent per year is the simple interest rate.

Compound Interest

L dollars invested for T years becomes

$$L[1 + (i/m)]^{mT} \qquad (2.3b)$$

where i percent per year is the compound interest rate and m is the number of times the interest is compounded every year.

Continuously Compounded Interest

L dollars invested for T years becomes

$$Le^{rT} \qquad (2.3c)$$

where r percent per year is the continuously compounded interest rate and e is the exponential function.

2.4 | Discounting (PV) and Compounding (FV): Moving Money across Time

We can use interest rates to find the dollar return or to price a zero-coupon bond. If we invest a dollar today and it continues to earn interest that we do not withdraw, then the final amount on the maturity date is the **dollar return**. The dollar return measures how an invested dollar grows over time. In real life, you can earn a dollar return by investing in a **money market account** (**mma**), which earns the risk-free rate in each period.

The inverse of a dollar return is the price of a zero-coupon bond. A **zero-coupon bond** (or **zero**) sells at a discount, makes no interest (or coupon) payments over the bond's life, and pays back the **principal** (or the **par value**) on the maturity date.

A zero-coupon bond and a mma are closely related securities; *the price of a zero-coupon bond (B) and the dollar return $(1 + R)$ obtained from investing in a mma are inverses of one another,* $B \equiv 1/(1 + R)$. Both mmas and zeros help us move funds across time. Example 2.2 shows how to compute a dollar return and the price of a zero.

EXAMPLE 2.2: Computing a Dollar Return, Pricing a Zero, and Moving Funds across Time

- Suppose that the simple interest rate is 6 percent per year. Today is time 0, and the bond matures at time $T = 1/2$ year. Then the dollar return after six months of investing in a mma is

$$1 + R = 1 \times [1 + 0.06(1/2)] = \$1.03$$

This dollar return is the future value of $1 invested today.

- Today's price of a zero-coupon bond that pays $1 after six months is

$$B \equiv 1/(1 + R) = 1/1.03 = \$0.9709 = \$0.97$$

This is the present value of $1 received after six months.

RESULT 2.3

Compounding and Discounting Cash Flows with Dollar Returns and Zero-Coupon Bonds

Consider cash flows $C(0)$ available today (time 0) and $C(T)$ available at some later date (time T). Then multiplication of today's $C(0)$ by the dollar return (or equivalently, division by a zero-coupon bond price) gives the future value

$$C(0)R = C(0)/B \qquad (2.4\text{a})$$

Multiplication of the future $C(T)$ by a zero-coupon bond price (or division by the dollar return) gives the present value (or discounted value)

$$BC(T) = C(T)/(1 + R) \qquad (2.4\text{b})$$

where $(1 + R)$ is the dollar return at time T from investing \$1 today, $B \equiv 1/(1 + R)$ is today's price of a zero-coupon bond that pays \$1 at time T, and T is the time to maturity in years. See Figure 2.2.

In the case of simple interest,

$$1 + R = (1 + i \times T) \qquad (2.4\text{c})$$

where i is the simple interest rate per year.

In the case of continuously compounded interest,

$$1 + R = e^{rT} \qquad (2.4\text{d})$$

where r is the continuously compounded interest rate per year.

You can easily extend this result to move multiple cash flows across time, which may occur at different time periods (see Extension 2.2). Example 2.3 demonstrates how to compound and discount when a continuously compounded risk-free interest rate (r) is given.

EXAMPLE 2.3: Computing Present Values Using a Continuously Compounded Rate

- Suppose that we receive \$100 after six months. Let the continuously compounded risk-free interest rate r be 6 percent per year. Consequently, $C(T) = \$100$, $r = 0.06$, and $T = 0.5$ year. Using expressions (2.4b) and (2.4d), the present value (PV) of \$100 is

$$100\, e^{-0.06 \times 0.5} = 97.0446 = \$97.04$$

- Using the notation defined previously, $B = \$0.970446$. If you invest this at a continuously compounded rate of 6 percent, you will get \$1 in 6 months. Hence we can also write the PV of \$100 in six months as $100B$.

- Notice that $(1 + R) = 1/B = 1.0304545$. Consequently, expressions (2.4a) and (2.4d) give the future value (FV) of \$100 after six months as

$$100(1 + R) = \$103.045$$

Continuous compounding will be useful in powerful options pricing models like the Black–Scholes–Merton model. If you are trying to compute options prices and you know the market price of a zero, then, as explained in the following Example 2.4, you can extract the risk-free continuously compounded rate and plug it into the Black–Scholes–Merton model.

EXTENSION 2.2: Moving Multiple Cash Flows across Time

Moving cash flows across time is a fundamental tool that we use throughout the book. One can use interest rates, zero-coupon bonds, and mma values to do this.

EXAMPLE 1: Moving Multiple Cash Flows across Time

- Suppose you graduate a year from now and expect to get a job from which you squirrel away $5,000 at year's end. Moreover, you expect a year-end bonus of $10,000. Assuming that we can commit "several sins"—(1) disregard the basic principle that risky cash flows must be discounted by risky discount rates and (2) operate under the assumption that the same interest rate applies to loans of different maturities—let us borrow against these future cash flows and use the funds to help pay your college tuition.

- Your bank offers you a loan at 6 percent interest, compounded daily. Approximating this by continuous compounding, we let $r = 6$ percent be the continuously compounded risk-free interest rate. Then the price of a zero-coupon bond maturing in $t = 2$ years is given by $B(2) = 1/e^{rt} = e^{-rt} = e^{-0.06 \times 2} = \$0.8869$ (rounded to 4 decimal places). Writing $C_1(2) = \$5,000$ and $C_2(2) = \$10,000$, discounting the individual cash flows and adding them up gives $B(2)C_1(2) = 0.8869 \times 5,000 = \$4,434.60$ and $B(2)C_2(2) = 0.8869 \times 10,000 = \$8,869.20$, whose sum is

$$B(2)C_1(2) + B(2)C_2(2) = \$13,303.81 \tag{1}$$

- Alternatively, you can add up the cash flows and then discount by multiplying by the zero-coupon bond price:

$$B(2)[C_1(2) + C_2(2)] = 0.8869 \times (5,000 + 10,000) = \$13,303.81 \tag{2}$$

Both approaches give the same answer. In the actual calculations, $B(1)$ and $B(2)$ are not rounded to 4 decimal places (see Extension 2.1).

- The equality of expressions (1) and (2) can be generalized to yield a formula for discounting cash flows belonging to a particular time period, $t = 2$:

$$B(2)C_1(2) + B(2)C_2(2) = B(2)[C_1(2) + C_2(2)] \tag{3}$$

You can express this compactly by using the summation sign (Σ). Then expression (3) can be written as

$$B(2)\left[\sum_{s=1}^{2}C_s(2)\right] = \sum_{s=1}^{2}B(2)C_s(2) \tag{4}$$

- What about extending this result to cash flows available at different time periods? Continuing with our previous example, suppose your grandparents have been saving for your college education by investing in a tax-favored education savings account. Your paternal grandparents will gift you $C_1(1) = \$12{,}000$ and your mother's parents will give you $C_2(1) = \$10{,}000$ at time $t = 1$. Assuming that the interest rate r is 6 percent, and the price of a zero-coupon bond maturing in one year is $B(1) = e^{-0.06 \times 1} = \$0.9418$, the present value of these cash flows is

$$B(1)[C_1(1) + C_2(1)] = 0.9418 \times (12{,}000 + 10{,}000) = \$20{,}718.82 \tag{5}$$

- Suppose you want to determine how much of a loan you can take out today based on these future cash flows. For this you need to compute the present value of the four cash flows, two after one year and two after two years. They have the same value, $\$34{,}022.63$, irrespective of how you add them up:

$$B(1)C_1(1) + B(1)C_2(1) + B(2)C_1(2) + B(2)C_2(2)$$
$$= B(1)[C_1(1) + C_2(1)] + B(2)[C_1(2) + C_2(2)]$$

- A generalization yields our next result.

RESULT 1:

The Sum of a Present Value of Cash Flows Is Equal to the Present Value of the Sum

Suppose that there are S securities, which provide s cash flows ($s = 1, 2, \ldots, S$), some of which could be zero. These cash flows can occur at times t ($t = 1, 2, \ldots, T$), so that the cash flow from security s at time t is $C_s(t)$. Then the sum of the present value of each cash flow is equivalent to (1) adding up the cash flows from all securities at a particular time t, (2) computing the PV of this sum, and (3) adding up these cash flows across time. This can be expressed as

$$\sum_{t=1}^{T}\sum_{s=1}^{S}B(t)C_s(t) = \sum_{t=1}^{T}B(t)\left[\sum_{s=1}^{S}C_s(t)\right] \tag{5}$$

where $B(t)$ is the price of a zero-coupon bond that pays $\$1$ at time t.

FIGURE 2.2: Compounding and Discounting Cash Flows using the Dollar Return $(1+R)$ or the Zero-Coupon Bond Price (B)

Now (Time 0)	Future (Time T)

$C(0)$ ────────────────────────▶ $C(0)(1 + R) = C(0)/B$

$BC(T) = C(T)/(1 + R)$ ◀-------------------- $C(T)$

EXAMPLE 2.4: Finding the Continuously Compounded Rate from a Zero-Coupon Bond

- Suppose a zero-coupon bond that is worth $0.90 today pays $1 after two years. Assuming that money grows at the continuously compounded rate of r percent per year, we have

$$0.90e^{2r} = 1$$
$$\text{or, } e^{2r} = 1/0.90$$

- Taking natural logarithms and remembering that $log(e^X) = X$,

$$2r = \log(1/0.90)$$
$$\text{or } r = (1/2) \log(1/0.90) = 0.0527 \text{ or } 5.27 \text{ percent}$$

Replacing numbers with symbols in the preceding expression ($2 = T$ and $0.90 = B = 1/[1 + R]$) gives us Result 2.4, which allows us to move from a notional variable (a posted interest rate) to a traded asset price (a zero-coupon bond or a dollar return), and vice versa.

> **RESULT 2.4**
>
> -
>
> ## Computing Continuously Compounded Interest Rates from a Zero-Coupon Bond Price or a Dollar Return
>
> The continuously compounded interest rate per year r can be computed from a zero-coupon bond price B (or a dollar return $1 + R$) by
>
> $$r = (1/T) \log (1/B) = (1/T) \log (1 + R) \qquad (2.5)$$
>
> where T is the time to maturity in years.

Now that you have seen how to price zero-coupon bonds (B), move funds across time (T), find dollar returns ($1 + R$), and compute continuously compounded interest (r), you may wonder where zero-coupon bond prices come from. This brings us to the Treasury securities market, where debts of the US government trade.

2.5 | US Treasury Securities

Modern finance has made **Treasury securities (Treasuries)** interesting and exciting by developing a whole range of derivatives that depend on them. Although seemingly ordinary, Treasuries are the bedrock on which the world of finance is built. Following are five reasons why:

1. Five characteristics make Treasuries particularly important: (1) these debt securities have no default risk as they are backed by the full faith and credit of the US government; (2) they trade in a market with some of the smallest bid/ask spreads in the world, which is the transaction cost of buying and selling Treasuries (only 1 or 2 basis points for the most active issues, a **basis point** being 1/100th of 1 percent); (3) their interest payments are free from state and local taxes; (4) they have low minimum denominations starting at $1,000; and (5) they offer a spectrum of maturities that range from one day to thirty years.

2. The prices of Treasuries can help us determine borrowing and lending rates for future dates. What is the forward rate for borrowing money for two years starting 10 years from today? As Chapter 21 shows, the answer can be easily determined from Treasury prices.

3. We will study options and futures that are written on Treasuries. Remember the T-bond futures that we mentioned in the first chapter? They are one of the most actively traded futures contracts. The world has become a more volatile place, and derivatives based on fixed-income securities (bonds) can be very useful for hedging interest rate risks.

4. Interest rate options pricing models like the Heath–Jarrow–Morton model relax the constant interest rate assumption of the Black–Scholes–Merton model. They often use Treasury rates of different maturities as the necessary inputs.

5. Moreover, in part of a growing trend, financial firms convert many individual loans and debts into a package of securities using a process called **securitization** and sell them to third-party investors. Your mortgage loans, car loans, and credit card loans may have been financed that way. Loan access to wider markets generates more competitive rates that benefit consumers. The interest rates on these **asset-backed securities** are determined by adding a basis point spread to comparable maturity Treasury rates. We will revisit securitization in chapter 26 and explain how it played a critical role in the financial crisis of 2007–9.

2.6 | US Federal Debt Auction Markets

When former US president Ronald Reagan was asked for his thoughts on the growing federal deficit, he replied, "The deficit is big enough to take care of itself!" No matter which party held power in Washington, D.C., the last several decades have seen government spending exceed taxes. Years of **budget deficits** (= Government receipts − Government expenditures) have led to a mountain of **federal debt**, standing at over $13 trillion at the end of the millennium (Figure 2.3 shows the level of public debt on an annual basis). This is hardly surprising. There is a natural tendency toward overspending in a democracy because elected politicians bring pork-barrel projects to help their constituencies.

Whatever the reason, the US national debt and deficit became alarmingly large in the 1990s and took center stage on the political arena. US citizens interpreted continuing deficits as implying higher future taxes. Supply-side tax cuts

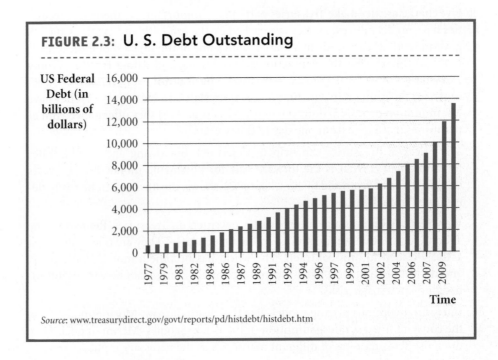

FIGURE 2.3: U. S. Debt Outstanding

US Federal Debt (in billions of dollars)

Source: www.treasurydirect.gov/govt/reports/pd/histdebt/histdebt.htm

of Reagan's era lost their appeal, and federal income tax rates were raised immediately. A robust economy also increased tax receipts. Consequently, the US government started paying off its debts at the turn of the new millennium. But the surpluses soon evaporated, and the budget deficit is back in the red.

As circumstances shape destiny, a huge federal debt has forced the Treasury to devise efficient ways of raising funds. Consequently, the United States has developed an extremely sophisticated system of selling Treasuries through **sealed bid auctions**, a model that has been adopted by many other nations. The buyers in such auctions submit **sealed bids**. These are written promises to buy a fixed number of Treasuries at a fixed price. The Treasury awards the securities to the highest bidders. In reality, these are **yield auctions**, in which the bidders specify a yield and the Treasury translates this interest rate into a price. Every year, the Treasury finances the public debt through over 150 auctions, each typically selling $10 to $20 billion worth of securities.

There were twenty-one **primary dealers** in the United States on October 31, 2011. Examples of primary dealers include BNP Paribas Securities; Barclays Capital; Cantor Fitzgerald and Company; Citigroup Global Markets; Credit Suisse Securities (USA); Daiwa Securities America; Deutsche Bank Securities Inc.; Goldman, Sachs; HSBC Securities (USA); J. P. Morgan Securities; Mizuho Securities USA; Morgan Stanley; RBS Securities; and UBS Securities. These are large securities firms with whom the New York Fed buys and sells Treasuries to conduct open-market operations that fine-tune the US money supply. These firms also actively bid in Treasury auctions, as do other direct and indirect bidders. These bidders tread cautiously because bidding incorrectly, even several basis points, can make a difference between millions of dollars in profits and losses. So players in the auction submit bids as near to the bidding deadline as possible using all available information.

Suppose you go to a Fed office just before a 1:00 PM Eastern Time auction deadline. You will see representatives of the bidders standing with heads glued to mobile telephones, holding near-completed auction bid forms, except for the yield (which translates into a price) and the quantity. At the very last minute, a flurry of activity begins, and each firm's trading desk relays the bid yield and the quantity demanded to their reps. The reps hurriedly scribble down this vital information and scramble to submit the bids as the last seconds tick away.

Do all investors in Treasuries take part in competitive bidding? No, because the Treasury allows noncompetitive bids for smaller amounts. These bids are always filled, and they pay the price determined by the competitive bidders. Historically, 10 to 20 percent of a typical Treasury auction has been awarded to noncompetitive bidders. Noncompetitive bids encourage the direct participation of regular folks in the auction process.

The quotes from competitive and noncompetitive bids are tallied, securities are allocated to the successful bidders, and the results of the auction are announced in a press conference. The *Wall Street Journal* and the other news providers carry the announcement. The process repeats itself over 150 times a year.

What about the auction itself? Are there particular auction formats that are better than others? Extension 2.3 examines the economics underlying the two main auction formats that the Treasury has used over the years.

EXTENSION 2.3: Discriminatory Auctions versus Uniform Price Auctions

Why auctions? Although Treasury bills have been sold through auctions since their appearance in 1929, long-term debt (Treasury notes and bonds) were traditionally sold through **fixed-price offerings,** where the price, the interest rate, and the maturity were announced beforehand. These fixed-priced offerings had a problem. If the terms of the offering were sweet, then many buyers would line up. If the terms were not sweet, few buyers would participate. Consequently, the security had to be underpriced to be attractive. This under pricing cost the Treasury an additional $100 million to $200 million in yearly payments. Auctions avoid this problem by letting the bidders correctly price the securities.

Auctions can be designed in many ways. In a seemingly never-ending venture, academics conceptually design and evaluate Treasury auctions to discover which (1) raise more money for the Treasury and thus cheaply finance the deficit and (2) are less susceptible to manipulations by roguish bidders and thus maintain the fair reputation of the market. Most of us frown on discrimination. Yet the Treasury used to sell securities through a **multiple price auction** (or a **discriminatory auction, DA**), in which the successful bidders paid different prices for the same security. This "what you bid is what you pay" process created a **winner's curse**, in which successful bidders (winners) paid more on average than the security was worth. The following example illustrates this phenomenon.

EXAMPLE 1: A Discriminatory Auction versus a Uniform Price Auction

- Suppose five bidders are trying to buy three identical silver cups with bids $100, $98, $96, $95, and $90.
  - The top three bids get the cups.
  - The average price is $98 in a discriminatory auction.
  - The highest bidder pays $100, which is more than the average price of $98.
  (For a summary, see Table 2.1 [Extension 2.3].)

- William Vickrey, a Nobel Prize–winning economist, came up with a new idea. In a classic paper from 1961, he introduced the concept of a **second price auction** (also called a Vickrey auction), in which the highest bid wins but the winner pays an amount equal to that of the next highest bid. This strange concoction made matters interesting. Milton Friedman applied this idea to the Treasury market. He testified before the US Congress in 1959 and argued in favor of a **uniform price auction (UPA)**, in which all successful bidders would pay the highest losing bid. He discredited discriminatory auctions because of the winner's curse as well as the potential for collusion and information sharing among the bidders.

- UPA ends discrimination and sounds fairer. But wouldn't it lower the Treasury's revenue? Perhaps not. A major lesson of finance and economics is that *the institutions matter and people's actions are influenced by the rules of the game.* Here the bidders might submit higher bids, which could lead to higher revenue than a discriminatory auction. It depends on the extent to which the demand curve under a uniform price auction shifts outward. Notice the trade-off between the extra revenue from discrimination and (possibly) higher revenue from aggressive bidding and greater participation in a UPA.

The US Treasury experimented using UPA in the 1970s, but the results were inconclusive. What about collusion? It was found in the 1980s that when Mexico moved from DA to UPA, it lowered the profits of colluding dealers. After Salomon Brothers manipulated the two-year note auctions in May 1991 (see this story in chapter 10), Friedman and other academics again clamored for a UPA. Most academic studies conclude that the UPA raises more revenue and lowers the chance of manipulation (Chatterjea and Jarrow 1998, p. 277). The US Treasury again started experimenting with UPA, was pleased with the wide participation it generated, and adopted it for all auctions after November 2, 1998.

TABLE 2.1: Selling Three Cups to Five Bidders

	Discriminatory Auction (DA)	Uniform Price Auction (UPA)
Bid 1 (highest)	100	105
Bid 2	98	103
Bid 3	96	100
Bid 4	95	99
Bid 5 (lowest)	90	95
Average price paid	98	99
Comments	Top 3 bidders get the cups and pay their bid prices	Top 3 bidders get the cups but pay the highest losing bid

2.7 | Different Ways of Investing in Treasury Securities

Bidding in auctions is not the only way to purchase Treasury securities. For example, you can buy Treasuries (1) in the when-issued and secondary markets, (2) through the repo and reverse repo markets, or (3) via interest rate derivatives. This section describes each of these alternative ways of buying Treasuries. Barring rare exceptions, these markets tend to be fairly liquid and are usually dominated by big **institutional investors** (institutions such as commercial banks, investment banks, pension funds, mutual funds, and hedge funds).

The Treasury Auction and Its Associated Markets

A week or so before an auction, the Treasury announces the size of the offering, the maturities, and the denominations of the auctioned Treasuries. The Treasury permits forward trading of Treasury securities between the announcement and the auction, and the to-be-auctioned issue trades **when, as, and if issued**. Traders take positions in this **when-issued** market, and a consensus price emerges. The when-issued market spreads the demand over seven to ten days, which leads to a smooth absorption of the securities by the market. The buyer and seller in the when-issued market fulfill their commitments after the Treasuries become available through the auction.

Newly auctioned Treasuries are called **on-the-run** and have lower spreads than **off-the-run** securities issued in prior auctions. A very active **resale (secondary) market** exists for Treasuries, giving investors further chances to invest. The timeline for the three markets for buying Treasuries is shown in Figure 2.4.

The Repo and the Reverse Repo Market

Investment banks operate a security dealership business that makes profits by trading standard securities as well as custom-made products for clients. They do this by highly leveraging both the asset and liability sides of their balance sheets (see chapter 1 for a typical firm's balance sheet). For example, believing that buying Treasuries will gain in value and borrowing Treasuries will decline in value, the firm may support $100 billion worth of purchased securities and $95 billion worth

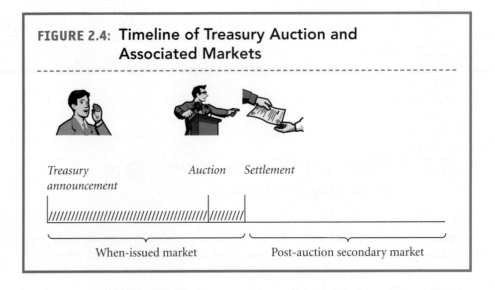

FIGURE 2.4: Timeline of Treasury Auction and Associated Markets

Treasury announcement

Auction   Settlement

When-issued market   Post-auction secondary market

of borrowed securities using only $5 billion of capital. Leverages like this are usually accomplished through repo and reverse repo markets, examples of which are given in Extension 2.4.

Partially contributing to the immense popularity of repos was the fact that they initially provided the only method of short selling Treasuries and corporate debt securities (see Extension 2.4). This short selling technique became antiquated when interest rate derivatives arrived. Derivatives facilitate the same transaction but far more efficiently. We will explore how this works in the final part of the book. Although this particular economic role of repos is now less important, the repo market still thrives and is an important element of Treasury markets.

EXTENSION 2.4: A Repurchase Agreement

Suppose that Repobank has purchased a large quantity of Treasury securities and it needs an overnight loan to finance the purchase. Repobank expects to sell the Treasuries on the market the next day, so an overnight loan is sufficient. To finance its position, it enters into a **repurchase agreement** ("does a repo") with RevRepobank (another fictitious name), who enters into a **reverse repo** ("does a reverse") transaction. The next example outlines the mechanics of this transaction in simple terms.

EXAMPLE 1: Example of a Repo and a Reverse Repo

- As per standard industry norms, Repobank takes, say, $10 million from RevRepobank and sells RevRepobank Treasury securities worth a little more. The next day, Repobank repurchases those securities at a slightly higher price—the extra amount determines an annual interest rate known as the **repo rate**. Though it involves a purchase and a repurchase, a repo is basically a short-term loan that is backed by high-quality collateral (see Figure 2.5 [EXTENSION 2.4]).

- If Repobank defaults, then RevRepobank keeps the securities. If RevRepobank **fails to deliver** the securities instead, then Repobank keeps the cash longer. In that case, the repo is extended by a day, but the terms remain the same—Repobank pays the day after tomorrow the amount it was supposed to pay tomorrow, essentially keeping the funds for an extra day at zero interest. And this is repeated day after day until the cash and the securities are exchanged. You may find that holders of scarce securities are able to borrow funds in the repo market at close to a zero percent rate of interest.

- Repos provide a way of **short selling** Treasuries and corporate debt securities. After acquiring the securities, RevRepobank can short sell them to a third party. Later, it can buy these securities in the market, at a lower price if the bet is successful, and return them to Repobank and close out the repo.

- Entering into a repo agreement is equivalent to borrowing cash and using the short maturity Treasury security as collateral. The repo rate is the effective borrowing rate for Repobank and the lending rate for RevRepobank.

■ Repos are usually for overnight borrowing and are known as **overnight repos**. If Repobank wants to borrow funds for another night, then the whole process must be repeated. Alternatively, **term repos** are set up for a fixed period that lasts longer than overnight, whereas **open repos** have no fixed maturity and may be terminated by a notice from one of the sides. The market is huge. Major players include heavyweights like the Federal Reserve Bank, state and local governments, commercial and investment banks, mutual funds, and large companies.

Interest Rate Derivatives

Derivatives whose payoffs depend on Treasury (or closely related) securities are called **interest rate derivatives**.[4] There are derivatives like futures on Treasuries

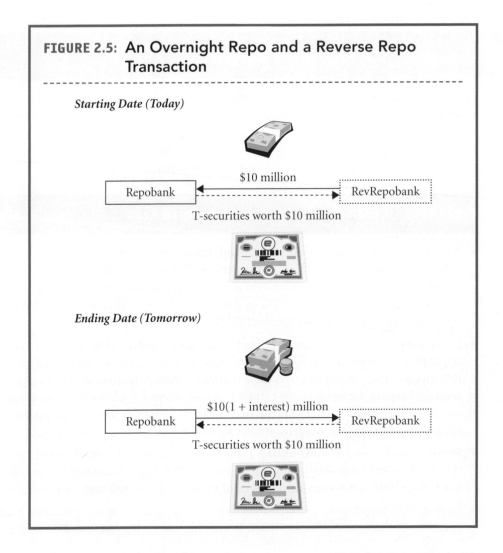

FIGURE 2.5: An Overnight Repo and a Reverse Repo Transaction

Starting Date (Today)

Repobank ←---- $10 million ---- RevRepobank

T-securities worth $10 million

Ending Date (Tomorrow)

Repobank ←---- $10(1 + interest) million ---- RevRepobank

T-securities worth $10 million

[4] Closely related to Treasury securities are Eurodollar deposits, which are discussed later in this chapter.

and options on futures on Treasuries that allow investors to place leveraged bets or set up hedges on interest rates. We will discuss interest rate derivatives and their pricing models in Part IV of the book.

2.8 Treasury Bills, Notes, Bonds, and STRIPS

The Treasury sells two types of marketable debts: (1) **coupon bonds** that pay interest (**coupons**) every six months and a *principal amount* (*par* or *face value*) at maturity and (2) *zero-coupon bonds* that don't pay interest but pay back the principal at maturity. The United States issues bonds with maturities of one year or less in the form of zero-coupon bonds and calls them **Treasury bills** (or **T-bills**). Coupon bonds have two names: those with original maturity of two to ten years are called **Treasury notes** (or **T-notes**), whereas those with original maturity of more than ten years up to a maximum of thirty years are called **Treasury bonds** (or **T-bonds**). The notes and bonds make coupon and principal payments that remain fixed over the security's life.

There is an exception. In 1997, the Treasury started selling a new class of securities called **inflation-indexed bonds** or **TIPS** (Treasury Inflation Protected Securities). These bonds guarantee a fixed real rate of return, which is the nominal rate of return in dollar terms minus the inflation rate as measured by the CPI over their life. This is accomplished by raising the principal of the bond each year by changes in the US CPI. Each year, the coupon payment is computed by multiplying the adjusted (and increasing) principal by the real rate of return.

The name "coupon" may sound strange to your ears. In days gone by, bonds had coupons attached to them. The bearer of the bond detached the coupon and sent it to the issuer, who mailed back interest payments. Coupons are rare these days. In fact, since 1983, all Treasury securities are kept in book entry form at the Federal Reserve Bank's computers, and the owner is given a receipt of ownership and receives deposits directly from the Fed. But the term *coupon* survives.

The Treasury does not issue zeros of long maturities. Still, a pure discount bond with a single payment at maturity appeals to many investors. Wall Street firms figured out a way of making money by selling what people demanded. Wall Street firms bought coupon-bearing Treasury securities, put them in a trust to make them safe, and issued claims against the principal and the different coupon payments. This was an arbitrage opportunity: the firms paid less for the original Treasury than what they collected by selling the artificially created zero-coupon bonds. In February 1985, the Treasury entered this activity by allowing Treasury securities to be STRIPped.

How do **STRIPS** (Separate Trading of Registered Interests and Principal of Securities) work? Although the Treasury does not issue or sell STRIPS directly to investors, it allows financial institutions as well as brokers and dealers of government securities to use the commercial book-entry system to separate a Treasury note or a bond's cash flows into strips and sell them as individual zero-coupon bonds. Claims to individual cash flows coming out of a Treasury security are synthetically created zero-coupon bonds of different maturities. Moreover, an investor can buy up the individual strips from the market and reconstruct the original T-bond or note. Figure 2.6 shows how thirty-one strips can be created from a newly issued fifteen-year T-bond.

A Treasury security can be stripped at any time from its issue date until its maturity date. For tracking purposes, each cash flow due on a certain date is assigned a unique Committee on Uniform Security Identification Procedures (CUSIP) number that depends on its source—consequently, they are categorized as coupon interest (ci), note principal (np), and bond principal (bp). Even though they may come from different Treasury securities, all ci due on a certain date have the same generic CUSIP and may be combined to create a coupon paying note or a bond. By contrast, np or bp is unique for a particular security and hence is not interchangeable.

The STRIPS program had been very successful:

1. STRIPS made Treasuries more attractive to investors, leading to greater demand, higher prices, lower yields, and cheaper financing of the national debt. For example, not many people would be interested in holding a thirty-year bond with sixty cash flows. But a newly issued thirty-year bond can be stripped into sixty semi-annual coupon payments and a final principal payment. These cash flows can be sold to different investors needing zeros of different maturities. For example, grandparents of a newborn may gift a strip for future education costs.

2. STRIPS help to identify the term structure of interest rates, a graph that plots the interest rate on bonds against the time to maturity. Earlier in this chapter, we talked about the benefits of knowing the risk-free rates of different maturities, an important input to the pricing of interest rate derivatives studied in Part IV of the book.

Once we get the price of a Treasury security, we know the cash flows that it generates. Particularly useful are T-bill and STRIPS prices for moving cash flows across time.

Prices of Treasuries can be found in financial newspapers like the *Wall Street Journal* and *Investor's Daily*. The quotes are collected from the over-the-counter market and are for transactions of $1 million or more. Notes, bonds, and strips are quoted in 32nds, so a quote of 93:08 (for bid) and 93:09 (for ask) for a strip maturing in one year means that $93 and 8/32 is the price the dealer will buy and $93 and 9/32 is the price the dealer will sell. These quotes are based on a par value equal to $100.

T-bill prices follow an entirely different convention. They are quoted in terms of a banker's discount yield. Before introducing this notion, it may be useful to see how the rate of return and the bond-equivalent yield are determined.

When the *annualized rate of return* (see Result 2.1) is applied to Treasury bills, we get its bond-equivalent yield. This is reported as the "ask yield" in the *Wall*

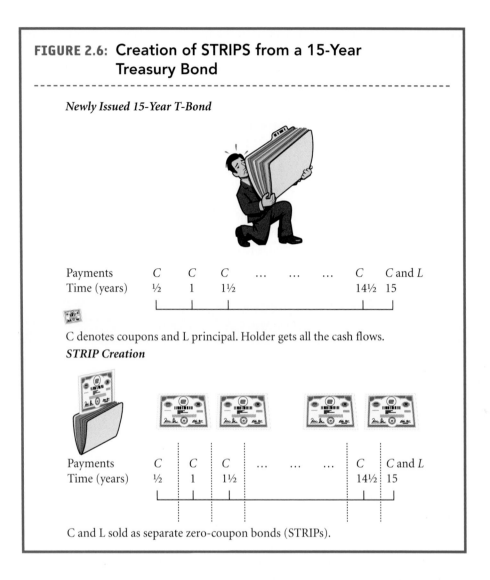

FIGURE 2.6: Creation of STRIPS from a 15-Year Treasury Bond

Newly Issued 15-Year T-Bond

Payments	C	C	C	...	...	...	C	C and L
Time (years)	½	1	1½				14½	15

C denotes coupons and L principal. Holder gets all the cash flows.

STRIP Creation

Payments	C	C	C	...	...	...	C	C and L
Time (years)	½	1	1½				14½	15

C and L sold as separate zero-coupon bonds (STRIPs).

Street Journal, which corresponds to the bond-equivalent yield earned when buying a T-bill from a dealer. The **bond-equivalent yield** for Treasury bill prices is

$$\text{Bond equivalent yield} = \left(\frac{365}{T} \right) \frac{(1 - B)}{B} \tag{2.6}$$

where B is the bill's price expressed as a bond that pays \$1 at maturity and T is the number of days from settlement to maturity.

However, Treasury bills are quoted in terms of a **banker's discount yield**, which is typically reported for both ask and bid prices. **Ask** is the price at which one can readily buy a security from a dealer, and **bid** is the price at which one can promptly sell. They are analogous to prices at which a car dealer will sell or buy a used car.

The banker's discount yield differs from the bond-equivalent yield in two ways: (1) the denominator has the face value instead of the price paid (note the 1 in the denominator) and (2) the interest rate is annualized on a 360-day basis. The banker's discount yield is given by

$$\text{Banker's discount yield} = \left(\frac{360}{T}\right)\frac{(1 - B)}{1} \tag{2.7a}$$

$$\text{or Bill price}, B = \left[1 - (\text{banker's discount yield})\left(\frac{T}{360}\right)\right] \tag{2.7b}$$

where 1 is the face value (par value) of the bill, B is bill price, and T is the number of days from settlement (the date ownership is transferred, time 0) to maturity. Example 2.5 applies these formulas to data from the financial press.

EXAMPLE 2.5: T-Bill Price Computation

■ The financial press reports the following:
  - Days to maturity 24
  - Bid 4.71 percent
  - Ask 4.67 percent
  - Change 0.01
  - Ask yield 4.75 percent

■ Using expression (2.7b) and assuming that the bill's principal is $1, the ask price for the bill is

$$= 1 - 0.0467 \times (24/360)$$
$$= \$0.996887$$

In other words, $0.996887 is the ask price of a zero-coupon bond that pays $1 in twenty-four days. Similarly, $0.996860 is the bid price of a zero that pays $1 in twenty-four days.

■ How much are we actually earning on our investment? This is given by the bond-equivalent yield (reported as ask yield because it is computed from the ask price). Using expression (2.6)

$$\text{Bond-equivalent yield (for ask yield)}$$
$$= (365/24) \times [(1/0.996887) - 1]$$
$$= 0.0475$$

This verifies the quote.

The inverse relationship between bond prices and interest rates leads to an inversion of the relation between the ask/offer and bid for interest rates. In most

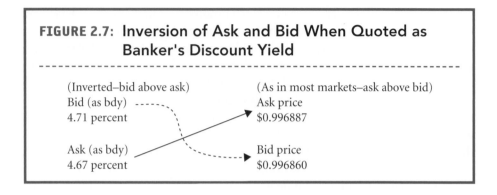

FIGURE 2.7: Inversion of Ask and Bid When Quoted as Banker's Discount Yield

(Inverted–bid above ask)
Bid (as bdy)
4.71 percent

(As in most markets–ask above bid)
Ask price
$0.996887

Ask (as bdy)
4.67 percent

Bid price
$0.996860

markets, the ask/offer is higher than the bid, but that's not the case for the ask and the bid when we quote them as a banker's discount yield. Using the numbers from Example 2.5, this situation is shown in Figure 2.7.

The banker's discount yield is important because it helps price a T-bill. Using the face value in the denominator or 360 days in the computation doesn't have any economic significance. It's just the way pricing conventions have developed in this market. Using 360 days for quoting interest rates and using 1 in the denominator (as in Formula 2.2) just make it easier to compute.

2.9 | Libor versus Bbalibor

Though US Treasury securities are fundamental to the international bond markets, there are other interest rates that are keenly followed and widely used. In particular, interest rates earned on dollar deposits in non-US banks are such an example. These rates are related to the London Interbank Offered Rate (**libor**, pronounced *lie-bore*), which is the interest rate used to determine cash payments on most swap contracts in the swap market. Swaps are discussed in chapters 7 and 22.

To understand how libor gets created, let us peek at the London interbank market. Owing to their business activities, banks and other financial institutions face deficit or surplus fund situations on a regular basis. Banks in the United States manage their cash by borrowing or lending in the interbank **federal funds market**. Major London banks handle those imbalances by borrowing or lending deposits of different maturities in the London interbank market. The most important of these deposits are **Eurodollars**, which, as you may recall from chapter 1, are US dollars held outside the United States in a foreign bank or a subsidiary of a US bank. Owing to the dual benefit of being dollar deposits free from US jurisdiction, Eurodollars have gained huge popularity among a whole range of holders, including central banks, financial institutions, companies, and retail individual investors.

Now a bank with surplus funds lends the funds to another bank for a fixed time period at the libor valid for that period. This is a **Eurodollar rate** (say, 5.02 percent per year for a three-month deposit) in case of Eurodollars. Alternatively, a bank pays the London Interbank Bid Rate (**libid**, pronounced *lie-bid*) for the privilege of borrowing money: three-month libid could be 5.00 percent for Eurodollars. These rates may change minute by minute, and they may vary from bank to bank, but competition ensures that they are almost nearly the same at any given point in time.

The British Bankers' Association (BBA) collects libor quotes from its panel of major banks for deposit maturities ranging from overnight to a year and computes **bbalibor**. For Eurodollar deposits, the BBA collects libor from sixteen banks, drops the two highest as well as the two lowest quotes for each maturity, averages the rest to compute the bbalibor, and releases it to the market shortly after 11:00 AM London time on every trading day. It does a similar exercise for deposits denominated in nine other currencies, announcing ten term structures in all. In this book, following market convention, we will use the term *bbalibor* for Eurodollar deposits.

Bbalibor is the most popular global benchmark for short-term interest rates, and it enters into numerous derivative contracts. An index is used instead of a particular bank's Eurodollar rate because an index is less prone to manipulation. As bbalibor has some credit risk, its values are higher than a similar maturity Treasury security, their difference being known as the **Treasury/Eurodollar (TED) spread**. Instead of Treasuries, many large financial institutions use bbalibor as a proxy for the risk-free interest rate in derivative pricing models. Like Treasury securities, Eurodollar interest computations assume 360 days in a year.

The Eurodollar market is now measured in trillions of dollars. In later chapters, we will study the vast interest rate derivatives market that uses Eurodollars as the underlying commodity.

2.10   Summary

1. An interest rate is the rate of return earned on money borrowed or lent. The annualized rate of return on an investment is given by

$$
\text{Rate of return} = \left(\frac{365}{T} \right)
$$

$$
\times \left(\frac{\text{Selling price} + \text{Income} - \text{Expenses} - \text{Buying price}}{\text{Buying price}} \right)
$$

$$
= \left(\frac{365}{T} \right) \times \left(\frac{\text{Profit or loss}}{\text{Buying price}} \right)
$$

where T is the time interval, measured by the number of days over which the investment is held, and Income and Expenses denotes any positive or negative cash flows, respectively, from the investment during this period.

2. There are many ways of computing interest. For a certain quoted rate, the realized interest can vary with (1) the method of compounding, (2) the frequency of compounding (yearly, monthly, daily, or continuously compounded), (3) the number of days in the year (52 weeks; 360 days, or 365, or 366 for a leap year), and (4) the number of days of the loan (actual or in increments of months).

3. The three basic methods of computing interest are simple, compound, and continuous compounding. In simple interest, an annual rate is used for the loan duration. When computed over several months, a fraction of that annual rate is used. In case of compound interest, interest is computed on both the original principal as well as the accrued interest. Continuous compounding involves paying interest on the principal and accrued interest on a continuous basis.

4. Interest rates help us find the price of a zero-coupon bond (zeros). These bonds sell at a discount and pay back the face value at maturity. They pay no interest otherwise. Multiply any dollar amount by a zero-coupon bond's price to get its present value, or divide the amount by it to get its future value.

5. US Treasury securities, whose payments are backed by the taxing power of the US government, are considered default-free. They help us determine the risk-free interest rate. They are sold through a sealed-bid uniform price auction, in which all successful bidders pay the same price as the lowest successful bid. One purchases a Treasury security by (1) trading in the auction and its associated markets, (2) entering into a repurchase (repos are short-term debts collateralized by high-quality debt securities) or a reverse repo transaction, or (3) investing in interest rate derivatives.

6. Marketable Treasury securities (Treasuries) are classified as bills, notes, and bonds. Treasury bills are zero-coupon bonds with original maturity of one year or less. Coupon bonds have two names: those with original maturity of two to ten years are called Treasury notes (or T-notes), whereas those with original maturity of more than ten years up to a maximum of thirty years are called Treasury bonds (or T-bonds).

7. Financial institutions and brokers and dealers of government securities can create zero-coupon bonds by segregating cash flows of Treasury notes and bonds and sell them to the public. These artificially created zeros are called STRIPS.

8. In the bond markets, the annualized rate of return is called the bond-equivalent yield. In case of Treasury bills,

$$\text{Bond equivalent yield} = \left(\frac{365}{T}\right)\frac{(1-B)}{B}$$

where B is the price of a T-bill that pays \$1 at maturity and T is the number of days from settlement (the date ownership is transferred, time 0) to maturity. But Treasury bills are quoted in terms of a banker's discount yield, which is given by

$$\text{Banker's discount yield} = \left(\frac{360}{T}\right)\frac{(1-B)}{1}$$

9. Besides Treasuries, major interest rates in the global financial markets include libor and repo rates. Libor and libid are the respective rates for the banks to lend and borrow surplus funds in the London interbank market. The BBA (1) collects libor quotes from major banks for deposits denominated in ten different currencies, (2) for each currency it collects quotes with maturities ranging from one day to one year, (3) computes a trimmed mean by dropping some of the highest and lowest rates, and (4) releases these rates to the market shortly after 11:00 AM London time on every trading day. This is called bbalibor.

10. Bbalibor for Eurodollar deposits (which are dollar-denominated deposits held outside the US and free from US banking laws and regulations) has emerged as the most popular global benchmark for short-term interest rates and enters into numerous derivatives contracts. Many large financial institutions are replacing Treasuries with bbalibor as a proxy for the risk-free interest rate. Many floating interest rates are set at a spread above the relevant Treasury security rate or bbalibor.

2.11 | Cases

Breaking the Buck (Harvard Business School Case 310135-PDF-ENG). The case educates students about how money market funds work and the challenges faced in managing these funds during the financial crisis of 2008–9.

Foreign Ownership of US Treasury Securities (Darden School of Business Case UV1366-PDF-ENG, Harvard Business Publishing). The case describes the workings of the US Treasury securities market and explores the implications of significant foreign holdings of US debt.

Innovation at the Treasury: Treasury Inflation-Protection Securities (A) (Harvard Business School Case 204112-HCB-ENG). The case explores the various risks as well as policy issues surrounding the introduction of a new financial security product.

2.12 | Questions and Problems

2.1. The interest rate is 5 percent per year. Compute the six-month zero-coupon bond price using a simple interest rate.

2.2. The interest rate is 5 percent per year. Compute the six-month zero-coupon bond price using a compound interest rate with monthly compounding.

2.3. The interest rate is 5 percent per year. Compute the six-month zero-coupon bond price using a continuously compounded interest rate.

2.4. The interest rate is 5 percent per year. Compute the six-month zero-coupon bond price using a banker's discount yield (the zero-coupon bond is a US T-bill with 180 days to maturity).

2.5. What is a fixed-income security?

The next three questions are based on the following table, where the interest rate is 4 percent per year, compounded once a year.

Time (in years)	Cash Flows (in dollars)
0 (today)	−105
1	7
2	9
3	108

2.6. Compute the present value of the preceding cash flows.

2.7. Compute the future value of the preceding cash flows after three years.

2.8. What would be the fair value of the preceding cash flows after two years?

2.9. If the price of a zero-coupon bond maturing in three years is $0.88, what is the continuous compounded rate of return?

2.10. What are the roles of the primary dealers in the US Treasury market?

2.11. What is the when-issued market with respect to US Treasuries? What role does this market play in helping the US Treasury auction securities?

2.12. What is the difference between on-the-run and off-the-run Treasuries?

2.13. What is a repurchase agreement? Explain your answer with a diagram of the transaction.

2.14. What is a Treasury STRIPS? What benefits do the trading of Treasury STRIPS provide?

2.15. Explain how bbalibor is computed by the BBA.

2.16. What is a Eurodollar deposit, and what is a TED spread?

2.17. What is the difference between Treasury bills, notes, and bonds? What are TIPS, and how do they differ from Treasury bills, notes, and bonds?

2.18. You bought a stock for $40, received a dividend of $1, and sold it for $41 after five months. What is your annualized arithmetic rate of return?

2.19. Using the standard demand–supply analysis of microeconomics, explain how a uniform price auction can generate more or less revenue than a discriminatory auction.

2.20. Suppose that you are planning to enroll in a master's degree program two years in the future. Its cost will be the equivalent of $160,000 to enroll. You expect to have the following funds:

- From your current job, you can save $5,000 after one year and $7,000 after two years.

- You expect a year-end bonus of $10,000 after one year and $12,000 after two years.

- Your grandparents have saved money for your education in a tax-favored savings account, which will give you $18,000 after one year.

- Your parents offer you the choice of taking $50,000 at any time, but you will get that amount deducted from your inheritance. They are risk-averse investors and put money in ultrasafe government bonds that give 2 percent per year.

The borrowing and the lending rate at the bank is 4 percent per year, daily compounded. Approximating this by continuous compounding, how much money will you need to borrow when you start your master's degree education two years from today?

3

Stocks

3.1 | Introduction

Institutions that play similar economic roles can differ widely in appearance. A farmer's market in a remote African village and a fancy shopping mall in a North American suburb are both markets. MBA degree–holding sellers of customized derivatives products and peddlers of Oriental rugs are both dealers. The man at the airport who helps you find a cheap hotel near an exotic beach and the realtor who arranges the purchase of a vacation home are both brokers. As these examples illustrate, seemingly diverse economic phenomena often have commonalities.

This leads to this chapter's theme—"unity in diversity"; here we try to understand the features common to different securities markets and their traders.[1] We introduce primary and secondary markets, exchanges and over-the-counter markets, brokers and dealers, and the bid and ask prices that dealers post. We also discuss market microstructure, a subfield of finance that studies how market organization and traders' incentives affect bid/ask spreads. We classify traders into different categories on the basis of their trading strategies. We describe how automation is transforming trading and the three-step process of execution, clearing, and settlement that is common when transacting exchange-traded securities. Next, we study the effect of dividends on stock prices and portfolios, paving the way for managing a portfolio that replicates a stock index and pricing derivatives written on it. Finally, we illustrate the process of short selling stock and margins.

The process of trading securities, the players who trade, and the facilitators who make trading possible are also present in the bond markets discussed in chapter 2. However, we discuss them with respect to stock markets first because these are the easiest markets to understand—trading of different derivatives can also be seen as extensions of this process.

3.2 | Primary and Secondary Markets, Exchanges, and Over-the-Counter Markets

As a small company grows, it needs more and more cash to finance its operations. After initial financing from founders and friends, and perhaps private equity from venture capitalists, the company becomes ready to tap the capital markets. A privately held company sells shares to the public for the first time in an **initial public offering** (**ipo**), which is the **primary market** for stocks. To issue stocks, you hire an investment banker who manages the process. Through cumbersome paperwork, publishing information brochures, and getting approval from government agencies, the investment banker burns a lot of your future proceeds in the process.

---

[1] The phrase "Unity in Diversity" is the official motto of the European Union ("United in Diversity"), Ghana, Indonesia, South Africa, and some other nations; it has also been used to describe India.

Soon after their birth in primary markets, stocks move on to **secondary markets**, where they change ownership through secondhand transactions. Exchanges and the over-the-counter (OTC) market are the two basic types of secondary markets. Traditionally, the main characteristic of an **exchange** was a central physical location where buyers and sellers gathered to trade standardized securities under a set of rules and regulations, the **New York Stock Exchange** (**NYSE**) being a prime example. But the information revolution of the 1990s changed that forever—most exchanges in the new millennium, especially those outside of the United States, do not have floor trading; instead, they have a centralized computer network that does trade matching.[2]

By contrast, any trade away from an exchange is called an **OTC transaction**.[3] The expression *over-the-counter* goes back to the early days of the United States, when banks primarily acted as dealers for stocks and bonds, which were sold at counters in their offices. There are organized markets for OTC transactions, where commercial and investment banks, institutional investors, brokers, and dealers participate. Such **OTC markets** (also called **interbank markets**) have no central location. Telephone, telex, and computer networks connect geographically dispersed traders and make trades possible in OTC markets. Exchanges used to handle the bulk of stock trading in the United States, but in recent times, organized OTC markets have taken on increased importance.

Exchanges operate under the basic assumption that if all trades take place in a central location, this provides a level playing field that leads to fair price formation. The privilege to trade on an exchange (by physically being present on the trading floor or by participating in the exchange's computerized network trading activities) comes from an **exchange membership**, also called a **seat**. The term *seat* was coined in the early days of the NYSE, when members sat in assigned chairs. Individuals own the seats. Seats being valuable assets of limited supply, they can be quite expensive, their prices reflecting profit opportunities on the floor. A seat price at the NYSE fluctuated wildly during the late 1990s and into the new millennium, reflecting uncertainty about the exchange's future. For example, seat prices reached a record high of $2.65 million in August 1999, but on August 3, 2004, a NYSE seat sold for only $1.25 million, a record low since December 1998 (see the *Wall Street Journal*, August 4, 2004). Then, in December 2005, NYSE seat prices again reached an all-time high of $4 million.[4] Although many exchanges still

---

[2] The **US Code** defines the term *exchange* to mean "any organization, association, or group of persons, whether incorporated or unincorporated, which constitutes, maintains, or provides a market place or facilities for bringing together purchasers and sellers of securities or for otherwise performing with respect to securities the functions commonly performed by a stock exchange as that term is generally understood, and includes the market place and the market facilities maintained by such exchange" (defined in Section 3[a][1] of the Securities Exchange Act of 1934 [15 USC 78c[a][1]]). The term *board of trade* means any organized exchange or other trading facility.

[3] Most OTC transactions involve a dealer who stands ready to buy and sell securities from an inventory that she maintains. The next section discusses dealers in greater detail.

[4] See "New York Stock Exchange Ends Member Seat Sales Today—Trading License Auction Occurs Next Wednesday, Jan. 4," www.nyse.com/press/1135856420824.html.

have seats, the NYSE merged in 2007 with Euronext to create a public company, **NYSE Euronext**, that has abolished seats and separately sells trading licenses.

US stock exchanges are regulated by the **Securities and Exchange Commission (SEC)**, a federal government agency whose job is to protect investors, punish violators, and prevent fraud. Before the SEC's formation in 1934, the stock exchanges were considered a hotbed of shady activity that routinely hurt the ordinary investor. Mark Twain famously said in Pudd'nhead Wilson's tale (1894), "October. This is one of the peculiarly dangerous months to speculate in stocks. The others are July, January, September, April, November, May, March, June, December, August and February." Interestingly, many folks no longer consider stock exchanges as bad or risky; rather, they are now viewed as venues where respectable investors pursue wealth by taking acceptable levels of risk. The derivatives exchanges, riding a wave of mysticism and intrigue, have easily snatched the disrepute.

All exchange-traded securities, including derivatives, must satisfy government requirements before they can be sold to the public or traded on an exchange. For example, a federal government regulatory agency called the **Commodity Futures Trading Commission (CFTC)** approves every kind of futures contract before it sees daylight. Moreover, for a security to trade on an exchange, the issuing company must satisfy some **listing requirements** in terms of the company's assets, annual earnings, shareholder interests, and audit requirements, among other factors. The NYSE has the steepest requirements among the American exchanges, and the US listing requirements are generally stricter than those in Asia or Europe.

Exchanges tend to have strict rules and regulations, codes of conduct for members, and self-governance procedures. By lowering the likelihood of market manipulation and fraud, exchanges make traders comfortable, which increases trade volume (business). No exchange likes to have a government regulator at close heels, and a good self-governance program keeps them away. Moreover, self-regulation can stave off legal actions by angry customers who may otherwise feel cheated. Self-regulation is costly, but like a vaccination, its benefits outweigh the costs.

Most exchanges also have a system of mediating disputes (**arbitration**) that handles problems early in the process and lowers the chances of lawsuits. Although small offenses may avoid detection, the big ones tend to get punished. Regulators and exchanges regularly report names of guilty individuals and their punishments. The press disseminates this information to the general public.

OTC contracts require no regulatory approval. Organized OTC markets, being an electronically connected network of spatially separated traders, have fewer restrictions than an exchange. They offer investors greater investment choices but little transaction safety. For many OTC markets, when the going gets tough, the tough may skip town—there is risk of a counterparty failing to honor his side of the contract. In OTC markets, as in life, you need to remember the adage "know your customer."

Table 3.1 lists some major exchanges and OTC markets around the world. Most securities that you will encounter in this book trade on one of the following US exchanges—the NYSE (now a part of NYSE Euronext), the NASDAQ Stock Market (NASDAQ, now part of the NASDAQ OMX Group), the Chicago Board Options Exchange (CBOE), or the CME Group (which includes the Chicago Mercantile

Exchange [CME]). The CME Group was created on July 9, 2007 when the CME and the Chicago Board of Trade (CBOT) cast aside their longtime rivalry and merged to create a single electronic trading platform and a single trading floor. The CME Group has similar plans for the New York Mercantile Exchange (NYMEX), which it acquired in August 2008.

3.3 | Brokers, Dealers, and Traders in Securities Markets

Want to buy a house or get insurance protection? Call a broker. Need a new car or planning to purchase a fancy electronic gadget? See a dealer. Because people trade at different times, and they desire to see a collection of goods to make their pick, dealers are useful. Dealers intermediate across time by maintaining an inventory of goods.

Buyers can buy from and sellers can sell to a dealer. The **dealer** sells a commodity at the **offer** or the *ask price* and buys the commodity at the *bid price*. Ask and bid prices were defined in chapter 1. (Write *a* [for ask] *above* and *b* [for bid] *below*; Ask is the Buying price for the Customer [abc].) For example, a used car dealer sets two prices: the retail (or the ask) price at which he sells cars and a wholesale (or the bid) price at which he buys cars.

The dealer earns a living from the difference between these two prices, which is known as the **bid/ask (bid/offer) spread**. In finance, **spread** has four different uses: (1) the gap between bid and ask prices of a stock or other security, (2) the simultaneous purchase and sale of separate futures or options contracts for the same commodity for delivery in different months (also known as a straddle), (3) the difference between the price at which an underwriter buys an issue from a firm and the price at which the underwriter sells it to the public, and (4) the price an issuer pays above a benchmark fixed-income yield to borrow money. These spread definitions (except for the third definition, which is more relevant in a corporate finance course) will be used throughout the book.

Paucity of information concerning trading opportunities is an impediment to transactions. **Brokers** are intermediaries who help to overcome this hurdle and facilitate transactions. They match buyers and sellers and earn commissions for this service. Brokers have no price risk because they carry no inventory and do not trade on their own accounts. Dealers face price risks because they hold inventories.

In both exchanges and OTC markets, brokers and dealers play significant roles. They earn a living by maintaining smoothly functioning, orderly markets. Many exchanges designate specialized dealers as **market makers**. They make markets by posting ask and bid prices and stand ready to trade at those prices throughout the trading day—and enjoy enhanced trading privileges for their services. In OTC markets, some dealers take up market-making functions. Brokerage and dealership are risky business—charging too much will drive away customers, whereas charging too little will wipe the business out. Risks originate from many sources:

- *Set security/margin deposit levels.* Higher margins make brokers safer, but they are costlier to customers.

TABLE 3.1: Some Major Exchanges and OTC Markets

Name	Comments
US Exchanges	
Chicago Board of Trade (CBT or CBOT, now part of the CME Group)	US exchange for trading futures and options
Chicago Board Options Exchange (CBOE)	US exchange for trading options on equity, indexes, interest rates, and funds
Chicago Mercantile Exchange (CME, part of the CME Group)	Major US exchange for trading futures and options
New York Mercantile Exchange (NYMEX, now part of the CME Group)	Major physical commodity futures exchange
NASDAQ Stock Market (NASDAQ, now part of the NASDAQ OMX Group)	Major US electronic stock market
New York Stock Exchange (NYSE, part of NYSE Euronext)	Major US stock exchange
International Exchanges	
Australian Securities Exchange (ASE)	Australian exchange created by merger of Australian Stock Exchange and Sydney Futures Exchange
BM&FBOVESPA	Brazilian exchanges
Bourse de Montréal (Mx), ICE Futures Canada	Canadian derivatives exchange
Central Japan Commodity Exchange (C-COM), Fukuoka Futures Exchange (FFE), Kansai Commodity Exchange (KANEX), Osaka Securities Exchange (OSE), Osaka Mercantile Exchange (OME), Tokyo Commodity Exchange (TOCOM), Tokyo Grain Exchange (TGE), Tokyo International Financial Futures Exchange (TIFFE), Tokyo Stock Exchange (TSE), and Yokohama Commodity Exchange (Y-COM)	Japanese exchanges trading derivatives and other securities
Dalian Commodity Exchange (DCE), Shanghai Futures Exchange (SHFE), Zhengzhou Commodity Exchange (ZCE)	Major Chinese derivative exchanges
Eurex	A futures and options exchange for euro-denominated derivatives
Euronext (part of NYSE Euronext)	Pan-European exchange for trading basic securities and derivatives
Hong Kong Exchanges and Clearing Limited (HKEx)	Asian exchange for trading stocks and derivatives
Korea Exchange–Futures Market Division	World's largest exchange in terms of derivative trade volume in 2003 and 2004
London Metal Exchange (LME)	Major exchange for trading derivatives on nonferrous metals
Mercado Mexicano de Derivados (MexDer)	Mexican exchange for trading financial futures and options
National Stock Exchange (NSE) and Bombay Stock Exchange (BSE)	Indian exchanges for trading stocks, bonds, and derivatives

OMX Exchanges (now part of the NASDAQ OMX Group)	Integrated Nordic and Baltic marketplace for trading stocks, bonds, and derivatives
Singapore Exchange (SGX)	Asia-Pacific's first demutualized and integrated securities and derivatives exchange
South African Futures Exchange (SAFEX)	South African derivatives exchange
Taiwan Futures Exchange (TAIFEX)	Taiwanese futures exchange
Tel-Aviv Securities Exchange (TASE)	Israeli exchange for trading stocks and derivatives
OTC Markets	
Foreign exchange market	World's largest financial market
OTC Bulletin Board (OTCBB)	US quotation service for OTC securities
Pink Quote	OTC quotation system for unlisted US securities
Money market	US-centered OTC market for trading very high quality bonds that mature in one year or less
Swap market	London-centered OTC market

- *Inventory to maintain.* A larger inventory provides more to sell, but it's costlier to maintain and makes the dealer more vulnerable to price declines.

- *Bid and ask prices to post.* A narrower spread means more transactions but fewer profits per trade, while a widening of the spread has the opposite effect.

- *The amount of securities to bid or offer at those prices.* A higher amount at any price exposes the dealer to a greater risk of sharp price movements.

Brokers and the dealers understand these trade-offs and finely balance risks and expected returns to survive in ruthlessly competitive markets. The setting of bid and ask prices is the most important decision that a dealer faces. Market microstructure is the subfield of finance that studies these decisions (see Extension 3.1).

There are many ways of characterizing traders in security markets. One common practice is to distinguish them as *individual investors* or *institutional traders*. For our purpose, it is more useful to categorize them in terms of their trading strategies either as arbitrageurs, hedgers, or speculators. **Arbitrageurs** seek price discrepancies among securities and attempt to extract riskless arbitrage profits. **Hedgers** try to reduce risk by trading securities and are often cited as the chief reason for the existence of derivatives markets. **Speculators** take calculated risks in their pursuit of profits; they may be classified as scalpers, day traders, or position traders on the basis of how long they hold their trades:[5]

---

[5] The CFTC Staff Report on "Commodity Swap Dealers and Index Traders with Commission Recommendations" (2008) defines a fourth class of speculators in the context of commodity markets: **commodity index traders**. These long-term investors do not bet on market direction but add a commodity exposure to their portfolios for diversification purposes.

EXTENSION 3.1: The Market Microstructure of Securities Markets

What determines the bid/ask spread? **Market microstructure**, a subfield of financial economics, seeks to answer this question. At least three factors determine the bid/ask spread:

1. **Order processing costs** are the physical costs of trading, such as seat costs, accounting and computer costs, exchange fees, security deposits (margins), and taxes.

2. The **inventory theory of trading** argues that a dealer adjusts the bid/ask spread to maintain an optimal level of inventory. To understand this process, suppose that a dealer quotes $100.00 to $100.10 for a stock but finds that his inventory is rapidly growing—everybody is selling and nobody is buying. He should first lower the bid price from $100.00 to, say, $99.95 so that the sell orders fall and the inventory size stabilizes; then, he can lower the ask price to make the stock more attractive to customers. Conversely, if the inventory is shrinking, the dealer may first raise the ask price to $100.15 or $100.20 and then raise the bid so that customer buying slows down and a reasonably sized inventory results.

3. The **information theory of trading** assumes that some traders are better informed about a financial security's prospects than others. There are two types of traders: (1) **informed traders**, who have special information and trade strategically, and (2) **uninformed traders**, who trade to convert assets to cash or to rebalance their portfolios. The dealer is viewed as an uninformed trader.

Two kinds of gains and losses come from trading securities: (1) **market gains or losses** owing to the rise or fall of the market and (2) **trading gains or losses** owing to information costs. Only informed traders make trading gains, whereas the uninformed traders make trading losses. The dealer always loses when trading with an informed trader, who knows when to buy or when to sell or when not to trade.

To protect himself from the informed trader, the dealer (1) maintains a bid/ask spread and (2) offers to trade only a limited amount at the posted bid and ask prices. The dealer can widen the spread to make it harder for the informed trader to make money. The dealer recoups losses to informed traders by trading with uninformed traders. Uninformed traders include those who read the *Wall Street Journal* and think that they are making informed trades. In reality, that information has long been built into the prices. The more uninformed are the trades, the happier is the dealer. He can actually lower the bid/ask spread when the sheep outnumber the wolves.

In summary, (1) the dealer makes zero expected profits ("normal profit" in economics parlance), (2) the informed traders make positive profits, and (3) the uninformed traders make negative profits. The dealer acts as a conduit through which funds flow from the uninformed to the informed trader.

Market microstructure theory gives some plausible, commonsense explanations for several phenomena observed in financial markets:

1. *There is always a risk of trading with someone who is better informed.* Trading on nonpublic proprietary information about a company (**insider information**) is illegal in the United States and invites jail time; however, such restrictions are looser in many other countries with well-developed financial markets. When you are enthusiastic about loading up on foreign stocks, remember that few countries prosecute insider trading restrictions as zealously as the United States.[6] Even in the United States, informed trading may avoid detection.

[6] Bhattacharya and Daouk (2002) studied 103 countries and found that although 87 countries had laws restricting insider trading, only 38 of them had enforced such laws. They suggest that it is enforcement and not just the existence of law that matters—cost of equity is reduced by about 5 percent in countries where insider trading laws have been enforced.

2. *Actively traded stocks have small spreads.* Actively traded stocks are followed by many analysts and are widely held by investors. For example, stocks of giant companies like Walmart and General Electric have a much smaller spread than inactive NASDAQ stocks in both absolute and relative terms.

3. *Prices reflect information.* When bad things happen to a company, people trade on that information and sell stocks—this information soon gets built into the price. Further trades will not be rewarded—you cannot profit from stale information. Financial economists say that *the markets are "efficient" because security prices reflect information.* (The notion of market efficiency is discussed in chapter 6.) If the markets are efficient, then why would people trade? One reason is to invest surplus funds and earn a normal return consistent with the risk–return trade-off. Or perhaps people have different information and thus different beliefs about what the price should be. When somebody gets wildly enthusiastic about an investment prospect or identifies what she thinks is a surefire winning stock, financial academics caution, "Do you think you know more than the market?"

4. *Both the direction of trade and the trade size carry information.* Buy orders put upward pressure on prices, and large orders exert greater thrust than smaller ones. Suppose you are a dealer for a small stock that trades on the NASDAQ. No analyst follows the company and nobody is interested in the stock—a hundred shares trade on an average day. Suppose you suddenly see a buy order for ten thousand shares. You will immediately infer that good things are happening to the company and increase both the ask and bid prices to protect yourself.

Owing to insider trading restrictions, informed traders operate less in stock markets and more in the less regulated derivatives markets.

These concepts are quite relevant for analyzing securities, explaining markets, and understanding trader mentality.

1. **Scalpers** trade many times a day with the hope of picking up small profits from each transaction. They are physically present on an exchange's trading floor and pay very low trading costs. Scalpers' holding periods are often measured in minutes and seconds. Market makers are scalpers. Scalpers make markets more liquid by standing ready to buy and sell at posted prices. *Liquidity* is a desirable feature of securities markets. It's the ease with which an asset can be converted to cash, and vice versa.

2. **Day traders** try to profit from price movements within the day. They open their trading positions in the morning and close them out before going home at night.

3. **Position traders** (also called **trend followers**) maintain speculative trading positions for longer periods of time. Position traders often try to identify and capture the abnormal price differences between two assets (a spread), with the hope of reaping a profit when the spread is restored to its historical values.

These distinctions aren't ironclad, and traders sometimes flit from one role to another.

3.4 | Automation of Trading

Toward the turn of the century, rapid advancements in IT gave us revolutionary products and services, for example, cell phones, the Internet, and personal computers. Exchanges, brokers, and dealers exploiting these technologies have lowered trading costs and in many cases eliminated human labor from the trading process. IT has also revolutionized trading: innovations like electronic exchanges, online brokerage accounts, and network linkages among exchanges are now commonplace. There are three levels of technology adoption in the trading process, which we briefly describe (see Figure 3.1).

At **level I**, the traditional system of trading securities involves little mechanization. Transactions take place on an exchange's trading floor. A customer phones in a trade, which is recorded by a broker and passed on to a clerk, who in turn forwards it to a floor broker. To trade bonds, options, and stocks, brokers and dealers meet at specific **trading posts** on the exchange floor. To trade futures, they meet on a polygonal area on the exchange floor called a **pit** or a **ring**.

A trade is **executed** when the two sides agree on the terms and conditions and on the price and quantity and commit to transact. Trade information is disseminated by ticker tapes. **Ticker tapes** are running paper tapes or electronic panels displaying a variety of prices, quotes, and relevant news to subscribers located both in and off the exchange. You may have seen these on television business programs: an electronic band at the bottom of the screen flashing **ticker symbols** (e.g., GM for General Motors) and prices while an anchor reads business news. This was how the process worked before the IT revolution, and they continue to work this way in some exchanges even to this day.

At **level II**, the system uses computers to cut out personnel in the early part of the trading process and to take orders directly to brokers on the trading floor. The NYSE and some futures exchanges, including the big ones in Chicago, prefer this system.

At **level III**, electronic exchanges simplify the trading process by eliminating floor trading. Although electronic exchanges started in 1971 with the NASDAQ, they really took off during the 1990s with the IT revolution. Electronic exchanges use computer terminals to display anonymously placed buy and sell orders. Traders place orders by calling up the brokerage firm or through the firm's website. Next, the order goes to the firm's order processing center, then to the exchange's computer system, where sophisticated software matches the order to execute the trade.

Level III trading has facilitated "algo" and program trading. Suppose that a trader wants to quickly construct a portfolio of one hundred different stocks to take advantage of a price discrepancy. Assembling brokers and instructing them to immediately buy precise quantities of one hundred diverse stocks can be tricky business. To overcome this problem, a computer program can be written that places immediate buy orders for those stocks. This is an example of **program trading**. **Algorithmic trading** or **algo** uses an algorithm (which is a set of rules or sequence of steps) to rapidly identify patterns in real-time market data and quickly exploit potentially profitable trading opportunities. We discuss algorithmic and program trading in greater detail in chapter 6.

Electronic exchanges are gaining widespread acceptance. Many new exchanges, such as the Boston Options Exchange, Europe's Eurex, the Korea Futures Exchange, Mercado Mexicano de Derivados, the National Stock Exchange of India, and the International Securities Exchange of the United States, began as fully electronic exchanges. Many other exchanges, such as the London International Financial Futures and Options Exchange, the Hong Kong Futures Exchange, and the Tel-Aviv Stock Exchange, have replaced open-outcry pit trading with electronic systems.

FIGURE 3.1: Different Levels of Automation of Securities Trading

Level I Automation (Brokers and Dealers Involved)

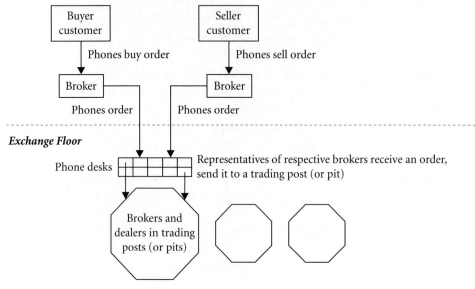

Exchange Floor

Phone desks — Representatives of respective brokers receive an order, send it to a trading post (or pit)

Level II Automation (Cuts Out Personnel, Takes Order Directly to Floor Broker)

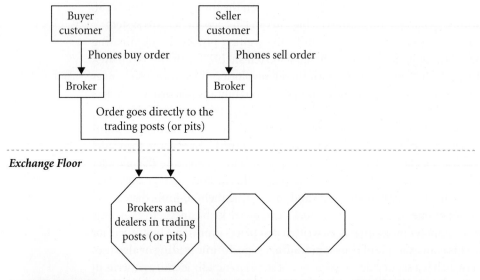

Exchange Floor

Level III Automation (Completely Computerized System – No Brokers and Dealers)

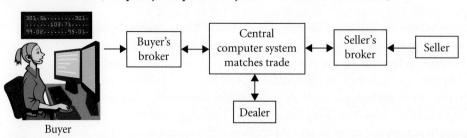

3.5   The Three-Step Process of Transacting Exchange-Traded Securities

Security trading on an organized exchange generally involves three steps: execution, clearing, and settlement. OTC transactions follow a similar approach, except that there is no clearing done by a third party (Figure 3.2 shows these three operations for a typical stock trade):

- *Execution.* As noted earlier, a trade is *executed* when the buyer (or her representative broker) and the seller (or his rep) "meet" on an exchange, physical or electronic; agree on price and quantity; and commit to trade.

- *Clearing.* Before the market reopens, an executed trade must clear through the exchange's clearinghouse. Some brokers and dealers become **clearing members**, who, besides clearing their own trades, clear trades for their clients and for nonclearing brokers and dealers. The clearinghouse **clears** a trade by matching the buy and sell orders, recognizing and recording the trade. The clearinghouse in a derivatives exchange performs the additional role of guaranteeing contract performance by becoming a seller to each buyer and a buyer to every seller.

- *Settlement.* Finally, a trade ends with a **cash settlement** when the buyer pays for and gets the securities from the seller. In the old days, this involved the exchange

---

FIGURE 3.2: Execution, Clearing, and Settlement in the Stock Market

- -

A) Execution

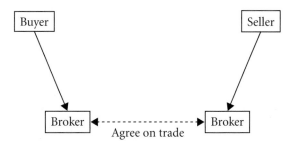

(Alternately, a dealer may replace a trader and her broker)

B) Clearing (after market closing but before market opening on next trading day)

Brokerage firm representatives meet with clearinghouse officials to "clear" (recognize and record) a trade.

C) Settlement (one or more business days after execution)

Buyer pays seller and gets ownership of the securities.

of an ownership certificate for cash or check. Nowadays, it is usually done through transfer of electronic funds for ownership rights between brokerage accounts.

IT advances have drastically reduced the time lag between these three steps. Trades can be executed in the blink of an eye and even settled on a real-time basis. While the NYSE and NASDAQ remain dominant venues for stock trading, there are more **execution choices** than ever before. Your broker has a "duty to seek the best execution that is reasonably available for its customers' orders."[7] For example, a broker may send your order:

- to trade an exchange-listed stock to a national exchange (like the NYSE), to a smaller regional exchange (like the Boston Stock Exchange), or to a firm called a **third market maker**, which stands ready to trade the stock at publicly announced prices
- to trade an OTC stock to a market maker in the OTC markets
- to an **electronic communications network** (**ECN**), which is an electronic system that automatically matches buy and sell orders at specified prices
- to another division of his firm to **internalize** the order by filling it from the firm's own inventory

You can also instruct the broker to route your order to a specific exchange, a particular dealer, or a predetermined ECN.

3.6 | Buying and Selling Stocks

Stocks have been trading in Europe for centuries. The oldest stock exchange opened in Amsterdam in 1602 with printed shares of the United East India Company of the Netherlands. The London Stock Exchange (now part of NYSE Euronext) traces its origins back to 1698, when a list of stock and commodity prices called "The Course of the Exchange and other things" was issued, and stock dealers, expelled from the Royal Exchange for rowdiness, started to operate in the streets and coffeehouses nearby (see the London Stock Exchange's website at www.londonstockexchange.com). The nineteenth century belonged to England—Britannia ruled the waves, the sun never set on the British Empire, and London was the commercial capital of the world. After World War I, the hub of commercial and trading activity shifted from London to New York and to the NYSE.

Trading at the New York Stock Exchange

Established in 1790 but acquired by the NASDAQ OMX Group in 2008, the Philadelphia Stock Exchange is the oldest stock exchange in the United States.

---

[7] This discussion is primarily based on the article "Trade Execution: What Every Investor Should Know," www.sec.gov/investor/pubs/tradexec.htm. *Best execution* means that "your broker must evaluate the orders it receives from all customers in the aggregate and periodically assess which competing markets, market makers, or ECNs offer the most favorable terms of execution."

However, the NYSE has long been the main venue for trading stocks. The NYSE began in 1792, when twenty-four prominent stockbrokers and merchants assembled under a buttonwood tree on Wall Street in Lower Manhattan and signed an agreement to trade charging a uniform commission rate. Eventually, the Big Board (a popular name for the NYSE) became the world's best known and one of the largest stock markets—its average trading volume exceeds a billion and a half shares each day. The market value of all stocks listed on the NYSE is in excess of a mind-boggling $13 trillion. The exchange heavily invests in technology and has pioneered many innovations such as the stock ticker, an automated quotation service, electronic ticker display boards, and electronic order display books.

The NYSE is often portrayed as a prototypical securities market. It has trading posts where **specialists** stand. They are dealer–broker market makers whose job is to make an orderly market in the stocks assigned to them. There could be some thirty to fifty stocks in which any particular specialist is the sole market maker. The NYSE allows **dual trading**, in which a specialist can act as a broker and as a dealer on the same day, though not in the same transaction. Many experts oppose dual trading because it leads to a conflict of interest and the potential cheating of customers by putting the customers' interests behind the specialist's self-interest. Supporters claim that dual trading helps ordinary traders by making markets more liquid. Example 3.1 discusses a hypothetical trade on the Big Board.

EXAMPLE 3.1: Exchange Trading of Stocks

Trade Orders

- Suppose Ms. Longina Long wants to buy a **round lot** (one hundred shares) of YBM, which is the abbreviation for Your Beloved Machines Inc., a fictitious company that we use throughout this book. Assume that like many major US companies, YBM trades on the Big Board. Ms. Long has opened a brokerage account and placed enough funds into it for trading. She places an order by calling up her broker or submitting the order through an Internet account.

- The broker's representative records and time stamps her order; web orders automatically record this information. Smaller orders go directly to the specialist via the Super DOT (Designated Order Turnaround) system. The representative relays regular orders to a clerk at the broker's desk on the trading floor, who fills out an order form and gives it to a runner. The runner hands this over to one of the firm's **floor brokers**, who takes it for execution to the specialist's post. **Block trades** that involve ten thousand shares or more are often negotiated away from the trading floor, with or without the help of brokers, in what is known as the **upstairs market**. Figure 3.3 shows how different orders are channeled.

- The specialist maintains a **limit order book** that records orders waiting to be filled. A **limit order** must be filled at the stated or a better price or not traded at all. By contrast, a market order must be immediately transacted at the best available price. A **liquid** stock is actively traded and has many

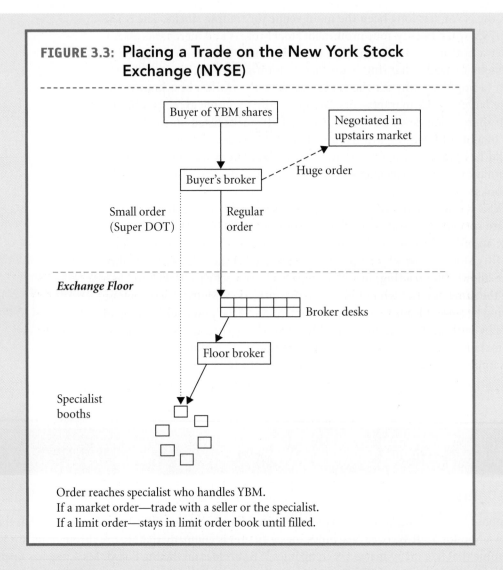

FIGURE 3.3: **Placing a Trade on the New York Stock Exchange (NYSE)**

Buyer of YBM shares

Negotiated in upstairs market

Buyer's broker → Huge order

Small order (Super DOT)

Regular order

Exchange Floor

Broker desks

Floor broker

Specialist booths

Order reaches specialist who handles YBM.
If a market order—trade with a seller or the specialist.
If a limit order—stays in limit order book until filled.

limit buy and sell orders around the market price. As such, reasonably sized stock positions can easily be converted into cash with a minimum loss of value. On the basis of outstanding limit orders, as well as what he thinks is a prudent price (he steps in to trade on his account if he can offer a better price than those in the order book), the specialist quotes a price of $100.00 to $100.10. This means that he is willing to buy stocks from you at $100.00 per share (the bid price) and sell stocks to you at $100.10 (the ask price or the offer price).[8]

---

[8] Following a tradition that goes back two centuries, share prices traded in increments of 1/32nd in the NYSE. The NYSE shifted to a decimal system in 2001 and started quoting stock as well as equity option prices in 1 cent increments. Other US exchanges implemented the same.

Trade Execution

- Suppose Long submits a *market order* and a **counterparty** is sought to take the other side of the trade. This could be another investor trading off the floor or a professional dealer on the floor. At the NYSE, if no one else arrives with the same or a superior price, the specialist steps in and sells Long 100 YBM stocks at the ask price of $100.10 per share, and the trade gets executed. Ms. Long pays $10,010 for shares plus brokerage commissions. A discount broker may charge her as little as $5, while a full-service broker will cost more.

Clearing and Settlement

- After execution, the NYSE transmits trade records via computer to a little known but powerful organization called the **National Securities Clearing Corporation** (**NSCC**) for clearance and settlement. They are sent as **locked-in** transactions, which already have trade details from buyers and sellers prematched by a computer. The NSCC also "nets trades and payments among its participants, reducing the value of securities and payments that need to be exchanged by an average of 98% each day."[9] It generally clears and settles trades on a three-business-day cycle ($T + 3$ basis). See Extension 3.2 for a discussion of today's efficient settlement system.

[9] www.dtcc.com/about/subs/nscc.php.

A specialist system is not the only way to trade. French Exchange MATIF (now part of NYSE Euronext) used to let stock buy and sell orders accumulate and then periodically set a price at which all orders would trade. Even today, some exchanges, including Euronext-Paris, open each day's trading using this method. Derivatives exchanges like the Chicago Board of Trade use an open-outcry method, where each transaction is cried out in a circular area of the exchange floor called the **trading pit**. Also, as discussed before, many older exchanges are scrapping floor trading and restructuring themselves as electronic exchanges.

Through a heavy investment in technology, the Big Board has built a system that can trade billions of shares a day. Their initial strategy was to develop everything around the specialist, as discussed under level II automation. However, being equipped with sophisticated technology that offers better value to customers, electronic exchanges are relentlessly seizing market share from older exchanges with specialists and floor trading. Faced with such threats, the NYSE took a number of bold steps: it merged with the fully electronic Archipelago Exchange (ArcaEx) on March 7, 2006, and formed a for-profit, publicly owned company known as the NYSE Group Inc. On April 4, 2007, it merged with Europe's leading cross-border

EXTENSION 3.2: Back-Office Operations in the New Millennium

Today's traders enjoy a superb trading environment with near-instantaneous execution, fast trade confirmation, speedy clearing, and near-flawless settlement. The Big Board's computers handled trading of 4.121 billion shares on February 27, 2007, without a glitch. This is a far cry from the late 1960s, when daily trading volume touching 10 million shares overwhelmed the *cages* (a popular nickname for the back-office system) of Wall Street firms and the NYSE had to shut down to clear the paperwork backlog.

Solution to the paperwork crisis involved holding all paper stock certificates in a central location and the establishment of the Central Certificate Service (CSS) in 1968, which eliminated physical handling and enabled electronic transfer of securities. CSS was succeeded by the **Depository Trust Company** (**DTC**) in 1973, which was reorganized as a subsidiary of the newly created **Depository Trust and Clearing Corporation** (**DTCC**) in 1999. The world's largest post-trade financial services company, DTCC is a user-owned company that, through its subsidiaries, provides clearing and settlement services for equities, fixed income securities, and over-the-counter derivatives.

A typical stock trade cleared and settled by DTCC's subsidiaries goes through the following process: "The post-trade clearance and settlement cycle begins on the date the trade is executed. On this date trade details are electronically transmitted to its subsidiary NSCC for processing, the majority of which are in real-time."[10] The **National Securities Clearing Corporation** (**NSCC**) was established in 1976 to provide clearing, settlement, risk management, and central counterparty services.

Trade Date (T)

Of equity transactions, 99.9 percent are sent as "locked-in" trades, which means that the marketplace has already compared them at the time of execution, confirming all details, including share quantity, price, and security. NSCC sends to participants automated reports, which are legally binding documents that show trade details. These reports confirm that transactions have entered the clearance and settlement processing stream.

T+1

NSCC's guarantee of settlement generally begins midnight between $T+1$ and $T+2$. At this point, NSCC steps into the middle of a trade and assumes the role of a central counterparty, taking on the buyer's credit risk and the seller's delivery risk. This guarantee eliminates uncertainty for market participants and inspires public confidence.

T+2

NSCC issues broker-dealers summaries of all compared trades, including information on the net positions of each security due or owed for settlement.

T+3

$T+3$ is settlement—the delivery of securities to net buyers and payments to net sellers. Broker-dealers instruct their settling banks to send or receive funds (through the Federal Reserve System) to and from DTC as NSCC's agent. Securities generally do not physically change hands because ownership is electronically recorded.

---

[10] www.dtcc.com/about/business/tplus3.php.

exchange, Euronext, to create the world's largest exchange group, NYSE Euronext. The NYSE has positioned itself to survive and thrive in this new world order.

Over-the-Counter Trading

Over-the-counter markets, along with regional exchanges, have always provided the major venue for trading small stocks and other securities that could not be listed on the Big Board. Since the 1970s, NASDAQ has been considered the major OTC market in the United States. However, a history on NASDAQ's website (www.nasdaq.com) shows how the distinction between exchanges and OTC markets can sometimes get blurred:

- *Formation of the SRO NASD.* The Securities Exchange Act of 1934 led to the creation of the Securities Exchange Commission and the self-regulatory organization the **National Association of Securities Dealers** (**NASD**), entrusted with the job of regulating the US securities industry. A **self-regulatory organization** (**SRO**) is made up of members of an industry or a profession and exercises some regulatory authority over it.

- *Launching of the NASDAQ, which became the first electronic exchange.* In 1971, NASD launched the **National Association of Securities Dealers Automated Quotations**, or **NASDAQ**, pronounced "naz-dack"). NASDAQ was a successor to OTC trading and was referred to as the OTC for many years. Initially, it was merely a computer bulletin board system that listed stock price quotes. It did not connect buyers and sellers. Actual trading took place over the telephone. Over the years, it became more of a stock market by adding automated trading systems. By the late 1980s, NASDAQ had evolved into the world's first true electronic stock exchange.

- *The SRO moves out of the NASDAQ.* In 2000, the NASD began divesting itself of the NASDAQ, which became a part of the publicly traded company the **NASDAQ Stock Market Inc**. (**NASDAQ**). NASDAQ is a registered national securities exchange in the United States for NASDAQ-listed securities.

- *The new SRO.* In 2007, the NASD and the member regulation, enforcement, and arbitration functions of the NYSE were consolidated to form a new SRO, the **Financial Industry Regulatory Authority** (**FINRA**).

- *The OTC market.* Following the Penny Stock Reform Act of 1990, the **OTC Bulletin Board** (**OTCBB**) began operations as "a regulated quotation service that displays real-time quotes, last-sale prices, and volume information in over-the-counter (OTC) equity securities."[11]

- *NASDAQ OMX Group.* In 2008, the NASDAQ Stock Market completed the purchase of a Swedish–Finnish financial company (that controlled seven Nordic and Baltic stock exchanges) to form the NASDAQ OMX Group.

Subsequently, the OTC market in the United States has shifted to the OTCBB and the Pink Quote OTCBB, which has expanded over the years, bringing greater

---

[11] www.otcbb.com/aboutOTCBB/overview.stm.

transparency to the OTC equities market. Only market makers can quote securities in the OTCBB, and FINRA rules prevent them from collecting any fees for this service. OTCBB displays market data through vendor terminals and websites. The **Pink Quote** (formerly known as Pink Sheets owing to the color of the paper on which the quotes used to be printed) is an electronic system that displays quotes from broker-dealers for some of the riskiest stocks trading in the OTC markets. The SEC website cautions potential traders, "with the exception of a few foreign issuers, the companies quoted in Pink Quote tend to be closely held, extremely small and/or thinly traded. Most do not meet the minimum listing requirements for trading on a national securities exchange. . . . Many of these companies do not file periodic reports or audited financial statements with the SEC, making it very difficult for investors to find reliable, unbiased information about those companies."[12] Caveat emptor, or "buyer beware," is the guiding principle in this market.

Alternative Trading Systems: Dark Pools and Electronic Communications Networks

The technology revolution has introduced securities trading in venues that are opaque. These new trading venues are called *alternative trading systems* (ATS). ATS such as dark pools and electronic communications networks (ECNs) are SEC-approved non-exchange-based markets for trading securities. Such nonexchange trading venues are a result of the SEC's 1998 **Regulation ATS** (Regulation of Exchanges and Alternative Trading Systems).[13]

Dark pools (or **dark pools of liquidity**) have several features. First, they are secretive trading networks that do not send an order directly to an exchange or display it in a limit order book. Second, an interested trader either negotiates with a potential counterparty or gets matched with one by the dark pool. Third, the market is a near-exclusive domain for institutional players with large orders. National exchanges like NYSE Euronext and NASDAQ Stock Market also route some of their orders to dark pools. A May 8, 2008 article in the *Wall Street Journal* titled "Boom in 'Dark Pool' Trading Networks Is Causing Headaches on Wall Street" reported the existence of forty-two active dark pool networks that accounted for about 10 percent of daily trading volume in the United States as compared to just

---

[12] www.sec.gov/answers/pink.htm.

[13] Regulation ATS defines an *alternative trading system* "as any system that: (1) constitutes, maintains, or provides a marketplace or facilities for bringing together purchasers and sellers of securities or for otherwise performing with respect to securities the functions commonly performed by a stock exchange under Exchange Act Rule 3b-16; and (2) does not set rules governing the conduct of subscribers other than the conduct of such subscribers' trading on such organization, association, person, group of persons, or system, or discipline subscribers other than by exclusion from trading." It defines (see footnote 38 of Reg ATS) a *crossing network* as a system "that allows participants to enter unpriced orders to buy and sell securities. Orders are crossed at specified times at a price derived from another market" (www.sec.gov/rules/final/34-40760.txt).

seven dark pools and less than 1 percent of the volume in 2003. Another article titled "Watch Out for Sharks in Dark Pools" (*Wall Street Journal*, August 19, 2008) warns about the "higher risk of shark encounters" for institutional investors in dark pools.

ECNs are alternate trading systems that are registered with the SEC as broker-dealers. An ECN's participants are subscribers, which include institutional investors, broker-dealers, and market makers. Individual traders can indirectly participate by opening an account and submitting trades through a broker-dealer subscriber. ECNs primarily trade stocks and currencies. Trades are usually submitted as limit orders, which get executed when the ECN matches buy and sell orders according to some protocol. If no matching order is found, an ECN may send it to another market center for execution. Unlike a dark pool, the orders are publicly displayed to all subscribers.

Founded in 1969 to provide electronic trading for institutions, Institutional Networks (Instinet) has been a pioneer in electronic trading and it became the first ECN in 1997. The NASDAQ (founded in 1971) may be considered an early ECN. ECNs were formally recognized and approved in 1998 when the SEC introduced Regulation ATS. By slashing trading fees and providing better execution, ECNs have enjoyed mind-boggling growth. For example, BATS Trading (Better Alternative Trading System), an ECN owned by eleven investment banks that was founded in June 2005, has become the third largest equity market in the United States after the NYSE Euronext and NASDAQ OMX.

3.7 | Dollar Dividends and Dividend Yields

"All men are ready to invest their money, but most expect dividends," observed T. S. Eliot in *Choruses from the Rock* in 1934. As Eliot observed, **dividend** payments in the form of cash (**cash dividend**) or additional shares (**stock dividend**) are a time-honored way for companies to reward their shareholders. For dividend payments, the ex-dividend date is an important day. If you buy the stock before the **ex-dividend date**, you get the share and the dividend (buying stock **cum-dividend**); however, if you buy it on or after this date, then you get the stock without the dividend (buying stock **ex-dividend**).

Let us analyze the behavior of the stock price on the ex-dividend date. Suppose the cum-dividend stock price is $100 and the company pays a $2 dividend. Then, we claim that the ex-dividend stock price should be $98. Why? If it were not, profit-hungry traders would take advantage of any deviation, and as profits and losses occur, this trading activity eventually eliminates the discrepancy from the market price.

To see how this works, suppose the ex-dividend stock price is $99 instead. Then, clever traders will buy this stock just before it goes ex-dividend. Their $100 investment will immediately become $101 (ex-dividend stock price $99 plus dividend worth $2), which they can sell and make $1 in instant profit. Conversely, if the stock price falls by more than $2, say, it falls to $97 after the stock goes ex-dividend, then the traders can "go short" (borrow and sell the stock) and buy back the stock after it goes ex-dividend, locking in $1 as instant profits. In this way, $98 is the only ex-dividend stock price consistent with no riskless profit opportunities.

We formalize this observation as a result.

RESULT 3.1

- -

The Relation between a Stock's Price Just Before and After It Goes Ex-Dividend

In a market free of riskless profit opportunities,[14]

$$S_{CDIV} = S_{XDIV} + \text{div} \qquad (3.1)$$

where S_{CDIV} is stock price cum-dividend, S_{XDIV} is stock price ex-dividend, and div is the amount of the dividend.

Dividends are paid in dollars. However, to compare dollar dividends across stocks with different valuations, one computes dividend yields. A **dividend yield** is the dividend expressed as a fraction of stock price. In this example, the dividend yield is $(2/98) = 0.0204$ or 2.04 percent. Dividing by the stock price normalizes the dollar dividend and makes a comparison possible across stocks on an apples-to-apples basis.

The dividend yield is also useful when dealing with **stock indexes** like the Standard and Poor's 500 Index (S&P 500), which is a weighted-price average of five hundred major US stocks (indexes are discussed in more detail in chapter 6). Accounting for hundreds of dividends (near two thousand dividends in the case of the S&P 500) and adjusting the index's value accordingly are daunting tasks. A simple technique for making this adjustment using the dividend yield involves the following steps: (1) add up all the dividends paid over the year and express this sum as a percentage of the index value generating a dividend yield, and call it δ; (2) assume that δ is paid out over the year on a continuous basis, proportional to the level of the index; and (3) assume that the dividend gets continuously reinvested in the index so that the index grows in terms of the number of units. An initial investment of one unit in this index then becomes e^{δ} units after one year and $e^{\delta T}$ units after T years. We illustrate this computation with Example 3.2.

---

[14] Later, we will call this an *arbitrage opportunity*. Formally, this result also depends on the stock price process having a continuous sample path (see Heath and Jarrow 1988). Of course, this result also depends on the market satisfying the standard frictionless and competitive market assumptions that are introduced in later chapters.

EXAMPLE 3.2: Dividend Yields

- Suppose that a fictitious stock index named "INDY Index" stands at 1,000 on January 1 and has a dividend yield of $\delta = 0.06$ or 6 percent per year. Assume that dividends are paid $m = 3$ times a year, where each payment is $\delta/m = 0.02$ times INDY's price at the dividend payment date. Let us buy one unit of the index "INDY Spot."

- Four months later, INDY stands at 1,100. The dividend payment is 0.02 times this amount, which equals 22. As we reinvest this dividend, the amount of the dividend is irrelevant—all we need to know is that we have $1 \times 1.02 = 1.02$ units of the index from now onward.

- Four more months later, we will get another 2.00 percent of the index level as a dividend. Because we were previously holding 1.02 units of INDY Spot, we now have $1.02^2 = 1.0404$ units of INDY Spot. Similarly, at the end of the year, we have $1.02^3 = 1.061208$ units of the index.

- Next, we modify the payout frequency and assume that the dividend is paid continuously and plowed back into the portfolio after each payment. Here an investment of one unit of INDY Spot will be worth $e^{\delta T}$ units after T years (see appendix A). Eight months later, we have

$$e^{\delta T} = e^{[0.06 \times (2/3)]} = 1.040811$$

units of the index.

This property is restated as Result 3.2.

RESULT 3.2

Valuing an Asset Paying a Continuously Compounded Dividend Yield

Consider an asset that pays a continuously compounded dividend yield of δ per year, which is reinvested back in the asset. Then, a unit investment in the asset today grows to $e^{\delta T}$ units after T years.

Note that Result 3.2 gives a quantity adjustment to the stock price to incorporate a dividend payment, while Result 3.1 is a price adjustment. These two modifications will be used later in the book when considering stocks paying dividends.

3.8 | Short Selling Stocks

There are two ways of selling shares: selling a stock from one's existing portfolio and selling short a share that one does not own. The first transaction is as straightforward as stock buying, whereas the second involves a more complex procedure. A **short seller** borrows shares from an existing stockholder and then sells them. He has the obligation to buy back the shares in the future and return them to the lender. Moreover, he owes the lender any dividends that the company pays.

Interestingly, the act of short selling artificially creates more long shares than were originally issued in the primary market. Later in the book, you will see that this can become a critical factor in market-manipulation trading schemes.

A stock buyer is **bullish** because she expects that the stock will go up in value. A stock seller is **bearish** because he expects the stock to fall in value. A short seller is much more aggressive in his bearish stance, unlike a seller, who simply gets rid of a stock. A short seller bets on his negative view by undertaking a fairly risky trade, which could be quite dangerous if the bet goes wrong. Chapter 10 discusses an example in which a manipulator corners the market and squeezes the shorts.

To see how short selling works, let's walk through a short sell example (Example 3.3).

EXAMPLE 3.3: Short Selling

- "Typically when you sell short, your brokerage firm loans you the stock. The stock you borrow comes from either the firm's own inventory, the margin account of other brokerage firm clients, or another lender," informs an article on the SEC's website.[15]

- Suppose Mr. Oldham owns one hundred shares of BUG (Boring Unreliable Gadgets, a fictitious company name), which are held in his account at Mr. Brokerman's firm. To make them available for short selling, the shares are held in "street name." Oldham doesn't gain anything from this—he is just helping Mr. Brokerman earn some commissions. For simplicity, let's assume that Mr. Brokerman is the only broker in town.

- Brokerman borrows one hundred shares from Oldham, lends them to Shorty Stock, and helps Shorty sell them short to Mr. Newman (see Figure 3.4). In the future, Shorty has to buy one hundred BUG shares, no matter what the price is, and give them back to Oldham. He owes any dividends paid over this period to Brokerman, who credits them to Oldham's account.

- The market is now long two hundred and short one hundred BUG stocks. Still, from BUG's perspective, there are only one hundred outstanding shares owned by Newman. The other one hundred shares held long by Oldham and the one hundred shares short sold by Shorty Stock are artificial creations, for they cancel one another. *Newman gets dividends from BUG and has the voting rights.*

- Strangely, Oldham's *original shares became artificial shares* during the short selling process. They are Shorty Stock's babies, which he has to look after. Thus Shorty has to match any cash dividends, stock dividends, and so on, that Oldham would have rightfully received.

- Dividends lower a stock's value and benefit Shorty Stock because he can now buy them more cheaply. A dollar dividend on a $50 stock will lower its value to $49, which will help Shorty earn a dollar if he now buys back the stock. Paying Oldham this dollar will keep everyone happy by making things fair.

[15] "Division of Market Regulation: Key Points about Regulation SHO" describes the short selling process for retail customers (see www.sec.gov). Before July 6, 2007, the SEC allowed short selling only when the last trade was at a price higher than the previous (this would be called an **uptick**) or when the last trade was at the same price as the previous, which in turn was higher than the previous (a **zero uptick**). Rules and regulations governing short selling in the United States remain in a state of flux and may undergo changes in the future.

- The only thing that Oldham really loses is voting rights because BUG will not recognize an extra owner. He doesn't mind that, unless he is planning to thrust major changes on BUG through proxy fights.

FIGURE 3.4: Short Selling Example

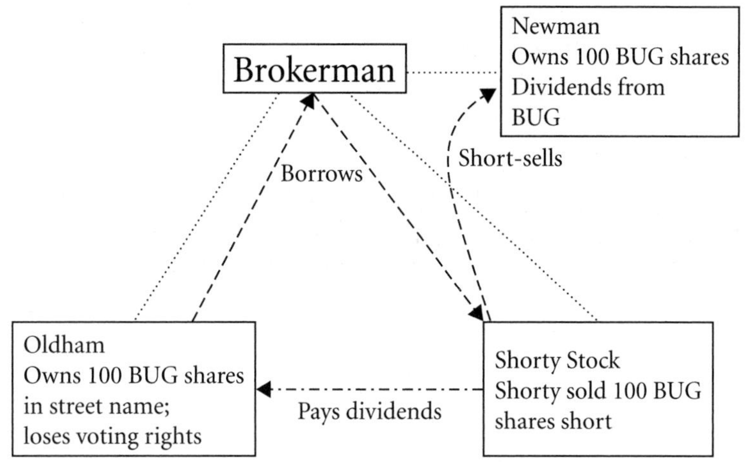

3.9 | Margin: Security Deposits That Facilitate Trading

The word *margin* has many meanings. In economics, the terms *margin* and *marginal* are often used to denote what happens as a result of a small or unit change. In accounting, the term *profit margin* (of a business) refers to the amount by which revenues exceed costs. In financial markets, **margin** means "a sum deposited by a speculator with a broker to cover the risk of loss on a transaction on account; now esp. in to buy (also trade, etc.) on margin" (according to the Oxford English Dictionary Online). Margins and collaterals are fundamental to any security market transaction involving explicit or implied borrowing.

Let's consider some examples:

- *Buying stocks on borrowed funds.* You decide to *leverage* (usually called **gearing** in Europe) your portfolio to increase your potential returns. Suppose you invest $10,000 of your own funds and take a loan of $8,000 from your broker to buy securities worth $18,000. You must open a **margin account** (also known as a **cash and margin account**) with your broker. Your stock investment of $10,000 is the margin or collateral, which acts like a security deposit. Now, a 10 percent return on your leveraged portfolio will be $1,800 earned on your investment, an

18 percent return. But leverage cuts both ways because losses also get magnified. Your actual return is lower because the broker charges you interest on the daily balance of your loan until you pay him back.

■ *Short selling stocks.* A short seller must also open a margin account. The broker requires you to keep the proceeds from the short selling plus additional funds as margin in this account. Remember that to short, you borrowed the stock first.

Before initiating a trade that requires margin, you must put up the **initial margin**. This could be in the form of cash or high-quality, low-risk securities. For the broker's protection, there is a **maintenance margin requirement**: the minimum amount that you must maintain in the account to keep it open. If your position loses value and the margin account balance declines to this thresh-old level, the broker will issue a **margin call** that requires you to promptly pro-vide enough cash (maintenance margin is always in the form of cash) to restore your account balance to the maintenance margin level. If you fail to do this, the broker liquidates your portfolio. Extension 3.3 shows how margin account adjustments work.

EXTENSION 3.3: Margin and Stock Trading

As a result of the great stock market crash of 1929, the US government would like to control the level of stock speculation and has entrusted the Federal Reserve Board with the job of setting minimum margin require-ments for securities trading. The exchanges and brokerage firms may set them at even higher (but not lower) levels. However, the real role of margin in financial transactions is to minimize counterparty credit risk.

Currently the Fed sets the initial margin requirement at 50 percent and the maintenance margin at 25 per-cent for stocks (and convertible bonds). This means that when initiating a margin trade, you must come up with at least 50 percent of your own funds and finance the rest with a loan from your broker. Your purchased securities will appear with a credit sign and the loan with a debit mark in your brokerage account, and the broker will charge interest on it. As it is a **secured loan** (a low-risk loan backed by collateral; the market value of the stock is much more than the amount borrowed), your broker will probably charge the **call loan rate** (or **broker's call**) and add a slight premium. Adding a spread to the benchmark bbalibor rate usually determines the **broker loan rate**. It is regularly published (along with other interest rates) in the "Money and Investing" section of the *Wall Street Journal* and in the business sections of many other newspapers. The following for-mula is used for margin computations.

Formula 1 (EXTENSION 3.3) Margin Computation for Stock Trading

The margin (or security deposit) computation in connection with buying stocks on margin (by taking a loan from a broker) or short selling is given by the formula

$$\text{Margin} = [(\text{Market value of assets} - \text{Loan}) / \text{Market value of assets}]$$

If maintenance margin is 25 percent, then your equity must be at least 25 percent of the portfolio value. If your equity has dropped below this level, you must respond to a margin call, deposit additional funds, and bring the equity back to the 25 percent level. Your firm may set its own margin requirements (often called "house requirements") at a higher level, say, 40 percent, for maintenance margin.

Margin adjustments can get very complicated (see Sharpe, Alexander, and Bailey 1999). The following example illustrates the computations involved.

EXAMPLE 1: Margin Account Adjustments for Stock Trading

Buying Stocks on Margin

- Suppose you buy two hundred YBM stocks at $100 each. The purchase price is $20,000, and you decide to borrow 50 percent of this amount, $10,000, from your broker. Your investment is $10,000. By our formula, initial margin is given by

$$(20,000 - 10,000)/20,000 = 0.5 \text{ or } 50 \text{ percent}$$

- Suppose YBM goes up to $110. Then
  - the market value of your assets is $200 \times 110 = \$22,000$
  - the loan amount is still $10,000
  - the investment in your account is (Market value of assets − Loan) = 22,000 − 10,000 = $12,000
  - the margin in your account = 12,000/22,000 = 0.5455

- Suppose YBM goes down to $60. Then
  - the market value of the portfolio is $200 \times 60 = \$12,000$, and your investment is 12,000 − 10,000 = $2,000
  - the margin = 2,000/12,000 = 0.1667
  - you will receive a margin call to come up with more cash, an extra $1,000, so that your margin meets the 25 percent requirement

Margin Account for a Short Seller

- Suppose you decide to sell YBM short instead and hope to use the $20,000 in proceeds to buy a new red car. However, the broker not only refuses to let you touch any of this money but also requires you to deposit an additional 50 percent, or $10,000, into your margin account. Isn't this outrageous?

- If you think carefully, the broker's actions are entirely justified. Consider what would happen if he keeps just $20,000 and the stock price goes up by just 1 cent. Your account now has a negative value of $-200 \times 100.01 + 20,000 = -\$2$. The 50 percent initial margin requirement provides the cushion he needs. Whereas a stock buyer may or may not open a margin account, a short seller is always required to do so.

- In contrast to a regular stock purchase, a short sale involves an initial sell and a subsequent buy. Consequently, any increase in the stock price will increase the liability and eat up margin in your account.

3.10 | Summary

1. This chapter has two themes: a study of securities trading in general and stock trading in particular. Institutional details matter in finance. Stock trading is the easiest type to understand, and the trading of different derivatives can be seen as extensions to this process.

2. Stocks first trade in primary markets and then in secondary markets.

3. Exchanges were characterized by central physical locations where buyers and sellers gathered to trade. Nowadays, many exchanges are completely electronic and have a central computer executing the trades.

4. Any trade away from an exchange is called an over-the-counter transaction. There are organized OTC markets (interbank markets), which are diffused networks of buyers and sellers, brought together by telecommunication connections.

5. Brokers match buyers and sellers and earn commissions for this service. Dealers trade on their own account and survive by posting a bid/ask spread.

6. Traders may be classified into three categories: hedgers who use securities for risk reduction, speculators who accept risky trades with profit expectations, and arbitrageurs who try to find price discrepancies and extract riskless arbitrage profits with strategies like buying low and selling high. Speculators can be further distinguished as scalpers, day traders, and position traders on the basis of how long they hold their trades.

7. The IT revolution has given us online brokerage accounts, electronic exchanges, and network links among exchanges and has equipped individual investors with unprecedented resources. Electronic exchanges minimize human involvement in the trading process and have eliminated floor trading altogether.

8. Security trading in an organized exchange generally involves three fundamental steps: execution, clearing, and settlement. There are more execution choices today than ever before. A trade may be sent to a national exchange, to a smaller regional exchange, to a third market maker, to a market maker in the OTC market, to an alternative trading system such as an electronic communications network, or to another division of the firm.

9. The NYSE is a prototypical securities market. Much of the trading is carried out on the exchange floor. Broker-dealers called specialists stand by their trading posts and help maintain an orderly market for trading stocks. Regulatory problems and competition from electronic exchanges forced NYSE to abandon its traditional model. It merged with an electronic exchange and demutualized and restructured itself as a for-profit company.

10. Dividend payments are a time-honored way of rewarding stock investors. When the stock goes ex-dividend, the cum-dividend stock price equals the ex-dividend stock price plus the dividend.

11. The concept of continuously compounded interest can be used to study an investment in a portfolio that mimics the cash flows from a stock index. Consider one unit investment in an asset that pays dividends according to a continuously

compounded yield δ per year, which is reinvested back in the asset (assume dividend δ/m is paid and compounded m times per year, where m becomes infinitely large). Then, after T years, the portfolio will contain $e^{\delta T}$ units of the asset.

12. A short seller borrows shares held in street name and sells them short. The original owner loses voting rights, and the short seller compensates the owner for dividends.

13. Although the concept of margin is similar for trading different securities, the transactions vary. Traders buying stocks open a margin account only if they would like to finance a part of their purchase with a loan from the broker. Margins are security deposits that can be in the form of cash or some high-quality security. Margin account holders must start with an initial margin. When the account balance falls below the maintenance margin level, the broker issues a margin call, at which time the account holder must come up with enough cash to restore the account balance to the maintenance margin level. Short sellers are always required to open margin accounts and must keep the entire sale proceeds plus some additional margin with the broker.

3.11 | Cases

Martingale Asset Management L.P. in 2008: 130/30 Funds and a Low Volatility Strategy (Harvard Business School Case 209047-PDF-ENG). The case discusses the mechanics and the economic implications of leverage and short selling for investment strategies and evaluates minimum volatility stock investment strategies and quantitative investing in general.

Deutsche Borse: (Harvard Business School Case 204008-PDF-ENG). The case explores the implications of Deutsche Borse's acquisition of a stake in a company specializing in clearing, settlement, and custody of securities across borders.

ICEX: Making a Market in Iceland (Harvard Business School Case 106038-PDF-ENG). The case examines the impact of increased performance on the international visibility and positioning of the Icelandic Stock Exchange and considers various options for stock exchange growth in the backdrop of the country's strong economic performance during the period.

3.12 | Questions and Problems

3.1. Explain the difference between a stock and a bond.

3.2. Explain the difference between an exchange and an OTC market.

3.3. Explain the difference between a broker and a dealer.

3.4. Explain the difference between a bid and an ask price.

3.5. Explain the difference between a market order and a limit order.

3.6. A forward market is trading for future purchase of a commodity, while a spot market is trading for immediate purchase. Is the stock market a spot or forward market?

3.7. For the stock market, can there be a difference between the total number of shares issued by a company and the total number of shares held by investors in the market? If yes, explain why.

3.8. Explain the difference between execution and settlement.

3.9. Explain the difference between bull and bear markets.

3.10. The SEC regulates American stock markets. However, NYSE members have committees that carry out a host of self-regulatory activities. NYSE members are profit seeking—why would they self-regulate themselves, when regulations only raise their cost of doing business?

3.11. Why does a dealer offer to trade only a fixed amount at the bid and ask prices?

3.12. You are a dealer and post a price of $50.00 to $50.50 for a stock. The buy orders outweigh sell orders, and your inventory is dwindling. How should you adjust the bid and the ask prices, and why?

3.13. What is the difference between an arbitrageur, a hedger, and a speculator?

3.14. What is program trading? Algorithmic trading?

3.15. What is the difference between a stock trading ex-dividend and cum-dividend?

3.16. Suppose that a stock pay a $5 dividend at time t. The dividend is announced at time $(t-1)$, when the stock trades cum-dividend at a price of $100. What should be the ex-dividend price at time t? Explain your answer.

3.17. Explain how to sell a stock short, assuming that you do not own the underlying stock. Why would one short sell a stock?

3.18. Consider the following data: YBM's stock price is $100. The initial margin is 50 percent, and the maintenance margin is 25 percent. If you buy two hundred shares borrowing 50 percent ($10,000) from the broker, at what stock price will you receive a margin call?

3.19. If the stock price is $105 and the company had paid in the previous year two quarterly dividends of $0.50 each and two more of $0.55 each, then what is the dividend yield?

3.20. Consider an asset that pays a continuously compounded dividend yield of $\delta = 0.05$ per year, which is reinvested back in the asset. If you invest one unit in the asset, how many units would you have after 1.5 years?

4

Forwards and Futures

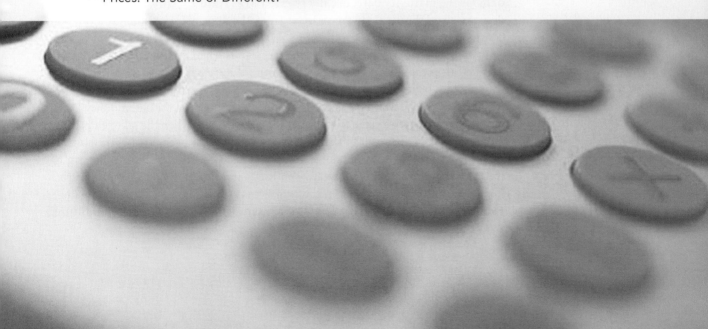

4.1 | Introduction

Surprisingly although many think of derivatives as new and sophisticated securities, this is hardly the case. Forward contracts are the oldest known derivatives, tracing their origins back to India (2000 BC), to ancient Babylonia (1894–1595 BC), and even to Roman merchants trading grains with Egypt.[1] Futures contracts are "the new kids on the block." The oldest futures contracts traded in Amsterdam, Netherlands, in the middle of the sixteenth century and on the first futures exchange, the Dojima Rice Exchange in Osaka, Japan, in 1688. As such, there must be good reason why these contracts have existed for millennia to facilitate trade across time. With respect to those who believe that derivatives are new innovations, we see that their timing is only off by three or four thousand years—but what are a few thousand years among friends?

We start our study with the simplest and the most basic derivatives, forwards and futures. First we introduce forward contracts that trade in the over-the-counter market. Next we discuss futures contracts. Forward and futures contracts are fraternal twins, for the two derivatives are very similar but not identical. We explore their similarities and differences, then we take a bird's-eye view of how a company uses forward (and futures) contracts for hedging input and output price risk, a topic discussed in greater detail in chapter 13.

4.2 | Forward Contracts

Intuitively, a forward contract locks in a price today for a future transaction—*contract now, transact later* is the mantra. More formally, a **forward contract** or a **forward** is a binding agreement between a buyer and a seller to trade some commodity at a fixed price at a later date. This fixed price is called the **forward price** (or the **delivery price**, usually denoted by F), and the later date is the **delivery date** (or the **maturity date**, usually referred to as **time T**). Forward contracts are derivatives as their values are derived from the spot price of some underlying commodity.

By market convention, no money changes hands when these contracts are created. Such an exchange can only happen if both sides are happy with the terms of the contract and believe the contract is fair, that is, *it has a zero value*. To understand why, suppose the forward had a positive value to the buyer of the commodity. Then it must have a negative value to the seller. This means that when the seller enters the forward contract, his wealth immediately declines. He has been hoodwinked by the buyer! A rational seller would not freely enter into such a contract. A similar argument holds in reverse if the forward contract has a negative value. Consequently, if no money changes hands when the contract is created, it must have a zero value. As such, the delivery price written into the contract must be a fair price for future

---

[1] See chapter 8 for an in-depth history.

trading of the asset. How do we find this delivery price? It's actually quite straight-forward. Chapters 11 and 12 will show how to find this price using some basic economic principles.

Derivatives trade on an exchange or in an over-the-counter (OTC) market. Like a magician pulling a hare out of his hat, derivatives also get created out of thin air! Indeed, they are created when one party wants to trade a particular derivative, finds another party to take the other side of the transaction, negotiates a price, and completes the deal. This observation highlights a classic characteristic of derivatives—they trade in **zero net supply** markets. A derivative does not exist until a trade takes place—unlike stocks, the buyer's and seller's positions net out, leaving the net supply of derivatives at zero. As such, trading derivatives is also a **zero sum** game. What one side of the contract gains, the other side loses, and vice versa.

Some market jargon is useful in understanding derivative transactions. If you agree to buy at a future date, then you take a **long position** or you are **going long**. If you agree to sell at a future date, then you are taking a **short position** or you are **going short**. A forward buyer is bullish while a forward seller is bearish about the direction of the price of the underlying commodity. Consider the following example of a forward contract.

EXAMPLE 4.1: The Life of a Forward Contract

- Today is January 1. Ms. Longina Long longs to buy some gold at a fixed price in the middle of the year. Forwards trade in the OTC (interbank) market, where Long's broker finds Mr. Shorty Short. Long and Short agree to trade fifty ounces of gold at a forward/delivery price of $1,000 per ounce on June 30 at a mutually convenient place (see Figure 4.1).

- When the contract begins, its delivery price is adjusted so that the contract is executed without exchanging cash. Consequently, the delivery price is fair, and the market value of the contract is zero at the start.

- *Thus a derivative (forward contract) gets created through mutual agreement.* The brokers collect commissions from the traders for their matching service.

- If Long and Short want, they can close out their positions early through mutual agreement. Theoretically speaking, they can sell their respective sides of the trade to other investors in the secondary market. Practically speaking, it's a hard task. Surely they can trade with others to stop price risk, but credit risk will remain. If they don't close out their positions early, Long and Short meet on the maturity date of June 30.

- What happens on June 30 depends on where the spot settles on that fateful day. Because they agreed on **physical delivery**, Short sells fifty ounces of gold to Long at $1,000 per ounce. Had they decided on **cash settlement** instead, the loser would have paid the price difference to the winner. If the spot price of gold is higher than the delivery price of $1,000 per ounce, then Long wins and Short loses— Long *pays less* for gold than it's worth in the spot market. Conversely, if the spot price of gold is lower than $1,000 per ounce on June 30, then Long loses and Short wins—she *pays more* for that gold than it's worth in the spot market. The forward contract terminates after delivery.

FIGURE 4.1: Timeline for a Forward Contract

Now (start date) (Time 0 = January 1)	*Intermediate dates*	*Delivery/maturity date* (Time T = June 30)
Long agrees to buy 50 ounces of gold on June 30, which Short agrees to sell.	Traders can close out positions by making a reverse trade (sell if long, buy if short).	Long buys gold for $1,000 from Short. If gold price >$1,000, Long wins. If gold price <$1,000, Short wins.
No money is paid now.	If they don't close out positions, they meet on June 30.	*Zero–sum game*-one's gain is the other's loss.
They negotiate the forward price F = $1,000 and contract terms.*		Long's payoff $S(T) - \$1,000$. Short's payoff $-[S(T) - \$1,000]$.

* Prices are per ounce

We will now summon the power of algebra to understand these concepts and develop formulas for Long's and Short's payoffs on the maturity date. Before doing so, though, let's adopt some conventions that will be useful (see boxed insert).

TABLE: Conventions

(used unless otherwise noted)

- Prices are for one unit of an asset or a commodity. Multiply by the contract size to get the total value of the transaction.

- We start at time 0.

- We will often suppress arguments like t and T to reduce clutter. For example, we denote $F(t, T)$ by $F(t)$ or F.

Figure 4.1 gives the key dates in a forward contract. Because there are no intermediate cash inflows or outflows to a forward contract, we can just focus on the beginning and the end. Suppose the forward starts today. Remember our mantra *contract now, transact later*—we need two symbols to capture "now" and "later." Let $F(t, T)$ be the forward price (or delivery price) that we decide now (time t) for a transaction later on the delivery date (T). The first symbol, t, indicates the date the forward price is quoted, and the second argument, T, gives the delivery date. To keep things simple, we will usually start our clock at time $t = 0$. The forward price is $F(0, T)$. To reduce clutter, we will often write $F(t, T)$ or $F(0, T)$ as F.[2]

How is the delivery price linked to the forward price? When the contract starts, by definition, the forward price equals the delivery price, denoted by F. *The delivery price remains fixed over the life of the contract.* The forward price, which is the delivery price of newly written contracts, can, of course, change. If we had waited a day and entered into a new forward contract tomorrow (date $t + 1$ or date 1) for buying gold at the same delivery date T, the price might be different. The new delivery price or the forward price is $F(t + 1, T)$ or $F(1, T)$. But that's not our price. We are committed to pay $F(0, T)$ at time T. Fair or foul, we have to live with our agreed on delivery price until the contract matures.

Let $S(.)$ be the *spot price* (or *cash price*) of the commodity for an immediate (spot) transaction. Generically, $S(t)$ is the spot price at any time t; it takes values $S(0)$ at date 0 and $S(T)$ on the delivery date T. We can call up a broker and easily get $S(0)$, but who can foretell what $S(T)$ will be on the delivery date? No one can exactly because the spot price on the delivery date is random and unknown. In fact, if you could predict stock prices correctly, using derivatives, you'd become a multimillionaire quickly.

As a result, standing in the present, we don't know the value of the forward contract to the long position holder at the delivery date (T). So we write

$$\text{Long's payoff at the delivery date } T = [S(T) - F] \tag{4.1}$$

If there's physical delivery, the long gets a commodity worth $S(T)$, which she can immediately sell. This is shown with a positive sign. She pays the delivery price F. This payment enters with a negative sign.

If there's cash settlement, the long gets $S(T) - F$ from the short when $S(T) > F$ and pays $F - S(T)$ if $S(T) < F$:

$$\begin{aligned}\text{Short's payoff at the delivery date } T &= -[S(T) - F] \\ &= F - S(T)\end{aligned} \tag{4.2}$$

---

[2] For simplicity, we ignore market imperfections like transaction costs, taxes, and convenience yields from holding a long position in the underlying asset. We will include these market imperfections in later chapters.

With physical delivery, the short gets paid the delivery price F, a cash inflow. He surrenders to the long an asset that's worth $S(T)$ in the market.

If the contract is cash settled, then the short gets $F - S(T)$ if $F > S(T)$; otherwise, she pays $S(T) - F$ to the long.

Notice that the long's and short's payoffs are exactly equal and opposite. As mentioned previously, forward contracts are *zero-sum games*—if you add up the two payoffs, the net result is zero.

EXAMPLE 4.1(Continued): Payoffs to a Long and Short Forward Contract

- We revisit Example 4.1 again, but this time using notation. Today is January 1 (date 0). The forward price on which Ms. Long and Mr. Short agree for delivery on June 30 (date T) is $F(0, T) = F = \$1,000$ (all prices are for an ounce of gold).

- Suppose the spot price on the delivery date T is $S(T) = \$1,005$. Long's forward payoff on delivery is $(1,005 - 1,000) = \$5$ or a gain of $5. Long pays $1,000 for gold worth $1,005 in the spot market. Short's forward payoff at time T is $-(1,005 - 1,000) = -\$5$ or a loss of $5. The contract forces short to accept this below-market price for gold on the delivery date.

- If, instead, $S(T)$ is $990 on the delivery date, then Long's payoff at delivery is $(990 - 1,000) = -\$10$ or a loss of $10. She pays $1,000 for gold worth only $990 in the market. Short's payoff at delivery is $-(990 - 1,000) = \$10$ or a gain of $10. Observe that for each possible spot price $S(T)$, the long's and the short's payoffs add to zero, confirming the zero-sum nature of this trade.

- The profit and loss for long's and short's forward positions on the delivery date (time T) are graphed on the **profit diagram** in Figure 4.2. The x axis plots the spot price of gold ($S[T]$) on the delivery date, while the y axis plots the profit or loss from the forward contract.

- The payoff to Long is a dashed straight line, making a 45 degree angle with the horizontal axis and cutting the vertical axis at a negative $1,000, which is the maximum loss. This happens when the spot (gold) is worthless, but Long still has to pay $1,000 for it. Above this, each dollar increase in the spot price cuts Long's loss by a dollar. If gold is worth $1, then Long's loss is $1,000 - 1 = \$999$. If it's worth $800, then the loss is $200. Ms. Long and Mr. Short break even at $1,000. If the gold price ends up higher than $1,000 on the delivery date, then Long sees profits. Figure 4.2 shows that the profit potential for a long forward position is unbounded above.

- The payoff to Short is the downward sloping dashed straight line, making a negative 45 degree angle with the horizontal axis. Considering the horizontal axis as a mirror, Short's payoff is the mirror image of Long's payoff. When gold is worth 0, Short makes $1,000, as worthless gold is sold for $1,000. Thus Short's payoff line touches the vertical axis at $1,000. For each dollar increase in gold's price, Short's profit declines by a dollar. If gold is worth $1, then Short's profit will be $1,000 - 1 = \$999$, and so on. If gold increases beyond $1,000, then Short starts losing money. Short's maximum loss is unbounded—if gold soars, Short plunges into the depths of despair! This shows the risks of **naked short selling** (short selling without holding an offsetting position in the underlying asset).

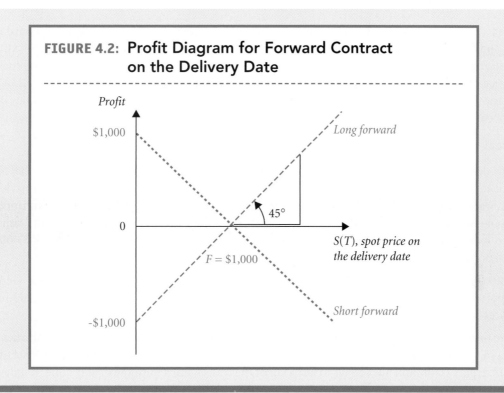

FIGURE 4.2: Profit Diagram for Forward Contract on the Delivery Date

4.3 | The Over-the-Counter Market for Trading Forwards

The OTC derivatives market has seen tremendous growth over the last four decades. Gigantic markets exist for foreign exchange ("forex") forwards, money market instruments, and swaps. This is a market for the "big guys"—the banks—with excellent credit ratings. As such, it is often called the *interbank market*. The participants trade by telephone, telex, and computer, and they tend to be located in the world's major financial centers such as London, New York, and Tokyo. Example 4.2 shows a typical transaction in the forex (foreign exchange) forward market.

EXAMPLE 4.2: Trading Currency Forward

The Contract

- Suppose a US company has bought a machine worth €3 million from a German manufacturer with payment due in three months. The treasurer of the US company feels that at $1.4900, the euro is attractively priced in the spot market.[3] But he doesn't know what will happen in three months time; for example, if a euro costs $1.6000, his company will pay an extra $330,000.

- The treasurer would like to pay today, but the company is short of cash. He checks the forward market and finds that DeutscheUSA (a fictitious name), a large commercial bank, bids euros for $1.5000 and offers euros for $1.5010 in three months' time (see Figure 4.3). He readily agrees and locks in a price of $1.5010 × 3,000,000 = $4,503,000 for the machine. This forward market trade allows the treasurer to eliminate exchange rate risk from the transaction so that the business can focus on its core competency.

The Dealer's Hedge

- How does DeutscheUSA protect itself? Having far-flung operations and diverse customer bases, big banks can often find another firm to take the other side of the transaction. Suppose DeutscheUSA has branches in Germany. Contacting its customer base, DeutscheUSA finds a German importer hoping to buy €3 million worth of computer parts from the United States in three months' time. To shed foreign exchange risk, the German importer agrees to buy €3 million for $1.5000 × 3,000,000 = $4,500,000.

- DeutscheUSA has done something cool. It has removed price risk for both the US and German importers and managed to earn a riskless spread of (1.5010 − 1.5000) × 3,000,000 = $3,000 in the process! Skillful dealers try to perfectly offset such OTC trades.

- In reality, such perfect offsets are unlikely, and DeutscheUSA may have residual price risk after netting out all of its foreign currency transactions. Moreover, DeutscheUSA has some credit risk if any counterparty fails, and it will have to keep tab of the transactions until the deal is done. If it desires, DeutscheUSA may hedge any residual net exposure with forex futures or by entering into a forward transaction with another dealer in the forex market.

---

[3] The **International Organization for Standardization,** or the **ISO,** has established three-letter codes for representation of currencies and funds. ISO's currency codes are USD for the US dollar, AUD for the Australian dollar, EUR for the euro, JPY for the Japanese yen, GBP for the UK pound sterling, etc. When no confusion arises, we will use commonly used expressions (and symbols) like dollar ($), euro (€), yen (¥), and pound sterling or pound (£).

OTC market participants may be classified as brokers, dealers, and their clients. Usual clients are banks, corporations, mutual funds, hedge funds, insurance companies, and other institutions. Many banks act as dealers and make markets in a variety of derivatives. Sometimes clients call up dealers for quotes. Typically a dealer's sales force makes regular cold calls to potential and existing clients, trying to sell their derivatives products. Owing to competition, simple derivatives like currency forwards aren't very lucrative. Banks' proprietary trading desks make more profits when they can identify some special client need and create a customized product. Big players have **trading** or **dealing rooms**, where trading desks dedicated to spot, forward, and options trading are located. Forward prices are quoted in terms of a bid and ask, and because there are no specified delivery months like June and September, forward prices get quoted for delivery in one, two, three, six, or more months from the current date. Recently, owing to new financial regulations, many banks are deemphasizing proprietary trading and focusing more on their dealership businesses.

FIGURE 4.3: Intermediary's Role in the Forward Transaction

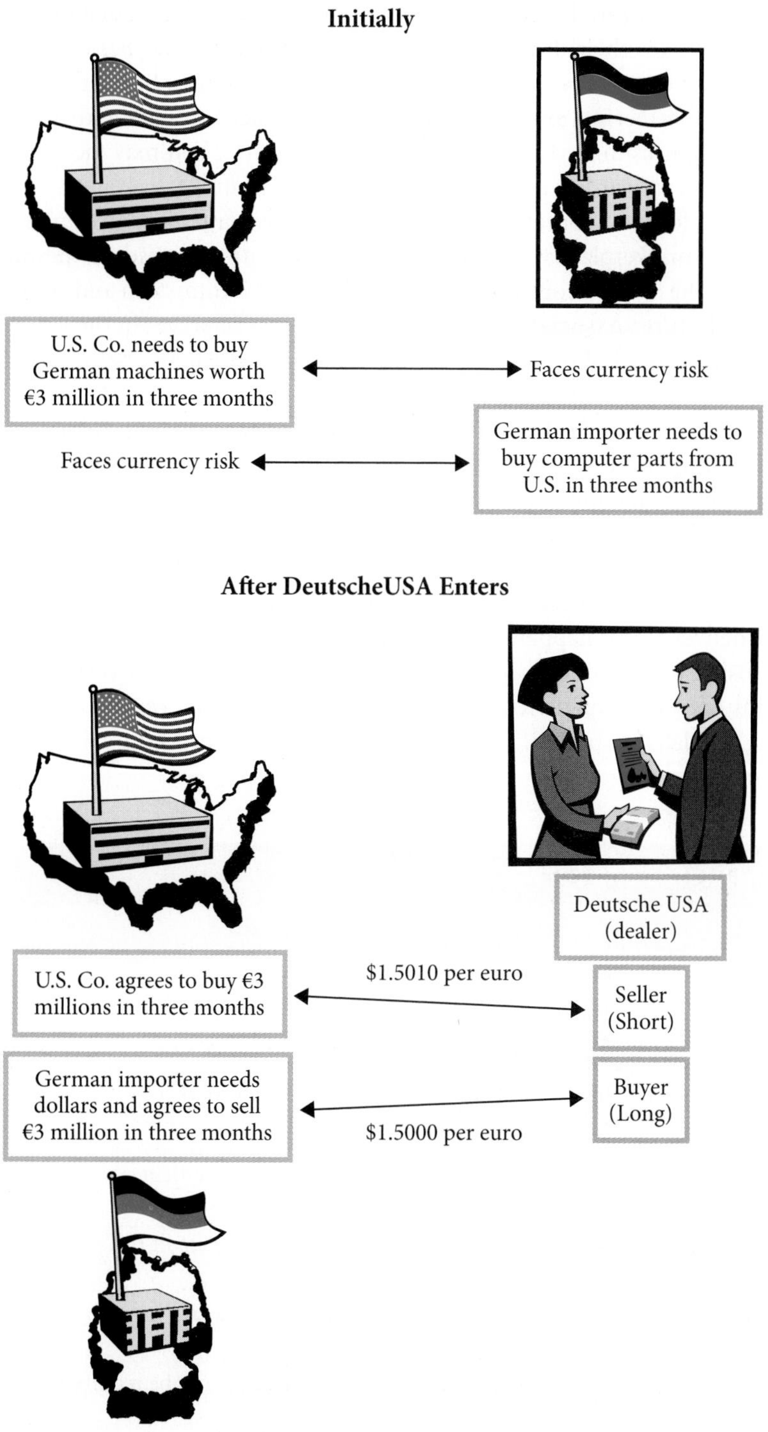

Initially

U.S. Co. needs to buy German machines worth €3 million in three months

Faces currency risk

Faces currency risk

German importer needs to buy computer parts from U.S. in three months

After DeutscheUSA Enters

U.S. Co. agrees to buy €3 millions in three months

$1.5010 per euro

Deutsche USA (dealer)

Seller (Short)

German importer needs dollars and agrees to sell €3 million in three months

$1.5000 per euro

Buyer (Long)

Deutsche USA has perfectly hedged its book and earns $3,000 spread. It has credit risk but no price risk.

4.4 | Futures Contracts

Forward and futures contracts are fraternal twins. Both involve an exchange of cash for an asset purchased at a later date but at prices negotiated at the start of the contract. Yet their differences (explored in Table 4.1 and Figure 4.4) make it hard to label them as identical. Just as a variety of features like air bags, antilock brakes, power steering, and seat belts make a car easier and safer to drive, a number of added features make futures easier and safer to use. You may view futures as a standardized forward or a forward as a customized futures.

Unlike a forward contract, a futures trades on an organized *exchange*, which is a regulated marketplace where buyers and sellers gather to trade a "homogeneous product." The federal Commodity Futures Trading Commission and the industry's **National Futures Association** regulate commodity exchanges in the United States. In contrast, a forward trades in the OTC market, where no regulator tells them the dos and don'ts.

An exchange standardizes futures contracts for easy trading. A trader only has to tell how many contracts to buy or sell and at what price. Standardization helps create a secondary market. It reduces transaction costs and makes futures markets more liquid. A short can easily close out her position before delivery by going long the same contract with another trader, who becomes the new short, while the original long position remains undisturbed. In fact, most futures are closed out before delivery. This happens because making physical delivery is a costly exercise, and closing out futures early avoids this expense. If, for some reason, a position remains open until maturity, then delivery must take place on one of several dates during the delivery period. The details of this delivery procedure are discussed in chapter 9.

TABLE 4.1: Comparison of Futures and Forward Contracts

	Futures	Forward
a.	Regulated	Largely unregulated
b.	Trades in an organized exchange	Trades in an OTC market
c.	Standardized	Customized
d.	Usually liquid and has a secondary market	Illiquid and has virtually no secondary market
e.	A range of delivery dates	Usually has a single delivery date
f.	Usually closed out before maturity to avoid taking physical delivery	Usually ends in physical delivery or cash settlement
g.	Guaranteed by a clearinghouse and has no credit (counterparty) risk	No such guarantee and has counterparty credit risk
h.	Trading among strangers; individual's creditworthiness is irrelevant	Forward traders know each other and usually have high credit rating or require collateral
i.	Requires margins (security deposits)	No margin requirements (but collateral may be required)
j.	Small transaction costs	Transaction costs are high
k.	Settled daily	Settled at maturity

FIGURE 4.4: A Diagram of a Futures Contract

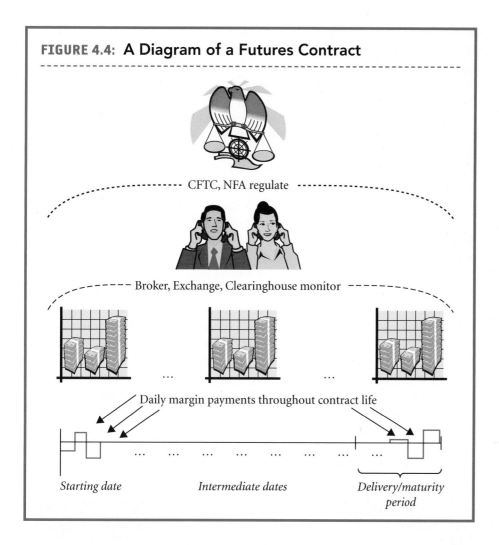

CFTC, NFA regulate

Broker, Exchange, Clearinghouse monitor

Daily margin payments throughout contract life

Starting date   *Intermediate dates*   *Delivery/maturity period*

Contrast this with a forward contract, which is privately negotiated between two traders. As such, the costs of transacting are high. Early termination requires the consent of both sides—you cannot unilaterally close out a position before delivery. Consequently, forwards are highly illiquid, have virtually no secondary market, and are usually held until maturity. Conversely, forwards are tailor-made to suit counterparties' needs and objectives. Forwards can be designed and traded even in situations when no futures contracts are available.

A futures exchange has associated with it a **clearinghouse** that clears executed trades and guarantees contract performance by becoming the counterparty to every trader. As such, it eliminates counterparty risk in the transaction. The clearinghouse controls its counterparty risk by requiring traders to keep a margin (security) deposit in their brokerage accounts, which are marked to market and settled at the end of each trading day. We discuss this in greater detail in chapter 9. By contrast, a forward contract fixes a price for a future transaction that remains locked in over the contract's life, and settlement only takes place on the delivery date.

Futures are primarily designed as risk management tools. They are poor instruments for buying and selling the commodity owing to the hassle of shipping to and from delivery points in specific locations like Chicago and New York, which may ill suit most traders. The US law takes this into consideration and distinguishes contracts on how they end. If delivery is planned and regularly happens, then the contract is likely to be classified as a forward; otherwise, it is a futures. During the 1960s and the early 1970s, some brokerage firms were offering off-exchange forward contracts that were standardized like futures (see Edwards and Ma 1992). Regulators tried to bring them under their jurisdiction, but in 1974, the US Congress denied such incursions by defining forwards as deferred delivery contracts that naturally end in delivery, thereby permitting them to trade away from the exchange floor.

Although institutional differences are important, forwards and futures are also different from an economic perspective because a futures contract has daily cash flows, whereas a forward only has a final cash flow. This payout feature implies that futures and forward prices are usually different (see Extension 4.1 on this issue), but more important, it implies that the risks from holding the contracts differ. Futures face cash flow reinvestment risk with changing interest rates, whereas forwards do not. Because interest rates are random and constantly changing, this reinvestment risk is important, and it affects both pricing and hedging considerations.

Futures (and exchange-traded options) have enjoyed enormous growth around the world. Table 4.2 lists global futures and options volumes for the years 2009 and 2010. Notice that in addition to the older US exchanges, many new international exchanges, including the Korean Options Futures Exchange (KOFEX), EUREX of Europe, the International Securities Exchange (IS) of the United States, MexDer of Mexico, the Dalian Commodity Exchange of China, National Stock Exchange (NSE) of India, and the Taiwan Futures Exchange (Taifex), rank high on this list.

4.5 | Exchange Trading of a Futures Contract

Next we sketch the trading of a futures contract, which has evolved over time to efficiently serve user needs. Moreover, this will also help us to understand options exchanges, which evolved from futures exchanges. We describe open-outcry pit trading, which is still used at the **Chicago Board of Trade** (**CBOT**), the **Chicago Mercantile Exchange** (**CME** or the **Merc**), the **New York Mercantile Exchange** (**NYMEX**), and the **Commodity Exchange**, which are *designated contract markets* (a technical name for futures exchanges—see chapter 10 for elaboration) operated by the **CME Group**. Many experts believe that electronic trading may eventually replace this method of floor trading.

EXTENSION 4.1: Forward and Futures Prices: The Same or Different?

Forward and futures prices are equal when interest rates are nonrandom and credit risk is absent, as proven by Cox, Ingersoll, and Ross (1981) and Jarrow and Oldfield (1981). In reality, interest rates are stochastic—they can wiggle and shift in unpredictable ways owing to myriad factors. This drives a wedge between futures and forward prices because a futures contract's cash flows face reinvestment risk, whereas a forward contract's do not. The reinvestment risk creates uncertainty as to the ultimate payment made for the commodity on the delivery date. This same uncertainty is not faced by a forward contract, and as such, it becomes a differentiating factor. Moreover, these contracts have different credit risks. OTC-traded forwards can have substantial counterparty default risk, but exchange-traded futures have significantly less, giving us yet another reason for a price difference.

What about the empirical evidence? Naturally a topic like this attracts academic study. An early study by Rendleman and Carabini (1979) concluded that differences between forward and futures prices on US Treasury bill contracts were insignificant. In foreign exchange markets, Cornell and Reinganum (1981) and Chang and Chang (1990) found little difference between forward and futures prices for five currencies— British pounds, Canadian dollars, German marks, Japanese yen, and Swiss francs. However, Dezhbakhsh (1994) studied these differences with a larger data set and found significant divergence between the prices of several currencies. In the case of commodities, Park and Chen (1985) studied gold, silver, silver coins, platinum, and copper and found significant differences between forward and futures prices. So what can one conclude? At least based on this sampling of empirical studies, the verdict is still out!

However, it's important to remember that the crucial distinction between these two contracts is not that their prices differ but that their risks aren't the same. The forward has a single cash flow at maturity, whereas futures have daily cash flows. Consequently, forwards and futures cash flows and values need to be hedged differently owing to the reinvestment risk. This implies that from a risk management perspective, they are different securities.

TABLE 4.2: Top Thirty Derivatives Exchanges Ranked by the Number of Futures and Options Traded in 2010

Rank	Exchange	January–December 2009	January–December 2010	% Change
1	Korea Exchange	3,102,891,777	3,748,861,401	20.8
2	CME Group (includes CBOT and NYMEX)	2,589,555,745	3,080,492,118	19.0
3	Eurex (includes ISE)	2,647,406,849	2,642,092,726	−0.2
4	NYSE Euronext (includes US and European Union markets)	1,729,965,293	2,154,742,282	24.6
5	National Stock Exchange of India	918,507,122	1,615,788,910	75.9
6	BM&FBOVESPA	920,375,712	1,422,103,993	54.5
7	CBOE Group (includes CFE and C2)	1,135,920,178	1,123,505,008	−1.1
8	NASDAQ OMX (includes US and Nordic markets)	815,545,867	1,099,437,223	34.8
9	Multi Commodity Exchange of India (includes MCX-SX)	385,447,281	1,081,813,643	180.7

TABLE 4.2: *(Continued)*

10	Russian Trading Systems Stock Exchange	474,440,043	623,992,363	31.5
11	Shanghai Futures Exchange	434,864,068	621,898,215	43.0
12	Zhengzhou Commodity Exchange	227,112,521	495,904,984	118.4
13	Dalian Commodity Exchange	416,782,261	403,167,751	−3.3
14	Intercontinental Exchange (includes US, UK, and Canadian markets)	263,582,881	328,946,083	24.8
15	Osaka Securities Exchange	166,085,409	196,350,279	18.2
16	JSE South Africa	174,505,220	169,898,609	−2.6
17	Taiwan Futures Exchange	135,125,695	139,792,891	3.5
18	Tokyo Financial Exchange	83,678,044	121,210,404	44.9
19	London Metal Exchange	111,930,828	120,258,119	7.4
20	Hong Kong Exchanges and Clearing	98,538,258	116,054,377	17.8
21	ASX Group (includes ASX and ASX 24)	82,200,578	106,386,077	29.4
22	Boston Options Exchange	137,784,626	91,754,121	−33.4
23	Tel-Aviv Stock Exchange	70,914,245	80,440,925	13.4
24	London Stock Exchange Group (includes IDEM and EDX)	77,490,255	76,481,330	−1.3
25	Mercado Español de Futuros y Opciones Financieros	93,057,252	70,224,176	−24.5
26	Turkish Derivatives Exchange	79,431,343	63,952,177	−19.5
27	Mercado a Término de Rosario	51,483,429	62,046,820	20.5
28	Singapore Exchange (includes Sicom and AsiaClear)	53,237,389	61,750,671	16.0
29	China Financial Futures Exchange	0	45,873,295	NA
30	Bourse de Montréal	21,937,811	30,823,273	40.5

Note. Ranking does not include exchanges that do not report their volume to the Futures Industry Association (FIA).
Source: "Annual Volume Survey" available at "Trading Volume Statistics" section of Futures Industry Association's website (www.futuresindustry.org/downloads/Volume-Mar_FI%28R%29.pdf).

EXAMPLE 4.3: Exchange Trading of Futures Contracts

Order Placement

- Today is January 1. Ms. Longina Long and Mr. Shorty Short are trying to do the transaction of Example 4.1 with exchange-traded futures contracts. They both want to trade fifty ounces of gold at a fixed price on June 30.

- Gold futures trade on the NYMEX and the CBOT, both divisions of the CME Group, and on other exchanges. During regular hours, transactions occur on the exchange's trading floor. Each regular contract is for one hundred troy ounces of gold, but there are also some mini-contracts of smaller size. No gold futures contract matures in June. There are contracts for April and July, but these months may not suit Long's buying needs or Short's selling desire. Standardization allows quick trading, but there is a trade-off in that it reduces available choices.

- Futures traders must first open margin accounts (security deposits in the form of cash or some acceptable securities) with a **Futures Commission Merchant** (**FCM**).[4] Old-fashioned Shorty calls up his FCM and dictates a market order to sell one July gold futures at the best available price. The FCM's representative records and time stamps his order and sends it to a clerk on the exchange's trading floor (see Figure 4.5).

- Technologically savvy Longina submits her market order through an FCM's website. Futures traders can place their orders in many other ways besides market orders (see Example 5.8 and Extension 5.2 of chapter 5 for different order placement strategies). From FCM's processing center, the web order is forwarded via computer to a clerk on the trading floor. The FCM's clerk then fills out an order form and sends it to the floor broker in the trading pit. A *floor broker* is a trader's agent and has a fiduciary responsibility to protect a client's interests. He earns a commission for his service.

- A *trading pit* or a *ring* has a circular or a polygonal shape with concentric rings of steps flowing inward to a central place. Inside the pit jostle a motley group of floor brokers, floor dealers, exchange officials, clerks, market analysts, journalists, and others. Rules require **open-outcry trading**—the floor broker or the dealer has to cry out the bid (a proposal to buy) or ask (or offer, a proposal to sell) in the trading pit so that others may participate. Usually this information is also conveyed by hand signals. In more advanced systems, prices are displayed via computer terminals and electronic boards.

- The objective of a single-location market with traders shouting is to give everybody a chance to participate, hoping that this will lead to greater transparency and better price discovery. Moreover, quote boards on the floor help with information dissemination.

Trade Execution

- Shorty's broker in the trading pit checks the quote board and sees that most trades are occurring at a little over $1,000. He senses the market and cries out an offer to sell one contract at $1,001. Standing in the crowd is Longina's broker, who signals the desire to take the other side of this trade. The trade is executed when they agree on terms.

---

[4] A **FCM** provides a one-stop service for all aspects of futures trading: it solicits trades, takes futures orders, accepts payments from customers, extends credit to clients, holds margin deposits, documents trades, and keeps track of accounts and trading records.

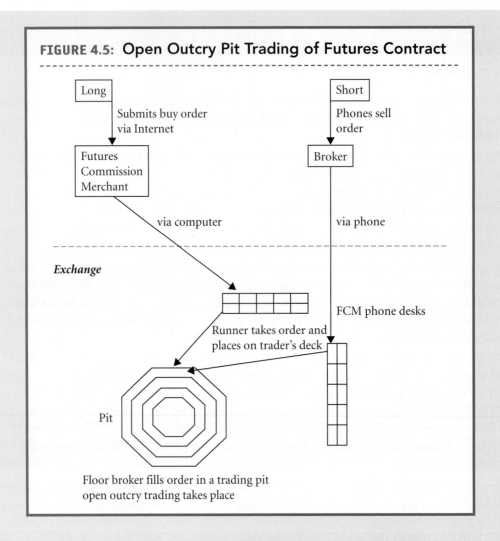

FIGURE 4.5: Open Outcry Pit Trading of Futures Contract

- Next the brokers quickly record the trade on an index card and give it to an exchange employee, who feeds this information into the exchange's computer system. Relevant information flashes up on the large electronic quote boards above the exchange floor and is simultaneously disseminated by ticker tapes around the globe.

- Long and Short pay their respective broker commissions on a **round-trip** basis. There is no charge when entering a position, but the full charge is due at the time the futures transaction is closed. The amount of commission varies from trader to trader. It could be as low as $10 per round trip trade for a discount broker but far more for a full-service brokerage firm.

Clearing a Futures Trade

- Before the market reopens, representatives of the clearing members take the trade records to the exchange's clearinghouse. The clearinghouse checks the records, and once the records match, the clearinghouse clears the trade by recognizing and recording it.

- The clearinghouse also guarantees contract performance by acting as a seller to every buyer and as a buyer to every seller (see Figure 4.6). The clearinghouse minimizes default risk by keeping margins for exchange members, who, in turn, keep margin for their customers.

Settling a Futures Trade

- A stock trade is **settled** when a buyer pays cash and gets the stock's ownership rights from the seller. In contrast, a futures trade has a special feature called **daily settlement**, by which profits and losses are paid out daily. At the end of each trading day, a futures position is **marked to market** by crediting or debiting the day's gain or loss, respectively, to a trader's margin account, an amount that equals the difference between yesterday's and today's futures prices. If the futures price goes up, Long wins; if it goes down, Short gains.

- Marking-to-market resets the delivery price at maturity for outstanding futures contracts to the current futures price in freshly minted futures. This process of marking-to-market also resets the value of a futures contract to zero at the end of each trading day.

- To understand marking-to-market, suppose Long buys one hundred ounces of gold from Short in July for $1,001 per ounce. Suppose the next day's settlement price is $1,004. Long would screech if you tell her that she now has to buy gold in July at $1,004 because she thought she locked a price of $1,001! However, she would agree to buy at $1,004 if you were to pay her the price difference between her earlier price and the new one: ($1,004 − $1,001) = $3 per ounce. To handle this payment, $3 × 100 = $300 is taken from Short's margin account and deposited into Long's margin account. Wouldn't $300 earn daily interest in a bank account? And wouldn't such daily receipts or payments happen in an unpredictable fashion? The answer to both questions is yes. As noted earlier, these observations are what differentiate futures from forward contracts. Chapter 9 explains how marking-to-market works in greater detail.

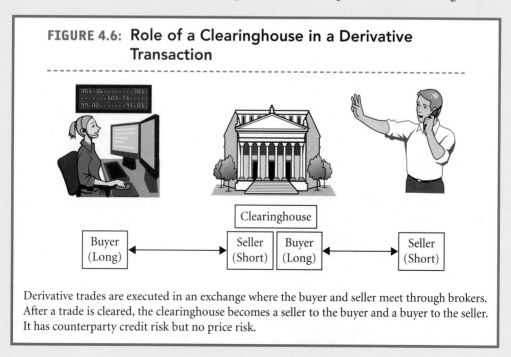

FIGURE 4.6: Role of a Clearinghouse in a Derivative Transaction

Derivative trades are executed in an exchange where the buyer and seller meet through brokers. After a trade is cleared, the clearinghouse becomes a seller to the buyer and a buyer to the seller. It has counterparty credit risk but no price risk.

Closing the Contract

- A month later, Longina sells one July gold futures to Miss Tallmadge, closes out her position, and clears her slate. Her effective selling price after all the marking-to-markets is close to $1,001. Taxes, interest charges on margin balances, and other market imperfections will make the realized price a bit different from $1,001. Tallmadge is the new long vis-à-vis Shorty's short.

- Shorty decides to physically deliver the gold during the contract's delivery period in July. He delivers one hundred ounces of gold as per exchange requirements and collects an amount close to $100,100 from Tallmadge.

Futures trading is becoming increasingly popular in different parts of the world, including in countries that were previously hostile to it. Extension 4.2 discusses futures trading in some developing countries, with particular focus on Ethiopia, modern futures exchanges in China, and village Internet kiosks that inform and empower India's farmers.

EXTENSION 4.2: Futures Exchanges in China, India, and Ethiopia, and E-Choupal in Village India

Moving Commodities from Farms to Consumers

When you read Grimm's fairy tales about the old days, you come across farmers who keep a portion of the crop for family consumption and sell the rest in the market. Even today, this is true in many parts of the world, where farmers' markets are held on a regular basis. But when food moves to towns and cities, you need a **supply chain**—a network of storage facilities, transporters, distributors, and retailers that take food from the farmer and deliver it to the consumer.

Advanced economies use sophisticated technology at each stage of the supply chain to minimize costs and maintain product quality. For example, fruits and vegetables are flash frozen, sent in refrigerated trucks, and kept in temperature-controlled warehouses to extend their shelf life. Owing to this process, restaurants can offer an incredible variety of "fish, flesh, and fowl" such as Maine lobster, Alaskan king crab, Hawaiian mahimahi, and Russian caviar. And as Walmart and many other companies have demonstrated, sophisticated supply chains can significantly lower costs that in competitive markets get passed on to consumers.

However, the story is different when commodities move from rural to urban areas in some of the poorest countries. Farmers sell their excess crops to a middleman, who acts as a broker or dealer. Visualize the farmers manually loading crops into sacks, putting them on a bullock-driven cart, taking them to the middleman's house for inspection, weighing and packaging, and selling at whatever price they are offered. The produce goes through several middlemen before it reaches retail outlets. Significant waste can occur during repackaging and reinspection by the middlemen, and poor handling and lack of refrigeration can further diminish the quantity. The farmers get only a small fraction of the final price. True, each of these intermediaries serves a useful economic function, but they are relevant only because the infrastructure is primitive and sophisticated risk management tools are absent.

Futures Trading in China

Consider China, a country home to over 1.3 billion people. During the 1980s and 1990s, China became interested in developing sophisticated financial markets and institutions. Futures trading began in China in 1993. However, during the first few years, "new exchanges opened with wild abandon, and speculative volume ballooned" (Qin and Ronalds, 2005). Eventually, the Chinese authorities closed more than forty of these exchanges. The **Dalian Commodity Exchange**, the **Shanghai Futures Exchange**, the **Zhengzhou Commodity Exchange**, and the **China Financial Futures Exchange** (founded in 2006) are the only operating futures exchanges remaining in China today. These exchanges are either fully electronic or use a combination of open-outcry and electronic trading. All four show up in the list of top thirty derivatives exchanges in the world (see Table 4.2 and Figure 4.7).

Interestingly, an October 12, 2009, article in the *Wall Street Journal* titled "China Targets Commodity Prices by Stepping Into Futures Markets" reported that the leaders of Communist China are planning to use futures exchanges "to fight back" foreign suppliers who "inflate [China's] commodity prices." China's rapid economic growth requires the importation of vast quantities of many commodities: the country buys 10 percent of the world's crude oil (making China the second largest importer of oil after the United States), 30 percent of its copper, and 53 percent of its soybean output. By developing the three commodities exchanges as "major players in setting world prices for metal, energy and farm commodities," China expects to be less susceptible to exchange prices elsewhere.

The article reported that China's ambitious plan, however, does not immediately threaten exchanges in Chicago, London, and New York, where benchmark prices for most commodities are set. This is because of restrictions on foreign participation in Chinese exchanges and the government's role as both a player and a policy maker in the markets. Futures traders joke that "China is second only to the weather in driving some commodity prices—but less predictable." Chinese futures prices have begun affecting global prices for many key commodities. For example, Chinese demand was a major contributor to huge swings in crude oil prices during 2008–9 (see Figure 4.7).

Futures Trading in India

At the start of the new millennium, India removed a four-decade-long ban on commodity futures trading, allowed resuscitation of moribund exchanges, and approved the opening of new ones. Soon afterward, during 2002–3, three major electronic multicommodity exchanges, the **National Multi Commodity Exchange of India Ltd.**, the **Multi Commodity Exchange (MCX)**, and the **National Commodity and Derivatives Exchange Limited** were formed. As Table 4.2 depicts, the Multi Commodity Exchange and the National Stock Exchange of India ranked among the world's top ten derivatives exchanges in terms of trading volume in the year 2010.

In yet another development, September 2010 saw the opening of the United Stock Exchange (USE) of India. Backed by government and private banks as well as corporate houses, the USE currently offers trading in currency futures (on-the-spot exchange rate of Indian rupees against the dollar, euro, pound sterling, and yen) and options (on the US dollar Indian rupee spot rate) but plans to expand its offerings to include interest rate derivatives.[5] Despite its limited product line, the USE was ranked thirteenth in terms of the total number of derivatives contracts traded during the first six months of 2011.[6]

---

[5] See www.useindia.com/genindex.php#.

[6] www.futuresindustry.org/downloads/Complete_Volume%2811-11_FI%29.pdf.

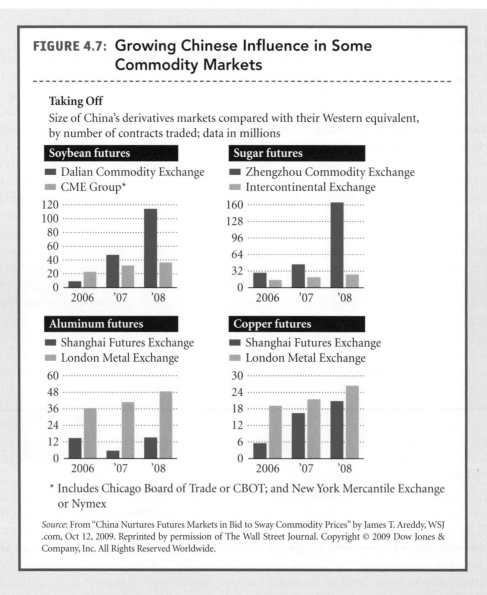

FIGURE 4.7: Growing Chinese Influence in Some Commodity Markets

Taking Off

Size of China's derivatives markets compared with their Western equivalent, by number of contracts traded; data in millions

Soybean futures
- Dalian Commodity Exchange
- CME Group*

Sugar futures
- Zhengzhou Commodity Exchange
- Intercontinental Exchange

Aluminum futures
- Shanghai Futures Exchange
- London Metal Exchange

Copper futures
- Shanghai Futures Exchange
- London Metal Exchange

* Includes Chicago Board of Trade or CBOT; and New York Mercantile Exchange or Nymex

Source: From "China Nurtures Futures Markets in Bid to Sway Commodity Prices" by James T. Areddy, WSJ .com, Oct 12, 2009. Reprinted by permission of The Wall Street Journal. Copyright © 2009 Dow Jones & Company, Inc. All Rights Reserved Worldwide.

Commodity futures exchanges have also been founded in many other countries, including those in Latin America, Eastern Europe, and Asia. However, Africa has been slow in adopting futures trading. Next we consider the inspiring story of an exchange in Ethiopia that opened for business in 2008. Notice that China's and India's stories mostly center around institutional players and other sophisticated traders. By contrast, the following two cases consider using derivatives to help improve the standard of living of rural folk.

An Ethiopian Commodity Exchange

Consider Ethiopia, whose fertile lands are capable of growing abundant wheat and corn. Yet it is one of the world's poorest countries. Ethiopian farmers failed to take advantage of soaring global grain prices. Low education, poor infrastructure, civil conflicts, and unstable neighbors like Sudan, Somalia, and Eritrea (with whom Ethiopia fought a war over border disputes) contribute to the country's woes.

As written in the *Wall Street Journal* ("Ethiopia Taps Grain Exchange in Its Battle on Hunger," February 27, 2008), Ethiopia opened the modern **Ethiopia Commodity Exchange** (**ECX**) in April 2008, the first of its kind in Africa and the only functioning commodities exchange outside South Africa. The $21 million project was inaugurated with the support of the Ethiopian government ($2.4 million), the World Bank, some United Nations agencies, the International Food Policy Research Institute (IFPRI), and individual countries such as the United States.[7] Eleni Zaude Gabre-Madhin, who worked for the World Bank before returning to her native Ethiopia as the program leader of Development Strategy and Governance for IFPRI, has been the driving force behind this exchange and has served as its first chief executive officer.

ECX's objective is to stop farmers from getting exploited by middlemen and to link them directly with global markets. Heavily influenced by the CBOT, ECX introduced a system of open-outcry floor trading for six agricultural commodities. The farmers take their crops to one of the many warehouses that ECX has set up across the nation, have them weighed and graded, and get a warehouse receipt (for the deposited grain), which they can sell immediately or at a later date at the commodities exchange. Electronic screens set up in twenty market towns disseminate real-time grain prices at several different places across the world (including Ethiopia's capital Addis Ababa and the exchanges in London and Chicago). The farmer's selling price becomes an informed choice.

Following the path trodden by the CBOT 160 years back, ECX began with spot trading and plans to add futures trading (see "Rising Prices and the Role of Commodity Exchanges," *Wall Street Journal*, April 17, 2008). The *Wall Street Journal* article reports that Gabre-Madhin saw strong parallels between the current situation in Ethiopia and the state of the American farm trade before the CBOT was formed. She expects ECX to bring "the same innovations the Board of Trade brought the US: uniform quality standards, fair 'price discovery' and futures contracts."

E-Choupal in India

What does India's largest cigarette maker have to do with Internet kiosks in rural India? Previously known as Imperial Tobacco Company of India Ltd., ITC Ltd. has annual revenue of over $5.1 billion and has "a diversified presence in Cigarettes, Hotels, Paperboards & Specialty Papers, Packaging, Agri-Business, Packaged Foods & Confectionery, Information Technology, Branded Apparel, Personal Care, Stationery, Safety Matches and other FMCG [Fast Moving Consumer Goods] products."[8] ITC's agri-business division, which is one of the largest exporters of agricultural commodities in India, runs e-Choupals in over six thousand villages and expects to reach one hundred thousand villages over the next decade.

Building on the term *choupal*, which refers to the meeting place in the village, **e-Choupal** is a desktop computer with an Internet connection that links farmers to a variety of services. It is the brainchild of ITC's

[7] Founded in July 1944 at the Bretton Woods conference, the **World Bank Group** consists of five closely associated institutions that are owned by their member countries. Their mission is to "fight poverty and improve living standards of the people in the developing world." Two of these five, the International Bank for Reconstruction and Development, which "makes loans and grants and provides analytical and advisory services to middle-income and creditworthy poorer countries," and the International Development Association, which "offers interest-free credits and grants to the world's 81 poorest countries," are referred to as the **World Bank** (www.worldbankgroup.org). The **United Nations** (**UN**) is a multipurpose international agency that was founded in 1945 with the aim of (see the UN Charter) ending wars, upholding fundamental human rights, establishing justice, honoring treaties and international law, and promoting "social progress and better standards of life in larger freedom" (www.un.org/aboutun/charter /index).

[8] www.itcportal.com/sets/itc_frameset.htm.

chairman Yogesh Chander Deveshwar. Wildly enthusiastic about the project, Deveshwar even predicted that e-Choupal would be more important to the company than cigarettes in five years' time.

Implementation of e-Choupal has been difficult owing to a shortage of "phone lines, electricity and literate farmers," notes an article titled "Cigarettes and Virtual Cathedrals" (*Economist*, June 3, 2004). ITC has overcome these problems with VSAT satellite links, solar batteries, and carefully chosen *sanchalaks*, or "conductors," who are educated local farmers in charge of running e-Choupals. The article describes e-Choupal's functioning in a village in the Indian state of Madhya Pradesh as follows:

In Badamungalaya, farmers use the e-CHOUPAL to check prices for their soya beans at the nearest government-run market, or even on the Chicago futures exchange. They look at weather forecasts. They order fertilizer and herbicide, and consult an agronomist by e-mail when their crops turn yellow. Some buy life insurance. The local shopkeeper orders salt, flour and sweets. Two wealthy villagers have even bought motorcycles. Others club together to rent tractors. School children check their exam results. "Distance has been killed," says Mr Nagodia [e-Choupal's *sanchalak*].

ITC's website states that the e-Choupal model has been specifically designed "to tackle the challenges posed by the unique features of Indian agriculture, characterised by fragmented farms, weak infrastructure and the involvement of numerous intermediaries, among others."

In futures trading, the terms *open interest* and *trading volume* need careful distinction: **trading volume** is the total number of contracts traded, whereas **open interest** is the total number of all outstanding contracts, which may also be counted as the total number of long (or short) positions. Trading volume is a measure of a market's liquidity: the more the volume is traded, the more active the market is. In contrast, the open interest is a measure of the market's outstanding demand for or exposure to a particular commodity at the delivery date. Example 4.4 further explores the distinction between these two concepts.

EXAMPLE 4.4: Volume versus Open Interest

- Suppose that a July gold futures just becomes eligible for trading. Heather buys twenty of those contracts from Kyle. Trade records will show the following (for convenience, they are also shown in Table 4.3):
  - Heather is long twenty contracts.
  - Kyle is short twenty contracts.
  - Trading volume is twenty contracts.
  - Open interest is twenty contracts.

- Heather decides to reduce her exposure. She sells ten contracts to Tate. As a result,
  - Heather is now long ten contracts.
  - Tate is long ten contracts.
  - Kyle is short twenty contracts, as before.

- Trading volume rises to thirty contracts.
- Open interest is twenty contracts, as before.

■ Kyle reduces his short position. He buys five contracts from Heather. Consequently,
  - After selling five contracts, Heather is long five contracts.
  - Tate is long ten contracts, as before.
  - Kyle is short fifteen contracts after this trade.
  - Trading volume, which adds up the number of trades, is thirty-five contracts.
  - Open interest, which is the sum total of all outstanding long positions (or short positions), is now fifteen contracts.

TABLE 4.3: Trade Records for Gold Futures Contracts

Kyle sells twenty contracts to Heather

Trader	Long	Short	Trading Volume	Open Interest
Heather	20		20	20
Kyle		20		

Heather sells ten contracts to Tate

Trader	Long	Short	Trading Volume	Open Interest
Heather	10		30	20
Kyle		20		
Tate	10			

Heather sells five contracts to Kyle

Trader	Long	Short	Trading Volume	Open Interest
Heather	5		35	15
Kyle		15		
Tate	10			

4.6 | Hedging with Forwards and Futures

Forwards and futures are widely used for hedging commodity price risks at future dates. Consider a typical firm, which uses inputs to produce one or more outputs. Input and output prices are susceptible to price fluctuations. Usually, a firm tries to shed price risk for both its inputs and outputs, provided it is not costly to do so. Then it can concentrate on production; in other words, it can focus on what it does best. Obviously, it is a judgment call to decide which risks to cure and which to endure.

Suppose that to reduce *input price risk*, a firm sets up a **long hedge** (or a **buying hedge**) by taking a *long position in a forward contract*. For example, a company that mines and refines gold in some remote area and uses natural gas to power its electricity generators may find it prudent to buy a forward contract on natural gas. If natural gas prices go up in the future, then the company pays more in the spot market, but the spot market loss is largely offset by the gain on the forward contract. On the flip side, if natural gas prices go down, the company will surrender some of its spot market gains through losses on the forward position. This is always the case when one employs a hedging strategy. Hedging with forwards (and futures) cuts both ways: it reduces the risk of financial loss from adverse price movements, but also takes away potential gains from favorable price changes.

Alternatively, to reduce *output price risk*, the company can establish a **short hedge** (or **selling hedge**) by taking a *short position in a forward contract*. If the company sells gold forward, then it will remove or lessen the potential for loss (as well as gains) from future spot price fluctuations. If the spot goes down, then the company loses money when it sells gold in the cash market, but it profits from the forward contract. The losses and gains are reversed when the spot price goes up.

Hedging is analogous to purchasing an insurance policy on the commodity's price. It pays off when prices move in an adverse direction. But as with all insurance policies, there is a cost—the premium. If the price does not move in an adverse way, you paid for insurance that you didn't use. This is the cost. Risk-averse individuals will often buy insurance despite this cost, and analogously, firms will often hedge their input or output price risk.

4.7 | Summary

1. The buyer and seller in a forward contract agree to trade a commodity on some later delivery date at a fixed delivery (forward) price. Forwards are zero net supply contracts. Forward trading is a zero-sum game. On the maturity date, the buyer's (or the long's) payoff is the spot price minus the delivery price. The seller's (or the short's) payoff is equal in magnitude but opposite in sign to the long's payoff.

2. There are organized OTC (interbank) markets for trading forwards, which are dominated by banks and other institutional traders. These markets are huge. For example, foreign currency forwards attract billions of dollars of trade every day and have outstanding obligations measured in trillions of dollars.

3. The buyer and seller of a futures contract agree to trade a commodity at a fixed delivery price on the maturity date. A futures contract is similar to a forward. The long position holder in both these contracts agrees to buy the commodity, while the short agrees to sell. The forward or futures price is set so that no cash changes hands when the contract is created. This implies that the contracts have zero initial value.

4. Exchange-traded derivatives are highly regulated contracts that trade in organized exchanges. A clearinghouse clears trades and guarantees contract performance. Traders are required to keep margins (security deposits) that are adjusted daily to minimize default risk. Exchanges also act as secondary markets where traders can take their profits or cut their losses and exit the market.

5. Futures are traded on the floor of older exchanges like the Chicago Board of Trade and the Chicago Mercantile Exchange using an open-outcry method. Offers to trade must be shouted in trading rings or pits so that other brokers and dealers can hear and join. Exchange employees are also present on the trading floor to report prices and ensure that the system works well.

6. Many firms reduce price risk by trading futures and forward contracts. A firm can lower input price risk by setting up a long hedge buying a forward and reduce output price risk by establishing a short hedge selling a forward.

4.8   Cases

The Dojima Rice Market and the Origins of Futures Trading (Harvard Business School Case 709044-PDF-ENG). The case blends business history with policy issues surrounding the introduction of rice futures at the Dojima Exchange, the world's first organized (but unsanctioned) futures market.

United Grain Growers Ltd. (A) (Harvard Business School Case 201015-PDF-ENG). The case considers how a Canadian grain distributor can identify and manage various risks.

ITC eChoupal Initiative (Harvard Business School Case 297014-PDF-ENG). The case discusses the use of Internet technologies and derivative contracts to help poor farmers in rural India.

4.9   Questions and Problems

4.1. Define a forward contract. If a forward contract on gold is negotiated at a forward price of $1,487 per ounce, what would be the payoff on the maturity date to the buyer if the gold price is $1,518 per ounce and to the seller if the gold price is $1,612 per ounce?

4.2. Define a futures contract.

4.3. Discuss the similarities and differences between forward and futures contracts.

4.4. What are the costs and benefits to a corn grower trading a forward contract? If she is expecting a harvest in three months, should she buy or sell the derivative?

4.5. Which contract has more counterparty risk, a forward contract or a futures contract? Explain your answer.

4.6. Discuss the benefits of standardization of a futures contract.

4.7. What are the two roles that a clearinghouse plays in the case of a futures contract?

4.8. Ang, Bong, Chong, and Dong are trading futures contracts. Carefully identify the trading volume and open interest for each trader from the following transactions:

   a. Ang buys five October silver futures from Bong.

   b. Chong sells nine December silver futures to Bong.

   c. Dong buys ten October silver futures from Chong.

   d. Bong sells five December silver futures to Ang.

   e. Ang sells three October silver futures to Chong.

4.9. Suppose you are a trader specializing in futures on corn, wheat, oats, barley, and other agricultural commodities. From the following list, which risks do you face (mark each with a yes or no): credit risk, market risk, liquidity risk, settlement risk, operational risk, legal risk.

4.10. For forward and futures contracts, what is the difference between physical delivery and cash settlement?

4.11. Why does a futures contract have zero value when it is first written?

4.12. What is marking-to-market for a futures? Why is this marking-to-market important for reducing counterparty risk?

4.13. Explain why a futures contract is a zero-sum game between the long and short positions.

4.14. Are forward contracts new to financial markets? Explain.

4.15. Can you think of a reason why forward prices and futures prices on otherwise identical forward and futures contracts might not be equal?

4.16. What is the OTC market for trading derivatives? How do OTC markets differ from exchanges?

4.17. When holding a futures contract long, if you do not want to take delivery of the underlying asset, what transaction must you perform? Explain.

4.18. If you are short a futures contract, why do you not have to borrow the futures contract from a third party to do the short sale?

4.19. Is the futures price equal to the value of the futures contract? If not, then what is the value of a forward contract when it is written? Explain.

4.20. Is the forward price equal to the value of a forward contract? If not, then what is the value of a forward contract when it is written? Explain.

5

Options

5.1 | Introduction

After introducing options in an intermediate finance class, a professor asked, "Is auto insurance an option?" A serious student from the front row replied, "It is not an option because state law requires it, but you have the option to choose from different insurance companies." Though the student was entirely correct, this was not the answer for which the professor was hoping. He took a deep breath and went on to explain that put options are very similar to insurance contracts because they restore an asset's value after a decline and that much of option jargon comes from the insurance industry—and he resolved to frame his questions more carefully in the future.

As the example illustrates, the word *option* has many meanings in daily life. Exchange-traded options are well-defined contracts with specific features. This chapter describes these option features and discusses how they trade. At the chapter's end, we discuss how traders buy or sell options for various strategic objectives.

5.2 | Options

Options come in two basic **types**: calls and puts, names you have heard before. A **call option** gives the **buyer**

the right, but not the obligation

to *buy* a specified quantity of a financial or real asset from the **seller**

on or before a fixed future **expiration date**

by paying an **exercise price** agreed on today

The buyer is also called the **holder** or the *owner*. The seller is known as the *grantor*, the *issuer*, or the **writer**. The known future expiration date is also called the **maturity date**, and the fixed price is known as the **exercise price** or **strike price**. The holder **exercises the call** when she exercises her right and buys the underlying asset by paying the exercise price; otherwise, she lets the call expire worthless.

By contrast, a put option gives the right to sell. Specifically, a **put option** gives the owner the right to *sell* the asset to the writer at the strike price until the expiration date. A buyer **exercises the put** when he sells the underlying asset and receives the strike price from the put writer; otherwise, he can let the put expire worthless. Options do not come free—the option buyer must pay the writer a fee (**option's price** or **premium**) for selling those rights.

The terms *call* and *put* come from what the buyer can do with these options. A call gives the option to buy, that is, to *call the asset away* from the writer. Conversely, a put gives the option to sell or to *put the asset to* the writer. In each case, the writer stands ready to take the other side of the buyer's decision. We say that a call buyer is *bullish* because she expects the underlying asset to go up in value, and a put buyer is *bearish* because he expects the asset price to decline. Naturally, their counterparties hold opposite market views: the call writer is bearish and the put writer is bullish. We also say that the option (call or put) buyer is **long** the option, so the writer ends up with a **short** position.

Notice that calls and puts have a lot in common with insurance policies and may be viewed as insurance contracts for hedging or risk reduction. If someone hits a car, the insurance company pays the owner enough money (subject to some deductibles) to restore the car to its original value. Likewise, a put pays the holder in case of a meltdown in the asset's value. A call buyer benefits from an asset price rise but does not suffer from its decline. The call buyer pays for insurance to avoid losses if the stock falls. The call writer provides this insurance. For these reasons, an option price is called a *premium*. A premium is what you pay for the insurance.

Calls and puts are examples of **plain vanilla** or **standard derivatives**. Later we will consider **nonstandard** or **exotic derivatives**, which are derivatives with more complex payoffs. Plain vanilla options are usually defined in one of two ways: American or European. A **European option** can only be exercised at the maturity date of the option, whereas an **American option** can be exercised at any time up to and including its expiration date. What we defined earlier were calls and puts of the American type. The adjectives *European* and *American* tell how the options differ in their exercise choices and have nothing to do with where they trade—in Europe, America, Africa, Asia, Australia, or even in Antarctica. European-style options trade in the United States and across the Atlantic, and American-style options transact in Europe.

Both American and European options have the same value on the expiration date, if the American option remains unexercised. Before expiration, however, American options are at least as valuable as their European counterparts. They duplicate what European options can do, but they also offer an early exercise feature, which is more. You don't pay less when you get more. Chapter 6 will show how the assumption of no arbitrage makes this happen. Such simple insights are useful when trading options.

The important question studied in later chapters is, *How do you find an option's premium*? This has bewildered academics for a long time. A breakthrough came in 1973 with the development of the seminal *Black–Scholes–Merton (BSM)* option pricing model (see chapter 19). The importance of the BSM model can hardly be overstated—it helped spawn the entire field of derivative pricing that we see today. However, option pricing still remains a Herculean task. For example, there is no generalized closed-form solution for finding an American option's premium.[1] This is important because most exchange-traded options are of the American type, and we need to price them. When closed-form solutions are not available, numerical procedures (computer programs) are used instead (see Wilmott 1998; Duffie 2001; Glasserman 2003). There remain many open questions, and option pricing remains an intellectually challenging field to which interesting contributions can still be made.

---

[1] A **closed-form solution** is an exact mathematical formula like $x = (a + b)^2$. If you know a and b, you can easily solve for x. The BSM model solves an option's price in terms of known variables and functions like the cumulative normal distribution.

5.3 | Call Options

Call Payoffs and Profit Diagrams

Option payoffs on the expiration date or at early exercise are easier to understand in a **perfect market**, where **market imperfections** like transaction costs, taxes, and trading restrictions are assumed away. In reality, the market contains such imperfections. The brokers who match option trades charge commissions for their services. A dealer will quote an ask price (say, $4) and a bid (say, $3.90) for the option premium. Large trades tend to have market impact, and the entire order may not be filled at the price posted by a dealer. Unfortunately, these real-world features detract from understanding the basic payoffs. Hence we study option payoffs under a perfect market structure. Once you know how these contracts work, you can adjust for these imperfections.

The next example considers a call buyer's and writer's payoffs and profit diagrams on the expiration date.

EXAMPLE 5.1: European Call Option Payoff and Profit Diagrams

Call Buyer's Payoff

- Today is January 1 (time 0). An April 100 European call option on the stock of Your Beloved Machines Inc. (YBM) is created when Ms. Longina Long pays the premium $c = \$4$ to Mr. Shorty Short, who becomes the writer. This call has a strike price of $K = \$100$, and it ceases trading on the third Friday of April. This is the only day this European call can be exercised (time T); see Figure 5.1 for this option's timeline.[2]

- Long's exercise decision depends on the stock price $S(T)$ on the fateful expiration date. If $S(T)$ is $106, then Long exercises the call because the stock is worth more than the strike (traders say that the option is **in-the-money**). She pays the strike, receives the stock worth $S(T)$, and makes $[S(T) - K] = \$6$ in the process. The $4 premium is a sunk cost and does not affect the exercise decision.

- Conversely, if the stock is worth less than the strike, then the option expires worthless—**out-of-the-money**, in traders' parlance. If Long is keen to acquire the stock, she should directly tap the stock market. It's imprudent to exercise out-of-the-money options. For example, if $S(T)$ is $92, she gets $92 - 100 = -\$8$ by exercising the call, an outcome she should avoid. And when $S(T)$ equals the strike price, the option is **at-the-money**, and the long is indifferent regarding exercise. In reality, a comparison of transaction costs for purchasing the stock is likely to influence her decision. For example, suppose Long is planning to purchase a thinly traded stock. If the stock's spread is too high, Long may exercise an at-the-money call (or even a call that is slightly out-of-the-money) to more cheaply acquire the stock.

---

[2] The OCC (www.optionsclearing.com/about/publications/expiration-calendar-2010.jsp) and exchange websites label the following Saturday as the expiration date. This is a technicality. The third Friday, which we label as time (date) T, is the relevant economic date for our purpose because it is (1) the day when the option stops trading, (2) the only day a European option can be exercised, and (3) the last day an American option may be exercised. For simplicity, we will use the terms *exercise date* and *expiration date* interchangeably.

■ True to the proverb "a picture says a thousand words," patterns emerge when we graph these payoffs in a **payoff diagram**. These diagrams plot the stock price at expiration, $S(T)$, along the horizontal axis and the option payoff (or *gross payoff*) along the vertical axis. Long call's payoff starts at 0 value when the stock price is zero and lies flat along the axis until the stock price reaches $K = \$100$ (see Figure 5.2). Beyond this, the payoff increases at a 45 degree angle, rising by a dollar for each dollar increase in $S(T)$.

Call Writer's Payoff

■ Because option trading is a zero-sum game, Short's call's payoff is the mirror image across the horizontal axis of Long's payoff. The writer loses nothing at expiration until $S(T)$ reaches \$100, beyond which his payoff declines at a negative 45 degree angle. When $S(T) = \$106$, Short loses \$6, which is Long's gain. When $S(T) = \$92$, Short loses nothing.

Call Buyer's Profit

■ Payoff diagrams fail to reveal why Short, who has a zero or negative payoff on the expiration date, will get into this venture. This limitation is overcome by a **profit diagram**, which adds the option's

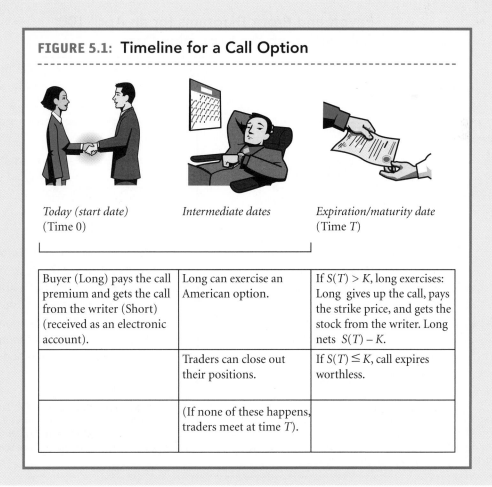

FIGURE 5.1: Timeline for a Call Option

Today (start date) (Time 0)	Intermediate dates	Expiration/maturity date (Time T)
Buyer (Long) pays the call premium and gets the call from the writer (Short) (received as an electronic account).	Long can exercise an American option.	If $S(T) > K$, long exercises: Long gives up the call, pays the strike price, and gets the stock from the writer. Long nets $S(T) - K$.
	Traders can close out their positions.	If $S(T) \leq K$, call expires worthless.
	(If none of these happens, traders meet at time T).	

premium to the trader's payoff. The profit diagram plots $S(T)$ along the horizontal axis but has profit (or loss) from option trading along the vertical axis. For convenience, we ignore any interest that the option premiums may earn in the margin account. This allows us to combine the cash flows at the option's initiation and expiration dates on the same diagram.

- If $S(T)$ does not exceed the strike price $K = \$100$, Long loses $c = \$4$, the premium she paid for the call. This is her maximum loss. When $S(T)$ exceeds \$100, Long will definitely exercise the call. A dollar increase in $S(T)$ raises the value of her position by a dollar and cuts her losses. Consequently, the profit graph is a horizontal straight line at −\$4 until it reaches the strike price, where it increases at a 45 degree angle. When $S(T) = \$104$, Long's \$4 gain exactly offsets her initial \$4 investment and gives "zero profit." When $S(T)$ goes beyond \$104, it's even sweeter. Technically speaking, the call holder has limitless profit potential (see Figure 5.2). Focusing on our familiar points, when $S(T) = \$106$, Long has a net gain of \$2 because he makes \$6 but he paid \$4 for the call. Conversely, when $S(T) = \$92$, Long does not exercise and loses only the \$4 premium.

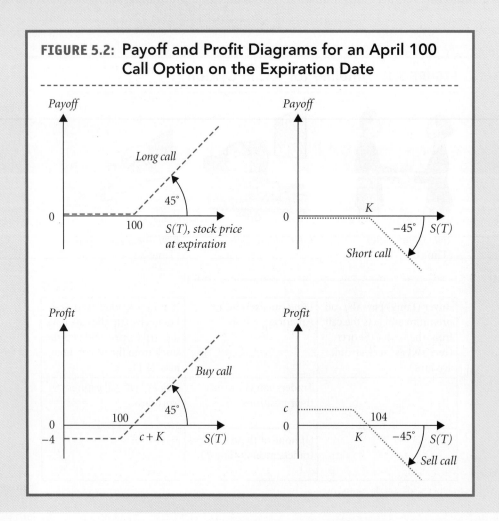

FIGURE 5.2: Payoff and Profit Diagrams for an April 100 Call Option on the Expiration Date

Call Writer's Profit

- When $S(T)$ does not exceed the strike, the call writer keeps the $4 premium collected up front. This is also the maximum profit. When $S(T)$ increases above $100, Long's exercise reduces this amount. Zero profits occur when $S(T) = \$104$. Below this level, Short plunges deeper into losses (see Figure 5.2). In the example considered, when $S(T) = \$106$, the writer has a loss of $2. When $S(T) = \$92$, Long does not exercise, and Short's profit is $4. Because option trading is a zero-sum game, the total gain of both traders is zero. In reality, brokerage commission lowers the profits accruing to each trader.

- Notice what the diagrams reveal: call writing can generate far larger losses than call buying. The maximum loss to the buyer is the premium. In contrast, the writer can literally fall into a bottomless abyss where the maximum loss is unbounded. Recognizing this asymmetry, the options exchange requires a call writer to hold more funds in a margin account than a buyer.

The Call's Intrinsic and Time Values

An American call is identical to a European call, except that it can be exercised any time until expiration. Remember that if an American call is not exercised early, then it has the same value as a European call on the expiration date so that the payoff diagrams are identical. And prior to expiration, the exercise strategy for an American option is guided by two facts: (1) one should never exercise an out-of-the-money option, and (2) when exercising an in-the-money call early, one receives the stock price minus the strike price. In other words, if an American call is exercised early, then its payoff looks like that of a European call on the expiration date.

We summarize these insights.

RESULT 5.1

Intrinsic (or Exercise) Value of a Call Option

A call holder's payoff at expiration or if exercised early is

$$\text{Call's intrinsic value} \equiv \begin{cases} S - K & \text{for } S > K \\ 0 & \text{otherwise} \end{cases} \quad (5.1a)$$

which may be written as

$$\text{Call's intrinsic value} = \max(S - K, 0) \quad (5.1b)$$

where S is the stock price on the exercise date, K is the strike price, and max means the maximum of the two arguments that follow.

This is a call option's boundary condition. The payoff is also referred to as the call's intrinsic or exercise value.

What does this mean? For $S < K$, the term $(S - K)$ is negative, the call is not exercised, and 0 is the value. When $S \geq K$, the call's value equals $S - K$. The profit is obtained by subtracting the call's premium from the preceding payoff.

This result has a simple corollary. It implies that if the stock price hits zero, then the call price is also zero. Indeed, if the stock hits zero, it has no future, and it is never going to take a positive value again. Consequently, a call, which gives the right to purchase the stock in the future, must also be zero.

The intrinsic value is only part of an option's premium. The remainder is the additional value accruing to an option because the stock price may increase further before maturity. Consequently, we define the **time value** of a European or American option as

$$\text{Time value of an option} = \text{Option price} - \text{Option's intrinsic value} \quad (5.2)$$

Time value declines as one approaches the expiration date and (by its definition) becomes zero when the option matures. Example 5.2 computes the time value of a call option.

EXAMPLE 5.2: Time Value of a Call Option

■ On some date t before expiration, suppose that YBM's stock price $S(t) = \$101$ and the call price $c(t) = \$2.50$. If the strike price $K = \$100$, then

Call option's time value

$= \text{Call price} - \text{Call's intrinsic value}$

$= c(t) - [S(t) - K]$

$= 2.50 - (101 - 100)$

$= \$1.50$

Price Bounds for American Calls

Although we are yet to price options, the boundary condition and some simple reasoning can determine what call option prices are admissible and what prices aren't.

EXAMPLE 5.3: Price Bounds for an American Call Option

■ As in Example 5.1, consider an American call option with a strike price $K = \$100$. Its price can never exceed the underlying stock's price. Indeed, the call is a security that gives the holder the right to buy the underlying stock by paying the strike price. If you have to choose between the two—a gift of the stock versus getting the stock by paying some money—which one would you prefer? Getting the gift, of course, which implies that the stock is worth more than the option.

- Consequently, a call's price can never exceed the underlying stock's price. Figure 5.3 plots today's stock price $S(t)$, written as S for simplicity, along the horizontal axis and has both the stock and the call price along the vertical axis. The upward sloping 45 degree line from the origin represents the stock price. The call price can never exceed this value, and the 45 degree line forms an upper bound. A rational investor will never let a call's price fall below the boundary condition given by Result 5.1, $\max(S - 100, 0)$, which forms a lower bound. This is the kinked line that starts at the origin and increases at a 45 degree angle when the stock price is $100.

- Let us illustrate these bounds with some numbers:
  - When the call is out-of-the-money, say, the stock price is $90, the time value prevents the call price from being zero. So it will lie above the horizontal axis. However, the call price can never exceed the stock price of $90, and hence it will lie below the 45 degree line emanating from the origin.
  - When the call is in-the-money, say, the stock price is $115, the call is worth at least $S - K = 115 - 100 = \$15$ if exercised. So the call price can never fall below the lower bound, and of course, it can never exceed $115, which lies on the upper bound.

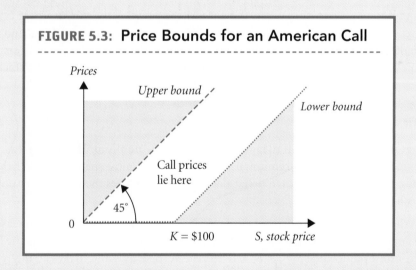

FIGURE 5.3: **Price Bounds for an American Call**

5.4 | Put Options

Put Payoffs and Profit Diagrams

We illustrate a put option's payoff and profit diagrams with an example.

EXAMPLE 5.4: European Put Option Payoff and Profit Diagrams

Put Option Payoffs

- Today is January 1 (time 0). Ms. Long pays Mr. Short $p = \$6$ and buys a May 50 European put option on Boring Unreliable Gadgets Corp (BUG). This put gives Long the right to sell BUG stocks on the exercise date, the third Friday of May (time T), at the strike price $K = \$50$.

- A put's timeline is similar to that for the call given in Figure 5.1. If the put is not closed out early, the traders meet on the expiration date T. If the stock price is less than the strike price (the put is **in-the-money**), Long exercises the put, receives K dollars, surrenders the stock worth $S(T)$, and makes $[K - S(T)]$ in the process. For example, if $S(T) = \$40$, then Long sells the stock for $50 and makes $10. Conversely, if $S(T)$ is greater than K (the put is **out-of-the-money**), it's unwise to exercise. For example, if $S(T) = \$55$, Long gets $(50 - 55) = -\$5$ if she exercises and zero if she doesn't. Exercise is irrelevant if BUG closes at $50 (the put is **at-the-money**).[3]

- These considerations enable us to draw the payoff diagrams. For large stock prices, the put holder's payoff has zero value, and it lies on the horizontal axis. As the stock price declines and dips below the strike, the payoff forms a kink at K and increases at a 45 degree angle, increasing by a dollar for each dollar decrease in the stock price (see Figure 5.4). The profit peaks when the stock is worthless, but Long can sell it for K dollars as per contract terms.

- Because option trading is a zero-sum game, the put writer's payoff is the mirror image across the x-axis of the buyer's payoff. When $S(T)$ is greater than $50, the put seller loses nothing, and the payoff coincides with the horizontal axis. When the stock goes below the strike, the payoff decreases below the horizon line at a 45 degree angle starting at K, and it reaches the nadir when the stock becomes worthless.

Put Option Profit

- The profit diagram adjusts the payoff diagram for an option's premium. If $S(T)$ is greater than the strike price $K = \$50$, Long loses the premium $p = \$6$, which is the most she can lose. When $S(T)$ falls below $50, Long exercises the put—each dollar decrease in $S(T)$ raises the value of her position by a dollar and cuts her losses.

- Consequently, the profit graph is a horizontal line at $-\$6$ for high values of $S(T)$. It increases upward at a 45 degree angle when $S(T)$ touches $K = \$50$ on its downward journey, and it cuts the horizontal axis at the zero-profit point when $S(T) = \$44$. It hits the vertical axis and makes an intercept of $44 when $S(T) = 0$ (see Figure 5.4). The profit graph for a put holder is the mirror image of the buyer's graph across the horizontal axis. Notice that both the maximum profit and the biggest loss are bounded for a put option.

- Next we illustrate these profit (or loss) computations. For $S(T) = \$40$, Long makes $(50 - 40) = \$10$ by exercising the put. However, he paid $6 for the option, netting a profit of $10 - 6 = \$4$, which is also Short's loss. For $S(T) = \$55$, Long does not exercise the put, and her loss is the $6 premium, which is also Short's profit.

---

[3] Transaction and liquidity costs may slightly modify this decision. If the long has a substantial holding in the underlying stock that is thinly traded and wants to sell, then she may exercise an at-the-money or slightly out-of-the-money put option to sell the stock at minimum transaction cost.

The Put's Intrinsic and Time Values

An American put may also be exercised before expiration. Of course, if an American put is not exercised early, then the American and European puts have identical value on the expiration date so that their payoff diagrams are identical. Before expiration, the exercise strategy for an American option is determined by two facts: (1) one should never exercise an out-of-the-money option, and (2) in case of early exercise of an in-the-money put, the value is the strike price minus the stock price. When exercised early, an American put's payoff looks like that of a European put on the expiration date.

These observations are summarized as Result 5.2.

RESULT 5.2

- -

Intrinsic (or Exercise) Value of a Put Option

A put holder's payoff at expiration or if exercised is

$$\text{Put's intrinsic value} \equiv \begin{cases} K - S & \text{for } S < K \\ 0 & \text{otherwise} \end{cases} \tag{5.3a}$$

which may be written as

$$\text{Put's intrinsic value} = \max(K - S, 0) \tag{5.3b}$$

where K is the strike price, S is the stock price on the exercise or expiration date, and max means the maximum of the two arguments that follow.

This is a put option's boundary condition. The payoff is also referred to as the put's intrinsic (or exercise) value.

For example, consider a put with a strike price of $K = \$50$. When $S(T) = \$55$, $K - S(T) = -\$5$. As the maximum of $-\$5$ and 0 is clearly 0, the put value $p(T) = 0$ at expiration. When $S(T) = \$40$, then $K - S(T) = \$10$ is the intrinsic value. For $S(T) < K$, the positive term $[K - S(T)]$ is the put's payoff. When $S(T) \geq K$, the term $K - S(T)$ is no longer positive, and zero becomes the put's intrinsic value.

The next example illustrates the computation of a put's time value.

EXAMPLE 5.5: Time Value of a Put Option

- At time t, let BUG's stock price $S(t) = \$48$ and its put price $p(t) = \$3$ for a strike price $K = \$50$. Then

$$\text{Put option's time value}$$
$$= \text{Put premium} - \text{Put's intrinsic value}$$
$$= p(t) - [K - S(t)]$$
$$= 3 - (50 - 48)$$
$$= \$1$$

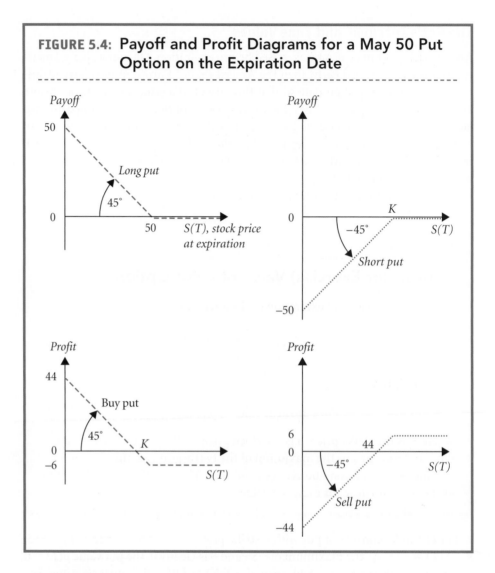

FIGURE 5.4: Payoff and Profit Diagrams for a May 50 Put Option on the Expiration Date

Price Bounds for American Puts

As with calls, we can use the boundary condition to determine price bounds for put options.

EXAMPLE 5.6: Price Bounds for an American Put Option

- As in Example 5.4, consider an American put option with a strike price of $K = \$50$. Its value can never exceed the strike price because the put gives the holder the right to sell the underlying stock at the strike price. Thus the maximum payoff from the put is the exercise price $K = \$50$. This forms an upper bound for the put price and is depicted by the horizontal line at $50 in Figure 5.5.

- The put's price can never fall below $\max(0, 50 - S)$, the boundary condition given by (5.3), which forms a lower bound. This is the line that originates at $50 on the vertical axis, decreases at a 45 degree angle until it hits $50 on the horizontal axis, and then continues along the horizontal axis.

- We illustrate these bounds with an example:
  - When the put is in-the-money, say, the stock price is $10, the put price cannot fall below its exercise value $50 - 10 = 40. Because the put price cannot rise above its upper bound of $50, it lies between $40 and $50.
  - When the put is out-of-the-money, say, the stock price is $60, the put price cannot fall below the horizontal axis because no one would exercise and lose money. Of course, it cannot exceed its upper bound: the flat line at $50 above the horizontal axis.

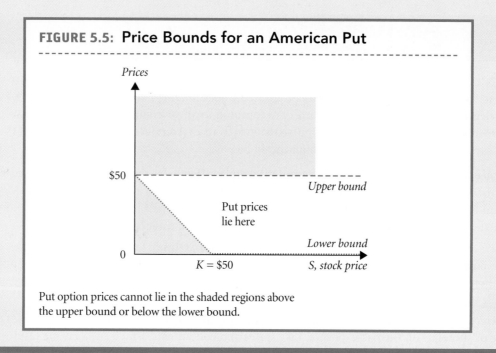

FIGURE 5.5: Price Bounds for an American Put

Put option prices cannot lie in the shaded regions above the upper bound or below the lower bound.

5.5 | Exchange-Traded Options

Relative to futures contracts, exchange-traded options are newcomers. They started trading in 1973 with the opening of the **Chicago Board Options Exchange** (**CBOE**). Today options trading is dominated by big exchange groups, which offer diverse product lines (stocks, bonds, options, futures, etc.). They include the New York Stock Exchange (NYSE), which has AMEX and Arca Options (the Pacific Exchange got merged into Arca), the CME Group, the NASDAQ OMX Group (which has BX, the former Boston exchange, and PX, the former Philadelphia exchange), the Eurex (whose wholly owned subsidiary is the International Securities Exchange), the CBOE (which has the C2 Options Exchange), and BATS (which grew from an electronic communications network).

The **Options Clearing Corporation** (**OCC**) clears the bulk of exchange-traded options. As such, the OCC becomes the guarantor of contract performance to each buyer and seller. As discussed before, a clearinghouse makes options safer to trade, helps develop a secondary market, allows anonymous trading, and eliminates the need to track one's counterparty. These benefits have greatly contributed to option market growth. Extension 5.1 discusses the benefits of exchange-traded options in greater detail. The exchanges clearing trades with the OCC in 2011 include the BATS Options Exchange, the C2 Options Exchange, the CBOE, the International Securities Exchange, NASDAQ OMX BX, NASDAQ OMX PHLX, the NASDAQ Stock Market, the NYSE Amex Options, and the NYSE Arca Options (see the OCC's website at www.theocc.com).

EXTENSION 5.1: Benefits of Exchange-Traded Options

The introduction of exchange-traded options fundamentally altered options markets. We list here many of the benefits of these contracts; for a more detailed list, see *Understanding Equity Options* (September 2007, www.optionsclearing.com). Some of these features are common to any exchange-traded derivative security, while others are unique to options. Although our discussion is from an American perspective, most of these benefits apply to exchange-traded options throughout the globe.

1. *Central marketplace.* An exchange is a central marketplace that helps the process of price discovery, collects and disseminates price information, and conducts surveillance and regulatory oversight. Moreover, the **Option Price Reporting Authority** links the various option markets in the United States and widely disseminates last sale reports, price quotes, and a variety of option trade–related data.

2. *Orderly, efficient, and liquid markets with low transaction costs.* Option features like contract size, strike price, and expiration date are preset by the exchange. Standardization enables quick collection of quotes and fast execution of trades. A well-organized market structure has helped develop orderly, competitive markets. For actively traded securities, spreads are small and information gets quickly reflected in prices.

3. *Flexibility.* Options are flexible, versatile investment tools that can be combined with a securities portfolio to hedge or speculate on the risk exposure. Like spices and condiments, which enhance the taste and flavor of food, options can do wonders when judiciously used. Option trading strategies are discussed in greater detail in chapter 15.

4. *Limited risk for most traders.* Option buyers and put traders have limited risk, but call sellers have unbounded risk. Whether the glass is half full or half empty depends on your perspective. Although the risk from most option positions is quite limited, many option traders lose their entire investments in a relatively short span of time.

5. *Guaranteed contract performance.* Although options on equities and indexes trade on different US exchanges, most trades are channeled through the OCC, a single clearinghouse that eliminates credit risk. Once the OCC is satisfied that an order matches, it clears the trade, delinks the buyer from the seller, and becomes the counterparty to each trade.

6. *Secondary market.* Exchange-traded options have active secondary markets where traders can enter or exit their positions with relative ease. For example, a seller can buy the option that she has written earlier and inform the exchange that this is a closing transaction—the exchange cleans the slate and frees her entirely from the trade.

7. *Overcome stock market restrictions.* Options can often avoid restrictions and limitations that may characterize the underlying's market. Recall from chapter 3 that stock markets sometime impose restrictions—for example, many countries prohibit short selling of stocks. To circumvent this restriction, you can buy a put option to bet on a stock's slide.

8. *Certificateless trading.* Stocks and bonds have ownership certificates, and they have moved to a virtually certificate-free existence in recent years. Options were certificateless from the very start, which reduced paperwork and trading costs. Options exist as computer entries, and a broker's confirmation is the evidence of ownership.

Because the CBOE grew out of the Chicago Board of Trade, it shares many of the same features of futures and stock exchanges. Example 5.7 considers a hypothetical options trade at the CBOE, illustrating these features.

EXAMPLE 5.7: Exchange Trading of a Call Option

Order Placement

- Today is January 1 (time 0). Ms. Longina Long and Mr. Shorty Short have opened margin accounts and have been approved for trading options with their respective brokers. Unbeknownst to each another, they simultaneously decide to trade ten April 100 call options on Your Beloved Machines Inc. (YBM). These American calls have a strike price of $K = \$100$ and an exercise date of the third Friday of April. Because each option **contract** is on one hundred shares, ten contracts reflect gains or losses from one thousand shares.

- Tech-savvy Longina flips open her laptop and logs onto her brokerage account. Finding that YBM April calls have a bid price of $4.00 and an ask–offer price of $4.05, she types in a *limit order* that instructs her broker to buy ten contracts at $4.00 or a lower price. Old-fashioned Shorty calls up his broker and places a *market order* that is immediately executed. Small orders are matched via computers and are filled and confirmed within a few seconds. Most option trades are executed on the exchange floor.

- Suppose Long's and Short's orders are sent via computer to their respective brokerage firms' representatives at booths on the trading floor. Hundreds of well-equipped booths rented out to clearing firm members line the walls of the exchange floor. Once the orders reach these booths, they are passed on to floor brokers, who take them to a trading station, where brokers and dealers gather to conduct business, for execution.

- A typical CBOE-like exchange has many trading posts on the exchange floor, with each post having some ten or more trading stations. A trading station is assigned several stocks, and all options on a particular stock trade only at that location. Typically, it is a raised counter behind which stands an **order book official** (or **board broker**) and his assistants. They write down transactions and maintain the **order book**, which contains all outstanding limit orders.

- Most of the time, buy and sell orders arrive randomly and do not synchronize well. A *market maker dealer* makes the option market liquid by maintaining an inventory and standing ready to trade. Each market maker is assigned some options and is required to make regular bids and offers for at least twenty—in many cases, fifty—option contracts.

- Different exchanges follow different conventions. The exchanges and trading mechanisms are constantly evolving due to technological advances and competition across the exchanges for trading volume. Most exchanges still have dealers to provide market making services, but electronic matching systems are playing a larger and larger role. For specific details, the reader should consult the exchanges' websites directly.

Trade Execution, Clearing, and Settlement

- Shorty's broker accepts Longina's limit order, and ten contracts are executed at $c = \$4.00$. Floor brokers send back trade information using a handheld computer. Longina sees the trade confirmation on her web page, and Shorty gets a confirmatory phone call from the broker's representative. Vital transaction data also go into the exchange's main computer system.

- Commission rates vary. A discount broker typically charges a fixed rate, which may be as small as $5 to $20 per trade, and a variable rate, which typically ranges from 50 cents to $2 for each option on one hundred shares. Many firms charge lower commissions for (1) Internet orders; (2) active traders; (3) the simplest orders like market orders; (4) small-sized orders, because they are unlikely to be based on privileged information; and paradoxically, (5) larger orders, to give customers a break. Brokers charge two commissions: one at the time of buying (or selling) and a second commission when selling (or buying back) or exercising the option.

- Suppose Long's discount broker charges her $10 for the trade plus a dollar per contract—$20 in all. Consequently, Long's brokerage account is debited an amount equal to the buying price plus commission:

$$\text{Price} \times 100 \times (\text{Number of contracts}) + \text{Commission}$$
$$= 4 \times 100 \times 10 + 20$$
$$= \$4{,}020$$

- Shorty has a full-service broker who charges $50 for the trade plus $3 per contract—$80 in all. Short's margin account is credited an amount equal to the selling price less the commission:

$$\text{Price} \times 100 \times (\text{Number of contracts}) - \text{Commission}$$
$$= 4 \times 100 \times 10 - 80$$
$$= \$3{,}920$$

Because selling options is a risky transaction, Short's broker requires him to keep the entire proceeds as well as some extra funds as a security deposit in the margin account.

Closing the Contract

- Being exchange-traded contracts, options have secondary markets. Traders retain the flexibility of taking their profits or cutting their losses and walking away. Long may sell the option to a third party and close out her position—she may win or lose in the process. Quite independently, Short can buy the option in a closing transaction, and a third trader then becomes the writer. Because this is an American call, Long can exercise at any time until the maturity date.

- Fluctuations in option prices affect the margin account's value. Suppose that YBM rallies tomorrow and the call price increases by $3. Then Long's margin account gains $3,000, and Short's margin account declines by the same amount. If his maintenance margin is breached, Shorty has to add funds to his margin account.

- Suppose that the option is neither exercised nor closed out early so that the counterparties meet again on the expiration date. To avoid the hassle of paying the broker a fee for exercising and yet another fee for trading YBM shares, they decide to close out their positions just before the option's expiration and trade at a $7 premium per option. Then Long's profits are

$$
\begin{aligned}
&\text{Sale proceeds} - \text{Cost} \\
&= (7 \times 100 \times 10 - 20) - 4{,}020 \\
&= \$2{,}960
\end{aligned}
$$

and Short's profit (remember, his brokerage costs are higher) is

$$
\begin{aligned}
&\text{Sale proceeds} - \text{Cost} \\
&= 3{,}920 - (7 \times 100 \times 10 + 80) \\
&= -\$3{,}160
\end{aligned}
$$

5.6 | Longs and Shorts in Different Markets

Market practitioners often use the terms *long* and *short* to convey the notions of buying and selling. But these terms have different meanings in different markets. For derivatives, *long* means "buy," and *short* means "sell." Derivatives trade in zero net supply markets, where each buyer has a matching seller. Long and short in the derivatives markets are just opposite sides of the same trade. Consequently, it is a zero-sum game because one trader's gain is the other's loss.

The short seller in the stock market does something more complex. She borrows shares, sells them, and buys back those shares at a later date to return them to the lender. For futures and forwards, both a long and a short have obligations to transact at a future date. The long agrees to buy the asset, and the short agrees to sell.

Options give the buyer the right to buy (call) or sell (put) at a fixed price until a fixed date. No matter whether it's a call or a put, the buyer who is long has an option. They decide to exercise or not. In contrast, the writer, who holds a short position, has an obligation. The short needs to fulfill the option's terms as chosen by the long. For this situation, the buyer pays the writer a premium at the start.

5.7 | Order Placement Strategies

All traders face the same dilemma: to trade immediately or to wait to see if one can get a better price. If you want to transact immediately, submit a *market order*; however, if you can wait for a better price, then submit **contingent orders** that depend on the price, time, and other relevant factors. But there is a trade-off: *market orders may get traded at a bad price, whereas price-contingent orders may never get filled.*

Example 5.8 considers different types of order placement strategies for trading stocks in fairy-tale (hypothetical) situations. These same order placement strategies also apply to futures and options. Let's start our discussion with stocks for easy illustration and then show how the argument extends to derivatives like options.

EXAMPLE 5.8: Order Placement Strategies

A Market Order

- A dealer quotes an ask–offer price of $100.10 and a bid price of $100.00 per share for YBM stock. Hoping that it will rally, you want to buy YBM in a hurry. You can place a **market buy order**, which gets executed immediately at the best price your broker can find—very likely at $100.10. You may be forced to pay a bit more or enjoy paying slightly less if a spate of buy or sell orders suddenly comes in. Unless there is a severe market breakdown, market orders are always filled.

- A market order is also the simplest way to buy options and futures. Recall in the previous example that Shorty placed a market sell order and sold the option for $4, which was the bid price. If gold futures prices are being cried out in the trading pit at $1,500.10 to sell and $1,500.00 to buy, then a market buy order is likely to get executed at $1,500.00.

A Price-Contingent Order

- Sometimes you may get a better price by waiting. You can place a *limit order* that must be executed at the stated or a better price or not executed at all. One must specify whether this is a day order or a good-until-canceled order. An unfilled **day order** automatically cancels at the day's end, while a **good-until-canceled (GTC) order** stays open almost indefinitely in the specialist's order book until it is closed. To eliminate stale orders, many brokers automatically cancel GTC orders after a significant time period has passed, for example 60 days.

- Suppose you place a **limit buy order** at $99.00. If the stock price decreases from $100.10 and your trade gets executed, then you obtained a $1.10 price improvement. However, you also run the risk that the stock may rally and the order may never be filled. Similarly for an option on YBM that is being quoted at a bid price of $4.00 and an ask price of $4.05, a trader hoping to benefit from market fluctuations may place a limit sell order at $4.50.

A Time-Contingent Order

- A **time-of-day order** specifies execution at a particular time or interval of time. For example, you may request execution at 2:00 PM in the afternoon, or you may request execution between 2:30 PM and 3:00 PM. More examples of orders that depend on time or other characteristics are given in Extension 5.2.

Combinations of Related Orders

- Sometimes traders place orders in combination. For example, a **spread** order may instruct the broker to execute the order when the price difference between two securities reaches a certain value. A **cancel order** or a **straight cancel order** completely cancels a previous order. A **cancel replace order** replaces an existing order with a new one. See Extension 5.2 for more examples of such order placement strategies.

Extension 5.2 augments Example 5.8 to include many more strategies. Our discussion also applies to options and futures trading, and we can similarly place such orders for bonds, the Treasury securities introduced in chapter 2.

EXTENSION 5.2: More Order Placement Strategies

Example 5.8 discussed some basic order placement strategies, but they form a small subset of the possible order placement strategies. We first show how minor variations in a simple limit order can create a whole range of strategies, and then we give more examples that depend on time and other factors as well as strategies placed in combination with other securities. Moreover, we enrich our examples by including order placement strategies for trading futures and options.

EXAMPLE 5.8: (Continued) Order Placement Strategies

Price-Dependent Orders

- Suppose that a dealer is quoting an ask–offer price of $100.10 and a bid price of $100.00 for YBM stock and that you have placed a good-until-canceled limit order to buy them for $99.00 per share. Even if YBM touches $99.00, your limit order may not be filled. This occurs when there are many outstanding limit orders at $99.00 and the price increases before your order gets filled. If you really want to trade at a price of $99.00, or something close, place a **market-if-touched order**, which becomes a market order as soon as a trade occurs at your specified price of $99.00.

- Suppose you want to buy YBM if a rally develops. Here you can place a **stop order to buy** (or **buy stop order**) for YBM at $101.00, which is above the current price of $100.10. This becomes a market order as soon as a bid or an offer or a trade price for YBM hits $101.00 or more.

- The opposite of a buy stop is a **stop-loss order** (or a **sell stop order**) that is placed below current market prices. Suppose that YBM has a big run-up to $120 after you buy it. You may desire to lock in your gain. If so, you can place a **stop order** to sell YBM if the price falls below $118. Should YBM rise further, you will profit more. If it falls, you can protect a big chunk of your earlier profit by selling the stock at $118.

- Another possibility is to place a **buy stop-limit order**. Suppose you place a stop-limit order to buy YBM stock at $101.00, which is above the current price. This order becomes a limit buy order as soon as a bid, an offer, or a trade price hits $101.00 or higher. This order has the risk of never being filled. For example, if the market pierces $101 and immediately shoots up, then your broker will be unable to buy at $101.00 or a lower price.

Owing to their complex nature, many exchanges do not accept stop-limit orders.

Time- and Other Factor-Dependent Orders

- Earlier we considered a **time of day order** that specifies execution at a particular time or interval of time. An example of such an order that has earned a separate name is the **market on close order** (**MOC order**), which becomes a market order during the last minute of trading. As you are likely to get a bad price when hurriedly winding up things at day's end (your potential counterparties know that you are trying to escape before the barn door gets bolted), the MOC has also earned the name "murder on close" order!

- A **fill or kill order** (**FOK order**) must be immediately filled or it is canceled. Don't place this order too far from the current price—it is unlikely to go through and will only irritate your broker. Expert traders sometimes use FOKs to test the market's strength or weakness.

- An **all or none order** (**AON**) must be executed in full. Suppose you place a limit order to buy three thousand shares of YBM. A trader is willing to sell you only one thousand shares. Normally the limit order will go through and you will get a partial execution. Someone else may sell you the remaining two thousand shares at your price, or those may never be filled. With an all-or-none order, your broker must get three thousand shares to match your three thousand buys; otherwise, this limit order will not be executed.

- A **good this week order** (**GTW**) is valid only for the week in which it is placed.

- A **discretionary order** (or **market-not-held** or **disregard tape order**; **DRT**) is a market order, but the filling broker may delay it in an attempt to get a better price. This can be useful for executing large trades as it gives the broker more leeway to do a better job.

Combination Orders

- A **spread order** involves a market order to buy one option and to sell another. For example, suppose that you have two calls trading on YBM with strike prices of $100 and $105. You can set up a spread order to buy the high strike and sell the other. Spread orders do not focus on the absolute price levels but instead on the difference between the two option prices. You will see more examples of spread strategies later in the book.

- A **scale order** requests a series of trades at staggered prices. Suppose you are buying April YBM calls with a strike price of $100. Although the last trade was conducted at $4, you are worried that the price impact of your trade will lead to partial fulfillment. Consequently, you may place a scale order to buy twenty-five contracts at a limit price of $4.00, twenty-five at $4.10, twenty-five at $4.20, and the final twenty-five at $4.25.

- We previously considered a **cancel order** or a **straight cancel order**, which completely cancels a previous order, and a **cancel replace order**, which replaces an existing order with a new one. Another variation is a **one cancels the other order** (**OCO order**) or an **alternative order**, which involves a group of orders where the execution of one cancels the other. Suppose you plan to buy put options on gold with a strike price of $1,000. If you place an OCO order to buy October puts at a limit price of $5 (which is currently trading at $6) or December puts at $7 (which is currently trading at $9), then the execution of any one order will nullify the other. An OCO helps to choose the contract that reaches the favorable price first.

- A **switch order** is a spread order that relates to a previous position. Suppose you buy December gold options hoping that gold will rally, but the rally never occurs. Nonetheless, you are still optimistic that the rally will occur before April. You can use a switch order to replace the maturing December option with one that matures in April.

5.8 | Summary

1. A call option gives the buyer (the "long") the right but not the obligation to buy a specified quantity of a financial or real asset from the seller (the "short") on or before a fixed future expiration date by paying an exercise price agreed today. A put gives the holder the right to sell. A put is similar to an insurance contract that pays in case of a decline in an asset's value. The writer is paid a premium for selling such rights.

2. A European option can only be exercised at the maturity date, whereas an American option can be exercised at any time up to and including the expiration date. The names "American" and "European" do not depend on where the option trades. Most exchange-traded options in the United States are of the American type.

3. A call holder's payoff at expiration or if exercised early, its intrinsic value, is the stock price minus the strike price when the stock price is greater than the strike (call is in-the-money) and zero otherwise (call is out-of-the-money). A put's intrinsic–exercise value is the strike price minus the stock price when the stock price is less than the strike and zero when the stock price is greater than or equal to the strike. Intrinsic value is only part of an option's value. The rest is the time value, which takes into account that the option's value may increase before it expires.

4. Payoffs to different option positions as a function of the stock price at expiration generate well-known patterns, which can be depicted in a payoff diagram. Profit diagrams adjust these diagrams for the option's premium.

5. Options started trading on organized exchanges in 1973 with the opening of the CBOE. Traditional exchanges have many trading posts on the exchange floor, where brokers and dealers gather to trade options of particular kinds. Today derivatives trade on exchanges around the globe. Technology is transforming the way derivatives trade. Several old exchanges have scrapped floor trading and moved to a fully automated electronic trading system, and newer ones often start as fully electronic exchanges.

6. Traders in a hurry place market orders that are immediately executed. Traders who can wait in the hope of a better price strategically submit limit orders that may be contingent on price, time, and other relevant factors or submitted in combination with other orders. There is a trade-off: market orders may get traded at a bad price, while price improvement orders may never be filled. Contingent orders are possible for trading stocks, options, and futures.

5.9 | Cases

Goldman, Sachs, and Co.: Nikkei Put Warrants—1989 (Harvard Business School Case 292113-PDF-ENG). The case illustrates how investment banks can design, produce (hedge), and price put warrants on the Nikkei Stock Average.

Nextel Partners: Put Option (Harvard Business School Case 207128-PDF-ENG). The case examines issues surrounding Nextel's shareholders' vote to exercise a put option that requires the company's largest shareholder, Sprint Nextel Corp., to purchase all the shares it does not already own.

Pixonix Inc.—Addressing Currency Exposure (Richard Ivey School of Business Foundation Case 908N13-PDF-ENG. Harvard Business Publishing). The case discusses the impact of exchange rate fluctuations on a firm's cash flows and how derivatives can be used to manage this risk.

5.10 | Questions and Problems

5.1. Explain the differences between an option's delivery and expiration dates.

5.2. Explain the differences between European and American options. How do the names relate to the geographical continents?

5.3. Explain the differences between call and put options. Are they just the exact opposites of each other?

5.4. Explain the differences between long and short in the stock market. Explain how one shorts a stock.

5.5. Explain the differences between long and short in the option market. What is the difference between an option buyer and writer?

5.6. Explain the differences between an option's intrinsic and time values. How do these relate to the option's price?

5.7. Explain the differences between an option's maturity and exercise date. When does exercise take place for a European option? For an American option?

5.8. Explain and carefully describe the following four security positions, drawing payoff diagrams wherever necessary to support your answer:

   a. short a forward contract with a delivery price of $100

   b. short selling a stock at $100

   c. going short on an option with a strike price of $100

5.9. Suppose that the current price of platinum is $400 per ounce. Suppose you expect that in three months the price will increase to $425. You are worried, however, that there is a small chance that platinum may fall below $390 or even lower. What securities can you use to speculate on the price of platinum?

5.10. Why is an American option worth at least as much an otherwise similar European option? Is there an exercise strategy that one can use to turn an American option into a European option? Explain.

5.11. You ask your broker for a price quote for (a fictional company) Sunstar Inc.'s March 110 calls. She replies that these options are trading at $7.00. If you want to buy three contracts, what would be your total cost, including commission? Assume that the broker charges a commission equal to a flat fee of $17 plus $2 per contract.

5.12. "Because a call is the right to buy and a put is the right to sell, a long call position will be canceled out by a long put position." Do you agree with this statement? Explain your answer.

5.13. The short position in a put option has the obligation to buy if the option is exercised. Isn't this counter to the notion that a short position indicates a "sell"? Explain your answer.

5.14. The following option prices are given for Sunstar Inc., whose stock price equals $50.00:

Strike Price	Call Price	Put Price
45	5.50	1.00
50	1.50	1.50
55	1.00	5.50

Compute intrinsic values for each of these options and identify whether they are in-the-money, at-the-money, or out-of-the-money.

5.15. Do you agree with the following statement: "An out-of-the-money option has an intrinsic value of zero and vice versa"? Explain your answer.

5.16. Compute the profit or loss on the maturity date for a short forward position with a forward price of $303 and a spot price at maturity of $297.

5.17. Compute the profit or loss on the maturity date for a December 45 call for which the buyer paid a premium of $3 and a spot price at maturity of $47.

5.18. Compute the profit or loss on the maturity date for a November 100 put for which the seller received a premium of $7 and a spot price at maturity of $96.

5.19. Because options are zero-sum games, the writer's payoffs are just the negatives of the sellers. Demonstrate the following (by algebraic arguments or by using numbers):

a. the call seller's payoff at expiration is $-\max(0, S - K) = \min(0, K - S)$
b. the put seller's payoff is $-\max(0, K - S) = \min(0, S - K)$

5.20. What is the difference between a market buy order and a limit order? When would you use a market versus a limit order?

6

Arbitrage and Trading

6.1 | Introduction

Once upon a time in days not too long ago, a venerable finance professor went with two of his graduate students to a McDonald's restaurant for a working lunch. One student noticed that the Big Mac sandwiches were on a buy-one-get-one-free special. Bubbling with excitement, the student ran to the mentor to share the news. His jaws dropped as he approached, for the master himself was sitting with two Big Macs, discussing the selling of one to the second student at half price: "You also know about this?" "Yes," the professor replied, "it's an arbitrage." Selling the second free sandwich at half price would indeed be an arbitrage opportunity!

Taking a cue from this story, we define **arbitrage** (**arb**) as a chance to make riskless profits with no investment. The concept of arbitrage is invaluable for building **pricing models**, which are mathematical formulas that price derivatives in terms of related securities. Since the 1970s, financial markets have been generating innovative derivatives by attaching extra features to simple financial securities, by designing entirely new derivatives with complicated payoffs, or by combining several derivatives into a single composite security. For this last example, the composite security's price must equal the sum of the prices of these simpler constituent derivatives. Otherwise, eagle-eyed traders can make arbitrage profits by buying the relatively cheaper of the two and selling the more expensive one. This observation leads one to recognize that a more general truth holds. *In the absence of arbitrage, all portfolios or securities with identical future payoffs must have identical values today.* This is the essence of the no-arbitrage principle that we discuss later in this chapter.

Easy arbitrage opportunities are hard to find. Still we start with them because they form the foundations of our study and help us understand the more complex arbitrages that appear in today's marketplace. The existence of arbitrage opportunities implies that the markets are somehow inefficient. We introduce the various notions of market efficiency and discuss what happens when they are violated. Next we talk about some pricing anomalies and the trading strategies that profit from them. Finally, we take a bird's-eye view of hedge funds. Hedge funds have pioneered many advanced trading tools and techniques to search for arbitrage opportunities, and they continue to remain among the most sophisticated users of derivatives today.

6.2 | The Concept of Arbitrage

Financial markets exert a ruthless discipline on their players. No one advises a careless trader to modify bad quotes; instead, people grab such mispricings, and the misquoting trader sees his wealth disappear. Earlier we defined arbitrage as a chance to make riskless profits with no investments. This trivial description masks an activity that makes and takes millions of dollars every day. Eager traders pour over computer screens displaying prices from diverse markets and scan them for arbitrage opportunities. The act of arbitrage supports the livelihood of many. But gone are the days when one could sit in an armchair reading the financial press and find easy arbitrages. Today's arbitrageurs work very hard for their money.

Traders searching for arbitrage is rational and predictable behavior. Picking up a hundred dollar bill from the ground is normal behavior.[1] It is hard, if not impossible, to model behavior if one oftentimes picks up the bill, sometimes doesn't, and yet at other times picks up the bill but leaves a few bucks in its place for the person coming next! Therefore, for the subsequent theory, we assume that one never leaves money behind and relentlessly picks up even the tiniest of arbitrage opportunities. As we later see, this assumption has very powerful implications; indeed, it lies at the heart of the derivative pricing models presented in this book.

There are many types of arbitrage. Some arbitrage operations are easy to understand and implement but hard to find in practice, whereas others are just the opposite. All such arbitrages can be decomposed into one of three types involving mispricings across space, mispricings across time, or when the sum of the parts' prices differ from the price of the whole. Example 6.1 discusses these three types of arbitrage opportunities.

EXAMPLE 6.1: The Three Types of Arbitrage Opportunities

- *Arbitrage across space* (see Figure 6.1a). Suppose Your Beloved Machines Inc.'s (YBM) stock has an ask price of $100.00 on the Big Board and a bid price of $101.00 in Tokyo. If the brokerage cost is $0.10 per share, then one can buy stocks at a lower price in New York, simultaneously sell them at a higher price in Tokyo, and make 80 cents in arbitrage profits.

- *Arbitrage across time* (see Figure 6.1b). Free lottery tickets are an example of arbitrage across time. Result 3.1 of chapter 3, which states that a stock's price falls exactly by the amount of the dividend on the ex-dividend date, if violated, also represents an example of an arbitrage across time.

- *The sum of the parts' prices differs from the price of the whole* (see Figure 6.1c). Some people see arbitrage opportunities in conglomerates, which are huge companies with diverse lines of business. They claim that the share prices of conglomerates often fail to reflect the true value of the underlying assets and trade too low. Corporate raiders buy conglomerates, sell the constituent businesses or their assets, and more than recover their initial investments. "I saw the company and thought that the sum of the parts was worth more than what it was trading for," observed a notorious corporate raider Asher Edelman as he targeted a French conglomerate.[2] Investment bankers doing mergers and acquisitions believe the opposite. They believe that mergers create arbitrage opportunities where the sum of the parts is less than the whole. The idea that the same payoffs no matter how they are created, trade at the same price is known as the **law of one price**.

[2] Corporate raider Asher B. Edelman once taught a business course at Columbia University, in which he offered $100,000 to any student who would find a takeover target for him. However, the university banned the offer. In the late 1990s, he targeted Societe du Louvre, the French holding company to which the above comment applies (see "Champagne Taste: An American Raider in Paris Challenges an Old World Dynasty—Edelman Presses Taittingers to Choose Family Values or Shareholder Value—Free to Paint a Hotel Pink," *Wall Street Journal*, November 11, 1998).

---

[1] In an often-told tale, two finance professors are walking together, and they see a $100 bill lying on the ground. When one ponders whether he should pick it up, the other replies not to bother because the bill is not really there: "As markets are efficient, someone must have already picked it up before." This story is usually told to clarify the "ideal" notion of an efficient market, while teasing finance academics.

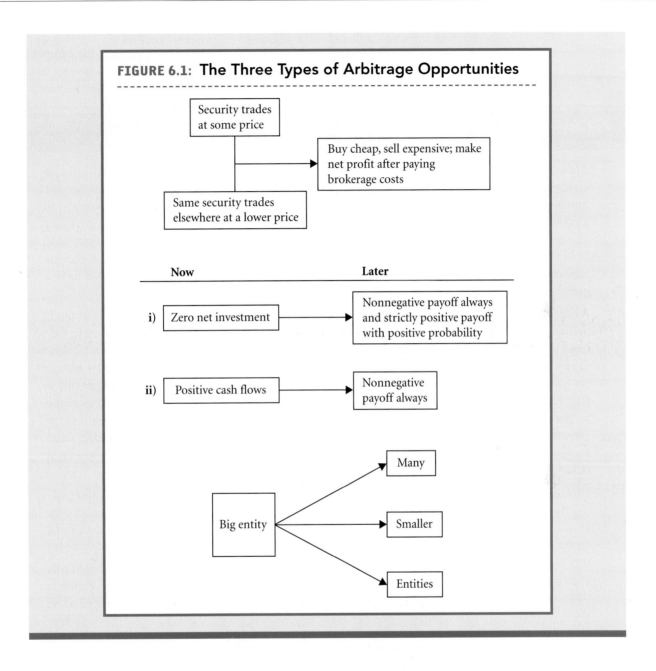

FIGURE 6.1: The Three Types of Arbitrage Opportunities

Are such arbitrage opportunities likely to exist in today's financial market, where technological advances have lowered brokerage costs and made it possible to move millions of dollars in a matter of seconds? Most economists believe that the answer to this question is no—and if they exist, it is especially hard to find them in well-functioning and efficient markets. Perhaps they can be found in some emerging markets, but they fade away quickly as traders start grabbing them. Sometimes what may seem like arbitrage opportunities in a **perfect world** (where **market imperfections** or **frictions** like transaction costs, bid/ask prices, taxes, and restrictions on asset divisibility are assumed away) cease to be so when market imperfections are included. In actual markets, market frictions are relevant and should always be taken into account when considering arbitrage opportunities. Let's discuss a few real-life examples of arbitrages.

EXAMPLE 6.2: Real-Life Arbitrages

- *Sports arbitrage.* Not too long ago the soccer World Cup finals had two powerhouse teams, Brazil and Germany, playing. Uncle Sanjoy relishes the story of how he visited a Wall Street firm and entered into two bets with acquaintances. First, he agreed to pay one person $10,000 if Brazil won but receive $5,000 otherwise. Then, uncle slyly adds that he visited another office, and bet with a second person to receive $11,000 if Brazil won but pay $4,000 otherwise. No matter which team won, uncle locked in $1,000. Although gambling exasperates his wife, uncle quietly commented that he had locked in arbitrage profits by exploiting inefficiencies in the system and that he truly enjoyed watching the game!

- *Airline miles arbitrage.* Airlines put all kinds of restrictions on tickets, serve scant morsels of food, manhandle baggage, make passengers endure long delays, and cancel flights. Those who have suffered in the sky at the hands of airlines will be amused by a story in the *Wall Street Journal*, "How Savvy Fliers Make the Most of Their Miles" (December 16, 2008), which related how some travelers got the best out of their frequent flier miles. Normally a ticket obtained by redeeming frequent flier miles would yield the value of approximately one cent per mile. Some folks figured out how to transform this once cent per mile into more. One gentleman paid about 1.3 cents per mile to "friends" through the Internet and then used the miles for business class tickets between China and the United States. "I call it airline miles arbitrage," said the savvy traveler, who created business class tickets for coach ticket prices and in the process, earned about six to nine cents per mile.

- *Uncle Sam's generosity.* The idea of arbitraging Uncle Sam (the US government) appeals to most people, but few succeed in doing so. However, an article in the *Wall Street Journal*, "Miles for Nothing: How the Government Helped Frequent Fliers Make a Mint—Free Shipping of Coins, Put on Credit Cards, Funds Trip to Tahiti; 'Mr. Pickles' Cleans Up" (December 7, 2009), reported a story where this happened. What happened? Because a paper dollar lasts only about twenty-one months in circulation, dollar coins save a country money as they can last for thirty years or more. To promote their use, the US Mint offered to sell presidential and Native American $1 coins at face value, ship them for free, and buyers could charge the purchase to their credit cards without handling fees. However, well-intentioned plans sometimes have unintended consequences. Arbitrageurs bought large quantities of coins from the mint, paid for them with credit cards that offered frequent flier miles for free air travel (typically, one cent for each dollar charged in purchases), and immediately deposited the coins in the bank to pay for the credit card coin purchase. The story states that one software consultant ordered $15,000 worth of coins and even had the delivery person deposit the coins directly in his car's trunk so that he could take them to the bank. Discovering such activities, US Mint officials sent letters to prospective buyers seeking the reasons for their purchase and denied further access to those who did not respond. The mint also warned on its website that credit card companies should consider such purchases as cash advances, which aren't eligible for earning airline miles. A mint official summarized the situation this way: "Is this illegal? No. Is it the right thing to do? No, it's not what the program is intended to do."

6.3 | The No-Arbitrage Principle for Derivative Pricing

Modern finance theories use the idea that arbitrage opportunities do not exist in well-functioning markets to derive many important results. This was pioneered by the **Miller and Modigliani (M&M) propositions** in corporate finance, which state that if market imperfections like taxes are assumed away, then the choice of debt or dividend policy does not affect the value of a firm. (Taxes are imperfections! Who says finance jargon is boring?) In our case, the absence of arbitrage opportunities lies at the heart of derivative pricing models, including the celebrated Black–Scholes–Merton and the Heath–Jarrow–Morton models included in this text. This section explains how.

The Law of One Price

Suppose one wants to price a market-traded derivative, which we label as "portfolio A." Assume that there are no cash flows on this traded derivative before maturity so that there are only two dates of concern—today and when the derivative matures. Now let us create portfolio B, a collection of different traded securities with known prices and no intermediate cash flows, to match portfolio A's payoffs on the maturity date (see Figure 6.2). The values of these two portfolios are linked by a **no-arbitrage principle**: *to prevent arbitrage, two portfolios with identical future payoffs must have the same value today.*[3] Using this principle, the cost of creating portfolio B is the "fair" or "arbitrage-free" value of the traded derivative portfolio A.[4] This is known as the **law of one price**.

Nothing Comes from Nothing

Continuing with the previous discussion, if we subtract portfolio A from portfolio B, then we get the second representation, which will be one of our main methods for proving results (see Figure 6.2). By construction, the value of this new portfolio is zero for sure on the maturity date. To prevent arbitrage profits, it must also have zero value today. The derivative's price can be solved from this condition. This insight can be paraphrased as *nothing comes from nothing.*[5] When identical cash flow securities are subtracted, yielding zero at a future date, the result is emptiness, nothing, nada, zero now!

---

[3] Suppose this principle does not hold. If portfolio A is cheaper than portfolio B today, "buy low, sell high": buy A and sell B. You will have a zero cash flow in the future because the cash inflow will cancel the outflow, and the price difference you capture today becomes arbitrage profit. If B is cheaper than A, just reverse the trades to capture the arbitrage profit.

[4] The same argument works when the price of the derivative is known but there is an unknown variable in the payoff. For example, a forward contract has a zero value on the starting date, but the unknown forward price is in the payoff. The solution to this equation is the arbitrage-free forward price.

[5] "Nothing comes from nothing" (or *ex nihilo nihil fit* in Latin) is a philosophical expression of a thesis first advanced by the Greek philosopher Parmenides of Elea, who lived in the fifth century BC.

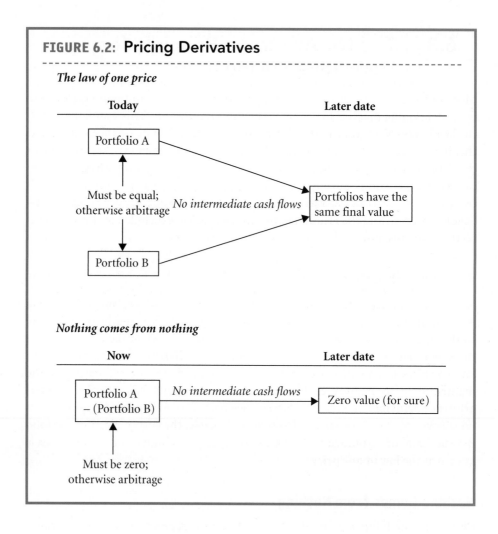

FIGURE 6.2: Pricing Derivatives

The law of one price

Today   Later date

Portfolio A

Must be equal;   *No intermediate cash flows*   Portfolios have the
otherwise arbitrage   same final value

Portfolio B

Nothing comes from nothing

Now   Later date

Portfolio A
– (Portfolio B)   *No intermediate cash flows*   Zero value (for sure)

Must be zero;
otherwise arbitrage

These are the two standard techniques used for pricing derivatives from chapter 11 onward in this book.

As we have often observed, arbitrage opportunities are likely to be absent in well-functioning and efficient markets—but what do we really mean by an "efficient market"? Well, read on.

6.4 | Efficient Markets

The word *efficient* has many different meanings in economics (see Extension 6.1). However, to a finance academic there is only one meaning. When a finance academic states that "markets are efficient," she means an **informationally efficient market**: a market where asset prices quickly absorb and "fully" reflect all relevant information. But what relevant information is this referring to?

The **efficient markets hypothesis** (**EMH**) is presented with respect to three different information sets:

1. **Weak-form efficiency** asserts that stock prices reflect all relevant information that can be gathered by examining current and past prices. If this is true, then **technical analysis** (which involves looking at price patterns to predict whether a stock's price will go up or down) will not generate returns in excess of the risk involved. In addition, and more relevant to us, *if the market is weak-form efficient, then there are no arbitrage opportunities*. Why? Because finding arbitrage opportunities only depends on the information contained in current and past prices. It is this connection that relates an efficient market to the arbitrage-free pricing of derivatives.

2. **Semistrong-form efficiency** asserts that stock prices reflect not only historical price information but also all publicly available information relevant to those particular stocks. If this holds, then fundamental analysts (**fundamental analysis** involves reading accounting and financial information about a company to determine whether a share price is overvalued or undervalued) would be out of business.

3. **Strong-form efficiency** asserts that stock prices reflect all relevant information, both private and public, that may be known to any market participant. If this is true, then even **insiders** (who have privileged, yet to be made public information about the company) will not make trading profits in excess of the risk involved.

There is a never-ending debate on whether markets are efficient with respect to these three different information sets. The preponderance of evidence tends to accept weak-form efficiency, and strongly reject strong-form efficiency, especially given the numerous insider-trading lawsuit convictions historically obtained by the Securities and Exchange Commission (SEC). The evidence with respect to semistrong-form efficiency is mixed.

The assumption of no arbitrage underlying the models developed in this book is very robust. Indeed, *if markets are weak-form efficient, then no arbitrage opportunities exist.* Hence the weakest form of market efficiency justifies the assumption of no arbitrage. But don't get confused. Assuming there are no arbitrage opportunities in subsequent modeling does not imply that we are assuming that the market is weak-form efficient. As just discussed, the assumption of no arbitrage is a much weaker notion than even a weak-form efficient market. Hence it is more likely to be satisfied in actual markets, and thus it provides a more robust model than market efficiency does.

EXTENSION 6.1: The Efficient Markets Hypothesis

Economic Efficiency

Efficiency has numerous different meanings in economics. A first course in microeconomics introduces the notion of Pareto efficiency. Named after the Italian economist Vilfredo Pareto, a market is **Pareto efficient** when no person can be made better off without making someone else worse off (see Varian 2003). Production efficiency means producing the maximum possible output for a given set of inputs. One can talk about efficient factories, efficient manufacturing processes, and efficient laborers. In contrast, finance focuses on *informational efficiency*, that is, how quickly information gets absorbed and reflected in asset prices. The belief that markets are informationally efficient is called the *efficient markets hypothesis.*

The notion of an informationally efficient market traces back to Louis Bachelier, the French mathematician who is recognized as the founder of option pricing theory (see chapter 17 for a brief biographical sketch of Bachelier). Economists Alfred Cowles, Holbrook Working, Harry Roberts, and Eugene Fama; astrophysicist M. F. Maury Osborne; and statistician Maurice Kendall were among the pioneers studying the empirical characteristics of security prices. These early researchers found that stock prices exhibited no predictable price patterns. In 1965, Paul Samuelson published a groundbreaking paper titled "Proof That Properly Anticipated Prices Fluctuate Randomly" in the *Industrial Management Review,* which provided a theoretical justification for this observed stock price randomness in an informationally efficient market.

The 1992 edition of Professor Burton Malkiel's book *A Random Walk Down Wall Street* (as quoted in Campbell, Lo, and MacKinlay 1997, 20–21) provides a nice definition of *efficiency*:

> A capital market is said to be efficient if it fully and correctly reflects all relevant information in determining security prices. Formally, the market is said to be efficient with respect to some information set . . . if security prices would be unaffected by revealing that information to all participants. Moreover, efficiency with respect to an information set . . . implies that it is impossible to make economic profits by trading on the basis of [that information set].

This definition implies that one can test market efficiency by studying the price reactions caused by information released to the market. If prices do not change on an information release, then the market is efficient with respect to that information. Furthermore, one can also test market efficiency by seeing whether trading on the basis of information can make economic profits. If so, then the markets are inefficient. The **efficient markets hypothesis** (**EMH**) is presented with respect to three different information sets:

1. **Weak-form efficiency** asserts that stock prices reflect all relevant information that can be gathered by examining current and past prices. If this is true, then technical analysis is not profitable. Moreover, it implies that no arbitrage opportunities exist because arbitrages are based on current and past price data. This is the key insight that relates market efficiency to derivatives pricing. Consider an example of what happens when the market is weak-form efficient. Suppose that you have studied Your Beloved Machine Inc.'s (YBM) price patterns and found that whenever the stock falls to $90, it rallies and shoots up to $95. You notice that YBM has hit $90, and you contact your broker to capitalize on your discovery. However, by the time you are ready to trade, the price has already moved up to $95, and your "discovery" is useless for obtaining profits. Technicians would call $90 a **support level** because when prices fall to that level, there are lots of buyers waiting on the sidelines to rush in and cause the price to move up. Support levels are an example of *technical analysis.* In a weak-form efficient market, technical analysis is useless for generating economic profits (as this example illustrates). Academic studies tend to support weak-form efficiency because prices seem to reflect information that can be gleaned by observing current and past price data. *In particular, this supports the assertion that markets rarely contain arbitrage opportunities.*

2. **Semistrong-form efficiency** asserts that stock prices reflect not only historical price and volume information but all publicly available information relevant to a particular stock. Thus any effort to dig up publicly available information for profitable trading is fruitless. If this form of market efficiency holds, then fundamental

analysts are out of business. For example, suppose you read in the morning newspaper that YBM has entered into a highly profitable partnership with another company that, in your estimate, would increase the stock price by $4. Eager to profit from this fundamental analysis, you rush in a buy order. However, you find that the price has already increased by $4, wiping out your anticipated profits. Semistrong-form efficiency implies that **fundamental analysis** cannot generate profits in excess of the risk involved. Academic studies testing semistrong-form efficiency are mixed. This suggests that fundamental analysis may sometimes work.

3. **Strong-form efficiency** asserts that *stock prices reflect all relevant information, both private and public,* that may be known to a market participant. If this is true, then even **insiders** (who have privileged information about the company) cannot make trading profits. Academic empirical studies strongly reject strong-form efficiency. This means that prices do not reflect *all* available information and that insiders can and do make money by trading on their information. Consider an extreme example: suppose that you are the chief executive officer of a major public company and we are enjoying a round of golf together. Amid the fresh air of our county club, you share with me information that your company is about to be purchased by YBM. The market does not know this yet, and the stock price does not reflect this information. This is inside information. Trading on this information will certainly generate profits in excess of the risk involved —and send you to jail as well! Many countries have laws preventing insider trading. Regulators carefully study trading behavior of people who are likely to possess such information, and they take special delight in levying fines on insiders and putting them behind bars.

An interesting paradox exists in an efficient market, as pointed out by Professors Sanford Grossman and Joseph Stiglitz (1980) in "On the Impossibility of Informationally Efficient Markets." They argue that markets can only be efficient if analysts dig up, uncover, and analyze information on companies. But if prices already reflect this information, then there are no incentives for analysts to do this research, and if analysts cease doing this research, prices stop reflecting this information, and markets are not efficient. Hence the paradox! But all is not lost for the efficient markets hypothesis. Information acquisition costs break this paradox. Given that there are costs to obtaining information, the market can be efficient up to the point where the economic profits of gathering information just equal its costs.

6.5 | In Pursuit of Arbitrage Opportunities

Well-resourced, astute players trade for the purpose of exploiting arbitrage opportunities. As the next section illustrates, academics have uncovered phenomena that seem to suggest the existence of such arbitrages.

The Closed-End Fund Puzzle

Closed-end fund share prices are often claimed to represent arbitrage opportunities. To understand this claim, we must first understand closed-end funds, and to understand closed-end funds, we need to first understand investment companies.

An *investment company* sells shares to investors, invests the funds received in various securities according to a stated objective, and passes the profits and losses back to the investors after deducting expenses and fees. Federal securities law classifies investment companies into three basic types: mutual funds (legally known as **open-end companies**), closed-end funds (legally known as **closed-end companies**), and **UITs** (legally known as **unit investment trusts**). *Mutual funds*, like those offered by Fidelity and Vanguard, are open ended and take new investments at any time. A shareholder can redeem his shares directly from the fund whenever he desires. **Closed-end funds** issue shares at their creation but none thereafter. Just like regular stocks, the shares of closed-end funds trade on organized exchanges. Closed-end funds are not redeemed by the fund for cash. To close out an investment, an investor must sell her shares on the secondary market. Finally, unit investment trust shares can be redeemed like mutual funds; moreover, they have a termination date when the fund's assets are sold and the proceeds are paid out to investors.

Redemptions in mutual funds and UITs pay the company's net asset value per share. **Net asset value** (**NAV**) is the value of the company's total assets minus its total liabilities, often expressed on a per share basis. For example, if an investment company has securities and other assets worth $110 million and has liabilities of $5 million, its NAV would be $105 million. If the investment company has issued 1 million shares, then $105 would be its NAV per share. NAV changes daily due to market fluctuations. Mutual funds and UITs are usually required to compute its NAV at least once per business day (which they usually do after the market closes). Closed-end funds, however, are exempted from this requirement.

For reasons that are doubted and debated, the shares in most closed-end funds trade at a discount from their asset value. This is known as the **closed-end fund puzzle**.[6] These discounts represent potential arbitrage opportunities. To see this, suppose that a closed end fund is worth $100 million in the market, but the underlying securities have a net asset value of $105 million. What can one do? One can buy all the shares, open up the fund, and sell the underlying securities to make $5 million in arbitrage profits (see Figure 6.1c). However, not all closed-end funds trade at a discount. Some trade at premiums over their underlying asset values, like the legendary Warren Buffett's Berkshire Hathaway Company at the end of the twentieth century. Why? Again, a puzzle.

Spread Trading

At the heart of many arbitrage strategies is spread trading. **Spread trading** involves buying and selling one or more similar securities when their price differences are large, with the aim of generating arbitrage profits as their price differences later converge to some target value.

---

[6] Sharpe et al. (1995) notes three of the most prominent "puzzles" concerning the typical pricing of closed-end funds: (1) initially, shares sell at a premium of roughly 10 percent of their net asset value, which falls to a discount of roughly 10 percent soon afterward; (2) the size of this discount fluctuates widely over time; and (3) it seems possible to earn abnormally high returns by purchasing funds with the biggest discounts.

For example, suppose that Your Beloved Machines Inc. (YBM) has two classes of shares with different voting rights. You find that class A shares are trading at $100 and class B shares are trading at $85. This is a spread of $100 − 85 = \$15$. However, you've discovered that the spread has historically been $10, and you expect it to return to that level.

To take advantage of this price discrepancy, you can buy the underpriced class B shares and sell the overpriced class A shares. If your bet is correct and the spread returns to $10, you can reverse the trades and capture $5 in profits. Notice that you are betting on the movement of a spread and not on the direction of the stock prices themselves. Spread trading is one of the most common arbitrage trading strategies used in financial markets. The next section discusses one such widely used strategy, called *index arbitrage*.

Index Arbitrage

A **stock index** is an average of stock prices that are selected by some predetermined criteria. For example, the **Dow Jones Industrial Average** (also called the **DJIA, Dow 30,** the **Dow industrials**, the **Dow Jones**, or simply the **Dow**) and the **Standard and Poor's 500 Index** (**S&P 500**) are stock indexes created by using a *price-weighted* average of thirty major US stocks and the *market value–weighted* average of five hundred major US companies, respectively (see Extension 6.2 for a discussion of indexes).

Sometimes the value of a stock market index gets disjointed from the arbitrage-free price of a futures contract written on the index. In such situations, the potential for **index arbitrage** exists. Suppose the traded futures contract on an index is overvalued. The arbitrage is to short the traded futures contract and go long a *synthetic* futures contract constructed to have the same cash flows as the traded futures contract. The synthetic futures contract is constructed using the portfolio of the traded stocks underlying the index. This strategy will lock in the price difference at time 0 and have zero cash flows thereafter. The arbitrage is a violation of the nothing comes from nothing principle. Extension 6.3 illustrates index arbitrage via a simple example.

Big Board officials are often concerned that index arbitrage may cause large price swings. After the market crash of October 1987, the New York Stock Exchange (NYSE) set up a trading restriction called a **circuit breaker**, which prohibits buying or selling stocks when the index moves by more than a certain number of points.[7] Futures traders and exchanges have long railed against circuit breakers, arguing that they reduce volume and liquidity in their markets. Like the daily limits for futures price movements, circuit breakers invoke strong arguments from both proponents and opponents.

---

[7] For the Dow index, the current circuit breaker can be found at usequities.nyx.com/markets/nyse-equities/circuit-breakers.

EXTENSION 6.2: Stock Indexes

There are two basic types of stock indexes: price-weighted and value-weighted indexes. We illustrate both using examples.

EXAMPLE 1: A Price-Weighted Index (PWI)

■ Summing the share prices and dividing by the number of shares creates a price-weighted index. Consider the hypothetical stock price data in Table 6.1. Here YBM's share price is $100 today and $110 tomorrow. BUG's price is $50 today and $45 tomorrow. The equal average PWI is equal to

$$\text{Sum of stock prices / Number of stocks}$$
$$= (100 + 50)/2 = 75 \text{ today and } (110 + 45)/2 = 77.5 \text{ tomorrow}$$

The weights (percentage holdings of each stock) in the index are equal to one-half for both YBM and BUG.

■ While one stock went up and the second went down, the PWI index registered a 2.5 point gain or

$$\text{(Tomorrow's index value} - \text{Today's index value)/Today's index value}$$
$$= (77.5 - 75)/75 = 0.0333 \text{ or a } 3.33 \text{ percent increase}$$

■ This is called a **price-weighted average** because when viewed as a portfolio, each stock's return is weighted by a percentage proportionate to the price of the stock relative to the value of the portfolio.

The DJIA is computed by creating a price-weighted average of thirty high-quality blue chip stocks from diverse industries. The component stocks are selected at the discretion of the editors of the *Wall Street Journal*. The membership list is periodically modified so that the index continues to accurately reflect the general US stock market. Such revisions are imperative because companies go through mergers, acquisitions, and bankruptcy.

TABLE 6.1: Stock Price Data

Stock	Today's Price	Tomorrow's Price	Shares Outstanding (millions)	Today's Market Value (millions)	Tomorrow's Market Value (millions)
YBM	$100	$110	50	$5,000	$5,500
BUG	$50	$45	20	$1,000	$900
Total				$6,000	$6,400

EXAMPLE 2: A Value-Weighted Index (VWI)

■ Multiplying the stock price by the shares outstanding (which gives the stock's total **market capitalization**) and then summing across all stocks creates a value-weighted index. Using the data from Table 6.1, we get a VWI equal to

Sum of stock price times shares
$$= (100 \times 50 + 50 \times 20) = 6,000 \text{ today and } (110 \times 50 + 45 \times 20) = 6,400 \text{ tomorrow}$$

The weights (percentage holdings of each stock) in the index are

$$\text{for YBM} = \$5,000/\$6,000 = 0.8333$$
$$\text{for BUG} = \$1,000/\$6,000 = 0.1667$$

- The percentage change in the VWI is

$$(\text{Tomorrow's index value} - \text{Today's index value})/\text{Today's index value}$$
$$= (6,400 - 6,000)/6,000 = 0.0667 \text{ or a 6.67 percent increase}$$

- In practice, the index is often normalized to make its value equal to some arbitrary number at a given date. This is for convenience in reporting the index. For example, the VWI index's value could be normalized to be 100 today by dividing by 60. The number 60 must also divide the index's value at all future dates. In this case, the index value tomorrow would be $6,400/60 = 106.67$.

- This is called a value-weighted index because when viewed as a portfolio, each stock's return is weighted by its market value relative to the total value of the stock market.

The S&P 500 is a market-value-weighted index of five hundred large-sized US companies. A value-weighted index is sometimes called a **market-cap weighted index**.

A History of Stock Indexes

In 1882, three young reporters, Charles Dow, Edward Jones, and Charles Bergstresser (who later became a partner), founded a news agency, the Dow Jones and Co., in a basement office on 15 Wall Street. The company prospered, and in 1889, it introduced the *Wall Street Journal*, a four-page newspaper that sold for two cents a copy. Over time, the journal grew into the world's premier business newspaper.

Charles Dow also pioneered the creation of stock market indexes. The story underlying this creation provides insight into why indexes are important, even in today's complex world. In the nineteenth century, companies were veiled in a cloak of secrecy and made little disclosure to the general public. Moreover, their stocks were risky and subject to frequent manipulations, often by company management working in concert with powerful brokers and dealers.[8] Prices exhibited erratic movements, and it was hard to understand market trends. To help investors see these trends, in 1884, Dow Jones and Co. started reporting the average price of eleven leading stocks, nine of which were railroad companies. In response to criticism that the index was not representative of the entire stock market, in 1896, the company started separate reporting of a railroad index and a price average of twelve "smokestack" companies known as the Dow Jones Industrial Average. The railroad index eventually became the Dow Jones Transportation Average, which currently includes twenty stocks of the airline, trucking, railroad, and shipping businesses.

From this meager beginning, indexes now abound. Following is a listing of some of the different indexes and index providers today:

---

[8] These problems, however, continued to linger until a federal regulatory body, the SEC, was founded in 1934. President Franklin D. Roosevelt appointed as the SEC's first chairman Joseph P. Kennedy (1888–1969), who founded the powerful Kennedy clan of American politics. He was a shipbuilder, a motion picture mogul, and a master stock market manipulator who, on becoming chairman, banned many of the market manipulative practices that made him rich!

- Dow Jones Indexes develops, maintains, and licenses over three thousand indexes. They are classified as blue chip indexes (indexes of blue chip stocks), Dow Jones Wilshire indexes (indexes that measure the US real estate market), benchmark indexes (such as hedge fund strategy indexes, total market indexes, and portfolio indexes), specialty indexes (such as the Corporate Bond Index, DJ-AIG commodity indexes, the DJ-CBOT Treasury Index, Internet indexes, Islamic market indexes, microsector indexes, and REIT indexes), China indexes, custom indexes, and credit derivative indexes (see www.djindexes.com).

- Standard and Poor's Financial Services LLC maintains numerous indexes. S&P indexes belong to the categories equity (which has subcategories like S&P global indexes, US indexes, European indexes, Chinese indexes, Hong Kong indexes, Indian indexes, and emerging markets), the S&P Commodity Index (an index computed from seventeen commodity futures prices), the S&P Composite Spreads, S&P hedge fund indexes, the S&P Europe-Registered Funds Index Series, structured finance, and S&P Investortools municipal bond indexes (see www.spglobal.com).

- The National Association of Securities Dealers Automated Quotation System maintains market indexes like the NASDAQ Composite Index (index of over three thousand securities listed on the NASDAQ Stock Market), the NASDAQ-100 Index (index of one hundred of the largest companies listed on the NASDAQ Stock Market), and many sector indexes such as the NASDAQ Financial-100 Index and the NASDAQ Industrial Index (see www.nasdaq.com).

- Morgan Stanley Capital International Inc. is another leading provider of equity (international and US), fixed-income, and hedge fund indexes (see www.msci.com/overview).

- The FTSE group calculates sixty thousand indexes daily. FTSE's flagship product is FTSE (popularly called "footsie") 100, which is a value-weighted index of the "100 most highly capitalised blue chip companies, representing approximately 80 percent of the U.K. market" (see www.ftse.com).

- Nihon Keizai Shimbun Inc. ("Nikkei") provides several indexes, including the Nikkei 225 Stock Average, which includes 225 of the most actively traded issues on the Tokyo Stock Exchange. It also provides the Nikkei 300 Stock Average, which is an index of three hundred major issues (see www.nni.nikkei.co.jp).

Algos

The IT revolution has given rise to **algorithmic trading** (nicknamed **algos**), sometimes called **high-frequency trading**. These are computer program–driven trades that try to profit from fleeting mispricings or arbitrage opportunities. "High-frequency trading now accounts for 60 percent of total US equity volume, and is spreading overseas and into other markets."[9]

Clearly the securities market has bifurcated. Complex customized securities require careful comprehension and more human involvement in trading. Yet the

[9] hft.thomsonreuters.com/2009/11/20/quiet-evolution-drawn-into-the-light/.

time to execute standardized security trades has gone down drastically. Algos try to reduce **latency**, the time duration between order placement and execution. Huge investments are made to develop technology for algos. With this obsession for speed, even location counts—servers that are placed nearer to the trading venue can cut latency by milliseconds (one millisecond is 1/1,000th of a second) and help the computer trader react nearly instantaneously to changing market information.

In today's world, algos are used to pick up information quickly from news stories and trade based on them. Latency reduction is critical in black-box and statistical-arbitrage trading, in which computer programs try to capture price distortions that may last for only a fraction of a second. Order-handling algorithms divide large trades into smaller parts and move extremely fast to fetch the best price in electronic markets.

Algos aren't for ordinary retail traders. They require considerable capital for computers, programs, and data feeds. The world of investments is not a level playing field. High-frequency trading has friends and foes. Proponents argue that such trading increases liquidity and market efficiency. Opponents argue that such computer trades, because they are given priorities in execution, "rip off" ordinary traders and cause market distortions and increased volatility. The debate is currently heated and unresolved.

Hedge Funds

Historically, hedge funds have been at the cutting edge of financial industry practices and have pioneered the use of many fancy derivatives and complex trading strategies, including taking advantage of arbitrage opportunities.

What is a hedge fund? *Hedge funds* are a special type of investment company in which only wealthy individuals can invest. Wealthy investors are considered to be more sophisticated, and therefore where they invest requires less regulatory supervision. Consequently, unlike mutual and closed-end funds, they are less regulated entities (they are not required to register with the SEC or the Commodity Futures Trading Commission [CFTC]). Like mutual and closed-end funds, hedge funds collect money from investors, invest them in securities, and pass on gains and losses to investors on a proportionate basis. The key differences between mutual funds and hedge funds are detailed in Table 6.2.

Hedge funds are organized as **limited partnerships**, where the investors are limited partners and the fund managers are general partners. Hedge funds are structured to avoid direct regulation and taxation in most countries. Hedge fund managers generally specialize in a particular type of investment strategy, and they enjoy broad investment flexibility (Extension 6.4 discusses many of the major hedge fund investment strategies). Hedge funds have a penchant for secrecy and disclose little information to the public. Because they often adopt complex strategies that are hard to unwind, many hedge funds put restrictions on when investors can pull their money out of the fund.

EXTENSION 6.3: Index Arbitrage

This extension explains index arbitrage. To simplify the presentation, the discussion replaces futures with forward contracts. For the purposes of this demonstration, this difference is not important. The differences between forward and futures contracts, which were discussed in chapter 4, will be further clarified in subsequent chapters.

Index arbitrage generates riskless profits by putting the no-arbitrage principle to work. We illustrate it with a simple example.

EXAMPLE 1: The No-Arbitrage Principle

■ Let a PWI be created by computing an average of the stock prices of YBM and BUG worth $100 and $50 today, respectively. This gives an index value of $75 today.
  - Suppose that a dealer quotes a forward price of $80 on a forward contract on PWI that matures in one year.
  - Let the simple interest rate be 6 percent per year. And suppose that neither stock will pay any dividends over the next year.

■ Next, suppose that a trader believes the forward price is too high. Intuitively, she wants to sell the traded forward contract and create a synthetic forward contract by buying the PWI index portfolio, borrowing the funds to do so, and holding the portfolio until the traded forward contract matures. She performs the following steps:
  - She sells two forward contracts to the dealer, whereby she locks in a selling price of $80 per unit of the index: $160 in all.
  - Simultaneously, she buys one share of each stock for a total cost of $150 and finances this purchase by borrowing. Notice that she has a zero cash flow today because the traded forward requires no cash flows on its initiation date.
  - One year later, she gives two units of the index to the dealer who sold her the forward. This costs nothing because she made allowance for this by purchasing the stocks earlier. She gets $160 from him in return.
  - But she has to repay the loan with interest. This entails an outflow that equals

$$\text{Today's index purchase price} \times (1 + \text{interest cost})$$
$$= 150 \times 1.06$$
$$= \$159$$

  - She pays out $159 but receives $160, and makes $1 in arbitrage profits. She makes this profit no matter where the index moves a year from today.

We make extensive use of this technique to develop cost-of-carry models in chapters 11 and 12.

TABLE 6.2: Comparison of Mutual Funds and Hedge Funds

	Mutual Funds	Hedge Funds
a.	Regulated; have to register with the SEC	Largely unregulated; usually not required to register with the SEC
b.	Narrowly focused investment policy	Hedge fund managers tend to specialize in one investment strategy but enjoy broad investment flexibility
c.	Limited leverage, limited derivatives usage	Can heavily leverage their portfolio; no restrictions on derivative usage
d.	Investors can usually redeem their shares and quickly get their money back	Cash is usually locked in for substantial periods
e.	No limits on who can invest; pool together funds of many investors so as to invest in diversified assets	Investors are high net worth individuals or institutions who seek to benefit from the asset-picking talents of the hedge fund managers
f.	Investments are generally less risky; volatility also depends on the stated investment policy	Investments are usually more risky, but it depends on strategy used
g.	Returns are generally correlated with market-wide indexes	Returns are often loosely correlated with the general markets
h.	Charges, expenses, and fees that investors pay generally constitute a small percentage of the asset value	Charges, expenses, and fees are generally much higher than for mutual funds, with a significant component dependent on how the fund has performed

EXTENSION 6.4: Hedge Fund Investment Strategies

Hedge funds do not constitute a homogeneous asset class. Although the bulk of hedge funds describe themselves as long or short equity, many different investment strategies are used:

- **Long** or **short equity** is a generic term covering portfolios that buy underpriced stocks and short sell overpriced stocks. The first hedge fund, founded by Alfred Winslow Jones in 1949, pioneered this strategy (www.awjones.com).
  - An **equity market–neutral** strategy involves maintaining a close balance in market value between long and short positions.
  - A **short bias** strategy involves a larger market value in short selling.

- **Global macro strategy** hedge funds seek assets that are mispriced relative to their alternatives in global markets based on macroeconomic considerations. An expert of this style of investing, billionaire George Soros, became one of the world's best-known speculators during the last two decades of the twentieth century. He made money by placing aggressive, leveraged bets on the direction of currencies, stocks, bonds, and other markets.

- An **arbitrage strategy** fund seeks arbitrage opportunities:
  - **Convertible arbitrage** involves the simultaneous purchase of convertible securities and the short sale of the issuer's common stock. This is considered a **market-neutral strategy** because it avoids market risk (or price risk) by hedging.

- **Fixed-income arbitrage** involves detecting and exploiting mispricing in bond prices.
- **Statistical arbitrage** (or **StatArb**) involves trading securities that have deviated from a statistical relationship. A popular strategy is a **pairs trade** in which stocks are put into pairs by fundamental or market-based similarities. When one stock in a pair outperforms the other, the poorer performing stock is bought with the expectation that it will climb toward its outperforming partner, which is sold short.
- **Derivative arbitrage** exploits mispricings between a derivative and the underlying security.

■ **Stale-price arbitrage** takes advantage of prices from closed markets. A major scandal erupted in 2003, when it was revealed that many mutual funds granted such arbitrage opportunities to selective clients, including some hedge funds (see "Trading Scandal's Legacy, Five Years On; 'Stale-Price' Deals Cost Small Investors, but Led to Reforms," *Wall Street Journal*, August 26, 2008). On days when the broad US market had sharply risen, speculators moved into mutual funds with big international exposure just before the market's close. They had the expectation that foreign markets, which were already closed for the night, would have a rally on the following day, and they were buying the fund shares cheap because the foreign company shares in those mutual funds were valued at the foreign day's closing price, which did not reflect the later development in US markets.

■ **Event-driven** strategies involve specializing in particular events.
- A **distressed securities** strategy involves investing in distressed stocks.
- **Risk arbitrage** involves trading shares of an acquiring and a target public company to earn profits if the merger is completed.

6.6 | Illegal Arbitrage Opportunities

Arbitrage is a broad concept. You can bring under its umbrella dubious, socially unfavorable, and illegal trading activities. Medical students first learn how a healthy body functions before they study abnormalities and diseases. We follow a similar approach. Previously we introduced legal arbitrage opportunities that facilitate market efficiency. Now we shift gears and study nefarious arbitrage opportunities. These illegal arbitrage opportunities occur in malfunctioning securities markets and remain a major problem that regularly appears in the national, local, and financial press. Trading abuses and manipulations are forms of illegal arbitrage opportunities that we now discuss.

Floor Trading Abuses

Regulatory oversight is intended to prohibit deception and fraud. Nonetheless, there are numerous examples where individuals have violated these rules and conspired to manipulate the market. Such trades are arbitrages but of an illegal form. We look at both the rules and these trading violations.

To protect customers, the Commodity Exchange Act (CEA) and exchange rules ban **fictitious trading**. This is a broad category of transactions in which no bona fide, competitive, open-outcry trade takes place. The following floor-trading practices violate the CEA:

■ **Accommodation trades** allow others to benefit at the expense of a floor broker's customer. Examples include **busting** or undoing a customer's already executed order to help another customer, **cuffing** trades by delayed filling of a customer's order to benefit another trader, and deliberately depriving a customer of profits.

- **Bucketing** happens when a broker directly or indirectly takes the opposite side of a customer's trade without an open and competitive execution of the order on an exchange.

- **Cross trading** is an offsetting or noncompetitive match of the buy order of one customer against the sell order of another. Normally banned, this is permitted in special cases when executed in accordance with the CEA and CFTC regulations and rules of the contract market.

- **Curb** (**kerb**) **trading** takes place by telephone or by other means after the official market has closed. It is so named because originally, it took place in the street, on the curb outside the market.

- **Ginzy trading** happens when a floor broker, in executing an order—particularly a large order—fills a portion of the order at one price and the remainder at another price to avoid the exchange's rule against trading at fractional increments or "split ticks."

- **Prearranged trading** takes place when two brokers agree on a price beforehand.

- A **wash sale** is a sell and buy transaction for the same commodity initiated without the intent to make a bona fide transaction. These trades generally do not result in any change of ownership, and are often used to avoid paying taxes.

Most US commodity exchanges operate under a **free crowd system**, where floor members simultaneously bid and offer either for their own or customer accounts. Transactions often take place simultaneously at different places in the trading ring. By contrast, the NYSE operates under a **specialist system** that allows **dual trading**—the specialist or market maker can act as a dealer in some transactions and as a broker in others. This works fine in the NYSE, where the specialist's trades are carefully audited and scrutinized, but noisy and confusing trading pits provide a very different setting, where brokers can easily put their interests ahead of the customer's.

In commodity markets, *dual trading* occurs when, in the same day, (1) a floor broker executes customer orders and also trades for his own account (or an account in which he has an interest) or (2) a futures commission merchant carries customer accounts and also trades or permits its own employees to trade in accounts with a proprietary interest. Dual trading has the potential for abuse because two simultaneously pursued interests—one's own interest as a trader and the best interest of the customer—can collide with each other. One such abuse is **front running**, which is trading based on an impending transaction by another person. For example, a floor trader may buy on his own account in front of his customer's buy order. Then, he makes unscrupulous gains by selling the shares he bought to the customer at a higher price when executing the customer's buy order.

In 1993, the CFTC banned dual trading in commodities markets: on a given day, a floor trader must tell the exchange whether he wants to be a pit broker or a local (dealer) for that trading day. However, it allows exceptions. For example, dual trading is allowed for contracts with small trading volume and in exchanges with well-developed audit systems.

Market Manipulation

A chronic problem facing free markets is that individuals often try to manipulate prices to their advantage. Manipulation has long been a concern in the securities market. For example, in its report on the [Securities] Exchange Act of 1934, the Senate Committee wrote, "The purpose of the act is . . . to purge the securities exchange of these practices which have prevented them from fulfilling their primary function of furnishing open markets for securities where supply and demand may fully meet at prices uninfluenced by manipulation or control."[10] The Commodity Exchange Act states that it is illegal to manipulate or attempt to manipulate a commodity's future delivery price, yet proving manipulation in a court of law is not easy.

The law requires that to prove **manipulation**, the manipulator (1) must be shown to have the *ability* to set an artificial futures price, (2) must have *intended* to set an artificial price, and (3) must have *succeeded* in setting such a price. But what is an "artificial futures price"? One can reply that it does not reflect normal demand and supply. But what, then, is "normal demand and supply"? This line of argument leaves significant room for interpretation; therefore, in the United States, manipulation is left to the courts to decide.

Next we discuss some well-known examples of market manipulation.

EXAMPLE 6.5: Painting the Tape or Portfolio Window Dressing

- Unlike mutual funds that compute prices daily, hedge funds report performance on a monthly or quarterly basis. Reporting is a big event because performance figures determine a fund manager's remuneration. They also influence investors' decisions to seek or shun the fund—bad numbers often create a mad rush to the door.

- Assume that the time has come to do the books but that the fund is doing poorly. What to do? Take a small company whose shares the fund already owns in substantial numbers and start buying more of them to push the price higher. Then, all shares have higher values, and the fund's performance is spruced up. This is called **portfolio window dressing** or **painting the tape**.

- A *Wall Street Journal* story, "Long and Short: Lifting the Curtains on Hedge-Fund Window Dressing" (September 7, 2005), notes that tape painting usually takes place in low-daily-volume, small-market capitalization stocks, whose prices can be moved by a large buyer with relative ease.

A bear raid is a market manipulation strategy generating arbitrage profits that was widely prevalent in US stock markets in the nineteenth and early twentieth centuries. Remember from chapter 2 how short selling works—a short seller borrows shares, accepts the obligation to pay dividends to the lender, and agrees to return the security to the lender at a future date. Traders organizing a **bear raid** take large short positions in a company's stock, spread unfavorable rumors that

---

[10] Report of the Committee on Banking and Currency, "Stock Exchange Practices," U.S. Senate Report No. 1455, 73d Cong., 2d Sess., 1934 (the "Fletcher Report"). The quote appears in Chapter I "Securities Exchange Practices," Section 11 "The government of the exchanges," Subsection (b) "Necessity for regulation under the Securities Exchange Act of 1934."

depress the stock further, and buy back those shares when other shareholders panic and unload their stock holdings at depressed prices.

Short sellers can get severely burned if they get caught in a market corner and a short squeeze, which was also a pervasive problem in the early days of stock markets. The next example shows how a market corner and short squeeze works.

EXAMPLE 6.6: A Market Corner and Short Squeeze

- Suppose a company has ten thousand outstanding shares, which sell for $50 in the market. This is the **deliverable supply**, of which Alexander owns three thousand shares, Bruce owns three thousand shares, and Caesar owns four thousand shares. The shares are held in street name with their common broker, Mr. Brokerman, so that short sellers can borrow (see Figure 6.3).

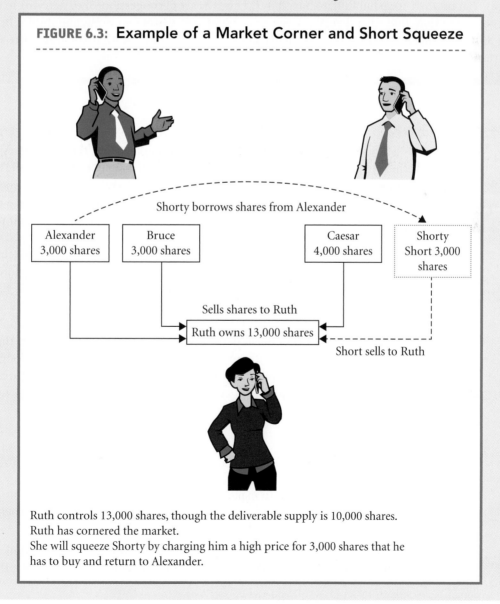

FIGURE 6.3: Example of a Market Corner and Short Squeeze

Shorty borrows shares from Alexander

| Alexander 3,000 shares | Bruce 3,000 shares | | Caesar 4,000 shares | Shorty Short 3,000 shares |

Sells shares to Ruth

Ruth owns 13,000 shares

Short sells to Ruth

Ruth controls 13,000 shares, though the deliverable supply is 10,000 shares.
Ruth has cornered the market.
She will squeeze Shorty by charging him a high price for 3,000 shares that he has to buy and return to Alexander.

- Shorty is bearish on the company and expects the share price to decline from $50 to $40. He **short sells** three thousand shares, which his broker, Mr. Brokerman, borrows from Alexander. They are sold at $50 per share to Ruth, who happens to be a "ruthless manipulator."

- Ruth now buys all the shares from Alexander, Bruce, and Caesar. She now has a monopoly position and has bought three thousand more shares than the deliverable supply of ten thousand shares, making it thirteen thousand in all. Ruth has **cornered the market**.

- At the time of settlement, Alexander does not have shares to give to Ruth. He asks Mr. Brokerman to return his three thousand shares. Since Ruth owns them all, nobody is willing to lend shares. Normally, Shorty can keep his short position open as long as he likes. As scarcity is preventing Alexander's trade from getting settled, Brokerman informs Shorty that he has to return the borrowed shares at once.

- Shorty has nowhere to go but Ruth to buy shares. This is a case of **congestion**: Shorty, trying to **cover his short position**, finds that there is an inadequate supply of shares to borrow, and Ruth is unwilling to sell her shares, except at sharply higher prices. In other words, Ruth is **squeezing the short**. She can easily bankrupt Shorty.

This example easily extends to futures market. First the trader goes long the futures contract in excess of the immediately deliverable supply. Then she keeps her long position open, eventually acquires all the deliverable supply, and ends up in a monopoly position. After she has cornered the market, a short squeeze develops. She demands delivery, but the short cannot find any supply to cover their positions, except from her—and she extracts her price.

These undesirable situations are in violation of the Commodity Exchange Act statute. To stop short squeezes, the CFTC can suspend trading and force settlement at a "fair" price set by the exchange issuing the contract. This happened, for example, with the Hunt brothers' holdings of silver futures in 1979 and 1980. Contract provisions are also designed to increase the deliverable supply, which minimizes the likelihood of manipulation, by allowing variation in the quality of the asset delivered (with appropriate price adjustments) and a longer delivery period. Still, manipulations happen. We discuss additional futures market manipulations in chapter 10.

6.7 | Summary

1. Arbitrage is a chance to make riskless profits with no investment. Arbitrage profits can be generated in several ways—across time, across space, and when the sum of the parts' prices differ from the price of the whole.

2. The no-arbitrage pricing principle involves skillfully creating a portfolio of assets that replicates the payoff to a traded derivative and then arguing that the cost of

this portfolio is the "fair" or "arbitrage-free" value of the traded derivative. This is the standard technique used for pricing derivatives.

3. Arbitrage profits do not exist in an efficient market where market prices reflect all past and current price information. However, markets aren't always efficient, and sophisticated traders use advanced tools and techniques to make arbitrage profits.

4. Hedge funds have emerged as some of the most prominent users and promoters of sophisticated derivatives and complex trading strategies. These unregulated investment vehicles collect money from wealthy investors and institutions, invest in diverse securities, and pass on the gains or losses to investors after deducting substantial fixed as well as performance-based fees.

5. There are a number of floor trading abuses that exchanges ban, which go by fancy names like "fictitious trading," "busting," "cuffing," "bucketing," "cross trading," "curb trading," "ginzy trading," and "wash sales." Dual trading, in which an exchange member acts as both a dealer and a broker on the same day, is generally banned owing to the possibility of abuse in the trading pits.

6. A chronic difficulty with free markets is that traders try to manipulate prices to their advantage. Market manipulation is an example of an illegal arbitrage opportunity. Manipulation has long been a problem in futures markets, but it is hard to prove. The courts in the United States judge manipulation on a case-by-case basis.

7. A market corner and short squeeze is a common manipulation technique that has a checkered past in futures markets. It involves a trader going long in the futures market and squeezing the shorts subsequently in the cash market, when they scramble to cover their short positions.

6.8 | Cases

Arbitrage in the Government Bond Market? (Harvard Business School Case 293093-PDF-ENG). The case examines a pricing anomaly in the large and liquid Treasury bond market, where the prices of callable Treasury bonds seem to be inconsistent with the prices of noncallable Treasuries and an arbitrage opportunity appears to exist.

RJR Nabisco Holdings Capital Corp.—1991 (Harvard Business School Case 292129-PDF-ENG). The case explores a large discrepancy in the prices of two nearly identical bonds issued in conjunction with a major leveraged buyout and considers how to capture arbitrage profits from the temporary anomaly.

Nikkei 225 Reconstitution (HBS Premier Case Collection Case 207109-PDF-ENG). The case considers how an institutional trader who may receive several billion dollars of customer orders in connection with a redefinition of the Nikkei 225 index can provide liquidity for the event and pick up arbitrage profits.

6.9 | Questions and Problems

6.1. What is an arbitrage opportunity across space? Give an example.

6.2. What is an arbitrage opportunity across time? Give an example.

6.3. What is the law of one price?

6.4. Explain the pricing principle "nothing comes from nothing."

6.5. Suppose a two-year Treasury note is trading at its par value $1,000. You examine the cash flows, and if you sell them individually in the market, you get $47.85 for the six-month coupon, $45.79 for the one-year coupon, $43.81 for the one-and-a-half-year coupon, $41.93 for the two-year coupon, and $838.56 for the principal.

    a. Are these prices correct?

    b. If not, show how you can capture arbitrage profit in this case.

6.6. Suppose a two-year zero-coupon bond has a price of $0.90 and a three-year zero has a price of $0.85. A bank allows you to borrow or lend at 4 percent, compounded once a year. Show two ways that you can make arbitrage profits from these prices.

6.7. You can trade Boring Unreliable Gadget Inc.'s stock for $77 per share in the United States and for €50 in Europe. Assume a brokerage commission of $0.10 per share in the United States and €0.10 in Europe. A foreign exchange dealer quotes a bid price of $1.5000 for each euro and offers them for $1.5010.

    a. Are these prices correct?

    b. If not, show how you can capture arbitrage profit by trading BUG stock.

6.8. What is an efficient market, and what does it mean for a market to be weak-form, semistrong-form, and strong-form efficient?

6.9. If the market is weak-form efficient, do arbitrage opportunities exist? Explain your answer. Do you think arbitrage opportunities exist? Explain your answer.

6.10. What is a closed-end fund, and what is the "closed-end fund puzzle"?

6.11. Suppose that Boring Unreliable Gadget Inc. has two classes of shares with different voting rights. You find that class A and class B shares are trading at $49 and $37, respectively. However, historically, the spread has been $15, and you expect the price difference to reach that level.

    a. Explain how you would set up a spread trade and how much profit you expect to make once the prices correct themselves.

    b. Would the preceding strategy work if class A stock goes up to $75 per share?

6.12. What is a stock index? Describe the differences between the Dow Jones Industrial Average and the S&P 500 stock price indexes.

6.13. What is algorithmic trading, and how can it be used to make profits? How does this relate to program trading?

6.14. Explain the differences between a hedge fund and a mutual fund. Can anyone invest in a hedge fund? If not, who can, and why the difference?

6.15. What is a wash sale? Can you explain why the IRS (tax authorities) prohibits the use of wash sales?

6.16. What is front running? Explain why an investor should be concerned if his stockbroker front runs his trades.

6.17. What is dual trading? Why should an investor be concerned about a specialist dual trading?

6.18. What are the three conditions that the law requires to prove manipulation? Are these hard or easy to prove?

6.19. What is a short squeeze, and under what circumstances does it occur?

6.20. What is a bear raid? How does a bear raid relate to trading on inside information?

7

Financial Engineering and Swaps

7.1 | Introduction

In January 1993, the French chemical and pharmaceutical giant Rhône-Poulenc offered its employees an opportunity to buy discounted shares as part of its forthcoming privatization plan. With an eye toward "wide employee participation," the scheme involved a dizzying array of features, including minimum investment incentives, price discounts, free shares, interest-free loans, tax benefits, an option to opt in or out of dividends, and an installment plan to pay for the shares over time. Despite the best intentions of this intricate scheme, the plan badly flopped. Then came Bankers Trust, an American bank famous for its derivatives and trading prowess (and infamous for widely publicized losses incurred by its clients Procter & Gamble and Gibson Greetings). Bankers Trust streamlined the terms of the Rhône-Poulenc plan and also added a critical safety feature—the investment would earn a guaranteed minimum return but surrender some gains if the stock price increased. The modified plan was a success.

How could they guarantee a minimum return? Armed with your derivatives knowledge, you can now understand what happened. The plan protected Rhône-Poulenc from the downside (by buying a put option), and it financed this plan by removing some of the upside (by selling a call option). This is an example of financial engineering.

Financial engineering studies how firms design derivatives to solve practical problems and exploit economic opportunities. This vast subject is taught at varying depths in many universities around the world. After presenting some simple examples, we introduce swaps, which were among the first uses of financial engineering. We briefly discuss applications and uses of swaps and illustrate the basic workings of interest rate swaps, forex swaps, currency swaps (including a valuation formula), commodity swaps, equity swaps, and the highly useful but much maligned credit default swaps. Chapter 22 discusses swap markets and interest rate swaps again in greater detail. We conclude with a quick look at the dazzling variety of available swaps and derivatives contracts.

7.2 | The Build and Break Approach

Sometimes children snap together plastic blocks to build beautiful toys. At other times, they rip apart their creations into simpler structures. We adopt a similar **build and break approach**. Sometimes we combine derivatives and financial securities to create new derivatives tailored to meet investment needs, and at other times, we break down a complex derivative into its simpler components. This is important for two reasons.

The first reason is that it provides an approach for pricing derivatives—*break a derivative into simpler parts, price the simpler parts, and sum to get the original derivative's price*. Arbitrage, like adhesive, binds the parts' prices together to equal the price of the whole and makes sure that the technique works. For example, you can price a **convertible bond** as the sum of a regular bond and an option to convert the bond into a fixed number of stocks. An **extendible bond** may be valued as the price of a straight bond plus an option to extend the bond's life. So when a rocket scientist tries to sell you a complex derivative at an exorbitant price, you can value it by this method and prevent yourself from being gouged.

The second reason is that it enables the use of derivatives to modify a portfolio's return to meet various investment objectives. For example, suppose a company is considering issuing fixed rate debt when interest rates are high to finance an investment project. The company is worried about getting stuck with an expensive debt issue if interest rates go down. To avoid this problem, the company can issue **callable bonds**. In the case that interest rates decline, the company can exercise the call provision in the callable bonds and buy back the bonds at a predetermined price. Where does the company get the funds to buy back the bonds? It issues new fixed rate bonds at the lower interest rate.

7.3 | Financial Engineering

Toward the end of the twentieth century, financial engineering emerged as a vibrant, new subfield of finance and operations research.[1] **Financial engineering** applies engineering methods to finance. At the simplest level, financial engineering and risk management puts our build and break approach to work. The best way to understand this approach is through some examples of financial engineering in practice.

Cash Flows versus Asset Values

To a beginning student, when forming and liquidating portfolios, the signs of the cash flows and asset values may be confusing. To preempt such confusion, we make the following observations. When constructing a portfolio, a positive value means that you are purchasing an asset, hence there is a negative cash flow. For example, if you are buying Your Beloved Machine stock, it shows up as a positive value in the portfolio, but you spend $100, a negative cash flow, in acquiring it. If the value is negative, you are creating a liability, and there is a positive cash flow. For example, borrowing $90 gives a positive cash inflow of $90. The $90 is a liability because you must pay it back in the future. Note that when a portfolio is constructed, *the signs of the cash flows and asset values are opposite.*

At liquidation, this relationship changes. When liquidating a positive value position, you are selling an asset; hence there is a positive cash flow. For example, YBM has a positive value in your portfolio, and selling it for $120 will generate a

---

[1] Cornell University offered the first financial engineering degrees. It states on the Cornell University website (www.orie.cornell.edu/orie/fineng/index.cfm) that "Robert Jarrow and David Heath advised students for several years before formalizing the program in 1995, making Cornell one of the very first universities to have a graduate program in Financial Engineering, and arguably the oldest such program in the world."

positive cash flow. If the value is negative before liquidation, then the cash flow is negative because you are closing a liability. For example, your $90 loan, being a liability, has a negative value in the portfolio. Repaying it on the liquidation date, say, for $94, incurs a negative cash flow. Note that at liquidation, *the signs of the cash flows and asset values are the same*. We will often call both the cash flows and values at liquidation the *payoffs*. As they have the same sign, no confusion should result.

When proving results, for some arguments we will consider cash flows and for others asset values. As long as you keep these relationships in mind, there should be no confusion. The key is to "follow the money!"

Examples

Our first example considers a commodity derivative—a bond whose payoff is indexed to gold prices.

EXAMPLE 7.1: A Bond Indexed to Gold Prices

- Goldmines Inc. (fictitious name) is a gold mining company. It sells a highly standardized product, pure gold, in the world market. It needs money for exploring, for setting up a mine, for running a mine, and for refining operations. The company's fortune ebbs and flows with the price of gold.

- The company decides to raise cash by selling bonds. This is attractive because interest payments are tax deductible. But debt makes a company vulnerable to financial distress—a debt-free company, by definition, can never go bankrupt!

- An investment banking firm designs a bond with the following payoff on the maturity date T:
  - A payment of $1,000
  - An additional amount tied to gold's price per ounce, $S(T)$, which is

$$
\begin{array}{ll}
0 & \text{if } S(T) < \$950 \\
10[S(T) - 950] & \text{if } \$950 \le S(T)
\end{array}
$$

- This payoff is given in Table 7.1 and graphed in Figure 7.1. You can generate the first payment synthetically by investing in zero-coupon bonds. The second payoff looks similar to a long call option position: buying ten calls with a strike price of $950 does the trick. Consequently, the cash flows from the traded bond may be obtained synthetically by forming a portfolio consisting of (1) a zero-coupon bond worth $1,000B$, where B is today's price of a zero-coupon bond that pays $1 at maturity, and (2) buying ten European calls, each with a price of c and a strike price of $950 (see Table 7.2).

- The no-arbitrage principle assures that the replicating portfolio must have the same value as the traded bond. Therefore the bond's value is $(1,000B + 10c)$. In later chapters, you will learn how to price this call option with the binomial or the Black–Scholes–Merton model.

■ Why sell a security like this? First, it will raise more cash up front. Second, it hedges some of the output price risk that Goldmines Inc. faces. If gold prices are high at maturity, it shares some of its profits—that's not too bad. And if gold prices decline, only the principal is repaid.

TABLE 7.1: Payoffs for a Traded Bond Indexed to Gold

Bond Payoff	Time T (Maturity Date) Cash Flow	
	$S(T) < 950$	$950 \leq S(T)$
	1,000	1,000
	0	$10[S(T) - 950]$
Net cash flow	1,000	$1,000 + 10[S(T) - 950]$

TABLE 7.2: Cash Flows for the Synthetic Bond Indexed to Gold

Portfolio	Time T Cash Flow	
	$S(T) < 950$	$950 \leq S(T)$
Long zeros (face value 1,000)	1,000	1,000
Long 10 calls (strike price 950)	0	$10[S(T) - 950]$
Net cash flow	1,000	$1,000 + 10[S(T) - 950]$

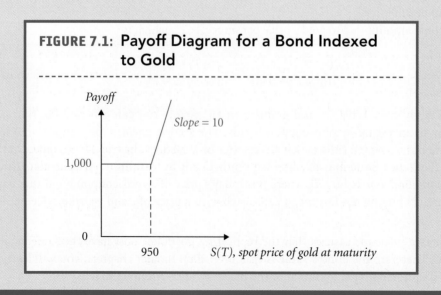

FIGURE 7.1: Payoff Diagram for a Bond Indexed to Gold

The example just discussed is a **commodity-indexed note**, which has its return tied to the performance of a commodity (like platinum, gold, silver, or oil) or a commodity index (like Bridge/CRB Futures Index, a commodity futures index that goes back to 1957). Sometimes the holder can get unlimited benefits from price rises (as in this example), but at other times, the payoffs are capped.

Close cousins of these derivatives are **equity-linked notes** (**ELN**). An ELN is a combination of a zero-coupon (or a low coupon) bond whose return is based on the performance of a single stock, a basket of stocks, or a stock index (see Gastineau and Kritzman [1996] for definitions and discussions). These come in numerous variations and have fancy trade names like ASPRINs, EPICs, GRIP, SIR, and SUPER. This extra kicker from the equity component makes these securities attractive to buyers, helps the issuers raise more cash up front, and also hedges some of the inherent risks in their business.

Our next example shows a hybrid security created to achieve a tax-efficient disposal of a stock that has appreciated in value.

EXAMPLE 7.2: Hybrid Securities

- Suppose you are the chief executive officer of Venturecap Co. (a fictitious name) that has bought 1 million shares in a start-up company Starttofly Inc. at $3 per share. The start-up has done very well and is about to go public. Because Venturecap bought these shares through a **private placement**, securities laws prevent selling those shares for two years. However, you want to dispose of these shares because finance academics report that high prices achieved after an initial public offering usually disappear after six months.

- What should you do? One alternative is for Venturecap to issue **hybrid debt** (also called a **structured note**), which is a combination of a bond and a stock. Your investment banker can design premium equity participating securities (PEPS) that allow you to get the benefits of a sale without actually selling Starttofly's stock.

- How does this work? Suppose the investment banker designs a three-year bond that pays interest at an annual coupon rate of 4 percent per year on the PEPS selling price of $20. The buyer of each PEPS also gets a share of Starttofly after three years. Many investors like the idea of buying Starttofly for $20 in the future and getting the coupon payments over the intermediate years, and the *no-arbitrage principle* ensures that this security is equivalent to buying a bond and selling the stock.

- Venturecap sells 1 million PEPS and raises $20 million up front. Moreover, it pays capital gains taxes only when it sells the Starttofly stock, which is three years from now, and it gets to deduct the interest payments of $800,000 from its taxes every year.

- Hybrids have been sold in the United States, Asia, Europe, and Australia. Two representative examples of PEPS are the following:
  - In March 1996, the media giant Times Mirror Co. issued 1,305,000 shares of PEPS due in five years. This debt paid a low interest rate of 4.25 percent per year on a $39.25 issue price, or $1.668 per year. The underlying stock was AOL Common, received in five years.

- On September 29, 1999, Kansas City–based UtiliCorp United sold 10 million units of PEPS at $25 per unit with a yield of 9.75 percent. Holders of the PEPS received UtiliCorp stock on November 16, 2002, based on the then current common stock price. The PEPS matured two years after that date. UtiliCorp used the net proceeds of about $250 million "to reduce short-term debt and other short-term obligations incurred for acquisitions, construction and repayment of long-term debt and for general corporate purposes" (reported in First Mover, UtiliCorp United's news magazine, 1999 third quarter).

The knowledge of financial engineering can help in many finance-related jobs: as a *corporate financial manager* issuing securities; as a *banker* designing, pricing, and trading securities; as an *investment manager* running an actively managed securities portfolio; and as a *financial regulator* overseeing markets, understanding firms' behavior, and preventing financial catastrophes. Risk managers are in demand these days, and their importance is likely to increase in the foreseeable future.

7.4 | An Introduction to Swaps

Swaps are one of the most successful uses of financial engineering. A **swap** is an agreement between two counterparties to exchange ("swap") a series of (usually) semiannual cash flows over the life (**tenor** or **term**) of the contract. Salomon Brothers arranged the first swap between International Business Machines Corp. and the World Bank in 1981. Swaps have been wildly successful. A quarter century later, the swap market is over $250 trillion in outstanding principal.[2]

A swap contract specifies the underlying currencies, applicable interest rates, payment timetable, and default contingencies. Being over-the-counter (OTC) instruments, swaps do not enjoy the same level of protection as exchange-traded derivatives. You must carefully document them and, if necessary, add collateral provisions to mitigate credit risk (see chapter 22 for a detailed discussion of swap documentation).

As swaps are customized, they come in many flavors and varieties. The simplest swaps go by the fancy name of **plain vanilla**, whereas more complex varieties are called **exotics**. Parties in a **plain vanilla interest rate swap** exchange fixed for floating interest payments, while those in a **plain vanilla currency swap** exchange fixed payments in one currency for fixed payments in another

[2] www.bis.org.

currency. The bbalibor rate for eurodollars (see chapter 2) has traditionally been used as a reference rate for the cash payments on most swap contracts. Nowadays, a large number of swaps are denominated in the European Union's euro as well as other major currencies like the Japanese yen and the pound sterling. Swaps have flourished because they provide an efficient way of *transforming one cash flow to another* with very low transaction costs. Our discussion of how the pursuit of lower transaction costs is shaping the global markets is relevant here (see Extension 1.1).

7.5 Applications and Uses of Swaps

Swaps have many financial engineering uses:

- *Transforming loans.* A company can transform a fixed interest rate loan into a floating interest rate loan and vice versa through a plain vanilla interest rate swap.

- *Hedging currency risk.* A Japanese manufacturer repatriating profits from its US subsidiary can convert dollars into yen through a cross-currency swap and thereby protect itself from currency risk.

- *Altering asset/liability mix.* The 1970s showed that a sharp rise in interest rates can bankrupt a **savings and loan bank** (S&L) specializing in home mortgage lending. A rate hike increases the value of the liabilities (because the deposits must be paid higher interest) but has little immediate impact on the assets (which primarily consist of fixed rate mortgage loans). An S&L can hedge this risk via an interest swap, in which the S&L pays a fixed rate but receives a floating rate. This swap lowers the mismatch in cash flows from both the S&L's floating rate liabilities (deposits) and fixed rate assets (mortgage loans).

- *Creating payoffs that are hard to attain.* As there are no exchange-traded derivatives on jet fuel, an airline can hedge its fuel costs by entering into a commodity swap that pays the average aviation fuel price computed over a month in exchange for a fixed payment.

- *Avoiding market restrictions.* An international investor who is prevented from investing in a country's stocks by local governmental rules can go around this restriction by entering an equity swap that pays her an amount tied to the return on the local stock index.

7.6 Types of Swaps

As in other financial markets, the swap market has its own financial intermediaries. These **swap facilitators** (also called **swap banks** or just **banks**) either act as a broker (which is becoming less common these days) or perform the role of a dealer. For simplicity, we omit these dealers from our examples. This hardly alters the story. Just think of these dealers as intermediaries who siphon off a few basis points from the cash flows without affecting the basic nature of the transactions.

Interest Rate Swaps

A **plain vanilla interest rate swap** exchanges fixed for floating interest rate payments at future dates. As all payments are denominated in the same currency, a notional principal is used to determine the payments, and cash flows are netted. Interest rate swaps alone constituted more than 50 percent of the global market for OTC derivatives contracts in 2011.[3] Example 7.3 shows the setup and cash flows from a plain vanilla interest rate swap (see chapter 22 for a valuation formula).

EXAMPLE 7.3: A Plain Vanilla Interest Rate Swap (Fixed-for-Floating)

Contract Setup

- Suppose that Fixed Towers Inc. borrowed $100 million for three years at a floating rate of one-year bbalibor, but it now wants to switch to a fixed interest rate loan. Floating Cruisers Co. raised the same sum and for the same period at a fixed rate of 6 percent but now wants to switch to a floating rate, the one-year bbalibor.

- They swap. They work out a deal in which Fixed agrees to pay Floating 6 percent and receive bbalibor on the $100 million notional. This will go on for three years, which is the swap's tenor or term. The swap is shown in Figure 7.2.

- Though swaps often have quarterly payments, let's assume for simplicity that they exchange cash flows at year's end. As a result of this agreement, Fixed's cash flows are (−bbalibor + bbalibor − 6 percent =) −6 percent times the notional, whereas Floating's cash flows are (−6 percent + 6 percent − bbalibor =) −bbalibor times the notional. The swap switched each of their existing loans to the other type.

- It makes no sense to simultaneously exchange $100 million for $100 million. That's why $100 million is called the *notional*—it exists as a notion, never changes hands, and is only used for computing payments.

The Cash Flows

- We compute the net payments assuming that bbalibor takes the values 5, 6, and 7.50 percent, respectively, over years 1, 2, and 3.

---

[3] See www.bis.org/publ/qtrpdf/r_qs1112.pdf.

(1st year, bbalibor = 5 percent)
Fixed owes Floating 6 percent times the notional.
Floating owes Fixed 5 percent times the notional.
Fixed will pay Floating 1 percent of $100 million or $1,000,000 at the end of the first year.

(2nd year, bbalibor = 6 percent)
Net payment is 0.

(3rd year, bbalibor = 7.50 percent)
Fixed owes Floating 6 percent times the notional.
Floating owes Fixed 7.50 percent times the notional.

FIGURE 7.2: Example of a Plain Vanilla Interest Rate Swap Transforming a Fixed Rate Loan Into a Floating Rate Loan

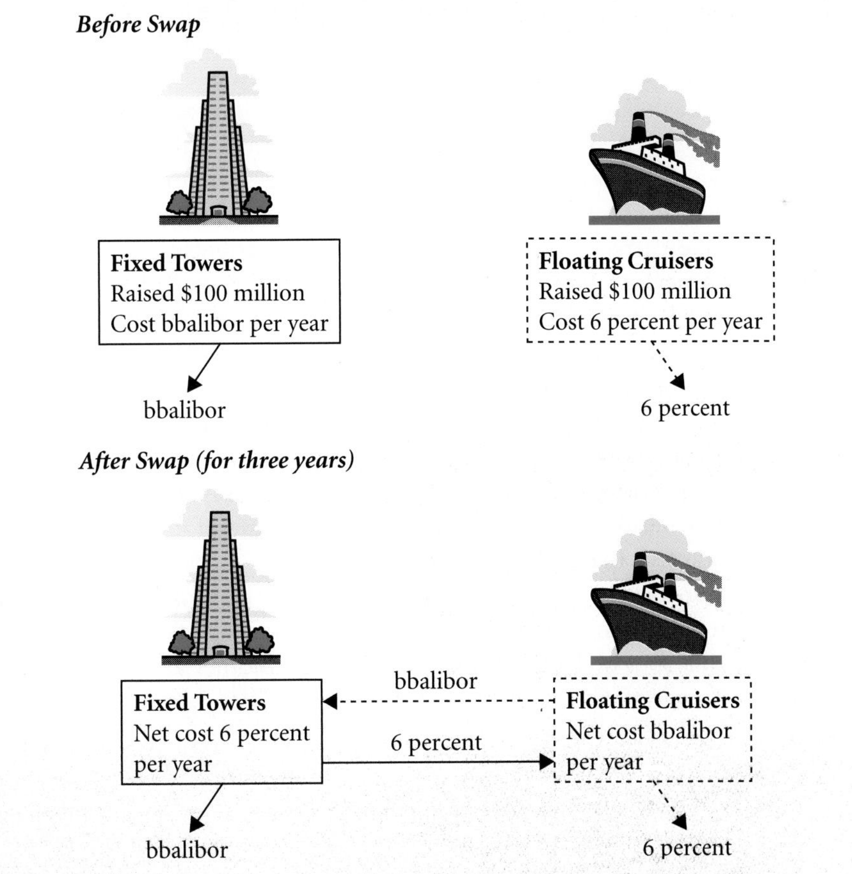

Before Swap

Fixed Towers
Raised $100 million
Cost bbalibor per year

bbalibor

Floating Cruisers
Raised $100 million
Cost 6 percent per year

6 percent

After Swap (for three years)

Fixed Towers
Net cost 6 percent per year

bbalibor

6 percent

Floating Cruisers
Net cost bbalibor per year

bbalibor

6 percent

Fixed receives from Floating 1.50 percent of $100 million or $1.5 million at the end of the third year.

Then the contract ends.

- In reality, counterparties in swaps and other OTC derivatives contracts sign detailed bilateral agreements. Since its founding in 1985, the **International Swap Dealers Association** (later renamed the International Swaps and Derivatives Association) has been instrumental in developing convenient documents for these contracts.

Forex Swaps

"Rule, Britannia, rule the waves."[4] After attaining supremacy in the early eighteenth century, the Royal Navy remained the world's most powerful navy for over two hundred years, and the British pound reigned supreme. However, the pound lost some of its luster in the mid-twentieth century, when the Bretton Woods system established the dollar as the standard currency. As such, global trade and economic transactions became increasingly denominated in dollars.

The dollar's dominance is seen in the **foreign exchange (forex) market**, where most transactions involve exchange of foreign currencies for dollars, and vice versa.[5] The forex market is the world's largest financial market, where a trillion dollars of currencies change hands daily. The term **exchange rate** denotes the price of one currency in terms of another. The currencies are quoted either in **direct** or **American terms** as dollars per unit of foreign currency (say, $2 per pound sterling) or in **indirect** or **European terms** as foreign currencies per unit of dollar (say, £0.5 per dollar). An exchange rate between two currencies other than US dollars is referred to as a **cross-rate**.

Just as you buy an ounce of gold by paying dollars, think of foreign currencies as tradable goods with dollar prices. If the price goes up and you have to spend more dollars to buy one unit of a foreign currency (say, £1 = $3), then we say that the **dollar has depreciated**. Fewer dollars for a unit of foreign currency (say, £1 = $1) means that the **dollar has appreciated**.

Forex swaps are widely used in forex markets for managing currency risks. A **forex swap** (or **FX swap**) is a single transaction with two legs: (1) the contract starts with a spot exchange of one currency for another and (2) it ends with a reverse exchange of these currencies at a subsequent date. Example 7.4 shows the basic idea behind a forex swap.

---

[4] "Rule, Britannia!" is a patriotic British national song, which originated from the poem with the same name written by Scottish poet James Thomson in the mid-eighteenth century.
[5] See international finance textbooks like Krugman and Obstfeld (2000) for a description of the forex market.

EXAMPLE 7.4: A Forex (FX) Swap

- Suppose that Americana Bank has $200 million in excess funds for which Britannia Bank (both fictitious names) has an immediate need. They enter into a forex swap with a tenor of one month.

- The spot exchange rate S_A is $2 per pound sterling in American terms, and its inverse $S_E = 1/2 = £0.50$ per dollar in European terms. Americana gives $200 million to Britannia and receives (Dollar amount × Spot exchange rate in European terms) = $200 × £0.50$ per dollar = £100 million today.

- The annual simple interest rates are $i = 6$ percent in the United States and $i_E = 4$ percent in the United Kingdom. After one month (using a monthly interest rate computation for simplicity), Britannia repays Americana,

$$\text{Dollar amount} \times \text{Dollar return}$$
$$= \$200 \times [1 + (0.06/12)]$$
$$= \$201 \text{ million}$$

and Americana repays Britannia,

$$\text{Foreign currency amount} \times \text{Value of one pound invested for one month}$$
$$= £100 \times [1 + (0.04/12)]$$
$$= £100.3333 \text{ million}$$

Forex swap trading has its own characteristic features, market conventions, and jargon.[6] Instead of beginning immediately, a forex swap may start at a future date. A majority of forex swaps have lives that are measured in weeks rather than months. These versatile instruments have many uses such as (1) managing cash flows in connection with imports and exports, (2) managing borrowings and lendings in foreign currencies, (3) handling foreign exchange balances, and (4) temporarily exchanging excess amounts of one currency for another.

---

[6] Online Trading.hk's website states, "If both dates are less than one month from the deal date, it is a **short-dated swap**; if one or both dates are one month or more from the deal date, it is a **forward swap**. . . . In practice, a limited number of standard maturities account for most transactions. The first leg usually occurs on the spot value date, and for about two-thirds of all FX swaps the second leg occurs within a week. However, there are FX swaps with longer maturities." It also notes that "if, for example, a trader [Americana in our example] bought a fixed amount of pounds sterling spot for dollars (the exchange) and sold those pounds sterling six months forward for dollars (the re-exchange), that would be called a **buy/sell sterling swap**" (www.onlinetrading.hk/fx-swaps.html).

Currency Swaps

A plain vanilla **currency swap** (or a **cross-currency swap**) is an arrangement between two counterparties involving (1) an exchange of equivalent amounts in two different currencies on the start date, (2) an exchange of interest payments on these two currency loans on intermediate dates, and (3) repayment of the principal amounts on the ending date. Because it's an OTC contract, the counterparties can modify the terms and conditions at mutual convenience. Some currency swaps skip the exchange of principal and just use them as notional amounts for computing interest. Interest payments are made in two different currencies and are rarely netted.

Although currency swaps were the first swaps to exist, they have since fallen behind interest rate swaps in terms of trading volume. Still, on June 30, 2011, currency swaps and currency forwards stood at $53,341 billion in terms of notional outstanding and $2,005 billion in terms of gross market value in the global OTC derivatives markets.[7] To get an idea of the size of this market, remember that the gross domestic product of the United States was a little over $15 trillion in June 2011.

Corporations use currency swaps to exchange one currency into another. They do this to repatriate profits and to set up overseas factories. Our next example shows how such a swap works.

EXAMPLE 7.5: A Plain Vanilla Currency Swap (Fixed-for-Fixed)

- Suppose that Americana Auto Company wants to build an auto plant in the United Kingdom and Britannia Bus Corporation (both fictitious names) wants to do the same in the United States. To open a factory, you need local currency. Often a manufacturer can more easily raise cash at home because it has relationships with local banks. Americana and Britannia both plan to do this, and seeing a large spread between foreign exchange buying and selling rates, they decide to do the currency conversion via a currency swap. This is a generic **fixed-for-fixed currency swap** that involves regular exchange of fixed payments over the swap's life.

The Swap Contract

- The automakers enter into a swap with a three-year term on a principal of $200 million. The spot exchange rate S_A is $2 per pound. Americana raises $100 \times 2 = \$200$ million and gives it to Britannia, which, in turn, raises £100 million and gives it to Americana. Assuming annual payments, Americana pays Britannia 4 percent on £100 million and Britannia pays Americana 6 percent on $200 million at the end of each year for three years. The companies are basically exchanging their borrowings.

The Cash Flows

- The swap ends after three yearly payments, and the principals are handed back. Figure 7.3 shows these cash payments.

---

[7] See www.bis.org/publ/qtrpdf/r_qs1112.pdf. The **notional or nominal amounts outstanding** give a "measure of market size and a reference" from which derivatives payments are determined. But the amount at risk may be much smaller. **Gross market values** are defined as the "sums of the absolute values of all open contracts with either positive or negative replacement values evaluated at market prices on the reporting date." See Bank for International Settlements (2005).

Extension 7.1 provides a valuation formula for fixed-for-fixed currency swaps.

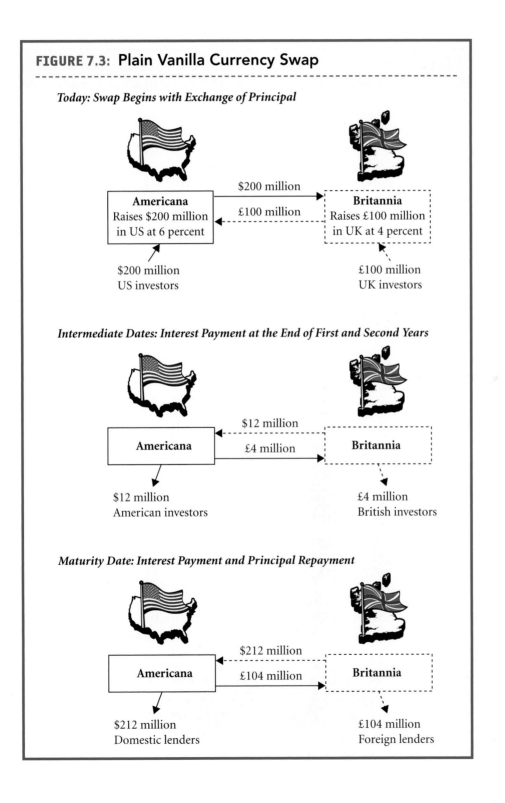

FIGURE 7.3: Plain Vanilla Currency Swap

Today: Swap Begins with Exchange of Principal

$200 million

Americana
Raises $200 million
in US at 6 percent

£100 million

Britannia
Raises £100 million
in UK at 4 percent

$200 million
US investors

£100 million
UK investors

Intermediate Dates: Interest Payment at the End of First and Second Years

$12 million

Americana

£4 million

Britannia

$12 million
American investors

£4 million
British investors

Maturity Date: Interest Payment and Principal Repayment

$212 million

Americana

£104 million

Britannia

$212 million
Domestic lenders

£104 million
Foreign lenders

EXTENSION 7.1: Valuing Fixed-for-Fixed Currency Swaps

We continue Example 7.5 to develop a valuation formula for currency swaps.

EXAMPLE 7.5: (Continued) A Valuation Formula for a Currency Swap

Contract Setup

- The situation and the terms guiding this swap are as follows:
  - Consider the US dollar as the domestic currency and pounds sterling as the foreign currency.
  - The swap's tenor T is three years, and it involves annual interest payments.
  - The spot exchange rate S_A is $2 per pound in American terms, which is $S_E = 1/S_A = £0.50$ per dollar in European terms.
  - Americana raises the principal amount $L = \$200$ million at the coupon rate i of 0.06 or 6 percent per year.
  - Britannia raises an equivalent sum at the coupon rate i_E of 0.04 or 4 percent per year. The principal amount L_E is calculated by multiplying the dollar principal by the spot exchange rate: $L \times S_E = L_E = 200 \times 0.50 = £100$ million.

- Americana pays US investors:

$$C = \text{Principal (in domestic currency)} \times \text{Interest rate (on dollar principal)}$$
$$= L \times i$$
$$= 200 \times 0.06$$
$$= \$12 \text{ million}$$

  at the end of each year for three years.
  - Britannia pays UK investors an annual amount:

$$C_E = \text{Principal (in "European" currency)} \times \text{Interest rate (on foreign currency principal)}$$
$$= L_E \times i_E$$
$$= 100 \times 0.04$$
$$= £4 \text{ million}$$

The Cash Flows

- The swap generates the following cash flows (see Figure 7.3):

  Time 0: Today
  The swap begins with an exchange of the principals. Americana pays $L = \$200$ million (shown with a solid line arrow) and gets $L_E = £100$ million from Britannia (shown with a broken line arrow).

  Time 1 (after one year) and Time 2 (at the end of the second year)
  Interests are paid at year's end. Americana pays C_E of £4 million to Britannia (see solid line arrow), which passes it on to the original British investors (see broken line arrow). Britannia pays C of $12 million to Americana (broken line arrow), which passes it on to the original American investors (solid line arrow). The companies have exchanged their borrowings. Americana has

transformed a dollar liability into a sterling liability, while Britannia has done the opposite and accepted a dollar loan.

Time 3 (after three years)
The swap ends when the companies return their principals and final interest payments. Americana pays £4 million in interest and repays the principal of £100 million to Britannia and receives $212 million.

A Pricing Model

- Today's cash flows cancel and do not affect the swap valuation. As Americana will be receiving dollars and paying sterling, we can value this swap to Americana by adding up the present value of all the dollar payments that the company receives and subtracting from this sum the present value (in dollar terms) of all the sterling payments that the company makes.

- To compute present values, first find the zero-coupon bond (or "zero") prices in the two countries. They come from the government securities in the United States and the United Kingdom. The UK government–issued bonds are called **gilt securities**. Like their American cousins, gilts have a whole range of maturities, semiannual coupon payments, STRIP features, callable issues, and the presence of inflation-protected securities. The UK has even issued **consols**, which are perpetual bonds that never mature.

- Denote US zero prices by $B(t)$ and UK zero prices by $B(t)_E$, where $t = 1, 2$, and 3 years are the times to maturity (see Table 7.3).

- Discount the cash flows by multiplying them by the respective zero-coupon bond prices (Result 1, Extension 2.1 shows how this works). Multiplying the dollar receipts by the US zero prices, we get the following:

> Present value of Americana's dollar receipts
> = PV of dollar interest payments + PV of dollar principal
> = [(Price of a US zero-coupon bond maturing in one year × Interest payment) +
>   (Price of a zero-coupon bond maturing at time 2 × Cash flow)
> + (Price of a zero-coupon bond maturing in year 3 × Interest)]
> + (Price of a zero-coupon bond maturing in three years × Principal)
> = $[B(1)C + B(2)C + B(3)C] + [B(3)L]$
> = $(0.95 + 0.89 + 0.82) \times 12 + (0.82 \times 200)$
> = \$195.92 million
> = PV   (1)

TABLE 7.3: Zero-Coupon Bond Prices in the United States (Domestic Country) and the United Kingdom (Foreign Country)

Time to Maturity (in years)	US (Domestic) Zero-Coupon Bond Prices (in dollars)	UK (Foreign) Zero-Coupon Bond Prices (in pounds sterling)
1	$B(1) = \$0.95$	$B(1)_E = £0.96$
2	$B(2) = 0.89$	$B(2)_E = 0.91$
3	$B(3) = 0.82$	$B(3)_E = 0.85$

Multiplying the sterling payments by UK zero prices, we get the present value of Britannia's sterling receipts, which equals Americana's payments. Consequently,

$$
\begin{aligned}
&\text{Present value of Americana's sterling payments} \\
&= \text{PV of interest payments in pounds sterling} + \text{PV of sterling principal} \\
&= [B(1)_E C_E + B(2)_E C_E + B(3)_E C_E] + [B(3)_E L_E] \\
&= (0.96 + 0.91 + 0.85) \times 4.00 + 0.85 \times 100 \\
&= \text{£95.88 million} \\
&= \text{PV}_E
\end{aligned}
\tag{2}
$$

■ Convert this into US dollars by multiplying it by the spot exchange rate:

$$
\begin{aligned}
&\text{Present value of Americana's sterling payments in terms of today's dollars} \\
&= \text{PV}_E \times S_A \\
&= 95.88 \times 2 \\
&= \$191.76 \text{ million}
\end{aligned}
\tag{3}
$$

■ The dollar value of the foreign-currency swap to Americana Auto Company is

$$
\begin{aligned}
&\text{Value of the currency swap to the domestic investor} \\
&= (\text{Present value of Americana's dollar receipts}) \\
&\quad - [\text{Present value of Americana's sterling payments (in dollar terms)}] \\
&= \text{PV} - \text{PV}_E \times S_A \\
&= 195.92 - 191.76 \\
&= \$4.16 \text{ million}
\end{aligned}
\tag{4}
$$

This means Americana must pay Britannia $4.16 million to enter into the swap.

■ Owing to credit risk, it is prudent to avoid any upfront payment and make this a **par swap**, which has a zero value. You can do this by tweaking the interest rates until this happens. For example, if you keep i fixed, you will find that $i_F = 0.047647$ makes this a par swap.
We restate this as a result.

RESULT 1

Valuing a Plain Vanilla Currency Swap

A currency swap begins at time 0, when
1. a domestic counterparty ("American") pays the principal L dollars to a foreign counterparty ("European" or "Foreigner") and receives an equivalent sum L_E in foreign currency
2. American agrees to pay a fixed interest on L_E to Foreigner in exchange for a fixed dollar interest on L at the end of each period (times $t = 1, 2, \ldots, T$)
3. the counterparties repay the principals on the maturity date T

Then,

> The value of the swap to American, V_{SWAP}
> = Present value of dollar receipts − Present value of foreign currency payments (converted into US dollars at the spot rate)
> $$= PV − PV_E \times S_A \qquad (5)$$

where PV is the present value of future dollar cash flows received by American, PV_E is the present value of future foreign currency payments, and S_A is today's spot exchange rate in American (dollar) terms. The present value of the cash flows is computed as

$$PV = \sum_{t=1}^{T} B(t)C + B(T)L \qquad (6)$$

$$= \left[\sum_{t=1}^{T} B(t)i + B(T) \right] L \qquad (7)$$

where $B(t)$ is today's price of a US zero-coupon bond that pays one dollar at time t and C is the coupon or the interest on the dollar principal that is paid at times $t = 1, 2, \ldots, T$ (computed as dollar principal times the simple interest rate or $L \times i$).

PV_E is similarly computed by attaching a subscript E and by replacing domestic by foreign currency cash flows and zero-coupon bond prices in the preceding formula.

Currency swaps have several interesting features. First, a swap's value depends on two sets of interest rates: domestic as well as foreign interest rates of different maturities.[8] Second, although our example assumes annual payments, most swaps involve semiannual payments. You can easily add this feature. Notice that Result 1 of Extension 7.1 is quite general and does not depend on whether we have annual or semiannual cash flows. Third, the swap value is arbitrage-free. If an errant dealer quotes a different price for the same swap, then you can buy "the cheaper and sell the more expensive swap" and create arbitrage profits. Fourth, anything goes in the swaps markets—these OTC contracts can be designed to satisfy the whims and fancies of the counterparties.

Commodity and Equity Swaps

Example 7.6 illustrates a simple commodity swap.

---

[8] Using the covered interest rate parity formula (see Result 12.3), you can eliminate the foreign interest rate and rewrite the formula in terms of the spot and the currency forward rate.

EXAMPLE 7.6: Hedging Airline Fuel Costs with a Commodity Swap

- Aviation fuel is a major cost for airlines (see Extension 13.1 for a discussion of airlines and their fuel costs). Some airlines hedge this price risk by entering into a *commodity swap* in which they pay a fixed price and receive the average aviation fuel price computed over the previous month.

- Suppose HyFly Airlines (fictitious name) needs 10 million gallons of aviation fuel per month, which it buys on a regular basis from the spot market. Seeing a huge rise in oil (and aviation fuel prices) in recent years, HyFly is scared that a continued run-up will ruin the airline, and it decides to hedge its exposure by entering into a commodity swap.

- The swap is structured as follows (see Figure 7.4 for a diagram of this swap):
  - The notional is 10 million gallons of aviation fuel.
  - The swap has a two-year term, and the payments are made at the end of each month.
  - HyFly pays the dealer a fixed price of $1.50 per gallon or $10,000,000 \times 1.50 = \$15$ million each month.
  - The dealer pays a floating price that is the average spot price of fuel during the previous month.
  - The payments are net.

- Suppose last month's average price is $1.60 per gallon.
  - Then the dealer pays $10,000,000 \times 1.60 = \$16$ million at the end of the this month.
  - As the payments are netted, the airline receives $1 million.
  - This extra payment helps alleviate the airline's higher aviation fuel price paid in the spot market.

- Suppose oil prices fall unexpectedly and last month's average fuel price was $1.30. The savings that HyFly generates from the lower price have to be surrendered to the dealer, who must be paid $2 million by the terms of the contract.

This commodity contract is hard to price because it involves an average price (see Jarrow and Turnbull [2000] for a valuation formula for this swap).

Equity swaps are similar to the swaps previously discussed. The simplest **equity swaps** involve counterparties exchanging fixed rate interest payments for a floating payment that is tied to the return on a stock or a stock index. The payments are computed on a notional and exchanged at regular intervals over the swap's term. The index may be a broad-based index (such as the Standard and Poor's 500) or a narrowly defined index (such as for a specific industry group like biotechnology). Equity swaps allow money managers to temporarily change the nature of their portfolios and bet on the market. Suppose that we find two portfolio managers who hold completely opposite views about the direction of the stock market. They can enter into an equity swap in which the bullish manager receives a floating rate tied to the market index and pays the bearish manager a fixed interest rate.

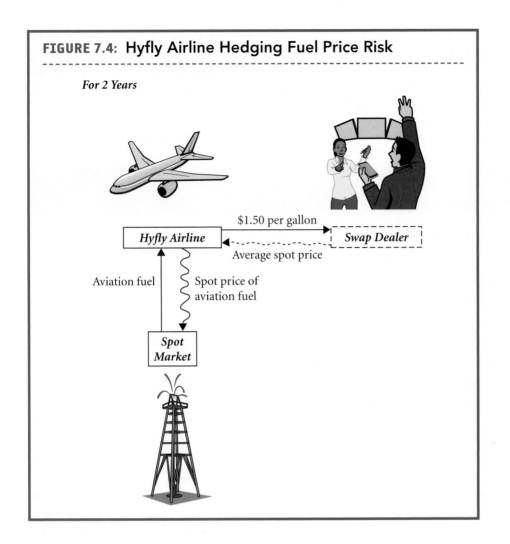

FIGURE 7.4: Hyfly Airline Hedging Fuel Price Risk

Credit Default Swaps

Credit default swaps (**CDS**) have been hailed during good times as a "wonder of modern finance" and vilified during the financial crisis of 2007 as a "'Ponzi scheme' that no self-respecting firm should touch" (see "Credit Derivatives: The Great Entangling," *Economist*, November 6, 2008). A discussion of the role played by CDS in the credit crisis is contained in chapter 26. Designed during the 1990s (by J. P. Morgan), CDS combine the concepts of insurance and swaps to create a contract that plays a useful economic role. It enables the holder of a risky bond to sell the credit risk embedded in the bond to a counterparty willing to bear it. Let's consider how a CDS works.

A CDS is a term insurance policy on an existing corporate or government bond. A typical CDS matures in one to five years and has a notional amount equal to the face value of the bond being insured, with most CDS being in the $10 to $20 million range. The seller of a CDS (the insurer) receives a periodic premium payment (usually quarterly) for selling the insurance. If a **credit event** occurs—the bond defaults—then the buyer of the CDS (the insured) receives the face value of the debt from the seller but hands over the bond in return.[9] The CDS contract ends if a credit event occurs.

The premium payment is quoted as a **CDS spread** (say, 100 basis points per annum). The actual dollar payment is the prorated spread (adjusted for the length of the payment period) times the notional. The CDS spread is quoted in the market so that no cash is exchanged when the CDS is written. This implies that the CDS has zero value at initiation. The next example illustrates the working of a CDS.

EXAMPLE 7.7: Hedging Default Risk

- The Worried Borrowers Fund (a fictitious name) has purchased a bond issued by Candyfault Enterprises (CE) (another fictitious name). The bond has five years until it matures, pays a 5.5 percent annual coupon, and has a notional of $5 million. The pension fund manager is concerned that Candyfault might default on its interest payments over the next year owing to the current recession. She wants to hedge its default risk but does not want to sell the bond.

- To hedge the default risk on CE over the next year, it buys a one-year CDS on CE with a notional of $5 million. The CDS quoted spread is 400 basis points per year, paid quarterly. The Worried Borrowers Fund buys this CDS.

- The quarterly premium payment made by the Worried Borrowers Fund is

$$0.04 \times (1/4) \times \$5 \text{ million} = \$50,000$$

- The CDS seller gets this payment quarterly until the CDS expires or until CE defaults on its bond, whichever comes first. In the event of default, the CDS seller pays the Worried Borrowers Fund $5 million, and it takes possession of the CE bond.

Pricing of this simple contract, however, is a difficult task. A valuation formula for a standard CDS is given in chapter 26. CDS are also written on asset back securities, called **ABS CDS**, but their cash flows are somewhat different (see Jarrow 2011).

7.7 | Summary

1. We emphasize a build and break approach, in which derivatives can be broken down into component parts or combined with other derivatives to create new ones.

2. Once the building blocks are understood, one can venture into financial engineering, a new discipline that applies engineering methods to financial economics.

---

[9] This is the case of physical delivery. If cash delivery occurs instead, the swap buyer receives the difference between the face value of the debt and the market price of the defaulted debt issue (usually determined through an auction).

3. A swap is an agreement between two counterparties to exchange a series of cash payments over its life. Swaps are successful vehicles for transforming one kind of cash flow to another. Swaps are OTC contracts that can be customized to the counterparties. The simplest kinds of swaps have the following structure:

   a. A plain vanilla interest rate swap exchanges fixed for floating rate payments. The principal, called the notional principal, never changes hands but is used only for computing cash flows. Payments are netted because the cash flows are denominated in the same currency.

   b. A forex swap involves a spot exchange of foreign currencies that is followed by a reverse exchange of equivalent amounts (principal plus relevant interest) at a future date.

   c. A plain vanilla currency swap (or a cross-currency swap) is an arrangement between two counterparties involving (1) an exchange of equivalent amounts of two different currencies on the starting date, (2) an exchange of interest payments on these two currency loans on intermediate dates, and (3) repayment of the principal on the ending date.

   d. A commodity swap involves an exchange of an average price of some notional amount of a commodity in exchange for a fixed payment.

   e. An equity swap exchanges fixed rate interest payments for a floating payment that is tied to the return on a stock or a stock index.

   f. A credit default swap is a term insurance policy on a bond.

7.8 | Cases

Times Mirror Company PEPS Proposal Review (Harvard Business School Case 296089-PDF-ENG). The case examines the design of a premium equity participating security for tax-efficient disposal of an appreciated common stock.

Privatization of Rhone-Poulenc—1993 (Harvard Business School Case 295049-PDF-ENG). The case illustrates how a recently privatized French company can use financial engineering to design an investment plan for employees that would enhance their ownership of company shares.

Advising on Currency Risk at ICICI Bank (Harvard Business School Case 205074-PDF-ENG). The case studies how a large Indian bank can hedge risks from multiple interest rates and currencies by using a variety of derivatives like swaps, options, and futures contracts on interest rates and currencies.

7.9 | Questions and Problems

7.1. Briefly describe a plain vanilla interest rate swap. Is the notional principal paid out at the swap's beginning and maturity?

7.2. Briefly describe a currency swap. Is the notional principal paid out at the swap's beginning and maturity?

7.3. How does a plain vanilla interest rate swap differ from a currency swap?

The next two questions use the following information:

American Auto enters into a plain vanilla currency swap deal with European Auto. American raises $30 million at an 8 percent fixed interest rate, while European raises an equivalent amount of €33 million at 9 percent. They swap these two loans. The swap lasts for three years, and the payments take place at the end of each year.

7.4. What is the principal? Does it change hands at the beginning and end of the swap?

7.5. Calculate the gross payments involved and indicate who pays what in this swap deal.

The next two questions use the following information:

Esandel Bank enters into a plain vanilla interest rate swap with a swap facilitator Londoner Inc. Esandel pays a fixed amount of 8 percent per year to Londoner, which in turn pays a floating amount bbalibor + 1.50 percent. The principal is $15 million. The swap lasts for five years, and the payments take place at the end of each year.

7.6. What is the notional principal? Does it change hands at the beginning and end of the swap?

7.7. Who is in the "receive fixed" situation? Who is in the "pay-fixed" situation?

7.8. Calculate the net payments involved and indicate who pays what in this swap deal if the bbalibor takes on the values 7.00 percent, 6.50 percent, 7.00 percent, 7.50 percent, and 6.00 percent at the end of the first, second, third, fourth, and fifth year, respectively.

Consider the swap in Examples 7.6 and 7.6 (continued) from Extension 7.2.

- The automakers enter into a swap with a three-year term on a principal of $200 million.

- The spot exchange rate S_A is $2 per pound. Americana raises $100 \times 2 = $200 million and gives it to Britannia, which in turn raises £100 million and gives it to Americana.

- Americana pays Britannia 4 percent per year on £100 million and Britannia pays Americana 6 percent per year on $200 million at the end of each year for three years.

Now assume that the companies make payments *every six months*: the swap ends after six semiannual payments, and the principals are handed back after three years.

7.9. Using zero-coupon bond prices (maturing every six months) given below, compute the value of this swap.

Zero-Coupon Bond Prices in the United States (Domestic Country) and the United Kingdom (Foreign Country)		
Time to Maturity (in years)	US (Domestic) Zero-Coupon Bond Prices (in dollars)	UK (Foreign) Zero-Coupon Bond Prices (in pounds sterling)
0.5	$B(0.5) = \$0.99$	$B(0.5)_E = £0.98$
1	$B(1) = 0.97$	$B(1)_E = 0.96$
1.5	$B(1.5) = 0.95$	$B(1.5)_E = 0.93$
2	$B(2) = 0.93$	$B(2)_E = 0.91$
2.5	$B(2.5) = 0.91$	$B(1.5)_E = 0.88$
3	$B(3) = 0.88$	$B(3)_E = 0.85$

7.10. How can one use a currency swap to hedge currency risk?

7.11. How can one use an interest rate swap to change a fixed rate loan into a floating rate loan?

7.12. How can a savings and loan bank use an interest rate swap to match its long-term fixed rate investments with the risks of its short-term floating rate demand deposit obligations?

7.13. What is an equity swap? What is a commodity swap?

7.14. Suppose an investor is precluded from investing in a country's stocks by government regulations but can invest in the country's government bonds. Design a swap to overcome these regulations.

7.15. What is a forex swap? Explain how it works.

7.16. In chapter 2, we described how the US Treasury STRIPS worked. Explain how Wall Street firms had financially engineered a product similar to STRIPS.

7.17. What is a callable bond? When would it be used?

7.18. What is a putable bond? When would it be used?

7.19. What is a convertible bond? How would you break it down into simpler parts and price it?

7.20. Check the Internet or other sources and answer the following questions:

a. Briefly describe the Troubled Asset Relief Program (TARP) program of the US government.

b. What was the derivative used in the program? Why would the US government trade such a "toxic thing" as a derivatives contract?

c. How would you approach the pricing of the security used in the TARP?

d. Discuss the success of the program to date.

Forwards and Futures

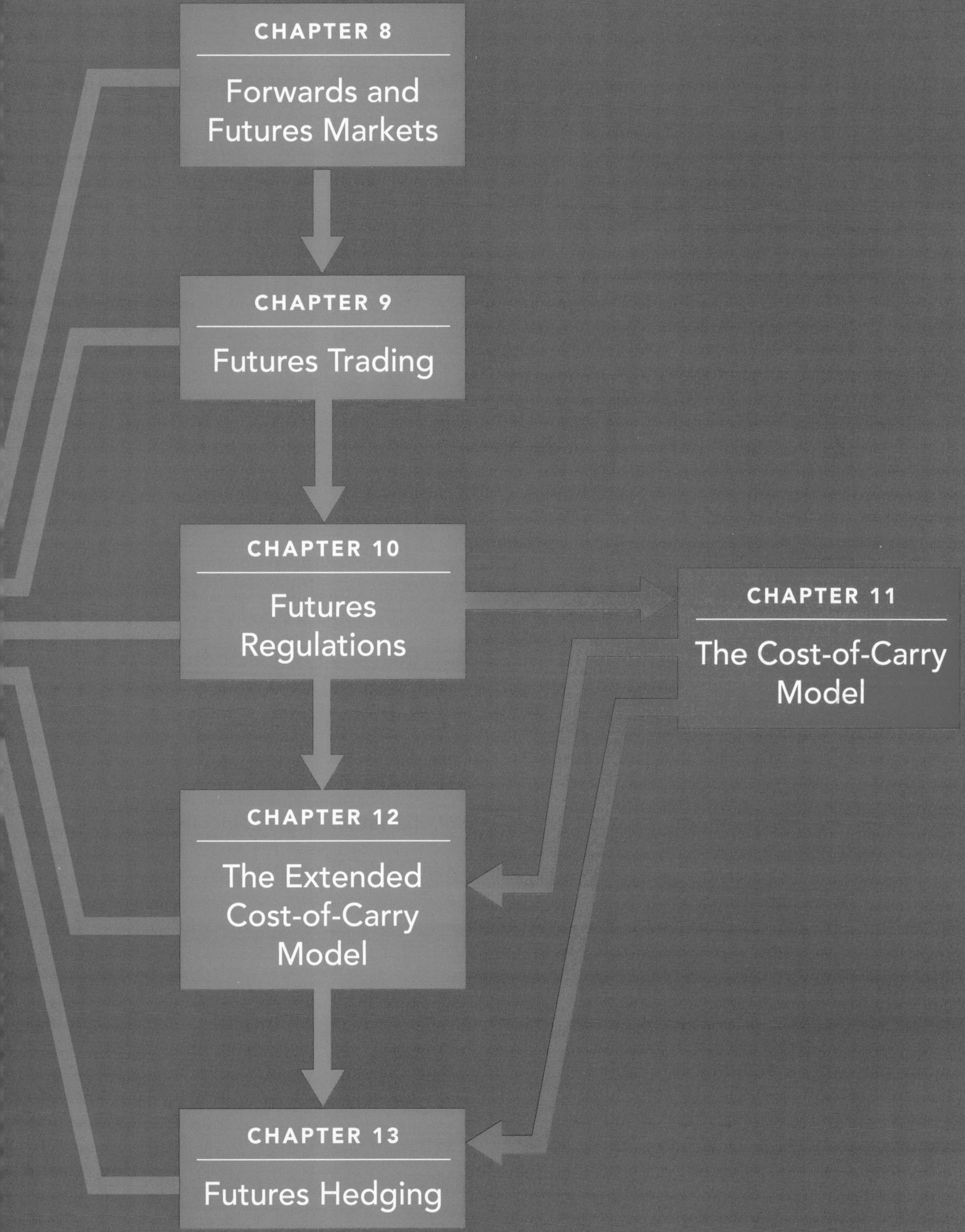

CHAPTER 8

Forwards and
Futures Markets

CHAPTER 9

Futures Trading

CHAPTER 10

Futures
Regulations

CHAPTER 11

The Cost-of-Carry
Model

CHAPTER 12

The Extended
Cost-of-Carry
Model

CHAPTER 13

Futures Hedging

8

Forwards and Futures Markets

8.1 | Introduction

In 1688, the world's first futures exchange, the Dojima Rice Exchange, opened its doors. It was located in Osaka, which was Japan's commercial center at the time known as the "country's kitchen." In those days, if you controlled rice, then you controlled the Japanese economy. The Dojima Exchange devised a fairly advanced system of trading that has many commonalities with the way futures trade today. A day's trading time was determined by a firebox system. The market would open in the morning with the lighting of a wick in a hanging wooden box, and it would close when the wick was completely burned down. If the wick was extinguished early, then all trades of that day were canceled. You can imagine how losing traders tried to puff out the fire early, while winning traders and exchange officials attempted to foil such plans. Raw emotions would sometimes get expressed through brawls and fistfights (see Alletzhauser 1990; West 2000). Such skirmishes occasionally break out on trading floors of futures exchanges even today.

As this story relates, emotions (and stakes) can run high at futures exchanges, the workings of which are described in this chapter. We take up forward and futures contracts from where we left off in chapter 4. We discuss the usefulness of forward and futures contracts and present a brief history. Although futures-type contracts have traded in many times and places, the evolution of the modern futures contract really began in mid-nineteenth-century Chicago and was completed in about seventy-five years. After decades of relative calm, the 1970s saw a period of astonishing changes in futures markets. These developments can be classified into four categories: (1) introduction of new futures contracts, (2) the opening of new exchanges, (3) consolidation and greater linkages among exchanges, and (4) the automation of trading. Finally, we examine a gold futures contract and study how futures prices get reported in the financial press and quoted by vendors.

8.2 | Applications and Uses of Forwards and Futures

As forward and futures markets are growing by leaps and bounds (and huge securities markets don't exist without good reason), they must be serving a useful role in the economy. And this growth is not just in futures on commodities like corn and gold. The 1970s saw the introduction of **financial futures** ("**financials**"), which are futures contracts based on financial assets (such as foreign currencies) and on economic or financial variables (such as interest rates). These contracts have become very popular.

What is the utility of forward and futures contracts including those written on financial assets and financial variables? Futures and forwards take investors far beyond the realm of ordinary stocks and bonds and, in the language of Star Trek, "where no man has gone before." Consider the following observations:

1. By purchasing forwards and futures in advance, a trader can smooth unexpected future price fluctuations that can come from demand–supply mismatches.

2. Forwards are useful for acquiring a commodity at a fixed price at a later date. Futures are seldom used for trading assets because of the costs involved with physical delivery. However, their features make them excellent tools for managing price risk.

3. Forwards and futures help make the market more "complete." In a **complete market**, sufficient securities trade such that investors can construct portfolios to obtain all possible probability distributions over future payoffs.

4. They help traders to speculate. Speculators have a beneficial presence in most futures markets. Speculators increase liquidity and enhance market efficiency, but destabilizing speculation can also take place, and we look at several manipulation cases in chapter 10.

5. They allow investors to leverage their capital and hold large trading positions without tying up cash. However, like speculation, leverage cuts both ways and can sometimes do more harm than good. For example, futures bets destroyed Barings PLC, a venerable British bank that had existed for over two hundred years.

6. The process of trading forwards and futures generates useful information about future price expectations called **price discovery**, an important function discussed in greater detail in chapter 10.

8.3 | A Brief History of Forwards and Futures

Forward trading began early in the dawn of civilization (see Table 8.1) and thrives to this day. It is estimated that current forward markets are several times the size of futures markets. To get some idea of why this is true, note that foreign exchange ("forex") forwards form a big chunk of the foreign exchange market, which is one of the world's largest financial markets. Swaps, which may be viewed as a series of forward contracts, have a market size measured in trillions of dollars.

The history of forwards and exchange-traded futures may be divided into three phases:

1. *Early trading of forward and futures-type contracts.* Forward contracts evolved separately in many parts of the world. Sometimes they traded in centrally located

TABLE 8.1: Early History of Trading Forward and Futures-Type Contracts

Year	Development
2000 BC and onward	Forward contracts traded in Greece, India, and the Roman Empire
Eleventh and twelfth centuries AD and onward	Medieval fairs
1531	The first commodities exchange in Antwerp, Belgium
1550s onward	Futures and options contracts traded in Amsterdam, Netherlands
1571	Royal Exchange for trading commodities in London, England
1688	Dojima Rice Exchange in Osaka, Japan

markets with standardized trading rules and contract terms that prompted some scholars to label them as futures contracts.

2. *Evolution of the modern futures contract.* Today's futures contracts started taking shape in the United States during the nineteenth century and arrived at its present form over the next seventy-five years.

3. *Developments since the 1970s.* An astonishing variety of futures were conceived and marketed during the last three decades of the twentieth century. Exchanges merged, new exchanges emerged, and exchanges became connected. Furthermore, trading became increasingly automated, often removing brokers and dealers from the matchmaking process to let traders interact through an electronic interface.

Early Trading of Forward and Futures-Type Contracts

Forward contracts have been used to reduce risk for eons. Forwards traded in India around 2000 BC, in ancient Greece and Rome, in medieval Europe, and in Japan during the seventeenth century (see Table 8.1).

Coming out of the rubrics of the Roman Empire, medieval Europe evolved into city-states. In the second millennium, states set up trade fairs at which merchants from different regions came to sell their wares. Trade benefited all: businesses prospered, kingdoms flourished, and the monarch collected tax revenues. Mercantile laws were developed to regulate and coordinate trade, standardize contract terms, and resolve disputes. Trades were done in the spot market, where goods got exchanged for metallic currency or other products.

Over time, fair letters were developed. A **fair letter** specified delivery of a commodity at a future date and at a fixed place. This was a great convenience. Gone was the hassle of dragging a big bulk of merchandise from place to place. Fair letters provided proof of ownership of goods held safely in warehouses. Moreover, they became **negotiable** and changed hands several times before settlement. The fair letter is a forward contract and a precursor of today's futures.

But fairs were held only a few times a year. An inevitable development was setting up an exchange where buyers and sellers gathered regularly to trade. This was pioneered in the Belgian city of Antwerp. The city built an exchange in 1531, adopted a set of rules for contract enforcement the following year, and created a legislative framework to support financial transactions later in the decade. Financial and commercial transactions flourished, derivatives contracts developed, speculation (including wagers on political events and bets through foreign exchange options) grew rampant, and manipulation of commodity prices became a threat to the markets.

Meanwhile, Amsterdam was becoming the major market for grain, herring, and other bulk commodities (see Gelderblom and Jonker 2005). Fearing that speculators could use derivatives to manipulate prices and that manipulated food prices would cause social unrest, the government often switched between banning and allowing forward trading. But the markets did not disappear when they were banned. Markets simply went underground. Records indicate that Amsterdam grain dealers used both futures and options in the 1550s and the decades that followed. Subsequently, the markets expanded to include forwards, futures, and call and put options on equities.

One of the earliest commodities exchanges was the Royal Exchange of London, which was inaugurated by Queen Elizabeth I in 1571. Today the original location houses an upscale shopping mall. The renowned London Metal Exchange and the London Stock Exchange both trace their ancestry back to the Royal Exchange.

The world's oldest stock exchange, as noted in chapter 2, opened in Amsterdam in 1602. Soon futures and options contracts started trading. This was a time when the tulip was gaining popularity in Holland. A few decades later, the Dutch got involved in an extraordinary speculative fervor over rare tulip bulbs, and futures and options were devised to help the speculating public. As with other price bubbles, the famous tulip bulb price bubble ended when prices came crashing down and derivatives trading dried up.

As noted at the beginning of this chapter, Osaka's Dojima Rice Exchange opened its doors in 1688. It is considered the world's first organized futures market because the contracts were standardized, had fixed life, required margin payments, and involved clearinghouses. Over 1,300 exchange members traded rice receipts, which gave holders ownership of rice kept in warehouses. Trading took place by a firebox system, as earlier described. West (2000) suggests that this firebox system encouraged mutual monitoring of trading and discouraged price manipulation. The exchange operated for centuries and was closed down in 1939 because of wartime controls.

US Futures Exchanges and the Evolution of the Modern Futures Contract, 1848–1926

Despite interesting developments elsewhere, modern futures trading really began in Chicago in the mid-nineteenth century with the establishment of the **Chicago Board of Trade** (**CBOT** or **CBT**). Why Chicago? Located on the windswept shores of Lake Michigan, the "Windy City" is close to the fertile farmlands of the great Midwest. Nineteenth-century Chicago became America's major transportation and distribution center for agricultural produce. Farmers shipped their grains to Chicago, much of which then moved eastward to where most Americans lived.

But agriculture is a seasonal business. Prices crashed at harvest times as farmers flooded Chicago with grains and rose again as the grain was used and became scarce. A need was felt for a central marketplace to smooth such demand–supply imbalances. The futures market was devised to fill this void.

To standardize the quality and quantity of grains traded, eighty-two merchants founded the CBOT in 1848. Spot market trading began immediately, and more developments followed. Table 8.2 shows how US futures trading evolved to reach its present-day perfection. It all began in a modest way between 1849 and 1850 with the trading of to arrive contracts, simple forward contracts that traded in a particular place. A **to arrive** contract allowed a farmer to sell grains at a later date at a price fixed in advance. These contracts were negotiated for delivery at weekly intervals starting around harvest time. The CBOT flourished.

In the mid-1860s, the CBOT streamlined trading and further standardized contracts in terms of size, quality of commodities, delivery dates, and places. The contracts came to be called **futures**. Most important, the CBOT also required

TABLE 8.2: Evolution of Today's Futures Contract (1848–1926)

Year	Development
1848	The CBOT was established to standardize grains trading
1849–50	To arrive contracts started trading at the CBOT
1865	General rules were developed at the CBOT that standardized futures contracts; traders were required to post margins
1874	The Chicago Produce Exchange was formed to trade farm products; it became the Chicago Butter and Egg Board in 1898, and in 1919, it became the CME, with its own clearinghouse
1877	Speculators were allowed to trade at the CBOT
1882	NYMEX was established
1925	A clearinghouse was established at the CBOT

performance bonds called **margins** from both buyers and sellers. This eliminated counterparty risk. In 1877, the CBOT allowed speculators to trade. Prior to this time, only producers or purchasers could trade. In contrast, speculators trade for profits and not for hedging purposes.

Meanwhile there was a need to organize the trading of butter, eggs, poultry, and other farm products. Merchants trading these commodities founded the Chicago Produce Exchange in 1874; this became the Chicago Butter and Egg Board in 1898 and emerged as the **Chicago Mercantile Exchange** (**CME** or **the Merc**) in 1919. It became widely known for trading traditional futures contracts on dairy, meat, and poultry products.

These developments made Chicago the US center for commodities trading. New York City lagged behind Chicago. In the nineteenth century, New York City was growing furiously, but it had a poor infrastructure for storing, pricing, and transferring agricultural, dairy, and meat products. To help alleviate this problem, a group of merchants founded the Butter and Cheese Exchange of New York, renamed the **New York Mercantile Exchange** (**NYMEX**) in 1882. Another major US futures exchange, the **Commodity Exchange** (**COMEX**), was founded in 1933 from the merger of four smaller exchanges. The COMEX later became a major venue for trading gold, silver, and copper futures.

Another innovation came when clearinghouses were established by the CBOT in 1925 and by the CME after its reorganization in 1919. As noted earlier, in exchange-traded derivatives markets, a clearinghouse plays the crucial role of *clearing* a trade by matching the buyer and seller, recognizing and recording trades, and (nearly) eliminating counterparty default risk. These developments almost created the futures contract as we know it today.

Recent Developments, 1970 Onward

Futures markets have undergone significant changes since 1970 (see Table 8.3). We classify these changes into four categories: (1) the introduction of new futures contracts, (2) the opening of new exchanges, (3) the consolidation and greater linkages among exchanges, and (4) the automation of trading.

TABLE 8.3: Milestones in the History of Futures Trading since 1970

Year	Development
1972	The first successful financial futures, foreign currency futures, started trading at the newly created IMM at the CME
1973	The CBOE was founded by members of the CBOT
1974	US Congress passed the Commodity Futures Trading Commission Act that created the CFTC
1975	The first interest rate futures, GNMA futures contracts, started trading at the CBOT
1977	Treasury bond futures began trading at the CBOT
1981	The first cash-settled contract, the eurodollar futures, started trading at the CME
1982	The NFA, a self-regulatory organization made up of firms and people who work in the futures industry, was established
1982	Options on US Treasury bond futures started trading at the CBOT
1982	The first index futures contract, the Value Line index futures, started trading at the Kansas City Board of Trade; within months, the S&P 500 stock index futures started trading at the CME
1984	The first international futures link, the CME/SIMEX mutual offset trading link, was established
1992	A postmarket global electronic transaction system, Globex, was launched by the CME and Reuters

NEW FUTURES CONTRACTS When exchange rates are stable, no one needs to hedge foreign exchange (forex) risks. The end of the Bretton Woods System in 1971, however, moved the world from fixed to floating exchange rates. This immediately created a demand for derivatives to hedge forex risk. In 1972, the CME responded by creating the **International Monetary Market (IMM) division** for trading forex futures. The seven foreign currency futures that started trading at the IMM became *the first successful financial futures traded*. Financial futures now form a majority of the ten most actively traded contracts. The century-long dominance of corn, wheat, and other agricultural futures quickly faded away.

The creation of the IMM is an interesting story about the interplay between academic thought and market practice (see "New Game in Town," *Wall Street Journal*, May 16, 1972). Economics professor and Nobel laureate Milton Friedman played a pivotal role in the founding of the IMM. His free-market views had many supporters, including Merc chairman Leo Melamed. A staunch opponent of the Bretton Woods system of fixed exchange rates, Friedman felt in 1967 that the British pound was overvalued, and he approached three Chicago banks in an attempt to sell the pound forward, offering to post the necessary collateral. But the amused bank officials turned down the professor's offer because he did not have the necessary "commercial interest" for dealing in foreign currencies. On November 13, 1971, Melamed met Friedman for breakfast and sought his opinion about starting a currency futures market. Friedman emphatically supported the idea and was commissioned to do a feasibility study titled "The Need for a Futures Market in Currencies." Friedman's seminal study and steadfast support helped overcome the regulatory resistance. The IMM opened its doors on May 16, 1972, and the CME became the first exchange to successfully build a financial futures market.

But exchanges don't always succeed. Credit for the first currency futures exchange goes to the **International Commercial Exchange**, an exchange founded by the members of the New York Produce Exchange in 1970 but that closed its doors in 1973. Its failure has been attributed to several causes: (1) bad timing (as it was founded when the Bretton Woods agreement was still in force), (2) limitations of a small exchange, (3) small contract size, (4) a failure to adequately promote itself, (5) high margin requirements, and (6) high brokerage fees (see "New Game in Town," *Wall Street Journal*, May 16, 1972).

The 1960s were a prosperous time in the United States. Bountiful harvests depressed farm prices, but US government price supports propped them up[1]—and there was no price volatility. As volatility is the lifeblood of derivatives, agricultural futures markets went completely dry. To explore new ways of augmenting their income, members of the CBOT opened the world's first options exchange, the **Chicago Board Options Exchange** (**CBOE**).

Novel products and new markets generate a need for greater regulatory oversight. In 1974, the US Congress passed the **Commodity Futures Trading Commission** (**CFTC**) **Act**, which created the CFTC as the "federal regulatory agency for futures trading." In 1982, the **National Futures Association** (**NFA**), an industry body, was established. NFA does a slew of self-regulatory activities, which (remember from chapter 1) enhances the reputation of the futures markets and reduces the need for greater federal oversight.

In the 1970s, oil shocks and other supply-side disturbances hiked up the inflation rate, causing interest rates to be more volatile. In 1975, the CBOT launched the Government National Mortgage Association (GNMA) futures, which protected mortgage holders from interest rate risk. This was the first interest rate derivative. The contract died a natural death because the introduction of US Treasury bond futures in 1977 proved to be a better hedge for the same risk (see Johnston and McConnell 1989; Duffie 1989). Despite its demise, the Ginnie Mae futures contract was the spark that ignited the creation of the vast global market for interest rate derivatives, one of which was the eurodollar futures introduced by the CME in 1981.

Eurodollar futures were the world's first cash-settled futures contracts. Normally, when a futures contract is carried to delivery, the short collects the futures price and delivers the underlying commodity. A **cash-settled futures contract** has no such physical delivery provision. If taken to maturity, a cash payment equal to the difference between the settlement price at the contract's end and the previous day's settlement price closes out the contract.

Cash settlement allows a futures contract to end, in T. S. Eliot's words, "not with a bang but a whimper." Without cumbersome delivery, it became possible to design an extraordinary range of derivatives based on notional variables like indexes, interest rates, and other intangibles.

The year 1982 saw the introduction of options both on futures and on stock index futures. In chapter 5, we introduced **options on spot**, which are options

---

[1] See recollections of Joseph Sullivan (1988). Nicknamed Mr. Options, Sullivan was responsible for the development of the Chicago Board Options Exchange—initially as vice president for planning at the CBOT and then as the first president of the CBOE.

contracts based on an underlying asset or a notional variable. Equity options on blue chip stocks like Ford and International Business Machines are its simplest examples. By contrast, **options on futures** or **futures options** have a futures contract as the underlying. This market started in 1982 with US Treasury bond futures. Most futures options now trade side by side with their underlying futures contracts on their respective exchanges.

Index futures came as a natural next development. These are cash-settled futures contracts that have an index as the underlying variable. America's second oldest futures exchange, the **Kansas City Board of Trade** (opened in 1856), won the race to start index futures trading. In 1982, it got regulatory approval to trade futures on the **Value Line Index**. This is an average of over 1,700 stocks tracked by Value Line Incorporated, a well-known provider of investment advice. Months later, the CME introduced the Standard and Poor's 500 index futures (S&P 500), which soon overtook the former. Index futures are very popular for implementing different trading strategies, including hedging, speculation, and index arbitrage.

Subsequent years saw the introduction of an assortment of new contracts. Futures contracts on interest rates in major currencies like dollars (eurodollars), the euro, the Japanese yen, and the pound sterling are offered by major exchanges including the CME Group and the NYSE Euronext. Moreover, they trade on short-term interest rate benchmarks, which are often determined by a method similar to bbalibor (see chapter 2) and use the suffix **IBOR** or **BOR** (for "interbank offered rate"). Examples include interest rate futures on BUBOR in Budapest, HIBOR in Hong Kong, KORIBOR in Korea, MOSIBOR in Moscow, and STIBOR in Stockholm. The emergence of the European Community has also created the need for euro-based futures. Just open the "Money and Investments" section of the *Wall Street Journal* or go to the website of one of the futures exchanges to get an idea of this diversity.

NEW EXCHANGES In terms of trading volume, some of the world's largest futures and options exchanges have opened in recent years. For example, new exchanges such as Eurex of Europe, the International Securities Exchange of the United States, MexDer of Mexico, the Shanghai Futures Exchange of China, the National Stock Exchange of India, and the Taifex of Taiwan have joined the ranks of the CME Group and the London Metal Exchange, as shown in Table 4.2. There are futures exchanges even in countries with emerging financial markets like Bangladesh, Honduras, Latvia, and Tunisia. In all, nearly a hundred futures exchanges operate today. Many of them are modeled after US futures exchanges, and they even relied on American technical expertise to be set up (recall Extension 4.2).

The new millennium saw challenges to the long-standing US dominance of the derivatives industry. Across the Atlantic, Europe created a common market under the banner of the European Community. To position itself for this momentous change, in mid-1998 two prominent European exchanges, Germany's Deutsche Terminbörse AG (DTB itself was started as an all-electronic futures exchange in 1989) and the Swiss Options and Financial Futures Exchange (SOFFEX), started trading and clearing derivatives transactions through **Eurex**, a uniform technical platform. Eurex is a completely decentralized system that operates very much like an over-the-counter market. Members can access it electronically from anywhere, creating a global network. Armed with a vast selection of derivatives, Eurex overtook the CBOT and the CME, and became the first derivatives exchange to shatter both the 300 million contracts a year mark in 1999 and the 400 million mark in 2000.

In 2000, the merger of the Amsterdam, Brussels, and Paris Bourses created **Euronext N.V.** In 2002, it acquired the London International Financial Futures and Options Exchange (LIFFE) and merged with the Portuguese Exchange BVLP. Euronext. The company's global derivatives business (Euronext had since merged with the NYSE and acquired other exchanges) is ranked among the world's top five derivatives exchanges in Table 4.2. The *Korea Futures Exchange (KOFEX)* ranks first. Since January 27, 2005, KOFEX has become a division of the newly formed **Korea Exchange**. While Eurex was annually trading a little over a billion contracts, KOFEX traded a mind-boggling 2.9 billion contracts in 2003 and 2.5 billion in 2004, grabbing over a 25 percent share of global contract volume. In 2010, the Korea Exchange traded an astounding 3.748 billion futures and options contracts at a time when the second-ranked CME group was trading 3.080 billion contracts (see Table 4.2). Much of their volume comes from trading options on the Korea Composite Stock Price Index (KOSPI).

CONSOLIDATION AND LINKAGES The European Union's motto "United in Diversity" is an apt description of today's financial world: numerous exchanges with diverse product lines in distant lands have proliferated with customers linked through a single electronic terminal. The first international futures link was established in 1984 when the **Singapore International Monetary Exchange** (**SIMEX**), the first financial futures exchange in Asia, set up a mutual offset trading arrangement with Chicago's CME. There has been no looking back.

Recent years have seen a trend toward extended trading hours. The year 1992 saw the launching of **Globex**, a postmarket global electronic transaction system. It is an automated order entry and matching system operated by Britain's Reuters Limited, a global news vendor. Originally developed for the CME, Globex participants include Brazilian Exchange BM&FBOVESPA, Bursa Malaysia (BMD), GreenX, the Dubai Mercantile Exchange (DME), the Korean Exchange (KRX), and the Minneapolis Grain Exchange (MGEX). Globex links hundreds of terminals into an instantly interactive, worldwide network. Globex links hundreds of terminals into an instantly interactive, worldwide network. It begins shortly after and ends a little before CME's regular trading hours, facilitating a twenty-three-hour trading day for many CME-listed futures and options. The term "regular trading hours" has lost some of its meaning. Many futures contracts are truly global and trade around the clock.

In the last decade of the twentieth century, mergers and acquisitions, long common in the corporate world, occurred in futures markets. On April 4, 2007, Euronext merged with the NYSE Group to create **NYSE Euronext**. For many years, the CME and the CBOT fought intensely for the top position among the US futures exchanges. However, they merged their companies in 2007 to form the **CME Group**. Earlier in 1994, the NYMEX had merged with the COMEX. In 2008, NYMEX became a wholly owned subsidiary of the CME Group. Currently the CME Group operates four *designated contract markets*, which is a technical name for entities that are similar to traditional futures exchanges that operate under the oversight of the CFTC (see discussions under the Commodity Futures Modernization Act [2010] of chapter 10).

AUTOMATION OF TRADING   As discussed in chapter 3, IT advances have revolutionized securities trading by making innovations like electronic exchanges, online brokerage accounts, and network linkage fairly commonplace. For convenience, we divided technology adoption in the trading process into levels I, II, and III. Level I is the traditional system of trading securities with little mechanization; level II is an intermediate model in which trading involves computers that cut out personnel only in the early part of the process by taking orders directly to brokers on the trading floor; and level III is completely electronic trading. Many new exchanges, such as the Boston Options Exchange, Eurex, and the Korea Futures Exchange, began as fully electronic exchanges. Many old exchanges, such as the Liffe of the NYSE Euronext group and the Tel-Aviv Stock Exchange, ended pit trading and became completely computerized. Seeing these developments, it's no surprise that automation and a complete replacement of floor trading by electronic trading is predicted by market observers.

| 8.4 | **Futures Contract Features and Price Quotes** |

This section discusses a futures contract's specifications and how prices and trades are recorded.

Commodity and Financial Futures Contracts

Futures contracts are divided into those on commodities or financial futures. **Commodity futures** usually refer to futures contracts on commodities like cattle, coffee, copper, and corn. **Financial futures** refer to futures contracts on financial assets like bonds, currencies, or even on notional variables like stock indexes and interest rates (see Table 8.4).[2]

Greater connectivity among exchanges has considerably expanded the menu of choices available for trading futures. Most futures have similar features, especially those trading on US exchanges. As "seeing one is seeing them all," we select a popular contract and examine its specifications. Gold is the natural choice since gold futures trade on several US exchanges and on at least ten foreign ones.

---

[2] Legally the term *commodity* has a broader definition that includes nearly all goods and services (see Title 7 [Agriculture], chapter 1 [Commodity Exchanges], Section 1a of the US Code), and under this legal definition, financial futures are considered commodity futures.

The Gold Futures Contract

Let us examine the specifications of the gold futures contract that trades on the COMEX division of the CME Group (see Example 8.1).[3]

EXAMPLE 8.1: The Gold Futures Contract Traded on the COMEX Division of the CME Group

- A **trading** or **ticker symbol** identifies the futures contract. The gold futures contract has the ticker symbol GC.

- A **trading month** identifies the contract's delivery month. At any time, GC contracts trade with "delivery during the current calendar month; the next two calendar months; any February, April, August, and October falling within a 23-month period; and any June and December falling within a 60-month period beginning with the current month."[4] Table 8.5 gives actual price quotes for these contracts and shows some months that trade. The choice of trading months is crucial for many commodities. As gold is produced steadily throughout the year, it makes sense to have delivery months spaced at regular intervals throughout the year. Futures on agricultural commodities often have delivery months clustered around harvest times.

- The **trading unit** or **contract size** (also called **even lot**) is one hundred troy ounces per contract. Some commodities have futures contracts of multiple sizes. The CME Group also offers COMEX-traded mini-sized miNY fifty-ounce gold futures contracts (ticker symbol QO) and Globex-traded E-micro gold futures based on ten troy ounces of gold (ticker symbol MGC).

- **Trading hours** (all these times are U.S. Eastern Standard Time) are 8:20 AM to 1:30 PM for the open-outcry session taking place on the exchange floor. Electronic trading is conducted from 6:00 PM until 5:15 PM via the CME Globex trading platform, Sunday through Friday. There is a forty-five-minute break each day between 5:15 PM (current trade date) and 6:00 PM (next trade date). The contract also trades in the **CME ClearPort**, a system for clearing over-the-counter trades, where the trading hours are identical to those of Globex.

- The **price quotation** is in US dollars and cents per troy ounce. If the quoted price is $500, then the **position size** for one contract is $500 \times 100 = \$50,000$.

- The **minimum price fluctuation** or **tick size** measures the minimum price jump. GC has a tick size of 10 cents ($0.10) per troy ounce or $10 per contract. For example, if the gold futures price is $500.00, the next higher price would be $500.10, the next would be $500.20, and so on. The long position gains and the short position loses by $10 for each of these jumps. If the price falls from $500.00 to $498.50, then the long loses $150 per contract.

- The **maximum daily price fluctuation** or **daily price limit** is the maximum price change allowed in a day. Some commodities have price limits (see the relevant exchange websites for details). If

---

[4] January 7, 2012, www.cmegroup.com/trading/metals/precious/gold_contract_specifications.html.

[3] January 7, 2012, www.cmegroup.com/trading/metals/precious/gold_contract_specifications.html.

TABLE 8.4: Examples of Futures Contracts That Trade in the United States

Category	Examples of Commodities
Commodity Futures	
Grains and oilseeds	Corn, soybean, wheat, canola, . . .
Livestock and meat	Cattle, pork belly, hogs, . . .
Food and fiber	Coffee, orange juice, sugar, cotton, . . .
Metals	Copper, gold, platinum, silver, . . .
Energy	Gasoline, heating oil, natural gas, electricity, . . .
Other products	Ammonia, lumber, plywood, . . .
Financial Futures	
Interest rates	Canadian bonds, euribor, eurodollars, Treasury securities, . . .
Currencies	Euro, peso, pound, Swiss franc, . . .
Indexes	Dow, Nasdaq, Nikkei, S&P 500, . . .

the futures price moves up by the limit, the contract is **limit up**; if it hits the lower limit, then it is **limit down**. Trading stops if such **limit moves** occur. Why set price limits? Proponents (including most regulators) take the view that price limits reduce "hysteria" and lowers price volatility by forcing traders to "cool off" after dramatic price moves. Opponents (including most economists and finance academics) believe that price limits create artificial barriers that interfere with the normal forces of demand and supply without serving any useful purpose.

- The **last trading day is the third to last business day** of the delivery month. This is the last day on which a GC contract maturing in that month can trade.

- **Delivery** is the traditional way of ending a futures contract. Gold delivered against a GC contract must bear a serial number and an identifying stamp of a refiner approved and listed by the exchange. Delivery must be made from a depository that has been licensed by the exchange.

- Besides delivery, a contract may end with an **exchange of physicals** (**EFP**) for the futures contract. In this case, the buyer and the seller privately negotiate the exchange of a futures position for a physical position of equal quantity. EFPs take place at locations that are away from the exchange floor.

- The **delivery period** is the time period during which delivery can occur. The **first delivery day** is the first business day of the delivery month, while the **last delivery day** is the last such day. Like most futures, the GC seller decides if a delivery should take place, and if so, when to start the process and what grade to deliver. This makes sense because historically, sellers were hedgers who held the physical commodity for sale.

- **Trading at Settlement** allows traders to trade any time during trading hours but at a delivery price that is the settlement price determined at the day's close. This is only allowed for certain months.

- Regarding **grade and quality specifications**, in case of delivery, the seller must deliver 100 troy ounces of gold, subject to various specifications regarding assaying fineness, the form in which it can be delivered, and acceptable refiners (details are available from the exchange on request.)

- The **position limit** restricts the number of contracts that a speculator can hold in particular commodities (see the relevant exchange websites for details). Position limits try to prevent traders from manipulating by accumulating huge long positions and then squeezing short sellers. Several forward and futures market manipulation cases discussed in chapter 10 show that this risk is real.

- **Margins are security deposits** required to open and maintain futures positions. A nonmember opening a speculative position has to keep an **initial margin** (security deposit needed to open a futures position) per contract. The **maintenance margin** is the amount that if the account value falls to this level, the trader has to supply more funds to bring the margin back to the initial margin. For the exact dollar margins required, see the relevant exchange websites.

Gold Futures Price Quotes

Wire news services, websites, and many major daily newspapers carry futures price quotes. As there are some differences in how they report, we discuss price quotes for the COMEX gold futures. Table 8.5 gives these prices for Thursday, August 24, 2007, from the NYMEX website (this contract currently trades on the CME Group's COMEX division; quotes are available online[5]). Newspapers provide basic information like where the contract trades, the size of the contract, and how prices are quoted. This redundant information is not reported on the NYMEX website.

The first column lists the delivery months. The **last trade price** is reported next: this was $678.00 for the December 2007 contract. Many exchanges begin each day's trading with an **opening call** period for each contract month. The first few bids, offers, and traded prices during this initial time period establish an **opening price** or an **opening range**. This can give rise to different **open high** and **open low** prices, which were $671.20 and $670.90, respectively, for December 2007. Regular trading begins after everyone gets a chance to execute trades at the opening call.

High and **low** are the highest and the lowest traded prices per contract per day. The high price for December 2007 gold was $679.00, while the low was $666.70. The difference between the high and the low prices determines the trading **range** for the trading session.

Like the opening, trading ends in a special way. The closing minutes are usually the busiest because this is when many traders close out their open trades to avoid margins for overnight positions. During the brief ending period, called the **market close**, or the last minute of trading, known as the **closing call**, a **closing price** or a **closing range** is established.

For actively traded contracts with few price fluctuations, the exchange's Settlement Committee picks a **settlement price** from this closing range, often the last traded price. The settlement price (abbreviated **settle**) is the fair value of the contract at market close. For December 2007, the most recent settlement price was $677.50. The task is harder for thinly traded contracts. For example, April 2008

---

[5] See www.cmegroup.com/trading/metals/precious/gold_quotes_globex.html.

TABLE 8.5:   COMEX Gold Futures Prices at Market Close on Thursday, August 24, 2007

GOLD (Comex Division, NYMEX) 100 troy oz.; $ per troy oz.

	Last	Open High	Open Low	High	Low
Aug 2007	668.10	n/a	662.10	668.80	662.10
Sep 2007	667.00	659.60	659.60	667.00	659.60
Oct 2007	671.20	665.00	664.00	673.10	661.00
Nov 2007	n/a	n/a	n/a	n/a	n/a
Dec 2007	678.00	671.20	670.90	679.00	666.70
Feb 2008	683.00	n/a	673.90	683.10	673.00
April 2008	679.40	679.40	679.40	679.40	679.40
June 2008	694.00	685.00	685.00	694.00	685.00
Aug 2008	n/a	n/a	n/a	n/a	n/a
Oct 2008	n/a	n/a	n/a	n/a	n/a
Dec 2008	710.00	n/a	701.30	710.00	701.30
Feb 2009	n/a	n/a	n/a	n/a	n/a
April 2009	n/a	n/a	n/a	n/a	n/a
June 2009	n/a	n/a	n/a	n/a	n/a
Dec 2009	n/a	n/a	n/a	n/a	n/a
June 2010	n/a	n/a	n/a	n/a	n/a
Dec 2010	n/a	n/a	n/a	n/a	n/a
June 2011	n/a	n/a	n/a	n/a	n/a
Dec 2011	n/a	n/a	n/a	n/a	n/a
June 2012	n/a	n/a	n/a	n/a	n/a

traded nine contracts, which may have traded hours before the close. Moreover, many contracts, like February, April, and June for the year 2009, did not trade at all. In this case, the Settlement Committee considers the spreads relative to other futures prices. The spreads between different maturity futures prices are generally quite stable. For example, the spread between the April and February 2008 settlement prices was $5.70, between June and April $5.60, and between August and June $5.40. Here the spreads between the February and April 2009 and the April and June 2009 settlement prices (contracts with no current trading volume) were set at $5.60.

The next column reports the **change** in the settlement price from the day before. For example, the December 2007 settlement price rose by $0.50 to end at $677.50.

Some tables report **lifetime highs** and **lows**, which refer to the highest and the lowest traded prices recorded for a contract month since it began trading. This information is absent here.

Recent Settle	Change	Open Interest	Estimated Volume	Last Updated
668.00s	+0.10	261	204	8/24/2007 2:57:39 PM
668.70s	−1.70	234	41	8/24/2007 2:58:42 PM
671.50s	−0.30	35815	2069	8/24/2007 3:32:29 PM
n/a	0	n/a	n/a	n/a
677.50s	+0.50	188352	59490	8/24/2007 3:41:59 PM
683.40s	−0.40	16264	659	8/24/2007 1:49:42 PM
689.10s	−9.70	17710	9	8/24/2007 1:41:15 PM
694.70s	−0.70	14606	37	8/24/2007 1:42:53 PM
700.10s	0	7541	47	8/24/2007 1:41:15 PM
705.50s	0	1469	n/a	8/24/2007 1:41:15 PM
710.90s	−0.90	15978	181	8/24/2007 1:41:15 PM
716.60s	0	11076	n/a	8/24/2007 1:41:15 PM
722.20s	0	1630	n/a	8/24/2007 1:41:15 PM
727.80s	0	10983	n/a	8/24/2007 1:41:15 PM
744.90s	0	2566	n/a	8/24/2007 1:41:15 PM
762.30s	0	2569	n/a	8/24/2007 1:41:15 PM
780.10s	0	2585	n/a	8/24/2007 1:41:15 PM
798.10s	0	1724	n/a	8/24/2007 1:41:15 PM
816.50s	0	1035	n/a	8/24/2007 1:41:15 PM
835.90s	0	0	n/a	8/24/2007 1:41:15 PM

Open interest is the number of outstanding contracts for a particular maturity month. December 2007 has 188,352 open contracts. Each of these contracts must end through a closing trade, a delivery, or a physical exchange.

The **estimated trading volume** during the current session is 59,490 contracts for December 2007, and the **last updated** gives the time of the last trade.

The Exchange and Clearinghouse

US securities exchanges are governed by a tight set of rules and regulations. Traditionally, they have been organized as voluntary, nonprofit institutions. Individual traders hold exchange memberships or seats. *Seats* give members valuable privileges such as the right to earn a living as a pit broker, the privilege of trading in the pit as a local ("right where the action is"), lower commissions on trades, and the ability to take part in exchange governance. Consequently, seats are bought, sold, and rented like any other asset. Seat prices reflect profit opportunities on the trading floor. In the past, seats in the larger US derivatives exchanges have fetched over $400,000 each.

Futures exchanges in the United States have clearinghouses affiliated with them. Sometimes the exchanges are organized as a nonprofit corporation whose stockholders are the exchange's clearing members, for example, the Board of Trade Clearing Corporation used to act as a clearinghouse for the CBOT's transactions. At other times, they are set up as departments within an exchange, for example, the **CME Clearing** clears all CME trades. Sometimes several exchanges share a common clearinghouse: the International Commodities Clearing House clears trades for many futures exchanges in the United Kingdom, and the Options Clearing Corporation does the same for many options exchanges in the United States.

A clearinghouse forms the foundation on which a futures exchange is built. As noted before, it serves several useful functions: it clears trade (and collects a **clearance fee** for each contract cleared), it guarantees contract performance to all traders, and it collects margin from clearing members. A clearinghouse has matched books; therefore it has no market risk, but it does have counterparty risk. To alleviate this credit risk, it has several layers of financial protection. On top of margins, a member must keep guarantee funds with the clearinghouse. In case a member defaults, the clearinghouse first pays from his margin, then from the member's guarantee fund, subsequently from the surplus fund of clearance fees, and finally from the guarantee fund of all members according to some prespecified formula.

A wave of privatization has recently hit futures exchanges. Many US futures exchanges are converting themselves into shareholder-owned, for-profit corporations. In November 2000, both the CME and the NYMEX successfully demutualized and became public companies incorporated in Delaware, a tiny state that attracts many companies by its friendly corporate laws and statutes. Members then become shareholders. Instead of leading, the United States is playing catch-up because many exchanges around the world are already organized as profit-seeking firms.

8.5 | Commodity Price Indexes

We have used equity market indexes, the Dow Jones Industrial Average, and the S&P 500 index to understand the history of stock markets, to gauge market sentiments, to evaluate portfolio performance, and even as the underlying for derivatives. Can indexes also play such roles in commodity markets? The answer is yes.

Consider Figure 8.1, which graphs the Reuters/Jefferies CRB index, a commodity price index discussed later. During the 1950s and 1960s, inflation was low, commodity prices were relatively stable, and volatility was not a matter of concern. The 1970s, 1980s, and 1990s exhibited more volatility but no discernable trend in the index. A dramatic upward trend began in 2003 with increased volatility. Not surprisingly, this increased volatility has been accompanied by an increase in the trading of commodity futures. Extension 8.1 presents an interesting debate concerning the direction of future commodity prices between the doomsters and the boomsters.

Several commodity price indexes have been created. The most popular commodity price index, the **Reuters/Jeffries CRB index** (RJ/CRB), is computed by averaging the futures prices of nineteen different commodities. First computed in 1957 by the Commodities Research Bureau, the RJ/CRB index has since been revised ten times to provide "a more liquid and economically relevant benchmark that will provide a timely and accurate representation of commodities as an asset class."[6] The tenth revision (2005) discontinued the previous practice of equal weighting and classified the commodities under four groups. The first group consists of three petroleum products, while the rest consist of various commodities that provide liquidity as well as diversification benefits.

Several other commodity price indexes are popular in the United States. Standard and Poor's publishes world production–weighted **S&P GSCI indexes** based on twenty-four commodities, which consist of four separate but related S&P GSCI indexes: the spot index, the excess return index, the total return index, and a futures price index. Introduced in 1998, the **Dow Jones–AIG Commodity Index Family** (DJ-AIGCI) is composed of indexes based on futures contracts on nineteen physical commodities. DJ-AIGCI indexes are computed on an excess and total return basis, report spot as well as forward indexes, and are available in US dollar

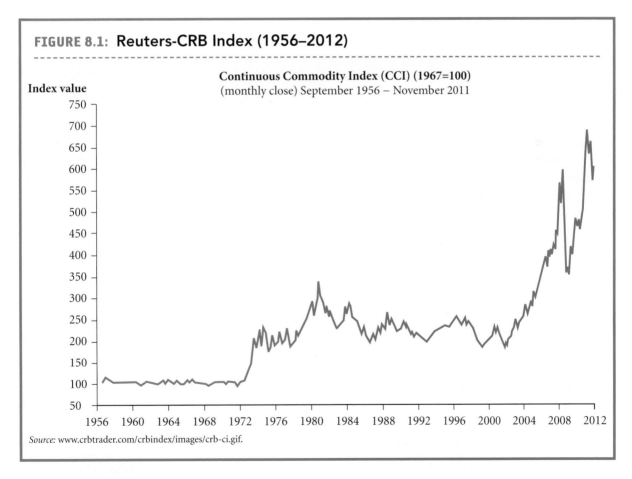

FIGURE 8.1: Reuters-CRB Index (1956–2012)

Continuous Commodity Index (CCI) (1967=100)
(monthly close) September 1956 – November 2011

Index value

Source: www.crbtrader.com/crbindex/images/crb-ci.gif.

[6] See page 6 of the booklet "CRB: Thomson Reuters/Jefferies"; available at www.jefferies.com/pdfs/ TRJCRB_Index_Materials.pdf.

and several foreign currency versions. The **Rogers International Commodity index** (RICI) was developed in 1998 by commodity investor James B. Rogers (see RICI Handbook 2008). Covering more commodities than other indexes, RICI is a dollar-based total return index that corresponds to a collection of commodities representing the global economy including futures traded in different exchanges, in different countries, and quoted in different currencies.

Notice the following about these indexes. First, as these indexes are weighted averages, the booming energy sector gets high weights, ranging from 30 plus percent for RJ/CRB and DJ-AIGCI to over 70 percent for the S&P GSCI index in 2008. Second, because these indexes are based on short-lived futures contracts that mature on a regular basis, the managers of the index must periodically **roll the futures index** by replacing the expiring futures with similar new contracts. Third, many derivatives have been created based on these indexes. For example, there are exchange-traded funds or exchange-traded notes based on these indexes, and futures or options on futures trade on these indexes. **Exchange-traded funds** (**ETFs**) are similar to mutual funds but trade in an exchange on a real-time basis (see Extension 12.2 for a discussion of ETFs). **Exchange-traded notes** are bonds issued by an underwriting bank, which promises to pay a return (minus any fees) based on the performance of a market benchmark (like a commodity price index) or some investment strategy.

EXTENSION 8.1: Doomsters and Boomsters

Two Opposing Views on the Future Direction of Commodity Prices

The first camp, popularly known as **doomsters**, owes its intellectual origins to the great English economist Thomas Malthus, whose ideas on the economics of population growth came to be known as the **Malthusian doctrine**.[7] It argues that as productivity increases and new lands are discovered, the food supply increases in arithmetic proportions, such as 1, 2, 3, ... However, due to the population's propensity to reproduce, it increases geometrically, such as 1, 2, 4, 8, ... Consequently, events like war, famine, and pestilence check the population growth relative to the food supply so that people always stay just at the subsistence level. No wonder economics has been called the *dismal science*!

Building on this intellectual foundation, the doomster school argues that a growing number of humans rely on a limited supply of natural resources, and scarcity will force commodity prices to rise through time.

A prominent proponent of this neo-Malthusian view is Stanford University professor Paul R. Ehrlich. His 1968 book *The Population Bomb* warned, "The battle to feed all of humanity is over. In the 1970s and 1980s hundreds of millions of people will starve to death in spite of any crash programs." Although this and many other dire predictions failed to materialize, the book sold over 3 million copies and earned praise for raising the awareness of environmental matters.

The opposite camp, popularly referred to as **boomsters**, espouses **free-market environmentalism**, which argues that free markets, property rights, and a good legal system will take care of the environment. They

---

[7] Born into a prosperous and enlightened English family, Thomas Robert Malthus (1766–1834) was home-schooled by his father and a series of tutors, won prizes and scholarships as a student at the University of Cambridge, took the holy orders, became a professor of history and political economy at East India Company College at Haileybury, was elected a fellow of the prestigious Royal Society of London and of the Royal Academies in France and Berlin, and cofounded the Statistical Society of London.

dismiss the other side's gloom and doom. They cite that after the high-inflation days of the 1970s, commodity prices failed to show a pronounced upward trend implied by increasing scarcity.

The champion of the second group was Julian L. Simon (b. 1932), a professor at the University of Maryland when he died in 1998. His 1981 book *The Ultimate Resource* challenged the notion of Malthusian catastrophe and offered an alternate explanation. He argued that the power of human beings to invent and adapt is the ultimate resource. Simon showed that after adjusting for inflation and wage increases, most raw material prices fell over the past decades. To quote from a song by the Beatles, "It's getting better all the time."

A Bet between Professor Doomster and Professor Boomster

Boomster Simon and doomster Ehrlich entered into a wager based on their views (see "When the Boomster Slams the Doomster, Bet on a New Wager—Clash of Eco-Titans Rekindles a Rancorous Core Debate over Future of the Earth," *Wall Street Journal*, June 5, 1995). The bet's conditions were as follows: on September 29, 1980, Ehrlich would buy on paper $200 worth of each of five strategically important metals (chromium, copper, nickel, tin, and tungsten). If, ten years later, their inflation-adjusted prices went up, then Simon would pay the inflation-adjusted value increase for each of these portfolios. If they declined, Simon would receive a payment instead. Note that the professors were trading a derivative that was essentially a combination of five forward contracts with some price adjustments.

Ehrlich and his colleagues saw *an arbitrage opportunity*: "I and my colleagues, John Holdren (University of California, Berkeley) and John Harte (Lawrence Berkeley Laboratory), jointly accept Simon's astonishing offer before other greedy people jump in." Ten years later, they were in for a rude surprise—for a variety of reasons, the real prices for all these metals and the nominal prices for three declined. *Wired* magazine ("The Doomslayer," www.wired.com/wired/archive/5.02/ffsimon_pr.html) reports that the drubbing was particularly hurtful because Simon had given Ehrlich and his colleagues a priori advantage by letting them select the five metals. A month after the bet ended, Professor Ehrlich quietly mailed Professor Simon a check for $576.07.

8.6 | Summary

1. Both a forward and a futures contract fix a price for a later transaction. They have many differences: unlike a forward, a futures contract is (1) regulated, (2) exchange traded, (3) standardized, (4) liquid, (5) guaranteed by a clearinghouse, (6) margin adjusted, (7) daily settled, (8) usually closed out before maturity, and (9) has a range of delivery dates.

2. Futures and forwards have many uses: (1) they help smooth out price fluctuations that can come from demand–supply mismatches, (2) they help create a complete market, (3) they help people to speculate, (4) they allow traders to leverage their capital, (5) they make efficient trading possible, and (6) they help generate information and aid in price discovery.

3. Forward trading is as old as antiquity. Today's futures contract started in nineteenth-century Chicago and more or less arrived at its present-day form over the next eighty years. An astonishing variety of futures were introduced since the

1970s—financial futures being a major innovation. Moreover, exchanges merged, new exchanges emerged, and electronic trading replaced the traditional open-outcry method of pit trading throughout the world.

4. As futures are standardized, they allow quicker transactions. Futures contract specifications are available on an exchange's website.

5. Many vendors carry futures price quotes. A typical quote table gives the opening price, the day's high and low, the settlement price, the change in settlement price from the previous day, lifetime high and low, open interest for each contract, and other information like the estimated volume and open interest for all contracts on that particular commodity.

6. Several commodity price indexes like the Reuters/Jeffries CRB index, S&P GSCI indexes, Dow Jones–AIG Commodity Index Family, and Rogers International Commodity index are used to gauge the direction of commodity prices and to create derivatives that allow investors to add a commodity price exposure to their portfolios.

8.7 | Cases

CME Group (Harvard Business School Case 711005-PDF-ENG). The case describes the CME Group, the world's largest commodities exchange, futures and options on futures contracts, history, regulation, and the strategic choices the company faced.

Bringing OTC Back to the Exchange: Euronext.liffe's Launch of ABC (Harvard Business School Case 706489-PDF-ENG). The case examines value creation, market design, and competitive positioning issues for a derivatives trading exchange in the context of launching matching, clearing, and confirmation services for the over-the-counter market.

Lessons Learned? Brooksley Born and the OTC Derivatives Market (A) (Harvard Business School Case 311044-PDF-ENG). The case studies a proposal to regulate the over-the-counter derivatives market, whose lack of implementation might have been one of the factors that contributed to the financial crisis of 2007–9.

8.8 | Questions and Problems

8.1. Where and when was the world's first modern futures exchange founded? Explain how trading took place on this exchange.

8.2. Discuss the four different categories into which the history of futures contracts since 1970 has been classified, giving two examples of some of the major developments under each of the four categories.

8.3. What are the three different levels of mechanization of futures trading? Give examples of each such system.

8.4. Briefly explain the pros and cons of daily price limits in futures markets.

8.5. Consider a fairly illiquid futures contract that has not traded for days. Do you still need a settlement price for this contract? If so, how would the exchange go about determining this settlement price?

8.6. Explain the difference between closing price and settlement price. Are they the same or different? Which price is used for marking-to-market?

8.7. Why were the early regulators of US commodity futures markets directly under the control of the US Department of Agriculture? How did this change in 1974?

8.8. If regulation is bad for business, why does the National Futures Association put a significant amount of regulation on its members?

8.9. Consider the gold futures contract traded in the COMEX division of the CME group. What is the trading unit size and minimum tick size?

8.10. Using Table 8.5, what is the last price on the June 2008 futures contract? What does the last price mean?

8.11. Using Table 8.5, what is the open interest on the June 2008 futures contract? What does the open interest mean?

8.12. Using Table 8.5, looking at the open, high, and low prices on the June futures contract, what can you tell about the trend of futures prices on this contract during the day?

8.13. Using Table 8.5, which three futures contracts have the most trading activity?

8.14. Briefly discuss the history of the first interest rate derivatives contract.

8.15. What were the first cash-settled futures contracts and are they still trading today?

8.16. Where and when were the first index futures contracts traded? Discuss the factors that contributed to the success or failure of this contract.

8.17. Today, are futures contracts only traded on US exchanges? Explain your answer.

8.18. Is trading in futures contracts mainly for hedging, or speculation, or both? Explain your answer.

8.19. Explain why forward contracts have been trading for centuries. What economic function do they perform? What improvement did futures contracts provide over forward contracts? Explain your answer.

8.20. The following questions concern the doomsters and the boomsters.

    a. What were the opposing views promoted by Professors Ehrlich and Simon?

    b. Describe the wager between Professors Doomster and Boomster and the outcome of this bet.

9

Futures Trading

9.1 | Introduction

The movie *Trading Places* made a caricature of futures trading. In a particular sequence, Dan Aykroyd and Eddie Murphy entered the trading pit, visibly nervous and yet pumped up to speculate by shorting orange juice futures. They suddenly realized that the powerful Duke brothers were trying to corner the OJ futures market. This was in anticipation of crop damage from a frost in the orange-growing states. Some traders thought that the Duke brothers had inside information on the extent of the losses and joined the fray. Futures prices increased. Dan, Eddie, and other sellers soon felt that they were sliding down a bottomless pit. Suddenly it all changed. The commerce secretary announced on television that the frost had bypassed the orange-growing regions. This implied a rich harvest with soft prices. Dan and Eddie were ecstatic: OJ futures prices rapidly fell, and they made a ton of cash; the Duke brothers went completely broke—and all of this happened in an hour! Although the movie is fictionalized, it does capture the dark side of futures trading (it is suspiciously similar to the Hunts brothers' silver manipulation story in the next chapter).

To put this movie in context, this chapter describes the mechanics of trading futures contracts. We discuss brokers, dealers, and others who work in the industry, then we list various ways of moving in and out of futures. This is followed by a description of margins and daily settlement. Next we explore various properties of futures and forward prices. We end with a discussion of futures spread trading strategies.

9.2 | Brokers, Dealers, and the Futures Industry

Brokers match buyers and sellers in futures and earn commissions for this service. They also represent their customers to the exchanges and clearinghouse. Dealers step in and take the other side of trade when no one else offers a better price. Like a used car dealer who maintains an inventory and posts a retail price for trading cars, dealers in futures markets keep an inventory of futures contracts and quote bid and ask prices to maximize income. Moreover, brokers and dealers also act as first-level regulators because they have a duty to report irregularities and fraud to the exchange authorities and government regulators.

Brokers and dealers in futures markets may do business as individuals, or they may be organized as associations, partnerships, corporations, or trusts. They must register with the Commodity Futures Trading Commission (CFTC). In 2009, the CFTC registered and regulated over sixty-six thousand individuals who helped retail customers trade futures or transact trades for their own accounts.[1]

---

[1] See www.cftc.gov/reports/par/2009/2009par050104.html.

To open a futures trading account, one must go through a **futures commission merchant (FCM)** or an **introducing broker (IB)** registered with an FCM. An IB's role and responsibilities are limited: an IB may seek and accept orders but must pass them on to a carrying broker (usually an FCM) for execution, and an IB cannot accept funds—funds must be directly deposited with the carrying broker. In contrast, an FCM provides a one-stop service for all aspects of futures trading: solicit trades, take futures orders, accept payments from customers, extend credit to clients, hold margin deposits, document trades, and maintain accounts and trading records. Also known as *commission houses* or *wire houses*, FCMs employ others who are variously called **account executives**, **associated persons (APs)**, **registered commodity representatives**, or **customer's men**. Actually an AP is a catchall category of individuals who deal with customers in the offices of an FCM, an IB, or an agricultural trade option merchant.[2]

Floor brokers (FBs or **pit brokers)** stand on exchange floors in trading pits to execute clients' trades. Also present on the exchange floor are **floor traders (or locals)** who trade for their own accounts. To further their business interests, brokers often band together to form a **broker association**. Members of such **broker groups** have access to each other's unfilled orders and share responsibility for executing orders. Several hands can better handle big orders, particularly complex orders involving several different futures. Moreover, group members share revenues and expenses as well as profits or losses from trading activities.

Where does one go for trading advice? There are **commodity trading advisors** who dispense wisdom through newsletters or advise clients on an individual basis. Most of them are technical analysts who use past price patterns to predict future price movements.

To invest with professional managers, one can go to **commodity pool operators (CPOs)**. They run **commodity pools (funds)**, which are mutual fund–type operations speculating in futures. Rarely are these pools stellar performers: the returns are often negative, and when positive, they often underperform the market on a risk-adjusted basis. Moreover, they charge large management fees and require big margin deposits.

9.3 | Floor Trading of Futures Contracts

Although electronic exchanges are fast gaining market share, pit trading is still the dominant trading method at major US futures exchanges. Example 9.1 discusses several aspects of pit trading.

---

[2] The CFTC glossary (www.cftc.gov/ConsumerProtection/EducationCenter/CFTCGlossary/index.htm) defines an **agricultural trade option merchant** as "any person that is in the business of soliciting or entering option transactions involving an enumerated agricultural commodity that are not conducted or executed on or subject to the rules of an exchange."

EXAMPLE 9.1: Pit Trading of Futures

The Trading Pit

- On the exchange floor, futures trading occurs in a *trading pit* or a *ring*. It's a circular or polygonal stage with concentric rings of steps that flow from outside to inside. Looking from the outside, the steps first rise a little and then steadily go down into a center hole. On the outer steps of a typical exchange stand clerks (deck holders) who are assistants to floor brokers. The inside steps are occupied by floor brokers and dealers. The most active contract may be the one with the nearest delivery date, and it may trade on the topmost step of the pit, where it is closest to the phone desks of the FCMs. Other contracts trade on other steps. Some pits may be divided into wedgelike slices with different delivery months trading in their respective slices. Each exchange has many trading pits for trading different futures contracts—gold may trade in one pit, silver in another, and so on.

- After receiving a trade order, the FCM's clerk on the trading floor fills out an order form and gives it to a runner. The runner takes it to the trading pit and gives it directly to the floor broker or his deck holder.

- If it is a *market order*, it gets filled fairly quickly, and the runner takes back the information to the phone clerk, who communicates it back to the originating broker. If it is a *contingent order*, such as a limit order, the deck holder puts it in the proper place on a deck, where a floor broker fills it at the appropriate time.

- Trading takes place by an *open-outcry method*, whereby the floor broker or the floor dealer has to cry out the *bid* (a buy proposal) or *ask/offer* (a sell proposal) on the exchange's trading floor so that others may join. The information may also be simultaneously conveyed by hand signals. This is a method of trading that communicates a trader's intentions with her hands. For example, the palm stretches outward if the trader wants to sell and inward if she wants to buy. Different ways of stretching and closing fingers indicate numbers. More advanced systems may display prices via computer terminals and electronic boards. The idea behind trading at a single location with traders shouting out orders is that it gives everyone an opportunity to participate, which leads to greater transparency and better price discovery.

- What traders articulate and gesticulate is *how many* contracts to *buy or sell* and at what *price* (per unit). An *ask* or *offer* to sell gold futures may be vocalized as "1 at 1,000.8," meaning that the trader wants to sell one contract at a futures price of $1,000.80 per ounce. A *bid* may be cried out as "1,000.3 for 3," indicating that she wants to pay $1,000.30 per ounce for three contracts. This reverse order of calling price and quantity is necessary to prevent confusion arising from the shouts and noises in the trading pit. If the *tick size* or minimum price fluctuation is 10 cents per ounce (as it is for gold futures trading at the New York trading floor of the CME Group), the numbers are reported one place after the decimal instead of the conventional practice of reporting two places after the decimal.

The Quote Board

- Exchanges have one or more **quote boards** placed in a visible location on the trading floor. These are electronic displays with large lettering that disseminate vital trade information. Figure 9.1 shows a sample quote board and a sample ticker tape with hypothetical data for gold futures at a particular time during a trading day.

- The ticker symbol for the traded contract is given on top of the table.
- The top two entries give the opening range; 995.1 (dollars per ounce) was the highest and 994.0 the lowest price when the market opened.
- The third and fourth rows give the day's highest (1,002.5) and lowest (994.0) recorded prices.
- The fifth row reports the estimated trading volume—so far, 143 contracts have traded.
- From the sixth row until the thirteenth row, the board displays the last seven prices or asks or bids before the last recorded price (1,000.4). An A next to a price denotes an ask, a B denotes a bid, and all other prices are for actual trades. If a new trade takes place or a bid/ask price is cried out in the pit, then it moves into the last position on the thirteenth row, and all existing prices shift upward. The previous last price, 1,000.4, is now placed next to 1 (it gets depicted as 00.4 in short), and so on, and the top entry 1,000.3 is dropped.
- The fourteenth row gives the net change (+5.4), which is the difference between the last price and the settlement price of the previous trading day. The settlement price is close to the contract's closing price and is used for computing margin payments.
- The fifteenth row gives the previous trading day's settlement price, 995.0.
- Finally, the last two rows of our sample board display the highest (1,655.0, which may be a trade price or a bid) and the lowest (867.5, a trade price or an ask) recorded price since the contract started trading.

■ Figure 9.1 also displays a portion of a sample ticker tape. It's a running tape that reports the contract's ticker symbol, the last traded price 1,000.4, and the time of the trade. Many tapes also display additional information, including volume and bid/ask quotes.

■ What happens when a trading frenzy builds up? In such situations, price reports may lag and the exchange may declare a **fast market**. People understand that during chaotic conditions, the prices and the information displayed on the board may not be accurate. Fewer prices may show up on the board, say, four instead of seven, with other slots displaying the word "FAST" instead.

Trade Execution

■ A trade is *executed* when two brokers or dealers agree to terms and complete a transaction. Then they record the price, quantity traded, delivery month, name of the clearing firm, and the initials of the counterparty on an index card. They give the card to a price reporter, who records the trade in the computer system, where it is displayed on large electronic quote boards above the exchange floor and simultaneously disseminated by ticker tape around the world.

Clearing Futures Trades

■ After trading ends, it's time to *clear* trades. Before the market reopens, representatives of the clearing members as well as those of nonclearing members take their trade records to submit them to the exchange's clearinghouse. Once the records match, the clearinghouse clears the trade by recognizing and recording it. This is similar to a clearinghouse's role in stock trading; however, clearinghouses at derivatives exchanges play another crucial role. Clearinghouses guarantee contract performance by acting as a seller to every buyer and a buyer to every seller (see Figure 4.6). The clearinghouse

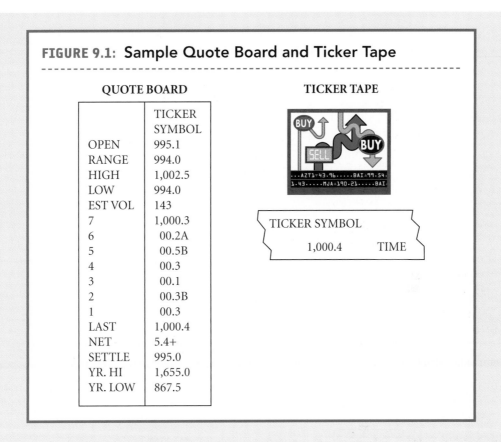

FIGURE 9.1: Sample Quote Board and Ticker Tape

QUOTE BOARD

	TICKER SYMBOL
OPEN	995.1
RANGE	994.0
HIGH	1,002.5
LOW	994.0
EST VOL	143
7	1,000.3
6	00.2A
5	00.5B
4	00.3
3	00.1
2	00.3B
1	00.3
LAST	1,000.4
NET	5.4+
SETTLE	995.0
YR. HI	1,655.0
YR. LOW	867.5

TICKER TAPE

...AZT1▾43.96.....BAI▴99.54.
1.43.....MJA▴190.21.....BAI.

TICKER SYMBOL

1,000.4   TIME

guarantees execution by requiring margin from the clearing members, who in turn require margin from their own clients and the nonclearing members who submitted trades through them; and of course, the nonclearing members require margin from their customers. It's a pyramid structure throughout (see Figure 9.2). With the clearinghouse as the watchdog, traders can focus on trading strategies without worrying about possible snags in contract performance or default risk.

■ Things do go wrong: a trader's identification may be incorrectly recorded or a wrong price may get jotted down. In that case, the trade does not clear and is declared an **out-trade**. To help resolve this problem, each brokerage house employs **out-trade clerks**, who pore over records at the time of clearing and, through several rounds of reconciliation, match the trades. Most out-trades are voluntarily corrected before trading restarts. Unresolved out-trades are tackled by arbitration or through the exchange's judicial procedures. Of course, electronic trading does not have this problem, but punishments there can be severe because order entry errors cannot be rectified.

Settling Futures Trades

■ Remember that futures trade at a fair price where no cash changes hands when the contract is initiated. Profits and losses are realized at the end of each trading day and are credited or debited, respectively, to traders' margin accounts through a process called *daily settlement*. Later in this chapter, we show how these adjustments work.

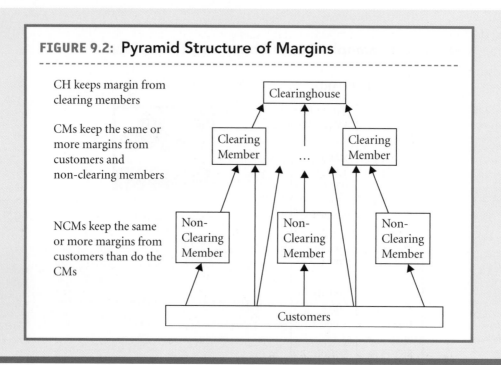

FIGURE 9.2: Pyramid Structure of Margins

CH keeps margin from clearing members

CMs keep the same or more margins from customers and non-clearing members

NCMs keep the same or more margins from customers than do the CMs

Clearinghouse

Clearing Member   ...   Clearing Member

Non-Clearing Member   Non-Clearing Member   Non-Clearing Member

Customers

9.4 Entering and Ending a Futures Position

Entering into a long or a short futures position is easy: one calls a broker and places an opening order. One can also easily close a position before maturity by placing an opposite trade on the same contract and informing the broker that this is a closing order.

As you have seen before in chapter 1, there are many ways of placing orders to open or close futures positions and also to buy or sell exchange-traded securities. Closing before maturity is not the only way to end a futures contract. There are four ways of ending a futures position, glimpses of which you have seen before: a closing transaction, physical delivery, cash settlement, or an exchange for physicals (see Figure 9.3):

1. *A closing transaction.* Suppose you go long a December gold futures. You are obliged to *buy gold at the futures price* during the December delivery period. A futures position can be ended earlier. You can do this by an offsetting transaction called a **closing transaction** or a **reversing trade**. Just take a short position in the same December gold futures. You are now obliged to *sell gold at that day's futures price* during December. This cancels the initial position. Tell your broker that the second trade was a closing transaction, and he will wipe your slate clean. Over 95 percent of futures contracts close before maturity.

2. *Physical delivery*. This was the only way of closing futures in the past. In a physical delivery, the short gets cash from the long and obtains a **warehouse receipt** that gives ownership of goods held in a licensed warehouse or a **shipping certificate** that is a promise by an exchange-approved facility to deliver the commodity under specified terms. A futures contract specifies (1) acceptable deliverable grades (some contracts allow substitution of inferior grades with price discounts and superior grades with price premiums), (2) acceptable delivery dates (usually within the last trading month, i.e., the month that includes the last trading day), and (3) acceptable delivery places (with price adjustments for different locations). Though conceptually similar, the delivery methods vary slightly from exchange to exchange. For most contracts, the short has the privilege of initiating a delivery notice. The exchange usually matches him with the oldest existing long position. In a typical delivery process, there would be a first notice day, a last notice day, and a last trading day. The **first notice day** is the first day on which a short can

---

FIGURE 9.3: Four Methods of Ending a Futures Position

- -

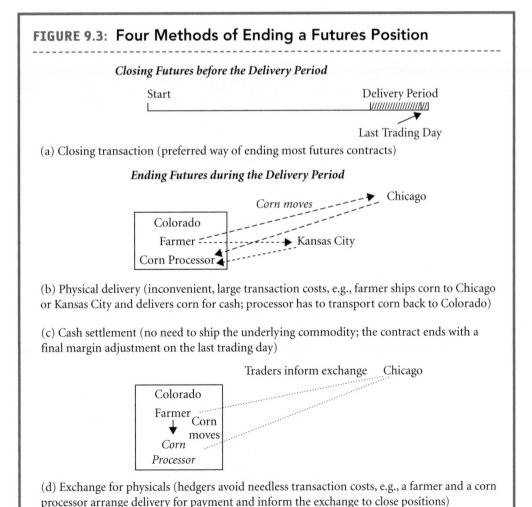

Closing Futures before the Delivery Period

(a) Closing transaction (preferred way of ending most futures contracts)

Ending Futures during the Delivery Period

(b) Physical delivery (inconvenient, large transaction costs, e.g., farmer ships corn to Chicago or Kansas City and delivers corn for cash; processor has to transport corn back to Colorado)

(c) Cash settlement (no need to ship the underlying commodity; the contract ends with a final margin adjustment on the last trading day)

(d) Exchange for physicals (hedgers avoid needless transaction costs, e.g., a farmer and a corn processor arrange delivery for payment and inform the exchange to close positions)

submit a notice of intention to make delivery, and the **last notice day** is the last such day. The **last trading day** is usually one or more days before the last notice day. Exchanges generally do not make or take delivery of the actual commodity; they only specify how the delivery process occurs. Table 9.1 shows important dates regarding maturity and delivery of the CME Group's New York floor traded 100-ounce gold futures contracts (ticker GC) maturing in the months of June, August, and October of the year 2013.

3. *Cash settlement.* In case of a *cash settlement*, a final adjustment is made to the margin accounts of the buyer and seller equaling the difference between the last trading day's settlement price and the settlement price of the previous day[3]—and then the contract ends.

4. *Exchange for physicals.* Another possibility is a spot market trade between two parties who have genuine buying and selling needs for the underlying commodity and have already hedged their prices by establishing futures positions. This is called an **exchange for physicals** (**EFP**) transaction. Afterward, they notify the exchange and the clearinghouse about the transaction, and their slates are rubbed clean. The next example shows how this works.

EXAMPLE 9.2: An Exchange for Physicals

- Suppose a farmer grows corn in Colorado. She sells short fifty corn futures to fix a selling price for her produce. A corn processing plant is located five miles up the road from the farmer. It buys, processes, and sells corn to the cereal maker who makes cornflakes. The corn processor goes long fifty corn futures and fixes a buying price for the input. Both traders are hedgers: the farmer genuinely needs to sell corn, while the processing plant legitimately needs to buy it.

- At delivery time, why ship 250,000 (= 50 contracts $\times$ 5,000 bushels/contract) bushels of corn all the way to Chicago or Kansas City and then ship it back to Colorado as per CME Group's contract stipulations? This will incur needless transportation costs and time delays.

- It would be much better to do the transaction directly: the farmer ships corn to the processing plant and receives the day's settlement price (although provisions allow EFPs at a mutually agreed price). Both report the price and the quantity traded to the Chicago Board of Trade, which then checks that these reports match and closes the fifty long and short positions.

EFPs have grown in popularity in recent years. Most oil futures are settled by EFPs, and their use is increasing in both gold and silver futures markets.

---

[3] For the Standard and Poor's 500 index futures contract, the opening price on the morning after the last trading day is used for cash settlement. This feature was added to avoid extraordinary price volatility associated with the **triple witching hour**, which is the last hour of trading on the third Friday of the months of March, June, September, and December—the day when stock index futures, stock index options, and options on stock index futures simultaneously expire.

TABLE 9.1: Important Dates Regarding Termination of Trading and Delivery of a COMEX Gold Futures Contract of the CME Group

Important Dates	Delivery Month		
	June 2013	August 2013	October 2013
First trading day	June 30, 2008	September 30, 2011	November 30, 2011
Last trading day	June 26, 2013	August 28, 2013	October 29, 2013
First notice day	May 31, 2013	July 31, 2013	September 30, 2013
First delivery day	June 3, 2013	August 1, 2013	October 1, 2013
Last notice day	June 27, 2013	August 29, 2013	October 30, 2013
Last delivery day	June 28, 2013	August 30, 2013	October 31, 2013

9.5 | Margin Accounts and Daily Settlement

To buy and sell futures, one must open a **futures account** with a broker. To open a futures position, one must post **initial margin** (or **performance margin**), which acts as a performance bond. Most exchanges allow initial margins to be paid with cash, bank letters of credit, or short-term Treasuries. The broker, if she is a clearing member, keeps margin deposits with the exchange's clearinghouse; if she is not, she keeps them with a clearing member, who in turn keeps margin with the exchange. This earnest money ensures that when the going gets tough, the tough do not leave town!

Daily Settlement

When futures prices increase, a long position gains value. This makes sense: if you buy something at a fixed price and the new purchase price increases, then you must make a profit. The seller's situation is just the opposite. So when the futures price increases, the long's account is credited with **variation margin**, which is the change in the settlement price from the previous trading day, and the short's account is debited the same. These additions (*collects*) or subtractions (*pays*) of variation margins at the end of each trading day are known as *daily settlement*. When this is done, the margin account is said to be *marked-to-market*. Traders can keep only a small amount as margin, often 5 percent or less of the position size (e.g., if the gold futures price is $1,000 and the initial margin is $5,000, then it is only $5,000/(1,000 \times 100) = 5$ percent), and still trade.

Marking-to-market substantially lowers credit risk and makes futures safer to use than forward contracts. The reason is simple. With futures, the largest loss to the contract is a one-day movement in the futures price. In contrast, with forwards, the largest loss is the movement in the forward price over the entire life of the contract. Margins buffer this smaller loss for futures, whereas collateral buffers this larger loss for forwards.

The next example shows how daily settlement works for a futures contract.

EXAMPLE 9.3: Daily Settlement of a Gold Futures Contract

- On Monday, Ms. Longina Long buys three gold futures contracts from Mr. Shorty Short. Both traders have margin accounts. We refer to Monday as time 0, Tuesday as time 1, and so on. The futures contract matures on Friday (time T or 4) when the day's trading ends. For convenience, we use the end of the day's spot and settlement prices. All prices and computations are on a per ounce basis.

- Monday (time 0)
  - The spot price on Monday, $S(0)$, is $1,000.00.
  - The futures price on Monday for the contract maturing on Friday is $\mathcal{F}(0,4) = \$1,000.60$. For simplicity, we suppress T from the notation for the futures price $\mathcal{F}(0,T)$ and write it as $\mathcal{F}(0)$. We will reintroduce it later when considering contracts maturing at different dates. Table 9.2 records the trading day as the first column and futures prices as the second column.
  - Because futures contracts always clear at fair prices, no cash changes hands when the position is entered at the close of Monday's trading.

- Tuesday (time 1)
  - $S(1) = \$1,006.00$
  - $\mathcal{F}(1) = \$1,006.40$
  - Yesterday, Ms. Long locked in a price of $1,000.60 for buying gold on Friday. Now she is asked to pay $1,006.40 instead. She is understandably upset. However, she will be indifferent if Mr. Short pays her the price difference. By daily settlement, this amount, $\mathcal{F}(1) - \mathcal{F}(0) = 1,006.40 - 1,000.60 = \$5.80$, is credited to Long's margin account (and it is debited to Short's margin account) after Tuesday's close. This is reported in the third column of Table 9.2. Long's contract now has a futures price of $\mathcal{F}(1) = \$1,006.40$.

- Wednesday (time 2)
  - $S(2) = \$996.00$
  - $\mathcal{F}(2) = \$996.20$
  - Long would be happy to buy gold for $996.20 on Friday, while Short would be unhappy to sell at that price. To mark-to-market the contract, Long's account is debited by a variation margin of $\mathcal{F}(2) - \mathcal{F}(1) = 996.20 - 1,006.40 = -\$10.20$. Short's account is credited the same amount. Values become fair again.

- Thursday (time 3)
  - $S(3) = 988.00$
  - $\mathcal{F}(3) = 988.20$
  - Long's cash flow is $\mathcal{F}(3) - \mathcal{F}(2) = 988.20 - 996.20 = -\$8$.

- Friday (time T or time 4)
  - $S(4) = 995.00 = \mathcal{F}(4)$
  - The spot and futures prices equal each other at the end of Friday's trading. They should because a futures contract maturing in an instant is the same as a spot market transaction and therefore the futures price must be the same as the spot price.
  - Long gets $\mathcal{F}(4) - \mathcal{F}(3) = 995.00 - 988.20 = \$6.80$ from Short.

TABLE 9.2: Futures Prices and Margin Account for Longina Long

Day	Futures Settlement Price	Change in Futures Settlement Price	Daily Futures Gain or Loss (Last Column ×300)	Interest Earned on Previous Balance	Margin Account Balance	Margin Call	Margin Account Balance (After Adjustment)
Mon	$\mathcal{F}(0) = 1,000.60$				15,000.00		15,000.00
Tues	$\mathcal{F}(1) = 1,006.40$	5.80	1,740	1.50	16,741.50		16,741.50
Wed	$\mathcal{F}(2) = 996.20$	−10.20	−3,060	1.84	13,683.34		13,683.34
Thurs	$\mathcal{F}(3) = 988.20$	−8.00	−2,400	1.64	11,284.98	3,715.02	15,000.00
Fri	$\mathcal{F}(4) = 995.00$	6.80	2,040	1.50	17,041.50		17,041.50

How are these adjustments actually made? If your futures position gains value, you may remove funds that are in excess of the initial margin, but if it loses value, the broker gets uncomfortable. So there is a mandatory amount called a *maintenance margin* (usually set at 75 percent of the initial margin) that must be maintained in the account at all times. If the account value touches or drops below this level, then the broker places a margin call and requests that you come up with enough variation margin *in cash* to bring your account to the initial margin level. If you fail to meet a margin call, your broker can close out your positions. You may be liable for more cash if your position is liquidated at a loss. To avoid this hassle, traders often keep more funds than the required initial margin.

In reality, other issues must also be reckoned with. For example, there are transaction costs, and the margin account earns interest. As this discussion can get complicated quickly, to simplify the presentation we embrace the old maxim "follow the money!" Following this maxim, we take an accountant's perspective and keep track of the margin account's cash flows, including daily interest.

EXAMPLE 9.4: A Margin Account's Cash Flows Including Interest Earned

- Continuing with the previous example, let us track the margin account of Ms. Longina Long, who buys three gold futures contracts on Monday at a futures price of $\mathcal{F}(0) = \$1,000.60$ per ounce. We write the number of contracts as $n = 3$, the contract size as $\kappa = 100$ ounces, and the margin account's balance as Bal(t), where $t = 0, 1, 2, 3, 4$ are the days over which the futures contract lasts.

- As a speculator who is not an exchange member, Long must keep the commodity exchange mandated initial margin of $5,000 per contract or $15,000 in total, which we write as Bal(0). Long's margin account balances are plotted in Figure 9.4. Her maintenance margin is $4,000 per contract.

The margin account balance *earns interest*. Assume that the interest rate $i(0)$ is 1 basis point for Monday. This overnight interest rate changes randomly across time and gets declared at the start of each trading day.

- On Tuesday, the gold futures settlement price goes up to $\mathcal{F}(1) = 1{,}006.40$. Long's margin account gets credited for the increase in the position's value and earns interest on the previous day's balance, values reported in the fourth and fifth columns of Table 9.2, respectively. Tuesday's margin account balance is

$$\begin{aligned}
\text{Bal}(1) &= [\text{Futures(Tues)} - \text{Futures(Mon)}] \times \text{Number of contracts} \times \text{Contract size} + \\
&\quad (1 + \text{Daily interest}) \times \text{Margin account balance (Mon)} \\
&= [\mathcal{F}(1) - \mathcal{F}(0)] \times n \times \kappa + [1 + i(0)] \times \text{Bal}(0) \\
&= 5.80 \times 3 \times 100 + (1 + 0.0001) \times 15{,}000 \\
&= 1{,}740 + 15{,}000 + 1.50 = \$16{,}741.50
\end{aligned}$$

- This amount is noted in the sixth column. As there is no margin call, we repeat this in the eighth column. Long can remove the **excess margin** of $1,741.50 if she wants. We assume that she keeps it in the margin account.

- On Wednesday, the gold futures price falls to $\mathcal{F}(2) = \$996.20$ and Long's futures position loses value. Assuming Tuesday's interest rate $i(1)$ is 0.00011 for the day, the new margin balance is

$$\begin{aligned}
\text{Bal}(2) &= [\mathcal{F}(2) - \mathcal{F}(1)] \times n \times \kappa + [1 + i(1)]\text{Bal}(1) \\
&= -10.20 \times 300 + 1.00011 \times 16{,}741.50 \\
&= \$13{,}683.34
\end{aligned}$$

- Her account is now **under-margined** as it has fallen below the initial margin level. The broker is uncomfortable but does nothing.

- On Thursday, the gold futures price falls by another $8. Assuming $i(2)$ is 0.00012 for the day, the new margin balance is Bal(3) = $11,284.98. As this is below the maintenance margin level of $3 \times 4{,}000 = \$12{,}000$, the broker issues a margin call instructing her to come up with $3,715.02 in cash (which is reported in the seventh column of Table 9.2 and also shown in Figure 9.4). She does this and her account balance is restored to the initial margin account level of $15,000, and this figure is reported in the last column. Notice that futures traders are required to bring the margin account balance up to the initial margin level and not to the maintenance margin level as required in stock markets.

- On Friday, the gold futures price goes up by $8. If $i(3) = 0.0001$, her margin account balance is $17,041.50.

- Suppose Mr. Shorty Short took the other side of the transaction. His daily futures gains and losses would be the opposite of Long's, but his margin account balance would earn different interest. Also, as the futures price did not move too much against Short, he will not get any margin calls.

- As noted in Table 9.2, for the magnitude of these investments, the interest earned is small (approximately $1.50) and perhaps unimportant. However, consider a futures position with a notational in the tens of millions of dollars. In that case, the interest earned per day is considerable and not so easily ignored.

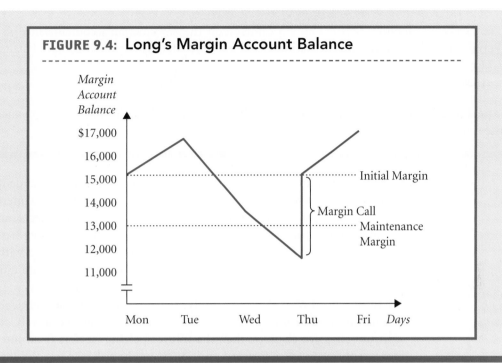

FIGURE 9.4: Long's Margin Account Balance

9.6 | Futures and Forward Price Relations

What is the relation between futures and forward prices? Before addressing that question, let's consider an example that computes a futures contract's payoffs when positions may be entered and exited early.

EXAMPLE 9.5: Futures Payoffs When Positions Are Closed Out Early

- Consider the data from Example 9.4. Ms. Long bought gold futures on Monday. Her payoff on Tuesday due to daily settlement is

$$\text{Futures(Tues)} - \text{Futures(Mon)}$$
$$+ \text{One day's interest on Monday's margin account balance}$$
$$= \mathcal{F}(1) - \mathcal{F}(0) + \text{Interest}$$
$$= \$5.80 + \text{Interest}$$

per ounce. If Ms. Long were to decide to close out on Tuesday, she would take a profit of $5.80 plus the interest on the margin account balance.

- Instead of on Monday, if Ms. Long buys futures on Tuesday and closes out her position with a reversing trade on Thursday, then her payoff is

[Futures(Wed) − Futures(Tues) + One day's interest on Tuesday's margin account balance] +
[Futures(Thurs) − Futures(Wed) + One day's interest on Wednesday's margin account balance]
$= \mathcal{F}(3) - \mathcal{F}(1) + \text{Interest}$
$= -18.20 + \text{Interest}$

on a per ounce basis. The interest earned on the margin account balance is unknown in advance and hence random.

As indicated in this example, the interest earnings are dependent on the futures price changes. Furthermore, interest rate changes affect the interest earnings on the margin account as well. In conjunction, these two effects modify the risk of holding a futures contract relative to a forward contract that has no such cash flows. Indeed, if interest rate changes are positively correlated with futures price changes, then the futures position benefits from interest rate movements because as cash flows are received, more interest is earned. In this case, the risk of a futures position is reduced slightly relative to an otherwise identical forward contract position. Conversely, if interest rate changes are negatively correlated with futures price changes, then the futures position suffers from interest rate movements relative to a forward position. Here the risk is increased. It is important to note that *this interest rate risk is priced into the market clearing futures prices, driving a wedge between futures and forward prices.* Recall that forward contracts have no intermediate cash flows and therefore no explicit interest earnings risk.

A generalization of this example gives a useful result for computing a futures trader's profits and losses. Let date 0 be the initiation date of a futures contract and date T be its delivery date. Suppose a trader enters a long futures position at time t_1 (which can be as early as date 0) when the futures price is $\mathcal{F}(t_1)$ and closes out her position at a later date t_2 (which can be as late as date T) when the futures price is $\mathcal{F}(t_2)$. A futures trader's profit or loss is the sum of daily variation margins and interest earned on the margin account balance for the time period over which the futures position is held:

$$\text{Long's payoff} = \text{Closing futures price} - \text{Initial futures price} + \text{Interest}$$
$$= \mathcal{F}(t_2) - \mathcal{F}(t_1) + \text{Interest} \tag{9.1a}$$

and

$$\text{Short's payoff} = -(\text{Closing futures price} - \text{Initial futures price}) + \text{Interest}$$
$$= -[\mathcal{F}(t_2) - \mathcal{F}(t_1)] + \text{Interest} \tag{9.1b}$$

on a per ounce basis. Of course, the interest earned on the long and short positions differ.

These results make sense and ease the task of computing margin account balances (see Example 9.6). Remember that futures prices are determined in the market so that a trader entering a position pays nothing at the start. If the underlying commodity increases in value, then futures prices also move up. Long benefits because the fixed price at which she agreed to buy has increased in value, and Short loses because what he agreed to sell at a fixed price has become more expensive.

EXAMPLE 9.6: Margin Payments for a Portfolio of Futures Contracts

- Pearl is a speculator. Trading at the prices given in Table 9.3a, she went long two contracts of gold on January 20, short three platinum contracts on January 21, and long five silver contracts on January 23. She then liquidated all her futures positions on January 26. Her gains and losses are computed in Table 9.3b. Her net gain is

    Long gold futures payoff + Short platinum futures payoff + Long silver futures payoff
    $= 2,200 - 1,785 + 4,975$
    $= \$5,390$

    where we have ignored the interest earned on the margin account balances for simplicity.

Let us continue with Examples 9.3 and 9.4 to explore several important properties of forward and futures prices.

TABLE 9.3A: Futures Prices

Trading Date	June Gold Futures, 100 troy oz/Contract (dollars/ounce)	April Platinum Futures, 50 troy oz/Contract (dollars/ounce)	March Silver Futures, 5,000 troy oz/Contract (cents/ounce)
Jan 20	989.1	1,149.0	2,542.1
Jan 21	992.8	1,153.3	2,600.0
Jan 22	989.4	1,154.1	2,553.3
Jan 23	1,007.0	1,169.5	2,623.3
Jan 26	1,001.0	1,165.2	2,643.2
Jan 27	1,008.4	1,175.0	2,651.8

TABLE 9.3B: Margin Account for Pearl

Portfolio	Computation of Profits/Losses	Dollar Amount
Long 2 June gold futures on Jan 20	$(1,000.1 - 989.1)$ per ounce $\times$ 100 troy ounce per contract $\times$ 2 contracts	\$2,200
Short 3 April platinum futures on Jan 21	$-(1,165.2 - 1,153.3) \times 50 \times 3$	−1,785
Long 5 March silver on Jan 23	$(2,643.2 - 2,623.3) \times 5,000 \times 5 \div 100$	4,975
Net profit		5,390

Equality of Futures and Spot Price at Maturity

In Example 9.3, suppose that at Friday's close, the futures price is $995 but the spot price is $997. Then anyone can buy the futures, acquire gold for $995, and sell it immediately in the open market for $997 to pick up an arbitrage profit of $2. The buying pressure raises the futures price, the selling pressure lowers the spot price, and the two converge. If instead the futures price is higher than the spot price, then an arbitrageur can sell futures, make a delivery, and take an arbitrage profit. To prevent arbitrage opportunities, the *futures price must equal the spot price at the maturity of the contract.* Of course, we need to make assumptions such as that there are no **market frictions** (such as transaction costs [brokerage commissions, bid/ask spread], margin requirements, short sales restrictions, taxes that may be levied at different rates, and assets that are not perfectly divisible), that spot and futures can be simultaneously traded, and that the futures mature on a single day.

Equality of Forward and Futures Prices before Maturity

Are forward and futures prices equal before maturity? They are equal only under a restrictive set of assumptions such as constant interest rates, no market frictions, and no credit risks, but not otherwise. Our next example explores this and related issues.

EXAMPLE 9.7: Equality of Forward and Futures Prices

- Consider the gold futures contract introduced in Example 9.3. Next, consider a gold forward contract that is similar to this futures contract. It begins on Monday, matures on Friday, and has one hundred ounces of pure gold as the underlying. We compare two trades by Ms. Longina Long entered at Monday's close: buying one forward contract versus buying one futures contract.

- First, assume an idealistic setting in which interest rates are assumed to be zero, market frictions are assumed away, and counterparties have no credit risk. Now let us compare the payoffs on a per ounce basis from forward and futures trades.

- At Friday's close, Ms. Long's payoff from a long forward trade is

$$= \text{Spot(Fri)} - \text{Forward(Mon)}$$
$$= 995 - F(\text{Mon}) \tag{9.2a}$$

where $F(\text{Mon})$ is the forward price for the contract maturing on Friday.

- At Friday's close, Ms. Long's payoff from a long futures trade is

$$= [\text{Futures(Tues)} - \text{Futures(Mon)}] + [\text{Futures(Wed)} - \text{Futures(Tues)}]$$
$$+ [\text{Futures(Thurs)} - \text{Futures(Wed)}] + [\text{Futures(Fri)} - \text{Futures(Thurs)}]$$
$$= 995 - \mathcal{F}(\text{Mon}) \tag{9.2b}$$

where $\mathcal{F}(\text{Mon})$ is the futures price on Monday. This happens because Futures(Fri) = Spot(Fri) = $995 at Friday's close.

- The two payoffs must be equal because they acquire the same asset on the same date while requiring no cash when initiated. Hence, comparing expressions (9.2a) and (9.2b), we get

$$F(\text{Mon}) = \mathcal{F}(\text{Mon}) = \$995 \qquad (9.3)$$

This example demonstrates that under the assumption of zero interest rates, forward and futures prices are equal. But what happens if interest rates are non-zero? In this case, it can be shown (see Jarrow and Turnbull [2000] for a proof) that forward and futures prices are equal, but only if interest rates are nonrandom. This is an improvement over the first assumption, but it is still an unreasonable one. Interest rates are random and wiggle unpredictably across time.

If one allows interest rates to be random, which is the truth, then the equality between forward and futures prices no longer holds. The primary reason is that futures earn interest on the margin account, while forward contracts do not. The equality argument that gave us expression (9.3) does not apply. This is demonstrated by continuing the previous example.

EXAMPLE 9.7 (CONTINUED): Equality of Forward and Futures Prices

- Let us allow interest rates to be random, while holding the other assumptions the same. Again, let's compare payoffs from a forward and futures trade.
  - At Friday's close, Ms. Long's payoff from a long forward trade is

$$= 995 - F(\text{Mon}) \qquad (9.4a)$$

  - At Friday's close, Ms. Long's payoff from a long futures trade is

$$= 995 - \mathcal{F}(\text{Mon}) + \text{Interest earned on margin account balance over the time period during which futures position is held} \qquad (9.4b)$$

on a per ounce basis.

  - Equate the payoffs as before and rearrange terms to get

$$\mathcal{F}(\text{Mon}) = F(\text{Mon}) + \text{Interest} \qquad (9.5)$$

- Expression (9.5) shows that futures and forward prices are structurally different. This is because a futures trader earns interest on her margin account balances but a forward trader does not.

- Introducing additional market imperfections such as transaction costs serves to complicate the relation between forward and futures prices even more.

- In addition, forward and futures contracts face different risks, on top of the market risks discussed earlier. Let us consider the three additional risks stated in chapter 1 (credit, liquidity, operational) and see how each affects forward and futures contracts differently.
  - Being exchange traded, a futures contract is essentially free from credit risk; a forward contract may not be. It depends on the collateral relationships prearranged between the relevant counterparties.

- Over-the-counter traded forwards are more illiquid than are the exchange-traded futures, introducing greater liquidity risk in forward contracts.
- Being an over-the-counter instrument, a forward also has more operational risk than does an exchange-traded futures contract.

The moral of the story is that forward and futures contracts are different securities and, consequently, have different prices. They are fraternal twins, not identical!

Convergence of the Basis

The spot price minus the futures price is called the **basis**. Although it randomly changes across time, it eventually becomes zero at maturity. This well-known property of futures prices is known as **convergence of the basis**.

Looking back, we see this in Example 9.4 where the basis takes on the values −0.60 (Monday), −0.40 (Tuesday), −0.20 (Wednesday), −0.20 (Thursday), and 0 (Friday). Figure 9.5a plots the spot and futures prices from Examples 9.3 and 9.4, and Figure 9.5b shows the behavior of the basis over time.

9.7 | Trading Spreads

Futures traders trade naked futures or establish various hedge positions. They also trade spreads whereby they try to exploit relative movements between two futures prices that usually track one another for economic, historical, and other reasons.

One can set up an **intracommodity spread** in the futures market by simultaneously buying and selling futures contracts on the *same commodity* but with *different maturity months* or an **intercommodity spread** by simultaneously buying and selling futures contracts on *different commodities* with the *same or different* delivery months. When delivery dates differ, it is called a **time spread** or a **calendar spread**.

Why trade spreads? If you are placing directional bets with futures, you need to have expectations about future spot prices. Alternatively, market forces sometimes create abnormal differences between two futures prices that should closely track one another. People speculate with spreads in such situations, hoping to profit when the price difference corrects itself. Notice that when trading spreads, there is no risk from the direction in which the futures prices move.

Spread trading can be tricky because spreads may vary with the seasons. For example, although since 1970 wheat has on average cost a dollar more per bushel than corn, an article titled "Corn, Wheat Swap Roles as Prices Surge" (*Wall Street Journal*, August 9, 2011) noted the opposite: corn was trading higher than wheat, a gap that grew to 66.75 cents in July 2011. This reversal was caused by low supply as well as rising demand for corn from China, while wheat prices fell as many countries had bumper crops. If futures prices move together with spot prices, this is an ideal setting for an intercommodity spread trade that sells corn and buys wheat futures.

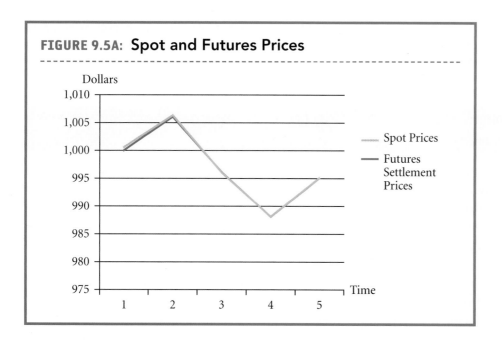

FIGURE 9.5A: **Spot and Futures Prices**

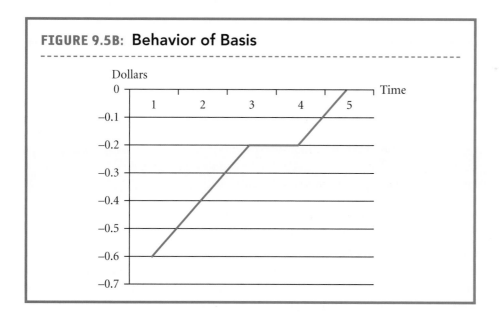

FIGURE 9.5B: **Behavior of Basis**

This strategy was adopted by many traders at the time hoping for "wheat gaining on corn, since the main wheat harvest is over and more corn supplies are poised to hit the market." But many traders also avoided this strategy in 2011 because, as observed an agricultural consultant, "the seasonal reliability is not there."

Still, spreads are usually safer than an outright long or short position. For this reason, brokers tend to require less margin for spread positions than for naked positions. When closing out a futures or an option position, they regularly ask, Is this part of a spread position? The next two examples illustrate hypothetical spread trading when the futures prices are narrower (Example 9.8) or wider (Example 9.9) than expected.

EXAMPLE 9.8: An Intracommodity Spread

- Suppose you notice that the April gold futures price is $1,008, whereas that for December is $1,014 (all prices are per ounce). In traders' jargon, the spread is $6 to the December side. Sensing a mispricing, you consult your extensive collection of past price data and find that this intracommodity spread has historically hovered around $8.

- Set up a spread trading strategy: buy the relatively underpriced December futures contract and simultaneously sell the relatively overpriced April futures contract (see Figure 9.6). Traders say that you are **buying the spread** for $6. No money changes hands because you are trading futures, but you have to keep margin deposits with your broker.

- Suppose that next month, the April futures price stays the same, but the December futures price rises to $1,016, as predicted. Close out your positions by **selling the spread** for $8: sell December and buy the April gold futures contract. You make no profit on the April contract but $2 on the December. Stated differently, you make $2 by buying the spread for $6 and selling it for $8.

Example 9.9 considers an intercommodity spread.

EXAMPLE 9.9: An Intercommodity Spread

- Suppose that the platinum futures price is $1,080 per ounce and the gold futures price for a contract expiring in the same month is $1,000 per ounce.

- Suppose you become a technical analyst, put on green goggles, and gaze intently at price charts on the computer screen. You note that the charts reveal that the intercommodity spread should narrow to $50. You can speculate on this insight by selling the spread for $80: sell the relatively overpriced platinum futures and buy the relatively underpriced gold futures contract.

- Gold futures prices can rise, stay level, or fall, and so can platinum futures prices. Suppose that a month from now, the spread magically narrows to $50. You earn a profit of $30.

When trading spreads, remember the wry warning (attributed to renowned economist John Maynard Keynes) that "the market can remain irrational longer than you can remain solvent."

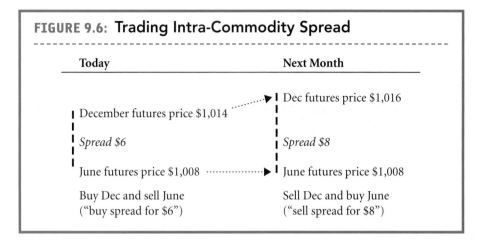

FIGURE 9.6: Trading Intra-Commodity Spread

Today	Next Month
	Dec futures price $1,016
December futures price $1,014	
Spread $6	*Spread $8*
June futures price $1,008	June futures price $1,008
Buy Dec and sell June ("buy spread for $6")	Sell Dec and buy June ("sell spread for $8")

9.8 │ Summary

1. Commodity trading advisors advise clients, commodity pool operators run commodity pools, while futures commission merchants and introducing brokers help investors trade. On the trading floor, floor brokers handle customer orders and floor traders trade on their own behalf, making the market liquid in the process.

2. One can initiate a futures position by calling a broker and placing an opening order. There are many order placement strategies, the simplest being a market order that is immediately executed. One can move out of a futures position by (1) a closing transaction, (2) physical delivery, (3) cash settlement, or (4) an exchange for physicals.

3. To open a futures position, one must keep an initial margin to guarantee contract performance. When a futures price goes up, a long position gains and a short position loses profits. Through a process called daily settlement, the long's account is credited with variation margin (which is the change in the settlement price from the previous trading day) and the short's account is debited the same. The opposite happens when a futures price goes down—long loses and short makes a profit. After daily settlement adjustments are made, the brokerage account is said to be marked-to-market. This substantially lowers credit risk and makes futures safer to use.

4. Futures prices have a number of useful properties. For example, the futures price must equal the spot price at the contract's maturity. As the contract maturity approaches, the basis (= Spot − Futures price) converges to zero. Forward and futures prices are unequal under random interest rates.

9.9 │ Cases

Investment Linked to Commodity Futures (Harvard Business School Case 293017-PDF-ENG). The case examines an investment linked to an index of commodity futures prices and explores how the index is constructed, how commodity futures behave, and what the portfolio impacts of such an investment might be.

Futures on the Mexican Peso (Harvard Business School Case 296004-PDF-ENG). The case considers the issues that the Chicago Mercantile Exchange faces regarding how to design, and whether and when to introduce, a futures contract on the Mexican peso.

Alcoma: The Strategic Use of Frozen Concentrated Orange Juice Futures (Harvard Business School Case 595029-PDF-ENG). The case explores price risk management in the orange juice industry when an increase in orange tree production led to a surplus production of orange juice.

9.10 | Questions and Problems

9.1. On an exchange floor, what is a floor broker?

9.2. What is the open-outcry method of trading futures contracts? What are the benefits of the open-outcry method relative to a computer-based transaction?

9.3. How is a futures contract trade executed on an exchange?

9.4. What is a closing transaction on a futures contract? Do you need to take delivery to terminate a futures contract position?

9.5. For physical delivery of a futures contract, explain the three-day delivery process.

9.6. What does marking-to-market mean?

9.7. What risk do margin accounts on futures contracts and marking-to-market minimize? Explain your answer.

9.8. What is the difference between initial margin and variation margin of a futures contract? Provide a simple example to explain your answer.

9.9. Explain what a margin call is and when it occurs on a futures contract.

9.10. Ignoring credit risk, if interest rates are constant and equal to zero, do forward prices equal futures prices? Why?

9.11. What is the basis of a futures contract? Give a simple example to explain your answer. What does convergence of the basis mean with respect to a futures contract?

9.12. Ignoring credit risk, when interest rates are random, must forward prices and futures prices be equal? Explain why or why not.

9.13. Suppose you notice that the April gold futures price is $1,518, while that for December is $1,535 (all prices are per ounce). Historically, this spread has been around $10. Explain the workings of a spread strategy that you may set up in the hope that the spread would revert to its historical level.

9.14. In January, May futures for sugar (world) trades for 7 cents per pound, while sugar (domestic) trades for 22 cents per pound. You consult technical charts and conclude that their spread is going to widen to 20 cents per pound.

a. Suggest a trading strategy for exploiting such opportunities.

b. If the spread indeed widens as predicted, what is your trading profit if you trade seven contracts of each type, with 112,000 pounds in each contract?

9.15. Suppose you go short one contract of gold at today's closing futures price of $1,300 per ounce. Suppose that your brokerage firm requires an initial margin of 5 percent of the position size ($130,000 in this example) and sets the maintenance margin at 80 percent of the initial margin. Contract size is one hundred ounces. Keep the margins constant throughout this example. Track the value of your margin account if the closing futures prices are as follows. Clearly identify any margin call received and the amount of variation margin that you have to produce.

Day	Closing Futures Price (dollars/ounce)
0 (today)	1,300
1	1,303
2	1,297
3	1,290
4	1,297

The next two questions are based on the following data:

The euro FX (currency) futures contract that trades in the Merc has the following features:

Euro FX Contract Highlights	
Ticker symbol	EC
Trading unit (underlying)	Euro 125,000
Quotation	US$ per euro
Minimum price fluctuation (tick)	$.0001/euro = $12.50/contract
Contract months	March, June, September, December
Regular trading hours (RTH)	7:20 AM–2:00 PM (Chicago Time)
GLOBEX 2 trading hours	2:30 PM–7:05 AM (Chicago Time); on Sundays, trading begins at 5:30 PM
Last trading day	Second business day before the third Wednesday of the contract month

Assume initial margin is $2,511 and maintenance margin is $1,860 per contract (the exchange periodically revises these numbers).

9.16. Track margin account payments to a trader holding long position in two contracts when the euro takes the following values (in terms of US dollars): 0.8450, 0.8485, 0.8555, 0.8510, 0.8480, 0.8423, 0.8370, 0.8300, 0.8355.

9.17. Track the margin account payments to a trader holding short position in one contract when the euro takes the following values (in terms of US dollars): 0.8450, 0.8485, 0.8555, 0.8510, 0.8480, 0.8423, 0.8370, 0.8300, 0.8355.

9.18. Suppose that the platinum futures price is $1,580 per ounce and the gold futures price for a contract expiring in the same month as platinum is $1,500 per ounce (see Example 9.9). Hoping that the spread will narrow to $50 in a month's time, set up a spread trading strategy, discuss all possible outcomes for the futures prices after a month, and illustrate these outcomes in a diagram.

9.19. Explain the difference between cash-settled and physical-settled futures contracts.

9.20. Who pays the counterparty when a futures trader defaults?

Futures Regulations

10.1 | Introduction

Price discovery is an important function of futures markets. Even so, US citizens became upset in July 2003 when the Defense Advanced Research Projects Agency (DARPA), a research wing of the US Department of Defense, announced plans for a "Policy Analysis Market," where anonymous individuals could trade futures whose payoffs would depend on a terrorist indicator (see Extension 10.1 for an elaboration). The proposal that the US government set up an online betting parlor for terrorist activities enraged both legislators and the public. The project was killed soon after it was unveiled. Despite its ethical problems, it was hailed as a good idea by some economists, who noted that futures prices have done an excellent job of predicting conventional as well as nonconventional events. DARPA argued that futures markets usually fare better than experts in predicting events like elections, and this project's mission was to tap the collective wisdom in market prices—price discovery—to understand the probabilities of terrorist activities. But this argument from the Department of Defense didn't quite fly.

This chapter discusses the price discovery role of futures markets, regulations, and market manipulation. First, we explore the market conditions needed for futures to trade. Next, we look at futures market regulations. Finally, we discuss futures trading abuses and market manipulation: colorful stories of powerful players who sought quick gains by cornering the market and squeezing the shorts until regulators foiled their ploys.

10.2 | Which Markets Have Futures?

When is a futures market for a particular commodity likely to succeed? Three conditions—*competitive markets, standardization*, and *volatile prices*—seem to be among the key ingredients needed.

A **competitive market** is one in which each investor's trades are too insignificant to influence prices and traders act as price takers (see Varian 2003). Economists view competitive markets as the ideal setting. Markets cease to be competitive when some participants gain market power and manipulate prices to their benefit. When markets can be manipulated, traders are reluctant to trade knowing that they can lose significant wealth to the manipulators. For example, consider the following:

- When a monopoly (a single seller), an oligopoly (a small band of sellers), or a cartel fixes commodity prices, futures trading may not develop. This is the case for diamonds but not for oil. Extension 10.1 tells a tale of the spectacularly successful diamond cartel and a less successful but immensely influential joint venture by the oil-producing nations.

- When a sole buyer or a small number of buyers drive the market, futures markets for the commodity are unlikely. There are no futures markets for missiles and weapons where the government is the sole buyer.

Standardization refers to the ability of a commodity to be sold in standardized units. For example, gold and silver are easy to standardize in terms of quantity and quality. As such, one can easily write contracts on future purchases or sales of these commodities in large quantities. In contrast, automobiles are not so easily standardized. There are hundreds of different car models available, distinguished by manufacturer and other features like manual or automatic, electric, gas, or diesel, and so on. Consequently, it is no surprise that automobile futures do not exist.

Volatile prices are commodity prices that change randomly across time in an erratic (up and down) fashion. Volatile prices create risk for producers in determining both their input costs and output sales. Volatile prices therefore generate a demand to hedge these price risks and also a need to forecast future prices. Futures markets exist to fulfill these two needs. Let us explore both these roles filled by futures markets, price discovery, and hedging in more detail.

Price Discovery

Price discovery is related to the notion of market efficiency (see chapter 6). In efficient markets, prices accurately reflect available information. Such information includes past and current prices (weak-form efficiency), publicly available information (semi-strong-form efficiency), and private information (strong-form efficiency). This concept is not only true for spot markets but for futures markets as well. Because futures market traders include producers who have private knowledge of supply and demand conditions, futures markets are widely believed to be (semistrong-form) efficient, thereby generating prices that reflect more information and provide better price forecasts—*price discovery*—than any ordinary trader's information could. This is the motivation underlying the US Department of Defense's July 2003 proposal to set up a futures market in terrorism indicators. Although well intentioned, the plan was shelved following heavy criticism concerning its ethical considerations (see Extension 10.1). Price discovery helps futures buyers and sellers of commodities. For example, firms that process and distribute corn can fix the buying and/or selling price by trading futures, or the retail seller, which may be your neighborhood supermarket chain, can do the same.

EXTENSION 10.1: Pentagon's Plan for a Futures Market on Terrorism

Price discovery was the motivation for a futures market on terrorism. The US Department of Defense (known as the Pentagon because it is headquartered in a pentagon-shaped building in Washington, D.C.) has a research wing named DARPA, whose mission, as noted on its website, is "to develop imaginative, innovative and often high-risk research ideas offering a significant technological impact that will go well beyond the normal evolutionary developmental approaches." DARPA was instrumental in the development of the Internet. With their mandate to "think outside the box," DARPA submitted in July 2003 a proposal to Congress to create a "Policy Analysis Market," which would be a futures market on terrorist indicators.

It was to be an online market where anonymous speculators could "bet on forecasting terrorist attacks, assassinations and coups.[1]"

The market was proposed to work as follows: suppose you have information that the president of a country will be removed by a certain date. Current futures prices do not yet reflect this information. To profit from your information, given that current futures prices are priced too low, say, at $0.30, you buy a futures on that event. If more traders also believe the event will occur, then futures prices may increase to $0.60 or $0.70. If the president is out of office by the designated date, then you are paid $1 per futures contract. Otherwise, you lose your investment of $0.30. Hence the futures price reflects the market's aggregate belief regarding the probability of the event (after adjusting for risk; see chapter 17 and the notion of risk-neutral probabilities). By looking at the futures price, one can infer an *informed* probability of the event occurring—this is price discovery. In the preceding situation, if the final futures price is $0.60, then the futures price–based probability of the event occurring is 60 percent.

The Pentagon defended the program: "Research indicates that markets are extremely efficient, effective and timely aggregators of dispersed and even hidden information. . . . Futures markets have proven themselves to be good at predicting such things as elections results; they are often better than expert opinions."[2] The program was not entirely novel because online betting sites were quite common prior to this proposal.

Members of the US Senate were upset. Many voiced concern that since the trading was anonymous, potential terrorists could profit from the trading, and there was also the potential problem that some lunatic would place huge bets and then actually try to carry out the nefarious act. The moral and ethical dimensions of the proposal were a concern.

The plan was quashed within two days after its announcement. Economist Hal Varian commented in the *New York Times* "A Good Idea With Bad Press" on July 31, "It was a good idea, killed by terrible public relations." He explained how markets have done a superb job of gleaning information in many nonconventional settings and explained that many of the objections raised by politicians were generally based on misunderstandings of what was actually proposed (e.g., the maximum gain from trade was limited to less than $100, making it unlikely for a potential terrorist to raise large sums in this market; no assassination futures was actually proposed; and if there was evidence of "insider trading" by potential terrorists, then intelligence agencies like the Central Intelligence Agency would pursue their trails). Varian's arguments were not persuasive.

---

[1] "Threats and Responses: Plans and Criticisms; Pentagon Prepares A Futures Market On Terror Attacks" in the *New York Times* dated July 29, 2003.

[2] ibid.

Hedging

Hedging in the *New Oxford Dictionary of English* is defined as to "protect (one's investment or an investor) against loss by making balancing or compensating contracts or transactions." If you hedge with futures (for which you pay nothing to start), then you get protection from price swings. You benefit when the spot adversely moves but surrender gains when the spot moves in your favor. Hedging with futures is beneficial to firms for minimizing input and output price risks, thereby smoothing costs and profits. This is true for both producers (e.g., farmers, manufacturers) and suppliers (e.g., gold and copper mines). Hedging is the motivation for the existence of oil futures markets, despite that the oil producers form a pricing cartel known as the **Organization of the Petroleum Exporting Countries** (OPEC) (see Extension 10.2).

Speculation

In contrast to hedging, the term **speculation** carries a negative connotation. The humorist Mark Twain said, "There are two times in a man's life when he should not speculate: when he can't afford it, and when he can." But speculation is really the flip side of hedging. Hedgers are buying insurance against adverse price movements. Speculators are selling the insurance: gambling that the adverse price movements will not occur.

For futures markets to work, both hedgers and speculators are usually needed, and both play a crucial role. The reason is that it is unusual for hedgers on both sides of the market (suppliers and users) to have exactly offsetting demands. As such, hedging demands for a commodity are often one-sided. In such circumstances, speculators provide the liquidity needed for a successful futures market to exist.

In addition to their role in providing market liquidity—being the insurance sellers—speculators also play a second important role in futures markets: they facilitate the price discovery role because they often trade based on private information, obtained by costly investigation. Speculators trading on the basis of their private information increase market efficiency because as they trade, their information gets reflected in market prices.

Without speculators, futures markets would be both less liquid and less efficient, and sometimes, without speculators, futures markets would not exist. An example is the market for precious diamonds, in which the Diamond Cartel removed the speculators' incentives to participate (see Extension 10.2).

EXTENSION 10.2: When Sellers Have Market Power—A Tale of Two Cartels

Cartels

An oligopoly is a market that is dominated by a handful of sellers, more than one but not too many. For example, Boeing of the United States, Airbus of Europe, and some fringe suppliers like Ilyushin and Tupolev (now divisions of Russia's United Aircraft Corporation) dominate the production of large passenger airplanes. Members of an oligopoly sometimes join to form a cartel. A **cartel** is a coalition of producers that monopolizes a commodity's production and sale. A cartel tries to maximize joint profits by controlling supply—it allocates a share of the common market to each member, sets sales quotas, regulates production, and fixes prices. By eliminating competition, a cartel raises prices for consumers and profits for the producers. In the process, it may keep inefficient companies in business. Cartels are banned in the United Kingdom and the United States. However, they are legal in many parts of the world, including highly industrialized nations like France, Germany, Italy, and Japan.

By controlling the supply of a commodity, and therefore prices, cartels can potentially eliminate the benefits of both hedging and price discovery in futures markets. In such circumstances, futures markets will not exist. This is the case with the Diamond Cartel, but it is not the case with oil and OPEC. Consider the tale of these two cartels.

De Beers and the Diamond Cartel

There is a quote on the South African diamond manufacturing conglomerate De Beers Group's website: "For more than a century, the name 'De Beers' has been synonymous with diamonds." Cecil Rhodes founded this enterprise during the 1880s by consolidating several diamond mines in Southern Africa.[3] Around the same time, he formed the London Diamond Syndicate to control the world's diamond trade. This was later transformed by Sir Ernest Oppenheimer into the Central Selling Organization, a group of marketing organizations that controlled much of the world's diamond trade until the last decade of the twentieth century.

A February 2001 *Fortune* magazine article ("The De Beers Story: A New Cut on an Old Monopoly") reported that De Beers entered agreements with most major diamond producers (including the former Soviet Union) and led a very effective cartel. In the 1990s, about 45 percent of the global diamond production was mined by De Beers and another 25 percent went through its hands. In 2000, De Beers announced that it would stop manipulating the supply by buying and storing diamonds. Afterward, De Beers focused on selling diamonds from its own mines after branding them with a "Forevermark" to guarantee their integrity. These steps strengthened the demand for diamonds à la De Beers. Despite this announcement, the effectiveness of the diamond cartel did not disappear. A *New York Times* article dated August 9, 2008, titled "Talking Business: Diamonds Are Forever in Botswana," reported that "today, De Beers has about 40 percent of the diamond market—but it is far more profitable than under the old regime, when it controlled 80 percent of the market."

The strong control of the supply of diamonds by the De Beers Group destroyed the price discovery role of a diamond futures market as documented because diamond prices do not reflect supply and demand but the activities of De Beers. Although hedging demands certainly exist for firms using diamonds in production, there

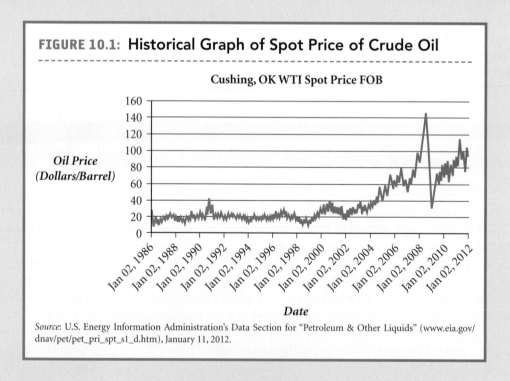

FIGURE 10.1: Historical Graph of Spot Price of Crude Oil

Cushing, OK WTI Spot Price FOB

Oil Price
(Dollars/Barrel)

Source: U.S. Energy Information Administration's Data Section for "Petroleum & Other Liquids" (www.eia.gov/dnav/pet/pet_pri_spt_s1_d.htm), January 11, 2012.

---

[3] A son of a vicar and a graduate of the University of Oxford, Cecil J. Rhodes (1853–1902) built a vast fortune by investing in diamond and gold mines in southern Africa. After his death, the bulk of his fortune was bequeathed for the establishment of the Rhodes scholarship that helps educate future leaders of the world by awarding scholarships at Oxford to young people from the British Commonwealth, the United States, and Germany.

are no offsetting hedging demands from the suppliers (the cartel). For a diamond futures market to work, speculators need to provide the missing liquidity, but the strong control of the market supply by De Beers removed the desire for speculators to participate in such a market. Consequently, no diamond futures markets exist today.

OPEC

For many years, OPEC seemed to glimmer faintly beside the glittering De Beers diamond cartel. Founded in 1960 by five oil-rich nations, Iraq, Iran, Kuwait, Saudi Arabia, and Venezuela, OPEC currently has seven other members: Algeria, Angola, Ecuador, Libya, Nigeria, Qatar, and the United Arab Emirates. OPEC states that its objective is to "co-ordinate and unify petroleum policies among Member Countries, in order to secure fair and stable prices for petroleum producers; an efficient, economic and regular supply of petroleum to consuming nations; and a fair return on capital to those investing in the industry."[4] The oil and energy ministers of these countries meet at least twice a year in OPEC headquarters in Vienna and decide on the organization's output level.

OPEC came into prominence during the 1970s, when members curtailed production and jacked up oil prices. The price per barrel of oil rose from $3 in 1973 to $30 in 1980. However, every now and then, some members surreptitiously produce more, and the price drops.

FIGURE 10.2: OPEC Share of World Crude Oil Reserves (2010)

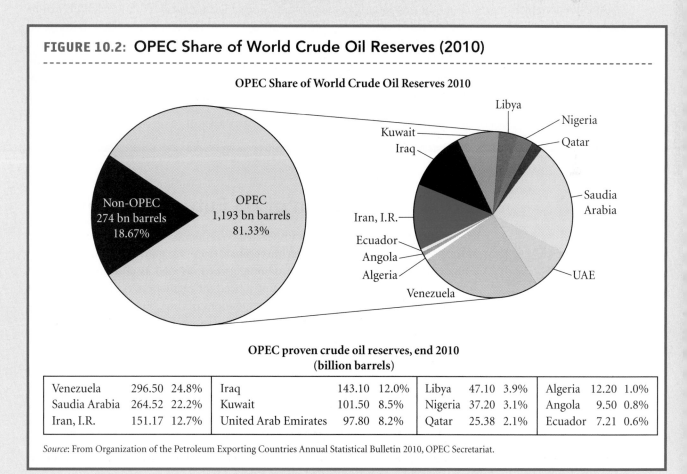

OPEC Share of World Crude Oil Reserves 2010

OPEC proven crude oil reserves, end 2010
(billion barrels)

Venezuela	296.50	24.8%	Iraq	143.10	12.0%	Libya	47.10	3.9%	Algeria	12.20	1.0%
Saudia Arabia	264.52	22.2%	Kuwait	101.50	8.5%	Nigeria	37.20	3.1%	Angola	9.50	0.8%
Iran, I.R.	151.17	12.7%	United Arab Emirates	97.80	8.2%	Qatar	25.38	2.1%	Ecuador	7.21	0.6%

Source: From Organization of the Petroleum Exporting Countries Annual Statistical Bulletin 2010, OPEC Secretariat.

[4] www.opec.org/opec_web/en/about_us/24.htm.

OPEC maintained a low profile during the decades that followed. Oil prices generally stayed low even though demand increased. For reasons that are still being debated, crude oil prices began a huge run-up in January 2004. Spot prices smashed the $50 mark in mid-2005 and the $100 mark in early 2008, before somewhat cooling down (see Figure 10.1 for a graph of historical crude oil prices). Of course, a host of factors affect oil prices: economic growth, political events, or natural calamities like hurricanes. Commodity price speculators have also attracted significant blame.

What role has OPEC played in all this? In the FAQs section of its website, OPEC claims that it does not control the oil market and gives the classic economics textbook answer "high or low oil prices are determined by interactions between demand and supply." However, it acknowledges that it has market power, because although its member countries "produce about 42 per cent of the world's crude oil [which hovered around 30 million barrels per day during September–November 2011[5]] and 18 per cent of its natural gas," OPEC's exports constitute about 55 percent of global crude oil trade (see Figure 10.2), and it can strongly affect the oil market, especially if it decides to change its production levels. By December 2008, the oil price had retreated to below $40 per barrel again. A global recession that lowered energy demand, and a curb in speculation owing to vigilant regulators are possible reasons for this dramatic fall. Since that time, oil prices have climbed and are currently (December 2011) around $100 per barrel.

As evidenced by Figure 10.2 and the previous discussion, oil prices are highly volatile. Although OPEC exhibits market power, it is not the only force affecting prices (this is in contrast to the diamond cartel). Because oil is a key input to so many production processes (users), and because there are also so many small suppliers, the hedging demands on both sides of the market are quite large. As noted earlier, speculators are eager to participate in these markets. Combined, despite the existence of OPEC, these conditions explain the existence of successful oil futures markets, serving both the price discovery and hedging functions previously described.

[5] See www.opec.org/opec_web/static_files_project/media/downloads/data_graphs/MI112011.pdf.

10.3 | Regulation of US Futures Markets

Futures markets are not for the fainthearted. Wild price swings have been common since inception, and there have been numerous attempts to manipulate futures prices. Competitive markets can lead to economic growth as well as efficiency. However, sometimes they fail to function, creating a need for regulation. As is often the case with regulations, many of the rules and regulations of the US securities market have arisen to fix problems evidenced within financial markets during a financial crisis.

Major Regulatory Acts

Regulation of the US futures markets began on a cold winter's day in February 1859, when the governor of Illinois signed a legislative act that granted a corporate charter to the Chicago Board of Trade (CBOT). The charter, among other things, granted the exchange self-regulatory authority over its members, standardized commodity grades, and provided for CBOT-appointed grain inspectors whose decisions were binding on members. This was a critical early step in the evolution of futures contracts.[6]

[6] See "History of the CFTC: US Futures Trading and Regulation Before the Creation of the CFTC" from www.cftc.gov/About/HistoryoftheCFTC/history_precftc.

Another major step was taken in October 1865, when formal trading rules were introduced at the CBOT, including margin requirements and delivery procedures. Three years later, the exchange adopted a rule to deter manipulation by banning "'corners' (defined as 'making contracts for the purchase of a commodity, and then taking measures to render it impossible for the seller to fill his contract, for the purpose of extorting money from him')."[7] In 1877, the CBOT began publishing futures prices on a regular basis, and in 1883, the first organization was formed to clear CBOT contracts on a voluntary basis.

US federal regulations with respect to futures markets began in the 1880s when the first bills "to regulate, ban, or tax futures trading in the U.S."[8] were introduced in Congress. About two hundred such bills were introduced over the next forty years (see Table 10.1 for a list of some major US futures regulations). As agricultural futures dominated the markets in the early days, regulations primarily focused on grain (such as corn, wheat, oats, and rye) trading, and the regulatory controls were placed in the hands of the US Department of Agriculture (USDA).

In 1922, the **Grain Futures Act** was passed. It regulated grain futures trading, banned "off-contract-market futures" trading, created (an agency of the USDA) the Grain Futures Administration for administering the act, and established the Grain

TABLE 10.1: Some Major Milestones in the Federal Regulation of US Futures Markets

Year	Development
1880s	The first bills are introduced in Congress to regulate futures markets.
1922	The Grain Futures Act was passed. The Grain Futures Administration was created as a department of the US Department of Agriculture.
1936	The Commodity Exchange Act, an amendment of the 1922 Act, was passed. The Commodity Exchange Administration was created as the first federal regulator of futures markets.
1974	The Commodity Futures Trading Commission Act was passed. This created the Commodity Futures Trading Commission as an independent "federal regulatory agency for futures trading."
1978, 1982	The Futures Trading Acts were passed.
1982	The National Futures Association, a self-regulatory agency for the futures industry, was established.
2000	The Commodity Futures Modernization Act of 2000 was passed.
2010	The Dodd–Frank Wall Street Reform and Consumer Protection Act was passed. This significantly increased regulatory oversight of the over-the-counter derivatives market.

[7] See "History of the CFTC: US Futures Trading and Regulation Before the Creation of the CFTC" from www.cftc.gov/About/HistoryoftheCFTC/history_precftc.

[8] ibid.

Futures Commission (consisting of the secretaries of agriculture and commerce and the attorney general), which had the broad power of suspending or revoking a contract market's designation. In 1923, the Grain Futures Administration implemented "a large trader reporting system," which required reporting "on a daily basis the market positions of each trader exceeding a specified size." This evolved into the Commitments of Traders reports, which "remains an integral part of the CFTC's oversight scheme to this day."[9]

The **Commodity Exchange Act of 1936** amended and extended the 1922 act. It replaced references to "grains" with the term "commodities," and it expanded the approved list to include commodities like butter, cotton, and eggs. The Grain Futures Commission became the Commodity Exchange Commission and was granted the authority to establish federal speculative position limits. The act also required futures commission merchants to keep customer funds separately in margin accounts and "prohibited fictitious and fraudulent transactions such as wash sales and accommodation trades, and banned all commodity option trading"[10]; the ban on options trading on commodities was lifted only in 1981. In 1947, this commission evolved into the Commodity Exchange Authority (also an agency of the USDA). It continued to administer the Commodity Exchange Act until the mid-1970s. This broad regulatory framework, with some minor modifications over the years, supported futures trading in the United States for four decades. But all this changed with the passing of the **Commodity Futures Trading Commission (CFTC) Act of 1974**.

As noted before, the futures markets went through a rapid expansion during the 1970s: financial futures started trading and futures were introduced on more commodities than ever before. Congress responded by passing the CFTC Act. This created the CFTC as the independent, ultimate "federal regulatory agency for futures trading," taking responsibility for regulating futures trading in 1975. The CFTC Act also proposed creation of a self-regulatory organization. Subsequently, an industry body called the **National Futures Association (NFA)** was established in 1982, which works with the CFTC to help regulate the markets. More legislation followed in 1978 and 1982. This whole body of legislation is known as the amended **Commodity Exchange Act (CEA)**. The Commodity Exchange is discussed in Title 7 ("Agriculture"), chapter 1 ("Commodity Exchanges") of the US Code.

A landmark legislation that substantially altered the CEA, the **Commodity Futures Modernization Act of 2000 (CFMA)**, was passed by Congress and signed into a law in December 2000. The major changes included the following:

1. *Lifting of a long-standing ban by the CFMA, which made it possible to trade* **security futures products**, *which are futures contracts based on single securities and narrowly based stock indexes.* The CFTC and the Securities and Exchange Commission (SEC) jointly regulate security futures products.

---

[9] See "History of the CFTC: US Futures Trading and Regulation Before the Creation of the CFTC" from www.cftc.gov/About/HistoryoftheCFTC/history_precftc.

[10] ibid.

2. *Easing up on regulations for swaps, other over-the-counter (OTC) derivatives, and trading facilities for these products.* Although there was a push by Brooksley Born, the CFTC's chairperson, to more closely regulate OTC swaps, owing to a unified opposition to more regulation by Alan Greenspan (the Federal Reserve chairman) and Robert Rubin (the Treasury secretary), the push failed and the OTC derivatives markets remained largely unregulated by this act.

3. *Streamlining of regulation and the creation of three types of markets*: (1) *designated contract markets (DCMs)*, which were the only type that existed before (examples of DCMs include the Chicago Mercantile Exchange [CME], the CBOT, the NYMEX, and the COMEX of the CME Group), (2) **derivative transaction execution facilities**, which have fewer regulations but more restrictions on who and what trades, and (3) **exempt boards of trade** with restrictions similar to (2) but exempt from CFTC regulation, except for antifraud and antimanipulation provisions.

4. Establishment of new derivatives clearing organizations that make it easier to clear OTC derivative transactions.

The CFMA regulations reflected the deregulatory mood prevalent at the time. The loosely regulated OTC derivative markets seemingly worked well until the financial crisis of 2007–9, where it was documented that trading in OTC derivatives helped cause the crisis (see chapter 26 for an elaboration of this role). In response to this lack of regulation, in 2010, Congress passed the **Dodd–Frank Wall Street Reform and Consumer Protection Act**. This massive 849-page act[11] was the largest effort to regulate US financial markets since the 1930s Great Depression. It introduced numerous significant changes to bank and financial market regulation. Some key features of the Dodd–Frank Act related to derivatives are as follows:[12]

- *Increased regulation.* Provides the SEC and CFTC authority to regulate OTC derivatives so that irresponsible practices and excessive risk taking no longer escape regulatory oversight.

- *Central clearing and exchange trading.* To require central clearing and exchange trading for more derivatives, this act replaced derivatives transaction execution facilities with a new type of entity, the *swap execution facility*. Neither exempt boards of trade nor *exempt commercial markets* (another category of trading organization with fewer regulations) are active as of January 2012.

- *Market transparency.* This requires data collection by clearinghouses and swap repositories to improve market transparency and provide regulators the necessary information for monitoring and responding to systemic risks.

- *Financial safeguards.* These add safeguards by ensuring that dealers and major swap participants have adequate financial resources to guarantee the execution of derivatives contracts.

[11] See www.gpo.gov/fdsys/pkg/PLAW-111publ203/pdf/PLAW-111publ203.pdf.

[12] See http://banking.senate.gov/public/_files/070110_Dodd_Frank_Wall_Street_Reform_comprehensive_summary_Final.pdf.

The details of the rules are to be determined by various committees, and as of January 2012, the rules are still under formulation.

The CFTC, the NFA, and the Regulatory Role of Exchanges

In establishing the CFTC, Congress recognized that futures markets are important to economic growth. The CFTC has five commissioners appointed by the president, with the advice and consent of the Senate, to serve staggered five-year terms, and it has seven major operating units: the Office of the General Counsel, the Office of the Executive Director, the Division of Swap Dealer and Intermediary Oversight, the Division of Clearing and Risk, the Division of Market Oversight, the Division of Enforcement, and the Office of the Chief Economist.[13] They help the CFTC carry out its mission: (1) to regulate futures so that the participants are protected from manipulation, abusive trading practices, fraud, and systemic risk and (2) to foster financially sound and competitive markets. To fulfill these responsibilities, the CFTC carries out a variety of activities:

- *The CFTC must approve new contracts and changes to existing contracts.* Each new futures contract is evaluated with respect to three issues: (1) justification of individual terms and conditions, which thoroughly examines the details of the contract to ensure that there will be sufficient supply of the underlying commodity to prevent market manipulation; (2) an economic purpose test, which requires exchanges to show that the proposed contract will be useful for price discovery or hedging; and (3) other public interest requirements.

- *The CFTC develops rules and regulations that govern the NFA and all futures exchanges.* These rules and regulations define the requirements for registration, disclosure, minimum financial standards, daily settlement, separation of customer funds, supervision and internal controls, and other activities.

- *The CFTC requires companies and individuals who handle customer funds or give trading advice to register with them.* Actually, the NFA handles the registration process on the CFTC's behalf.

- *The CFTC ensures compliance of its rules and regulations as well as the Commodity Exchange and Dodd–Frank acts.* It conducts trade practice surveillance and audits selected registrants. It investigates and prosecutes alleged violations of CFTC regulations. Whenever necessary, the CFTC files court cases.

- *The CFTC detects and prevents manipulation, congestion, and price distortions.* It conducts daily market surveillance. It can intervene and take corrective action if it believes manipulation is present.

- *The CFTC oversees training of brokers and their representatives and other industry professionals.* It can force brokers and representatives to take competency tests. The CFTC also makes sure that all registrants complete ethics training.

---

[13] www.cftc.gov/About/CFTCOrganization/index.htm.

- *The CFTC does research on futures markets and provides technical assistance.* It makes economic analyses for enforcement investigations and gives expert help and technical aid with case development and trials to US attorney's offices, other federal and state regulators, and international authorities.

- *The CFTC helps coordinate global regulatory efforts.* It develops policies and regulations governing foreign and cross-border transactions.

- *The CFTC handles customer complaints against registrants.* It hears and decides enforcement cases. The CFTC offers a reparations procedure for persons who have reason to believe that they have suffered a loss due to a violation of the Commodity Exchange Act or CFTC regulations in their dealings with a CFTC registrant.

The SEC regulates securities and the CFTC regulates futures, but who regulates options? Following an intense turf battle between these two regulators, the agreement is that the SEC regulates options on stocks, while the CFTC regulates those on futures. The fight relapses whenever new derivatives are introduced that carry joint characteristics. The issue of overlapping jurisdiction remains unresolved at this time.

On the next rung of the regulatory ladder are the commodity exchanges and the National Futures Association. These self-regulatory organizations (SROs) must, among other things outlined in the CFTC's regulations, enforce minimum financial and reporting requirements for their members.

As a registered futures association under the Commodity Exchange Act, the NFA is an SRO composed of futures commission merchants, commodity pool operators, commodity trading advisors, introducing brokers, leverage transaction merchants, commodity exchanges, commercial firms, and others who work in the futures industry.[14] Banks and exchanges may join the NFA, but they are not required to do so. Because pit brokers and locals do not deal directly with the public, they are exempted from joining and are just guided by exchange rules and regulations. The NFA is involved in a range of activities that include the following:

- On behalf of the CFTC, the NFA registers all categories of persons and firms dealing with futures customers.

- The NFA screens and tests registration applicants and determines their qualifications and proficiency.

- The NFA requires futures commission merchants (FCMs) and introducing brokers to keep sufficient capital and maintain good trading records.

- The NFA tracks financial conditions, retail sales practices, and the business conduct of futures professionals, and it ensures compliance with the requirements.

- The NFA provides a variety of regulatory services and programs to electronic exchanges to help them treat customers fairly and to maintain orderly markets.

---

[14] www.nfa.futures.org.

- The NFA audits, examines, and conducts financial surveillance to enforce compliance by members.

- The NFA maintains an arbitration program that helps to resolve trade disputes.

Commodity exchanges complement federal regulations with their own rules. These rules cover many aspects of futures trading such as the clearance of trades, trade orders and records, position limits, price limits, disciplinary actions, floor trading practices, and standards of business conduct. Obviously, SROs have strong incentives to do a good job because a positive reputation brings more business. An effective self-regulation program lowers the chances of the CFTC's interfering. Clearinghouses also take part in regulatory activities. At the lowest level of the regulatory ladder are the brokers and dealers. Their job is to enforce regulations and report fraud, market manipulation, and abnormalities to the exchange and other relevant authorities.

Enforcement Actions by the CFTC and the NFA

The NFA has comprehensive compliance rules "covering a wide variety of areas such as advertising, telephone solicitations, risk disclosure, discretionary trading, disclosure of fees, minimum capital requirements, reporting and proficiency testing."[15] The NFA takes disciplinary action against violators, ranging from issuing warning letters to filing formal complaints that can result in penalties that include "expulsion, suspension for a fixed period, prohibition from future association with any NFA Member, censure, reprimand and a fine of up to $250,000 per violation."

The CFTC's Division of Enforcement investigates and prosecutes alleged violations of the Commodity Exchange Act and Commission regulations. The CFTC takes enforcement action against individuals and firms registered with the commission, those who are engaged in commodity futures and option trading on designated domestic exchanges, and those who improperly market futures and options contracts. Enforcement actions during 2008–9 include the following cases:

- The CFTC fined a foreign currency broker $200,000 for allowing customer confidential personal information to appear on the Internet, and the CFTC required the broker to establish systems to protect against such future incidents.

- The CFTC fined an energy trading company $175,000 for failing to properly and accurately prepare trading cards involving NYMEX natural gas futures.

- The CFTC fined $5 million and permanently banned a futures commission merchant and its principals to settle an undercapitalization and a false statements charge.

- The CFTC fined $50,000 and banned a broker for fraudulently allocating trades to his personal account.

---

[15] www.nfa.futures.org.

- The CFTC banished forever from the industry a former NYMEX compliance department clerk for disclosing nonpublic information "regarding investigations and proposed regulatory" actions to NYMEX floor brokers.

- The CFTC ordered a foreign national to pay over $279 million in restitution and a $12 million civil penalty for defrauding commodity pool participants in four pools that he managed and banned him from the industry.

- The CFTC filed an enforcement action against a foreign couple who made fraudulent representations to raise $650,000 from at least nine hundred people in the United States and other countries with the promise of participation in a commodity pool and used the pool's assets for personal expenses, including gambling!

The CFTC has also been vigorously investigating and prosecuting Ponzi schemes.[16] Named after the notorious swindler Charles Ponzi, a **Ponzi scheme** is a scam that pays early investors returns from the cash coming in from subsequent investors. A common technique is to start a commodity pool and lure unwary, unsophisticated investors by promising them a generous return. Eventually, the whole scheme unravels and leaves behind a trail of cheated customers. Ponzi schemes have attracted special attention since 2008, when it was revealed that prominent stockbroker and financial adviser Bernard Madoff ran a giant Ponzi scheme that bilked investors for tens of billions of dollars.

10.4 | Manipulation in Futures Markets

In 1869, notorious financiers Jay Gould, James Fisk, and their co-conspirators tried to corner the gold market.[17] As told in "Gold at 160. Gold at 130" (*Harper's Weekly*, October 16, 1869), at that time, US currency was redeemable for gold. The federal government bought and sold gold to manage the money supply. Its trading essentially fixed the price in the relatively small $15 million gold market. Anticipating access to inside information on gold trading policy from the highest levels of the government through kickbacks and bribes, the conspirators bought up huge amounts of gold and attempted a market corner. The result was a two-week period of turmoil in the gold market that brought America's foreign trade, which used gold as the medium of exchange, to a virtual standstill. To defuse a looming economic

[16] On May 21, 2009, the CFTC's acting director of enforcement Stephen J. Obie said, "The CFTC continues to devote substantial enforcement resources to bring to justice Ponzi schemesters who mercilessly steal from those who often times cannot afford to lose their investment. . . . We have seen an avalanche of Ponzi cases and have thus far in 2009 filed 23 such cases, and I expect more to be forthcoming." From www.cftc.gov/PressRoom/PressReleases/pr5659-09.

[17] Although this was not a market corner by our previous definition (see chapter 6), where shorts have difficulties in fulfilling their obligations to acquire and return the scarce securities, this was, nonetheless, considered a corner because many people needed to buy gold for a variety of purposes (like foreign trade), and they were forced to do so at the manipulated high price.

panic and restore normal conditions in the gold market, President General Ulysses Grant ordered the sale of gold to buy bonds. On September 24, 1869, minutes after the Treasury secretary's telegram instructing a sale of $4 million worth of gold reached the "Gold Room," the price of gold, which had earlier ranged between $160 and $162, fell to $133 per ounce. The day went down in history as Black Friday, and the speculators got a severe jolt.

This was just one incident. As we noted in chapter 6, market corners and short squeezes have a long history in financial markets. Market structure, the creation of shorts as futures get transacted, and supply variability for many of the underlying commodities make futures markets especially prone to price manipulation and trading abuses. We now discuss some well-known cases of manipulation in these markets. These cases give a sense of the range and types of manipulations that have occurred and may occur again in the future.

Great Western Food Distributors and Egg Futures

A court found Great Western Distributors Inc. guilty of manipulating the December 1947 egg futures contract at the CME. The key developments were as follows:

- The closing price of the December 1947 egg futures price was abnormally high compared to the January 1948 futures. Moreover, both the December 1947 futures price and the cash price of refrigerator eggs were abnormally high relative to the cash price of fresh eggs in December 1947. So *price abnormality* was determined largely based on historical price spreads.

- Near the end of the contract's closing, Great Western had 60 to 75 percent of the open interest and 45 to 50 percent of the cash deliverable supply. The court concluded that the company had *market dominance* in both futures and cash markets. Interestingly, the court excluded fresh eggs and out-of-town refrigerator eggs from the deliverable supply because the short would have to pay very high transportation costs to ship them to Chicago to satisfy delivery requirements.

- The trickiest part in any manipulation case is establishing intent. Here testimony of an employee of Great Western stating that he had instituted the whole scheme in the hope of making a profit was key.

How Onion Futures Got Banned

Onions smell and make you cry, but that's not the reason why onion futures do not trade in the United States. During the 1950s, farmers lobbied to pass legislation for banning these contracts because they were prone to manipulation. Here's the full story behind the onion futures ban.[18]

- On June 18, 1956, the CEA issued a complaint charging a New York onion grower, Vincent W. Kosuga, a Chicago produce distributor, Sam S. Siegel, and

---

[18] "History of the CFTC: Futures Regulation before the Creation of the CFTC," www.cftc.gov.

National Produce Distributors with: (1) an attempted upward manipulation of a November 1955 onion futures contract, (2) an attempted price stabilization manipulation of the November and December 1955 contracts, and (3) successful downward manipulation of a March 1956 contract (which began trading at $2.75 per fifty-pound bag in August 1955 but fell to 10 cents by mid-March 1956).

- An article titled "Odorous Onions" (*Time*, July 2, 1956) reports that the CEA asserted that:
  - In fall 1956, Kosuga and Siegel bought 928 carloads of onions and shipped them to and stored them in Chicago (this was 98 percent of the deliverable supply for onion futures in Chicago).
  - Then, Kosuga and Siegel asked thirteen onion growers to buy onions and threatened that they would dump their onion holdings and force prices down if the growers refused. The growers complied and bought 285 carloads for $168,000. In return, the manipulators promised to keep their onion stocks off the market until March 1956, thus supporting the long side of the market.
  - Next, Kosuga and Siegel double-crossed the farmers and switched to a short position in the market, to the extent of 1,148 carloads, in February 1956. The price fell to $1.02 a bag—they were engaging in "a conspiracy to depress the prices in order to cover their short position" in the March onion futures. They even "shipped some of their aging onions out of Chicago, had them culled, resorted and repacked, and then sent back to Chicago #151 to make it appear as though large quantities of new onions were pouring into town." The growers were stuck with onions that they had bought at a high price.

- On June 3, 1960, a USDA judicial officer found that the respondents performed the attempted stabilization and successful downward manipulation (cases [2] and [3]) but found insufficient evidence for the upward manipulation (case [1]). The duped onion growers' losses prompted the House Agriculture Subcommittee to hold a hearing, which eventually led to the Onion Futures Act of 1958, which banned onion futures trading.

The Hunts Silver Case

A Peruvian government firm Minpeco SA sued the Hunt brothers and "co-conspirators (including Arab sheiks)" for $150 million, charging that they conspired to corner the silver market. A jury found them guilty, and the Hunt brothers were given huge fines. A class-action suit was also filed on behalf of seventeen thousand investors. Eventually, in the late 1980s, two of the Hunt brothers filed for bankruptcy. The details were as follows (see Duffie [1989], pp. 335–9 and Edwards and Ma [1992], p. 198–9):

- Oil magnate H. L. Hunt, one of world's richest persons, had two wives. One of his wife's sons (referred to here as the Hunt brothers or the Hunts) had a mind-boggling net worth of over $5 billion in 1980 but ended bankrupt after the Silver Crisis.

- Several times during the 1970s, the Hunts took large long positions in both silver spot and futures markets and rolled their hedge forward (i.e., closed out a position in an expiring futures and then took an identical position in a distant-month futures contract). They also invested in a number of silver producers.

- This pattern was repeated in 1979–80 on a grander scale. The Hunt brothers (1) held large long positions in silver futures (at times reaching nearly 250 million ounces—an amount equivalent to fifty thousand COMEX contracts [that traded in the Commodity Exchange] and much more than US domestic silver consumption), (2) held dominant long positions in many near-month contracts, (3) demanded delivery when contracts matured, and (4) made supply scarce by holding huge quantities of silver bullions and coins. Some twenty futures commission merchants helped the Hunt brothers, and the firms Bache Halsey Stuart Shields and Merrill Lynch handled over 80 percent of the Hunt brothers' spot and futures trading.

- Silver prices shot up. Historically, silver prices rarely crossed $10 per ounce, but the spot and futures price of silver rose from about $9 per ounce in July 1979 to $35 per ounce at year's end, peaking at over $50 per ounce in January 1980. Apparently, the Hunts had cornered the market.

- The exchanges consulted the CFTC and took steps to break the squeeze. Margin requirements were increased, stricter position limits were imposed, and the Hunts were forced to implement **liquidation-only trading**. They could not increase their silver position unless it was for hedging purposes. They also had to exit the market as contracts expired. By the end of March, silver prices dropped to $11 per ounce. It was this decline in silver prices that destroyed the Hunts' wealth.

Salomon Brothers and US Treasury Securities

The US Treasury securities market is one of the world's largest and most liquid securities markets. Legal scholars like Easterbrook (1986) and Fischel and Ross (1991) have opined that it is nearly impossible to corner the supply of Treasuries. Unfortunately, the impossible occurred as Salomon Brothers Inc., a major player in the Treasury securities market, admitted deliberate and repeated violations of Treasury auction rules beginning in 1990.

Here is how the Salomon short squeeze in the May 1991 auction of the two-year US Treasury note worked:

- There are three related markets for buying Treasuries: (1) the sealed bid Treasury auction, (2) the preauction when-issued market, and (3) the postauction resale market (see chapter 2).

- Salomon took considerable pride in its trading prowess and boasted itself to be the greatest bond trading firm in the world. To ensure broad participation (read stop Salomon's dominance!) in its auction of Treasury securities, the Treasury enacted **the 35 percent rule** for each auction: a single bidder cannot bid more than 35 percent of the offering at any particular yield or be awarded more than 35 percent of the offering.

- Many Wall Street firms sell Treasuries to their clients in the when-issued market, enter the auction with a net short position, and buy securities in the auction to fulfill their obligations. This is a profitable business because the price usually goes down slightly from the when-issued price owing to greater supply in the auction—but not in this auction. Salomon submitted aggressive bids at a yield of 6.81 percent when the notes were trading on a when-issued basis at approximately 6.83 percent directly prior to the auction (which means Salomon paid more for the auctioned securities).

■ Salomon evaded the 35 percent rule by submitting multi-billion-dollar bids on behalf of clients and then transferred those securities to its own account at cost. Salomon ended up controlling 94 percent of the competitively auctioned securities. Having cornered the market, Salomon squeezed the shorts from the when-issued market by charging them a premium price for these notes when they came to cover their short positions in the postauction resale market.

■ Academics have tried to measure how much Salomon stood to gain from this squeeze. Studies estimate that this ranged between $5 million and $30 million (for details, see Jegadeesh 1993; Jordan and Jordan 1996).

■ The penalties to Salomon were enormous. Its reputation was badly bruised. Soon after the cornering allegations surfaced and federal agencies started investigating, regulators barred Salomon from making a market in various federal and state government securities, cutting off a major source of the company's income. Salomon stock, which was trading in the $50 to $60 range, soon plunged to $30. Billionaire Warren Buffett, a major shareholder of Salomon, flew in from Nebraska and took control. Several top executives lost their jobs, and many talented personnel left. Salomon admitted no wrongdoing other than violating Treasury auction rules and paid a staggering $290 million in fines. The once-feared Salomon now belongs to the past. It went through mergers and acquisitions and is now part of Salomon Smith Barney, which is a subsidiary of Citigroup. Even the name Salomon has been phased out.

Buying Cheese to Manipulate Milk Futures

Manipulation may involve separate but related markets. On December 16, 2008, the CFTC ordered Kansas City, Missouri–based dairy marketing cooperative Dairy Farmers of America (DFA) and two of its former top executives to pay $12 million to settle charges of attempted manipulation and speculative position limit violations:[19]

■ The CFTC found that from May 21 through June 23, 2004, DFA and its chief executive and chief financial officers tried to manipulate the price of the CME's Class III milk futures contracts maturing in June, July, and August 2004. They did this by buying block cheddar cheese on the CME cheese spot market.

■ These intermarket trades were found to be manipulative because the CME block cheese price plays a significant role in establishing Class III milk futures prices—a fact that is well known throughout the industry. Moreover, DFA's speculative holding of Class III milk futures contracts exceeded the CME's

[19] From www.cftc.gov/PressRoom/PressReleases/pr5584-08.

speculative position limit on several days in 2004, which ran afoul of the Commodity Exchange Act.

- The commission barred the executives and DFA from trading futures for several years and required DFA to implement a compliance and ethics program. The CFTC also fined two former executives of a DFA subsidiary $150,000 for aiding and abetting DFA's position limit violations.

Banging the Close

Technology has opened up new ways of manipulating prices. On July 24, 2008, the CFTC filed a complaint against Netherlands-based Optiver Holding, two of its subsidiaries, and three Optiver employees in a US district court, charging that the defendants had manipulated or attempted to manipulate NYMEX crude oil, gasoline, and heating oil futures contracts on nineteen separate instances in March 2007 and succeeded in creating artificial prices in at least five of those cases.[20]

The defendants traded three NYMEX energy futures contracts: the Light Sweet Crude Oil futures contract (Crude Oil, also referred to as West Texas Intermediate [WTI]), the New York Harbor Heating Oil futures contract (Heating Oil), and the New York Harbor Reformulated Gasoline Blendstock futures contract (New York Harbor Gasoline).

The CFTC alleged that the defendants employed a practice popularly known as **banging** (or **marking**) **the close**, which involves manipulating the prices by trading a large position leading up to the close followed by offsetting the position before the end of trading. The scheme had the following ingredients:

- It involved *Trading at Settlement* (TAS) contracts for crude oil, heating oil, and gasoline contracts. These are special futures contracts in which the counterparties decide at the time of trading that the contract price will be the day's settlement price plus or minus an agreed differential.[21] If you trade a TAS contract, you can offset it by trading a futures contract on the other side of the market.

- Computing settlement prices is tricky in many futures markets because of potential manipulation. The settlement prices for each of these three energy futures

---

[20] The CFTC filed a "Complaint for injunctive and other equitable relief and civil monetary penalties under the Commodity Exchange Act" on July 24, 2008, in the US District Court, Southern District of New York, demanding a jury trial against Netherlands-based Optiver Holding BV, two Optiver subsidiaries, and three Optiver employees. Our discussion is based on "Complaint: Optiver US, LLC, et al.," "CFTC Charges Optiver Holding BV, Two Subsidiaries, and High-Ranking Employees with Manipulation of NYMEX Crude Oil, Heating Oil, and Gasoline Futures Contracts" and "Case Background Information re CFTC v. Optiver US, et al." (www.cftc.gov/PressRoom/PressReleases/pr5521-08).

[21] NYMEX introduced *trading at settlement* contracts on heating oil and unleaded gasoline futures in March 2002 on a pilot basis and then expanded it to other energy futures. Initially available only for the spot month, TAS is usually available for the front two months. No TAS contracts are traded on the last trading day. In other words, for contracts that allow TAS trading, you have a choice—you can either decide to trade a regular futures contract (which would lock in that moment's futures price) or a TAS contract (which would trade at TAS price plus a price adjustment). See www.cmegroup.com for more information on TAS contracts. Other exchanges such as the Intercontinental Exchange also offer TAS contracts on many commodities, including cotton, oil, and orange juice.

contracts are determined using **the volume-weighted average prices** (**VWAP**) of futures trades occurring during the closing period (the **close**) for the contracts, which lasts from 2:28 to 2:30 PM. The defendants planned to control the VWAP and wrote about "bullying the market" in their recorded conversations and e-mails.

- The traders concocted a three-step system to make manipulative profits:
  - First, they would accumulate substantial positions in TAS contracts by trading at different times of the trading day.
  - Second, they would enter closing trades for approximately 20 to 30 percent of their contracts during the **pre-close** period, which are the dying minutes before the market enters the close.
  - Third, Optiver would sell 70 to 80 percent of its holdings during the close, which lasts from 2:28:00 to 2:29:59.

  In conjunction, these three steps manipulated prices so that Optiver could obtain profits from its trades.

- The CFTC alleged that the defendants had forced the futures prices lower on three instances and higher in two cases and made approximately $1 million in the process.

10.5 | Managing Commodity Markets

The economic definition of a speculator is someone who is trading and not hedging. For example, a trader who is short gold futures but does not hold gold in inventory is speculating. In contrast, if this trader holds gold in inventory for production purposes, then she is a hedger. Futures regulations regard speculators as "evil" and impose size limits on their positions—to preclude the accumulation of market power for the purposes of manipulative trading strategies. In contrast, they view hedgers as "saintly" and impose no such size limit restrictions. Although the economic definition of a speculator and hedger is unambiguous, in practice, it is not always so easy to tell speculators from hedgers.

Prior to the 1990s, the CFTC and exchanges classified futures traders like farmers, manufacturers, and commodities dealers (with legitimate hedging needs) as **commercial traders**, and the CFTC allowed them to trade virtually any number of exchange-traded futures contracts desired. These were the hedgers. By contrast, they imposed speculative position limits on all other traders, who were viewed as **noncommercial traders**. These were the speculators. Obviously, noncommercial traders could be hedgers using the economic definition, but they were not considered as such.

However, beginning in the 1990s, two new kinds of traders, commodity index traders and swap dealers, entered the markets and changed these traditional classifications. **Commodity index traders** include institutional players like endowment funds and pension funds. They diversify their portfolios by adding commodity exposures through passive long-term investment in commodity indexes. **Swap dealers** play a more complex role—on one hand, they compete with the futures markets by offering customized derivatives to their clients, but on the other hand, they also trade in the futures markets to hedge risks in their swap books. Typically affiliated with a bank or other large financial institution, swap dealers operate as market makers by being ready to act as the counterparty to both commercial and noncommercial traders.

A change in the regulatory framework took place in 1991, when the CFTC granted a Goldman Sachs subsidiary J. Aron the same exemption from specula-tive position limits as those allowed to commercial traders (see "A Few Speculators Dominate Vast Market for Oil Trading," *Washington Post*, August 21, 2008). J. Aron was into commodity merchandising and traded swaps as a part of its business. It planned to sell to a large pension fund a commodity swap based on an index that included wheat, corn, and soybeans, all of which fell under federal specula-tive position limits. To hedge this short commodities exposure, it planned to buy exchange-traded futures contracts on those commodities. The CFTC classified this as a bona fide hedge because the swap dealer had demonstrated that the positions were "economically appropriate to the reduction of risk exposure attendant to the conduct and management of a commercial enterprise." Once the door was opened, more exemptions followed.

10.6 | Summary

1. Futures contract trading in the United States is a highly regulated activity. It is governed by the Commodity Exchange Act. The Commodity Futures Modern-ization Act of 2000 made substantial changes to the existing legislation. It made it possible to trade security futures products, it eased up on regulations of OTC derivatives, it allowed new types of futures trading facilities and products, and it facilitated clearing of OTC derivative trades. In 2010, the Dodd-Frank Wall Street Reform and Consumer Protection Act was passed to increase OTC deriva-tive market regulation in response to the financial crisis of 2007–2009.

2. Market regulation in the United States is implemented at the highest level by the federal regulatory agency, the Commodity Futures Trading Commission, and then by a self-regulatory organization, the National Futures Association, the exchanges themselves, and finally, at the grassroots level, by brokers handling customer accounts.

3. The Commodity Futures Trading Commission monitors the markets, inves-tigates and prosecutes alleged violations of the Commodity Exchange Act and commission regulations, and punishes violators with fines and (temporary or permanent) banishment from the futures industry.

10.7 | Cases

Amaranth Advisors: Burning Six Billion in Thirty Days (Richard Ivey School of Business Foundation Case 908N03-PDF-ENG, Harvard Business Publishing). The case provides students with (1) a deeper understanding of commodity futures markets in general and of natural gas markets in particular, (2) an introduction to hedge funds and an insight into the largest hedge fund collapse in history, and (3) an introduction to such concepts as liquidity risk, value-at-risk, spread trades, and the use of derivatives.

Mylan Lab's Proposed Merger with King Pharmaceutical (Harvard Business School Case 209097-PDF-ENG). The case considers how hedge funds and other investors may use derivatives to separate votes from shares and the legal, moral, and economic implications of this ability.

Rogue Trader at Daiwa Bank (A): Management Responsibility under Different Jurisprudential Systems, Practices, and Cultures (University of Hong Kong Case HKU442-PDF-ENG, Harvard Business Publishing). The case examines the importance of complying with regulations in the context of a major foreign bank operating in the United States.

10.8 | Questions and Problems

10.1. Give two reasons why futures markets may not be started on a commodity. Give an example of such a commodity to support your answer.

10.2. What is price discovery with respect to the trading of a futures contract? Give an example of its use.

10.3. Explain why hedging and speculation are like "two sides of the same coin."

10.4. Why were the early regulators of US commodity futures markets directly under the control of the US Department of Agriculture? How did this change in 1974?

10.5. What is the CFTC's mission?

10.6. What is the National Futures Association and how does it differ from the CFTC?

10.7. If regulation is bad for business, why does the National Futures Association put a significant amount of regulation on its members?

10.8. Suppose that you are an economist working for the CFTC and an exchange has proposed to introduce futures trading on individual stocks. Would you accept this proposal? Give reasons for your answer.

10.9. Suppose that it is five minutes to the close of trading for the day and you are a trader on the exchange floor. Your client gives you a sell order for one thousand contracts. You are holding one hundred contracts long. How can you take advantage of this situation?

10.10. Summarize what happened in the Great Western Food Distributors manipulation case.

10.11. Summarize what happened in the Hunts silver case.

10.12. Summarize what happened in the Salomon Brothers manipulation.

10.13. Why is the possibility of manipulation bad for the trading of futures contracts? Give an example of what can go wrong.

10.14. Given the existence of the OPEC cartel, is the market for the spot price of oil a competitive market, or not? Do you think the OPEC cartel activities affect the futures price of oil? Explain why or why not.

10.15. Why are onion futures not traded?

10.16. Is selling an insurance contract speculating? Is buying an insurance contract hedging? Are insurance contracts a benefit to society? Explain why or why not.

10.17. Explain why speculation in futures trading is analogous to selling insurance contracts. Does this imply that speculation with futures is beneficial or harmful to the economy? Explain your answer.

10.18. Do futures contracts need to be regulated? If yes, what can go wrong without regulation? Give an example to explain your answer.

10.19. Can you identify common features in the three manipulation stories involving forward or futures markets? How can "authorities" intervene and break squeezes in a typical situation?

10.20. Briefly describe the events and developments that led to a spectacular increase in oil prices in the new millennium. In your answer, discuss the role of speculators.

11

The Cost-of-Carry Model

11.1 | Introduction

To trade a forward contract on a spot commodity and not get ripped off, one needs to know the *fair* forward price. But how can one determine this price? We claim that if you understand the concepts of present and future value introduced in chapter 2, then you should already be able to guess the answer. Give up? The answer is that the forward price should be the *future value* of the spot commodity today! Why? If all's right with the world, then this should be today's price for buying the spot commodity in the future. This chapter shows that under a reasonable set of assumptions, including the assumption of no arbitrage studied in chapter 6, this guess is correct.

The technique we use to prove this guess is called the **cost-of-carry model**, and it is the simplest and first application of the arbitrage-free pricing methodology studied in chapter 6. Later chapters will use the same no-arbitrage approach to price more complex derivatives such as options.

The *cost-of-carry model* is derived via a **cash-and-carry argument** whereby the underlying commodity is purchased with borrowed cash and held until the forward contract's maturity date, thereby it is carried into the future. When held, various **costs-of-carry** (or **carrying charges**) such as interest on the borrowed cash and storage costs for the commodity are paid. At the forward contract's maturity, the borrowing is repaid, yielding unfettered ownership of the commodity. The cost of purchasing the commodity in the future by the cash-and-carry strategy is easily determined. All of the ingredients are known at the start (the spot price, interest rates, storage costs). Because this strategy generates the same payoff as the forward contract, the forward price can be determined from the cost of constructing the strategy today; otherwise, an arbitrage opportunity exists. All's right with the world after all!

The reasonable assumptions underlying the cost-of-carry model are frictionless markets, no cash flows to the underlying commodity, no counterparty credit risk, and competitive markets. Interest rates and commodity prices are random. Financial assets that satisfy the no cash flow assumption include stocks that pay no dividends over the forward's life and zero-coupon Treasury bonds that mature after the delivery date. The final results of this chapter use the cash-and-carry argument to value a forward contract at an intermediate date and to establish a link between two different maturity forward prices on the same commodity. We adopt a data–model–arbitrage approach that is used throughout the book. This approach starts with a numerical example (data). Next, we replace numbers with symbols (model). Finally, we generate arbitrage profits when securities are mispriced (arbitrage).

11.2 | A Cost-of-Carry Example

"Home is where one starts from," wrote T. S. Eliot in *Four Quartets*. The cost-of-carry model uses the concept of no arbitrage as our home. We develop the basic cost-of-carry model via either of two equivalent techniques, which we labeled the *law of one price* and *nothing comes from nothing* in chapter 6. These simple techniques rest on several key assumptions. We discuss the assumptions after illustrating the ideas involved.

Example 11.1 uses the law of one price. It considers two different ways of buying a stock in the future: buying a forward contract or buying the stock in the spot market and carrying it to the future. We create these two positions so that we can extract the forward price by equating their values today. We replace numbers with symbols to obtain the basic cost-of-carry model.

EXAMPLE 11.1: Finding the Forward Price Using the Law of One Price

The Data

- Today is January 1. Suppose that we go to the *forward market* and buy a one-year forward contract on Your Beloved Machine Inc. (YBM) stock. Unless noted otherwise, all computations are on a per stock basis. No cash changes hands today because the forward price F is the fair price. At maturity, we receive one YBM stock worth $S(T)$ from the forward's seller by paying him the forward price F dollars. Record the cash flows (in Table 11.1a) as 0 today (time 0) and $S(T) - F$ on the delivery date (time T). This is portfolio A, which we label as the market traded forward.

- Alternatively, one can buy one share of YBM in the *spot market* today and carry it to the future. Assuming that YBM pays no dividends over the forward's life, the cash flows (in Table 11.1b) are -100 today and $S(T)$ on December 31.

- To create a future liability equal to the forward price, borrow its present value by shorting zero-coupon bonds. This cash inflow reduces today's net payment. If the interest rate is fixed at 6 percent per year, the cash flows are $F/(1 + \text{interest}) = F/1.06$ today and $-F$ a year later (see Table 11.1b). These long stock and short bond positions make up portfolio B, which is our synthetic forward.

- By the law of one price, to prevent arbitrage, portfolios A and B with identical future payoffs must have the same value today. Consequently,

$$-100 + F/1.06 = 0$$

$$\text{or } F = 100 \times 1.06 = \$106 \tag{11.1}$$

The forward price equals the amount repaid on the loan for the stock purchase.

Table 11.1: Creating Portfolios with Equal Payoffs

TABLE 11.1A: Portfolio A: Long Market Traded Forward

Portfolio	Today (Time 0) Cash Flow	Delivery Date (Time T) Cash Flow
Long forward (forward price F)	0	$S(T) - F$
Net cash flow	0	$S(T) - F$

TABLE 11.1B: Portfolio B: Long Stock and Short Bonds (Long Synthetic Forward)		
Portfolio	Now (January 1)	Maturity Date (December 31)
Buy YBM in the spot market (stock price $S = \$100$)	-100	$S(T)$
Short zero-coupon bonds to borrow the present value of the forward price F (interest rate is 6% per year)	$F/1.06$	$-F$
Net cash flow	$-100 + F/1.06$	$S(T) - F$

The Model

- Use symbols to generalize. Replace 100 with S and 0.06 with R to get our first result (stated later as Result 11.1):

$$F = S(1 + R) \tag{11.2a}$$

$$\text{or } S = BF \tag{11.2b}$$

where $(1 + R)$ is the future value of $1 invested today (which is also known as the dollar return) and $B \equiv 1/(1 + R)$ is today's price of a zero-coupon bond that pays $1 at maturity.

A Graphical Approach

- One can also develop the cost-of-carry model using payoff diagrams. Recall from chapter 5 that these diagrams plot "Payoffs" (or gross payoffs) along the vertical axis and the "stock price on the delivery date," $S(T)$, along the horizontal axis.

- First, buy one YBM stock. Its payoff is a straight line starting at the origin and rising at a 45° angle. If the stock is worthless on the forward's delivery date, then you get 0; if it's worth $5, then you get $5, and so on (see Figure 11.1). Next, draw another diagram under this depicting the payoff from a short bond position with a future liability of F dollars. This is a line parallel to the horizontal axis that begins at $-F$ on the vertical axis.

- Now, vertically add up the payoffs from these two graphs. The short bond trade lowers the long stock's payoff by a parallel downward shift of F dollars. Consequently, the combined payoff starts at $-F$ along the vertical axis, rises at a 45° angle to the horizontal axis at F, and keeps increasing. The combined position is a *synthetic forward* because its payoff on the maturity date is identical to that of a market-traded forward contract. Because the forward price F is chosen so that the traded forward contract's value is zero, to prevent arbitrage, the synthetic forward must also have zero value. Setting the synthetic forward's cost of construction $(S - BF)$ to zero yields the cost-of-carry model.

Arbitrage Profits

- What would you do if the forward price differs from the arbitrage-free price? Suppose that an errant trader quotes a forward price of $110. As this is higher than $106, sell the overpriced forward, buy the stock, and borrow the present value of $110. Then

$$-100 + 110/1.06 = \$3.77$$

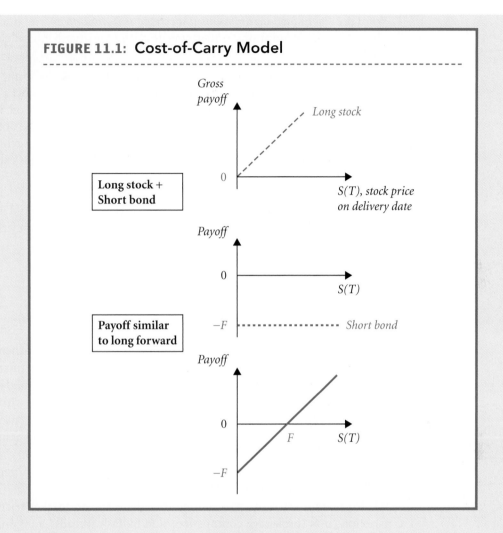

FIGURE 11.1: Cost-of-Carry Model

is your immediate arbitrage profit—and you have no future cash flow because the short traded forward and the long synthetic forward's cash flows exactly offset each other. If the trader quotes $100 instead, reverse the trades and make $-100/1.06 + 100 = \$5.66$. Any forward price other than the arbitrage-free price of $106 creates an arbitrage opportunity.

Instead of using the law of one price, if we subtract portfolio A from portfolio B, we could use the nothing comes from nothing principle instead. This technique creates a new portfolio that has a zero value in the future and therefore must also have zero value today.

This example illustrates that there is nothing magical about the forward price. The forward price is linked to today's spot price via the cost-of-carry model, which only includes the interest cost in this simple setting. This simple model raises several questions:

1. *What are the hidden assumptions underlying this argument?* The next section discusses the assumptions underlying this and most other models in this book.

2. *Is the cost-of-carry model useful in other contexts?* In its simple form, it generates the forward prices for **investment assets** like currencies and stocks. Forward prices for **consumption or production assets** like corn, copper, and oil, which are primarily held for consumption or as inputs to production, may be obtained by modifying this model to incorporate additional carrying charges such as transportation and storage costs as well as *convenience yield* benefits. This extension is presented in chapter 12.

The remainder of this chapter generalizes this example to build the cost-of-carry model. First, we need to introduce the hidden assumptions underlying our arguments.

11.3 | The Assumptions

A **model** is a simplified or idealized description, often expressed mathematically, that helps us understand and explain reality. Financial models serve this purpose. Being abstractions, models rely on simplifying assumptions. To understand a model, one needs to understand the assumptions. First, they show when to use, when not to use, and how not to abuse a model. Second, they give a sense of when the model fails and the biases that may result. Understanding the assumptions changes a model from a black box to an open box.

We need the following assumptions for derivative pricing models in general and for forward pricing models in particular.

A1. No market frictions. We assume that there are no market frictions like transaction costs (brokerage commissions and bid/ask spreads), margin requirements, short sale restrictions, taxes that may be levied at different rates, and assets that are not perfectly divisible.

The frictionless market assumption helps us create a benchmark model against which other models can be compared. Once you understand this ideal setting, you can add back frictions to better capture reality. In addition, it's a reasonable first approximation for many institutional traders. For example, professional traders at major investment banks have far lower transaction costs than do small investors. Professionals often trade within the bid/ask spread, they have less stringent margin requirements, they can avoid short sale restrictions, and their trading profits are taxed at a uniform rate. Of course, there are large start-up costs for maintaining such operations, but we do not focus on these costs here. To quote an economics professor's pet expression, "They are important but not directly relevant for our purpose." Furthermore, frictionless markets may now be a reasonable first approximation for small traders in some markets because of the accumulated advances in information technology that have drastically reduced trading costs.

A2. No credit risk. Also known as **default risk** or **counterparty risk**, this is the risk that the counterparty to a transaction will fail to perform on an obligation. We assume that there is no credit risk.

If credit risk exists, cash flows become less predictable, and we stumble at the onset. No credit risk is a reasonable approximation for exchange-traded derivatives, whose performance is guaranteed by a clearinghouse. Vigilant exchange officials, alert brokers and dealers, the customer's margin account, and the exchange's capital minimize this risk. Over-the-counter derivatives, however, may possess substantial credit risks. In practice, prudent actions, such as trading only with counterparties that have high credit ratings, having well-documented legal contracts, and requiring parties to keep collateral, reduce this risk. Pricing derivatives in the presence of credit risk is an area of active research. Jarrow and Turnbull (1995) developed a popular model for pricing credit derivatives that is used in industry, known as the reduced form approach. This extension is discussed in chapter 26.

A3. Competitive and well-functioning markets. In a competitive market, traders' purchases or sales have no impact on the market price; consequently, traders act as price takers. In a well-functioning market, traders agree on zero-probability events, and price bubbles are absent. We assume competitive and well-functioning markets.

In a competitive market, a trader is individually too small for his trades to have a quantity impact on the price and to possess market power. Consequently, he acts as a price taker vis-à-vis the market. The competitive markets assumption is the workhorse of modern economics, and many powerful results are derived from it. As illustrated via the futures market manipulations described in chapter 10, this assumption does not always hold. Pricing securities when traders have market power and when prices can be manipulated is a difficult exercise. One must take into account bargaining and strategic interactions—ideas and concepts that are outside the scope of this book. Consequently, the cost-of-carry model is a poor model in such a setting. Focusing on competitive markets avoids these complications.

By agreeing on zero-probability events, we mean that traders must agree on events relevant to the commodities price movements that *cannot happen*. For example, an event might be "the commodity's price exceeds $1,000 in two weeks' time." If one trader believes that this event cannot happen, then all traders must all agree that this event cannot happen. When traders disagree on such **zero-probability events**, they cannot come to a consensus regarding what is considered an arbitrage opportunity. This destroys our key argument for proving results (see assumption 5).

We also assume that there are no asset price bubbles. A **price bubble** happens when an asset's price deviates from its intrinsic or fundamental value. The **fundamental** or **intrinsic value** can be defined in two equivalent ways. The first is the present value of its future cash flows. The second is the price one would pay if, after purchase, you had to hold the asset forever. If you reflect on these, it becomes clear that they are equivalent definitions. A difference between the market price and the fundamental value only occurs if one believes that selling (retrading) can generate a higher value than holding forever—this difference is the bubble. The terminology reflects the popular belief that such deviations are short-lived and surely burst, like a soap bubble. It has been shown that many Internet stocks exhibited a price bubble during the 1990s, when they reached astonishingly high values despite an absence of dividend payments and continued reports of zero or negative earnings. We rule out price bubbles because our pricing arguments fail to hold in this context.

Pricing derivatives in noncompetitive markets and in the presence of bubbles is a daunting task and a hot area of research. We return to this topic again in chapter 19, when we discuss pricing options.

A4. No intermediate cash flows. As a first pass, we assume that the underlying commodity has no cash flows over the forward contract's life. This is a simplification that we will need to relax.

When considering stocks, most companies reward their shareholders by paying dividends. US companies tend to be fairly conservative about their dividend policies. They pay fixed dividends and dislike tinkering with either the payment date or the amount, lest the market infers something negative from their actions. In addition, many commodities receive income or cash flows—coupon-paying bonds or consumption/production assets that provide convenience yields are prime examples. Moreover, consumption/production assets tend to incur transaction, storage, insurance, and other costs. For the present, we ignore these costs.

A5. No arbitrage opportunities. This assumption's meaning is self-evident.

These five assumptions form the bedrock of our analysis, and they determine the validity of our models. Talented traders regularly monitor the market and check whether the assumptions are satisfied. If the assumptions aren't satisfied, the pricing models and trading strategies may fail to work. In such a situation, one should not rely on the model's implications. If one is using the model to hedge, the hedge may no longer work. An optimal strategy may be to close out the position, rethink, and come back another day. As in Kenny Rogers's song, "you got to know when to hold 'em, know when to fold 'em, know when to walk away, know when to run."

11.4 | The Cost-of-Carry Model

We now assemble the different components that we have developed to formally derive our forward pricing model. If the notations seem abstract, remember the data from our example (S is \$100, $1 + R = 1/B = \$1.06$) to get a numerical feeling for the argument.

The Model Setup

The **cost-of-carry forward pricing model** has the following structure:

- There are two dates. At time 0 (which is today), we start the clock, trade, and create one or more portfolios of securities. The clock stops at some later time T. We collect the cash flows from the traded securities, compute our gains and losses in dollar terms, take the cash, if any, and go home. We measure time in years. Note that $(T - 0) = T$ is also the time to maturity, or the life of the contract, computed in terms of years or its fraction.

- Three securities trade: a stock, a forward on the stock, and a zero-coupon bond. Unless specified otherwise, we use the terms *asset, commodity, stock,* and *spot* somewhat interchangeably. Spot trading and a cash market transaction also have the same meaning.

- The stock price is $S(0) \equiv S$ today and $S(T)$ at time T. The forward contract starts today and a forward price $F(0, T) \equiv F$ is determined in the market such that no cash changes hands. This is the fair price. To understand why this price is fair, suppose the contrary. If it were not fair, then one side of the contract would be entering into the contract with an immediate loss and with no additional compensation. Conversely, the other side of the contract is entering with an immediate gain and at no additional cost. This is an arbitrage opportunity and, thus, an unfair price.

- The contract ends on the *delivery or maturity date* by cash settlement or physical delivery (we view them as equivalent transactions for payoff computations). The long's payoff is $S(T) - F$ and the short's payoff is $-[S(T) - F]$, which are equal and opposite.

- Traders can borrow or lend funds at the risk-free rate by shorting or buying zero-coupon bonds. Let $B(0, T) \equiv B$ be today's price of a zero-coupon bond that pays one dollar at time T. Let $1 + R \equiv 1 + R(0, T)$ be the dollar return obtained at time T from investing one dollar in the zero today. Notice that it's the inverse of the zero's price: $1 + R \equiv 1/B$.

- As in chapter 2, we will use R and B to move funds across time—multiplying today's cash flows by $1 + R$ gives their future values (compounding), whereas multiplying future cash flows by B gives their present values (discounting).

We utilize the law of one price (from chapter 6) to formally derive the cost-of-carry model.

Using the Law of One Price

To find the arbitrage-free forward price F, let's consider two different ways of buying the stock in the future without a cash flow today. First, buy a forward contract. This cashless trade obliges you to acquire the stock by paying the forward price on the delivery date (this is our portfolio A). Second, buy the stock today and finance this purchase by borrowing. This costless transaction gives you the stock and a liability equal to today's stock price with its accrued interest on the same maturity date (this is our portfolio B). These transactions are summarized as follows:

> Portfolio A (*buy forward*): Zero-cost portfolio (today) → Get the stock, pay the forward price F (write this as $S[T] - F$) (maturity date)

> Portfolio B (*buy the stock, sell the zero-coupon bonds to finance the stock purchase*): Zero-cost portfolio (today) → Get the stock, repay the loan (write this as $S[T] - S[1 + R]$) (maturity date)

Note that these two final payoffs only differ by the constant $[F - S(1 + R)]$ and that this constant is known today. These two portfolios with identical initial values (zero) must also have the same value on the delivery date (see Figure 11.1). If one of these values differs, it opens up an arbitrage opportunity that will be exploited by vigilant traders standing ready to pick up money lying on the street—they will trade until the two prices are equal and no arbitrage remains. This implies that *the forward price must equal to today's stock price repaid with accrued interest*, that is, $[F = S(1 + R)]$.

Because this is such an important technique, we formalize this argument in Extension 11.1 using the nothing comes from nothing principle.

EXTENSION 11.1: A Formal Derivation of the Cost-of-Carry Model

The formal derivation shows the arbitrage opportunity underlying the cost-of-carry model if the result is violated. Assuming no arbitrage, then, precludes such violations. There are two possible violations of the cost-of-carry model, yielding two opposite inequalities. Using these inequalities, it is then easy to show the arbitrage opportunity that results, and our argument applies.

This more formal approach to proving the cost-of-carry model is useful when considering market frictions like taxes, transaction costs, different borrowing and lending rates, and short selling restrictions. Chapter 12 provides an example of this.

We demonstrate the formal argument using the nothing comes from nothing principle.

Using Arbitrage Tables for the Zero-Value Portfolio

One can create a zero-value portfolio by subtracting portfolio B from portfolio A. We do this in an arbitrage table (see Tables 11.2a and 11.2b). This approach has the advantage that it reveals the links between the fair cost-of-carry price and the trading strategy that captures arbitrage profits from mispricings.

- *Buy a forward contract.* This trade has zero cash flow today (time 0) and a payoff of $S(T) - F$ on the delivery date (time T). You get an asset worth $S(T)$ and incur a liability equal to the forward price F dollars, which is denoted by $-F$. Jot down these cash flows in Table 11.1a.

- *Eliminate the stock by selling it short.* You receive S today and obtain a future liability $-S(T)$ on the maturity date (Table 11.1b records these cash flows, and Figure 11.2 shows this chain of reasoning).

TABLE 11.2A: Arbitrage Table for Reverse Cash-and-Carry

Portfolio	Today (Time 0) Cash Flow	Maturity Date (Time T) Cash Flow
Buy forward	0	$S(T) - F$
Short sell stock	S	$-S(T)$
Invest proceeds from short selling by buying risk-free zero-coupon bonds	$-S$	$S(1 + R)$
Net cash flow	0	$S(1 + R) - F$

TABLE 11.2B: Arbitrage Table for Cash-and-Carry

Portfolio	Today (Time 0) Cash Flow	Delivery Date (Time T) Cash Flow
Sell forward	0	$-[S(T) - F]$
Buy stock	$-S$	$S(T)$
Borrow to finance spot purchase	S	$-S(1 + R)$
Net cash flow	0	$F - S(1 + R)$

- *Invest the proceeds from short selling in the bond market.* Buy zero-coupon bonds to lock in an interest rate. This gives $S(1 + R)$ on the delivery date, where $(1 + R)$ is the dollar return.

This portfolio is costless to create and worth $[S(1 + R) - F]$ on the delivery date. To prevent arbitrage, a portfolio that is worthless today with a constant value at delivery must also have zero value on the delivery date. We can prove this by showing the arbitrage opportunities that result if the value at delivery is not zero. This requires considering two cases, when the value at delivery is positive and when it is negative.

Establishing a Lower Bound

Suppose the portfolio given in Table 11.1a takes a positive value on the delivery date. This positive inflow is an arbitrage opportunity—a costless portfolio rewarding you with a positive payoff. Thus, when today's spot price plus the carrying charge is greater than the forward price, you can capture arbitrage profits by buying the relatively underpriced forward contract and selling the relatively overpriced replicating portfolio (by short selling stock and buying bonds).

The process is called a **reverse cash-and-carry** because our chain of reasoning involves short selling the asset and making good on this obligation in the future. Consequently, to rule out arbitrage, the portfolio cannot take a positive value in the future so that the payoff

$$S(1 + R) - F \leq 0$$

$$\text{or } S(1 + R) \leq F \tag{1}$$

Thus $S(1 + R)$ is a lower bound to the forward price F.

Establishing an Upper Bound

What if our zero-cost portfolio takes a negative value on the delivery date instead? This turnabout requires a reversal of the argument. If today's spot price plus carrying cost is less than the forward price, you can capture arbitrage profits by selling the relatively overpriced forward contract and buying the relatively underpriced replicating portfolio. The new payoff has the same magnitude but with a positive sign on the delivery date (see Table 11.1b).

This process is called **cash-and-carry** because we purchase the spot and carry it to the future by paying the necessary carrying costs. Therefore, to prevent arbitrage, the new portfolio's payoff cannot take a positive value on the delivery date:

$$F - S(1 + R) \leq 0$$

$$\text{or } F \leq S(1 + R) \tag{2}$$

Thus $S(1 + R)$ forms an upper bound to the forward price F.

The Pricing Model

The only way $S(1 + R)$ forms both an upper and a lower bound to F (i.e., inequalities [1] and [2] jointly hold) is when they are equal, or

$$F = S(1 + R) \tag{3}$$

This is our cost-of-carry model. It states that the *forward price is the future value of the spot price*.

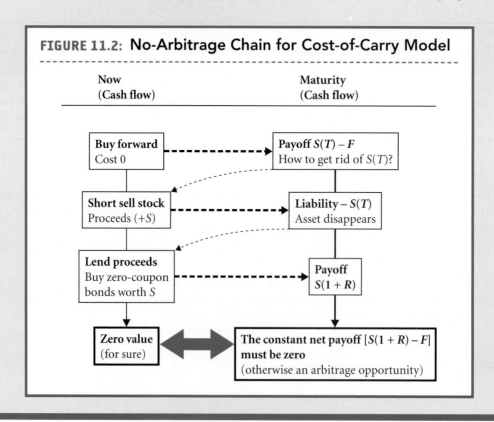

FIGURE 11.2: No-Arbitrage Chain for Cost-of-Carry Model

Different Methods for Computing Interest

Remember from chapter 2 that we can compute B and R by using various discrete or continuous compounding methods. So far, we have computed B by using simple interest, which is the easiest case. We can also use continuous compounding by writing the zero-coupon bond price B or dollar return $1 + R$ as

$$B = e^{-rT} \text{ and } 1 + R = 1/B = e^{rT}$$

where r is the continuously compounded interest rate.

We gather all our results together.

RESULT 11.1

- -

Cost-of-Carry Model

Consider a forward contract on a commodity beginning at time 0 (today) and maturing at time T. Then

$$F = S(1 + R) \tag{11.2a}$$

Equivalently,

$$S = BF \tag{11.2b}$$

where $F \equiv F(0, T)$ is today's forward price for delivery at time T, $S \equiv S(0)$ is today's spot price of the underlying commodity, R is the dollar return at time T from investing \$1 in a zero-coupon bond today, and $B \equiv 1/(1 + R)$ is today's price for a zero-coupon bond that pays \$1 at time T.

Dollar returns are computed by the formulas

$$\text{Simple interest: } 1 + R = (1 + i \times T) \tag{11.2c}$$

$$\text{Continuously compounded interest: } 1 + R = e^{rT} \tag{11.2d}$$

where i is the simple interest rate per year and r is the continuously compounded interest rate per year.

Continuously compounded interest rates give a better approximation than do simple interest rates when compounding is computed daily. Moreover, we will show in the next chapter that this assumption lays the foundation for developing a variety of cost-of-carry models, including those written on indexes and commodities that incur storage costs and have convenience yields. The next example uses this formula to compute forward prices and capture arbitrage profits.

EXAMPLE 11.2: Finding Forward Prices and Capturing Arbitrage Profits

The Forward Price

- Consider the data from Example 11.1. The YBM stock price S is $100 today, a newly written forward on YBM matures in one year, and the simple interest rate is 6 percent per year. Then expression (11.2c) gives

$$\text{Dollar return } 1 + R = (1 + 0.06 \times 1) = \$1.06 \text{ and the}$$

$$\text{zero-coupon bond price } B = 1/1.06 = \$0.9434$$

By expression (11.2a), the forward price is

$$F = S(1 + R) = \$106.00$$

which is the same price as in Example 11.1.[1]

Capturing Arbitrage Profits

- Suppose that an errant trader quotes a forward price of $110. Then the spot and forward prices are too far apart. The spot is $100, while the discounted forward price $BF = \$103.77$ so that $S - BF = -\$3.77$.

- One can profit by doing a cash-and-carry arbitrage. Simultaneously buy the relatively underpriced stock, sell the relatively overpriced forward, and short zero-coupon bonds with a maturity value of $110 to balance the portfolio. Immediately collect $3.77. The net payoff will be zero for sure on the maturity date.

- Want to take your profits at maturity? Modify the bond position—short only enough zero-coupon bonds to finance the spot purchase, and make $F - S(1 + R) = \$4$ on December 31.

- Now, consider a different scenario—use the same data as before, except let the forward price be $100. Here $S - BF = \$5.66$, suggesting that either the stock price is too high or the forward price is too low (or both). Do a reverse cash-and-carry arbitrage by selling the stock, buying the forward, and buying zero-coupon bonds. As before, the bond position can be tinkered with to take the profit now or later. If you buy zero-coupon bonds with a face value of $100, then you will make $-BF + S = \$5.66$ of arbitrage profits today.

[1] If this is continuously compounded interest, r is 6 percent, and then by (11.2a) and (11.2d), the forward price is $F = S(1 + R) = 100 \exp(0.06 \times 1) = \$106.18$.

The Arbitrage Table Approach

The previous examples motivate an arbitrage table approach for solving problems and proving results. By systematically recording cash flows at different dates, an arbitrage table enables direct comparison, which makes proofs easier. Although there are no set rules, we suggest three possible methods:

1. *Understand the problem, using numbers if necessary.* What do the different variables mean? Which security generates what cash flows? When? Draw a timeline. Plug dates and variable values into the formula to get a feel for the result to prove

or how to make arbitrage profits. Use your intuition to sense which variables are overvalued or undervalued, using our "buy low, sell high" dictum.

2. *Interpret cash flows.* If the cash flows are positive today and zero on the delivery date, then you have made arbitrage profits. Alternatively, if cash flows are zero today and have a positive value on the delivery date, then you also have made arbitrage profits.

3. *Gather variables to one side of the equality and set the net cash flows at one of the dates to zero.* It is inconvenient to work with nonzero cash flows at both the starting and ending dates. Life is easier if you gather variables to one side of an equality so that you can set today's or the delivery date's net cash flows to zero. Then, to prevent arbitrage, the other net cash flow must also be zero.

11.5 | Valuing a Forward Contract at Intermediate Dates

Suppose you bought a forward contract some time back, but it still has remaining life. How much it is worth today? If the spot price soars or plunges, how would it affect the forward's value?

We use a cash-and-carry argument to develop a formula that answers these questions. The model may be used for **mark-to-model accounting**, which requires the valuation of assets and liabilities on a daily basis, a practice that is increasingly becoming popular with companies and regulators. Example 11.3 introduces a numerical example that is then generalized to obtain the relevant result.

EXAMPLE 11.3: Valuing a Forward Contract at an Intermediate Date

The Data

- Suppose that you bought a forward on January 1. Three months have passed. Meanwhile, the underlying price has increased. Of course, your long position has gained value because you entered into a contract to buy the underlying at a fixed price, but the underlying has become more valuable. What is the exact value of your long position today? Let us consider an example that uses some of our previous data:
  - On January 1 (time 0), YBM's stock price $S(0)$ was $100.
  - The simple interest rate i was 6 percent per year.
  - You purchased a newly written forward contract on YBM that matures in a year on December 31 (time T).
  - The forward price was set at $F(0) = S(1 + R) = \$106$.

- Three months have passed; today is April 1 (time t). YBM has rallied and the new stock price $S(t) \equiv S$ is $120. You are still obliged to buy YBM by paying $F(0)$ in nine more months ($T - t$ is 0.75 years). But what about the value of your forward, $V(t) \equiv V$? If you sell your position, how much should you get paid?

- Draw a timeline to keep track of the cash flows (see Figure 11.3). The stock price increase has made the long forward position more valuable, the exact amount of which is determined by the arbitrage table (see Table 11.3).

- Begin the portfolio construction as if you are buying the forward position by paying V. This has a payoff of $S(T) - F(0) = S(T) - 106$ on December 31. Next, short sell the stock. This gives $120 today but creates a liability $-S(T)$ on the delivery date. The stock disappears, but you still have to come up with $106. This can be arranged by lending the present value of $106 via buying zero-coupon bonds. Notice that on April 1, the price of a zero-coupon bond that pays $1 on December 31 is

$$B \equiv B(t, T) = 1/(1 + 0.06 \times 0.75) = \$0.9569^2$$

- The portfolio has a zero value on December 31. To prevent arbitrage,

$$-V + 120 - 0.9569 \times 106 = 0 \qquad (11.3)$$
$$\text{or } V = \$18.56$$

The Model

- Replace numbers with symbols in expression (11.3) to get

$$-V + S - BF(0) = 0$$
$$\text{or } V = S - BF(0)$$

---

[2] Instead, if we assume a continuously compounded interest rate r of 6 percent per year fixed, then $F(0) = SR = 100 \times \exp(0.06 \times 1) = \$106.18$, $B(t, T) = \exp(-0.06 \times 0.75) = \$0.9560$, and $V = 120 - 0.9560 \times 106.18 = \$18.49$. There is a 7 cent difference in value of a forward contract because of the different ways of computing interest.

This is Result 11.2, which is formally stated as follows.

RESULT 11.2

- -

Valuing a Forward Contract at an Intermediate Date

Consider a forward contract created at time 0 and that matures at time T. On an intermediate date t (today),

$$V = S - BF(0) \qquad (11.4a)$$

where $F(0)$ is the forward price at time 0 for a contract maturing at time T, $V \equiv V(t)$ is today's value of a long forward position, $S \equiv S(t)$ is today's spot price of the underlying commodity, and $B \equiv B(t, T)$ is today's (time t) price of a zero-coupon bond that pays one dollar at time T.

In the case of simple interest, B is $1/[1 + i(T - t)]$, where i is the interest rate per year. In the case of continuously compounded interest, B is e^{-rt}, where r is the interest rate per year.

TABLE 11.3: Valuing a Forward Contract That Began Earlier

Portfolio	Today, April 1 (Time t) Cash Flow	Delivery Date, December 31 (Time T) Cash Flow
Buy forward (worth $V[t]$ or V to long), forward price $F(0) = \$106$	$-V$	$S(T) - 106$
Short sell spot ($S = 120$)	120	$-S(T)$
Lend present value of forward price $BF(0)$	$-(1/1.045)106$	106
Net cash flow	$-V + 120 - 0.9569 \times 106$	0

This is a more general version of our first result. If we set $V = 0$, as happens on a forward contract's starting date, then Result 11.1 becomes a special case of Result 11.2. Using Results 11.1 and 11.2 together, we can obtain another insight. First, we note that Result 11.1, when applied to the time t forward price, implies that $S = BF(t)$. Second, substitution of this fact into expression (11.4a) and some

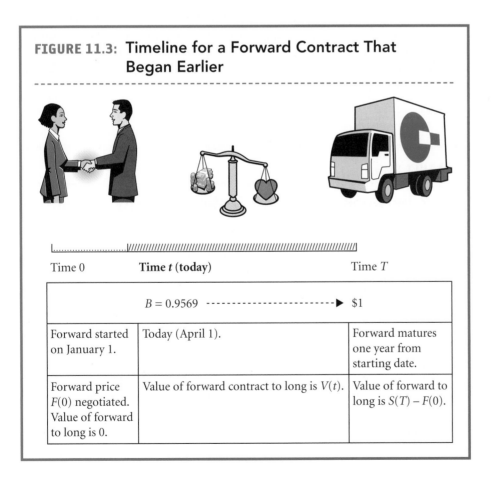

FIGURE 11.3: Timeline for a Forward Contract That Began Earlier

Time 0	**Time t (today)**	Time T
	$B = 0.9569$ ----------------------▶ $1	
Forward started on January 1.	Today (April 1).	Forward matures one year from starting date.
Forward price $F(0)$ negotiated. Value of forward to long is 0.	Value of forward contract to long is $V(t)$.	Value of forward to long is $S(T) - F(0)$.

simple algebra yields an alternative expression for the value of the forward contract at time t:

$$V = B[F(t) - F(0)] \tag{11.4b}$$

This expression shows that the value of the forward contract increases by the present value of the change in the new delivery price, $F(t)$, relative to the original delivery price, $F(0)$. The present value is needed to reflect the fact that the payments are not made until the delivery date, time T.

11.6 | Linking Forward Prices of Different Maturities

Consider a market in which the cost-of-carry model determines forward prices with high accuracy. If we change the delivery date, the model gives us a series of forward prices corresponding to contracts maturing on those different dates. We can also use the cash-and-carry argument to develop a formula linking these prices. This enables us to find one forward price when only the carrying cost and another forward price are known. When several forward contracts exist on the same commodity, this model also enables us to determine whether all the forward prices are correct or some of them are out of line. The model is given as our Result 11.3. A simple proof follows the result.

RESULT 11.3

- -

Link between Near- and Distant-Maturity Forward Prices

Consider two forward contracts that begin at time 0 (today), mature on the near-maturity date (time n) and the distant-maturity date (time d), respectively. Then, standing at time n,

$$F(0, n) = \frac{B(0, d)}{B(0, n)} \times F(0, d) \tag{11.5}$$

where $F(0, n)$ and $F(0, d)$ are the forward prices negotiated at time 0 for forward contracts maturing at times n and d, respectively, and $B(0, t)$ is the price of a zero-coupon bond at time 0 that pays \$1 at times $t = d$ and $t = n$.

The zero-coupon bond price B is $1/(1 + it)$ for simple interest and e^{-rt} for continuously compounded interest, where i and r are the respective annual interest rates.

Although we view this result as an application, it's also a generalization. If you set the near-maturity forward to be at its delivery date n, then by convergence of the basis, $F(0, n)$ becomes the spot price $S(n)$, $B(n, n) = 1$, and expression (11.5) gives back Result 11.1 at time n.

To prove Result 11.3, we just use Result 11.1 twice, once for time n and once for time d, getting the two equations

$$S(0) = B(0, d) \times F(0, d)$$
$$S(0) = B(0, n) \times F(0, n)$$

Setting these two equations equal and solving for $F(0, n)$ gives the result.

11.7 | Summary

1. We use no arbitrage via the law of one price and the principle that nothing comes from nothing introduced in chapter 6 to develop a forward pricing model. First, we create a securities portfolio to replicate a market-traded forward's payoff. To avoid arbitrage, the cost of the replicating portfolio must equal to the forward contract's arbitrage-free value. Equivalently, an alternative portfolio going long the forward contract and selling short the replicating portfolio (or vice versa) will have a zero value both now and in the future. Both approaches give the same price.

2. A portfolio consisting of a long stock, a short forward, and short some zero-coupon bonds can be created so that it has zero value on the forward's maturity date. To prevent arbitrage, it must also have a zero value on the starting date. The forward price is determined from this condition. This gives Result 11.1, which is the basic cost-of-carry model. It states that the forward price is the future value of the spot price or $F = S(1 + R)$.

3. The cost-of-carry model makes a number of assumptions: no market frictions, no credit risk, competitive and well-functioning markets, no dividends over the contract's life, and no arbitrage opportunities.

4. There are several ways of developing cost-of-carry models and solving arbitrage problems. We primarily use arbitrage tables, which systematically record cash flows at different dates.

5. We use the cash-and-carry argument to build more complex models. Result 11.2 states that the value of a forward contract at an intermediate date equals the spot price minus the discounted value of the old forward price or $V = S - BF(0)$. Result 11.3 states that when two different forward contracts are written on the same commodity but with different maturity dates, the near-maturity forward price is a fraction of the distant-maturity forward price or $F(0, n) = B(0, d)/B(0, n) \times F(0, d)$.

11.8 | Cases

American Barrick Resources Corp.: Managing Gold Price Risk (Harvard Business School Case 293128-PDF-ENG). The case discusses derivative usage for hedging by a gold mining company.

Banque Paribas: Paribas Derives Garantis (Harvard Business School Case 295008-PDF-ENG). The case explores issues connected with a broker-dealer setting up a derivatives subsidiary to achieve a credit rating.

Hedging Currency Risks at AIFS (Harvard Business School Case 205026-PDF-ENG). In this case a company considers managing foreign currency risks with derivatives.

11.9 | Questions and Problems

11.1. Today's price of gold in the spot market is $1,500 per ounce. The price of a zero-coupon bond maturing in one year is $0.95. What will be the one-year forward price for gold?

11.2. The current price of Your Beloved Machine's stock is $109. The continuously compounded interest rate is 5.25 percent per year. What will be the five-month forward price for YBM stock?

11.3. The spot price of silver is $30 per ounce. The simple interest rate is 6 percent per year. The quoted six-month forward price for silver is $31.

  a. What should be the arbitrage-free forward price for silver for a forward contract maturing in six months?

  b. Demonstrate how you can make arbitrage profits in this market.

11.4. Today's spot price of silver is $30 per ounce. The simple interest rate is 6 percent per year. The quoted six-month forward price for silver is $32. Transaction costs are $0.10 per ounce whenever spot silver is traded and a $0.25 per ounce one-time fee for trading forward contracts but no charges for trading bonds.

  a. Demonstrate how you can make arbitrage profits in this market if there are no transaction costs.

  b. If you have to pay transaction costs, demonstrate how you will make arbitrage profits or explain why you cannot make any such profits.

11.5. Suppose that the continuously compounded interest rate is 6 percent per year, and the nine-month forward price for platinum is $1,750. What is today's spot price of platinum?

11.6. What does the assumption of no market frictions mean? Is this assumption true in current commodity markets?

11.7. If the assumption of no market frictions is not true, then why should we study models using this assumption?

11.8. What is the competitive market assumption, and what adverse market behavior does it exclude?

11.9. What are the five assumptions underlying the cost-of-carry model for pricing forward contracts? Which of these assumptions are most likely to be satisfied in current commodity markets?

11.10. State the key result of the cost-of-carry model in your own words.

11.11. Today is January 1. Forward prices for gold forward maturing on April 1 is $1,500 per ounce. The simple interest rate is 6 percent per year. What would be the forward price for a forward contract on gold maturing on August 1?

11.12. Today is January 1. Forward prices for contracts maturing on April 1 and on October 1 are $103 and $109, respectively. The simple interest rate is 8 percent per year. Assuming the spot price is $100 today, demonstrate two ways in which you can make arbitrage profits from these prices.

11.13. Today is January 1. Forward prices for contracts maturing on April 1 and on October 1 are $103 and $109, respectively. On April 1, the price of a zero-coupon bond maturing on October 1 is $0.97. Assuming that the underlying interest rate is a constant interest rate, demonstrate one way of making arbitrage profits from these prices.

11.14. State the equation for the valuation of a forward contract in your own words.

11.15. Suppose you bought a forward on January 1 that matures a year later. The forward price was $214 at that time, and the simple interest rate was 7 percent per year. Six months have passed, and the spot price is now $150. What is the value of your forward contract today?

11.16. Suppose you trade a forward contract today that matures after one year. The forward price is $105, and the simple interest rate is 7 percent per year. If, after six months from today, the spot price is going to be $150 and the value of the forward contract is $20, demonstrate how you can make arbitrage profit from these prices.

11.17. The value of a forward contract that you have been holding for the last six months is $50 today. It matures in 3 more months. If today's spot price is $100 and the underlying interest rate is 5 percent, what was the forward price that you had negotiated when you purchased the contract six months back?

11.18. Explain the difference between the forward price and the value of a forward contract. How are they related?

11.19. What is the relation between forward prices of different maturities on the same underlying?

11.20. (Excel) For gold and silver, collect from the internet today's spot prices as well as futures prices for futures contracts maturing up to one year. Also collect Treasury bill prices of different maturities. Using the above data, perform the following for three of the most actively traded futures contracts for gold as well as for silver:

a. Assuming that interest is the only cost of carry, use Result 11.1 (Cost-of-Carry Model) of Chapter 11 to compute forward prices that correspond to the maturities of three of the most actively traded contracts for the two metals.

b. Compare these prices to the traded futures prices. Do they seem significantly different? If so, explain why.

Hints and Suggestions:

- New York spot price for gold and silver can be found on a metal dealer's (such as Kitco's) website.

- Futures prices can be obtained from an exchange's (such as the CME Group's) website www.cmegroup.com/market-data/index.html

- Daily Treasury bill rates data can be found from the US Treasury's website www.treasury.gov/resource-center/data-chart-center/interest-rates/Pages/TextView.aspx?data=billrates

- Use settlement prices wherever possible. If ask and bid prices are quoted for the spot or futures, take the average of the two.

- Exclude futures contracts maturing in the current month as they can have liquidity problems.

12

The Extended Cost-of-Carry Model

12.1 | Introduction

Cornell University is situated in rural upstate New York. The university campus is built on a hill overlooking beautiful Lake Cayuga and the city of Ithaca. The landscape is scenic, dotted with hills, valleys, and even a few gorges formed during the ice age. The winters are cold, snowy, and icy, which makes driving the roads treacherous. When choosing a car to own in Ithaca, a resident has many options to consider. Key among these options is the choice of rear-wheel, front-wheel, or four-wheel drive. To safely navigate the wintry roads, four-wheel drive is the preferred selection. Consequently, four-wheel drive cars are in great demand.

Analogous to an Ithacan deciding which car to buy in hilly Ithaca, when constructing a forward pricing model, one needs to consider the market setting carefully. Commodities differ in whether they have cash flows, storage costs, or convenience yields. Choosing the correct model for proper pricing and hedging requires matching the model's assumptions with market conditions. To do so otherwise leads to "treacherous driving" when using the model in practice.

Chapter 11 presented the arbitrage-free forward pricing model under the assumption that the underlying commodity has no cash flows, storage costs, or convenience yields over the forward contract's life. However, stocks and stock indexes pay dividends, bonds make coupon payments, foreign exchange prices are affected by both domestic and foreign interest rates, and physical commodities like corn or gold incur storage costs but may receive a convenience yield. The model in chapter 11 also assumed frictionless markets and equal borrowing and lending rates, but trading involves brokerage commissions as well as the bid/ask spread, and borrowing and lending rates differ. How does one modify the forward pricing model when these assumptions are relaxed to get a better approximation? The purpose of this chapter is to answer this question. We do this by relaxing assumptions A1 and A4 of chapter 11 and thereby incorporate dividends, storage costs, convenience yields, and market imperfections into our framework.

Although this additional complexity appears daunting, it isn't. The basic logic of the cost-of-carry model still applies, but with bells and whistles attached. Most of these extensions can be easily handled with only minor modifications to the basic model. By the end of this chapter, one should be able to choose the safest "vehicle" for forward pricing in realistic market "landscapes."

12.2 | A Family of Forward Pricing Models

The last chapter's cost-of-carry model includes interest as the only cost-of-carry and invokes a cash-and-carry argument to express the forward price as the future value of the spot price (Result 11.1). As in chapter 11, unless specified otherwise, we use the terms *asset*, *commodity*, *stock*, and *spot* interchangeably. Spot trading and a cash market transaction also have the same meaning. The cost-of-carry model relied on several critical assumptions that we repeat here for convenience:

A1. No market frictions

A2. No credit risk

A3. Competitive and well-functioning markets

A4. No intermediate cash flows

A5. No arbitrage opportunities

This chapter studies the determination of forward prices in a variety of settings. Figure 12.1 provides a road map for the family of forward pricing models considered. We first generalize the model by relaxing the fourth assumption with the introduction of dividends. This gives the first three extended models of this chapter:

- The simplest dividend model assumes that the underlying stock pays fixed dollar dividends on known dates (Result 12.1a). This model is useful for finding forward prices for contracts written on equities and coupon-bearing Treasury bonds that mature after the delivery date.

- The second dividend model assumes that the underlying stock pays continuous dividends (Result 12.1b). It's helpful for finding forward prices when the underlying is a stock index.

- An important application of the second model is to determine forward prices for foreign currency forward contracts (Result 12.2).

The dividend model paves the way for richer models. One such extension is storage costs for holding a commodity mainly used for consumption or production like copper, corn, or crude oil. Storing the physical commodity may also provide a *convenience yield* like the ability to keep a production process running in times of temporary shortages. We include these costs and benefits to build further extensions of the model (Results 12.3 and 12.4). Last, we introduce market frictions such as brokerage costs, differential borrowing and lending rates, and limited access to proceeds from short sales. Here buys and sells are no longer symmetric. Well-defined prices give way to ranges within which arbitrage-free forward prices must lie (Result 12.5).

12.3 | Forwards on Dividend-Paying Stocks

Most mature US companies pay their shareholders regular dividends (see chapter 3 for a discussion of dividends). Companies dislike tinkering with the payment date or the dividend amount to minimize the possibility that markets will

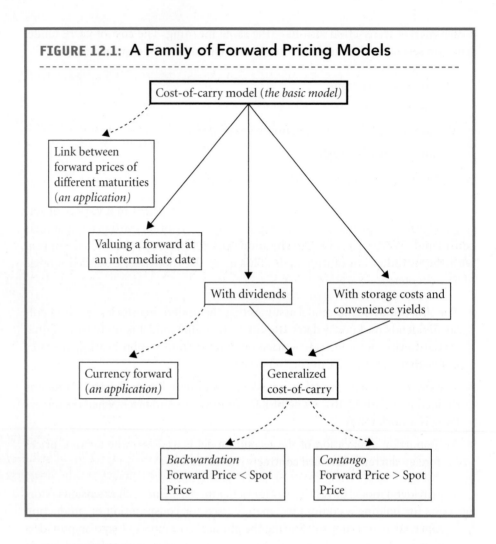

FIGURE 12.1: A Family of Forward Pricing Models

ascribe negative reasons for these actions and penalize the stock price. Firms like to wear the face of an English monarch from which you can read nothing (see Extension 12.1 for a discussion of some of the issues connected with dividend policy). Consequently, fixed payment dates and fixed dollar dividends are reasonable assumptions for mature companies. Many assets, such as Treasury notes and bonds, have highly predictable cash flows and may be similarly modeled.

The Cost-of-Carry Model with Dollar Dividends

Consider a company that pays a fixed dollar dividend on a future date decided in advance. A dividend payment actually involves several dates including the declaration date and the report date (see Extension 12.1). For our purposes, we only need to focus on the ex-dividend date, which is the cutoff for buying the stock with the dividend. Recall our discussion from chapter 3.

- Buying the stock before it goes ex-dividend date gives the share plus the dividend; purchasing after this deadline gives the share without the dividend.

- On the ex-dividend date, the cum-dividend stock price equals the ex-dividend stock price plus the dividend (see Result 3.1).

Dividends create an extra cash flow from holding the stock. If one adjusts the stock price for this cash flow, the standard argument follows. Example 12.1 shows how to do this. The resulting pricing model is identical to our cost-of-carry model, except that the stock price net the present value of the dividend replaces the stock price in the basic model.

EXAMPLE 12.1: The Forward Price when the Underlying Pays a Fixed Dollar Dividend

The Data

- Consider the data from Example 11.1. Your Beloved Machine Inc.'s (YBM) stock price S is $100 today (January 1, time 0), and the simple interest rate is 6 percent per year. Consider a newly written forward contract on YBM that matures in one year (December 31, time T).

- Now, assume that the stock pays a dividend div of $1 in three months (April 1, time t_1). Figure 12.2 gives the timeline for these cash flows. Table 12.1 accommodates this dividend by adding an extra column to our arbitrage table.

- To determine the forward price, we use the nothing for nothing arbitrage principle. We create a portfolio that has zero net payoffs on all future dates. To handle the dividend, we need to borrow cash to generate a future liability just equal to the dividend payoff. Here are the details:
  - Buy one share of YBM. This gives a dividend div = $1 after three months and a stock worth $S(T)$ after one year.
  - Zap the dangling dividend by borrowing its present value. As $B_1 = 1/(1 + 0.06 \times 0.25) = \$0.9852$ is the price of a zero-coupon bond maturing in three months, record the cash flows as $B_1 \text{div} = \$0.9852$ today and $-\$1$ on the ex-dividend date.
  - Sell YBM forward to eliminate it from the portfolio on the maturity date.
  - Finally, get rid of the forward price F by borrowing its present value. Jot down the cash flows as $BF = (1/1.06)F$ today and $-F$ after one year.

- To prevent arbitrage, today's net cash flow must also be zero:

$$-100 + 0.9852 \times 1 + 0.9434F = 0 \qquad (12.1)$$
$$\text{or, } F = \$104.96$$

The Model and Arbitrage Profits

- Replace numbers with symbols in (12.1) and rearrange terms to get

$$S - B_1 \text{div} = BF \qquad (12.2)$$

- Suppose a dealer forgets to adjust for the dividend and quotes a forward price of $106. To obtain arbitrage profits, create the portfolio given in Table 12.1. This has a short position in the overpriced dealer-quoted forward and a long position in the synthetic forward. Then

$$-S + B_1 \text{div} + BF$$
$$= -100 + 0.9852 + (106/1.06)$$
$$= \$0.9852$$

The present value of the dividend is the immediate arbitrage profit.

- If the quoted forward price is less than the arbitrage-free price, reverse the trades to capture the arbitrage profit.

Formalizing this example gives our first result.

RESULT 12.1A

Cost-of-Carry Model with Dividends

Consider a forward contract written today on a stock that pays a fixed dollar dividend div on a known future date. Then

$$S - B_1 \text{div} = BF \qquad (12.2)$$

where today (time 0) $\leq$ ex-dividend date (time t_1) $\leq$ maturity date (time T), S is today's spot price, F is today's forward price for time T, and $B_1 \equiv B(0, t_1)$ and $B \equiv B(0, T)$ are today's prices of zero-coupon bonds maturing on the ex-dividend and the delivery dates, respectively.

The zero-coupon bond price B is $1/(1 + iT)$ in the case of simple interest and e^{-rT} for continuously compounded interest, where i and r are the annual interest rates. B_1 is computed by replacing T with t_1 in these expressions.

EXTENSION 12.1: Dividend Policy

Quarterly dividend payments are a regular feature for US corporations. A quarterly stock dividend involves multiple dates. The dividend **declaration date** is when a company's board of directors announces that a dividend will be paid to all shareholders registered on some future **record date**. To reduce the possibility of mailing dividend checks to the wrong person, brokers and the exchange set up an **ex-dividend date**, usually two business days before the record date. If you buy the stock before it goes ex-dividend, you get the share along with the dividend (also called buying the share *cum-dividend*). If you buy after this deadline, then you get the stock without the dividend (also called buying the share *ex-dividend*).

In 1956, a study based on a survey of major US industrial companies by Professor John Lintner found that the dividend decision was guided by well-established policies and practices and not by a company's retained earnings. Most managers believe that the market prefers a stable or gradual growth in dividends. Hence managers try to avoid changes in dividend rates that might be reversed within a year or two, and they pay dividends to attain target dividend payout ratios. The **payout ratio** is the ratio of dividends to earnings per share. These empirical findings support the fact that most US companies dislike tinkering with the date or the amount of the dividend.

A seminal 1958 paper by Nobel laureates Franco Modigliani and Merton Miller, known as Modigliani–Miller or M&M, argued that dividend policy should not affect firm value because dividend payments can be replicated, at no extra cost, by an investor selling some stocks in an otherwise identical, non-dividend-paying firm. To prevent arbitrage, these firms must have equal values. To prove these results, one needs to assume that a firm's investment policy is fixed and known to investors, there are competitive and frictionless markets, and so on. Aren't these similar to the assumptions needed for developing derivative pricing models by the no-arbitrage principle? Of course they are (and this is not by chance!).

Since the early 1960s, economists have been relaxing the various M&M assumptions and studying security prices and dividend behavior. Brickley and McConnell (1987, 1989) state that these studies address three related questions:

1. Does the level of dividends affect firm value?

2. Do changes in the dividend level affect firm value?

3. Does the choice of payout method (cash payout vs. share repurchase vs. stock dividend or any other form of payment) affect firm value?

For example, a dividend increase may have a number of possible effects. Some countries like the United States tax dividends twice: once on corporate profits and once again on personal income. Higher dividends may mean a loss of value to shareholders because more money is being paid to the government. But what happens if shares are held by tax-exempt individuals and institutions or by people whose income is so low that they do not pay income taxes? Then the issue of double taxation does not arise, and a dividend change would be greeted with an indifferent shrug.

Yet another possibility is signaling. Following the pioneering works of Akerlof, Spence, and Stiglitz, the ideas of asymmetric information, adverse selection, and signaling have been applied to study dividend policy. Given cautious dividend policy, a dividend increase could signal rosy prospects: a company is likely to raise dividends only if it can sustain the new level in future years. You may have noticed that this argument is similar to that given by managers in Lintner's 1956 study. What about deliberately raising dividends to signal higher profitability to investors who may be imperfectly informed about the firm? Wouldn't this jack up the stock price? No—this cannot happen in a signaling equilibrium. For the signal (like "raising dividend") to be meaningful, it must have a cost (such as "higher tax burden"). A credible signal is hard to mimic and costly to do. Only those "good" firms who can bear the cost will increase dividends; "bad" firms who cannot bear the cost will not. Investors realizing this react appropriately.

Dividend policy is a highly debated and much researched area in modern corporate finance. We know a lot about dividend policy, and yet there is much that we do not understand. In the last chapter of their classic text *Principles of Corporate Finance*, Richard Brealey and Stewart Myers (2003) give a list of "10 Unsolved Problems in Finance." The sixth unsolved problem stares glaringly back at us: *how can we resolve the dividend controversy?*

We can easily extend this to accommodate more dividends. Suppose that the stock pays another dividend div_2 at time t_2 before the forward matures. Then, the result gets modified to

$$S - (B_1\text{div}_1 + B_2\text{div}_2) = BF \tag{12.3}$$

where div_1 has a subscript to link it with the payment date and B_2 is today's price of a zero maturing on the second ex-dividend date. In its most general form,

$$S - (\text{Present value of all dividends over the forward's life}) = BF \tag{12.4}$$

Why adjust for dividends? We do these adjustments because dividends differently impact the stock and the forward: the long stock earns dividends but the long forward doesn't. Once you take out the dividends accruing to the stock, it puts both positions on the same footing, and our familiar cost-of-carry argument

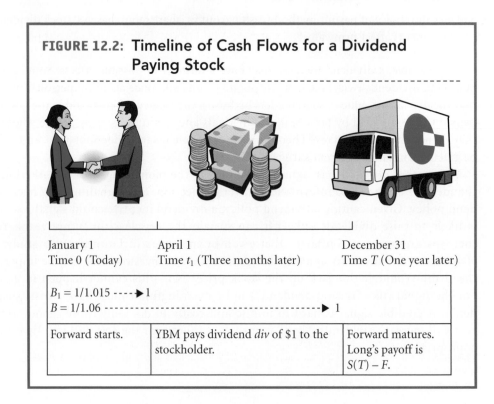

FIGURE 12.2: Timeline of Cash Flows for a Dividend Paying Stock

January 1 Time 0 (Today)	April 1 Time t_1 (Three months later)	December 31 Time T (One year later)
$B_1 = 1/1.015$ ---▶ 1 $B = 1/1.06$ ------------------------▶ 1		
Forward starts.	YBM pays dividend *div* of $1 to the stockholder.	Forward matures. Long's payoff is $S(T) - F$.

TABLE 12.1: Arbitrage Table for Finding the Forward Price of a Dividend-Paying Stock

Portfolio	Today, January 1 (Time 0) Cash Flow	Dividend Date, April 1 (Time t_1) Cash Flow	Delivery Date, December 31 (Time T) Cash Flow
Buy stock, get dividend div after three months	-100	1	$S(T)$
Borrow present value of the dividend B_1div today	$(1/1.015) \times 1$	-1	
Sell forward	0		$-[S(T) - F]$
Borrow present value of forward price BF	$(1/1.06)F$		$-F$
Net cash flow	$-100 + 0.9852 \times 1 + 0.9434F$	0	0

applies. Next, we introduce forwards on indexes. For these contracts, the dividend adjustment is more complex.

The Cost-of-Carry Model with a Dividend Yield

This section studies forward contracts on indexes. Modern portfolio theory (MPT; say it quickly and it comes out as "empty!") pioneered the idea of investing in diversified portfolios that replicate the returns on stock market indexes. An **index mutual fund** (or a **stock index fund**) pursues this objective by holding a basket of securities in the same proportion as the index. The fund's share price is usually determined at day's end. An **exchange traded fund** (**ETF**) strives to do the same, but it trades continuously on an exchange (see Extension 12.2 for a discussion of these funds).[1] Indexes and index funds underlie a large number of derivative securities, including forward contracts.

What is the arbitrage-free forward price of such an indexed portfolio? Unfortunately, the dividend adjustment method outlined in the previous section, which assumes that the dividends and their payment dates are nonrandom, works poorly for an index because there are too many dividends. This section, therefore, develops an alternative approach that accommodates random dividends and random payment dates. This modification uses dividend yields and the continuously compounded version of the cost-of-carry model (see chapters 3 and 11, respectively). To apply this modification, we first need to understand how to adjust an index's value for continuously paid dividends. And this, in turn, requires a discussion of synthetic index construction.

---

[1] Extension 6.1 of chapter 6 discusses indexes in greater detail. The purpose and scope of ETFs have broadened over time. For example, one can now find ETFs that match the performance of an index focusing on an industry sector (such as biotechnology or computer) and replicate the returns from holding a commodity (such as silver or gold).

EXTENSION 12.2: Index Mutual Funds and Exchange-Traded Funds—"Can a Monkey Do It?"

Index Mutual Funds

In April 2000, Vanguard Group's passively managed 500 Index Fund overtook Fidelity Investment's actively managed Magellan Fund to become the largest mutual fund in the United States. Since its inception in 1976, its objective has been to match the performance of the S&P 500 index. In an amusing anecdote, an investor once mistook the fund manager George "Gus" Sauter for a phone representative and said, "Listen, you and I both know a monkey could run an index fund" (see "The Match Game: Can a Monkey Do It? Index-Fund Managers Still Get No Respect—As Billions Flow In or Out, Equaling S&P 500 Results Becomes Tricky Business—Beating the Stock Pickers," *Wall Street Journal*, January 28, 1997). In reality, creating and maintaining such a replicating portfolio, called **indexing**, is a challenging endeavor. Consider indexing the S&P 500. Such a portfolio has to invest in five hundred US stocks in the same proportions as contained in the index. For a total dollar investment, indivisibility of share units may make it difficult to match exactly the proportions. In addition, the managers of the index often change its composition for reasons such as improving the index and accounting for mergers and acquisitions. Mimicking these changes in real time (to match exactly the index's performance) is a difficult task.

Some index funds modify the index-matching strategy to boost performance. Such index-modifying strategies include (1) buying futures instead of stocks when futures are cheaper, (2) picking up extra income by lending securities, (3) temporarily holding a bit more of a thinly traded stock than is called for in a benchmark, (4) waiting a day or two to make a purchase if there are lots of buyers scrambling for shares, and (5) buying stocks being added to an index in advance of the effective date of those changes. Detractors point out that such strategies may not always work. For example, a Vanguard bond-market index fund trailed its benchmark by 2 percent in 2002 when the strategy of varying sector weightings backfired.

Professional money managers frown on indexing and deride it as guaranteeing average performance. However, there is a fly in the ointment. Despite all the resources that go into professional stock selection, empirical research has found that most money managers fail to consistently beat a broadly defined index on a risk-adjusted basis. Paradoxically, it's the money spent on research and transaction costs from trading that drags performance down.

In contrast, index funds have been quite successful in keeping down these costs. For example, in fall 2004, expense ratios for large mutual funds tracking the S&P 500 index were 0.18 percent or 18 basis points at the Vanguard Group and 7 to 10 basis points at Fidelity Investments, while an average comparably sized fund investing in similar stocks charged an expense ratio of 1.21 percent. The **expense ratio** measures the funds expenses as a percentage of its net asset value. Expenses include management and administrative fees but exclude transaction costs.

Exchange-Traded Funds

Barring some exceptions (like Fidelity's sector funds, which are hourly priced), mutual funds are priced after the market closes. Consequently, they aren't nimble enough for arbitrage trading purposes. This impediment is overcome by *ETFs*, which are securities giving the holder fractional ownership rights over a basket of securities. The Securities and Exchange Commission (SEC) legally classifies ETFs as open-end companies or unit investment trusts (which we defined in Chapter 6, section 6.5), but they trade on exchanges like closed-end funds. ETFs behave like regular stocks. They trade continuously during trading hours, they can be shorted, they may be traded on margin, and they can even have derivatives written on them.

Although ETFs are simple, elegant, and easily traded securities, their creation and maintenance is a complex process:

- The process is managed by a **fund sponsor** or **manager** who submits a detailed plan to the SEC and gets its approval. The sponsor manages the fund, reinvests dividends, and maintains oversight. Sponsors are usually big firms like Barclays Global Investors, State Street Global Advisors, and Vanguard Group.

- Next, an **authorized participant** buys a large portfolio of securities, places them in a custodial bank, and gets a **creation unit** in exchange. Many creation units are usually constructed.

- Creation units are decomposed into ETF shares, typically twenty-five thousand or more. ETF shares are sold on exchanges, where retail investors like you and me can buy them.

- ETF shares are sold in two ways: (1) in the secondary market or (2) by collecting enough ETF shares to assemble a creation unit and then selling the creation unit back to the ETF, to get the basket of securities that underlies the unit. This limited ability to redeem shares is a reason why ETFs cannot describe themselves as mutual funds.

ETFs put the no-arbitrage principle to work—arbitrage ensures that an ETF's price will not stray too far from its net asset value. For example, if the demand for an ETF slackens and it sells at a discount to net asset value, arbitrage profits can be created by buying up ETF shares to make up a creation unit, exchange them for the underlying securities, and sell those securities at a profit.

Although the SEC has allowed the creation of actively managed ETFs since 2008, most ETFs seek to match some market index. In this respect, they are similar to index mutual funds. ETFs tend to have lower annual expenses than mutual funds. A brokerage fee is charged when an ETF is purchased or sold. In contrast, most mutual funds do not charge fees for initial investments. However, ETFs are more tax-efficient than mutual funds. If an investor sells a large number of shares, then the fund manager must sell securities in the fund to raise money, resulting in capital gains for all investors. But redemption of ETFs is just like selling a stock—it will not burden other investors with unwanted capital gains. For these reasons, it is hard to compare ETFs and index mutual funds in terms of their superiority as an investment vehicle.

The first exchange-traded fund, Toronto Index Participation Units (TIPS 30), was introduced in 1990. The first US ETF, Spider (Standard & Poor's depositary receipt or SPDR), whose objective was to match the returns on the S&P 500, was introduced in 1993. Since the 1990s, ETFs have proliferated and taken the industry by storm. Popular ETFs like the Nasdaq 100 and Spider have since joined the ranks of the largest investment funds in the United States.

A Synthetic Index

An index is a portfolio of stocks (or assets) formed according to some rules. A **synthetic index** is a portfolio created for the purpose of replicating the returns on a traded index. Indexes come in two varieties: those that adjust for dividends and those that do not. **Total return indexes**, like Merrill Lynch's TRAKRS and Germany's DAX, assume that all disbursements from the portfolio's stocks, including regular dividends, get reinvested in the index portfolio. For total return indexes, the reinvestment assumption effectively removes the dividends from consideration because there are no cash flows. In this case, forwards on total return indexes can be priced using the no cash flow assumption, and the results of chapter 11 apply.

However, most indexes, including the Dow Jones Company's and Standard and Poor's, make no adjustment for regular cash dividends. In this case, dividends need to be explicitly considered. The trick is to compute the value of the index today (time 0), excluding the present value of the dividends paid over the life of the forward contract. To compute this adjustment, it is helpful first to consider how such an index's value changes if all dividends are reinvested, as in a total return index.

Let the value of the index today without reinvestment be $S(0)$ and its value at time T be denoted $S(T)$. Assume that it pays a continuous dividend yield of δ percent per year. For comparison purposes, consider an otherwise identical index with the same time 0 value $I(0) = S(0)$. For this index, however, assume that all of the continuously paid dividends are reinvested back into this index. Let us call this the synthetic total return index. Because the dividends are reinvested into $I(T)$, its value at time T will exceed that for the index where dividends are not reinvested, that is, $I(T) > S(T)$. In fact, using Result 3.2, we know that

$$I(T) = S(T)\, e^{\delta T}$$

Note that $S(0)$ represents the present value of the index at time T *plus the dividends*. To get the present value of the index, less the continuously paid dividends over the life of the forward contract, we just remove the dividend yield term; that is,

$$\text{present value of } S(T) = S(0)\, e^{-\delta T}$$

This expression gives us the modified "stock price" to use in the forward pricing model.

The proof that this represents the present value of the time T index value without the dividends consists in showing that this equals the *cost of constructing* a trading strategy in the index with no intermediate cash flows that gives a payoff exactly equal to $S(T)$ at time T. To obtain no intermediate cash flows, just buy the index at time 0 and reinvest all dividends back into the index. This creates a synthetic total return index. But we are not quite done. We need also to adjust the initial number of units purchased so that we get the right payoff at delivery, after reinvesting the dividends. If we purchase $e^{-\delta T} < 1$ units of the index at time 0, for a value of $e^{-\delta T} S(0)$ then the time T value of the position in the synthetic total return index will be

$$\text{(Units) Price} = e^{-\delta T} I(T) = e^{-\delta T} S(T)\, e^{\delta T} = S(T)$$

This is the desired result. *Notice that this is a quantity adjustment in contrast to the price adjustment used previously for dollar dividends.*

This modification assumes that the dividends on the index are paid over the year at a uniform rate (see Figure 12.3). Although some dividends are smaller, while others are larger, this is a reasonable assumption if there are sufficiently many stocks in the index and dividends are paid randomly over time. Newspapers and other information vendors regularly report these dividend yields. For example, on May 25, 2007, the Dow Jones Industrial Average, Nasdaq 100, and Standard and Poor's 500 (S&P 500) had dividend yields of 2.25 percent, 0.48 percent, and 1.89 percent, respectively.[2]

Example 12.2 uses this stock price modification to determine the forward price on an index. In practice, an index derivative usually has a multiplier, for example, the Chicago Mercantile Exchange's S&P 500 futures is $250 times the S&P 500 index level, and if the previous day's futures price is 1,000 and today's price is 1,000.10, then the long would have $250(1,000.10 - 1,000) = \$25$ credited to her brokerage account. As we have done before, we ignore the multiplier and do calculations on a per unit basis.

EXAMPLE 12.2: The Forward Price for an Index with a Dividend Yield

The Data

- Consider a fictitious "INDY index" obtained by averaging stock prices and a synthetic index "INDY spot" that replicates its performance. INDY's current level S is 1,000, and the index does not reinvest dividends. A newly written forward contract on the index matures in a year (time T). Let the continuously compounded interest rate r be 6 percent per year.

- Stocks constituting INDY index paid $20 of dividends last year and are expected to pay the same this year. Then, the dividend yield $\delta = 20/1,000 = 0.02$ or 2 percent per year.

- If you buy $e^{-\delta T} = e^{-0.02 \times 1} = 0.9802$ units of INDY spot *and reinvest the dividends on a continuous basis*, then you will have one unit of the index worth $S(T)$ at year's end.

- Table 12.2 records the following trades in an arbitrage table:
  - Sell the forward contract on the INDY index. This gives a zero value at time 0 and $-[S(T) - F]$ on the delivery date T.
  - Buy 0.9802 units of INDY spot, and record the cash flows as $-0.9802 \times 1,000 = -980.20$ today. Reinvest all dividends until delivery back into the index to get $S(T)$ on the maturity date.
  - Borrow the present value of F. A zero-coupon bond maturing one year later is worth $B = e^{-rT} = e^{-0.06} = \$0.9418$ today. Record the cash flows as $BF = 0.9418F$ on January 1 and $-F$ on December 31.

- The resulting portfolio has a zero payoff on the delivery date. To prevent arbitrage, the net payoff is zero today. Consequently,

$$-0.9802 \times 1,000 + 0.9418F = 0$$
$$\text{or } F = \$1,040.81 \tag{12.5}$$

---

[2] www.indexarb.com/dividendAnalysis.html.

The Model and Arbitrage Profits

- Replace the numbers with symbols in (12.5) to get

$$-e^{-\delta T}S + e^{-rT}F = 0$$
$$\text{or } F = Se^{(r-\delta)T}$$

- Suppose an errant dealer quotes \$1,020 as the forward price for INDY index. As this is less than the arbitrage-free price, buy the relatively underpriced traded forward and sell short the synthetic forward as in Table 12.2. This gives an immediate arbitrage profit of

$$-e^{-rT}F + e^{-\delta T}S$$
$$= -0.9418 \times 1,020 + 0.9802 \times 1,000$$
$$= \$19.60$$

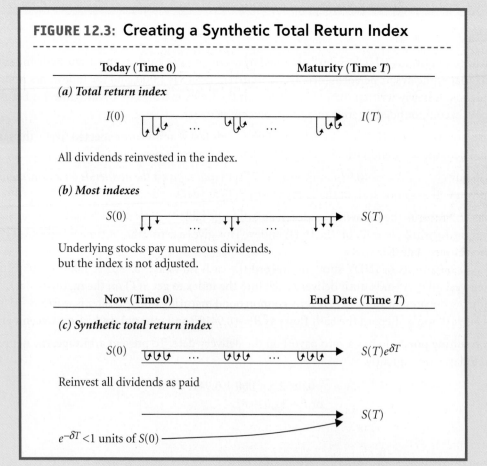

FIGURE 12.3: **Creating a Synthetic Total Return Index**

Today (Time 0)	Maturity (Time T)

(a) Total return index

$I(0)$ $I(T)$

All dividends reinvested in the index.

(b) Most indexes

$S(0)$ $S(T)$

Underlying stocks pay numerous dividends, but the index is not adjusted.

Now (Time 0)	End Date (Time T)

(c) Synthetic total return index

$S(0)$ $S(T)e^{\delta T}$

Reinvest all dividends as paid

      $S(T)$

$e^{-\delta T} < 1$ units of $S(0)$

This example gives our next result.

> **RESULT 12.1B**
>
> ---
>
> ## The Cost-of-Carry Model with a Known Dividend Yield
>
> Consider a forward contract today (time 0) with delivery at time T. The underlying stock index pays dividends at a continuous rate δ that are not reinvested. Then,
>
> $$F = Se^{(r-\delta)T} \qquad (12.6)$$
>
> where S is today's price of the stock index, F is today's forward price for time T, r is the continuously compounded interest rate per year, and δ is the dividend yield, which is the sum of all dividends paid over one year expressed as a fraction of the stock index's price.

Why bother about such small adjustments for the dividend yield? Although tiny, these adjustments are needed to determine the forward price for a stock index. If you trade without such adjustments, you are vulnerable to being arbitraged. Second, they can be used to understand foreign currency forward prices, which are discussed next.

TABLE 12.2: Cost-of-Carry Arbitrage with an Index That Pays Dividends at a Continuous Rate

Portfolio	Today (Time 0) Cash Flow	Delivery/Maturity Date One Year Later (Time T) Cash Flow
Sell one forward contract on INDY index	0	$-[S(T) - F]$
Buy 0.9802 units of INDY stock worth S	$-0.9802 \times 1{,}000$	$S(T)$
Borrow the present value of F	$e^{-0.06}F$	$-F$
Net cash flow	$-980.20 + 0.9418F$	0

The Foreign Currency Forward Price

As currencies have negligible storage costs, we can analyze them in the cash-and-carry framework. Currencies earn risk-free returns in their home countries through investments in their respective government securities. Consequently, they are like financial securities that earn dividends, and as our next example shows, Result 12.1b can be applied.

EXAMPLE 12.3: The Cost-of-Carry Model for Foreign Currency Forward Contracts

The Data

- Top management of Americana Auto have asked the treasurer to repatriate to the United States £100 million from its operations in the United Kingdom and to make this money available in a year's time. The treasurer considers two choices: (1) *convert now* (with the help of the spot exchange rate and then invest in domestic bonds) or (2) invest in foreign bonds and *convert later* (with the help of a forward exchange rate or a forward contract).

- Today's spot exchange rate S_A is $2 per pound in American terms, and its inverse $S_E = 1/2 = £0.50$ per dollar in European terms. The continuously compounded annual risk-free interest rates are $r = 6$ percent in the United States (domestic) and $r_E = 4$ percent in the United Kingdom (foreign).

Using a Forward Exchange Rate (Investments/International Finance Course Approach)

- (see Figure 12.4) To convert now, multiply £100 million by the spot exchange rate S_A. Invest this dollar amount in one-year US Treasury bills. As the dollar return $(1 + R)$ is $e^{rT} = e^{0.06} \times 1 = \$1.0618$, the value after one year is

$$\text{Initial sterling amount} \times \text{Spot exchange rate in American terms} \times \text{Dollar return}$$
$$= £100 \times \$2 \text{ per pound} \times 1.0618$$
$$= \$212.3673 \text{ million} \tag{12.7}$$

- For the second choice, invest in the United Kingdom's risk-free Treasury gilt securities for one year. One pound gives $1 + R_E = e^{r_E T} = e^{0.04 \times 1} = 1.0408$. Consequently, £100 million would be worth after one year:

$$\text{Initial sterling amount} \times \text{Value of one pound invested in zeros for one year}$$
$$= 100 \times 1.0408$$
$$= £104.0811 \text{ million} \tag{12.8a}$$

- Unless you find a magician like those of the "rare oul' times" who can gaze at a crystal ball and foretell the future, the spot exchange rate that prevails in the future is unknown. However, the treasurer can fix the price for converting dollars into pounds sterling in one year's time. She can do this in the forward currency market, where a dealer stands ready to commit to converting in one year at the fair price $F_A(In)$, where "In" indicates a link to an investment or an international finance course. Multiply £104.0811 million by this quantity to get its dollar value:

$$(\text{Initial sterling amount} \times \text{Value of one pound invested in zeros}) \times F_A(In)$$
$$= \$104.0811 \times F_A(In) \text{ million} \tag{12.8b}$$

- To prevent arbitrage, they should be equal:

$$\$212.3673 = \$104.0811 \times F_A(In)$$
$$\text{or, } F_A(In) = \$2.0404 \text{ per pound} \tag{12.9}$$

The Model

- Replacing numbers with symbols in expression (12.9) and remembering that the initial sterling amount cancels, we get

$$F_A(In) = S_A e^{(r - r_E)T} \tag{12.10}$$

This is similar to our previous result (Result 12.1b).

Finding the Forward Price Using a Forward Contract

■ Alternatively, she can convert pounds sterling to dollars by using a currency forward contract. Table 12.3 shows the trades that generate the arbitrage-free forward price:

- Buy one foreign zero-coupon bond whose price is $B_E = 1/(1 + R_E) = 1/1.0408 = £0.9608$ in the United Kingdom. Obtain the dollar cost by multiplying it by the spot exchange rate in American terms, $-B_E \times S_A = -0.9608 \times 2 = -\$1.9216$. The bond is worth one pound at maturity, whose dollar value is obtained by multiplying it by the spot rate $S(T)_A$ prevailing after one year.

- Remove the spot exchange rate from the portfolio on the delivery date by selling a forward contract on pounds sterling with the forward price F_A. This gives an immediate payoff of 0 and a future payoff of $-[S(T)_A - F_A]$ in American terms.

- Borrow the present value of this forward price by multiplying it by the one year Treasury bill price $B = 1/(1 + R) = 1/1.0618 = \$0.9418$. This gives $B \times F_A = 0.9418 F_A$ today and $-F_A$ in the future.

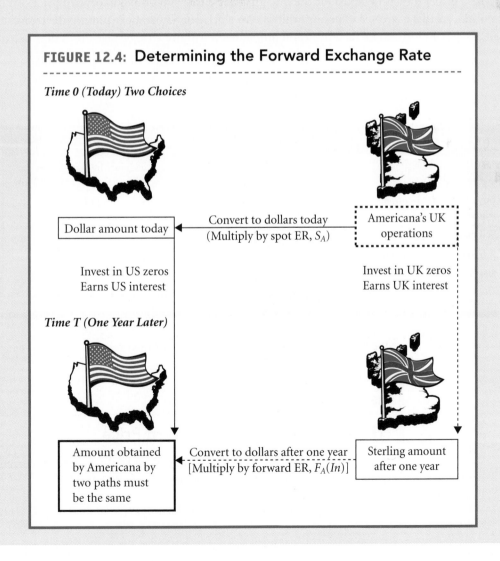

FIGURE 12.4: Determining the Forward Exchange Rate

Time 0 (Today) Two Choices

| Dollar amount today | ← Convert to dollars today
(Multiply by spot ER, S_A) | Americana's UK
operations |

Invest in US zeros
Earns US interest

Invest in UK zeros
Earns UK interest

Time T (One Year Later)

| Amount obtained
by Americana by
two paths must
be the same | ← Convert to dollars after one year
[Multiply by forward ER, $F_A(In)$] | Sterling amount
after one year |

- As the portfolio's payoff is zero on the delivery date, to prevent arbitrage, it must also have a zero value today. Consequently,

$$-0.9608 \times 2 + 0.9418 F_A = 0$$
$$\text{or } F_A = \$2.0404 \text{ per pound} \tag{12.11}$$

The Model

- Replacing numbers with symbols in expression (12.11), we get

$$F_A = S_A B_E / B = S_A e^{(r - r_E)T} \tag{12.12}$$

- Compare and you will discover that the two forward prices are the same. The forward price in an investments or international finance course is the same as the arbitrage reinforced price that we obtain with the help of a forward contract! This result is known as **covered interest rate parity**.

Arbitrage Profits

- Suppose a dealer forgets to adjust for the foreign interest rate and quotes a forward price of $2.1237 per pound. As this is greater than our arbitrage-free price of $2.0404 per pound, the treasurer can create the portfolio given in Table 12.3 and immediately capture an arbitrage profit of

$$-B_E \times S_A + B \times F_A$$
$$= -1.9216 + 0.9418 \times 2.1237$$
$$= \$0.0784$$

TABLE 12.3: The Arbitrage Table for the Currency Forward Price		
Portfolio	Now (Time 0) Cash Flow	Delivery/Maturity Date One Year Later (Time T) Cash Flow
Buy one UK zero-coupon bond whose price is $B_E S_A$ today	-1.9216	$S(T)_A$
Sell pound sterling forward	0	$-[S(T)_A - F_A]$
Borrow the present value of F_A	$0.9418 F_A$	$-F_A$
Net cash flow	$-0.9608 S_A + 0.9418 F_A$	0

We restate the pricing model (12.12) as our next result.

RESULT 12.2

- -

The Foreign Currency Forward Price

Consider a forward contract today (time 0) for trading a foreign currency at time T. Then the forward exchange rate is given by

$$F_A = S_A (B_E / B) = S_A e^{(r - r_E)T} \tag{12.12}$$

where F_A and S_A are the forward and today's spot exchange rates in American terms, $B \equiv B(0, T)$ is today's price of an American (domestic) zero-coupon bond that pays a dollar at time T, $B_E \equiv B_E(0, T)$ is today's price of a "European" (foreign) zero-coupon bond that pays one unit of foreign currency at time T, and r and r_E are the continuously compounded domestic and foreign risk-free interest rates, respectively.

12.4 | Extended Cost-of-Carry Models

Consider a commodity that is primarily used for consumption or production, like copper, corn, or crude oil. If one holds a long position in these commodities, she incurs insurance costs, shipping costs, and storage costs. We call all of these **storage costs**. Alternatively, the availability of the physical stock may enable someone to keep a production process running smoothly or earn extra cash by lending them in times of temporary shortages. These benefits are commonly known as the **convenience yield** (or **convenience value**) of the commodity.[3] They aren't directly observed but may be implicitly computed from market data. By contrast, forward traders do not acquire these benefits or incur these costs. However, they exist, and Example 12.4 shows how to incorporate them in our framework.

EXAMPLE 12.4: The Cost-of-Carry Model for Commodities with Storage Costs and Convenience Yields

The Data

- Consider a fictitious commodity Alloyum that is costly to store but has a convenience yield. Let the simple interest rate be 6 percent per year. Consider a newly written forward contract that matures in a year. We create the portfolio shown in Table 12.4:
  - Buy Alloyum for $S = \$100$ today. It costs $\$0.05$ per month to store an ounce of this commodity. This storage cost G is 12 months $\times$ 0.05/month $= \$0.60$ for the year, which is paid up front. This expense does not show up on the delivery date, but you have to borrow this amount today in addition to the commodity's price. At maturity, repay $(S + G)(1 + R) = 100.60 \times 1.06 = \$106.6360$.
  - As the holder of Alloyum, collect the convenience yield Y of $\$0.50$ at time T.
  - Borrow to finance the purchase and sell forward to eliminate the spot.

---

[3] Using tools of modern option princing theory, Jarrow (2010) concludes that convenience yields do not exit as a separate concept and argues that it is best understood as a label given to certain cash flows generated from storing a commodity. These cash flows have two embedded options, which he calls the scarcity and usage options.

The Model and Arbitrage Profits

- The portfolio has zero value today and a known (or a constant) value at maturity. To prevent arbitrage, it must have a zero value on the delivery date. Replace numbers with symbols to get the pricing model:

$$F - 106.6360 + 0.50 = F - (S + G)(1 + R) + Y = 0$$
$$\text{or } F = (S + G)(1 + R) - Y = \$106.1360 \tag{12.13}$$

- If an errant dealer quotes F as \$107, then the portfolio in Table 12.4 gives an arbitrage profit of

$$107 - 106.1360 + 0.50$$
$$= \$0.8640$$

on the delivery date.

TABLE 12.4: The Arbitrage Table for Forward Contract Commodities with Storage Costs and Convenience Yields		
Portfolio	Today (Time 0) Cash Flow	Delivery Date One Year Later (Time T) Cash Flow
Buy commodity (pay asset price S and storage cost G)	$-100 - 0.60$	$S(T)$
Get convenience value Y at maturity		0.50
Borrow to finance purchase	100.60	-106.6360
Sell forward	0	$-[S(T) - F]$
Net cash flow	0	$F - 106.6360 + 0.50$

We write the result.

RESULT 12.3

- -

The Cost-of-Carry Model with Storage Costs and Convenience Yields

Consider a forward contract written today (time 0) on a commodity that incurs storage costs (which are collected up front) but also gives a convenience yield (which is received at the maturity date T). Then,

$$F = (S + G)(1 + R) - Y \tag{12.13}$$

where $1 + R$ is the dollar return, S is today's spot price, F is today's forward price for time T, G is the storage cost, and Y is the convenience yield.

This model introduces storage costs and convenience yield on arbitrary dates. Why up front and at the back end, respectively? If benefits and costs happen often enough, you can avoid this problem by using a continuously compounded version of the model. Assume that all holding costs (like the storage cost and the interest rate) as well as the benefits (like the dividend yield and the convenience yield) are accrued or disbursed at a continuous rate over the life of the forward. Using a quantity adjustment, start your trade with $e^{-(\delta + y - g)T}$ units of the commodity. Following a path trodden before, you can develop a generalized version of the cost-of-carry model.

RESULT 12.4

- -

An Extended Cost-of-Carry Model

Consider a forward contract today (time 0) that matures at time T. The underlying asset pays cash flows at a continuous rate δ. Then,

$$F = Se^{[(r+g) - (\delta + y)]T} \tag{12.14}$$

where r is the risk-free rate per year, g is the rate of continuously paid storage costs per year, and y is the rate of continuously paid convenience yields per year.

The basic tenets of the extended cost-of-carry model are as follows:

- There is some deliverable amount of the spot commodity that is carried across time and traded at a later date.
- The spot price equals the forward price in the absence of costs and benefits to the physical holder of the asset (see Figure 12.5).
- Various "costs" increase while benefits decrease the forward price.

12.5 | Backwardation, Contango, Normal Backwardation, and Normal Contango

"I can call spirits from the vasty deep," said Glendower, in Shakespeare's *King Henry VI*. To this, Hotspur replied, "Why, so can I, or so can any man; But will they come when you do call for them?" We can keep adding features and build fancier cost-of-carry models that give deeper results. But are they useful? If you are interested in determining fair value, then the answer is yes, but if you are interested in determining risk premium or whether forward prices are unbiased predictors of future spot prices, then the answer is no. To answer these later questions, we need to discuss backwardation, contango, normal backwardation, and normal contango.

When the forward price is higher than the spot price, we say that the market is in **contango**. This is the usual situation because for most commodities, using the cost-of-carry model (consider the extended cost-of-carry model of Result 12.4), the costs exceed the benefits. When the reverse happens, the market is in **backwardation** (see Figure 12.5). The cost-of-carry model using convenience yields is how a financial engineer understands pricing.

Economists, alternatively, seek explanations via the demand and supply mechanism.[4] Their aim is to understand **risk premium**, the compensation for risk, and they are interested in the relation between forward prices and expected future spot prices. For forwards, economists often consider a market where hedgers and speculators interact.

Consider a market where all traders expect that in three months from today, the spot price for corn will be $5 per bushel. Suppose that the market is dominated by corn processors who want to hedge. They are interested in fixing a price for procuring corn in the future to make corn oil, breakfast cereal, and other corn products. They are willing to pay a higher price than $5 per bushel to reduce their risk for buying an input into their production process. The demand curve for the producers (whom we label as net hedgers) is given in Figure 12.6. Notice that this is a relatively steep demand curve, indicating insensitivity of these hedgers to the forward price because they need forwards to set up their hedge.

Now there are speculators who take the other side of the transaction and expect a profit. They are willing to short forward if they receive a forward price that is higher than the expected spot price (and go long if the opposite happens). Consequently, they have a relatively flat demand curve that passes through the expected spot price. Notice that we have extended the horizontal axis to the left side of the vertical axis to accommodate short positions. Suppose that at $5.05 per bushel, the net hedging demand from the long equals the number of contracts the speculators are willing to go short, which is 500 in this example. *This creates a situation in which the forward price is greater than the expected future spot price.* The difference is a risk premium, the compensation to the speculators for the risk they bear. To avoid confusion with the definition of contango, we call this **normal contango**.

Consider another scenario where corn farmers, who want to hedge by selling forward and fix a selling price for their corn, dominate the forward market. These hedgers would like to go short. Their demands are met by speculators who are willing to go long only if the expected spot price exceeds the current forward price. This is because for the speculators to be in the market, their

---

[4] "Give me a one-handed economist! All my economists say, 'On the one hand . . . on the other,'" exclaimed Harry S. Truman (1884–1972), who was the thirty-third president of the United States (1945–53).

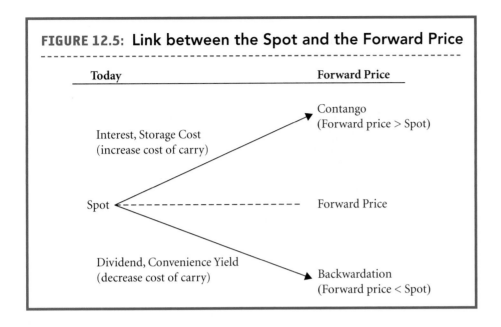

FIGURE 12.5: Link between the Spot and the Forward Price

Today   Forward Price

Contango
(Forward price > Spot)

Interest, Storage Cost
(increase cost of carry)

Spot   Forward Price

Dividend, Convenience Yield
(decrease cost of carry)

Backwardation
(Forward price < Spot)

expected return must be positive. By selling at a price below the expected future spot price, hedgers entice the speculator to go long, and this transfers the unwanted risk to the speculator. *This creates a **normal backwardation** because the forward price is less than the expected future spot price.* And, the risk premium is reversed.

The concepts of normal contango and normal backwardation are, thus, exactly the notions needed to understand risk premium and whether the forward price exceeds or is less than the expected futures spot price of the commodity. Our cost-of-carry models cannot answer these more subtle questions. The trade-off is that the cost-of-carry model gives a price, but the economic approach doesn't.

12.6 | Market Imperfections

How does the cost-of-carry model get modified if we start considering market "imperfections" such as transaction costs, different borrowing and lending rates, and restrictions on short selling? Here the cash-and-carry arbitrage and the reverse cash-and-carry are no longer symmetric. Consequently, we get price ranges within which the forward price lies. These bounds are likely close because it's the trader with the lowest transaction costs (and not retail traders like us) who take advantage of arbitrage opportunities and determine the price bounds. Example 12.5 introduces brokerage commissions into our basic cost-of-carry model.

FIGURE 12.6: Normal Contango and Normal Backwardation

Normal Contango

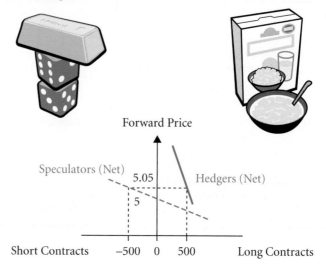

Forward Price

Speculators (Net)   5.05   Hedgers (Net)

5

Short Contracts   −500   0   500   Long Contracts

Expected spot price is $5
Forward price is $5.05 in equilibrium
(net demand = net supply)

Normal Backwardation

Farmer

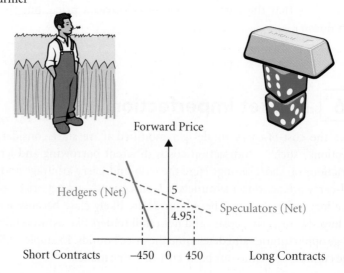

Forward Price

Hedgers (Net)   5

4.95   Speculators (Net)

Short Contracts   −450   0   450   Long Contracts

Expected spot price is $5
Forward price is $4.95 in equilibrium

EXAMPLE 12.5: Forward Price Bounds in the Presence of Market Imperfections

- Consider the data from Example 11.1. YBM's stock price S is $100 today (January 1, time 0), and the dollar return $(1 + R)$ is $1.06. Consider a newly written forward on YBM that matures in one year (time T).

- Assume that when trading YBM, a brokerage commission is charged that equals $TC = 1$ percent of the stock price. For simplicity, assume that there are no transaction costs on the maturity date. Now we need two tables, Tables 12.5a and 12.5b, for an arbitrage portfolio.

- Table 12.5a shows, to prevent arbitrage,

$$-101 + 0.9434F \leq 0$$
$$\text{or } F \leq 107.0596 \qquad (12.15a)$$

This gives an upper bound for the forward price.

- Table 12.5b shows the no-arbitrage portfolio for a reverse cash-and-carry. Here

$$-0.9434F + 99 \leq 0$$
$$\text{or } 104.9396 \leq F \qquad (12.15b)$$

This gives a lower bound for the forward price.

- Combining expressions (12.15a) and (12.15b),

$$104.9396 \leq F \leq 107.0596 \qquad (12.15c)$$

The forward price lies between $104.9396 and $107.0596.

- Replacing numbers with symbols gives the formula

$$S(1 + R)(1 - TC) \leq F \leq S(1 + R)(1 + TC) \qquad (12.16a)$$

TABLE 12.5A: Arbitrage Table for Cash-and-Carry

Portfolio	Today (Time 0) Cash Flow	Maturity Date (Time 1) Cash Flow
Buy spot (pay 1 percent transaction cost today)	$-100 \times (1 + 0.01)$	$S(T)$
Sell forward	0	$-[S(T) - F]$
Borrow present value of F	$0.9434F$	$-F$
Net cash flow	$-101 + 0.9434F$	0

TABLE 12.5B: Arbitrage Table for Reverse Cash-and-Carry

Portfolio	Today (Time 0) Cash Flow	Delivery Date (Time 1) Cash Flow
Sell spot (deduct transaction costs from short sale proceeds)	$100 \times (1 - 0.01)$	$-S(T)$
Buy forward	0	$S(T) - F$
Lend present value of F	$-0.9434F$	F
Net cash flow	$-0.9434F + 99$	0

Besides brokerage commissions, there may be a bid/ask spread.[5] As transaction costs increase, the price bounds become farther apart. However, different traders may have different transactions costs. This opens up quasi-arbitrage (near-arbitrage) opportunities for the lowest cost trader.

One can introduce more market frictions in a similar fashion. For example, with unequal borrowing and lending rates, the relation becomes

$$S(1 + R_{\text{LEND}}) \leq F \leq S(1 + R_{\text{BORROW}}) \tag{12.16b}$$

where $1 + R_{\text{LEND}}$ is the dollar return from lending and $1 + R_{\text{BORROW}}$ is that for borrowing. Several of these relations may be combined.

RESULT 12.5

- -

The Cost-of-Carry Model in the Presence of Brokerage Commissions and Unequal Borrowing and Lending Rates

When stock trades are charged a brokerage commission of TC on today's trade, and the borrowing rates are higher than the lending rates, then the forward price F satisfies:

$$S(1 + R_{\text{LEND}})(1 - TC) \leq F \leq S(1 + R_{\text{BORROW}})(1 + TC) \tag{12.16a}$$

where S is today's stock price, F is today's forward price for time T, and $1 + R_{\text{LEND}}$ and $1 + R_{\text{BORROW}}$ are the dollar returns for lending and borrowing, respectively.

Like playing with children's blocks, you can combine Results 12.4 and 12.5 to build even more general models. To apply the cost-of-carry model in practice requires a good understanding of the market and matching the market's structure to the model's assumptions. For financial commodities like stock indexes or Treasury securities, convenience yields and storage costs are not relevant, so the simpler models apply. In contrast, for agricultural commodities like corn or wheat, convenience yields and storage costs are extremely important and need to be included. Given the previous discussion, all that is left for a correct application of these models is experience and market savvy. Both of these will come in good time, and the old saying is especially relevant in this regard: "practice makes perfect."

---

[5] And when you sell short, the brokerage firms may not allow you the full proceeds—you may only earn interest on part of the funds kept with the broker. When there are restrictions on short selling, you may have an inequality like $S(1 + q \times \text{Interest}) \leq F \leq S(1 + R)$, where q is the fraction of usable funds derived from the short sale. Notice that this arbitrage only works in one direction because long and short positions have asymmetric payoffs. This relationship is less important because rules of short selling tend to vary from country to country.

12.7 | Summary

1. We extend the basic cost-of-carry model to incorporate market frictions (relax assumption A1 of chapter 11) and dividends (ease A4) into the framework.

2. Assuming that interest is the only relevant carrying charge, we get three forward pricing models for assets that generate income:

   a. The simplest dividend model assumes that the underlying stock pays fixed dollar dividends on known dates. This gives Result 12.1a, which states that the stock price net of the present value of dividend is the discounted forward price or $S - B_1 \text{div} = BF$. This is useful for finding forward prices for contracts written on dividend-paying stocks and coupon-bearing Treasury bonds that mature after the delivery date.

   b. When the underlying stock pays dividends at a continuous rate δ, we get Result 12.1b: the forward price is the compounded value of the stock price, where compounding is done at a net rate equal to the difference between the interest rate and the dividend yield or $F = Se^{(r-\delta)T}$. This is useful for finding forward prices when the underlying is an index portfolio.

   c. A modification of the previous model gives covered interest rate parity, which expresses the forward exchange rate as the spot exchange rate compounded at a net rate equal to the difference between the domestic and the foreign interest rates. Result 12.2 states that $F_A = S_A (B_E / B) = S_A e^{(r-r_E)T}$.

3. For commodities mainly used for consumption or production, storage costs can be important. However, holders of the physical commodity may also get a convenience yield. We include these costs and benefits to build a generalized cost-of-carry model (Result 12.4): the forward price is the compounded value of the spot price, where compounding is done at a net rate equal to the costs (interest rate r plus the storage cost rate g) minus the benefits (dividend yield δ plus the convenience yield y) or $F = Se^{[(r+g)-(\delta+y)]T}$.

4. Contango is a market where the forward price is higher than the spot price. This happens when the net cost-of-carry is positive in the generalized cost-of-carry model. The market is in backwardation when the reverse happens.

5. Normal contango happens when a majority of the hedgers want to set up a long hedge. Speculators assume the other side of the trade, but they require a risk premium for supplying liquidity: the forward price is greater than the expected future spot price. When the net hedgers are short, the risk premium is reversed, and a normal backwardation market is created where the forward price is less than the expected future spot price.

6. Buys and sells are no longer symmetric when market imperfections like brokerage costs, differential borrowing and lending rates, and short selling restrictions are introduced. Well-defined prices give way to ranges within which forward prices lie.

12.8 | Cases

Diva Shoes Inc. (Darden School of Business Case UV0265-PDF-ENG, Harvard Business Publishing). The case studies a US-based manufacturer's currency risk exposure and considers whether hedging via a forward contract or a currency option is advisable.

Leveraged Buyout (LBO) of BCE: Hedging Security Risk (Richard Ivey School of Business Foundation Case 908N23-PDF-ENG, Harvard Business Publishing). The case considers an equity partnership's currency risk exposure and evaluates various derivative instruments for hedging those risks.

Risk Management at Apache (Harvard Business School Case 201113-PDF-ENG). The case evaluates a company's hedging strategy and the derivatives used for this purpose.

12.9 | Questions and Problems

12.1. a. Explain the cost-of-carry model with dollar dividends in your own words.

   b. Justify why the spot price considered in the model is net of the present value of all future dividends paid over the life of the contract.

   c. Why don't we adjust for dividends that are paid after the forward's maturity date?

12.2. Boring Unreliable Gadget Inc.'s stock price S is $50 today. It pays a dollar dividend after two months. If the continuously compounded interest rate is 4 percent per year, what is the forward price of a six-month forward contract on BUG?

12.3. Boring Unreliable Gadget Inc.'s stock price S is $50 today. It pays dividends of $1 after two months and $1.05 after five months. If the continuously compounded interest rate is 4 percent per year, what is the forward price of a six-month forward contract on BUG?

12.4. Boring Unreliable Gadget Inc.'s stock price S is $50 today. The company, however, reliably pays quarterly dividends to shareholders. For example, BUG paid $0.95 dividend one month back; it will pay $1 dividend two months from today, $1.05 after five months, $1.10 after eight months, and $1.15 after eleven months. If the continuously compounded interest rate is 4 percent per year, what is the forward price of a six-month forward contract on BUG?

12.5. Boring Unreliable Gadget Inc.'s stock price S is $50 today. It pays dividends of $1 after two months and $1.05 after five months. The continuously compounded interest rate is 4 percent per year. If the six-month forward price is $51, demonstrate how you can make arbitrage profits or explain why you cannot.

12.6. Boring Unreliable Gadget Inc.'s stock price S is $50 today. It pays dividends of $1 after two months and $1.05 after five months. The continuously compounded interest rate is 4 percent per year. Transactions costs are $0.10 per stock traded, a $0.25 one-time fee for trading forward contracts, and no charges for trading bonds. If the six-month forward price is $51, demonstrate how to make arbitrage profits or explain why you cannot.

12.7. Explain how the cost-of-carry model with dollar dividends differs from the cost-of-carry model with dividend yields.

12.8. What is a convenience yield for a commodity and why is it important to include in the cost-of-carry model? Give an example of a commodity that has a convenience yield.

12.9. What are exchange-traded funds? How are they structured? Are they better than mutual funds? Explain your answer.

12.10. a. What is a stock index? What happens to stock indexes when dividends are paid?

 b. What is a synthetic index? Why is it useful?

12.11. Consider SINDY Index obtained by averaging stock prices and a synthetic index SINDY spot that replicates its performance. (1) SINDY's current level I is 10,000, and the synthetic index's price S is $10,000. (2) A newly written forward contract on the index matures after $T = 0.5$ years. (3) The continuously compounded interest rate r is 5 percent per year. (4) Stocks constituting SINDY spot paid $190 of dividends last year and are expected to pay the same this year.

 a. Compute the dividend yield δ on SINDY spot.

 b. Compute the forward price F.

12.12. Consider the data given in problem 12.11 for futures contracts on SINDY Index. If the forward price is $F = \$10,231$, show how you can make arbitrage profits or explain why you cannot.

12.13. Consider the data given in problem 12.11 for futures contracts on SINDY Index. Suppose you have to pay transaction costs: (1) When you go long or sell short a portfolio of stocks, transaction costs (brokerage fees plus the price impact of the trade) equal 10 basis points of the synthetic index's price. (2) There is a one-time fee of $15 for trading forward contracts but no charges for trading bonds. If the forward price is $F = \$10,231$, show how you can make arbitrage profits or explain why you cannot.

12.14. Today's spot exchange rate S_A is $1.30 per euro in American terms. The continuously compounded annual risk-free interest rates are $r = 4$ percent in the United States (domestic) and $r_E = 3$ percent in the Eurozone. What is the four-month forward rate in American terms if the cost-of-carry model holds?

12.15. The current dollar/Swiss franc spot exchange rate is 0.5685. If you invest one dollar for ninety days in the US domestic riskless asset, you earn $1.0101, and if you invest one franc for ninety days in the Swiss riskless asset, you earn 1.0113 francs (assume continuous compounding). A broker offers you a ninety-day forward contract to buy or sell 1 million francs at the exchange rate of 0.55 dollars/franc. Are there arbitrage profits to be made here? If so, compute them.

12.16. Alloyum costs $0.10 per month to store (which is paid upfront) but gives a convenience yield of $0.12 per month (which is received on the maturity date). If its spot price S is $200 per ounce and the continuously compounded interest rate r is 5 percent per year, what is the five-month forward price for Alloyum?

12.17. In the previous example, suppose a trader quotes a five-month forward price of $206 per ounce. Demonstrate how you can make arbitrage profits from these prices; if you cannot, explain your answer.

12.18. COMIND Index is computed by averaging commodity prices. Compute the five-month forward price for this index if the spot price is 1,000 and the continuously compounded annual rates for various costs and benefits are 5 percent for the interest rate, 3 percent for the dividend yield, 4 percent for the storage cost, and 3 percent for the convenience yield.

12.19. Find the price bounds for the five-month forward price for Boring Unreliable Gadgets when

    a. BUG's stock price S is $50 today

    b. a trader can borrow money at 5 percent and lend money at 4 percent, where the interest rates are annual simple interest rates

    c. a brokerage commission of 0.5 percent of the stock price is charged today but your broker waives transaction costs on the maturity date

12.20. Forward prices for April and June forward contracts for platinum are $400 per ounce and $410 per ounce, respectively. The interest rate is 1 percent for the April–June period. There is a 1 percent transaction cost whenever you trade (buy or short sell) the spot in June, but the broker is waiving any transaction costs for trading forward contracts and brokerage costs for trading the spot in April. Can you generate arbitrage profits? Explain your answer. (Assume that the spot price of platinum in June lies between $400 and $500.)

13

Futures Hedging

13.1 | Introduction

The novelist Dostoyevsky perceptively observed in *The Gambler*: "as for profits and winnings, people, not only at roulette, but everywhere, do nothing but try to gain or squeeze something out of one another." This aptly defines a zero-sum game of which, excluding transaction costs, futures trading is an excellent example. There is a pool of talented futures traders who earn a living from this business thereby depressing the chances of winning for ordinary traders who lose money on average. Then, why trade futures?

Cynics give a facile explanation: people are "into commodities" because it's as thrilling as going to the casinos. True to circus-owner P. T. Barnum's immortal quote that "there's a sucker born every minute," these gamblers gladly lose for the joy of the ride. Perhaps others believe that they really can win the futures game. We know no surefire strategy. Even if you stumble on such a strategy, repeated use will destroy its efficacy. So, why trade futures?

In reality, most futures contracts are traded to hedge risks that preexist in some line of business, and hedgers are willing to give up expected returns as payment for this "insurance." We discussed this issue in the context of normal backwardation in chapter 12. For example, Figure 13.1 shows a man selling goods on some tourist spot, perhaps a beach. If he chooses his wares wisely, say, by carrying an assortment of umbrellas and sunglasses, then he has hedged well. Come rain or come shine, he has something to sell. If this is not possible, he could use futures to manage these risks. For example, he could sell only umbrellas and buy futures on a sunglass company's stock, instead of selling sunglasses.

Who hedges? A majority of the Fortune 500 companies and a growing number of smaller firms hedge risk. Farmers often hedge the selling price of their produce. Many producers hedge input as well as output price risk—chapter 1 gave us an inkling of derivatives usage by the consumer product giant Procter & Gamble.

This chapter explores the reasons for hedging, discusses its cost and benefits, and introduces futures hedging strategies. We discuss perfect and cross hedges, long and short hedges, and risk-minimization hedging using standard statistical techniques.

13.2 | To Hedge or Not to Hedge

Unfortunately, there is no general answer to what may be phrased as (with apologies to the immortal William Shakespeare) *to hedge or not to hedge—that is the question*. We can only discuss hedging's benefits and costs.

Should the Firm or the Individual Hedge?

The classic Modigliani and Miller (M&M) papers argued that debt policies do not affect firm value. This irrelevance follows because a shareholder can replicate such policies herself by trading stocks in otherwise identical firms. Therefore the no-arbitrage principle ensures that these companies, differing only in their debt

FIGURE 13.1: Wisely Hedged: Come Rain, Come Shine, He Has Something to Sell*

Inspired by a 1980s newspaper advertisement.

policies, must have equal value. The same argument can be applied to a firm hedging its balance sheet risks giving intellectual support to the irrelevance of hedging. However, the M&M results rely on several key assumptions, including no market frictions (including bankruptcy costs), no taxes, and no information asymmetry. In the real world, these assumptions fail to hold. Consequently, if reducing the firm's risk is in the shareholders' best interest, then a firm can usually do a better job of hedging than individual investors. Indeed, a company (1) is likely to have lower transaction costs; (2) can trade larger contracts than a shareholder; (3) can dedicate competent personnel to hedging; (4) can hedge by issuing a whole range of securities, which individuals cannot; (5) may have private information about the company's risks; and (6) can hedge for strategic reasons that lie beyond an ordinary investor's knowledge. In all these cases, a company creates more value than an individual investor hedging on her own. But hedging is costly to implement, both in developing and retaining the relevant expertise within the firm, and in executing the transactions.

The Costs and Benefits of Corporate Hedging

A hedged business has fewer risks to worry about, but exactly why is this an advantage? Aren't businesses supposed to take risks? We answer these questions next, and although we focus on the use of futures, many of these same benefits can be obtained with other derivatives such as forwards, options, and swaps:

1. *Hedging locks in a future price.* Recall chapter 8, in which we discussed the establishment of the Chicago Board of Trade. The CBOT built orderly markets for grain trading to avoid price crashes at harvest times and booms afterward. Hedging with futures helps smooth such demand–supply imbalances. It allows traders to lock in stable prices and plan production and marketing activities with greater certainty.

2. *Hedging permits forward pricing of products.* For example, many airlines routinely hedge aviation fuel prices, which is a major input cost. If fuel costs can be fixed (and other costs, such as staff salary, airplane depreciation, airport gate rental charges, and travel agents' commissions, can be estimated in advance), then the airline can better set a profit margin and determine future seat prices. Customers like knowing travel costs far in advance.

3. *Hedging reduces the risk of default and financial distress.* **Default** means a failure to pay a contractual payment, such as debt, when promised. Default triggers unfavorable outcomes such as lawyer fees, potential bankruptcy costs and liquidation fees, losing control over the company's assets, and increased costs of doing business because suppliers fear that they may not be paid and customers may worry about quality and service. These are called *financial distress costs*. A company can reduce the likelihood of incurring these costs by hedging some of the risks it faces.

4. *Hedging facilitates raising capital.* Because of the decreased risk of default, bankers allow hedgers to borrow a larger percentage of a commodity's value at a lower interest rate than nonhedgers. This same logic applies to firms.

5. *Hedging enables value-enhancing investments.* Froot et al. (1994) argue that if external sources of funds (like stock and bond issuances) are costlier to corporations than internally generated funds, then hedging can help stabilize internal cash flows and make them available for attractive investment opportunities.

6. *Hedging reduces taxes.* A hedge may be used to capture the benefits of a tax loss or take advantage of a tax credit. The basic intuition is simple. Because one can use a tax loss or a credit only when the company has positive profits, it may be worthwhile to smooth out profits by hedging rather than letting them fluctuate. See Extension 13.2 for an example that illustrates this notion.

However, hedging also incurs costs. When trading with a speculator, a hedger often pays an implicit fee by trading at a price inferior to the expected future payoff. Of course, brokers must also be paid. The presence of these trading costs constitutes a basic argument against futures hedging. Moreover, businesses must allocate valuable personnel to devise hedging strategies, set up adequate checks and balances to prevent rogue employees from ruinously speculating with the firm's money, ensure compliance with the laws of the land, and meet the government's accounting requirements in this regard.[1]

Hedging is analogous to purchasing an insurance policy on some commodity's spot price. It pays off when spot prices move in an adverse direction. However, as with all insurance policies, there is a cost—the premium. If the spot price does not move adversely, one pays for insurance not used. Risk-averse individuals buy insurance despite this cost, and analogously, firms often hedge.

To hedge or not to hedge remains an unsettled question that must be resolved on a case-by-case basis. One often hears any number of catchy maxims: "no risk, no gain" alongside "risk not thy whole wad." Which to choose requires expertise, finesse, and knowledge, which are acquired through study and experience.

EXTENSION 13.1: Airlines and Fuel Price Risk

In August 2006, US president George W. Bush gathered his economic team in the picturesque retreat of Camp David. Although the economic outlook was strong, the newly appointed secretary of the treasury, Henry M. Paulson Jr., previous chairman and CEO of the Wall Street firm Goldman Sachs, was worried about the likelihood of a financial crisis. "If you look at recent history, there is a disturbance in the capital markets every four to eight years," observed Paulson, as he painted a picture of how an enormous amount of leverage and risk had accumulated in the financial system. In reply to a presidential query as to how this risk can be reduced, the secretary gave "a quick primer on hedging." He cited as an example that "airlines might want to hedge against rising fuel costs by buying futures to lock in today's prices for future needs" (Paulson, 2010).

Indeed, fuel costs can hit the airlines hard. Fuel is a major cost of the airline business; it can be between 10 percent (in good times) and more than 35 percent (in bad times) of their average expenses.[2]

"When the going gets tough, the tough get going" goes a familiar saying. As the oil price went up, the airlines adopted a wide range of measures, some prudent and others drastic, to reduce fuel consumption. Most of these approaches aimed at lowering the aircraft's weight because a lighter plane is cheaper to fly. Other steps included flying more fuel-efficient planes and reducing the time that plane engines stay on. Some started trading commodities. Many commercial airlines as well as companies like FedEx (which uses its extensive fleet to quickly deliver packages to numerous locations around the globe) use derivatives on crude oil to hedge. The hedged amount varies. Sometimes they hedge little or none of their exposure; at other times they hedge much more (see Table 13.1 for a description of the fuel hedging situation in early 2005 for major US airlines, ranked in terms of passenger traffic).

Annual reports of companies mention their derivatives exposure. Southwest Airlines maintained its long track record of profitability into the new millennium by extensive hedging even at a time when many other airlines were reeling from losses and operating under bankruptcy protection. Consider the 2007 annual report of Southwest Airlines, which gleefully gloats,

[2] www.iata.org/index.htm.

---

[1] Barings Bank, one of England's oldest and most prestigious merchant banks, founded in 1762 by Sir Francis Baring, collapsed in 1995 after a rogue employee, Nick Leeson, lost $1.4 billion of company money speculating in futures contracts. Nowadays, most companies have stronger oversight of the firm's overall risk situation through the office of a chief risk management officer, who often reports directly to the chief executive officer.

TABLE 13.1:   Fuel Hedge and Potential Impact of Fuel Price Increases for Leading US Airlines (Ranked by Size in Terms of Passenger Traffic) in 2005[a]

Airlines	Hedging Situation (2005)	Impact of Fuel Price Increase (2005 or Earlier)
American Airlines	15% hedged in first quarter, not at all in remaining quarters	Negative impact on fuel costs from 33.7 cent per gallon increase in jet fuel in 2004: $1 billion
United Airlines	11% hedged for 2005, at about $1.27 per gallon, excluding taxes	
Delta Airlines	Not hedged	Every 1 cent rise in the average jet fuel price per gallon increases its liquidity needs by about $25 million per year
Northwest Airlines	Hedged about 25% for the first quarter and 6% for the full year	A 1 cent change in the cost of each gallon of fuel impacts operating expenses by about $1.6 million per month
Continental Airlines	Not hedged	Annual fuel costs will increase by $40 million for each $1 increase in crude oil prices (rose by about $14 a barrel in 2005); also liable to pay regional carrier ExpressJet's fuel costs above 71.2 cents a gallon
Southwest Airlines	85% hedged with derivatives that cap prices at $26 a barrel (current market price: over $57 a barrel)	Expects first-quarter fuel costs with hedge to exceed fourth quarter's 89.1 cents average price per gallon
US Airways	No fuel hedged as of December 31, 2004	About a $2 million increase per month, representing about 4% of its 2005 jet fuel requirements
America West Airlines	45% hedged for the rest of this year and 2% hedged for 2006	A 1 cent per gallon increase in jet fuel prices increases its annual operating expense by $5.7 million
Alaska Airlines	50% hedged for 2005	A 1 cent per gallon increase in jet fuel prices increases its annual operating expenses by about $4.0 million
JetBlue Airways	22% hedged for 2005	

[a] Based on "US Airlines Face Billions in Extra Fuel Costs," *Airwise News*, March 17, 2005.

We were well prepared and recorded our 35th consecutive year of profitability, a record unmatched in commercial airline history. . . . Jet fuel prices have been rising every year for the last five years. Our fuel hedging program has consistently mitigated such price increases dating back to year 2000. Since then, in each year, we have striven to hedge at least 70 percent of our consumption. In 2007, we were approximately 90 percent protected at approximately $51 a barrel. That protection saved us $727 million last year and limited us to an 11.3 percent increase in the economic cost per gallon, year-over-year. . . . A year ago, crude oil was hovering around $50 a barrel. By fourth quarter 2007, crude oil prices had skyrocketed to $100 a barrel. Fortunately, we are again well hedged for 2008 with approximately 70 percent of our fuel needs protected at approximately $51 a barrel.

Buoyed by a successful derivatives hedging program, Southwest did a brand-strengthening exercise in 2008 that hit the competition hard. It ran newspaper ads boasting its low airfare with no hidden fees, and its website took snipes at the rivals by proudly proclaiming, "Low fares. No hidden fees. No first checked bag fee. No second checked bag bee. No change fee. No window or aisle seat fee. No curbside check-in fee. No phone reservation fee. No snack fee. No fuel surcharge."[3]

It's hard to question successful hedging programs! But Southwest is also a very well-run company. The annual report notes that its on-time performance, few flight cancellations (less than 1 percent of flights scheduled), and small number of complaints filed with the US Department of Transportation placed it in the front rank in the airline industry.

Unfortunately, the tables turned. For the first quarter of 2009, Southwest reported a net loss of $91 million, including special charges totaling $71 million (net), relating to "non-cash, mark-to-market and other items associated with a portion of the Company's fuel hedge portfolio."[4] The company's CEO, Gary C. Kelly, stated in a press release dated April 16, 2009,

> We benefited from significantly lower year-over-year economic jet fuel costs in first quarter 2009. Even with $65 million in unfavorable cash settlements from derivative contracts, our first quarter 2009 economic jet fuel costs decreased 16.2 percent to $1.76 per gallon. With oil prices rising, we have begun to rebuild our 2009 and 2010 hedge positions, using purchased call options, to provide protection against significant fuel price spikes.

The press release also noted about Southwest:

> The Company has derivative contracts in place for approximately 50 percent of its second quarter 2009 estimated fuel consumption, capped at a weighted average crude-equivalent price of approximately $66 per barrel; approximately 40 percent for the remainder of 2009 capped at a weighted average crude-equivalent price of approximately $71 per barrel; and approximately 30 percent in 2010 capped at a weighted average crude-equivalent price of approximately $77 per barrel. The Company has modest fuel hedge positions in 2011 through 2013.

Southwest's "hedging" experience demonstrates the difficulties in distinguishing hedging from speculation and illustrates that even well-considered actions do not always deliver favorable outcomes.

[3] www.southwest.com.

[4] "Southwest Airlines Reports First Quarter Results," www.southwest.com.

EXTENSION 13.2: A Hedged Firm Capturing a Tax Loss

Hedging with derivatives expands a company's choices and may allow it to take advantage of tax situations. The next example shows how futures contracts can be used to stabilize earnings so that a company can utilize past losses to reduce current taxes.

EXAMPLE 1: Hedging to Capture a Tax Loss

- Goldmines Inc. (fictitious name) mines, refines, and sells gold in the world market. The company's profits move in tandem with gold price movements. Assume that the pretax profit is $100 million when gold prices go up (which happens with a 50 percent chance) and 0 if gold prices go down (which also happens with a 50 percent chance). Alternatively, Goldmines can hedge with gold futures and have a known profit of $48 million.

- Figure 13.2 shows these payoffs. We label them as event 1 (profit $100) and event 2 (profit $0). These events are shown in a binomial tree, where the payoff $100 is placed on the upper branch of the tree, while $0 is placed on the lower branch.

Computing an Expected Value

- To compute the company's expected profit multiply each event's payoff by its respective probability and then add across events:

> The expected payoff
> = [(Probability of high gold price) × (Payoff $100)] + [(Probability of low gold price)
> × (Payoff $0)]
> = 0.50 × $100 + 0.50 × 0
> = $50

for the unhedged company.

- We can show the superiority of the hedging strategy by computing the expected after-tax profits for the unhedged and hedged firm under different scenarios.

After-Tax Expected Profits (Simple Case)

- Assume that the tax rate is 30 percent. When the gold price is high, $100 million pretax profit gives an after-tax profit of 100 × (1 − tax rate) = $70 million. When the gold price is low, the pretax profit is 0, and so is the after-tax profit. After-tax profits are shown in Figure 13.2.

> Expected after-tax profit for unhedged firm
> = [(Probability of high gold price) × (After-tax profit when the gold price is high)]
> + [(Probability of low gold price) × (After-tax profit when the gold price is low)]
> = 0.50 × 70 + 0.50 × 0
> = $35 million

- The *hedged firm* makes a profit of $48 million irrespective of the gold price:

> After-tax profit for hedged firm
> = 48 × 0.7
> = $33.6 million

- The company can choose either. The actual choice depends on the risk preferences of the company's management and shareholders.

After-Tax Expected Profits (When $25 Million Tax-Deductible Loss Is Carried Forward)

- Now suppose that the company has accumulated losses totaling $25 million. It can deduct this loss from this year's profit and thus lower the tax burden. Such strategies of tax reduction are known as **tax shields**.

- Assume that if unutilized, this one-shot opportunity disappears. We will show that the hedged firm can always utilize the losses to lower its taxes, but the unhedged firm can only do this half the time.

- For the unhedged firm, total tax when the gold price is high is

> (Pretax profit − Loss deducted) × (Tax rate)
> = (100 − 25) × 0.3
> = $22.5 million

FIGURE 13.2: **Profits of a Hedged and an Unhedged Firm**

Pre-Tax Profit

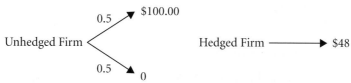

Expected profit of the unhedged firm = 0.5 × 100 + 0.5 × 0 = $50 million

Expected After-Tax Profit (with No Loss Carried Forward)

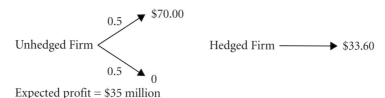

Expected profit = $35 million

Expected After-Tax Profit (with $25 Million Tax Deductible Loss)

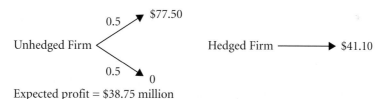

Expected profit = $38.75 million

The total tax when the gold price is low is 0. Consequently, the after-tax profit is (100 − 22.5) = $77.5 million when the gold price is high and zero when it is low (see Figure 13.2):

> Expected after-tax profit for the unhedged firm
> = [(Probability of high gold price) × (After-tax profit when gold price is high)]
>   + [(Probability of low gold price) × (After-tax profit when gold price is low)]
> = 0.50 × 77.5 + 0.50 × 0
> = $38.75 million

■ By contrast, the total tax for the *hedged firm* is (48 − 25) × 0.3 = $6.90:

> After-tax profit for the hedged firm
> = (48 − 6.90)
> = $41.10 million

■ Clearly hedging is a superior strategy: not only does the hedged firm generate greater after-tax profit but it also removes swings and stabilizes this amount.

13.3 | Hedging with Futures

Chapter 4 gave us an inkling of how a company can use forward contracts for hedging input and output price risks. Now that you are more familiar with the workings of a futures contract (which are easier to use than forward contracts), let us explore hedging with futures.

Perfect and Imperfect Hedges

Ours is an imperfect world, in which it is hard to find perfect hedges. A **perfect hedge** completely eliminates spot price risk for some commodity. This happens when (1) the futures is written on the commodity being hedged, (2) the contract matures when you are planning to lift the hedge, and (3) the contract size and the other characteristics of a futures unerringly fit the hedger's need. **Imperfect or cross hedges** occur when these three conditions are not satisfied. For example, a bank may reduce the price risk of its loan portfolio, which is vulnerable to interest rate changes, by trading Treasury bond futures contracts. This is a cross hedge because the futures is written on US Treasury bonds, whereas the loans being hedged consist of, say, house mortgages, car loans, and certificates of deposit. Even when futures on the same commodity are available, the issue of a timing mismatch may occur. Consequently, basis risk emerges as a paramount concept in analyzing, setting, and managing a futures hedge.

Basis Risk

Basis risk is a focal point in understanding futures hedges. The **basis** is defined as the difference between the spot and the futures price. It is written as Basis = Cash price − Futures price. The next example shows how crucial basis risk is when hedging a commodity's spot price risk. We illustrate this in the context of two companies using buying and selling hedges to offset input and output risks, respectively.

EXAMPLE 13.1: A Gold Futures Basis Risk

- Today is January 1, which is time 0. Consider the gold futures contract trading on the COMEX Division of the CME Group described in chapter 8. The prices are reported on a per ounce basis. Figure 13.3 gives the timeline and the various prices. For simplicity, we assume that no interest is earned on margin account balances.

- On today's date, the spot price of gold $S = \$990$, and the June contract's futures price $\mathcal{F}(0) = \$1,000$. The basis is

$$b(0) = \text{Spot price } S(0) - \text{Futures price } \mathcal{F}(0)$$
$$= 990 - 1,000$$
$$= -\$10$$

FIGURE 13.3: **Timeline and Prices for Gold Futures Hedging Example**

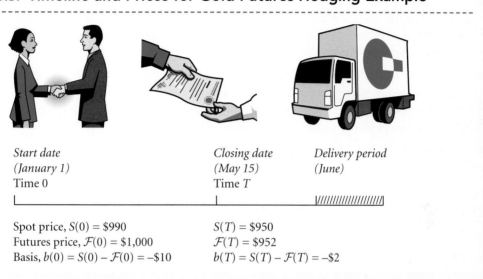

Start date	Closing date	Delivery period
(January 1)	(May 15)	(June)
Time 0	Time T	

Spot price, $S(0) = \$990$ $S(T) = \$950$
Futures price, $\mathcal{F}(0) = \$1,000$ $\mathcal{F}(T) = \$952$
Basis, $b(0) = S(0) - \mathcal{F}(0) = -\$10$ $b(T) = S(T) - \mathcal{F}(T) = -\$2$

- The delivery period for the contract is in June. For the subsequent discussion, suppose that on May 15, time T, the spot price $S(T)$ is \$950 and the June futures price $\mathcal{F}(T)$ is \$952. The new basis is

$$b(T) = S(T) - \mathcal{F}(T)$$
$$= 950 - 952$$
$$= -\$2$$

Goldmines Inc. Sets Up a Short Hedge

- Suppose that the mining company Goldmines Inc. goes short June gold futures contracts on January 1 to hedge its output price risk. The company sells gold and lifts the hedge by closing out the futures position on May 15.

- Goldmines sells gold for \$950, but it makes $-[\mathcal{F}(T) - \mathcal{F}(0)] = -(952 - 1,000) = \$48$ on the futures position. So the effective selling price on May 15 is (see expression [9.1b] of Chapter 9)

$$\text{Spot cash flow} + \text{Futures cash flow}$$
$$= 950 + 48$$
$$= \$998$$

- One can rewrite this as

$$\text{Spot} - (\text{Change in futures prices})$$
$$= S(T) - [\mathcal{F}(T) - \mathcal{F}(0)]$$
$$= [S(T) - \mathcal{F}(T)] + \mathcal{F}(0)$$
$$= \text{New basis} + \text{Old futures price} \qquad (13.1)$$

No matter when the company closes its position, *the old futures price is fixed, and only the new basis affects profits.*

Jewelrygold Inc. Sets Up a Long Hedge

- Now look at the same problem from the perspective of a jewelry maker, Jewelrygold Inc. As discussed in chapter 4, the company can reduce input price risk by setting up a long hedge (a buying hedge) and going long gold futures. When it is time to buy gold in the spot market, the company sells these futures and removes the hedge.

- On January 1, Jewelrygold goes long a June gold futures contract to hedge input price risk. On May 15, the company buys gold for $950 and simultaneously sells futures for $952 to end the hedge. Although Jewelrygold pays less for gold, it has to surrender nearly all of its gains through the hedge. The cash flow from the futures position is $[\mathcal{F}(T) - \mathcal{F}(0)] = 952 - 1,000 = -\$48$.

- Jewelrygold's effective price on May 15 is $998. By looking at the cash flows, the buying price is

$$
\begin{aligned}
&= -\text{Spot} + (\text{Change in futures prices}) \\
&= -S(T) + [\mathcal{F}(T) - \mathcal{F}(0)] \\
&= -[S(T) - \mathcal{F}(T)] - \mathcal{F}(0) \\
&= -(\text{New basis} + \text{Old futures price}) \quad\quad\quad (13.2)
\end{aligned}
$$

This is the same value as in the previous example, except for the minus sign.

This example shows that a futures hedged spot commodity's portfolio value can always be viewed as the sum of the old futures price and the new basis. Consequently, hedgers are interested in how the basis evolves randomly through time. This randomness gives rise to **basis risk** in hedging, which is often measured by computing the basis's variance (or standard deviation). Basis risk is, thus, fundamental to futures hedging, and hedgers often talk about the widening or narrowing of the basis in passionate terms. Many of them have extensive charts depicting the historic behavior of the basis, looking for a crystal ball to foretell the future.

Guidelines for Futures Hedging

Real life is far more complex than textbook examples. Exchanges offer only a handful of futures, whereas there are thousands of commodities. The specter of an imperfect hedge visits us again. When setting up a hedge, it's natural to ask, which contract and for what maturity? The next example discusses the issues involved in answering this question.

EXAMPLE 13.2: Hedging by Selecting a Futures from Several Competing Contracts

Suppose that a new alloy Alloyum (a fictitious name) is developed that can replace precious metals in industrial and ornamental use. Let Alloyum trade in the spot market. Alloyum futures may or may not trade, and we discuss both possibilities. If you produce thirty thousand ounces of Alloyum, how would you hedge output price risk?

Alloyum Futures Trade, and You Know When to Lift the Hedge

This case happens when the Alloyum futures contract's maturity date exactly matches the delivery date of the spot commodity commitment. Then, sell [(Spot position)/(Alloyum futures contract size)] = 30,000/50 = 600 Alloyum futures, assuming a contract size of fifty ounces. Basis risk eventually disappears because the spot converges to the futures price at maturity. This can be shown by setting $S(T) = \mathcal{F}(T)$ in Expression (13.1). With zero basis risk, you fix the selling price at maturity, which is none other than today's futures price. Congratulations, you have set up a perfect hedge. (This perfect hedge ignores the interest rate risk from marking-to-market. Such reinvestment risks will be considered later in the chapter.)

Alloyum Futures Trade, and You Do Not Know When to Lift the Hedge

In this case, one way to proceed is to compute the variance of the basis for different maturity futures contracts on Alloyum and select the one that scores the lowest. Lower basis risk means that the futures price deviates less from the spot price. You are likely to find that the futures contract maturing in the same month as the spot sale is the best candidate. In this case, hedge with the smallest basis risk futures contract. The number of contracts to be shorted may be found by the risk-minimization hedging strategy discussed later in this chapter.

Alloyum Futures Do Not Trade, and You Know When to Lift the Hedge

In this case, you may first like to select a similar commodity on which a futures contract is written and decide on the maturity month. Collect price data for Alloyum and for contender commodity futures contracts maturing in the same month as the spot sale, and compute correlations of price changes as in Tables 13.2a and 13.2b. On the basis of these tables, we select the platinum futures because it has the highest correlation to Alloyum each year as well as in the overall period.

Alloyum Futures Do Not Trade, and You Do Not Know When to Lift the Hedge

This is the worst case for hedging. First, select a commodity futures contract as in the previous case. Then, select a maturity month, and find the futures contract with the largest correlation with Alloyum spot price changes and that minimizes the variance of the basis. Consider the data given in Table 13.2a (Example 13.4 shows how to compute correlations) and Table 13.2b. The futures contract that matures in the spot sale month is the best performer both in terms of the largest correlation and the lowest variance of the basis. It is closely followed by the futures contract maturing a month after the spot sale date.

The preceding analysis recommends the spot sale month futures contract. There is, however, a famous saying in economics that "there are no solutions, only trade-offs" (Sowell 1995, p 113). The other futures contracts may have lower transaction costs. Liquidity is another concern because it often increases as the contract approaches maturity, but dries up in the delivery month. Furthermore, if you happen to be holding a long futures position during the delivery month, then you run the risk of accepting a truckload of the underlying commodity if the short decides to deliver. Thus the next month's futures contract, despite (slight) inferiority in terms of correlation and variance of the basis, may be the better choice.

TABLE 13.2a: Correlations between Alloyum Spot and Precious Metal Spot Month Futures Price Changes[5]

Futures	Years 1–3	Year 1	Year 2	Year 3
Platinum futures	0.78	0.73	0.89	0.83
Gold futures	0.70	0.72	0.73	0.70
Silver futures	0.59	0.58	0.65	0.58

TABLE 13.2b: Correlations between Alloyum Spot and Platinum Price Changes and the Variance of the Basis for Platinum Futures Contracts[6]

Futures Contracts	Correlation of Price Changes	Variance of Basis
Previous-month futures	0.79	3.20
Spot-month futures	0.89	0.88
Next-month futures	0.87	0.99
Sixth-month futures	0.71	9.80

[5] You can create Table 13.2a by (1) recording on a specific day of each month the Alloyum spot price and the precious metal futures price for contracts that mature on that month (this will give four series of observations), (2) noting month-to-month price differences for each of these four series, and finally, (3) computing (by a computer program such as Excel or by hand calculation) the correlations among the Alloyum price and futures price differences for each of these series (this will give three correlations). Alternatively, you can use daily or weekly data for computations.

[6] You can create Table 13.2b by recording on a specific day of each month the Alloyum spot price and the four futures prices (for contracts that matured in the previous month, will mature in the spot month, will mature the following month, and will mature six months from the current month, respectively) and then proceeding as in Table 13.2a. There will be four different series for each basis, each of which is created by subtracting from the Alloyum spot price the relevant futures price.

13.4 | Risk-Minimization Hedging

Suppose that you want to hedge a long spot commodity position by shorting futures contracts. Using a statistical or econometric model, assuming that past price patterns repeat themselves enables you to find the optimal number of contracts to minimize the variance of the hedging error. This section discusses this statistical approach to hedging.

The Mean-Variance Approach

The **mean-variance approach** to risk-minimization hedging (or optimal hedging) determines the optimal number of contracts needed to minimize the variance of the portfolio's price changes. The intuition of this approach can be understood by first considering a perfect hedge:

- *A perfect hedge.* Suppose you are holding a long position in the spot commodity. You need to short futures contracts to hedge the spot commodity's price risk. In the pristine world of a perfect hedge, any change in the spot position will be exactly offset by an equal and opposite change in the futures position. Consequently,

$$
\begin{aligned}
&\text{Change in portfolio value} \\
&= \text{Change in spot position} - \text{Change in futures position} = 0 \qquad (13.3)
\end{aligned}
$$

The minus sign before the change in the futures position is because we are short the futures contract and the spot and futures prices move in the same direction. With minor modifications, we can recast the problem to focus on how changes in the spot and futures prices per unit are related. Using data from Example 13.2, we can hedge a long position of thirty thousand ounces of Alloyum production by selling [(Cash position)/(Alloyum futures contract size)] = 30,000/50 = 600 Alloyum futures. We can write this as follows:

$$
\begin{aligned}
\text{Change in portfolio value} &= (30{,}000 \times \text{Change in spot price per ounce}) \\
&\quad - (600 \times 50 \times \text{Change in futures price per ounce}) \\
&= 0 \qquad (13.4)
\end{aligned}
$$

There is no change in the portfolio value because the spot and the futures price changes exactly match.

- *An imperfect hedge.* In reality, the hedge will be imperfect because the spot and the futures price changes do not exactly match. Here you can find the risk-minimizing number of futures contracts. Consider hedging our spot exposure of n ounces by selling q futures contracts of size f ounces per contract. Then we can rewrite the left side of expression (13.4) as

$$
\begin{aligned}
\text{Change in portfolio value} &= (n \times \text{Change in spot price per ounce}) \\
&\quad - (q \times f \times \text{Change in futures price per ounce}) \\
&= n[S(t) - S] - qf[\mathcal{F}(t) - \mathcal{F}] \\
&= n\Delta S - qf\Delta\mathcal{F} \qquad (13.5)
\end{aligned}
$$

where $S(t)$ and S are the spot prices per ounce on some future date (time t) and today (time 0), $\mathcal{F}(t)$ and $\mathcal{F}$ are futures prices per unit on those same respective dates, and Δ compactly denotes the price change. Note that this change does not equal zero because it is an imperfect hedge. To find the number of contracts to sell to risk-minimize hedge the spot portfolio, compute the variance of the portfolio and select n to minimize this variance. You can do this by taking the partial derivative of the portfolio variance with respect to q, setting it equal to zero, and solving for q (see the appendix to this chapter). This leads to the following result.

RESULT 13.1

The Risk-Minimizing Number of Futures Contracts for Hedging a Spot Commodity Position

To minimize the risk of a long portfolio of a spot commodity, sell short q contracts where

$$q = (n/f)h \tag{13.6}$$

and n is the size of the spot position, f is the number of units of the underlying commodity in one futures contract, and h is the optimal hedge ratio (or minimum-variance hedge ratio or risk-minimized hedge ratio).

The optimal hedge ratio is given by

$$h = \frac{cov_{S,F}}{var_F} = \frac{sd_S}{sd_F} corr_{S,F} \tag{13.7}$$

where $cov_{S,F}$ is the covariance between changes in the spot price (ΔS) and the futures price ($\Delta \mathcal{F}$), var_F is the variance of the change in the futures price, sd_S is the standard deviation (or volatility) of the change in the spot price (standard deviation is the positive square root of the variance), sd_F is the standard deviation of change in the futures price, and $corr_{S,F}$ is the correlation coefficient between ΔS and $\Delta \mathcal{F}$.[7]

---

[7] The second part of the formula follows from the result: "covariance equals the product of the standard deviations and the correlation coefficient" or $cov_{S,F} = sd_S \times sd_F \times corr_{S,F}$.

Considering various cases reveals the intuition behind this result. Suppose that the price changes for the spot commodity and the futures contract are perfectly correlated (i.e., $corr_{S,F}$ equals 1) and their standard deviations match (i.e., $sd_S = sd_F$). Then the optimal hedge ratio h equals 1. This is the holy grail of a perfect hedge, which is nearly impossible to attain in practice but is useful as an illustration.

Next assume that there is a high correlation between the price changes ($corr_{S,F}$ is close to one) and the spot price change has a lower volatility than the futures price change (i.e., $sd_S < sd_F$). Then a unit of spot is hedged with less than a unit of futures. Conversely, if the spot price change fluctuates more than the futures price change (i.e., $sd_S > sd_F$), then one unit of spot needs more than one unit of the futures to hedge.

The optimal hedge ratio gives us an easy formula for setting up a futures hedge. Example 13.3 shows how to implement this by utilizing spot and futures price data, which can be easily collected from business newspapers or Internet data sources.

EXAMPLE 13.3: Setting Up a Risk-Minimization Hedge with Price Data

- Suppose that you are planning to sell thirty thousand ounces of Alloyum at some future date. To start, you collect Alloyum spot price and platinum futures price data for sixteen consecutive trading days (see Table 13.3).

- Begin by computing the price differences for each of these two series of price observations. Next use a spreadsheet to compute the parameter estimates needed for the optimal hedge ratio. (The appendix to this chapter discusses related issues and demonstrates how to find h with the help of a simple calculator; section 13.6 shows how to do these calculations using the spreadsheet program Microsoft Excel.) We get

  the standard deviation of changes in the futures price per unit, $sd_F = 14.3368$
  the standard deviation of changes in the spot price $sd_S = 15.5002$
  the correlation coefficient between the spot and futures price changes, $corr_{S,F} = 0.7413$

- Use these estimates in the second part of expression (13.7) of Result 13.1 to compute the minimum-variance hedge ratio:

$$h = \frac{sd_S}{sd_F} corr_{S,F} = \frac{15.5002}{14.3368} 0.7413 = 0.8015^8$$

- To hedge $n = 30{,}000$ ounces of Alloyum with a platinum futures contract (contract size $f = 50$), you need to sell

$$q = (n/f)h$$
$$= (30{,}000/50)0.8015$$
$$= 480.9 \text{ or } 481 \text{ contracts (with integer rounding)}$$

---

[8] Or, you can use the first part of Result 13.1 to determine the optimal hedge ratio, $h = cov_{S,F}/var_F = 18.3048/22.8381 = 0.8015$.

Alternatively, you can compute the hedge ratio by suitably framing the problem and estimating a linear regression (see the appendix to this chapter).

Limitations of Risk-Minimization Hedging

Comedian Rodney Dangerfield often chuckled, "I don't get no respect." Doesn't this comment apply to risk-minimization hedging? It is purely computational, and except for some ad hoc adjustments, it is a single-shot exercise with no prescription for modifying the hedge over time. It works well if a closely related commodity can be found and you know when to lift the hedge. It works less well otherwise and if the hedge needs to be rolled over or rebalanced.

TABLE 13.3: Alloyum Spot and Platinum Futures Price Data

Day t	Alloyum Spot $S(t)$	Platinum Futures $\mathcal{F}(t)$
0	1,215	1,233
1	1,209	1,236
2	1,239	1,245
3	1,245	1,254
4	1,254	1,272
5	1,227	1,254
6	1,230	1,248
7	1,224	1,242
8	1,239	1,260
9	1,251	1,263
10	1,227	1,254
11	1,215	1,227
12	1,209	1,221
13	1,203	1,230
14	1,185	1,203
15	1,194	1,209

The idea of rebalancing is related to the concept of (exact) **dynamic hedging**, which involves regular adjustments to a perfect hedge over time. Dynamic hedging requires sophisticated analytical tools, and it applies in a complete market. It is impossible to implement in an incomplete market (see Duffie [1989] and Jarrow and Turnbull [2000] for examples and issues related to dynamic hedging). In complete markets (remember chapter 8), all kinds of securities trade that generate future payoffs contingent on all possible future events. In reality, the markets are incomplete, and it may be difficult to develop good futures pricing models to which dynamic hedging applies. Consequently, risk-minimization hedging, despite all its limitations, starts looking respectable again. In incomplete markets, it continues to attract serious research interest.

13.5 | Futures versus Forward Hedging

It's common practice in many circles to treat forwards and futures as equivalent and interchangeable contracts. However, this is incorrect for many reasons. Although a forward is easy to price, ordinary investors rarely trade in the "organized" forward market. Big banks, large corporations, and other institutions with excellent credit ratings dominate this market, and to guarantee execution of the contracts, these financial institutions usually need to post collateral. These trading restrictions are imposed to reduce "counterparty credit risk"—the nonexecution of the contract terms. Counterparty credit risk is a big concern in the trading of over-the-counter derivatives, as recently evidenced by the related regulatory reforms following the

2007 credit crisis in the Dodd–Frank Wall Street Reform and Consumer Protection Act (see chapter 26 for more discussion of these issues). Second, given that forward contracts are bilateral negotiated agreements, forward markets are illiquid and subject to significant liquidity risk. For example, if a counterparty closes a forward contract early, significant closing costs are incurred.

By contrast, a futures (1) is an exchange-traded, standardized contract; (2) has margins and daily settlement, which makes it safer than a forward due to the absence of credit risk; (3) allows small traders, weaker credits, and complete strangers to participate; and (4) usually trades in a liquid market, where traders can enter or unwind their positions with ease.

But there is another important difference between futures and forward contracts due to the marking-to-market of a futures contract. Marking-to-market a futures contract introduces risks involved with reinvesting the cash flows before the contract matures. These same reinvestment risks are not faced by a forward contract. Tracking the cash flows to these contracts, the futures trader, unlike the forward trader, earns random and uncertain interest on margin balances.

As discussed in chapter 9, the interest earned on a futures margin account is dependent on the futures price changes. In addition, interest rate changes also affect the interest earnings. Indeed, if interest rate changes are positively correlated with futures price changes, then the futures position benefits from interest rate movements because as cash flows are received, more interest is earned. In this case, the risk of a futures position is reduced slightly. Conversely, if interest rate changes are negatively correlated with futures price changes, then the futures position suffers from interest rate movements. In this latter case, the risk is increased. This interest rate risk affects hedging performance because of the random cash flows received. This same risk is not present in a forward contract.

13.6 | Spreadsheet Applications: Computing *h*

You can easily compute the optimal hedge ratio (*h*) by using a standard spreadsheet program such as Microsoft Excel. Next we demonstrate this for Example 13.3.

EXAMPLE 13.3: Computing the Optimal Hedge Ratio (Solved Using Microsoft Excel)

Generating the Inputs

Consider the same data as in Example 13.3. Type in the numbers and the terms exactly as follows in an Excel spreadsheet (see Table 13.4):

- Type *Day t* in cell A1, 0 in A2, 1 in A3, 2 in A4, and so on up to 15 in cell A17. You may speed up data entry by using the Auto Fill feature: type 0 in A2 and 1 in A3, highlight the cells A2 and A3, and then drag down the bottom right hand corner of the cursor so that the desired values get filled in cells A4 to A17.

- Type $S(t)$ in B1 and then fill out the Alloyum spot prices as given in Table 13.3: 1,215 in B2, 1,209 in B3, and so on, up to 1,194 in B17.

- Type $\mathcal{F}(t)$ in C1 and then fill out the platinum futures prices $\mathcal{F}(t)$ as given in Table 11.2 for sixteen consecutive trading days.

- Type $\Delta S(t)$ in D1 and then type "= B3 − B2" in D3, "= B4 − B3" in D4, and so on. You may speed this up by using the Auto Fill feature: type "= B3 − B2" in D3 and then drag down the bottom right hand corner of the cursor so that the desired values fill in cells D4 to D17.

- Type $\Delta \mathcal{F}(t)$ in E1 and then type "= C3 − C2" in E3. Use Auto Fill as we have just mentioned and fill out the desired values in cells E4 to E17.

TABLE 13.4: Computing h Using Microsoft Excel

A	B	C	D	E	F	G	H
					$\Delta S(t) \times$	$\Delta \mathcal{F}(t) \times$	$\Delta S(t) \times$
Day t	$S(t)$	$\mathcal{F}(t)$	$\Delta S(t)$	$\Delta \mathcal{F}(t)$	$\Delta S(t)$	$\Delta \mathcal{F}(t)$	$\Delta \mathcal{F}(t)$
0	1,215	1,233					
1	1,209	1,236	−6	3	36	9	−18
2	1,239	1,245	30	9	900	81	270
3	1,245	1,254	6	9	36	81	54
4	1,254	1,272	9	18	81	324	162
5	1,227	1,254	−27	−18	729	324	486
6	1,230	1,248	3	−6	9	36	−18
7	1,224	1,242	−6	−6	36	36	36
8	1,239	1,260	15	18	225	324	270
9	1,251	1,263	12	3	144	9	36
10	1,227	1,254	−24	−9	576	81	216
11	1,215	1,227	−12	−27	144	729	324
12	1,209	1,221	−6	−6	36	36	36
13	1,203	1,230	−6	9	36	81	−54
14	1,185	1,203	−18	−27	324	729	486
15	1,194	1,209	9	6	81	36	54
Sums			−21	−24	3,393	2,916	2,340
VARA			240.2571	205.5429			
STDEV			15.50023	14.33677			
COVAR			164.7429				
CORREL			0.74134				
h			0.801501	0.801501			

Computing Estimates from the Sample and the Minimum-Variance Hedge Ratio

The entries in columns D and E are the two data series with which we work. You can do the computations as follows (and verify that these are the same as the sample variances that you computed in Example 13.3):

- Type in a name for the sample variance such as VARA in cell A20, type "= VARA(D3:D17)" in D20 and hit return to get 240.2571, and type "= VARA(E3:E17)" in E20 and hit return to get 205.5429.

- Type STDEV in A21, type "= STDEV(D3:D17)" in D21 and hit return to get 15.50023, and type "= STDEV(E3:E17)" in E21 and hit return to get 14.33677.

- As Excel's covariance formula is given for the population, you need to multiply the estimator by $n/(n-1)$ to get the sample estimate. Accordingly, type COVAR in A22, and type "= COVAR(D3:D17,E3:E17)*(15/14)" in D22 and hit return to get 164.7429.

- Type CORREL in A23 and "= CORREL(D3:D17,E3:E17)" in D23 and hit return to get 0.74134.

- Type h in A24 and "= D22/E20" in D24 and hit return to get 0.801501. This is the expression (13.6) given in Result 13.1. You may also get h via the second result in (13.6) by typing "= D23*D21/E21" in E24 and hitting return—it's the same answer.

13.7 │ Summary

1. Most futures contracts are traded to hedge spot commodity price risk. Producers may set up a long hedge (or a buying hedge) to fix the buying price for an input and a short hedge (or a selling hedge) to fix the selling price of an output.

2. As with any other derivatives, the costs and the benefits must be carefully weighed before hedging a spot commodity with futures. They involve direct and indirect costs: the brokers must be paid, and a trade may fetch a bad price. But hedging also has many potential benefits: it can stretch the marketing period, protect inventory value, permit forward pricing of products, reduce the risk of default and financial distress costs, and perhaps facilitate taking advantage of a tax loss or tax credit.

3. A perfect hedge completely eliminates price risk. It happens when (1) the futures is written on the commodity being hedged and (2) the contract matures when you are planning to lift the hedge. Generally, there is basis risk. The basis is defined as the difference between the spot price and the futures price.

4. For a seller of a futures contract who hedges output price risk, the effective selling price is (new basis + old futures price). For a buyer of a futures contract who hedges input price risk, the effective buying price is the negative of (new basis + old futures price).

5. We can use a statistical model, assuming past price patterns repeat themselves, to set up a risk-minimization hedge. To minimize the risk of a long portfolio

of the spot commodity, sell short $q = (n/f)h$ contracts, where n is the size of the spot position, f is the contract size, and h is the optimal hedge ratio (or minimum-variance hedge ratio) defined as $cov_{S,F}/var_F$, where $cov_{S,F}$ is the sample covariance between the change in the spot price (ΔS) and the change in the futures price per ($\Delta \mathcal{F}$) and var_F is the variance of the change in the futures price.

13.8 | Appendix

Deriving the Minimum-Variance Hedge Ratio (h)

Suppose you are planning to sell n units of a spot commodity at some future date and decide to hedge this exposure by selling short q futures contracts today.

- Rewrite the change in the portfolio value between today (time 0) and some future date (time t) as

$$\Delta \text{Portfolio}$$
$$= (n \times \text{Change in spot price}) - (q \times f \times \text{Change in futures price})$$
$$= n[S(t) - S(0)] - qf[\mathcal{F}(t) - c(0)]$$
$$= n\Delta S - qf\Delta\mathcal{F} \tag{13.8}$$

where f is the number of units of the futures contract, $S(t)$ is the spot price at date t, $\mathcal{F}(t)$ is the futures price at date t, and Δ denotes a price change.

- Select q so as to minimize the change in the portfolio value. First, use statistics to compute the variance of the portfolio's price change:

$$\text{variance}(aX - bY) \equiv a^2 variance(X) + b^2 variance(Y) - 2ab[covariance(X, Y)] \tag{13.9}$$

where a and b are constants and X and Y are random variables. As n, q, and f are constant parameters, set $a = n$, $b = qf$, $X = \Delta S$, and $Y = \Delta\mathcal{F}$ in expression (13.9) to get

$$var(\Delta \text{Portfolio}) = n^2 var_S + (qf)^2 var_F - 2nqf \times cov_{S,F} \tag{13.10}$$

where var_S is the variance of change in the spot price (ΔS), var_F is the variance of change in the futures price ($\Delta\mathcal{F}$), and $cov_{S,F}$ is the sample covariance between the change in the spot and futures prices.

- Using calculus, we minimize expression (13.10) by taking the partial derivative with respect to q and setting it equal to zero:

$$\frac{\partial}{\partial q}[var(\Delta \text{Portfolio})] = 2qf^2 var_F - 2nf\, cov_{S,F} = 0$$

The second partial derivative is a positive number, which indicates that this minimizes the expression. Rearrange terms to get the number of futures contracts to sell short (or go long in case you are setting up a buying hedge):

$$q = (n/f)h \qquad (13.11)$$

where the optimal hedge ratio h equals $(cov_{S,F}/var_F)$.

Computing the Minimum-Variance Hedge Ratio (h)

Example 13.3 shows how to input the values into a business calculator or a computer to determine the minimum variance hedge ratio (h). Here we show how to directly calculate h.

Statistical Approach

Start by deciding how frequently and over what time interval you collect your data. Standard practice is to fix a time interval (daily, weekly, or monthly) and use the end of the interval's settlement prices.

DATA SERIES

- To cross-hedge Alloyum spot with platinum futures, we need their prices as basic inputs. These are reported in Table 13.5 (Appendix), whose first three columns are as follows:
  - The first column is labeled *Day t*, and it keeps track of the days. There are $(T + 1) = 16$ observations corresponding to sixteen consecutive trading days, where t "runs" from day 0 to day $t = 15$.
  - Columns 2 and 3 record the Alloyum spot price $S(t)$ and the platinum futures price $\mathcal{F}(t)$, respectively, for these sixteen consecutive trading days. All prices are reported for one unit of the respective commodity.

PRICE DIFFERENCES

- Compute price differences for each price series.
  - Column 4 reports changes in the value for Alloyum spot. Denote the spot price change from date $(t - 1)$ to date t as $\Delta S(t) \equiv S(t) - S(t - 1)$. Label column 4 as $x(t)$ for convenience. For example, when $t = 6$,

$$x(6) \equiv \Delta S(6) \equiv S(6) - S(5) = 1{,}230 - 1{,}227 = 3$$

  - Column 5 does the same for platinum futures. Label this as $y(t)$. For example,

$$y(6) \equiv \Delta\mathcal{F}(6) = \Delta\mathcal{F}(t) \equiv \mathcal{F}(t) - \mathcal{F}(t - 1)$$
$$= \mathcal{F}(6) - \mathcal{F}(5) = 1{,}248 - 1{,}254 = -6$$

- Notice that when computing the "difference," you lose the first observation. We now have $T = 15$ observations. We denote them by t, where $t = 1, 2, \ldots, 15$.

- We can now forget our second and third columns. We use the fourth and fifth columns to compute the minimum-variance hedge ratio h.

TABLE 13.5: Price Data and Calculations for the Minimum-Variance Hedge Ratio (h)

Day t	Alloyum Spot $S(t)$	Platinum Futures $\mathcal{F}(t)$	$\Delta S(t) \equiv S(t) - S(t-1) \equiv x(t)$	$\Delta\mathcal{F}(t) \equiv \mathcal{F}(t) - \mathcal{F}(t-1) \equiv y(t)$	$[\Delta S(t)]^2 \equiv x(t)^2$	$[\Delta\mathcal{F}(t)]^2 \equiv y(t)^2$	$\Delta S(t) \times \Delta\mathcal{F}(t) \equiv x(t)y(t)$
0	1,215	1,233					
1	1,209	1,236	−6	3	36	9	−18
2	1,239	1,245	30	9	900	81	270
3	1,245	1,254	6	9	36	81	54
4	1,254	1,272	9	18	81	324	162
5	1,227	1,254	−27	−18	729	324	486
6	1,230	1,248	3	−6	9	36	−18
7	1,224	1,242	−6	−6	36	36	36
8	1,239	1,260	15	18	225	324	270
9	1,251	1,263	12	3	144	9	36
10	1,227	1,254	−24	−9	576	81	216
11	1,215	1,227	−12	−27	144	729	324
12	1,209	1,221	−6	−6	36	36	36
13	1,203	1,230	−6	9	36	81	−54
14	1,185	1,203	−18	−27	324	729	486
15	1,194	1,209	9	6	81	36	54
Sums			$\Sigma x = -21$	$\Sigma y = -24$	$\Sigma x^2 = 3,393$	$\Sigma y^2 = 2,916$	$\Sigma xy = 2,340$

Some values useful for the computations follow:

$$\sum_{t=1}^{T} x(t) = -21$$

$$\sum_{1}^{15} y(t) = -24$$

$$\sum x(t)^2 = 3,393$$

$$\sum y^2 = 2,916$$

$$\sum_{t=1}^{15} x(t)y(t) = 2,340$$

COMPUTATION-SIMPLIFYING TECHNIQUES

- Three more columns are introduced to help simplify our calculations.
  - Columns 6 and 7 record the square of the price changes reported in columns 4 and 5, respectively. Finally, column 7 reports the product of the values in columns 5 and 6. For example, when $t = 6$, we get

$$[x(6)]^2 = 3^2 = 9$$
$$[y(6)]^2 = (-6)^2 = 36$$
$$x(6)y(6) = -18$$

STATISTICAL ESTIMATES

- To compute h from historical data, modify our formulas for covariance and variance by replacing the T with $(T-1)$ in the denominator to get an unbiased estimate.[9]

- We get the following parameter estimates to help us compute h (see Table 13.6 [Appendix]):

   sample covariance, $cov_{S,F} = 164.7429$
   sample variance of ΔS, $var_S = 240.2571$
   sample variance of ΔF, $var_F = 205.5429$
   sample standard deviations, $sd_S = 15.5002$ and $sd_F = 14.3367$
   correlation coefficient between ΔS and $\Delta \mathcal{F}$, $corr_{S,F} = 0.7413$

- These estimates are used to compute the minimum-variance hedge ratio h. The first part of equation (13.7) of Result 13.1 gives

$$h = \frac{cov_{S,F}}{var_F} = \frac{164.7429}{205.5429} = 0.8015 \tag{13.12}$$

while the second part verifies the same result:

$$h = \frac{sd_S}{sd_F} \, corr_{S,F} = \frac{15.5002}{14.3367} \, 0.7413 = 0.8015 \tag{13.13}$$

- If you are estimating these values over a longer period, then you run the risk that a futures contract may mature and no longer trade. Suppose you are hedging with the "nearest maturity" futures contract, whose price changes are likely to have the best correlation with the spot price changes. Suppose this contract stops trading on day 12. Select the futures contract that is going to mature next, get its futures prices for days 12 and 13, and write the price difference $\Delta \mathcal{F}(13) \equiv \mathcal{F}(13) - \mathcal{F}(12)$ in the first table in the cell corresponding to day 13's price difference.

Econometric Approach: A Linear Regression Model

Econometrics is the branch of economics that studies relationships between economic variables using mathematics and statistics. A staple of econometrics is the **linear regression model**,[10] in which a dependent variable may be determined

---

[9] Such adjustments make the estimator BLUE, and statisticians love "BLUEs" (Best Linear Unbiased Estimators). See DeGroot and Schervish (2011), or Mood et al. (1974).

[10] See standard econometrics textbooks like Amemiya (1994) or Johnston and DiNardo (1997) for a discussion of the linear regression model.

TABLE 13.6: Statistical Estimates and Computation of the Optimal Hedge Ratio h

Statistical Estimate	Formula	Computations	Estimated Value
a. Sample mean, $\bar{x}$	$\dfrac{1}{T}\sum_{t=1}^{T}x(t)$	$-21/15$	-1.4000
b. Sample mean, $\bar{y}$	$\dfrac{1}{15}\sum_{t=1}^{15}y(t)$	$-24/15$	-1.6000
c. Sample covariance of ΔS and $\Delta \mathcal{F}$, $cov_{S,F}$	$\dfrac{1}{T-1}\sum_{t=1}^{T}\left[x(t)-\bar{x}\right]\times\left[y(t)-\bar{y}\right]$ $=\dfrac{1}{14}\left\{\left[\sum_{t=1}^{15}x(t)y(t)\right]-15\bar{x}\bar{y}\right\}$	$\dfrac{1}{14}\left[2{,}340-15\left(\dfrac{-21}{15}\right)\left(\dfrac{-24}{15}\right)\right]$	164.7429
d. Sample variance of ΔS, var_S	$\dfrac{1}{T-1}\sum_{t=1}^{T}\left[x(t)-\bar{x}\right]^2$ $=\dfrac{1}{14}\left[\sum_{t=1}^{15}x(t)^2-15\bar{x}^2\right]$	$\dfrac{1}{14}\left[3{,}393-15\left(\dfrac{-21}{15}\right)^2\right]$	240.2571
e. Sample variance of $\Delta \mathcal{F}$, var_F	$\dfrac{1}{T-1}\sum_{t=1}^{T}\left[y(t)-\bar{y}\right]^2$	$\dfrac{1}{14}\left[2{,}916-15\left(\dfrac{-24}{15}\right)^2\right]$	205.5429
f. Sample standard deviation of ΔS, sd_S	$+\sqrt{var_S}$	$+\sqrt{240.2571}$	15.5002
g. Sample standard deviation of $\Delta \mathcal{F}$, sd_F	$+\sqrt{var_F}$	$+\sqrt{205.5429}$	14.3367
h. Correlation coefficient between ΔS and $\Delta \mathcal{F}$, $corr_{S,F}$	$\dfrac{cov_{S,F}}{sd_S\times sd_F}$	$\dfrac{164.7429}{15.5002\times 14.3367}$	0.7413
i. Minimum-variance hedge ratio, h	$\dfrac{cov_{S,F}}{var_F}$	$\dfrac{164.7429}{205.5429}$	0.8015
j. h (alternate computation)	$\dfrac{sd_S}{sd_F}corr_{S,F}$	$0.7413\left(\dfrac{15.5002}{14.3367}\right)$	0.8015

from the values of one or more independent variables, under the assumption that these variables are linearly related. In this case, the model takes the form

$$\Delta S(t)=\alpha+\beta\Delta\mathcal{F}(t)+u(t) \qquad (13.14)$$

where α and β are unknown parameters and $u(t)$ are independent and identically distributed error terms with an expected value of 0 and a constant variance.

Next you have to estimate these parameters. The most popular approach is the **least squares method**, in which α and β are chosen so that the sum of squared errors $\Sigma[\Delta S(t)-\alpha-\beta\Delta\mathcal{F}(t)]^2$ is minimized. Interestingly, the value of β obtained is identical to the hedge ratio h in Result 13.1. This makes life easy. Estimate the regression equation (13.12) by hand or by using a standard statistical package like MATHEMATICA, MINITAB, SAS, or TSP, and the estimated value of β will give you the hedge ratio. Spreadsheet programs like Microsoft Excel can also run regressions.

13.9 | Cases

Lufthansa: To Hedge or Not to Hedge . . . (Richard Ivey School of Business Foundation Case 900N22-PDF-ENG-PDF-ENG, Harvard Business Publishing). A short case that explores the costs and benefits of hedging and the derivatives that may be used for hedging purposes.

Enron Gas Services (Harvard Business School Case 294076-PDF-ENG). The case considers the risks and opportunities of selling a variety of natural gas derivatives by a financial services subsidiary of the largest US integrated natural gas firm.

Aspen Technology Inc.: Currency Hedging Review (Harvard Business School Case 296027-PDF-ENG). The case examines how a small, young firm's business strategy creates currency exposure and how one can manage such risks.

13.10 | Questions and Problems

13.1. Define a long hedge and a short hedge and give examples of each kind of hedge.

13.2. What are the benefits of a corporation's hedging? In your answer, explain why the corporation and not the corporation's equity holders must do the hedging. Are there any costs to a corporation's hedging?

13.3. What is the difference between a perfect hedge and a cross hedge? Give examples to clarify your answer.

13.4. If one cannot create a perfect hedge, what are the alternatives? Give an example to explain your answer.

13.5. What is the basis for a futures contract? What happens to the basis on the delivery date?

13.6. There is no futures contract on aviation fuel. Combo Air Inc. has to buy 3 million gallons of aviation fuel in three months. Suppose you are in charge of Combo Air's hedging activities. You gather the following data:

TABLE 13A: Jet Fuel Cash Prices vs. Near Month Energy Futures Prices: Correlations of Price Changes

	1986–88	1986	1987	1988
Heating oil futures	0.54	0.76	0.89	0.32
Gasoline futures	0.41	0.74	0.73	0.19
Crude oil futures	0.45	0.70	0.72	0.25

a. Which energy futures contract will you choose for hedging jet fuel purchase?

b. Is this a long hedge or a short hedge?

13.7. The *variance* of monthly changes in the spot price of live cattle is (in cents per pound) 1.5. The *variance* of monthly changes in the futures price of live cattle for the April contract is 2. The correlation between these two price changes is 0.8. Today is March 11. The beef producer is committed to purchasing four hundred thousand pounds of live cattle on April 15. The producer wants to use the April cattle futures contract to hedge its risk. What strategy should the beef producer follow? (The contract size is forty thousand pounds.)

13.8. Are hedging with forwards and futures contracts the same, or are there different risks to be considered when using these two contracts? Explain your answer.

13.9. When you hedge a commodity's price risk using a futures contract, give an example where the counterparty is also hedging. Give an example where the counterparty is speculating.

13.10. Kellogg will buy 2 million bushels of oats in two months. Kellogg finds that the *ratio* of the standard deviation of change in spot and futures prices over a two-month period for oats is 0.83 and the coefficient of correlation between the two-month change in price of oats and the two-month change in its futures price is 0.7.

   a. Find the optimal hedge ratio for Kellogg.

   b. How many contracts do they need to hedge their position? (The size of each oats contract is five thousand bushels; oats trades in the CME Group.)

13.11. Explain why hedging is like buying an insurance policy. To buy an insurance policy, you need to pay a premium; what is the corresponding premium in hedging? Give an example to clarify your answer.

13.12. Suppose that after you graduate, you plan to be a stock analyst for a major financial institution. You know that if the stock market increases in value, you will get a job with a good salary. If the stock market declines, you will get a job, but the salary will be lower. How can you hedge your salary risk using futures contracts? Is this a perfect or imperfect hedge?

13.13. Your company will buy tungsten for making electric light filaments in the next three to six months. Suppose there are no futures on tungsten. How would you hedge this risk? (Discuss the type of hedge, general hedging approach, and guidelines that you would like to follow.)

13.14. You are the owner of a car rental business. If gasoline prices increase, your car rental revenues will decline. How can you hedge your car rental revenue risk using futures contracts? Is this a perfect or imperfect hedge?

13.15. What commodity price risk does Southwest Airlines hedge, and why? Has it always been successful in its hedging program?

13.16. What is risk-minimizing hedging? Briefly outline how you would set up a risk-minimizing hedge. Is a risk-minimizing hedge a perfect or imperfect hedge? Explain your answer.

13.17. Canadian American Gold Inc. (CAG) has half its gold production from mines located in Canada, while the other half is from those in the United States. CAG uses a quarter of its production for making gold jewelry sold at a fixed price through stores in the two nations, and the rest is sold on the world market, where the gold price is determined in US dollars. Canadian profits are repatriated to the United States, where CAG's headquarters are located. CAG's chief executive officer wants to use futures contracts to hedge the entire production of ten thousand ounces of gold and as many other transactions as possible. He communicates his desire to you but seeks your opinion one last time before the orders go out. Devise a sensible hedging strategy that would still be in line with the CEO's wishes (assume x is the quantity used for making gold jewelry in the United States).

13.18. The spot price of gold today is $1,505 per ounce, and the futures price for a contract maturing in seven months is $1,548 per ounce. Suppose CAG puts on a futures hedge today and lifts the hedge after five months. What is the futures price five months from now? Assume a zero basis in your answer.

13.19. Suppose that Jewelry Company is planning to sell twenty thousand ounces of platinum at some future date. The standard deviation of changes in the futures price per ounce sd_F is 12.86, that for changes in the spot price per ounce sd_S is 14.38, and the correlation coefficient between the spot and futures price changes $corr_{S,F}$ is 0.80.

a. Compute the optimal hedge ratio for Jewelry Co.

b. How many contracts do they need to hedge their position? (The contract size is fifty ounces.)

c. Will this be a buying or a selling hedge?

13.20. (Microsoft Excel) Given the following data, compute the hedge ratio for a risk minimizing hedge.

Day t	Alloyum Spot $S(t)$	Platinum Futures $\mathcal{F}(t)$
0	1,233	1,245
1	1,219	1,256
2	1,118	1,130
3	1,246	1,264
4	1,250	1,280
5	1,219	1,223
6	1,230	1,248
7	1,227	1,280
8	1,249	1,260
9	1,225	1,289
10	1,227	1,254
11	1,223	1,255
12	1,211	1,223
13	1,203	1,267
14	1,189	1,213
15	1,199	1,219

Options

14

Options Markets and Trading

14.1 | Introduction

Believe it or not, governments trade derivatives. Distinguished economist Lawrence Summers recounted an interesting experience when he was deputy secretary of the US Treasury (see Summers 1999, p. 3):

> Any doubt I might have had about the globalization of economic thinking was shattered when I met with Chinese Premier Zhu Rhongji in early 1997 in the same pavilion where Chairman Mao had received foreign visitors. After being offered a Diet Coke, I was asked a variety of searching questions about the possible use of *put options* [emphasis added] in defending a currency, and how they might best be structured.

A communist leader dabbling in derivatives!

A more recent example of derivative securities being used to support a government's fiscal and monetary policy occurred in the United States during the 2007 credit crisis. To reduce the cost of the capital infusion by the US Treasury into financial institutions under the Troubled Asset Relief Program (TARP), warrants—a type of call option—were used. These warrants, issued to the US Treasury by the banks receiving the TARP funds, provided additional upside potential to the US Treasury. After the banks recovered, the US Treasury made significant profits on its warrant positions, reducing the cost of the TARP program. Exactly as hoped!

This chapter continues our discussion of options and their markets started in chapter 5. First, we review the history of options trading, which is divided into two phases around the watershed year of 1973. Next we describe some features of options contracts. We end the chapter with regulatory issues, including market manipulation. Although our discussions primarily revolve around **equity options**, many of the features discussed here are similar to other options encountered later in this book and elsewhere in life.

14.2 | Exchange-Traded Options

Why trade options? Unlike futures, options have asymmetric payoffs, a special feature that allows users to carve out richer payoff structures than what's otherwise obtainable. This makes options valuable tools for hedging, speculation, and risk management. Because the holder is rewarded when the underlying moves favorably but has no loss when it moves adversely, options are similar to insurance contracts and require a premium payment at their onset. But regular use of options can get expensive, and one must carefully weigh the costs and benefits before trading an option. We skip discussing the applications and uses of options because of its similarity with our earlier discussion of the applications and uses of derivatives (see section 1.3), swaps (see section 7.5), and forwards and futures (see section 8.2).

Although options have traded over the counter (OTC) for hundreds of years, the market really took off when exchange-traded options were introduced on the Chicago Board Options Exchange (CBOE) in 1973. The reasons are twofold. First, an exchange creates a central marketplace: an orderly, efficient, and liquid market with low transaction costs where traders can enter or exit positions with ease. Second, a clearinghouse for the exchange guarantees contract performance and makes trades virtually free from credit risk. The resulting popularity of plain vanilla exchange-traded options paved the way for the development of the now gigantic OTC market for trading customized, complex options. The causation did not happen in reverse. Although OTC options have traded for centuries, their market remained small and inefficient, fraught with credit and legal risks, never catching on with the investing public until after exchange traded options became popular. Why did it happen this way? To find out, read on.

14.3 | A History of Options

"History has many cunning passages, contrived corridors," wrote T. S. Eliot in the poem "Gerontion." This describes the history of options. Option-like contracts arise naturally in economic life. One enters a call-like agreement when you pay a deposit in advance of buying a house with the provision that your failure to complete the purchase forfeits this amount; you enter into a put-like contract when you buy insurance by paying a premium. The term *premium* also denotes the price of an option, which reinforces the close link between options and insurance.

Despite these similarities, the options and insurance markets went their separate ways. Insurance contracts have enjoyed popular support for centuries, but options' acceptance has waxed and waned over the years. Options and futures traded side by side in Amsterdam during the Dutch golden age of the seventeenth century. They have traded for over two hundred years in small OTC markets in London, New York, and several cities of Continental Europe. Options traded as bilateral contracts that were loaded with credit, legal, and liquidity risks. They were viewed as tools for speculation that served no worthwhile economic purpose. In fact, the US Securities and Exchange Commission (SEC; created after the great stock market crash of 1929) repeatedly tried to outlaw options. The market ebbed and flowed depending on the participants. It expanded when big financiers wrote options because their reputation and deep pockets assuaged the buyers about credit risk.

The opening of the CBOE in 1973, support from academic economists, and the Black–Scholes–Merton pricing model helped options reach the mainstream and remove their stigma of gambling. The information technology revolution of the 1990s ushered in the era of electronic exchanges and web-based trading. Insurance and options markets have converged again. Nowadays options are viewed as risk management tools that "complete the markets" by allowing traders to carve out different portfolio payoffs. They trade on many exchanges around the globe, and traders can transact through a single electronic platform.

Despite this convergence, the history of options trading is sufficiently different from that of futures trading to merit further discussion. We divide the history into two phases:

1. *Early trading of options.* Option-like contracts have traded since antiquity, with options trading in organized OTC markets in Amsterdam, London, and New York City in past centuries.

2. *The year 1973: the watershed year and after.* The Nobel Prize–winning Black–Scholes–Merton model gave traders a vital tool for pricing and hedging options. The opening of the CBOE ended the old, inefficient OTC markets and brought numerous innovations. Post-1973 saw the development of a variety of contracts, the opening of new exchanges, the automation of trading, and the consolidation and linkages among exchanges. This story is akin to the history of futures trading discussed in chapter 8. That's hardly surprising because economic, political, regulatory, and technological changes similarly affected the options markets.

Early Trading of Options

Confusions and *Delusions*? These catchphrases come from the titles of two books that appear in a list of the "10 Best Books Ever Written on Investment" ("Investing by the Book: Richard Lambert Picks the 10 Best Books Ever Written on Investment," *Financial Times,* January 28, 1995). These books tell us, among other things, how options and futures traded in Western Europe over four centuries ago. Before exploring that history, however, we mention that the first recorded option usage occurred when Greek intellectuals were still laying the foundations of Western civilization. There is a story telling how Thales the Milesian (624–545 BC) purchased an option to buy the use of olive presses in the next harvest year, which he was sure would yield a bountiful harvest. His prediction was correct, and he profited handsomely from exercising his option.[1]

Let us move forward two millennia, whiz past medieval Italy (where the European Renaissance and the double-entry accounting system began), and arrive in Belgium and the Netherlands. Gelderblom and Jonker (2005) tell the story of how sophisticated financial markets developed in these Western European nations, which, nonetheless, were vexed by problems that continue to afflict us to this day (see Table 14.1 for a timeline of options trading and Extension 14.1 for a discussion of the history of derivatives in the Netherlands during 1550–1700).

It was in Antwerp, Netherlands, where trading migrated from periodic medieval fairs (discussed in chapter 8) to a permanent home. The city built an exchange in 1531, adopted a set of rules for contract enforcement in the following year, and created a legislative framework to support financial transactions later in the decade. Financial and commercial transactions flourished, derivatives contracts developed, speculation (including wagers on political events and bets through foreign exchange options!) grew rampant, and manipulation of commodity prices became a threat to markets.

Meanwhile, Amsterdam became the major market for grain from the Baltic region, herring, and other bulk commodities. Records from the period document how grain dealers in the city used both futures and options in the 1550s and the following decades. Fearing that speculators could use derivatives to manipulate

---

[1] This story is from Jowett's translation of chapter 11 of Book 1 of Aristotle's Politics (etext.library. adelaide.edu.au/a/aristotle/a8po/). The story and its link to options is mentioned in Professor Henry Crosby Emery's 1896 PhD thesis at Columbia University titled "Speculation on the Stock and Produce Exchanges of the United States."

staple food prices and cause social unrest, the authorities repeatedly banned forward trading. However, the market did not disappear; it simply went underground and was confined to the insiders. Subsequently, the market again became public, expanding to include forwards, futures, and call and put options on equities. The 1630s saw an extraordinary speculative frenzy over rare tulip bulbs, with futures and options helping hedgers and the speculating public. We discuss this episode later in this chapter.

A small options market for sophisticated traders continued to operate in Continental Europe, London, and New York for over two centuries (see Malkiel and Quandt 1969). For example, during the 1690s, a well-organized options market existed in London, and it continued to exist despite the ban on options and futures promulgated under Barnard's Act of 1733. In 1821, the London Stock Exchange Committee proposed a rule that would forbid members from dealing in options. Loud protest came from a large number of members; they even raised money to build a rival stock exchange building. The ban was never implemented, option trading continued (restricted but) uninterrupted, and Barnard's Act itself was repealed in 1860. The European options market remained small because many prominent firms refused to participate.

A New York City–options market became active during the last four decades of the nineteenth century, when Russell Sage operated as a financier, securities trader, options writer, and broker on a vast scale (see Extension 14.2). Russell Sage's financing and trading activities relate to several important features of financial markets:

1. *The importance of collateral.* An article titled "Russell Sage" (*New York Times*, August 5, 1903), attributed Sage's success to his being "an excellent judge of collateral." It noted that "crises and panics have passed him unharmed, and when others were eager to borrow he was as eager to lend—if the collateral was satisfactory."

2. *Financing, brokering and dealership.* "I keep more ready money at my command than any bank" was one of Sage's favorite sayings. He supplied funds for mergers, acquisitions, and stock price manipulations and charged handsome interest on these loans. He became a broker and dealer for stocks, bonds, and options. "For a longer period than the business men of the present generation can remember he was an extensive operator in puts, calls, and straddles, and has dealt in securities on a scale of magnitude almost without precedent," noted the 1903 *Times* article.

TABLE 14.1: Early History of Options Trading

Year	Development
600 BC onward	Thales of Miletus traded optionlike contracts.
1550–1650	Birth of options and futures trading in Amsterdam
1630s	Futures and options traded on tulips in the Netherlands
1860–1900	Russell Sage extensively traded calls, puts, spreads, and straddles
1910	The Put and Call Brokers and Dealers Association was founded

EXTENSION 14.1: Derivatives Trading in the Netherlands (1550–1700)

Sixteenth-century Netherlands was growing prosperous through trade and commerce and readying itself for the Dutch golden age. The Dutch golden age was an era of cultural, economic, political, and scientific achievements that spanned the entire seventeenth century and made this tiny seafaring nation one of the most powerful countries on earth. Gelderblom and Jonker's (2005) article titled "Amsterdam as the Cradle of Modern Futures and Options Trading, 1550–1650" traces back organized derivatives trading to this distant time and place.

Modern Financial Market in Medieval Amsterdam

The markets that developed in Amsterdam have many common features with today's sophisticated financial markets:

- *Price transparency.* Amsterdam required wheat and rye prices to be quoted daily. In 1556 the city formalized the practice that all grain trades over a certain amount must be reported to one of the two town's bellmen, who would both announce the price to other grain dealers and present a sample of the merchandise.

- *Standardization.* Between 1582 and 1584, the Board of the Great Fisheries standardized herring trading in terms of age, time of year caught, and the way the fish was processed. Forward and options trading on herring soon followed.

- *Price volatility, speculation, and market manipulation.* Antwerp and Amsterdam had enough price volatility for derivatives to develop. In 1556, Amsterdam's sheriff accused German and Flemish merchants of "the great evil" of driving up prices through forward contracts.

- *Contract enforcement and credit risk.* When prices escalated in the second half of 1556, Amsterdam grain dealers tried to cancel existing forward contracts. But Antwerp merchants argued before the authorities that the preexisting bans on forward trading did not apply to foreign grains and managed to get their counterparties to honor the contracts. Besides governmental and legal support, peer pressure was yet another mechanism that forced traders to honor contract terms.

- *Rules and regulations, clearing and settlement.* Laws of the land, rules and regulations governing transactions, and a system of clearing (called *rescontre*) kept credit risks low and helped markets grow. Brokers played a critical role in most transactions. They were required to keep a register of all arranged transactions and to help organize the clearing of claims on a regular basis.

Two major sources of foreign trade were the Dutch East and West India companies (VOC and WIC, respectively), which sent ships to trade in Asia and the Americas. They were organized as joint-stock companies with transferable shares. The companies prospered and paid decent dividends. Their volatile share prices rapidly rose to dizzying heights. Speculators were attracted to these shares. Forward and options contracts started trading on these shares, and repo transactions and pledging shares as loan collateral developed. As merchants tore up the original contracts after a transaction was consummated, the frequency and extent of trading of these OTC instruments remains unknown.

De la Vega's Confusión de Confusiones

In 1688, a successful merchant Joseph Penso de la Vega published a book entitled *Confusión de Confusiones* (*Confusions of Confusions*). It vividly portrays Amsterdam's financial markets and makes insightful observations on the psychology and motives of the market participants:

- *Exchange and the trading process.* After trading in "The Dam" (a square faced by the town hall) in the morning, the traders proceeded to the "Exchange" (an enclosed building surrounded by columns), where business was conducted from 12 noon to 2 PM. Handshakes or hand slaps signified the execution of a trade.

- *Different kinds of traders.* The stock exchange had three kinds of traders: (1) financial lords and big capitalists, who held shares for their dividends and were indifferent to stock price movements; (2) merchants who sometimes speculated but generally tried to keep risks low; and (3) gamblers and speculators, who put up "wheels of fortune" and undertook complicated schemes in pursuit of profits.

- *Bulls and bears.* The speculators could be classified as bulls and bears. The bulls began their operations with a purchase and the hope that prices would rise. The bears always began their operations with sales, and they were "completely ruled by fear, trepidation, and nervousness." De la Vega warned that one must take bearish positions only on "extraordinary occasions" to take advantage of a "chance for a quick profit, a chance that will flutter away from you if you do not grasp it promptly."

- *Different ways of taking a position (and short selling was disliked by the regulators).* Much the same way as today, traders could buy stocks in the spot market, on margin; trade futures contracts with specified settlement dates; and trade options. They could also sell shares short—a practice (like other risky transactions) frowned on by the authorities, who, much like present-day regulators, periodically issued edicts to ban them altogether.

- *Two kinds of brokers and dual trading.* Because of dual trading concerns, there were two kinds of brokers. Municipal authorities appointed a limited number of "sworn" brokers who took an oath that they would not do business on their own account. The rest were "free" brokers, who roamed free in large numbers, the profession being the refuge of many ne'er-do-wells and failures in life.

- *Coffeehouses.* Starbucks had ancestors! Speculators frequently visited coffeehouses, where they would meet other people, read books and play board games, sip drinks (choice of chocolate, coffee, milk, or tea), enjoy a smoke, and relish the well-heated rooms during the winter months. The visitors would network with people, collect news, and negotiate transactions, without incurring great costs.

Characterizing them "as sails for a happy voyage during a beneficent conjuncture and as an anchor of security in a storm," de la Vega explains the workings of *opsies* (Dutch name for options) on Dutch East India Company's shares as follows:[2]

> The price of the shares is now 580, [and let us assume that] it seems to me that they will climb to a much higher price because of the extensive cargoes that are expected from India, because of the good business of the Company, of the reputation of its goods, of the prospective dividends, and of the peace in Europe. Nevertheless I decide not to buy shares through fear that I might encounter a loss and might meet with embarrassment if my calculations should prove erroneous. I therefore turn to those persons who are willing to take options and ask them how much [premium] they demand for the obligation to deliver shares at 600 each at a certain later date. I come to an agreement about the premium, have it transferred [to the taker of the options] immediately at the Bank, and then I am sure that it is impossible to lose more than the price of the premium. And I shall gain the entire amount by which the price [of the stock] shall surpass the figure of 600.

De la Vega had accurately captured the benefits of options three centuries before our time!

[2] De la Vega notes that *opsies* is derived from the Latin word *optio*, "which means choice, because the payer of the premium has the choice of delivering the shares to the acceptor of the premium or of demanding them from him [respectively]."

EXTENSION 14.2: Russell Sage: The Old Straddle

Born in Oneida County, New York, **Russell Sage** (1816–1906) was the seventh son in a family that was moving westward from Connecticut in search of a better life. Although he received little formal education and began working as an errand boy in his brother's grocery store at age twelve, Sage studied arithmetic and bookkeeping during his spare time, bought and expanded his brother's business, and became successful in several trading ventures. He invested in the telegraph and came to own large sections of the nation's railroad infrastructure. He entered politics and served two terms in the US Congress. Eventually, he settled in New York City, bought a seat in the New York Stock Exchange, and became a key player in the world of finance.

An article title "Russell Sage" in the *New York Times* (August 5, 1903), written on the occasion of the secretive multimillionaire's eighty-eighth birthday, attributed his success to the following: "he is extremely shrewd and knows how to bet discreetly and he is *an excellent judge of collateral* [emphasis added]." Although Sage would deliberately cast the impression that he was a slow learner, anecdotes reveal a razor-sharp mind capable of handling enormous amounts of detail that remained quick and lucid until the last years of his life. He used his talents to run a gigantic financing, securities trading, and brokerage business.

Running an Options Business

A biography by Paul Sarnoff (1965) vividly portrays how Russell Sage conducted his options business. On a typical day, the frugal multimillionaire would take the train to work (using the free travel pass that he got as the president of the Metropolitan Elevated Railroad Company). Sage would then settle down in his office, read his mail, and check the ticker tape to sense the market. Then he would turn to options:

> Sage would return to his desk, where as if by a silent signal, his brother-in-law, Colonel John J. Slocum, would hand him a bulky folio of "sheets"—legal size manila that indicated his stock-market position and inventory of puts and calls. Sage would then carefully and quickly scan the sheets, altering and making offering-price changes commensurate with the changing prices in the market. The corrections and code marks that earmarked the "papers" he wanted disposed of having been noted on the sheaf of yellow pages, Sage would hand the folio to Slocum, who in turn passed it on to Johnny McCann. McCann then went out into the hall to hold his matinee.

> This performance consisted of an oral offering of the "merchandise" Sage had earmarked for his horde of street-hawkers to dispose of. At the end of Johnny's rendition, there customarily ensued a wild clamor as Sage's army vied for his merchandise. Having unloaded the inventory, McCann would back into the office and return to the "cage" [cashier's window] while Sage's minions piled out into the financial districts to sell the merchandise themselves at a profit. (Sarnoff 1965, 241)

He devised options strategies like spreads and straddles and earned the nickname "Old Straddle"!

Honoring His Contracts

Sage rarely lost money in the financial markets, but was reported to have lost between $4 million and $8 million during the Grant and Ward Crash of 1884. Initially, the word was spread that Sage would "lay down" (i.e., renege) on his puts, calls, spreads, and straddles. An angry crowd of impatient holders of his papers thronged outside his office and smashed the glass in his partition door. Sage's *New York Times* obituary dated June 23, 1906, reported that he was "at his office the next morning at the usual hour and met his losses promptly and without a murmur."

Sage scaled back his options writing for a couple years but then returned with gusto. A story titled "Some Hit and Miss Chat" (*New York Times,* November 15, 1886), reported that "the old-time activity is seen again in Russell Sage's office, and put-and-call brokers are again crowding the corridors. Mr. Sage is issuing privileges with a freedom that is astounding the Street. . . . The brokers say that Mr. Sage's terms now are more liberal than he ever made before." Overall, he did very well. The *New York Times* obituary reported that one year Sage was said to have earned $10 million in his options business.

Sage used his vast capital to make lucrative loans and run a highly profitable derivatives business. The options market went dormant after Sage retired in 1903, but it picked up again in 1904, when another frugal multimillionaire, Amos M. Lyon (who began his life on a Vermont farm and was estimated to have been worth $25 million at the time), entered the fray. Thus, in the absence of the safeguards that characterize today's exchange-traded derivatives, only financiers with top reputations and deep pockets could enter the highly profitable options writing business.

3. *Role of the writer in the development of OTC options markets and credit risk concerns.* Because the writer has the onus of making future payments, the OTC options market expanded when the writer's role was played by a major financier, whose wealth and reputation allayed the buyer's credit risk fears (on the demand side, there seems to be no shortage of people willing to wager a small amount in the hope of bigger future payoffs, in Sage's day or in our times!).[3]

4. *The invention of straddles and spreads.* Sarnoff gave Sage credit for inventing the spread and the straddle and suggested that his extensive dealing in calls and puts as well as these two creations led to the development of the "modern system of selling stock-option contracts."[4] These activities earned him the nickname "Old Straddle."

5. *Dual trading and manipulation.* An obituary in the *New York Times* (dated July 23, 2006) observed, "Mr. Sage's money has assisted manipulations, but, except in his earlier years, the conditions were those of safety for Mr. Sage, and he was not the manipulator." Conflicts of interest between Sage's brokerage and dealership business had surfaced in lawsuits. For example, a client successfully sued Sage in a dual-trading case discussed later in this chapter.

6. *Dividend adjustments.* A dividend lowers the value of an asset; consequently, a dividend lowers the value of a call and raises the price of a put. A client once took the aged Sage to court in a dispute about dividend adjustments and an option's value (see "Dividends and Puts," *New York Times*, April 6, 1887). Dividend adjustments to option contracts is a relevant issue in today's markets, and options exchanges have well-defined policies for these adjustments (see section 14.4 and Example 14.4 for further discussions).

7. *Put–call parity.* Much like today's credit card companies, Sage was adept at extracting money from his debtors under various guises like slapping late fees and

---

[3] The OTC option contracts that Sage sold went by the name of **privileges**. They usually expired three months after their purchase date, had a strike price close to the market price on the day or week that the option was bought, and had no secondary markets. Colloquially, these options were referred to as **papers**.

[4] A *spread* is created by buying one call and selling another on the same underlying with different strike prices, different maturity dates, or both. Spreads can be similarly created with puts. A *straddle* is created by buying (or selling) a call and a put option on the same underlying, with the same strike price and the same maturity date. The next chapter discusses these strategies in detail.

service charges on top of the 7 percent interest rate ceiling set by New York's usury laws. In 1869, Sage and several other people were arrested when the government made a raid on the "Usury Ring." Sage had violated the law when he added an extra 1 percent late charge fee on top of the existing interest rate to a loan that a stockbroker was unable to repay on time. Although intense maneuvering saved him from jail time, Sage was badly shaken by this incident. Eventually, he devised *conversions*, where he created synthetic loans by using the put–call parity principle and effectively charged interest rates higher than what the usury laws would allow (see Extension 16.1 for a description of this strategy). This also illustrates Merton Miller's assertion stated in chapter 1 that financial securities help issuers make money by innovating around government regulations that prohibit otherwise profitable transactions.

The OTC option market in the nineteenth and the early twentieth centuries wasn't too different from that in historic Amsterdam. Options contracts were written in printed forms where traders filled in the details and had them notarized. The dealers sold options by word of mouth or by advertising in the newspapers. **The Put and Call Brokers and Dealers Association** was established in 1910 to organize options trading in the United States.

The government continued to view options trading with suspicion for good reasons. Particularly in the early twentieth century, speculators would often use options to manipulate stock prices. After the stock market crash of 1929, the US Congress sought to ban options trading. The newly founded SEC's initial recommendation was "not knowing the difference between good and bad options, for the matter of convenience, we strike them all out." The mantle of defending options trading fell on industry veteran broker-dealer Herbert J. Filer (see Filer 1959). Concerned about the vast number of options contracts that expire worthless, the congressional committee asked, "If only 12 1/2 percent are exercised, then the other 87 1/2 percent of the people who bought options have thrown money away?" Filer replied, "No sir. If you insured your house against fire and it didn't burn down you would not say that you had thrown away your insurance premium." Filer's arguments helped the SEC to endorse the view that if properly used, options could be a valuable investment tool. Options trading volume (in terms of shares), which was about half of 1 percent of the New York Stock Exchange (NYSE) reported stock trading volume in 1937, rose to around 1 percent in 1955 and hovered around that number during the 1960s; however, trading remained anemic, and the stigma of gambling prevented the options market from enjoying vigorous growth.

The Year 1973: The Watershed Year and After

This landscape began to change in 1973 with the opening of the CBOE and the publication of the Black–Scholes–Merton options pricing model. We describe here the circumstances that led to the founding of the CBOE and the options markets that developed afterward.

EARLY INFLUENCES Perhaps surprising, the birth of the first options exchange was facilitated by academic writings. In the 1960s, options valuation was already in the air, and many economists did research on options. Economic professors

Malkiel and Quandt (1969) wrote a book titled *Strategies and Rational Decisions in the Securities Options Markets* that discussed various early options pricing models, explored sixteen trading strategies (you will see most of these strategies in the next chapter), and concluded that option trading is beneficial to the economy. They recommended the clearing of all bids and offers for options in a central marketplace, the establishment of secondary markets with full public reporting, and the homogenization of contract terms.

MacKenzie and Millo (2003) believe that after reading an article by Malkiel and Quandt (1969), the CBOT vice chairman Edmund O'Connor became interested in establishing an options exchange. CBOT chairman Charles P. Carey stated, "The original concept was actually written on the back of a napkin by the CBOT Vice Chairman Ed O'Connor during a dinner meeting with CBOT Chairman Bill Mallers and President Henry Hall Wilson."[5]

THE OPENING OF THE CHICAGO BOARD OPTIONS EXCHANGE   The CBOE opened its doors on April 26, 1973. Just 911 call options contracts traded on sixteen stocks on the inaugural day. The trading floor was set up in the previous Chicago Board of Trade members' smoking lounge. Some questioned the wisdom of starting a new exchange during a bad bear market. Others doubted whether Chicago grain traders could successfully introduce a new trading instrument that was ascertained too complex for the public by the NYSE. Members griped that they were pouring money down the drain by buying a seat for $10,000 at the exchange's leadership's insistence. However, what began gingerly under the watchful eyes of nervous regulators soon enjoyed robust growth. The daily trading volume at the end of the first month exceeded the average daily volume in the old, OTC options market.

Despite its ups and downs, a remarkable expansion of options markets followed the opening of the CBOE—see Table 14.2 for some milestones in this extraordinary march. The mid-1970s saw the introduction of options trading on several US exchanges and in other nations. In 1975, the clearing facility of the CBOE was reorganized as the *Options Clearing Corporation (OCC)*, which functions as the common clearinghouse for most exchange-traded listed options in the United States and has virtually eliminated credit risk. The same year, computerized price reporting was also introduced in the CBOE.

During the three-year period 1977–80, the SEC put a moratorium on additional listings pending a review of the options industry's growth. The stock market crash in October 1987 led to a temporary waning of interest in options. Still the innovations continued, and a variety of new contracts were introduced. The IT revolution of the 1990s led to several key developments similar to the ones described in chapter 8: automation lowered transaction costs, many exchanges introduced partial or complete electronic trading, greater links were established among exchanges, and a wave of mergers and consolidations transformed the markets.

Today the CBOE is a huge marketplace where options on more than fifty thousand series trade on more than 1,332 stocks and 41 indexes. Over fifteen hundred

---

[5] "CBOT Chairman Speaks at Business Leaders Program on Innovation," see: www.mondovisione.com/media-and-resources/news/cbot-chairman-speaks-at-business-leaders-program-on-innovation/.

competing market makers trade more than 1 million options contracts representing over $25 billion in value trade on a typical day. The CBOE's 45,000-square-foot trading floor is housed in a 350,000-square-foot, seven-storey-tall building that has over four thousand phone lines, thirty-four hundred personal computers, and more computer screens (twenty-four hundred price information display terminals and forty-five hundred monitors) under "one roof than any other building in the world, including the NASA Space Center in Houston."[6] The building has over fifty thousand miles of wiring and cable, which is "enough to wrap around the world twice."[7] Seat prices exceeded the $3 million mark in 2007–8, as the exchange was readying itself for demutualization.[8]

A VARIETY OF OPTIONS Most options varieties were introduced during the 1970s and 1980s. In 1977, put options started trading at the CBOE. The year 1982 saw the beginning of currency options trading on the Philadelphia Stock Exchange and Treasury bond futures options on the Chicago Board of Trade, which brought futures exchanges into the options business (see Extension 14.3). The following year, cash-settled options on broad-based stock indexes (including options on the Standard and Poor's [S&P] 500 index) were launched at the CBOE. As with futures, cash settlement allowed the creation of new kinds of options with rich payoff structures.

By mid-1983, exchange-traded options were available for hedging and speculating on equity, commodity, currency, interest rates, and stock indexes. Many options were subsequently introduced in these categories. For example, the CBOE introduced long-lived equity options, **LEAPS** (**Long-Term Equity AnticiPation Securities**), with up to three years' life in 1990, options on sector indexes in 1992, **FLEX options** (which allow traders to modify some key specifications) in 1993, and options on country indexes in 1994. On the basis of academic research by Professor Robert Whaley, the CBOE unveiled in 1993 the **VIX** (**CBOE Volatility Index**), which measures the market's estimate of near-term volatility as implied by the S&P 500 stock index option prices. The VIX index was modified in 2003 from measuring an implied volatility to that of an expected volatility. Colloquially known as the "Fear Gauge," VIX is a widely used barometer of investor sentiment and market volatility. The CBOE introduced futures contracts on VIX in 2004 and option contracts on VIX in 2006—we discuss the VIX in chapter 20.

NEW EXCHANGES AND THE AUTOMATION OF TRADING Many existing exchanges embraced options trading, and new options exchanges were formed. In 1975, call options commenced trading at the **American Stock Exchange**, the **Philadelphia Stock Exchange**, and the **Montreal Stock Exchange** in Canada. In 1976, they were introduced on the **Pacific Exchange** in San Francisco and in the **Australian**

---

[6] www.cboe.com.

[7] ibid.

[8] As the CBOE was moving from a member-owned organization to a for-profit business, seat prices exceeded $3 million in several instances during 2007–8 and fetched a record $3.2 million on June 17, 2008 (see "CBOE Seat Sells for New High of $3.2 Million," www.cboe.com/AboutCBOE/ShowDocument.aspx?DIR=ACNews&FILE=cboe_20080617.doc&CreateDate=17.06.2008).

Options Market, which became the first options market outside North America. In 1978, two of the world's oldest exchanges introduced options trading in Europe: the **European Options Exchange** was founded by the members of the **Amsterdam Stock Exchange**, and the **London Traded Options Market** was established as a part of the London Stock Exchange. By the end of the decade, **BOVESPA** became the first exchange to introduce options trading in Brazil.

During the 1980s, the exchanges worked on expanding the market and jockeyed for greater market share. An article titled "Too Many Trading Places" in *The Economist* magazine (June 19, 1993) reports the status of European exchanges. Many of the regional exchanges got merged. For example, on January 1, all German exchanges were grouped under a firm called **Deutsche Borse AG**. Still, at the time the twelve member nations of the European Community had thirty-two stock exchanges and twenty-three futures and options exchanges as compared to eight stock exchanges and seven futures and options exchanges in the United States. Although the European Options Exchange was the first derivatives exchange in Europe, it surrendered its lead to the **London International Financial Futures and Options Exchange**. Established in 1982, the exchange clearly benefited from the "Big Bang" deregulation of 1986 (which opened London's stock exchange to banks and foreigners and introduced SEAQ, a screen-plus-telephone-based securities

TABLE 14.2: Some Milestones in Options Markets, 1973 and After

Year	Development
1973	First options exchange, the Chicago Board Options Exchange (CBOE), was founded, with call options trading on sixteen underlying stocks
1975	Call options began trading in the American Stock Exchange, the Philadelphia Stock Exchange, and the Montreal Stock Exchange in Canada; the Options Clearing Corporation (OCC) was established for exchange-traded options in the United States
1976	Calls began trading on the Pacific Exchange and the Australian Options Market
1977	Put options were introduced at the CBOE
1977–80	The Securities and Exchange Commission put a moratorium on the options market
1978	The European Options Exchange and London Traded Options Market were established
1982	Currency options started trading at the Philadelphia Stock Exchange
1982	Options on US Treasury bond futures started trading at the CBOT
1983	Options on broad-based stock indexes started trading at the CBOE
1987	Stock Market crash in October 1987 set back the options market, from which it took years to recover
1993	Introduction of the CBOE Volatility Index (VIX), a key measure of market expectations of near-term volatility conveyed by Standard and Poor's index options prices
1998	Deutsche Borse AG and Swiss Exchange started Eurex, a joint platform for trading and clearing derivatives trade
2000	Euronext was founded through the merger and consolidation of several European exchanges
2000	First all-electronic exchange in the United States, the International Securities Exchange, was founded

EXTENSION 14.3: Options on Futures

Why trade options on futures? Recall the observation from chapter 1 that *trading gravitates to the most liquid markets with minimum transaction costs*. As the stock market is very liquid with minimal transaction costs, it's no surprise that we have bustling markets for equity options. But storage costs and convenience yields for many commodities in the spot market make it easier for traders to hedge and speculate on commodities in the more liquid futures markets. Consequently, it's natural for options on futures to trade on such commodities.

For **options on spot** (also called **spot options**), the spot commodity is obtained when the option is exercised. By contrast, exercise of a **futures option** gives the holder a position in the underlying futures. In the United States, active futures as well as futures options markets exist for diverse commodities such as cattle, cotton, corn, crude oil, gold, and silver. These options trade on the same exchange where the futures contracts trade, whether it's a trading pit or electronic exchange. Simultaneous trading of futures and futures options helps the price discovery process.

Example 1 shows how a futures option works. Notice that both spot options and futures options behave similarly in response to a movement in the underlying.

EXAMPLE 1: Call and Put Options on Futures

- Today is January 1. Suppose the April gold futures price is $1,515 per ounce. Futures options with a contract size of one hundred ounces and for $1,490, $1,495, $1,500, $1,510, $1,520, $1,530, and several other strike prices (per ounce) trade in the New York Mercantile Exchange of the CME Group.[9]

- Consider a **call option on a commodity futures**. If you exercise this option, you will receive a long position in the underlying futures contract and a cash payment equal to the excess of the futures price over the strike price. For example, if you exercise an April 1,500 call, you end up long an April futures and receive a payment of (1,515 − 1,500) = $15 per ounce, $1,500 in all. If the payment is negative, do not exercise—enter the futures at zero cost in the market instead.

- The exercise of a **put option on a commodity futures** puts the holder into a short position in the underlying futures and brings in a cash amount equal to the strike price minus the futures settlement price. For example, if you exercise a December 1,520 put, you end up being short December futures and receive a payment of (1,520 − 1,515) = $5 per ounce.

- Obviously, the long has to pay premiums for these options. A modified version of the Black–Scholes–Merton model can be used to price futures options. More advanced models like the Heath–Jarrow–Merton model (developed in 1987, published in 1992) can also be used for this purpose (see Amin and Jarrow 1991).

---

[9] Options are available for the nearest six of the following contract months: February, April, June, August, October, and December. Additional contract months—January, March, May, July, September, and November—will be listed for trading for a period of two months. A sixty-month options contract is added from the current calendar month on a June/December cycle. On the first day of trading for any options contract month, there will be thirteen strike prices each for puts and calls. Strike prices are set $10 per ounce apart for strike prices below $500, $20 per ounce apart for strike prices between $500 and $1,000, and $50 per ounce apart for strike prices above $1,000. For the nearest six contract months, strike prices will be $5, $10, and $25 apart, respectively (based on contract specifications on www.cmegroup.com/trading/metals/precious/gold.html).

Notice that if you replace the futures price $\mathcal{F}(T)$ with the stock price $S(T)$, then futures options payoffs are similar to equity options payoffs. For example, consider a call futures option and a regular equity call option on a stock with the same strike price K. If you exercise the equity call, your payoff is $[S(T) - K]$. If you exercise the call futures option, you receive $[\mathcal{F}(T) - K]$ and a long futures position on the stock. As the futures contract has a zero value, it can be liquidated at no cost. Exercise of a put futures option leads to a short position in the underlying futures plus the strike minus the futures price $\equiv [K - \mathcal{F}(T)]$, and a similar argument holds.

trading system) and a merger with the London Traded Options Market in 1992. American options and futures exchanges continued to maintain the lion's share of the market.

The global options market suffered a severe setback during the stock market crash of October 1987, and it took over a decade for the volume to return to pre-crash levels. Despite being home to some of the largest stock exchanges in terms of market capitalization, Japan was a latecomer to the world of derivatives. Derivatives markets began in Japan with the trading of ten-year Japanese government bond futures on the **Tokyo Stock Exchange** in 1985. Introduction of other derivatives took place with the inauguration of the Osaka Stock Futures 50 in the rival **Osaka Stock Exchange** in 1987, options on stock indexes in 1989, and equity options in 1997 on both these exchanges.

As the 1990s progressed, several discernible patterns emerged, which we discussed in the context of futures in chapter 8. Competition put relentless pressure to cut costs, and IT advances made that possible. Exchanges dismantled floor trading or began as completely electronic exchanges. With their commitment to floor trading, US exchanges kept falling behind. Wake-up calls came when Eurex and Euronext were founded, the Korea Futures Exchange traded an astonishing 2.9 billion contracts in 2003, and mergers and acquisitions were transforming the marketplace. Forsaking the traditional nonprofit structure, most exchanges demutualized, and many new exchanges started as for-profit concerns. Established in 2000 as an all-electronic options exchange, the **International Securities Exchange** became the world's largest equity options exchange. Stiff competition came from the OTC derivatives markets, which grew faster than the exchanges. Fed chairman Alan Greenspan (recall chapter 10) used this fact to justify less regulation and a hands-off policy toward the OTC markets.

The US exchanges regrouped and rethought their options (no pun intended!) and strategies. Seeing that electronic trading was the wave of the future for trading plain vanilla securities, they acquired or merged with organizations that focused on electronic trading or developed their own automated trading systems (see chapters 3 and 8). Automation, mergers, and acquisitions helped them regain some of the largest volumes in futures and options trading in 2008.[10] Today options markets exist in most major financial centers around the world. Even deep discount brokerage firms allow customers to open an options trading account with only a modest outlay.

---

[10] "Annual Volume Survey 2008: A Wild Ride," www.futuresindustry.org.

14.4 | Option Contract Features

Let us examine the contract specifications for CBOE equity options.[11] The CBOE trades options from 8:30 AM to 3:00 PM Central Time (Chicago time). CBOE equity options are American, and they can be exercised any time from purchase until the option's last trading day, which is the third Friday of the expiration month. If the third Friday is a legal holiday, then the option expires the day before. Each option is for one hundred shares of the underlying stock. If exercised, the stock share is delivered three business days later.

The minimal tick size is $0.05 for options trading below $3 and $0.10 for options trading above. However, through a pilot program inaugurated on January 26, 2007, options series are quoted in pennies ($0.01) for options prices below $3 and in nickels ($0.05) for higher options prices.[12]

Maturity Dates

For a particular stock, options belong to an assigned quarterly **cycle**, either the January, February, or March cycle. *With respect to a particular cycle, options maturities are listed for the next two months plus two additional maturities, selected three months apart.* An example explains this procedure.

EXAMPLE 14.1: Determining the Expiration Months

- The *January cycle* has the months January, April, July, and October. The *February cycle* has February, May, and so on. Each stock approved for options trading belongs to one of the cycles. For example, IBM has a January cycle, Hewlett Packard has a February cycle, and Walmart Stores has a March cycle.

- Consider the expiration months for traded options on IBM starting January 1.
  - On January 1, IBM has options expiring in January, February (the two near-term months), April, and July (the next two months from the quarterly cycle).
  - After the third Friday of January, one can trade IBM options maturing in February, March, April, and July.
  - After the third Friday of February, one can trade options maturing in March, April, July, and October.

- Different kinds of options have different expiration dates. For example, LEAPS are issued with three-year maturities and expire on the third Friday of the expiration year. **Quarterly options** (or the "**quarterlies**"), which can be written on some indexes and exchange-traded funds, expire on the last business day of each calendar quarter.

---

[11] See www.cboe.com.

[12] See "Options Exchanges Begin Penny Quoting Pilot: Similar Move for Stocks Has Meant Better Prices for Investors," www.sec.gov/news/press/2007/2007-10.htm.

Strike Prices

When an option with a particular maturity starts trading, strike prices for in-, at-, and out-of-the-money are listed. If the stock price is over $200, the strikes are issued $10 apart. Between $200 and $25, the strikes are issued $5 apart, and below $25, only $2.50 apart. Strike prices are adjusted for stock dividends and stock splits but not for cash dividends. If the stock price moves significantly before the option expires, then new strikes are listed to maintain the balance with respect to in-, at-, and out-of-the-money. The next example illustrates this process.

EXAMPLE 14.2: Determining the Strike Prices

- Suppose the stock opens at $21 on Monday following the third Friday of the month, when new long-maturity options are listed. This is the first trading day after the shortest maturity option expires. Newly listed options (both calls and puts) have strike prices of $20 and $22.50, immediately above and below the current stock price. Additional in- and out-of-the-money strikes are also listed at this time.

- Next, suppose that only the $20 and $22.50 options are listed, and the stock rallies. When it reaches $22.51, options with a strike price of $25 are introduced. If it goes beyond $25, options with the next higher strike of $30 start trading, and so forth. Of course, one can still trade options with strike prices $20 and $22.50, which were listed earlier, until these contracts expire.

- Liquidity is usually the greatest for options with strike prices near the current stock price. Trading volume and the number of contracts outstanding tend to decline as the stock goes deeper in- or out-of-the-money.

Margin Requirements and Position Limits

The margin (borrowing) restrictions for long positions in options can be summarized as follows: (1) short-term options (nine months or less) must post the full purchase price with zero borrowing and (2) long-term options (more than nine months) can borrow up to 25 percent of the purchase price. Options sellers are usually required to keep the full purchase price plus some extra cash as a cushion against risk.[13] An example illustrates these restrictions.

---

[13] For writers of options on equity and "narrow-based index," the Fed has set the margin requirements as follows: margin account initial requirement, "100% of option proceeds plus 20% of underlying security/index value less out-of-the-money amount, if any, to a minimum of option proceeds plus 10% of underlying security/index value for calls; 10% of the put exercise price for puts"; margin account maintenance requirement, "For each short option, 100% of option market value plus 20% of underlying security/index value less out-of-the-money amount, if any, to a minimum of option mkt. value plus 10% of underlying security/index value for calls; 10% of the put exercise price for puts" (www.cboe.com/micro/margin/strategy.aspx).

EXAMPLE 14.3: Margin Account Adjustments

■ *Long call or long put (maturing in less than nine months).* For example, from Figure 14.1, if Ms. Long is buying five IBM March 2009 (IBMCR) calls worth $2.30 per share, she will need to keep (Ask price × Number of contracts × Contract size) = 2.30 × 5 × 100 = $1,150 in her margin account.

■ *Long call or long put (maturing in over nine months).* The initial (maintenance) margin requirement is 75 percent of the cost (market value). For example, if Ms. Long wants to buy ten IBM January 2010 (WIBAR) contracts worth $12.50, she will have to keep at least 75 percent of 12.50 × 10 × 100 = 0.75 × 12,500 = $9,375 of her own money as margin and borrow up to $3,125 from her broker.

■ *Options writer.* Suppose Mr. Short is selling ten IBM October 95 (IBMVS) put options (see Figure 14.1). Then margin would be computed as follows:

- 100 percent of contract proceeds (13.30 × 10 × 100)	$13,300
- Plus 20 percent of aggregate contract value (0.2 × 90.42 × 1,000)	18,084
- Minus the amount by which out-of-the-money [(90.42 − 95) × 1,000]	(−)4,580
- TOTAL amount (13,300 + 18,084 − 4,580)	$26,804

Also compute

- Put option proceeds (13.30 × 10 × 100)	$13,300
- Plus 10 percent of aggregate exercise price (0.1 × 95 × 1,000)	9,500
- TOTAL amount (13,300 + 9,500)	$22,800

The margin Short has to keep is $26,804, which is the larger of the two.

If the options holder-writer has positions in other options or the underlying, the CBOE adjusts these margin restrictions, taking into account the portfolio's overall risk. For example, the margin required for a long stock plus a long put position is significantly lower than a long put position alone. The adjusted margin takes into account the reduced risk from the long stock hedging the long put position.

Options position limits are imposed to reduce the potential for market manipulation. For actively traded stocks with large capitalizations (e.g., IBM or Microsoft), the position limit is 250,000 contracts. Stocks with smaller capitalizations have smaller position limits. Exemptions may be granted for qualified hedging strategies.

Dividends and Stock Splits

Options are not adjusted for cash dividends or stock distributions that do not exceed 10 percent of the stock's value. When a stock splits or pays large stock dividends, the option's strike price is adjusted on the ex-dividend day or the ex-split day. The adjustment depends on whether the split or stock dividend is an integer multiple such as 3 for 1 or a fractional such as 3 for 2. The OCC has developed these rules and procedures in an attempt to guarantee that options traders do not suffer losses from these events (see Extension 14.3 for a historical perspective on these adjustments).

EXAMPLE 14.4: Options Adjustment for Stock Splits and Stock Dividends

IBM's stock price is $90.42 (see Figure 14.1). Consider the April 90 call contract.

An Integer Multiple Split

- Suppose IBM has a 3 for 1 split. An investor who held one share would now have three shares worth $30.14 per share. On the ex-distribution day, the number of options will increase by a factor of 3, and the strike price will be reduced by a factor of 3.

- The aggregate exercise price before the split was $100 \times \$90 = \$9,000$. After the split, it equals $3 \times 100 \times \$30 = \$9,000$. They are the same—the adjustment makes the option neutral with respect to a stock split.

A Fractional Split

- Suppose IBM has a 3 for 2 split. An investor holding two shares will now own three shares. To prevent arbitrage, the new share's price will be $90.42/1.5 = 60.28$, where $3/2 = 1.5$ is the **split ratio**.

- In this case, instead of adjusting the number of contracts, the number of shares in each contract is multiplied by the split ratio: $100 \times 1.5 = \$150$. The new strike price is obtained by dividing the old strike price by the split ratio. Thus the new exercise price after the split is $90/1.5 = \$60$.

- Notice that the aggregate exercise price before the split was $9,000. After the split, the aggregate exercise price is $150 \times \$60 = \$9,000$. Again, this adjustment makes the option neutral with respect to the stock split.

Stock Dividends

- Large stock dividends (greater than 10 percent of the stock's price) are called stock splits and are treated accordingly. For example, a 3:1 split is really a 200 percent stock dividend, and a 3:2 split is a 50 percent stock dividend.

Reverse Split

- If IBM has a 1 for 2 reverse split, the stock price would become $180.84. The contract is adjusted so each original option is now an IBM April 180 call covering fifty shares.

14.5 | Options Trading, Exercising, and the Expiration Process

The Trading Process

Options trading involves the three-step process of execution, clearing, and settlement inherent to exchange-traded securities. As with futures, only a clearing member can clear trades. A clearing member must be a member of an options exchange, satisfy OCC's minimum capital, and meet other requirements. He must maintain efficient operations on the trading floor and in the back office. Clearing members pay both the exchange and the OCC a fee for each traded contract. They recoup these expenses from the fees charged to their customers.

Exercising the Option

The process begins when the holder conveys her intention to exercise the option to her broker. To ensure exercise on a particular day, the notification must be given before the broker's daily cutoff time. Next, the broker submits an exercise notice to the OCC. The OCC sends the notice to one or more clearing members holding short positions on the same contract. The clearing member, in turn, assigns it (either randomly or on a first-in, first-out basis) to one or more customers who hold short positions in the contract. The clearing member representing the short is obligated to sell (in the case of a call) or buy (in the case of a put) the underlying shares at the specified strike price. The OCC then arranges for the delivery of the shares of stock and the exchange of strike price funds.

The Expiration Process

The expiration date is the last day an option trades. For listed stock options, this is the third Friday of the expiration month. Brokerage firms must submit exercise notices to the OCC.

The OCC has developed a procedure known as **exercise by exception** (also called **ex-by-ex**) to expedite the handling of the exercise of expiring options. Every contract in-the-money will be automatically exercised unless the clearing member advises OCC otherwise. Currently equity and index options that are in-the-money by at least 1 cent are automatically exercised. Nonetheless, most brokers still require their customers to notify their intention to exercise even if an option is in-the-money.

When an equity option is exercised or assigned and it is not covered by stock holdings in the account, sufficient purchasing power must be in the account to make or take delivery of the shares. Otherwise, the broker may close your expiring options positions, even without notification, on the option's last trading day. If the expiring position is not closed and there is insufficient purchasing power, the broker may submit "do not exercise" instructions to the clearing member without notification.

14.6 | Options Price Quotes

Wire news services, websites, and many major daily newspapers carry options price quotes. Because each stock has calls and puts that differ in terms of exercise price and expiration months, an exchange typically has tens of thousands of options trading. All options contracts of the same type written on the same underlying stock belong to the same **option class**. For example, different IBM calls belong to one option class, whereas different IBM puts belong to another. Within a particular class, all options with the same strike price and expiration date belong to an **option series**; for example, IBM March 100 calls belong to one option series, IBM April 90 calls belong to another option series, and IBM April 100 puts belong to yet another option series. Example 14.6 illustrates IBM's options price quotes.

EXAMPLE 14.5: IBM Options Price Quotes

- Figure 14.1 gives the IBM options "chain table" data from March 12, 2009, compiled from the CBOE website (the figure has been condensed and all quotes are twenty minutes delayed). Calls are written on the left side and puts are written on the right side of the figure, with the strike price in the middle. The first set of numbers reports call and put prices for March 2009, with the shaded region reporting options that are in-the-money.

- Consider the tenth entry under "Calls," for which $90 is the strike price. The row contains the following data, moving from left to right:
  - This option is also identified by IBMCR—C stands for the third month, March, and R stands for the strike $90.[14]
  - The price $2.27 is recorded under "Last Trade," which stands for an option's last reported trade price.
  - The 0.56 denotes the price change from the previous settlement price.
  - The bid price $2.25 and the ask price $2.30 are reported per option on one IBM share. Options trade in increments of 5 cents for low options prices and 10 cents for higher options prices.
  - The 6,516 under "Volume" is the number of contracts that have traded so far during the trading day.
  - "Interest" 14,198 is the open interest, which is the total number of outstanding contracts.

FIGURE 14.1: IBM Options Quote from CBOE Website

(IBM) International Bus Mach Corp Com

March 2009

	Calls							Puts					
Symbol	Last Trade	Change	Bid	Ask	Volume	Interest	Strike Price	Symbol	Last Trade	Change	Bid	Ask	Volume	Interest
IBMCX	43.40	2.40	45.20	45.60	n.a.	n.a.	45.00	IBMOX	0.10	0.00	0.05	0.05	35	123
IBMCU	36.00	−6.60	40.30	40.60	n.a.	n.a.	50.00	IBMOU	0.05	0.00	0.05	0.05	148	2,350
IBMCV	33.40	4.40	35.20	35.60	n.a.	5	55.00	IBMOV	0.05	0.00	0.05	0.05	7	325
IBMCL	25.20	1.20	30.20	30.60	7	92	60.00	IBMOL	0.05	0.00	0.05	0.05	7	827
IBMCM	20.90	−3.00	25.30	25.60	4	117	65.00	IBMOM	0.05	0.00	0.05	0.05	34	1,309
IBMCN	19.60	0.60	20.30	20.60	14	218	70.00	IBMON	0.05	0.00	0.05	0.10	20	3,153
IBMCO	12.80	−1.70	15.40	15.60	30	578	75.00	IBMOO	0.09	−0.01	0.05	0.10	307	7,409
IBMCP	10.45	1.35	10.50	10.70	116	2,874	80.00	IBMOP	0.20	−0.05	0.15	0.20	828	10,548
IBMCQ	5.90	1.10	5.80	6.00	1,200	10,054	85.00	IBMOQ	0.50	−0.40	0.50	0.55	5,373	14,901
IBMCR	2.27	0.56	2.25	2.30	6,516	14,198	90.00	IBMOR	1.85	−1.05	1.80	1.90	2,741	12,079
IBMCS	0.50	0.15	0.45	0.50	3,078	14,336	95.00	IBMOS	5.00	−1.00	5.00	5.10	426	4,213
IBMCT	0.05	−0.01	0.05	0.10	148	10,760	100.00	IBMOT	10.10	−1.49	9.50	9.70	62	1,913
IBMCA	0.05	0.00	0.05	0.15	2	4,150	105.00	IBMOA	15.30	−4.10	14.50	14.80	6	75
IBMCB	0.03	−0.02	0.05	0.05	16	3,473	110.00	IBMOB	18.30	−7.00	19.40	19.80	26	10

[14] Some vendors also denote where the option was traded in the following way: no hyphen or letter present, Composite; E, CBOE (Chicago Board Options Exchange); A, AMEX (American Stock Exchange); P, PCX or PSE (Pacific Stock Exchange); X, PHLX (Philadelphia Stock Exchange); b, BOX (Boston Options Exchange); 8, ISE (International Securities Exchange).

IBMCC	0.05	0.03	0.05	0.05	n.a.	410	115.00	IBMOC	n.a.	n.a.	24.30	24.70	n.a.	n.a.
IBMCD	0.03	−0.04	n.a.	0.05	n.a.	81	120.00	IBMOD	n.a.	n.a.	29.50	29.80	n.a.	n.a.
IBMCE	n.a.	n.a.	n.a.	0.05	n.a.	n.a.	125.00	IBMOE	34.00	0.00	34.40	34.70	1	n.a.

Apr 2009

| | Calls | | | | | | | | Puts | | | | | |
Symbol	Last Trade	Change	Bid	Ask	Volume	Interest	Strike Price	Symbol	Last Trade	Change	Bid	Ask	Volume	Interest
IBMDP	11.8	0.90	11.60	11.80	458	3,221	80.00	IBMPP	1.30	−0.25	1.25	1.35	1,527	12,260
IBMDQ	7.80	0.99	7.70	7.90	2,381	9,649	85.00	IBMPQ	2.40	−0.23	2.40	2.45	1,060	13,098
IBMDR	4.60	0.73	4.50	4.70	1,672	11,644	90.00	IBMPR	4.20	−0.75	4.10	4.30	2,145	10,644
IBMDS	2.40	0.60	2.30	2.40	3,405	21,552	95.00	IBMPS	6.90	−1.20	6.80	7.00	254	14,501
IBMDT	1.05	0.30	0.95	1.05	992	15,196	100.00	IBMPT	12.01	−3.19	10.50	10.70	1	2,553

Jul 2009

| | Calls | | | | | | | | Puts | | | | | |
Symbol	Last Trade	Change	Bid	Ask	Volume	Interest	Strike Price	Symbol	Last Trade	Change	Bid	Ask	Volume	Interest
IBMGP	14.23	0.83	14.50	14.70	88	1,605	80.00	IBMSP	4.70	−0.26	4.60	4.70	58	3,457
IBMGQ	11.40	1.00	11.20	11.40	317	1,883	85.00	IBMSQ	6.30	−0.60	6.30	6.40	264	4,300
IBMGR	8.50	0.80	8.40	8.50	600	5,110	90.00	IBMSR	8.67	−0.53	8.40	8.60	93	5,381
IBMGS	6.10	0.80	6.00	6.10	168	8,500	95.00	IBMSS	11.00	−0.70	11.00	11.20	27	1,283
IBMGT	4.22	0.62	4.10	4.20	274	6,417	100.00	IBMST	15.31	−0.19	14.10	14.30	n.a.	848

Oct 2009

| | Calls | | | | | | | | Puts | | | | | |
Symbol	Last Trade	Change	Bid	Ask	Volume	Interest	Strike Price	Symbol	Last Trade	Change	Bid	Ask	Volume	Interest
IBMJP	16.23	2.33	16.30	16.60	20	397	80.00	IBMVP	7.00	−1.86	6.60	6.80	2	162
IBMJQ	13.40	2.70	13.20	13.50	3	202	85.00	IBMVQ	9.30	−1.70	8.50	8.70	12	345
IBMJR	10.59	2.29	10.50	10.70	48	119	90.00	IBMVR	11.32	−0.18	10.70	10.90	n.a.	387
IBMJS	7.40	1.10	8.10	8.30	44	519	95.00	IBMVS	14.40	−0.60	13.30	13.60	44	257
IBMJT	6.00	0.40	6.10	6.30	13	273	100.00	IBMVT	17.90	−2.30	16.30	16.60	43	98

Jan 2010

| | Calls | | | | | | | | Puts | | | | | |
Symbol	Last Trade	Change	Bid	Ask	Volume	Interest	Strike Price	Symbol	Last Trade	Change	Bid	Ask	Volume	Interest
WIBAP	17.70	2.30	17.60	18.30	15	1,744	80.00	WIBMP	8.60	−1.80	8.40	8.70	n.a.	5.576
WIBAQ	14.10	2.30	14.60	15.20	1	1,151	85.00	WIBMQ	11.70	−0.90	10.40	10.70	8	2,616
WIBAR	11.63	1.23	12.20	12.50	n.a.	7,696	90.00	WIBMR	13.20	−1.60	12.70	13.00	2	6,936
WIBAS	9.50	1.70	9.90	10.10	3	3,383	95.00	WIBMS	15.70	−0.90	15.30	15.70	47	2,008
WIBAT	7.74	0.27	7.80	8.10	6	10,373	100.00	WIBMT	19.60	−3.70	18.30	18.60	22	5,714

(continued)

FIGURE 14.1: Continued

	Calls								Puts				
							Jan 2011						
Symbol	Last Trade	Change	Bid	Ask	Volume	Interest	Strike Price	Symbol	Last Trade	Change	Bid	Ask	Volume	Interest
VIBAU	n.a.	n.a.	69.30	70.80	n.a.	n.a.	20.00	VIBMU	0.45	0.00	0.30	0.45	50	358
VIBAX	n.a.	n.a.	67.00	68.20	n.a.	n.a.	22.50	VIBMX	0.55	−0.25	0.45	0.60	100	204
VIBAE	n.a.	n.a.	64.50	65.80	n.a.	n.a.	25.00	VIBME	0.80	−0.12	0.65	0.75	2	105
VIBAV	n.a.	n.a.	59.30	60.80	n.a.	n.a.	30.00	VIBMV	1.20	−0.25	1.05	1.25	n.a.	883
VIBAG	49.50	1.00	54.70	55.90	n.a.	25	35.00	VIBMG	2.10	−0.08	1.65	1.90	20	163
VIBAW	47.70	1.90	50.10	51.30	1	41	40.00	VIBMW	2.95	0.05	2.40	2.60	1	236
VIBAI	42.90	−6.20	45.80	47.00	2	7	45.00	VIBMI	3.40	−0.10	3.20	3.60	n.a.	147
VIBAZ	39.20	−6.60	41.60	43.00	10	207	50.00	VIBMZ	4.70	−0.80	4.20	4.60	10	407
VIBAK	35.40	0.00	37.80	39.00	2	2	55.00	VIBMK	6.30	0.24	5.40	5.90	10	135
VIBAL	31.50	−0.10	34.30	35.40	3	92	60.00	VIBML	7.00	−0.80	6.80	7.20	1	323
VIBAM	28.20	−5.30	31.40	31.90	2	21	65.00	VIBMM	9.60	−0.70	8.30	8.70	44	293
VIBAN	24.80	−0.70	28.00	28.80	n.a.	254	70.00	VIBMN	11.60	0.00	10.00	10.60	25	331
VIBAP	20.20	−2.84	22.00	22.90	6	293	80.00	VIBMP	16.70	1.50	14.10	14.70	40	439
VIBAQ	18.50	0.96	19.90	20.30	50	479	85.00	VIBMQ	18.80	−0.96	16.30	16.90	117	748
VIBAR	15.80	0.40	17.20	17.90	10	1,079	90.00	VIBMR	22.40	1.40	18.80	19.40	n.a.	1,107
VIBAS	14.30	1.20	14.90	15.70	45	521	95.00	VIBMS	22.60	−1.90	21.50	22.20	11	636
VIBAT	13.00	0.40	13.00	13.70	1	1,424	100.00	VIBMT	27.00	0.10	24.40	25.20	n.a.	676
VIBAB	9.80	0.30	9.50	10.10	4	812	110.00	VIBMB	35.50	0.10	30.70	31.60	24	512
VIBAD	6.60	−0.20	6.90	7.50	34	638	120.00	VIBMD	42.90	2.10	37.70	38.70	11	196
VIBAF	4.80	0.40	4.90	5.30	16	407	130.00	VIBMF	47.00	−4.00	45.40	46.20	3	193
VIBAH	3.60	0.60	3.20	3.70	1	599	140.00	VIBMH	54.80	−0.10	53.60	54.70	47	257
VIBAJ	2.25	0.05	2.25	2.50	67	672	150.00	VIBMJ	66.50	−2.00	62.30	62.90	42	227

Source: http://delayedquotes.cboe.com/options/options_chain.html?ASSET_CLASS=STO&ID_OSI=85502&ID_NOTATION=1551887

14.7 | Regulation and Manipulation in Options Markets

In the movie *Mission: Impossible II* (2000), a fictional character, Sean Ambrose, plans to release a virus and then profit by selling the antidote. "I want stock!" Sean thunders. "Stock options, to be precise." And in the James Bond movie *Casino Royale* (2006), a fictional banker, Le Chiffre, provides a guerrilla group a safe haven for its funds. But Le Chiffre's investments actually involve considerable risk.

He buys puts on a successful company and then engineers a terrorist attack to sink the stock values. Stock options and market manipulation have entered pop culture!

Options have long been associated with market manipulation. For example, during the 1920s, options gained notoriety when they were used in conjunction with stock price manipulation schemes. One abusive practice was for speculators with large holdings of the underlying stock to grant call options to stockbrokers (see Overby 2007). In return, brokers would recommend their clients purchase the stock. The resulting demand would benefit brokers and speculators, who would sell at an increased price. This was done on a large scale by creating **option pools**, which "acquired options directly from major stockholders of a company, including directors, banks, and the company itself."

Dual trading is another problem that has long plagued options markets (see chapter 6). A client Robert D. "Pop" Vroom successfully sued Russell Sage in a case of dual trading. Vroom bought several puts from Sage. On May 9, 1901, a day of panic in the local market, Vroom noticed that the share prices underlying the puts were quite low. He instructed Sage, who was also his broker, to buy the shares. Vroom then planned to sell the stocks back to Sage by exercising the puts. But the broker who represented Sage on the floor told the court, "The Exchange was in a great uproar, the amount of selling being unprecedented. He had a lot of trouble getting what he wanted, and had to rush around the floor for some time before he could find a seller. By that time the prices had gone up, but he bought them anyway, for those were his orders—to buy at the market price." Vroom argued that if "Mr. Sage could not execute his order on the Stock Exchange as given, he should have so reported."[15] The court awarded a $17,000 judgment in Vroom's favor.

Another market manipulation scheme is buying out-of-the-money options and simultaneously buying the underlying shares to artificially increase the stock price so that the options end up in-the-money. Traders on the other side, who were getting ready to go out and celebrate happy hour on a late Friday afternoon, may suddenly find that their short out-of-the-money call options, which were seemingly worthless, suddenly end up in-the-money (see the discussion of portfolio window dressing in chapter 6)!

We introduced the notion of a price bubble in chapter 11, which happens when the stock price substantially deviates from its intrinsic or fundamental value. Bubbles typically involve a dramatic price rise followed by a drastic decline. Bubbles are associated with the dotcom boom of the 1990s and the recent real estate rise and collapse, and options are often connected with such episodes. A classic case was the tulip bulb bubble in seventeenth-century Holland. Dutch tulips are famous to this day, but their early history was fraught with speculation, greed, and fraud (see Dash 2001; Overby 1999; Malkiel 2003).

The tulip bulb bubble story begins in 1593, when a botany professor brought tulip bulbs from Turkey to Holland, hoping to vend them at high prices. This market flourished, and tulips traded actively in the Netherlands in the years that

---

[15] "Suit against Russell Sage," *New York Times*, June 19, 1901; "Russell Sage Must Pay $14,603 to Vroom," *New York Times*, March 19, 1904; "Russell Sage Loses Suit," *New York Times*, March 4, 1906.

followed. Some time later, many bulbs caught a benign virus that patterned their petals with bright stripes of contrasting colors. The public adored these "bizarres" and bid their prices up. Tulip bulb prices increased to a peak during the mid-1630s, when people from all walks of life, from noblemen to chimney sweeps, joined the fray. Some even bartered or pawned personal belongings to buy tulip bulbs with the hope of selling them at ever-increasing prices.

Derivatives sprang up to feed the frenzy, and speculators used these derivatives (including options) for leverage—but they also helped the hedgers. Tulip growers and retailers bought calls and futures for protection against price increases. Such hedging strategies are practiced by many businesses even today. After months of outrageous prices and tumultuous trading, the market suddenly crashed in February 1637. Bad regulation and poor quality control have been blamed as the reasons for the crash.

It's no surprise that the regulators have historically been hostile to options. MacKenzie and Millo (2003) note that the proposal for the establishment of the CBOE was met with "instinctual hostility, based in part upon corporate memory of the role options had played in the malpractices of the 1920s." CBOE's first president, Sullivan, was told by one leading SEC official that he had "never seen a [market] manipulation" in which options were not involved. A former SEC chairman even compared options to "marijuana and thalidomide." In a twist of fate, today's regulators support options exchanges and consider them the lesser evil compared to the unregulated OTC derivatives markets.

14.8 | Summary

1. Options trade because they provide payoffs different from forwards, futures, and the underlying stock.

2. Historically, options have been looked at with suspicion because of a cumbersome transaction process, small trading volume, high fees, counterparty risk, and the bad repute of market participants. The result was that investors surreptitiously traded a small number of contracts or shunned them altogether. The government's response ranged from a grudging acceptance to an outright ban.

3. Options markets got a boost in 1973 with the publication of the Black–Scholes–Merton model and the opening of the CBOE. Options trading has seen tremendous growth in the years that followed. This includes trading in options on interest rates, sector funds, exchange-traded funds, and indexes.

4. Equity options traded on the CBOE have the following features:
   a. *Nature*: American physical delivery options
   b. *Contract size*: one hundred shares
   c. *Last exercise date*: the third Friday of the expiration month
   d. *Quotes*: usually quoted in pennies ($0.01) for options prices below $3 and in nickels ($0.05) for higher options prices

e. *Strike prices intervals*: $2.50 when the strike price is between $5 and $25, $5 between $25 and $200, and $10 for points over $200; strikes are adjusted for splits and recapitalizations but not for cash dividends

f. *Strike prices*: in-, at-, and out-of-the-money strike prices are initially listed; new series are generally added when the underlying trades through the highest or lowest strike price available

g. *Expiration months*: two near-term months plus two additional months from the January, February, or March quarterly cycles

h. *Margin*: short-term options buyers post the full price; long-term options buyers (maturing in more than nine months) can borrow up to 25 percent of the purchase price; options sellers are required to keep the full purchase price plus extra funds as cushion against risk

14.9 | Cases

Chicago Board Options Exchange (CBOE) (Harvard Business School Case 205073-PDF-ENG). The case discusses institutional details behind how options trade at the CBOE.

International Securities Exchange: New Ground in Options Markets (Harvard Business School Case 203063-PDF-ENG). This case examines the equity options market, the major parties involved, and the options trading process.

Milk and Money (Kellogg School of Management Case, Case KEL343-PDF-ENG, Harvard Business Publishing). This case considers how a family dairy firm can use regression analysis to choose the best hedges for its dairy products.

14.10 | Questions and Problems

14.1. Briefly describe options trading that took place in 1500–1700 Amsterdam and in nineteenth-century London and New York City.

14.2. Who was Joseph Penso de la Vega?

14.3. a. Who was Russell Sage?

   b. Why was Sage called "The Old Straddle"?

   c. Briefly describe four aspects of Sage's financial operations that remain of current interest.

14.4. a. Why did options trading fall into disrepute in the United States during the early decades of the twentieth century?

   b. What was the SEC's original stance towards options trading?

   c. What was the options industry participants' response to the SEC's views?

14.5. During the nineteenth century, futures trading in the United States steadily gained acceptance while options trading was associated with suspicion.

   a. Can you explain why this happened?

   b. How and when did this view of options trading get changed?

14.6. Briefly describe the events and developments that led to the founding of the CBOE.

14.7. Describe two developments that took place in 1973 that made it a watershed year in the history of options.

14.8. What is an option on a futures? Explain the workings of this derivative contract.

The next two questions are based on the following data from the CME Group's website (prices as of 6:59:36 PM Central Standard Time on August 26, 2011).

Strike	Call	Put
1,820	85.20	107.80
1,825	83.20	110.90
1,830	81.30	113.90
1,835	79.40	217.10
1,840	77.50	120.20

Spot price of gold is $1,830 per ounce. Contract size is one hundred ounces. Prices are per ounce.

14.9. a. Identify which calls are in-the-money, at-the-money, and out-of-the-money.

   b. If you exercise a call with a strike price of $1,820, what is your payoff, and what are your holdings of the futures contracts?

   c. For this call option on gold futures, what is the intrinsic value, and what is the time value?

14.10. a. There is an obvious mistake in the put price data—correct that first.

   b. Identify which puts are in-the-money, at-the-money, and out-of-the-money.

   c. If you exercise a put with a strike price of 1,835, what is your payoff, and what are your holdings of the futures contract?

   d. For this put option on gold futures, what is the intrinsic value, and what is the time value?

14.11. Suppose Your Beloved Machines Inc. has a February cycle for options trading. State the months for which regular equity options on YBM (which expire on the third Friday of the month) trade on the following dates:

   a. January 1

   b. January 27

   c. March 1

14.12. State the dollar amount of margin you are required to keep with a broker when trading one contract (on one hundred shares) of the following options on Your Beloved Machines Inc. YBM's current stock price is $103.

    a. A long put worth $6 for an option maturing in six months

    b. A long call worth $8 for an option maturing in ten months

    c. A short call worth $3 for an option maturing in two months if the strike price is $105

14.13. A long is generally associated with buying and a short with selling. Is it counterintuitive that the put holder gets the right to sell? Explain your answer.

14.14. Your Beloved Machine's current stock price is $90. YBM December 100 calls trade for $6.

    a. Adjust the options prices and terms of the contract for a 4:1 split.

    b. Adjust the options prices and terms of the contract for a 3:2 split.

14.15. Are options on the CBOE adjusted for cash dividends or stock dividends or both?

14.16. Use Figure 14.1.

    a. For the IBM April 2009 calls, is the call value increasing or decreasing in the strike price?

    b. For the IBM April 2009 puts, is the put value increasing or decreasing in the strike price?

    c. For the IBM March 2009 calls, which strikes are the most actively traded?

    d. For the IBM March 2009 puts, which strikes are the most actively traded?

14.17. What is exercise by exception with respect to CBOE options?

14.18. What is an options class? What is an options series? Give examples to illustrate your answer.

14.19. What is open interest for a traded options contract? What does this tell you about the trading interest in a particular options contract?

14.20. Give two examples of market manipulation in the options market.

15

Option Trading Strategies

15.1 | Introduction

While teaching options and futures for the first time, one of us (Chatterjea) was sharing some frustrations with a colleague, Mike Goldstein, about the difficulties in motivating students. Mike advised, "That's not the way to teach derivatives. You should cover the interesting stuff, and show how to implement option trading strategies. Suppose that a takeover is going on, and explain how to set up a straddle to bet on the outcome." He had hit the nail on the head! Focusing on equations like $C(K_1) - C(K_2) \leq K_1 - K_2$ for $K_1 \geq K_2$ is not the best way to attract interest. Moreover, this gives a false sense of mathematical sophistication while achieving little substance. It's far more exciting to take options where the action is and discuss their role for speculating on takeover battles, placing leveraged bets on the markets, and protecting portfolios from market crashes. This is the approach we take here.

This chapter studies some popular options trading strategies. We present profit diagrams for the basic options trades, hedged and spread strategies, including "butterflies" and "condors," followed by strategies involving combinations of options. Along the way, we discuss how options relate to insurance contracts and present a bird's-eye view of taxation and reporting requirements. After this chapter, you should be able to understand "Options Report" stories in *The Wall Street Journal*. The strategies we discuss are relevant to all players in the options market: the individual trader, the financial institution, the nonfinancial corporation, and even the government.

15.2 | Traders in Options Markets

Bill Lipschutz, who had taken one of the world's first options courses from one of us (Jarrow) at Cornell University, joined Salomon Brothers Inc. in 1981, a prestigious Wall Street investment banking firm at the time.[1] Though Salomon prided itself as one of the world's most powerful trading companies, Lipschutz was disappointed to find options trading to be nonquantitative. He found that no one seemed to know the Black–Scholes–Merton model. Trading strategies were based on ad hoc criteria, for example, the head of the proprietary options trading desk said, "'I went to buy a car this weekend and the Chevrolet showroom was packed. Let's buy GM calls.' That type of stuff." Then, one day, a trader pulled him aside and gave away the great secret: "Look, I don't know what Sidney is teaching you, but let me tell you everything you need to know about options. You like 'em, buy calls. You don't like 'em, buy puts."

In the early 1980s, many Wall Street firms placed "leveraged outright bets" and prayed to the "Bitch-Goddess Success."[2] As the decade unfolded, however, most

---

[1] This story is taken from the interview "Bill Lipschutz: The Sultan of Currencies" in Jack Schwager's (1992) book *The New Market Wizards: Conversations with America's Top Traders*. Lipschutz developed an early expertise in trading currency options, which began trading on the Philadelphia Stock Exchange in 1982. During his eight-year stint at Salomon, he routinely traded billions of dollars' worth of currencies and became the "largest and most successful currency trader" in the firm.

[2] Professor William James of Harvard University used the expression "Bitch-Goddess Success" in a letter to the British writer H. G. Wells.

investment banks started assembling a team of derivative experts and running proprietary trading desks to make profits. Goldman Sachs and Company, a key player in this transformation, lured Professor Fischer Black from the Massachusetts Institute of Technology and made him a partner. Black helped usher in the migration of many finance professors and numerous talented PhDs in the natural and engineering sciences into Wall Street firms. The most mathematical of these recruits came to be variously viewed as "quants" and "rocket scientists" whose job was to apply their math mastery to make profits. Salomon did not lag behind. It pioneered the mortgage-backed securities market during the 1970s, arranged the world's first swap contract in 1981 (see chapter 22), and built an active derivatives shop. Its consultants included Nobel laureate Robert Engle, who was hired to develop volatility forecasts and devise trading strategies based on cutting-edge econometrics.

Much of our discussion of options strategies in this chapter will be from the perspective of an individual investor. Financial institutions also trade options to bet on the markets and capture arbitrage profits. Hedge funds and proprietary trading desks at investment banks also implement the strategies we describe. For example, a senior portfolio manager at Fidelity Investments, Anthony Bolton, correctly timed the market when he bought a put option on UK stocks in April 2006, a few weeks before the FTSE 100 index declined 10 percent (see "Oracle of U.K. Has New Worry," *Wall Street Journal*, May 29, 2008). Warren Buffett noted in his 2008 chairman's letter in the annual report of Berkshire Hathaway Inc. that his company had entered into 251 derivatives contracts, including writing fifteen- and twenty-year maturity European put options on four major indexes (the Standard and Poor's [S&P] 500, London's FTSE 100, Europe's Euro Stoxx 50, and Tokyo's Nikkei 225). He believed that each of these contracts was "*mispriced at inception* [emphasis added], sometimes dramatically so." Doesn't this smack of arbitrage? Affirming his belief that "the CEO of any large financial organization *must* be the Chief Risk Officer as well," Buffett declared that he had initiated these positions, would continue to monitor them, and would take full responsibility if the company lost profits on these derivatives trades.

We discuss later in the chapter how traders (including insurance companies) use options to hedge and speculate on catastrophic risks. Many foundations and endowments, mutual funds, and pension funds actively trade options. Options oftentimes underlie financial engineering techniques used by nonfinancial companies, which buy inputs to produce outputs. Sometimes governments use options. Recall the example at the beginning of chapter 14, in which Lawrence Summers and Zhu Rongji discussed the feasibility of using put options to defend the value of the Chinese currency and how the US government used warrants to design a highly effective financial rescue package for troubled banks. Options trading strategies adopted by different kinds of traders get regularly mentioned in the financial press and addressed in case studies. For simplicity, we begin our discussion from the perspective of a retail trader.

15.3 | Profit Diagrams

As pictures say a thousand words, we use profit diagrams as our primary tool for discussing options trading strategies. Recall that *profit diagrams* place the stock price on the expiration date $S(T)$ on the horizontal (x) axis and the net profits from trades on the vertical (y) axis. The profit or loss is computed by vertically adding up the profits and losses for each security within the trade. Wherever convenient, we show the strike price K, the maximum profit (or loss), and the stock price corresponding to the **breakeven point** (**BEP**; or the **zero-profit point**), where the trader recoups the option premium. Absent market frictions, the zero-sum nature of options trading ensures that the BEP is the same for both the buyer and the writer.

Profit diagrams have some limitations. First, you can only draw them for European options. American options have the risk that one or more legs of the strategy may get exercised early and disappear from the diagram. Second, they do not apply before expiration because the time value of the options (see chapter 5) moves their profits away from those on the expiration date. Third, we must have just one stock as the underlying. You cannot draw profit diagrams for a portfolio of options on different stocks.

Still these diagrams are quite useful. If American options remain unexercised until expiration, they have the same payoffs as European options. Although most exchange-traded options in the United States are American options, early exercise isn't very common. The next chapter will demonstrate that options are usually worth more alive (i.e., unexercised) than dead (exercised). Profit diagrams provide a useful snapshot of the possibilities on the option's maturity date.

We focus on equity options. With minor modifications, you can similarly analyze other options, including those on commodities, indexes, and even futures and forwards. For now, we examine simple options trading strategies. Along with these strategies come stories of options users and their uses. Some are fairy tales illustrating the important aspects of a trade, whereas others are real-world examples.

15.4 | The Nitty-Gritty Details of Options Trading

When you apply for options trading privileges, your brokerage firm will ask you detailed information about your assets and liabilities, liquid net worth, and prior trading experience. On the basis of this information, the broker assigns you an appropriate trading level out of the four or five possible. An example of option trading levels is:

- "Level 1 is the safest strategies, just covered calls.

- Level 2 is all strategies in Level 1 plus riskier strategies like long calls, long puts, long straddles, long strangles, covered puts, married puts, and synthetic puts.

- Level 3 is all strategies from Levels 1 and 2 plus even riskier strategies like debit spreads, credit spreads, calendar/diagonal spreads, and short puts.

- Level 4 allows the broadest flexibility including adoption of the riskiest strategies: all strategies from prior levels plus short calls."[3]

The broker must furnish a copy of an options disclosure document "Characteristics and Risks of Standardized Options," prepared by the **Options Clearing**

[3] http://us.etrade.com.

Corporation. Just as commercial airplanes will not fly until the flight attendants have demonstrated the safety procedures and advised the passengers to read the safety cards, your options trading account will not be approved unless you have been provided with this document and advised to read it carefully.

After understanding the mechanics of trading, which we described in chapter 5, an investor is ready to place an options trade. Suppose you want to trade five IBM January 130 calls maturing in the year 2011. This American call on IBM's stock has a strike price of $130, stops trading on the third Friday of January (which is the last day it can be exercised), covers one hundred shares, and trades on the Chicago Board Options Exchange (CBOE) and elsewhere. You can submit your order in one of three ways: via Internet, through an automated system that can be accessed by a telephone, or by calling and dictating the order to a live operator. If you are trading via the broker's website, you need to fill out some standard information:

- *Symbol: IBM110122C130.* Here IBM is the underlying stock's ticker symbol, 11 for the year 2011, 01 for January, 22 for the expiration date, which is the twenty-second day of the month, C for call, and 130 for the strike price.

- *Order type.* Indicate whether this is a basic order (like the current trade), a complex order (such as a spread), or a buy–write order (buy IBM and sell a call against it). Select from buy open, sell open, buy close, or sell close.

- *Number of contracts.* Input 5 in this case.

- *Execution type.* Choose one of the following: market, limit, stop, stop limit, or trailing stop $ order.[4] See chapters 3 and 5 for a discussion of different order placement strategies.

- *Term.* Indicate whether this will be good for the day, good for sixty days, immediate or cancel, or fill or kill (FOK). The last two types of orders must be immediately executed with immediate or cancel, allowing for partial execution (with the rest being canceled), while an FOK order must be filled in its entirety or killed.

- *All-or-none.* This indicates that you do not accept partial execution. If the order is executed, it must be filled in its entirety.

15.5 | Options Strategies

A story titled "Options Trading Grew Up in 2009" (*Wall Street Journal*, January 4, 2010) reported that many new options traders entered the market in 2009, with the OCC having a record volume of over 3.6 billion contracts. What attracted these options traders? The article identified several factors. Many investors traded options to better manage their portfolio's risks after suffering losses. Some adopted complex strategies that "helped them to reduce trading costs and limit the impact

---

[4] A **trailing stop order** has a stop feature that changes with the moving (or trailing) activation price, hence the name. For example, suppose you buy IBM stock at $120 and immediately place a trailing stop sell order with a $1.00 trailing stop, which is reset with a $5 change in stock price. This sets the stop price to $119.00. Say IBM falls to 119.01; then the stop will not be executed. If it reaches $125, then the stop is reset at $124; if it continues to rally and reaches $130, the stop is reset at $129; and if it then falls to $129, it hits the stop and the order becomes a market order.

of 'decay,' which describes the pace at which options lose value as they approach expiration." To prevent losses, they bought put options or "put spreads," and to generate income, they tended to sell "covered calls." This and the next two sections discuss these options trading strategies.

Common Options Price Data

Most of our options trading strategy examples will use the following common options pricing data (COP data) for a fictitiously named company, OPSY, which is the Dutch name for options:

- The current stock price S is $22.50.
- The time to maturity T is six months.
- The strike prices K are $17.50, $20, $22.50, and $25.
- The continuously compounded, risk-free interest rate r is 5 percent per year.
- The European options prices are given in Table 15.1.

TABLE 15.1: European Option Price Data for OPSY		
Strike Price	**Call Price**	**Put Price**
$K_0 = \$17.50$	$5.50	$0.10
$K_1 = 20.00$	3.50	0.50
$K_2 = 22.50$	2.00	1.50
$K_3 = 25.00$	1.00	3.00

Stock price $S = \$22.50$; time to maturity $T = 6$ months; risk-free interest rate $r = 5$ percent per year.

We ignore market imperfections such as transaction costs and also interest earned on the option's premium. Usually these are small. Of course, you can easily add them to the profit or loss amounts.

Naked Trades: The Basic Building Blocks

The basic option trading strategy building blocks are stand-alone positions containing a single option. Traders refer to these as **naked trading strategies** (who said options are boring?). Long naked trades are **outright purchases** because you are not holding an offsetting position in the underlying stock. Short naked trades are also known as **uncovered** strategies because you are not **covering** (by reducing the risk of) the trade by simultaneously taking a position in the underlying stock.

EXAMPLE 15.1: Going Long and Selling Short: Stocks and Options

Before illustrating the four uncovered positions for European call and put options (with strike prices of $22.50), we draw profit diagrams for long and short stock trades (see Figure 15.1). You can evaluate option trades vis-à-vis these key references. Naked option trading strategies are popular among traders.

Long and Short Stock

■ As stocks are limited liability assets, the maximum loss is the price paid. Long OPSY's profit diagram is a straight line that emanates from a loss of $22.50 along the vertical axis. It rises at a 45 degree angle, cuts the horizontal axis at the breakeven point of $22.50, and continues upward with infinite profit potential.

■ The short stock's profit diagram is the mirror image of the long stock across the *x* axis. An oft-quoted Wall Street saying attributed to the notorious financier Daniel Drew explains the riskiness of short selling: "He who sells what isn't his'n, buys it back or goes to prison."

Long Call

■ Buying OPSY 22.50 European calls for $2 gives the right to buy the stock for $22.50 at time *T*. Recall from chapter 5 that the profit diagram is a horizontal line starting from (a maximum loss of) $2 on the vertical axis. Then, at the strike price of $K = \$22.50$, it shifts upward at a 45 degree angle, breaks even where the stock price $S(T)$ equals the strike price plus call premium (BEP = $24.50), and increases with an unbounded profit potential.

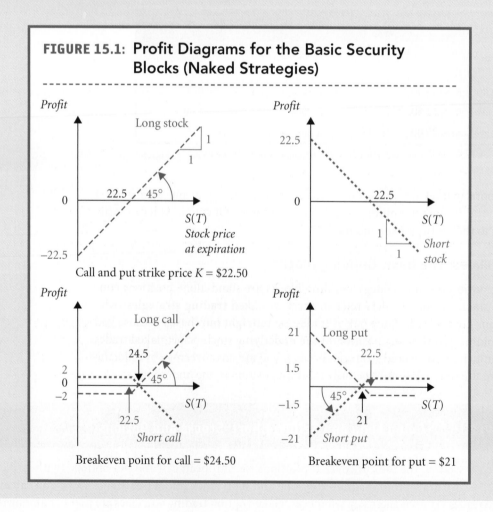

FIGURE 15.1: Profit Diagrams for the Basic Security Blocks (Naked Strategies)

- Applications and uses follow:
  - Buy calls to benefit if the stock goes up while limiting losses to the premium if the stock goes down. You can buy OPSY stocks for $22.50 per share. Alternatively, you can buy OPSY 22.50 six-month calls for $2 per share. Each trade has its pros and cons. Action on the call happens during its short life span. By contrast, you can hold on to the stock forever in the hope of a price increase. If OPSY goes down to $15, you lose $7.50 per share but just $2 on the call. If OPSY goes up, you immediately start benefiting on the long stock, but you have to wait until the stock price crosses the breakeven point of $24.50 before profiting on the call.
  - Let's look at percentage returns. A $7.50 decline is a 33.33 percent loss on the stock investment, but a $2 loss on the premium is a 100 percent loss on the option. If the stock goes up to $30, then there is a 33.33 percent profit on the stock but a $(30 - 24.50)/2 = 275$ percent profit on the call. *The dollar gain or loss is higher for the stock, but the percentage gain or loss is higher for the option.* This happens because options are leveraged investments.
  - Buy calls to speculate on events, corporate developments, and sector and economic performance. For example, the *Wall Street Journal* ("Traders Bet on Departure of Citigroup's CEO," October 18, 2007) reported that traders purchased calls in the expectation that the banking giant Citigroup's chief executive officer would soon depart, a move that was expected to boost the company's stock.

Short Call

- Selling a call option is also known as shorting or writing a call. A short call's profit diagram is the mirror image across the *x* axis of that for a long call.

- Naked call writing is one of the riskiest strategies, and only seasoned option traders with sufficient financial resources are allowed to employ this strategy.

- The financial press has regular stories on call writing. For example, "Merck, Schering Active" (*Wall Street Journal*, April 1, 2008) reported that on March 31, 2008, shares of pharmaceutical companies Merck and Co. and Schering-Plough Corp. fell 15 percent and 26 percent, respectively, after a panel of cardiologists urged doctors to decrease the use of a cholesterol drug that these companies jointly sell. Hoping that the stock prices would stay in a narrow range after this decline, some options traders sold both calls and puts.

Long Put

- A put buyer loses the entire premium of $1.50 if the stock price stays above the strike but starts recouping his investment when $S(T)$ dips below this mark. The breakeven point is at $21, where the $1.50 gain exactly offsets the premium paid. Profit is maximized when $S(T)$ hits zero. Here a worthless stock is sold for $22.50, and deducting the premium arrives at a profit of $21.
  - Put purchasers bet on the downside but limit their losses in case the bet goes wrong. As with calls, a long put has similar pluses and minuses vis-à-vis a short stock trade.
  - Put buying also gets regular press coverage, for example, see the *Wall Street Journal* ("GM Puts Are Active amid Sales Worries," November 20, 2007). On November 19, 2007, options traders bearish on General Motors sold over 107,700 puts, which was more than twice the volume for the call.

Short Put

The uncovered put writer has the obligation to buy OPSY for $22.50 on assignment of an exercise notice. A put writer is **uncovered** if he does not have a short stock position or has not deposited cash equal to the strike to form a **cash-secured put**.

Naked put sellers take losses during market crashes. One of the most notorious examples happened during the Black Monday crash of October 19, 1987. Buoyed by the large stock market gains during the mid-1980s, naked put sellers viewed put premiums as free cash. But when the Dow fell 22.61 percent on this fateful day, many of these put sellers were wiped out.

- Naked put writers often have two objectives: to receive premium income and to acquire stock at a cost below its market price at some future date.

- Short put strategies are bullish. For example, the *Wall Street Journal* ("Spread on Countrywide Shows Futures Is Anybody's Guess," December 1–2, 2007) stated that at the end of November 2007, traders sold puts on Countrywide, which was the largest independent US home lender. This bullish strategy was adopted when the mortgage market was declining and it was reported that a government-sponsored plan might be introduced to aid distressed home mortgage holders.

To summarize, naked options trades generate profits that are similar to those created by trading stocks without their downsides. But they are created for a limited time and require regular payment of premiums to maintain the position over long time periods.

15.6 | Hedged Strategies

Hedged strategies combine options and stocks in ways that reduce the overall risk of naked option trades. They are usually **covered strategies** because they hedge option transactions with the stocks that protect (cover) them.

EXAMPLE 15.2: Hedged and Covered Strategies

Covered Call Writing (Long Stock plus Short Call)

- Covered call writing combines a short call with the underlying stock. An article titled "Covered Calls Prove Popular Strategy" (*Wall Street Journal*, January 2, 2010) reported that this popular strategy was used at the time by a staggering 84 percent of options investors at the huge brokerage firm Charles Schwab and Co. Inc. Figure 15.2 illustrates this 1:1 hedge strategy.

- At the origin, the long OPSY trade incurs the maximum loss ($22.50), but the short call retains the entire call premium of $2. The combined profit is $-22.50 + 2 = -$20.50$.
- As the stock price increases, the short call's profit graph (a dotted line parallel to the horizontal axis) remains constant at $2, but the long stock's profit graph (an upward sloping dashed line) rises by a dollar for each dollar increase in $S(T)$. The resulting profit diagram (shown by a solid line) rises at a 45 degree angle, until the breakeven point at $20.50.
- At the strike price of $22.50, the profit is $2 (from short call) + 0 (from long stock) = $2. For higher values of $S(T)$, the short call's profit decreases at a negative 45 degree angle, which neutralizes the long stock position's increase. Consequently, the covered call's profit diagram is a flat line for all higher values of OPSY.

- Doesn't the profit diagram for this concoction look like the diagram for a short put position? Using the words of Horatio in Shakespeare's immortal play *Hamlet*, "season your curiosity for a while." The next chapter will explain why this happens.

- The timing of the trades gives this strategy different names. It's called a **buy–write** if one *simultaneously* buys the stock and sells the call, but it's an **overwrite** if one sells the call *after* purchasing the share.

- Buy–write's popularity prompted the CBOE to develop an innovative benchmark for measuring the performance of such strategies. Released in April 2002, the award-winning **CBOE S&P 500 BuyWrite Index** (**BXM**) is based on the total returns from hypothetically holding the S&P 500 stock index portfolio and writing a slightly out-of-the-money, one-month maturity call option on the S&P 500 index. A 2006 study by Callan Associates found that over an eighteen-year period ending in 2006, BXM's return lagged slightly behind that of the S&P 500 but with only two-thirds of the risk. Although BXM usually trailed behind the S&P 500 index in bull markets, the premium income from the hedge helped it to consistently outperform the S&P 500 during the bear markets.

- Traders who write covered calls generally have two objectives: collecting a premium or hedging a stock trade. By accepting the premium, the writer surrenders the opportunity to benefit from a stock price rise above the exercise price. The call premium gives the writer some cushion against a stock price fall, but he remains vulnerable to losses from a deep decline in the stock. Covered call writing works well in neutral markets, particularly when the volatility is high, which translates into higher call prices.

- Covered call writing is a more conservative strategy than an outright stock purchase. An article, "Warming Up to Options," in the October 1981 issue of *Institutional Investor* magazine reported that a growing number of pension funds were using or contemplating using the covered call strategy. A director of investments at a pension fund went as far as to comment that covered call writing is one of the most conservative strategies possible.

- Even the government views covered call writing as a less risky strategy. You can write covered calls in some tax-advantaged retirement savings accounts. In June 2009, the Securities and Exchange Commission approved allowing employees to sell calls against unexercised holdings of **employee stock options** (which are call options on the stock that are granted by the company as a form of noncash compensation; see "Stock Options Opened for 'Call Writing,'" *Wall Street Journal*, June 26, 2009).

■ A *Wall Street Journal* article ("Cheap Stocks Give Investors Options," September 26, 2008) reported a clever use of covered writing. Traders bought shares of government-sponsored enterprises Fannie Mae and Freddie Mac for about $2 and sold out-of-the-money calls. The strategy possessed several interesting features. First, at the time the article was written, the US government had announced an agreement for a $700 billion bailout plan to aid major financial firms. Second, this news coupled with the fact that the Treasury hadn't eliminated the common stock of these organizations (which, nonetheless, were ready "to be put in a conservatorship by the U.S. government") led the traders to perceive that the stock was unlikely to crash to zero, thus limiting the strategy's downside risk.

Covered Put Buying (Long Stock plus Long Put)

■ Another highly popular strategy, covered put buying has long been used to justify the trading of options: to buy insurance by hedging a long stock with an option. Figure 15.2 illustrates this strategy.
- At the origin, the long OPSY trade loses $22.50 but the long put position has a gain of $21, giving a profit of $-\$1.50$, which is the maximum loss.
- For each dollar increase in $S(T)$, the long put decreases the covered put strategy's profit by a dollar, giving a profit parallel to the horizontal axis.
- When $S(T)$ reaches $K = \$22.50$, the long put's profit changes and becomes parallel to the x axis, but the long stock position keeps increasing. As a result, the profit rises at a 45 degree angle, signifying boundless profit potential.

■ As with the previous strategy, the timing of the trades gives the strategy different names. It is called a **married put** (from an old Internal Revenue Service ruling, states the Options Industry Council website) if one *simultaneously* buys the put and the stock, but a **protective put** if one buys the put to protect the downside risk of a stock *previously purchased*.

■ Again, the profit diagram looks like another option trade, a long call position. We will explain this in the context of put–call parity in the next chapter.

■ Traders employ covered put strategies for several reasons:
- *Establishing a minimum selling price for the stock*. No matter how far the stock declines, your loss is limited to the put premium plus the difference, if any, between the stock's purchase price and the put's exercise price. In this case, the minimum selling price is (Strike price − Put premium) = $22.50 − 2 = \$20.50$.
- Microsoft and Dell have long been selling puts on their own stocks in conjunction with their stock repurchase programs. Their aims are to control the volatility of their shares, keep them in a trading range, and earn premium income (see "Internet Companies Consider Options," *Risk*, August 1999; "Hedging Option Plans: Good for Who?" *Risk*, September 2000).
- *Buy puts to protect unrealized profit in a long stock position*. Suppose you bought OPSY when it was trading for $15 and it has now reached $22.50. You can set up a protective put position to hedge your profit against short-term price declines. No matter how far the stock falls, you can always exercise the put and sell the stock at the strike price $22.50. Your profit never falls below [(Strike price − Stock purchase price) − Put premium) = $(22.50 − 15) − 1.50 = \$6$.

FIGURE 15.2: 1:1 Hedges: Covered Call Writing (Buywrite or Overwrite) and Covered Put Buying (Married Put or Protective Put)

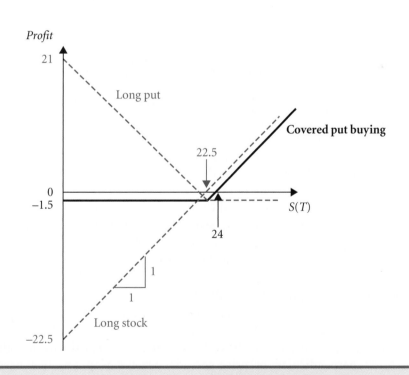
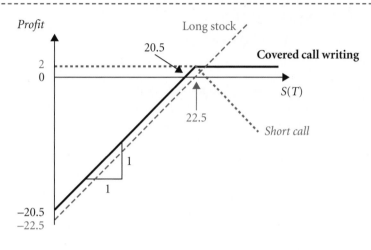
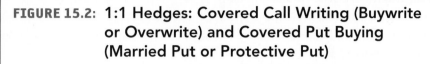

Covered Call Buying (Short Stock plus Long Call)

Suppose you are bearish and sell OPSY short. This is a high-risk strategy. What's your protection if the stock rallies instead? One can hedge the risk by buying a call (perhaps an out-of-the-money call like OPSY 25, which has a price of $1).

Covered Put Writing (Short Stock plus Short Put)

A less popular strategy, covered put writing tries to generate some income for the short sellers.

The 1:2 Hedge

The previous four strategies considered 1:1 hedges (see Figure 15.2), in which one option was covered by one stock. You can also create hedged strategies by combining unequal numbers of options. A 1:2 hedge combines a long stock with two short calls (see Figure 15.3) or two long puts. The profit diagram looks similar to the diagram of a straddle discussed later in this chapter. These strategies have long been used by dealers who write options; for example, when options are at-the-money, a call writer may buy half a share for each call sold, whereas a put writer may sell half a share for each put sold. The precise quantity of stocks to hedge options trades to remove all of the portfolio's price risk is given by the stock's delta, which is discussed in chapters 17, 18, and 19 and in considerable detail in chapter 20.

15.7 | Spread Strategies

Oxford University professor John L. Austin asserted during a lecture that although there are many languages in which a double negative makes a positive, no language uses two positives to express a negative statement. Seated in the audience was another eminent philosopher, Sidney Morgenbesser. He dismissively dissented, "Yeah, yeah," and the tone of his voice disproved the claim.[5] In finance, we can use a variation of this venerable philosopher's assertions to describe a spread strategy in which two risky trades combine to form a less risky portfolio. This happens because a **spread strategy** subtracts "similar" risks, making the end product safer than either of the two originals. Because spreads are two-sided hedges that combine two options of the same type but on opposite sides of the market, the exchanges allow spreads to have lower margins than naked trades. A spread gives a smaller profit if the underlying moves in one direction but a tiny loss otherwise. Choice of which option to buy and which to sell determines whether it is a bullish or a bearish spread.

Spreads come in three basic types: (1) **vertical spreads** (also called **money**, **perpendicular**, or **price spreads**) involving options that have different strike

---

[5] A professor at Columbia University for a half-century, **Sidney Morgenbesser**'s (1921–2004) scholarship and quick wit made him an influential philosopher. (Based on the *New York Times* obituary dated August 4, 2004.)

FIGURE 15.3: Long Stock and Two Short Calls (1:2 Hedge)

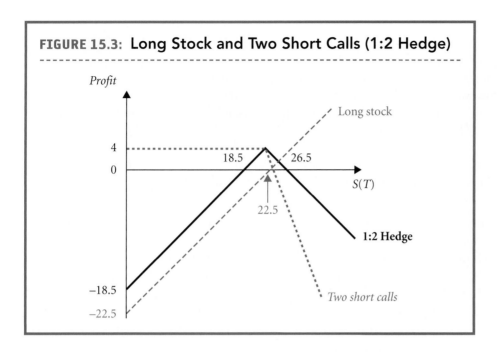

prices but expire on the same date; (2) **horizontal spreads** (or **time** or **calendar spreads**) involving options that have the same strike but different maturity dates; and (3) **diagonal spreads** involving options that differ both in terms of strike price and maturity date. Different maturity dates prevent representing diagonal and horizontal spreads in standard profit diagrams. Instead, traders compute options sensitivities to understand the behavior of such portfolios. Chapter 20 explains these tools.

EXAMPLE 15.3: Bull and Bear Spreads

Bull Spread

- You can create a **bullish vertical spread** by buying an option and simultaneously *selling an option of the same type but with a higher strike price*, where both options have the same underlying security and the same date of maturity.[6] Traders set up bull spreads when they are optimistic about the underlying stock. We create a **bull call spread** by trading OPSY calls from our COP data, as follows:
  - Buy the OPSY call with a strike price $K_1 = 20$ for \$3.50 and sell a call with $K_2 = 22.50$ for \$2 and draw their profit graphs (see Figure 15.4).

[6] For a *bullish horizontal spread*, buy an option and sell another option of the same type and strike but with shorter life. For a *bullish diagonal call spread*, buy an option with a lower strike price and longer time to maturity than the one that is sold. Do the opposite for bearish spreads.

- If the stock price at expiration is zero, the loss of $3.50 on the first call is partially offset by a $2 gain on the second call, giving a loss of $1.50.
- The loss stays constant until $S(T)$ reaches $20. Beyond this, the long call's profit graph increases at a 45 degree angle, while the short call's profit graph remains flat. Consequently, the profit graph for the bull spread, which was $1.50 below the horizontal axis, moves up dollar for dollar for each dollar increase in $S(T)$, cuts the x axis at the BEP = $(20 + 1.50) = 21.50$, and reaches $1 when $S(T)$ reaches $22.50.
- Beyond $22.50, the short call position decreases at a negative 45 degree angle. This decline neutralizes the upward rise from the long call, and the net result is a flat line that is $1 above the x axis.

■ This is a **debit spread** because it costs money to create the spread, as opposed to in a **credit spread**, where you receive money in the creation process. You create a credit spread when you enter into a **bullish put spread** by buying a put and simultaneously *selling another put with a higher strike price*. For example, by buying the OPSY 20 put and selling the OPSY 22.50 put, you create a bull spread that has a maximum loss of $1.50, a BEP at $21.50, and a maximum profit of $1—a profit graph that happens to be identical to the graph of our previous bull call spread (see Figure 15.4).

■ Options traders often placed bearish bets on banking stocks during the 2008–9 credit crisis. They include bearish put spreads (see below) on Wells Fargo and Inc. on July 23, 2008, SunTrust Banks Inc., and again on Wells Fargo on August 25, 2008.[7]

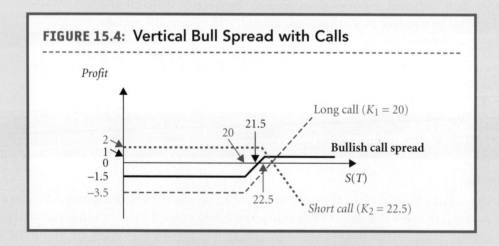

FIGURE 15.4: Vertical Bull Spread with Calls

[7] *Wall Street Journal* articles "WaMu Is Seized, Sold Off to J.P. Morgan, in Largest Failure in U.S. Banking History," September 26, 2008; "Options Volatility Gauge Puts Better Light on Financial Firms," July 24, 2008; "SunTrust Banks, Wells Fargo See Elevated Activity in Puts," August 26, 2008.

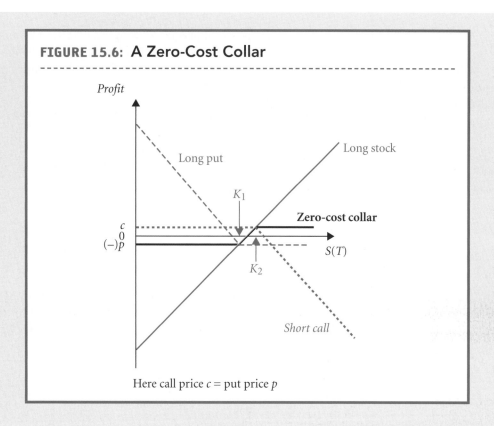

FIGURE 15.6: A Zero-Cost Collar

Here call price c = put price p

EXAMPLE 1: Examples of a Call Spread, a Ratio Spread, Butterflies, and Condors

Bull Call Spread

One can create a bull call spread similar to the one in Example 15.3 by buying one OPSY 17.50 call for $5.50 and selling one OPSY 20 call for $3.50. The profit diagram is initially a flat line with a loss of $2, rises at a 45 degree angle as the stock price goes from $17.50 to $20, breaks even at $19.50, and again becomes a flat line at a profit of $0.50 when $S(T)$ exceeds $20 (see Figure 15.7).

Ratio Spread

- Now sell another OPSY call with strike price $20. By selling two calls, you collect a premium of $3.50 × 2 = $7, and the profit diagram declines by $2 for each dollar increase in $S(T)$ beyond $20. This creates a **ratio spread**, which is defined as an options trading strategy in which the number of calls (or puts) purchased is different from the number of calls (or puts) sold. The profit graph for this **one-by-two call spread** is a flat line emanating from $(-5.50 + 7) = 1.50 on the vertical axis, which then rises at 45 degrees when $S(T)$ exceeds $17.50 and attains the peak value of $(1.50 + 2.50) = 4 when $S(T)$ is $20 (see Figure 15.7).[10] Beyond this, the long call moves the graph up, but the two short calls drag it down twice as fast, resulting in a line that declines at a negative 45 degree angle.

- Market professionals use spreads for a variety of purposes. Suppose you bought OPSY for $50 and now it has fallen to $22.50. What can you do? Perhaps you can adopt a **hope and hold** strategy: hold OPSY with the hope that it will bounce back to the price at which you bought it! Alternatively, you can **double up** by buying the same number of shares at the now "lower price" or by purchasing an equivalent number of calls to the shares held. This lowers the breakeven point if the stock rallies. On the negative side, it requires additional funds and increases the downside risk. Yet another possibility is a **repair strategy**: for every stock held, buy one call with a strike price close to the current stock price and sell two calls with a higher strike price, where all the calls expire on the same date and the strike prices are chosen to minimize the cost of this strategy. This imposes a ratio call spread on a long call position. A profit diagram reveals that the breakeven point for the original stock trade gets lowered but does not benefit if the stock has a sharp increase.

Butterfly Spread

- A **butterfly spread** is created by trading four options of the same type (all calls or all puts) with three different strike prices: two options with extreme strike prices are bought (written) and two options are written (bought) with the middle strike price (see Figure 15.7).

- A butterfly spread is a two-sided hedge that bets on the volatility of the underlying security: a long butterfly spread makes a small profit if the volatility is low and a small loss otherwise. The profit graph for this long butterfly call spread starts at a maximum loss of $(-5.50 + 7 - 2) = -\$0.50$ along the vertical axis. Initially a line parallel to the horizontal axis, the profit graph starts increasing when $S(T)$ exceeds 17.50, breaks even at 18, attains a maximum value of 2 when $S(T)$ is 20, declines and cuts the x axis again at 22, falls to $-\$0.50$ at 22.50, and again becomes a line parallel to the x axis for all higher values of $S(T)$.

- A butterfly spread is so named because the profit diagram looks like a butterfly's wings. If you reverse the preceding trades, you will create a short butterfly spread. You can also create butterfly spreads with puts.

Condor

- Thinking that OPSY might fluctuate more than anticipated, you decide to expand the region over which you want to profit. You modify the butterfly spread by (1) keeping a long call with $K_0 = 17.50$ as before, (2) (instead of two short calls at the same strike) selling one call at the next higher strike price $K_1 = 20$ and another at $K_2 = 22.50$, and finally, (3) buying a call with the uppermost strike $K_3 = 25$ (see Figure 15.7). This creates a **condor spread**, which has four options with four strike prices: long two options with extreme strikes and short two options with strike prices in the middle, and vice versa. The wings of the condor, the largest flying land bird in the western hemisphere, inspire the name.

- Our condor's profit diagram begins on the y axis at $(-5.50 + 3.50 + 2 - 1) = -\$1$, the amount obtained by adding up the premiums. Initially, it's a line parallel to the x axis because the profits from the calls are flat at this point. When $S(T)$ goes beyond 17.50, the call with the lowest strike becomes active and increases the payoff. The profit graph reaches a maximum value of 1.50 when $S(T)$ is 20. It becomes a flat line for $S(T)$ lying between 20 and 22.50 because the call with a strike of $K_0 = 17.5$ pulls it up but the call with $K_1 = 20$ pushes it down. Beyond 22.50, the third call (with $K_2 = 22.50$) kicks in, and the profit graph falls. Finally, when $S(T)$ exceeds 25, the fourth option (with $K_3 = 25$) also becomes active and increases the payoff: with two calls pulling it up and two pushing it down, it again becomes a flat line. You can also create a condor with puts.

---

[10] A *call ratio spread* typically involves buying calls and selling a greater number of calls at a higher strike price. If you sell calls and buy a greater number of calls at a higher strike price, then you create a *call backspread*.

FIGURE 15.7: Bull Call Spread, Ratio Spread, Butterfly, and Condor

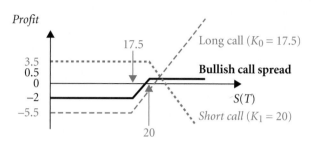

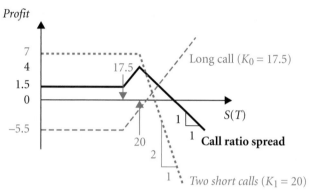

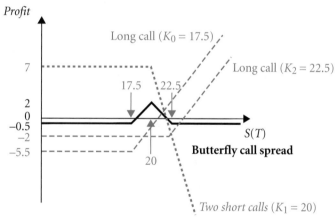

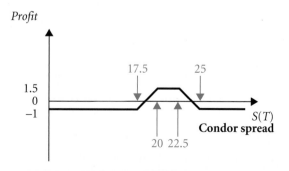

EXTENSION 15.2: Reinsurance Contracts and Call Spreads

Reinsurance contracts on a loss causing event (e.g. hurricanes) are equivalent to a call spread in which the call options are written on the losses of the insured event. To understand this equivalence, let us first discuss insurance and then reinsurance markets.

For millennia, insurance contracts have been used as a mechanism for pooling, sharing, and mitigating the financial impact of risky events. Some five thousand years back, the Babylonians developed a system of maritime loans that exempted the debtor from repayment in case the ship sank. In Europe, **Bottomry bonds** were forgiven if the ship was lost, and **burial societies** paid funeral expenses in case a member died.

The basics of **insurance** may be described as follows: an **insurance company** (or the **insurer**, say, State Farm Insurance) accepts risks faced by individuals or businesses (the **insured**) by underwriting an insurance contract (a **policy**, such as an auto insurance policy) that states the various terms and conditions under which the company accepts certain risks (like paying for damages to a car that was involved in an accident) and what risks it does not accept (the **exclusions**, such as refusal to pay if the car was used for racing or stunt show activities).

The insurer collects a small amount (the **premium**, say, $500 every six months) on a regular basis but makes relatively large but infrequent payouts to the policyholders who have suffered losses. Insurance provides compensation for losses (like payment in case of a car accident).

Insurance comes in many stripes and shades, including the familiar ones like accident, auto, health, home, life, property, travel, and unemployment. **Lloyd's of London**, a marketplace for underwriters that began more than three centuries back in Edward Lloyd's Coffee House, has been a leader in selling unusual insurance policies. Lloyd's underwriters have insured a coffee taster's tongue, actress America Ferrera's smile, Rolling Stones guitarist Keith Richards's fingers, actress Marlene Dietrich's legs, and the beard of a man who plays Santa Claus in New York's Macy's department store ("Costa Coffee Taster: Ten of the Weirdest Insurance Policies," *The Telegraph* (UK), March 9, 2009)!

Risks Facing the Insurance Industry

Insurance is a high-risk business. Consider some of the risks in this regard:

- *Dearth of natural hedges.* Insurance is a high risk business that cannot be hedged using traded financial securities. Insurance companies employ applied mathematics and statisticians called **actuaries**, who calculate the likelihood of loss events and fair premiums for insuring these risks.

- *Diversification and the law of averages.* Diversification is the industry's key mantra. Insurers try to manage risks by diversifying their losses across a large number of policyholders. The business survives on the **law of large numbers**, which says that as more and more independent and identically distributed observations are collected, the average gets closer and closer to the mean value for the population. Although no one can foretell whether any particular insured entity will suffer a loss, actuaries can estimate with reasonable accuracy the expected losses in a large population. They compute fair premiums based on these expected losses. Insurance companies often lose money when the realized losses exceed the expected losses.

- *Reinsurance.* For catastrophic events like major earthquakes and hurricanes, the law of large numbers does not apply because these events are not independent and identically distributed across the population. Insurance companies hedge their losses on such catastrophies by buying their own insurance. This is called **reinsurance**. We discuss reinsurance after the following example.

- *Insurance and hedging.* Because of the close association between these two concepts, we can define, broadly speaking, buying insurance as hedging and selling insurance as speculation.

EXAMPLE 1: Hedging Hurricane Risk

- Catastrophic Insurance Corporation (CatIns Corp., a fictitious name) sells homeowner's insurance contracts to one hundred thousand homes along the shores of the Gulf of Mexico in the states of Florida, Alabama, Mississippi, Louisiana, and Texas. The contract provides protection against **hurricane risk**, which is the risk of losses coming from powerful storms, and it has the following features:
  - Annual premium $15,000.
  - Fixed-amount deductible $10,000.
  - Maximum coverage amount $300,000 (which is less than the value of each home).
  - Contract pays for losses from one hurricane in a given year. For simplicity, assume that if a hurricane hits, it does the same dollar damage to all homes covered by the insurance policy. These losses manifest the inability of the insurance company to diversify these losses in a large pool of the insured. Also assume that underwriting costs and investment income net out to zero.

- We draw the payoff for CatIns in a modified profit diagram in which "profit per contract" for the insurance company is plotted (as before) along the vertical axis and the underlying "loss per home" (instead of underlying asset price) is depicted along the horizontal axis. Of course, you can draw the payoff in a usual profit diagram. However, this representation is more natural in the context of insurance, where losses are key. We determine the payoff as follows (see Figure 15.8; both variables are graphed in thousands of dollars).

No Hurricane

CatIns keeps the entire premium of $15,000, which is shown as 15 in the diagram. For one hundred thousand homes, this turns out to be $1.5 billion.

If Hurricane Damage Happens

For the first $10,000 in losses, the company pays nothing. The payoff (shown by a shaded line) remains parallel to the horizontal axis at $15,000. For higher losses, the company pays a dollar for each dollar increase in loss. The payoff line declines at a 45 degree angle and cuts the x axis when the total loss reaches $25,000, shown as 25 in the diagram. Beyond this, the payoff declines until the total loss on each home reaches the maximum loss of $300,000, where CatIns pays $275,000. This is a payout of $27.5 billion, a staggering sum considering that the company earned only $1.5 billion in premiums.

Insurer Buys Reinsurance

CatIns can buy reinsurance that pays for losses to a home over $100,000 for a premium of $3,000 payable to a reinsurance company. Then, the new payoff line emanates from the y axis at (15,000 − 3,000) = $12,000, stays parallel to the x axis until "loss per home" reaches $10,000, goes down thereafter at a 45 degree angle, cuts the horizontal axis at $22,000, reaches a maximum loss of (100,000 − 22,000) = $78,000 when "loss per home" reaches $100,000, and again becomes parallel to the x axis because the reinsurance company pays for the higher losses.

Equivalence to a Call Spread

This loss diagram shows that the payoffs to CatIns with reinsurance are equivalent to a call spread on the hurricane losses. The company makes a limited profit if the hurricane's losses are mild, and the company incurs losses that are capped at $7.8 billion when large hurricanes hit homeowners.

Reinsurance Markets

Reinsurance has a long history. One of the earliest known reinsurance contract agreements was written in Latin and signed by Italian merchants on July 12, 1370. In *A System of the Law of Marine Insurances*, James Allen Park (1799, 276-77) defined *reinsurance*: "Re-assurance, as understood by the law of England, may be said to be a contract, which the first insurer enters into, in order to relieve himself from those risks which he has incautiously undertaken, by throwing them upon other underwriters, who are called re-assurers." Reinsurance helps insurance companies manage **tail risk**, which refers to the risk of occurrence of infrequent events that cause large losses when they occur. Tail risk is so named because these large loss events lie on the extreme end ("tail end") of a probability distribution of such loss events.

Today giant reinsurers such as Munich Re and Swiss Re, who earned net premiums of $27.3 and $24.3 billion, respectively, in 2008, dominate the reinsurance market. A distant third was Warren Buffet's Berkshire Hathaway ($12.1 billion net premium), which, nonetheless, was far more profitable than the top two. Lloyd's of London has long been an innovator and a major player in the field of specialized insurance and reinsurance. In 2008, Lloyd's was ranked fifth in terms of net premium earned ($6.7 billion) on reinsurance contracts.

As illustrated by the example, an insurance company's profit diagram under a typical reinsurance contract is equivalent to a call option spread. The call options are written with a one-year maturity on the aggregate losses realized by the insurance company, where the strikes correspond to the initial deductible and the payment cap. Given the call spread analogy, reinsurance contracts can be priced using the option pricing methodologies presented in chapters 17–20.

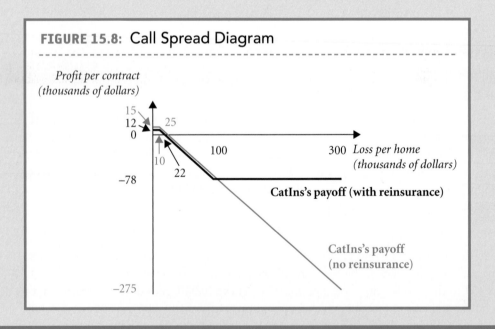

FIGURE 15.8: Call Spread Diagram

15.8 | Combination Strategies

"A double privilege pays a profit, no matter which way the market goes, and costs $212.50," declared an advertisement in 1875 in the book *Secrets of Success in Wall Street* by Tumbridge and Co., Bankers and Brokers, which had its office on 2 Wall Street, New York City at that time. An ancestor to today's booklets that aim at informing and attracting traders to options, this forty-eight-page volume describes the workings of the New York Stock Exchange and the over-the-counter options market. The traded contracts went by the name **stock privileges** and were essentially American options: calls, puts, spreads, and straddles that were customarily written on one hundred shares of stock and matured in thirty days. Tumbridge charged $100 as the premium for a call or a put and a $6.25 broker's commissions for each leg of the trade. **Double privilege** referred to spreads and strangles, which were created by trading two options, and hence charged two commissions.

Straddles and strangles are examples of **combination strategies** that combine options of different types on the same underlying stock and expiring on the same date, where the options are either both purchased or both written. For example, buying a call and a put with the same strike price creates a **straddle** (called a **put-to-call strategy** in London); if their strike prices are different, you get a **strangle**.

Straddles and strangles are volatility plays. Options traders use them to bet on risky future events affecting a company that can impact the stock price in either a positive or negative direction. Traders sometimes write them when they expect neutral markets.

EXAMPLE 15.4: Straddles and Strangles

Straddle

- You **buy a straddle** (a **long straddle** or a **bottom straddle**) by buying a call and a put as follows:
  - Buy OPSY 22.50 options, the call for $2 and the put for $1.50, and draw the profit diagram (see Figure 15.9).
  - If the stock price at expiration is zero, the long put makes $21, but the long call loses $2, giving a gain of $19. As $S(T)$ increases, the long call's payoff remains parallel to the horizontal axis, but the long put drags the straddle's payoff down at 45 degrees. The payoff cuts the x axis at the breakeven point $19, keeps declining, and reaches the nadir—a loss of $3.50.
  - For values of $S(T)$ higher than $22.50, the long put's payoff becomes parallel to the x axis, but the long call pulls the straddle's payoff up at 45 degrees, which cuts the x axis again at the BEP = (22.50 + 2 + 1.50) = $26. For higher values of $S(T)$, the payoff increases at 45 degrees, reflecting infinite profit potential.

- If you reverse the preceding trades and sell a call and put, then you **sell a straddle** (establish a **top straddle** or a **short straddle**), a bet on low future volatility whose payoff is the mirror image of the bottom straddle across the horizontal axis.

Strangle

- A **long strangle** is created by buying options with different strike prices, where the strike price of the put is lower than the strike price of the call. Though it's a volatility bet like a straddle, a strangle does have some differences:

- Buy the OPSY 22.50 call for $2, and buy the OPSY 20 put for $0.50. Plot these two strategies in a profit diagram (see Figure 15.9).
- At the origin, the payoff for the strangle is $19.5 - 2 = 17.5$. For higher values of $S(T)$, it declines at a 45 degree angle until it reaches -2.5 when $S(T)$ is $20. For the stock price lying between $20 and $22.50, the payoff is flat because both the call's and put's payoffs are parallel to the horizontal axis. Beyond $22.50, the long put's payoff stays flat, but the long call pulls up the strangle's payoff, which cuts the x axis at 25 and keeps increasing at a 45 degree angle, indicating an unlimited profit potential.

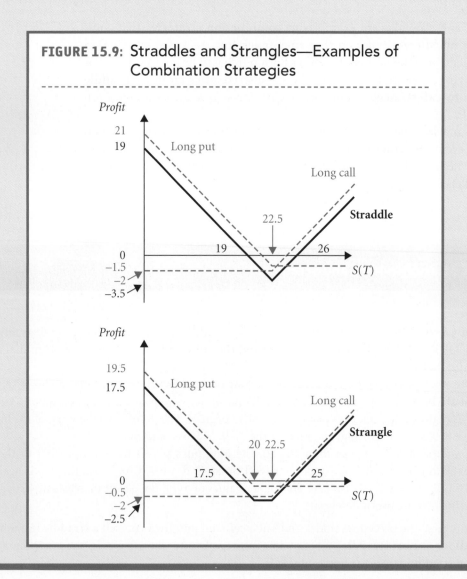

FIGURE 15.9: Straddles and Strangles—Examples of Combination Strategies

"The tax straddle rules are extremely complex," warns the booklet *Taxes and Investing* (January 2009), prepared by none other than the Options Industry Council, the industry body that promotes options trading. This statement foretells what to expect when you undertake the daunting task of understanding the tax rules for derivatives trades. Extension 15.3 briefly discusses some of the issues in connection with taxation, accounting, and reporting requirements for options and derivatives trades.

EXTENSION 15.3: Taxation of Options Trades and Summaries of FASB 133 and 161

Individual Traders

Individuals in the United States pay taxes at the ordinary income tax rate for **short-term capital gains** (i.e., capital gains from assets held for one year or less) and at a reduced rate for **long-term capital gains** (i.e., assets that have been held for more than one year and sold at a profit). Consider some of the guidelines for taxation of options trades.

Long Calls

- Calls that are bought and sold through a closing sale are taxed as just discussed.

- An expired call gets treated as a sale.

- If the call is exercised, the call's holding period becomes irrelevant, and the capital gain or loss is computed on the stock trade. Taxes are paid on (Stock's selling price − Stock's basis), where Stock's basis = (Call premium + Commissions paid at the time of call purchase and exercise + Strike price). The stock's holding period begins on the day after the call is exercised. Gains or losses are short term or long term, depending on how long the stock is held.

Short Calls

- The call premium received by the writer does not immediately get counted as income. It is held in suspension and adjusted against a closing call trade or a stock trade that results from an assignment.

- Irrespective of how long the call is outstanding, the premium for expired calls and the gain or loss from the termination of a short call position through a closing transaction are treated as short-term capital gains or losses.

- When a call is assigned, the call's holding period becomes irrelevant. The stock's holding period gets treated in a similar fashion as that for long calls.

Long Puts

- As with long calls, profits or losses on purchased puts that end with a closing trade are classified into long-term or short-term capital gains or losses.

- As with the long call, the put's expiration is considered a sale. The holding period determines whether this qualifies for a long-term or short-term capital loss.

- When a put gets exercised, the put premium and commission on the stock sale reduce the amount realized from the stock sale.

Short Puts

- As with short calls, the put premium is held in suspension until the writer's obligation ends.

- As with short calls, the premium for expired puts and the gain or loss from ending a short put position through a closing transaction are treated as short-term capital gains or losses, regardless of the period over which the put has been outstanding.

- Put assignment leads to a process similar to a call assignment with the appropriate adjustments.

Tax Straddles

■ The Internal Revenue Service considers trades to be **tax straddles** if they involve "offsetting positions" with respect to actively traded stocks, bonds, commodities, and currencies. **Offsetting positions** are those that substantially reduce the risk of loss associated with holding one or more other positions. The tax code has a large set of rules for tax loss deferral, classification of short-term versus long-term capital gains and losses, and other relevant factors that affect the taxation of profit or loss.

Covered Calls

■ Tax straddle rules, however, do not apply to "qualified cover calls." They have their own extensive set of rules. Taxes depend on what securities are involved, the time left for the call to expire (less than thirty days, more than thirty days, thirty-one to ninety days, or more than ninety days to expiration), the previous day's closing stock price level ($25 or less, $25.01 to $50, $50.01 to $150, or more than $150), and so on, with special rules for long-dated options.

Institutional Traders

Rules and regulations governing taxation and reporting requirements for an institution's options trading are even more complicated than for individual traders. Taxation of derivatives in the United States is guided by the Financial Accounting Standards Board's **Statement of Financial Accounting Standards No. 133: Accounting for Derivative Instruments and Hedging Activities** (**FASB Statement No. 133** or **FAS 133** or **SFAS 133**; issued June 1998), which established "accounting and reporting standards for derivative instruments, including certain derivative instruments embedded in other contracts, (collectively referred to as derivatives) and for hedging activities." FASB 133 was amended in March 2008 by **FASB No. 161: Disclosure about Derivative Instruments and Hedging Activities—An Amendment of FASB Statement No. 133**, which enhanced the derivatives disclosure framework. The summaries and essence of FASB 133 and 161 are available on the FASB website. We leave it to your accounting professor to explain them to you!

15.9 | Summary

1. Potential options traders must submit detailed financial information and a history of their trading experiences to a brokerage firm. The broker uses this information to assign the trader to an appropriate trading level to open an options account.

2. Options trading strategies' performances are drawn in profit diagrams for European options with a single stock as the underlying. The basic building blocks for options trading are simple naked (or uncovered) strategies that are stand-alone positions buying or selling a single call or put option.

3. Hedged strategies combine options and stocks in a way that dampens the overall risk as compared to a naked option trade. They are usually covered strategies because they tend to back the option transaction with a stock that protects (or covers or collateralizes) it. Hedged strategies include covered call writing (long stock plus short call) and covered put buying (long stock plus long put).

4. Spread strategies combine several options of the same type (either both calls or both puts) on the same underlying but on different sides of the market. These

two-sided hedges give a small profit if the underlying moves in one direction but suffer a small loss otherwise.

5. Spreads come in three basic types: (1) vertical spreads involve options that have different strike prices but expire on the same date, (2) horizontal spreads involve options that have the same strike but different maturity dates, and (3) diagonal spreads involve options that differ both in terms of strike price and maturity date.

6. Several other categories of spread strategies can be created by adding options of the same type, with the same or different strike prices, to a spread strategy:
   - A ratio spread has the number of calls (or puts) bought different from the number of calls (or puts) sold.
   - A butterfly spread has four options of the same type (all calls or all puts) with three different strike prices: buy (sell) two options with extreme strike prices and write (purchase) two options with a middle strike price.
   - A condor spread has four options with four strike prices: purchase (write) the two extreme options and sell (buy) two options with strike prices in the middle.

7. Combination strategies combine options of different types on the same underlying stock and expiring on the same date, where both options are either purchased or written. A straddle combines a call and a put with the same strike price. A strangle combines a call and a put with different strike prices.

15.10 | Cases

Cephalon Inc. (Harvard Business School Case 298116-PDF-ENG). The case introduces students to the use of equity derivatives as part of a risk-management strategy, examines the application of cash flow hedging in a corporate context, and explains the pricing of a derivative security with large jump risk.

National Insurance Corp. (Harvard Business School Case 296036-PDF-ENG). The case considers whether a major reinsurer should use exchange-traded insurance derivatives for managing catastrophic risk.

Compensation at Level 3 Communications (Harvard Business School Case 202084-PDF-ENG). The case analyzes a compensation plan that rewards managers for the firm's performance only if the firm's stock price movement exceeds a benchmark.

15.11 | Questions and Problems

The next eleven questions are based on the following data for a fictitiously named company, OOPS.

- Current stock price S is $22.
- Time to maturity T is six months.
- Continuously compounded, risk-free interest rate r is 5 percent per year.
- European options prices are given in the following table:

Strike Price	Call Price	Put Price
$K_1 = \$17.50$	$5	$0.05
$K_2 = 20$	3	0.75
$K_3 = 22.50$	1.75	1.75
$K_4 = 25$	0.75	3.50

15.1. Use options with strike $K_2 = 20.00$:

   a. Draw a long call profit diagram.

   b. Draw a short call profit diagram.

   c. Draw a long put profit diagram.

   d. Draw a short put profit diagram.

15.2. Use options with strike $K_2 = 20.00$:

   a. Draw a covered call (long stock plus short call) profit diagram.

   b. Give a reason why a trader might want to hold a covered call position.

   c. Explain the difference between a buy–write and an over-write strategy.

15.3. Use options with strike $K_2 = 20.00$:

   a. Draw a covered put (long stock plus long put) profit diagram.

   b. Give a reason why a trader might want to hold a covered put position.

   c. Explain the difference between a married put and a protective put.

15.4. Use options with strike $K_3 = 22.50$:

   a. Draw the profit diagram for a long call and a short put position for options with the same strike and maturity date.

   b. Draw the profit diagram for a long stock and two short calls.

15.5. Using options with strike price $K_3 = 22.50$, draw the profit diagram for a long call, a short stock, and a short put position for options with the same strike and maturity date. What other investment has this profit diagram?

15.6. a. What is a bullish vertical spread?

   b. Draw a bullish vertical spread by trading put options with strike prices $K_2 = 20$ and $K_4 = 25$.

15.7. a. What is a bearish vertical spread?

   b. Draw a bearish vertical spread by trading call options with strike prices $K_1 = 17.50$ and $K_3 = 22.50$.

15.8. Draw a butterfly spread by going long calls with strike prices $K_1 = 17.50$ and $K_3 = 22.50$ and selling short two calls with a strike price in the middle.

15.9. Draw a condor spread by going long calls with strike prices $K_1 = 17.50$ and $K_4 = 25$ and selling short two calls with each strike price in the middle.

15.10. a. What is the aim of a long (or bottom) straddle strategy?

   b. Create a long straddle by buying a call and a put with strike price $K_3 = 22.50$.

15.11. **a.** What is the aim of a short (or top) strangle strategy?

   b. Create a short strangle by writing a call with strike price $K_3 = 22.50$ and a put with strike price $K_1 = 20$.

The next five questions are based on the following options price data for Tel Tales Corporations (fictitious name), where the options expire on the same date in May. Draw profit diagrams in each case, clearly showing the stock price corresponding to zero profit, the maximum profit and loss, and so on.

Stock	Strike (K)	Call Price	Put Price
$29	$25	$5	$1
	30	2	3
	35	1	6

15.12. A 3:1 reverse hedge (buy three May 30 calls and short the stock).

15.13. A bullish spread (long call with strike price of 25 and short call with strike price of 30).

15.14. A butterfly spread (long put with strike prices 25 and 35 and short two puts in the middle).

15.15. A strangle (buy call with $K = 30$ and buy put with $K = 25$).

15.16. A straddle (buy a call and a put with $K = 30$).

15.17. Goldminers Inc. mines and refines ore and sells pure gold in the global market. To raise funds, it sells a derivative security whose payoff is as follows:

- Part of the security is a zero-coupon bond (which is sold at a discount and makes no interest payments) that pays a principal of $1,000 at maturity T.

- Goldminers also pays an additional amount that is indexed to gold's price (per ounce) at maturity $S(T)$:

$$
\begin{array}{ll}
0 & \text{if } S(T) \le \$1,350 \\
30[S(T) - 1,350] & \text{if } \$1,350 < S(T) \le \$1,400 \\
1,500 & \text{if } \$1,400 < S(T)
\end{array}
$$

Analyze this derivative as a combination of bond and put options.

15.18. **a.** What is a collar in the options market?

   b. How would you create a zero-cost collar?

   c. Why might a copper manufacturer find it useful to employ this strategy?

15.19. **a.** Describe how insurance works.

   b. What is reinsurance?

15.20. An insurance company has insured oil fields in the Middle East. Next, it purchases reinsurance to manage its "tail risk." How can the reinsurance company hedge some of its risks by trading derivatives?

16

Option Relations

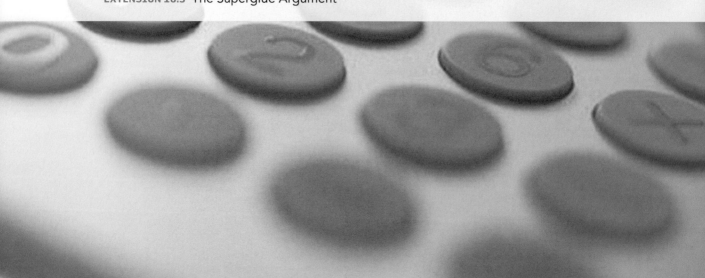

16.1 | Introduction

Eager to find how the options on Palm Inc.'s stock were performing on their inaugural trading day, he switched on his computer, entered the Internet, and logged on to his online brokerage account. Like Alice in Lewis Carroll's children's classic *Alice's Adventures in Wonderland*, he grew "curiouser and curiouser" and could hardly believe his eyes. Market-traded put options were trading $4 higher than the arbitrage-free price predicted by put–call parity. Filled with enthusiasm, he established a game plan based on the textbook prescription to exploit the mispricing, but he stumbled at the outset. He could not find Palm shares to borrow and sell short, a critical step in constructing the arbitrage. He (one of us) did not make millions that morning but acquired knowledge and, most important, a story to share with you! Later in this chapter, we will discuss the Palm arbitrage in greater detail.

The last chapter analyzed various options trading strategies using their profit diagrams on the maturity date. Determining an option's price prior to expiration is a far more difficult task. Although it's easy to find the forward price using the no-arbitrage argument because of the forward's linear payoff, the nonlinear option payoffs complicate the argument. In fact, to get an exact value, one needs to assume an evolution for the underlying stock price (which indicates how the stock price evolves through time), the most popular being a lognormal distribution. This is studied in subsequent chapters. But what can you learn about options properties without assuming such an evolution? This is the topic studied in this chapter.

Here we study three different categories of options price relations. First, we establish put–call parity for European options. This fundamental relation stitches together the stock, a bond, and call and put options. Put–call parity is not new: financier Russell Sage used it to circumvent New York State usury laws in the late 1800s. Next, we examine some restrictions that options prices must satisfy under the no-arbitrage assumption. These provide the key steps to our final topic: the early exercise of American options. As early exercise features are embedded in various other financial securities, it is important to understand this topic well.

Throughout this chapter, we maintain our standard assumptions: *no market frictions, no credit risk, competitive and well-functioning markets, no intermediate cash flows (such as cash dividends)*, and *no arbitrage*. However, we will occasionally need to relax the assumption of "no intermediate cash flows" below.

16.2 | A Graphical Approach to Put–Call Parity

In *The Put-and-Call*, published in London in 1902, Leonard R. Higgins describes the workings of London's over-the-counter options market. In this book, he makes the following intriguing observation: that "a put can be turned into a call by *buying* all the stock" and that "a call can be turned into a put by *selling* all the stock." As observed by Higgins, a clever arrangement of stocks and European options establishes put–call parity (PCP). Initially, we illustrate this result with payoff diagrams in the next example, and later by other methods.

EXAMPLE 16.1: Establishing Put–Call–Parity by Payoff Diagrams (Replicating a Call)

- We can replicate a European call option by trading the underlying stock, a European put option, and zero-coupon bonds. The options on the stock need to have a common strike price and a common expiration date. For simplicity we use the common options pricing data (COP data) from chapter 15.

- First, buy an OPSY 20 put option whose time T payoff diagram is drawn in Figure 16.1a. Next, buy one OPSY stock and place its payoff diagram below that of the put. Now create a third payoff diagram that sums the first two payoffs for each value of $S(T)$. This payoff graph for the long put plus the stock starts at a value of $K = \$20$ on the vertical axis. When $S(T)$ exceeds $20, the graph rises at a 45 degree angle to the x axis.

- For convenience, we redraw this portfolio payoff in Figure 16.1b. Draw another diagram underneath this depicting the payoff from shorting a bond with a future liability of $20. The present value of this cash flow today is $20B$, where B is today's price of a zero-coupon bond that pays a dollar after six months. The short bond's payoff is a line parallel to the x axis at $-\$20$.

- Now sum the payoffs of the previous positions (Long put + Long stock) and short bonds. The portfolio (Long put + Long stock + Short bonds) replicates the payoff to a long call option with strike price K.

- As the time T payoffs are the same, the law of one price equates the value of the two portfolios today:

$$\text{Long call} = \text{Long put} + \text{Long stock} + \text{Short bond} \tag{16.1}$$

Expression (16.1) is put-call parity (PCP) for European options. We can view the left side, the call, as a market-traded asset and the portfolio on the right side as a synthetic call (a portfolio that synthetically constructs the traded call's payoffs).

16.3 | Put–Call Parity for European Options

We follow the data–model–arbitrage approach to establish put-call parity (PCP) for European options. As in the previous section, we consider a market-traded call and construct a synthetic call with identical future payoffs. By the law of one price, the traded and the synthetic call must have the same value today. This yields the PCP relation. In this example, instead of the law of one price, we use the equivalent nothing comes from nothing principle instead.

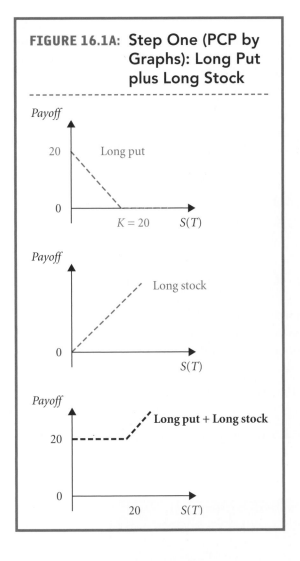

FIGURE 16.1A: Step One (PCP by Graphs): Long Put plus Long Stock

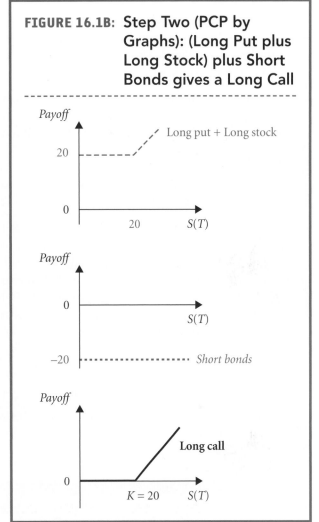

FIGURE 16.1B: Step Two (PCP by Graphs): (Long Put plus Long Stock) plus Short Bonds gives a Long Call

EXAMPLE 16.2: Put–Call Parity for European Options

The Data

- Consider the COP data of section 15.5 of chapter 15.
  - OPSY's stock price S is $22.50 at time 0.
  - The European options on OPSY have a common strike price $K = \$20$ and mature in $T = 6$ months. Today's put price p is $0.50. The call price c is to be determined.
  - The continuously compounded risk-free interest rate r is 5 percent per year. Today's price of a zero-coupon bond paying $1 at time T is $B = e^{-rT} = \$0.9753$.
  - No dividends are paid on OPSY's stock over the option's life.

- All trades are recorded in an arbitrage table. The first column of Table 16.1 gives the trade description and the second column records today's cash flows. The expiration date payoffs are presented in the last two columns. The third column reports the payoffs when $S(T)$ is less than or equal to $20, and the last column gives the payoffs when it's greater than $20.

- We first implement a stock purchase plan portfolio.
  - Buy the stock in the *spot market* for $22.50. The cash flow is recorded as −22.50 in the second column. The stock is worth $S(T)$ after six months. Jot down $S(T)$ in both the third and fourth columns.
  - Tap the *bond market* to borrow the present value of the strike price $K = \$20$ by shorting zero-coupon bonds. This cash flow reduces today's payment. Record 0.9753×20 today and the liability −20 in the last two columns.

- Next, using the *options market*, we create a synthetic short stock portfolio.
  - Sell one OPSY 20 call. Record this trade as $-c$ in the second column. The call expires worthless if $S(T)$ is less than or equal to $20. For higher values of $S(T)$, the future payoff is a liability. Surrender the stock worth $S(T)$ and receive $20 in return, for a cash flow of $[20 - S(T)]$.
  - Buy an OPSY 20 put. The premium $p = \$0.50$ is written as a positive cash flow today. If $S(T)$ is less than or equal to $20, then the put holder receives $20 but has to surrender the stock worth $S(T)$. Record the put payoff as $[20 - S(T)]$ in this case. The put expires worthless when $S(T)$ exceeds $20.

- The first two trades (Long stock + Short bond) have the payoff $[S(T) - 20]$ at expiration. The last two trades (Short call + Long put) create an equal but opposite payoff on the expiration date.

- The final row of Table 16.1 considers net cash flows. The portfolio's payoff is always zero on the expiration date.

TABLE 16.1: Arbitrage Table for Put–Call Parity

Portfolio	Today (Time 0) Cash Flow	Expiration Date (Time T) Cash Flow	
		$S(T) \leq 20$	$20 < S(T)$
Stock purchase plan			
Long stock	−22.50	$S(T)$	$S(T)$
Short bonds to borrow the present value of strike ($K = \$20, B = \$0.9753$)	0.9753×20	−20	−20
Synthetic short stock			
Short call	c	0	$20 - S(T)$
Long put	−0.50	$20 - S(T)$	0
Cash flows	$-22.50 + 0.9753 \times 20 + c - 0.50$	0	0

- The portfolio of stocks, bonds, and options created has a zero value for sure in the future. To prevent arbitrage, using the nothing comes from nothing principle, it must have zero value today. Consequently,

$$-22.50 + 0.9753 \times 20 + c - 0.50 = 0$$
$$\text{or } c = \$3.49$$

This is the European call option's arbitrage-free price.

The Model

- Use symbols to generalize. Replace $22.50 with S, 0.9753×20 with $B \times K$, and $0.50 with p to get the PCP for European options:

$$-S + BK + c - p = 0 \tag{16.2}$$

Arbitrage Profits

- A violation of PCP leads to arbitrage. Suppose you find an errant trader who quotes a call price of $4. As this is higher than the arbitrage-free price from PCP, create the portfolio in Table 16.1: buy the stock, short the bonds, buy the put, and sell the relatively overpriced call. This gives the cash flows

$$-S + BK + c - p$$
$$= -22.50 + 0.9753 \times 20 + 4 - 0.50$$
$$= \$0.51$$

as your immediate arbitrage profit.

- If the trader quotes $3 instead, reverse the trades and make $0.49 as an arbitrage profit.

We use expression (16.2) to formally state our result.

RESULT 16.1

Put–Call Parity for European Options

$$c = p + S - BK \tag{16.3}$$

where c and p are today's prices of European calls and puts, respectively, that have strike price K and expiration date T, B is today's price of a zero-coupon bond that pays a dollar at time T, and S is today's price of the underlying stock.

PCP is a useful tool for understanding how to use options in forming trading strategies. We start with the put because it is the easiest option to understand. Indeed, a put option is like an insurance policy because it insures the value of the underlying stock at its strike price. With this insight, we can rewrite PCP as

$$\text{Call} = \text{Insurance} + \text{Stock} + \text{Borrowing} \qquad (16.4)$$

We see that a call option is equivalent to buying the stock on margin (by borrowing) and protecting the stock purchase with an insurance policy.

This intuition can help us to understand how to trade on information using options. For example, suppose that you are the only person in the market who knows that the stock is going to rise above the strike price. (Note: this is a thought experiment—we are not considering issues like whether trading on inside information will attract jail time!) What is the best way to trade on this information: buying a call? No. This is the wrong answer because by buying the call, you are also paying for the put, which is insurance on the stock that you do not need. Recall that you are certain that the stock price will rise. In this case, the optimal strategy is to buy the call and sell the put. Using PCP again, we also see that this is equivalent to buying the stock and financing the purchase with borrowed cash, which creates leverage (called *gearing* in Europe).

Now suppose that you expect that the stock is likely to increase but you are unsure. In this case, is buying the call the best strategy? Maybe. The answer really depends on your risk tolerance. Pay for the put if you like the downside insurance protection but not otherwise.

16.4 | Market Imperfections

Market imperfections introduce difficulties, but they may also create opportunities. Merton Miller's observation that financial securities can help overcome rules and regulations becomes pertinent. Options and PCP can provide tools to work around these imperfections. In the article "The Ancient Roots of Modern Financial Innovation: The Early History of Regulatory Arbitrage," Michael Knoll (2008) cited ancient examples of merchants using PCP to get around restrictions on interest payments. For example, two millennia back, Israeli financiers used PCP in this way. English financiers did the same five hundred years ago, and interestingly, the transaction they devised led to the development of the modern mortgage. These examples illustrate **tax** or **regulatory arbitrage**, which involves unpackaging and rebundling cash flows with the aim of profiting from otherwise prohibited transactions. Extension 16.1 discusses two additional examples of PCP in action.

One can tinker with PCP to generate two extensions: (1) to accommodate dividends and (2) for American options. These extensions are shown in Extension 16.2.

EXTENSION 16.1: Put–Call Parity in Imperfect Markets

How Russell Sage Overcame Usury Laws

In his biography of Russell Sage, Paul Sarnoff (1965) credits the multimillionaire with discovering PCP. Sage used it to overcome New York State's usury law restrictions. In 1869, after a stockbroker failed to repay a one-month loan of $230,000 at 7 percent per year, Sage agreed to extend the loan for another month but slapped on (much like today's credit card companies who are adept in levying all sorts of fees and charges on customers!) another 1 percent "late charge." However, this pushed the interest above the New York usury law–mandated cap of 7 percent, which was the maximum amount a private individual could charge on loans. Russell Sage was picked up in a "raid" on the "Usury Ring," and the judge sentenced him with a fine of $250 and to a confinement in the city prison for five days.

Some intense maneuvering helped Sage avoid jail time. Afterward, he closed his "usury business" of loaning money to clients at high interest rates and devised an alternative strategy using PCP. The ingenious financier bought a put and shares of a stock from the client and sold him a call. Sage's portfolio would be (Long stock + Long put + Short call), which is equivalent to a long bond portfolio by PCP (see expression [16.2]). The client's position was the opposite. The client was short a synthetic bond, which is equivalent to taking a loan.

As no law in New York State limits the amount one can charge for a call, the crafty "Dean of Wall Street" was free to charge any call price desired. If he charged a high price for the call, then the portfolio (Long stock + Long put + Short call) would have a low value. A low value meant that Sage paid less today for the same principal amount at maturity, which translates into a higher interest rate earned.

PCP Violations for Palm Shares

Sometimes PCP fails because of market imperfections. This happened with Palm Inc. options in an incident discussed at the chapter's start.

On March 2, 2000, 3Com did an **equity carve-out** of its subsidiary Palm, which had made the world's first successful handheld computer, the PalmPilot, in 1992. Accordingly, 3Com sold 5 percent of Palm shares to the general public in an initial public offering and declared that later in the year, it would distribute the remaining shares in a **spin-off** to its existing shareholders (who would get 1.525 shares of Palm for every share of 3Com they held). The mispricing that resulted in the equity and options markets got extensive press coverage and academic study (see Lamont and Thaler 2003).

A hot company during the days when tech stocks led the dotcom stock market craze, Palm had an unbelievable initial public offering (IPO). Its stock closed at the end of the first day's trading at $95.06 per share. This implied that 3Com's stock price, which would equal 1.5 Palm shares plus the value of 3Com's other assets and businesses was −$63 per share, or −$22 billion. The mishmash confused options traders. They adopted strategies like writing call options and short selling 3Com stock to buy Palm stock, whose market capitalization then exceeded the parent company's valuation! "There is absolutely no rationale behind it," interjected a trader. Predictably, Palm started declining after the IPO.[1]

When options began trading on March 16, 2000, Palm stock traded around $55. The at-the-money (strike price $K = \$55$) call price $c = \$5$ and the put price $p = \$9$. These numbers are illustrative. The bid/ask spread was

---

[1] "Palm IPO Soars, Then Retreats a Bit, Pushing Traders to Unwind Options in Parent 3Com," *Wall Street Journal*, March 3, 2010.

large, and the market was in a state of confusion, making it hard to find accurate prices. A zero-coupon bond price paying $1 after one month was worth $0.995. A quick check of put–call parity suggests

Synthetic put price = Call price + Present value of strike − Stock price
= 5 + 0.995 × 55 − 55
= $4.725

And yet the price of the market-traded put was $9. Isn't this an arbitrageur's dream come true? Wouldn't this mean that if you sell the market-traded put and buy the synthetic put (see expression [16.2]), you can immediately capture an arbitrage profit of 9 − 4.725 = $4.275 in one trade? Repeat a million times, and you become a millionaire four times over!

Unfortunately, a market imperfection disrupted this trade. To create the arbitrage portfolio, an "arbitrageur" needs to sell the relatively overpriced market-traded put and "buy" the relatively underpriced synthetic put via buying the call, shorting the stock, and lending the present value of the strike. In this circumstance, however, the broker could not supply the Palm shares for short selling (by borrowing them from another investor). The scarcity of shares for short selling prevented the realization of the arbitrage profits and led to the divergence between theory and practice. The situation did not last long. The price anomaly disappeared within days; however, a lesson was learned. *Paper profits can differ from actual realizable profits, and market imperfections do matter.*

EXTENSION 16.2: Dividends and American Options

Put–Call Parity Adjusted for Dividends

The parallels are eerie. One can easily modify the basic PCP by using the tools developed in chapter 12 for adjusting the cost-of-carry model for dividends. The intuition remains the same as before. A dividend lowers the cost of a stock purchase, and replacing the stock price with the "stock price net of all dividends over the life of the derivative" modifies the formula.

Assuming that a fixed-dollar dividend div is paid on a known future date t_1 and B_1 is today's price of a zero-coupon bond maturing on the ex-dividend date (recall Result 12.1a), **put–call parity for European options** (with a known dollar dividend) can be written as

$$c = p + (S - B_1 \text{div}) - BK \tag{1}$$

As before, this can be easily generalized to accommodate multiple dividends.

For options on indexes, we can use the insights from Result 12.1b. If the underlying pays dividends at a continuous rate δ, then **put–call parity for European options** (with a known dividend yield) can be written as

$$c = p + e^{-\delta T}S - e^{-rT}K \tag{2}$$

A Put–Call Parity Inequality for American Options

The basic PCP does not work for American options because the option may get exercised before the expiration date. However, a PCP inequality for American options does hold. For these inequalities, we add the assumption that interest rates are nonnegative, or equivalently, that a zero-coupon's price is always less than or equal to 1.

EXAMPLE 1: A Relation between American Calls and Puts

The Data

- The stock price is S today. Assume that the stock pays no dividends over the life of the options.

- American calls and puts worth c_A and p_A, respectively, trade on the stock. They have the same strike price K and expire at time T but may get exercised early at time t.

- Interest is compounded continuously at the risk-free rate r percent per year. You can invest in zero-coupon bonds or a money market account (mma). B is today's price and $B(t)$ is the price at time t of zeros that mature at time T. An investment of \$1 in a mma today grows to $[1 + R(t)]$ on the intermediate (exercise) date t and to $(1 + R)$ on the expiration date.

When the Portfolio Involves a Long Put (and Short Call)

- Create a portfolio similar to the basic PCP: buy one put, write one call, buy one stock, and short bonds to borrow the present value of the strike. Today's portfolio value is

$$p_A - c_A + S - BK \tag{3}$$

You decide when to exercise the put. Your counterparty decides when to exercise the American call. Thus two things can happen in the future: the holder of the American call exercises early, or she does not. Your response depends on Long's decision on the call.

- *If the American call is not exercised early*, then the American call becomes equivalent to the European call worth c. You can write $c_A = c$. Now, if you don't exercise your American put early, then it behaves like a European put, which means $p_A = p$. With $c_A = c$ and $p_A = p$, expression (3) becomes equal to 0 by PCP for European options. But you can exercise your American put before it expires. This flexibility makes the American put worth at least as much as the European put. Thus (3) becomes

$$p_A - c_A + S - BK \geq p - c + S - BK = 0 \tag{4a}$$

- *If your counterparty exercises the American call early*, then portfolio (3) has a payoff on the exercise date t (when you buy back the bonds by paying $B[t]$ for each zero):

$$p_A(t) - [S(t) - K] + S(t) - B(t)K = p_A(t) + [1 - B(t)]K \geq 0 \tag{4b}$$

This is nonnegative because a put cannot have a negative value and $B(t)$ is worth less than or equal to a dollar.

- Thus the portfolio $(p_A - c_A + S - BK)$ has a value greater than or equal to zero. Combining (4a) and (4b) and moving c_A to the right side, we get our first inequality:

$$p_A + S - BK \geq c_A \tag{5}$$

When the Portfolio Involves a Short Put (and Long Call)

- Create the portfolio: sell the put, buy the call, short the stock, and invest K dollars in a mma. Notice that this differs from the basic PCP portfolio because more dollars are kept in case the put is exercised early. This portfolio's value today is

$$-p_A + c_A - S + K \tag{6}$$

Here the buyer determines whether to exercise the American put. As before, we will act in response to Long's decision.

- *If there is no early exercise*, then the American put is the same as the European put, $p_A = p$. If you don't exercise the American call early, then it behaves like the European call, which means $c_A = c$. With $c_A = c$ and $p_A = p$, (6) becomes equal to KR on the maturity date (you can verify this in a payoff table). Because the last quantity is greater than zero, (6) cannot be less than zero today:

$$-p_A + c_A - S + K \geq 0 \qquad (7a)$$

Because you can exercise your American call early, this makes it even more valuable, which reinforces the relationship in (7a).

- *If the buyer exercises early the American put*, then portfolio (6) has a payoff on the exercise date t (when K has grown to $K[1 + R(t)]$):

$$\begin{aligned} &= -[K - S(t)] + c_A - S(t) + K[1 + R(t)] \\ &= KR(t) + c_A(t) \geq 0 \end{aligned} \qquad (7b)$$

because both the call and $R(t)$ are nonnegative.

- Thus the portfolio $(-p_A + c_A - S + K)$ cannot have a negative value today. Combining (7a) and (7b) and rearranging terms, we get our second inequality:

$$c_A \geq p_A + S - K \qquad (8)$$

- *For the PCP inequality for American options*, combining (5) and (8), we get the **relation between the stock, the bond, and the American options**:

$$p_A + S - K \leq c_A \leq p_A + S - BK \qquad (9)$$

16.5 | Options Price Restrictions

This section explores various options price restrictions for several reasons:

- They hone intuition and enhance understanding.

- They generate arbitrage opportunities when the bounds are violated.

- Just as you stretch before you sprint, a discussion of options price relations forms the stepping-stone to understanding early exercise of options, which is the final topic of this chapter.

To facilitate understanding, we establish the options price restrictions in several different ways: (1) a *diagrammatic approach* with profit diagrams; (2) an *arbitrage table approach*, where cash flows are recorded in a table and no arbitrage yields the result; and (3) a *superglue argument*, which is our name for comparing the original security with a "restricted" but otherwise identical security and then proving the result by arguing that "less cannot be worth more." Why "superglue?" Read extension 16.3.

We begin with the simple and then move to the complex. We use our standard notation and assumptions, except one: *we allow the underlying stock to pay dividends.* This is an important extension because most stocks pay dividends.

RESULT 16.2

American Options Are Worth More Than European Options

2a.
$$c_A \geq c \geq 0 \qquad (16.5a)$$

2b.
$$p_A \geq p \geq 0 \qquad (16.5b)$$

This result holds because European and American options are identical, except for their exercise features. European options can only be exercised at expiration, whereas American options can be exercised anytime. As "more cannot be worth less," an American option can never be priced less than an otherwise identical European option. This simple yet robust principle underlies the superglue argument, which is used later to prove some results (see Extension 16.3). Of course, an option's price must be nonnegative because the holder can always discard the option without exercising it.

The next two results restate the option price bounds established earlier in chapter 5.

RESULT 16.3

Call Price Boundaries

3a. An American call's price is less than or equal to the stock price, that is,

$$c_A \leq S \qquad (16.6)$$

3b. When the stock price is zero, the call price is also zero.

Result 16.3a also holds for European calls because they are less valuable than American calls. Notice that an American call's price cannot fall below the boundary condition stated earlier in chapter 5. These are depicted in the first diagram in

Figure 16.2, which reproduces Figure 5.3. Result 16.3b follows by setting $S = 0$ in Result 16.3a and recognizing that the call's value must always be nonnegative.

RESULT 16.4

- -

Put Price Boundaries

An American put's price is less than or equal to the strike price K, and a European put's price is less than or equal to the present value of the strike price:

4a. $$p_A \leq K \tag{16.7a}$$

4b. $$p \leq BK \tag{16.7b}$$

where B is today's price of a zero-coupon bond that pays \$1 at the option's maturity.

A put option entitles the holder to receive the strike price, but he has to surrender the stock in return. Thus the put price cannot exceed the strike price, which forms an upper bound. Because a European put's maximum payoff is the strike and only on the expiration date, today's put price must be less than or equal to the present value of the strike price.

RESULT 16.5

- -

Call Price Bound before Expiration

Before expiration, a European call's price is greater than or equal to the larger of the stock price minus the present value of the strike or zero:

$$c \geq \max(S - BK, 0) \tag{16.8}$$

We will prove this result with payoff diagrams, by an arbitrage table, and using the superglue argument (see Extension 16.3). The result also holds for American options, which are more valuable than otherwise identical European options.

Figure 16.3 shows two payoff diagrams on the expiration date. The first diagram is for a stock purchase plan that consists of buying the stock and shorting K zero-coupon bonds. The second diagram, which is placed beneath the first, is for a long call. Visual inspection shows that the stock purchase plan pays off less than the long call. A consideration of today's value of these two payoffs establishes that

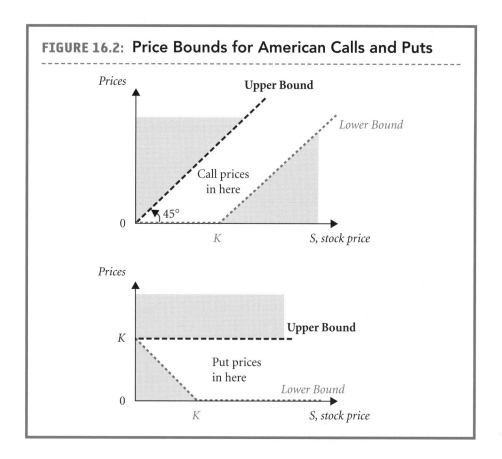

FIGURE 16.2: Price Bounds for American Calls and Puts

$c \geq S - BK$. Because the call's value must also be nonnegative, we get expression (16.8).

Our next example uses a variant of our data–model–arbitrage approach to establish the relation.

EXAMPLE 16.3: Establishing Result 16.5 with an Arbitrage Table

The Data, Arbitrage, and Diagram

- Consider the data from Example 16.2 with a slight modification. OPSY's stock price S is $22.50, the six-month $20 strike European call price c is $2 and the put price p is $0.50, and the zero-coupon bond price B is $0.97531.

- Does Result 16.5 hold? We have $S - BK = 22.50 - 0.97531 \times 20 = \$2.9938$. This is greater than the call price of $2, and the inequality in (16.8) is violated. Transferring the right side terms to the left side, we get the expression $c - S + BK = 2 - 2.9938 = -\$0.9938$.

- Buy low, sell high. Create an arbitrage portfolio by buying the underpriced call and selling the overpriced portfolio $(S - BK)$ by shorting the stock and buying the bonds. Record these cash flows in Table 16.2. You immediately get $0.9938. At expiration, the portfolio has a 0 payoff when the call is in-the-money and a nonnegative payoff of $[20 - S(T)]$ otherwise.

■ You can also see this arbitrage possibility by drawing the profit diagram for the portfolio in Table 16.2. Take $0.9938 and invest it in bonds. As the inverse of B is the dollar return $(1 + R)$, the future value of $0.9938 is $0.9938 \times (1/0.97531) = \$1.0190$ after six months. The portfolio payoff after six months is $[20 - S(T)]$ when the call is out-of-the-money, and 0 otherwise. Adding $1.02 (after rounding) to this shifts the whole curve up (see the diagram in Figure 16.4). This confirms the arbitrage opportunity.

To establish the result, one simply replaces the numbers with algebraic symbols. Writing $S = \$22.50$, $K = \$20$, $B = \$0.97531$, and $c = \$2$, the last row in the second column of Table 16.2 shows that $-c + S - BK = 0.9938$. You can generalize the last row, as $c < S - BK$ leads to a cash inflow today and a nonnegative payoff $[K - S(T)]$ when $S(T) \le K$, and 0 otherwise. This is an unstable situation. To prevent arbitrage, we must have

$$c \ge S - BK \tag{16.9}$$

This is Result 16.5 when combined with the fact that $c \ge 0$.

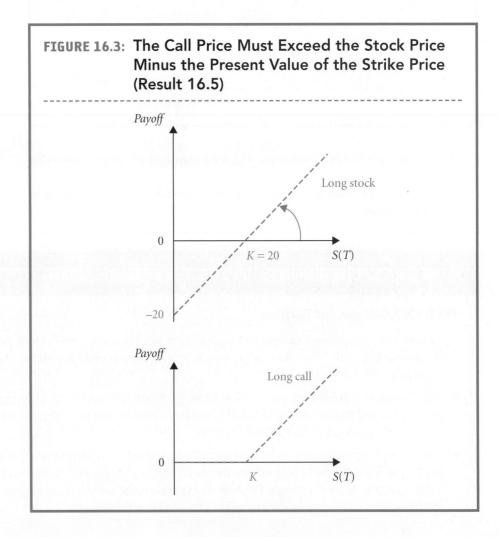

FIGURE 16.3: **The Call Price Must Exceed the Stock Price Minus the Present Value of the Strike Price (Result 16.5)**

TABLE 16.2: Arbitrage Table Showing How a Violation of $c \geq S - BK$ (Result 16.5) Creates an Arbitrage Opportunity

Portfolio	Today (Time 0) Cash Flow	Expiration Date (Time T) Cash Flow	
		$S(T) \leq 20$	$20 < S(T)$
Buy call	−2	0	$S(T) - 20$
Short sell stock	22.5	$-S(T)$	$-S(T)$
Buy bonds to lend the present value of strike ($K = \$20$, $B = \$0.97531$)	-0.97531×20	20	20
Cash flows	0.9938	$20 - S(T)$	0

Figure 16.4 also demonstrates an easy way to identify an arbitrage portfolio by drawing a profit diagram and checking to see whether you can make arbitrage profits.

- If the profit graph for a portfolio lies entirely above (or with some portions of it lying along) the horizontal axis, then you have created an arbitrage portfolio.
- If the profit graph lies entirely below (or with some portions of it lying along) the horizontal axis, just reverse the trades to capture arbitrage profits.
- A profit graph that crosses the axis leads to both trading profits and losses, which can never represent an arbitrage opportunity.

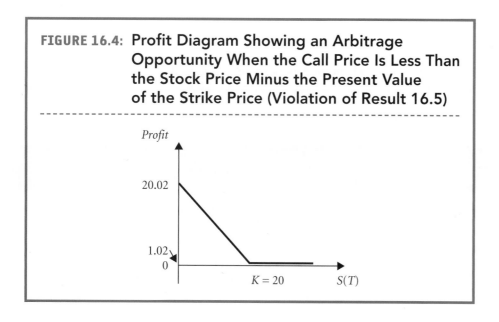

FIGURE 16.4: Profit Diagram Showing an Arbitrage Opportunity When the Call Price Is Less Than the Stock Price Minus the Present Value of the Strike Price (Violation of Result 16.5)

Result 16.5 has its counterpart for put options.

RESULT 16.6

Put Price Bound before Expiration

6a. Before expiration, a European put's value must be greater than or equal to the larger of the present value of the strike price minus the stock price or zero:

$$p \geq \max(BK - S, 0) \tag{16.10a}$$

6b. Before expiration, an American put's value must be greater than or equal to its intrinsic value:

$$p_A \geq \max(K - S, 0) \tag{16.10b}$$

Result 16.6a follows easily using the superglue argument (see Extension 16.3). Result 16.6b follows from the boundary condition because you can always exercise an American put early and collect the strike price by surrendering the stock.

RESULT 16.7

Relation between Options with Different Strike Prices

7a. The lower the strike price, the more valuable the European call:

$$c(K_2) \leq c(K_1) \text{ for } K_1 < K_2 \tag{16.11}$$

7b. The higher the strike price, the more valuable the European put:

$$p(K_1) \leq p(K_2) \text{ for } K_1 < K_2 \tag{16.12}$$

Both these results hold for American options as well.

Extension 16.3 proves Result 16.7 using the superglue argument.

EXTENSION 16.3: The Superglue Argument

Remember superglue, the unusually strong adhesive that advertisements claim can hang a car and lift two thousand pounds per square inch? Our use of superglue is different—we take the idea, but not the product! Consider two identical securities, which we name Sec. We attach a "restriction" to one of these securities, something unfavorable or adverse that removes one of its provisions, and assume that it gets fastened with superglue (see Figure 16.5). As such, the restriction is permanent, and the security's provisions are changed forever.

The essence of the **superglue argument** is this: consider a security Sec and an otherwise identical security with the restriction attached, which we call Sec_R (short for Security$_{RESTRICTED}$). A long position in Sec_R cannot have a greater value than Sec because *less cannot be worth more*, that is, Price of Sec_R ≤ Price of Sec.

This is a no-arbitrage condition. If it happens otherwise, then buy the security, add the restriction (with superglue at no cost), and sell it for more to make arbitrage profits. We can use this principle to derive all of our options price bounds and relations. We illustrate just a few of these below.

Consider the proof of result 16.2 (directly below). Let Sec be an American option. Next, we attach a restriction to this option with superglue: "it cannot be exercised early." Then, by no arbitrage, we know that the price of the restricted security—equivalent to a European call—must be less than the price of the unrestricted security—the American call. (Figure 16.5 illustrates this approach).

Result 16.2 American Options Are Worth More Than European Options

Proof:

Sec: American option.

Sec_R: American option + Restriction "No early exercise allowed"

Because Sec_R has become an otherwise identical European option, the superglue argument gives:
European option price ≤ American option price.

FIGURE 16.5: The *Superglue* Argument for Options

- -

| Sec | Sec_R |

Security

Security + Restriction

Sec_R is identical to Sec except for a restriction that is attached by superglue. Then, price of Sec_R ≤ price of Sec.

Result 16.3b $c_A \leq S$

Proof:

Sec: Stock

Sec_R: Stock + Restriction "Pay an additional K dollars to maintain possession, otherwise throw away, and the decision must be made before time T." Of course, with this restriction attached, the restricted stock is an American call.

Hence American call price $\leq$ Stock price.

Result 16.5 $c \geq S - BK$

Proof:

Sec: European call.

Sec_R: European call + Restriction "Always exercise the call even if it is out-of-the money." Today's price of Sec_R is $S - BK$.

The superglue argument gives the result. Result 16.2 tells us that this argument also holds for American calls.

Result 16.7a $c(K_1) \geq c(K_2)$ for $K_1 < K_2$

Sec: European call with strike price K_1.

Sec_R: European call with strike price K_1 + Restriction "Must pay the extra amount $(K_2 - K_1)$ in case of exercise." The restricted security is equivalent to a European call with strike price K_2.

The superglue argument gives the result.

A similar argument holds for American calls.

EXAMPLE 16.4: Result 16.7b by the Modified Data–Model–Arbitrage Approach

- Consider the COP data from chapter 15 with minor modifications. Puts trade on OPSY that mature in six months. The premiums are $p(20) = \$2$ for strike price $K_1 = \$20$ and $p(22.50) = \$1.50$ for $K_2 = \$22.50$. These numbers violate inequality (16.12). We use the arbitrage opportunity in the data to justify our model, which is relation (16.12).

When Both Puts Are European

- As shown in Table 16.3, we create the arbitrage portfolio by selling the overpriced OPSY 20 put and buying the underpriced OPSY 22.50 put. This gives a cash flow of $+2 - 1.50 = \$0.50$ today. The puts' payoffs on the expiration date depend on the stock price.
  - If $S(T)$ is less than or equal to $\$20$, the short put has a payoff of $-[20 - S(T)]$ and the long put has a payoff of $[22.50 - S(T)]$. This gives a payoff of $\$2.50$.
  - For $20 < S(T) \leq 22.50$, the OPSY 20 put has a 0 payoff while the long OPSY 22.50 put has a payoff of $[22.50 - S(T)]$. For this range for $S(T)$, the payoff is nonnegative.
  - When $S(T)$ is greater than $\$22.50$, both options are out-of-the-money and have 0 payoffs.

- We showed that

$$p(20) = \$2 > p(22.50) = \$1.50$$

leads to an arbitrage opportunity. The no-arbitrage requirement dictates that $p(20) \leq p(22.50)$.

- Replace numbers with symbols and you get the result

$$p(K_1) \leq p(K_2) \text{ for } K_1 < K_2$$

When Both Puts Are American

- Suppose the mispricing holds and the prices reflect those for American puts instead. As with European puts, create an arbitrage portfolio by selling the OPSY 20 American put and buying the OPSY 22.50 American put. This gives $0.50 today. In the future, if the short put is not exercised against you, hold on to the long put. The payoff on the expiration date is given in Table 16.3. By contrast, if the OPSY 20 put is exercised against you, exercise the OPSY 22.50 put to eliminate the stock position, and you are left with $2.50 on the exercise date. This trade is an arbitrage opportunity. Hence, the only American put prices consistent with no arbitrage must satisfy result 16.7b.

TABLE 16.3: Arbitrage Table for Result 16.7b: The Higher the Strike Price, the More Valuable Is the Put

Portfolio	Today (Time 0) Cash Flow	Expiration Date (Time T) Cash Flow		
		$S(T) \leq 20$	$20 < S(T) \leq 22.50$	$22.50 < S(T)$
Sell 20 put	2	$-[20 - S(T)]$	0	0
Buy 22.50 put	-1.50	$22.50 - S(T)$	$22.50 - S(T)$	0
Cash flows	0.50	2.50	$22.50 - S(T)$	0

RESULT 16.8

Option Prices and Time to Maturity

A shorter maturity American option cannot have a larger value

8a.	$c_A(T_1) \leq c_A(T_2) \text{ for } T_1 < T_2$	(16.13)
8b.	$p_A(T_1) \leq p_A(T_2) \text{ for } T_1 < T_2$	(16.14)

The results need not hold for European calls (because of dividends) or European puts.

The next example establishes this result.

EXAMPLE 16.5: Establishing Result 16.8a

- Suppose that the OPSY call with strike price $20 maturing in $T_1 = 6$ months has a price of $c_A(T_1) = c_A$ (6 months) = \$3.50 but the call maturing in $T_2 = 1$ year is worth $c_A(T_2) = c_A$ (12 months) = \$3. Exploit this situation by selling the relatively overpriced six-month call for \$3.50 and use the proceeds to buy the relatively underpriced one-year call for \$3. This leaves \$0.50.

- If c_A (6 months) is exercised against you before expiration, exercise c_A (12 months) to satisfy the short call provisions. And you still have your 50 cents.

- If c_A (6 months) is never exercised, you can make more money by selling c_A (12 months), which has six months left, or you can hold on to the call. Remember that all we need to show is that we can make arbitrage profits—there is no need to demonstrate how to maximize profits.

- Replace numbers with symbols to establish the result.

Longer-maturity European calls need not be more valuable than their shorter-maturity counterparts. You can easily see this with a counterexample. Consider six-month and twelve-month European calls on the OPSY stock with a common strike price of $20. Suppose we know today that the stock will pay a liquidating dividend and have zero value after one year but no dividends will be paid earlier. Then, c(12 months) = 0. But c(6 months) > 0 because it's possible for OPSY to close higher than $20 after six months. This is true because the stock price today is $22.50. If we knew that its price would never exceed $20 in six months' time, then its price must be less than $20 today to avoid immediate arbitrage. Notice that the shareholders will not scream foul because they are not suffering any loss of value owing to the liquidating dividend. It's only the call holders who are losing out because options are not protected for cash dividends in the United States.

Result 16.8b need not hold for European puts. We illustrate this with an example. A money manager who had previously taught finance classes at the University of Nebraska used the following one-hundred-year put option example in a 2008 chairman's letter to the shareholders of his company. His name? Warren Buffett.

Consider three out-of-the-money European put prices when OPSY's stock price is $22.50 and the strike price is $20. One of these options will mature in a second. The put price is obviously 0. Alternatively, if the time to maturity is six months, this option has a premium of $0.50, as given in our COP data (or some other number that's greater than zero because a lot can happen to the stock in six months' time). Now consider a really long maturity European put. Using Result 16.4b, if the interest rate r is 5 percent, discounting gives the present value of $20 as $0.1348 when the time to maturity is one hundred years. The longer-maturity European put has a smaller value than the six month option. By considering out-of-the-money very short maturity puts and very long maturity puts (both of which are close to zero), you can see that the European put's premium does not necessarily increase with time to maturity.

16.6 | Early Exercise of American Options

Although some traders do not bother about early exercise, professional traders routinely exercise options early when it's optimal to do so. Early exercise is important because if you do not exercise when it's optimal, you are giving away profits to the writer. Empirical studies have found instances of both rational and irrational early exercise decisions. Extension 16.4 discusses several of these studies.

Following two simple rules yields the optimal early exercise strategy.[2]

RESULT 16.9

Rules of Thumb for Early Exercise

9a. Exercise an American call the first time its price is equal to the stock price minus the strike price:

$$c_A = S - K \qquad (16.15)$$

9b. Exercise an American put the first time its price is equal to the strike price minus the stock price:

$$p_A = K - S \qquad (16.16)$$

The first time early exercise is optimal, the traded option's price will equal its exercise value. These results are independent of the stock price evolution or dividend payout policy. They depend, however, on the assumption that the markets are arbitrage-free and well functioning, where c_A and p_A reflect the "true" option prices. Note that neither option's price can be strictly less than (16.15) or (16.16) without generating an arbitrage opportunity (hence the equality).

---

[2] The formal proof of the optimality of these rules involves solving the optimal stopping problem; see Jarrow and Protter (2008).

It is very easy to use these rules of thumb to decide when to exercise early. Just simultaneously monitor the stock price and the option's price across time. If this expression becomes satisfied, then exercise; otherwise, do not exercise. Following these simple rules of thumb will generate maximum value for your option positions and frustrate professional traders hoping that the options are irrationally exercised (see Extension 16.4).

No Dividends

Let us start with an American option on OPSY, where the stock doesn't pay any dividends. Our first result is as follows.

RESULT 16.10

Early-Exercise Decisions for American Options on No-Dividend Stocks

Assume the stock pays no dividends over the option's life.

10a. An American call becomes identical to a European call. It should never be exercised early.

10b. An American put should be exercised if the stock price is small enough relative to the strike price and the time remaining to maturity.

To prove Result 16.10a, let's consider what happens to the value of a call if it is exercised early. If you exercise the American call before it expires, you get on the exercise date t:$[S(t) - K] = [S(t) - 20]$ dollars, where $S(t)$ is OPSY's stock price and $K = \$20$ is the strike. By contrast, if you sell the call, Result 16.5 ensures that you get at least $[S(t) - BK] = [S(t) - 20B]$. This is a larger amount because the zero-coupon bond price B is less than 1. So do not exercise the American call—the value of your position in the market is larger. If you do not want to hold the option, *sell it, but do not exercise it*.

Result 16.10a may be difficult to believe at first sight. To understand why it is true, let us perform a thought experiment. Consider holding an American call option on OPSY with a strike price of $20 when the stock is trading at $22.50. Let the option mature in one year's time. Now, assume that everyone in the market believes (including yourself) that the stock is going to crash and be worth only $1 in a year's time (see Figure 16.6; the stock price crash is shown by the dashed line starting from today, time t). Shouldn't you exercise the call today? After all, if you hold it to expiration, it will be worth zero dollars, and if you exercise the call today, you get $2.50.

The answer is, yes, you should exercise it today under this scenario. But doesn't this contradict Result 16.10a? The answer is no. The reason is that Result 16.10a holds only under the assumption of no arbitrage. Our initial supposition creates an immediate arbitrage opportunity, violating the assumption of no arbitrage underlying the result. Indeed, if everyone believes the stock is worth $1 a year from now, its price today must be less than $1 and not $22.50; otherwise, the arbitrage is to short the stock and buy it back after the price declines.

Next, let us consider a related thought experiment that does not violate the no-arbitrage assumption. Suppose instead that you have inside information (recall our earlier warning: this is just a thought experiment!), and only you know the stock is going to crash and be worth $1 in a year's time. Here, because only you have this information, the stock price of $22.50 is consistent with no arbitrage. Shouldn't you exercise this call today? The answer is no! Although you could exercise it now to get an immediate $2.50, you can make more money by selling it in the market. The market price of the American call exceeds $2.50 by Results 16.2 and 16.5:

$$c_A \geq c \geq S - BK = 22.50 - 20B > 2.50$$

because $B < 1$.

Given these thought experiments, we now better understand Result 16.10a. It says that you can make more profits by selling the OPSY call rather than by exercising it. Thus, if no dividends are paid to the stockholder over the option's life, then the call option is always worth more alive than dead. Do not exercise such a call: sell it. *Sell it!* SELL IT!!

Puts, though, have a different story. Unlike calls that have an unbounded profit potential, put payoffs are capped by the strike price, the maximum payoff possible. This leads to Result 16.10b. To understand why Result 16.10b is true, consider the following hypothetical example. Consider a six-month original maturity put on OPSY that began two months back. If OPSY's stock price is $S(t) = \$0.0001$ today, an immediate exercise gives $K - S(t) = (20 - 0.0001) = \$19.9999$. If the interest rate r is 6 percent per year, investing the proceeds in a money market account over the next day yields

$$[K - S(t)]e^{rT}$$
$$= [19.9999] \, e^{0.06 \times (1/365)}$$
$$= \$20.003$$

FIGURE 16.6: Illustration of Result 16.10a

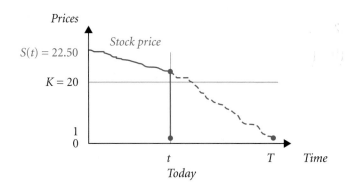

If everyone believes in the dashed line, the stock price will crash now and fall below $1.
If only you believe in the dashed line, do not exercise (get $2.50), but sell the call for more.

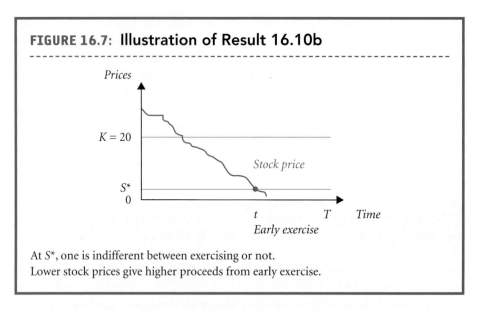

FIGURE 16.7: Illustration of Result 16.10b

At S^*, one is indifferent between exercising or not.
Lower stock prices give higher proceeds from early exercise.

Waiting one day and then deciding to exercise yields at most $20, and if one waits, the stock price may rise and even less of a payoff may occur. So early exercise is optimal today. Of course, this is a pathological example selected to make our point, but it does prove that early exercise is sometimes optimal if the stock price is low enough and interest rates are high enough.

This pathological example also illustrates another observation. It is easy to believe that as the stock price rises, there is some stock price S^* where you are just indifferent between exercising today or not. The S^* just balances the interest earned on the proceeds of early exercise with the chance of the stock price declining more (see Figure 16.7). Such an S^* does in fact exist. Unfortunately, to prove this observation and to determine the S^* precisely, we need a model for the stock price evolution. This analysis will be pursued in chapter 18. For now, we can only prove Result 16.10b.

Dividends and Early Exercise

Dividends change the optimal exercise decision for American options. Recall that when dividends are paid, the stock price falls. We characterized this dividend-induced price drop as Result 3.1:[3]

$$S_{\text{CDIV}} = S_{\text{XDIV}} + \text{div} \tag{3.1}$$

where S_{CDIV} is stock price cum-dividend, S_{XDIV} is stock price ex-dividend, and div is the amount of dividend. A natural place to investigate early exercise is around the time a stock goes ex-dividend. This leads to our next result.

---

[3] Exceptions to this statement can happen. We need some technical assumptions about the process underlying stock price changes. The statement in (3.1) holds, for example, if the stock price process follows a lognormal distribution, which underlies the Black–Scholes–Merton model. It does not hold, for example, if the stock price process allows discrete jumps and the jump happens at the same time as the stock goes ex-dividend; see Heath and Jarrow (1988) for a formal discussion.

RESULT 16.11

Optimal Times for Exercising American Calls

The only times when it may be optimal to exercise early is just before a stock goes ex-dividend.

The next example establishes this result with an application of Result 16.5.

EXAMPLE 16.6: Establishing Result 16.11

- Consider a six-month OPSY 20 call. Let the next dividend div_1 be paid at time t_1, which is two months from today (time 0). Should you exercise this call at a time t, anytime over the next two months?

- Consider the two possible strategies: early exercise at time t or wait and exercise at time t_1. If you exercise at time t, the value of your position is $S(t) - 20$, but if you exercise an instant before OPSY goes ex-dividend at time t_1, even if the option is out-of-the-money, then you get $S_{CDIV} - 20$. The present value at time t of waiting until time t_1 to exercise is

$$S(t) - 20B$$

where B is the time t price of a zero-coupon bond that pays \$1 at time t_1.

- Because B is less than 1, the second strategy gives you more value than the first. Thus exercising the American call just before the stock goes ex-dividend is better than exercising it anytime between now and the first dividend date.

- This result follows because exercising earlier than these ex-dividend dates leads to an early surrender of the strike price—an action that loses interest but does not generate any additional benefit. Hence, if the call is exercised early to obtain the dividend on the stock, it will be exercised just an instant before the stock goes ex-dividend. This is depicted in Figure 16.8. See Jarrow and Turnbull (2000) and other finance textbooks for a discussion of how big the dividend needs to be to trigger early exercise.

FIGURE 16.8: Timeline for Exercise of American Options

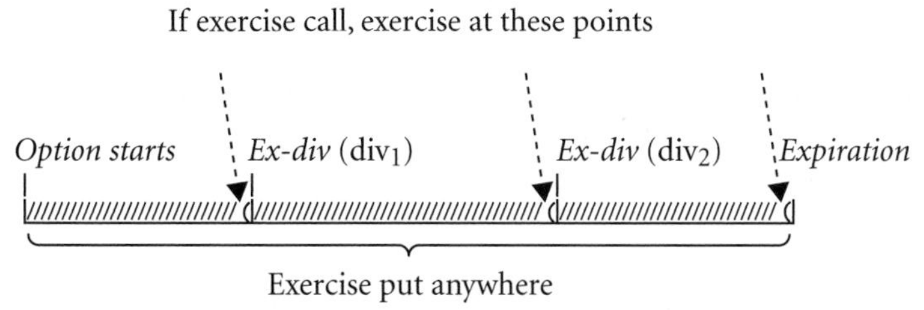

If exercise call, exercise at these points

Option starts   *Ex-div* (div_1)   *Ex-div* (div_2)   *Expiration*

Exercise put anywhere

If exercising an American call early, exercise just before the stock goes ex-dividend. An American put may be exercised anytime (but dividends tend to delay exercise).

And what about developing early exercise results for puts? Puts can get exercised early even without dividends. As dividends would cause the stock price to drop further, their presence is likely to delay early exercise. To get more precise insight, we need to model the stock price evolution. Again, we address this in later chapters.

EXTENSION 16.4: Studies of Put–Call Parity, Price Bounds, and Early Exercise

Earlier in this chapter, we examined violations of put–call parity and discussed Lamont and Thaler (2003), who documented the violation of PCP for some stocks through equity carve-outs. Ofek et al. (2004) find violations of PCP that depend on short sales constraints. Both these papers identify market imperfections where our assumptions and results no longer apply.

Many academic papers have studied violations of option price bounds and restrictions. For example, an early study by Bhattacharya (1983) using transaction data found small and infrequent violations of the rational boundary conditions. Many papers have studied optimal exercise strategies. For example, a study by Finucane (1997) examined equity call options over the two-year period 1988–89 and found that approximately 20 percent of early call exercise occurs at times other than ex-dividend dates (when, as we have explained, you do not expect early exercise to happen). Although he found that most of the non-dividend related early exercise can be understood with transactions costs, he concluded that a significant number of options appeared to be irrationally exercised.

Many call holders neglect to exercise the option just before it goes ex-dividend, even though it is optimal to do so. Hao et al. (2010) estimate that during the period 1996–2006, more than 40 percent of exchange-traded equity options in the United States that should have been optimally exercised weren't. There are some market makers and arbitrageurs who watch these actions and employ a **dividend play** (or **dividend spread arbitrage strategy**) to pick up the money left on the table when the call owners leave the options unexercised.

A dividend play can be implemented in several ways. The strategies are implemented on the last cum-dividend day, which is the day before the stock goes ex-dividend. Notice that if all the calls are optimally exercised, then all calls disappear from the market! But if some traders do not exercise when it is optimal, those unexercised calls decline in value. Traders take advantage of this price pattern by short selling calls on the day before a company's stock goes ex-dividend and then buying those calls back after the stock has gone ex-dividend when the calls have declined in value. Moreover, they can delta hedge their position by trading stocks, which is a strategy that we discuss in chapter 20.

Another sophisticated version of the dividend play strategy involves market markers trading among themselves to establish a long and a short call position in the same option. As the long and the short cancel out, the position is riskless and requires no capital investment. These market makers exercise all their long calls. The long stock position enables them to capture dividends. Later, they buy back any unexercised calls at a cheaper price (see "Playing Options? Get Versed First—Complex Call Trade Pits Sophisticated Traders Against Individuals," *Wall Street Journal*, October 20, 2009).

16.7 | Summary

1. Put–call parity for European options (see Result 16.1) states that the call price plus the present value of strike equals the stock price plus the put price, or $c + BK = S + p$, where B is today's zero-coupon bond price paying a dollar on the options' common maturity date and K is the common strike price.

2. PCP has a number of applications and uses:
   - PCP can be used to create synthetically an option, a stock, or a bond.
   - PCP can be easily modified to adjust for known dividends.

3. Option prices satisfy restrictions that can be derived using the no-arbitrage principle. These theorems hone intuition and enhance understanding, lead to arbitrage profits in case of violations, and form a stepping-stone to understanding the early exercise of options.

4. Options price restrictions can be established in several different ways: (1) a diagrammatic approach with profit diagrams, (2) an arbitrage table approach, where cash flows are recorded in a table and no arbitrage yields the result, and (3) a superglue approach, which is our name for comparing the original security with a "restricted" but otherwise identical security and then proving the result by arguing that "less cannot be worth more."

5. Some options price properties for stocks that may pay dividends are as follows:
   - Result 16.2—American options are worth more than European options: $c_A \geq c$ and $p_A \geq p$.
   - Result 16.3—Call price boundaries
     3a. An American call's price is less than or equal to the stock price: $c_A \leq S$.
     3b. When the stock price is zero, the call price is also zero.
   - Result 16.4—Put price boundaries
     4a. An American put's price is less than or equal to the strike price K: $p_A \leq K$.
     4b. A European put's price is less than or equal to the present value of the strike price: $p \leq BK$.
   - Result 16.5—Before expiration, a European call price must exceed the stock price minus the present value of the strike price: $c \geq S - BK$.
   - Result 16.6a—Before expiration, a European put must be greater than or equal to the present value of the strike price minus the stock price: $p \geq BK - S$.
   - Result 16.6b—Before expiration, the value of an American put must be greater than or equal to its intrinsic value: $p_A \geq K - S$.
   - Result 16.7a—The lower the strike price, the more valuable is the European call: $c(K_1) \geq c(K_2)$ for $K_1 < K_2$.
   - Result 16.7b—The higher the strike price, the more valuable is the European put: $p(K_1) \leq p(K_2)$ for $K_1 < K_2$.
     Both these results hold for American options as well.

- Result 16.8—Option prices and time to maturity: the longer the time until expiration, the greater the price of an American call or a put.
  8a. $c_A(T_1) \leq c_A(T_2)$ for $T_1 < T_2$.
  8b. $p_A(T_1) \leq p_A(T_2)$ for $T_1 < T_2$.
  However, these results need not hold for European calls or European puts.

6. Early-exercise considerations begin with the following:
   Result 16.9a—Exercise an American call the first time its price is equal to the stock price minus the strike price: $c_A = S - K$.
   Result 16.9b—Exercise an American put the first time its price is equal to the strike price minus the stock price: $p_A = K - S$.

7. Dividends play a critical role in early-exercise decisions:
   - Assume the stock pays no dividends over the option's life:
     Result 16.10a—The American call becomes identical to a European call. It should never be exercised early.
     Result 16.10b—The American put should be exercised if the stock price is small enough relative to the strike price and the time to maturity.
   - Absent market frictions, dividends cause the stock price to drop by the amount of the dividend (Result 3.1). This is used to establish the following:
     Result 16.11—The only times when it may be optimal to exercise an American call early is just before a stock goes ex-dividend.
     Puts can get exercised early even without dividends, but dividends are likely to delay early exercise.

16.8 | Cases

Boston Properties (A and B) (Harvard Business School Cases 211018 and 211041-PDF-ENG). The case introduces options pricing, payoff diagrams, and the law of one price and explains arbitrage as well as no-arbitrage bounds.

Smith, Barney, Harris Upham and Co. Inc. (Darden School of Business Case UV0074-PDF-ENG, Harvard Business Publishing). The case approaches put–call parity from the trader's perspective and examines the practical aspects of doing arbitrage in the options markets.

Sleepless in L.A. (Richard Ivey School of Business Foundation Case 905N11-PDF-ENG, Harvard Business Publishing). The case discusses the Black–Scholes–Merton model for options pricing, the concept of implied volatility, and put–call parity. It also shows how options pricing can be used to value corporate liabilities of a financially distressed company.

16.9 | Questions and Problems

The next two questions are based on the following data for European options:

Call price = $5, risk-free continuously compounded interest rate $r = 5$ percent per year, stock price $S = \$55$, strike price $K = \$55$, time to maturity $T = 1$ month.

16.1. If the put price $p_Q = \$9$, show how to capture arbitrage profits in this market.

16.2. Suppose short selling of stocks is not allowed in this market. Can you still make arbitrage profits? Explain your answer.

16.3. Do the following data satisfy put–call parity for European options? If they don't, show how you can create a portfolio to generate arbitrage profits. Call price = $6, put price = $3, stock price $S = \$102$, strike price $K = \$100$, time to maturity $T = 3$ months, and risk-free continuously compounded interest rate $r = 5$ percent per year.

16.4. How can you adjust put–call parity for known dividends on a single known date?

16.5. Prove put–call parity for European options in the case of a single known dividend:

$$c + PV(Div) + Ke^{-rT} = p + S$$

where S is stock price, K is strike price, T is maturity date for the option, r is risk-free interest rate, c is European call price, p is European put price, and $PV(Div)$ is the present value of dividends.

16.6. Using put–call parity, given $c = \$2$, $PV(Div) = \$1$, $p = \$1$, $S = K = \$100$, $r = 0.05$ per year, and $T = 0.25$ years, can you make arbitrage profits? Explain.

16.7. Explain the relation between a put option (with strike price K and maturity date T years from today) and a T-period insurance policy that insures the stock for K dollars.

16.8. Different countries, different customs, different market practices! Suppose you go to a country where traders with inside information can easily trade. There, you have inside information that the stock price is going to increase for sure (no chance that it will decline), and it is legal to trade on this information. What is the best strategy to use?

16.9. Does put–call parity always hold in financial markets? If not, give a few reasons why it may not hold.

16.10. On the day options on Palm began trading, the share prices grossly violated the put–call parity. Describe and explain why this happened.

16.11. a. How did Russell Sage violate New York State's usury laws?

b. How did Sage use put–call parity to overcome these market restrictions?

c. Can you link Russell Sage's actions with a distinguished economist's view on what drives financial innovation?

16.12. Is it true that the lower the exercise price, the more valuable the call? Explain your answer.

16.13. Is a European put on the same stock with the same maturity worth more or less if the strike price increases? Explain your answer.

16.14. Is it true that the more the time until expiration, the less valuable an American put? Explain your answer.

16.15. Can you make arbitrage profits from the following European call prices? If so, give two such examples of arbitrage, neatly showing the portfolio construction as well as the various cash flows. The stock price is $40.

Strike Price	Expiration Month		
	April	July	September
35	1	6	3
40	2	5	6

16.16. The following prices are given for American put options on a stock whose current price is $100:

Strike Price	Expiration Month	
	March	June
95	1	11
100	7	5

Construct three portfolios for making arbitrage profits, showing the cash flows from each portfolio.

16.17. The following prices are given for American call options on a stock whose current price is $100:

Strike Price	Expiration Month	
	March	June
95	11	10
100	8	8
105	2	5

Construct three portfolios for making arbitrage profits, showing the cash flows coming from each portfolio.

16.18. If a European call is written on a stock that never pays a dividend, would you ever exercise the call option early? Explain your answer.

16.19. If an American put is written on a stock that never pays a dividend, would you ever exercise the put option early? Explain your answer.

16.20. a. Is there a simple rule of thumb that you can use to know when to exercise an American call early? If yes, explain the rule.

b. Is there a simple rule of thumb that you can use to know when to exercise an American put early? If yes, explain the rule.

17

Single-Period Binomial Model

17.1 | Introduction

"Once in Hawaii I was taken to see a Buddhist temple," wrote physicist Richard Feynman in *The Meaning of It All: Thoughts of a Citizen Scientist*. "In the temple a man said, . . . 'To every man is given the key to the gates of heaven. The same key opens the gates of hell.'"[1] Derivatives may be viewed as such a key. When the financial crisis of 2007 hit many countries, including the United States, numerous commentators, and even the lay public, blamed it on derivatives. Indeed, credit rating agencies failed to correctly rate complicated derivatives, and the losses on these derivatives brought down many financial institutions. Conversely, the growth of the derivatives market has been praised as improving economic welfare by shifting risks from those who fear it to those who profit from it. And derivatives help solve financial problems. They were even used by governments during the crisis to help resolve it.

For example, the US Treasury started the **Troubled Asset Relief Program** during the financial crisis to commit up to "$700 billion to rescue the financial system," notes the July (2009) Oversight Report of the Congressional Oversight Panel, "TARP Repayments, Including the Repurchase of Stock Warrants." TARP purchased stock in the stressed banks with "troubled assets," but in addition, they received ten-year warrants. Warrants are call options—derivatives! After the banks recovered, the US government sold these warrants back to the banks or to others at a "fair price," determined with the help of the Black–Scholes–Merton (BSM) and binomial models. In doing so, they profited substantially. Note the use of the binomial model!

This chapter develops the single-period binomial model with an eye toward understanding the major tenets of options pricing. We provide an illustrative example, give the model's intuition, and state the necessary assumptions. To value the option, we construct a synthetic option with identical payoffs using the stock and a money market account. This takes us to martingale pricing and risk-neutral valuation, which lies at the heart of modern theory and which enables us to understand the more complex option pricing models (OPMs) that follow. Chapter 18 extends this chapter to a multiperiod setting and makes the binomial model practical and useful. The subsequent two chapters adopt a similar pattern: chapter 19 introduces the BSM model, and chapter 20 discusses the model's practical use.

17.2 | Applications and Uses of the Binomial Model

Options pricing bewildered and baffled academics until Fischer Black, Myron Scholes, and Robert Merton developed an analytic pricing model for European

---

[1] Feynman, Richard P., 1998. *The Meaning of It All: Thoughts Of A Citizen-Scientist*. Reading, Massachusetts : Perseus Books, 6.

options in 1973. The mathematics underlying the model's derivation is difficult. Nobel laureate William Sharpe (1995, p. 185) wrote,

> The basis for the important Black–Scholes option valuation formula was, for me, hard to understand and virtually impossible to explain, since it was grounded in the difficult mathematics of continuous processes. Surely, I thought, there must be a discrete-time, discrete-state counterpart. Happily, there was. Moreover, numeric experiments showed that values obtained with the resultant *binomial process* converged quite rapidly to those of the continuous form as the number of discrete steps increased. I presented this (*binomial*) approach in 1978 in my textbook.

To more simply derive the model, as Sharpe noted, one can use a binomial model and then take limits. Although the binomial model had been used as a teaching tool at the Massachusetts Institute of Technology (MIT) and other places before its publication, it was first printed in Sharpe's classic textbook *Investments*. Subsequently, Cox, Ross, Rubinstein, Rendleman, Bartter, Jarrow, and Rudd developed popular versions of the binomial model.

The model gets its name **binomial** (*bi* means "two") from the assumed stock price evolution. From any point in time onward, over the next time step, the stock price can take only one of two possible values. This raises two immediate questions: (1) why do we need to make an assumption about stock price movements, and (2) is it reasonable to assume that stock prices can only take two values?

The last chapter explicitly answered the first question. There we pushed as far as we could without imposing a model for the stock price evolution. Although we got many results, we could not obtain a pricing model. One needs to assume a model for the stock price evolution like the binomial (which we do in this and the next chapter) or a lognormal (chapter 19) to develop an exact OPM.

As for the second question, do stocks really only take one of two values at each time step? No. But we need to start somewhere. We start with the simplest model to facilitate understanding and then add the necessary layers of complexity. The simple binomial OPM possesses some desirable features:

- *It approximates the BSM model.* The binomial OPM can be repeated at each time step in a multiperiod tree. When the parameters are properly chosen (see Extension 18.1) and the model is run over many small time intervals, the multiperiod binomial OPM prices closely approximate BSM model prices.

- *It illustrates martingale pricing, the central idea of derivatives pricing.* The binomial approach utilizes "martingale pricing," a powerful technique for valuation. Once you understand this approach, you will find it easier to understand more complex OPMs.

- *It provides a useful numerical approximation technique.* The binomial model is a versatile tool that gives numerical values to approximate solutions to exact pricing models (like the BSM model) or provides answers when no explicit analytical solutions exist (as in the case of an American put). Later chapters show how to use the binomial model to price interest rate derivatives. Even proprietary trading desks of Wall Street firms sometimes use sophisticated versions of the binomial pricing model.

17.3 | A Brief History of Options Pricing Models

The history of OPMs has two phases: before and after 1973.

Option Pricing Pre-1973

BACHELIER, SAMUELSON, AND ITO It all started more than a century ago, when a young French mathematician, Louis Bachelier (1900), wrote a dissertation titled "The Theory of Speculation" that developed a prototype OPM (see the biographical sketch of Bachelier). Despite some shortcomings, it was the forerunner of the BSM model. Bachelier was the first to model stock prices as a random walk.[2] But fate was unkind, and he did not get the recognition he deserved during his lifetime.[3] Within a decade after Bachelier's death, his work resurfaced and influenced two major fields. First, it led to the creation of the field of options pricing. It attracted the attention of Professor Paul Samuelson, the first American to win the Nobel Prize in Economics (see the biographical sketch of Samuelson). During the 1960s, Samuelson and others worked on improving Bachelier's model (see Figure 17.1 and Table 17.1 for a summary of landmark achievements in this field). Second, Bachelier's work inspired the development of stochastic calculus by Professor Kiyosi Ito. This mathematics was used in the derivation of the BSM model and in the subsequent development of mathematical finance.

PREPARING THE GROUND FOR THE BLACK–SCHOLES–MERTON MODELS "Science moves, but slowly, slowly, creeping on from point to point," lamented the narrator in Lord Alfred Tennyson's poem "Locksley Hall." This was true of options pricing. In the decades that followed World War II, economists improved Bachelier's

---

[2] The view that Bachelier was the first to model stock prices as a random walk has been challenged by Franck Jovanovic and Philippe Le Gall of the University of Paris. Their 1999 paper argued that this honor goes to a French economist, Jules Regnault (see Jovanovic and Le Gall 1999, p. 362).

[3] A renewal of interest in Bachelier's work in the late twentieth century was followed by the founding of the Bachelier Finance Society in 1996. The society's activities promote advancing the "discipline of finance under the application of the theory of stochastic processes, statistical and mathematical theory." www.bachelierfinance.org/.

model and set the stage for the BSM model. The early improvements included the following:

- *The lognormal distribution for stock prices*. Samuelson (and physicist M. F. M. Osborne) introduced the lognormal distribution that gave a better description of stock prices than the normal distribution (used by Bachelier) because it avoided the possibility of negative stock prices.

- *The no-arbitrage principle*. Although arbitrage was widely used in stock, options, and foreign currency markets for over a hundred years (see Nelson 1904), Professors Modigliani and Miller's (1958, 1961) seminal papers in corporate finance successfully applied the no-arbitrage principle in an academic setting. No arbitrage is a critical assumption underlying the BSM model. You have seen this principle in earlier parts of this book.

- *Hedging an option with a stock*. This idea also has a long history in practice. Nelson (1904) describes how an options writer in the sophisticated London options market would hedge: "straightaway buy half the stock against which the Call is sold." In their book, Thorp and Kassouf's (1967) numerical approach utilized the same idea and was a forerunner to the idea of a "perfect hedge," which is the key insight underlying the BSM model introduced by Robert C. Merton.

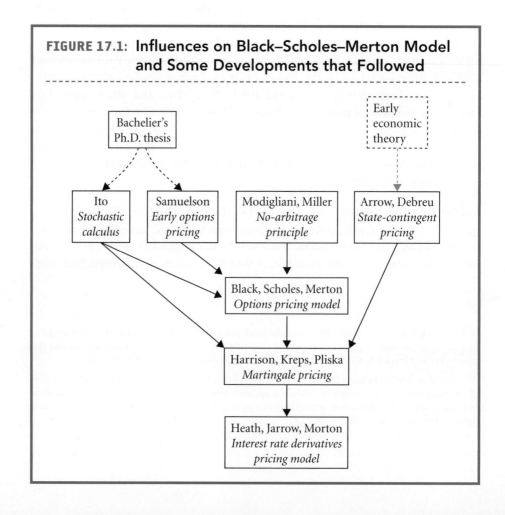

FIGURE 17.1: Influences on Black–Scholes–Merton Model and Some Developments that Followed

TABLE 17.1: Some Milestones in the History of Option Pricing Models

Year	Development
1900	Bachelier developed the first option pricing model (OPM).
1950s	Ito developed stochastic calculus and Ito's formula. Modigliani and Miller (M&M) introduced the no-arbitrage principle. Arrow and Debreu developed state-contingent pricing.
1960s	Samuelson and other scholars improved Bachelier's model.
1973	The Black–Scholes and Merton models were published.
1970s, 1995	Merton (1974, 1977) and Jarrow and Turnbull (1995) models for pricing derivatives with credit risk were introduced.
1978–82	The binomial model was presented in Sharpe (1978), Cox et al. (1979), Rendleman and Bartter (1979), and Jarrow and Rudd (1982).
1979 and 1981	Harrison and Kreps (1979) and Harrison and Pliska (1981) developed the martingale pricing methodology.
1987 and 1992	The Heath–Jarrow–Morton model (introduced in 1987, published in 1992), an interest rate OPM, was introduced.
1997	Merton and Scholes, the surviving co-originators of the BSM model, won the Sveriges Riksbank Prize in Economic Sciences in Memory of Alfred Nobel.

TABLE 17.A: Biographical Sketch: Louis J.-B. A. Bachelier

Louis Jean-Baptiste Alphonse Bachelier (1870–1946) was born into a respectable bourgeois family in Le Havre, France. His maternal grandfather was a banker and a poet. His father was a wine merchant, a vice consul for Venezuela, and an amateur scientist. After his parents' death, Louis became the head of the family enterprise Bachelier fils, which acquainted him with the world of financial markets.

Louis Bachelier studied mathematics at the prestigious Sorbonne in Paris. Courtault et al. (2000, p. 344) states that his doctoral dissertation, "Théorie de la Spéculation" (defended on March 29, 1900), can be viewed as the "origin of mathematical finance and of several important branches of stochastic calculus such as the theory of Brownian motion, Markov processes, diffusion processes, and even weak convergence in functional spaces." Bachelier's mentor mathematician Jules Henri Poincaré strongly supported the dissertation, encouraged further development of the ideas contained therein, and authorized "M. Bachelier to have his thesis printed and to submit it."

Louis Bachelier remained mathematically active and continued writing articles and books, including popular books on the stock market. Bachelier's work was occasionally noted during his lifetime. Although the Russian probabilist Andrei Kolmogorov and the British economist John Maynard Keynes referenced his work, he passed away in relative obscurity.

TABLE 17.B: Biographical Sketch: Paul A. Samuelson

Paul Anthony Samuelson (1915–2009) was the first American Nobel laureate in economics and has been hailed as "the foremost academic economist of the 20th century" (see his obituary, *New York Times*, December 14, 2009). After graduating from the University of Chicago, he wrote a seminal PhD dissertation at Harvard University, which was embellished and published as the *Foundations of Economic Analysis* (1947). The influential *Foundations*, over five hundred academic papers, thousands of magazine columns, and a textbook created Samuelson's prominence. At his death, Samuelson

(*continued*)

TABLE 17.B: (Continued)

held the highest ranked institute professorship at MIT. Samuelson left his mark on numerous areas within economics: revealed preference, welfare economics, gains from trade, public goods, factor proportions trade theory, exchange rates, the balance of payments, overlapping generations, and random-walk finance ("The Incomparable Economist," December 15, 2009, http://krugman.blogs.nytimes.com/2009/12/15/the-incomparable-economist/). However, many believe that Samuelson's textbook *Economics* was his greatest contribution. *Economics* sold an astonishing 4 million plus copies in eighteen editions in over six decades.

Paul Samuelson also influenced mathematical finance, the story of which is narrated in Jarrow and Protter (2004). During the mid-1950s, the statistician L. Jimmie Savage stumbled on Bachelier's book by chance and alerted Samuelson about the work. Samuelson remarked, "Bachelier seems to have had something of a one-track mind. But what a track!" Samuelson's major contributions to options pricing were his two (Samuelson 1965a, 1965b) papers and one with Robert Merton (Samuelson and Merton 1969). These papers developed several influential ideas:
- Samuelson (1965b) proved that stock prices must fluctuate randomly sixty-five years after Bachelier had assumed such a random walk. We discussed Samuelson's contribution to the efficient markets hypothesis in Extension 6.1.
- Samuelson (1965a) and Samuelson and Merton (1969) developed formulas for pricing warrants using an equilibrium model requiring the estimation of a risk premium.

TABLE 17.C: Biographical Sketch: Kiyosi Ito

Kiyosi Ito (1915–2008) developed *stochastic calculus* (or Ito calculus), which uses concepts from traditional calculus, probability theory, and the theory of *stochastic processes*. His research found application in many fields, including engineering, genetics, and mathematical finance. Ito's lemma was critical to the derivation of the Black–Scholes–Merton model. Stochastic calculus continues to play a central role in the development of mathematical finance.

On graduation from the prestigious University of Tokyo, Ito worked for Japan's Cabinet Statistics Bureau (1938–43), where he devoted his free time to studying probability. Building on the works of American, French, and Russian mathematicians, Ito devised a theory of *stochastic differential equations*. Afterward, he joined Nagoya University, got a PhD from the University of Tokyo (1945), and spent the bulk of his career as a Kyoto University professor (1952–79).

He worked with many collaborators and spent time visiting at foreign universities. One of his collaborators, Professor Daniel Stroock of MIT, observed (see Ito's obituary, *New York Times*, November 23, 2008), "Ito had an intense curiosity, whether focused on math theory or world affairs or shoeing horses." The obituary noted that Ito had learned Chinese, German, French, and English, but "he mastered them as written languages instead of conversationally."

Kiyosi Ito came to probability theory when few mathematicians worked in this area. Eventually, his work gained global acceptance. Ito was recognized with many professional honors, including the Wolf Prize of Israel and the Kyoto Prize of Japan, and he was the first recipient of Germany's Carl Friedrich Gauss Prize.

Options Pricing, 1973 and After

During the late 1960s, two young PhDs, Fischer Black and Myron Scholes, teamed up to work on options pricing. Around the same time, Robert Merton, a PhD student of Paul Samuelson, started working on the same problem. Joining the previous three insights, 1973 saw the publication of the *Black–Scholes–Merton* model (chapter 19 provides a more detailed history), which forms the foundation for today's OPMs. Their work stands as a towering achievement not only in finance but also in the field of economics.

After the watershed year of 1973, a race began to build better pricing models. Numerous OPMs resulted. These models priced different kinds of derivatives and relaxed the BSM model's assumptions. The race continues to this day with unabated fury.

Why develop better OPMs? There are many reasons. The opening of options exchanges and the expansion of over-the-counter options trading created a need for better hedging. Brokers and dealers need OPMs to make effective markets. Further fueling the need for OPMs, macroeconomic changes occurred with the demise of the Bretton Woods system of fixed exchange rates. Spikes in inflation and the end of stable interest rates increased volatility in these markets. This increased volatility created a demand for derivatives to hedge the risks. Investment banks became eager innovators developing an attractive array of interest rate derivatives products to better serve clients' needs and to make profits. Hedging these derivatives required new OPMs.

The OPM extensions can be classified under five headings:

1. *Improving the BSM model and using it for different underlyings.* Soon after the publication of the BSM came a slew of models that improved the original. They included Black's model to price commodity contracts and Roll's model to value American options with dividends (see Jarrow and Turnbull 2000). The stock price evolution was generalized, and market imperfections like short selling restrictions and transaction costs were included as well.

2. *Including a term structure of random interest rates.* A major drawback of the BSM model is its constant interest rate assumption. Early attempts at pricing interest rate options required estimating risk premia (e.g., Vasicek 1977; Brennan and Schwartz 1979) that made the models difficult to use. The removal of the need to estimate interest rate risk premia came in 1992 when the Heath–Jarrow–Morton (HJM) model was published. All arbitrage-free interest rate OPMs are special cases of the HJM model.[4] A discrete time precursor to HJM is the Ho and Lee (1986) model.

3. *A rigorous mathematical foundation.* Harrison, Kreps, Pliska, and others generalized the mathematics behind the BSM model. They developed martingale pricing, which soon became the most widely used technique for pricing derivatives. This employed the concept of *state-contingent pricing*, which originates in the classic papers on general equilibrium by Arrow and Debreu (1953, 1954).

4. *Pricing derivatives with credit risk.* Merton (1974, 1977) pioneered the pricing of derivatives with credit risk with the *structural approach*. Jarrow and Turnbull (1995) developed an alternative method that relaxes some restrictive assumptions inherent in Merton's formulation. The Jarrow–Turnbull approach is called the *reduced-form* credit risk model. See chapter 26 for additional discussion.

5. *Numerical methods.* With more complex pricing models came the need to compute their values quickly and efficiently on computers. The binomial model was one of the first successful numerical methods (see Sharpe 1978; Cox et al. 1979; Rendleman and Bartter 1979; Jarrow and Rudd 1982). Others include numerical methods for solving partial differential equations and Monte Carlo simulation techniques.

To understand options pricing theory, we begin with an example that illustrates the key ideas.

---

[4] Baxter and Rennie (1996) state, "In the interest-rate setting, Heath–Jarrow–Morton is as seminal as Black–Scholes. By focusing on forward rates and especially by giving a careful stochastic treatment, they produced the most general (finite) Brownian interest-rate model possible. Other models may claim differently, but they are just HJM with different notations." Baxter and Rennie's book presents a nice exposition of the HJM model. See also chapters 23–25 of this book.

17.4 | An Example

This section illustrates the binomial options pricing approach through an example.

A Binomial Lattice

The essential idea of a binomial lattice is explored first.

EXAMPLE 17.1: The Expected Value (Mean) and Variance

- Consider a lottery that pays $100 with probability 0.01 (a 1 percent chance) and $0 with probability of $1 - 0.01 = 0.99$ (a 99 percent chance).

- The future outcomes of this lottery are called the **states of nature**. For convenience, we label the event "$100" as the up state and the event "$0" as the down state. These two possible events are shown in a binomial lattice or binomial tree (see Figure 17.2), where the payoff $100 is placed on a node reached by the upper branch of the tree, while $0 is placed on a node reached by the lower branch.

- The lottery's expected value and variance are computed by standard techniques. The **expected (or mean) payoff**,

$$\mu = \sum_{i=1}^{2} (\text{Probability of event } i) \times (\text{Payoff in event } i)$$

$$= (\text{Probability of event 1}) \times (\text{Payoff in event 1}) + (\text{Probability of event 2}) \times (\text{Payoff in event 2})$$

$$= (\text{Probability of \$100}) \times (\$100) + (\text{Probability of \$0}) \times (\$0)$$

$$= 0.01 \times \$100 + 0.99 \times 0$$

$$= \$1.00$$

The **variance** of the payoff

$$\sigma^2 = \sum_{i=1}^{2} (\text{Probability of event } i) \times (\text{Payoff in event } i - \text{Mean payoff})^2$$

$$= 0.01 \times (100 - 1)^2 + 0.99 \times (0 - 1)^2$$

$$= 98.01 + 0.99$$

$$= \$99$$

The **standard deviation** (or **volatility**)

$$\sigma \equiv +\sqrt{\text{variance}}$$

$$= \$9.9499$$

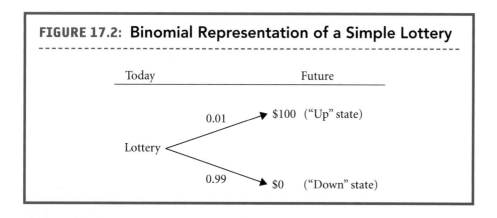

FIGURE 17.2: Binomial Representation of a Simple Lottery

Today   Future

                    0.01 → $100 ("Up" state)

Lottery

                    0.99 → $0   ("Down" state)

The mean measures a variable's average and the variance measures its fluctuations. We often work with the **standard deviation (s.d., or volatility)**, the positive square root of the variance, because it has the same units as the original observations. The mean and the variance are invaluable for doing any serious work in finance. Our OPMs utilize the volatility σ as a key input. Using standard statistical tools, we estimate these parameters using market data. Real-world data are generated by nature drawing the outcomes using the actual probabilities (which we refer to as q and $[1 - q]$ for the stock going up and down, respectively).

A Single-Period Example

Example 17.2 presents the single-period OPM.

EXAMPLE 17.2: European Call Pricing

■ Your Beloved Machine Inc.'s (YBM) stock price S is $100 today (time 0). After one year (time T), the stock price $S(1)$ can either go up to $120.00 or down to $90.25. Let the actual probability of the stock going up $q = 3/4$; then that of YBM going down is $(1 - q) = 1/4$.

■ Consider a European call option with strike price $K = \$110$ and maturity date time 1. The call's payoff at time 1 is $\max[S(1) - 100, 0]$, that is, it is $10 = \max[120 - 110, 0]$ if the stock goes up and $0 = \max[90.25 - 110, 0]$ if the stock goes down.

■ Let a money market account (mma) cost $1 per unit at time 0. A dollar invested in the mma grows to $1.0513 (see Figure 17.3).

Synthetic Call Construction

■ Form a portfolio V with m shares of the stock and b units of the mma. Its value today is

$$V(0) = m100 + b \tag{17.1}$$

■ We want to choose (m, b) such that the portfolio's payoffs at time 1, $V(1)$, equal those of the traded call on the expiration date. This holds if the following two equations are satisfied:

$$m120.00 + b1.0513 = 10 \tag{17.2}$$
$$m90.25 + b1.0513 = 0 \tag{17.3}$$

■ Solving these equations gives $m = 0.3361$ and $b = -28.85$, where a positive sign indicates a long and a negative sign a short. We call this portfolio the *synthetic call*.

■ Plugging the solutions into expression (17.1) gives $V(0) \equiv m100 + b = \$4.76$. This is the *cost of constructing* the synthetic call at time 0. To avoid arbitrage, this must be today's price for the *traded call, c*.

■ It is interesting to note that the option's value was determined without using the actual up probability $q = 3/4$. This is an important observation. We will explain the reasons for this shortly.

■ Note that expression (17.1) also has a *hedging interpretation*. If you buy $V(0)$ (a call option) and want to hedge the stock price risk, then sell m shares of the stock. This creates the hedged call portfolio $V(0) - m100 = b$, which is riskless because it's equivalent to a position in the mma. We will also explain this hedging interpretation more completely later in this chapter.

Arbitrage Profits

■ What happens when the traded call's price differs from the price of the synthetic call? Seize the opportunity and make arbitrage profits by buying low, selling high, or as the British would say, buying cheap, selling dear.

■ Suppose an errant trader quotes $7 for the traded call. As the traded call is more expensive, sell it and buy the synthetic call. Let's do the accounting to see if it all works out.
  - Sell the overpriced traded call for $7 and purchase the underpriced synthetic call by buying 0.3361 shares for $33.61 and borrow $28.85 by shorting the mma at a net cost of $4.76.
  - Today's cash flow is $+7 - 4.76 = \$2.24$. This is the immediate profit.
  - You have no liabilities in the future. If the stock rises at maturity, you owe $10 as the writer of the traded call. This is offset by the $10 that you get as the buyer of the synthetic call. Both calls expire worthless if the stock falls instead.

■ If a trader quotes $3 for the call, simply reverse your strategy: buy the traded call and simultaneously sell the more expensive synthetic call by short selling 0.3361 shares for $33.61 and lending $28.85 by buying the mma. You immediately make $1.76, and there is no future net exposure as the assets and liabilities perfectly match.

Put Pricing

■ Consider a European put with a strike price of $K = \$110$ and a maturity of one year. As with the call, set up a portfolio to match the put's time 1 value of $0 = \max(110 - 120, 0)$ in the up state and $\$19.75 = \max(110 - 90.25, 0)$ in the down state. This yields two equations in two unknowns (m, b):

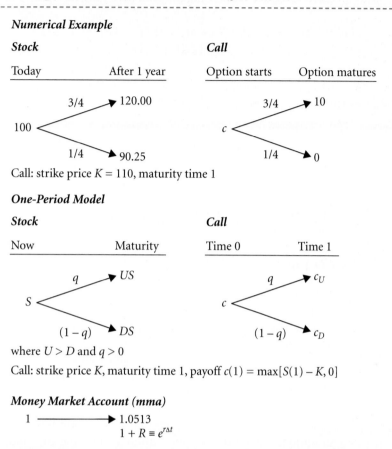

FIGURE 17.3: Single Period Binomial Example and Model

Numerical Example

Stock   *Call*

Today	After 1 year

Option starts	Option matures

Call: strike price $K = 110$, maturity time 1

One-Period Model

Stock   *Call*

Now	Maturity

Time 0	Time 1

where $U > D$ and $q > 0$

Call: strike price K, maturity time 1, payoff $c(1) = \max[S(1) - K, 0]$

Money Market Account (mma)

$1 \longrightarrow 1.0513$

$1 + R \equiv e^{r\Delta t}$

$$m120.00 + b1.0513 = 0$$
$$m90.25 + b1.0513 = 19.75$$

- Solve the two equations to get the stock shares $m = -0.6639$ and the number of mmas needed $b = 75.78$.

- As the stock and put prices move in opposite directions, it makes intuitive sense that the replicating portfolio combines a short position in the stock and a long position in the mma.

- The European put option's price p is equal to the cost of construction at time 0, that is,

$$V(0) \equiv m100 + b = -0.6639 \times 100 + 75.78 = \$9.39$$

Put–Call Parity

- Alternatively, you can derive the put's value using put–call parity for European options:

$$
\begin{aligned}
\text{Put price} &= \text{Call price} + \text{Present value of strike} - \text{Stock price} \\
&= 4.76 + 110 \times (1/1.0513) - 100 \\
&= \$9.39
\end{aligned}
$$

Any other put price will open up arbitrage opportunities.

17.5 | The Assumptions

Consider the opening lines of economic Nobel laureate Robert Solow's (1956, p. 65) classic paper on growth theory:

> All theory depends on assumptions which are not quite true. That is what makes it theory. The art of successful theorizing is to make the inevitable simplifying assumptions in such a way that the final results are not very sensitive. A "crucial" assumption is one on which the conclusions do depend sensitively, and it is important that crucial assumptions be reasonably realistic. When the results of a theory seem to flow specifically from a special crucial assumption, then if the assumption is dubious, the results are suspect.

Solow's characterization applies to the assumptions underlying our OPMs. The assumptions are the key to understanding and using any model. Recall our discussion of the cost-of-carry model and its assumptions from chapter 11. We need those same assumptions (A1 to A5) plus two more (A6 and A7). One is needed to describe the behavior of interest rates, and the other is needed to characterize the binomial stock price evolution. For emphasis as well as a better understanding of the model, we repeat our discussion of assumptions A1–A5.

A1. No market frictions. We assume that trading involves no *market frictions* such as transaction costs (brokerage commissions, bid/ask spreads), margin requirements, short sale restrictions, and taxes (which may be levied on different securities at different rates). Moreover, assets are perfectly divisible.

This helps us to create a benchmark model to which one can later add frictions. In addition, it's a reasonable approximation for many traders such as institutions. Moreover, political changes, regulatory changes, and the information technology revolution have substantially reduced market frictions.

A2. No credit risk. We assume that there is no *credit risk*. Also known as *default risk* or *counterparty risk*, this is the risk that the counterparty will fail to perform on an obligation.

The absence of credit risk is a reasonable assumption for exchange-traded derivatives. Over-the-counter derivatives, however, may possess substantial credit risks, unless there are adequate collateral provisions.

A3. Competitive and well-functioning markets. In a competitive market, traders' purchases or sales have no impact on the market price; consequently, traders act as price takers. In a well-functioning market, traders agree on zero-probability events, and price bubbles are absent.

The competitive markets assumption is the workhorse of modern economics. Spot, forward, and futures markets for many agricultural commodities and precious metals behave like competitive markets. Pricing securities when counterparties have market power and traders can manipulate prices is a difficult exercise. One must take into account bargaining and strategic interactions, which are outside the scope of this book.

By agreeing on zero-probability events, we mean that traders must agree on events relevant to the stock's price movements that *cannot happen*. For example, an event might be "the stock's price exceeds $1,000 in two weeks' time." If traders disagree on zero-probability events, then they cannot come to a consensus regarding what is considered an arbitrage opportunity. This destroys our key tool for proving results (see assumption A5).

A *price bubble* happens when an asset's market price deviates from its intrinsic or fundamental value. The *fundamental or intrinsic value* is the price paid if, after purchase, you have to hold the asset forever. A difference between the market price and fundamental value only occurs if one believes that selling can generate a higher value than holding it forever. The difference is the price bubble. Recent research shows that bubbles can invalidate the methodology we employ for pricing options. Fortunately, however, one can show that there are no price bubbles possible in a discrete time binomial model (see Jarrow et al. 2010).

A4. No intermediate cash flows. Many assets reward their holders with income or cash flows such as dividends for stocks and coupon income for bonds. For now, we assume that the underlying asset has no cash flows over the option's life. The next chapter will show how to relax this assumption by introducing dividends.

A5. No arbitrage opportunities. This is self-explanatory.

These five assumptions are a repetition of the assumptions used in the cost-of-carry model of chapter 11. Next we introduce two additional assumptions needed for deriving the binomial OPM.

A6. No interest rate uncertainty. We assume that interest rates are constant across time. This assumption only works for short-lived options whose underlyings are not interest rates. It does not work well for long-dated options whose underlying assets' prices are correlated with interest rate changes, like long-term options on foreign currencies. But long-dated options and interest rate derivatives are important in today's markets, and their pricing is a prime challenge for researchers and practitioners. We relax this assumption in part IV of the book.

Recall that we did not require this assumption for our cash-and-carry models. It wasn't necessary because forwards are essentially valued in a single-period setting. However, we will soon be introducing multiperiod and continuous time models in which bond investments have reinvestment risks. To avoid this problem, we assume a constant interest rate. Assumption A6 will be maintained for all OPMs in part III of the book.

A7. Binomial process. We assume that the stock trades in discrete time and that its price evolves according to a binomial process. For a current stock price, next period's stock price will either get multiplied by an up factor $U > 1$ and take a higher value $U \times$ Stock price or it will be multiplied by a down factor D and take a lower value $D \times$ Stock price. We let $q > 0$ denote the actual probability of going up. We also assume $U > D$. Otherwise, we have mislabeled up and down.

Assumption A7 will be with us in this and the next chapter. It will eventually be replaced by the assumption of "continuous trading" and the evolution of the stock price according to a "lognormal process" in the context of the BSM model.

17.6 | The Single-Period Model

To develop the model, we proceed through a sequence of steps. First, we explain the no-arbitrage principle used in the example. Second, we show how to build a binomial tree that is arbitrage-free. Next comes the martingale representation of stock prices, which helps us to develop fancy entities called *pseudo-probabilities*. Then we obtain the call's value by building on Example 17.2. Finally, we introduce an alternative perspective on options pricing called *risk-neutral valuation*. The next chapter will extend this to develop a multiperiod binomial OPM that approximates the BSM model.

The No-Arbitrage Principle

Let's summarize the no-arbitrage principle used in the previous example to find the option's value.

- We considered a market in which both a stock and an option traded.
- The stock took one of two possible values at the maturity date, and so did the option because the option's payoff is completely determined by the stock's ending value and the strike price.

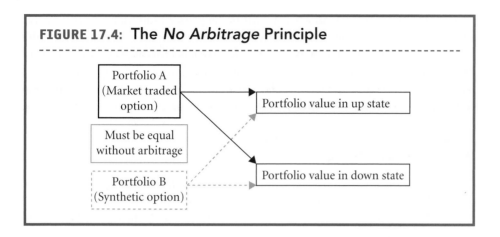

FIGURE 17.4: **The *No Arbitrage* Principle**

- We created a portfolio of the stock and mma to match the option's payoffs in each of these time 1 states. This replicating portfolio is called the **synthetic option**.

- By the law of one price—the no-arbitrage principle—the cost of constructing the synthetic option must equal the price of the traded option.

- Why should they be the same? If the traded option and the synthetic option differ in price (see Figure 17.4), then you have two distinct ways of getting the same cash flows. Shrewd traders will make arbitrage profits by buying the cheaper option and selling the dearer option until their prices converge.

- This pricing methodology has an interesting by-product. A portfolio that holds one of these options long and the other short should be entirely riskless. This kills two birds with one stone: *pricing and hedging problems are solved in a single stroke!*

Building Binomial Trees

We need some notation to build a binomial tree. Today at time 0, the stock price is $S(0)$ or S. At time 1, it can move up to $S(1)_{UP}$ or slide down to $S(1)_{DOWN}$. Let's write $S(1)_{UP} = SU$ and $S(1)_{DOWN} = SD$, where the positive numbers $U > D$ are called the **up and down factors**, respectively (Figure 17.5 shows how a stock price path looks in a single-period tree).

This **multiplicative binomial model** has the advantage of ruling out negative stock prices. Moreover, in the multiperiod setting, it makes life easier by insuring that the tree's branches recombine. To reduce clutter, we drop the dollar sign from the tree.

The other traded security is an mma. It earns the risk-free rate in each period. A dollar gives $(1 + R) = \exp(r\Delta t) \equiv e^{r\Delta t}$ at the end of each period, where r is the continuously compounded yearly interest rate and Δt is the length of the time period. In Figure 17.3, a single arrow is used to show the mma's value because it earns a fixed return.

Consider a European call option with strike price K and maturity time 1. Let $c(0)$ or c denote its time 0 value. Given the call's boundary condition, the call's values at date 1 are given by $\max[0, S(1) - K]$. We label this as $c(1)_{\text{UP}} \equiv c_U$ when the stock price goes up and $c(1)_{\text{DOWN}} \equiv c_D$ when it goes down (we drop some letters to reduce clutter). Figure 17.3 shows this model under the binomial tree example. Put values p_U and p_D could have been similarly introduced.

Arbitrage-Free Trees

"House built on a weak foundation, will not stand oh no," sang "King of Calypso" Harry Belafonte, who popularized Caribbean music. The same can happen with a model. Because we price options with a binomial tree using the no-arbitrage principle, the tree must be arbitrage-free for logical consistency. Otherwise, the whole approach collapses, like a house without a strong foundation.

A simple condition **Up factor > Dollar return > Down factor** ($U > [1+R] > D$) is both necessary and sufficient to rule out arbitrage profits in the binomial tree (see the appendix to this chapter for a proof). It states that neither the stock's nor the mma's returns dominate the other, a necessary condition for an economic equilibrium—and this makes intuitive sense. If one security is superior to the other, why invest in the inferior asset? This common sense arbitrage-free condition is trivial to impose and easy to understand. It must also hold in the multiperiod binomial tree, and it can be generalized. For example, even if U, $(1+R)$, and D depend on the node in the tree, the same condition must hold for all nodes. This will prove useful in part IV of the book, when we price interest rate options.

Stock Prices and Martingales

Before pricing options, let us study the no-arbitrage condition to see if we can obtain any additional insights. Suppose that $U > (1 + R) > D$ holds in the stock price tree so that arbitrage is ruled out. Algebra tells us that $U > [1+R] > D$ holds if and only if we can find a unique number π between 0 and 1 such that

$$(1 + R) = \pi U + (1 - \pi)D \tag{17.4}$$

(You can see this intuitively: as U is large and D is small, you can alter π to create any number that lies between them.)

Dividing both sides of expression (17.4) by $(1 + R)$ and multiplying by S gives

$$S = \frac{\pi US + (1 - \pi)DS}{1 + R} \tag{17.5}$$

This expression has a useful interpretation. Look at the stock tree in Figure 17.3. Suppose we say that the "probability" of the stock going up is π, and that of going down is (1 − π). Then, the stock's expected payoff computed with these probabilities and discounted to the present by the riskless rate (1 + R) is today's stock price! This gives us a simple method for computing the stock's present value that is consistent with no arbitrage.

Given a stock price tree, it is easy to determine π. Indeed, solving expression (17.4) gives

$$\pi = \frac{(1 + R) - D}{(U - D)} \text{ and } (1 - \pi) = \frac{U - (1 + R)}{U - D} \tag{17.6}$$

What have we done? Our no-arbitrage condition implies the existence of some numbers, π and (1 − π), which we have interpreted as probabilities, and we have used them to compute the stock's present value. However, it is important to emphasize that they are not the actual probabilities of the stock going up or down (which are $q = 3/4$ and $[1 - q] = 1/4$ in this case), so we call them **pseudo-probabilities** (or **martingale probabilities** or **risk-neutral probabilities**). The last two names will make sense shortly.

Next we rewrite expression (17.5) two more times. Why? Because after it is rewritten, it is easier to see how the binomial model relates to the BSM OPM studied in chapter 19. We thus rewrite expression (17.5) as (with $T = 1$)

$$S = E^{\pi}\big[S(T)\big]e^{-rT} \tag{17.7a}$$

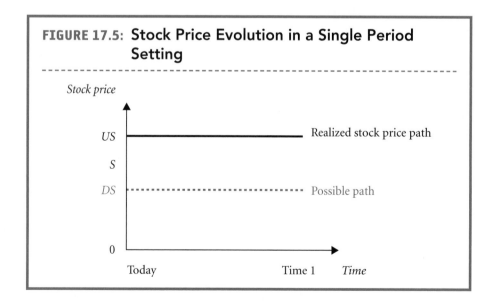

FIGURE 17.5: Stock Price Evolution in a Single Period Setting

where $E^\pi(.)$ is shorthand for denoting that we are computing an expected value by using the probabilities π and $(1 - \pi)$, and we replaced $(1 + R)$ with e^{rT}.

This method of computing the stock's present value as its expected payoff using the pseudo-probabilities and discounting it backward through time with the mma's value (expression [17.6]) is also known as **martingale pricing**. To see this interpretation, we need to rewrite this expression using the notation for a mma's value. Let A and $A(1) = e^r$ be the time 0 and time 1 value, respectively, of the mma. Then, expression (17.7a) is

$$\frac{S}{A} = E^\pi\left[\frac{S(T)}{A(T)}\right] \tag{17.7b}$$

This expression shows that $S(t)/A(t)$ is a martingale under the pseudo-probabilities. What is a **martingale**? It's a stochastic process $X(t)$ whose time t value equals the expected value of $X(T)$ at some later time T. Martingales are associated with "fair gambles" because what you have today is what you expect to have tomorrow. In finance, this sense of fairness gives us a pricing system with no arbitrage opportunities. Because of expression (17.7b) the pseudo-probabilities are often called the *martingale probabilities*.

The Pricing Model

Inspired by the example, we create a synthetic call using a replicating portfolio $V(0)$ $[\equiv mS + b]$ with m shares of the stock worth S per share and b units of the mma priced at a dollar each.

At time 1, we want to find (m, b) to match the portfolio's value to the traded call's value in each state. This yields two equations in two unknowns:

in the "up" state: $\qquad V(1)_{\text{UP}} = mUS + b(1 + R) = c_U$ $\qquad$ (17.8a)

in the "down" state: $\qquad V(1)_{\text{DOWN}} = mDS + b(1 + R) = c_D$ $\qquad$ (17.8b)

where

$$c_U = \max(US - K, 0) \text{ and } c_D = \max(DS - K, 0) \tag{17.8c}$$

A solution exists and solving them gives

$$m = (c_U - c_D)/(US - DS) \tag{17.9a}$$

$$b = (Uc_D - Dc_U)/[(U - D)(1 + R)] \tag{17.9b}$$

m is known as an *option's delta* or the *hedge ratio*. We will soon show why it is the holy grail of options pricing.

The cost of constructing this portfolio is

$$V(0) \equiv mS + b$$

$$= \frac{c_U - c_D}{(U - D)S}S + \frac{Uc_D - Dc_U}{(U - D)(1 + R)}$$

$$= \frac{1}{1 + R}\left[\left(\frac{(1 + R) - D}{U - D}\right)c_U + \left(\frac{U - (1 + R)}{U - D}\right)c_D\right] \qquad (17.10)$$

Now to prevent arbitrage, the synthetic call's cost of construction, $V(0)$, must equal the traded call's price, c. This is the option's arbitrage-free price! As seen in expression (17.10), this value depends only on (S, U, D, R, K), which we refer to somewhat flippantly as KRUDS. These are the current stock price (S), the up and down factors (U, D), the dollar return on the mma $(1 + R)$, and the contract's strike price (K). Missing from the call's value are q and $(1 - q)$, the actual probabilities of the stock going up or down.

This omission is important and it occurs because, in the derivation of the option's price, we use an exact replication argument. No matter which node of the tree the stock price moves, the synthetic call's payoffs exactly duplicate the option's payoffs. Hence we don't care what the actual probability is of moving up or down.

The omission of the actual probabilities from the option's price is important because it implies that if two investors agree on the KRUDS, but they disagree on q, they will still agree on the call's price. Of course, disagreement about the probability q might lead to disagreement about the stock price S when (U, D, R) are fixed. But if agreement about S occurs (which you can readily see for actively traded liquid stocks), then the call's price is fixed by our no-arbitrage argument.

The Hedge Ratio

Classical myths depict the **Holy Grail** as the cup used by Jesus Christ at the Last Supper. Believed to possess miraculous powers, it has been lost and sought for centuries. Indeed, the quest for the lost Holy Grail features prominently in the tales of the legendary knights of King Arthur's court. Options pricing theory also has its holy grail, the **hedge ratio**, the number of shares of the stock to hold for each written call to form a perfect hedge. This hedge ratio has miraculous powers because with it one can construct a synthetic call to obtain the arbitrage-free price of a traded option. Without it, our argument fails.

The hedge ratio for the binomial model is given by expression (17.9a):

$$m = \frac{c_U - c_D}{(U - D)S}$$

To prove this, consider a portfolio consisting of the short call and m shares of the stock. The initial value of this portfolio is

$$-c + mS$$

The values of this portfolio at time 1 in the up and down states are:

$$-c_U + mUS = \frac{c_U D - c_D U}{(U - D)}$$

$$-c_D + mDS = \frac{c_U D - c_D U}{(U - D)}$$

Because these values are equal, the covered call is riskless—and we have found the holy grail! To reemphasize, the hedge ratio works perfectly if the world behaves according to our single-period model. Finding a hedge ratio that works for more complex and realistic OPMs is a much harder task. Our quest for the holy grail (of options pricing) continues in the coming chapters for these more complex OPMs.

Risk-Neutral Valuation

Another interesting insight can be obtained using some additional algebra on expression (17.10). We can use the pseudo-probabilities to rewrite the call's value in another form, which has a nice economic interpretation. Recall that expression (17.6) gave $\pi = [(1 + R) - D]/(U - D)$ and $(1 - \pi) = [U - (1 + R)]/(U - D)$. Using them, we can rewrite the call's arbitrage-free value (17.10) as

$$c = [\pi c_U + (1 - \pi)c_D]/(1 + R) \tag{17.11}$$

This expression is an example of the **risk-neutral valuation** procedure. The option's value is its expected payoff using the pseudo-probabilities and discounted using the mma's rate. As the legendary baseball coach Yogi Berra said, "it's like déjà vu, all over again!" The pseudo-probabilities π and $(1 - \pi)$ are back to give us a simple way of computing present values! This interpretation gives the pseudo-probabilities an alternative name: *risk-neutral probabilities*.

Using (17.8c), we can write (17.11) compactly (using $T = 1$) as

$$c = E^\pi\{\max[0, S(T) - K]\}\, e^{-rT} \tag{17.12}$$

which will be shown later to be similar to an expression used to express the BSM model in chapter 19.

EXAMPLE 17.3: Risk-Neutral Pricing of European Options in a Single-Period Binomial Model

- Consider the data from Example 17.2. The model starts at date 0 (time 0) and ends at date 1 (time T).
- Three securities trade:
  - YBM's stock price S is $100 today. The up factor U is 1.2000 and the down factor D is 0.9025.[5]
  - A dollar invested in the mma earns $r = 5$ percent per year and gives a dollar return of $(1 + R) = e^{rT} = e^{0.05 \times 1} = \$1.0513$ in one year.
  - As the strike price K is $110, the option prices at maturity are $c_U = \max[120 - 110, 0] = 10.00$ and $p_U = \max[110 - 120, 0] = 0$ when the stock goes up to $120.00 and $c_D = \max[90.25 - 110, 0] = 0$ and $p_D = \max[110 - 90.25, 0] = 19.75$ when the stock goes down to $90.25.
- Expression (17.5) gives the pseudo-probability of an up movement $\pi = [(1 + R) - D]/(U - D) = 0.5001$.
- The risk-neutral pricing equation (17.9) gives today's option prices:

$$c = [\pi c_U + (1 - \pi)c_D]/(1 + R) = \$4.76$$
$$p = [\pi p_U + (1 - \pi)p_D]/(1 + R) = \$9.39$$

These are the same prices that we got in Example 17.2.

[5] We derive them by using $\sigma = 0.142470$ in Jarrow–Rudd specification (see Extension 18.1).

Actual versus Pseudo-probabilities

We noted that the pseudo-probabilities (π and $[1 - \pi]$) for up and down movement in the stock prices, respectively, differ from the actual probabilities (q and $[1 - q]$). But how are they related?

Because the two sets of probabilities denote positive fractions, we can link them by introducing two positive terms ϕ_U and ϕ_D that denote an adjustment for risk:

$$\pi = \phi_U q \tag{17.13a}$$

$$(1 - \pi) = \phi_D(1 - q) \tag{17.13b}$$

The appendix to this chapter shows why ϕ_U and ϕ_D are an adjustment for risk. The intuition is simple. To compute present values, it is well known that one can take expected future values (using the actual probabilities) and discount to the present using a *risk-adjusted rate*. The larger the risk, the larger is the risk-adjusted discount rate. However, if one uses the pseudo-probabilities instead to compute a present value as in the risk-neutral valuation expression (17.11), then the discount rate becomes the riskless rate. Because risk-neutral valuation does not adjust the discount rate for risk, to get the same present value, the adjustment for risk must occur in the use of the pseudo-probabilities (as distinct from the actual probabilities). This is indeed the case. Building on this insight, the appendix also discusses how these two sets of probabilities and the risk premium can be estimated using market data.

We note that each set of probabilities has its own use: the actual probabilities contribute (in conjunction with historical data) to the estimation of the volatility, while the pseudo-probabilities (which we manufacture by using the risk-free interest rate, the length of a time interval, and the volatility; see Extension 18.1) are used for computing option prices. These actual and pseudo-probabilities will stay with us in the chapters that follow.

Next, we combine the different components that we have introduced to see the big picture with the help of the "Trick."

Robert Merton's "Trick"

In the early days of options pricing, Robert Merton used to give the intuition of risk-neutral valuation to MIT students with an argument that he called the "Trick." He explained that one could consider two worlds: the *real world* and a *pseudo-world* (see Figure 17.6). Because most people abhor risk, we assume that the investors in the real world are *risk averse* but that those in the pseudo-world are *risk neutral*.[6] The same securities, (1) a mma, (2) a stock, and (3) an option, trade in both worlds and evolve randomly across time. An investment of a dollar in the mma grows to $(1 + R)$ dollars at the end of a period in both worlds. The stock takes the same time 0 and time 1 values in both worlds. However, the probabilities of going up and down, which are given by the pseudo-probabilities in the pseudo-world and the actual probabilities in the real world, are different.

In the risk-neutral world, the stock's expected return must equal the expected return of the mma. This happens because risk does not matter. In addition, the call option's return must also equal that of the mma. This implies that the call's value must equal its discounted expected value using π, which is the risk-neutral valuation expression (17.11).

In the actual world, however, risk does matter in valuation. The **Trick** results from creating a riskless portfolio consisting of a long call and short stock by using the option's delta, as in the synthetic call. This hedged long call portfolio, being riskless, will have the same value in both worlds. Hence, the option's price (which is extracted from the cost of constructing the synthetic call) must be the same in both worlds as well! The "valuation" Trick is to move from the real world to the pseudo-world, where things are tractable, price the option there, and bring that price back to the real world.

Risk-neutral valuation gets its name because we compute an expected payoff in an otherwise identical economy in which traders are risk neutral and they "believe" in the pseudo-probabilities and not in the actual ones. But remember that this is a hypothetical economy, a trick used for valuation, and does not represent the real world. In the real world, most investors are risk averse.

---

[6] How you view risk is important in economic analysis. In our Example 17.1, the expected payoff from the lottery was $1. A **risk-neutral** trader focuses only on the expected $1 payoff and does not bother about risk. A **risk-averse** trader prefers a sure dollar over any risky lottery that expects to pay the same, while the opposite holds for a **risk-lover** trader. Modeling the last two types of traders is a complex task, and the economists use utility functions for that purpose.

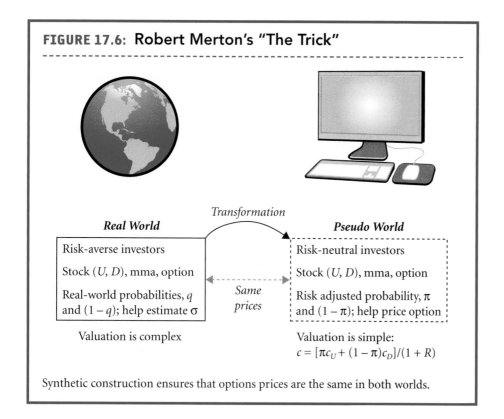

FIGURE 17.6: Robert Merton's "The Trick"

Transformation

Real World

| Risk-averse investors |
| Stock (U, D), mma, option |
| Real-world probabilities, q and $(1 - q)$; help estimate σ |

Valuation is complex

Same prices

Pseudo World

| Risk-neutral investors |
| Stock (U, D), mma, option |
| Risk adjusted probability, π and $(1 - \pi)$; help price option |

Valuation is simple:
$$c = [\pi c_U + (1 - \pi)c_D]/(1 + R)$$

Synthetic construction ensures that options prices are the same in both worlds.

17.7 | Summary

1. In 1973, Fischer Black, Myron Scholes, and Robert Merton revolutionized the field of derivatives pricing by publishing the BSM model. Since 1973, options pricing developed along four, somewhat interlinked directions: (1) improving the BSM model and using it for different underlyings, (2) developing models that allow for random interest rates, (3) putting derivatives pricing on a rigorous mathematical foundation, and (4) using computational methods, including the binomial framework.

2. The binomial model has several advantages: (1) it is a great teaching aid that gives a simple, intuitive introduction to options pricing, (2) it can be repeated to build a multiperiod tree, which gives prices that closely approximate the BSM model, (3) it utilizes martingale pricing, the paramount technique of derivatives valuation, and (4) it is a versatile model that prices standard European and American options and other derivatives.

3. The binomial OPM makes some key assumptions: no market frictions, no credit risk, competitive and well-functioning markets, no interest rate uncertainty, no intermediate cash flows, and no arbitrage. In addition, it assumes that the underlying trades at discrete time intervals and follows a binomial process.

4. The OPM constructs a synthetic option that replicates a traded option's payoff. Next, if no arbitrage opportunities exist, the two must have the same value. An option's arbitrage-free price is the cost of constructing the synthetic option.

5. The binomial OPM is set up as follows:
   - Three securities trade: a stock, a riskless mma, and a European (call or put) option.
   - The stock price goes up and down by the factors of U or D, respectively.
   - A dollar invested in the mma gives a dollar return of $(1 + R)$ after one period.
   - As the strike price is given, the option's payoffs at maturity are determined by the stock prices on the tree. Solve for the option price by the formula

$$\text{Option price} = [\pi \times (\text{Option payoff})_{\text{UP}} + (1 - \pi) \times (\text{Option payoff})_{\text{DOWN}}]/(1 + R)$$

   where $\pi = [(1 + R) - D]/(U - D)$ is the pseudo-probability of an up movement, and option payoffs "up" and "down" are considered at the up and down nodes.
   - The method of computing the expected payoff with pseudo-probabilities and discounting with the mma's value is known as risk-neutral valuation.

17.8 | Appendix

Proving the No-Arbitrage Argument

The no-arbitrage condition $U > (1 + R) > D$ proves useful in many contexts.

1. *Single-period binomial model:* $U > (1 + R) > D$ ("*Bounded Dollar Return*"): This is a necessary and sufficient condition for no arbitrage in a single-period tree. This is the result proven in this extension.

2. *Multiperiod binomial model:* This result must hold at every node in the multiperiod binomial tree.

3. *Binomial interest rate derivatives pricing model:* A generalized version of this result is required for pricing interest rate derivatives in a binomial framework: if U, $(1 + R)$, and D depend on the node in the tree, then the bounded dollar return condition must hold for all nodes (see Jarrow 2002b).

4. *Pseudo-probabilities:* We will soon see that this condition is intimately connected with the existence of pseudo-probabilities (or equivalent martingale probabilities or risk-neutral probabilities) in binomial models.

Thus the condition that we establish is linked to the core ideas at the heart of options pricing. Next, we prove our result in two steps:

- First, we show that a violation of $U > (1 + R) > D$ leads to arbitrage profits, which means that this is a necessary condition for no arbitrage.

- Next, we show that arbitrage profits lead to a violation of $U > (1 + R) > D$, which means that this is a sufficient condition for no arbitrage.

RESULT 1 (APPENDIX)
- -
No-Arbitrage Condition

The condition $U > (1 + R) > D$ is equivalent to no arbitrage.

PROOF OF PART I: NO ARBITRAGE IMPLIES $U > (1 + R) > D$. Assume the condition $U > (1 + R) > D$ fails. We show that this gives arbitrage profits. A violation of $U > (1 + R) > D$ can happen in one of two ways—either $(1 + R)$ is to the left side of $U > D$ (i.e., $[1 + R] \geq U > D$) or to its right (i.e., $U > D \geq [1 + R]$).

- Suppose $(1 + R) \geq U > D$. This makes the mma a better investment than the stock, irrespective of the stock's going up or down. Suppose the stock price is $100 today. Short sell the stock and invest the 100 proceeds in the mma. At the end of the period, your arbitrage profit is $100[(1 + R) - U] \geq 0$ if the stock goes up or $100[(1 + R) - D] > 0$ if the stock goes down. This is an arbitrage strategy.

- Suppose $U > D \geq (1 + R)$. This makes the mma an inferior investment to the stock. Borrow at the risk-free rate by short selling the mma, invest the proceeds in the stock, and collect arbitrage profits.

PROOF OF PART II: $U > (1 + R) > D$ IMPLIES NO ARBITRAGE. Assume that there is arbitrage. We show that this leads to a violation of $U > (1 + R) > D$. Recall from chapter 6 that arbitrage can be expressed as a costless strategy that nonetheless pays something in the future. With two assets, a stock, and a mma, how would you obtain a zero-investment portfolio? Obviously, you cannot buy or sell both assets simultaneously (how would you finance such trades?). You must buy one asset and short the other. However, you cannot make arbitrage profits if $U > (1 + R) > D$ holds. Why? Because in one of the up or down nodes, the payoff to the portfolio will be negative.

To see this, suppose that you buy the stock and short the mma obtaining a zero initial investment portfolio. The payoff at time 1 if you go up is $U - (1 + R) > 0$. The payoff if you go down at time 1 is $D - (1 + R) < 0$. This portfolio is not an arbitrage opportunity. Conversely, if you short the stock and long the mma, the zero initial investment portfolio has a negative payoff in the up node and a positive payoff in the down node. This zero investment portfolio is also not an arbitrage opportunity. Hence the only way you can make arbitrage profits is when $U > (1 + R) > D$ fails to hold.

The Probabilities and Risk Premium

RELATING ACTUAL AND PSEUDO-PROBABILITIES Let us further explore the concepts of the actual probabilities $(q, 1 - q)$ and the pseudo-probabilities $(\pi, 1 - \pi)$ in the context of our single-period model and compute the risk premium that connects them.

First, the probabilities must agree on zero-probability events. If one of the actual probabilities is zero, the stock price tree will fail to branch out and the stock becomes a riskless asset. The condition $q > 0$ if and only if $\pi > 0$ prevents this collapse.

Next, recall that we linked the pseudo- and actual probabilities by (17.13a) and (17.13b):

$$\pi = \phi_U q \tag{1a}$$

$$(1 - \pi) = \phi_D (1 - q) \tag{1b}$$

where ϕ_U and ϕ_D are positive numbers that adjust for risk. You can write them as two values taken by the random variable $\tilde{\phi}$. To summarize, today's stock price is S, and the parameters take on the following values after one period:

$$S(1) = \begin{cases} US \text{ is associated with } q > 0, \pi > 0, \text{ and } \tilde{\phi} = \phi_U \\ DS \text{ corresponds to } (1 - q) > 0, (1 - \pi) > 0, \text{ and } \tilde{\phi} = \phi_D \end{cases}$$

It follows from this definition that the expectation of the random variable $\tilde{\phi}$ *computed using the actual probabilities* is given by

$$E(\tilde{\phi}) \equiv \phi_U q + \phi_D (1 - q) = \pi + (1 - \pi) = 1 \tag{2}$$

THE RISK PREMIUM Expression (17.5) allows us to write the present value of the stock price at time 0 as the discounted expected payoffs using the pseudo-probabilities:

$$S = \frac{\pi US + (1 - \pi)DS}{1 + R} \tag{3}$$

Using (1a) and (1b), we rewrite this as

$$S = \frac{q(\phi_U US) + (1 - q)(\phi_D DS)}{1 + R} \tag{4}$$

Notice that we are adjusting for risk via the cash flows in the numerator. This contrasts with the traditional way of computing a present value. The traditional method is to adjust the denominator. You may have taken courses in capital budgeting or project evaluation, in which you learned to compute the **net present value** by discounting risky cash flows, positive or negative, with a risk-adjusted discount rate.

Interestingly, π and q are related by a risk premium. Using algebra and statistics, we show that the risk premium is given by $\text{cov}(-\tilde{\phi}, S(1)/S)$. To establish this, first, note from (4) that we have

$$S = \frac{E(\tilde{\phi}S(1))}{1 + R}$$

$$\text{or } 1 + R = \frac{E(\tilde{\phi}S(1))}{S} \tag{5}$$

where $E(.)$ denotes the expectation computed by using the actual probabilities q and $(1 - q)$.

A familiar result in statistics (for two random variables x and y, $\text{cov}[x, y] = E[xy] - E[x]E[y]$) gives

$$\text{cov}(\tilde{\phi}, S(1)) = E(\tilde{\phi}S(1)) - E(\tilde{\phi}) E(S(1)) \tag{6}$$

Using (2) and transferring the last expression to the left-side, we get

$$\text{cov}(\tilde{\phi}, S(1)) + E(S(1)) = E(\tilde{\phi} \, S(1)) \tag{7}$$

We can write (5) using (7) and another result from statistics $[\text{cov}(ax, y) = a\text{cov}(x, y)]$ as

$$1 + R = \frac{E(\tilde{\phi}S(1))}{S} = \text{cov}\left(\tilde{\phi}, \frac{S(1)}{S}\right) + \frac{E(S(1))}{S} \tag{8}$$

Rearrangement of expression (8) gives

$$\frac{E(S(1))}{S} = 1 + R - \text{cov}\left(\tilde{\phi}, \frac{S(1)}{S}\right) = 1 + R + \text{cov}\left(-\tilde{\phi}, \frac{S(1)}{S}\right)$$

$$\text{or } S = \frac{E(S(1))}{\left[1 + R + \text{cov}\left(-\tilde{\phi}, \frac{S(1)}{S}\right)\right]} \tag{9}$$

We rewrite expression (9) as the following result.

> **RESULT 2 (APPENDIX)**
> --
> ## The Risk Premium Linking Actual and Pseudo-probabilities
>
> In a single-period model, the actual and pseudo-probabilities are linked by a risk premium $\operatorname{cov}(-\tilde{\phi}, S(1)/S)$, which is given in the following expression:
>
> $$S = \frac{q(US) + (1-q)DS}{1 + R + \operatorname{cov}\left(-\tilde{\phi}, \dfrac{S(1)}{S}\right)} \qquad (10)$$
>
> where $\operatorname{cov}(\ ,\ )$ is the covariance operator.

Thus the risk premium is $\operatorname{cov}(-\tilde{\phi}, S(1)/S)$. As shown, the risk premium depends explicitly on the pseudo-probabilities, proving they give an adjustment for risk. The risk premium can be explicitly derived in an equilibrium model. **Equilibrium models** (such as the capital asset pricing model) require the equality of demand and supply, the presence of utility functions and endowments, which determine risk premium (defined as the expected risky return less the risk-free rate). By contrast, **arbitrage models** (like our options pricing models) do not need such features and use only the no-arbitrage condition to derive the results. Notice that the difference in the two approaches to computing present values is that we only need to use arbitrage pricing for expression (3), but for expression (10), we need to compute both ϕ_U and ϕ_D, which requires an equilibrium model.

ESTIMATING PROBABILITIES How would you compute the probabilities? As noted before, the computation of the pseudo-probabilities $(\pi, 1-\pi)$ is given in expression (17.6). The actual probabilities can be computed using historical data and statistics for a single-period binomial distribution. First, using historical data, estimate the expected return $\hat{E}(\text{return})$; then set it equal to the theory's expected return, $\hat{E}(\text{return}) = qU + (1-q)D$, and solve for q. Remember that this is a toy model, and although we have shown how to solve for q, the estimation issues become more involved in the case of more complex models—but they use the same ideas as shown here!

17.9 | Cases

Leland O'Brien Rubinstein Associates Inc.: Portfolio Insurance (Harvard Business School Case 294061-PDF-ENG). The case studies the rise and fall of Leland O'Brien Rubinstein Associates' portfolio insurance selling business.

Leland O'Brien Rubinstein Associates Inc.: SuperTrust (Harvard Business School Case 294050-PDF-ENG). The case examines Leland O'Brien Rubinstein Associates' attempts to rebuild itself after the 1987 stock market crash by creating new products to meet the unsatisfied needs of equity investors.

Tata Steel Limited: Convertible Alternative Reference Securities (B) (Richard Ivey School of Business Foundation Case 910N32-PDF-ENG, Harvard Business Publishing). The case considers valuation of a convertible bond offering by a global top ten steel producer.

17.10 | Questions and Problems

17.1. Why is the binomial model a useful technique for approximating options prices from the Black–Scholes–Merton model? Describe some applications and uses of this model.

17.2. How is the no-arbitrage principle used in the binomial model to find options prices?

17.3. In the binomial options pricing model, it is assumed that the stock price follows a binomial process.

  a. Is this a reasonable description of the actual stock price process?

  b. If not, why should one study this model?

17.4. a. In the binomial options pricing model, what assumptions are made about dividends and interest rates?

  b. In the binomial stock price tree, what restrictions are needed on the up and down factors, relative to the risk-free rate, to avoid arbitrage? Explain.

17.5. In the binomial options pricing model, what is the hedge ratio?

17.6. a. In the binomial options pricing model, what are the pseudo-probabilities?

  b. In the binomial options pricing model, what does risk-neutral valuation mean? Explain.

17.7. a. When pricing an option using risk-neutral valuation, one is assuming that all investors are risk neutral. Hence, if one believes that investors are risk averse, risk-neutral valuation cannot be used. True or false? Explain your answer.

  b. Explain Robert Merton's "Trick" in the context of options pricing.

The next eight questions are based on the following data for a single-period binomial model:

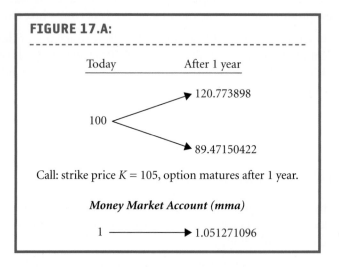

FIGURE 17.A:

	Today	After 1 year

100 →
  120.773898
  89.47150422

Call: strike price $K = 105$, option matures after 1 year.

Money Market Account (mma)

1 ⟶ 1.051271096

Note:

In this problem:

The up factor U is $US/S = 120.773898/100 = 1.2077$.

The down factor D is $DS/S = 89.471504/100 = 0.8947$.

Dollar return $1 + R = 1.0513$.

We report numbers to four places and the final answer to two places after the decimal point although calculations consider ten places after the decimal point.

17.8. a. Given the preceding data, set up a perfect hedge and compute the call option's value.

   b. What is the hedge ratio? What does it signify?

17.9. a. What are the pseudo-probabilities?

   b. Show that the stock price is its discounted expected value using these pseudo-probabilities.

17.10. Compute the call option's value using risk-neutral valuation.

17.11. Suppose the market price of the call option is $6. Is there an arbitrage opportunity? Show how you can take advantage of this price to make arbitrage profits.

17.12. a. Set up a perfect hedge and compute the put option's value. Let the put have the same strike price $K = \$105$.

b. What is the hedge ratio? What does it signify?

17.13. Compute the put option's value using risk-neutral valuation.

17.14. Using the data from questions 17.8 and 17.11, verify that put–call parity holds.

17.15. For the data in question 17.13, suppose the market price of the put option is $3. Is there an arbitrage opportunity? Explain how one would trade to exploit this arbitrage.

The next four questions are based on the following data for a single-period binomial model:

- A stock's price S is $50. After six months, it either goes up by the factor $U = 1.22095341$ or it goes down by the factor $D = 0.79881010$.

- Options mature after $T = 0.5$ year and have strike price $K = \$45$.

- A dollar invested in the money market account earns continuously compounded risk-free interest at 2 percent per year.

17.16. Compute the call's value.

17.17. Suppose the market price of the call option is $5. Is there an arbitrage opportunity? Explain how one would trade to exploit this arbitrage.

17.18. Consider the following exotic option whose payoff at expiration is given by the stock price squared less a strike price if it has a positive value, zero otherwise:

$$\max[S(1)^2 - K, 0]$$

Assuming that the strike price K is $2,500, determine the value of this exotic option under the assumption of no-arbitrage. If the market price of the call is $600, how would you trade to exploit this arbitrage opportunity?

17.19. Consider the following exotic option whose payoff at maturity is given by the square root of the stock price less the strike price if it has a positive value, zero otherwise:

$$\max\left[\sqrt{S(1)} - K, 0\right]$$

Assuming that the strike price K is $7, determine the value of this exotic option under the assumption of no-arbitrage. If the market price of the call is $0.10, how would you trade to exploit this arbitrage opportunity?

17.20. (Microsoft Excel) Implied Volatility

Consider the following data for computing option prices given to you by your professor.

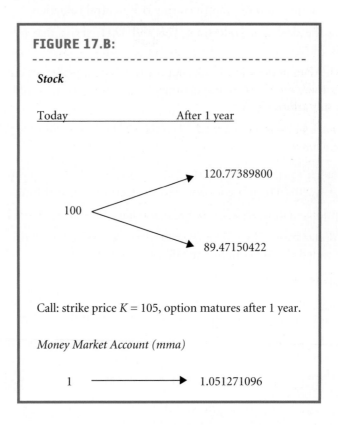

FIGURE 17.B:

- -

Stock

Today | After 1 year

120.77389800

100

89.47150422

Call: strike price $K = 105$, option matures after 1 year.

Money Market Account (mma)

1 ⟶ 1.051271096

You want to know how this data was generated. The professor, when asked, apologizes and says, "I used a Jarrow-Rudd approximation but I lost the data. You are an Excel expert—why don't you use 'Goal Seek' and determine what the volatility is?"

18

Multiperiod Binomial Model

18.1   Introduction

Not too many years back, a large US consulting company valued some options for a client. Two groups within the company were given the job. One of them used the celebrated Black–Scholes–Merton (BSM) option pricing model (OPM), which gives a neat analytical solution. This team argued that the BSM model is useful because a formula enables the computation of changes in the option price in response to changes in the stock price (later, you will see how this helps traders to hedge and manage an options portfolio). The rival group used a multiperiod binomial OPM with thirty time periods and thirty-one branches in an Excel spreadsheet. They argued that the binomial model is easier for clients to understand and that it gives prices close to the BSM values. Both claims are correct, yet ease of understanding carried the day.

This chapter extends the binomial model to a multiperiod setting and shows how to set the parameters to get prices that closely approximate the BSM. First, we develop a two-period binomial OPM repeating concepts and methods used earlier. Risk-neutral valuation, when generalized, takes us to the multiperiod model. We also show the versatility of this numerical approximation technique when it is used to price American options and for including dividends. Finally, we discuss setting up the binomial model in a spreadsheet program like Microsoft Excel.

18.2   Toward a Multiperiod Binomial Option Pricing Model

To construct the multiperiod binomial OPM, we first need to understand the assumed stock price process.

The Stock Price Evolution

Figure 18.1 shows how a stock price path looks under the binomial assumption. The first figure shows the path in the single-period binomial model, which is the model from chapter 17. It's a line parallel to the horizontal axis. Here it corresponds to the value US. Alternatively, it could have taken the value DS. In looking at this graph, one can easily reject the single-period model as a good approximation over, say, a one-year horizon when compared to the actual stock price path given in the next figure.

The next figure also shows the stock price path in a multiperiod binomial setting. You can still reject this evolution just by observation, but what happens if these periods shrink and become really small? We have superimposed a realistic looking stock price path on this graph. When the time steps become small, the multiperiod binomial price process approximates this actual price path quite well! Here the multiperiod binomial model may not be so easily rejected. In fact, choosing the actual probability of going up q, the up factor U, and the down factor D appropriately, the multiperiod binomial evolution approaches the lognormal distribution that we use in the next chapter to obtain the BSM model.

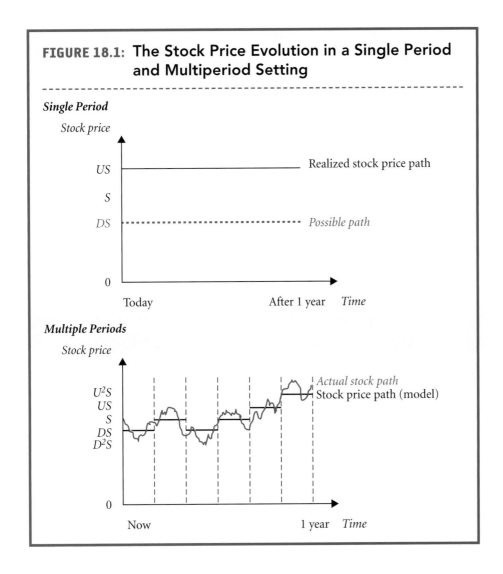

FIGURE 18.1: **The Stock Price Evolution in a Single Period and Multiperiod Setting**

Binomial Option Price Data

Our examples will use the binomial option pricing data (BOP data!) for Your Beloved Machines Corp. (YBM), which are the same data used in Example 17.2 in the last chapter.

- YBM's current stock price S is $100.

- We consider a European call on YBM with strike price $K = \$110$ and maturity time $T = 1$ year.

- The model starts today (time 0) and ends after one year at time $T = 1$.

- The stock price return volatility σ is 0.142470.

- The number of periods n varies; it can be 1, 2, 3, or more. If n is 2, we divide the time to maturity T into two periods of length $\Delta t = T/n = 0.5$ year each. If n is 3, then $\Delta t = 1/3 = 0.3333$ year, and so on.

- We let the continuously compounded risk-free interest rate r be 5 percent per year. In the one-period model, the dollar return $1 + R = e^{0.05} = \$1.0513$ after one year. In the two-period model, the dollar return $1 + R = e^{r\Delta t} = e^{0.05 \times 0.5} = \$1.0253$ after one period and $(1 + R)^2 = 1.0253^2 = \$1.0513$ after two periods—at year's end. This is a benefit of continuous compounding. No matter how you slice and dice the time intervals, your investment still grows by the same amount over a year. Recall that all of our computations are performed to 16 decimal place accuracy, although for clarity in exposition, we report rounded numbers up to either 2 or 4 decimal places.

The Stock Price Tree

The next step is to price options in a two-period binomial model. Example 18.1 presents the stock price tree and the money market account used for options pricing.

EXAMPLE 18.1: A Stock Price Tree and Option Prices at Maturity

- As before, a stock, a money market account, and a European call option trade. We use the BOP data. The model has three dates: today is the starting date (time 0), six months later is date 1, and the maturity is date 2 (time $T = 1$ year), when the call expires. As the number of periods n is 2, there are two time periods of length $\Delta t = T/n = 0.5$ years each.

- The asset price evolution is shown in Figure 18.2. The dollar return is $1 + R = \$1.0253$ after one period. YBM's stock price evolves according to a multiplicative binomial model. From any node in the binomial tree, the next period's stock price is obtained by either multiplying the current stock price by the up factor U or by the down factor D. We compute these factors using specification 1 in Table 18.1 (see Extension 18.1): $U = 1.1282$ and $D = 0.9224$.
  - Starting from a price of $S = \$100$ at date 0, the stock can either go up to $US = 1.1282 \times 100 = \$112.82$ or down to $DS = \$92.24$ at the end of the first period.
  - If the stock price is US at date 1, then it either goes up to $U(US)$ or down to $D(US)$ at date 2. If it has a value of DS at date 1, then it subsequently goes up to $U(DS)$ or down to $D(DS)$. Hence

$$U(US) = 1.1282 \times 112.82 = 127.29$$
$$D(US) = 0.9224 \times 112.82 = 104.07 = U(DS)$$
$$D(DS) = 0.9224 \times 92.24 = 85.08$$

  - Notice that the "up and then down" dotted path combines with the "down and then up" dashed route because $D(US) = U(DS)$. The branches combine because we use a multiplicative model. This feature is very useful when there are many periods. For example, if the branches recombine, a two-period model would have three instead of four separate nodes. However, in a 10-period model, there would be $10 + 1 = 11$ separate nodes in a recombining tree but $2^{10} = 1,024$ separate nodes if the branches do not recombine.
  - A generalization of the result $(U > 1 + R > D)$ of chapter 17 is essential to make the tree arbitrage-free. We assume that this condition holds at every node in the tree.

- The actual probability of the stock going up is $q = 3/4$ and that of YBM going down is $(1 - q) = 1/4$. Multiplying the probabilities together gives the probability of two up movements as $q^2 = 9/16$, an up and a down movement as $2q(1 - q) = 3/8$, and two down movements as $(1 - q)^2 = 1/16$.

- You can easily compute the options prices at date 2.
  - The call's value at maturity is given by $\max[0, S(2) - K]$. Consider the topmost node in Figure 18.2. The stock price there is U^2S. Thus when the stock goes "up and then up," the call value at time 2 is $c(2)_{UP,UP} \equiv c_{UU} = \max(U^2S - K, 0)$. Note that "$UU$" appears as a subscript in the call price. Also note that we drop "(2)" to reduce clutter. The call has a strike price $K = \$110$. Hence $c_{UU} = \max(127.29 - 110, 0) = 17.29$. The call finishes out-of-the-money at the other two nodes on date 2, so $c(2)_{UP,DOWN} \equiv c_{UD} = 0$ and $c(2)_{DOWN,DOWN} \equiv c_{DD} = 0$.
  - The put's value at date 2 is $\max[K - S(2), 0]$. Using this formula, $p_{UU} = 0$, $p_{UD} = 5.93$, and $p_{DD} = 24.92$.

18.3 | A Two-Period Binomial Model

We will utilize the previous data to compute European options prices using a technique called *backward induction*.

Backward Induction

In Sir Arthur Conan Doyle's first novel *A Study in Scarlet* (1887), Sherlock Holmes made a classic comment about his crime detection technique: "In solving a problem of this sort, the grand thing is to be able to reason backward. That is a very useful accomplishment, and a very easy one, but people do not practise it much." Interestingly the approach used by Sherlock Holmes is called **backward induction**, a mathematical technique where one starts at the end and then solves a problem by working backward through time. We use it to solve the multiperiod binomial option pricing. The steps are as follows:

- Create the binomial stock price tree by repeatedly attaching the single-period structure to the end of each node until the tree reaches the option's maturity date.

- Starting at the last date in the tree, given the strike price, you can easily compute the option's values on the expiration date for all possible final nodes.

- At the end of the last period, consider the option values ordered from the top node to the bottom node. Select the top two option values and apply the risk-neutral pricing formula to get the topmost option price at the previous date. Next, move down one node at the final time, and repeat this computation for the next two option values. Continue moving down the final nodes of the tree in this fashion, until the bottommost node is reached. When reached, this process generates all the option prices at the beginning of the last period from the top to the bottom of the tree.

- Step back one time step (toward date 0), and compute the option values at the beginning of the current period, using the procedure just described. Continue doing this period by period, working backward through time. Eventually you come to today and then the process ends. The solution is today's option price.

FIGURE 18.2: Two-Period Binomial Model for Pricing a European Option

Numerical Example

Stock Today	Stock 6 months	Stock 1 year	Call 1 year	Put 1 year	Pseudo Prob 1 year	Actual Prob 1 year
		127.29	17.29	0	0.25	9/16
	112.82					
100.00		104.07	0	5.93	0.50	6/16
	92.24					
		85.08	0	24.92	0.25	1/16

Two-Period Model

Stock Date 0	Stock Date 1	Stock Date 2	Call Date 2	Put Date 2	Pseudo Prob Date 2	Actual Prob Date 2
		U^2S	c_{UU}	p_{UU}	π^2	q^2
	US					
S		UDS	c_{UD}	p_{UD}	$2\pi(1-\pi)$	$2q(1-q)$
	DS					
		D^2S	c_{DD}	p_{DD}	$(1-\pi)^2$	$(1-q)^2$

Money Market Account (mma)

Date 0	Date 1	Date 2
1	1.0253	1.0513
	1	1.0253

Today	6 months	1 year
1	$1+R$	$(1+R)^2$

Option Pricing via Synthetic Construction (Method 1)

This section uses data from Example 18.1 to demonstrate how to price options in a two-period binomial framework. We begin by setting up a dynamic hedge using the stock and a money market account to replicate the call's value. Dynamic hedging is the extension of our synthetic construction to a multiperiod setting.

We use a **dynamic, self-financing trading strategy** to construct a portfolio that replicates the traded option's payoffs. This portfolio is **dynamic** because it changes over the multiple periods, and it is **self-financing** because there are no net cash flows at intermediate dates. When no arbitrage is allowed, the cost of constructing this synthetic option must equal the price of the traded option.

EXAMPLE 18.2: Pricing a Call via Synthetic Construction

- When solving the model, like Sherlock Holmes, we have to work backward from the end. Inspired by the example, we create at date 1 (one date before the last date) a portfolio $V(1) \equiv m(1)S(1) + b(1)$ with $m(1)$ shares of the stock worth $S(1)$ and $b(1)$ units of the money market account priced $1 each. This portfolio is constructed to replicate the option's values at date 2. It is the synthetic call option. Its cost of construction must equal the traded call value at date 1, or else arbitrage opportunities arise.

- We have to do the replication exercise twice: once when the stock goes up to US and once more when it goes down to DS. In each case, we have to solve two equations in two unknowns to find the share holdings $m(1)$, $b(1)$.

- We use the same data as in Example 18.1 (see Figure 18.2 for a summary of this information) to illustrate this method. To reduce clutter, we use U and D in the subscripts instead of UP and DOWN, for example, $V(2)_{UP,UP}$ is expressed as $V(2)_{UU}$. At date 2, when the stock is at US ($= 112.82$) on date 1,

$$\text{In the ``up, up'' state,} \qquad V(2)_{UU} = m(1)U^2S + b(1)(1+R) = c_{UU}$$
$$\text{In the ``up, down'' state,} \qquad V(2)_{UD} = m(1)UDS + b(1)(1+R) = c_{UD}$$

Solving these equations, we get

$$m(1)_U = (c_{UU} - c_{UD})/(U^2S - UDS) = 17.29/(127.29 - 104.07) = 0.7445$$
$$b(1)_U = (Uc_{UD} - Dc_{UU})/[(U-D)(1+R)]$$
$$= -(0.9224 \times 17.29)/[(1.1282 - 0.9224)1.0253]$$
$$= -75.57 \tag{18.1}$$

Thus the cost of constructing the synthetic call at date 1 in the up state is $V(1)_U = m(1)_U US + b(1)$ $= 8.4345 = \$8.43$. To rule out arbitrage, this must equal the traded call's price c_U on date 1 in the up state. At date 2, when the stock is at DS ($= 92.2363$) on date 1, either solve the two equations to find that the call is worthless at date 1, or infer that if the call is sure to be worthless at date 2, then it must also be worthless at date 1. So when the stock goes down to 92.24, $m(1)_D = 0$ and $b(1)_D = 0$, giving the synthetic option a value of $c_D = 0$ at date 1 in the down state.

- Finally, let us now move back to date 0. Construct a portfolio $V(0) \equiv m(0)S(0) + b(0)$ with $m(0)$ shares of the stock worth $S(0)$ and $b(0)$ units of a money market account worth $1 each. This portfolio's share holdings are constructed to match the synthetic call prices c_U and c_D at date 1, giving two equations in two unknowns. At date 1,

$$\text{In the ``up'' state,} \qquad V(1)_U = m(0)112.82 + b(0)1.0253 = 8.43 = c_U$$
$$\text{In the ``down'' state,} \qquad V(1)_D = m(0)92.24 + b(0)1.0253 = 0 = c_D$$

Solving these equations, we get $m(0) = 0.4097$ and $b(0) = -36.8536$, so the cost of constructing the synthetic call at date 0 is

$$V(0) = m(0)S(0) + b(0) = 4.1135 = \$4.11$$

This must equal $c(0) \equiv c$, the traded call's price today. Any other quoted price will create get-rich opportunities for vigilant arbitrageurs. The numbers from this exercise are summarized in Figure 18.3.

This simple example illustrates several important features of the multiperiod binomial OPM:

- *Prices differ from the single-period model prices.* Despite using the same BOP data, the single- and two-period models give different options prices: $4.76 and $4.11, respectively. This is because the two trees aren't identical. Compare the figures to notice that the stock and the option prices have different distributions at the maturity date.

- *Self-financing.* We show next that the dynamic trading strategy is self-financing. Initiate the trading strategy at date 0 by buying 0.4097 units of the stock priced at $100 and finance this by selling 36.8536 units of the money market account worth $1 each. You still need to invest $4.11, which is the call price. Suppose the stock goes up to $112.82 after six months. Then the portfolio's value is $8.43. Liquidate this portfolio and raise funds by selling 75.57 units of the money market account for $1 each. Use the total proceeds of $84 (= $8.43 + $75.57) to buy 0.7445 units of the stock. Obviously, this transaction is self-financing. After the up node, suppose the stock goes up again to $127.29 at the end of the year. Then the portfolio's value is $(0.7445 \times 127.29 - 75.57 \times 1.0513) = \$17.29$. If the stock goes down from there to $104.07, then the portfolio value is $(0.7445 \times 104.07 - 75.57 \times 1.0513) = 0$. These payoffs are identical to the call values at the corresponding nodes in the tree at date 2. Suppose the stock goes down to $92.24 at date 1 instead. Then the call becomes worthless. No trades are necessary. The call has zero value thereafter.

- *Dynamic market completion.* Just two assets, a stock and a money market account, replicate the three option values at maturity. Note that we have **dynamically completed** the market, where the term *complete* refers to the portfolio's ability to match all possible option values at maturity.

- *A hedging interpretation.* Notice the holy grail, the hedge ratios $m(0)$, $m(1)_U$, and $m(1)_D$ in the model. They tell us how to rebalance our portfolios to synthetically construct the option values in the nodes that follow.

- *Independent of actual probabilities.* Note that the actual probabilities of the stock moving up or down do not enter the valuation procedure. As in the single-period binomial model, this is because we exactly replicate the option's payoffs at

FIGURE 18.3: The Two-Period Binomial Model for Pricing European Call Options (Numerical Values)

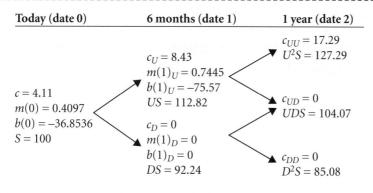

$1 becomes $1 + R = 1.0253$ after six months. Strike price $K = 110$.

every node in the tree on the expiration date. Hence the probabilities of reaching these nodes do not affect the option's values.

Repeat, Repeat: Risk-Neutral Pricing (Method 2)

Why crank out option values by solving linear equations when we can summon the power of algebra? Plug the algebraic values from expression (18.1) into the portfolio's value to get the synthetic call's value at date 1:

$$c_U = V(1) = m(1)S(1) + b(1) = \frac{c_{UU} - c_{UD}}{(U - D)US}US + \frac{Uc_{UD} - Dc_{UU}}{(U - D)(1 + R)}$$

Rearrange terms (keep R in the denominator, gather c_{UU} and c_{UD} and rewrite) to get

$$c_U = \frac{\left(\dfrac{(1 + R) - D}{U - D}\right)c_{UU} + \left(\dfrac{U - (1 + R)}{U - D}\right)c_{UD}}{1 + R} \tag{18.2}$$

Recalling Yogi Berra, "It's like déjà-vu, all over again!" Our pseudo-probabilities are back. As before, we write the pseudo-probability of going up as $\pi = [(1 + R) - D]/(U - D)$ and going down as $(1 - \pi) = [U - (1 + R)]/(U - D)$. Now you can compactly write the *binomial call OPM* as

$$c_U = [\pi c_{UU} + (1 - \pi)c_{UD}]/(1 + R) \tag{18.3}$$

One can develop similar formulas for call prices at the down node c_D and at today's date c. Moreover, replacing c with p gives the formula for pricing puts! Generalize this to get a formula for pricing European options.

RESULT 18.1

- -

A Formula for Pricing Options by Repeated Application of Risk-Neutral Pricing

$$c = [\pi \times c_U + (1 - \pi) \times c_D]/(1 + R) \tag{18.4}$$

where $\pi = [(1 + R) - D]/(U - D)$, U and D are the up and down factors, respectively, and $1 + R$ is the dollar return.
The same formula applies for puts.

The next example uses this formula.

EXAMPLE 18.3: Pricing a Call by Repeated Application of Risk-Neutral Pricing

Using the same data as in Examples 18.1 and 18.2, we get

$$\pi = (1.0253 - 0.9224)/(1.1282 - 0.9224) = \$0.50$$
$$c_U = [\pi c_{UU} + (1 - \pi)c_{UD}]/(1 + R) = (17.29 \times 0.50)/1.0253 = \$8.43$$
$$c_D = [\pi c_{UD} + (1 - \pi)c_{DD}]/(1 + R) = 0$$
$$c = [\pi c_U + (1 - \pi)c_D]/(1 + R) = (0.50 \times 8.43)/1.0253 = \$4.11 \tag{18.5}$$

which verifies today's call price.

One-Step Valuation: Prelude to the Multiperiod Model (Method 3)

For pricing European options, you can simplify further and do it all in one step. In expression (18.4), plug the expressions for c_U and c_D into the call value c and simplify to get

$$c = \frac{\pi c_U + (1 - \pi)c_D}{(1 + R)} = \frac{\pi^2 c_{UU} + 2\pi(1 - \pi)c_{UD} + (1 - \pi)^2 c_{DD}}{(1 + R)^2} \tag{18.6}$$

This is the **two-period binomial model**. The numerator computes the expected payoff using the pseudo-probabilities and the denominator discounts the cash flows. The model's description follows:

- As the pseudo-probability of going from S to US is π, and from US to U^2S is also π, the pseudo-probability of going from S to U^2S is π^2, which is the pseudo-probability of reaching c_{UU}. Similarly, the pseudo-probability of reaching UDS (which corresponds to the call price of c_{UD}) is $\pi(1-\pi)$. As there are two such paths, shown by the dotted and dashed lines in Figure 18.2, multiply by 2, giving an overall probability of $2\pi(1-\pi)$. The stock payoff D^2S (and call value c_{DD}) has the pseudo-probability $(1-\pi)^2$. These pseudo-probabilities are noted in the last column of the first figure.

- Once you have these pseudo-probabilities, compute expected payoffs by multiplying each option payoff by the pseudo-probability of reaching those nodes.

- Next, compute the overall expected payoff for the call by summing up the expected payoffs computed in the previous step.

- This gives the expected payoff at time T. Discount by the dollar return $(1+R)^2$ to get today's expected payoff.

EXAMPLE 18.4: A Two-Period Binomial Call Pricing Model

Using the pseudo-probabilities from Example 18.3 and the option payoffs from Example 18.1 in expression (18.6) gives today's call price:

$$c = (0.25 \times 17.29 + 0.50 \times 0 + 0.25 \times 0)/1.0253^2 = \$4.11$$

One can also price European puts by any one of these three methods.[1] Moreover, if you know the value of one option, you can price the other using put–call parity.

[1] For example, to replicate a put, set up a portfolio $V \equiv mS + b$, as before. Working backward with the second-period put prices $p_{UU} = 0$, $p_{UD} = \$5.93$, and $p_{DD} = \$24.92$, one gets $p_U = \$2.89$ and $p_D = \$15.05$ and, ultimately, today's put price $p = \$8.75$. Methods 2 and 3 work similarly.

EXAMPLE 18.5: European Put Pricing by Put–Call Parity

Using the BOP data and the call price from the previous example, put–call parity for European options (Result 16.1) gives the put price as

$$p = c + KB - S = 4.11 + 110 \times (1/1.0513) - 100 = \$8.75$$

18.4 # The Multiperiod Binomial Option Pricing Model

We can utilize the Binomial Theorem from mathematics to develop a generalized version of the option pricing model. Many distinguished scholars have worked on this theorem including Sir Isaac Newton, truly the first rocket scientist!

Binomial Coefficients and Pseudo-probabilities

The **binomial coefficient** (see the binomial theorem in Appendix A) provides a general formula for computing the number of ways of reaching a final payoff in the multiperiod stock price tree. The binomial coefficient $\binom{n}{j}$ (read "n choose j") gives the number of combinations of selecting j objects out of n objects:

$$\binom{n}{j} = \frac{n!}{j!(n-j)!} \tag{18.7a}$$

where the expression $n!$ (read **n-factorial**) is defined as

$$n! = n \times (n-1) \times (n-2) \times \ldots \times 2 \times 1$$
$$\text{and } 0! = 1 \tag{18.7b}$$

Because the number of up movements uniquely identifies the number of different paths reaching a particular end-period stock payoff (which automatically fixes the number of down movements), we can use the binomial coefficient to compute the number of such paths. Suppose the stock price at expiration is $U^j D^{n-j} S$. As this has j up movements and $(n-j)$ down movements, the number of paths is given by the binomial coefficient $\binom{n}{j}$. To compute the total pseudo-probability of reaching $U^j D^{n-j} S$, multiply the number of ways to reach this node by the probability of each path occurring $\pi^j (1-\pi)^{n-j}$. The product is given by

$$\left(\frac{n!}{j!(n-j)!} \right) \pi^j (1-\pi)^{n-j} \tag{18.8}$$

Next, we use this to dress up our two-period model in this binomial garb.

Recasting the Two-Period Example in the Multiperiod Framework

In the two-period binomial tree ($n=2$), the stock price reaches $U^2 S$ or UDS or $D^2 S$ at maturity. The topmost node $U^2 S$ is reached by two ups in the stock price. Using $n=2$ and $j=2$, we write the pseudo-probability of the outcome as

$$\binom{2}{2} \pi^2 (1 - \pi)^0 = \left(\frac{2!}{2!(2 - 2)!} \right) \pi^2 = \pi^2 \tag{18.9a}$$

(Note that $[1 - \pi]^0 = 1$.)

One reaches *UDS* in two ways: "up and then down" and "down and then up." Using $n = 2$ and $j = 1$, the total pseudo-probability of reaching *UDS* is

$$\binom{2}{1} \pi^1 (1 - \pi)^{2-1} = \left(\frac{2!}{1!(2 - 1)!} \right) \pi(1 - \pi) = 2\pi(1 - \pi) \tag{18.9b}$$

Two downs in a two-period tree is reached by a unique path. Using $n = 2$ and $j = 0$, the total pseudo-probability of reaching $D^2 S$ is

$$\binom{2}{0} \pi^0 (1 - \pi)^2 = \left(\frac{2!}{0!(2 - 0)!} \right) (1 - \pi)^2 = (1 - \pi)^2 \tag{18.9c}$$

One can compactly express expressions (18.9a)–(18.9c) as

$$\binom{2}{j} \pi^j (1 - \pi)^{2-j} = \left(\frac{2!}{j!(2 - j)!} \right) \pi^j (1 - \pi)^{2-j} \tag{18.9d}$$

where $j = 2$, 1, and 0, respectively.

These match the pseudo-probabilities determined earlier (for convenience, we also report these values in Figure 18.4). Recall that our two-period call valuation formula (18.6) was

$$c = \frac{\pi^2 c_{UU} + 2\pi(1 - \pi) c_{UD} + (1 - \pi)^2 c_{DD}}{(1 + R)^2}$$

Using expression (18.9a), rewrite the first expression in the numerator as

$$\pi^2 c_{UU} = \left[\binom{2}{2} \pi^2 (1 - \pi)^0 \right] \times \max(U^2 S - K, 0)$$

Notice that one can write the call payoff as $\max(0, U^j D^{2-j} S - K)$ with $j = 2$ in this particular instance.

Similarly, rewriting the other two terms in the numerator and using the summation notation yields a compact expression for the call's price:

$$c = \frac{1}{(1 + R)^2} \sum_{j=0}^{2} \left\{ \left[\binom{2}{j} \pi^j (1 - \pi)^{2-j} \right] \times \left[\max(0, U^j D^{2-j} S - K) \right] \right\} \tag{18.10}$$

FIGURE 18.4: Two-Period Binomial Model for Pricing European Options

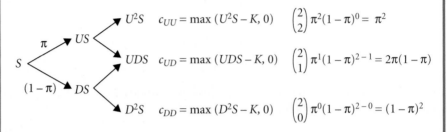

Money Market Account (mma)

Date 0	Date 1	Date 2
$1 \longrightarrow$	$1 + R \longrightarrow$	$(1 + R)^2$

The *n*-Period Binomial Option Pricing Model

Replace 2 by *n* in expression (18.10) to get the general multiperiod binomial model, which is the main result of this chapter.

RESULT 18.2

The *n*-Period Binomial Option Pricing Model

$$c = \frac{1}{(1 + R)^n} \sum_{j=0}^{n} \left\{ \left[\binom{n}{j} \pi^j (1 - \pi)^{n-j} \right] \times \right.$$

$$\left. \left[\max(0, U^j D^{n-j} S - K) \right] \right\} \qquad (18.11)$$

where *n* is the number of time periods, T is the option's maturity date, $\Delta t \equiv T/n$ is the length of each time period, $1 + R \equiv e^{r\Delta t}$ is the dollar return from the money market account for a time period, j is the numbers of up movements in *n* periods (thus $[n - j]$ is the number of down movements),

$\binom{n}{j} = \dfrac{n!}{j!(n - j)!}$ is the number of ways of choosing j "ups" out of *n* movements, π is the pseudo-probability for the up movement ($[1 - \pi]$ is the same for the down movement), U is the up factor for the stock price movement and D is the down factor, S is the initial stock price, and K is the strike price.

Replacing the call payoff by $\max(0, K - U^j D^{n-j} S)$ gives the formula for pricing a European put option.

Who but its creator would appreciate such a hideous-looking construct? In its defense, expression (18.11): (1) is a generalization of the simpler formulas introduced earlier, (2) it just uses high school algebra (of course, with some notations), and (3) it is easily programmed into a spreadsheet program such as Microsoft Excel (see the example at the chapter's end).

To reiterate, expression (18.11) generalizes our simple formula for European call pricing developed in the previous section. The first expression within parentheses uses dollar returns to discount the cash flows. Next comes the summation sign, which adds up the "option payoffs" multiplied by the "pseudo-probability of reaching those payoffs" for all possible cases. The result is the option's price!

As in the last chapter, we can rewrite Result 18.2 more abstractly to get an expression similar to the one used in the context of the BSM model (which is explained in the next chapter):

$$c = E^\pi[c(T)]e^{-rT} \tag{18.12}$$

where $E^\pi(.)$ denotes computing the expectation under the pseudo-probability π.

Note, as emphasized before, that the option price does not depend on the actual probabilities of the stock price evolution but only on the pseudo-probabilities. Extension 18.1 shows how to choose the up and down factors to obtain a model that approximates the BSM model when the time steps are small. In the limit, this approximation generates a lognormal distribution that underlies the BSM model.

You can use Result 18.2 for the one-step valuation of European options in multiperiod binomial trees. The next example demonstrates how to do this when the model has four periods.

EXAMPLE 18.6: A Four-Period Binomial Example

- This four-period example uses the same BOP data. Given the number of time periods n is 4, divide the time to maturity T into four periods of length $\Delta t = T/n = 0.25$ years each.

- Using specification 1 in Table 18.1, we get $U = 1.08458539$, $D = 0.94056717$, $\pi = 0.50001507$, and $(1 - \pi) = 0.49998493$. Moreover, $1 + R = e^{r\Delta t} = e^{0.05 \times 0.25} = \$1.0126$ after one period and $(1 + R)^4 = 1.0126^4 = \$1.0513$ after four periods.

- Using expression (18.11), we get today's European call price:

$$c = \frac{1}{(1 + R)^4}\left\{\binom{4}{4}\pi^4(1 - \pi)^0 \max(0, U^4 D^0 S - K) + \binom{4}{3}\pi^3(1 - \pi)^1 \max(0, U^3 D^1 S - K)\right\}$$

$$= \left(\frac{1}{1.0513}\right)(0.5000^4 \times 28.3742 + 4 \times 0.5000^4 \times 10)$$

$$= 4.0653 \text{ or } \$4.07$$

What happens to the option values if we keep on increasing the number of periods in our numerical example? This is explored in Table 18.2, where we generate options prices by applying specification 1 of Extension 18.1 using finer and finer time intervals. Here Table 18.2a contains some of the Excel workings (for the binomial model for $n = 1, 2, 4, 8, 16,$ and 32; the second panel is a continuation of the computations in the first panel), and Table 18.2b reports call and put prices

EXTENSION 18.1: Linking the Binomial Model to the Black–Scholes–Merton Model

The binomial model is easy to understand and simple to implement, but will it give prices that one can comfortably quote in real markets? The answer is yes! The binomial OPM can be used to approximate the BSM model. The approximation works through approximating the probability distribution for the underlying asset's price, which the BSM model assumes is a lognormal distribution. The distribution for the binomial process quickly approaches this when the parameter values are properly specified and the model is run over many small intervals. Consequently, options values from the multiperiod binomial models converge to the BSM model.

There are several ways of achieving this convergence. "The finance literature has revealed no fewer than 11 alternative versions of the binomial option pricing model for options on lognormally distributed assets," wrote Chance (2008, p. 38), who noted that the three most widely used versions are Cox et al. (1979), Rendleman and Bartter (1979), and Jarrow and Rudd (1982).

The last specification, known as the **Jarrow–Rudd binomial model**, was developed by Jarrow and Rudd (1982). It builds on Rendleman and Bartter's approach and was further modified in Jarrow and Turnbull's (1996) book. In their specification, as the time interval diminishes, the pseudo-probability approaches 0.50 (see Table 18.1).

Another specification is the **Cox–Ross–Rubinstein binomial model.** Though widely used in practice, it gives erroneous results for large time intervals or small volatilities (see Table 18.1). For both specifications, the greater the number of intervals, the better will be the approximation. One must use at least fifty periods to generate good options prices in the binomial models.

Which specification is superior? The answer is, they are all equivalent, because they all approach the same BSM model prices as n goes to infinity. Chance (2008, p. 54) concludes that the (binomial) "model is not a single model but a family of interpretations of a discrete-time process that converges to the continuous Brownian motion process [which underlies the BSM models] in the limit and accurately prices options."

TABLE 18.1: Setting Up the Factors and the Pseudo-Probabilities to Link the Binomial and BSM Models

	Specification 1 (Jarrow–Rudd)	Specification 2 (Cox–Ross–Rubinstein)
Up factor (U)	$U = e^{r\Delta t - \frac{\sigma^2}{2}\Delta t + \sigma\sqrt{\Delta t}}$	$e^{\sigma\sqrt{\Delta t}}$
Down factor (D)	$D = e^{r\Delta t - \frac{\sigma^2}{2}\Delta t - \sigma\sqrt{\Delta t}}$	$1/U$
Pseudo-probability of stock going up (π)	$\dfrac{(1+R)-D}{U-D}$	$\dfrac{(1+R)-D}{U-D}$
Pseudo-probability of stock going down ($1-\pi$)	$\dfrac{U-(1+R)}{U-D}$	$\dfrac{U-(1+R)}{U-D}$

where Δt is the length of the time interval, r is the continuously compounded annual risk-free interest rate, $1 + R = \exp(r\Delta t) \equiv e^{r\Delta t}$, and σ^2 is the variance of the continuously compounded return.

TABLE 18.2: Convergence of Binomial Option Prices to the Black–Scholes–Merton Model Values

a. Excel Workings (Binomial Model for $n = 1, 2, 4, 8, 16$, and 32)

S	K	T	n	$\Delta t = T/n$	r	1 + R	σ
100	110	1	1	1	0.05	1.0512711	0.14247
100	110	1	2	0.5	0.05	1.02531512	0.14247
100	110	1	4	0.25	0.05	1.01257845	0.14247
100	110	1	8	0.125	0.05	1.00626957	0.14247
100	110	1	16	0.0625	0.05	1.00312989	0.14247
100	110	1	32	0.03125	0.05	1.00156372	0.14247

U	D	π	$(1-\pi)$	Call	Put
1.199999511	0.90247088	0.500120656	0.499879344	$4.75727159	$9.39250829
1.128249231	0.92236346	0.500042629	0.499957371	4.113492	8.7487287
1.084585393	0.94056717	0.500015067	0.499984933	4.065304709	8.7005414
1.056912736	0.95562533	0.500005326	0.499994674	3.944816311	8.58005301
1.038843626	0.96741588	0.500001883	0.499998117	3.813430739	8.44866743
1.026783114	0.97634426	0.500000666	0.499999334	3.767810681	8.40304738

b. Options Prices

Number of Intervals	Call Option Price	Put Option Price
1	$4.757272	$9.392508
2	4.113492	8.748729
4	4.065305	8.700541
8	3.944816	8.580053
16	3.813431	8.448667
32	3.767811	8.403047
64	3.803293	8.438853
BSM model	3.783772	8.419009

for these periods (plus that for $n = 64$). The resulting values converge to the BSM model prices; however, you will have to wait until the next chapter to learn how the BSM model values are obtained.

18.5 | Extending the Binomial Model

The multiperiod binomial model is an all-purpose tool useful for pricing derivatives more complex than the options studied to this point. As such, it is useful to think of the multiperiod model as a computational procedure for valuing arbitrary derivative securities. We illustrate two extensions: (1) including dividends and (2) valuing American options.

Known Dividends

US options exchanges do not alter the strike price or make adjustments for cash dividends. Such dividends lower the value of a call but raise the value of a put. Pricing options in the presence of dividends is tricky business. We consider two relatively straightforward ways of adjusting the binomial model for known dividends.

As in chapters 3 and 11, the ex-dividend date is the cutoff date for a dividend payment, and we assume that arbitrage ensures that the ex-dividend stock price falls by the dividend (see Result 3.1). Fixed-percentage dividends are easier to model in the binomial framework because the tree still recombines. Unfortunately, fixed-dollar (not fixed-percentage) dividends are the norm among US corporations. Corporations try to hold steady both the dividend date and the dollar amount (see Extension 12.1 for a discussion of dividend policy of US companies). Example 18.7 shows how to adjust the model for both fixed-dollar and fixed-percentage dividends.

EXAMPLE 18.7: Adjusting for Known Dividends (Based on Example 18.2)

Known Dividend Date and a Percentage Dividend Rate

- In Example 18.2, assume that the stock pays a dividend of $\delta = 5$ percent just before six months. Then the stock price at time 1 needs to be adjusted to reflect this dividend. Accordingly, the revised stock prices at time 1 are

$$US(1 - \text{dividend rate}) = 112.824923(1 - 0.05) = 107.18$$
$$DS(1 - \text{dividend rate}) = 92.2363(1 - 0.05) = 87.62$$

- Proceed as before. Use these revised stock prices to create the binomial tree. Six-month as well as subsequent stock prices are multiplied by $(1 - \text{dividend rate})$. The tree recombines as before, and our option valuation technique works. Verify that the call value is $2.60 and the put value is $12.23.

Known Dividend Date and a Dollar Dividend

- Suppose that in Example 18.2, the stock pays the dividend div = $5 just before six months. In that case, compute the stock price on date 1 as US or DS as before, and then subtract $5 from it. Now create the binomial tree with these revised prices and solve for the options values as before (see Figure 18.5). Note that the tree does not recombine. There are four nodes after one year in a two-period tree (had this been a 10-period tree, you would have 1,024 final nodes!). Solve for the options values by working backward through time, and verify that the call value is $2.77 and the put value is $12.28.

Valuing American Options

American options can be easily valued in a binomial model using the following steps:

- Create a binomial stock price tree as for the European option and find the option values after n periods when the option matures.

- Using the risk-neutral valuation formula, compute (1) the European option's value at the "last but one" period (i.e., $[n - 1]$ periods) and (2) the option's payoff if it is immediately exercised. Retain the larger of these two as the American option's value and use it in future computations.

- Work backward period by period. At each node, determine whether the option is worth more alive (computed value) or dead (exercised value), and retain the larger of these two values. The procedure ends when you reach today's date. The option's value at time 0 gives the solution. By following this algorithm, you have created the American option price tree.

- Note that a by-product of the valuation is a description of whether to exercise or not at every node in the tree. Hence the valuation technique also provides the optimal exercise strategy.

- Result 16.10 of Chapter 16 tells us that an American call on a stock that pays no dividends over the option's life is never exercised early: you get more by selling the call rather than exercising it. Such an American call is equal to a European call, and they have identical binomial trees. In contrast, American put options may be exercised early, and they differ from European puts. Next, we use Examples 18.1–18.3 to create an American put option tree in Example 18.8.

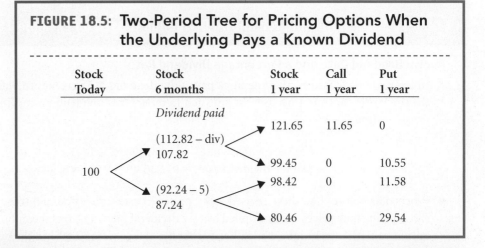

FIGURE 18.5: Two-Period Tree for Pricing Options When the Underlying Pays a Known Dividend

Stock Today	Stock 6 months	Stock 1 year	Call 1 year	Put 1 year
	Dividend paid			
		121.65	11.65	0
	(112.82 – div) 107.82			
100		99.45	0	10.55
		98.42	0	11.58
	(92.24 – 5) 87.24			
		80.46	0	29.54

EXAMPLE 18.8: American Option Pricing (Based on Examples 18.1–18.3)

- Remember that a call option on a stock that pays no dividends over the option's life is never exercised early. Consequently, the European and American call option trees are the same as in Example 18.2. You can verify this by performing the calculations based on the procedure stated earlier.

- The story is different for American put options. For convenience, the first tree in Figure 18.6 gives the European put. The second tree shows the American put.

- Six months before maturity, the European put's value in the up state is 2.8942. If the put is exercised, the payoff is

$$110 - 112.8249 = -2.8249$$

The put is worth more alive than dead—don't exercise. Retain the value 2.8942 in the American put option tree.

- Six months before maturity, the put option's value in the down state is 15.0494. If the put is exercised, the payoff is

$$\max(110 - 92.2363, 0) = 17.7637$$

Here the put is worth more dead than alive. Discard the existing value 15.0494 and replace it with 17.7637 in the tree.

- Move back to the present. For the American put, if the put is exercised, it gives

$$\max(110 - 100, 0) = 10$$

Using the American put values from time 1, we find at time 0

$$p = \frac{\pi p_U + (1 - \pi)p_D}{1 + R} = \frac{0.50 \times 2.8942 + 0.50 \times 17.7637}{1.0253} = \$10.0733$$

The last value being the largest is recorded as today's American put value, and the put is not exercised today.

FIGURE 18.6: Two-period Binomial Model for Pricing American Options

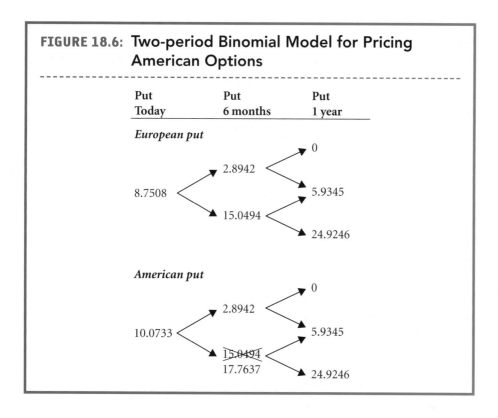

18.6 | Spreadsheet Applications

The binomial model can be implemented using spreadsheet programs like Microsoft Excel. This section demonstrates how to do this in two steps: First, we show how to solve a two-period binomial model, and second, we show how to solve a sixteen-period example.

A Two-Period Binomial Example

You can program the multiperiod binomial OPM in a Microsoft Excel workbook.

EXAMPLE 18.9: Solving Example 18.3 by Excel

Generating Inputs

- In an MS Excel worksheet, type in the following. This example uses the BOP data provided earlier in the chapter and used in Examples 18.2 and 18.3. See Figure 18.7 for the worksheet:
  - S in cell A1 and 100 in cell A2
  - K in B1 and 110 in B2
  - T in C1 and 1 in C2
  - n in D1 and 2 in D2
  - "$\Delta t = T/n$" in E1 and 0.5 in E2 (you can create Δ in Microsoft Office 2007 or later by going to the "Ribbon" at the top of the page, and then in Microsoft Excel by clicking on the tab "Insert"

and then on "Symbol," clicking on Δ, copying/cutting Δ, and pasting it into the Excel worksheet (alternatively, you can follow the same steps in Microsoft Word and copy and paste the symbol here); other Greek symbols can be similarly inserted)

- r in F1 and 0.05 in cell F2
- R in G1 and "=EXP(F2*E2)" in G2 and then hit return to get 1.025315 (you can also get this by going to the Ribbon, clicking on the tab "Formulas," clicking on "f_x Insert Function" and then choosing EXP from the menu of functions, typing (or selecting with the mouse) "F2*E2" in the Number window that will open up, and then clicking on OK).
- σ in A4 and 0.142470 in A5

■ Choose the up and down factors according to one of the specifications connecting the binomial model with the BSM model (see Extension 18.1). We use the Jarrow–Rudd specification:

- Type U in B4. For the up factor $U = \exp\left[(r - \sigma^2/2)\Delta t + \sigma\sqrt{\Delta t}\right]$, type "=EXP(((F2-(A5*A5/2))*E2)+(A5*SQRT(E2)))" in B5 and hit return to get 1.128249.
- Type D in C4. For the down factor $D = \exp\left[(r - \sigma^2/2)\Delta t - \sigma\sqrt{\Delta t}\right]$, type "=EXP(((F2-(A5*A5/2))*E2)-(A5*SQRT(E2)))" in C5 and hit return to get 0.922363.

■ Type π in D4 and then "=(G2-C5)/(B5-C5)" in D5 and hit return to get 0.500043. Type $(1 - \pi)$ in E4 and then "=1-D5" in E5 and hit return to get 0.499957.

Creating Binomial Stock Tree and Computing Options Prices and Pseudo-probabilities at Maturity

■ To create the stock tree, type the headings "Stock $(t = 0)$" in A8, "Stock $(t = 1)$" in B8, and "Stock $(t = 2)$" in C8 and then type the following expressions after "=" in each cell; follow up by hitting the return key at the end:

- type "=A2" in cell A11 and hit return to get 100
- A11*B5 in B10 to get 112.824923
- A11*C5 in B12 to get 92.236346
- B10*B5 in C9 to get 127.294633
- B10*C5 in C11 to get 104.065586
- B12*C5 in C13 to get 85.075435

■ For call prices at maturity, type the heading "Call $(t = 2)$" in D8 and then type the following after "=" in each cell and hit return at the end:

- MAX(C9-B2,0) in D9 to get 17.294633
- MAX(C11-B2,0) in D11 to get 0
- MAX(C13-B2,0) in D13 to get 0

■ For put prices at maturity, type in the label "Put $(t = 2)$" in E8 and then type the following after "=" in each cell and hit return at the end:

- MAX(0,B2-C9) in E9 to get 0
- MAX(0,B2-C11) in E11 to get 5.934414
- MAX(0,B2-C13) in E13 to get 24.924565

■ To create the pseudo-probabilities of reaching these option values at maturity, type in the label "Pseudo-probability" in F8 and then type and hit return:

- D5*D5 in F9 and hit return to get 0.2500043
- 2*D5*E5 in F11 to get 0.500000
- E5*E5 in F13 to get 0.249957

Notice that these pseudo-probabilities sum to 1.

FIGURE 18.7: Two-Period Binomial Example with Excel (Example 18.3)

	Column A	B	C	D	E	F	G
Row 1	S	K	T	n	$\Delta t = T/n$	r	R
2	100	110	1	2	0.5	0.05	1.025315
3							
4	σ	U	D	π	$(1 - \pi)$		
5	0.142470	1.128249	0.922363	0.500043	0.499957		
6							
7							
8	Stock ($t = 0$)	Stock ($t = 1$)	Stock ($t = 2$)	Call ($t = 2$)	Put ($t = 2$)	Pseudo Probability	
9			127.294633	17.294633	0.000000	0.250043	
10		112.824923					
11	100		104.065586	0.000000	5.934414	0.500000	
12		92.236346					
13			85.075435	0.000000	24.924565	0.249957	
14							
15							
16	EUROPEAN OPTION TREES (METHOD 2)						
17							
18	*Call tree*						
19	Call ($t = 0$)	Call ($t = 1$)	Call ($t = 2$)				
20			17.294633				
21		8.434532					
22	4.113492		0.000000				
23		0.000000					
24			0.000000				
25							
26	*Put tree*						
27	Put ($t = 0$)	Put ($t = 1$)	Put ($t = 2$)				
28			0				
29		2.893700					
30	8.748729		5.934414				
31		15.047745					
32			24.924565				
33							
34							
35	EUROPEAN OPTION PRICES (METHOD 3)						
36	call =	4.113492					
37	put =	8.748729					

European Call and Put Valuation (Method 2)

- Type "EUROPEAN OPTION TREES (METHOD 2)" in A16, "Call Tree" in A18
- You can create the call tree through a repeated application of expression (18.4) of Result 18.1:
  - Type in the headings "Call ($t = 0$)" in A19, "Call ($t = 1$)" in B19, and "Call ($t = 2$)" in C19.
  - Copy call values at date 2—type D9 in C20, D11 in C22, and D13 in C24 to get $c_{UU} = 17.294633$, $c_{UD} = 0$, and $c_{DD} = 0$, respectively.

- To solve for call values at date 1, type "=(D5*C20+E5*C22)/G2" in B21 and "=(D5*C22+E5*C24)/G2" in B23.
- Solve and plug in "=(D5*B21+E5*B23)/G2" in cell A22 to get today's call value 4.113492 or $4.11.

■ This completes the "call tree" that has all possible call values in the binomial tree. The two-period "put tree" is similarly created below the call tree and gives a put value of 8.748729 or $8.75.

European Call and Put Valuation (Method 3)

■ Type "EUROPEAN OPTION PRICES (METHOD 3)" in A35, "call=" in A36, and "put=" in A37. Using (18.6), we type "= (F9*D9+F11*D11+F13*D13)/(G2^2)" in B36 to get today's call value 4.113492 or $4.11.

■ Using a variant of (18.6), where calls are substituted with put values, we type "=(F9*E9+F11*E11+F13*E13)/(G2^2)" in cell B37 to get today's put value 8.748729 or $8.75.

A Sixteen-Period Example

Next we extend the preceding example to build a sixteen-period model using the same BOP data.

EXAMPLE 18.10: A Sixteen-Period Example (Excel Application)

■ We use the BOP data: S is $100, K is $110, T is 1 year, r is 5 percent per year, and σ is 0.142470. This time, we slice up T into sixteen periods of length Δt each so that $\Delta t = T/n = 1/16 = 0.0625$ years. Table 18.3a reports the values obtained by using specification 1 (Jarrow–Rudd) of Table 18.1:

$$U = 1.038843626$$
$$D = 0.96741588$$
$$\pi = 0.500001883$$
$$(1 - \pi) = 0.499998117$$

■ The detailed workings are reported in Table 18.3b.
- Column A has j, the number of up movements.
- Column B has the call symbols (e.g., in the row corresponding to $j = 14$, we indicate the call symbol by U14D2S-K; this has stock price for fourteen ups and two downs, from which is subtracted the strike price).
- Column C has the call values at expiration.
- Column D has the combination, the number of ways of getting j up movements $\binom{16}{j}$.
- Column E has the pseudo-probability of the up movements π^j.
- Column F has the pseudo-probability of the down movements $(1 - \pi)^{16-j}$.
- Column G has the pseudo-probability of the particular path $D \times E \times F$.
- Column H has the "expected payoff" $C \times G$.

- Summing all the values in column H, discounted by $(1 + R)^{16}$, gives the call option value, $c = \$3.81$. As we have done the hard work for the call, we can use put–call parity to obtain the put premium:

$$p = c + KB - S$$
$$= 3.81 + (110/1.0513) - 100$$
$$= \$8.45$$

TABLE 18.3: A Sixteen-Period Binomial Example (Solved Using Microsoft Excel)

a. Basic Data, Computations, and European Call and Put Values

S	K	T	n	$\Delta t = T/n$	r	$1 + R$	σ	U	D
100	110	1	16	0.0625	0.05	1.00313	0.14247	1.038843626	0.96741588

π	$(1 - \pi)$	Call	Put
0.500001883	0.499998117	\$3.813430739	\$8.448667

b. Excel Workings

A	B	C	D	E	F	G	H
j	Call Symbol	Call Values at Expiration	Combination	Pseudo-Probability of Up Jumps π^j	Pseudo-Probability of Down Jumps $(1 - \pi)^{(16-j)}$	Pseudo-Probability of Particular Path D*E*F	Expected Payoff C*G
16	U16S-K	73.993666	1	1.52597E-05	1	1.52597E-05	0.001129122
15	U15DS-K	61.342818	16	3.05193E-05	0.4999981	0.000244153	0.014977064
14	U14D2S-K	49.561804	120	6.10384E-05	0.2499981	0.001831137	0.090754475
13	U13D3S-K	38.590817	560	0.000122076	0.1249986	0.008545244	0.329767937
12	U12D4S-K	28.374162	1,820	0.000244152	0.0624991	0.027771833	0.788002483
11	U11D5S-K	18.859973	4,368	0.000488301	0.0312494	0.066651897	1.257052981
10	U10D6S-K	9.9999511	8,008	0.000976599	0.0156246	0.122194223	1.221936262
9	U9D7S-K	1.7491174	1,1440	0.001953191	0.0078123	0.174561862	0.305329191
							Sum/1.051271= 3.81343074

18.7 | Summary

1. The basic binomial OPM is described by the following:

   a. Three securities trade: a stock, a riskless money market account, and a European (call or put) option.

   b. The stock price goes up by factors of U or D from each node. The stock price tree repeats this single-period structure at the end of each node.

   c. A dollar invested in the money market account gives a dollar return of $1 + R \equiv e^{r\Delta t}$ after one period.

   d. Given the strike price, you can compute the option's payoffs at maturity from the stock tree. Then solve the previous period's option price by repeatedly applying the formula

   $$\text{Option price} = [\pi \times (\text{Option price})_{\text{UP}} + (1 - \pi) \times (\text{Option price})_{\text{DOWN}}]/(1 + R)$$

   where $\pi = [(1 + R) - D]/(U - D)$ is the pseudo-probability of an up movement and the options prices "up" and "down" are considered at the next up and down nodes.

2. The n-period multiplicative binomial OPM is

   $$c = \frac{1}{(1 + R)^n} \sum_{j=0}^{n} \left\{ \left[\binom{n}{j} \pi^j (1 - \pi)^{n-j} \right] \times \left[\max(0, U^j D^{n-j} S - K) \right] \right\}$$

   where $\binom{n}{j} \equiv n!/[j!(n-j)!]$ is the number of ways of choosing j "ups" out of n movements and $n! = n \times (n-1) \times (n-2) \times \ldots \times 2 \times 1$ is the n-factorial.

3. An American option may be valued in the binomial framework as follows:

   a. Create a binomial stock price tree as in the case of the European option and find the option values at time n, which is the maturity date.

   b. Using the risk-neutral valuation formula, compute (1) the European option's value at time $(n-1)$ and (2) the option's payoff if it is immediately exercised. Retain the larger of these two as the American option value and use it in future computations.

   c. Work backward period by period. At each node, determine whether the option is worth more alive (computed value) or dead (exercised value), and retain the higher of these two values. Stop when you reach today's date. By following this process, you have created the American option price tree.

18.8 | Cases

Leland O'Brien Rubinstein Associates Inc.: Portfolio Insurance (Harvard Business School Case 294061-PDF-ENG). The case studies the rise and fall of Leland O'Brien Rubinstein (LOR) Associates' portfolio insurance selling business.

Leland O'Brien Rubinstein Associates Inc.: SuperTrust (Harvard Business School Case 294050-PDF-ENG). The case examines LOR Associates' attempts to rebuild itself after the 1987 stock market crash by creating new products to meet the unsatisfied needs of equity investors.

The Value of Flexibility at Global Airlines: Real Options for EDW and CRM (Kellogg School of Management Case, Case KEL266-PDF-ENG, Harvard Business Publishing). The case evaluates real options for technology projects using a binomial model.

18.9 | Questions and Problems

18.1. Why is a multiperiod binomial model a better approximation to the actual stock price process than the single period binomial model?

The next seven questions are based on the following data for a two-period binomial model

- A stock's price S is $100. After three months, it either goes up and gets multiplied by the up factor $U = 1.163287$, or it goes down and gets multiplied by the down factor $D = 0.861785$.
- Options mature after $T = 0.5$ years and have a strike price $K = \$110$.
- A dollar invested in the money market account grows to $R = \$1.012578$ after three months.

The stock price tree is:

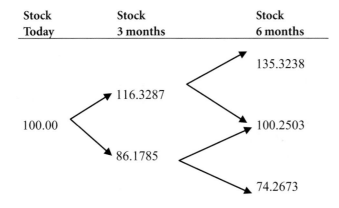

Stock Today	Stock 3 months	Stock 6 months
		135.3238
	116.3287	
100.00		100.2503
	86.1785	
		74.2673

18.2. Compute the call value in the above tree using synthetic construction.

18.3. Demonstrate how you can make arbitrage profits when a trader quotes a call price of $2.

18.4. Compute the value of the call option using risk neutral valuation.

18.5. Compute the put value in the above tree using synthetic construction.

18.6. Suppose the market price of the put option in question 18.5 is $10, how would you take advantage of this mispricing? Explain your answer.

18.7. Given the data in question 18.5, compute the value of the put option using risk neutral valuation.

18.8. Consider the call and put options in questions 18.2 and 18.5. Show that they satisfy put–call parity.

The next five questions are based on the following data for a four period binomial model
- Options mature after $T = 2$ years and have a strike price $K = \$75$.
- The price of the underlying stock price is $50. The stock price evolves according to the Jarrow–Rudd specification in this 4-period model with volatility $\sigma = 0.3$.
- The continuously compounded risk-free interest rate r is 5 percent per year.

18.9. a. Compute the up and down factors for the stock price movements and the dollar return $(1 + R)$ for each period.

  b. Use these up and down factors to create a 4-period tree for the stock price movements.

18.10. Find the value of all call options in the tree by repeated application of risk neutral valuation.

18.11. Explain the European call option formula at time 0 based on an n-period binomial option pricing model.

18.12. Find the value of all put options in the tree by repeated application of risk-neutral valuation.

18.13. Explain the European put option formula at time 0 based on an n-period binomial option pricing model.

The next eight questions are based on the following data for a two-period binomial model
- Options mature after $T = 0.5$ year and have strike price $K = \$45$.
- The price of the underlying stock price is $50. The stock price evolves according to the Jarrow–Rudd specification in this 2-period model with volatility $\sigma = 0.2$.
- The continuously compounded risk-free interest rate r is 2 percent per year.

18.14. Compute the up and down factors, the dollar return $(1 + R)$, and the stock price lattice.

18.15. Compute today's call option price in this 2-period tree.

18.16. Compute today's put option price in this 2-period tree.

18.17. Consider an otherwise identical American call option with the preceding data, maturing at time 2. Compute its value. How do the American and European call prices compare?

18.18. Consider an otherwise identical American put option with the preceding data, maturing at time 2. Compute its value. How do the American and European put prices compare?

18.19. Compute today's American put option price in this 2-period tree if the strike price is $70. Does early exercise occur?

18.20. Consider the following exotic option whose payoff at maturity is given by the stock price squared less a strike price if it has a positive value, zero otherwise:

$$\max[S(2)^2 - K, 0].$$

Assuming that the strike price is $2,000, determine the value of this exotic option under the assumption of no-arbitrage.

18.21. Consider the following exotic option whose payoff at maturity is given by the square root of the stock price less the strike price if it has a positive value, zero otherwise:

$$\max\left[\sqrt{S(2)} - K, 0\right].$$

Using the preceding data except for assuming a new strike price is $5, determine the value of this exotic option under the assumption of no-arbitrage.

(Microsoft Excel) The next question is based on the following data for a three period binomial model

- Options mature after $T = 0.5$ year and have strike price $K = \$65$.
- The price of the underlying stock S is $63. The stock price evolves according to the Jarrow–Rudd specification in this 3-period model with volatility $\sigma = 0.3$.
- The continuously compounded risk-free interest rate r is 0.045 per year.

18.22. **a.** Using Excel, compute today's call option value with the preceding data.

b. Using Excel, compute today's put option value with the preceding data.

19

The Black–Scholes–Merton Model

19.1 | Introduction

The year 1973 saw the publication of the Black–Scholes–Merton (BSM) option pricing model (OPM) and the birth of the first modern options exchange, the Chicago Board Options Exchange. Professor Rubinstein declared in his 1994 American Finance Association presidential address, "This model [BSM model] is widely viewed as one of the most successful in the social sciences and has perhaps been (including its binomial extension) the most widely used formula, with embedded probabilities, in human history." We share the professor's enthusiasm, but we are a little less sure about the usage data.[1]

This chapter presents the BSM model. First, we consider some applications and uses. Next, we provide a brief history of the events that led to its development and publication. We describe the model's assumptions, present the Black–Scholes formula for valuing European options, and discuss the theory underlying the model's structures. We discuss how to gather the inputs, including the most elusive, the "volatility." Finally, we show how to extend the BSM model to adjust for dividends, to price foreign currency options, and we discuss the pricing of American options. An insert presents a bird's-eye view of exotic options.

19.2 | Applications and Uses

In an essay titled "In Honor of the Nobel Laureates Robert C. Merton and Myron S. Scholes: A Partial Differential Equation That Changed the World," one of us (Jarrow 1999, p. 243) wrote,

> The insights of Robert C. Merton, Myron Scholes and Fischer Black on option pricing have had a substantial impact in many areas. In the social sciences, their insights initiated derivatives, a new field of research. Within economics, these insights have illuminated areas of corporate finance, financial markets and institutions, industrial organizations, labor economics, international economics, and general equilibrium. In the financial industry, these insights enabled the growth and expansion of derivative markets in equities, foreign currencies, interest rates, and commodities. They also enabled the creation of new firms and organizational structures within firms with respect to trading opportunities and risk management. In society at large, these innovations improved the efficiency of financial markets and facilitated a more optimal allocation of resources.

The "demand" for trading options, both on the long and the short side of the market, for hedging or speculative purposes, arises in the course of the "ordinary

---

[1] In George Bernard Shaw's play "O'Flaherty V. C.," an English general told an Irish war hero, "Well, in recruiting a man gets carried away. I stretch it a bit occasionally myself. After all, it's for king and country. But if you won't mind my saying it, O'Flaherty, I think that story about your fighting the Kaiser and the twelve giants of the Prussian guard singlehanded would be the better for a little toning down. I don't ask you to drop it, you know; for it's popular, undoubtedly; but still, the truth is the truth. Don't you think it would fetch in almost as many recruits if you reduced the number of guardsmen to six?"

business of life."[2] We can classify traders into three categories on the basis of their tools, techniques, and trading approaches:

1. *mathematical modelers*, who construct OPMs using differing assumptions characterizing markets; the prime example is the BSM model
2. *statistical modelers*, who construct their OPMs on the basis of historical price patterns and using statistical tools
3. *lottery buyers*, who play and pray in the hope of favorable outcomes

All three types of traders exist in our markets. When you listen to market gurus who instruct you to abandon models and rely solely on intuition, then you have inadvertently slipped into the third category, where (recall from chapter 15) Bill Lipschutz's former colleagues at Salomon Brothers dwelled. Many successful traders do rely on psychological impulses. However, they also employ models to help guide their decisions. The distinction between theory and statistical models will become crucial in the next chapter, when we discuss how to use the BSM model in practice.

The BSM model has several useful characteristics. First, it's easier to compute than is the binomial model because the modeler need not worry about the number of branches and how to construct them. Second, analytical hedge ratios and "Greeks" are more convenient than computing numerical derivatives, and despite its simplicity, the BSM model can be "made to work," even though some of the model's assumptions fail to hold. We discuss these robustness issues in the next chapter.

19.3 | Nobel Prize–Winning Works (1973)

During the late 1960s, a Harvard-trained applied mathematician, Fischer Black, was working as a consultant in Boston. Black applied the capital asset pricing model to value options and derived a partial differential equation that implicitly solved the option's value (see the biographical sketches of Black and Scholes). He teamed up with Massachusetts Institute of Technology (MIT) assistant professor Myron Scholes to solve the equation and derive the formula that bears their names. At the same time, a doctoral student of Paul Samuelson, Robert Merton, was pioneering the use of stochastic calculus to tackle a variety of problems, including portfolio theory and option valuation (see the biographical sketch of Merton). Why didn't Black, Scholes, and Merton work together?

---

[2] The expression comes from the economist **Alfred Marshall** (1842–1924), who began his classic text *Principles of Economics* (Marshall 1890, p. 12) with the following statement: "Political Economy or Economics is a study of mankind in the ordinary business of life; it examines that part of individual and social action which is most closely connected with the attainment and with the use of the material requisites of wellbeing."

A story made famous (or "notorious," in Merton's words) in Peter L. Bernstein's (1992) book *Capital Ideas* states that Merton "inconveniently overslept" and missed a seminar presentation by Black and Scholes. Scholes, who is a close friend of Merton, bluntly attributed their separate works to a "friendly rivalry" and wrote, "I guess we did not appreciate that each of us had an interest in this research area" (Scholes 1998, p. 353–6). Later they had long discussions and an exchange of ideas. Merton showed Black and Scholes how to derive their partial differential equation using a perfectly hedged portfolio consisting of the stock and the option.

The Black–Scholes paper had difficulty getting published, being rejected by both the *Journal of Political Economy* and the *Review of Economics and Statistics.* Professors Merton Miller and Eugene Fama used their personal influence to get the paper published in the *Journal of Political Economy* as "The Pricing of Options and Corporate Liabilities" in 1973. The same year also saw the publication of Merton's (1973a) "Theory of Rational Option Pricing" in the *Bell Journal of Economics and Management Science.* The rest is history. The Black–Scholes and Merton papers deeply influenced both academics and practice. The crowning academic glory came in 1997 when Merton and Scholes won the Bank of Sweden Prize in Economic Sciences in Memory of Alfred Nobel. Black, whose contributions were duly acknowledged in the Nobel citation, unfortunately died from cancer two years earlier and missed the honor.

How should we name these models? It was Merton who coined the name the "Black–Scholes model." He held off the publication of his own paper containing his derivation of the OPM until the Black and Scholes paper was published. Merton was luckier in terms of publication. The newly launched *Bell Journal of Economics and Management Science* not only published the paper but paid $500 for the manuscript, which was "an irresistible bait for a young assistant professor still earning a starting salary of only $11,500" (Bernstein 1992, p. 221). In honor of all three scholars, we refer to this work, in line with emerging practice, as the BSM model.

19.4 | The Assumptions

The BSM model, like its binomial approximation, requires several important assumptions. We repeat here assumptions A1–A6 of chapter 17, which are common to both models and restate much of the discussion. The last assumption (binomial trading process) is replaced by two assumptions (A7 and A8) that characterize the stock price evolution under continuous trading.

A1. No market frictions. We assume that trading involves no *market frictions* such as transaction costs (brokerage commissions and bid/ask spreads), margin requirements, short sale restrictions, and taxes (which may be levied on different securities at different rates). Moreover, assets are perfectly divisible. This helps create a benchmark model to which one can later add frictions, and it's a reasonable approximation for institutional traders.

Biographical Sketch: Fischer Black

Fischer Sheffey Black (1938–95) spent much of his early childhood in the Carolinas. Black graduated with an AB in physics (1959) from Harvard University. He also earned a PhD from Harvard in applied mathematics (1964), developing an interest in computers and artificial intelligence. He began his career as a finance consultant working for Arthur D. Little (1965–69).

He met Myron Scholes in 1968 and soon started collaborating on many research projects. Scholes introduced Black to the weekly finance workshops at MIT's Sloan School of Management. Black was bubbling with new ideas from the outset. His self-professed poor memory led to the practice of always writing down his ideas immediately, no matter what else was going on. He would even interrupt his own lectures with silent periods of note taking.

Fischer Black took his first academic job in 1971 as a visiting professor at the University of Chicago's business school, where he became a full professor after one year. He returned to Boston and joined the Sloan School in 1975. After nine years at MIT, Black joined the investment banking firm of Goldman Sachs and Company and rose to become a partner. One of the first "quants," he helped start the exodus of many talented PhDs (in economics, finance, mathematics, operations research, physics, statistics, etc.) into Wall Street firms, and he pioneered the idea of using computers for actual trading, which introduced a new type of arbitrage opportunity (Mehrling 2005).

Though never formally trained in economics and finance, Fischer Black made many outstanding contributions to the field (see Merton and Scholes [1995] for a discussion of his academic work). Besides options pricing, he contributed to (1) asset pricing, (2) the design of financial markets, (3) portfolio management, (4) taxes and economic behavior, and (5) business cycles and monetary theory.

Biographical Sketch: Myron Scholes[3]

Myron Samuel Scholes was born in 1941 in Timmins, Ontario, Canada, where his father practiced dentistry and his mother (and her uncle) established a chain of small department stores. He became interested at an early age in economics and, in particular, finance:

> During my teenage years, I was always treasurer of my various clubs; I traded extensively among my friends; I gambled to understand probabilities and risks; and worked with my uncles to understand their business activities. I invested in the stock market. . . . I was fascinated with the determinants of the level of stock prices. I spent long hours reading reports and books to gleam the secrets of successful investing, but, alas, to no-avail.

This was an early introduction to the efficient markets hypothesis for an academic who himself made numerous empirical contributions to this field.

On graduation from McMaster University, Scholes joined the University of Chicago's MBA program. Granted a junior computer-programming position that involved helping professors with their research, he worked day and night at the computer facility and became, in his words, "one of the first computer nerds." Scholes fell in love with economics and economics research. Eventually, he did his PhD in financial economics from Chicago under Nobel laureate Merton Miller's guidance and joined MIT's Sloan School as an assistant professor in 1968.

Subsequently, Scholes taught in business schools at the University of Chicago and Stanford University. Scholes had a highly productive research career. Besides developing the BSM model, he tested the capital asset pricing model and extensively studied the effect of taxation on asset pricing and incentives.

Biographical Sketch: Robert Merton

Robert Cox Merton (born 1944) grew up in Hastings-on-Hudson, a village of about eight thousand outside New York City. His father, Columbia University's renowned sociology professor Robert K. Merton (who coined everyday expressions like *role model*, *self-fulfilling prophecy*, and *unintended consequences*), introduced his son "to baseball, poker, magic, and the stock market (only magic didn't take root)."

[3] Unless otherwise noted, the quotes in these bios are from www.nobel.se/economics/laureates/1997.

Biographical Sketch: Robert Merton (Continued)

Following a BS in engineering mathematics from Columbia University and an MS in applied mathematics from the California Institute of Technology, Merton entered MIT's economics PhD program. Regarding his interest in finance, Merton recalls,

> In college, I spent time doing some trading, learning tape watching, and hearing the lore of the market from retail traders in brokerage houses. . . . At Cal Tech, many mornings I would get to a local brokerage house at 6:30 AM (9:30 AM in New York) for the opening of the stock market, spend a couple of hours watching the tape and trading, and then go to my classes. In addition to stocks, I traded warrants, convertible bonds, and over-the-counter options.

A graduate student under Samuelson, Merton soon found that "my 'after/before-hours' interest in such things could also be a legitimate part of my day-hours devoted to research." Focusing little on course work but intensely on research, Merton (who had published his first article in a history journal as an undergraduate) finished his PhD in three years. He joined MIT's Sloan School as an assistant professor of finance in 1970. After teaching there for eighteen years, Merton moved to the Harvard Business School, where he held a University Professorship, the highest professorial honor that Harvard grants. In 2010, he moved back to MIT with a distinguished professorship.

Robert Merton wrote many seminal papers. His contributions include (1) dynamic models of consumption and portfolio selection (Merton 1969, 1971, 1973), (2) linking corporate finance and options pricing (Black–Scholes independently made a similar observation) (also called the "structural approach"; see Merton 1974, 1977), and (3) a model for pricing options when the underlying stock returns have "jumps" (Merton's [1976] jump diffusion model). His later research focused on understanding the financial system, with special emphasis on the dynamics of institutional change.

A2. No credit risk. We assume that there is no *credit risk*. Also known as *default risk* or *counterparty risk*, this is the risk that the counterparty will fail to perform on an obligation. The absence of credit risk is a reasonable assumption for exchange-traded derivatives. Over-the-counter derivatives, however, may possess substantial credit risks, unless there are adequate collateral provisions.

A3. Competitive and well-functioning markets. In a competitive market, traders' purchases and sales have no impact on the market price; consequently, traders act as price takers. In a well-functioning market, traders agree on zero-probability events, and price bubbles are absent.

The competitive markets assumption is the workhorse of modern economics. The relaxation of this assumption is discussed in Extension 19.2, after we present the BSM model. When traders disagree on such *zero-probability events*, they cannot come to a consensus regarding what is considered an arbitrage opportunity. This destroys our key tool for proving results (see assumption A5).

A *price bubble* happens when an asset's price substantially deviates from its intrinsic or fundamental value. Recent research shows that bubbles can invalidate the methodology we employ for pricing options (see Extension 19.1).

A4. No intermediate cash flows. Many assets reward their holders with cash flows such as dividends for stocks and coupons for bonds. The BSM model assumes that the underlying asset has no cash flows over the option's life. Later in the chapter, we will show how to relax this assumption.

A5. No arbitrage opportunities. This is self-explanatory.

EXTENSION 19.1: Bubbles and Option Pricing

As discussed in chapter 17, a *price bubble* happens when an asset's price substantially deviates from its intrinsic or fundamental value. The *fundamental or intrinsic value* can be defined in two equivalent ways: the first is the present value of its future cash flows; the second is the price paid if, after purchase, you have to hold the asset forever. A difference only occurs if one believes that selling can generate a higher value. This difference is the bubble.

OPMs, like any other models, are valid under a given set of assumptions. When an assumption fails, the model may no longer be valid. If assumption A3 (competitive and well-functioning assumption) fails and a bubble exists, then many results of option pricing theory no longer hold (see Jarrow, Protter, and Shimbo 2010b).

Fortunately, with respect to the BSM model, assumption A8 is consistent with assumption A3. This is because the assumption that the stock price follows a lognormal distribution excludes bubbles. Thus, the lognormal distribution is a very strong assumption. If one believes that there are stock price bubbles, then the lognormal distribution assumption needs to be modified, and the BSM model no longer applies.

It can be shown that in a market with no arbitrage opportunities or dominated assets, asset price bubbles only exist when the market is incomplete. Because most option pricing theories assume a *complete market* (where, recall from chapter 8, securities trade that help investors attain any desired future payoffs), so that synthetic construction is possible, we see that the standard approach to option pricing excludes bubbles. Again, this is a good result, as long as one believes that there are no stock price bubbles.

But how do you price options when there are asset price bubbles in an incomplete market? In such markets, alternative pricing methodologies need to be invoked. The two common approaches are using indifference/utility-based pricing and identifying the risk-neutral probabilities from traded derivatives. Because exact hedging is no longer possible, we cannot price by synthetic construction; however, risk-neutral valuation may still apply. When there are bubbles in the underlying asset, pricing is subtle. Recent research suggests that some results stay the same while others change:

- Put–call parity still holds for European options in the presence of bubbles.

- Risk-neutral valuation works for the put's price because it has a bounded payout, but it does not work for the call; it turns out that if the underling asset has a price bubble, so does the call.

- Forwards and futures both inherit the underlying's price bubble, and even more interesting, futures prices can have their own price bubbles.

Bubbles are a thorn in the side of the policy makers, a source of problems for asset holders, an opportunity for hedge fund managers, and a hot research area for professors. The three witches in William Shakespeare's *Macbeth* sang together, "Double, double, toil and trouble/Fire burn and cauldron bubble." Perhaps we should rephrase: "Bubble, bubble, toil and trouble!"

A6. No interest rate uncertainty. We assume that interest rates are constant across time. This assumption works for short-lived options whose underlying asset isn't sensitive to interest rate movements. This assumption is relaxed in part IV of the book.

Next, we introduce two assumptions that are crucial for developing the BSM model

A7. Trading takes place continuously in time. This assumption gives a realistic description of transacting actively traded stocks. Stocks do not trade only on a fixed time grid but rather at any time instant during the trading day. This is particularly true in today's markets, where a significant amount of trading volume is attributed to *high-frequency* computerized trading strategies pursuing fleeting profit opportunities in the blink of an eye.

A8. The stock price follows a lognormal probability distribution. This assumption means that the continuously compounded returns on the stock follow a normal distribution. We will explain this assumption in two ways: first, by some diagrams, and second, by adding more structure to the continuously compounded rate of return concept familiar from chapter 2.

Does the lognormal assumption give a realistic model of stock price behavior? As pictures say a thousand words, let's go back to our diagrams. In Figure 19.1, the first two diagrams repeat possible stock price evolutions from Figure 18.1, for the single period and multiperiod binomial models, respectively. As "seeing is believing," you can easily surmise, "These don't look like stock price paths!" The multiperiod binomial evolution diagram leaves open the intriguing possibility that it might start looking like a stock price path if the time step shrinks to zero. This brings us to the third figure, which depicts a stock price path for the lognormal distribution. Here you can no longer rule out the evolution just by visual inspection. A rejection of this evolution now requires the use of formal statistical procedures. Hence it is the first "real" or "realistic" stock price evolution that we have considered.

Next, let's use Result 2.1c (with slightly enhanced notation): an investment of $L(0) \equiv L$ dollars in a risk-free account today grows to $L(T) \equiv L(0)e^{rT}$ dollars after T years, where r is the continuously compounded risk-free rate of return per year. Is there a similar result for stocks? Yes. We can write

$$S(T) = S(0)e^{yT} \tag{19.1}$$

where $S(T)$ and $S(0)$ are the stock prices at times T and 0, respectively, and y is the continuously compounded rate of return on the stock per year.

However, this return is not risk-free. To characterize its properties, we need a model of returns that (1) generates prices that look like the stock price patterns observed in financial markets, (2) never allows *stock prices to be negative* (because they are of limited liability), (3) but allows *stock price returns to be positive, zero, or negative* (as you find in the markets), and (4) provides a mathematically tractable model. Samuelson, Merton, and other researchers achieved these objectives in one stroke by replacing Bachelier's arithmetic Brownian motion with a geometric Brownian motion. The modification gives us a structure similar to (19.1).

The *geometric Brownian motion* assumption is that y is normally distributed with mean $(\mu - \sigma^2/2)T$ and standard deviation $\sigma\sqrt{T}$. This is expressed as

$$S(T) = S(0)e^{\mu T - \frac{\sigma^2}{2}T + \sigma\sqrt{T}z} \tag{19.2}$$

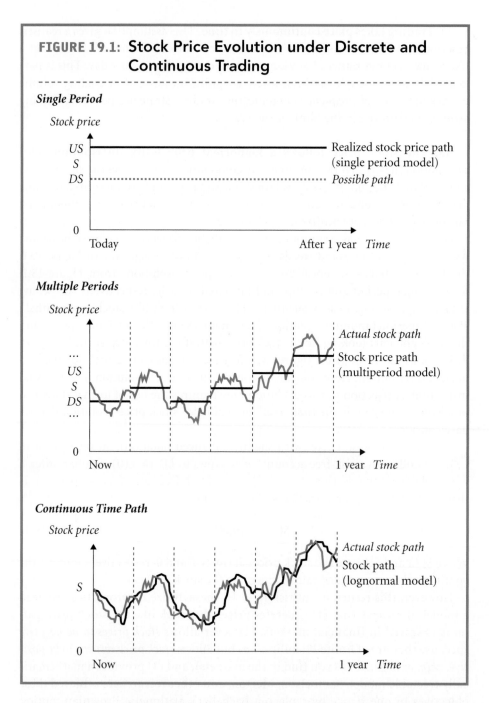

FIGURE 19.1: Stock Price Evolution under Discrete and Continuous Trading

Single Period

Multiple Periods

Continuous Time Path

where μ is the expected return on the stock per year, σ is the standard deviation or volatility of the stock's return per year, and z is a **standard normal random variable** with mean 0 and variance 1; that is, z has the probability density function (a plot of which gives the familiar bell curve)

$$q(z) = \frac{1}{\sqrt{2\pi}} e^{-\frac{z^2}{2}}$$

(19.3)

The probability $q(z)$ is the actual probability of the random variable z, which generates the randomness in the stock price $S(T)$.

Note that expression (19.2) satisfies properties 1, 2, and 3 trivially. Property (4) follows because the normal distribution is so well studied. The appendix to this chapter provides an axiomatic justification for modeling the stock price with a lognormal distribution based on the efficient markets hypothesis.

19.5 | The Pricing and Hedging Argument

The original proof of the BSM model utilizes the idea of hedging an option position with an opposing stock trade, a notion used by options writers in London more than a century ago (Nelson 1904). An understanding of this hedging argument is essential to understanding the BSM model. The intuition is easily explained in three steps (see Figure 19.2).

Step 1

- Call prices and the underlying stock price move together. This happens because as the stock price goes up, the call has a higher chance of ending up in-the-money, which makes the call more valuable today.

- Consequently, the call value is a function of the underlying stock price, and because the option eventually matures, its price must also depend on time.

Step 2

- If a long call and a long stock position move together, then a long call and a short stock position must move in opposite directions. Recall from chapter 15 that this creates a partial hedge because the increase in one is offset by a decrease in the other.

- But they don't perfectly balance, so it is not a perfect hedge.

Step 3

- We can modify the partially hedged position in the long call and short stock to make it a perfect hedge. One can do this by short selling a fraction of a stock for each long call. Then, for any movement in the stock price, the change in the call value exactly offsets the change in the short stock position.

- The perfectly hedged portfolio uniquely identifies the option's arbitrage-free price. This happens because the hedged portfolio requires a known initial investment, and it is riskless over the next time period. To avoid arbitrage, it must earn the risk-free rate. The equation implied by this restriction, a partial differential equation, when solved yields the option's price. The mathematics for this argument is contained in the appendix to chapter 20.

The replication argument as just described utilizes the *hedge ratio*, which we called the holy grail of option pricing. Jarrow (1999, p. 233) notes that "the idea of

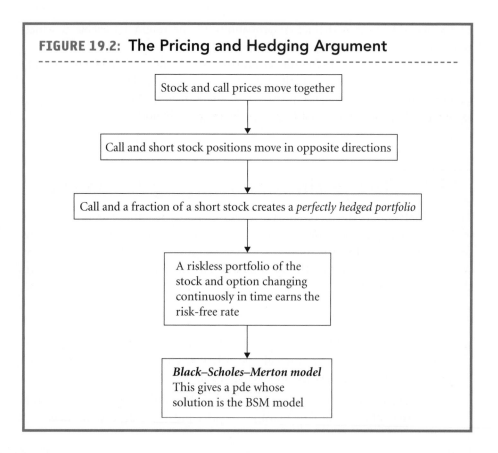

FIGURE 19.2: The Pricing and Hedging Argument

Stock and call prices move together

↓

Call and short stock positions move in opposite directions

↓

Call and a fraction of a short stock creates a *perfectly hedged portfolio*

↓

A riskless portfolio of the stock and option changing continuosly in time earns the risk-free rate

↓

Black–Scholes–Merton model
This gives a pde whose solution is the BSM model

constructing a perfectly hedged portfolio is the key insight of the Black–Merton–Scholes model, more important than the valuation formula itself. Indeed, if one considers the meaning of a perfectly hedged portfolio, it becomes apparent that *it implies that a position in the stock and the riskless asset can be created that exactly duplicates the changes in value to the call option*" [emphasis added]. The creation of *synthetic options* is the basis for most OPMs and will be used throughout this book.

19.6 | The Black–Scholes–Merton Formula

Under assumptions A1–A8, one can derive the Black–Scholes–Merton formula for pricing European options. There are three ways of proving this formula: (1) taking the limit of the multiperiod binomial model of chapter 18 as the time steps go to zero, (2) directly applying risk-neutral valuation, and (3) using the hedging argument of the previous section to obtain a *partial differential equation (pde)* whose solution yields the formula. The appendix to this chapter provides the proof using the multiperiod binomial model, the simplest derivation, and the proof using risk-neutral valuation, the paramount technique of modern derivatives pricing. The appendix to chapter 20 provides the pde proof, the derivation originally used by Black and Scholes (1973) but the least extendable methodology of the three.

The formula is given by the following result.

RESULT 19.1

- -

The Black–Scholes–Merton Formulas for Pricing European Options

The European call price is

$$c = SN(d_1) - Ke^{-rT}N(d_2) \qquad (19.4a)$$

where $S \equiv S(0)$ is today's spot price, $N(\,.\,)$ is the cumulative standard normal distribution function which has mean 0 and standard deviation 1,

$$d_1 = \frac{\log\left(\frac{S}{K}\right) + \left(r + \frac{\sigma^2}{2}\right)T}{\sigma\sqrt{T}}$$

$$d_2 = d_1 - \sigma\sqrt{T}$$

K is the strike price, r is the continuously compounded risk-free interest rate per year, T is the time to maturity measured in years (time 0 is today), and σ is the stock return's volatility per year, which is the square root of the stock return's instantaneous variance.

The European put price is given by

$$p = Ke^{-rT}N(-d_2) - SN(-d_1) \qquad (19.4b)$$

One can show that the put price follows from the call's price using put–call parity for European options along with the result that $N(d) + N(-d) = 1$.

The first observation to make about the BSM formula is that the call's value depends on the stock price (S), the strike price (K), the time to maturity (T), the riskless interest rate (r), and the stock return's volatility (σ). It does not depend, surprisingly, on the stock's expected return (μ). This omission is significant and has two important implications.

First, the stock's expected return is the most difficult input to estimate. The estimation of the other inputs is easier and discussed in a subsequent section. In fact, had the option's value depended on μ, the formula would not have been used. Estimating μ is equivalent to estimating the stock's risk premium, and no two financial economists agree on how to do this. This is a well-known problem in portfolio theory. Consequently, avoiding the estimation of μ is a blessing in disguise.

The second implication is that because the option value does not depend on μ, two traders who agree on (S, K, T, r, σ) but disagree on the stock's expected return, μ, will still agree on the call's value. Of course, if they disagree on the stock's expected return, μ, the traders will probably disagree on the stock price S. However, if they agree on S, regardless of their views of μ, they agree on the call's value.

Our next example demonstrates how to use Result 19.1, assuming that you are given all of the inputs.

EXAMPLE 19.1: Using the Black–Scholes–Merton Formula

Consider the binomial option pricing (BOP) data of chapter 18:

- YBM's current stock price S is $100.
- The strike price K is $110.
- Time to maturity $T = 1$ year.
- The volatility σ of the stock's return is 0.142470 per year.
- The continuously compounded risk-free interest rate r is 5 percent per year.

The European Call Price

- Compute d_1 and d_2:

$$d_1 = \frac{\log\left(\frac{S}{K}\right) + \left(r + \frac{\sigma^2}{2}\right)T}{\sigma\sqrt{T}} = \frac{\log\left(\frac{100}{110}\right) + \left[0.05 + \frac{(0.14247)^2}{2}\right](1)}{0.14247\sqrt{1}} = -0.2468$$

$$d_2 = d_1 - \sigma\sqrt{T} = -0.2468 - 0.14247 = -0.3893$$

- One can get the cumulative normal distribution function from (1) a spreadsheet program such as Excel or Lotus Notes, (2) a calculator, or (3) a table of values for the standard normal distribution (appendix A at the end of the book shows how to read this table)[4]. Using Excel, we get

$$N(d_1) = N(-0.2468) = \text{NORMSDIST}(-0.2468) = 0.4025$$
$$N(d_2) = N(-0.3893) = \text{NORMSDIST}(-0.3893) = 0.3485$$

- The zero-coupon bond price is $B = e^{-rT} = e^{-0.05} = 0.9513$.
- The European call price using the BSM formula is

$$c = SN(d_1) - Ke^{-rT}N(d_2)$$
$$= 100 \times 0.4025 - 110 \times 0.9513 \times 0.3485$$
$$= \$3.78$$

The European Put Price

- For European puts, we need different values from the cumulative normal distribution function:

$$N(-d_1) = N[-(-0.2468)] = N(0.2468) = \text{NORMSDIST}(0.2468) = 0.5975$$
$$N(-d_2) = \text{NORMSDIST}(0.3893) = 0.6515$$

- The European put price is

$$p = Ke^{-rT}N(-d_2) - SN(-d_1)$$
$$= 110 \times 0.9513 \times 0.6515 - 100 \times 0.5975$$
$$= \$8.42$$

[4] In Excel, the command "= NORMSDIST(z)" gives the standard normal cumulative distribution function (in Lotus Notes, use the command @NORMAL[z,0,1,0]). The distribution has a mean of 0 and a standard deviation of 1.

The European Put Price (by Put–Call Parity)

- We can double-check our computations using put–call parity:

$$p = c + Ke^{-rT} - S = 3.78 + 110 \times 0.9513 - 100 = \$8.42$$

19.7 | Understanding the Black–Scholes–Merton Model

To better understand the BSM model, we apply the same argument used to obtain the binomial model in chapter 17. This argument starts by introducing an analogous notion to that of the pseudo-probability.

Stock Prices and Martingales

In an arbitrage-free market, it can be shown (as in the binomial model) under the lognormal assumption that there exist pseudo-probabilities such that the stock price today is its discounted expected value at time T, that is,

$$S(t) = E^\pi \big[S(T) \big] e^{-r(T-t)} \qquad (19.5)$$

where $\pi(z)$ are the pseudo-probabilities. This is analogous to expression (17.7).

Expression (19.5) is a present value formula. In this formula, the adjustment for risk occurs in the use of the pseudo-probabilities when taking the expectation and not in the discount rate, which is riskless. Rearranging terms in expression (19.5), we get

$$\frac{S(t)}{e^{rt}} = E^\pi \left[\frac{S(T)}{e^{rT}} \right] \qquad (19.6)$$

In this form, analogous to chapter 17, we see that the stock price normalized by the price of a money market account is a martingale under the pseudo-probabilities. As noted in chapter 17, martingales in probability theory are associated with fair games, that is, games in which the gambler has an equal chance of losing or winning. In our context, this is an implication of the no arbitrage assumption. In fact, although not proven here, the implication also goes in the reverse direction. These insights are the basis for many generalizations of the BSM formula. Next we apply this approach to value a European call option.

Risk-Neutral Valuation

Under the lognormal distribution assumption, the market is complete, and we can construct a portfolio in the stock and money market account that exactly replicates the payoffs to the traded call option. As before, the cost of constructing this synthetic option yields the arbitrage-free price of the traded call, and exactly as in chapter 17, this implies that the call price can be computed as its discounted expected payoff using the pseudo-probabilities and the risk-free rate; that is, *risk-neutral valuation* applies:

$$c = E^\pi\big\{\max\big[0, S(T) - K\big]\big\}e^{-rT} \tag{19.7a}$$

It is shown in the appendix to this chapter that one can rewrite this expression in the following way:

$$c = E^\pi\big\{S(T)\,|\,S(T) \geq K\big\}\text{Prob}_\pi\big\{S(T) \geq K\big\}e^{-rT} \\ - K\text{Prob}_\pi\big\{S(T) \geq K\big\}e^{-rT} \tag{19.7b}$$

Making the identification of the terms in expression (19.7b) with those in the BSM formula (19.4), we see that

$$S(0)N(d_1) = E^\pi\big\{S(T)\,|\,S(T) \geq K\big\}\text{Prob}_\pi\big\{S(T) \geq K\big\}e^{-rT} \\ KN(d_2)e^{-rT} = K\text{Prob}_\pi\big\{S(T) \geq K\big\}e^{-rT} \tag{19.8}$$

The identifications help explain the meaning of the BSM formula.

We now see that the first term in the BSM formula, $S(0)N(d_1)$, can be interpreted as the discounted expected stock price at maturity, given that it ends up in-the-money multiplied by the probability of being in-the-money. This interpretation makes intuitive sense. Of course, as just noted, the expectation is computed using the pseudo-probabilities to adjust for the risk of the cash flows.

The second term in the BSM formula, $KN(d_2)e^{-rT}$, can be interpreted as the discounted strike price (Ke^{-rT}) times the pseudo-probability of ending up in the money, that is, $N(d_2) = \text{Prob}_\pi\{S(T) \geq K\}$. Again, this interpretation makes intuitive sense. This explains why the hedge ratio $N(d_2)$ is always between zero and 1, because the probability of being in-the-money is always between 0 and 1. It is 0 only when the stock price will never be in-the-money, and it is 1 only when the stock price will be in-the-money for sure.

Actual versus Pseudo-probabilities

Are the actual ($q[z]$) and pseudo- ($\pi[z]$) probabilities linked? Interestingly, and not surprisingly, they are linked by a risk premium. The argument is a simple generalization of our discussion in chapter 17. The details are given in the appendix to this chapter.

First, note that

$$\pi(z) > 0 \text{ if and only if } q(z) > 0 \tag{19.9a}$$

that is, the actual and pseudo-probabilities must agree on zero-probability events. This follows from the no arbitrage assumption. Consistent with this, one can show that the pseudo-probabilities equal

$$\pi(z) = \phi(z)q(z) \tag{19.9b}$$

where $\phi(z) = e^{-(\theta^2/2)+\theta z} > 0$ and $\theta = -[(\mu - r)/\sigma]\sqrt{T}$.

The quantity $\phi(z)$ in expression (19.9b) represents an adjustment for risk, and θ is, in fact, the stock's risk premium. The appendix to this chapter provides the justification for these statements. Notice that the result looks identical to that from chapter 17.

19.8 | The Greeks

We can gain a better understanding of the BSM model by understanding how its prices change when we change the inputs. This is easily accomplished by taking partial derivatives (given in Result 19.1) with respect to the stock price (S), time to maturity (T), the riskless interest rate (r), and the stock return's volatility (σ). In addition, we also compute the second partial derivative with respect to the stock price. These partial derivatives are called the **Greeks** because they are often written using the Greek alphabet—although one of them has a fictitious Greek name! These Greeks are given in Table 19.1. They are also useful for hedging and portfolio risk management, which are discussed in chapter 20.

Interpreting the Greeks

We first consider the **delta**, which measures the change in the option's value when there is a small change in the underlying stock price. For the call, we have

$$\text{Delta} \equiv \frac{\partial c}{\partial S} = \frac{\text{Change in the value of the call}}{\text{Change in the value of the stock}} = N(d_1) \qquad (19.10a)$$

The term on the right side of this expression is defined in Result 19.1. This shows that the delta, the hedge ratio, is a number strictly between zero and one. We can similarly compute the delta for a put.

The sensitivity of the delta to changes in the underlying stock price is called the **gamma**. This is the second partial derivative of the BSM call price formula with respect to the stock price, that is

$$\text{gamma} \equiv \frac{\partial(\text{Delta})}{\partial S} = \frac{\text{Change in the delta}}{\text{Change in the value of the stock}} = \frac{\partial^2 c}{\partial S^2}$$

$$= \frac{1}{S\sigma\sqrt{T}}N'(d_1) > 0 \qquad (19.10b)$$

where $N'(.)$ is the standard normal density function and all of the remaining symbols are defined in Result 19.1. The gamma shows that as the stock price increases, the delta increases. The gamma for the put is similarly computed by taking the partial derivative with respect to the underlying stock price of the delta for the put. The gamma for the put and the call are identical. The next example illustrates these computations.

EXAMPLE 19.2: Deltas and Gammas for European Options

- Consider the BOP data (see Example 19.1): $S = \$100$, $K = \$110$, $T = 1$ year, $\sigma = 0.142470$ per year, and $r = 0.05$ per year. Using the formulas from Table 19.1 and computations from the previous example, we get $d_1 = -0.2468$. Then,

$$\text{For the call, delta}_C = N(d_1) = 0.4025$$
$$\text{For the put, delta}_P = -N(-d_1) = -0.5975$$

- We use Microsoft's Excel spreadsheet program for computing deltas and plotting their values. The deltas are computed using the NORMSDIST function for stock prices S at $5 intervals ranging from $50 to $150 (see Table 19.2) and are drawn in Figure 19.3a, where the stock price is depicted on the horizontal axis and the delta values are along the vertical axis. Notice that both the deltas are upward sloping curves.

- To understand these figures, consider the behavior of the option's price for extreme stock price values.
  - For stock prices near 150, the call is deeply in-the-money and increases by almost a dollar for a dollar increase in the stock price, which gives a delta close to 1. In contrast, the put is deeply out-of-the-money and has a near-zero response to any stock price movement, signifying that the put's delta is close to 0.
  - For very low stock prices, the call's delta is almost 0, while the put option's price decreases by almost a dollar for each dollar increase in the stock price, yielding a delta close to −1.

- The gamma is the same for calls and puts. Using the NORMDIST function in Microsoft Excel's spreadsheet to compute $N'(d_1)$, we get

$$\text{gamma} = N'(d_1)/(S\sigma\sqrt{T}) = 0.0272$$

We compute the gammas for stock prices $S = 50, 55, \ldots, 145, 150$; report them in Table 19.2; and plot them in Figure 19.3b.

TABLE 19.1: Partial Derivatives of the Black–Scholes–Merton Model

Derivative	Call Option	Put Option
Delta $\equiv \dfrac{\partial BS}{\partial S}$	$0 < N(d_1) < 1$	$-1 < -N(-d_1) < 0$
Gamma $\equiv \dfrac{\partial^2 BS}{\partial S^2}$	$\dfrac{1}{S\sigma\sqrt{T}}N'(d_1) > 0$	Same as for European call
Theta $\equiv \dfrac{\partial BS}{\partial t}$	$-\dfrac{SN'(d_1)\sigma}{2\sqrt{T}} - rKe^{-rT}N(d_2) < 0$	$-\dfrac{SN'(-d_1)\sigma}{2\sqrt{T}} + rKe^{-rT}N(-d_2) \gtrless 0$
Vega $\equiv \dfrac{\partial BS}{\partial \sigma}$	$S\sqrt{T}N'(d_1) > 0$	Same as for European call
Rho $\equiv \dfrac{\partial BS}{\partial r}$	$TKe^{-rT}N(d_2) \geq 0$	$-TKe^{-rT}N(-d_2) \leq 0$

BS denotes European option prices c and p as obtained from Result 19.1; $N(\cdot)$ is the cumulative normal distribution function with mean 0 and variance 1; and $N'(\cdot)$ is the normal density function.

The sensitivity of the option value to changes in the time to expiration is called **theta**:

$$\text{theta} \equiv \frac{\partial c}{\partial t} = \frac{\text{Change in the value of the option}}{\text{Decrease in the time to expiration}}$$

$$= -\frac{SN'(d_1)\sigma}{2\sqrt{T}} - rKe^{-rT}N(d_2) < 0$$

The theta of the call is negative. This makes intuitive sense because as time passes (which means Δt is positive) and the time to maturity decreases, the option becomes less valuable. This follows for two reasons: first, the variance of the stock's return (given by $\sigma^2 T$) decreases, and second, the present value of the strike (which is the *cost of exercising*) increases, and both changes work in the same direction to make the call less valuable. The put's theta has an ambiguous sign. Here the first effect is similar to that of a call. However, as time passes, the present value of the strike price the put holder pays increases, which increases the put's value. In a given context, it's hard to tell which of these two opposing effects dominate.

TABLE 19.2: Deltas and Gammas for Calls and Puts

Stock Price, S	Call delta$_C$	Put delta$_P$	Gamma
50	0.0000	−1.0000	0.0000
55	0.0000	−1.0000	0.0000
60	0.0001	−0.9999	0.0000
65	0.0005	−0.9995	0.0002
70	0.0030	−0.9970	0.0009
75	0.0117	−0.9883	0.0029
80	0.0349	−0.9651	0.0068
85	0.0826	−0.9174	0.0126
90	0.1620	−0.8380	0.0191
95	0.2720	−0.7280	0.0245
100	0.4025	−0.5975	0.0272
105	0.5381	−0.4619	0.0265
110	0.6636	−0.3364	0.0233
115	0.7686	−0.2314	0.0186
120	0.8492	−0.1508	0.0137
125	0.9065	−0.0935	0.0094
130	0.9446	−0.0554	0.006
135	0.9685	−0.0315	0.0037
140	0.9828	−0.0172	0.0021
145	0.9909	−0.0091	0.0012
150	0.9953	−0.0047	0.0006

The sensitivity of the option value to changes in the volatility is called **vega** (which is not in the Greek alphabet but has found popular usage nonetheless!):

$$\text{vega} \equiv \frac{\partial c}{\partial \sigma} = \frac{\text{Change in the value of the option}}{\text{Change in the volatility}}$$

$$= S\sqrt{T}N'(d_1) > 0 \qquad (19.10\text{d})$$

As the volatility increases, the value of the call increases. The same is true for the put option. Increased volatility is a good thing for the option's value! The larger the volatility, the more spread out the stock price distribution is and the larger is the tail probability that the option ends up in-the-money. It's no wonder that most traders view options as "volatility bets"!

Last, the sensitivity of the option value to changes in the interest rate is called **rho**:

$$\text{rho} \equiv \frac{\partial c}{\partial r} = \frac{\text{Change in the value of the option}}{\text{Change in the value of the interest rate}}$$

$$= TKe^{-rT}N(d_2) \geq 0 \qquad (19.10\text{e})$$

As the interest rate increases, the call's value declines. This is due to the decrease in the present value of the strike price paid at time T if the option ends up in-the-money. But a European put's rho is negative. This happens because a rise in the interest rate lowers the present value of the exercise price that the holder might receive at expiration, and this reduces the put's value.

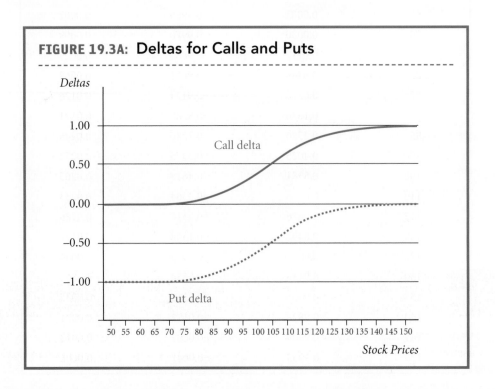

FIGURE 19.3A: **Deltas for Calls and Puts**

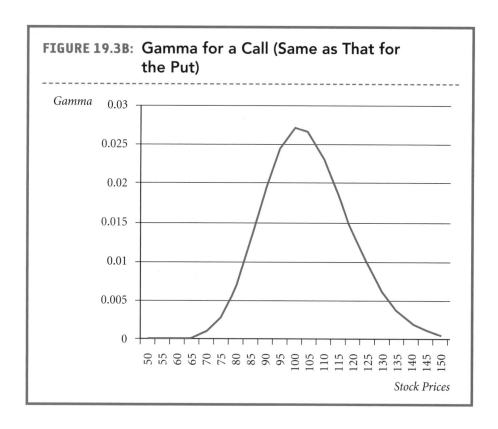

FIGURE 19.3B: Gamma for a Call (Same as That for the Put)

Some Road Bumps Ahead

The Greeks are useful for understanding the sensitivity of option values to changes in the inputs. Sometimes the Greeks are also used for hedging option price risks caused by changes in these parameters. A warning needs to be raised at this time! We will show in chapter 20 that delta and gamma hedging are valid procedures when the BSM assumptions are satisfied (Extension 19.2 shows what happens when the competitive markets assumption is violated and market manipulation is possible). However, even if the BSM assumptions are valid, rho hedging (which has been largely abandoned by the practitioners) and vega hedging (which should also disappear but exists today in many institutions) have serious conceptual problems. Let us drop a hint. We held volatility and interest rates constant throughout our derivation of the BSM formula, so the risk of their changing was not included in the price. This is in contrast to the stock price, whose risk was explicitly considered. Now, all of a sudden, we cannot start tinkering with something that we kept fixed. We will return to these issues in chapter 20.

EXTENSION 19.2: Market Manipulation and Option Pricing

In the derivation of the BSM model, assumption A3, the competitive and well-functioning markets assumption is crucial. Extension 19.1 already discussed how option pricing changes when stock price bubbles exist that violate the well-functioning assumption. This extension discusses the difficulties in pricing options when the competitive markets assumption is relaxed.

A competitive market is one in which traders' trades do not affect the stock price. When this assumption is relaxed and traders' trades change the price, stock market manipulation is possible. In a market that can be manipulated, the BSM model is no longer valid. In fact, the BSM value and delta can be completely wrong. We illustrate such a dramatic failure of the BSM model with a simple example.

Let us consider a European call option with strike price K and maturity T written on a stock with time t price $S(t)$, and volatility σ.

Suppose that the stock price has evolved across time, as graphed in Figure 19.4, and that currently we are standing at time $T - \varepsilon$ for a small $\varepsilon > 0$, where the stock price is out-of-the-money, that is,

$$S(T - \varepsilon) < K$$

Using the BSM formula, it can easily be shown that the value of the call option and its delta are approximately zero, that is,

$$c \sim 0 \text{ and delta} \sim 0 \tag{1}$$

This is because the stock is trading out-of-the-money, and with so little time remaining before the option expires, it is unlikely to move much above the strike price.

Now suppose that trades can change the stock price. This is the violation of the competitive market assumption. Furthermore, suppose that a manipulator purchases a large quantity of the stock's shares purposely to cause the stock price to jump to $S^* > K$. In light of this manipulation, the true price of the call option and its delta are easily seen to be

$$c = S^* - K \text{ and delta} = 1 \tag{2}$$

As indicated, these values are dramatically different from those predicted by the BSM model. If a risk manager had used the BSM model to hedge an option position using a delta value near zero (see chapter 20 for

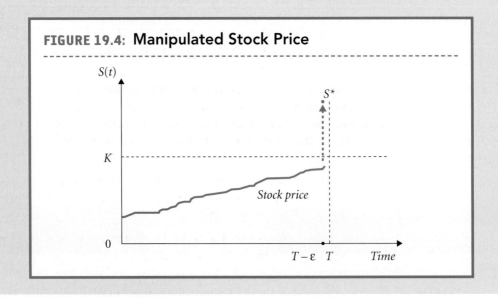

FIGURE 19.4: Manipulated Stock Price

an elaboration on delta hedging), he would have lost significant wealth because of the market manipulator's actions.

As this example illustrates, the BSM model no longer applies when the competitive markets assumption is relaxed. Pricing options in a world in which the stock price can be manipulated is a fruitful area for research (see Bank and Baum 2004; Jarrow 1994).

19.9 | The Inputs

Most of the inputs for the BSM formula are easily obtained. The most elusive input to measure is the volatility. Because of its importance, volatility estimation is discussed in this section and also in the next chapter. This chapter concentrates on historical volatility, the next chapter on calibration and implied volatilities.

Observable Inputs

The strike price (K) and time to maturity (T) are specified in the option contract. The stock price (S) is easy to obtain. For actively traded stocks, use the last transaction price, and for less liquid stocks, use the average of the bid and ask prices.

The continuously compounded risk-free interest rate (r) is computable from Treasury security prices. Select the Treasury bill that matures closest to the option's expiration date, take the average of the bid and ask yields, and compute the Treasury bill's price. Last, solve for the continuously compounded annual interest rate from this zero-coupon bond price (see chapter 2). This is the interest rate to use in the BSM formula.

Volatility: The Elusive Input

Volatility is the hardest input to estimate. There are two standard methods for estimating the volatility: an explicit method using past stock prices, called the *historical volatility*, and an implicit method using option market prices, called the *implied volatility*.

HISTORICAL VOLATILITY The volatility when estimated using statistical methods and past price data is called a **historical volatility**. An estimate of the volatility is the stock return's sample standard deviation, although numerous other estimators can also be used. Historical volatility estimation, using actual stock price realizations, is based on nature's "draws" from the actual probability distribution expression (19.1). This implies, of course, that the estimates of both the stock's expected return μ and volatility σ are obtained under the actual probability q. The next example illustrates how to estimate the stock's volatility using the return's sample standard deviation.

EXAMPLE 19.3: Computing Historical Volatility

■ Stock price data are available from newspapers or the Internet.

■ *The data.* Table 19.3 reports closing stock prices for Your Beloved Machines Corp. (YBM). Column 1 is labeled Week(t). There are $(n + 1) = 17$ observations corresponding to 17 consecutive weeks, where t runs from week 0 to week $t = 16$. Column 2 records weekly closing prices for YBM. Seventeen observations are chosen to illustrate the computation. In practice, a larger number of observations are recommended. This issue is discussed after the example.

■ *The price relative.* The **price relatives** of the stock prices are reported in column 3. This is given by $S(t)/S(t-1)$, where $S(t)$ is week t's closing price. For example, when $t = 6$, the price relative is

$$S(6)/S(5) = 103/100 = 1.03$$

Notice that when computing the "difference," the first observation is lost. We now have $n = 16$ data points, which we denote by $t = 1, 2, \ldots, 16$.

■ *The logarithm of the price relative.* The natural logarithm of the price relative, $\log[S(t)/S(t-1)]$, is computed and recorded in the fourth column. For example, we have

$$\log[S(6)/S(5)] = \log(1.03) = 0.029558802$$

For simplicity, write this as $\log[S(t)/S(t-1)] = x(t)$.

■ *Computing the sample variance.* One can proceed in several ways:
  - If the data are input into a spreadsheet or a computer program, the sample variance is computed in one step. For example, running Excel command VARA over the sixteen observations in cells D4 = 0.019802627 to D19 = 0.029852963 gives VARA(D4:D19) = 0.000390218.
  - Alternatively, one can plod through the calculations by hand, first computing the sample mean,

$$\hat{\mu} = \frac{1}{n}\sum_{t=1}^{n} x(t) = 0.019802627/16 = 0.001237664$$

and then reporting in column 5 the deviations of the $x(t)$'s values from the mean, squared, and then computing the average of these squared deviations using $(n-1) = 15$ in the denominator to get the sample variance:

$$\hat{\sigma}^2 = \frac{1}{n-1}\sum_{t=1}^{n}\left[x(t) - \hat{\mu}\right]^2 = 0.005853263/15 = 0.00390218$$

■ *Computing the annualized volatility.* To convert the computed sample variance to the annualized variance, because the variance is proportional to the time period (see Result 1 in the appendix to this chapter), we need only multiply by the number of weeks in a year, that is,

$$\hat{\sigma}^2_{Annual} = \hat{\sigma}^2_{Week}(\text{Number of weeks}) = 0.00390218 \times 52 = 0.02029131$$

TABLE 19.3: Computing σ from Weekly Price Data

Week (t)	Stock Price $S(t)$	Price Relative $\dfrac{S(t)}{S(t-1)}$	Log of Price Relative $\log\left[\dfrac{S(t)}{S(t-1)}\right] \equiv x(t)$	$\displaystyle\sum_{t=1}^{16}\left[x(t)-\hat{\mu}\right]^2$
0	100			
1	102	1.02	0.019802627	0.000344658
2	99	0.970588235	−0.029852963	0.000966627
3	100	1.01010101	0.010050336	7.76632E-05
4	101	1.01	0.009950331	7.59106E-05
5	100	0.99009901	−0.009950331	0.000125171
6	103	1.03	0.029558802	0.000802087
7	104	1.009708738	0.009661911	7.09679E-05
8	101	0.971153846	−0.029270382	0.000930741
9	101	1	0	1.53181E-06
10	100	0.99009901	−0.009950331	0.000125171
11	101	1.01	0.009950331	7.59106E-05
12	100	0.99009901	−0.009950331	0.000125171
13	102	1.02	0.019802627	0.000344658
14	102	1	0	1.53181E-06
15	99	0.970588235	−0.029852963	0.000966627
16	102	1.03030303	0.029852963	0.000818835
Sums			$\Sigma x = 0.019802627$	0.005853263
Mean			$\Sigma x/16 = 0.001237664$	

The positive square root is the annualized volatility $\hat{\sigma} = 0.14245$.

■ *Converting to annualized figures.* Suppose you compute the volatility using daily data instead. How would you annualize this? Although people initially used 365 days, empirical studies suggest that a better volatility estimate is obtained if one uses the number of trading days instead (see French 1980; French and Roll 1986).[5] Assuming there are 250 trading days in a year, one gets

$$\hat{\sigma}^2_{Annual} = \hat{\sigma}^2_{Daily}(250)$$

[5] If you compute sigma using monthly data (one stock price data per month), then use the square root of 12 as the adjustment factor to compute annualized volatility.

In computing the sample variance, a number of choices need to be made. First, how many observations should you use? Theoretically speaking, more observations will give a better estimate, everything else held constant. But everything else is almost never constant! A long time series of prices may not be stationary because the underlying structure of the company may change, and consequently, so, too, the stock's volatility. A good rule of thumb is to get a minimum of fifty observations (where the central limit theorem from statistics kicks in, which enables the use of the normal distribution for hypothesis testing). Second, what should the time interval be between stock price observations? Shorter intervals imply more price observations, but at short intervals, market frictions and market microstructure issues can introduce significant noise into the estimation. Daily or weekly intervals have less of these microstructure problems. A good rule of thumb is to use daily or weekly data.

IMPLIED VOLATILITY   The volatility estimated using an OPM in conjunction with contemporaneous option market prices, instead of past stock prices, is called an **implied volatility**. This section explains how to obtain such an estimate using the BSM formula.

For the purposes of this estimate, we can rewrite the BSM call price as $BSM(\sigma)$, where σ is the volatility. The *implied volatility* σ_{Imp} is defined as the volatility that solves the following equation:

$$c_{Market} = BSM(\sigma_{Imp}) \qquad (19.11)$$

In words, the implied volatility is that volatility that equates the market price for an option equal to its BSM value.

Thus, for the implied volatility, we use (S, K, r, T) and c_{Market} as *inputs* and then compute the volatility σ by solving this equation. Technically, since the BSM formula is an increasing function of the volatility, a solution always exists. Unfortunately, no closed form solution is available. However, using numerical approximation techniques, the option's implied volatility σ_{Imp} can be easily determined.

This estimation method is an example of **calibration**, in which one estimates a parameter from a model by using market prices as inputs rather than outputs. Calibration and implied volatilities are often misused, so care should be exercised when employed. Chapter 20 discusses the use and misuse of calibration and implied volatilities in detail.[6]

19.10 | Extending the Black–Scholes–Merton Model

This section extends the BSM model in three key directions: one is to dividends, two is to foreign currency options, and three is to American options. All these extensions are important applications of the BSM model.

---

[6] Note that because implied volatility estimation uses market prices and the BSM formula, this estimation is done under the pseudo-probabilities π and does not depend on the actual probabilities.

Adjusting for Dividends

The assumption that the underlying stock pays no dividends underlies the BSM model. But most stocks pay dividends, which lowers the price of calls and raises the price of puts. Fortunately, one can adjust the basic model for dividends. We present two such approaches. The first adjusts the BSM formula for a known dollar dividend, whereas the second allows the stock to pay random dividends at a continuous rate. Here the discussion of dividend adjustments presented in the cost-of-carry model (chapter 12) and the multiperiod binomial model (chapter 18) are relevant.

When *the dividend date and dollar dividend are known*, replace the actual stock price with the current stock price minus the present value of all the dividends paid over the option's life. Then continue with business as usual: employ the BSM model with this modified stock price. Thus expression (19.4a) gets modified to

$$c = [S - \text{PV(Dividends)}]N(d_1) - Ke^{-rT}N(d_2) \qquad (19.12)$$

where

$$d_1 = \frac{\log\left[\dfrac{S - PV(\text{Dividends})}{K}\right] + \left(r + \dfrac{\sigma^2}{2}\right)T}{\sigma\sqrt{T}}$$

$$d_2 = d_1 - \sigma\sqrt{T}$$

When the *dividend rate is known*, again the stock price is replaced by the current stock price less the present value of the dividends paid over the option's life, but here there is a fractional reduction ($e^{-\delta T}$), that is,

$$c = Se^{-\delta T}N(d_1) - Ke^{-rT}N(d_2) \qquad (19.13a)$$

$$p = Ke^{-rT}N(-d_2) - Se^{-\delta T}N(-d_1) \qquad (19.13b)$$

where δ is the dividend yield:

$$d_1 = \frac{\log\left(\dfrac{S}{K}\right) + \left(r - \delta + \dfrac{\sigma^2}{2}\right)T}{\sigma\sqrt{T}}$$

$$d_2 = d_1 - \sigma\sqrt{T}$$

The dollar dividend is random in this case because the random stock price is multiplied by a constant dividend rate, yielding a random dollar dividend payment. This model, originally derived by Robert Merton (1973a), is particularly useful for valuing index and currency options for the reasons we had discussed before (see chapter 12). In the special case when $\delta = 0$, this model reduces to the BSM model. The next example illustrates their use.

EXAMPLE 19.4: Pricing a European Option on an Index

The Data

- Consider the data from chapter 12:
  - INDY index's current level $I = 1,000$.
  - The continuously compounded interest rate r is 6 percent per year.
  - The dividend yield $\delta = 20/1,000 = 0.02$ or 2 percent per year because the stocks constituting INDY paid $20 in dividends last year.

The European Call Price

- Consider a European call on INDY with maturity $T = 1$ year and a strike price of $K = 1,100$. Let the index's return volatility σ be 0.142470 per year. The payoff to the call on the maturity date is $100[S(T) -1,100]$ dollars if it ends in-the-money, and is zero otherwise, where 100 is the contract multiplier. This call is valued using expression (19.13a), as follows:
  - Compute d_1 and d_2:

$$
d_1 = \frac{\log\left(\dfrac{S}{K}\right) + \left(r - \delta + \dfrac{\sigma^2}{2}\right)T}{\sigma\sqrt{T}}
$$

$$
= \frac{\log\left(\dfrac{1,000}{1,100}\right) + \left[0.06 - 0.02 + \dfrac{(0.14247)^2}{2}\right](1)}{0.14247\sqrt{1}}
$$

$$
= -0.3170
$$

$$
d_2 = d_1 - \sigma\sqrt{T} = -0.3170 - 0.14247 = -0.4595
$$

  - Using the NORMSDIST function of Excel, we get the cumulative standard normal distribution function values

$$
N(d_1) = N(-0.3170) = 0.3756
$$
$$
N(d_2) = N(-0.4595) = 0.3223
$$

  - The zero-coupon bond price is $B = e^{-rT} = e^{-0.06} = 0.9418$.
  - The present value of the dividend yield $e^{-\delta T} = e^{-0.02} = 0.9802$.
  - The European call price for the index option is therefore

$$
c = e^{-\delta T}SN(d_1) - Ke^{-rT}N(d_2)
$$
$$
= 0.9802 \times 1,000 \times 0.3756 \times 1,100 \times 0.9418 \times 0.3223
$$
$$
= \$33.6286
$$

  - Using the contract multiplier 100, the European call's price is $3,362.86.

Foreign Currency Options

Pricing foreign currency options using the BSM formula is just a clever use of the BSM model with a dividend yield. We illustrate this application with an example.

EXAMPLE 19.5: Pricing a European Option on a Currency

The Data

- Consider the data from chapter 12:
  - Let today's spot exchange rate S_A be $2 per pound (in American terms).
  - Let the continuously compounded annual risk-free interest rates be $r = 6$ percent in the United States (domestic) and $r_E = 4$ percent in the United Kingdom (foreign). The UK rate is interpreted as the "dividend yield" δ in this context.

The European Call Price

- Consider a European call on pound sterling with maturity $T = 1$ year and a strike price of $K = \$2.10$. Let the pound's volatility σ be 0.10 per year. The payoff to the call on the maturity date is $100[S(T) - 2.10]$ dollars if it ends in-the-money, and zero if otherwise, where 100 is the contract multiplier. This call is valued using expression (19.14a):
  - Compute d_1 and d_2:

$$d_1 = \frac{\log\left(\dfrac{2}{2.1}\right) + \left[0.06 - 0.04 + \dfrac{(0.1)^2}{2}\right](1)}{0.1\sqrt{1}} = -0.2379$$

$$d_2 = d_1 - \sigma\sqrt{T} = -0.2379 - 0.1 = -0.3379$$

  - Moreover, we get
$$N(d_1) = N(-0.2379) = 0.4060$$
$$N(d_2) = N(-0.3379) = 0.3677$$

  The zero-coupon bond price (US) is $B = e^{-rT} = e^{-0.06} = 0.9418$. The zero-coupon bond price (foreign) $B_E = e^{r_E T} = e^{-0.04} = 0.9608$.
  - The European call price for the currency option is therefore

$$c = e^{-r_E T} S N(d_1) - K e^{-rT} N(d_2)$$
$$= 0.9608 \times 2 \times 0.4060 - 2.1 \times 0.9418 \times 0.3677$$
$$= \$0.0529$$

Using the contract multiplier 100, the European currency call's price is $5.29.

Valuing American Options

The BSM formula and its dividend modifications only hold for European options. Yet American options trade. We know from chapter 16 that when there are dividends, American options are more valuable than European options because of an early exercise premium. Unfortunately, we can only obtain formulas for American call options in some very special cases, and there are no closed-form solutions for pricing American put options. This implies that to price American options in practice, we need to turn to numerical procedures. Numerical procedures compute values using the computer instead of plugging into an analytic formula.

You have already been introduced to numerical procedures in chapter 18 when pricing American calls and puts using the binomial model. Because the multiperiod binomial model can be used to approximate a lognormally distributed stock price, the multiperiod binomial model provides an important tool for approximating American call and put values in the BSM model as well. This approach works well but can be computationally time consuming.

Other numerical procedures for pricing American call and put options are available as well. Numerical approximation techniques can be divided into two categories: (1) methods that numerically solve the partial differential equation (pde) implied by the option's price (see chapter 20 for a discussion of the BSM pde) and (2) those that approximate the stock price evolution to compute the option's risk-neutral value (a discounted expectation). To solve pdes, numerical techniques like finite difference methods and numerical integration can be employed. To compute discounted expectations, the binomial model and Monte Carlo simulation techniques are useful. Unfortunately, both methods are beyond the scope of this textbook and are left for more advanced courses (see Glasserman [2003] for Monte Carlo methods, Wilmott [1998] for pdes, and Duffie [2001] for a discussion of both).

EXTENSION 19.3: Exotic Options

Exotic options are derivative securities that differ from the simple, plain vanilla forwards, futures, and European and American call and put options that we have encountered so far. There are many exotic options with names like "digital options," "gap options," "options on the maximum or minimum," "down-and-out options," "down-and-in options," and "average options." The defining characteristic of any such exotic option is its payoff at maturity or at an intermediate time, conditional on certain events related to the path of the underlying stock price being satisfied. The easiest method of pricing such options is to use risk-neutral valuation and compute the discounted expected payoffs to these options under the pseudo-probabilities. We illustrate this general approach with two examples under the BSM assumptions.

Digital Options

A **digital put option** has a maturity date T and a strike price K. Its payoff at maturity is

$$\text{digital}(T) = \begin{cases} 1 & \text{if} \quad S(T) < K \\ 0 & \text{if} \quad S(T) \geq K \end{cases}$$

This payoff is similar to an ordinary European put, except in its payoff, which equals just \$1 if the option ends up in-the-money.

Using risk-neutral valuation, the time 0 value of a digital put option is

$$\text{digital}(0) = E^\pi\{\text{digital}(T)\}e^{-rT} = e^{-rT}N(d - \sigma\sqrt{T})$$

where

$$d = \frac{\log\left(\dfrac{S}{K}\right) - rT}{\sigma\sqrt{T}} + \frac{\sigma}{2}\sqrt{T}$$

Barrier Options

Barrier options are similar to European options, except the payoffs depend on whether the stock price hits some barrier over the option's life. We illustrate one such option.

A **down-and-out call option** has a maturity date T and a strike price K. Its payoff at maturity is that of an ordinary European call option, but only if a lower barrier (b) is not hit over the option's life. If the lower barrier is hit, the option expires worthless, regardless of its value at maturity. The payoff can be written as follows:

$$\text{down\&out}(T) = 1_{\{\tau > T\}}\max\left[S(T) - K, 0\right]$$

where

$$1_{\{\tau > T\}} = \begin{cases} 1 & \text{if} \quad \min S(t) > b \text{ for all } t \in [0,T] \\ 0 & \text{otherwise} \end{cases}$$

Using risk-neutral valuation, the time 0 value of a down-and-out call option is

$$\text{down\&out}(0) = E^\pi\{\text{down\&out}(T)\}e^{-rT}$$

A complex analytic formula for this expression exists; see Jarrow and Turnbull (2000).

19.11 | Summary

1. The year 1973 saw the publication of the Black–Scholes–Merton option pricing model. The BSM model forms the foundation of more advanced derivatives pricing models.

2. As with the binomial model, the BSM model assumes no market frictions, no credit risk, competitive and well-functioning markets, no interest rate uncertainty, no intermediate cash flows, and no arbitrage. Here, however, we introduce a different assumption for the stock price evolution. The BSM model assumes continuous trading and that the stock price returns follow a lognormal distribution.

3. The BSM formula for pricing a European call option is

$$c = SN(d_1) - Ke^{-rT}N(d_2)$$

where $S \equiv S(0)$ is today's spot price, $N(\dots)$ is the cumulative standard normal distribution function which has mean 0 and standard deviation 1,

$$d_1 = \frac{\log\left(\frac{S}{K}\right) + \left(r + \frac{\sigma^2}{2}\right)T}{\sigma\sqrt{T}}$$

$$d_2 = d_1 - \sigma\sqrt{T}$$

K is the strike price, r is the continuously compounded risk-free interest rate per year, T is the time to maturity measured in years, and σ is stock return's volatility per year.

4. As in chapter 17, it can be shown that the stock price, normalized by the price of a money market account, is a martingale under the pseudo-probabilities. This is an implication of our no arbitrage assumption. Under the lognormal distribution assumption, the market is complete, and risk-neutral valuation holds using the pseudo-probabilities and gives the call price as

$$c = E^\pi\{\max[0, S(T) - K]\}e^{-rT}$$

5. To understand the BSM formula, we compute the option sensitivities (popularly known as the Greeks) by taking partial derivatives with respect to the stock price (S) to get delta, the time to maturity (T) to get theta, the riskless interest rate (r) to get rho, and the stock return's volatility (σ) to get vega. In addition, the second partial derivative with respect to the stock price is the gamma. The Greeks are useful for options hedging and portfolio risk management, a topic we address in chapter 20.

6. Volatility is the hardest input to estimate. There are two standard methods for estimating the volatility: an explicit method using past stock prices, called the historical volatility, and an implicit method using option market prices, called the implied volatility. The implied volatility is discussed in chapter 20.

7. Three common extensions of the BSM model are to adjust for dividends, to price foreign currency options, and to price American options. American options don't have analytical solutions. They can be solved by numerical methods belonging to one of three types: (1) a multiperiod binomial option pricing model, (2) partial differential equations, and (3) Monte Carlo simulation techniques.

19.12 | Appendix

Modeling the Stock Price Evolution

This appendix justifies the widely used lognormal assumption for stock prices using fundamental axioms for stock price changes. We build this argument in several steps: we (1) divide the time horizon into shorter periods over which stock prices follow a continuously compounded (logarithmic) return, (2) introduce uncertainty via additional assumptions on these returns, and (3) apply the central limit theorem to show that stock prices are lognormally distributed.

Continuously Compounded (Logarithmic) Return

We introduce a discrete time multiperiod structure like the one introduced in chapter 18. We do this by chopping up the time horizon $[0, T]$ into n shorter time periods of length $T/n = \Delta t$ each (see Figure 19.5). Let us assume that over any time interval $[t - \Delta t, t]$, the stock price has a continuously compounded return z_t that is inspired by expression (19.1):

$$S(t) = S(t - \Delta t)e^{z_t} \qquad (1)$$

The stock price grows by continuous compounding. Setting $t = \Delta t, 2\Delta t, \ldots$ gives relations like

$$S(\Delta t) = S(0)e^{z_1} \text{ over } [0, \Delta t],$$
$$S(2\Delta t) = S(\Delta t)e^{z_2} \text{ over } [\Delta t, 2\Delta t], \ldots$$
$$S(T) = S(T - \Delta t)e^{z_T} \text{ over } [T - \Delta t, T]$$

We can use the preceding relations to write the stock price at the end of the time horizon as

$$S(T) = \left[\frac{S(T)}{S(T - \Delta t)} \frac{S(T - \Delta t)}{S(T - 2\Delta t)} \cdots \frac{S(\Delta t)}{S(0)} \right] S(0)$$

$$= e^{z_T} e^{z_{T-1}} \ldots e^{z_1} S(0)$$

$$= S(0) e^{z_1 + \ldots + z_{T-1} + z_T} \qquad (2)$$

Now, if we define the sum of these continuously compounded stock price returns over the short intervals as $Z(T)$, that is,

$$z_1 + \ldots + z_{T-1} + z_T \equiv Z(T) \qquad (3a)$$

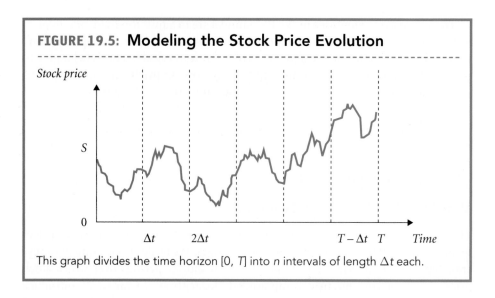

FIGURE 19.5: Modeling the Stock Price Evolution

This graph divides the time horizon [0, T] into n intervals of length Δt each.

then we can simply rewrite (2) as

$$Z(T) = \log[S(T)/S(0)] \qquad (3b)$$

Thus $Z(T)$ corresponds to the continuously compounded (or logarithmic) return over the time horizon $[0, T]$. Notice that (3a) is a linear relationship that has a number of attractive features and makes the model amenable to mathematical analysis.

Introducing Uncertainty

Next, we introduce *uncertainty* in our model. We do this by adding two assumptions, which are often-used statistical properties for a collection of random variables.

A1. The returns $\{z_t\} \equiv \{z_1, z_2, \ldots, z_T\}$ are independent. Early empirical studies suggested that stock price returns over successive intervals are independent of each other.

A2. The returns $\{z_t\}$ are identically distributed. Early empirical studies also suggested that stock price returns over successive intervals tend to follow the same distribution.

Notice that we have not specified any probability distribution for the continuously compounded stock price returns. These two assumptions yield the property that is often referred to by the abbreviation **iid** (for independent and identically distributed). Any process satisfying these assumptions is called a **random walk**. Stock prices following a random walk are linked with the efficient markets hypothesis introduced in chapter 6 because random walks occur when information comes in randomly and gets immediately reflected in stock prices.

Next, we introduce two more assumptions to ensure that stock prices behave as the time interval shrinks and approaches zero. We do this by assuming that the expected return and the variance of the return are proportional to the length of the time interval.

A3. The expected continuously compounded return can be written as

$$E(z_t) = \mu \Delta t \qquad (4)$$

where μ is a constant that corresponds to the expected continuously compounded return per year.

A4. The variance of the continuously compounded return can be written as

$$\text{var}(z_t) = \sigma^2 \Delta t \qquad (5)$$

where σ^2 is a constant that corresponds to the variance of the continuously compounded return per year.

Assumptions A1-A4 allows us to write

$$
\begin{aligned}
E[Z(T)] &= E(z_1 + \ldots + z_{T-1} + z_T) \\
&= \mu(\Delta t + \Delta t + \ldots + \Delta t) \\
&\quad [\text{because, by A3, the returns have identical mean } \mu] \\
&= \mu T \qquad\qquad\qquad (6a)
\end{aligned}
$$

and

$$
\begin{aligned}
\text{var}[Z(T)] &= \text{var}(z_1 + \ldots + z_{T-1} + z_T) \\
&= \text{var}(z_1) + \text{var}(z_2) + \ldots + \text{var}(z_T) \qquad [\text{by assumption A1}] \\
&= \sum_{j=1}^{n} \sigma^2 \Delta t \qquad [\text{by assumption A4}] \\
&= \sigma^2 T \qquad\qquad\qquad (6b)
\end{aligned}
$$

We used expression (6b) earlier in the chapter when estimating the stock's historical volatility.

The Central Limit Theorem

Next, we apply the **central limit theorem** (**CLT**). It states that the average of iid random variables (provided it has a well-defined mean and variance), when "standardized" (by subtracting from the average the common mean and dividing the expression by the standard deviation of the average), starts behaving like a standard normal distribution (see Mood et al. 1974; Cox and Miller 1990). An application of this theorem yields the following result.

RESULT 1 (APPENDIX)
- -
Lognormal Distribution of Stock Price Returns

Stock prices are lognormally distributed with mean μT and variance $\sigma^2 T$ over the time horizon $[0, T]$.

Hence we can write the continuously compounded return as

$$Z(T) = \log\left(\frac{S(T)}{S(0)}\right) = \left(\mu - \frac{\sigma^2}{2}\right)T + \sigma\sqrt{T}z \tag{7}$$

where z is a standard normal random variable with mean 0 and variance 1. Because z is normally distributed, $Z(T)$ is normally distributed, and hence $S(T)$ is said to have a lognormal distribution. This result is reported as expression (19.2) in the text, and it is used in Example 19.3.

First Derivation of the Black–Scholes–Merton Formula (as a Limit of the Binomial Model)

This appendix provides a formal derivation of the BSM formula based on the intuition obtained from Figure 19.1, the second graph of the multiperiod binomial model. In this figure, you can see that as the time interval becomes smaller, the multiperiod model appears more and more realistic. In fact, it can be shown that it approaches the lognormal distribution! Not surprisingly, this gives us a way to derive the BSM formula.

MULTIPERIOD BINOMIAL PARAMETERS FOR THE LOGNORMAL APPROXIMATION

- To formalize this intuition, we start with assumption A7 of chapter 17 as applied to the multiperiod binomial model. We divide our time interval $[0, T]$ into subintervals of length Δt, yielding $T/\Delta t = n$ intervals.

- Next, we use the Jarrow–Rudd specification of the parameters

$$U = e^{r\Delta t - \frac{\sigma^2}{2}\Delta t + \sigma\sqrt{\Delta t}} \text{ and } D = e^{r\Delta t - \frac{\sigma^2}{2}\Delta t - \sigma\sqrt{\Delta t}} \tag{8a}$$

given in Extension 18.1. Because the option value does not depend on the actual probability of moving up, we leave the actual probability unspecified, and work under the pseudo-probabilities. We choose the pseudo-probability $\pi = 1/2$. This choice guarantees that the binomial process for the log return on the stock over $[0,T]$ has an expectation and volatility equal to $rT - (\sigma^2/2)T$ and $\sigma^2 T$, respectively. Using expression (8a), the stock price process is

$$S(T) = S(0)U^j D^{(n-j)} \tag{8b}$$

- Taking logarithms of expression (8b) yields

$$\log S(T) = \log S(0) + j\log U + (n - j)\log D \tag{9a}$$

Next, substitution of U and D into this expression gives

$$\log S(T) = \log S(0) + j\left(r\Delta t - \frac{\sigma^2}{2}\Delta t + \sigma\sqrt{\Delta t}\right)$$

$$+ (n - j)\left(r\Delta t - \frac{\sigma^2}{2}\Delta t - \sigma\sqrt{\Delta t}\right) \tag{9b}$$

Substituting $\Delta t = T/n$ and simplifying this is transformed to

$$\log S(T) = \log S(0) + 2j\left(\frac{\sigma\sqrt{T}}{\sqrt{n}}\right)$$
$$+ \left(rT - \frac{\sigma^2}{2}T\right) - \sqrt{n}\sigma\sqrt{T} \tag{9c}$$

Last, rearranging terms gives

$$\frac{\log\frac{S(T)}{S(0)} - \left(rT - \frac{\sigma^2}{2}T\right)}{\sigma\sqrt{T}} = \frac{\left(j - \frac{n}{2}\right)}{\frac{\sqrt{n}}{2}} \tag{9d}$$

TAKING LIMITS

■ The famous de Moivre–Laplace theorem states that a binomial random variable approaches a normally distributed random variable as the number of realizations (time intervals) approaches infinity, that is,

$$\text{Prob}\left(\frac{j - \frac{n}{2}}{\frac{\sqrt{n}}{2}} \le x\right) \to N(x) \text{ as } n \to \infty \tag{10a}$$

Hence, by substitution of expression (9d), we see that the logarithm of the assumed stock price process approaches a normally distributed random variable, that is,

$$\text{Prob}\left(\frac{\log\frac{S(T)}{S(0)} - \left(rT - \frac{\sigma^2}{2}T\right)}{\sigma\sqrt{T}} \le x\right) \to N(x) \text{ as } n \to \infty \tag{10b}$$

In simpler notation, this implies that as $n \to \infty$,

$$S(T) = S(0)e^{(r-\frac{\sigma^2}{2})T+\sigma\sqrt{T}z} \tag{11}$$

where z is a standard normal random variable with mean zero and unit variance under the pseudo-probability $\pi(z)$. This is our lognormally distributed stock price!

MARTINGALE PRICING

■ The normal distribution has the property that

$$E^\pi[e^{\sigma\sqrt{T}z}] = e^{\frac{\sigma^2}{2}T} \tag{12a}$$

Taking the expectation of expression (11) yields

$$E^\pi[S(T)] = S(0)e^{(r-\frac{\sigma^2}{2})T}E^\pi\left[e^{\sigma\sqrt{T}z}\right] \tag{12b}$$

The use of expression (12a) in (12b) yields, after rearranging terms, the martingale pricing relation expression (19.6) given earlier in the text, that is,

$$S(0) = E^{\pi}[S(T)]e^{-rT} \tag{13}$$

where $E^{\pi}(\,.\,)$ is expectation using the pseudo-probabilities $\pi(z)$ associated with the lognormal distribution; that is, the current stock price $S(0)$ is the expected discounted value of the stock price at time T. This is analogous to expression (17.5).

RISK-NEUTRAL VALUATION

■ Next, using the multiperiod binomial call option formula from chapter 18, expression (18.11), with the Jarrow–Rudd parameters, we have

$$c_n = e^{-rT}\sum_{j=0}^{n}\left\{\left[\binom{n}{j}\pi^{j}(1-\pi)^{n-j}\right] \times \left[\max\left(0, U^{j}D^{n-j}S(0) - K\right)\right]\right\} \tag{14}$$

■ Using expression (8b) again, this can also be written as (see [18.12])

$$c_n = E^{\pi}\left\{\max\left[0, S(T) - K\right]\right\}e^{-rT} \tag{15}$$

This is called *risk-neutral valuation*.

TAKING LIMITS AGAIN

■ Taking the limit as $n \to \infty$, one gets

$$c_n \to E^{\pi}\left\{\max\left[0, S(T) - K\right]\right\}e^{-rT} \tag{16}$$

where $\pi(z)$ are the pseudo-probabilities associated with the random variable z as in expression (11). This follows from interchanging the limit and expectation operations (see Billingsley 1995, p. 291).

The next section shows that this yields the BSM formula.

Second Derivation of the Black–Scholes–Merton Formula (Using Risk-Neutral Valuation)

Using expression (16) above, we have

$$c = E^{\pi}\left\{\max\left[0, S(T) - K\right]\right\}e^{-rT} \tag{17}$$

EVALUATING THE EXPECTATION Taking conditional expectations, one can write the call value as the sum of two terms:[7]

$$\begin{aligned}
c = {}& E^{\pi}\{\max[S(T) - K, 0]|S(T) \geq K\}\,\text{Prob}_{\pi}\{S(T) \geq K\}e^{-rT} \\
& + E^{\pi}\{\max[S(T) - K, 0]|S(T) < K\}\,\text{Prob}_{\pi}\{S(T) < K\}e^{-rT}
\end{aligned} \tag{18}$$

---

[7] This follows from the fact that $E(X) = \sum_{Y} E(X\,|\,Y)\,\text{Prob}(Y)$, where X and Y are random variables.

Recognizing that if $S(T) \geq K$, $\max[0, S(T) - K] = S(T) - K$, and if $S(T) < K$, $\max[0, S(T) - K] = 0$, we can rewrite the last expression as

$$c = E^\pi\{S(T)|S(T) \geq K\}e^{-rT}\text{Prob}_\pi\{S(T) \geq K\} - K\text{Prob}_\pi\{S(T) \geq K\}e^{-rT} \quad (19)$$

One can show using the properties of normal distributions (see Jarrow and Rudd 1982) that

$$E^\pi\{S(T)|S(T) \geq K\}\,\text{Prob}_\pi\{S(T) \geq K\}e^{-rT} = S(0)N(d_1)$$
$$K\text{Prob}_\pi\{S(T) \geq K\}e^{-rT} = KN(d_2)e^{-rT} \quad (20)$$

Combined, these give the BSM formula. This completes the derivation.

The Probabilities and the Risk Premium

In our derivation of the BSM formula, we showed that one could write the stock price today as its discounted value using the pseudo-probabilities, that is,

$$S(0) = E^\pi\big[S(T)\big]e^{-rT} \quad (21)$$

where E^π represents expectation using $\pi(z)$.

Recall that the actual and pseudo-probabilities are related by the expression

$$\pi(z) = \phi(z)q(z) \quad (22)$$

where $\phi(z) = e^{-(\theta^2/2)+\theta z} > 0$ and $\theta = -\big[(\mu - r)/\sigma\big]\sqrt{T}$. Using $\phi(z)$, we can rewrite

$$S(0) = E\big[\phi(z)S(T)\big]e^{-rT}$$

$$= \left[\int_{-\infty}^{\infty}\phi(z)S(T)q(z)dz\right]e^{-rT} \quad (23)$$

This expression transforms the expectation taken in terms of the pseudo-probabilities to an expectation taken in terms of the actual probabilities.

There are two ways to compute a present value. One is as given in expression (21). Here the present value is computed by taking an expectation using the pseudo-probabilities and discounting at the risk-free rate. The adjustment for risk occurs in the use of the pseudo-probabilities when taking the expectation. The second and traditional way of computing a present value is to take the expectation using the actual probabilities and adjust the discount rate for risk. Expression (23) can be manipulated to generate this second method of computing a present value. Indeed, as proved immediately, this expression can be equivalently written as

$$S(0) = \left[\int_{-\infty}^{\infty}S(T)q(z)dz\right]e^{-(rT+\text{cov}[\log(\frac{S(T)}{S(0)}),-\log\phi(z)])}$$

$$= E[S(T)]e^{-(rT+\text{cov}[\log(\frac{S(T)}{S(0)}),-\log\phi(z)])} \quad (24)$$

where the discount rate is adjusted instead by the covariance term $\text{cov}(\log[S(T)/S(0)], -\log[\phi(z)])$, a risk premium. We see that the risk-adjusted discount rate depends on $\phi(z)$, which provides an alternative confirmation that $\phi(z)$ is an adjustment for risk.

Proof of (24)

This proof just uses simple calculus and knowledge of normal distributions. We start with

$$S(0) = \left[\int_{-\infty}^{\infty} \phi(z)S(T)q(z)dz\right]e^{-rT} \qquad (25)$$

Plugging in $\phi(z)$ and $S(T)$ gives

$$S(0) = S(0)\int_{-\infty}^{\infty} e^{-\frac{\theta^2}{2}+\theta z}e^{\mu T - \frac{\sigma^2}{2}T+\sigma\sqrt{T}z}\frac{e^{-\frac{z^2}{2}}}{\sqrt{2\pi}}dz\,e^{-rT}$$

$$= S(0)e^{\mu T - rT+\sigma\sqrt{T}\theta}\int_{-\infty}^{\infty} e^{-(\sigma\sqrt{T}+\theta-z)^2\frac{1}{2}}\frac{dz}{\sqrt{2\pi}}$$

which we get by completing the square. However,

$$\int_{-\infty}^{\infty} e^{-(\sigma\sqrt{T}+\theta-z)^2\frac{1}{2}}\frac{dz}{\sqrt{2\pi}} = 1$$

since this is normal with mean $(\sigma\sqrt{T}+\theta)$ and variance 1. Hence $S(0) = S(0)e^{\mu T - rT+\sigma\sqrt{T}\theta}$, which implies

$$\mu T - rT + \sigma\sqrt{T}\theta = 0$$
$$\text{or } \theta = -[(\mu - r)/\sigma]\sqrt{T}$$

Last,

$$\text{cov}\left(\log\left[\frac{S(T)}{S(0)}\right], -\log[\phi(z)]\right)$$

$$= \text{cov}\left[\mu T - \frac{\sigma^2}{2}T + \sigma\sqrt{T}z, \frac{\theta^2}{2} - \theta z\right]$$

$$= -\sigma\sqrt{T}\theta\text{cov}(z, z)$$

$$= -\sigma\sqrt{T}\theta$$

because $\text{cov}(z, z) = \text{var}(z) = 1$. Thus

$$\mu T = rT + \text{cov}\left(\log\left[\frac{S(T)}{S(0)}\right], -\log[\phi(z)]\right)$$

Finally, note that under $q(z)$, from expression (13) above

$$S(0) = E\big[S(T)\big]e^{-\mu T}$$

and substitution completes the proof.

19.13 | Cases

MW Petroleum Corp. (A and B) (Harvard Business School Cases 295029 and 294050-PDF-ENG). The cases focus on evaluation and execution of a creative financing structure that allows reallocation of oil price risk in the context of an acquisition.

MoGen Inc. (Darden School of Business Case UV1054-PDF-ENG, Harvard Business Publishing). The case shows how to price a convertible bond offering as a straight bond plus the conversion option.

Sara's Options (Harvard Business School Case 201005-PDF-ENG). The case studies the valuation of stock options in pay packages offered to a graduating MBA student.

19.14 | Questions and Problems

19.1. Explain why pricing and hedging go hand in hand in the Black–Scholes–Merton option pricing framework.

19.2. What does the Black–Scholes–Merton model assume about the evolution of the stock price, about dividends paid on the stock, and about interest rates?

19.3. Do you think the Black–Scholes–Merton model assumptions of no dividends paid on the stock and constant interest rates are reasonable assumptions? If not, why do you think they are imposed?

19.4. Briefly describe the seventy-three years of history behind the development of the Black–Scholes–Merton model, outlining some of the major advances that overcame critical hurdles and led to the development of the BSM model.

19.5. In the assumption of the Black–Scholes–Merton model,

    a. what is the stock's return volatility?

    b. what is assumed about the stock's return volatility? Is this assumption reasonable or not? If not, why do you think it is used?

The next two questions use the following information for pricing European options.

Special Motors Corporation's stock price S is \$59, the strike price K is \$60, the maturity T is forty-four days, the implied volatility σ is 30 percent per year, and the risk-free interest rate r is 3.3 percent per year.

19.6. Using the Black–Scholes–Merton formula, find the price of a call option.

19.7. **a.** Using the Black–Scholes–Merton formula, determine the price of a put option.

   b. Verify whether the options prices obtained in this and the previous question satisfy put–call parity.

19.8. Consider two investors who agree on the stock's price and volatility but who do not agree on the stock's expected return. One believes that the stock price will earn 15 percent over the next year, while the second believes that it will have a negative 5 percent return. Will they agree or disagree on the value of a one-year call option on the stock when using the Black–Scholes–Merton model? Explain your answer.

19.9. Explain how to compute the Black–Scholes–Merton model using the pseudo-probabilities. What is this principle called?

19.10. What is the difference between the actual probabilities and the pseudo-probabilities, and on what does it depend? Explain your answer.

19.11. What are the Greeks in the Black–Scholes–Merton formula? Which two Greeks correspond to changes in the stock price?

19.12. Comment on the following questions, carefully explaining your answers.

   a. As the stock price input increases, everything else constant, does a call option's price increase or decrease?

   b. As the volatility input increases, everything else constant, does a call option's price increase or decrease?

19.13. Given the data for Special Motors Corp. given earlier (i.e., S is $59, K is $60, T is forty-four days, σ is 30 percent per year, and r is 3.3 percent per year), compute the call option's delta and gamma.

19.14. **a.** Which inputs to the Black–Scholes–Merton model are observable and which need to be estimated?

   b. Describe some of the difficulties in estimating the unobservable input.

19.15. What is the implied volatility when using the Black–Scholes–Merton model? Does this estimate depend on the stock's time series of past stock prices? Explain your answer.

19.16. FunToy's stock has the following weekly closing prices: 40, 41, 43, 42, 42, 46, 43, 44, 47. Assuming fifty-two trading weeks in a year, compute the annualized, sample standard deviation (volatility) σ.

19.17. Fallstock Inc.'s stock price S is $45. European options on Fallstock have a strike price $K = $50, a maturity $T = 180$ days, the risk-free interest rate $r = 5$ percent per year, and the let the volatility $\sigma = 0.25$ per year. The company is going to pay a dividend of 50 cents after 125 days.

   a. Compute the price of a call option using the Black–Scholes–Merton model.

   b. Compute the price of a put option.

19.18. SINDY index is currently at $I = 11,057$. European options on SINDY have a strike price $K = \$11,000$, a maturity $T = 45$ days, a dividend yield $\delta = 1.5$ percent per year, the risk-free interest rate $r = 5$ percent per year, and the estimated implied volatility $\sigma = 16$ percent per year.

    a. Compute the price of a call option using the Merton formula.

    b. Compute the price of a put option using the appropriate version of put–call parity (see chapter 16).

19.19. A European call on euro matures after $T = 6$ months. The call pays on the maturity $100[S(T) - 1.30]$ dollars if it ends in-the-money, and zero is otherwise, where 100 is the contract multiplier and $\$1.30$ is the strike price K. Euro's volatility σ is 12 percent per year. Today's spot exchange rate S_A is $\$1.4$ per euro (in American terms). The continuously compounded annual risk-free interest rates are $r = 5$ percent in the United States (domestic) and $r_E = 4.5$ percent in the Eurozone. Compute the price of the call option using the Merton formula.

19.20. How would you value an American call option in the Black–Scholes–Merton model?

20

Using the Black–Scholes–Merton Model

20.1 | Introduction

More than a century ago, financiers who sold options for strategic and manipulative purposes dominated the New York City options market. In contrast, London dealers acted more like insurance agents employing a "model" to estimate the option's premium as the stock's average price less the strike price plus various costs and profits. These sellers would also often "delta hedge" their positions. New Yorker Samuel A. Nelson (1904, p. 14) remarked that the London options market, "where the business is more of a science" prospered more than its Wall Street counterpart. Isn't it interesting that a model helped organize a trader's thinking, placed trading on a more scientific footing, and helped the market grow more than a century before our time!

Today, models are actively used in financial markets. In fact, *model misuse and abuse* significantly contributed to the 2007 financial crisis. Many financial institutions misused models and, consequently, underestimated the risk of their positions. These errors led to insufficient equity capital in the economy, resulting in the failures of numerous financial institutions. If the financial institutions had better understood the model subtleties, perhaps this credit crisis could have been avoided. Understanding the content of this chapter will set you on the path to avoiding such errors.

This chapter explains how to use the Black–Scholes–Merton (BSM) model to facilitate risk management. First we present a brief history of option model usage. We consider the century-old technique of delta hedging and the post-1973 practice of gamma hedging. These hedging strategies utilize the Greeks. We show that both delta and gamma hedging are consistent with options pricing theory. We also explain why two other once popular techniques, the now-discarded rho hedging and the still-practiced vega hedging, are not. Next we revisit the knotty problem of volatility estimation via the computation of implied volatilities. This is an example of calibration, a popular technique that also has significant scope for abuse. We end this chapter with a discussion of the BSM model's extensions and generalizations.

20.2 | A Brief History of Model Usage

A brief history clarifies how models helped to shape the options markets (see Table 20.1 for milestones). This history can be divided into two phases: the early history and after 1973. Interestingly, in the early days of derivative pricing, practice was ahead of academic research, which was virtually non-existent. After the BSM model, the roles reversed, and markets followed the theory. Nowadays, it's fair to say that it has become a two-way street—practice and theory influence and enrich each other.

The Early History

The early option pricing models (OPMs) used in the London market were statistical models heavily influenced by insurance industry pricing practice. Still these models spurred market growth (see Extension 20.1). The late nineteenth century's "Dean of Wall Street," Russell Sage, used put–call parity to skirt New York State usury laws (see Extension 16.1). He used it to cleverly charge a higher interest rate than the

TABLE 20.1: Some Milestones in the History of Models and Their Use in Options Markets

Year	Development
Late nineteenth century	London dealers used statistical models based on past price movements to determine option premiums.
1870s	Russell Sage used put–call parity to circumvent New York state's interest rate usury laws.
1900	Louis Bachelier's thesis at Sorbonne in Paris.
1973	The Black–Scholes–Merton model was published.
1987	Portfolio insurance fails during the US stock market crash.
1987 and 1992	The Heath–Jarrow–Morton model was introduced in 1987 and published in 1992.

7 percent ceiling rate mandated. Not only was Sage a pioneer model user but he also conducted *tax* (or *regulatory*) *arbitrage* a century before Merton Miller argued (recall chapter 1) that regulations and taxes spur financial innovation. And although the French mathematician Louis Bachelier published a pioneering OPM in 1900, that model and its successors saw virtually no use until some seven decades later.

EXTENSION 20.1: London and New York Options Markets in the Nineteenth Century

Toward the end of the nineteenth century, options were traded in the over-the-counter markets in New York and some major European cities. Books from the era, *The Theory of "Options" in Stocks and Shares* by Charles Castelli (1877), *Secrets of Success in Wall Street* by Tumbridge and Co. (1878), *The Put-and-Call* by Leonard R. Higgins (1902), and *The A B C of Options and Arbitrage* by Samuel A. Nelson (1904), have left interesting descriptions of these markets.

In the vast resource-rich United States, powerful financiers nicknamed "robber barons" frequently manipulated stocks and options in which they held controlling interest. The "Old Straddle," Russell Sage, would sell calls on the stocks he possessed and would write puts to increase his holdings in case the price declined. Because New York options dealers employed "judgment" or "shrewd guessing" to determine option values, Nelson (1904, p. 30) surmised that "*value, then not being ascertainable at the time of sale, would not govern the price* [emphasis added], which is a gamble if having no object other than the expectation that the buyer will lose."

Great Britain developed a sophisticated insurance industry for protection against a variety of risks. Options were traded in London, and Castelli (1877) observed,

> The *Premium*, which is payable when the Option expires, fluctuates according to the variations of the Stock to be contracted: if the fluctuations are violent and numerous, and its future course liable to a great rise or great fall, then the premium asked is very heavy; if, however, the stock has evenly kept its quotations, Options can be negotiated for a very trifling premium. Thus, Options on Russians are more costly than those on Spanish Stocks.

Nelson (1904, p. 15) noted about the London options dealer that "he works by a rule of thumb, but he has an exact theory behind it." The dealer's approach was similar to that of a life insurance seller who knew that although he might have to pay large sums to particular claimants, the actuaries tables indicate that "if he can only get enough business of the kind [provided "he makes no bad bets" and wisely diversifies], the law of averages will bring him out with expenses and a legitimate profit" (pp. 15–6). Nelson also noticed a significant decline in options trading on Wall Street over a twenty-year period. He ascribed this to three factors: first, an unwillingness on the part of American firms to "sell options on the insurance plan as in London" (p. 23); second, a reluctance to sell options in small lots; and third, a Spanish War tax, though temporary, which cut into the profits of options dealers. For these reasons, "the option business for a time was to an extent degraded by its associations," and most of the business was "diverted to the London market, where dealing in options is an important part of the securities' trade" (pp. 23–4).

It's no surprise that the London Stock Exchange recognized many kinds of options trading. In contrast, the New York Stock Exchange refused to legitimize options contracts negotiated on the exchange floor (despite that many New York Stock Exchange members regularly traded options).

After 1973

After its development, the BSM model facilitated the derivatives markets expansion.

- *The BSM model tempered the Securities and Exchange Commission's opposition to options trading.* The Securities and Exchange Commission (SEC) was founded in 1934 during the tumultuous years that followed the Great Stock Market Crash of 1929. Focused on cleaning up the stock market, the SEC tried to ban options trading, which had been historically associated with stock price manipulation, speculation, and gambling. MacKenzie and Millo (2003, p. 114) report that one SEC official compared options to "marijuana and thalidomide." The SEC's attitude shifted after 1973, and it stopped associating options trading with gambling.

- *Leland–O'Brien–Rubinstein and portfolio insurance.* During the 1980s, Leland–O'Brien–Rubinstein Associates developed a profitable business helping clients protect their portfolios through **portfolio insurance**, synthetic put options created by trading in stock index futures and Treasury securities. Unfortunately, this business came to a screeching halt after the market crash of 1987, when the model failed to work as theorized. This happened because several of the model's assumptions (such as *competitive markets*), which are good approximations under normal market conditions, failed to hold during severe market stress. Studies cited portfolio insurance as a major cause of the crash because portfolio insurance required traders to sell shares when the market was declining, thereby fueling the drop. The experience with portfolio insurance gave a severe jolt to the blind belief in the BSM model.

- *The Heath–Jarrow–Morton model.* Because of double-digit inflation in the late 1970s and the 1980s, interest rates became large and volatile. This increased interest rate volatility generated a demand for securities and models to help manage these risks. Unfortunately, the BSM model was not designed for this application, given its constant interest rate assumption. A number of models relaxing the constant interest rate assumption were developed to overcome this failing, but unlike the BSM model, they all depended on interest rate risk premium. In contrast, Cornell University's David Heath, Robert Jarrow, and Andrew Morton developed an interest rate derivatives pricing model, which analogous to BSM did not depend on these risk premiums. This model, called the HJM model (we discuss this model in part IV of this book), was widely distributed as a working paper in 1987 and shortly thereafter utilized in the financial industry. The model was finally published in an academic journal in 1992. Generalizations of the HJM model have been applied to stochastic volatility options pricing, foreign currency derivatives, commodity futures, and Treasury Inflation Protected securities, among other instruments. These extensions helped facilitate the exponential growth of the derivatives markets in the following years.

20.3 | Hedging the Greeks

Hedging the Greeks is a risk management technique used to eliminate market risks from a stock or options portfolio. Borrowing terms from the title of the classic western movie *The Good, the Bad and the Ugly*, we label delta and gamma hedging as "the good" and faulty practices like vega and rho hedging as "the bad and the ugly." Both delta and gamma hedging are "the good" because they are consistent with the theory (and assumptions) underlying the BSM model. In contrast, vega and rho hedging are "the bad and the ugly" because they are inconsistent with the theory. Hence, as argued later, they do not and, in fact, cannot fulfill their desired objectives.

Delta Hedging

The **delta** (or **hedge ratio**) is the number of shares of the stock to trade for each option held to remove all price risk from an option position. For this reason, in earlier chapters, we characterized the hedge ratio as the *holy grail* of options pricing.

To construct a delta-hedged position, we consider a portfolio $V(t)$ at time t consisting of a long call with price $c(t)$ and n shares of the underlying stock worth $S(t)$ each. Suppressing the time symbol t for simplicity, the initial value of the portfolio is

$$V = c + nS \qquad (20.1a)$$

The change in this portfolio's value over a small time interval $[t, t + \Delta t]$ can be written as

$$\Delta V = \Delta c + n\Delta S \qquad (20.1b)$$

where $\Delta V \equiv V(t + \Delta t) - V(t)$, $\Delta c \equiv c(t + \Delta t) - c(t)$, and $\Delta S \equiv S(t + \Delta t) - S(t)$.

The goal of delta hedging is to choose n such that the variance of the change in the portfolio's value is equal to zero, that is, $\text{var}(\Delta V) = 0$, where $\text{var}(\,.\,)$ denotes variance. Then, the portfolio will be riskless.

Recognizing that the call's price is a function of time and the underlying stock price, using a Taylor series expansion from first-year college calculus, one can solve for this n (see the appendix to this chapter). The solution is the option's delta. We state this observation as a result.

RESULT 20.1

- -

Delta Hedging in the Black–Scholes–Merton Model

To remove price risk from a long call position, short

$$\text{delta}_C \equiv \frac{\partial c}{\partial S} = N(d_1) \text{ shares of stock} \qquad (20.2a)$$

where

$$d_1 = \frac{\log\left(\frac{S}{K}\right) + \left(r + \frac{\sigma^2}{2}\right)T}{\sigma\sqrt{T}} \qquad (20.2b)$$

$N(\,.\,)$ is the cumulative standard normal distribution function (which has mean 0 and standard deviation 1), S is the stock price, K is the strike price, r is the continuously compounded risk-free interest rate, T is the time to maturity, and σ is the stock return's volatility (see Result 19.1).

To delta hedge a long put position, buy $\text{delta}_P \equiv N(-d_1)$ stocks.

We illustrate the effectiveness of this result with a numerical example.

EXAMPLE 20.1: Delta Hedging

The purpose of this example is to show the effectiveness of delta hedging.

- Suppose we buy a European call option on Your Beloved Machine's (YBM) stock at time t by paying a price c. We assume that the stock price S is \$100, the strike price K is \$110, the time to maturity T is 1 year, the volatility σ of the stock's return is 0.142470 per year, and the continuously compounded risk-free interest rate r is 5 percent per year.

- To hedge one long call position, short delta_C shares of YBM. This gives a *delta-neutral* portfolio $V = c - (\text{delta}_C)S$. We compute the values of $\Delta V = \Delta c - (\text{delta}_C)\Delta S$ for various stock prices in Table 20.2 to see how the delta hedge works. For simplicity, we assume that the stock price can magically change without changing any of the other inputs to the model![1]

[1] This gives a rough-and-ready estimation of hedging performance. For better approximations, you can track ΔV over a longer period (such as a day) and make allowance for the interest cost $Vr\Delta t$.

TABLE 20.2: Delta Hedging Errors for Calls and Puts

S	d_1	Delta$_C$ = $N(d_1)$	Delta$_P$ = $-N(-d_1)$	Call	Put	ΔV (Call)	ΔV (Put)
90	−0.9863	0.1620	0.8380	1.0294	15.6646	1.2709	1.2709
95	−0.6068	0.2720	0.7280	2.1030	11.7382	0.3319	0.3319
99	−0.3173	0.3755	0.6245	3.3948	9.0300	0.0135	0.0136
100	**−0.2468**	**0.4025**	**0.5975**	**3.7838**	**8.4190**	**0**	**0**
101	−0.1770	0.4298	0.5702	4.1999	7.8351	0.0136	0.0136
105	0.0957	0.5381	0.4619	6.1367	5.7719	0.3403	0.3403
110	0.4222	0.6636	0.3364	9.1477	3.7829	1.3386	1.3386

- Row 6 reports $S = \$100$ in column 1, $d_1 = -0.2468$ in column 2, $N(d_1) = $ delta$_C = 0.4025$ in column 3, and the call price $\$3.7838$ in column 5 (see Example 19.2).
- Column 5 reports call values corresponding to the stock prices recorded in column 1.
- Column 7 reports changes in the hedged portfolio's value for different stock prices:

$$\Delta V = \Delta c - (\text{delta}_C)\Delta S$$
$$= [c(t + \Delta t) - c(t)] - (\text{delta}_C)[S(t + \Delta t) - S(t)]$$
$$= (\text{New call price} - 3.7838) - 0.4025(\text{New stock price} - 100)$$

For example, for $S = \$95$, we get $\Delta V = (2.1030 - 3.7838) - 0.4025(95 - 100) = \$0.3319$.

■ As seen in Table 20.2, *delta hedging works well for small movements in the stock price.* Indeed, ΔV is smaller when the new stock price is close to the original stock price (e.g., when $S = 99$, $\Delta V = 0.0135$), and it has larger values when it deviates further (e.g., when $S = 110$, $\Delta V = 1.3386$).

■ Following the same approach, one can make a long put trade delta-neutral by buying

$n = -\text{delta}_P = -[-N(-d_1)] = 0.5975$ shares. This is reported in row 6 of Table 20.2.

- We get a delta-neutral portfolio $V = p + (\text{delta}_P)S$ at time t.
- Using values from column 6 of Table 20.2, the change in value of this portfolio over $[t, t + \Delta t]$ is

$$\Delta V = \Delta p + (\text{delta}_P)\Delta S$$
$$= (\text{New put price} - 8.4190) + 0.5975(\text{New stock price} - 100)$$

For $S = \$95$, we get $\Delta V = (11.7382 - 8.4190) + 0.5975(95 - 100) = \$0.3319$. As before, the hedge works well for small fluctuations in the stock price.

Aren't these delta-neutral trades akin to the simple 1:2 hedges (which combine a long stock with two short calls or two long puts) that we discussed in chapter 15? In terms of actual implementation of the position, delta hedges are minor variants of such trades. However, the difference lies in the trader's objective as well as in her performance. Delta hedging, in theory, creates portfolios that are riskless for small fluctuations in the underlying stock price, as the previous example illustrates, whereas the 1:2 hedges are not riskeless.

Who delta hedges? Dealers who sell options regularly delta hedge their positions. The *Wall Street Journal* occasionally reports stories of delta hedging.[2] For example, on October 8, 2008, a large trader established a delta-neutral position by purchasing Kraft Foods Inc.'s stock and selling calls. On December 11, 2009, a trader implemented a massive delta-neutral trade by selling shares of J. P. Morgan Chase while buying calls.

Gamma Hedging

"In theory, there is no difference between theory and practice. But, in practice, there is," mused baseball player Yogi Berra. This quote applies well to delta hedging. If the world behaved as per the BSM assumptions, then hedging using delta is sufficient to make an option position riskless. One can continuously rebalance the hedge to perfectly replicate the option's payoff. The theory assumes, as noted, that the time between rebalancing, Δt, is infinitesimal, and therefore the corresponding changes in the stock price are small. But continuous trading is impossible. For weekly or even daily hedging, changes in the stock price are not small, and the hedging error can be significant. In addition, there are the familiar transaction costs that accompany any trade, which also makes continuous trading prohibitively expensive.

To address this problem, we need to hedge both small and large changes in the stock price over the hedging interval. We do this by also hedging the risk from changes in the "stock price squared." The second hedge uses the option's gamma, obtained by taking the second derivative of the BSM call price with respect to the stock price. The objective of the second hedge is to anticipate changes in the delta itself (the delta changes with changes in the underlying stock price) and to compensate for these changes.

To hedge these two risks, we need two securities so that we can establish a gamma-hedge in addition to a delta hedge. We can hedge a short call by trading the underlying stock and another option on the same stock. Consider forming a portfolio $V(t)$ consisting of one long call with price $c_1(t)$, n_1 shares of the stock with price $S(t)$, and n_2 units of the second option with price $c_2(t)$. The value of the portfolio is

$$V = c_1 + n_1 S + n_2 c_2 \tag{20.3a}$$

The change to this portfolio's value over the time interval $[t, t + \Delta t]$ is

$$\Delta V = \Delta c_1 + n_1 \Delta S + n_2 \Delta c_2 \tag{20.3b}$$

The objective of delta and gamma hedging is to choose n_1 and n_2 such that the variance of the position is zero, that is, $\text{var}(\Delta V) = 0$. Using a Taylor series expansion, the appendix to this chapter shows that the solution is as follows.

---

[2] The following are from the *Wall Street Journal* articles "Bullish Traders Take Positions in Colgate-Palmolive, P&G" (October 9, 2008) and "J. P. Morgan Chase Is Active on Treasury's Warrant Sale" (December 14, 2009).

RESULT 20.2

Delta and Gamma Hedging a Long Call Position

To remove delta and gamma price risk from a long call with price c_1, buy n_1 shares of stock with price S and sell n_2 shares of another option on the same stock with price c_2, where

$$n_1 = (\text{gamma}_{C1}/\text{gamma}_{C2})\text{delta}_{C2} - \text{delta}_{C1} \qquad (20.4a)$$

$$\text{and } n_2 = -\text{gamma}_{C1}/\text{gamma}_{C2} \qquad (20.4b)$$

The Greeks are defined by the general formulas

$$\text{delta}_C \equiv \frac{\partial c}{\partial S} = N(d_1) \text{ where } d_1 = \frac{\log\left(\dfrac{S}{K}\right) + \left(r + \dfrac{\sigma^2}{2}\right)T}{\sigma\sqrt{T}} \qquad (20.4c)$$

$$\text{and gamma}_C \equiv \frac{\partial^2 c}{\partial S^2} = \frac{1}{S\sigma\sqrt{T}}N'(d_1)$$

where $N(\,.\,)$ is the cumulative standard normal distribution function and $N'(\,.\,)$ is the standard normal density function.

The next example illustrates the effectiveness of both gamma and delta hedging.

EXAMPLE 20.2: A Gamma- and Delta-Neutral Portfolio

This example illustrates the increased effectiveness of gamma hedging.

- Suppose we buy a European call on YBM at time t for c_1 dollars. From the previous example, $S = \$100$, $K = \$110$, $T = 1$ year, $\sigma = 0.142470$ per year, and $r = 0.05$ per year.

- Let us delta and gamma hedge this position by trading n_1 shares of YBM and n_2 shares of a second call also on YBM. Let the second European call's price be c_2, with a strike price of $\$105$ and a maturity of nine months.

- The change in this portfolio's value over the time interval Δt is given by $\Delta V = \Delta c_1 + n_1\Delta S + n_2\Delta c_2$. We show the performance of this hedge in Table 20.3.

- In row 4, columns 2–5 use $S = 100$, $K = 110$, $T = 1$, $\sigma = 0.142470$, and $r = 0.05$ to compute the relevant values for call 1: $(d_1)_{C1} = -0.2468$ in column 2, $\text{delta}_{C1} = N(d_1)_{C1} = 0.4025$ in column 3, $\text{Call}_1 = 3.7838$ in column 4, and $\text{gamma}_{C1} = N'(d_1)/(S\sigma\sqrt{T}) = 0.0272$ in column 5.

- In row 4, columns 6–9 do the same for call 2 with the strike price 105 and time to maturity 0.75 years: $(d_1)_{C2} = -0.0298$ in column 6, $\text{delta}_{C2} = N(d_1)_{C2} = 0.4881$ in column 7, $\text{Call}_2 = 4.4000$ in column 8, and $\text{gamma}_{C2} = N'(d_1)/(S\sigma\sqrt{T}) = 0.0323$ in column 9.

TABLE 20.3: Delta and Gamma Hedging Errors for Calls

S	$(d_1)_{C1}$	$\text{Delta}_{C1} = N(d_1)_{C1}$	Call_1	Gamma_{C1}	$(d_1)_{C2}$	$\text{Delta}_{C2} = N(d_1)_{C2}$	Call_2	Gamma_{C2}	ΔV
90	−0.9863	0.1620	1.0294	0.0191	−0.8837	0.1884	1.0857	0.0243	−0.0092
95	−0.6068	0.2720	2.1030	0.0245	−0.4455	0.3280	2.3630	0.0308	−0.0048
99	−0.3173	0.3755	3.3948	0.0269	−0.1113	0.4557	3.9281	0.0325	−0.0001
100	**−0.2468**	**0.4025**	**3.7838**	**0.0272**	**−0.0298**	**0.4881**	**4.4000**	**0.0323**	**0**
101	−0.1770	0.4298	4.1999	0.0273	0.0508	0.5203	4.9043	0.0320	0.0000
105	0.0957	0.5381	6.1367	0.0265	0.3656	0.6427	7.2344	0.0288	0.0117
110	0.4222	0.6636	9.1477	0.0233	0.7427	0.7712	10.7826	0.0223	0.1154

- Using the formulas in Result 20.2, we compute

$$n_1 = (\text{gamma}_{C1}/\text{gamma}_{C2})\text{delta}_{C2} - \text{delta}_{C1} = 0.007684$$
$$n_2 = -\text{gamma}_{C1}/\text{gamma}_{C2} = -0.840422$$

- Column 10 reports changes in the delta- and gamma-hedged portfolio's value for different stock prices over a short time interval:

$$\begin{aligned}\Delta V &= \Delta c_1 + n_1\Delta S + n_2\Delta c_2 \\ &= [c_1(t+\Delta t) - c_1(t)] + n_1[S(t+\Delta t) - S(t)] + n_2[c_2(t+\Delta t) - c_2(t)] \\ &= (\text{New call price}_1 - 3.7838) + 0.007684(\text{New stock price} - 100) \\ &\quad - 0.840422(\text{New call price}_2 - 4.4000)\end{aligned}$$

For $S = \$95$, we get $\Delta V = (2.1030 - 3.7838) + 0.007684(95 - 100) - 0.840422(2.3630 - 4.4000) = -\$0.0048$.

- This is less than the hedging error 0.3310 that we found for a corresponding stock price in Example 20.1 where we only delta hedged.

- A comparison of the last columns in Tables 20.2 and 20.3 indicates the *superiority of delta and gamma hedging over delta hedging alone*.

20.4 | Hedging a Portfolio of Options

The magic of finance is that what works for a single security can usually be extended to a portfolio of securities. Using this magic, we extend the idea of delta and gamma hedging to a portfolio of options on one or more underlying stocks. Let's begin with a simple example.

EXAMPLE 20.3: Computing the Delta of a Portfolio Consisting of Two Options on a Single Stock

Suppose that you create a diagonal spread (see chapter 15) by buying a hundred one-year YBM 110 calls and writing the same number of nine-month YBM 105 calls. When the stock price is $100, we compute their deltas, as reported in the previous example, where $delta_{C1} = 0.4025$ and $delta_{C2} = 0.4881$, respectively. The portfolio delta is the number of options times the deltas, then summed, that is,

$$delta_{Port} = 100 \times 0.4025 - 100 \times 0.4881 = -8.5575$$

The portfolio's delta implies that the portfolio's value will decline by approximately $8.56 for a dollar increase in stock price.

We can generalize this example to develop rules for portfolio risk management.

- *Computing the delta (and gamma) of an option portfolio on a single stock.* Suppose that you are holding n_i options (n_i is positive for long holdings, negative for short) where $i = 1, \ldots, N$ denotes N European calls or puts on YBM with different strikes and expiration dates. The delta of this portfolio is just the number of shares of each option times the deltas of each of the options summed across all the options:

$$delta_{Port} = \sum_{i=1}^{N} n_i \times delta_i \qquad (20.5)$$

You can similarly compute the gamma of an option portfolio on a single stock as the weighted sum of the individual gammas, where the weights are the share holdings.

- *Delta (and gamma) hedging an option portfolio on multiple stocks.* In this case, you need to delta hedge the option portfolio with respect to each of the different underlying stocks.
  - First, partition the portfolio based on the underlying stocks into subportfolios.
  - Next, compute the delta of each subportfolio by using expression (20.5).
  - Finally, delta hedge each subportfolio with respect to its underlying stock.
  - Analogously, you can extend this line of argument to gamma hedge a portfolio of options.

20.5 | Vega Hedging

When constructing the BSM model, by assumption, there is only one risk: the risk of stock price changes. Consequently, the OPM reflects the pricing of this risk. No other risks are present in the model's formulation.

Delta and gamma hedging using the BSM model are consistent with the theory underlying the BSM model because these quantities reflect the sensitivity of the option's value to stock price risk. The inability to trade continuously is what makes gamma hedging useful. All the other inputs to the BSM model, the interest rate (r) and the volatility (σ), are assumed to be constant. The risks of changing interest rates and volatility are therefore not reflected in the BSM formula. It is nonsensical to hedge changes in these constant parameters using the Greeks derived from the BSM formula. A simple example illustrates why this statement is true. After studying the example, we will apply this insight to vega hedging.

EXAMPLE 20.4: Errors in Hedging a Constant Parameter

- Consider a European call with strike price K and expiration date T that trades on Your Beloved Machines (YBM). We will trade YBM stocks to delta hedge a long position in this call option.

A Stock Growing at a Constant Rate

- Let us perform a thought experiment and introduce an *unrealistic assumption*. Let's assume that today's stock price $S(t)$ is nonrandom and grows at the risk-free rate r. We agree that this assumption is silly, but is it any more silly than assuming that the stock's return has a constant volatility?

- Continuing, given this assumption, at time t, we know whether the option is going to end in-the-money. Discounting the call's known time T payoffs at the risk-free rate gives the arbitrage-free call price:

$$c = \max\left[S - Ke^{-r(T-t)}, 0\right] \tag{20.6}$$

- There is no need to hedge our option position because there is no risk.

Delta Hedging Using Expression (20.6)

- We notice, however, that when applied to market data, the stock price is stochastic and our nonhedge doesn't work. The hedging error is the entire change in the option's price Δc.

- As an ad hoc fix, we attempt to hedge the Greek. In this case, the stock price is the relevant parameter, so we want to delta hedge using expression (20.6).

- As justification, we employ the Taylor series expansion of the call formula (20.6) around the stock price over $[t, t + \Delta t]$, as discussed previously. We delta hedge by choosing n shares of the stock to short for each long call, where

$$n = \frac{\partial c}{\partial S} \tag{20.7}$$

For this model, expression (20.6), we can compute the option's delta:

$$n = \frac{\partial c}{\partial S} = \begin{cases} 1 & \text{if } S - Ke^{-r(T-t)} > 0 \\ 0 & \text{otherwise} \end{cases} \tag{20.8}$$

- Here the delta hedge is to hold n shares of the stock as in expression (20.8). This implies that if the stock is currently in-the-money, $n = 1$, and if it is out-of-the-money, $n = 0$.
  - If the call is out-of-the-money, then delta hedging using expression (20.8) is equivalent to not hedging! In this case, hedging the Greek based on expression (20.8) is useless.
  - If the call is in-the-money, then delta hedging using expression (20.8) is equivalent to shorting the entire stock. In this case, let us investigate the improvement, if any, in the hedging based on expression (20.8) versus doing nothing at all.

Hedging Based on Expression (20.8) Does Not Work

- To prove that delta hedging based on the formula in expression (20.8) doesn't work when the call is in-the-money, we need to know the true random evolution of the stock price.

- Because we are now familiar with the BSM model, let's assume that the stock price actually satisfies the BSM lognormal distribution assumption from chapter 19. Then, the "true" price of the option is the BSM value, and we can approximate the change in the true option value using the BSM delta and a Taylor series expansion, that is,

$$\Delta c = \frac{\partial c}{\partial t}\Delta t + \frac{\partial c}{\partial S}\Delta S = \frac{\partial c}{\partial t}\Delta t + N(d_1)\Delta S$$

- Suppose that we delta hedge using expression (20.8) with one share of the stock. By direct substitution, we see that change in the value of the delta-hedged portfolio is

$$\Delta V = \Delta c - \Delta S = \frac{\partial c}{\partial t}\Delta t + \frac{\partial c}{\partial S}\Delta S - \Delta S = \frac{\partial c}{\partial t}\Delta t + [N(d_1) - 1]\Delta S \qquad (20.9)$$

If the delta hedge works, then the change in this portfolio's value should be just $(\partial c/\partial t)\Delta t$. Why? Because this term is deterministic, and it would imply that $\text{var}(\Delta V) = 0$. In contradiction, expression (20.9) shows that the hedging error of the hedged portfolio V is $[N(d_1) - 1]\Delta S$.

- Now if we didn't hedge at all, the change in the value of the portfolio would equal the change in the value of the option, that is,

$$\Delta V = \Delta c = \frac{\partial c}{\partial t}\Delta t + \frac{\partial c}{\partial S}\Delta S = \frac{\partial c}{\partial t}\Delta t + N(d_1)\Delta S \qquad (20.10)$$

- We can now see that delta hedging has really not improved our situation very much!
  - The hedging errors are $[1 - N(d_1)]\Delta S$ in expression (20.9) versus $N(d_1)\Delta S$ in expression (20.10).
  - For just in-the-money options, $N(d_1) \approx 0.6$. So the delta-hedged portfolio change (expression [20.9]) and the naked call portfolio (expression [20.10]) are quite close because $[1 - N(d_1)] \approx 0.4$ and $N(d_1) \approx 0.6$.

Summary

- Why does delta hedging work for the BSM model and not for this example? Because in the BSM model, the stock price is stochastic and its risk is priced within the model. Hedging its Greek is appropriate. In our example, however, the stock price is nonrandom, so its risk is not priced within the model. Hedging its Greek, the delta, using this call model doesn't work.

Now let us turn to vega hedging in the BSM model. Just as in our previous example, because the BSM model from which the vega is obtained has no volatility risk included, volatility risk is not priced within the model. The Taylor series expansion is irrelevant because the volatility is constant ($\Delta\sigma = 0$) in the derivation of the BSM model. In the BSM model, vega measures how the BSM's price changes if the volatility is changed *once and forever constant thereafter*. This is not the case with stochastic volatility. Hence vega hedging is meaningless in this context and will not work. The magnitude of the error in vega hedging, like our example, is understood by looking at an OPM that relaxes the constant volatility assumption. These are called **stochastic volatility option models**. Extension 20.2 illustrates the bias in vega hedging and provides a brief look into stochastic option volatility models.

EXTENSION 20.2: Stochastic Volatility Option Models

This extension shows the magnitude of the errors that occur in vega hedging when using the BSM formula. To see the bias, we consider a more general stochastic volatility OPM in which the stock's volatility is stochastic. In this more general model, in which volatility risk is priced, we can compute the correct vega and compare it to the vega from the BSM model. The difference between the two vegas characterizes the error in using the BSM vega.

For a *stochastic volatility option pricing model*, we need to change the constant volatility assumption A8 of chapter 19. This is done by retaining the same structure as expression (19.2) of chapter 19 but by modifying the volatility term from a constant σ to a new expression $\sigma(t)$, which is random. The stock price evolution is given by

$$\log S(t + \Delta t) = \log S(t) + \left(\mu - \frac{\sigma(t)^2}{2}\right)\Delta t + \sigma(t)\sqrt{\Delta t}z \tag{1}$$

where $S(t + \Delta t)$ is the stock price at time $t + \Delta t$, μ is the expected return on the stock per year, z is a standard normal random variable with mean 0 and variance 1, and the evolution of the volatility is given by

$$\sigma(t + \Delta t) = \sigma(t) + \eta(t)\Delta t + \beta_1(t)\sqrt{\Delta t}z + \beta_2(t)\sqrt{\Delta t}w \tag{2}$$

where $\eta(t)$ is the expected change in the volatility per year, $\beta_1(t)$ and $\beta_2(t)$ are volatilities of the volatilities, and w is another standard normal random variable with mean 0 and variance 1 that is independent of z.

In this model, both the stock price and the stock's volatility follow stochastic processes. It can be shown (see Eisenberg and Jarrow 1994) that the price of a European call option with strike price K and maturity T is

$$c(0) = \int_0^\infty \mathrm{BSM}(\theta_0)\pi(\theta_0 \,|\, \sigma_0)d\theta_0 \tag{3}$$

where $\mathrm{BSM}(\theta_0)$ is the BSM formula,

$$\theta_0 = \int_0^T \sigma_s ds$$

and the pseudo-probability of θ_0 conditional on σ_0 is

$$\pi(.|\sigma_0)$$

We see that the call option's true price is a weighted average of BSM values. The correct hedge ratio is therefore

$$\frac{\partial c(0)}{\partial \sigma_0} = \int_0^\infty \left[\frac{\partial BSM(\theta_0)}{\partial \theta_0} \frac{\partial \theta_0}{\partial \sigma_0} \pi(\theta_0|\sigma_0) + BSM(\theta_0) \frac{\partial(\pi(\theta_0|\sigma_0))}{\partial \theta_0} \right] d\theta_0 \tag{4}$$

Clearly this is different from the BSM vega, which is $\partial BSM(\sigma_0)/\partial \sigma_0$ in the notation of this extension. As such, the difference between these two vegas documents the error in using the BSM vega when the volatility is stochastic. The result is that hedging using the BSM vega when volatility is stochastic doesn't work.

20.6 | Calibration

In the world of applied sciences and engineering, *calibration* is the process of setting a device's measurements in tune with the measurements of another device with a known magnitude. For example, the unit of distance *meter* was measured from 1889 to 1960 in terms of a prototype "meter bar" kept in the International Bureau of Weights and Measures in France. To calibrate a second rod equal to one meter, one needs to compare it with the meter bar and mark off an identical distance.

In derivatives pricing, **calibration** is a technique that estimates a derivatives pricing model's parameters by equating the model's price to the market price of a derivative. Before understanding the use and misuse of calibration, especially with respect to the BSM model, we need to refine our understanding of economic models. There are two types of models: theoretical and statistical.[3]

Theoretical and Econometric Models

- A **theoretical model** relies on assumptions regarding the structure of the economy and economic theory to derive a set of outputs (Figure 20.1 shows the basic structure of such models). The purpose is to understand *cause and effect*. For example, the BSM model is a theoretical model. In this case, we have discussed the assumptions underlying the model. Its parameters are estimated using historical stock price data, as described in chapter 19, and the outputs are the option values and the Greeks (delta and gamma). The model is designed to understand the impact of the inputs (cause) on the outputs (effect).

- A **statistical model** or, equivalently, an **econometric model** (because our model arises in an economic context) identifies patterns in historical data—*correlations*—that are expected to continue into the future. Econometric models

---

[3]See pp. 2–3 of *Applied Time Series Analysis for Managerial Forecasting* by Charles R. Nelson (1973) for a discussion of *theoretical models* (which have mathematical functions to represent "causal relationships" in some economic environment) vs. statistical (econometric) models.

use statistical techniques to model the patterns in historical data. Recall that more than a century ago, London dealers used a very simple statistical model to price options. A similar statistical model for pricing options can be generated as follows. Using historical option prices, compute the average call price conditioned on the strike price, the time to maturity, the stock's volatility, and the level of the stock price. Use this conditional average call price as an estimate of the traded option's value. Here the conditional averages are capturing the correlations between the inputs (strike, maturity, volatility, stock price) and the output (option value). A more sophisticated statistical model for pricing call options is discussed later, which uses implied volatilities.

Both types of models have their advantages and disadvantages. Models are designed to understand the structural shifts in a dynamic and changing economy. Theoretical models hope to understand the casual relationships in these structural changes. If modeled correctly, a theoretical model is useful both before and after the structural shifts. The disadvantage of a theoretical model is that it is hard to get it right. In contrast, statistical models are often easier to construct, but they frequently do not capture structural shifts. Consequently, if a structural shift occurs, the statistical model will be in error until it is reestimated.

Statistical models are indispensable when no theoretical models can be built (we discussed an example of this in the context of risk minimization hedging in chapter 13). Sometimes, as we illustrate later in this chapter, a theoretical model can degenerate into a statistical model.

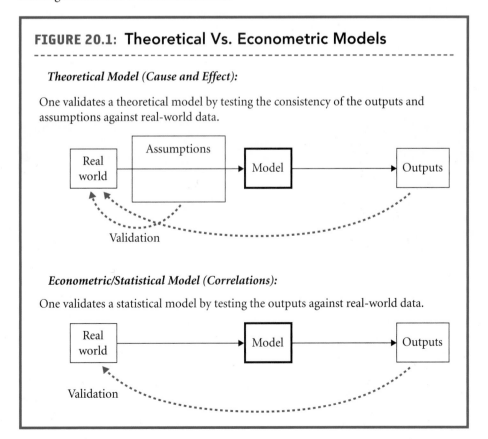

FIGURE 20.1: Theoretical Vs. Econometric Models

Theoretical Model (Cause and Effect):

One validates a theoretical model by testing the consistency of the outputs and assumptions against real-world data.

Econometric/Statistical Model (Correlations):

One validates a statistical model by testing the outputs against real-world data.

Using Calibration

Calibration has two uses with respect to derivatives pricing models. These two uses depend on whether the model is accepted or rejected when it is tested with respect to historical data.

DERIVATIVES PRICING MODEL ACCEPTED If the derivatives pricing model is accepted (consistent with historical data), then calibration can be used as a quick method for estimating the model's parameters. Note that in this case, the estimated model's parameters will be the same regardless of whether they are estimated using historical data or via calibration. However, this is not the usual circumstance under which calibration is used. The more usual circumstance is when the derivatives pricing model is rejected by historical data.

DERIVATIVES PRICING MODEL REJECTED If the derivatives pricing model is rejected (inconsistent with historical data), then *calibration is used to make the model's price consistent with the market price*. Note that in this case, calibration is used to fix or overcome a pricing error embedded in the derivatives pricing model. *The process of calibration thus transforms a theoretical model into an econometric model.* This econometric model provides a nonlinear estimate of the derivative's price. The nonlinear estimator results from the use of the inverse of the derivatives pricing formula.

Given that calibration generates a statistical model formulated to match market prices, the derivatives model should be used for no other purpose.[4] In this case, the calibrated model should only be used to price derivatives. The theoretical model, being rejected, can no longer be used to perform delta and gamma hedging. We will return to this comment later, when we discuss implied volatilities, but before this, we provide a simple example to illustrate these insights.

EXAMPLE 20.5: Calibration and Hedging Errors

To illustrate the incorrectness of using a calibrated derivatives pricing model to hedge when the underlying model is rejected by the data, we return to Example 20.4, in which the stock price $S(t)$ is non-random and grows at the risk-free rate r. This model is easily rejected using historical stock price data.

- Recall that under this assumption, the value of a European call option with strike price K and maturity T is

$$c(t) = \max\left[S(t) - Ke^{-r(T-t)}, 0\right] \tag{20.11}$$

and the option's delta is

$$\frac{\partial c}{\partial S} = \begin{cases} 1 & \text{if } S - Ke^{-r(T-t)} > 0 \\ 0 & \text{otherwise} \end{cases} \tag{20.12}$$

---

[4] Thomas J. Sargent of New York University discusses similar problems in macroeconomic models; see "An Interview with Thomas J. Sargent by George W. Evans and Seppo Honkapohja" in *Macroeconomic Dynamics* 9 (2005).

If we were to use this model to price options, we would discover that the model price does not match the market price. This is not surprising.

- Nonetheless, we can still use the model as a statistical model for pricing options if we use calibration. In this case, the parameter to calibrate is the stock price itself. We use calibration to find an implicit stock price, that is, that stock price S^* that equates the model price to the market price:

$$c_{Mkt}(t) = S^* - Ke^{-r(T-t)}$$

Such an implied stock price S^* always exists, and of course, the implied stock price will not equal the market price of the stock. However, this is not a concern because the purpose for using the model is to match options prices (not stock prices). Note the analogy of the implied stock price to an implied volatility in the context of the BSM model, in which volatility is held constant.

- Interestingly, we can then use this statistical model with the implied stock price to value different strike and different maturity options, and it will fit them reasonably well. *This is a valid use of the calibrated statistical model.*

- *An improper use would be to use the statistical model, with the implied stock price, to hedge an option.* The option's delta is either 1 or 0, which as noted before provides a very poor hedge.

Implied Volatilities

Computing an implied volatility with respect to the BSM model is the prime example of calibrating a derivatives pricing model. Hence we can apply our insights from the previous discussion of calibration to this situation. Before that, however, we recall the definition of the BSM implied volatility.

Consider a European call option on a stock with strike price K, maturity T, continuously compounded risk-free rate r, and stock return volatility σ. Denote the BSM model of chapter 19 by $BSM(t, S, \sigma, r, K, T)$. The implied volatility is that σ_{IV} such that the model call price matches the market price; that is, σ_{IV} is chosen to make the following equation hold:

$$BSM(t, S, \sigma_{IV}, r, K, T) = c_{Mkt} \qquad (20.13)$$

Thus, for implied volatility, we use (t, S, r, K, T) and c_{Mkt} as inputs and then compute σ_{IV} by solving this equation. Technically, since the BSM formula is an increasing function of the volatility, a solution always exists. Because the equation has no explicit analytical solution, numerical approximation techniques are used to compute the implied volatility σ_{IV}. We can rewrite the implied volatility in a more abstract form as

$$\sigma_{IV} = BSM^{-1}(c_{Mkt} : t, S, r, K, T) \qquad (20.14)$$

where $BSM^{-1}(\cdot)$ denotes the inverse function. As indicated, this expression gives a nonlinear estimator for the option's volatility as a function of the inputs (c_{Mkt}, t, S, r, K, T).

Next, we illustrate the computation of an implied volatility.

EXAMPLE 20.6: Computing Implied Volatilities

■ Table 20.4 reports closing option prices for International Business Machine Corp. (IBM) on February 3, 2011, along with relevant input data:
- Column 1 reports six strike prices $155 to $175 at $5 intervals.
- Column 2 reports the closing stock price on IBM.
- Column 3 reports the continuously compounded risk-free interest rate $r = 0.10$ per year (chapter 2 shows how to compute r from Treasury bill prices).
- Column 4 reports the time to maturity. Because options expire on February 19, there are sixteen days remaining before maturity. Thus, $T = 16/365 = 0.0438$ years.
- Column 5 reports the call prices from the market. We assume that these options are European.
- Column 6 reports the implied volatility. The implied volatility in column 6 are obtained in Excel by first guessing a value for the implied volatility, using this and the other inputs to determine

TABLE 20.4: Implied Volatilities

K	S	r	T	c_{Mkt}	Implied Volatility
150	163.53	0.001	0.0438	13.575	0.1944
155	163.53	0.001	0.0438	8.6	0.1409
160	163.53	0.001	0.0438	4.0	0.1235
165	163.53	0.001	0.0438	1.08	0.1249
170	163.53	0.001	0.0438	0.17	0.1325
175	163.53	0.001	0.0438	0.055	0.1654

FIGURE 20.2: Implied Volatility Smiles

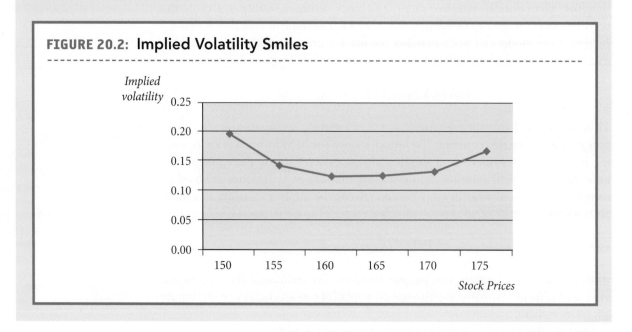

c_{BSM}, and then using Excel's "Goal Seek" command to solve for the implied volatility that would set the difference $(c_{Mkt} - c_{BSM})$ to zero.[5]

- Figure 20.2 plots the strike prices (column 1) along the horizontal axis and implied volatilities corresponding to each strike along the vertical axis. This gives a pattern that is referred to as a **volatility smile**.

- When computing implied volatilities, if the BSM model were consistent with the data, then for all strikes, one would get the same value. The graph would be a flat line. The implied volatilities are not equal, hence the BSM model is rejected by this example's data.

[5] You can solve for implied volatility by (1) trial and error, (2) by a spreadsheet program as outlined above (see problem 20.20 at the end of this chapter for more details), or (3) by using our Priced! software.

To understand the proper use of the calibrated BSM with an implied volatility, we first need to determine if the BSM model is accepted or rejected by historical data. Unfortunately, it is *well known that the BSM model is rejected by historical data*. The most direct verification of this rejection has been studies computing implied volatilities (as in the previous example). When computing implied volatilities, if the BSM model were correct, then for all the other inputs (t, S, K, r, T), one would get the same value for the volatility, and it would be equal to the historical volatility.

Unfortunately, when estimating implied volatilities from equity options, the evidence shows that (1) implied volatilities differ across strikes and maturities (the pattern is a smile or sneer; see Figure 20.2 for a typical pattern); (2) implied volatilities differ across time, stock prices, and interest rates; and (3) implied volatilities do not equal historical volatilities (see Bakshi et al. 1997; Pan 2002). This evidence strongly rejects the BSM model's validity.

Given that the BSM model is rejected, one can still use a calibrated BSM as a *nonlinear statistical model* for estimating options prices. This is typical industry practice. A common procedure is to estimate the implied volatility using a subset of the available options and then to use the resulting implied volatility estimate to price the remaining set of options or options at a later date. *This is a perfectly valid use of the BSM model.*

However, because the BSM model is rejected by historical data, *it is incorrect to use a calibrated BSM to delta or gamma hedge*. This is a common misuse of the BSM model. The hedging implications of the theoretical model are no longer valid. To hedge in this circumstance, one needs to employ either an alternative and more complex theoretical model or a purely statistical model (as was done for futures prices in chapter 13). Vega hedging will not work, contrary to common belief, for two reasons: first, it is a wrong Greek to hedge because it was held constant in the original BSM model (volatility risk is not reflected in the BSM price), and second, the BSM model is rejected by historical data, hence its partial derivatives—the Greeks—are irrelevant. For a study showing the poor hedging that results from using the BSM model with delta, gamma, and vega hedging, see Engle and Rosenberg (2000).

EXTENSION 20.3: VIX: The Fear Index

If you think implied volatility is scary, it has been used to develop something even scarier—the "fear index," called the **VIX**. The Chicago Board Options Exchange introduced the VIX in 1993 "to measure the market's expectation of the 30-day volatility implied by at-the-money S&P 100 Index (OEX) option prices."[6] In 2003, the VIX index was modified to represent an expected volatility instead of an implied volatility. Today, the VIX has developed into a widely watched barometer of stock market volatility, reflecting investor anxiety. The VIX index increases during financial crises (see Figure 20.3). Today, various derivatives trade on VIX, yielding investors and financial institutions a method to hedge or speculate on stock market volatilities.

FIGURE 20.3: The VIX Index (in percentage) across Time

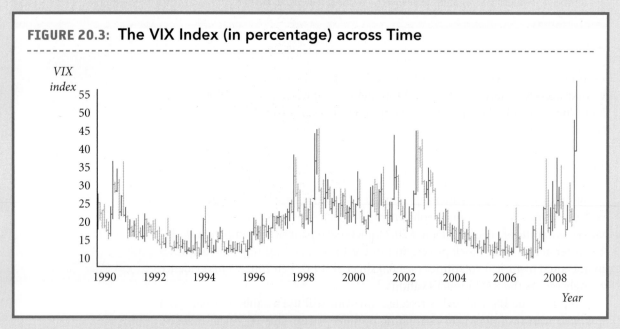

[6]See "The CBOE Volatility Index – VIX" (www.cboe.com/micro/vix/vixwhite.pdf), page 2.

20.7 The Black–Scholes–Merton Model: A Postscript

As shown, because the BSM model is rejected by historical data, although a calibrated BSM model is still useful for pricing options, it is not useful for hedging. A calibrated BSM model is a statistical model in which the implied volatility estimate captures any model errors into its magnitude. These model errors, however, invalidate its use for hedging. So what can one do to overcome the hedging limitation of the BSM model?

There are two approaches. First, one can build a statistical model relating changes in the option's price to changes in the stock's price, analogous to that used in chapter 13 for futures prices. Such a statistical model will inherit all the advantages and disadvantages of such models in predicting the future. Second, one can build a better mousetrap! The better mousetrap would generalize the assumptions so that the option model is no longer rejected by historical data.

A preliminary guide to these extensions is as follows. Extension 20.2 discusses how to extend the BSM model to include volatility risk. Chapters 21–25 of this book discuss how to include interest rate risk in OPMs. Asset price bubbles and their impact on option pricing were discussed in chapter 19. Finally, credit and liquidity risk extensions of OPMs are discussed in chapter 26. Transaction costs and trading restrictions are also worthy of study, but we leave their discussion to more advanced textbooks and the academic literature.

20.8 | Summary

1. Option models and option deltas have been used since the early 1900s to trade options. The year 1973 saw the publication of the Black–Scholes–Merton model, which changed financial markets thereafter.

2. Delta hedging is removing the price risk from a long call position by selling short

$$\text{delta}_C \equiv \frac{\partial c}{\partial S} = N(d_1) \text{ shares of stock}$$

where

$$d_1 = \frac{\log\left(\frac{S}{K}\right) + \left(r + \frac{\sigma^2}{2}\right)T}{\sigma\sqrt{T}}$$

A delta hedge works well when the time interval over which the hedge is executed is small.

3. Delta and gamma hedging removes the price risk from a long call with price c_1 by buying n_1 shares of stock with price S and selling n_2 shares of another option on the same stock with price c_2, where

$$n_1 = (\text{gamma}_{C1}/\text{gamma}_{C2})\text{delta}_{C2} - \text{delta}_{C1}$$

$$\text{and } n_2 = -\text{gamma}_{C1}/\text{gamma}_{C2}$$

The Greeks are defined by the general formulas

$$\text{delta}_C \equiv \frac{\partial c}{\partial S} = N(d_1) \text{ and gamma}_C \equiv \frac{\partial^2 c}{\partial S^2} = \frac{1}{S\sigma\sqrt{T}}N'(d_1)$$

where $N(\,.\,)$ is the cumulative standard normal distribution function and $N'(\,.\,)$ is the standard normal density function. Delta and gamma hedging are designed to overcome the errors introduced when the hedging interval is not small.

4. Vega hedging is a nonsensical procedure because it is based on an option valuation formula, the BSM model, that assumes volatility is a constant. Hence volatility risk is not embedded in the BSM formula, so the formula's sensitivity to changes in the stock's volatility, the vega, does not capture volatility risk in an option's price.

5. Calibration is an often-misused estimation procedure. In the context of the BSM formula, implied volatility estimation is an example of calibration. Because the BSM is rejected by historical data, using a calibrated BSM model transforms the theoretical BSM model into a statistical model. This statistical model can be used to estimate options prices, but it is invalid to use a calibrated BSM model to delta (and/or gamma) hedge an option position.

20.9 | Appendix

The Mathematics of Delta, Gamma, and Vega Hedging

Hedging using the Greeks is based on a Taylor series expansion. A **Taylor series** expresses a well-behaved function as a sum of terms involving its derivatives computed at a single point. For a function f of two variables x and y, the Taylor series about the point (a, b) can be written as (where $[x - a]$ is Δx, $[y - b]$ is Δy, $f[x, y] - f[a, b]$ is Δf; see appendix A)

$$\Delta f = \frac{\partial f}{\partial x} \Delta x + \frac{\partial f}{\partial y} \Delta y + \frac{1}{2}\left[\frac{\partial^2 f}{\partial x^2} \Delta x^2 + \frac{\partial^2 f}{\partial y^2} \Delta y^2 + 2\frac{\partial^2 f}{\partial x \partial y}\Delta x \Delta y \right] + \text{error}$$

where the higher-order terms of the expansion are considered insignificant "error terms" when Δx and Δy are small.

DELTA HEDGING Suppose one can trade quickly enough so that the infinitesimal time change dt is approximately equal to the small time change Δt that we consider in practice, that is, $dt \approx \Delta t$. Then the BSM theory implies that delta hedging removes all of the stock price risk from an option position. We now explain how this happens.

■ *The option and the stock portfolio.* Consider a portfolio consisting of one European call option with time t price $c(t)$. We want to trade n shares of a stock worth $S(t)$ to remove the stock price risk from this option position. Denote the time t value of the portfolio as $V(t)$. In symbols, we can write the evolution of the change in the portfolio's value over a small time interval $[t, t + \Delta t]$ as

$$\Delta V = \Delta c + n \Delta S \tag{1}$$

where $\Delta V \equiv V(t + \Delta t) - V(t)$ and the other terms are similarly defined.

- *The Taylor series expansion for a delta hedge.* Because the BSM call price is a function of time t and the stock price $S(t)$ (other terms like the volatility, the interest rate, and the strike price are constant parameters and not variables), we can use a Taylor series expansion to write

$$\Delta c = \frac{\partial c}{\partial t} \Delta t + \frac{\partial c}{\partial S} \Delta S + \text{error} \qquad (2)$$

where (error/Δt) goes to zero as the time interval shrinks to zero ($\Delta t \to 0$). This last observation implies that for small changes in time, Δt, the error term is small and can be ignored. Ignoring these terms, substitution of expression (2) into expression (1) gives the change in the value of our portfolio as

$$\Delta V = \frac{\partial c}{\partial t} \Delta t + \frac{\partial c}{\partial S} \Delta S + n \Delta S \qquad (3)$$

- *Determining the hedge ratio and constructing the delta-neutral portfolio.* To make this portfolio riskless for small changes in the stock price, choose n so that the term involving ΔS disappears. This is the only random term in expression (3). This is obtained by setting

$$\frac{\partial c}{\partial S} \Delta S + n \Delta S = 0 \qquad (4)$$

Solving for n yields

$$n = -\frac{\partial c}{\partial S} = -N(d_1) \equiv -\text{delta}_C \qquad (5)$$

The number of shares held has the opposite sign to the option position. Because we began with one long call, we need to short $\text{delta}_C \equiv N(d_1)$ shares of the underlying stock to hedge the exposure.

- *The delta is the holy grail of options pricing.* The hedge ratio n represents the number of shares of the stock to trade for each call to construct a riskless portfolio. Being riskless, this portfolio is equivalent to a position in a money market account. To see this, substituting n into expression (3) gives

$$\Delta V = \frac{\partial c}{\partial t} \Delta t \qquad (6)$$

Thus the change in the portfolio's value equals $\partial c / \partial t$ (which equals the call's theta; see Table 19.1) times the time interval Δt. This term is nonrandom, and hence it has zero variance. To avoid arbitrage, this portfolio must earn the riskless rate. This observation (combined with an extension of this approach, as described in the next section in the context of gamma hedging) leads to an alternative derivation of the BSM model. The portfolio V that we have constructed is said to be **delta neutral**.

Notice that delta hedging involves the first-order derivatives. Such approximations work well over small time periods, during which the stock price does not move much.

GAMMA HEDGING How does one remove the price risk of an option position over a time interval that is longer than what we had considered earlier: a day, or perhaps even a week (in other words, the hedging interval Δt is significantly larger than the infinitesimal time interval dt considered in the model)? We can achieve this by adding a gamma hedge to the delta hedge.

- *The Taylor series expansion for delta and gamma hedging.* Suppose that we are long one European call option and we want to remove the stock price risk from our portfolio over the time interval $[t, t + \Delta t]$. As before, we start with a Taylor series expansion of the call's value, but this time, we include the second-order term:

$$\Delta c = \frac{\partial c}{\partial t} \Delta t + \frac{\partial c}{\partial S} \Delta S + \frac{1}{2} \frac{\partial^2 c}{\partial S^2} (\Delta S)^2 + \text{error} \tag{7}$$

where (error/Δt) goes to zero as $\Delta t \to 0$. In the calculation, we ignore the error term because it is small.

- *Adding a stock and another option to the option portfolio.* Notice that there are "two" risks in the call's price movements—one comes from the change in the stock price and the other from the change in the stock price squared. To hedge two risks, we need two securities. We can use the underlying stock as one security and another option on the same stock as the second. At time t, we create a portfolio $V(t)$ consisting of one long call whose price is c_1, n_1 shares of the stock whose price is $S(t)$, and n_2 number of the second option whose price is c_2:

$$V(t) = c_1 + n_1 S + n_2 c_2 \tag{8a}$$

- *Constructing the delta- and gamma-neutral portfolio.* To determine the portfolio's composition, we write its value change over $[t, t + \Delta t]$ as

$$\Delta V(t) = \Delta c_1 + n_1 \Delta S + n_2 \Delta c_2 \tag{8b}$$

  - Substitution of expression (7) into (8b) for the change in the two calls' values gives

$$\Delta V = \frac{\partial c_1}{\partial t} \Delta t + \frac{\partial c_1}{\partial S} \Delta S + \frac{1}{2} \frac{\partial^2 c_1}{\partial S^2} (\Delta S)^2 + n_1 \Delta S$$

$$+ n_2 \frac{\partial c_2}{\partial t} \Delta t + n_2 \frac{\partial c_2}{\partial S} \Delta S + n_2 \frac{1}{2} \frac{\partial^2 c_2}{\partial S^2} (\Delta S)^2 \tag{9}$$

- To make this portfolio have zero risk, we want to choose n_1 and n_2 such that the coefficients of the terms involving ΔS and $(\Delta S)^2$ disappear. This gives two equations in two unknowns:

$$\frac{\partial c_1}{\partial S} + n_1 + n_2 \frac{\partial c_2}{\partial S} = 0 \tag{10a}$$

$$\frac{\partial^2 c_1}{\partial S^2} + n_2 \frac{\partial^2 c_2}{\partial S^2} = 0 \tag{10b}$$

Notice that expression (10a) involves the Greek deltas and that the second expression (10b) involve the Greek gammas (see Table 19.1).
- Rearrange terms in (10b) to get

$$n_2 = -\left(\frac{\partial^2 c_1}{\partial S^2}\right) \bigg/ \left(\frac{\partial^2 c_2}{\partial S^2}\right) \tag{11a}$$

The negative sign indicates that we need to sell short n_2 options. Alternatively, you can write n_2 as $-\text{gamma}_{C1}/\text{gamma}_{C2}$.
- Plug this value into (10a) and rearrange terms to get

$$n_1 = \left[\left(\frac{\partial^2 c_1}{\partial S^2}\right) \bigg/ \left(\frac{\partial^2 c_2}{\partial S^2}\right)\right] \frac{\partial c_2}{\partial S} - \frac{\partial c_1}{\partial S} \tag{11b}$$

This can also be written as $(\text{gamma}_{C1}/\text{gamma}_{C2})\text{delta}_{C2} - \text{delta}_{C1}$. The hedge involves going long n_1 shares of the stock if the preceding expression is positive and selling them short if the expression is negative.
- Substituting these shares into the portfolio's value shows that the resulting portfolio is riskless:

$$\Delta V = \frac{\partial c_1}{\partial t} \Delta t - \left[\left(\frac{\partial^2 c_1}{\partial S^2}\right) \bigg/ \left(\frac{\partial^2 c_2}{\partial S^2}\right)\right] \frac{\partial c_2}{\partial t} \Delta t \tag{12}$$

Such a portfolio, which consists of nonrandom terms, is said to be **delta and gamma neutral.**

VEGA HEDGING As we discuss in the text, vega hedging is "the bad and the ugly" and should not be used. To see why this is an invalid procedure, let us begin by following the logic that we employed for both delta and gamma hedging.

■ *The Taylor series expansion for a delta and vega hedge.* We start with the BSM formula, which depends on the stock price, time, and volatility, written $c[S(t), t, \sigma]$.

To hedge both the delta and vega over $[t, t + \Delta t]$, we proceed to use a Taylor series expansion, as before:

$$\Delta c = \frac{\partial c}{\partial t} \Delta t + \frac{\partial c}{\partial S} \Delta S + \frac{\partial c}{\partial \sigma} \Delta \sigma + \text{error} \tag{13}$$

where $(\text{error}/\Delta t)$ goes to zero as $\Delta t \to 0$. Because the error term is small, we ignore it in the subsequent calculations.

■ *Adding a stock and another option to the portfolio.* There are two risks in the call's price movements: one is the change in the stock price and the other is the change in the stock's volatility. As before, we hedge them using the underlying stock and a second option on the same stock. This gives the portfolio's value at time t:

$$V(t) = c_1 + n_1 S + n_2 c_2 \tag{14}$$

■ *Constructing the delta- and vega-neutral portfolio.* We write the change in the portfolio's value over $[t, t + \Delta t]$ as

$$\Delta V(t) = \Delta c_1 + n_1 \Delta S + n_2 \Delta c_2 \tag{15}$$

Substitution of the change in the call's value gives an expression analogous to expression (9):

$$\Delta V = \frac{\partial c_1}{\partial t} \Delta t + \frac{\partial c_1}{\partial S} \Delta S + \frac{\partial c_1}{\partial \sigma} \Delta \sigma + n_1 \Delta S$$
$$+ n_2 \frac{\partial c_2}{\partial t} \Delta t + n_2 \frac{\partial c_2}{\partial S} \Delta S + n_2 \frac{\partial c_2}{\partial \sigma} \Delta \sigma \tag{16}$$

- To make this portfolio have zero risk, we choose n_1 and n_2 such that the terms involving ΔS and $\Delta \sigma$ disappear. This is accomplished by requiring

$$\frac{\partial c_1}{\partial S} + n_1 + n_2 \frac{\partial c_2}{\partial S} = 0 \tag{17a}$$

$$\frac{\partial c_1}{\partial \sigma} + n_2 \frac{\partial c_2}{\partial \sigma} = 0 \tag{17b}$$

- Rearrange terms in (17b) to get

$$n_2 = -\left(\frac{\partial c_1}{\partial \sigma}\right) \Big/ \left(\frac{\partial c_2}{\partial \sigma}\right) \tag{18a}$$

A negative sign indicates that we need to sell short $vega_{c1}/vega_{c2}$ options.
- Plugging this value into expression (17a) and rearranging terms yields

$$n_1 = \left[\left(\frac{\partial c_1}{\partial \sigma}\right) \Big/ \left(\frac{\partial c_2}{\partial \sigma}\right)\right] \frac{\partial c_2}{\partial S} - \frac{\partial c_1}{\partial S} \tag{18b}$$

- However, there is a conceptual problem in this application. We have kept the parameter σ fixed throughout our derivation of the BSM model, and now we want to change it! This is nonsensical because the risk of a changing volatility is not reflected in the option's value. Consequently, *vega hedging is an invalid procedure that should never be used.*

A Third Derivation of the Black–Scholes–Merton Formula

The original derivation of the BSM formula in 1973 for valuing a European option was obtained as the solution to a partial differential equation. It follows from the Taylor series expansion used for delta and gamma hedging, with one small twist. Of course, this approach needs the underlying assumptions given in chapter 19.

Assume that the European call option's value depends *only on the price of the stock and time*, that is, $c(t) = c[t, S(t)]$. Then, you can create a "hedged position" by combining a long position in the stock with a short position in the option. Letting the short position in the stock be $(\partial c / \partial S)$ shares, the portfolio's value is

$$V = c - \frac{\partial c}{\partial S} S \tag{19}$$

- Suppose that the stock price changes by $\Delta S \equiv S(t + \Delta t) - S(t)$ over a small interval $[t, t + \Delta t]$ and the call price changes by Δc. Then, the change in the value of our portfolio is

$$\Delta V = \Delta c - \frac{\partial c}{\partial S} \Delta S \tag{20}$$

- *Use of Ito's lemma and stochastic calculus.* We can use stochastic calculus to develop an alternate expression for the change in the portfolio's value:
  - If the option position changes continuously, Ito's lemma yields

$$\Delta c = \frac{\partial c}{\partial t} \Delta t + \frac{\partial c}{\partial S} \Delta S + \frac{1}{2} \frac{\partial^2 c}{\partial S^2} (\Delta S)^2 \tag{21}$$

This is similar to equation (7).
  - Expression (18) can be further simplified by using another result from stochastic calculus, which allows us to write the squared change in the stock price as $(\Delta S)^2 = \sigma^2 S^2 \Delta t$. This is the "one small twist" mentioned earlier.
  - Substituting into (21) and applying it to (20) yields

$$\Delta V = \frac{\partial c}{\partial t} \Delta t + \frac{\partial c}{\partial S} \Delta S + \frac{1}{2} \frac{\partial^2 c}{\partial S^2} \sigma^2 S^2 \Delta t - \frac{\partial c}{\partial S} \Delta S$$

$$= \frac{\partial c}{\partial t} \Delta t + \frac{1}{2} \frac{\partial^2 c}{\partial S^2} \sigma^2 S^2 \Delta t \tag{22}$$

- *A riskless hedge.* Because all terms on the right side of (22) are deterministic, no arbitrage necessitates that the hedged portfolio V must earn the risk-free rate over the time period Δt, that is, $rV\Delta t$. Substitution and canceling Δt from both sides gives

$$rV = \frac{\partial c}{\partial t} + \frac{1}{2} \frac{\partial^2 c}{\partial S^2} \sigma^2 S^2 \tag{23}$$

- *Black–Scholes–Merton partial differential equation.* Substituting (19) into (23) and rearranging terms gives the famous BSM partial differential equation (pde)

$$\frac{\partial c}{\partial t} = rc - rS\frac{\partial c}{\partial S} - \frac{1}{2}\sigma^2 S^2 \frac{\partial^2 c}{\partial S^2} \tag{24}$$

- *Derivation of the Black–Scholes–Merton formula.* Using the call option's boundary condition $c(T) = \max[S(T) - K, 0]$, the solution to this pde is the BSM formula.

20.10 | Cases

J&L Railroad (Darden School of Business Case UV0251-PDF-ENG, Harvard Business Publishing) and **J&L Railroad: The Board Meeting** (Darden School of Business Case UV2566-PDF-ENG, Harvard Business Publishing). The first case studies a railroad company's decision to hedge next year's expected fuel demand. The second case, which may be done in conjunction with the first case, considers these issues in greater detail.

Pine Street Capital (Harvard Business School Case 201071-PDF-ENG). The case examines issues faced by a technology hedge fund in trying to decide whether and/or how to hedge equity market risk by short selling and trading options.

Sleepless in LA (Richard Ivey School of Business Foundation Case 905N11-PDF-ENG, Harvard Business Publishing). The case discusses the Black–Scholes–Merton model for options pricing, the concept of implied volatility, and put–call parity. It also shows how options pricing can be used to value the corporate liabilities of a financially distressed company.

20.11 | Questions and Problems

20.1. a. How did options dealers in nineteenth-century London approach options writing?

  b. How did it compare with options writers in New York City during the same period?

  c. Describe three probable causes as to why the options market in nineteenth-century London flourished while that in New York City lagged behind.

20.2. a. Why were the US regulators in the twentieth century opposed to options trading?

  b. What role did the Black–Scholes–Merton model play in changing regulators' views?

The next five questions use the following information for pricing European options.

Special Motors Corporation's stock price S is $59, the strike price K is $60, the maturity T is forty-four days, the implied volatility σ is 30 percent per year, and the risk-free interest rate r is 3.3 percent per year.

20.3. a. Given the preceding data, compute the call option's delta using the Black–Scholes–Merton model.

  b. Given the preceding data, compute the put option's delta using the Black–Scholes–Merton model.

20.4. a. Describe how to set up the delta hedge for a long call option position based on the computations in problem 20.3.

  b. If the stock price changes to $60 over the next trading day, what is the delta hedging error? Assume the Black–Scholes–Merton model accurately describes movements in the call's value.

20.5. a. Describe how you will set up the delta hedge for a short put option position based on computations in problem 20.3.

  b. If the stock price changes to $60 over the next trading day, what is the delta hedging error? Assume the Black–Scholes–Merton model accurately describes movements in the call's value.

20.6. a. Given the data in question 20.3, compute the call option's gamma on the basis of the Black–Scholes–Merton model.

  b. Given the data in question 20.3, compute the put option's gamma on the basis of the Black–Scholes–Merton model.

20.7. a. Consider a portfolio consisting of 50 shares of the stock, long 10 calls and short 30 puts. What is the portfolio's delta? (Use delta values from question 20.3.)

20.8. a. What is vega hedging?

   b. Describe some conceptual problems with this once-popular practice.

20.9. If you want to hedge volatility risk in a call option position, how would you go about doing so?

20.10. What is calibration with respect to the BSM model? Explain how to use calibration correctly. When is calibration used incorrectly?

20.11. Briefly describe the two types of models that we introduced, highlighting their strengths and weaknesses.

20.12. When constructing a theoretical model for pricing a derivative, if the theoretical model is rejected by historical data, can one still use the model to price derivatives? Explain your answer using the BSM as an example.

20.13. Complete the following table using the following information:

- Column 1 reports six strike prices $155 to $175 at $5 intervals.
- Column 2 is for the closing stock price on YBM, $160.
- Column 3 is for the risk-free interest rate $r = 10$ percent per year.
- Column 4 is for the time to maturity, which is twenty days ($20/265 = 0.054795$ years).
- Column 5 reports European call option prices from the market.
- Column 6 reports the implied volatility that you need to calculate.

Implied Volatilities		
K	c_{Mkt}	**Implied Volatility**
150	13.00	
155	8.00	
160	3.75	
165	1.00	
170	0.20	
175	0.05	

Comment on what this implies about the validity of the Black–Scholes–Merton model?

20.14. a. When using historical prices, is the Black–Scholes–Merton model accepted or rejected by the data?

   b. If the model is accepted, explain why. If the model is rejected, give one probable cause of rejection.

20.15. If historical data rejects the Black–Scholes–Merton model,

    a. can the model still be used for pricing options? Explain your answer.

    b. can the model be used for hedging option positions? Explain your answer.

20.16. What is a volatility smile with respect to the Black–Scholes–Merton model?

20.17. a. What is delta hedging? If the Black–Scholes–Merton model is correct, do you need delta hedging?

    b. What is gamma hedging? Under what conditions do you need gamma hedging on top of delta hedging?

20.18. In hedging using the Black–Scholes–Merton model, we used the phrase "the good, the bad, and the ugly." Identify "the good," and "the bad and the ugly" and explain why these descriptions are accurate or may be inappropriate.

20.19. Given the evidence supports that the stock's volatility is stochastic and the BSM model is rejected by the data, how can one hedge options?

20.20. (Microsoft Excel Project) We thank Professor Craig W. Holden of Indiana University, Bloomington, for providing a similar problem (copyright-free) on his website (www.kelley.iu.edu/cholden). His website www.excelmodeling .com has several books teaching hands-on practical finance with the help of Microsoft Excel.

Overview

The purpose of this assignment is to introduce you to the science of pricing options. The project has two parts:

- You will calculate and graph the value of European-style calls and puts using the built-in spreadsheet functions, such as the cumulative normal.

- Using actual options data from the *Wall Street Journal*, you will also calculate the implied volatilities using the solver module and graph the "smile" pattern of implied volatility.

Data (from the *Wall Street Journal*, March 3, 2000)

The closing price for the Standard and Poor's 500 (S&P 500) index (symbol SPX) was 1,381.76. As options expire on the third Friday of the expiration month (17th for March contracts, 21st for April contracts), choose the (annualized) ask yield rate for the Treasury bill that matures nearest to the expiration date. Express T as fraction of a year: 14/365 for March options and 49/365 for April options.

T-Bill Prices

Maturity	Days to Maturity	Ask Yield
Mar 16	13	5.28
Mar 23	20	5.13
Mar 30	27	5.30
Apr 06	34	5.31
Apr 13	41	5.48
Apr 20	48	5.61
Apr 27	55	5.76

S&P 500 Index Put Option Prices

Strike	Last (Price)	Strike	Last (Price)	Strike	Last (Price)
Mar 1325c	67	Mar 1375c	27	Mar 1425c	6 1/4
Mar 1325p	5 1/2	Mar 1375p	17	Mar 1425p	47 1/2
Apr 1325p	18 3/8	Apr 1375c	51	Apr 1425c	24
Mar 1350c	44	Apr 1375p	32	Apr 1425p	54
Mar 1350p	10	Mar 1400c	13 7/8	Mar 1450c	2 1/4
Apr 1350c	62 1/2	Mar 1400p	29	Mar 1450p	67
Apr 1350p	24	Apr 1400c	35 1/4	Apr 1450c	14 1/2
		Apr 1400p	44	Apr 1450p	72 1/2

A "c" denotes call price and a "p" denotes put price.

The Project

Do the project in Excel worksheets. Print out and turn in all of your results. Deliverables are noted below.

a. Cumulative Normal and Normal Density Graphs

Examine a standard normal distribution. Find the cumulative normal and the normal density for values of d from -3.0 to 3.0 in increments of 0.1. Record this in a table in your Excel worksheet. Then graph both the cumulative normal and the normal density on the same diagram with d on the x axis.

Deliverable: (1) The table with cumulative normal distribution function and the standard normal density function's values.

(2) The graph generated.

b. Option Pricing Using Black–Scholes–Merton Formula and Intrinsic Value Computation

Use the Black–Scholes–Merton formula to estimate the call price and the put price for options with the following data:

> Strike price $K = 10$
> Risk-free interest rate $r = 3$ percent or 0.03 per year
> Volatility $\sigma = 60$ percent or 0.6 per year
> Time to maturity $T = 1$ year
> $S(0)$ ranging from 0 (actually 0.0000001, a very small value) to 20, in increments of 2

Record these numbers and computations in a table.

Deliverable: (3) Table with various inputs and corresponding call and put prices estimated using the BSM model.

c. Intrinsic Value Computation and Graph

Now calculate call intrinsic values and put intrinsic values for the same options ($K = 10$ and $S(0)$ ranging from 0 to 20 in increments of 2).

Graph both the call price and the call intrinsic value on the same diagram with $S(0)$ on the x axis.

Similarly, graph both the put price and the put intrinsic value on the same diagram with $S(0)$ on the x axis.

Deliverable: (4) Table with the call price and the call intrinsic value, and the put price and the put intrinsic value. (You may combine (3) and (4) and present it in a single table.)

(5) The call graph.

(6) The put graph.

d. Implied Volatility Computation and Graph

Given data from the March 3, 2000, issue of the *Wall Street Journal*, calculate the implied volatility from S&P 500 index *put* options (not index call options) for K (strike) values of 1325, 1350, 1375, 1400, and 1425 for the March contract.

Then calculate the implied volatility from S&P 500 index *put* options (not index call options) for K values of 1325, 1350, 1375, 1400, and 1425 for the April contract.

Graph the implied volatility diagram with the exercise price X on the x axis and the March and April implied volatilities on the y axis.

<u>Deliverable</u>: (7) The table with the implied volatilities.

(8) The graph with the implied volatilities.

(Suggestions and useful information, relevant excel commands, and implied volatility computation)

Goal	Excel Command
1. To calculate the natural log:	= LN(A1)
3. To calculate the normal density:	= NORMDIST(A1,0,1,FALSE)
3. To calculate the cumulative normal:	= NORMDIST(A1,0,1,TRUE)
4. To calculate the exponential:	= EXP(A1)
5. To solve implied volatility:	Goal Seek

To estimate implied volatilities using Goal Seek command in Excel 2007 or later versions:

- In an Excel sheet, record different strike prices for March in one column and the various model inputs in other columns.

- In the column with the heading "Implied volatility," start with an arbitrary volatility number (say 0.2) and use it to compute March put price.

- Record market-traded March put prices corresponding to the different strike prices. In another column, note the "Put Price Difference" to record the difference between "market traded put price" and the "model generated put price" solved from the model.

- Next, select a cell under "Put Price Difference." On the Data tab, in the Data Tools group, click What-If Analysis, and then click Goal Seek.
  - In the "Set cell" box, record the current cell box.
  - In the "To value" box, type in 0.

- In the "By changing cell" box, type in the location of the cell corresponding to the implied volatility from the same row.
- Click OK to get the implied volatility in its own column. (In this case, the zero-price difference is obtained by changing the standard deviation.)

Hold and drag the mouse down to similarly solve implied volatilities corresponding to March put options corresponding to different strike prices.

IV

Interest Rate Derivatives

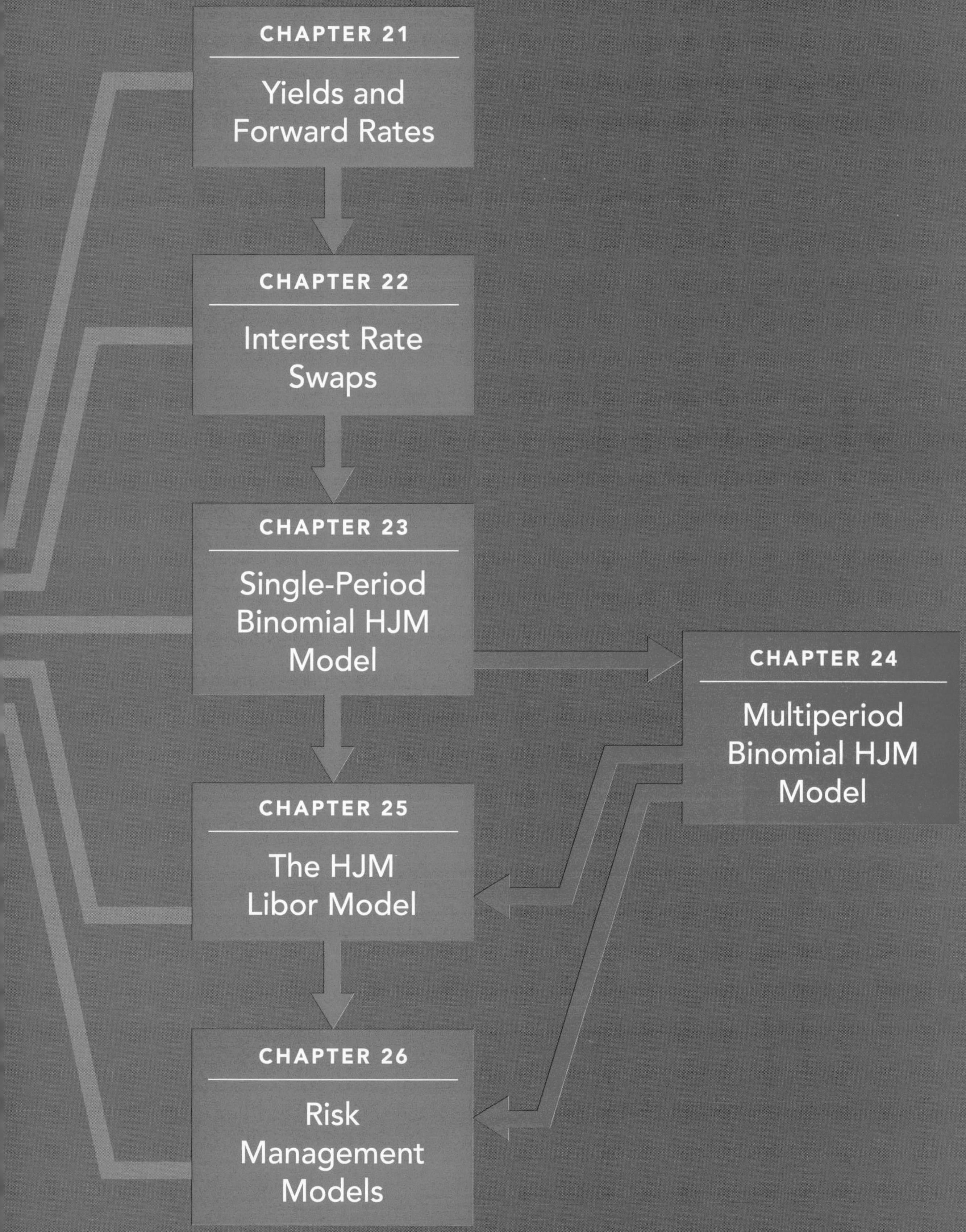

CHAPTER 21
Yields and
Forward Rates

CHAPTER 22
Interest Rate
Swaps

CHAPTER 23
Single-Period
Binomial HJM
Model

CHAPTER 24
Multiperiod
Binomial HJM
Model

CHAPTER 25
The HJM
Libor Model

CHAPTER 26
Risk
Management
Models

21

Yields and Forward Rates

21.1 | Introduction

In 1909, the founder of Ford Motor Company, Henry Ford, announced that the company would build only one car, the Model T, and famously declared, "Any customer can have a car painted any colour that he wants so long as it is black."[1] Similarly, mortgage loans used to be simple as well. In the 1950s and 1960s, home mortgages were typically made by savings and loans (S&Ls), whose standard offering was a no-frill thirty-year, fixed-rate loan. S&Ls were known as 3-6-3s because they paid depositors 3 percent, charged borrowers 6 percent, and the managers went to play golf at 3:00 PM! But times have changed.

Today home mortgages come with a variety of embedded options and complicated provisions (see Extension 21.1). There is a bewildering assortment of fixed- and adjustable- rate mortgages. Some have teaser rates with ceilings and floors on interest rates charged. Some don't pay principal in the early years, whereas others are extendible. Most can be repaid without penalty. To understand these provisions—the embedded options—one needs to understand interest rate derivatives (IRDs). This is the purpose of this and the remaining chapters.

Who uses IRDs? All players in the economy: individuals, corporations, governments, and financial institutions:

1. *Individuals.* A family's assets and liabilities are all sensitive to interest rate movements. On the liability side, interest rates affect payments on home mortgages, car loans, personal loans, and credit card balances. On the asset side, they affect earnings on savings accounts, certificates of deposit, and money market funds.

2. *Corporations and governments.* Corporations routinely use IRDs to structure their interest rate–sensitive liabilities and assets. Mutual funds, hedge funds, pension funds, insurance companies, and college and university endowments use IRDs to manage their investments. Last, they are essential for managing the complex treasury operations of local, state, and federal government.

3. *Financial institutions.* Financial institutions use advanced knowledge of IRDs to develop products for their clients and to manage their own interest rate risks.

Our discussion of IRDs parallels our earlier presentation of spots, forwards, futures, and options on commodities and equities; however, there's a twist. For IRDs, an *array* of different maturity default-free zero-coupon bonds replace the *single* commodity or stock price as the underlying asset. This small change raises some major hurdles for IRD pricing models. Still, despite its reputation for complexity, this subject is easy to understand if it is introduced gradually and with forethought. Magically, and perhaps without your awareness, the early chapters have already built this foundation for you!

For simplicity, we focus on Eurodollar IRDs. They are simpler than derivatives on Treasury securities. Moreover, Eurodollar IRDs attract the greatest trading volume, and you can have your cake and eat it too. Once you understand Eurodollar IRDs, it is easy to comprehend derivatives based on Treasuries.

---

[1] See Chapter IV of *My Life and Work* (1922) by Henry Ford in collaboration with Samuel Crowther from Project Gutenberg website www.gutenberg.org/dirs/etext05/hnfrd10.txt, February 23, 2011.

EXTENSION 21.1: Home Ownership and Derivatives

Suppose you find your dream house and submit an offer to buy the house for $500,000. A flurry of activity now begins. If the seller accepts the offer, the two of you first create an option contract. The seller's broker requires you to place a deposit, say, $5,000, with them. Should you decide to back out, the $5,000 will be forfeited; otherwise, it goes toward the purchase price. This deposit creates a *call option* to buy the house.

You now go to a bank or a mortgage broker to arrange a loan. They obtain your credit score indicating how you have handled debt in the past: credit card as well as other loan payments. Your credit score helps determine whether you get the loan plus the magnitudes of the down payment required and the interest rate charged.

On the basis of this evaluation, suppose that the lender agrees to loan you $450,000 for the house. This loan is called a **mortgage**. You have to pay this principal back in fifteen or thirty years with interest paid in monthly installments, and you have to come up with a $50,000 down payment. This 10 percent down payment provides a cushion against a decline in the house's value if you decide to leave town without a forwarding address! Unless you make a 20 percent down payment, the lender sometimes requires you to pay for mortgage insurance, which is a *put option* on the risk of your not repaying the principal (a credit derivative!).

Mortgages come in two varieties. A **fixed-rate mortgage (FRM)** charges a fixed interest rate over the loan's life. For a FRM, you have to pay back the loan in equal monthly installments over fifteen or thirty years. An **adjustable-rate mortgage (ARM)** usually charges a lower initial interest rate for one to five years, with the remaining payments adjusted depending on future interest rates. ARM mortgages come with caps and floors on the interest paid per period to protect both the lender and the borrower from adverse interest rate movements. These caps and floors are *call and put options* on interest rates—more IRDs!

Your expertise in modern finance should come in handy. If you are planning to stay in your home for a short period, or if you are betting that interest rates will remain low, or if you are anticipating a significant increase in your personal wealth in the near future, then an ARM may make sense. In addition, in the United States, most loans come without a prepayment penalty, so you can *choose* to pay back the loan before it matures. If interest rates fall, you also have the *option* of refinancing your home and locking in a cheaper interest rate.

In years past, the major players in the mortgage market were banks and savings and loan associations (S&Ls). The money for mortgage loans was raised and lent in local markets. Thanks to *modern finance,* a mortgage broker can now lend you the money for a house mortgage and immediately sell that loan in a national market. Typically, a loan is split into two parts. The right to service the loan is held by entities like the Bank of America or JP Morgan Chase, which regularly collects your mortgage payments and coaxes you to buy other products. The loan itself may be combined with other mortgage loans and sold to Wall Street wizards, who then combine these mortgage loans into a pool and sell bonds against the pool to cover the cost of their purchases. These bonds are called *asset-backed securities* or, in this case, **mortgage-backed securities**.

Did you really think the mortgage business was staid and stodgy?

On our journey to understanding IRDs, this chapter introduces yields and forward rates, which are fundamental concepts. We start by revisiting zero-coupon bonds, from which we extract yields, and the yield curve, concepts that are often introduced in basic finance and investment courses. We also discuss the once-popular but now fading techniques of duration and convexity based interest rate risk management. Then, we introduce forward rates, which are at the heart of modern interest rate risk management. We wrap up this chapter with a discussion of forward rate agreements (FRAs) and interest rate futures, which are analogous to forwards and futures on commodities and equities.

21.2 | Yields

To understand IRDS, we need to start at the beginning and understand yields. Yields are obtained from zero-coupon bond prices.

Revisiting Zeros

Our basic building blocks are risk-free zero-coupon bonds of different maturities. US Treasury bills and STRIPS and Eurodollar deposits fit our description of zeros. We introduced Treasuries and Eurodollars in chapter 2. Although derivatives on the Treasuries ruled the markets during the early days (1970s and 1980s), derivatives on Eurodollars took over thereafter, and became the dominant market with the greater trading volume. Moreover, IRDs on Eurodollars are often simpler than IRDs on Treasuries.

Recall that *Eurodollars* are dollar deposits in European banks (or European subsidiaries of US banks) that earn interest in dollars. They were concocted during the 1950s to evade the jurisdiction (and thus regulatory controls) of the US government. Moreover, unlike Treasury securities, for which large auctions affect the available supply, the larger supply of dollars changes less frequently and is less "lumpy." Less regulation and a less managed supply enable Eurodollar rates to adjust more freely to market forces than do Treasuries. This makes Eurodollar markets attractive to hedgers and speculators. These factors have contributed to the tremendous growth of Eurodollar markets, which are measured in trillions of dollars.

Recall from chapter 2 that there are three major interest rates relevant to Eurodollars. First is the *Eurodollar rate*, which is the interest rate paid on Eurodollar deposits. Second is the generic *London Interbank Offer Rate*, which is popularly known as *libor*. It is the interest rate at which major London banks offer to lend funds (in different currencies) to each other. Libor quotes on Eurodollars are among the most popular rates in the interest rate markets. Third is an international interest rate index based on average libor rates. Since January 1986, the British Bankers' Association (BBA) has been officially computing this index once a day at 11:00 AM London time. Using Telerate (who in turn collects the information from a number of data vendors such as Reuters, Thomson Financial, and *Bloomberg*), BBA gets quotes from sixteen banks as to their offer rates on Eurodollar deposits of all maturities ranging from one day to one year. For each maturity deposit, the two highest and lowest quotes are dropped, and the rest are averaged to compute what they have trademarked as *bbalibor* (see BBA's website at www.bbalibor.com). This rate is computed for ten currencies, with fifteen maturities for each.

The bbalibor rate for Eurodollars is the most widely used benchmark or reference rate for short-term interest rates worldwide. As it has some credit risk, bbalibor exceeds the corresponding rate on a similar maturity Treasury security, their difference being known as the **Treasury–Eurodollar (TED) spread**. Because an index is harder for any single financial institution to manipulate, bbalibor is used as the reference rate for over-the-counter interest rate derivatives contracts.[2] Like Treasury securities, Eurodollar interest rate computations assume 360 days in a year.

Yields and the Yield Curve

In chapter 2, we introduced zero-coupon bonds for the primary purpose of moving cash across time. Now we employ zeros for extracting the necessary interest rates. We only consider zero-coupon bonds that are default-free. Extensions of these insights to risky bonds are discussed briefly in chapter 26.

For simplicity, we denote time as progressing in unit increments $t = 0, 1, 2, 3, \ldots$. Of course, in practice, one needs to replace the unit increment with the actual days between the relevant cash flows.

From now on, we also need to attach time notations to our familiar symbols. For example, the price at time t of a zero-coupon bond that pays a dollar at time T is denoted $B(t,T)$. A zero-coupon bond's price at time 0 is denoted $B(0,T)$. This notation is illustrated in Figure 21.1.

The **yield** (or **yield to maturity** or **internal rate of return**) on a zero-coupon bond is that interest rate that equates the discounted bond's cash flows to its current

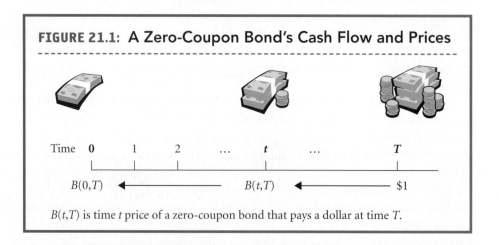

FIGURE 21.1: A Zero-Coupon Bond's Cash Flow and Prices

Time   **0**   1   2   ... t ... T

$B(0,T)$ ◄——————— $B(t,T)$ ◄——————— \$1

$B(t,T)$ is time t price of a zero-coupon bond that pays a dollar at time T.

[2] However, a study by the *Wall Street Journal* reported that even the bbalibor may have been manipulated during the financial crisis of 2007. Comparing libor rates quoted by major banks with another key rate (the premium on *credit default swaps [CDS]*, which gives the cost of insuring against default on debt issued by the bank), the *Wall Street Journal* concluded that some banks, such as Citigroup Inc., WESTLB, HBOS plc, JP Morgan Chase & Co., and UBS AG, were deliberately quoting low libor to hide their financially distressed situation (see "Study Casts New Doubt on Libor" and "How the Journal Analyzed Libor," *Wall Street Journal*, May 29, 2008).

price. It is the interest rate earned each period if the zero-coupon bond is held until maturity. The yield of a default-free zero is sometimes called the *spot rate*, although this terminology is fading in usage.

In symbols, the *yield* $R(0,T)$ at time 0 (today) is defined by the expression

$$B(0,T) = \frac{1}{[1 + R(0,T)]^T} \qquad (21.1)$$

Notice that yields generalize the concept of a dollar return used before. Our next example shows how to compute yields and create a **yield curve** that plots the zero-coupon bonds' yields (on the vertical axis) as a function of maturity (on the horizontal axis). This example also introduces the Common Zero-Coupon Bond Price Data utilized in this and subsequent chapters.

EXAMPLE 21.1: Computing the Yield Curve

- Today is time 0. Consider zero-coupon bonds with different maturity dates time T denoted by $B(0,T)$, where $T = 1, 2, 3, 4$. The common zero-coupon bond price data are shown in Table 21.1.
  - The first column reports the various times to maturity $T = 1, 2, 3, 4$. The longest-term zero-coupon bond matures at time 4.
  - The second and third columns give today's zero-coupon bond prices: $B(0,1) = \$0.97$, $B(0,2) = \$0.93$, and so on.

- These numbers are used to compute the yields in the fourth and fifth columns. A rearrangement of expression (21.1) gives the yield as

$$R(0,T) = \frac{1}{[B(0,T)]^{1/T}} - 1.$$

  - For example, the yield on the two-period zero is $R(0,2) = 1/[B(0,2)]^{1/2} - 1 = 0.0370$.
  - A plot of these yields against maturities gives the yield curve. In this case, it is also called the **zero-coupon yield curve** (or **zero curve**): see Figure 21.2.

TABLE 21.1: The Common Zero-Coupon Bond Price Data and Yields

Times to Maturity T	Today's Zero-Coupon Bond Prices, $B(0,T)$		Yields, $R(0,T)$	
1	$B(0,1)$	0.97	$R(0,1)$	0.0309
2	$B(0,2)$	0.93	$R(0,2)$	0.0370
3	$B(0,3)$	0.88	$R(0,3)$	0.0435
4	$B(0,4)$	0.82	$R(0,4)$	0.0509

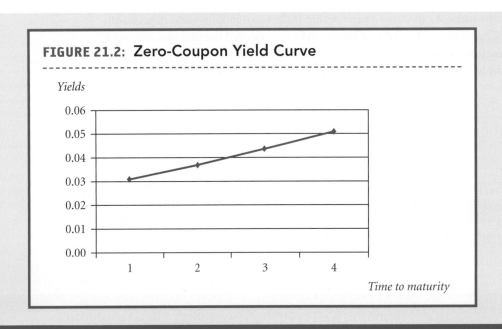

FIGURE 21.2: Zero-Coupon Yield Curve

Several concepts are related to yields.

- Standing at time t, the yield on the shortest-maturity zero-coupon bond maturing at time $(t+1)$ has a special name: the **spot rate of interest (or the spot rate)**. Using our notation for the yield, this is $R(t,t+1)$, but for simplicity, we write it as $R(t)$. We emphasize that whenever the second argument of the yield notation is missing, it will always denote the spot rate of interest.

- For future reference, we note that a *riskless money market account earns the spot rate of interest.* Standing at time t, a money market account's return is known over the next time step $[t,t+1]$. Of course, we do not know at time t what the time $(t+1)$'s or any future time period's spot rate will be. Future spot rates of interest are random.

- The graph of the yield curve is called the **term structure of interest rates**. Figure 21.3 graphs the yield curve at five different dates for Treasury securities. Note that the yield curve can be flat or upward or downward sloping. The shape of the yield curve reflects various factors such as (1) expectations of the market participants regarding the future movement of interest rates, (2) risk aversion of traders, and (3) the supply and demand considerations of the underlying zero-coupon bonds. The hypothesis that the shape of the yield curves only reflects expectations regarding the future movements of interest rates is known as the **expectations hypothesis**. Extension 21.2 provides a brief discussion of the expectations hypothesis as well as several other competing theories explaining the term structure of interest rates.

Consider a default-free *coupon* bond that trades in the market at time 0. The **yield** (or **yield to maturity**, also called the **internal rate of return**) on the coupon bond is the interest rate that equates the discounted coupon bond's cash flows to the bond's current price P_T. In symbols, the yield y satisfies

$$P_T = \frac{C}{(1 + y)} + \frac{C}{(1 + y)^2} + \ldots + \frac{C}{(1 + y)^{T-1}} + \frac{C + L}{(1 + y)^T}$$

$$= \sum_{t=1}^{T} \left[\frac{C}{(1 + y)^t} \right] + \frac{L}{(1 + y)^T} \tag{21.2}$$

where C denotes the yearly coupon, L denotes the principal (or par or face value), and T denotes the time to maturity in years.[3]

One can interpret the yield as the interest rate earned per period if (1) one invests today in a coupon bond that matures at time T, (2) one holds the bond until maturity, and (3) all the coupons received get reinvested (in the future) at today's yield y. Of course, of these three conditions, the third is the most unreasonable because future interest rates are random, and they will be unlikely to equal today's yield.

FIGURE 21.3: Yield Curves for Treasury Securities at Selected Dates

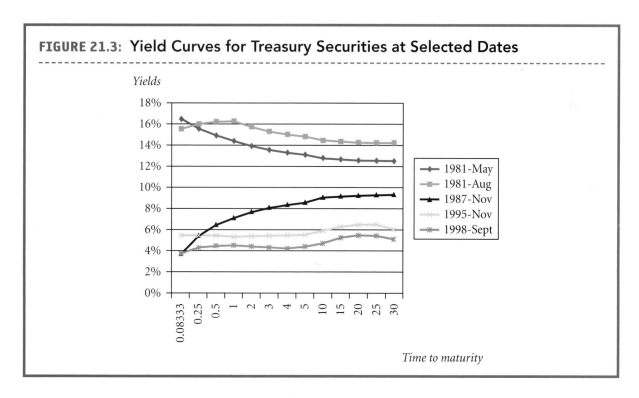

[3] We assume annual coupon payments for simplicity. When coupons are paid every six months, the formula is modified with $C/2$ replacing C, the expression in the denominator becoming $(1 + y/2)$, and the annual yield is written as $(1 + y/2)^2 - 1$.

EXTENSION 21.2: The Expectations Hypothesis

The classical (macro) economics term structure of interest rate literature characterizes the risk premium embedded in the term structure of interest rates according to hypotheses about investor behavior: the market segmentation hypothesis, the liquidity preference hypothesis, and the expectations hypothesis. Recall that *risk premia* are the compensation (in terms of an increase in expected returns above the spot rate) paid for the risks embedded in different securities. Given an understanding of risk premia, one can both price zero-coupon bonds and forecast future spot rates of interest.

The **market segmentation hypothesis**, which is normally associated with Professor John M. Culbertson (1957), states that the different maturity equilibrium zero-coupon bond prices are determined in isolation of each other by distinct market clienteles demanding payoffs at different horizons. Thus there is market segmentation across different future time horizons. This implies that the risk premia paid for bonds of different maturities are determined in isolation of the risk premia paid for the other maturity bonds, and that there might be arbitrage across market segments.

In contrast, Nobel laureate economist Sir John Richard Hicks's (1946) **liquidity preference hypothesis** is that the equilibrium zero-coupon bond prices of different maturities are jointly determined by supply and demand considerations, in particular, liquidity needs across time, and the interest rate risk premia reflect these considerations. Professors Franco Modigliani and Richard Sutch's (1966) **preferred habitat theory** argues that borrowers and lenders have their own preferred maturity habitats (as suggested by market segmentations hypothesis) and would only move to another habitat if they were given an increased premium to compensate for the risk and cost of moving. Modern equilibrium models of the term structure of interest rates can be viewed as the representation of the liquidity preference (or preferred habitat) hypothesis in a continuous time framework (see Cox et al. 1985; Dunn and Singleton 1986; Sundaresan 1984).

The *expectations hypothesis* is associated with economists Irving Fisher (1930) and Friedrich A. Lutz (1940). It has as its basic premise that zero-coupon bonds of different maturities are *perfect substitutes*. In the literature, this perfect substitutes hypothesis has been formalized (in terms of the mathematics) in three distinct ways. Each of these formalizations can be characterized by a formula for the zero-coupon bond's price. Jarrow (1981) and Cox et al. (1981) independently discovered this critique of the various expectations hypotheses. The following discussion is presented for the general case in terms of today (time 0), an intermediate date (time t), and the maturity date for a long-term bond (time T).

The **local expectations (LE) hypothesis** is that

$$E\left[\frac{B(t + 1, T) - B(t, T)}{B(t, T)}\right] = R(t) \tag{1a}$$

where $E[.]$ denotes expectation, $B(t, T)$ is the time t price of a zero-coupon bond that pays a dollar at maturity date T, and $R(t)$ is the spot rate at time t (which is the one-period rate for immediate borrowing or lending; see expression [21.1]).

This formalization interprets "perfect substitutes" as meaning that the different maturity zero-coupon bonds earn no risk premia, that is, the expected return on all zero-coupon bonds is equal to the spot rate of interest.

Equivalently, in terms of bond prices, the LE hypothesis can be written as:

$$B(0,T) = E\left\{\frac{1}{[1 + R(0)][1 + R(1)]\ldots[1 + R(T - 1)]}\right\} \tag{1b}$$

This implies, as in expression (1a), that the T-maturity bond's price is its expected discounted payoff using the spot rate of interest with no adjustment for risk.

The **return-to-maturity expectations (RME) hypothesis** is that

$$\frac{1}{B(0,T)} - 1 = E\{[1 + R(0)][1 + R(1)]\ldots[1 + R(T - 1)]\} - 1. \tag{2a}$$

This formalization of the "perfect substitutes" condition is that the T-period holding period return from a zero-coupon bond (the left side of expression [2a]) is equivalent to the expected return from holding the money market account over the same horizon (the right side of expression [2a]). To understand this second assertion, looking at the right side of expression (2a), the first term corresponds to the expected interest earned by investing a dollar in a money market account at time 0 and letting it roll over until time T. Interest is earned on interest. Subtracting the original dollar gives us the expected percentage return on the money market account over $[0, T]$.

Equivalently, in terms of bond prices, the RME hypothesis can be written as

$$B(0,T) = \frac{1}{E\{[1 + R(0)][1 + R(1)]\ldots[1 + R(T - 1)]\}} \tag{2b}$$

It can be shown that the LE and RME hypotheses are mutually exclusive (unless interest rates are deterministic) by Jensen's inequality.

The **unbiased expectations (UE) hypothesis** is that

$$f(0,t) = E\{R(t)\}. \tag{3a}$$

where $f(0,t)$ is a one-period borrowing or lending rate that you can contract at time 0 for the time interval $[t, t + 1]$; see expression (21.9) later in the text. Here the perfect substitutes condition is formalized to mean that forward rates provide an unbiased estimate of the expected future spot rate.

Equivalently, in terms of bond prices, the UE hypothesis can be written as

$$B(0,T) = \frac{1}{[1 + R(0)][1 + E\{R(1)\}]\ldots[1 + E\{R(T - 1)\}]}. \tag{3b}$$

It can also be shown that the LE and UE hypotheses are mutually exclusive.

If the term structure of interest rates has risk premia, then all three forms of the expectations hypotheses are not true, and the pricing of zero-coupon bonds becomes more complex. Unfortunately, empirical evidence strongly supports the existence of interest rate risk premium and the rejection of all three forms of the expectations hypothesis. But they are interesting hypotheses none-the-less because they help us to better understand the pricing of zero-coupon bonds. Knowing what is not true sometimes helps us understand what is, and why!

EXAMPLE 21.2: Computing a Coupon Bond's Yield

■ Consider a two-year coupon bond with price $P_2 = \$101.86$, principal $L = \$100$, and a yearly coupon of $C = \$6$. Using expression (21.2), the coupon bond's yield y is the solution to the equation

$$101.86 = \frac{6}{(1+y)} + \frac{106}{(1+y)^2},$$

or, $101.86y^2 + 197.72y - 10.14 = 0$.

■ Solving this quadratic equation (analytically, by trial and error, or by numerical methods) gives[4]

$$y = 0.05 \text{ or } 5 \text{ percent.}$$

■ Microsoft Excel enables you to compute the yield with one formula, which has the syntax:

YIELD(settlement,maturity,rate,pr,redemption,frequency,basis).

■ The inputs are as follows:
- *Settlement* is the bond's settlement date—the day from which the bond earns interest. Let us assume it is January 15, 2012, which is input into Excel as DATE (2012,1,15).
- *Maturity* is the date the bond expires, or January 15, 2014.
- *Rate* is the annual coupon rate, or 6 percent.
- *Pr* is the bond's price per $100 face value, which is $101.86.
- *Redemption* is the bond's redemption value per $100 face value, which is $100.
- *Frequency* is the number of coupon payments per year, 1 for annual payments, 2 for semiannual payments, 4 for quarterly payments, and so on.
- *Basis* is the type of day count basis to use. Here we use 0 to denote that we are assuming 30 days in a month and 360 days in a year. Other examples of basis are actual/actual, actual/360, and so on.

The yield is given by

YIELD(DATE(2012,1,15),DATE(2014,1,15),6%,101.86,100,1,0) = 0.049999687

---

[4] A quadratic equation $ax^2 + bx + c = 0$ has the solutions $x = [-b \pm \sqrt{(b^2 - 4ac)}]/2a$. Select the positive value for y.

A special case when computing a yield should be noted. If the price of the bond were 100 instead (equal to par), then the yield would equal the coupon rate of 0.03. When this happens, the coupon rate is the same as the yield and is called the **par bond yield**.

Yields are often used to select bonds for inclusion into an investment portfolio. However, this approach to bond portfolio selection is problematic. Just like warnings on cigarette cartons that alert one to the dangers of smoking, a warning needs to be posted at this point with respect to using yields for bond portfolio management. As noted earlier, the yield on a coupon bond is equivalent to the *internal rate of return (IRR)*. The IRR is a well-studied object in *capital budgeting*, which is the science of choosing among investment alternatives (in our case, bonds). The recommendation in early texts was to select projects with the highest IRR (read as yields). However, in their classic *Principles of Corporate Finance*, Brealey and Myers (2003) debunk IRR's desirability and point out several pitfalls. The most critical pitfall from our point of view is that when using IRR in making investment decisions, one is assuming that the reinvestment rate for future cash flows is non-random and equal to the IRR. Of course, in actual markets, interest rates are random, and this assumption is violated. Brealey and Myers therefore recommend not using the IRR when making investment decisions, and they provide suitable alternatives.

As a consequence, astute readers like you are also warned against using a bond's yield (the IRR) as the sole determinant for choosing among different bonds to hold in an investment portfolio. We will provide suitable alternative strategies for bond selection in chapters 23–25, in the context of the Heath–Jarrow–Morton (HJM) framework.

Spread Trading

Recall that a *spread* is the difference between rates or prices of two closely related securities. Market participants often trade spreads when they deviate from normal values. Spread trades are highly popular in futures, options, and bond markets.

An article titled "Playing the 'Yield Curve'" (*Wall Street Journal,* February 26, 2011) discussed new speculative products that allowed speculation on steepening (i.e., widening of the spread) or flattening (i.e., narrowing of the spread) of the yield curve. A steep yield curve is often seen at the beginning of an economic expansion, when the Federal Reserve (the Fed) keeps short-term interest rates low to help economic growth and investors expecting higher growth (and concomitant higher inflation) sell longer-term bonds (which drives down their prices), pushing up their yields.

At the time of this story, the US economy was coming out of a recession, and the yield curve was steep. The difference between the two- and ten-year Treasury securities was at a near-record level of about 3 percentage points (as compared to an average spread of 0.84 percentage points since 1976). Traders were betting that the yield curve would further steepen or flatten using **exchange-traded notes** (which are unsecured, exchange-traded, debt-like securities issued by investment banks and other financial companies) such as Barclay PLC's iPath US Treasury Steepener ETN, which profits from a steepening yield curve, and iPath US Treasury Flattener ETN, which pays off when the opposite happens.

The next example illustrates a spread trade with Treasury securities. The nature of this trade is similar to a spread trade with futures prices (see chapter 9).

EXAMPLE 21.3: Spread Trading in Bond Markets

- A story titled "Treasury Prices Fall on Rate-Cut Outlook" (*Wall Street Journal*, April 3, 2008) reported that investors reversed their spread trades as they "scaled back expectations for further rate cuts." As this was a bet on the macro-economy, some background information helps.

- The Fed responded to the 2007 financial crisis by aggressively cutting interest rates. Since September 2007, the Fed had lowered short-term rates from 5.25 percent to 2.25 percent.

- Many traders believed that the yield curve would become even steeper. They bought two-year Treasury notes and sold both the ten-year notes and thirty-year Treasury bonds. The bet was that the economy would continue to worsen. The traders planned to reverse their trades after the spread widened and lock in profits (see Figure 21.4).

- However, the economic outlook improved earlier than expected. Traders discarded their hope of a further 50 basis point interest rate cut by the Fed. They closed out their spread by reversing the earlier trade.[5]

- The trade is easy to see using STRIPS with face value $100. Suppose two-year STRIPS and ten-year STRIPS have yields $y_2 = 0.0180$ (or 1.80 percent) and $y_{10} = 0.0355$, respectively. Using expression (21.1), we get the STRIPS prices:
  - The two-year STRIPS price is $P_2 = 100B(0,2) = 100/(1.018)^2 = \$96.49$.
  - The ten-year STRIPS price is $P_{10} = 100B(0,10) = 100/(1.0355)^{10} = \$70.55$.
  - The spread between the interest rates is

$$y_{10} - y_2 = 0.0355 - 0.0180 = 0.0175 \text{ or } 1.75 \text{ percent}$$

  - If you expect this spread to widen to 2 percent, then your strategy is to buy the relatively underpriced two-year Treasury STRIPS and sell the relatively overpriced ten-year STRIPS. This has a cash flow of

$$-P_2 + P_{10} = -96.49 + 70.55 = -\$25.94$$

This is the cost of constructing the strategy.

- Suppose the spread widens as expected. For simplicity, assume that the ten-year STRIPS price stays the same but that the yield on the two-year STRIPS declines to 1.55 percent.
  - Now the two-year STRIPS price $P_2(new) = 100/(1.0155)^2 = \$96.97$.
  - Next, close out the spread by reversing the trades: sell the two-year and buy the ten-year STRIPS. This generates a cash flow of

$$P_2(new) - P_{10} = 96.97 - 70.55 = \$26.42$$

The net profit is the sum of the initial and final cash flows = 26.42 − 25.94 = $0.48.

---

[5] The article reports that the two-year note price fell 7/32 points (recall that Treasury note and bond prices trade in 1/32 point increments) and the yield went up from 1.786 percent to 1.890 percent. Ten-year Treasury notes also went down, by 11/32 point or $3.4375 for every $1,000 invested, and their yield went up from 3.545 percent to 3.585 percent. Notice that the yield change for a ten-year note was much less than that for a two-year note.

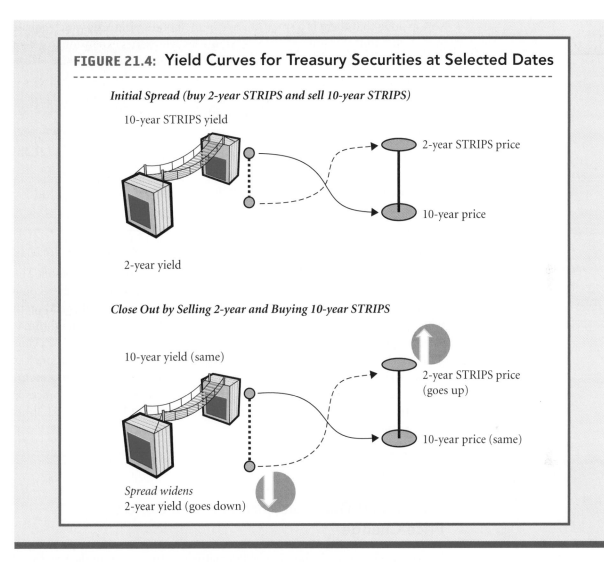

FIGURE 21.4: Yield Curves for Treasury Securities at Selected Dates

Initial Spread (buy 2-year STRIPS and sell 10-year STRIPS)

10-year STRIPS yield

2-year STRIPS price

10-year price

2-year yield

Close Out by Selling 2-year and Buying 10-year STRIPS

10-year yield (same)

2-year STRIPS price
(goes up)

10-year price (same)

Spread widens
2-year yield (goes down)

21.3 | The Traditional Approach

In 1938, Frederick R. Macaulay proposed the concept of duration (also known as Macaulay's duration), which led to the development of the traditional approach to interest rate risk management. We next discuss how duration and its related concept, convexity, are used for fixed-income securities portfolio management.

Duration

First, using expression (21.2), we write the bond's price as

$$P = \sum_{t=1}^{T} \frac{C}{(1 + y)^t} + \frac{L}{(1 + y)^T} \qquad (21.3a)$$

where y is the bond's yield.

Now assume that there is a small change in the bond's yield, Δy, which equals the new yield minus the original yield. Next, use a Taylor series expansion to get an expression for the approximate change in value of the bond's price:[6]

$$\Delta P \approx -\frac{1}{1+y}\left[\sum_{t=1}^{T}\frac{C \times t}{(1+y)^t} + \frac{L \times T}{(1+y)^T}\right]\Delta y$$

$$= -PDur\frac{\Delta y}{1+y} \qquad (21.3b)$$

where $\approx$ denotes approximation and Dur is duration, where

$$Dur = \frac{1}{P}\left\{\sum_{t=1}^{T}\left[\frac{C}{(1+y)^t}\right] \times t + \left[\frac{L}{(1+y)^T}\right] \times T\right\} \qquad (21.4)$$

A bond's duration (expression [21.5]) has a useful economic interpretation. The terms in the braces in expression (21.4) are the discounted cash flows. They become "weights" when expressed as a fraction of the bond price. These weights add up to 1, giving expression (21.4) the interpretation of a weighted average. In the summation, the weights are averaging the times to the cash payments $t = 1, 2, \ldots T$. Thus duration can be interpreted as *the bond's average life*. Using this interpretation, it is easy to see that the *duration of a zero-coupon bond is the same as the time to maturity* because there are no early cash flows and the expression within the braces is just the zero-coupon bond's price times the time to maturity. Expression (21.3b) is rewritten as the following result.

RESULT 21.1

- -

A Modified Duration Formula for a Bond's Price Change

For a small change in the bond's yield to maturity y, the change in the bond's price is

$$\Delta P \approx -PDur_M\Delta y \qquad (21.5)$$

where P is the original bond price,

ΔP is the change in the bond price (Δ denotes New value $-$ Original value),
$Dur_M \equiv Dur/(1+y)$ is the modified duration, and
Δy is the change in the yield to maturity.

---

[6] A Taylor series expansion allows us to write the change in the bond price as

$$P(y+\Delta y) - P(y) = (dP/dy)(\Delta y) + (1/2)(d^2P/dy^2)(\Delta y)^2 + \ldots$$

This relation is an approximation because only the first term on the right side is retained. We get a better approximation if the second derivative is used. This takes us to the notion of "convexity" (which we introduce later), but it also increases computational complexity.

Expression (21.4) shows that when yields change, the change in the bond's price can be approximated as minus the change in the bond's yield times the product of the bond's price and its modified duration. The negative sign in expression (21.5) reflects the fact that prices and yields move in opposite directions. The formula also shows that all else constant, a bond with a higher modified duration will have a greater price change for a given change in the yield. As such, modified duration can be interpreted as a "risk measure" for the bond.

The next example shows how to compute duration, modified duration, and to approximate changes in the bond's price when yields change only slightly.

EXAMPLE 21.4: Using Modified Duration to Approximate a Bond's Price Change

- Let a newly issued two-year coupon bond have a par value of $100, a coupon rate of 6 percent ($6), and a yield $y = 0.05$ or 5 percent per year. We present the following computations in Table 21.2:
  - Columns 1 and 2 record the timing and magnitude of the cash flows.
  - Column 3 reports the present value of the cash flows. They are computed by dividing $6 by $(1 + y) = 1.05$ and $106 by $(1 + y)^2$, respectively. Sum these numbers to get the bond's price, $101.8594. This is the same as the bond price P_2 in Example 21.2.
  - Column 4 is presented for computational convenience. The entries in each cell are derived by multiplying the present value of the cash flow by its timing (column 3 times column 1). Their sum equals $198.0045. Dividing this number by the bond price gives the duration:

$$Dur = \frac{198.0045}{101.8594} = 1.9439 \text{ years}$$

- Suppose that the yield increases by 25 basis points. Discount the bond's cash flow by the new rate 5.25 percent to get the new bond price of $101.3896. The bond price change equals

$$\Delta P = \text{New price} - \text{Old price}$$
$$= -\$0.4698$$

- Using expression (21.5)instead, we compute the bond's price change as

$$\Delta P \approx -P \, Dur_M \Delta y$$
$$= -101.8594 \times \frac{1.9439}{1.05} \times 0.0025$$
$$= -\$0.4714.$$

Comparing the two changes, the bond price actually declines to $0.4698 but the duration-based measure approximates a decline of $0.4714. The error is a little over 0.15 cents on a principal amount of one $100.

TABLE 21.2: Bond Price and Duration Computation

Time t (years)	Cash Flows	Present Value of Cash Flows	Present Value of Cash Flow $\times t$
1	6	5.7143	5.7143
2	106	96.1451	192.2902
Sum		$101.8594 (= bond price)	198.0045

Duration, $Dur = 198.0045/101.8594 = 1.9439$ years.

Notice an analogy. Just as we had used delta to get a linear approximation to changes in options prices for small changes in stock prices, we use modified duration to get a linear approximation to changes in bond prices for small changes in the yield. Both of these approaches are based on a first-order Taylor series expansion, and just as we improved the approximation in the case of options by incorporating the second derivative gamma, we can do the same and get a better approximation to the price-yield curve by introducing the second derivative with respect to the bond's yield. This gives a price change formula that uses both duration and convexity. Because the convexity approximation is identical to that obtained when using an option's gamma, we omit the details and refer the reader to the relevant discussion in chapter 20.[7]

Modified Duration Hedging

Consider a bond portfolio consisting of n_i units of the coupon bond with coupon payment C_i, maturity T_i, principal L_i, and price P_i for bonds $i = 1, \ldots N$. The time 0 value of this portfolio is

$$V = \sum_{i=1}^{N} n_i P_i. \tag{21.6a}$$

The bond portfolio's **modified duration** is[8]

$$Dur_{MV} = \sum_{i=1}^{N} w_i Dur_{Mi} \tag{21.6b}$$

---

[7] The new price change formula is $\Delta P \approx -P Dur_M \Delta y + (P/2) Convexity (\Delta y)^2$, where we define
$$Convexity = \frac{1}{P(1+y)^2} \left\{ \sum_{t=1}^{T} \left[\frac{t(t+1)C}{(1+y)^t} \right] + \frac{T(T+1)L}{(1+y)^T} \right\}.$$

[8] One can derive expression (21.6b) as follows. Define y to be the yield on portfolio V, viewing V as a "single bond" whose coupons differ across time. Take the derivative of both sides of expression (21.6a) with respect to y. This uses expression (21.3), which gives P as a function of an arbitrary yield y. Next, use expression (21.5) for each bond, including V when viewed as a "bond" by itself, and algebra to obtain (21.6b). In expression (21.6b), each bond's modified duration is evaluated at the portfolio's yield y, and not their own yields.

where $w_i = \dfrac{n_i P_i}{V}$ and Dur_{Mi} is the modified duration of bond i. Note that the weights sum to 1, that is $\sum\limits_{i=1}^{N} w_i = 1$.

The bond portfolio's modified duration is just the weighted average of the individual bond's modified durations, where the weight for bond i corresponds to the percentage of the portfolio's value represented by the position in that bond.

Given an existing bond portfolio, **modified duration hedging** is the process of modifying the composition of the bond portfolio through buying, selling, and/or shorting bonds such that the new portfolio has a zero-modified duration. Under certain conditions (to be shown below), duration hedging will remove the interest rate risk from a bond portfolio.

During the last few decades of the twentieth century, duration hedging was a widely used technique for managing the interest rate risk of a bond portfolio. However, it is currently being supplanted by the more sophisticated hedging techniques based on the HJM model.

To understand the conditions under which traditional duration hedging removes the interest rate risk from a bond portfolio, let's consider the simplest bond portfolio consisting of: (1) a single coupon-bond with coupon payment C, maturity T, principal L, and price P and (2) n zero-coupon bonds with maturity T and price B. We note that the coupon bond has a modified duration of Dur_M and that the T-period zero-coupon bond has a modified duration of $T/(1 + y_B)$, where y_B is the yield on the zero-coupon bond.

The portfolio's value is

$$V = P + nB. \tag{21.7a}$$

To duration hedge we choose n such that the right side of expression (21.7a) is zero, which implies that the modified duration of the portfolio is approximately zero,[9] that is

$$Dur_{MV} \approx \left(\frac{P}{V}\right) Dur_M + \left(\frac{nB}{V}\right) \frac{T}{1 + y_B} = 0. \tag{21.7b}$$

Algebra gives the number of zero-coupon bonds to trade as:

$$n = -\frac{P \times Dur_M \times (1 + y_B)}{B \times T}. \tag{21.7c}$$

This is called the **modified-duration hedge ratio**.

---

[9] The duration of the portfolio V is only approximately equal to zero because we replace the portfolio's yield y on the right side of expression (21.7b) with both the bond's and zero-coupon bond's yields, respectively, when computing their durations. The hedge ratio in expression (21.7c) is the appropriate one to remove interest rate risk, as shown below.

Now let's study the conditions under which this *zero-modified duration* portfolio's value does not change when interest rates change. First, we can write the change in the portfolio's value as

$$\Delta V = \Delta P + n\Delta B. \tag{21.8a}$$

Second, using the modified-duration approximation given in Result 21.1 for both the coupon and zero-coupon bonds, we can rewrite this as

$$\Delta V \approx -PDur_M\Delta y_P - nB\,\frac{T}{1 + y_B}\,\Delta y_B \tag{21.8b}$$

where Δy_P is the change in the yield on the coupon-bond P and Δy_B is the change in the yield on the zero-coupon bond B. Last, substitution of the modified-duration hedge ratio n from expression (21.7c) yields:

$$\Delta V \approx -PDur_M(\Delta y_P - \Delta y_B). \tag{21.8c}$$

This is the result for which we were looking! Examining this equation, we see that the zero-modified-duration bond portfolio's value will be neutral to changes in interest rates if and only if the coupon- and zero-coupon bonds' yields are equal when interest rates change, that is $\Delta y_P = \Delta y_B$. This is a very strong condition. It implies that *modified-duration hedging is effective if and only if the yield curve shifts in a parallel fashion*.

At this point, you can rightly sound an alarm. If you recall Figure 21.3, you see that the yield curve does not evolve through time via parallel shifts! Consequently, modified-duration hedging doesn't really work, especially when the long and short ends of the term structure of interest rates behave differently.

But modified-duration hedging has another problem as well. Recall that modified-duration hedging only uses the first-order approximation from the Taylor series expansion of the bond's price as a function of the yield. The first order approximation only works well when yield changes are small. If yield changes are large, then the second-order approximation in the Taylor series expansion needs to be included. This is called **convexity hedging**. Because convexity hedging with bonds is analogous to gamma option with options, we omit the remaining details and refer the reader to the relevant discussion in chapter 20. Unfortunately, convexity hedging does not solve the non-parallel shifting yield curve problem. For this reason, we do not recommend its use.

Applications and Limitations

Duration, its modifications and extensions, has been widely used in the past to manage interest rate risk.

1. *Active bond portfolio management.* One can modify a portfolio's duration to bet on the direction of future interest rate movements. For example, if one believes

that interest rates are going to fall (which would increase the value of a bond portfolio because bond prices will rise), just increase the portfolio's duration by eliminating low duration bonds and buying high duration bonds. High duration bonds are more sensitive to interest rate changes, so that an increase in the portfolio's duration will increase profits as interest rates fall. Do the opposite to soften the blow of an interest rate hike.

If desired, one can construct the portfolio to be **duration neutral**, that is, to have zero duration. As noted previously, making a bond portfolio delta neutral reduces, but does not eliminate, interest rate risk from the bond portfolio.

2. *Matching assets and liabilities.* A typical bank has liabilities (like checking and savings accounts) with very low duration (because customers can remove them at a moment's notice) and assets (like loans to consumers and businesses) with high durations (because they are typically for longer periods). In its natural state, a bank holds a speculative position in terms of the shape of the yield curve. A bank can reduce this vulnerability by managing the gap between the assets' and liabilities' durations. For example, it can increase the duration of the liabilities by encouraging customers to invest in long-term deposits, and it can lower the duration of the assets by issuing floating-rate loans such as adjustable-rate mortgages and lines of credit that charge variable rates tied to short-term interest rates.

Duration-based hedging has many shortcomings that limit its efficacy. Duration hedging strategies do not completely eliminate interest rate risk from a bond portfolio because of the inherent weaknesses of this approach. First, it only works for small changes in interest rates, and in reality, interest rates sometimes change by larger magnitudes before one can rebalance the portfolio. Second, it only works for parallel shifts of the yield curve, which assumes that all of the bonds' yields change by the same amount. However, this rarely happens in practice because short-term interest rates are much more volatile than long-term interest rates (see Figure 23.1). Combined, these two weaknesses greatly reduce the effectiveness of duration hedging.

Although some traders may still use the concept of duration to manage a bond portfolio's interest rate risk, duration-based hedging is on its way out. Term structure modeling, which we develop in this and the subsequent chapters, is a far superior method for interest rate risk management because it works for all possible evolutions of the yield curve.

21.4 | Forward Rates

"The old order changeth, yielding place to new," reflected a dying King Arthur [in Alfred Lord Tennyson's poem *Le Morte D'Arthur* (1845). So is it with respect to duration and traditional interest rate risk management. Newer techniques have been developed that overcome all of duration hedging's limitations. These techniques consider the impact of the changing shapes of the term structure of interest rates on bond prices. The approach is based on the HJM model discussed in chapters 23–25.

This section introduces the concept of a forward rate, which forms the basis of modern interest rate risk management. Forward rates are handy for several reasons.

1. *Forward rates are unit-free.* Rates provide a better measure to compare across bonds than do bond prices. To see this, consider a dollar increase in two identical stocks where one had a 2:1 split the day before. Does a dollar stock price increase convey the same meaning after the split as it did before? The answer is no because the benefit of a $1 increase in the stock's price depends on its initial price. Yet a 1 percent change for both stocks either before or after the split is comparable because it is unit-free. The same is true for forward rates when considering changes in bond prices.

2. *Forward rates are more stable than bond prices.* Again, that rates are unit-free becomes relevant. Consider a stock that earns 10 percent return per year, a stable rate. Its prices are $100 today, $110 after one year, $121 after two years, $133.10 after three years, and so on. The price changes differ across time and are not stable; however, the 10 percent return is constant. Similarly, zero-coupon bond prices change across time, yet forward rates can be stable. These considerations become important in estimating and modeling the term structure of interest rates in chapters 23–25.

3. *Versatility of forward rates.* The building blocks of modern interest rate management theory are interlinked:

$$\text{Zero-coupon bond prices} \leftrightarrow \text{Yields} \leftrightarrow \text{Forward rates}$$

where we use $\leftrightarrow$ to indicate that given one of these quantities, the others can be computed. Since all of these quantities are interchangeable, we select the simplest for analysis. This takes us to forward rates.

The Definition

To understand the definition, let us first study an example. Consider two zero-coupon bonds trading today (time 0) with maturities at times 3 and 4, and with prices $B(0,3) = \$0.88$ and $B(0,4) = \$0.82$, respectively. Their price ratio adjusted by subtracting 1 is $B(0,3)/B(0,4) - 1 = 0.0732$, or 7.32 percent. This adjusted ratio captures the implicit interest earned on the four period bond between times 3 and 4. Indeed, the extra interest earned over the time period [3, 4] is the only difference between the three and four period zero-coupon bonds.

Extending this example, we can formally define the time 0 **forward rate** for the future time period $[T-1, T]$ as

$$f(0,T-1) = \frac{B(0,T-1)}{B(0,T)} - 1 \qquad (21.9)$$

where $B(0, T-1)$ and $B(0, T)$ are today's zero-coupon bond prices for bonds maturing at times $(T-1)$ and T, respectively.[10]

As in the example, one can understand the forward rate by looking at Figure 21.5. This figure shows that the forward rate $f(0, T-1)$ isolates the implicit interest earned on the longer maturity bond over the last time period $[T-1, T]$. Example 21.5 illustrates this computation.

EXAMPLE 21.5: Computing Forward Rates

Table 21.3 uses the data from Example 21.1.

- The first column reports the various zero-coupon bond maturities denoted by $T = 0, 1, 2, 3, 4$. The second and third columns give today's zero-coupon bond prices. $B(0,0)$ is trivially 1.

- These numbers are used to compute the forward rates, reported in the fourth and fifth columns. By expression (21.9), $f(0,0) = B(0,0)/B(0,1) - 1 = 0.0309$. Similarly, one can compute the other rates such as $f(0,2) = [B(0,2)/B(0,3)] - 1 = 0.93/0.88 - 1 = 0.0568$, and so on.

- Figure 21.6 plots the **forward rate curve** that depicts the forward rates versus time to maturity. For comparison, also shown is the zero-coupon bond yield curve (from Example 21.1).

- We will often use the zero-coupon bond prices, forward rates, and yields to maturity from this table in subsequent numerical examples.

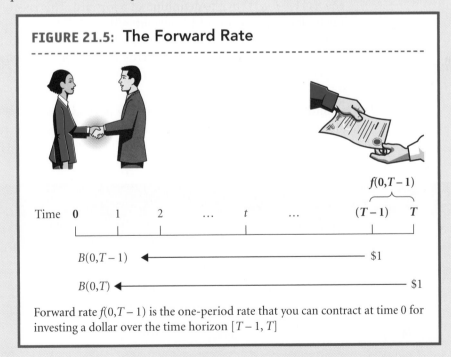

FIGURE 21.5: The Forward Rate

Forward rate $f(0, T-1)$ is the one-period rate that you can contract at time 0 for investing a dollar over the time horizon $[T-1, T]$

---

[10] We could have written the symbol as $f(t, T-1, T)$ to denote the forward rate, but we do not need the last symbol T because this is a one-period rate.

Understanding Forward Rates

We can understand forward rates in three related ways:

1. The first interpretation follows from the definition, which is the conventional approach in the academic lit erature and finance industry. Taking the ratio of two consecutive zero-coupon bond prices gives the implicit interest rate earned over the relevant future time period.

2. A second interpretation is as the rate one can contract today on riskless borrowing or lending over the future time period $[T - 1, T]$. One can see this interpretation using a payoff table (see Table 21.4), where the numbers from Example 21.5 are employed to illustrate how to replicate the borrowing rate over a future time period by trading in zero-coupon bonds today. The procedure is as follows:

   a. Today is time 0 and the longest bond's maturity date is $T = 4$.
   b. Today short one unit of the three-period zero-coupon bond worth $B(0,3) = \$0.88$ and buy $[B(0,3)/B(0,4)] = 0.88/0.82 = 1.0732$ units of the four-period zero-coupon bond worth $B(0,4) = \$0.82$.
   c. This portfolio has zero value today and hence zero cash flow.
   d. The first cash flow occurs at time 3 and is a negative dollar. This is the same as borrowing \$1 at time 3.
   e. The next cash flow is at time 4, when the four-period zero-coupon bond matures. This is a positive cash flow of $[B(0,3)/B(0,4)] = \$1.0732$, which equals $[1 + f(0,3)]$ by the definition of a forward. This is equivalent to paying back the borrowing of \$1 plus interest.

   To obtain the general result, replace time 4 by time T. This substitution shows that the cash flows obtained from the zero-coupon bond portfolio in the payoff table exactly replicate the cash flows from contracting at time 0 to risklessly borrow a dollar over $[T - 1, T]$.

3. The third interpretation is presented in the next section, where we show that the forward rate corresponds to the rate quoted on a forward rate agreement contract.

TABLE 21.3: Zeros, Forward Rates, and Yields

Maturity	Today's Zero-Coupon Bond Prices		Today's Forward Rates		Yields, $R(0,T)$	
0	$B(0,0)$	$1	$f(0,0)$	0.0309	$R(0,1)$	0.0309
1	$B(0,1)$	0.97	$f(0,1)$	0.0430	$R(0,2)$	0.0370
2	$B(0,2)$	0.93	$f(0,2)$	0.0568	$R(0,3)$	0.0435
3	$B(0,3)$	0.88	$f(0,3)$	0.0732	$R(0,4)$	0.0509
4	$B(0,4)$	0.82				

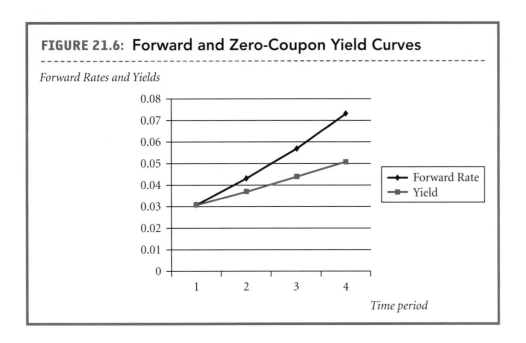

FIGURE 21.6: Forward and Zero-Coupon Yield Curves

Forward Rates and Yields

Using Forward Rates

This section shows how you can express other rates and prices in terms of forward rates. The next chapter will show you how to do the same with swaps, and chapters 23–25 will reveal the critical role forward rates play in modern interest rate derivatives pricing models. We start with an example.

TABLE 21.4: Payoff Table for a Portfolio of Zero-Coupon Bonds That Generates the Forward Rate

Portfolio	Time 0	Time $T-1=3$	Time $T=4$
Short one unit of a three-period zero-coupon bond worth $B(0,3)$ today	$B(0,3)$	-1	
Buy $\dfrac{B(0,3)}{B(0,4)} = \dfrac{0.88}{0.82} =$ 1.0732 units of a four-period zero-coupon bond worth $B(0,4)$ today	$-\dfrac{B(0,3)}{B(0,4)}B(0,4)$		$\dfrac{B(0,3)}{B(0,4)}$
Sum	0	-1	$1.0732 = \dfrac{B(0,3)}{B(0,4)} = f(0,3)+1$

EXAMPLE 21.6:   Computing a Zero-Coupon Bond Price Using Forward Rates

- Continuing with our previous example, using definition (21.9), we can write the first zero-coupon bond's price in terms of forward rates:

$$f(0,0) = \frac{1}{B(0,1)} - 1,$$

$$\text{or } B(0,1) = \frac{1}{1 + f(0,0)} \tag{21.10a}$$

where $f(0,0)$ is also the spot rate of interest.

- Considering a forward rate that starts one period later, at time 1, we get

$$f(0,1) = \frac{B(0,1)}{B(0,2)} - 1,$$

$$\text{or } B(0,2) = B(0,1)\frac{1}{1 + f(0,1)} = \frac{1}{\left[1 + f(0,0)\right]\left[1 + f(0,1)\right]} \tag{21.10b}$$

where the last term on the right uses the value of $B(0,1)$ from expression (21.10a).

- We can generalize by continuing these successive substitutions to derive an expression for a longer-maturity zero-coupon bond.

The generalization of this example is our next result.

RESULT 21.2

A Zero-Coupon Bond's Price and Yield in Terms of Forward Rates

$$B(0,T) = \frac{1}{\left[1 + f(0,0)\right]\left[1 + f(0,1)\right] \ldots \left[1 + f(0,T-1)\right]} \tag{21.11a}$$

$$R(0,T) = (\left[1 + f(0,0)\right]\left[1 + f(0,1)\right]$$
$$\ldots \left[1 + f(0,T-1)\right])^{\frac{1}{T}} - 1 \tag{21.11b}$$

where $B(0,T)$ is the time 0 price of a zero-coupon bond maturing at time T,
$R(0,T)$ is the zero-coupon bond's yield to maturity, and
$f(0,t)$ represents the forward rate contracted at time 0 for $[t, t+1]$.

Expression (21.11a) expresses a zero-coupon bond's price $B(0,T)$ as the discounted value of a dollar received at time T, where the discounting is done by the relevant forward rates. Expression (21.11b) states that a zero coupon bond's yield is the geometric average of the corresponding forward rates minus 1. This result follows readily from the definition of a zero coupon bond's yield as given in expression (21.1) at the start of this chapter. Expression (21.11b) also provides an additional insight: the *spot rate of interest* (denoted by $R[0]$) is the forward rate for immediate borrowing and lending for one period, that is,

$$R(0) = R(0,1) = f(0,0). \tag{21.12}$$

Although zero-coupon bonds are easier to work with, they don't often trade. In this case one can determine forward rates from coupon bond prices. This method is demonstrated in Extension 21.3.

The concepts of forward rates and yields are useful for understanding the basic interest rate derivatives, forward rate agreements, and interest rate futures, which are discussed in the next section.

EXTENSION 21.3: Computing Forward Rates from Coupon Bond Prices

Computing the forward rates from coupon bond prices is a simple exercise in solving a system of linear equations for a collection of unknowns. First we need the following no-arbitrage relation for a coupon bond.

Consider a coupon bond with price P_T, principal L, maturity date T, and a coupon payment C paid every period. To avoid arbitrage, in a frictionless and competitive market, it must be true that

$$P_T = CB(0,1) + CB(0,2) + \ldots + CB(0,T-1) + (C+L)B(0,T). \tag{1}$$

This follows by noting that the cash flows from a portfolio of zeros consisting of C units of $B(0,1)$, C units of $B(0,2), \ldots, C$ units of $B(0,T-1)$, and $(C+L)$ units of $B(0,T)$ are the same as from the coupon bond. Hence the cost of constructing this portfolio must equal the price of the traded coupon bond, or else there is an arbitrage opportunity. The right side of expression (1) is the cost of constructing the portfolio.

Next, suppose we are given a collection of T distinct coupon bond prices. Then, each coupon bond has an equation similar to expression (1). This gives us T equations in the T unknowns $\{B(0,1), B(0,2), \ldots, B(0,T)\}$. One can solve this system of linear equations using linear algebra to obtain the zero-coupon bond prices. If the system does not have a solution, one can find the zero-coupon bond prices that minimize the sum of errors squared between the right side of expression (1) and the coupon bond prices on the left side. Finally, one can input the zero-coupon bond prices obtained into expression (21.9) to get the forward rates.

EXAMPLE 1: Computing Forward Rates from Coupon Bond Prices

■ Today is time 0. Consider three US Treasury securities trading with par value $L = \$100$.
- The one-year Treasury bill has a price of $P_1 = \$97$.
- The two-year Treasury note has a price $P_2 = \$100.60$ and pays a coupon $C_2 = \$4$ annually.
- The three-year Treasury note has a price $P_3 = \$101.90$ and pays a coupon $C_3 = \$5$ annually.

Computing Zero-Coupon Bond Prices

- Fortunately, the first T-bill gives the zero's price. Expression (1) gives

$$P_1 = LB(0,1)$$
$$97 = 100B(0,1)$$
$$\text{or } B(0,1) = 0.97 \qquad \text{(2a)}$$

- Using the two-year T-note, expression (1) gives

$$P_2 = C_2 B(0,1) + (C_2 + L)B(0,2)$$
$$100.60 = 4 \times 0.97 + (4 + 100)B(0,2)$$
$$\text{or } B(0,2) = (100.60 - 3.88)/104 = 0.93 \qquad \text{(2b)}$$

- Finally, for the three-year T-note, expression (1) gives

$$P_3 = C_3 B(0,1) + C_3 B(0,2) + (C_3 + L)B(0,3)$$
$$101.9 = 5 \times 0.97 + 5 \times 0.93 + (5 + 100)B(0,3)$$
$$\text{or } B(0,3) = (101.90 - 4.85 - 4.65)/105 = 0.88 \qquad \text{(2c)}$$

Computing Forward Rates

As these zero-coupon bond prices are the same as the corresponding values in Example 21.5, we have already computed the forward rates and reported them in Table 21.3.

Once you have determined the zero-coupon bond prices, you can easily compute their yields and plot them against time to maturity to obtain the zero-coupon bond price curve.

21.5 The Basic Interest Rate Derivatives Contracts

A Brief History

Interest rate derivatives (IRDs) were created during the 1970s when the placid world of sluggish interest rates gave way to an era of unprecedented interest rate volatility. Recall from our discussions in chapter 8 that this happened because oil shocks and other supply-side disturbances hiked up inflation, making interest rates more volatile than before. Businesses started seeking tools for managing interest rate risks, which generated innovations in exchange-traded IRDs:

- In 1975, the Chicago Board of Trade (CBOT) launched the first IRD, the GNMA (Government National Mortgage Association) futures, which could be used to hedge long-term interest rate risk.

- In 1976, thirteen-week Treasury bill futures contracts started trading. Currently these are the oldest exchange-traded interest rate futures contracts.

- During the late 1980s, GNMA futures contracts became obsolete because US Treasury bond futures, which the CBOT introduced in 1977, provided a better hedge for the same risk.

- In 1981, the Chicago Mercantile Exchange (CME) introduced the world's first cash-settled derivative, Eurodollar futures. It provided a hedge for short-term interest rate risk, and thirteen years later, it replaced the T-bond futures as the world's most actively traded futures contract.

- In 1982, the CBOT introduced options on T-bond futures, whose pricing and hedging are discussed in chapters 23–25.

- In 1992, the CME launched a post-market global electronic transaction system Globex. Operated by the CME Group (which was created through the merger of the CBOT, the CME, and the New York Mercantile Exchange in 2007–8), today's Globex is a behemoth that operates twenty-four hours a day, can be accessed from almost anywhere on the globe, and carries more than 80 percent of the group's trading volume.[11] It has helped the growth of the IRD market, which has long been a twenty-four-hour market owing to the influence of world events on interest rates.

Diverse IRDs trade in today's markets. Recall that the basic equity (and commodity) derivatives on an underlying stock (or commodity) are forward contracts, futures contracts, European calls, and European puts. Analogous contracts trade for IRDs. In this case, the underlying "asset" is the spot interest rate, which is an index and not a traded security. The basic derivatives are the same but this time they have different names: forward rate agreements (FRAs), interest rate futures, caplets, and floorlets.

Not all of these basic securities trade, however. Traded are over-the-counter FRAs and exchange-traded futures. Caplets and floorlets trade only as parts of portfolios called caps and floors, respectively. Moreover, portfolios of FRAs and zero-coupon bonds also trade. These are interest rate swaps, which were introduced in chapter 7. This fact is demonstrated in the next chapter.

The next section introduces FRAs and interest rate futures contracts. We first present FRAs, which are easy to understand, and related to forward rates. Next follow Eurodollar futures, which are immensely popular and similar to T-bill futures (which are discussed in extension 21.4).

Forward Rate Agreements

A forward rate agreement is analogous to a forward contract and is sometimes simply known as a "forward." Just as a forward fixes a price for buying a commodity at a later date, a **forward rate agreement** fixes an interest rate for borrowing (or lending) over some future time period. The largest market for this over-the-counter contract is in London, where various dealers quote FRA rates for loans denominated in eurodollars, *euribor (Euro Interbank Offered Rate,* a bbalibor-like

---

[11] "Growth of CME Globex Platform: A Retrospective" (August 10, 2008); A publication of the CME Group. available at cmegroup.mediaroom.com/index.php?s=114&item=119.

interest rate index computed on euro interbank term deposits), pounds sterling, Swiss francs, and Japanese yen, among others.[12] The next example illustrates the workings of an FRA.

EXAMPLE 21.7: A Forward Rate Agreement

■ Today is January 1 (time 0). International Treats and Restaurants Inc.'s (INTRest, a fictitious name) treasurer plans to borrow $100 million five months from today to build a factory. She likes the current interest rate and decides to lock it in by entering into a long position in a forward rate agreement.

■ London based Dealerbank Corp. (fictitious name) quotes on a 5×8, 100–million-Eurodollar FRA a rate of 5.95 percent to 6 percent. Figure 21.7 shows the workings of this FRA (where we have simplified some market conventions related to the settlement date).
  - The 5×8 means that the FRA begins five months from today (June 1) and terminates on the eighth month.
  - The notional principal L_N is $100 million. This amount never changes hands but is used for computing interest payments. This is a Eurodollar FRA because the interest rates are computed in terms of bbalibor rates for eurodollars.
  - The treasurer decides to *buy* the FRA from the dealer at the f_{FRA} rate of 6 percent. This becomes the fixed borrowing rate that the company locks in. Alternatively, if INTRest wants to loan funds, it can sell the FRA for 5.95 percent, which becomes the effective lending rate.

■ Five months later, on June 1, the British Bankers Association announces the bbalibor rate for the next three months to be 8 percent per year. The buyer of the FRA collects a payment because this floating three-month bbalibor rate (known as the **reference rate**) is higher than the fixed FRA rate contracted in advance.

■ The treasurer gets paid on the payment date September 1 (which is the *termination date*)

$$\text{Notional principal} \times (\text{Reference rate} - f_{FRA}) \times \text{Time period}$$
$$= 100,000,000 \times (0.08 - 0.06) \times (92/360)$$
$$= \$511,111.11 \tag{21.13a}$$

■ *Some FRAs pay on the* **settlement date**, *which is the day the reference rate is announced* (five months from today in this example). In that case, to get the payment, discount the cash flow in expression (21.13a)

---

[12] Founded in 1999 with the launch of the Euro, **Euribor-EBF** (European Banking Federation) is an international non-profit association. Euribor-EBF owns and announces key benchmark rates: Euribor, Eonia, Eurepo, and Eonia Swap Index. The **euribor** (Euro Interbank Offered Rate) is the lending rate between banks in the EMU (European Monetary Union). Similar to bbalibor, *euribor* is a truncated mean of offer rates quoted by a collection of banks which is released to the market by the information company Thomson Reuters at around 11:00 AM Central European Time. **Eonia** (Euro OverNight Index Average) is an index of overnight lending rates between banks in the euro area collaterized with high quality securities, and the **EONIA SWAP INDEX** is the mid market rate of EONIA swap quotations between prime banks.

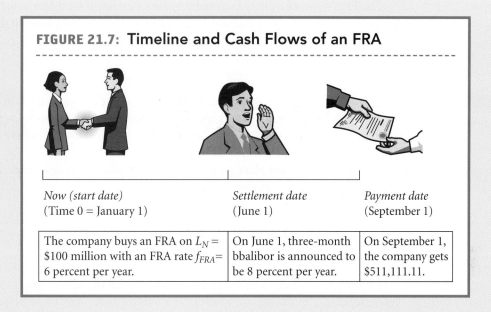

FIGURE 21.7: Timeline and Cash Flows of an FRA

Now (start date) (Time 0 = January 1)	*Settlement date* (June 1)	*Payment date* (September 1)
The company buys an FRA on $L_N =$ $100 million with an FRA rate $f_{FRA}=$ 6 percent per year.	On June 1, three-month bbalibor is announced to be 8 percent per year.	On September 1, the company gets $511,111.11.

using 8 percent, which is the market interest rate for this ninety-two-day period. Then Long's company collects on June 30:

$$\frac{511,111.11}{\left(1 \ + \ 0.08 \ \times \ \dfrac{92}{360}\right)} = \$500,871.08. \tag{21.13b}$$

- INTRest will have to pay 8 percent if it borrows money in June. The effective borrowing cost is only 6 percent because of the payment received on the FRA.

- The protection lasts only for three months. To hedge cash flows for a longer time horizon, INTRest can enter into a series of forward rate agreements of different maturities. The company would pay 6 percent and receive the floating reference rate for the relevant periods. Fortunately, this contract trades in the market as a package. As you may guess, this is the interest rate swap contract that we introduced in Chapter 7! The next chapter will formalize this intuition and show why an interest rate swap is a collection of FRAs.

Notice the following features of an FRA:

1. The FRA uses the actual/360-day count convention. Interest is computed over the actual number of days in the period, assuming there are 360 days in the year. FRAs on Eurodollars and Euribors follow this convention, while FRAs on pounds sterling follow the actual/365-day count convention.

2. The payment is discounted with the realized bbalibor rate by using simple interest rates.

3. We have assumed that there is no risk of default on the part of the writer of the FRA, implying that the payment contracted is the payment received. As an FRA is an over-the-counter instrument, collateral is needed to support the transaction, which the counter-parties negotiate.

4. As with a forward contract, the payoff from an FRA may be positive, zero, or negative. Thus, an FRA is a "bet" on the future movements of the bbalibor rate.

The FRA's payoff in this example can be formalized. Consider a forward rate agreement with notional principal L_N, settlement date t_{Set}, and payment date T. The forward rate agreement's payoff on the **payment date** (time T) is

$$L_N \times (Ref - f_{FRA})\ (T - t_{Set})/360 \qquad (21.14a)$$

where Ref is the reference rate (bbalibor or Euribor in most cases) determined at time t_{Set} that applies over the time period $(T - t_{Set})$ in days and where f_{FRA} is the FRA rate.

If the cash flow takes place on the day the reference rate is determined, then the FRA payoff on the **settlement date** (time t_{Set}) is

$$\frac{L_N \times (Ref - f_{FRA})(T - t_{Set})/360}{\left[1 + Ref \times (T - t_{Set})/360\right]} \qquad (21.14b)$$

where the payoff in expression (21.14a) is discounted to the settlement date by the reference rate.

In our discrete time model, the FRA payoff at time T simplifies to

$$L_N \times [R(T - 1) - f_{FRA}] \qquad (21.14c)$$

because the reference rate is $R(T - 1)$, the spot rate of interest at time $(T - 1)$, and the time period has unit length (not 360 days).

Interest Rate Futures

As you may guess, an **interest rate futures** contract is the exchange-traded "fraternal twin" of an FRA. This is because it's also a contract that fixes a borrowing (or a lending) rate at some future date. It differs from an FRA in the same way that a futures contract differs from a forward. A host of features distinguish them such as standardization, a clearinghouse, margins, and daily settlements. Some interest rate futures (like those on Treasuries) end in physical delivery, whereas others (like those on Eurodollars) end in cash settlement.

Futures prices get quoted the same way as the underlying security's prices are quoted. Consider some highly popular interest rate futures contracts that trade at the CME Group's exchanges. Futures prices for Treasury bonds, notes, and STRIPS are quoted in 32nds, with $100 as the par value. By going long a futures contract on one of these securities, you are promising to buy the underlying bond at a fixed price at a future date. However, Eurodollar futures, like Treasury bill futures, follow a different quoting convention. We discuss this in the context of Eurodollar futures, which are free from the complications related to the embedded options present in the physical delivery feature of T-bill futures contracts (Treasury futures are discussed in Extension 21.4).

Eurodollar futures contracts' payoffs are based on the three-month bbalibor rate at the future delivery date of the contract, but instead of directly quoting futures interest rates, Eurodollar futures contracts are quoted in terms of **futures prices**, which are defined as

$$Quoted\ futures\ price = 100 - Futures\ interest\ rate. \qquad (21.15)$$

For example, a quoted futures price of 94 implies a futures interest rate of $(100 - 94) =$ 6 percent.

Notice the following features of Eurodollar futures.

1. Obviously, dividing the futures interest rate by 100 gives the interest rate as a decimal, 0.06 in this case. The decimal point format is used in subsequent computations.

2. Ninety-four is the quoted futures price for a Eurodollar deposit with $100 par value paid three months after the contract matures. The quoted Eurodollar futures price, a number between 0 and 100, sets the market value of a newly created Eurodollar futures contract to zero.

3. This method of quoting futures prices has yet another benefit: it restores the familiar relation between ask and bid prices seen in other markets. Recall that in most markets the ask price (which is the buying price for the customer, *abc*) is higher than the bid price (which is the selling price of the customer). The same relationship holds in the interest rate market in term of prices: the ask price paid to buy a bond is higher than the bid price at which it is sold. However, bonds usually get quoted in terms of an interest rate: the yield. Due to an inverse relationship between a bond's price and its yield, the ask yield rate is lower than the bid yield rate. Similarly the quoted futures price, as Example 21.8 illustrates, places the quoted ask futures price higher than the quoted bid futures price (see Figure 21.8), and the ask futures interest rate is lower than the bid rate.

EXAMPLE 21.8: A Eurodollar Interest Rate Futures Contract

Eurodollar Futures Contract

- Suppose today is January 1, and the June Eurodollar futures has a quoted ask price of 94.00 and a quoted bid price of 93.99. This means the ask futures interest rate is $100 - 94 = 6$ percent per annum, while the bid futures interest rate is $100 - 93.99 = 6.01$ percent (see Figure 21.8). The underlying asset is a ninety-day 1 million Eurodollar three-month deposit. One million dollars is the notional amount, and the contract is cash-settled. The futures interest rate is always computed over a ninety-day period (see Table 21.5 for the CME Group–traded Eurodollar futures contract's specifications).

- It is important to note that the quoted futures price (94 for ask) is the convention that the market uses to determine the futures interest rate. Here, the ask futures interest rate is 6 percent or $i_{fut} = 0.06$ in decimal terms.

- The futures interest rate is used to determine the payments to the futures contract. The time t quantity that determines the payments to the futures contract is given by the formula

$$1,000,000 \times \left(1 - i_{fut} \times \frac{90}{360}\right) \tag{21.16a}$$

where i_{fut} is the futures interest rate expressed as a decimal. For convenience, we call this quantity the **futures-contract-price**.

- The difference between the quoted futures price and the futures-contract-price is an adjustment for the notional amount (from 100 to 1 million dollars) and an adjustment for the three-month time period over which the simple interest rate applies (note in expression 21.15 that the quoted futures price is implicitly for a one-year time period).

- The ask futures-contract-price is $1,000,000 \times [1 - 0.0600 \times (90/360)] = \$985,000$, and the bid futures-contract-price is $1,000,000 \times [1 - 0.0601 \times (90/360)] = \$984,975$ (see Figure 21.8). Notice that if the futures price goes down by one basis point, or 0.0001, then the Eurodollar futures-contract-price goes down by $25.

- The futures-contract-price on the delivery date is

$$1,000,000 \times \left(1 - i \times \frac{90}{360}\right) \tag{21.16b}$$

where i is the bbalibor spot interest rate at the delivery date expressed as a simple interest rate. Note that on the delivery date, we get convergence of the futures interest rate to the spot rate.

- The futures-contract-price on the delivery date represents the value on that date of a Eurodollar deposit paying a million dollars in three months time. This computation uses a simple interest rate (bbalibor) based on the 360 day year convention. For example, if $i = 0.03$ on the delivery date, then the futures contract price is $1,000,000 \times [1 - 0.03 \times (90/360)] = \$992,500$. This is the purchase price on the delivery date of a Eurodollar deposit that pays one million dollars after three months.

Hedging Example

- Let us tailor this contract to meet INTRest's hedging needs as enumerated in the previous example:
  - INTRest needs one hundred contracts to match the $100 million.
  - INTRest must *sell* Eurodollar interest rate futures contracts to fix the borrowing cost: if the interest rate increases, the futures price declines, the futures generates a negative payment, and being short INTRest receives a positive cash payment.
  - For example, if the futures price for the ask declines to 91.99 (which corresponds to a futures interest rate of $100 - 91.99 = 8.01$ percent), then the new futures-contract-price is $1,000,000 \times [1 - 0.0801 \times (90/360)] = \$979,975$.

- Being short one hundred contracts, INTRest has a cash flow of

$$-100 \times [\text{New contract value (for ask)} - \text{Old contract value (for bid)}]$$
$$= -100 \times (979,975 - 984,975)$$
$$= \$500,000$$

The contract's performance is similar to that of the FRA contract (see payoff in expression 21.13b).

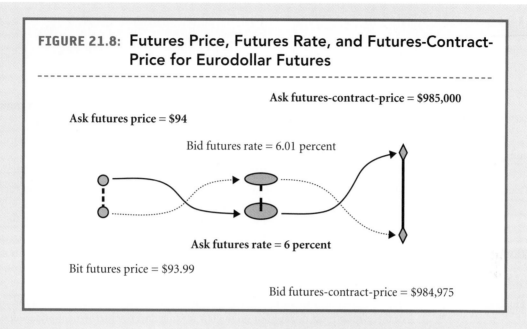

FIGURE 21.8: Futures Price, Futures Rate, and Futures-Contract-Price for Eurodollar Futures

Ask futures-contract-price = $985,000

Ask futures price = $94

Bid futures rate = 6.01 percent

Ask futures rate = 6 percent

Bit futures price = $93.99

Bid futures-contract-price = $984,975

Margins

- We have considered the bid/ask spread but neglected the other transactions costs (such as brokerage commissions) as well interest earned or paid on the margin account. Margin requirements for Eurodollar futures are complex. They depend on the trading strategy as well as other factors, and speculators have higher margin requirements than do hedgers or exchange members. As the following example shows, margin account adjustments are similar to those in Example 9.3.

- January 1
  - Ms. Long buys one June Eurodollar contract at a futures price of 94. As noted earlier, this corresponds to a futures-contract-price of $985,000.
  - No money changes hands today. Long keeps $1,000 initial margin with her broker. Her maintenance margin is $750 per contract.

- January 2
  - Settlement for the futures price is 94.05. The futures interest rate is $100 - 94.05 = 5.95$ percent or 0.0595 as a decimal. The futures-contract-price is
    $1,000,000 \times [1 - 0.0595 \times (90/360)] = \$985,125$.
  - The margin account adjustment
    = Futures-contract-price (Jan 2) − Futures-contract-price (Jan 1)
    $= 985,125 - 985,000 = \$125$. Her margin account balance is $1,000 + 125 = \$1,125$.
  - Notice that with the futures price increasing, the long position has gained value.

- January 3
  - Settlement for the futures price is 93.75. The futures-contract-price is
    $1,000,000 \times [1 - 0.0625 \times (90/360)] = \$984,375$.
  - The margin account adjustment $= 984,375 - 985,125 = -\$750$.
  - As her margin account's value $1,125 + (-750) = \$375$ has fallen below the maintenance margin level, she gets a margin call from her broker to deposit $(1,000 - 375) = \$625$ or more in cash.

TABLE 21.5: Eurodollar Futures Contract Specifications

Specification	Description
Underlying instrument	Eurodollar time deposit having a principal value of $1 million with a three-month maturity
Price quote	Quoted in IMM three-month labor index points or 100 minus the rate on an annual basis over a 360-day year
Tick size (minimum fluctuation)	One-quarter of one basis point (0.0025 = $6.25 per contract) in the nearest expiring contract month; one-half of one basis point (0.005 = $12.50 per contract) in all other contract months
Contract months	March, June, September, December, extending out ten years (total of forty contracts) plus the four nearest serial expirations (months that are not in the March quarterly cycle). The new contract month terminating ten years in the future is listed on the Tuesday following expiration of the front quarterly contract month
Last trading day	The second London bank business day prior to the third Wednesday of the contract expiry month; trading in the expiring contract closes at 11:00 AM London time on the last trading day
Final settlement	Expiring contracts are cash settled to 100 minus the British Bankers' Association survey of three-month US dollar libor on the last trading day; final settlement price will be rounded to four decimal places, equal to 1/10,000 of a percent or $0.25 per contract
Position limits	None
Trading hours (Central Time)	Open outcry, Monday–Friday: 7:20 AM–2:00 PM; CME GLOBEX, Sunday–Friday: 5:00 PM–4:00 PM

Source: www.cmegroup.com/trading/interest-rates/stir/eurodollar_contract_specifications.html

The Eurodollar's futures-contract-price in the preceding example can be formalized. Consider a Eurodollar futures contract at time t with delivery at time T and notional value $L_N = \$1$ million on a three-month Eurodollar deposit. The futures-contract-price of the Eurodollar futures at time t is given by the formula

$$\mathcal{F}(t) = L_N \times \left[1 - i_{fut}(t) \times \frac{90}{360} \right] \tag{21.16c}$$

where $\mathcal{F}(t)$ is the time t futures-contract-price and $i_{fut}(t)$ is the time t futures interest rate expressed as a decimal. Note that the quoted futures price does not explicitly appear in this expression. The futures price is just the convention used by the market to quote the futures interest rate.

Marking to market over the time period $[t, t+1]$ is given by the change in the futures-contract-prices, that is

$$\mathcal{F}(t+1) - \mathcal{F}(t) = -L_N \times \left[i_{fut}(t+1) - i_{fut}(t) \right] \times \frac{90}{360}. \tag{21.16d}$$

As the futures interest rate increases, the futures-contract-price declines, as indicated by the minus sign in this expression. This is intuitive because futures-contract-prices and futures interest rates move inversely to each other.

The settlement futures-contract-price for the futures contract on the delivery date is

$$\mathcal{F}(T) = L_N \times \left[1 - i(T) \times \frac{90}{360} \right] \qquad (21.16\text{e})$$

where $\mathcal{F}(T)$ is the time T futures-contract-price and $i(T)$ is the ninety-day bbalibor spot rate at time T expressed as a simple interest rate.

As we approach the delivery date, note that we get convergence of the futures interest rate $i_{fut}(t)$ to the spot rate of interest; that is, as t goes to T, $i_{fut}(t)$ approaches $i(T)$.

In our discrete time model, setting the notional value of the Eurodollar futures contract to a dollar, the futures-contract-prices at time t and the delivery date time T simplify to

$$\mathcal{F}(t) = [1 - i_{fut}(t)] \qquad (21.16\text{f})$$

and

$$\mathcal{F}(T) = [1 - R(T)] \qquad (21.16\text{g})$$

because the time period has unit length, and the spot rate of interest [see expression (21.12)] is also the simple interest in this case.

We note that in this discrete time case, the quoted futures price is the futures-contract-price expressed as a percentage (multiplied by 100). For our subsequent modeling, therefore, the distinction between the quoted futures price and the futures-contract-price is no longer needed.

EXTENSION 21.4: Treasury Futures

Treasury Bill Futures Price

Introduced in 1976, the thirteen-week Treasury bill futures contract is the oldest exchange-traded interest rate derivative. A highly popular contract for hedging and speculating on short-term interest rate risk, it shares many common features with the Eurodollar futures contract: both contracts are written on a notional principal of $1 million, both assume that interest applies over 90 days, both use 360 days in a year, and both are structured so that a one–basis-point movement in the index translates into a $25 change in the futures-contract-price. The key difference is that a T-bill futures contract has a T-bill as the underlying asset, which must be delivered physically if the short delivers, while a Eurodollar futures contract is cash-settled with no future delivery requirement.

To see how a 13-week T-bill futures works, let us start with an ask futures price of $94.00. Similar to the Eurodollar futures (see Example 21.8), this translates into an interest rate of $100 - 94 = 6$ percent per year. This is the banker's discount yield that you saw in expression (2.7b). Using this interest rate as the ask, expression (2.7b) gives an ask futures-contract-price for the bill with a face value of $1 million and ninety days to maturity:

$$P_{Ask} = 1{,}000{,}000B = 1{,}000{,}000\left[1 - (banker's\ discount\ yield)\left(\frac{T}{360}\right)\right]$$

$$= 1{,}000{,}000\left(1 - 0.06 \times \frac{90}{360}\right)$$

$$= 985{,}000$$

If the quoted futures price is $94.01, then the banker's discount yield is 5.99 percent, and the bond's ask futures-contract-price is $985,025. Similar to the Eurodollar futures, a rise in the futures price by one basis point is associated with a $25 increase in the thirteen-week Treasury bill futures-contract-price, a gain that will accrue to the buyer of the T-bill futures.

The physical delivery requirement makes the contract more cumbersome than Eurodollar futures. At the maturity of the T-bill futures, a newly issued T-bill becomes available with thirteen weeks to maturity. The CME Group allows the substitution of ninety-one-day and ninety-two-day T-bills with appropriate price adjustments to enhance the liquidity of the deliverable security.

Treasury Note and Bond Futures

Longer-maturity Treasury futures work similar to T-bill futures, but they are quoted differently. Treasury bonds, notes, and STRIPS are quoted in 32nds with $100 as the par value. By going long a futures contract on one of these securities, you are promising to buy the underlying bond at a fixed price at a future date.

As with T-bill futures, the short initiates the delivery and decides on which bond to deliver. The contracts allow substitution among several possible bonds with appropriate price adjustment via conversion factors. This gives the short a valuable embedded option in the form of providing the **cheapest-to-deliver bond**. Moreover, the short has another "option," known as the **wild card option,** because the T-bond futures stop trading at 2:00 PM. (Central Time), while bonds trade until 4:00 PM and the short has until 8:00 PM to issue the notice of intention to deliver. These embedded options significantly complicate the valuation of Treasury futures contracts.

The Equivalence between Forward and FRA Rates

Both forward rates and forward rate agreements lock in an interest rate for borrowing or lending starting at some future date. Is there a link between the two? The answer is yes, they are equal. Let us illustrate this with a simple example.

EXAMPLE 21.9: Forward and FRA Rates

- Using the assumption of no arbitrage, we will determine the FRA rate and demonstrate that it is equivalent to the forward rate.
  - Consider a forward rate agreement written at time 0 that starts at time 3 and matures at time 4.
  - Denote the FRA rate by $f_{FRA}(0,3) \equiv f_{FRA}$. The contract is on a notional principal of $L_N = \$100$ million.
  - The FRA contract is written on the spot interest rate's value at time 3, $R(3)$. This spot rate becomes known at time 3 and is effective over the time interval [3,4] (see expression [21.14c]).

At the FRA's Maturity Date, Time 4

■ The cash payoff at the FRA's maturity date is

$$[R(3) - f_{FRA}]100$$
$$= [1 + R(3) - (1 + f_{FRA})]100 \qquad (21.17a)$$

where we rewrite the payoff by adding and subtracting 1.

At Time 3

■ Moving back one period and computing the time 3 present value gives

$$[1 - (1 + f_{FRA})B(3,4)]100. \qquad (21.17b)$$

The first term is 1 because we get $[1 + R(3)]$ at time 4 by investing a dollar in a money market account at time 3, and the second term is obtained by multiplying $(1 + f_{FRA})$ at time 4 by the zero-coupon bond price $B(3,4)$ to get its present value at time 3.

At Time 0, When the FRA is Negotiated

■ To compute the time 0 present value, note two facts (see Figure 21.1): the time 0 present value of a dollar at time 3 is $B(0,3)$; similarly, the time 0 present value of $B(3,4)$ is $B(0,4)$. The present value of the preceding cash flow is therefore

$$[B(0,3) - (1 + f_{FRA})B(0,4)]100 \qquad (21.17c)$$

■ As with a conventional forward contract, the FRA rate sets the value of the FRA to zero on the day it is written (time 0). Equating expression (21.17c) to zero and solving for the FRA rate gives:

$$[B(0,3) - (1 + f_{FRA})B(0,4)]100 = 0$$
$$\text{or } f_{FRA}(0,3) \equiv f_{FRA} = [(B(0,3)/B(0,4)] - 1 \equiv f(0,3) \qquad (21.17d)$$

where the last term follows from the definition of the forward rate as given in expression (21.9).

The argument in the previous example works more generally. Replacing time 4 by T in expression (21.17d) yields the following result.

RESULT 21.3

The FRA Rate and Forward Rates

Consider an FRA with notional L_N, maturity date T, and settlement date $T - 1$ in the discrete time model. Then,

the FRA rate, $f_{FRA}(0, T - 1) = f(0, T - 1)$, the forward rate   (21.18)

This result is just as it should be. Recall from the previous section that the forward rate with maturity $(T-1)$ is that rate one can contract at time 0 for riskless borrowing and lending over $[T-1, T]$. In contracting, the borrower is betting that the spot rate of interest will be greater than the forward rate—but this is the same bet made when going long an FRA. When going long an FRA, one is betting that the reference rate, here the spot rate of interest, is greater than the FRA rate. Therefore, the two rates must be the same. This is a powerful insight: the abstract forward rate that we had defined earlier is the same as the interest rate that emanates from the market-traded forward rate agreement rate. The power of forward rates is further illustrated in the context of other derivatives in the next three chapters.

21.6 | Summary

1. The discussion of interest rate derivatives (IRDs) parallels the earlier presentation of spots, forwards, futures, and options on commodities and equities. For IRDs, an array of different maturity default-free zero-coupon bonds replace the single commodity or stock price as the underlying asset. Yields and forward rates extracted from the zeros are foundational concepts. We focus on Eurodollar IRDs, which are simpler than derivatives on Treasury securities and attract the greatest trading volume.

2. Eurodollars are dollar deposits in European banks (or a European subsidiary of a US bank) that earn interest in dollars. There are three major interest rates for Eurodollars: the Eurodollar interest rate paid on Eurodollar deposits, the generic libor at which London banks offer to lend dollars to each other, and the British Bankers' Association computed interest rate index bbalibor (which is an average of libor quotes collected from major London-based banks and released to the market around 11:00 AM).

3. Assuming a discrete framework in which time progresses in unit increments $t = 0, 1, 2, 3, \ldots$, the yield (or yield to maturity or internal rate of return) on a zero-coupon bond is the interest rate that equates the discounted bond's cash flows to its current price:

$$B(0,T) = \frac{1}{[1 + R(0,T)]^T}$$

where $B(0,T)$ is the time t price of a zero-coupon bond that pays a dollar at time T, and $R(0,T)$ is the yield at time t on a zero-coupon bond with maturity T.

4. Standing at time t, the yield on the shortest-maturity zero-coupon bond that matures at time $(t+1)$ has a special name—the spot rate of interest $R(t)$. A riskless money market account earns the spot rate of interest each period.

5. The yield curve plots the zero-coupon bonds' yields as a function of each bond's time to maturity. This graph is called the term structure of interest rates. A yield curve can take various shapes influenced by factors such as (1) the expectations of the market participants regarding the future movement of interest rates, (2) risk aversion, and (3) supply and demand considerations for the underlying zero-coupon bonds.

6. A default-free coupon bond's yield (or yield-to-maturity, also called the internal rate of return) y is defined by

$$P_T = \frac{C}{(1 + y)} + \frac{C}{(1 + y)^2} + \cdots + \frac{C}{(1 + y)^{T-1}} + \frac{C + L}{(1 + y)^T}$$

$$= \sum_{t=1}^{T}\left[\frac{C}{(1 + y)^t}\right] + \frac{L}{(1 + y)^T}$$

where P_T denotes the coupon bond price, C denotes the yearly coupon, L denotes principal (or par or face value), and T denotes time to maturity in years.

If the yield equals the coupon rate, the bond's price is identical to the par value, and the yield is called the par bond yield.

7. Traditional interest rate management involves computing Macaulay's duration and using it to approximate a bond's price change for a given change in the yield. Result 21.1 states that for a small change in the bond's yield to maturity y, the change in the bond's price is approximately

$$\Delta P \approx - P\, Dur_M \Delta y$$

where P is the original bond price, ΔP is the change in bond price, $Dur_M \equiv Dur/(1 + y)$ is the modified duration, and Δy is the change in the yield-to-maturity. The duration is computed by

$$Dur = \frac{1}{P}\left\{\sum_{t=1}^{T}\left[\frac{C}{(1 + y)^t}\right] \times t + \left[\frac{L}{(1 + y)^T}\right] \times T\right\}$$

where C is yearly coupon, L is the bond's par (or principal) value, T is the bond's maturity, and y is the original yield to maturity. The price approximation can be improved by a convexity adjustment, which uses the second-order term in a Taylor series expansion for the price change formula.

8. Duration is a weighted average of the time periods to the receipt of the cash flows. A bond with higher duration undergoes a greater price change given a change in the interest rate. The duration of a zero-coupon bond is the same as the time to maturity. A bond portfolio's duration is a weighted average of the durations of the individual bonds.

9. Duration-based hedging has many shortcomings that limit its efficacy. It only works for small changes in interest rates and for parallel shifts of the yield curve, which means that all yields change by the same amount. The yield curve rarely changes by parallel shifts.

10. The time 0 forward rate for the future period $[T - 1, T]$ is defined as

$$f(0, T - 1) = \frac{B(0, T - 1)}{B(0, T)} - 1$$

where $B(0, T - 1)$ and $B(0, T)$ are today's zero-coupon bond prices for bonds maturing at times $(T - 1)$ and T, respectively.

11. The zero-coupon bond price and yield can be expressed in terms of forward rates as

$$B(0,T) = \frac{1}{[1 + f(0,0)][1 + f(0,1)] \dots [1 + f(0,T-1)]}$$

$$R(0,T) = ([1 + f(0,0)][1 + f(0,1)] \dots [1 + f(0,T-1)])^{\frac{1}{T}} - 1.$$

where $B(0,T)$ is the time 0 price of a zero-coupon bond maturing at time T, $R(0,T)$ is the zero-coupon bond's yield to maturity, and $f(0,t)$ represents the forward rate contracted at time 0 for time t.

12. The spot rate of interest (denoted by $R[t]$) is also the forward rate for immediate borrowing and lending for one period, that is, $R(t) = f(t,t)$.

13. A forward rate agreement (FRA) is an over-the-counter contract that fixes the interest rate for borrowing (or lending) over some future time period. It has several features: (1) an FRA uses the actual/360-day count convention, (2) the payment is discounted with the realized bbalibor rate using simple interest, and (3) like a forward, the payoff from an FRA can be positive, zero, or negative. The FRA rate is the same as the forward rate.

14. Consider an FRA with notional principal L_N, settlement date t_{Set}, and payment date T. The payoff on the payment date is

$$L_N \times (Ref - f_{FRA})\,(T - t_{Set})/360$$

where Ref is the reference rate (bbalibor or euribor in most cases) determined at time t_{Dec} that applies over the time period $(T - t_{Set})$ in days, and where f_{FRA} is the FRA rate.

15. An interest rate futures is an exchange-traded contract that fixes a borrowing (or a lending) rate at some future date. It differs from an FRA in the same way as a futures contract differs from a forward. A host of features distinguish them such as standardization, a clearinghouse, margins, and daily settlements.

16. Eurodollar futures prices, like Treasury bill futures, get quoted in terms of an index, which is defined as

$$Futures\ price = 100 - Futures\ interest\ rate$$

17. The asset underlying a Eurodollars futures contract is a ninety-day 1 million Eurodollar three-month deposit. The futures interest rate is always computed over a ninety-day period, and the contract is cash-settled. The Eurodollar futures-contract-price at time t, which determines the payments to the futures contract, is given by the formula

$$1{,}000{,}000 \times \left[1 - i_{fut} \times \frac{90}{360}\right]$$

where i_{fut} is the futures interest rate obtained from the preceding formula for the futures price expressed as a decimal.

18. Consider an FRA with notional L_N, maturity date T, and settlement date $T-1$ in our discrete time model. Then,

the FRA rate, $f_{FRA}(0,T-1) = f(0,T-1)$, the forward rate.

21.7 | Cases

Pension Plan of Bethlehem Steel—2001 (Harvard Business School Case #202088-PDF-ENG). The case analyzes the company's pension fund assets and liabilities by using the traditional tools of interest rate risk management.

Union Carbide Corp.: Interest Rate Risk Management (Harvard Business School Case #294057-PDF-ENG). The case studies how the firm can manage its exposure to interest rates by matching the duration of its liabilities to the duration of its assets.

Deutsche Bank: Finding Relative Value Trades (Harvard Business School Case #205059-PDF-ENG). The case considers how the bank can find yield curve trades that are of interest to clients as well as to its proprietary trading desk.

21.8 | Questions and Problems

21.1. What is the difference between a Eurodollar, a Eurodollar rate, and the US T-bill rate?

21.2. What is libor? Explain how it is similar or not similar to bbalibor.

21.3. Compute the yield curve for the following zero-coupon bond prices.

Times to Maturity T	Today's Zero-Coupon Bond Prices $B(0,T)$	
1	$B(0,1)$	0.98
2	$B(0,2)$	0.96
3	$B(0,3)$	0.94
4	$B(0,4)$	0.90

21.4. How does the bond's yield relate to an internal rate of return? Is the bond's yield a good measure for its expected return over the next year?

The next three questions use the following information.
Bondy Bond (fictitious name) is a coupon bond that matures in 10 years. The coupon rate is 5 percent per year. The bond's principal is $10,000 and the market price is $8,500.

21.5. (Microsoft Excel) Compute the yield for Bondy Bond, showing how you use the Excel program for this purpose.

21.6. Compute Bondy Bond's duration using the yield computed in the previous problem.

21.7. Suppose the yield increases by 0.0005 over a week.

   a. Compute the new price of Bondy Bond.

   b. Compute the actual change in bond prices.

   c. Use a duration based formula to predict the change in Bondy Bond's price. How does this compare with the actual change?

21.8. A coupon bond has a life of 5 years, makes semiannual coupon payments at the rate of 6 percent per year, has a principal of $100, and a market price of $95.

   a. Using Excel, compute this bond's yield to maturity.

   b. Compute the duration of the bond.

21.9. At time 0, what is the duration of a zero-coupon bond with maturity T? Prove your answer using the definition of duration.

21.10. What are the two problems with using duration as a risk measure for changes in bond prices?

21.11. Compute the forward rates for the following zero-coupon bond prices.

Times to Maturity T	Today's Zero-Coupon Bond Prices $B(0,T)$	
1	$B(0,1)$	0.98
2	$B(0,2)$	0.96
3	$B(0,3)$	0.94
4	$B(0,4)$	0.90

21.12. Compute the forward rates and yields for the following zero-coupon bond prices.

Times to Maturity T	Today's Zero-Coupon Bond Prices $B(0,T)$	
1	$B(0,1)$	0.93
2	$B(0,2)$	0.90
3	$B(0,3)$	0.88
4	$B(0,4)$	0.85

21.13. Using a payoff table similar to Table 21.4 in the text, explain the portfolio of zero-coupon bonds that generates the forward rate $f(0,3)$.

21.14. Compute the zero-coupon bond prices from the following forward rates.

Times to Maturity T	Today's forward Rates $f(0,T)$	
1	$f(0,1)$	0.02
2	$f(0,2)$	0.03
3	$f(0,3)$	0.04
4	$f(0,4)$	0.05

21.15. What is the spot rate of interest $R(t)$? Explain how it relates to forward rates and yields.

21.16. What is a forward rate agreement? Give a numerical example to demonstrate the timing and magnitude of the payoffs to an FRA.

21.17. What is an interest rate futures? Give examples of two popular interest rate futures.

21.18. What are the differences between a forward rate agreement and an interest rate futures contract? In your answer, consider both the institutional differences and the economic differences.

21.19. Given the difference between forward rate agreements and interest rate futures contracts, would you expect the FRA rate to equal the futures interest rate, for otherwise identical contracts? Explain your answer.

21.20. What is the relation between an FRA rate for a contract that matures at time T and a forward rate of interest for time $T-1$?

22

Interest Rate Swaps

22.1 | Introduction

"*Trust* you couldn't; *gamble* you shouldn't." This characterizes the lessons learned from a fixed-for-floating interest rate swap deal struck in 1993 between Bankers Trust and Procter & Gamble (P&G). Enticed by the fact that the swap would pay a low floating rate, P&G apparently downplayed the importance of a "spread" in its payment terms, which could potentially increase its liability. Interest rates rose, the company suffered huge losses, and it sued, arguing it didn't understand the complex swap. Suffering a serious erosion of trust, the bank eventually forgave most of the money due and settled the suit. The moral of this story is clear: don't transact in derivative securities that you do not understand, especially those with complicated terms like an exotic interest rate swap! Understanding such swaps is a purpose of this chapter.

Although you have seen swaps before in chapter 7, we discuss them here in greater detail. The chapter begins with a brief history of swaps. Next, we discuss institutional features of swap contracts. Swaps enjoy great flexibility because they trade in the over-the-counter markets, but the trades are guided by standardized rules. We then develop a valuation formula for plain vanilla interest rate swaps. Last, we demonstrate how to construct swap curves, and we link swaps to forward rate agreements (FRAs) and forward rates.

The swap valuation formula presented in this chapter is obtained in a world with stochastic interest rates. But the valuation formula is derived without specifying a particular model for the evolution of the term structure of interest rates. This is due to the linear structure of the swap's payoffs in both the underlying fixed and floating rate cash flows. The swap's value is shown to only depend on the current term structure of zero-coupon bond prices. This is analogous to the option pricing relations obtained in chapter 16, prior to the study of the binomial option pricing model of chapters 17 and 18 or the Black–Scholes–Merton model of chapters 19 and 20. If you recall, the nonlinear payoffs of call and put options required the specification of a stock price process to obtain valuations. The same is true for the more general interest rate derivatives discussed in the chapters that follow. The nonlinear payoff structure of interest rate derivatives require the specification of an evolution for the term structure of interest rates, a key element in understanding the Heath–Jarrow–Morton (HJM) model.

22.2 | A Brief History

In 1981, the Wall Street firm Salomon Brothers Inc. organized a transaction between the World Bank (often referred to as "the Bank") and the International Business Machines Corporation (IBM) hailed as the first swap (see Extension 22.1 for the details of this swap transaction). The World Bank found that interest rates in West Germany and Switzerland were lower than in the United States, but the bank had already borrowed the maximum amount it could in these markets. IBM had loans denominated in Deutsche marks and Swiss francs. An appreciation of the dollar lowered the value of these loans, and IBM wanted to convert them into dollar loans. So, the Bank borrowed dollars by selling Eurobonds and converted them into marks and francs in the spot market. The deal was that the World Bank and IBM embraced each other's loan obligations. The net result was the first swap because it involved an exchange of cash flows at future dates.

The swap market has enjoyed phenomenal growth—Table 22.1 lists some milestones. We classify the market developments into four categories: (1) the introduction of new swap contracts, (2) the shift from a brokerage business to a dealership market, (3) the founding of the International Swaps and Derivatives Association (ISDA) and the standardization of contracts, and (4) the use of technology and the automation of trading.

The Introduction of Swap Contracts

The year 1982 saw a financial arrangement usually recognized as the first interest rate swap (see Johnson 2004; Greenbaum and Thakor 2007). You may have heard of Sallie Mae, a US government–sponsored enterprise that owns or manages student loans for over 10 million accounts.[1] To conduct its business, Sallie Mae buys floating-rate student loans from banks and other institutions where the interest rate on the loan is reset quarterly at the ninety-one day Treasury bill rate. It finances these purchases and hedges its exposure by selling short-term bonds paying interest rates correlated with this T-bill rate. However, being government sponsored, Sallie Mae can borrow cheaply at intermediate-term fixed rates. Conversely, there are companies that can raise money at favorable floating rates but that prefer fixed-rate loans. The first interest rate swap cleverly matched these two parties—Sallie Mae issued an intermediate fixed-rate loan, ITT Corporation issued a floating-rate note—and they swapped their payment obligations.

This deal opened the flood gates with respect to swap creation and issuance. Besides developing exotic versions of interest rate and currency swaps, in 1986, Chase Manhattan Bank intermediated the first commodity swap based on oil prices; in 1989, Bankers Trust organized the first equity swap; and in 1995, J. P. Morgan issued the first credit default swap. Swap markets have enjoyed enormous growth, as documented in Table 22.2. As indicated, from 1987 to 2009 the swaps market has experienced exponential growth. Interest rate and currency swaps were actively traded almost 15 years before either the credit default swap or equity derivatives markets traded significant notional quantities, which happened in 2001 and 2002, respectively. The almost halving of the credit default swaps outstanding during the 2007 financial crisis was mostly a result of a new recording methodology that required netting of offsetting contracts by the same institution on the same credit entity. As indicated, interest rate and currency swaps still account for the majority of swap contracts traded.

---

[1] The **Student Loan Marketing Association** (nicknamed **Sallie Mae**) began as a federal government–sponsored enterprise in 1972 but was privatized under the registered name Sallie Mae in 2004. The company primarily provides federal and private student loans, including consolidation loans, to undergraduate and graduate students and their parents (www.salliemae.com).

TABLE 22.1: Some Milestones in the History of Swaps

Year	Development
1981	The first currency swap was arranged by Salomon Brothers between IBM and the World Bank.
1982	The first interest rate swap was arranged between Sallie Mae and ITT Financial.
1985	The International Swap Dealers Association (ISDA; later renamed the International Swaps and Derivatives Association) was chartered. ISDA introduced SWAPS, a document template useful for standardizing swap contracts.
1986	The first commodity swap was intermediated by Chase Manhattan Bank.
1987	ISDA published the first Master Agreement, newer versions of which were introduced in 1992 and 2002.
1989	The first equity-linked swap was organized by Bankers Trust.
1995	The first credit default swap was traded by J. P. Morgan.

TABLE 22.2: Notional Amounts Outstanding at Year's End, All Surveyed Contracts, 1987–2009 (Based on the ISDA Market Survey)

Year	Total Interest Rate and Currency Derivatives	Total Credit Default Swaps	Total Equity Derivatives
1987	$865.60		
1988	1,654.30		
1989	2,474.70		
1990	3,450.30		
1991	4,449.50		
1992	5,345.70		
1993	8,474.50		
1994	11,303.20		
1995	17,712.60		
1996	25,453.10		
1997	29,035.00		
1998	50,997.00		
1999	58,265.00		
2000	63,009.00		
2001	69,207.30	918.87	
2002	101,318.49	2,191.57	2,455.29
2003	142,306.92	3,779.40	3,444.08
2004	183,583.27	8,422.26	4,151.29
2005	213,194.58	17,096.14	5,553.97
2006	285,728.14	34,422.80	7,178.48
2007	382,302.71	62,173.20	9,995.71
2008	403,072.81	38,563.82	8,733.03
2009	426,749.60	30,428.11	6,771.58

Source: www2.isda.org/search?keyword = market + survey.

From a Brokerage to a Dealership Market

By 1983, investment banks were arranging one-off swap transactions for their clients on a fully matched basis. Banks earned substantial brokerage fees and had no credit risk—but there were road bumps along the way. Every transaction had to be separately negotiated with the counterparties and carefully documented. The front office (traders) wanted to proceed but the back office (accountants) moved at a snail's pace, and the trader's numbers would sometimes differ from the accountant's. In a particularly telling incident, acute back-office problems forced J. P. Morgan to scale down its swap business for about six months in 1987.

The *swap banks* (also known as *swap facilitators*) discovered that by becoming **swap dealers**, they could cut their back-office costs by standardizing the contracts and trading them like homogeneous commodities. The swap banks also started **warehousing swaps**. They would enter into different swaps on both the buy and the sell side of the

---

EXTENSION 22.1: The First Swap Deal

"In some ways, the history of derivatives is the history of the World Bank," begins an article in the twentieth anniversary issue of *Risk* magazine. The article points out that the World Bank pioneered swaps and structured products and was one of the first institutions to embrace modern risk management practices. The story of the first swap deal provides useful insights. Consider the background of the first swap (see Sawyer 2007; Park 1984).

- During the early 1980s, the World Bank found that interest rates in West Germany and Switzerland were lower than those in the United States. Unfortunately, it had already borrowed the maximum amount it was allowed to raise in West Germany and Switzerland.

- Conversely, IBM had issued loans denominated in Deutsche marks (DM) and Swiss francs (SFr) during the 1970s but realized that the US dollar (USD) had risen against those currencies and had lowered the dollar value of the loans. IBM wanted to change these loans to dollars because it would (1) take fewer dollars to repay them, (2) hedge its currency risk exposure, and (3) match the payments with cash flows in the domestic market.

You can sense that both sides would have been better off if they bartered their liabilities through a transaction known as a *liability swap*—and that's what happened! In August 1981, Salomon Brothers organized the first swap on a notional principal of $290 million.

- The World Bank borrowed dollars by selling Eurobonds and converted this into marks and francs in the spot market. It had dollar liabilities but marks and francs in hand.

- The Bank and IBM exchanged each other's loan obligations.

This was a swap because it involved an exchange of cash flows at future dates (see Figure 22.1). If credit risk is ignored, IBM effectively converted its loans into dollar liabilities. By the same token, the World Bank's transaction was as good as raising cash in marks and francs.

Swaps are excellent examples of financial engineering. The fusion of two parallel loans creates a swap that reduces credit risk, avoids balance sheet impacts, and overcomes cumbersome capital market restrictions (remember Merton Miller's comment in Extension 1.1). Swaps have become a powerful tool in the hands of institutional investors as a low-cost instrument for transforming cash flows.

FIGURE 22.1: IBM World Bank Currency Swap, 1981

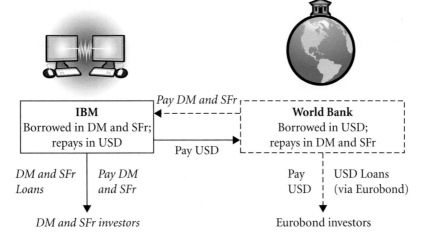

Before Swap

IBM
Borrows in DM and SFr;
wants to repay in USD

World Bank
Goal: to borrow in DM and SFr
but unable to do so

DM and SFr Loans   *Interest and principal in DM and SFr*

DM and SFr investors

World Bank raised dollars by selling Eurobonds.
The Bank converted dollars into marks and francs in the spot market.
IBM and the Bank exchanged future liabilities.

After Swap

Pay DM and SFr

IBM
Borrowed in DM and SFr;
repays in USD

World Bank
Borrowed in USD;
repays in DM and SFr

Pay USD

DM and SFr Loans   *Pay DM and SFr*

Pay USD   USD Loans (via Eurobond)

DM and SFr investors

Eurobond investors

IBM has dollar liabilities that hedge currency exposure and better match cash flows.
World Bank avoids market restrictions and accesses cheap financing in West German
and Swiss markets.

market and hedge the residual risk with interest rate derivatives. A banker from the early days summarized this progression: "First we were doing matched trades, then we realised that if we take on an interest rate swap and put on a Treasury hedge, we can actually protect against interest rate risk. The next logical step was to look at the entire book and just hedge the residual risk" (observation by Chris Goekjian, as reported in Sawyer 2007, p. 26). The next example illustrates how this works.

EXAMPLE 22.1: Managing a Swap Book

- Suppose that Swapbank Inc. (a fictitious name) enters into a plain vanilla interest rate swap on a notional principal of $100 million, where it receives floating-rate six-month bbalibor and pays a fixed rate per year. Like any other good dealer, Swapbank tries to *manage its books* by perfectly hedging its portfolio.

- The bank enters into an offsetting swap with matching terms, but it receives four basis points higher interest on a notional principal of $80 million. The bank has hedged its interest rate risk on $80 million and earns four additional basis points, which equals

  Principal amount $\times$ Spread $\times$ Time period over which interest is earned
  $= 80$ million $\times 0.0004 \times 0.5$
  $= \$16,000$ every six months

- Swapbank has counterparty credit risk. However, given the collateral agreements in the swap market, this risk is small.

- There is still risk from the remaining $20 million notional principal. Swapbank can enter into another offsetting swap to remove this risk. Swapbank can also remove this risk by trading other interest rate derivatives. We explain how to do this at the end of this chapter.

ISDA and Standardization of Contracts

As mentioned previously, to trade swaps quickly and to minimize transaction costs, standardized contracts were needed. Efforts at developing such documents began in 1984, when eighteen swap dealers joined together to form the *International Swap Dealers Association* (*ISDA*, pronounced "iz-da"; later renamed the *International Swaps and Derivatives Association* to reflect its broader scope). Chartered in 1985, ISDA published the **Code of SWAPS** (Code of Standard Wording, Assumptions, and Provisions for Swaps; the "Code"), which provides standardized documents known as the Master Agreements for over-the-counter (OTC) derivatives contracts. ISDA has grown with the swaps market. In 2008, ISDA had over eight hundred member institutions from fifty-six countries on six continents.[2]

The ISDA's **Master Agreement** establishes contract standards for privately negotiated derivatives so that legal uncertainty is reduced and credit risk is

---

[2] www2.isda.org.

lowered through collateral provisions, netting arrangements, and procedures to follow in the case of a default. The Master Agreement itself has two parts: (1) a preprinted form that cannot be amended and (2) a schedule that allows the two counterparties to note changes and amend provisions on the printed form (see Allen and Overy 2002). The Master Agreement establishes **noneconomic terms** (such as "representations and warranties, events of default, and termination events") that govern future OTC derivatives transactions between the two counterparties. Each time these two counterparties execute a future trade, all they need do is negotiate the economic terms and record them in a **Confirmation**. The Master Agreement, the confirmations, and other supporting documents make up the **ISDA Agreement Structure** (as of 2006). Since their creation, the Master Agreements have been updated in 1987, 1992, and 2002 to reflect changing market conditions.

22.3 | Institutional Features

It is instructive to follow a swap transaction from beginning to end and discuss the relevant institutional features met along the way (see Figure 22.2 for the timeline).

Entering a Swap Contract

Suppose Your Beloved Machines (YBM) decides to become a **swap issuer** (or a **swap initiator**). Then YBM contacts one or more swap providers who stand ready to be their counterparty. Of course, in selecting the swap bank, YBM needs to consider their credit rating, their prior experience with similar trading, the documentation they provide, and the price they quote.

There are three basic ways to initiate a swap contract:

1. The traditional way is by phone, during which the basic **economic terms of the transaction** (price or rate, principal amount, term, and frequency of payment) are negotiated and any **credit support** requirements (margin, or collateral, or a guarantee) are discussed. The counterparties are committed to transact as per this "oral agreement." Then, one counterparty (or broker, if involved) sends a letter containing the economic terms to the other and asks for a *confirmation*.

2. A second way is via a web-based trading platform, which displays a range of potential swaps. Once YBM has prearranged trading agreements with a bank, the company can check quotes and transact a plain vanilla swap in a matter of minutes. The bank has already made YBM sign the necessary paperwork and set up a system that allows it to trade quickly but safely.

3. A third way is by running an auction. This is more common in the case of **municipal swaps** that have a state, local, or municipal government as a counterparty.

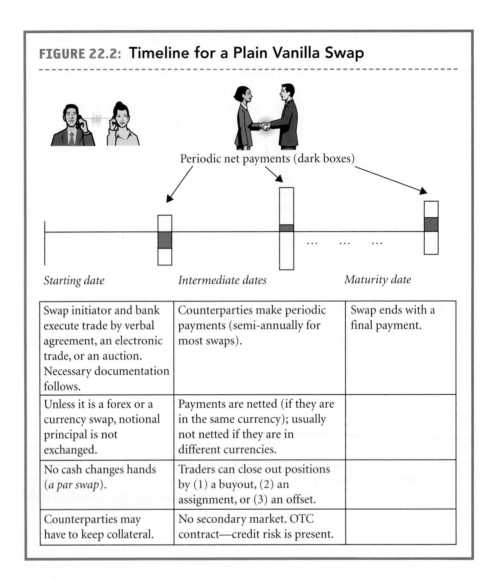

FIGURE 22.2: Timeline for a Plain Vanilla Swap

Periodic net payments (dark boxes)

Starting date   *Intermediate dates*   *Maturity date*

Swap initiator and bank execute trade by verbal agreement, an electronic trade, or an auction. Necessary documentation follows.	Counterparties make periodic payments (semi-annually for most swaps).	Swap ends with a final payment.
Unless it is a forex or a currency swap, notional principal is not exchanged.	Payments are netted (if they are in the same currency); usually not netted if they are in different currencies.	
No cash changes hands (*a par swap*).	Traders can close out positions by (1) a buyout, (2) an assignment, or (3) an offset.	
Counterparties may have to keep collateral.	No secondary market. OTC contract—credit risk is present.	

Documentation

"Partnerships often finish in quarrels" wrote Benjamin Franklin in his 1791 autobiography, "but I was happy in this, that mine were all carried on and ended amicably, owing, I think, a good deal to the precaution of having *very explicitly settled, in our articles, every thing to be done by or expected from each partner* [emphasis added], so that there was nothing to dispute, which precaution I would therefore recommend to all who enter into partnerships." This practical advice on partnerships, and by extension swaps, is the reason for documentation.

The swap contract's documentation must describe (1) the currencies of the cash flows, (2) the interest rates, (3) the principal amount, (4) whether the principal is exchanged, and (5) whether the counterparties make future cash payments in their entirety or through a net payment. Next comes a *timetable*: (6) the *tenor* (or *maturity*) of the swap and (7) the frequency of cash payments (every six months for a majority of simple swaps). Finally, the contract must specify *other issues* such as (8) how to terminate a swap early and (9) what to do if one side defaults. Of course, web-based trading platforms have most of this material prepackaged so that trades can be executed quickly.

Closing a Swap Position

If all contract terms are fulfilled, a swap terminates at its maturity date. But there are three ways of ending a swap before it matures. Suppose that YBM decides to close out an existing swap today and calculations show that the swap has a positive value of $1 million. Then, the process of closing is as follows:

1. **Buyout.** A buyout involves YBM's counterparty paying YBM $1 million and then ending the swap by mutual consent.

2. **Assignment.** With the counterparty's approval, YBM can assign the swap to a third party. The third party would pay YBM $1 million, replace YBM in the transaction, embrace all the benefits, and accept all the obligations for the swap's remaining life.

3. **Offset.** YBM can enter into an identical swap with equal but opposite terms as the original swap. YBM's counterparty in the new swap will have to pay YBM $1 million because that is the value of the swap. In the combined swap position, YBM will have zero net cash flows in the future. Notice that unlike the first two transactions, here YBM does not completely leave the market and will continue to have credit risk until both swaps mature.

22.4 | Valuation

This section values a *plain vanilla interest rate swap* when interest rates are stochastic. The valuation formula is derived without specifying a particular evolution of the term structure of interest rates. This is due to the linear structure of the swap's payoffs in both the underlying fixed and floating cash flows. This is analogous to the pricing of forward contracts in chapters 11 and 12.

Swap valuation involves a clever trick: (1) decompose the swap into a fixed rate and a floating rate loan corresponding to each leg of the swap, (2) compute the present value of each of these loans, and (3) take their difference. Of course, we know how to compute the present value of fixed cash flows, but how does one value the floating cash flows? We solve this problem with a simple observation.

The simple observation is that the *value of a floating rate loan is always equal to its par value on the payment and reset dates.*[3] This happens because the loan pays out the interest owed on these dates. For example, a floating rate loan of $100 million for three years pays out the relevant interests perhaps quarterly (by whatever method of interest computation devised) and at each quarterly payment date, the value of the loan outstanding is $100 million.

The clever trick in valuing a swap is to include the principal payments while valuing the fixed-rate and floating-rate cash flows. This inclusion does not matter because the principal payments cancel when taking the difference between the two loans' cash flows. And, it simplifies our task because it is easy to value both the fixed and floating rate loans. To see how this works, consider both a fixed rate loan paying interest for three years and then returning a principal of $100 million, and a three-year floating rate loan with a principal of $100 million. Next, value both of these loans. Now, if you take the difference between these values, the present value of the $100 million notional cancels, leaving just the present value of the fixed-rate payments less the floating rate payments. This is precisely the value of a swap.

Armed with these insights, let us value an interest swap.

EXAMPLE 22.2: Valuing a Plain Vanilla Interest Rate Swap (Fixed versus Floating)

A Numerical Example

- Consider the data from Example 7.4.
  - Fixed Towers Inc. borrowed $100 million for three years at a floating rate of one-year bbalibor but now wants a fixed-rate loan.
  - Floating Cruisers Co. raised the same amount, for the same time period, at a fixed interest rate of $i = 0.06$ or 6 percent per year and wants to switch to a floating-rate loan.
  - They do an interest rate swap by embracing each other's liabilities. Fixed Towers *buys the swap* by agreeing to pay the fixed rate of 6 percent to Floating Cruisers, who, in turn, *sells the swap* by agreeing to pay the one-year bbalibor rate to Fixed Towers (see Figure 22.3, which repeats Figure 7.2). A **swap buyer** pays a fixed rate and receives the floating rate, whereas a **seller** does the opposite.
  - The notional principal of $L_N = \$100$ million is used to compute interests that are paid at year's end.
  - We discount the fixed rate payments using the zero-coupon bond prices in Table 22.3.

---

[3] It is a simple matter to compute the present value of the next floating interest rate payment between the payment dates. *The present value of the next floating interest rate payment plus the par value is the value of the floating rate loan to the issuer between the payment dates.* The next floating interest rate payment (say, X) is known at the last repayment date (say, time a) and before it is due (say, time b). The next floating interest rate payment is equal to the current floating interest rate times the notional. Then, the present value at time a of the next floating interest rate payment at time b is $B(a, b)X$. At time b, when the interest is paid, the floating rate loan resets to par value.

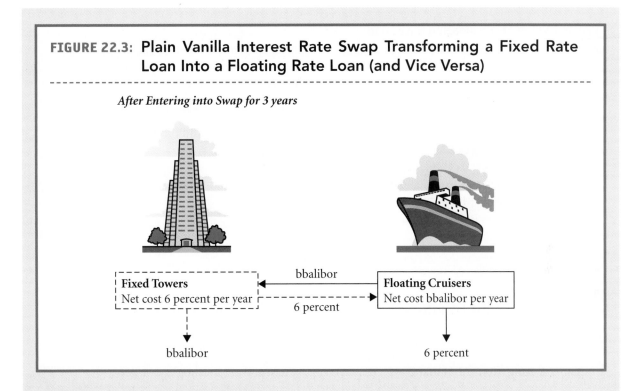

FIGURE 22.3: Plain Vanilla Interest Rate Swap Transforming a Fixed Rate Loan Into a Floating Rate Loan (and Vice Versa)

After Entering into Swap for 3 years

Present Value of the Fixed Rate Loan

- First, let us look at the fixed rate loan underlying the swap. The fixed rate loan has a coupon payment of C dollars per period plus a principal of L_N at the maturity date. The periodic payments are obtained by multiplying the notional principal by the fixed interest rate i. Therefore

$$\text{The fixed payment at the end of each period,}$$
$$C = L_N \times i$$
$$= 100 \times 0.06$$
$$= \$6 \text{ million} \tag{22.1}$$

The present value of the fixed rate loan is

$$PV_{Fix} = B(0,1) \times C + B(0,2) \times C + B(0,3) \times C + B(0,3) \times L_N$$
$$= (0.97 + 0.93 + 0.88) \times 6 + 0.88 \times 100$$
$$= \$104.68 \text{ million} \tag{22.2}$$

TABLE 22.3: Common Zero-Coupon Bond Price Data

Times to Maturity T	Today's Zero-Coupon Bond Prices $B(0,T)$	
1	$B(0,1)$	0.97
2	$B(0,2)$	0.93
3	$B(0,3)$	0.88
4	$B(0,4)$	0.82

Present Value of the Floating Rate Loan

- Recall our observation: the floating rate loan is always equal to its par value at the payment dates:

$$PV_{Float} = L_N = \$100 \text{ million} \tag{22.3}$$

Swap Valuation

- Consequently, the value of the swap to Fixed Towers, who pays fixed and receives floating, is computed by subtracting (22.2) from (22.3):

> Present value of the floating rate loan − Present value of the fixed rate loan
> $$= PV_{Float} - PV_{Fix}$$
> $$= 100 - 104.68 \text{ million}$$
> $$= -\$4.68 \text{ million} \tag{22.4}$$

- To enter the swap, Fixed Towers needs to be paid $4.68 million today.

- Alternatively, one can adjust the interest rate to make this a **par swap** with zero value. To do this, one needs to find the fixed rate that equates the present value of the two legs, that is,

$$L_N = B(0,1)C + B(0,2)C + B(0,3)C + B(0,3)L_N$$

Remembering from (22.1) that $C = L_N \times i$, rearranging terms, and canceling L_N, we get

$$\text{Swap rate } i_S = \frac{1 - B(0,3)}{B(0,1) + B(0,2) + B(0,3)} \tag{22.5}$$

The fixed interest rate for the par swap, i_S, is commonly referred to as the **swap rate**.

- Plugging in the values of the zero-coupon bonds, we get

$$i_S = (1 - 0.88)/(0.97 + 0.93 + 0.88) = 0.043165 \text{ or } 4.32 \text{ percent (approximately)}$$

This example motivates the following general result.

RESULT 22.1

- -

Valuing a Plain Vanilla Interest Rate Swap

Consider an interest rate swap between two counterparties starting today (time 0) and ending at time T. At the end of each period (at time t, where $t = 1, 2, \ldots, T$), the swap buyer pays a fixed amount $L_N \times i$ (where L_N is the notional principal and i is the fixed interest rate) and receives a floating payment known only at the beginning of that period.

The value of the swap to the buyer equals the present value of a floating-rate loan minus the present value of a fixed rate loan, that is,

$$V_{\text{Swap}} = \text{PV}_{\text{Float}} - \text{PV}_{\text{Fix}} \tag{22.6}$$

The present value of the floating rate loan at the payment dates always equals par, that is,

$$\text{PV}_{\text{Float}} = L_N \tag{22.7}$$

and the value of the fixed rate loan is the present value of the fixed cash flows, that is,

$$\text{PV}_{\text{Fix}} = [B(0,1) + B(0,2) + \ldots + B(0,T)]L_N \times i + B(0,T) \times L_N$$

$$= \left[\sum_{t=1}^{T} B(0,t) \right] L_N \times i + B(0,T) \times L_N \tag{22.8}$$

where $B(0,t)$ is the time 0 price of a zero-coupon bond that pays \$1 at time t.

In the case of a par swap, the fixed interest rate i_S (commonly known as the swap rate) is computed by setting $\text{PV}_{\text{Float}} = \text{PV}_{\text{Fix}}$.

For simplicity, our previous example assumed annual interest payments. Example 22.3 shows how cash flows are computed in the more realistic case of semiannual payments.

EXAMPLE 22.3: Plain Vanilla Interest Rate Swap with Semiannual Interest Payments

- Let us continue with the original swap in Example 22.2 but assume that the payments are made every six months. The fixed rate $i = 6$ percent is quoted on a **semiannual bond-equivalent basis**. It assumes a 365-day year and computes interest over the actual number of days in this period. If there are 182 days during the next six-month period, Fixed Towers pays after six months:

    Notional principal $\times$ Fixed interest rate $\times$ (Days in period/365)
    $= 100,000,000 \times 0.06 \times (182/365)$
    $= \$2,991,780.82$

- The floating side is quoted on a **money market yield basis**, which assumes 360 days in a year instead of 365. If the current six-month bbalibor rate is 5 percent per year, Floating Cruisers pays after six months

    Notional principal $\times$ Six-month bbalibor rate $\times$ (Days in period/360)
    $= 100,000,000 \times 0.05 \times (182/360)$
    $= \$2,527,777.78$

- Fixed Towers pays Floating Cruisers a net amount equal to

$$2,991,780.82 - 2,527,777.78$$
$$= \$464,003.04$$

- Every six months, Fixed Towers pays \$2,991,780.82 or a similar amount computed using the actual number of days over the previous six-month period. After six months are over, the counterparties check the market and finds the new six-month bbalibor rate that applies over the next six months. With this rate and the actual number of days in the period, the next floating payment is calculated.

22.5 | Interest Rate Swaps: A Postscript

We have viewed interest rate swaps primarily from the perspective of an institutional investor, but as we discuss next, interest rate swaps are also regularly used by government agencies. Following that, we study the complex interest rate swap issued by Bankers Trust and Deutsche Bank that led to lawsuits and raised numerous ethical questions. Finally, we explore the different kinds of interest rate swaps that can be created by adding features to plain vanilla interest rate swaps.

Municipal Swaps

Of course, you are familiar with the sophisticated financial operations of the US federal government that include managing the nation's money supply, regulating the banks and financial institutions, selling Treasury securities, and managing the public debt. But many state, local, and municipal governments raise funds by issuing **municipal bonds** (or **munis**), which pay interest at a fixed or a floating rate and enjoy a variety of tax-exemption benefits.[4] Many government entities also use swaps and other derivatives for managing the cash flows. Extension 22.2 discusses issues that government entities face in the municipal swap market. An article titled "US Local Governments Increase Derivatives Use" (*Risk*, September 2004) reported that because of low interest rates and changing laws, US local government agencies derivatives usage was "growing at well over 100 percent per year."

---

[4] Munis come in two major types: **general obligation bonds** that raise money for general purposes and **revenue bonds** that raise funds for specific projects like constructing a toll road whose future tolls will be used to pay interest and principal on these bonds. Interests earned on munis are usually exempt from federal income taxes and sometimes even from state and local government income taxes.

EXTENSION 22.2: Government Usage of Swaps

"The government should be regulating the derivatives markets and not using them" is a view held by many. But as we have discussed on several occasions, many governments trade derivatives. In particular, many government entities actively trade municipal swaps to manage interest risk in their receipts and expenditures. For example, a government entity that issued a fixed-rate coupon bond when rates were high can enter into a "receive fixed, pay floating" swap to take advantage of low interest rate environments. Swaps themselves do not necessarily affect an issuer's credit rating, but the major credit rating agencies do study how swaps relate to the issuer's overall asset–liability management policies and whether the issuer understands the terms, conditions, and risks of the swap.[5]

Municipal swaps possess familiar risks:

- *Counterparty risk*. This may be addressed by adopting prudent practices like setting up guidelines for exposure levels, ratings thresholds, and collateral requirements and by trading with counterparties who are rated AA or higher.

- *Basis risk*. This happens when the variable rate received on the swap (say, at the six-month bbalibor rate) does not match the variable rate that is being paid on the bonds (which may be tied to the SIFMA Municipal Swap Index, which is reset weekly).[6]

- *Termination risk*. This can be anticipated by assessing events that could trigger such an action.

- *Rollover risk*. This happens when the term of the bond being hedged (say, twenty years) is different from the term of the swap (say, five years), leaving the government entity unhedged at the swap's maturity.

- *Amortization risk*. This is the risk that the government entity may decide to retire the bond early, resulting in a mismatch between the expiration dates for the swap and the bond.

While public and private companies are likely to have Treasury Department personnel with expertise in swaps, a government agency issuing a swap may need more outside guidance. Want to advise government on swap related matters? Hired help may include (1) a *financial advisor* who reviews and analyzes various financing alternatives before entering into a swap; (2) a *swap advisor* who reviews and analyzes the swap alternatives, who helps in originating the swap (including arranging competitive pricing), who helps in monitoring the swap, and who helps the issuer formulate a swap policy; (3) a *swap/bond counsel* who helps comply with legal matters; and (4) a *swap insurer* who provides insurance in the event that the scheduled payments from the issuer to the swap bank do not occur.

Recurring incidents of financial follies, which get amplified during financial crisis, point to an urgent need to be very careful in these transactions. There's the old maxim worth remembering: "the law favors the vigilant and not the somnolent."

---

[5] The discussion is based on the issue briefs *The Fundamentals of Interest Rate Swaps* (October 2004) and available at the California Debt and Investment Advisory Commission's website (www.treasurer.ca.gov/cdiac/reports/questions.pdf).

[6] The Securities Industry and Financial Markets Association (SIFMA) produces the **SIFMA Municipal Swap Index**, which is a weekly computed market index consisting of high-grade, tax-exempt Variable Rate Demand Obligations (VRDOs) selected from SIFMA's extensive Municipal Market Data (MMD) database. **SIFMA** is an industry trade group representing securities firms, banks, and asset management companies in the United States, Europe, and Asia. **VRDOs** are bonds paying a floating interest that is periodically (daily, weekly, or monthly) adjusted; the holder has the option of redeeming a VRDO at the time of a rate change.

Legal and Ethical Issues

OTC swap contracts have attracted adverse publicity, bitterly fought lawsuits, and regulatory actions. An early controversy erupted around a publicized swap that we introduced at the beginning of the chapter with the comment "trust you couldn't, gamble you shouldn't." The actors in this high drama were seasoned players in the derivatives markets: Bankers Trust and P&G. The swap allowed P&G to pay a floating rate that was significantly lower than the market rate but where its payments could drastically rise if interest rates increased.

Interest rates increased unexpectedly (from P&G's perspective!), and the consumer products giant suffered over $100 million in losses on the swap. A lawsuit followed. P&G alleged that Bankers Trust had failed to properly disclose the risks and contract terms, that it had sold complex derivatives to other clients who also suffered heavy losses, and that its employees had cheated their customers. Facing a publicity nightmare and an erosion of trust by clients, Bankers Trust settled and forgave most of the debts (see Extension 22.3), but the once high-flying and hugely profitable bank had taken an irreparable hit to its reputation. In 1998, Deutsche Bank gobbled up Bankers Trust.

The Bankers Trust versus P&G saga had several ramifications. From a business point of view, it affected the growing use of derivatives by company treasuries. From a corporate governance and ethical perspective, it raised questions about how one should treat clients. From a risk management perspective, it stressed the importance of doing due diligence by carefully evaluating any derivative that a firm trades.

In another strange twist of fate, Germany's highest civil court ruled in 2011 that Deutsche Bank had improperly sold an interest rate swap to a client without adequately advising about the transaction's risks (see Extension 22.3). The ruling opened up a floodgate of suits because the bank had sold similar contracts to hundreds of clients, and many of them had lost money.

EXTENSION 22.3: Caveat Emptor versus Proper Disclosure

Bankers Trust versus Procter & Gamble

Bankers Trust New York Corporation began as a trust company in 1903, where the legendary financier John P. Morgan held controlling interest.[7] During the 1990s, Bankers Trust (BT) emerged as a leading dealer in the over-the-counter derivatives market. It sold complex derivatives to a number of its clients who wanted to manage (or speculate?) their interest rate risk. Many of these clients lost money. The most prominent of

---

[7] See Bankers Trust's history in *International Directory of Company Histories*, Volume 2, 1990, www.fundinguniverse.com/company-histories/bankers-trust-new-york-corporation-history.

them was the Procter & Gamble Corporation, which had long been using swaps and other derivatives for risk management (chapter 1 gave a brief description of P&G's derivative usage). We provide a brief description of some of the events that unfolded.

- The 1993 fixed-for-floating interest rate swap sold by P&G to BT possessed the following key features:
  - Notional principal $200 million
  - Contract date November 4, 1993; maturity date November 4, 1998
  - BT pays a fixed rate of 5.30 percent
  - P&G pays

$$\text{Commercial paper rate} - 0.75 \text{ percent} + \text{"Spread"} \tag{1}$$

This nonnegative spread was zero until November 4, 1994; afterward, it is computed by the formula

$$\begin{aligned}\text{Spread} = [(5\text{-year T-note yield} \times 98.5/5.78) - \text{Price of 6.25 percent} \\ 30\text{-year T-bond}]\end{aligned} \tag{2}$$

- Notice the sweetener in the first two expressions of the spread. P&G pays a floating rate that is 75 basis points lower than its market rate in the form of a commercial paper rate. A **commercial paper** is a promissory note sold by a company that is usually (1) unsecured, (2) matures in 270 days or less, and (3) like Treasury bills, sold as a zero-coupon bond. As the interest rate had been low during the past few years, P&G probably overlooked the other expression in its payment term, particularly the ration (98.5/5.78) in the spread, so that its interest expenses can rapidly increase beyond a threshold level.

- The Federal Reserve suddenly raised interest rates, and P&G lost over $150 million. Anguish, a gnashing of teeth, and a lawsuit against BT followed. Unlike another client, Gibson Greetings, that had sued BT complaining that it should never have let it engage in such risky deals, P&G alleged that BT did not properly explain potential costs of extricating itself from the swap. P&G's chairman declared that he agreed that end users of derivatives must be held accountable for their trades, "but only if the terms and risks are fully and accurately disclosed" (see "P. & G. Sues Bankers Trust Over Swap Deal," *New York Times*, October 28, 1994).

- P&G had a slim chance of successfully suing because caveat emptor, or "buyer beware," is a basic principle applicable to all aspects of life (including the over-the-counter derivatives market); a judge had ruled earlier that derivatives were not securities and were exempt from "more stringent securities laws;" and BT did not have a fiduciary obligation toward P&G in this trade (see "Bankers Trust Settles Suit with P. & G.," *New York Times*, May 10, 1996). However, its fortunes reversed when it was revealed that BT had sold complex derivatives to other clients who suffered similar losses, and some of its employees boasted how they had fleeced their customers by overcharging, which was caught on the bank's tape-recording system.

- BT's derivatives sales practices were investigated by the Securities and Exchange Commission, the Commodity Futures Trading Commission, and the Federal Reserve Bank of New York, who had "reprimanded or censured" the bank. Facing a publicity nightmare and an erosion of trust by clients, BT settled and forgave most of the debts. The damage to its reputation was enormous. Deutsche Bank acquired BT two years later.

Deutsche Bank

- History seems to have repeated itself. In the first decade of the new millennium, Deutsche Bank sold about seven hundred **spread-ladder swaps** to "German municipalities, community utilities and medium-size businesses." In these swaps, a client pays a floating rate (and receives a fixed rate) with the expectation that "long-term interest rates will increase while the short-term interest rates will decrease" (see "Deutsche Bank Awaits Verdict in Swaps Case—the Question Is, Were Its Clients Fairly Advised of Risks?," *Wall Street Journal,* March 22, 2011).

- In March 2011, Germany's highest civilian court ruled that Deutsche Bank had "failed to properly advise a client of the risks of interest-rate swaps" and instructed the bank to repay €541,000 ($769,000) to a client that had bought interest rate swaps on the bank's advice in an attempt to lower its interest payments (see "Global Finance: Court Deals Blow to Deutsche—Ruling That Bank Failed Client in Swaps Case May Lead to More Judgments," *Wall Street Journal,* March 23, 2011). The court ruled that the bank "had a particular duty to disclose all the risks to the company, as well as the bank's potential profit, because of its 'gross conflict of interest' in marketing a product whose risk was stacked to the bank's advantage and 'at the expense of the client.'" The ruling was particularly detrimental to the bank because it was likely to affect the outcome of many pending lawsuits filed against Deutsche bank by clients who had similarly lost money.

Variations of Interest Rate Swaps

Interest swaps have become quite sophisticated these days. Consider some examples created by adding various features to plain vanilla interest rate swaps:

- Setting a maximum value (or a **cap**) on the floating rate in a plain vanilla swap creates a **rate-capped swap**. Later you will see that this simple change embeds a call option into the swap. If a minimum value (or a **floor**) on the floating rate is also specified, then this security embeds an **interest rate collar**.

- A **yield swap**, which has both payments floating, may involve the exchange of a bond with a lower yield for one with a higher yield. Usually the higher-yield bond has a longer maturity and a lower credit rating, which implies a higher interest rate and credit risk.

- The notional principal in an **amortized swap** gets reduced over the swap's life according to a predetermined schedule. This is useful for hedging a portfolio of mortgages, which typically earns a fixed rate on the dollars invested and which amortizes over time owing to principal repayments.

- There are other swaps that involve changing notional principals. For example, **accreting swaps** have a notional principal increasing over time. These swaps are useful for hedging the risk associated with a construction project, where more money is invested over time. **Seasonal swaps** are useful in the retailing business, where the committed capital depends on the time of the year. The most general form of such a swap would be a **roller-coaster swap**, whose notional principal is structured by the dealer to suit the financing needs of the client's business.

- **A cancellable swap** gives one counterparty the right to cancel the swap without additional payments or penalties. They come in two types. A **callable swap** gives the *fixed-rate payer* the right to end the swap and is likely to be called when floating rates decline below a certain level. In contrast, a **putable swap** gives the *fixed-rate receiver* the right to put or cancel the swap and is likely to be put when floating rates rise above a threshold level.

- A **forward swap** (or a **deferred swap**) has its terms and conditions set at origination but begins only at a later date. This delaying tactic may be used for accounting or tax purposes.

- A **constant maturity swap** (or CMS) involves the exchange of fixed-rate payments for floating rate payments where the floating rate (which is the constant maturity rate) is reset at each period according to a fixed maturity market rate with a duration extending beyond that of the swap's reset period (such as the one-year constant maturity Treasury note rate).

To value and hedge these many variations of plain vanilla interest rate swaps, one needs the Heath–Jarrow–Morton model to price the embedded options, which is discussed in the next three chapters.

22.6 | Swaps and FRAs

The previous chapter noted that forward rates are the key rates underlying the valuation of interest rate derivatives. As the forward rate is identical to the FRA rate, it is not surprising that FRAs can be used to synthetically construct a swap. Let's see how.

Synthesizing Swaps with Eurodollars and FRAs

This section shows how to construct a synthetic swap as a portfolio of FRAs and zeros (Eurodollar deposits). Synthetic construction has several benefits: (1) it provides an alternative way for pricing a swap as the cost of this synthetic construction, (2) it shows how to hedge a swap's cash flows using FRAs and zeros, and (3) it provides a tool for identifying arbitrage opportunities across the FRA and swap markets. The next example demonstrates this construction.

EXAMPLE 22.4: Synthetic Construction of an Interest Rate Swap with FRAs and Eurodollar Deposits

The Construction

- A careful examination of a fixed-for-floating interest rate swap's cash flows reveals how the synthetic construction works. Consider the swap from Example 22.2.
  - The swap has a notional principal of $L_N = \$100$ million. It starts today (time 0) and matures after three years.
  - The fixed interest rate i is 0.06 per year.
  - The floating rate is the one-year bbalibor rate for Eurodollars, $R(t)$. These rates are known at the beginning of each period, that is, $R(0)$ is determined at time 0, $R(1)$ at time 1, and $R(2)$ at time 2.

- The swap buyer Fixed Towers pays fixed and receives floating. For example, its cash flow is

$$100[R(1) - 0.06] \tag{22.9a}$$

after two years. Figure 22.4 depicts the buyer's cash flows.

- Now, consider an FRA on a notional principal of $100 million that matures after two years. The FRA buyer's cash flow is given by expression (21.11c) of Chapter 21:

$$100[R(1) - f_{FRA}(0,1)] \tag{22.9b}$$

where $f_{FRA}(0,1)$ is the forward rate negotiated today that starts at the end of the first year and applies over the second year.

- Except for the last quantity in each expression, the cash flows in expressions (22.9a) and (22.9b) are the same. To adjust for this difference, add to the FRA trade a long position in $100[f_{FRA}(0,1) - 0.06]$ zero-coupon bonds maturing after two years. This could be a positive or

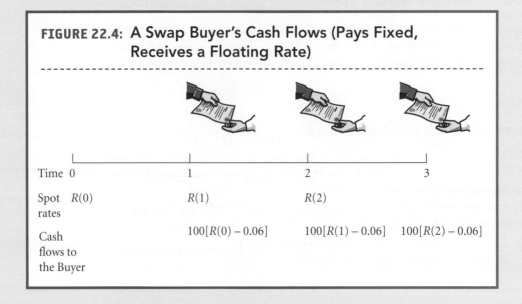

FIGURE 22.4: A Swap Buyer's Cash Flows (Pays Fixed, Receives a Floating Rate)

Time	0	1	2	3
Spot rates	$R(0)$	$R(1)$	$R(2)$	
Cash flows to the Buyer		$100[R(0) - 0.06]$	$100[R(1) - 0.06]$	$100[R(2) - 0.06]$

negative quantity, depending on whether the spot rate is greater than or less than the FRA rate. The long FRA and the long zeros' portfolio's payoff at time 2 will be

$$
\begin{aligned}
&100[R(1) - f_{FRA}(0,1)] + 100[f_{FRA}(0,1) - 0.06] \\
&= 100[R(1) - 0.06]
\end{aligned}
\tag{22.9d}
$$

This is the same as the swap's time 2 cash flow expression (22.9a).

- As this argument is not specific to time 2, you can synthetically construct each of the swap's cash flows at the other payment dates in an identical manner.

- Summing the FRAs and zeros across all the cash flow payment dates generates a portfolio of FRAs and zero-coupon bonds that yield the same cash flows as the swap.

We gather these ideas together as our next result.

RESULT 22.2

Synthetically Constructing a Swap Using FRAs and Zeros

Consider an interest rate swap starting today (time 0) and ending at time T. At the end of each period $t = 1, 2, \ldots, T$, the swap buyer pays a fixed amount $L_N \times i$ (where L_N is the notional principal and i is the fixed interest rate) and receives a floating amount, the spot rate $R(t-1)$.

The swap buyer's cash flows at time t are

$$
L_N \times [R(t-1) - i]
\tag{22.10}
$$

This swap's payoffs are identical to a long portfolio of FRAs with the same notional principal maturing at times $t = 1, 2, \ldots, T$ and $L_N[f_{FRA}(0, t-1) - i]$ zero-coupon bonds also maturing at times $t = 1, 2, \ldots, T$.

Given that swaps are portfolios of FRAs and zeros, it makes sense that one can use swap rates to extract forward rates. This extraction is demonstrated in Extension 22.4.

The Yield and Swap Curve

This section relates the Treasury (par bond) yield curve to the swap curve. Recall that the yield curve for US Treasury securities is obtained from T-bills for maturities of one year or less and from T-notes and T-bonds for maturities of more than one year. For the coupon-bearing bonds, the *par bond yields* are graphed. Recall that the par bond yields correspond to the yields on Treasury securities that are priced at par. Such a hypothetical Treasury yield curve is graphed in Figure 22.5.

EXTENSION 22.4: Computing Forward Rates from Swap Rates

Computing forward rates from swap rates is analogous to computing forward rates from coupon bond prices (see Extension 21.3). This is done by solving a system of linear equations for a collection of unknowns. The first step is to compute the zero-coupon bond prices.

Consider a par swap with value $V_{Swap} = 0$, notional (L_N), maturity date (T), and a swap rate (i_S) paid every period. Setting expression (22.7) equal to (22.8) in Result 22.1 and rearranging terms gives us an expression involving the zero-coupon bond prices, which are the unknowns, that is,

$$1 - B(0,T) = \left[\sum_{t=1}^{T} B(0,t) \right] \times i_S \qquad (1)$$

Next, suppose we are given a collection of T distinct maturity swap rates. Then, each swap has an equation similar to expression (1). This gives us T equations in the T unknowns $\{B(0,1), B(0,2), \dots, B(0,T)\}$. Solve them to obtain the zero-coupon bond prices. If the system does not have a solution, one can find those unknowns that minimize the sum of errors squared between the right side of expression (1) and the bond prices across all bonds.

EXAMPLE 1: Computing Forward Rates from Swap Rates

■ Today is time 0. Consider three plain vanilla fixed-for-floating swaps with swap rates $i_S = 0.0309$ for a swap maturing in one year, 0.0368 for a swap maturing in two years, and 0.0432 for a swap maturing in three years.

Computing Zero-Coupon Bond Prices

■ For the one-year swap, expression (1) gives

$$1 - B(0,1) = B(0,1)i_S$$

$$\text{or } B(0,1) = 1/(1.0309) = 0.97 \qquad (2a)$$

■ For the two-year swap, expression (1) gives

$$1 - B(0,2) = [B(0,1) + B(0,2)]i_S$$

$$\text{or } B(0,2) = (1 - 0.97 \times 0.0368)/(1 + 0.0368) = 0.9300 \qquad (2b)$$

■ Finally, for the three-year swap, expression (1) gives

$$1 - B(0,3) = [B(0,1) + B(0,2) + B(0,3)]i_S$$

$$\text{or } B(0,3) = (1 - 0.97 \times 0.0432 - 0.9300 \times 0.0432)/(1 + 0.0432) = 0.88 \qquad (2c)$$

These zero-coupon bond prices are the same as the corresponding values in Example 21.3, and we have already computed the forward rates in Example 21.5, completing this example.

Now let's construct a similar curve for the Eurodollar market. Recall that Eurodollar deposit rates are quoted for up to one year. These rates correspond to the T-bill yields and can be graphed directly. *Par swap rates* for swaps with maturities of more than one year complete the curve. Recall that a par swap rate is the rate that equates the present value of the cash flows from the swap's underlying coupon bond (expression [22.8]) to the face value of the bond (the present value of the swap's underlying floating-rate bond). Hence the par swap rate is equivalent to a par bond yield when viewed from this perspective. Such a hypothetical Eurodollar swap curve is also graphed in Figure 22.5.

Thus, when constructed in this manner, the swap curve is almost identical to the Treasury yield curve. The difference is not in the formulas for the rates graphed—they are the same and provide an apples-to-apples comparison. Rather, the difference is due to the differing credit risks between the Treasury and Eurodollar rates as measured by the *Treasury-Eurodollar (TED) spread*. If it were plotted on the same graph, the Eurodollar rate would exceed the Treasury rate by the TED spread. In fact, one reason for graphing the two curves together is to visually see their differences (the TED spread)! When markets are calm, the TED spread tends to be small in magnitude and relatively constant across maturities. When markets are in turmoil, however, the TED spread becomes large in magnitude, with the biggest differences on the short end of the curve. It is a useful statistic to gauge the market's pricing of credit risk for the largest European banks in times of calm and turmoil.

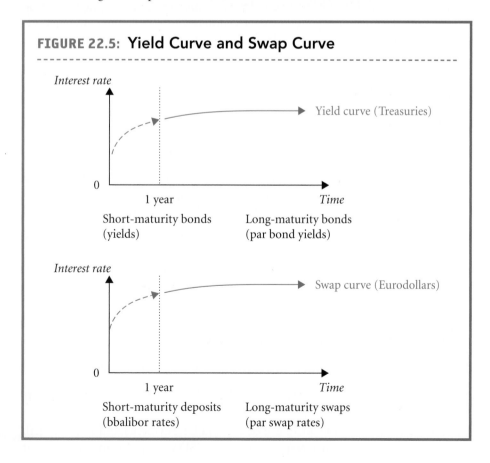

FIGURE 22.5: Yield Curve and Swap Curve

22.7 | Summary

1. The first swap was a currency swap arranged by Salomon Brothers between IBM and the World Bank. We divide the market developments into three categories: (1) the introduction of new swap contracts, (2) a shift from a brokerage business to a dealership market, (3) the founding of ISDA and the standardization of documents, and (4) the use of technology and the automation of trading.

2. There are three ways of initiating a swap contract: through phone calls, via a web-based platform, and by auctions. Auctions are more common in the case of municipal swaps. A swap position is closed through a buyout, through an assignment, or by entering into an offsetting swap.

3. A swap contract's documents must describe the cash flows, a timetable for the cash payments, and other relevant considerations like how to terminate a swap early and what to do if one side defaults.

4. The value of a plain vanilla interest rate swap to the fixed-rate payer equals the present value of the floating-rate note minus the present value of the fixed-rate loan implicit in the swap. A par swap sets the fixed interest rate so that the swap has a zero value.

5. A swap can be synthetically constructed as a portfolio of forward rate agreements and zero-coupon bonds.

6. The Treasury par bond yield curve and the Eurodollar swap curve graph identical rates, with the exception of credit risk. The difference between these two curves is called the Treasury over Eurodollar deposit rate (TED) spread.

22.8 | Cases

Procter and Gamble versus Bankers Trust: Caveat Emptor (Thunderbird Case A06-05-0001, European Case Clearing House). The case analyzes a complex interest rate swap between Procter & Gamble and Bankers Trust.

Wal-Mart's Use of Interest Rate Swaps (Harvard Business School Case 108038-PDF-ENG). The case studies Walmart's use of interest rate swaps to hedge the fair value of its fixed-rate debt against changing interest rates.

Banc One Corp.: Asset and Liability Management (Harvard Business School Case 294079-PDF-ENG). The case examines a bank's use of interest rate swaps to manage the sensitivity of its earnings to changes in interest rates and as an attractive investment alternative to conventional securities.

22.9 | Questions and Problems

22.1. If you enter a plain vanilla interest rate swap, what risks do you face?

22.2. a. To reduce counterparty risk in a swap, what conditions are written into the swap contract?

b. Consider both the structure of the regular payments and the notional. Are there any other restrictions in the ISDA swap documentation that reduce counterparty risk?

22.3. a. What are the three ways one can initiate a swap transaction?

   b. What are the four ways one can use to close a swap position?

22.4. Explain how a plain vanilla interest rate swap can change a fixed-rate loan into a floating-rate loan, and include a diagram to support your explanations.

22.5. What is the value of a floating-rate loan? Explain your answer.

22.6. a. What is the warehousing of swaps?

   b. Have swap dealers been successful in managing their books of plain vanilla interest swaps? Explain your answer.

22.7. Compute the value of a four-year fixed-rate loan with a coupon of 5 percent paid yearly on a principal of $100. Use the zero-coupon bond prices in the following table:

Times to Maturity T	Today's Zero-Coupon Bond Prices $B(0,T)$	
1	$B(0,1)$	0.97
2	$B(0,2)$	0.93
3	$B(0,3)$	0.88
4	$B(0,4)$	0.82

22.8. Explain why a cancellable swap might be of interest to a corporate treasurer.

22.9. Explain how to construct a swap using a floating-rate bond and a fixed-rate bond.

22.10. Explain why a swap has zero value when it is initiated. Why might this be a useful convention?

22.11. Based on the examples in the text, come up with an argument as to why plain vanilla interest rate swaps do not exchange principal, while a plain vanilla currency swap does.

22.12. Consider the swap in Example 22.2. Now, assume that the payments are made every six months. Zero-coupon bond prices (maturing every six months) are given in the following table:

Zero-Coupon Bond Prices		
Time to Maturity (in Years)	Zero-Coupon Bond Prices $B(0, T)$	
0.5	$B(0,0.5)$	0.99
1.0	$B(0,1.0)$	0.97
1.5	$B(0,1.5)$	0.95
2.0	$B(0,2.0)$	0.93
2.5	$B(0,2.5)$	0.91
3.0	$B(0,3.0)$	0.88

Compute the value of this swap.

22.13. How can one synthetically construct a swap using a portfolio of forward rate agreements and zero-coupon bonds?

22.14. Ignoring credit risk, is the swap rate on a *T*-year swap the same as the par-bond yield on a *T*-year Treasury bond? Explain your answer.

22.15. Describe the two different ways of synthetically constructing a swap. Which method is likely to be the easier to implement?

22.16. In the Bankers Trust versus Procter & Gamble situation, P&G argued that it did not fully understand the complex interest rate swap it had entered. Do you think it is prudent to enter a derivative that you do not completely understand? Explain your answer.

22.17. a. In chapter 1, we listed five different kinds of risks that were considered important by the Basel Committee on Banking Supervision and the International Organization of Securities Commissions. Pick three of these risks and explain why they are important to traders in the swap market.

b. Discuss the role played by the International Swaps and Derivatives Association in the swap and over-the-counter derivatives markets.

c. What is a Master Agreement?

22.18. Can you explain why an amortized interest rate swap might be a useful instrument for managing the risk of residential home mortgages?

22.19. After it is written and time has passed, will an interest rate swap always be equal to zero value? Explain.

22.20. Why are the swaps considered excellent examples of financial engineering?

23

Single-Period Binomial Heath–Jarrow–Morton Model

23.1 | Introduction

This chapter introduces the Heath–Jarrow–Morton (HJM) model for valuing interest rate derivatives in the context of a simple binomial model. This chapter is similar to yet different from the binomial option pricing model in chapter 17. It is similar in that the no-arbitrage and hedging arguments are invoked to value interest rate derivatives. It is different in that a key assumption is changed. No longer is there only one stock with random returns and one interest rate that is constant. Instead, we introduce a term structure of interest rates that fluctuates randomly across time. Just like Alice in her adventures in Wonderland,[1] we have fallen into a new world, the world of interest rate derivatives. It is similar to but different from our more familiar world of equity derivatives. In this new world, like the Cheshire Cat and Mad Hatter, there are strange and unusual characters—forward rates and zero-coupon bond prices—that will help us in searching for our white rabbit, which is the interest rate derivative's hedge ratio.

Although we considered interest rate derivatives (forward rate agreements [FRAs] and swaps) in chapters 21 and 22, they had linear payoffs. Consequently, we could value the derivatives without assuming a particular evolution for the term structure of interest rates. This and the next few chapters extend this analysis by considering the basic interest rate derivatives with nonlinear payoffs, including futures contracts as well as interest rate call and put options. In this new world, calls and puts are called *caplets* and *floorlets*. Portfolios of these options trade, called *caps* and *floors*. This chapter discusses caps and floors and their uses.

A brief history of interest rate derivatives models follows. Then, we study the single-period binomial HJM model. Because the purpose of the HJM model is to price interest rate derivatives, just as in the binomial option pricing model of chapter 17, we need to assume a stochastic evolution for the term structure of interest rates. The presentation of the material in this chapter purposely parallels the development of the binomial option pricing model (chapter 17). As such, this chapter piggybacks on that material to make our presentation simpler and easier to follow. First we state the necessary assumptions. Second, to value a traded caplet, we construct a synthetic caplet with identical payoffs using a zero-coupon bond and a money market account (mma). The cost of construction yields the caplet's arbitrage-free price. This takes us to determining the hedge ratio, martingale pricing, and risk-neutral valuation. To value a floorlet, we introduce caplet and floorlet parity, the analogue of put–call parity. A discussion of the valuation of alternative interest rate derivatives concludes the chapter. Chapter 24 picks up where this chapter ends by extending the single period to a multiperiod setting, thereby generating an HJM model that is useful in practice.

One last comment is necessary before reading chapters 23 and 24. All computations in the next two chapters are performed using our Excel-based software Priced!, which has more than sixteen digit accuracy. When reporting results in various formulas, however, we often round to four decimal places. The resulting

---

[1] *Alice's Adventures in Wonderland* is a classic book published in 1865 by Charles L. Dodgson under the pseudonym Lewis Carroll.

expressions, if evaluated using the reported (and rounded) numbers, may give different answers from those reported based on sixteen-plus digit accuracy. This is a typical problem when reporting numerical computations in this fashion (see Extension 2.1). Being forewarned, you should have no problems understanding the computations that follow.

23.2 | The Basic Interest Rate Derivatives

As seen earlier in this book, four basic derivatives are written on any underlying security or index: forwards, futures, call options, and put options. The same is true in the world of interest rate derivatives. In this context, the underlying "index" is the default-free spot rate of interest, and call and put options go by different names: caplets and floorlets, respectively. Yet in this strange new world, caplets and floorlets do not trade by themselves but only in portfolios called caps and floors, respectively. The reason these securities trade as portfolios is to economize on transaction costs. These securities, as will be shown, are useful for hedging fixed- and floating-rate coupon bonds. As coupon bonds have multiple cash flows, it makes sense that the basic hedging instruments need multiple cash flows as well. Interestingly, in this interest rate world, forwards trade separately as FRAs and also in portfolios, called interest rate swaps. We summarize these four basic derivatives in Table 23.1 and describe them subsequently.

TABLE 23.1: The Basic Interest Rate Derivatives

Today	Intermediate Date	Maturity Date
1. *Forwards*: forward rate agreements (FRAs) Buyer negotiates FRA rate (which is equivalent to the forward rate) and contract terms with the seller. No cash changes hands today.	No cash flows.	Short pays buyer the spot rate minus the FRA rate, applied on a notional amount and computed over a fixed time interval.
2. *Futures*: Eurodollar futures contracts Regulated, standardized contracts betting on a simple interest rate (bbalibor) to be realized at a future date. No cash changes hands today.	Marking-to-market cash flows.	Cash settlement based on a notional quantity computed over a fixed time period.
3. *Call options*: caplets A cap buyer pays a premium and buys a portfolio of European calls of different maturities on the same notional principal. The underlying is a simple interest rate (bbalibor). A caplet is one of those European calls.	Caplet buyer receives the spot rate less the cap rate if positive, or zero otherwise.	Same as in intermediate date.
4. *Put options*: floorlets A floor buyer pays a premium and buys a portfolio of European put options of different maturities on the same notional principal. The underlying is a simple interest rate (bbalibor). A floorlet is one of those European puts.	Floorlet buyer receives the floor rate minus the spot rate if positive, or zero otherwise.	Same as in intermediate date.

- *Forwards.* A *forward rate agreement* (FRA) is an over-the-counter (OTC) contract that fixes an interest rate for borrowing (or lending) over some future time period. The FRA rate is equivalent to the forward rate, which is the fundamental building block for our theory. An interest rate *swap* is a portfolio of zero-coupon bonds and FRAs (see chapter 22).

- *Futures.* An *interest rate futures* is an exchange-traded contract that fixes a borrowing (or a lending) rate at some future date. It differs from an FRA the same way that a futures contract differs from a forward contract. A host of features such as standardization, a clearinghouse, margins, and daily settlements make futures safe and easy to trade. Some interest rate futures (like those on Treasuries) end in physical delivery, while others (like those on Eurodollars) end in cash settlement.

- *Call options.* A **caplet** is a European call option on an interest rate that is effective for a single period. The buyer gets paid the spot rate minus the cap rate when it's positive, and nothing otherwise. A **cap** is a portfolio of caplets. Caps are cash settled contracts usually based on bbalibor.

- *Put options.* A **floorlet** is a European put option on an interest rate that is effective for a single period. The buyer is paid that period's floor rate minus the spot rate only when it's positive. A **floor** is a portfolio of floorlets. Floors are cash settled contracts usually based on bbalibor.

Of course, other, more exotic interest rate derivatives trade. One of these is a **swaption**, which is an option with an interest rate swap as the underlying. They come in two basic types: a **payer swaption** is an option to enter into a swap where the holder pays the fixed rate and receives the floating rate, while a **receiver swaption** is an option to enter into a swap where the holder pays the floating rate but receives the fixed rate.

Although the pricing of caps and floors is the primary goal in this chapter and the next two, we also discuss how to price swaptions. Before discussing pricing, let us consider how financial institutions use caps and floors.

Uses of Caps, Floors, and Collars

The next example illustrates how an interest rate cap can be used to speculate or hedge interest rate risk.

EXAMPLE 23.1: An Interest Rate Cap

Speculation

- International Treats and Restaurants Inc.'s (INTRest, a fictitious name) treasurer buys a cap today (time 0) with a cap rate $k = 5$ percent per year on a notional of $L_N = \$100$ million. This OTC contract matures in two years and has six-month bbalibor as the underlying floating rate of interest. This cap is a collection of four caplets, each of which makes payments based on the realized spot rates at six-month intervals.

- Figure 23.1 shows the cap's payoffs. The dotted line shows the six-month bbalibor rate. Spot rates are determined at the beginning of each time period, and payments based on these rates are made at the end of each time period.
  - Today's spot rate $R(0)$ is 0.06. The first caplet pays INTRest after six months:

$$L_N \times [R(0) - k] \times \text{Time period}$$
$$= 100 \times (0.06 - 0.05) \times 0.5 \text{ year}$$
$$= \$0.5 \text{ million} \tag{23.1a}$$

  - Six months later (time 1), the six-month bbalibor rate is $R(1) = 0.05$. The second caplet is at-the-money and no payment is made.
  - As $R(2) = 0.04$ is less than the cap rate, the third caplet also expires worthless at time 3.
  - The spot rate $R(3)$ is 0.07 after a year and a half. The fourth caplet gives INTRest a payoff of $100 \times (0.07 - 0.05) \times 0.5$ year = \$1 million at time 4.

Hedging

- A cap protects the holder against interest rate increases by putting a ceiling on the floating borrowing rate. To see this, suppose INTRest buys this cap and simultaneously issues floating rate debt paying bbalibor plus 50 basis points with $L = \$100$ million par value and with a similar payment date structure as the cap.
  - After six months, INTRest's cash flow is

$$\text{Cash flow from bond} + \text{Cash flow from first caplet}$$
$$= -L \times [R(0) + 0.005] \times \text{Time period} + L_N \times [R(0) - k] \times \text{Time period}$$
$$= -100 \times (0.005 + k) \times 0.5$$
$$= -2.75 \text{ million} \tag{23.1b}$$

  - The second and third cash out flows are just \$2.75 million and \$2.25 million, respectively, because INTRest benefits from the low floating rates at times 1 and 2, with $R(1) = 0.05$ and $R(2) = 0.04$.
  - At time 4, the total payment is again capped at \$2.75 million.

- The cap places a ceiling on INTRest's borrowing cost at the cap rate + 50 basis points.

The *cap's* payoff given in expression (23.1a) can be formalized as follows. Consider a cap consisting of T *caplets* with maturity dates $t = 1, 2, \ldots, T$. If the cap has a notional of L_N and a cap rate k per year, then a caplet maturing at time t has a payoff equal to

$$c_t = \max[0, R(t-1) - k] \times L_N \times \text{Time period} \tag{23.2a}$$

where $R(t-1)$ is the spot rate (bbalibor or euribor in most cases) determined at time $(t-1)$ that applies to the time period $[t-1, t]$. This time period is determined according to market conventions (such as actual/360 for Eurodollars and Euribor or actual/365 for pound sterling deposits). The cap's payoff is the sum of the individual caplet's payoffs.

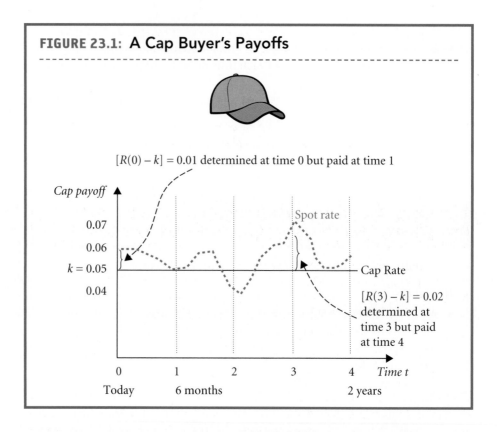

FIGURE 23.1: A Cap Buyer's Payoffs

In our discrete time model, the tth caplet's payoff at time t simplifies to

$$c_t = \max[0, R(t-1) - k] \tag{23.2b}$$

where we have assumed that the notional principal is \$1 and the time period has unit length.

A *floor* allows the holder to speculate or hedge on an interest rate decrease. A floor is a collection of *floorlets*, which are European put options on interest rates. A floor can ensure a minimum interest rate on an *existing bond holding* (which is analogous to a protective put strategy from chapter 15) or if one *simultaneously buys the bond and a floor* (which is analogous to a married put). Many endowment funds, hedge funds, mutual funds, pension funds, and financial institutions buy OTC traded interest rate floors to achieve a minimum return on their bond holdings while retaining the upside potential.

We can similarly describe a floorlet's payoff. Consider a floor consisting of T floorlets with maturity dates $t = 1, 2, \ldots, T$. If the floorlets have a notional of L_N and a floor rate k per year, then a floorlet maturing at time t has a payoff equal to

$$p_t = \max[0, k - R(t-1)] \times L_N \times \text{Time period} \tag{23.3a}$$

where $R(t-1)$ is the spot rate determined at time $(t-1)$ that applies to the time period $[t-1, t]$. Similarly, a floor's payoff is the sum of the individual floorlet's payoffs.

Analogously, a floorlet's payoff at time t in the case of our discrete model with a notional principal of $1 and a time period of unit length is

$$p_t = \max[0, k - R(t-1)] \qquad (23.3b)$$

A commonly used combination of interest rate derivatives is an **interest rate collar** that combines a cap and a floor with identical terms and conditions but with different strike rates. Let's consider an example.

EXAMPLE 23.2: An Interest Rate Collar

- Suppose that INTRest Inc.'s treasurer buys the interest rate cap of the previous example. It consists of four caplets each with a notional L_N of $100 million. The cap rate k_1 is 5 percent per year, the maturity date is 2 years, six-month bbalibor is the underlying floating rate of interest, and the payments are based on the realized spot rates at six-month intervals.

- Next, the treasurer thinks that she can save the company money by selling a floor with identical terms, except a floor rate of $k_2 = 2$ percent per year. The premium earned on the floor offsets the cap's cost and lowers the effective cost of the overall position.

- Now if the realized spot rate exceeds 5 percent, INTRest will receive a payment from the cap so that the company's effective rate is 5 percent. Conversely, if the spot rate falls below 2 percent, say, to 0.5 percent, INTRest will have to pay on the floor $-(k_2 - R) = -0.015$ or an outflow of 1.50 percent. The company has confined the interest rate paid to within the band of k_2 to k_1 or 2 to 5 percent. The short floor traded surrenders the opportunity to benefit from very low interest rates.

- This combination of caps and floors is similar to collars in the equity market introduced in chapter 15, and if the prices of the caps and floors match, then it is a *zero-cost collar*.

Before pricing interest rate derivatives like caps and floors, let us begin by providing a bird's-eye view of the historical development of interest rate derivatives pricing models.

23.3 | A Brief History of Interest Rate Derivatives Models

In their book *Financial Calculus—An Introduction to Derivatives Pricing*, Baxter and Rennie (1996, p. 203) wrote,

> In the interest-rate setting, Heath–Jarrow–Morton is as seminal as Black–Scholes. By focusing on forward rates and especially by giving a careful stochastic treatment, they produced the most general (finite) Brownian interest-rate model possible. Other models may claim differently, but they are just HJM with different notations.

To understand the relevance of these comments, we step back and look at the history of interest rate derivatives models.[2] Although the term structure has long been studied in the academic literature,[3] derivatives pricing models were only developed during the last quarter of the twentieth century. Pricing interest rate derivatives is a daunting task. *The key difficulty is in modeling the evolution of the term structure of interest rates.* This includes capturing the correlation between the long-, middle-, and short-term rates as they move randomly through time.

Interest rate derivatives pricing models began with a collection of papers focusing on the evolution of the *spot rate of interest*, called "spot rate" models, and it eventually ended with the HJM model.

- *Spot rate models.* This class of models focused on the evolution of the spot rate, $R(t)$. These models include those by Vasicek (1977), Brennan and Schwartz (1979), and Cox et al. (1985). Spot rate models have two major limitations. First, in these models, the values of interest rate derivatives depend on interest rate risk premia or, equivalently, on the expected return of default-free bonds. Recall that estimating a risk premium was the nagging problem facing option pricing in the pre–Black–Scholes–Merton (BSM) era, which the BSM model overcame. Second, these models can not easily match the initial yield curve. This yield curve matching is essential for accurate pricing and hedging of interest rate derivatives because any discrepancies in yield curve matching may generate "false" arbitrage opportunities in the priced derivatives.

- *HJM models.* To address the limitations of the spot rate model, the HJM model was developed. A precursor to the HJM model was a paper by Ho and Lee (1986), who imposed a simple binomial evolution on the zero-coupon bond price curve. Black et al. (1990) developed a related model. Hughston (1996, xxvii) wrote,

> Vasicek's paper, for all its accomplishments, does not actually address the problem of interest rate derivative valuation . . . all the necessary ingredients are in place, but this last step is not taken. Ten years have to pass before we come to the work of Heath, Jarrow and Morton (not published until 1992), who succeeded in putting together the pieces of the puzzle and built a general arbitrage-free model for discount bond dynamics and contingent claim valuation.

Motivated by consulting, Professor David Heath of Cornell University's School of Operations Research and Industrial Engineering and a PhD student, Andrew Morton, were working on this problem. Robert Jarrow, a professor of finance at

---

[2] See Hughston (1996) and Ho and Lee (2004), chapter 5, for additional histories of interest rate derivatives models.

[3] Shiller (1989) provides a comprehensive discussion of the fundamental concepts, theories, and empirical studies of the classical term structure literature.

Cornell's Johnson Graduate School of Management, joined them. Together they developed the HJM model, which was first presented as a working paper in 1987 and published as a series of papers in 1990 and 1992.

The HJM model is a continuous-time and multifactor model. It is very general. In fact, all of the previous spot rate models are special cases. Subsequent to its discovery, many papers were written studying special cases of the HJM model with nice analytic and computational properties. Not of all this research is in the public domain. Industry professionals acknowledge that they have proprietary versions of the HJM model implemented to make money for their firms!

A popular subcase of the HJM model known as the *libor model* (or the *market model* or the *BGM model*) is widely used by Wall Street for the pricing and hedging of caps, floors, and swaptions. Sandmann et al. (1995), Miltersen et al. (1997), and Brace et al. (1997) independently developed the libor model. A key feature of this model is that it uses simple bbalibor rates and not continuously compounded spot or forward rates. This model generates a formula for a caplet that is analogous to the BSM European call option formula. As such, it is familiar territory for derivatives traders, which explains its widespread popularity (see chapter 25 for a discussion of this model).

23.4 | The Assumptions

The assumptions underlying the single binomial HJM model are similar to those used to generate the binomial option pricing model of chapter 17, but with an important modification. The old assumption A6 that there is no interest rate uncertainty is now relaxed, and the old assumption A7 is replaced with a new assumption characterizing the random evolution of the term structure of interest rates. This new assumption is similar to, but more complex than, the old assumption A7 describing the evolution of stock prices.

For completeness, we first restate assumptions A1–A5.

A1. No market frictions. We assume that trading involves no *market frictions* such as transaction costs (brokerage commissions and bid/ask spreads), margin requirements, short sale restrictions, and taxes (which may be levied on different securities at different rates). Moreover, assets are perfectly divisible. This helps us to create a benchmark model to which one can later add frictions, and it's a reasonable approximation for institutional traders.

A2. No credit risk. We assume that there is no *credit risk*. Also known as *default risk* or *counterparty risk*, this is the risk that the counterparty will fail to perform on an obligation. The absence of credit risk is a reasonable assumption for both exchange-traded derivatives and many OTC derivatives because of collateral provisions.

A3. Competitive and well-functioning markets. In a competitive market, traders act as price takers and prices cannot be manipulated. In a well-functioning market, traders agree on *zero-probability events* so there is a consensus regarding what constitutes an arbitrage opportunity. Moreover, in such markets, price bubbles (which create a wedge between an asset's market price and its intrinsic or fundamental value) are assumed to be absent.

A4. No intermediate cash flows. Many assets reward their holders with cash flows such as dividends for stocks and coupon income for bonds. For now we assume that assets provide no such cash flows to their holders. As you will see later, such cash flows are easily incorporated into the model.

A5. No arbitrage opportunities. This is self-explanatory.

We now relax the old assumption A6 (of chapter 17) that there is no interest rate uncertainty. Instead, we allow the entire term structure of interest rates to fluctuate randomly through time. The relevant term structure is that of forward rates. Recall that expression (21.9) in chapter 21 gives the definition of the time t *forward rate* for the future period $[T-1, T]$ as

$$f(t, T-1) = \frac{B(t, T-1)}{B(t, T)} - 1 \tag{23.4}$$

where $B(t, T)$ is the time t price of a zero-coupon bond maturing at time T. When the time t forward rate corresponds to the immediate future period $[t, t+1]$, the forward rate gets a special name, the *spot rate*, and is denoted by $f(t, t) = R(t)$.

Given the term structure of forward rates, one can easily compute the term structure of zero-coupon bond prices as shown in chapter 21 (see Result 21.2). Conversely, given the term structure of zero-coupon bond prices, one can easily obtain the term structure of forward rates using expression (23.4). This equivalence implies that the term structure of forward rates and the term structure of zero-coupon bond prices contain the same information.

Thus one can describe the evolution of the term structure of interest rates by imposing an assumption on either the forward rates or the zero-coupon bond prices. In discrete time models, for pedagogical reasons—to see the economic reasoning more clearly—it is easier to impose the term structure evolution assumption on the zero-coupon bond prices. For parameter estimation, however, one must transform the zero-coupon bond price evolution to that of the forward rates because the forward rates' evolution is more time stationary, a property compatible with statistical estimation procedures (see chapter 21).

In continuous-time models, however, the situation reverses. It is easier to impose the term structure evolution assumption directly on forward rates. This is the approach taken in chapter 25 when discussing the HJM libor model. Of course, as we now know, these are equivalent ways of imposing the same assumption.

To model the term structure evolution, two changes are made to the binomial tree of chapters 17 and 18. First, the spot rate of interest is now random across time; call it $R(t)$. Second, stock prices are irrelevant and dropped from the model. Instead, each node now has a *vector* of zero-coupon bond prices $B(t,T)$ with maturities $T = 1, 2, 3, \ldots$ for times $t = 0, 1, 2, \ldots$. These zero-coupon bonds' prices have two arguments: one for today's date t and the other for the maturity date T. Given these insights, we now can state our final assumption.

A6. Single-period binomial process. The zero-coupon bond prices $B(t,T)$ for $t = 0, 1$ and $T = 1, 2, 3$ trade in discrete time, and their prices evolve according to a binomial process. After time 0, there are two states called "up" and "down." First, if the zero-coupon bond matures at time 1, then the current bond price goes to $1 regardless of the state. Second, the $T > 1$ maturity zero-coupon bond price is multiplied by the factor $u(0,T)$ in the up state and takes the price $u(0,T) \times B(0,T)$ with the actual probability $q(0) > 0$, or it is multiplied by the factor $d(0,T)$ in the down state and takes the price $d(0,T) \times B(0,T)$ with probability $1 - q(0)$. We assume that $u(0,T) > d(0,T)$.

The single-period evolution for the term structure of zero-coupon bond prices is given in Figure 23.2. We first explain this evolution via an example.

EXAMPLE 23.3: The Single-Period Term Structure Evolution

Let today be time 0. There are four securities in the model: three zero-coupon bonds and a money-market-account (mma). We describe their evolution over a one-year period.

The Zero-Coupon Bond Prices

- The time 0 prices of zero-coupon bonds maturing in 1 year (time 1), 2 years (time 2), and 3 years (time 3), respectively, are given in the following matrix:

$$\begin{bmatrix} B(0,3) = \$0.88 \\ B(0,2) = \$0.93 \\ B(0,1) = \$0.97 \end{bmatrix} \tag{23.5}$$

These prices are taken from the common zero-coupon bond price data used in Example 21.1. To reduce clutter, we drop the dollar signs from the tree.

- After one period, bond prices can move up or down. We assume that this happens with the actual probabilities $q(0) = 0.3$ and $[1 - q(0)] = 0.7$, respectively. The bond prices in the up state (labeled by the subscript u) are

$$\begin{bmatrix} B(1,3)_u = 0.9167 \\ B(1,2)_u = 0.9620 \\ B(1,1)_u = 1 \end{bmatrix} \tag{23.6a}$$

The bond prices in the down state (labeled by the subscript d) are

$$\begin{bmatrix} B(1,3)_d = 0.8977 \\ B(1,2)_d = 0.9555 \\ B(1,1)_d = 1 \end{bmatrix} \tag{23.6b}$$

Note that at time 1, the bond maturing at time 1 pays \$1 in both the up and down states and then disappears from the market.

Risky versus Riskless Securities

- In this evolution, there are two riskless securities, the bond that matures at time 1 and the mma. Both the two- and three-period maturity bonds are risky. This can be seen by computing their returns in both the up and down states and noticing that they are different:

$$\begin{bmatrix} [B(1,3)_u - B(0,3)]/B(0,3) = (0.9167 - 0.88)/0.88 = 0.0418 \\ [B(1,2)_u - B(0,2)]/B(0,2) = (0.9620 - 0.93)/0.93 = 0.0344 \\ [B(1,1)_u - B(0,1)]/B(0,1) = (1 - 0.97)/0.97 = 0.0309 \end{bmatrix} \tag{23.7a}$$

$$\begin{bmatrix} [B(1,3)_d - B(0,3)]/B(0,3) = (0.8977 - 0.88)/0.88 = 0.0201 \\ [B(1,2)_d - B(0,2)]/B(0,2) = (0.9555 - 0.93)/0.93 = 0.0274 \\ [B(1,1)_d - B(0,1)]/B(0,1) = (1 - 0.97)/0.97 = 0.0309 \end{bmatrix} \tag{23.7b}$$

This observation will prove useful later in this section.

The lower part of Figure 23.2 gives the formalization of this example using the symbols introduced in assumption A6.

THE ZERO-COUPON BOND PRICE EVOLUTION

- Today is denoted by time 0. The zero-coupon bond prices are given by $B(0,1)$, $B(0,2)$, and $B(0,3)$. They pay a dollar on their maturity dates: times 1, 2, and 3, respectively. Only time 1 is shown in this evolution.

- The actual probability of moving "up" is $q(0) > 0$.

- At time 1, the prices of the zeros move to the up state (in which case they get multiplied by the up factor) or the down state (where they get multiplied by the down factor).
  - If zero-coupon bond prices go up, the three-period bond has a new price of $B(1,3)_u$, which is obtained by multiplying $B(0,3)$ by the up factor $u(0,3)$.
  - Similarly, the two-period bond's price is $u(0,2)B(0,2) = B(1,2)_u$.
  - The one-period bond's price is $B(1,1)_u = 1$ because it matures, pays \$1, and disappears from the market.

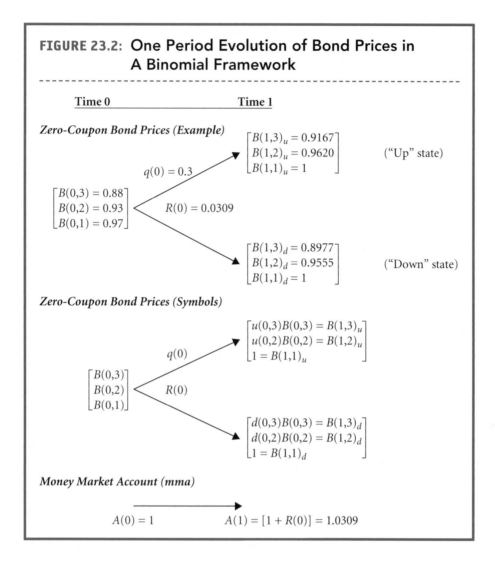

FIGURE 23.2: One Period Evolution of Bond Prices in A Binomial Framework

Time 0   Time 1

Zero-Coupon Bond Prices (Example)

$q(0) = 0.3$

$\begin{bmatrix} B(0,3) = 0.88 \\ B(0,2) = 0.93 \\ B(0,1) = 0.97 \end{bmatrix}$

$R(0) = 0.0309$

$\begin{bmatrix} B(1,3)_u = 0.9167 \\ B(1,2)_u = 0.9620 \\ B(1,1)_u = 1 \end{bmatrix}$ ("Up" state)

$\begin{bmatrix} B(1,3)_d = 0.8977 \\ B(1,2)_d = 0.9555 \\ B(1,1)_d = 1 \end{bmatrix}$ ("Down" state)

Zero-Coupon Bond Prices (Symbols)

$q(0)$

$\begin{bmatrix} B(0,3) \\ B(0,2) \\ B(0,1) \end{bmatrix}$

$R(0)$

$\begin{bmatrix} u(0,3)B(0,3) = B(1,3)_u \\ u(0,2)B(0,2) = B(1,2)_u \\ 1 = B(1,1)_u \end{bmatrix}$

$\begin{bmatrix} d(0,3)B(0,3) = B(1,3)_d \\ d(0,2)B(0,2) = B(1,2)_d \\ 1 = B(1,1)_d \end{bmatrix}$

Money Market Account (mma)

$A(0) = 1$ $A(1) = [1 + R(0)] = 1.0309$

- Note that the subscript u is attached to the prices of the zeros at time 1 to distinguish them from the down state prices.
- If zero-coupon bond prices go down, the three-period bond attains a new price of $d(0,3)B(0,3) = B(1,3)_d$. Similarly, $d(0,2)B(0,2) = B(1,2)_d$ and $B(1,1)_d = 1$. Here we use the subscript d for the down state.

THE SPOT RATE

- Irrespective of the state that occurs, the shortest-maturity bond pays $1 at time 1. This bond is thus riskless and earns the *spot rate*:

$$R(0) = [1 - B(0,1)]/B(0,1)]$$

$$= (1 - 0.97)/0.97$$

$$= 0.0309 \text{ or } 3.09 \text{ percent} \tag{23.8a}$$

THE MONEY MARKET ACCOUNT By definition, the mma grows at each period's spot rate of interest. If one invests \$1 in the mma at time 0, it pays a dollar return of $[1 + R(0)]$ at time 1. Hence the mma's values at times 0 and 1 are

$$A(0) = \$1 \text{ and}$$
$$A(1) = 1[1 + R(0)] = \$1.0309 \quad\quad (23.8b)$$

23.5 | The Single-Period Model

We now present the single-period binomial HJM model. We apply this model to price caplets, although as discussed later, the model is easily used to price other interest rate derivatives as well. The first step in this methodology is to guarantee that the assumed evolution is arbitrage-free.

Arbitrage-Free Evolutions

"The rain came down, the streams rose, and the winds blew and beat against that house; yet it did not fall, because it had its foundation on the rock," but the house built on sand "fell with a great crash" (see Matthew 7:25 and 7:27, King James New International Version). Similarly, we want to build a robust binomial tree that will not crumble when used to price interest rate derivatives. The tree (the method) crumbles if the tree's evolution admits arbitrage. Why? Because how can one determine the arbitrage-free price for a derivative when there exist arbitrage opportunities in the prices of the zero-coupon bonds themselves? Obviously, one cannot. Hence we need to guarantee that the assumed evolution is "built on rock" by being arbitrage-free. The task is far more complex than it was in the binomial model for pricing equity derivatives because here we have to ensure that a trader cannot make arbitrage profits by trading any combination of these zero-coupon bonds.

NECESSARY CONDITIONS We can use our insights obtained from the binomial model in chapter 17 to determine the arbitrage-free conditions. In chapter 17, there was only one risky asset's price on the binomial tree. Recall the no-arbitrage condition using the notation of this chapter:

$$\text{Up factor} > 1 + R(0) > \text{Down factor}$$

Here, however, we have two risky bonds at each node. Hence, if there is no arbitrage, then this condition must be true for both of the risky zero-coupon bonds $B(0,2)$ and $B(0,3)$. Otherwise, just as argued in chapter 17, one can form a portfolio of a risky zero-coupon bond and the mma to form an arbitrage opportunity.

This logic implies then that *a necessary condition for no arbitrage* is

$$u(0,T) > 1 + R(0) > d(0,T) \quad \text{for } T = 2, 3 \tag{23.9a}$$

where $u(0,T)$ and $d(0,T)$ are the T-period zero-coupon bond's up and down factors from time 0 to time 1.

But this condition is not sufficient to guarantee that the tree is arbitrage-free. The reason is because it only relates each risky bond to the mma. It does not compare the two risky bonds' returns to each other. Such a comparison will generate another necessary condition, which, in conjunction with expression (23.9a), will turn out to be sufficient. Before determining that remaining condition, however, it is useful to rewrite expression (23.9a) in an alternative form.

ALTERNATIVE NECESSARY CONDITIONS Simple logic shows that expression (23.9a) is true if and only if there exists a real number $\pi(0,T)$ with $0 < \pi(0,T) < 1$ such that

$$1 + R(0) = \pi(0,T)u(0,T) + [1 - \pi(0,T)]d(0,T) \tag{23.9b}$$

for $T = 2, 3$. That is, the dollar return on the mma is a weighted average of the up and down returns on the risky zero-coupon bonds. Note that the weight $\pi(0,T)$ depends on the current time (which is given by the first argument 0) and the particular risky bond under consideration (which is given by the second argument T). Solving expression (23.9b) gives a formula for this weight:

$$\pi(0,T) = \left(\frac{1 + R(0) - d(0,T)}{u(0,T) - d(0,T)} \right) \text{ and } 1 - \pi(0,T) = \left(\frac{u(0,T) - [1 + R(0)]}{u(0,T) - d(0,T)} \right) \tag{23.9c}$$

for $T = 2, 3$. With this formula, the necessary condition for no arbitrage simplifies to just checking to see if $0 < \pi(0,T) < 1$ for each T.

Last, we can rewrite expression (23.9b) one more time. Dividing both sides of (23.9b) by $[1 + R(0)]$ and multiplying both sides by $B(0,T)$ gives our final result:

$$B(0,T) = \frac{\pi(0,T)B(0,T)u(0,T) + [1 - \pi(0,T)]B(0,T)d(T)}{1 + R(0)} \text{ for } T = 2, 3 \tag{23.9d}$$

We will return to this condition shortly and explain its significance.

SUFFICIENT CONDITIONS The previous necessary conditions (23.9a)–(29.9d) do not compare the dollar returns of the two risky bonds. To compare these dollar returns, to see if there is any arbitrage embedded in their price evolutions, we can compare the cash flows to the traded two-period zero with a synthetic two-period zero, constructed using a portfolio of the three-period zero and the mma. If the price of the traded two-period zero equals the cost of constructing the synthetic two-period zero, then we know the dollar returns on the two- and three-period zeros admit no arbitrage. It is shown in the appendix to this chapter that for this to be true,

$$B(0,2) = \frac{\pi(0,3)B(0,2)u(0,2) + [1 - \pi(0,3)]\, B(0,2)d(0,2)}{1 + R(0)} \qquad (23.10)$$

Expression (23.9d) for the two-period zero is identical to expression (23.10) but with $\pi(0,2)$ instead of $\pi(0,3)$. This can only happen if

$$\pi(0,3) = \pi(0,2) \text{ with } 0 < \pi(0,2) < 1 \qquad (23.11)$$

which is our last necessary condition.

It turns out that expression (23.11) is also a sufficient condition for the tree to be arbitrage-free. The proof of this assertion is contained in the appendix to this chapter. We summarize this discussion as a result.

RESULT 23.1

Equal Pseudo-probability Condition

The single-period zero-coupon bond price evolution is arbitrage-free if and only if there exists a real number $\pi(0)$ strictly between 0 and 1 such that

$$\pi(0) = \pi(0,T) \text{ for } T = 2, 3 \qquad (23.12)$$

where $\pi(0,T) = ([1 + R(0) - d(0,T)]/[u(0,T) - d(0,T)])$, $R(0)$ is the time 0 spot rate, and $[u(0,T), d(0,T)]$ are the dollar returns on the T maturity zero-coupon bonds in the up and down states, respectively.

Because $\pi(0)$ is a number between zero and one, we can interpret it as a probability, and we call it the *pseudo-probability*. We call expression (23.12) the **equal pseudo-probability** condition. Fortunately, it greatly simplifies the task of checking to see if a zero-coupon bond price tree is arbitrage-free.

EXAMPLE 23.4: Verifying That a Single-Period Binomial Tree Is Arbitrage-Free

Consider the term structure evolution given in Example 23.2 and Figure 23.2. To check whether this evolution is arbitrage-free, we compute the up and down factors for the two zero-coupon bonds as they evolve from time 0 to time 1.

- For the zero-coupon bond maturing at time 3, we have

$$\text{up factor, } u(0,3) = B(1,3)_u/B(0,3) = 0.9167/0.88 = 1.0418 \text{ and}$$
$$\text{down factor, } d(0,3) = B(1,3)_d/B(0,3) = 0.8977/0.88 = 1.0201$$

- For the zero-coupon bond maturing at time 2, we have

$$\text{up factor, } u(0,2) = B(1,2)_u/B(0,2) = 0.9620/0.93 = 1.0344 \text{ and}$$
$$\text{down factor, } d(0,2) = B(1,2)_d/B(0,2) = 0.9555/0.93 = 1.0275$$

Next, we compute the pseudo-probabilities for the two- and three-period zeros:

$$\pi(0,3) = \left(\frac{1 + R(0) - d(0,3)}{u(0,3) - d(0,3)} \right) = \left(\frac{1.0309 - 1.0201}{1.0418 - 1.0201} \right) = 0.5$$

$$\pi(0,2) = \left(\frac{1 + R(0) - d(0,2)}{u(0,2) - d(0,2)} \right) = \left(\frac{1.0309 - 1.0275}{1.0344 - 1.0275} \right) = 0.5$$

- Because both these pseudo-probabilities are equal and strictly between 0 and 1, the single-period tree is arbitrage-free.

- For this tree, $\pi(0) = 0.5$ is the unique pseudo-probability of an up movement for zero-coupon bonds maturing at times 2 and 3.

Zero-Coupon Bond Prices and Martingales

Using the new notation, under the no-arbitrage condition (23.12), we can rewrite expression (23.9d) as

$$B(0,T) = \frac{\pi(0)B(1,T)_u + [1 - \pi(0)]B(1,T)_d}{1 + R(0)} \text{ for } T = 2, 3 \qquad (23.13a)$$

Suppose we view the "probability" of $B(0,T)$ going up as $\pi(0)$ and the probability of going down as $[1 - \pi(0)]$, where $T = 2$ and 3. Then, this expression shows that the zero-coupon bond's expected discounted payoff using the pseudo-probabilities is today's zero-coupon bond price! This gives a method for computing the present value of a zero-coupon bond.

Notice how similar this is to expression (17.5) in chapter 17. There the stock's price evolved as a martingale so that the stock price equaled its discounted expected payoff at time 1 using the pseudo-probabilities. Now we do the same for both zero-coupon bonds. The final step is applying the pseudo-probabilities to price interest rate derivatives. It is hoped that you are beginning to understand why martingale pricing lies at the heart of modern derivatives valuation.

EXAMPLE 23.5: Bond Prices as Expected Discounted Values

- Consider the term structure evolution given in Example 23.2 and Figure 23.2. At time 1, the three-period zero's price is $B(1,3)_u$ in the up state with pseudo-probability $\pi(0)$ and $B(1,3)_d$ in the down state with pseudo-probability $[1 - \pi(0)]$. As a dollar invested in the mma today gives $[1 + R(0)]$ at time 1, application of expression (23.13a) gives

$$\frac{\pi(0)B(1,3)_u + [1 - \pi(0)] B(1,3)_d}{1 + R(0)} = \frac{0.5 \times 0.9167 + 0.5 \times 0.8977}{1.0309} = 0.88$$

which matches $B(0,3)$, today's price of the zero-coupon bond maturing at time 3.

- Applying the same formula to the two-period zero whose prices at time 1 are $B(1,2)_u$ and $B(1,2)_d$ with pseudo-probabilities $\pi(0)$ and $[1 - \pi(0)]$, respectively, we get

$$\frac{\pi(0)B(1,2)_u + [1 - \pi(0)] B(1,2)_d}{1 + R(0)} = \frac{0.5 \times 0.9620 + 0.5 \times 0.9555}{1.0309} = 0.93$$

which matches $B(0,2)$, today's price of the zero-coupon bond maturing at time 2.

Using now familiar abstract notation, we rewrite these expressions as the following result.

RESULT 23.2

Risk-Neutral Valuation for Zero-Coupon Bond Prices

The time 0 value of a zero-coupon bond is

$$B(0,T) = \frac{E^{\pi}[B(1,T)]}{1 + R(0)} \quad \text{for } T = 2, 3 \qquad (23.13b)$$

where $E^{\pi}[\cdot]$ denotes expectation using the pseudo-probability $\pi(0)$, $R(0)$ is the time 0 spot rate, and $B(1,T)$ is the T maturity zero-coupon bond's price at time 1.

This result shows that the time 0 price of a zero-coupon bond equals its expected discounted time 1 price, where the discount rate is the spot rate and the expectation is computed using the pseudo-probabilities.

Finally, using the notation for the value of the mma also gives

$$\frac{B(0,T)}{A(0)} = E^\pi\left(\frac{B(1,T)}{A(1)}\right) \text{ for } T = 2, 3 \tag{23.13c}$$

This expression shows that the zero-coupon bond's price, normalized by the value of the mma, is a martingale under the pseudo-probabilities.

Alternatively stated, a necessary and sufficient condition for the tree to be arbitrage-free is the existence of a real number $\pi(0)$ strictly between 0 and 1 such that the normalized zero-coupon bond prices are martingales under this pseudo-probability. *It is this form of the no-arbitrage condition that readily generalizes to more complex models for the evolution of the term structure of interest rates.*

Understanding the Equal Pseudo-probability Condition

The equal pseudo-probability condition has a nice economic interpretation. To understand this interpretation, we note the obvious fact that

$$\pi(0,3) = \pi(0,2) \text{ holds if and only if } [1 - \pi(0,3)] = [1 - \pi(0,2)] \tag{23.14a}$$

Writing this expression out in full using Result 23.1, we see that the tree is arbitrage-free if and only if

$$\left(\frac{u(0,3) - [1 + R(0)]}{u(0,3) - d(0,3)}\right) = \left(\frac{u(0,2) - [1 + R(0)]}{u(0,2) - d(0,2)}\right) \tag{23.14b}$$

First, note that the numerator in expression (23.14b) is the compensation for bearing the risk of a zero-coupon bond versus holding the mma. This is because the possibility of receiving the larger return on the risky zero in the up state $u(0,T)$ is the reason one holds a risky bond instead of the mma. Figure 23.3 illustrates this difference.

Second, the denominator measures the spread, or the risk, of a zero-coupon bond. Indeed, the larger is the distance between the up and down returns on the zero-coupon bond, the riskier is the payoff, because both the gains and losses are magnified. Hence the distance between the largest and worst dollar returns on a zero-coupon bond is a measure of risk.

Combined, the ratio measures the reward per unit of risk, called the *risk premium*. The no-arbitrage condition can thus alternatively be stated as follows: *the tree is arbitrage-free if and only if all zero-coupon bonds earn the same risk premium.* This last observation makes good economic sense. If the zero-coupon bonds had different risk premiums, traders would desire to hold the zero with the largest compensation per unit of risk. In fact, if a trader also cleverly shorts a bond with a smaller compensation per unit of risk, all of the interest rate risk can be removed

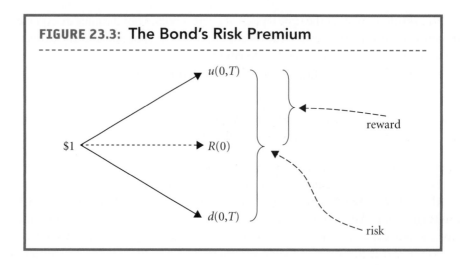

FIGURE 23.3: The Bond's Risk Premium

from the resulting portfolio to generate an arbitrage opportunity. This is the logic underlying Result 23.2.

Actual versus Pseudo-probabilities

As in chapter 17, the pseudo-probabilities $\pi(0)$ and $1 - \pi(0)$ for the up and down movements in the tree are both strictly positive if and only if the actual probabilities $q(0)$ and $1 - q(0)$ are strictly positive. This condition implies that there exist two strictly positive numbers ϕ_u and ϕ_d such that

$$\pi(0) = \phi_u q(0) \text{ and}$$

$$1 - \pi(0) = \phi_d [1 - q(0)]$$

These numbers ϕ_u and ϕ_d transform the actual probabilities to the pseudo-probabilities, which are useful for pricing derivatives using the technique of risk-neutral valuation (see below). The quantities ϕ_u and ϕ_d adjust the actual probabilities for the risk of the cash flows when computing the arbitrage-free price as a discounted expected value. The proof of this statement is identical to the proof given for the binomial model of chapter 17 (see the appendix to that chapter) and is therefore omitted.

Caplet Pricing

Having built this structure, it is now easy to price a caplet using the single-period HJM model. A caplet is a European call option on the spot rate of interest. Thus a caplet's payoff with maturity date 2 and strike rate k is given by

$$c(2) = \max[R(1) - k, 0] \tag{23.15a}$$

Note that the caplet's payoff at time 2 is based on the spot rate at time 1. This is by market convention.

Because this payoff is known at time 1, the present value of this payoff at time 1 is obtained by discounting (23.15a) by the spot rate $R(1)$:

$$c(1) = \frac{\max[R(1) - k, 0]}{1 + R(1)} \qquad (23.15b)$$

Thus, we can alternatively view the *caplet as having the maturity date 1 with this revised payoff*. This is justified because all of the payoff's uncertainty is resolved at date 1. As in this example, to facilitate computation, we introduce the following convention in this and the next chapter.

Caplet and Floorlet Maturity Convention: For valuation purposes, we consider a caplet's and floorlet's maturity as being one time step before the actual payment date with a payoff equal to the present value of the actual payment one time step later.

The caplet's payoffs are illustrated in Figure 23.4. We next show how to price this caplet, first with an example and then in general.

EXAMPLE 23.6: Pricing a Caplet

- As in the binomial model of chapter 17, we construct a portfolio consisting of a zero-coupon bond and mma to replicate the traded caplet's payoffs in both the up and down states. The cost of constructing this synthetic caplet is the arbitrage-free price of the traded caplet.

- Using the zero-coupon bond price evolution in Figure 23.2, we can compute the values for the spot rate at time 1 in the up and down states, $R(1)_u$ and $R(1)_d$, respectively:

$$R(1)_u = 1/B(1,2)_u - 1 = 1/(0.9620) - 1 = 0.0395$$

$$R(1)_d = 1/B(1,2)_d - 1 = 1/(0.9555) - 1 = 0.0465$$

The Caplet's Time 1 Payoffs

- Consider the caplet of Figure 23.4 maturing at time 1 with strike rate $k = 0.04$ per year. In the up state, the caplet ends out-of-the-money with zero value, as the following computation shows:

$$c_u = \max[(R(1)_u - k)/(1 + R(1)_u), 0]$$

$$= \max[(0.0395 - 0.04)/1.0395, 0] = 0 \qquad (23.16a)$$

In the down state, the caplet ends up in-the-money with value

$$c_d = \max[(R(1)_d - k)/(1 + R(1)_d), 0]$$

$$= \max[(0.0465 - 0.04)/1.0465, 0] = \$0.0062 \qquad (23.16b)$$

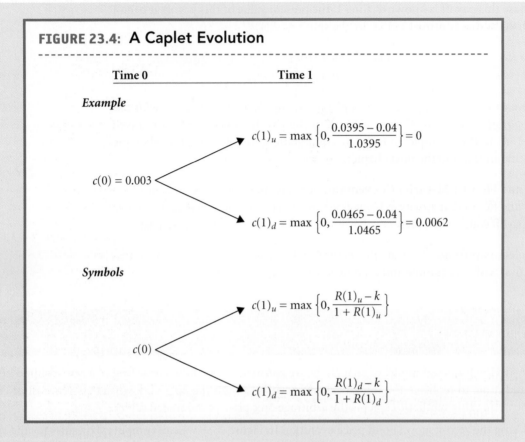

FIGURE 23.4: A Caplet Evolution

Constructing the Synthetic Caplet

- Form a portfolio using m shares of the two-period zero-coupon bond with price $B(0,2)$ and n units of the mma with value $A(0)$. The cost of construction is

$$V(0) \equiv mB(0,2) + nA(0) \qquad (23.17a)$$

- At time 1, we want to find (m, n) to match the portfolio's value to the traded caplet's value in each state. This yields two equations in two unknowns:

In the up state: $\qquad V(1)_u = mB(1,2)_u + nA(1) = c(1)_u$

$\qquad\qquad\qquad$ or $m0.9620 + n1.0309 = 0 \qquad (23.17b)$

In the down state: $\qquad V(1)_d = mB(1,2)_d + nA(1) = c(1)_d$

$\qquad\qquad\qquad$ or $m0.9555 + n1.0309 = 0.0062 \qquad (23.17c)$

Subtracting expression (23.17c) from expression (23.17b) gives

$$m \times (0.9620 - 0.9555) = -0.0062$$

$$\text{or } m = -0.9556$$

Plugging m's value into expression (23.17b) and solving we get

$$n = \frac{-m0.9620}{1.0309} = 0.8917$$

- So by going short 0.9556 of the two-period zero-coupon bond and buying 0.8917 units of the mma, we can construct a synthetic caplet. The cost of construction is

$$V(0) \equiv mB(0,2) + n$$

$$= -0.9556 \times 0.93 + 0.8917 = \$0.003$$

This is the arbitrage-free price of the traded caplet.

- One can repeat this construction using the mma and the three-period zero. Try it and see that since the term structure evolution is arbitrage-free, both approaches give the same caplet price.

The Hedge Ratio (the Holy Grail)

The holdings in the risky bond, m, is called the *caplet's delta* or the *hedge ratio*, the holy grail of option pricing. It is the ratio of change in the caplet's price to a change in the zero-coupon bond's price. Looking at expressions (23.17b) and (23.17c), we see that if one holds the traded caplet and shorts m units of the two-period zero-coupon bond, the resulting portfolio will be riskless and earn the mma's rate of return.

An Arbitrage Opportunity

Suppose that the market price of the caplet is \$0.005. Then, an arbitrage opportunity exists. The arbitrage opportunity is to sell the traded call for \$0.005 and buy the synthetic call at a cost of \$.003. At time 1, the payoffs to the short traded call and the long synthetic call are equal in magnitude and opposite in sign, so the net payoff is zero.

We can formalize this example to obtain some general conclusions regarding our method for pricing caplets.

THE CAPLET'S TIME 1 PAYOFFS First, we note that the caplet's time 1 payoffs are (see Figure 23.4)

In the up state:
$$c(1)_u = \max\left[0, \frac{R(1)_u - k}{1 + R(1)_u}\right] \qquad (23.18a)$$

In the down state:
$$c(1)_d = \max\left[0, \frac{R(1)_d - k}{1 + R(1)_d}\right] \qquad (23.18b)$$

CONSTRUCTING THE SYNTHETIC CAPLET We can create a synthetic caplet with cost of construction

$$V(0) = mB(0,2) + nA(0)$$

with m shares of the two-period zero worth $B(0,2)$ and n units of the mma priced at $A(0) = 1$.

Next, at time 1, we match this portfolio's value with that of the caplet's:

In the up state: $\quad V(1)_u = mu(0,2)B(0,2) + n[1 + R(0)] = c(1)_u \quad$ (23.19a)

In the down state: $\quad V(1)_d = md(0,2)B(0,2) + n[1 + R(0)] = c(1)_d \quad$ (23.19b)

Solving for m and n yields

$$m = \frac{c(1)_u - c(1)_d}{[u(0,2) - d(0,2)] \, B(0,2)} \tag{23.20a}$$

$$n = \frac{u(0,2)c(1)_d - d(0,2)c(1)_u}{[u(0,2) - d(0,2)] \, [1 + R(0)]} \tag{23.20b}$$

To avoid arbitrage, the cost of constructing the synthetic caplet portfolio must equal the traded caplet's price. Substitution of m and n into this expression and simplification, therefore, gives the arbitrage-free price of the caplet:

$$c(0) = mB(0,2) + n$$

$$= \frac{c(1)_u - c(1)_d}{[u(0,2) - d(0,2)] \, B(0,2)} B(0,2) + \frac{u(0,2)c(1)_d - d(0,2)c(1)_u}{[u(0,2) - d(0,2)] \, [1 + R(0)]}$$

$$\tag{23.21}$$

Notice that this caplet's value does not depend on the actual probability $q(0)$; it only depends on the up and down factors for the two-period zero $[u(0,2), d(0,2)]$, the two-period zero's price $B(0,2)$, and the spot rate of interest $R(0)$. This is similar to what we found in the binomial option pricing model in chapter 17.

This is an important observation. It implies that if two investors agree on these inputs, but disagree on the actual probability of going up, $q(0)$, they will still agree on the caplet's price. Of course, disagreement about the actual probability of going up $q(0)$ might lead to a disagreement about the initial zero's price $B(0,2)$ given fixed $[u(0,2), d(0,2), R(0)]$. However, if agreement about the zero's price $B(0,2)$ occurs, then the caplet's value is fixed by our no-arbitrage argument, and the two investors will agree on the caplet's price.

This omission occurs because in the derivation of the caplet's price, we use exact replication. No matter to which node of the tree the zero's price moves, the synthetic caplet's payoffs exactly duplicate the traded caplet's payoffs. Hence we are indifferent to what the actual probability is of moving up or down.

Finally, we note that the synthetic construction illustrated uses the two-period bond and the mma. An analogous synthetic construction could have been done using the three-period bond and the mma. This construction generates different holdings in the three-period bond and mma, as distinct from those in the two-period bond and mma, but the arbitrage-free price is identical. This is guaranteed by the equal pseudo-probability condition given by expression (23.12).

The Hedge Ratio (the Holy Grail)

The method for constructing the synthetic caplet also yields the method for hedging the risk of a long caplet position. Determining this hedge ratio, of course, is the holy grail of option pricing (see chapter 17). If one shorts m shares of the two-period zero for each caplet held long, the resulting portfolio is riskless. The holdings in the risky bond, m, is called the caplet's *delta or hedge ratio*. To see why the portfolio is riskless, we just need to rearrange the terms in expression (23.22) to obtain the time 0 hedged caplet portfolio:

$$c(0) - mB(0,2)$$

Its payoffs at time 1 are

In the up state: $\quad c(1)_u - mu(0,2)B(0,2) = c(1)_u - \dfrac{c(1)_u - c(1)_d}{[u(0,2) - d(0,2)]}u(0,2)$

$$= \frac{u(0,2)c(1)_d - d(0,2)c(1)_u}{[u(0,2) - d(0,2)]} = n[1 + R(0)]$$

In the down state: $\; c(1)_d - md(0,2)B(0,2) = c(1)_d - \dfrac{c(1)_u - c(1)_d}{[u(0,2) - d(0,2)]}d(0,2)$

$$= \frac{u(0,2)c(1)_d - d(0,2)c(1)_u}{[u(0,2) - d(0,2)]} = n[1 + R(0)]$$

In both the up and down states, the portfolio has the same value and is therefore riskless. As shown, it earns the spot rate of interest. The hedge ratio, m, given by expression (23.20a) therefore removes all of the interest rate risk from the hedged caplet portfolio.

Risk-Neutral Valuation

We can rearrange expression (23.21) for the caplet's arbitrage-free price to obtain another insight. Some algebra yields

$$c(0) = \frac{1}{[1 + R(0)]}\left[\left(\frac{1 + R(0) - d(0,2)}{u(0,2) - d(0,3)}\right)c(1)_u + \left(\frac{u(0,2) - [1 + R(0)]}{u(0,2) - d(0,2)}\right)c(1)_d\right]$$

Using the definition of the pseudo-probability in Result 23.1 under the no-arbitrage condition, we can rewrite this expression abstractly as

$$c(0) = \frac{\pi(0)c(1)_u + \left[1 - \pi(0)\right]c(1)_d}{1 + R(0)} \qquad (23.22a)$$

The caplet's arbitrage-free price is seen to be its expected discounted value using the pseudo-probabilities. This gives a present value formula. The pseudo-probabilities adjust for the risk of the caplet's payoff, and therefore one can use the riskless rate to discount to the present. As in chapter 17, if one uses this expression to value the caplet, then it is called *risk-neutral valuation*.

Using familiar abstract notation, we can summarize this result.

RESULT 23.3

Risk-Neutral Valuation for a Caplet

A caplet with strike rate k and maturing at time 1 is given by the formula

$$c(0) = \frac{E^\pi[c(1)]}{1 + R(0)} \qquad (23.22b)$$

where $E^\pi[\cdot]$ denotes expectation using the pseudo-probability $\pi(0)$, $R(0)$ is the time 0 spot rate, and $c(1)$ is the caplet's value at time 1.

As noted earlier, the caplet's value does not depend on the actual probability of moving to the up state. It only depends on the pseudo-probability. Because of expression (23.22b), the pseudo-probability is often called the **risk-neutral probability**.

We note in passing that this more abstract expression will prove useful in deriving a put–call parity theorem for caplets and floorlets analogous to that for ordinary calls and puts.

Risk-neutral valuation greatly simplifies the computation of the caplet's arbitrage-free price, as the following example shows.

EXAMPLE 23.7: Risk-Neutral Valuation

Using the binomial tree in Figure 23.2 and the caplet payoffs from Figure 23.4, we get

$$c(0) = \frac{\pi(0)c(1)_u + \left[1 - \pi(0)\right]c(1)_d}{1 + R(0)} = \frac{0.5 \times 0 + 0.5 \times 0.0062}{1.0309} = 0.003$$

As illustrated, using the risk-neutral valuation method is much easier than constructing the synthetic caplet and solving the two equations for the two unknowns—and it gives the same value, which should not be a surprise!

Valuing a Floorlet

Risk-neutral valuation can also be used to value a floorlet. Alternatively, the price of a floorlet can be obtained from that of a caplet by using a put–call parity relationship. This is given by the following result.

RESULT 23.4

- -

Caplet–Floorlet Parity

$$[f(0,1) - k]B(0,2) = c(0) - p(0) \qquad (23.23)$$

where time 0 is today, time 1 is the maturity date, $f(0,1)$ is the time 0 forward rate for date 1, $B(0,2)$ is today's price of a zero-coupon maturing at time 2, and $c(0)$ and $p(0)$ are today's prices of a caplet and a floorlet, respectively, with identical terms and conditions including strike rate k and maturity date 1.

This relation is proved in the appendix to this chapter. Caplet–floorlet parity shows that a position long a caplet and short a floorlet equals a long position in $[f(0,1) - k]$ zero-coupon bonds, represented by the left side of this expression. Given the value of a caplet, the value of the floorlet follows directly from this expression. The next example illustrates the use of caplet–floorlet parity for valuing a floorlet.

EXAMPLE 23.8: Valuing a Floorlet

- Consider a floorlet that has strike rate $k = 0.04$ per year and maturity date 2. Its time 2 payoff is

$$p(2) = \max[k - R(1), 0]$$

- The floorlet is a European put option on the spot rate of interest. Note that the caplet's payoff at time 2 is based on the spot rate at time 1. Because this payoff is known at time 1, the present value of this payoff at time 1 is obtained by discounting by the spot rate:

$$p(1) = \frac{\max\left[k - R(1), 0\right]}{1 + R(1)}$$

As with the caplet, since the floorlet's payoff is known at time 1, using our convention, we consider time 1 as the maturity of the floorlet.

- Let the term structure evolution be as in Figure 23.2 and Example 23.3. Consider a caplet with the same maturity and the same strike rate as the floorlet's. We determined the time 0 price of this caplet as $c(0) = 0.003$ dollars in Example 23.7. The forward rate at time 0 for date 2 is given by expression (23.4) as

$$f(0,1) = \frac{B(0,1)}{B(0,2)} - 1 = \frac{0.97}{0.93} - 1 = 0.0430$$

- Hence, using caplet–floorlet parity, we have that

$$p(0) = c(0) - [f(0,1) - k]B(0,2)$$

$$= 0.003 - (0.0430 - 0.04)0.93 = \$0.0002$$

which is the floorlet's value at time 0. You can check to see that using risk-neutral valuation gives the same answer, as it should!

Valuing Various Interest Rate Derivatives

The method we have developed for pricing caplets via risk-neutral valuation is surprisingly general. It can be applied to any interest rate derivative to obtain its arbitrage-free price. The only modification needed is to replace the caplet's time 1 payoff with that of the alternative interest rate derivative. We will show how to apply this technique to price American options, swaptions, and futures contracts after studying the two-period model in chapter 24. We cannot study them here because in a single period model, the complexity of these securities disappear: futures contracts become forward contracts, American options become European options, and swaptions become deterministic.

Multiple Factors

The single-period binomial HJM model is called a **one-factor model** because at each node of the tree, only one of two possibilities can happen: up and down. A **two-factor model** has three branches at each node in the tree: up, middle, and down; a three-factor model has four branches at each node, and so forth.

A *factor* corresponds to an economic shock affecting the evolution of the term structure of interest rates. Such shocks are due to the natural randomness in an economy resulting from the ordinary economic activities of production, consumption, technological advances, population growth, and government regulatory policy (monetary and fiscal). One can understand these random shocks by thinking about how to simulate an evolution through an HJM tree.

For a one-factor tree, starting at time 0 and progressing forward, flipping a single coin at each node generates a path through the tree. Of course, the coin would need to be biased with the probability of heads being the actual probability of moving up.

A coin is the simplest random generating device one can think of. Because only one random generating device is needed to create a path through a binomial tree, it is called a *one-factor model*. For a *two-factor model*, at each node in the tree, one needs to flip two coins to decide which branch to take. Recall that a two-factor model has three branches at each node. One coin is needed to decide between up and "the remaining two branches." A second coin is needed to choose between the remaining two branches: middle or down. Hence you need two of these simplest random generating devices to simulate an evolution through a two-factor HJM tree. Each random generating device is a "factor." The same logic extends for three or more factors.

The valuation and hedging methods for multifactor models are straightforward extensions of those illustrated for the one-factor model. The only difference is that more branches need to be considered, and hedging requires more zero-coupon bonds at each time step because there is more risk (see Jarrow 2002b).

When modeling the evolution of the term structure of interest rates, one should include enough factors to capture all of the relevant randomness affecting the economy. Macroeconomics can help in understanding the sources of this randomness, as discussed earlier. Researchers have estimated multifactor models and discovered that at least three or four factors are needed to provide term structure evolutions consistent with historical experience.

23.6 | Summary

1. The basic equity derivatives are forwards, futures, calls, and put options. The basic interest rate derivatives are forwards (called forward rate agreements), futures, call options (called caplets), and put options (called floorlets). Caplets and floorlets do not trade, but portfolios of caplets, called caps, and portfolios of floorlets, called floors, trade over-the-counter.

2. The single-period binomial HJM model assumes that the zero-coupon bond prices $B(t,T)$ for $T = 1, 2, 3$ and $t = 0, 1$ trade in discrete time and that their prices evolve according to a binomial process. First, if the zero-coupon bond matures the next period, that is, at time 1, then the current bond price goes to \$1 regardless of the state. Second, the current $T > t + 1$ maturity zero-coupon bond price either gets multiplied by an up factor $u(t,T)$ and takes the price $u(t,T) \times B(t,T)$ with the actual probability $q(t) > 0$, or it is multiplied by a down factor $d(t,T)$ and takes the price $d(t,T) \times B(t,T)$ with probability $1 - q(t)$.

3. The single-period zero-coupon bond price binomial tree is arbitrage-free if and only if there exist pseudo-probabilities $\pi(0)$ strictly between 0 and 1 such that

$$\pi(0) = \pi(0,T) \quad \text{for } T = 2, 3$$

$$\text{where } \pi(0,T) = \left[\frac{1 + R(0) - d(0,T)}{u(0,T) - d(0,T)} \right]$$

4. Consider a caplet maturing at time 2 with a strike rate of k. The present value of its payoff at time 1 is $c(1) = \max\left[0, (R(1) - k)/(1 + R(1))\right]$. Because this payoff is known at time 1, we consider the caplet's maturity as time 1, and not time 2. The arbitrage-free price of a caplet can be determined using risk-neutral valuation $c(0) = E^\pi[c(1)]/[1 + R(0)]$, where $E^\pi[\cdot]$ denotes expectation using the pseudo-probabilities. The hedge ratio $m = [c(1)_u - c(1)_d]/\{[u(0,2) - d(0,2)]B(0,2)\}$ can be used to form a riskless portfolio consisting of a long position in the caplet and shorting this number of two-period zero-coupon bonds.

5. Caplet–floorlet parity is

$$\left[f(0,1) - k\right]B(0,2) = c(0) - p(0)$$

where $f(0,1)$ is the time 0 forward rate for date 1, $B(0,2)$ is the time 0 zero-coupon price with maturity at time 2, and both the caplet with time 0 price $c(0)$ and the floorlet with time 0 price $p(0)$ have strike price k and maturity 1.

23.7 | Appendix

The Equal Pseudo-probability Condition

As with the binomial model for pricing equity options (see chapter 17), we can trade two assets to synthetically construct the price of a third asset. Closely related to this synthetic construction is the equivalence of the pseudo-probabilities, which the following proof shows.

Proof of Necessary Condition

- We first show how to construct the evolution of the traded two-period zero-coupon bond's price using a portfolio of the mma and the three-period zero-coupon bond.

- The payoffs to the traded two-period zero at time 1 in the up and down states are $u(0,2)B(0,2)$ and $d(0,2)B(0,2)$, respectively.

- Let us construct a portfolio consisting of n units of the mma and m shares of the three-period bond with time 0 value $V(0) \equiv mB(0,3) + nA(0)$ such that in both the up and down states, the portfolio's value matches the price of the two-period zero, that is,

$$V(1)_u = mB(1,3)_u + nA(1) = u(0,2)B(0,2)$$

and

$$V(1)_d = mB(1,3)_d + nA(1) = d(0,2)B(0,2)$$

- Using the notation from Figure 23.2, we can rewrite this system of equations as

$$mu(0,3)B(0,3) + n[1 + R(0)] = u(0,2)B(0,2)$$

$$md(0,3)B(0,3) + n[1 + R(0)] = d(0,2)B(0,2)$$

Solving this set of equations gives

$$m = \frac{[u(0,2) - d(0,2)]B(0,2)}{[u(0,3) - d(0,3)]B(0,3)} \quad \text{and} \quad n = \frac{[u(0,3)d(0,2) - u(0,2)d(0,3)]B(0,2)}{[u(0,3) - d(0,3)][1 + R(0)]}$$

Substituting these back into $V(0)$ gives the cost of construction as

$$V(0) = \frac{[u(0,2) - d(0,2)]B(0,2)}{[u(0,3) - d(0,3)]B(0,3)}B(0,3) + \frac{[u(0,3)d(0,2) - u(0,2)d(0,3)]B(0,2)}{[u(0,3) - d(0,3)][1 + R(0)]}A(0)$$

Algebra yields

$$V(0) = \frac{\left(\dfrac{1 + R(0) - d(0,3)}{u(0,3) - d(0,3)}\right)B(0,2)u(0,2) + \left(\dfrac{u(0,3) - (1 + R(0))}{u(0,3) - d(0,3)}\right)B(0,2)d(0,2)}{1 + R(0)}$$

Finally, using expression (23.9c), we can write the cost of construction as

$$V(0) = \frac{\pi(0,3)B(0,2)u(0,2) + [1 - \pi(0,3)]B(0,2)d(0,2)}{1 + R(0)} \tag{1}$$

- No arbitrage implies that the cost of constructing the synthetic two-period zero must equal the price of the traded two-period zero, that is,

$$B(0,2) = \frac{\pi(0,3)B(0,2)u(0,2) + [1 - \pi(0,3)]B(0,2)d(0,2)}{1 + R(0)} \tag{2}$$

Expression (2) is the third necessary condition (see expression [23.10]).

Proof of Sufficiency

- To prove sufficiency, we note that expression (23.12) implies that (23.13b) holds. We use this condition subsequently.

- Let condition (23.12) hold: $\pi(0) = \pi(0,T)$ for $T = 2, 3$ in our interest rate binomial tree. We suppose that an arbitrage opportunity exists and then generate a contradiction of (23.12), thereby proving that the evolution is arbitrage-free.

- Consider an arbitrage portfolio consisting of a units of the mma, b units of the two-period zero, and c units of the three-period zero-coupon bond. Then, by the definition of an arbitrage trading strategy this portfolio has a zero initial investment:

$$a + bB(0,2) + cB(0,3) = 0 \tag{3}$$

- After one period, the arbitrage portfolio's values must be non-negative always and one must be strictly positive, that is:

In the up state: $\qquad aA(1) + bB(1,2)_u + cB(1,3)_u \geq 0$

In the down state: $\qquad aA(1) + bB(1,2)_d + cB(1,3)_d \geq 0$

where at least one of the last two inequalities is strictly positive.

- Dividing the last two expressions by $A(1)$ and taking expectations using the pseudo-probability $\pi(0)$ gives

$$E^\pi \left(a + b\frac{B(1,2)}{A(1)} + c\frac{B(1,3)}{A(1)} \right) > 0 \tag{4}$$

But using expression (23.13b) on this last equation (which follows from [23.12]) yields a contradiction of expression (3):

$$a + bB(0,2) + cB(0,3) > 0 \tag{5}$$

Thus, when unique pseudo-probabilities exist, we cannot have an arbitrage opportunity in the tree.

Proof of Caplet and Floorlet Parity

To prove caplet and floorlet parity in the single-period model, consider a caplet and floorlet both with maturity 1 and strike rate k. Their time 2 payoffs are

$$c(2) = \max[0, R(1) - k] \text{ and}$$
$$p(2) = \max[0, k - R(1)]$$

where $R(1)$ is the spot rate.

It is easy to show that the following expression holds:

$$R(1) - k = \max[0, R(1) - k] - \max[0, k - R(1)] = c(2) - p(2) \tag{6}$$

One can easily verify that this identity is true by testing values for the spot rate that are greater than or less than the common strike rate k.

Add and subtract 1 on the left side and divide by the mma's time 2 value, $A(2)$. This gives

$$[1 + R(1)]/A(2) - (1 + k)/A(2) = \max[0, R(1) - k]/A(2) - \max[0, k - R(1)]/A(2)$$
$$\text{or } [1 + R(1)]/A(2) - (1 + k)/A(2) = c(2)/A(2) - p(2)/A(2) \tag{7}$$

Take expectations of (7) with respect to the pseudo-probability to get

$$E^\pi\left[\frac{1 + R(1)}{A(2)}\right] - (1 + k)E^\pi\left[\frac{1}{A(2)}\right] = E^\pi\left[\frac{c(2)}{A(2)}\right] - E^\pi\left[\frac{p(2)}{A(2)}\right] \tag{8}$$

The risk-neutral valuation method implies that

$$B(0,2) = E^\pi\left[\frac{1}{A(2)}\right] \tag{9a}$$

$$E^\pi\left[\frac{1 + R(1)}{A(2)}\right] = E^\pi\left[\frac{1}{A(1)}\right] = B(0,1) \tag{9b}$$

$$c(0) = E^\pi\left[\frac{c(2)}{A(2)}\right] \tag{9c}$$

$$p(0) = E^\pi\left[\frac{p(2)}{A(2)}\right] \tag{9d}$$

Substitution of expressions (9a)−(9d) in (8) yields the result

$$B(0,1) - (1 + k)B(0,2) = c(0) - p(0) \tag{10}$$

but the left side of this expression equals

$$\left[\frac{B(0,1)}{B(0,2)} - 1\right]B(0,2) - kB(0,2) = [f(0,1) - k]B(0,2)$$

where $f(0,1)$ is obtained from the definition of forward rate (see expression [23.4]). Substitution yields the final result:

$$[f(0,1) - k]B(0,2) = c(0) - p(0) \tag{11}$$

23.8 | Cases

Spencer Hall (A) (European Case Clearing House Case 9A95B045). The case analyzes issues surrounding the hedging of interest rate risk with instruments like interest rate swaps, caps, and collars.

Spencer Hall (B) (European Case Clearing House Case 9A97N004). An extension of the previous case (Spencer Hall [A]), the case considers issues surrounding the cancellation of an interest rate cap by accepting a premium payment.

Markborough Properties Inc. (Ivey Publishing Case 9A87B002, European Case Clearing House Case). The case examines how a company can hedge its interest rate risk by using derivatives like interest rate swaps and caps.

23.9 | Questions and Problems

23.1. Show that the following tree is not arbitrage-free.

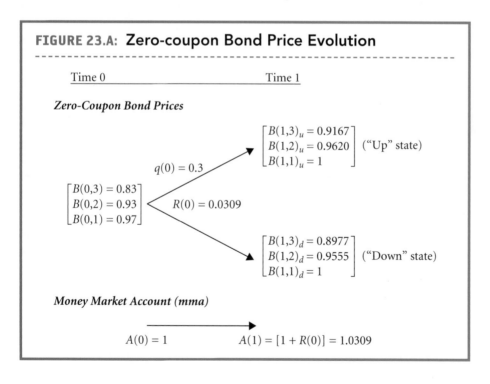

FIGURE 23.A: Zero-coupon Bond Price Evolution

Time 0   Time 1

Zero-Coupon Bond Prices

$$\begin{bmatrix} B(1,3)_u = 0.9167 \\ B(1,2)_u = 0.9620 \\ B(1,1)_u = 1 \end{bmatrix} \text{("Up" state)}$$

$q(0) = 0.3$

$$\begin{bmatrix} B(0,3) = 0.83 \\ B(0,2) = 0.93 \\ B(0,1) = 0.97 \end{bmatrix}$$

$R(0) = 0.0309$

$$\begin{bmatrix} B(1,3)_d = 0.8977 \\ B(1,2)_d = 0.9555 \\ B(1,1)_d = 1 \end{bmatrix} \text{("Down" state)}$$

Money Market Account (mma)

$A(0) = 1$ $A(1) = [1 + R(0)] = 1.0309$

23.2. Compute the forward rate evolution implied by Figure 23.2 (this is identical to the preceding tree with $B[0,3] = 0.88$).

23.3. In the caplet example 23.6, construct the synthetic caplet using the three-period zero and mma (the caplet has a strike rate of $k = 0.04$ or 4 percent). Show that the cost of construction is 0.003, the same as that with the two-period zero-coupon bond.

23.4. In the floorlet example 23.7, value the floorlet using risk-neutral valuation and show you get the same answer as in the text.

23.5. In the caplet example 23.6, suppose the traded caplet has a market price of $0.002. What is a trading strategy that will generate an arbitrage opportunity?

23.6. In the caplet example 23.6, suppose you have a long position in the caplet. Form a hedged portfolio of the caplet and the two-period zero-coupon bond that has no interest rate risk.

23.7. Use Figure 23.2. Consider a European call option on the three-period zero-coupon bond with maturity time 1 and strike price of $k = \$0.90$. Compute the value using risk-neutral valuation.

23.8. Use Figure 23.2. Consider a European put option on the 3-period zero-coupon bond with maturity time 1 and strike price of $k = \$0.90$. Compute the value using risk-neutral valuation.

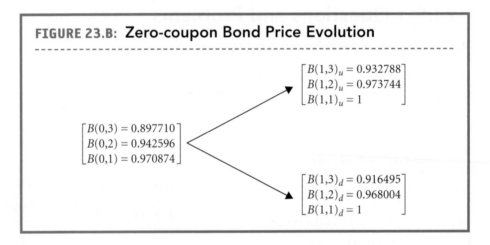

FIGURE 23.B: Zero-coupon Bond Price Evolution

$$\begin{bmatrix} B(0,3) = 0.897710 \\ B(0,2) = 0.942596 \\ B(0,1) = 0.970874 \end{bmatrix}$$

$$\begin{bmatrix} B(1,3)_u = 0.932788 \\ B(1,2)_u = 0.973744 \\ B(1,1)_u = 1 \end{bmatrix}$$

$$\begin{bmatrix} B(1,3)_d = 0.916495 \\ B(1,2)_d = 0.968004 \\ B(1,1)_d = 1 \end{bmatrix}$$

23.9. For the single period evolution in this figure, compute the spot rates at time 0 and at time 1 in both the up and down states. Prove that this tree is arbitrage-free (ignore round errors beyond two decimal places in the computation of the pseudo-probabilities).

23.10. For the single-period evolution in the preceding figure, consider a caplet with maturity time 1 with strike rate $k = 0.03$.

    a. What is the value of this caplet at time 0?

    b. What is the delta for this caplet in terms of the three-period zero-coupon bond?

23.11. For the single-period evolution in the preceding figure, what is the value of a floorlet with maturity time 1 and strike rate 0.03? Compute the value using risk-neutral valuation.

23.12. For the caplets and floorlets in examples 23.10 and 23.11, show that they satisfy caplet-floorlet parity.

23.13. For the single-period evolution given in the preceding figure, consider a European call option with maturity date 1 and strike price $k = \$0.92$ on the three-period zero-coupon bond. What is the arbitrage-free price of this call option?

23.14. For the single-period evolution given in the preceding figure, consider an American call option with maturity 1 and strike price $k = \$0.92$ on the three-period zero-coupon bond. What is the arbitrage-free price of this call option? Is early exercise (at time 0) optimal?

23.15. For the single-period evolution given in the preceding figure, consider a European put option with maturity 1 and strike price $k = \$0.92$ on the three-period zero-coupon bond. What is the arbitrage-free price of this put option?

23.16. For the single-period evolution given in the preceding figure, consider a European put option with maturity date 1 and strike price $k = \$0.94$ on the three-period zero-coupon bond. What is the arbitrage-free price of this put option?

23.17. For the single-period evolution given in the preceding figure, consider an American put option with maturity date 1 and strike price $k = \$0.94$ on the three-period zero-coupon bond. What is the arbitrage-free price of this put option? Is early exercise (at time 0) optimal?

23.18. Why do you think caps and floors trade as portfolios of caplets and floorlets in interest rate markets, whereas in equity markets, calls and puts directly trade?

23.19. Why is it that Eurodollar futures and forward rate agreement rates are not equal?

23.20. When one compares forward rate agreement contracts to Eurodollar futures contracts, which have greater counterparty risk? Do you think this might influence the difference between FRA and futures rates? If yes, why?

24

Multiperiod Binomial HJM Model

24.1 | Introduction

The single-period Heath–Jarrow–Morton (HJM) model is useful as a teaching tool to introduce the economic logic underlying the pricing and hedging methodology. However, even as a teaching tool, the single-period model has its limitations. Many interest rate derivatives need at least two periods to capture their complexity. For example, in a single-period setting, an American call option trivializes to a European call, a futures contract simplifies to a forward, and a swaption sheds its uncertainty and becomes a deterministic security! Therefore, even for pedagogical reasons, one needs to extend the HJM model to a multiperiod setting.

More important, the real limitation of a single-period model is that just as in the binomial option pricing model of chapter 18, the term structure evolution only becomes realistic when the time periods become small and the number of periods becomes large. To obtain a model useful for practice, one must extend the HJM model to a multiperiod setting. The two-period model of this chapter starts us along this path. The multiperiod extension just involves more complicated computations as the number of periods increase, easily done on a computer, once the economic logic of the two-period model is mastered (see Jarrow 2002b).

This chapter presents the multiperiod binomial HJM model. We start with the term structure of interest rate evolution in a two-period setting. Next, the two-period HJM valuation model is presented. The extension to multiple periods and the approximation to the continuous time HJM libor model, the topic of chapter 25, is discussed. Finally, the multiperiod model is applied to the pricing of caplets, floorlets, forward rate agreements (FRAs), Eurodollar futures, and swaption contracts. For ease of presentation, the material parallels the presentation used in the multiperiod binomial model of chapter 18. The next chapter presents a continuous time analogue to the Black–Scholes–Merton model for pricing caplets and floorlets.

24.2 | The Assumptions

We retain assumptions A1–A5, which have been with us since chapter 17, repeated here for convenience:

A1. No market frictions

A2. No credit risk

A3. Competitive and well-functioning markets

A4. No intermediate cash flows

A5. No arbitrage opportunities

We extend assumption A6 to two periods.

A6. Two-period binomial process. The zero-coupon bond prices $B(t,T)$ for $t = 0, 1, 2$ and $T = 1, 2, 3$ trade in discrete time, and their prices evolve according to a binomial process. At each time in the tree, there are two states "up" and "down." First, if the zero-coupon bond matures in the next period, that is, $T = t + 1$, then the current bond price goes to \$1 regardless of the state. Second, standing at time t, the current $T > t + 1$ maturity zero-coupon bond price either gets multiplied by the factor $u(t,T)$ in the up state and takes the price $u(t,T) \times B(t,T)$ with the actual probability $q(t) > 0$ or it is multiplied by the factor $d(t,T)$ in the down state and takes the price $d(t,T) \times B(t,T)$ with probability $1 - q(t)$. We assume that $u(t,T) > d(t,T)$.

Note that the verbal description is almost identical to that in the single-period model. The only difference is in the number of time steps considered. The two-period evolution is given in Figure 24.1. It is the same as the single-period evolution up to time 1 in both the up and down states. The difference occurs after time 1. For this reason, when describing the evolution, we focus only on discussing what happens after the first period.

EXAMPLE 24.1: The Two-Period Term Structure Evolution

Zero-Coupon Bond Prices

- *If we are in the up state at time 1*, then zero-coupon bond prices can go up again, or they can go down. The actual probability of going up is $q(1)_u = 0.2$. The prices of the zeros in the up and down states are identified by the subscripts uu and ud, respectively.
  - Consider the longest-maturity zero-coupon bond. If the up state occurs, then this zero's price is $B(2,3)_{uu} = 0.9555$. If the down state occurs, then the price of this zero is $B(2,3)_{ud} = 0.9504$.
  - Consider the two-period bond. If either state occurs, the bond pays off a dollar. Thus $B(2,2)_{uu} = B(2,2)_{ud} = 1$.

- *If we are in the down state at time 1*, the actual probability of going up is $q(1)_d = 0.6$. The prices of the zeros in the up and down states are identified by the subscripts du and dd, respectively.
  - Consider the three-period zero. If the up state occurs, then this zero's price is $B(2,3)_{du} = 0.9440$. If the down state occurs, then the zero's price is $B(2,3)_{dd} = 0.9349$.
  - Consider the two-period bond. If either state occurs, the bond pays off a dollar. Thus $B(2,2)_{du} = B(2,2)_{dd} = 1$.

- Note that over the time period $(1,2)$, there is one less zero-coupon bond trading in the term structure of zeros. This is because the one-period bond at time 0 matures at time 1 and disappears from the market.

- We note that the binomial tree, unlike that in the binomial model of chapter 17, does not recombine to form a lattice. This is because this example is based on a discrete approximation to the HJM libor model that does not recombine (see the appendix to this chapter).

The lower part of Figure 23.3 gives the formalization of this example using the symbols introduced in assumption A6.

Zero-Coupon Bond Prices

- If we are in the up state at time 1, and if up occurs again, then the three-period bond's price is $u(1,3)_u B(1,3)_u = B(2,3)_{uu}$. If down occurs instead, then the three-period bond's price is $d(1,3)_u B(1,3)_u = B(2,3)_{ud}$. The two-period bond pays \$1 regardless of the state at time 2.

- If we are in the down state at time 1, and if up occurs again, then the three-period bond's price is $u(1,3)_d B(1,3)_d = B(2,3)_{du}$. If down occurs instead, then the three-period bond's price is $d(1,3)_d B(1,3)_d = B(2,3)_{dd}$. The two-period bond pays \$1 regardless of the state at time 2.

The binomial tree in its most general form does not recombine to form a lattice. It could be designed to do so. Subcases of the HJM model where the tree recombines to form a lattice include the Ho and Lee (1986) and Vasicek (1977) models.

The Spot Rate

- If we are in the up state at time 1, then the spot rate is

$$R(1)_u = [1 - B(1,2)_u]/B(1,2)_u$$
$$= (1 - 0.9620)/0.9620 = 0.0395 \text{ or } 3.95 \text{ percent} \qquad (24.1a)$$

- If we are in the down state at time 1, then the spot rate is

$$R(1)_d = [1 - B(1,2)_d]/B(1,2)_d$$
$$= (1 - 0.9555)/0.9555 = 0.0465 \text{ or } 4.65 \text{ percent} \qquad (24.1b)$$

The Money Market Account

- The money market account (mma) earns the spot rate each period:

$$A(2) = [1 + R(0)] \times \begin{cases} 1 + R(1)_u & \text{if up} \\ 1 + R(1)_d & \text{if down} \end{cases}$$

$$= \begin{cases} 1.0717 & \text{if up} \\ 1.0788 & \text{if down} \end{cases} \qquad (24.2)$$

At this point, it is easy to understand how to extend the two-period model to three or more periods. Starting at time 0, the number of zero-coupon bonds trading at each node should exceed the number of periods in the model by at least one. Then, one just adds more time steps. At each time step, the shortest-maturity bond matures, pays \$1, and then disappears from the tree. Otherwise, the tree's structure is no different than the two-period evolution.

FIGURE 24.1: Two-Period HJM Evolution

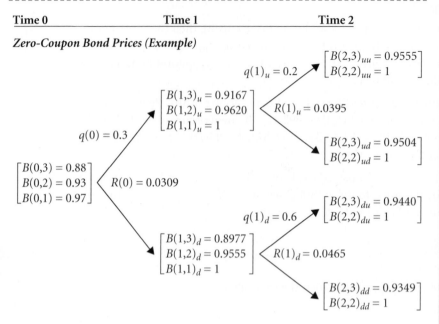

Zero-Coupon Bond Prices (Example)

Time 0	Time 1	Time 2

$q(1)_u = 0.2$

$\begin{bmatrix} B(2,3)_{uu} = 0.9555 \\ B(2,2)_{uu} = 1 \end{bmatrix}$

$\begin{bmatrix} B(1,3)_u = 0.9167 \\ B(1,2)_u = 0.9620 \\ B(1,1)_u = 1 \end{bmatrix}$ $R(1)_u = 0.0395$

$\begin{bmatrix} B(2,3)_{ud} = 0.9504 \\ B(2,2)_{ud} = 1 \end{bmatrix}$

$q(0) = 0.3$

$\begin{bmatrix} B(0,3) = 0.88 \\ B(0,2) = 0.93 \\ B(0,1) = 0.97 \end{bmatrix}$ $R(0) = 0.0309$

$q(1)_d = 0.6$

$\begin{bmatrix} B(2,3)_{du} = 0.9440 \\ B(2,2)_{du} = 1 \end{bmatrix}$

$\begin{bmatrix} B(1,3)_d = 0.8977 \\ B(1,2)_d = 0.9555 \\ B(1,1)_d = 1 \end{bmatrix}$ $R(1)_d = 0.0465$

$\begin{bmatrix} B(2,3)_{dd} = 0.9349 \\ B(2,2)_{dd} = 1 \end{bmatrix}$

Zero-Coupon Bond Prices (Symbols)

Time 0	Time 1	Time 2

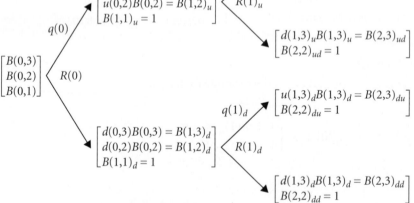

$q(1)_u$

$\begin{bmatrix} u(1,3)_u B(1,3)_u = B(2,3)_{uu} \\ B(2,2)_{uu} = 1 \end{bmatrix}$

$\begin{bmatrix} u(0,3)B(0,3) = B(1,3)_u \\ u(0,2)B(0,2) = B(1,2)_u \\ B(1,1)_u = 1 \end{bmatrix}$ $R(1)_u$

$\begin{bmatrix} d(1,3)_u B(1,3)_u = B(2,3)_{ud} \\ B(2,2)_{ud} = 1 \end{bmatrix}$

$q(0)$

$\begin{bmatrix} B(0,3) \\ B(0,2) \\ B(0,1) \end{bmatrix}$ $R(0)$

$q(1)_d$

$\begin{bmatrix} u(1,3)_d B(1,3)_d = B(2,3)_{du} \\ B(2,2)_{du} = 1 \end{bmatrix}$

$\begin{bmatrix} d(0,3)B(0,3) = B(1,3)_d \\ d(0,2)B(0,2) = B(1,2)_d \\ B(1,1)_d = 1 \end{bmatrix}$ $R(1)_d$

$\begin{bmatrix} d(1,3)_d B(1,3)_d = B(2,3)_{dd} \\ B(2,2)_{dd} = 1 \end{bmatrix}$

Time 0	Time 1	Time 2

Money Market Account (mma)

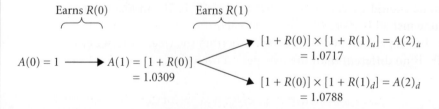

Earns $R(0)$ Earns $R(1)$

$[1 + R(0)] \times [1 + R(1)_u] = A(2)_u$
$= 1.0717$

$A(0) = 1 \longrightarrow A(1) = [1 + R(0)]$
$= 1.0309$

$[1 + R(0)] \times [1 + R(1)_d] = A(2)_d$
$= 1.0788$

24.3 | The Two-Period Model

The two-period binomial HJM model is analogous to the single-period model, once one employs the backward induction argument used in the multiperiod binomial option pricing model of chapter 18. The term structure evolution for the two-period economy is given in Figure 24.1 and was previously described.

Let us introduce some simplifying notation. At time 2, we see there are four states possible corresponding to the branches (up, up), (up, down), (down, up), and (down, down). We write the prices at time 2 as $B(2, T)_{su}$ and $B(2, T)_{sd}$, where $s \in \{u, d\}$ (which is a compact way of writing that s takes on either the value u or d) and $T = 2$, 3. For example, if $s = d$ and $T = 3$, then the first expression takes the value $B(2,3)_{du}$. This is the time 2 price of a three-period zero-coupon bond at the node reached by going down at time 1 and then up at time 2. Figure 24.1 shows that this zero has a price of 0.9440. Notice that the time paths are read from left to right: in du, the letter d denotes that the first movement is down, and the next letter u denotes that the second movement is up.

Arbitrage-Free Evolutions

Just as in the single-period model, we need to determine necessary and sufficient conditions for the two-period binomial tree to be arbitrage-free.

NECESSARY AND SUFFICIENT CONDITIONS It is clear that if the tree is arbitrage-free, then at each node and time, the single-period evolution at that node must be arbitrage-free. Thus Result 23.1 must hold at every node in the tree—and it turns out that if Result 23.1 holds at every node in the tree, then the tree is arbitrage-free. The proof of this last statement is identical to the sufficiency proof for Result 23.1 in chapter 23 and is therefore omitted. Consequently, we have obtained the following result.

RESULT 24.1

Equal Pseudo-Probability Condition

The two-period zero-coupon bond price evolution is arbitrage-free if and only if there exists real numbers $\pi(0)$, $\pi(1)_u$, $\pi(1)_d$ strictly between 0 and 1 such that the pseudo-probabilities at any node must be identical, that is,

$$\pi(0) = \pi(0,T) \text{ for } T = 2, 3 \tag{24.3a}$$

$$\pi(1)_s = \pi(1,3)_s \text{ for } s \in \{u,d\} \tag{24.3b}$$

where $\pi(0,T) = [1 + R(0) - d(0,T)] / [u(0,T) - d(0,T)]$; $\pi(1,3)_s = [1 + R(1)_s - d(1,3)_s] / [u(1,3)_s - d(1,3)_s]$; $R(0)$ and $R(1)_s$ are the time 0 and time 1 spot rates, respectively; and $u(0,T), d(0,T), u(1,3)_s, d(1,3)_s$ are the dollar returns on the zero-coupon bond in the up and down states at times 0 and 1, respectively.

In this characterization result, the no-arbitrage condition at time 0 is the same as in the single-period model. Note that at time 2, the last period in the tree, there is only one pseudo-probability. This is because there is only one risky zero-coupon bond trading over the last time step. Hence, over the last time step, the no-arbitrage condition is the same as in chapter 17. The pseudo-probability just needs to be strictly between zero and one.

When considering models with more than two time steps, both of these observations will always be true. First, for every time step except the last, there will be multiple pseudo-probabilities, all of which must be equal and strictly between zero and one for these nodes to be arbitrage-free. Second, over the last time step, there is only one pseudo-probability that must be strictly between zero and one.

The next example shows that this arbitrage-free condition is satisfied by the two-period binomial evolution in Figure 24.1.

EXAMPLE 24.2: An Arbitrage-Free Two-Period Binomial Tree

This example verifies that the term structure evolution in Figure 24.1 is arbitrage-free.

- First, we have already checked the node at time 0 in Example 23.4 and verified that it is arbitrage-free. Hence we only need to check the two nodes at time 1 in the up and down states. We need to compute the up and down returns on the three-period zero-coupon bond for all possible states at time 1. These are as follows:

$$u(1,3)_u = B(2,3)_{uu}/B(1,3)_u = 0.9555/0.9167 = 1.0423$$
$$d(1,3)_u = B(2,3)_{ud}/B(1,3)_u = 0.9504/0.9167 = 1.0367$$
$$u(1,3)_d = B(2,3)_{du}/B(1,3)_d = 0.9440/0.8977 = 1.0516$$
$$d(1,3)_d = B(2,3)_{dd}/B(1,3)_d = 0.9349/0.8977 = 1.0415$$

- Then, using expression (24.3), we compute the pseudo-probabilities:

$$\pi(1,3)_u = \left(\frac{1 + R(1)_u - d(1,3)_u}{u(1,3)_u - d(1,3)_u} \right) = \left(\frac{1.0396 - 1.0367}{1.0423 - 1.0367} \right) = 0.5$$

$$\pi(1,3)_d = \left(\frac{1 + R(1)_d - d(1,3)_d}{u(1,3)_d - d(1,3)_d} \right) = \left(\frac{1.0465 - 1.0415}{1.0516 - 1.0415} \right) = 0.5$$

Since this is the last time step and each of these pseudo-probabilities is between zero and one, the tree is arbitrage-free. We denote the value of these pseudo-probabilities as $\pi(1)_u$ and $\pi(1)_d$ in the up and down states, respectively.

Zero-Coupon Bond Prices and Martingales

Assuming that each node in the tree is arbitrage-free, just as in the single-period model, we can show that the zero-coupon bond prices must equal their expected discounted $1 payoff, using the pseudo-probabilities. To do this, we use backward induction.

Standing at time 1 in state $s \in \{u,d\}$, because the node is arbitrage-free, by definition of $\pi(1)_s$, algebra yields

$$B(1,T)_s = \frac{\pi(1)_s B(2,T)_{su} + \left[1 - \pi(1)_s\right] B(2,T)_{sd}}{1 + R(1)_s} \text{ for } T = 2, 3 \quad (24.4a)$$

or, more abstractly,

$$B(1,T)_s = \frac{E^\pi[B(2,T)]}{1 + R(1)_s} \text{ for } T = 2, 3 \quad (24.4b)$$

This is analogous to the single-period model, but viewed from time 1 in state s.

Next, stepping back to time 0, the logic used for the one-period model shows that

$$B(0,T) = \frac{\pi(0)B(1,T)_u + \left[1 - \pi(0)\right]B(1,T)_d}{1 + R(0)} \text{ for } T = 2, 3 \quad (24.5a)$$

Substitution of expression (24.4a) into this expression and algebra yields

$$B(0,T) = \pi(0)\pi(1)_u \frac{B(2,T)_{uu}}{\left[1 + R(0)\right]\left[1 + R(1)_u\right]}$$

$$+ \pi(0)\left[1 - \pi(1)_u\right] \frac{B(2,T)_{ud}}{\left[1 + R(0)\right]\left[1 + R(1)_u\right]}$$

$$+ \left[1 - \pi(0)\right]\pi(1)_u \frac{B(2,T)_{du}}{\left[1 + R(0)\right]\left[1 + R(1)_d\right]}$$

$$+ \left[1 - \pi(0)\right]\left[1 - \pi(1)_u\right] \frac{B(2,T)_{dd}}{\left[1 + R(0)\right]\left[1 + R(1)_d\right]} \quad (24.5b)$$

or, more abstractly, we get our final result.

RESULT 24.2

- -

Risk-Neutral Valuation for Zero-Coupon Bond Prices

The time 0 value of the zero-coupon bonds can be written as

$$B(0,2) = E^\pi\left(\frac{1}{\left[1 + R(0)\right]\left[1 + R(1)\right]}\right) \quad (24.6a)$$

and

$$B(0,3) = E^\pi\left(\frac{B(2,3)}{\left[1 + R(0)\right]\left[1 + R(1)\right]}\right) \quad (24.6b)$$

where $E^\pi(\cdot)$ denotes expectation using the pseudo-probabilities $[\pi(0),$ $\pi(1,s)]$; $R(0)$ and $R(1)$ are the time 0 and 1 spot rates, respectively; and $B(2,3)$ is the three-period zero-coupon bond's price at time 2.

These two expressions show that the zero-coupon bond's price is its expected discounted $1 payoff using the pseudo-probabilities.

Result 24.2 proves that the *local expectations hypothesis*, introduced in chapter 21 (see Extension 21.2), holds under the pseudo-probabilities and not the actual probabilities. The local expectations hypothesis states that all zero-coupon bonds earn the same expected return over any time period. Essentially, all zero-coupon bonds are equally risky. We see that the local expectations hypothesis is true under the pseudo-probabilities, and as seen later, because the pseudo-probabilities differ from the actual probabilities via a risk adjustment, the local expectations hypothesis cannot hold under the actual probabilities.

Last we note that the denominators in expressions (24.6a) and (24.6b) correspond to the time 2 value of the mma $A(2)$. As such, this immediately implies that the price of a zero-coupon bond normalized by the price of the mma, $B(t,T)/A(t)$, is a martingale under the pseudo-probabilities, generalizing the same result proven in the single-period model. The next example applies risk-neutral valuation to zero-coupon bonds.

EXAMPLE 24.3: Risk-Neutral Valuation for Zero-Coupon Bonds

Using the two-period evolution given in Figure 24.1, we can check to see if the risk-neutral valuation formula holds for the zero-coupon bonds maturing at time 2. The formula is

$$\pi(0)\pi(1)_u \frac{B(2,2)_{uu}}{[1 + R(0)][1 + R(1)_u]} + \pi(0)[1 - \pi(1)_u]\frac{B(2,2)_{ud}}{[1 + R(0)][1 + R(1)_u]}$$

$$+ [1 - \pi(0)]\pi(1)_u \frac{B(2,2)_{du}}{[1 + R(0)][1 + R(1)_d]}$$

$$+ [1 - \pi(0)][1 - \pi(1)_u]\frac{B(2,2)_{dd}}{[1 + R(0)][1 + R(1)_d]}$$

$$= 0.25\frac{1}{[1.0309][1.0396]} + 0.25\frac{1}{[1.0309][1.0396]}$$

$$+ 0.25\frac{1}{[1.0309][1.0465]} + 0.25\frac{1}{[1.0309][1.0465]}$$

$$= 0.97 = B(0,2)$$

validating the result in the two-period example. As shown, the price of the three-period zero is equal to its value in the four states at time 2 multiplied by the pseudo-probability of each state occurring and discounted to time 0 using the spot rates of interest. This is expression (24.6b) written out in longhand.

Caplet Pricing

We are now ready to price a caplet in this two-period economy. Although they are not shown on the two-period tree, the spot rate at time 2 in each state can be computed as

$$R(2)_{us} = \frac{1 - B(2,3)_{us}}{B(2,3)_{us}} \tag{24.7a}$$

and

$$R(2)_{ds} = \frac{1 - B(2,3)_{ds}}{B(2,3)_{ds}} \text{ for } s \in \{u,d\} \tag{24.7b}$$

Consider a caplet maturing at time 3 with strike rate k. The caplet's time 3 payoff is $c(3) = \max[0, \ R(2) - k]$. This value is known at time 2, hence the time 2 present value of this payoff is

$$c(2) = \max\left[0, \ \frac{R(2) - k}{1 + R(2)}\right] \tag{24.8}$$

Using the convention introduced in the previous chapter, for valuation purposes, we will consider the caplet's maturity as time 2. These are the payoffs used in the tree to compute the time 0 value of this caplet.

BACKWARD INDUCTION Let us recall the (fictional) super sleuth Sherlock Holmes, who popularized the method of backward induction: start at the end, work backward through time, eventually solving the problem at the beginning. To price the caplet using this method of backward induction, we pretend we are standing at time 1 and value the caplet at that time. Then, having the time 1 values, we move back to time 0 and value the caplet at that date, which gives our answer.

METHOD 1: CONSTRUCTION OF THE SYNTHETIC CAPLET AT TIME 1 Standing at time 1 at state $s \in \{u,d\}$, we want to construct the portfolio of the three-period zero and mma account such that the payoffs to the portfolio match the payoffs to the traded caplet. The method is identical to that used in the one-period model, except the notation is now different. We choose n shares of the three-period zero and m shares of the mma with cost

$$V(1)_s = mB(1,3)_s + n A(1)$$

such that at time 1,

in the up state: $V(2)_{su} = mu(1,3)_s B(1,3)_s + nA(1)[1 + R(1)_s] = c(2)_{su} \tag{24.9a}$

in the down state: $V(2)_{sd} = md(1,3)_s B(1,3)_s + nA(1)[1 + R(1)_s] = c(2)_{sd} \tag{24.9b}$

Solving for m and n yields

$$m = \frac{c(2)_{su} - c(2)_{sd}}{\left[u(1,3)_s - d(1,3)_s\right]B(1,3)_s} \tag{24.10a}$$

$$n = \frac{u(1,3)_s c(2)_{sd} - d(1,3)_s c(2)_{su}}{\left[u(1,3)_s - d(1,3)_s\right]A(1)\left[1 + R(1)_s\right]} \tag{24.10b}$$

Substitution of m and n into the cost of construction and simplification gives the arbitrage-free price of the caplet:

$$c(1)_s = mB(1,3)_s + nA(1)$$

$$= \frac{c(2)_{su} - c(2)_{sd}}{\left[u(1,3)_s - d(1,3)_s\right]B(0,2)} B(0,2) + \frac{u(1,3)_s c(2)_{sd} - d(1,3)_s c(2)_{su}}{\left[u(1,3)_s - d(1,3)_s\right]\left[1 + R(1)_s\right]}$$

$$\tag{24.11a}$$

METHOD 2: RISK-NEUTRAL VALUATION AT TIME 1   Using the arbitrage-free condition and the pseudo-probabilities, algebra yields

$$c(1)_s = \frac{\pi(1)_s c(2)_{su} + \left[1 - \pi(1)_s\right]c(2)_{sd}}{1 + R(1)_s} \tag{24.11b}$$

or, more abstractly,

$$c(1)_s = \frac{E^\pi[c(2)]}{1 + R(1)_s} \tag{24.11c}$$

We note again that this is the same method we used in the single-period model, except the time and state notation has changed. This gives a present value formula. The caplet's time 1 value is its discounted expected payoff at time 2 using the pseudo-probabilities.

PRICING THE CAPLET AT TIME 0   Having priced the caplet at time 1 in both the up and down states, we now move back to time 0 to price the caplet. Note that this is the same problem solved in the single-period model, except that we replace the previous payoffs with expression (24.11c). The arbitrage-free price of the caplet is therefore

$$c(0) = \frac{\pi(0)c(1)_u + \left[1 - \pi(0)\right]c(1)_d}{1 + R(0)} \tag{24.12a}$$

Substitution of the caplet's time 1 values from expression (24.11b) and algebra yields

$$c(0) = \pi(0)\pi(1)_u \frac{c(2)_{uu}}{[1 + R(0)][1 + R(1)_u]}$$

$$+ \pi(0)[1 - \pi(1)_u] \frac{c(2)_{ud}}{[1 + R(0)][1 + R(1)_u]}$$

$$+ [1 - \pi(0)]\pi(1)_u \frac{c(2)_{du}}{[1 + R(0)][1 + R(1)_d]}$$

$$+ [1 - \pi(0)][1 - \pi(1)_u] \frac{c(2)_{dd}}{[1 + R(0)][1 + R(1)_d]}$$

(24.12b)

Using more abstract notation, we can alternatively write this as our next result.

RESULT 24.3

Risk-Neutral Valuation Formula for a Caplet

A caplet with strike rate k and maturity date 2 is given by

$$c(0) = E^\pi \left(\frac{c(2)}{[1 + R(0)][1 + R(1)]} \right) \qquad (24.13)$$

where $E^\pi(.)$ denotes expectation using the pseudo-probabilities $[\pi(0), \pi(1,s)]$; $R(0)$ and $R(1)$ are the time 0 and 1 spot rates, respectively; and $c(2)$ is the caplet's value at time 2.

Expression (24.13) illustrates risk-neutral valuation for pricing a caplet, and it gives a present value formula! Today's price is the expected discounted value of the caplet's time 2 payoff, where the expectation uses the pseudo-probabilities. The pseudo-probabilities adjust for risk, consequently discounting is with the riskless spot rate of interest. For the purposes of computing the arbitrage-free price of a caplet, expression (24.13) is easy to use, as illustrated in the next example.

EXAMPLE 24.4: Pricing a Caplet

This example uses the risk-neutral valuation method to price a caplet with maturity time 2, strike rate $k = 0.05$, and notional of \$1.

- First, we need to compute the caplet's payoffs at time 2 in all states. To do this, we must first compute the spot rate of interest at time 2 in all states. Using Figure 24.1, we get

$$R(2)_{uu} = \frac{1 - B(2,3)_{uu}}{B(2,3)_{uu}} = \frac{1 - 0.9555}{0.9555} = 0.0465$$

$$R(2)_{ud} = \frac{1 - B(2,3)_{ud}}{B(2,3)_{ud}} = \frac{1 - 0.9504}{0.9504} = 0.0522$$

$$R(2)_{du} = \frac{1 - B(2,3)_{du}}{B(2,3)_{du}} = \frac{1 - 0.9440}{0.9440} = 0.0593$$

$$R(2)_{dd} = \frac{1 - B(2,3)_{dd}}{B(2,3)_{dd}} = \frac{1 - 0.9349}{0.9349} = 0.0696$$

- The caplet's payoffs at time 2 are

$$c(2)_{uu} = \max\left[0, \frac{R(2)_{uu} - k}{1 + R(2)_{uu}}\right] = \max\left[0, \frac{0.0465 - 0.05}{1.0465}\right] = 0$$

$$c(2)_{ud} = \max\left[0, \frac{R(2)_{ud} - k}{1 + R(2)_{ud}}\right] = \max\left[0, \frac{0.0522 - 0.05}{1.0522}\right] = 0.0021$$

$$c(2)_{du} = \max\left[0, \frac{R(2)_{du} - k}{1 + R(2)_{du}}\right] = \max\left[0, \frac{0.0593 - 0.05}{1.0593}\right] = 0.0088$$

$$c(2)_{dd} = \max\left[0, \frac{R(2)_{dd} - k}{1 + R(2)_{dd}}\right] = \max\left[0, \frac{0.0696 - 0.05}{1.0696}\right] = 0.0183$$

These payoffs are illustrated in Figure 24.2.

- Finally, using the risk-neutral valuation formula, the caplet's time 0 value is

$$c(0) = \pi(0)\pi(1)_u \frac{c(2)_{uu}}{[1 + R(0)][1 + R(1)_u]}$$

$$+ \pi(0)[1 - \pi(1)_u] \frac{c(2)_{ud}}{[1 + R(0)][1 + R(1)_u]}$$

$$+ \left[1 - \pi(0)\right]\pi(1)_u \frac{c(2)_{du}}{\left[1 + R(0)\right]\left[1 + R(1)_d\right]}$$

$$+ \left[1 - \pi(0)\right]\left[1 - \pi(1)_u\right] \frac{c(2)_{dd}}{\left[1 + R(0)\right]\left[1 + R(1)_d\right]}$$

$$= 0.25 \frac{0}{\left[1.0309\right]\left[1.0396\right]} + 0.25 \frac{0.0021}{\left[1.0309\right]\left[1.0396\right]}$$

$$+ 0.25 \frac{0.0088}{\left[1.0309\right]\left[1.0465\right]} + 0.25 \frac{0.0183}{\left[1.0309\right]\left[1.0465\right]}$$

$$= 0.0068$$

Floorlet Pricing

The same method can be applied to price a floorlet. The arbitrage-free valuation formula will be expression (24.13), with the payoff of the floorlet replacing that of the caplet. Alternatively, given the price of the caplet, one can use caplet–floorlet parity to value the caplet. The next result gives caplet–floorlet parity in the two-period setting.

RESULT 24.4

Caplet–Floorlet Parity

$$[f(0, t-1) - k]B(0, t) = c(0) - p(0) \qquad (24.14)$$

where $f(0, t-1)$ is the time 0 forward rate for date $t-1$, $B(0, t)$ is the time 0 zero-coupon bond price with maturity at time t, and both the caplet with time 0 price $c(0)$ and the floorlet with time 0 price $p(0)$ have strike rate k and maturity date $t-1$ for $t = 2, 3$.

The proof is identical to that of the single-period model and is therefore omitted (see the appendix to chapter 23). The next example shows how to price a floorlet using caplet–floorlet parity.

FIGURE 24.2: Caplet Evolution

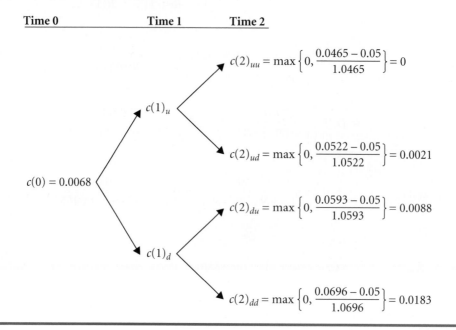

$$c(2)_{uu} = \max\left\{0, \frac{0.0465 - 0.05}{1.0465}\right\} = 0$$

$$c(2)_{ud} = \max\left\{0, \frac{0.0522 - 0.05}{1.0522}\right\} = 0.0021$$

$$c(2)_{du} = \max\left\{0, \frac{0.0593 - 0.05}{1.0593}\right\} = 0.0088$$

$$c(2)_{dd} = \max\left\{0, \frac{0.0696 - 0.05}{1.0696}\right\} = 0.0183$$

Time 0   Time 1   Time 2

$c(1)_u$

$c(0) = 0.0068$

$c(1)_d$

EXAMPLE 24.5: Valuing a Floorlet

- Consider a floorlet that has strike rate $k = 0.05$ and maturity time 2. Its time 3 payoff is

$$p(3) = \max[k - R(2), 0]$$

- The floorlet is a put option on the spot rate of interest. Note that the floorlet's payoff at time 3 is based on the spot rate at time 2. Because this payoff is known at time 2, the present value of this payoff at time 2 is obtained by discounting by the spot rate. For valuation purposes, this is the floorlet's maturity date.

$$p(2) = \frac{\max\left[k - R(2), 0\right]}{1 + R(2)}$$

- Let the term structure evolution be as in Figure 24.1. Consider a caplet with the same maturity and the same strike price as the floorlet's. We determined the time 0 price of this caplet as $c(0) = \$0.0068$ in Example 24.5.

- The forward rate at time 0 for date 2 is

$$f(0,2) = \frac{B(0,2)}{B(0,3)} - 1 = \frac{0.93}{0.88} - 1 = 0.0568$$

Hence, using caplet–floorlet parity (see expression [24.14]), we have that

$$p(0) = c(0) - [f(0,2) - k]B(0,3)$$
$$= 0.0068 - (0.0568 - 0.05)0.88 = 0.0008$$

The floorlet has a value of $0.0008 at time 0 on a notional of $1.

Valuing Various Interest Rate Derivatives

The same approach used for pricing a caplet can be used to price any interest rate derivative. The only modification is to replace the payoffs of the caplet with those of the interest rate derivatives under consideration. For American-type interest rate derivatives, just as in chapter 18, in the backward induction argument, one needs to make a decision regarding early exercise or not at each node of the tree. Otherwise, the procedure is identical to that illustrated earlier.

Multiple Factors

The extension to multiple factors in the two-period model is the same as in the single-period model. For example, a two-factor model has three branches at each node in the tree. The pricing methodology extends easily, see Jarrow (2002b) in this regard.

24.4 | The Multiperiod Model

The extension of the binomial HJM model to more than two time periods is computationally demanding but straightforward in terms of the ideas and concepts. When building the tree, more zero-coupon bonds are needed in the term structure as the time horizon in the model grows. There should be at least one more zero-coupon bond in the term structure than there are periods in the model. Except for the extended size of the bond price vectors at each node, the analysis is identical to that already presented. As the time progresses in the tree, one zero-coupon bond matures and leaves the term structure. When valuing interest rate derivatives, just as in the two-period model, backward induction is used. All of the previous results hold in a T-period model (see Jarrow [2002b] for more on this topic).

The multiperiod binomial HJM model can be used to approximate a continuous time HJM model by making the time steps small in size. The link between the multiperiod binomial HJM model and the HJM libor model discussed in the next chapter is provided in the appendix to this chapter. The appendix shows how to choose the up and down factors in the zero-coupon bond price evolution so that the implied simple forward rates have a lognormal distribution in the limit.

24.5 | Forwards, Futures, and Swaptions

Let us revisit FRAs, Eurodollar futures, and swaptions in the context of the two-period binomial model, although the results hold more generally in a multiperiod setting. As noted in the introduction to this chapter, the complexities of these contracts are only evidenced in multiperiod models.

Forward Rate Agreements

We previously discussed FRAs in chapter 21. Recall that in our discrete time model, the FRA payoff at time T can be written as

$$L_N \times [R(T-1) - f_{FRA}(0, T-1)] \qquad (24.15)$$

where L_N is the notional value of the contract and $f_{FRA}(0, T-1)$ is the time 0 FRA rate for time $T-1$. The payment on the FRA occurs one period after the uncertainty in the contract's payoff is determined.

Consider an FRA with maturity date 3 on a notional value of $1. Using the previous expression, we have that the FRA's time 3 payoff is

$$R(2) - f_{FRA}(0,2) \qquad (24.16)$$

A long position in the FRA receives at time 3 the difference between the spot rate and the agreed-on FRA rate $f_{FRA}(0,2)$. At time 0, the market-clearing FRA rate is determined such that the value of the FRA is zero. It was shown in chapter 21 that this market-clearing condition implies that the FRA rate is equal to the forward rate, that is,

$$f_{FRA}(0,2) = f(0,2) = \frac{B(0,2)}{B(0,3)} - 1 \qquad (24.17)$$

The forward rates at time 0 are easily computed from the zero-coupon bond prices at time zero in the two-period evolution of Figure 24.1:

$$\begin{bmatrix} f(0,2) = 0.0568 \\ f(0,1) = 0.0430 \\ f(0,0) = 0.0309 \end{bmatrix}$$

Eurodollar Futures

We previously discussed Eurodollar futures contracts in chapter 21 as well. Recall that in our discrete time model, a futures contract with delivery date T on a notional value of L_N has a futures price equal to

$$\mathcal{F}(t) = L_N \times \left[1 - i_{fut}(t)\right] \text{ at time } t \qquad (24.18a)$$

and

$$\mathcal{F}(T) = L_N \times \left[1 - R(T)\right] \text{ at time } T \qquad (24.18b)$$

where $i_{fut}(t)$ is the time t futures rate.

The cash flows over the life of the futures contract are determined by marking-to-market. We have that the cash flows at times $t = 1, 2, 3, \ldots$ are

$$\left[\mathcal{F}(t) - \mathcal{F}(t - 1)\right] = -L_N \times \left[i_{fut}(t) - i_{fut}(t - 1)\right] \quad (24.18c)$$

Consider a Eurodollar futures contract with maturity 2 on a notional value of $1. We can easily determine the arbitrage-free futures price in our two-period HJM model.

ARBITRAGE-FREE FUTURES PRICES We use backward induction in conjunction with the risk-neutral valuation formula to determine the arbitrage-free futures prices.

Standing at time 1, using the risk-neutral valuation formula, the value of the futures contract is

$$V(1) = \frac{E^\pi\left[\mathcal{F}(2) - \mathcal{F}(1)\right]}{1 + R(1)}$$

The time 1 futures price $\mathcal{F}(1)$ is set such that the contract has zero value. This implies that

$$0 = \frac{E^\pi\left[\mathcal{F}(2) - \mathcal{F}(1)\right]}{1 + R(1)}$$

Some simple algebra yields the result

$$\mathcal{F}(1) = E^\pi\left[\mathcal{F}(2)\right] \qquad (24.19)$$

The time 1 futures price is seen to be equal to the expected time 2 futures price, where the expectation is computed using the pseudo-probabilities.

Last, moving back to time 0, again using the risk-neutral valuation formula, the value of the futures contract is

$$V(0) = \frac{E^\pi[\mathcal{F}(1) - \mathcal{F}(0)]}{1 + R(0)}$$

As before, the time 0 futures price $\mathcal{F}(0)$ is set such that the contract has zero value. This implies that

$$0 = \frac{E^\pi[\mathcal{F}(1) - \mathcal{F}(0)]}{1 + R(0)}$$

or, equivalently,

$$\mathcal{F}(0) = E^\pi[\mathcal{F}(1)] \tag{24.20}$$

Similarly, the time 0 futures price is equal to the expected time 1 futures price under the pseudo-probabilities. Expressions (24.19) and (24.20) prove the fact that futures prices are a martingale under the pseudo-probabilities.

ARBITRAGE-FREE FUTURES RATES We can now determine the arbitrage-free futures interest rates using expressions (24.18a) and (24.18b). Substitution of these expressions into the arbitrage-free futures prices gives

$$1 - i_{fut}(1) = E^\pi[1 - R(2)] \text{ and } 1 - i_{fut}(0) = E^\pi[1 - i_{fut}(1)] \text{ or}$$

$$i_{fut}(1) = E^\pi[R(2)] \text{ and } i_{fut}(0) = E^\pi[i_{fut}(1)] \tag{24.21}$$

The futures rates are also seen to be martingales under the pseudo-probabilities.

One last computation gives us our final result. Using the notation of Figure 24.1, we can write expression (24.21) as

$$i_{fut}(1) = \pi(1)_s R(2)_{su} + [1 - \pi(1)_s] R(2)_{sd} \tag{24.22a}$$

for $s \in \{u, d\}$. Then, substitution of this expression into (24.21) gives

$$i_{fut}(0) = \pi(0) \{\pi(1)_u R(2)_{uu} + [1 - \pi(1)_u] R(2)_{ud}\}$$

$$+ [1 - \pi(0)] \{\pi(1)_d R(2)_{du} + [1 - \pi(1)_d] R(2)_{dd}\} \tag{24.22b}$$

Writing this expression more abstractly yields the following result.

RESULT 24.5

- -

Eurodollar Futures Rates

Consider a Eurodollar futures contract with maturity date 2 on a notional value of $1. The market clearing futures rate is

$$i_{fut}(0) = E^\pi[R(2)] \qquad (24.23)$$

where $E^\pi[\,\cdot\,]$ denotes expectation using the pseudo-probabilities $[\pi(0), \pi(1,s)]$ and $R(2)$ is the spot rate at time 2.

As evidenced by this result, the futures interest rate is the expected futures spot rate using the pseudo-probabilities. In contrast to common belief, the futures rate is not the expected future spot rate using the *actual probabilities*. Because the pseudo- and actual probabilities differ by a risk adjustment, we see that Eurodollar futures rates reflect both risk premia and the actual probabilities, generating a biased estimate of the future spot rate of interest.

Comparing Forward and Futures Rates

We can now compare the forward and futures interest rates. Using the definition of the spot rate $R(2)$, we can rewrite expression (24.23) as

$$i_{fut}(0) = E^\pi\left(\frac{1}{B(2,3)}\right) - 1 \qquad (24.24)$$

but

$$E^\pi\left(\frac{1}{B(2,3)}\right) = E^\pi\left(\frac{\frac{1}{A(2)}}{\frac{B(2,3)}{A(2)}}\right) > \frac{E^\pi\left(\frac{1}{A(2)}\right)}{E^\pi\left(\frac{B(2,3)}{A(2)}\right)} = \frac{B(0,2)}{B(0,3)} = 1 + f(0,2)$$

The first strict inequality is due to a well-known result in probability called *Jensen's inequality* (given a random variable x, $E[1/x] > 1/E[x]$). The second to last equality uses the risk-neutral valuation formulas for the zero-coupon bonds. The last equality is just the definition of the forward rate. Substitution of this insight into expression (24.24) shows that

$$i_{fut}(0) > f(0,2) \tag{24.25}$$

The futures rate is strictly greater than the forward rate. Both contracts are betting on the future spot rate of interest $R(2)$. However, interest rate futures contracts have marking-to-market, whereas FRAs do not. This implies that futures contracts have cash flow reinvestment risk that FRAs do not. Hence, to induce a speculator to enter a futures contract at zero value, a rate higher than the FRA rate needs to be included. This reinvestment risk difference between the two contracts is the cause of the inequality in expression (24.25). As stated many times before, futures and forward contracts are fraternal, not identical, twins! The next example illustrates the determination of eurodollar futures rates.

EXAMPLE 24.6: Eurodollar Futures Rates

■ This example computes the time 0 futures rates for a Eurodollar futures contract maturing at time 2 using the term structure evolution in Figure 24.1. Example 24.4 already computed the spot rates at time 2, which are: $R(2)_{uu} = 0.0465$, $R(2)_{ud} = 0.0522$, $R(2)_{du} = 0.0593$, and $R(2)_{dd} = 0.0696$. Then,

$$i_{fut}(0) = E^{\pi}[R(2)] = 0.25(0.0465 + 0.0522 + 0.0593 + 0.0696)$$
$$= 0.0569$$

■ For comparison, the time 0 forward rate for time 2 is

$$f_{FRA}(0,2) = f(0,2) = \frac{B(0,2)}{B(0,3)} - 1 = \frac{0.93}{0.88} - 1 = 0.0568$$

As the theory showed, the futures rate is greater than the corresponding FRA rate.

Swaptions

A **swaption** is an option (call or put) on the value of a swap at a future date. As an option, there is a strike price K and maturity date T, and the underlying—the swap—needs to be completely specified, receiving fixed and paying floating (or conversely). We illustrate the valuation of a swaption using the example in Figure 24.1.

EXAMPLE 24.7: Swaption Valuation

To value a swaption, one must first value the underlying swap.

- Consider a swap receiving floating and paying fixed with a notional of $100 million and maturing at time 2. Let the fixed rate on the swap be 0.04 per year. The floating rate is the spot rate $R(t)$.

- Using the valuation formula in chapter 22 (Result 22.1), the swap's value at time 1 can be written abstractly as the difference between the value of the floating-rate loan less the value of the fixed-rate loan:

$$V_{Swap}(1) = PV_{Float}(1) - PV_{Fixed}(1)$$

$$= 100 - [100 \times (0.04) \times B(1,2) + 100 \times B(1,2)]$$

Here a floating rate loan is always valued at par ($100 million), and the value of a fixed-rate loan is the present value of its coupon and principal payment at time 2. Using the zero-coupon bond prices from Figure 24.1, we obtain

$$V_{Swap}(1)_u = 100[1 - (0.04)\,0.9620 - 0.9620] = -0.0475$$
$$V_{Swap}(1)_d = 100[1 - (0.04)\,0.9555 - 0.9555] = 0.6248$$

- Consider a swaption written on this swap. Formally, let's consider a swaption that is a European call option on this swap with a maturity date time 1 and strike price $K = 0$. The payoff on the swaption at its maturity, time 1, is

$$\text{Swaption}(1) = \max[V_{Swap}(1), 0]$$

If the swap's value is greater than zero, the option is exercised and the long gets the underlying swap with value $V_{Swap}(1)$.

- Using the values of the swap computed earlier, the swaptions' values at time 1 in the up and down state are

$$\text{Swaption}(1)_u = \max[-0.0475, 0] = 0$$

$$\text{Swaption}(1)_d = \max[0.6248, 0] = 0.6248$$

- Finally, using the risk-neutral valuation formula, the time 0 value of the swaption is

$$\text{Swaption}(0) = \frac{\pi(0)\text{Swaption}(1)_u + [1 - \pi(0)]\text{Swaption}(1)_d}{1 + R(0)}$$

$$\frac{0.5 \times 0 + 0.5 \times 0.6248}{1.0309} = 0.3030$$

From an economic perspective, a swaption is an insurance policy that enables the long to enter a swap at a later date, at terms determined at time 0. Such a contract would be of interest to a corporate treasurer who entered into a floating-rate loan at time 0, and who may want to switch to a fixed-rate loan at a later date if interest rates increase, but at the fixed rates determined at time 0. If exercised at a later date, his floating-rate loan plus the swap changes the floating-rate loan into a fixed-rate loan, with the time 0 fixed rates—and there is no cost to exercise because the strike price is zero! This is a wonderful insurance product for the corporate treasurer, but as with all insurance contracts, it has a cost—premium—to be paid. The previous example demonstrated how to determine the arbitrage-free value of this premium.

24.6 | Summary

1. The binomial HJM model assumes that the zero-coupon bond prices $B(t,T)$ for $t = 0, 1, 2$ and $T = 1, 2, 3$ trade in discrete time and that their prices evolve according to a binomial process. First, if the zero-coupon bond matures the next period, that is, $T = t + 1$, then the current bond price goes to \$1 regardless of the state. Second, standing at time t, the current $T > t + 1$ maturity zero-coupon bond price either gets multiplied by an up factor $u(t,T)$ and takes the price $u(t,T) \times B(t,T)$ with the actual probability $q(t) > 0$ or it is multiplied by a down factor $d(t,T)$ and takes the price $d(t,T) \times B(t,T)$ with probability $1 - q(t)$.

2. The two-period zero-coupon bond price binomial tree is arbitrage-free if and only if there exist pseudo-probabilities $\pi(0)$, $\pi(1)_u$, $\pi(1)_d$ strictly between 0 and 1 such that

$$\pi(0) = \pi(0,T) \text{ for } T = 2, 3$$

and

$$\pi(1)_s = \pi(1,3)_s \text{ for } s \in \{u,d\}$$

where $\pi(0,T) = [1 + R(0) - d(0,T)]/[u(0,T) - d(0,T)]$ and $\pi(1,3)_s = [1 + R(1)_s - d(1,3)_s]/[u(1,3)_s - d(1,3)_s]$.

3. Consider a caplet maturing at time 2 with a strike rate of k. Its payoff at time 2 is $c(2) = \max\{0, [R(2) - k]/[1 + R(2)]\}$. The arbitrage-free price of a caplet can be determined using the risk-neutral valuation formula $c(0) = E^\pi(c(2)/([1 + R(0)][1 + R(1)]))$, where $E^\pi(\cdot)$ denotes expectation using the pseudo-probabilities.

4. Caplet–floorlet parity is

$$[f(0,1) - k]B(0,2) = c(0) - p(0)$$

where $f(0,1)$ is the time 0 forward rate for date 1, $B(0,2)$ is the time 0 zero-coupon bond price with maturity at time 2, and both the caplet with time 0 price $c(0)$ and the floorlet with time 0 price $p(0)$ have strike rate k and maturity 1.

5. Consider a Eurodollar futures contract maturing at time 2. The arbitrage-free futures rate at time 0 is $i_{fut}(0) = E^{\pi}[R(2)]$. The futures rate is always larger than the corresponding FRA rate.

24.7 | Appendix

Linking the Binomial HJM Model and the HJM Libor Model

The binomial interest rate model is easy to understand and to implement. But is it really useful? The answer is yes. In fact, the binomial model can approximate the popular HJM libor model, which is commonly used by financial institutions to price caps, floors, and swaptions. This appendix shows how to set the parameters of the binomial HJM model so that it approximates the HJM libor model of chapter 25.

With interest rate models, the specification is more complex than that used in the case of the binomial option pricing model in chapter 18 to approximate the Black–Scholes–Merton model. The logic of the procedures, however, is identical.

We provide the convergence parameters for a one-factor HJM model. These parameters are selected such that the simple forward rate $i(t,T)$ converges to a lognormal distribution, which yields the libor model.

First, impose a discrete time step of length Δt. Fix a partition of time such that $N\Delta t = \delta$. Let T^* be the maximum maturity zero-coupon bond under consideration with $t \leq T \leq T^*$, where $T^* = t + M\delta = t + M \cdot N \cdot \Delta t$. A total of $M \cdot N$ time steps of length Δt are in the time horizon.

The forward rate and spot rate over the time interval $[t, t + \Delta t]$ are defined by

$$f(t,T) = \left(\frac{B(t,T)}{B(t,T + \Delta t)} - 1 \right) \frac{1}{\Delta t}$$

and

$$R(t) = \left(\frac{1}{B(t,t + \Delta t)} - 1 \right) \Delta t$$

We would like to investigate the limit of the multinomial tree as $\Delta t \to 0$. We note that the forward rate $f(t,T)$ will converge to the continuously compounded forward rate $f(t,T)$ over the time period $[t, t + dt]$.

We are interested in the limit distribution of the simple forward rate, defined by

$$i(t,T) = \left(\frac{B(t,T)}{B(t,T + \delta)} - 1 \right) \frac{1}{\delta} \text{ for } 0 \leq t \leq T \leq T^*$$

where $[T, T + \delta]$ corresponds to the time interval in the future over which the forward rate applies; δ is a fixed time period, say, 0.25 years.

Choose at each time step t (see Jarrow 2002b, p. 286)

$$\pi_t = 1/2$$

$$u(t,T) = \frac{\left[1 + R(t)\right]}{\cosh\left(\displaystyle\sum_{j=t+\Delta t}^{T-\Delta t} \gamma(t,j)\Delta t^{3/2}\right)} e^{\displaystyle\sum_{j=t+\Delta t}^{T-\Delta t} \gamma(t,j)\Delta t^{3/2}}$$

$$d(t,T) = \frac{\left[1 + R(t)\right]}{\cosh\left(\displaystyle\sum_{j=t+\Delta t}^{T-\Delta t} \gamma(t,j)\Delta t^{3/2}\right)} e^{-\displaystyle\sum_{j=t+\Delta t}^{T-\Delta t} \gamma(t,j)\Delta t^{3/2}}$$

where $\cosh(x) \equiv (e^{-x} + e^{x})/2$ and the volatility functions for the continuously compounded forward rates satisfy

$$\gamma(t,T + \delta) = \gamma(t,T) + \frac{\partial\left(\dfrac{\delta \cdot i(t,T)\sigma(t,T)}{1 + \delta \cdot i(t,T)}\right)}{\partial T} \tag{1}$$

for the given inputs $\{B(t,T): T \geq t\}$ and $\{\sigma(t,T): T \geq t\}$, where $\sigma(t,T)$ is a deterministic function of time t (see Shreve 2004, p. 442).

The $\sigma(t,T)$ correspond to the instantaneous volatilities of the simple forward rates $i(t,T)$ in the libor model.

$$\text{Define } X(t,T) = \left(\frac{\delta \cdot i(t,T)\sigma(t,T)}{1 + \delta \cdot i(t,T)}\right)$$

Approximate $\partial X(t,T)/\partial T$ on the partition by its backward-looking derivative, that is,

$$\frac{\partial X(t,T)}{\partial T} \approx \frac{X(t,T - \Delta t) - X(t,T)}{\Delta t}$$

where $X(t,t - \Delta t) \equiv 0$.

The solution to expression (1) is given by the following. Let $T = t + j\Delta t + K\delta$, where $j = 0, \ldots, N$ and $K = 1, \ldots, M - 1$. Then, for fixed δ, and for each $j = 0, \ldots, N - 1$,

$$\gamma(t,T) = \gamma(t,t + j\Delta t) + \sum_{k=0}^{K} \frac{\partial X(t,t + j\Delta t + k\delta)}{\partial T} \tag{2}$$

To specify a process, $\gamma(t,t + j\Delta t)$ for $j = 0, \ldots, N - 1$ can be arbitrarily specified. We suggest setting them equal to zero.

Given are $B(t,T)$, $\sigma(t,T)$ for $T = t + n\Delta$ for $n = 0, \ldots, MN$. From $B(t,T)$, one computes $R(t)$ and $i(t,T)$. From $i(t,T)$, $\sigma(t,T)$, one computes $\gamma(t,T)$. Finally, substitution gives $u(t,T)$, $d(t,T)$. Then, the distribution for simple forward rates $i(T,T)$ $- i(t,T)$ converges to a lognormal distribution as $\Delta t \to 0$.

For implementation, to estimate the parameters, one often chooses

$$\sigma(t,T) = \sigma(T - t)$$

to be deterministic functions of time to maturity.

It is important to note that the binomial tree generated by this approximation is not a lattice. The nonlattice structure results from the desire to obtain lognormally distributed simple forward rates in the limit. To extend this approximation to a multifactor model, see Jarrow (2002b).

24.8 | Cases

Liability Management at General Motors (Harvard Business School Case 293123-PDF-ENG). The case studies issues related to managing the liability structure of General Motors using interest rate derivatives.

Columbia River Pulp Company Inc.—Interest Rate Hedging Strategy (Ivey Publishing Case 9A90B037, European Case Clearing House Case). The case examines issues related to hedging interest rate risk in a company's floating rate debt using interest rate derivatives like caps, collars, and swaps.

Spencer Hall (A) (European Case Clearing House Case 9A95B045). The case analyzes issues surrounding the hedging of interest rate risk with instruments like interest rate swaps, caps, and collars.

24.9 | Questions and Problems

24.1. Consider Figure 24.1 where $B(0,1) = \$0.95$ replaces $\$0.97$. Prove that the new tree is not arbitrage-free.

24.2. In the caplet example 24.4, suppose the strike rate $k = 0.06$. Value the caplet.

24.3. In the floorlet example 24.5, suppose the strike rate $k = 0.06$. Value the floorlet.

24.4. Show that the caplet and floorlet values obtained in problems 24.2 and 24.3 satisfy caplet–floorlet parity.

24.5. Use Figure 24.1. Consider a European call with maturity time 2 and strike price 0.95 on the three-period zero. What is the value of this call option?

24.6. Use Figure 24.1. Consider a European put with maturity time 2 and strike price 0.95 on the three-period zero. What is the value of this call option?

24.7. Consider the Eurodollar futures contract in example 24.6.

    a. Compute the time 1 futures rates in the up and down states s $[i_{fut}(1) = E^\pi[R(2)]]$.

    b. Compute the forward rate agreement rate at time 1 for maturity 2 in the up and down states. Show that these two are the same because both contracts mature in one period.

24.8. For the swap in example 24.7, let the strike price be $K = \$0.50$. Compute the value of the swap using risk-neutral valuation.

24.9. Why are swaptions a useful interest rate derivative? Give an example to explain your answer.

24.10. Suppose a borrower has a 10-year floating-rate loan but wants a fixed-rate loan. Explain how the borrower can change the floating-rate loan into a fixed-rate loan using caps and floors.

24.11. Suppose the term structures of Eurodollar futures rates are increasing for times 1, 2, 3, and 4. Does this mean that the spot rate of interest is expected to increase over the next four time periods?

The next questions are based on this figure.

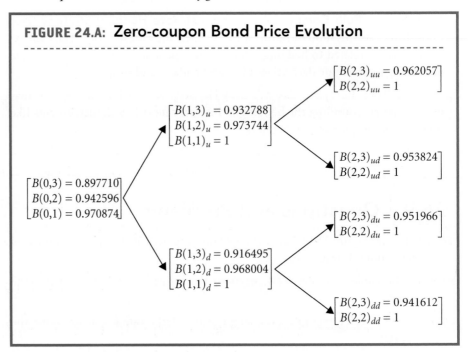

FIGURE 24.A: Zero-coupon Bond Price Evolution

24.12. Compute the spot rates of interest at every node in the tree.

24.13. Is the two-period evolution arbitrage-free? Prove your answer.

24.14. Consider a caplet with maturity date time 2 and strike rate $k = 0.03$. Compute the arbitrage-free value of this caplet.

24.15. Consider a floorlet with maturity date time 2 and strike rate $k = 0.03$. What is the value of this floorlet?

24.16. Using caplet–floorlet parity, verify the answers in problems 24.14 and 24.15.

24.17. Consider a European call with maturity time 2 and strike price $0.95 on the three-period zero. What is the value of this call option?

24.18. Consider a European put option with maturity date time 3 and strike price $0.93 on the three-period zero-coupon bond. What is the value of this put option?

24.19. Consider an American put option with maturity date time 3 and strike price $0.96 on the three-period zero-coupon bond. What is the value of this put option?

24.20. Compute the Eurodollar futures rates for a contract maturing at time 2 and compare them to the forward rate agreement rate for a contract maturing at time 3.

25

The Heath–Jarrow–Morton Libor Model

25.1 | Introduction

Once upon a time, an expert on interest rate derivatives and his wife went to a bank to open a certificate of deposit that would earn a fixed rate of interest. The bank gave them an option to change the interest rate once during the investment's lifetime and lock in the then-current rate. After explaining the various terms and conditions, the bank officer asked, "Do you understand this option?" The professor chuckled to himself and was tempted to reply, "Yes, and I even know how to value the option, do you?" But he just said yes, under his wife's glaring eyes. They finished the formalities and went on their way. As illustrated, even standard banking products contain interest rate derivatives requiring prudent handling!

This chapter continues our study of the Heath–Jarrow–Morton (HJM) model by extending the discrete time model of chapters 23 and 24 to a continuous-time model. You may recall that we assumed no interest rate risk in the continuous-time Black–Scholes–Merton (BSM) model. Now it is back with a vengeance! This chapter shows you how to price the most basic interest rate derivative, a caplet, in the continuous-time HJM libor model. Of course, a caplet is just a European call option on an interest rate, the same derivative studied in the BSM model. As such, this chapter is the analogue of chapters 19 and 20 on the BSM model.

The next section explains why pricing caplets is a significant milestone in our study of derivatives. After, we provide a brief history of caplet pricing models. Next are the assumptions underlying the HJM libor model, the caplet pricing formula, and a discussion of the inputs. Continuing, we reintroduce martingales, risk-neutral valuation, and the actual and pseudo-probabilities. The presentation is couched in terms of forward rates because of their desirable properties. The pricing of floorlets follows using caplet–floorlet parity. Then, we discuss delta and gamma hedging. The valuation of American options, futures contracts, swaptions, and other interest rate derivatives completes the chapter.

25.2 | Why Caplets?

Why does pricing a caplet in continuous time cap (pun intended!) our study of derivatives?

- Our mantra has been to focus on the key interest rate derivatives: forwards, futures, calls, and puts. Once you understand them well, you can understand most interest rate derivatives by applying the build and break approach (see chapter 7).

- We studied forwards in chapter 21. We discussed futures, calls, and puts on interest rates in chapters 23 and 24 in a discrete time model. This chapter repeats the discussion of futures, calls, and puts on interest rates in a continuous time setting.

- This takes us to *caplets*, which are call options on interest rates. Once one prices a caplet, a floorlet follows with *caplet–floorlet parity*. Futures are studied after caplets and floorlets.

So the time has come for the real stuff! First, let's take a peek at the history of caplet pricing models.

25.3 | A History of Caplet Pricing

Black's Model

The first widely used model for pricing caplets was based on Fischer Black's (1976) formula for pricing commodity options (see Extension 25.1 for a discussion of the model and Figure 25.1 for a diagram showing the evolution of these models). Black's model required the assumption of constant continuously compounded libor spot interest rates. Obviously this is an invalid assumption in a world with random interest rates. Nonetheless, the model was used in the beginning because little else was available. Today's traders use the libor model instead, which looks very similar to the original model but rests on thoroughly modern foundations that were developed almost twenty years later!

The Heath–Jarrow–Morton Model

Early interest rate option pricing models (OPMs), like the early equity OPMs, required the estimation of risk premium. The estimation of risk premium, which is equivalent to estimation of expected returns on zero-coupon bonds, is an impossible task. Just as the BSM model bypassed this thorny issue of risk premium estimation in the context of equity options, the HJM model did the same for interest rate derivatives. This insight enabled the market to price and hedge interest rate risk analogous to the way it is done for equity options. Consequently, it fostered the expansion of the swap and interest rate derivatives markets.

In *The Oxford Guide to Financial Modeling*, Ho and Lee (2004, p. 158) write, "We consider it [HJM] as a useful mathematical theorem or a model of interest rate models. . . . The theorem says that if we know the volatility surface, we can specify an arbitrage-free interest rate model." Thus the HJM model can be viewed as a "super-model" for pricing interest rate derivatives. As a special case of HJM, the libor model was discovered.

The HJM Libor Model

Black's model for pricing caplets admits arbitrage because it is impossible for both continuously compounded spot rates to be constant and simple forward rates to be random. This inconsistency was noted in the original HJM paper (Heath, Jarrow, and Morton 1992). Following this demonstration, a search began to overcome this flaw. The search was to find a stochastic evolution for interest rates where continuously compounded spot rates are random yet forward rates are lognormally distributed. The lognormal distribution was needed to maintain the essence of Black's formula.

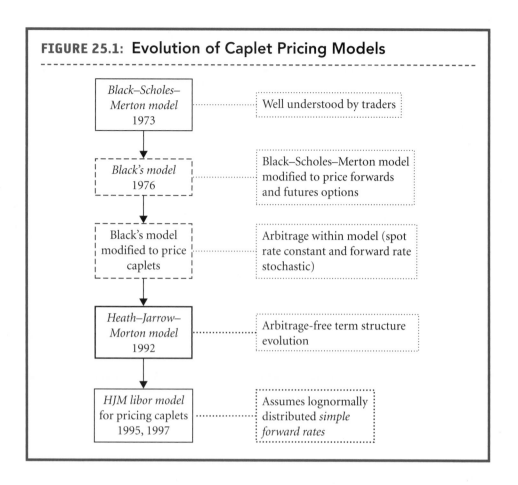

FIGURE 25.1: Evolution of Caplet Pricing Models

Black–Scholes–Merton model 1973 ⟶ Well understood by traders

Black's model 1976 ⟶ Black–Scholes–Merton model modified to price forwards and futures options

Black's model modified to price caplets ⟶ Arbitrage within model (spot rate constant and forward rate stochastic)

Heath–Jarrow–Morton model 1992 ⟶ Arbitrage-free term structure evolution

HJM libor model for pricing caplets 1995, 1997 ⟶ Assumes lognormally distributed *simple forward rates*

EXTENSION 25.1: Black's Model for Pricing Commodity Options and Caplets

In 1976, Black published "The Pricing of Commodity Contracts" in the *Journal of Financial Economics*. This paper extended the BSM model to price an option on commodity futures. Using notation similar to Result 19.1, Black's formula for a European commodity futures call option is

$$c = B(0,T)[FN(d_1) - KN(d_2)] \qquad (1)$$

where today is time 0, $B(0,T) \equiv e^{-rT}$ is today's price of a zero-coupon bond that matures at time T, r is the continuously compounded risk-free interest rate per year; T is the common maturity date for both the option and forward (or futures) contracts; F is the forward (or futures) price determined today; $N(\ldots)$ is the cumulative standard normal distribution function, $d_1 = \left[\log(F/K) + (\sigma^2 T/2)\right]/\sigma\sqrt{T}$ and $d_2 = d_1 - \sigma\sqrt{T}$; K is the strike price; and σ is the volatility of the continuously compounded forward (or futures) price.

As noted in part II of the book, forward and futures prices are the same if interest rates are constant. Note that formula (1) can be obtained by replacing the stock price S in the BSM model with $FB(0,T)$.

Black's model easily extends to price options on forward contracts where the option matures at date T but the forward matures at some later date. The new call price formula is the same as in expression (1), except that the zero-coupon bond price and the forward price correspond to the later date.

Next, to apply this model to caplets, one considers the forward rate $i(0,T)$ computed as simple interest (no compounding). Under this forward rate, Black's formula for pricing a caplet that matures at time T with strike rate k is

$$c = B(0,T+\delta)[i(0,T)N(d_1) - kN(d_2)]\delta \tag{2}$$

This is the formula in expression (1) with $i(0,T)$ replacing F, the volatility of the simple forward rate σ_B replacing σ, and an additional term δ denoting the time interval over which the caplet's interest payment applies. Note the similarity of this formula to the HJM libor caplet pricing formula of Result 25.1.

Unfortunately, Black's model does not satisfy our assumption A5 of no arbitrage. This happens because the model makes two assumptions that cannot both hold at the same time: first, the spot rate of interest (the riskless rate) is constant, and second, the forward rate is stochastic. These assumptions are mutually inconsistent. If the spot rate is always constant, then the forward rate must be nonrandom as well. Assuming that they hold together generates arbitrage opportunities within the model!

This inconsistency was the major motivation for the development of the HJM libor model. By giving an arbitrage-free justification for Black's formula (with modified inputs), the HJM libor model overcame these difficulties and allowed the pricing of caplets and floorlets.

Sandmann, Sondermann, Miltersen (1995); Miltersen, Sandmann, Sondermann (1997); and Brace, Gatarek, Musiela (1997) independently discovered the solution. They came up with the observation that *although continuously compounded forward rates cannot be lognormally distributed in an HJM model, simple forward rates can.* This basic insight enabled the easy pricing of caplets, floorlets, caps, and floors. This special case of the HJM model is known as the **libor model**. It also goes by the names *libor market model*, *forward libor model*, or the *market model*. The term *libor* is emphasized because of the practice of using the British Bankers' Association–determined London Interbank Offered Rate bbalibor as the underlying interest rate for caps and floors.

25.4 | The Assumptions

The first five assumptions underlying the HJM libor model are identical to those in chapter 19, and the sixth assumption is analogous to the lognormal assumption underlying the BSM model. This is no surprise because of the libor model's lineage to the BSM model via Black's (1976) model (see Figure 25.1).

Recall from the last two chapters that the caplet's underlying assets are the term structure of Eurodollar deposits (and swaps) or, equivalently, the term structure of Eurodollar zero-coupon bonds. The relevant assumptions from chapter 19 are assumed to hold for these traded zero-coupon bonds. They are repeated here for convenience (and emphasis).

A1. No market frictions. We assume that trading involves no market frictions and that the assets are perfectly divisible. This helps us to create a benchmark model to which one can add frictions, and it's a reasonable approximation for institutional traders. Furthermore, frictionless markets is even becoming a reasonable first approximation for small traders because the accumulated advances in information technology have drastically reduced trading costs.

A2. No credit risk. This is a reasonable assumption for exchange-traded derivatives but may be less so for over-the-counter (OTC) derivatives. In reality, OTC transactions often impose collateral provisions on the counterparties to lower such credit risk. We assume, as a first approximation, that the OTC collateral provisions remove credit risk from these OTC contracts. Interestingly, derivatives subject to credit risk are priced by extending this term structure modeling framework, which is studied in chapter 26.

A3. Competitive and well-functioning markets. In a competitive market, traders act as price takers. In a well-functioning market, traders agree on *zero–probability events* so that the meaning of an arbitrage opportunity is unambiguous. Price bubbles are also absent in such markets.

Despite this being a reasonable assumption, fines have been levied against Barclays bank for manipulating bbalibor rates during the financial crisis of 2007 (see Extension 25.2).

A4. No intermediate cash flows. As zero-coupon bonds do not have cash flows before they mature, this assumption is automatically satisfied.

A5. No arbitrage opportunities. This assumption is self-explanatory.

We discard old assumption A6, no interest rate uncertainty, and we now allow interest rates to fluctuate randomly. In this regard, we need to impose an assumption on the evolution of the term structure of interest rates.

To facilitate an understanding of this assumption, let us first revisit the concept of a forward rate from earlier chapters. Recall that expression (21.9) gives today's *forward rate* (for a discrete time interval) for the future period $[T, T+1]$ as

$$f(0,T) = \frac{B(0,T)}{B(0,T+1)} - 1 \qquad (25.1)$$

where $B(0,T)$ and $B(0,T+1)$ are today's (time 0's) prices for the zero-coupon bonds maturing at times T and $(T+1)$, respectively.

This definition is reasonably general. It holds irrespective of whether interest rates are stochastic or deterministic, but the limitation is that the time interval is discrete and of unit length. We need to generalize this aspect of the definition. The question is, how would you generalize this definition to compute a forward rate over any time period $[T, T+\delta]$, even for an infinitesimal time interval? An example helps to answer this question.

EXTENSION 25.2: Alleged Manipulation of Bbalibor during 2007–9

A Wall Street Journal Study

Bbalibor is elegant and simple. Once every business day, the British Bankers' Association (BBA) collects lending rates quoted by reputable, major London banks, discards extreme values, and computes a trimmed mean. Removal of the highs and the lows ensures that one or two banks cannot manipulate the index. As noted in chapter 8, this methodology is the basis for various interest rate indexes computed in numerous nations around the globe. But what if several banks submit false information to the rate determination panel? Articles in the *Wall Street Journal* suggest that this might have happened during the financial crisis of 2007–9.

Toward the end of 2007 and early 2008, many market observers complained that bbalibor was lower than what it should be and that it did not reflect the true cost of bank funds. Bbalibor's originator, the BBA, was initially defensive and denied any bias. Still the BBA bowed to pressure and conducted a review. Interestingly, the news of this review seemed to have pushed up libor (see "Libor Surges after Scrutiny Does, Too; Banks May Be Reacting As BBA Speeds Probe; Impact on Borrowers," *Wall Street Journal*, April 18, 2008).

Then, the *Wall Street Journal* also investigated the issue. It conducted a study showing that the index might have been deliberately underpriced during the financial crisis.[1] The study compared bbalibor to a similar rate that has historically moved in tandem, but was found to be out of sync during this period. The similar rate was an estimated borrowing rate computed using credit default swap rates, which we call *wsjlibor*.

The study's key findings included the following:

- Prior to the crisis, the two rates moved together, but they diverged in January 2008. On April 16, wsjlibor was 2.97 percent, 25 basis points higher than the actual bbalibor rate of 2.73 percent per year (see the last rectangle in Figure 25.2). This was consistent with a thirty- to forty-basis-point underpricing suggested by some analysts and strategists.

- The study attributed this gap to the underreporting of borrowing rates by several banks. Between late January and April 16, 2008, the study found that five banks had significant gaps between their reported libor rates and a similarly computed wsjloan rate: Citigroup (average 0.87 percent lower), JP Morgan Chase and Co. (0.43 percent), Germany's WESTLB (0.7 percent), the United Kingdom's HBOS (0.57 percent), and Switzerland's UBS (average 0.42 percent lower). Figure 25.2 shows the average gaps for these five banks in the Eurodollar libor panel.

- An examination of other borrowing rates such as the commercial paper rate led the study to conclude that these five banks were underreporting their borrowing costs to give the impression that they were healthier than they were.

- Payments on about $90 trillion in dollar-denominated interest rate derivatives depend on bbalibor. The journal's analysis computed that if the bbalibor was understated as estimated, it lowered interest payments by about $45 billion during the first four months of 2008. The winners include homeowners, companies, and investors, whereas the losers include other investors such as "mutual funds that invest in mortgages and certain hedge funds that use derivative contracts tied to Libor."[2]

---

[1] See "Study Casts Doubt on Key Rate; WSJ Analysis Suggests Banks May Have Reported Flawed Interest Data for Libor" and "Behind the Journal's Analysis," *Wall Street Journal*, May 29, 2008.

[2] "Study Casts Doubt on Key Rate; WSJ Analysis Suggests Banks May Have Reported Flawed Interest Data for Libor," *Wall Street Journal* (Eastern edition), May 29, 2008.

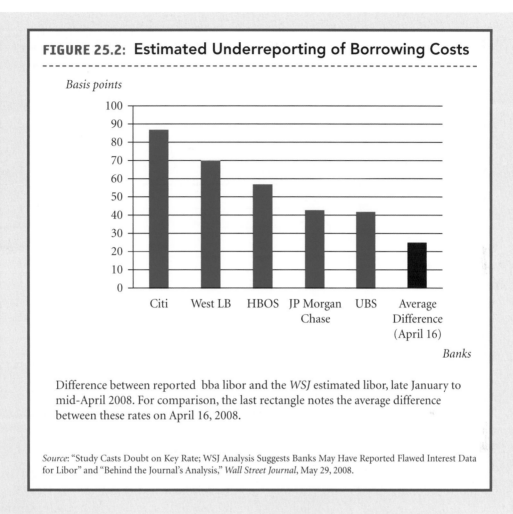

FIGURE 25.2: Estimated Underreporting of Borrowing Costs

Basis points

Difference between reported bba libor and the *WSJ* estimated libor, late January to mid-April 2008. For comparison, the last rectangle notes the average difference between these rates on April 16, 2008.

Source: "Study Casts Doubt on Key Rate; WSJ Analysis Suggests Banks May Have Reported Flawed Interest Data for Libor" and "Behind the Journal's Analysis," *Wall Street Journal*, May 29, 2008.

The Immediate Aftermath

During the first four months of 2008, the three-month and six-month dollar bbalibor rates were about twenty-five basis points lower than wsjlibor reported. After the news release concerning the BBA's review of bbalibor in mid-April, this difference fell to about fifteen basis points (see Figure 25.3). Following the publication of the *Wall Street Journal* articles, three-month bbalibor increased three basis points, its largest increase in more than two weeks (see "Under Watch, Libor Rises; Rate Hits 2.68% Ahead of Report on System Accuracy," *Wall Street Journal*, May 30, 2008).

Some subsequent studies have supported BBA's stance of no manipulation. In the Bank for International Settlements' March 2008 *Quarterly Review*, staff members Gyntelberg and Wooldridge found that bbalibor had moved away from "other reference rates to an unusual extent" during market turbulence but attributed "a deterioration in market liquidity, an increase in interest rate volatility and differences in the composition of the contributor panels" as the main causes of the divergence. In addition, the October 2008 issue of the International Monetary Fund's *Global Financial Stability Review* reported that "although the integrity of the US dollar LIBOR fixing process has been questioned by some market participants and the financial press, it appears that US dollar LIBOR remains an accurate measure of a typical creditworthy bank's marginal cost of unsecured US dollar term funding."

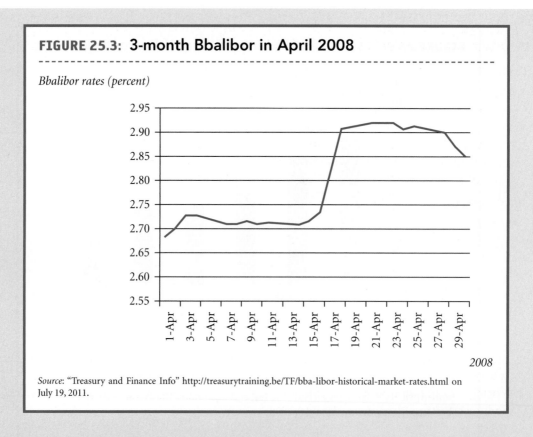

FIGURE 25.3: 3-month Bbalibor in April 2008

Bbalibor rates (percent)

Source: "Treasury and Finance Info" http://treasurytraining.be/TF/bba-libor-historical-market-rates.html on July 19, 2011.

Regulatory Probes and Lawsuits

Following the questions about bbalibor, the US Department of Justice, the Securities and Exchange Commission, and the Commodity Futures Trading Commission launched investigations (see "Regulators Probing Banks' Libor Reports," *Wall Street Journal*, March 16, 2011). Although some sixteen banks were initially contacted, the probe narrowed down to focus on a smaller group of banks.

Recall from chapter 6 that the law requires that to prove *manipulation*, the manipulator (1) must be shown to have the *ability* to set an artificial futures price, (2) must have *intended* to set an artificial price, and (3) must have *succeeded* in setting such a price. The regulators have a difficult task proving manipulation because "banks report and obtain borrowing costs in an opaque process that leaves a scant evidence trail" (see "Libor Probe's Hurdle—US Regulators Face Challenges Proving Wrongdoing," *Wall Street Journal*, March 18, 2011).

Antitrust and antifraud prosecutors pursued the Justice Department's case (see "UBS Aids Probe of Rate Collusion," *Wall Street Journal*, June 22, 2011). Investigated banks hired major corporate-defense law firms. The outcome of this case is yet to be determined.

Lawsuits followed. A hedge fund in Vienna, an investment firm in Miami, Eurodollar traders in London and Chicago, and a pension fund in Florida have filed lawsuits against the libor panel member banks (see "UBS Aids Probe of Rate Collusion," *Wall Street Journal*, June 22, 2011). The resolution of these cases awaits the passage of time. Recently, Barclays bank was fined $450 million by British and US regulators for manipulating bbalibor rates (see "Barclays fined for manipulation of Libor," *Washington Post*, June 27, 2012). Numerous other banks are still being investigated, and the saga is still unfolding.

EXAMPLE 25.1: Forward Rate Computations

Forward Rates (for a Discrete Time Interval)

■ We compute forward rates and report them in Table 25.1.
  - The first column reports time T: time 0 is today, time 1 is one year, and so on.
  - The second column reports today's prices of the zero-coupon bonds, $B(0,T)$, which mature at time T. Their numerical values are reported in the third column. For example, today's price of a zero that matures after one year is $B(0,1) = \$0.97$, after two years is $B(0,2) = \$0.93$, and so on (these numbers are taken from Table 21.3). $B(0,0) = \$1$ by definition.

■ We compute forward rates using definition (25.1).
  - The forward rate for the interval $[0,1]$ is $f(0,0) = B(0,0)/B(0,1) - 1 = 0.0309$ and is given in the fourth and fifth cells of the second row. Relation (21.12) tells us that this is also the spot rate, $R(0)$. Several of these computations are also reported in Table 21.3.
  - The forward rate over the interval $[1,2]$ is

$$f(0,1) = \frac{B(0,1)}{B(0,2)} - 1 = 0.0430 \qquad (25.2a)$$

■ We have two dates in the forward rate's notation: today (time 0), when the rate is quoted, and the date (time 1) when the rate becomes effective. Because we know the ending date (time 2), we skip writing it as a third argument. Although many of our examples consider the length of the time period to be one year, it need not be so in a continuous-time setting.

TABLE 25.1: Computing Different Types of Forward Rates (See Example 25.1)

Time T	Price of a Zero $B(0,T)$	$B(0,T)$ Values	Length of Interval	Forward Rates	Forward Rate Computations
0	$B(0,0)$	1	1	$f(0,0) \equiv R(0)$	$\dfrac{B(0,0)}{B(0,1)} - 1 = 0.0309$
1	$B(0,1)$	0.97	1	$f(0,1)$	$\dfrac{B(0,1)}{B(0,2)} - 1 = 0.0430$
1.0027	$B(0,1.0027)$	0.9699	$1/365 = 0.0027$	$i_{\frac{1}{365}}(0,1)$	$\left[\dfrac{B(0,1)}{B(0,1.0027)} - 1\right] \times 365 = 0.0421$
1.5	$B(0,1.5)$	0.95	0.5	$i_{0.5}(0,1)$	$\left[\dfrac{B(0,1)}{B(0,1.5)} - 1\right] \times 2 = 0.0421$
2	$B(0,2)$	0.93	1	$f(0,2)$	$\dfrac{B(0,2)}{B(0,3)} - 1 = 0.0568$
3	$B(0,3)$	0.88	1	$f(0,3)$	$\dfrac{B(0,3)}{B(0,4)} - 1 = 0.0732$

Simple Forward Rates (in Continuous Time)

- Suppose you want to compute a forward rate as in expression (25.2a) over a fixed but not a unit time interval such as six months. For this, we use the concept of simple interest, and we consider a *simple forward rate*. To compute this rate, we need a zero maturing at time 1.5: assume it has a price of $B(0,1.5) = \$0.95$. Considering the time interval $[1,1.5]$, we write the simple forward rate as

$$i_{0.5}(0,1) = \left(\frac{B(0,1)}{B(0,1.5)} - 1 \right) \frac{1}{0.5} = \left(\frac{0.97}{0.95} - 1 \right) 2 = 0.04210526 \qquad (25.2b)$$

per year. Note that in the definition of a simple interest rate, the time interval over which the interest rate applies needs to be indicated. The first time argument in the simple interest rate notation, $t = 0$, corresponds to the current date, while the second time argument corresponds to the start date of the future time interval $T = 1$. The subscript 0.5 following the symbol "i" indicates the length of the time interval over which the interest rate applies: half of a year. Finally, note that multiplication by 2 converts the 6 month interest rate into an annual rate.

- Why go back to the simple interest discussed in chapter 2? First, the Eurodollar market is a market in which the derivatives (such as swaps, caplets, and floorlets) use simple interest rates to compute cash flows, and second, it will enable us to price caplets using a modified Black's formula.

Continuously Compounded Forward Rates (in Continuous Time)

- Suppose instead that you want to compute the simple forward rate over an infinitesimal time interval one year into the future, $[1,1 + \Delta t]$, as $\Delta t \to 0$. Let us first approximate this by setting $\Delta t = 1/365 = 0.002740$ in expression (25.2b), which is one day measured in years. This requires a zero-coupon bond that matures after one year plus one day with a price of $B(0,1.002740) = \$0.969888$ today. Then, the simple forward rate over the small time interval $\Delta t = 1/365$ is

$$i_{\frac{1}{365}}(0,1) = \left(\frac{B(0,1)}{B(0,1.002740)} - 1 \right) \times 365 = 0.000115 \times 365 = 0.04214920 \qquad (25.2c)$$

per year. Notice that multiplication by 365 converts the daily interest rate into an annual rate.

- Using this rate, if you invest a dollar starting in one year for one day, then you get $1.000115 back in one year and one day.

- Taking smaller and smaller time intervals enables us to define the *continuously compounded forward rate* via (25.2c) as

$$\widetilde{f}(0,1) = \lim_{\Delta t \to 0} i_{\Delta t}(0,1) = \lim_{\Delta t \to 0} \left(\frac{B(0,1)}{B(0,1 + \Delta t)} - 1 \right) \frac{1}{\Delta t} \qquad (25.2d)$$

Here we introduce a different notation for the continuously compounded forward rate, as opposed to a simple interest rate over an infinitesimal time interval. This new notation avoids using a time interval subscript because the length of the time interval to which this forward rate applies is always fixed at an instant.

The example contains two important ideas that we rewrite for emphasis. First, we define the simple forward interest rate. Replacing 1 with T and 0.5 with δ in expression (25.2b) gives us the **simple forward rate** over $[T,T+\delta]$ (i.e., the forward rate expressed as a simple interest rate). We define this at time 0 for date T as

$$i(0,T) = \left(\frac{B(0,T)}{B(0,T + \delta)} - 1 \right) \times \frac{1}{\delta} \tag{25.3a}$$

Note that we delete the subscript because for the remainder of this chapter, the time interval over which the simple forward rate applies is fixed and always equals to δ. To reduce clutter, we started the clock at time 0, although our analysis holds even if the clock starts at time t.

Second, we define the continuously compounded forward rate by replacing 1 with T and $(1+ \Delta t)$ with $(T+ \Delta t)$ in expression (25.2d), where Δt is the time interval over which the interest rate applies. Taking limits as Δt goes to zero gives the **continuously compounded forward rate**:

$$\tilde{f}(0,T) = \lim_{\Delta t \to 0} \left(\frac{B(0,T)}{B(0,T + \Delta t)} - 1 \right) \frac{1}{\Delta t} \tag{25.3b}$$

Now, we add our assumption on the stochastic evolution of simple forward rates.

A6. The simple forward rate $i(T,T)$ over $[T,T+\delta]$ follows a lognormal distribution. This assumption is that the natural logarithm of the simple forward rate follows a normal distribution. In symbols,

$$i(T,T) = i(0,T)e^{\int_0^T \mu_s ds - \frac{1}{2}\nu_T^2(T) + \nu_T \sqrt{T} \cdot z} \text{ with probability}$$

$$q(z) = e^{-\frac{1}{2}z^2} / \sqrt{2\pi} \tag{25.4a}$$

where time 0 is today, time T is the maturity date, μ_T is the mean percentage change per year in the simple forward rate,

$$\nu_T^2 = \frac{\int_0^T \sigma_s^2 ds}{T} \quad (\nu \text{ is a Greek letter, pronounced "nu")} \tag{25.4b}$$

σ_s is the time $s-$ maturity simple forward rate $[i(0,s)]$'s volatility per year, $q(z)$ are the actual probabilities, and z is a standard normal random variable with zero mean and unit variance. Note that the relevant volatility in this evolution is ν_T, which is the "average" of the simple $s-$ maturity forward rates' instantaneous volatilities over the option's life. The mean is assumed to be a deterministic function of time to maturity T. The $s-$ maturity forward rate's volatility σ_s is assumed to be a constant.

This assumption is similar to the BSM model assumption A8 for the stock price's evolution presented in relationship (19.2). Here, however, the simple forward rate replaces the stock price as the variable with a lognormal distribution.

Other assumptions for the evolution of the simple forward rate will generate different term structure evolutions and different caplet pricing models. However, these alternative assumptions are usually imposed on the evolution of the continuously compounded forward rates $\tilde{f}(0,T)$ and not the simple forward interest rates as in the HJM libor model. Some of these alternative models go by the names of the assumed evolution: the Gaussian model, the extended Vasicek model, and the affine model (see Jarrow 2010). These alternative models are left for more advanced courses.

We complete our list of assumptions by retaining assumption A7 from chapter 19 with respect to the trading of the Eurodollar zero-coupon bonds.

A7. Trading takes place continuously in time. This assumption is self-explanatory.

These assumptions set the stage for introducing the HJM libor model.

25.5 | Pricing Caplets

Caplets are European call options on the simple forward rate. For many of our examples in this chapter, we use the following data.

Caplet and Floorlet Pricing (CFP) Data

- The caplets and floorlets start trading today (time 0) and expire after one year (time T).
- The notional principal L_N is $100 million.
- The strike rate (which may be the cap rate or the floor rate) k is 4 percent per year.
- The payoffs are based on six-month bbalibor, the simple forward rate $i(0,T)$. Assuming that this six-month period has 182 days, $\delta = 182/365 = 0.4986$ years is the investment period over which simple interest is computed.
- The average forward rate volatility ν_T is 0.15, or 15 percent per year.
- If the caplet (or the floorlet) is in-the-money, the payment is made 0.4986 years after the expiration date (at time $[T + \delta]$).
- The zero-coupon bond prices and simple forward rates are taken from the previous example (see Table 25.1).

Caplet Pricing Model

Before introducing the pricing model, let us illustrate the workings of a caplet in continuous time.

EXAMPLE 25.2: An Interest Rate Caplet's Payoffs

- International Treats and Restaurants Inc.'s (INTRest, a fictitious name) treasurer buys a caplet today (time 0) with maturity $T = 1$ year, a strike rate of $k = 4$ percent, and notional of $L_N = \$100$ million (see Figure 25.4 for a timeline).

- Suppose the six-month bbalibor rate realized after one year is 5 percent. This is the simple forward rate, $i(T,T) = i(1,1) = 0.05$.

- Use the caplet and floorlet pricing (CFP) data:
  - The caplet's payoff at time $(T + \delta) = 1.4986$ years is

$$c_{1.4986} = \max(0.05 - 0.04, 0) \times (182/365) \times 100 \text{ million}$$
$$= \$498{,}630.14 \qquad (25.5a)$$

  The payment is received δ years (a fraction of a year) after the caplet's maturity at time T. It equals the yearly simple interest rate difference $[i(T,T) - k]$ times the period δ over which the interest is earned times the notational.
  - The present value of the payment on the maturity date is obtained by multiplying it by the relevant zero-coupon bond's price. Suppose $B(1, 1.4986) = 0.9850$ is the price of a zero-coupon bond at time 1 (at time T) which matures after six more months (at time $[T + \delta]$). Then, the time 1 value of the caplet's payoff is

$$c_1 = 0.9850 \times \max(0.05 - 0.04, 0) \times (182/365) \times 100 \text{ million}$$
$$= \$491{,}150.68 \qquad (25.5b)$$

The caplet's payoff from this example can be easily formalized. Consider a caplet with notional principal L_N, strike rate k, maturity date T, and payment date $(T + \delta)$ and where the time period over which the simple interest rate is computed is δ years.

The caplet's payoff on the **payment date** is

$$c_{T+\delta} = \max[i(T,T) - k] \times \delta \times L_N \qquad (25.6a)$$

where the simple forward rate $i(T,T)$ is the interest rate at time T that applies over the time period $[T, T + \delta]$.

To obtain the value of this payoff at time T, discount this cash flow by multiplying it by the relevant zero-coupon bond's price. The caplet's value on the **maturity date** is

$$c_T = B(T, T + \delta) \max[i(T,T) - k] \times \delta \times L_N \qquad (25.6b)$$

where $B(T, T + \delta)$ is the time T price of a zero-coupon bond that pays a dollar at time $(T + \delta)$.

For computation, one can think of time T as both the *maturity date* and the *payoff date* of the caplet, but in this case, one needs to use expression (25.6b) as the caplet's payoff.

FIGURE 25.4: **Timeline for a Caplet (In Continuous Time)**

Start date	Intermediate dates	Maturity date	Payment date
Time 0		Time T	Time $(T + \delta)$
(Today)		(1 year)	(1.4986 years)

Time interval, $\delta = 0.4986$ year

Buyer and writer negotiate caplet's terms: the notional L_N, the strike rate k, the maturity date T	Long can exercise an American caplet	Bbalibor $i(T,T)$ determined for the period δ.	If $i(T,T) > k$, long's payoff is $c_{T+\delta} = L_N \times [i(T,T) - k] \times \delta$
			If $i(T,T) \leq k$, caplet expires out-of-the-money
Long pays premium and becomes owner of the caplet	Traders can close out their positions by reverse trades	Value of Long's payoff on this date, $c_T = B(T,T + \delta) \times L_N \times \max[i(T,T) - k] \times \delta$, where the zero-coupon bond pays \$1 at time $(T + \delta)$	*Zero-sum game—* Long's gain is Short's loss

Under the HJM libor model, it can be shown that the caplet's time 0 value is given by the following formula.

RESULT 25.1

HJM Libor Model Formula for Caplet Pricing

A caplet's price is

$$c = B(0,T + \delta) \, [i(0,T)N(d_1) - kN(d_2)] \times \delta \times L_N \qquad (25.7a)$$

where $B(0,T + \delta)$ is today's price of a zero-coupon bond that matures at time $(T + \delta)$, T is the caplet's maturity date, δ is the time period for interest computation, $i(0,T)$ is the simple forward rate per year that applies to the interval $[T,T + \delta]$, $N(\ .\ )$ is the cumulative standard normal distribution function (with mean 0 and standard deviation 1),

$$d_1 = \frac{\log\left[\dfrac{i(0,T)}{k}\right] + \dfrac{v_T^2 \times T}{2}}{v_T\sqrt{T}} \text{ and } d_2 = d_1 - v_T\sqrt{T} \quad (25.7b)$$

k is the strike rate (which is the cap rate), v_T is the average forward rate volatility over the caplet's life, and L_N is the notional principal.

We discuss the proof of this result later in this chapter when discussing risk-neutral valuation.

The caplet formula is similar in appearance to the standard BSM formula but applied to the simple forward rate at time T, $i(0,T)$, and not the stock price (which is irrelevant in the world of interest rate derivatives). The key difference from the standard BSM formula is that the stock price is replaced by the bond price $B(0,T + \delta)$ multiplied by the simple interest rate $i(0,T)$. This occurs because $B(0,T + \delta) \times i(0,T)$ corresponds to the present value of $i(T,T)$ dollars received at time $(T + \delta)$.

In addition to the simple forward rate $i(0,T)$, the caplet's value depends on the zero-coupon bond price $B(0,T + \delta)$, the strike rate k, the maturity date T, and the average forward rate volatility v_T. As with the BSM formula, the mean percentage change in the simple forward rate does not appear in this expression. Had it appeared, the thorny problem of risk premium computation would have remained with us. This "important omission" makes the formula usable. Analogous to the BSM model, this fact implies that if two traders agree on the inputs $[i(0,T), B(0,T + \delta), k, T, v_T]$ but disagree on the mean percentage change in simple forward rates, they will still agree on the caplet's price.

Our next example demonstrates Result 25.1.

EXAMPLE 25.3: Pricing a Caplet

- Consider the CFP data.
  - The caplet is traded today (time 0) and matures at $T = 1$ year.
  - The notional principal $L_N = \$100$ million and the strike rate $k = 4$ percent per year.
  - The contract applies to six-month bbalibor (which is the simple forward rate). The interest is computed over 182 days, or $\delta = 182/365 = 0.4986$ year.
  - The simple forward rate is $i(0,T) = i(0,1) = 0.0421$ (see the cell in the fifth row and fifth column in Table 25.1).

- - The average forward rate volatility v_T is 0.15, or 15 percent per year.
  - - A zero-coupon bond maturing after 1.4986 years is worth $B(0,T+\delta) = B(0,1.4986) = \$0.95$ today.
- ■ Compute d_1 and d_2:

$$d_1 = \frac{\log\left[\frac{i(0,T)}{k}\right] + \frac{v_T^2 \times T}{2}}{v_T\sqrt{T}} = \frac{\log\left(\frac{0.0421}{0.04}\right) + \frac{0.15^2 \times 1}{2}}{0.15\sqrt{1}} = 0.4170 \text{ and}$$

$$d_2 = d_1 - v_T\sqrt{T} = 0.4170 - 0.15 = 0.2670$$

- ■ Using Excel, we get cumulative standard normal distribution function values:

$$N(d_1) = N(0.4170) = \text{NORMSDIST}(0.4170) = 0.6616 \text{ and}$$
$$N(d_2) = N(0.2670) = \text{NORMSDIST}(0.2670) = 0.6052$$

- ■ The caplet's price using the HJM libor model formula (25.7a) for a $100 million notional is

$$
\begin{aligned}
c &= B(0,T+\delta)\,[i(0,T)N(d_1) - kN(d_2)] \times \delta \times L_N \\
&= B(0,1.4986)\,[i(0,1)N(0.4170) - 0.04N(0.2670)] \times 0.4986 \times 100 \text{ million} \\
&= 0.95 \times (0.0421 \times 0.6616 - 0.04 \times 0.6052) \times 0.4986 \times 100 \text{ million} \\
&= \$172,842.45
\end{aligned}
$$

25.6 | The Inputs

Collecting inputs for the HJM libor caplet pricing model is analogous to gathering the inputs for the BSM model. Most of the inputs are easily obtained, except for the average forward rate volatility.

Observable Inputs

The easiest inputs to obtain are the strike rate k, expiration date T, and time period for interest computation δ. These are written into the contract. What about the simple forward rate? Had the underlying been a Treasury security, one could observe zero-coupon bond prices from the market—but we are using Eurodollars and bbalibor rates. This difference only presents a minor complication.

As the forward rate is equivalent to the FRA rate (see Result 21.3), one can obtain the simple forward rate $i(0,T)$ by observing the rates from FRA contracts trading in the OTC markets. The quoted FRA rates are based on the simple interest rates as defined in expression (25.3a).[3]

---

[3] We point out that when we defined the forward rate in earlier chapters, for simplicity, we always fixed the time interval over which the rates applied to be equal to one unit of time. Here, to correspond to practice, it is necessary to make the time interval differ from one time unit. It is set equal to δ time units.

A Eurodollar zero-coupon bond's price can be created in several ways from these FRA rates. For example, you can use the FRA rates in the following formula to compute the zero-coupon bond prices:

$$B(0,T) = \frac{1}{[1 + i(0,0) \times \delta][1 + i(0,\delta) \times \delta] \cdots [1 + i(0,T - \delta) \times \delta]}$$

(25.8)

where $i(0,0)$ is the spot rate that applies over $[0,\delta]$, $i(0,\delta)$ is the simple forward rate computed over the next time period of length δ, and so on. This is a known relationship (expression [21.11a] of Result 21.2) that has been slightly modified to account for the time intervals not being of unit length, but equal to δ time units.

Alternatively, you can obtain these zero-coupon bond prices directly from Eurodollar rates (for maturities up to one year) and swap rates (for maturities beyond one year). The procedure for obtaining these zero-coupon bond prices from swap rates was given in Extension 22.4.

The Average Forward Rate Volatility

Like the thorny problem of volatility estimation encountered in the context of the BSM model, the average forward rate volatility is also the hardest input to estimate in the HJM libor model. As before, there are two standard methods for volatility estimation: an explicit method using past simple forward rates, yielding a *historical volatility*, and an implicit method—calibration—using caplet market prices, yielding an *implied volatility*.

Note that the expression for the volatility differs from that used for equity options. Here it equals the forward rate's average volatility over the caplet's life, that is,

$$\nu_T = \sqrt{\frac{\int_0^T \sigma_s^2 ds}{T}}$$

(25.9a)

where σ_s is the time s − maturity simple forward rate $i(0,s)$'s volatility per year.

To compute this expression, we need to estimate each individual s − maturity forward rate's volatility σ_s. The trick here is that we need to use *constant maturity* forward rates and compute their volatility just as we did the stock's return volatility in chapter 19. Except for these two differences, the methods for estimating the simple forward rate's volatility per unit time are analogous to those for equity options discussed in chapters 19 and 20.

The relevant expression to compute the s − maturity simple forward rate $i(t,s)$'s historical volatility is

$$\sqrt{\text{var}\left[\log\left(\frac{i(t + \Delta t,s + \Delta t)}{i(t,s)}\right)\right]\frac{1}{\Delta t}} = \sigma_s$$

(25.9b)

This is the standard deviation of the percentage change[4] in the s − maturity simple forward rate over $[t,t + \Delta t]$. Multiplication by $(1/\Delta t)$ annualizes the volatility estimate.

---

[4] The ratio $\log[i(t + \Delta t, s + \Delta t)/i(t,s)]$ gives the percentage change in the s − maturity simple forward rate over the time interval. Note that these forward rates correspond to the time intervals $[t,t + \delta]$ and $[t + \Delta t,t + \Delta t + \delta]$, respectively, where δ is fixed. In our example, δ corresponds to six months.

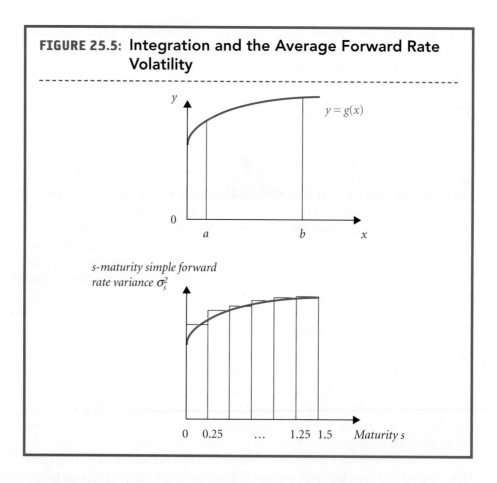

FIGURE 25.5: Integration and the Average Forward Rate Volatility

HISTORICAL VOLATILITY To compute the average forward rate volatility as given in expression (25.9a), we need to use some basic ideas from integral calculus. Consider a continuous function $y = g(x)$ as depicted in Figure 25.5, where x is plotted along the horizontal axis and y is plotted along the vertical axis. Calculus tells us that the integral $\int_a^b g(x)dx$ measures the area under this curve between $x = a$ and $x = b$. Recall that one can approximate this area using the set of rectangles lying below the curve (see Figure 25.2). Of course, the area of each rectangle equals its base times its height. The limit of the area covered by these rectangles as the bases go to zero yields the integral of $g(x)$ with respect to x from a to b. We use this simple approximation to compute the average forward rate volatility.

The procedure is as follows: (1) collect time series observations of the constant s — maturity forward rates for the entire term structure of maturities s ranging from 0 to time T, (2) compute the variance of the percentage changes in these simple forward rates using expression (25.9b), (3) add up the variances to get the approximation to the numerator of relationship (25.9a), and finally, (4) divide by the length of the entire time interval T to compute the average. Finally, taking the square root gives the average forward rate volatility.

As the historical volatility is estimated using actual forward rate realizations that nature "draws," this estimate is obtained under the actual probability distribution. Using our earlier terminology, we refer to this as "estimation under the probability q." The next example illustrates this method.

EXAMPLE 25.4: Computing the Historical Average Forward Rate Volatility

- Both the maturity of the caplet, time T, and the simple forward rate's investment interval, δ, are given by the contract's specifications. We choose $T = 1.25$ years and $\delta = 0.5$ years, representing a typical caplet's parameters.

- First, one must decide on the frequency (daily, weekly, or monthly) of the data. Then, one must collect the FRA quotes from dealers in the OTC markets for all maturity FRAs from time 0 to time T. Weekly observation intervals are a good choice, balancing microstructure noise versus providing a sufficient number of observations.

- Table 25.2 reports hypothetical constant maturity forward rates for maturities ranging from time 0 to $T = 1.25$ years, collected each week for twenty consecutive weeks. Each forward rate applies to a six-month investment period, that is, $\delta = 182/365 = 0.4986$ year.
  - The first column is labeled *Week n*, and it keeps track of the dates when the data points were collected.
  - The next six columns give the *constant s — maturity forward rates*. These simple forward rates always correspond to a constant s — years in the future. Each rate is for a six-month investment period. For example, on week 1, the forward rate for maturity time 0 (the spot rate) is 0.1000. The spot rate corresponds to the investment period [0,0.5]. Next, the forward rate for maturity time 0.25 is 0.1050, corresponding to the rate over the investment period [0.25, 0.75], and so forth.

- There are several ways to compute the sample variance:
  - There's the tedious way of hand computing. Although inefficient, it builds mental muscles. When computing by hand, one needs to compute both the mean and variance for each s — maturity forward rate time series:

$$\text{Mean:} \qquad \hat{\mu}_s = \frac{1}{N}\sum_{n=1}^{N} i(n,s) \qquad\qquad (25.10a)$$

$$\text{Variance:} \qquad \hat{\sigma}_s^2 = \frac{1}{N-1}\sum_{n=1}^{N} \left[i(n,s) - \hat{\mu}_s \right]^2 \qquad (25.10b)$$

  - Alternatively, one can use a programmable calculator, or a spreadsheet, or a statistical package on a computer. We input the data in Table 25.2 in Microsoft Excel and compute the variance in one step. For example, running Excel command VARA over the twenty observations in cells B2 = 0.1000 to B21 = 0.0920 gives VARA(B2:B21) = 0.00004779. We denote this by $\hat{\sigma}_0^2$ and

Table 25.2: Computing the Average Forward Rate Volatility Using Weekly Price Data

Week n	Constant Maturity Simple Forward Rate $i(n,s)$					
	$s=0$	$s=0.25$	$s=0.5$	$s=0.75$	$s=1.00$	$s=1.25$
1	0.1000	0.1050	0.1100	0.1150	0.1200	0.1150
2	0.1020	0.1060	0.1120	0.1160	0.1230	0.1160
3	0.1050	0.1070	0.1140	0.1160	0.1260	0.1190
4	0.1080	0.1090	0.1150	0.1180	0.1270	0.1230
5	0.1090	0.1110	0.1150	0.1210	0.1280	0.1250
6	0.1100	0.1130	0.1180	0.1210	0.1290	0.1280
7	0.1100	0.1150	0.1190	0.1250	0.1300	0.1310
8	0.1110	0.1150	0.1200	0.1240	0.1340	0.1310
9	0.1120	0.1160	0.1210	0.1270	0.1340	0.1350
10	0.1120	0.1170	0.1210	0.1280	0.1350	0.1360
11	0.1110	0.1180	0.1210	0.1270	0.1360	0.1310
12	0.1090	0.1170	0.1200	0.1260	0.1350	0.1280
13	0.1070	0.1130	0.1180	0.1230	0.1290	0.1210
14	0.1030	0.1090	0.1100	0.1200	0.1230	0.1240
15	0.0990	0.1050	0.1100	0.1160	0.1210	0.1210
16	0.0980	0.1030	0.1080	0.1180	0.1200	0.1190
17	0.0960	0.1010	0.1060	0.1090	0.1160	0.1160
18	0.0940	0.0990	0.1010	0.1050	0.1140	0.1110
19	0.0920	0.0970	0.1000	0.1030	0.1110	0.1090
20	0.0920	0.0950	0.0990	0.1010	0.1090	0.1080
Variance	0.00004779	0.00004984	0.00005241	0.00006542	0.00006747	0.00006940
Variance×0.25	0.00001195	0.00001246	0.00001310	0.00001635	0.00001687	0.00001735
Summed variance×0.25/ T	0.00007046					
Volatility× $\sqrt{52}$	0.060530					

T is 1.25 years; δ is 0.5 years.

record this below the three-month spot rate series. Similarly, we compute and record in the table $\hat{\sigma}_{0.25}^2 = 0.00004984$, $\hat{\sigma}_{0.5}^2 = 0.00005241$, and so on.

- Once we have these sample variances, it's easy to compute the average forward rate volatility.
  - Multiply each of these variance estimates by 0.25 (the base of the rectangle) and record them in the cell below in Table 25.2. Summing gives the area under the curve, that is,

$$\int_0^T \sigma_s^2 ds \approx \sum_s \hat{\sigma}_s^2 \times 0.25 = (\hat{\sigma}_0^2 + \hat{\sigma}_{0.25}^2 + ... + \hat{\sigma}_{1.25}^2) \times 0.25 = 0.00008808 \quad (25.10c)$$

- Dividing (25.10c) by the length of the time interval T gives

$$\nu_T^2 = \frac{\sum_s \hat{\sigma}_s^2 \times 0.25}{T} = 0.00007046 \tag{25.10d}$$

The positive square root is the average forward rate volatility $\nu_T = 0.008394$, or 0.8394 percent per week. To get the volatility per year, multiply by the square root of 52, to get 0.060530 or 6.0530 percent. This represents the average volatility (per year) of the constant maturity forward rates over the caplet's life.

In computing the historical average forward rate volatility, a number of issues still remain. First, how many observations should you use? Theoretically speaking, more observations will give a better estimate, but long time series data may not be "stationary." Second, how long should the time interval be between observation dates? If observations are collected at short intervals, then market frictions and market microstructure issues can significantly impact the estimation. Daily or weekly intervals have fewer of these problems. Finally, what should be the time interval between the maturities of the forward rates? The smaller the time interval, the better that the sum of the rectangles approximates the area under the curve. In practice, quarterly time intervals between the different maturity forward rates, as in Table 25.2, yield a reasonable approximation.

IMPLIED VOLATILITY Just as for the BSM formula, one can use market prices of caps, as portfolios of caplets, to find that average forward rate volatility ν_T that best matches market prices. This is *calibration*. The procedure yields an *implied volatility*.

In practice, just as in the BSM model, implied volatilities for caplets differ from historical volatilities, and when graphed across strikes and maturities, they exhibit a smile or sneer (see Jarrow et al. 2007; Rebonato 2002). This implies, as in the case of the BSM formula, that the HJM libor model is formally rejected by the data.

Nonetheless, the model can still be used with implicit volatilities but, in this case, only as a *statistical model* for pricing caplets. When used as a statistical model, its purpose must be restricted to pricing caplets (and floorlets) only, and its use as a hedging tool is no longer appropriate. This is because the *theoretical model* has been rejected (see chapter 20 for a detailed discussion of these issues). The comments and criticisms previously mentioned with respect to the BSM formula apply to the HJM libor model as well.

As with options in other markets, many dealers express their quotes in terms of volatilities, which they refer to as "vols." The other inputs being known, with the HJM libor model you can determine the caplet price.

25.7 | Understanding the HJM Libor Model

Recall martingales, pseudo-probabilities, and risk-neutral valuation from equity option pricing. We introduced them in part III of the book to provide an enriched understanding of the option pricing methodology. We do the same here. In addition, these concepts also enable us to provide a quick sketch of the proof for the caplet pricing formula in Result 25.1.

Forward Rates and Martingales

As discussed in the context of the binomial interest rate option pricing model of chapter 23, it can be shown (see Jarrow 2010)[5] that the no-arbitrage assumption implies the existence of pseudo-probabilities $\pi_{T+\delta}(z) > 0$ such that

$$i(0,T) = E^{\pi}_{T+\delta}[i(T,T)] \tag{25.11}$$

where $i(0,T)$ is today's (time 0) simple forward rate for the time interval $[T,T+\delta]$, T is the caplet's expiration date, δ is the time period over which the interest is applied, and $E^{\pi}_{T+\delta}[.]$ is expectation based on these pseudo-probabilities $\pi_{T+\delta}(z)$.

Here the pseudo-probabilities depend on the maturity of the forward rate. Expression (25.11) states that the current forward rate equals its expected time T value, when using the pseudo-probabilities. Interestingly, this shows that the unbiased expectations hypothesis (which was introduced in Extension 21.2) holds under the pseudo-probabilities. Because the pseudo-probabilities contain an adjustment for risk (see below), this also shows that the unbiased expectations hypothesis will not hold under the actual probabilities.

Risk-Neutral Valuation

To see how a caplet is priced by risk-neutral valuation, let us first note that the caplet's value can be written as

$$c(0) = B(0,T + \delta)E^{\pi}_{T+\delta}\big\{\max\big[i(T,T) - k,0\big] \cdot \delta\big\} \times L_N \tag{25.12}$$

where $E^{\pi}_{T+\delta}\{\cdot\}$ is expectation based on the pseudo-probabilities $\pi_{T+\delta}(z)$. In this expression, the caplet's payment date is time $(T+\delta)$.

This expression states that the caplet's time 0 value is equal to its discounted expected payoff, using the pseudo-probabilities. As such, it is analogous to the risk-neutral valuation procedure used with respect to the BSM model.

Expression (25.12) provides us with a convenient method for proving expression (25.7a) of Result 25.1. As noted earlier, under the pseudo-probabilities, the forward rate $i(T,T)$ has a lognormal distribution with mean zero and variance v_T^2. A direct

---

[5] It can be shown that the lognormally distributed simple forward rates imply a stochastic process for the corresponding continuously compounded forward rates. Condition (25.11) can then be used to show that the HJM arbitrage-free drift restriction holds for the continuously compounded forward rate process, proving that the implied term structure evolution is arbitrage-free.

evaluation of the expectation in expression (25.12) using this lognormal distribution gives the HJM libor formula. The proof is identical to that given for the BSM model, with the exception that only the inputs (and their interpretations) have changed.

Actual versus Pseudo-probabilities

The difference between the actual and pseudo-probabilities represents an adjustment for risk, just as for the BSM model. To see this, we start with assumption A5. Under assumption A5, the simple forward rate $i(0,T)$ at time 0 has a lognormal distribution. We can write this as

$$\log\left(\frac{i(T,T)}{i(0,T)}\right) = \int_0^T \mu_s ds - \frac{1}{2}v_T^2 T + v_T\sqrt{T}\cdot z \tag{25.13}$$

where z is a standard normal random variable with mean 0, variance 1, with probability $q(z) = e^{-\frac{1}{2}z^2}/\sqrt{2\pi}$. The expression (25.13) holds at any time t between time 0 and the expiration date T.

These $q(z)$s are the actual probabilities. As with the BSM model, it can be shown that the actual probabilities and the pseudo-probabilities must agree on zero-probability events, that is,

$$\pi_{T+\delta}(z) > 0 \text{ if and only if } q(z) > 0 \tag{25.14}$$

Otherwise, traders will not agree on what constitutes an arbitrage opportunity.

Second, this implies that the actual and pseudo-probabilities are related by:

$$\pi_{T+\delta}(z) = \varphi_{T+\delta}(z)q(z) \tag{25.15a}$$

where

$$\varphi_{T+\delta}(z) = e^{-\frac{\theta_{T+\delta}^2}{2}+\theta_{T+\delta}z} \text{ and} \tag{25.15b}$$

$$\theta_{T+\delta} = -\left(\frac{\int_0^T \mu_s ds}{v_T\sqrt{T}}\right) \tag{25.15c}$$

The quantity $\varphi_{T+\delta}(z)$ is an adjustment for risk. The justification for this statement is the same as that given for the BSM formula in chapter 19. This risk adjustment in the pseudo-probabilities is the reason that the risk-neutral valuation procedure works in our world with risk-averse traders!

25.8 | Caps and Floors

The HJM libor model for pricing caplets is all we need! One can use it to price a cap (which is a collection of caplets), a floorlet (via caplet–floorlet parity), and a floor (which is a collection of floorlets). Let's now see how to price these interest rate derivatives.

Caps

A *cap* is a financial security with a notional amount L_N, a strike rate k, an expiration date T, and a "payment" interval δ. The cap buyer receives the payment

$$\max[i(t-\delta, t-\delta) - k, 0] \times \delta \times L_N \qquad (25.16)$$

at the payment dates $t = \delta, 2\delta, \ldots, (T+\delta)$.

For example, the first payment happens at time δ, which is computed using the simple forward rate $i(0,0)$ that applies over the time interval $[0,\delta]$. Recall that this simple forward rate effective immediately is also the spot rate. The second payment happens at time 2δ and is based on the forward rate $i(\delta,\delta)$ known at time δ, and so forth.

Hence, a cap is a portfolio of caplets, with each caplet having the same strike rate k as the cap, and each with a different maturity date corresponding to the payment dates. We can find this cap's value by valuing each individual caplet and adding the resulting values.

Floorlets

A *floorlet* is a European put option on the spot rate of interest. As with a caplet, the payment is received δ years (a fraction of a year) after the floorlet's stated maturity at time T. The payment equals the notational times the simple interest rate $[k - i(T,T)]\delta$ adjusted for the time period δ over which the interest applies.

To dress this up in more formal terms, consider a floorlet with notional principal L_N, strike rate k, and expiration date T, where the time period over which interest is computed is δ years and the payment date is $(T+\delta)$. The floorlet holder's payoff on the *payment date* is

$$p_{T+\delta} = \max[k - i(T,T), 0] \times \delta \times L_N \qquad (25.17)$$

where the simple forward rate $i(T,T)$ is the interest rate determined at time T that applies over the time period $[T, T+\delta]$.

To obtain the value of this payoff on the floorlet's *maturity date*, multiply the preceding payoff by $B(T, T+\delta)$, which is the time T price of a zero-coupon bond that pays a dollar at time $(T+\delta)$. Once you have priced a caplet, it's easy to value a floorlet by using our old friend caplet–floorlet parity.

Caplet–Floorlet Parity

Just as the price of otherwise identical European calls and puts on the same underlying are related by put–call parity, so are the prices of caplets and floorlets. The following argument is a generalization of that given to derive caplet floorlet parity in the HJM binomial model. We start with a mathematical identity:

$$i(T,T) - k = \max[i(T,T) - k, 0] - \max[k - i(T,T), 0] \qquad (25.18a)$$

You can easily check that this identity is true by inputting values for the simple forward rate $i(T,T)$ that are greater than or less than the common strike rate k.

Notice that the payoffs on the right side are those at time $(T+\delta)$ for the caplet and floorlet, respectively. The left side represents the payments to an FRA with maturity time $(T+\delta)$. Next, we apply the risk-neutral valuation procedure: take expectations

$E^{\pi}_{T+\delta}\{\cdot\}$ using the pseudo-probabilities $\pi_{T+\delta}(z)$ and then discount the payoffs by multiplying by the zero-coupon bond's price that matures at time $(T+\delta)$. This gives

$$
\begin{aligned}
B(0,T + \delta)E^{\pi}_{T+\delta}&\left[i(T,T) - k\right] \times \delta \times L_N \\
&= B(0,T + \delta)E^{\pi}_{T+\delta}\left\{\max\left[i(T,T) - k,0\right]\right\} \times \delta \times L_N \\
&\quad - B(0,T + \delta)E^{\pi}_{T+\delta}\left\{\max\left[k - i(T,T),0\right]\right\} \times \delta \times L_N \qquad (25.18b)
\end{aligned}
$$

where we have also multiplied the expressions on both sides by $\delta \times L_N$, the time period over which interest is computed times the notional.

Because the expectation of $i(T,T)$ is today's simple forward rate, the expected value of the constant k is itself and the discounted expected value of the caplet's and floorlet's payoffs are today's prices, we get the final result.

RESULT 25.2

- -

Caplet–Floorlet Parity

$$
c - p = B(0,T + \delta)\ [i(0,T) - k] \times \delta \times L_N \qquad \textbf{(25.19)}
$$

where c and p are today's (time 0) prices of caplets and floorlets that have strike rate k and expiration date T, respectively, $B(0,T+\delta)$ is today's price of a zero-coupon bond that pays \$1 at time $(T+\delta)$, $i(0,T)$ is the simple forward rate that applies to the period $[T,T+\delta]$, and L_N is the notional principal.

Our next example uses caplet–floorlet parity to price a floorlet.

EXAMPLE 25.5: Pricing a Floorlet Using the HJM Libor Model

- Consider the CFP data.
  - Today is time 0, the floorlet's expiration date T is one year, interest applies over six months, a $\delta = 182/365 = 0.4986$ year period, and the payoff date is $(T+\delta)$.
  - The notional principal $L_N = \$100$ million and the strike rate $k = 4$ percent per year.
  - The simple forward rate applicable over δ is $i(0,T) = i(0,1) = 0.0421$.
  - The average forward rate volatility v_T is 0.15, or 15 percent per year.
  - A zero-coupon bond maturing after 1.4986 years is worth $B(0,T+\delta) = B(0,1.4986) = \$0.95$ today.

- Example 25.3 gave the caplet's price as

$$
\begin{aligned}
c &= B(0,T+\delta)\ [i(0,T)N(d_1) - kN(d_2)] \times \delta \times L_N \\
&= \$172,842.45
\end{aligned}
$$

- Using the caplet–floorlet parity relation (25.19), the floorlet's price is

$$
\begin{aligned}
p &= c - B(0,T+\delta)\ [i(0,T) - k] \times \delta \times L_N \\
&= 172,842.45 - 0.95 \times (0.0421 - 0.04) \times 0.4986 \times 100 \text{ million} \\
&= \$73,116.42
\end{aligned}
$$

Floors

A *floor* is a financial security on a notional amount L_N with a strike rate k, a maturity date T, and a "payment" interval δ. A floor holder receives payments

$$\max[k - i(t - \delta, t - \delta), 0] \times \delta \times L_N \tag{25.20}$$

at times $\delta, 2\delta, \ldots, T, (T + \delta)$. Thus a floor is a portfolio of floorlets, each with the same strike rate k as the floor but with different maturity dates corresponding to the payment dates. To value a floor, price the constituent floorlets and just add them up!

25.9 | Using the HJM Libor Model

Using a derivative pricing model really means "hedging." After all, a perfect hedge is the basis for derivatives pricing, and the holy grail of option pricing is the determination of the option's delta. Let's see how we can hedge in the HJM libor model.

Stepping back for one moment, hedging interest rate risk in an HJM model is very flexible because every traded security can be used to hedge anything else. However, because of the special structure of the HJM libor model, this section confines itself to a discussion of delta and gamma hedging for caplets and floorlets. There are several reasons for this.

1. Caplets and floorlets have closed-form solutions in the HJM libor model. This enables one to easily compute partial derivatives yielding exact formulas for delta and gamma hedges. Unfortunately, closed form solutions are not available for other interest rate derivatives.

2. Our discussion of the dangers in using vega hedging in a model where the volatility is nonrandom and not priced within the model applies to the HJM libor model. This is confounded by the fact that the HJM libor model is rejected by historical data, exactly analogous to the BSM model (see chapter 20).

3. The delta and gamma hedging techniques discussed here do not extend to more complex interest rate derivatives like American options and futures contracts, which do not have closed-form solutions. They must be hedged using numerical methods in a more complex HJM model, examples of which were discussed in chapter 24 in the context of a two-period binomial model. This is because the continuously compounded forward rates in an HJM libor model, which are needed to price interest rate derivatives that are not just simple extensions of caplets and floorlets, do not follow a simple probability distribution.

The Greeks

Hedging the Greeks is a risk management technique that uses the HJM libor model and a Taylor series expansion to hedge the interest rate risk of a cap or floor position. The approach is similar to the one discussed in chapter 20 in the context of the BSM model. Before introducing Greek hedging, let us first compute the deltas and gammas needed in the hedges.

- Taking the partial derivative of the caplet pricing formula in Result 25.1 with respect to $i(0,T) \equiv i$, it can be shown that the **caplet's delta** is

$$\text{Delta}_C \equiv \frac{\partial c}{\partial i} = B(0,T + \delta) \times N(d_1) \times \delta \times L_N > 0 \qquad (25.21a)$$

This makes sense because all else being equal, an increase in the simple forward rate raises a caplet's value.

- We can rewrite the definition of the simple forward rate given in expression (25.3a) as

$$B(0,T + \delta) = \frac{B(0,T)}{1 + i \times \delta} \qquad (25.21b)$$

Taking the partial derivative of this expression with respect to $i(0,T)$ gives

$$\frac{\partial B(0,T + \delta)}{\partial i} = -\frac{B(0,T)\delta}{(1 + i \times \delta)^2} < 0 \qquad (25.21c)$$

This expression also makes sense because an increase in the interest rate lowers a zero-coupon bond's value.

- Taking the second partial derivative of expression (25.21a), using (25.21c), and simplifying yields the **caplet's gamma**:

$$\text{Gamma}_C \equiv \frac{\partial^2 c}{\partial i^2} = \frac{B(0,T + \delta)}{i \times v_T \sqrt{T}} N'(d_1)\delta L_N - \frac{B(0,T)}{(1 + i \times \delta)^2} N(d_1)\delta^2 L_N$$

$$(25.21d)$$

where $N'(\cdot)$ is the standard normal density function.

Delta Hedging

The idea of a hedged portfolio is simple. Consider a portfolio consisting of a single caplet. Instead of selling the caplet, we want to take an offsetting position in another interest rate–sensitive security, to remove all the interest rate risk from our long caplet position. For this purpose, we can use some zero-coupon bonds. Hence we want to buy or sell some zero-coupon bonds to *delta hedge* the caplet so that the resulting portfolio becomes *delta-neutral*, and its value remains the same despite small fluctuations in the simple forward rate.

If we can trade quickly enough so that the time interval between trades Δt approximates an infinitesimal time interval dt, then the theory tells us that the delta hedge removes all interest rate risk from a caplet position. The result is a perfectly hedged portfolio that earns the risk-free rate under our assumptions (see the appendix of chapter 20 for a detailed discussion of this approach). Unfortunately, it is impossible to trade continuously as prescribed by the theory. Consequently, we must necessarily consider delta hedging over a finite but small time interval $[0, \Delta t]$.

To delta hedge a long caplet position, consider the resultant portfolio V consisting of the long caplet worth c and n shares of the zero-coupon bond worth

$B(0,T+\delta) \equiv B$. We implement this hedge at time 0, but you can do this at any time t. The initial value of the portfolio is

$$V(0) = c(0) + nB(0,T+\delta) \tag{25.22a}$$

In symbols, we can write the evolution of our portfolio's value over the time interval $[0,\Delta t]$ as

$$\Delta V = \Delta c + n\Delta B \tag{25.22b}$$

where $\Delta V \equiv V(\Delta t) - V(0)$ and $\Delta B \equiv B(\Delta t) - B(0)$.

Writing out the first-order terms in a Taylor series expansion in terms of changes in the simple forward rate Δi, we see that the portfolio is delta-neutral if we can find n such that

$$\Delta V = \frac{\partial c}{\partial i}\Delta i + n\frac{\partial B}{\partial i}\Delta i = 0 \tag{25.22c}$$

Note that the partial derivatives with respect to the model's other parameters are absent because they are fixed and do not change.

The preceding expression gives

$$n = -\frac{\dfrac{\partial c}{\partial i}}{\dfrac{\partial B(0,T+\delta)}{\partial i}} \tag{25.21d}$$

Using expression (25.21a) in the numerator and (25.21c) in the denominator yields

$$n = -\frac{B(0,T+\delta)N(d_1)\delta L_N}{-\left[\dfrac{B(0,T)\delta}{(1+i\times\delta)^2}\right]}$$

$$= N(d_1)(1+i\times\delta)L_N \tag{25.21e}$$

where we used expression (25.21b) to simplify further.

This gives the holy grail for the HJM libor model! The *hedge ratio n* represents the number of shares of the zero-coupon bond to hold for each caplet to construct a riskless portfolio (equivalent to a position in a money market account). Isn't it puzzling to see that a long position in a caplet is hedged by a long position in a zero-coupon bond? No. The reason is, of course, that bond prices and simple forward rates move in opposite directions, hence bond and caplet prices move in opposite directions too. It all makes sense!

RESULT 25.3

- -

Delta Hedging in the Libor Model

To remove the interest risk from a long caplet position, buy

$N(d_1)[1 + i(0,T) \times \delta]L_N$ shares of a zero-coupon worth $B(0,T+\delta)$ (25.23)

where $d_1 = (\log[i(0,T)/k] + v_T^2 T/2)/v_T\sqrt{T}$, $N(\ .\ )$ is the cumulative standard normal distribution function, today is time 0, $i(0,T)$ is the simple forward rate, T is the expiration date, δ corresponds to the period over which interest applies, L_N is the notional principal, $B(0,T+\delta)$ is today's price of a zero-coupon bond, k is the strike rate, and v_T is the average forward rate volatility.

The next example illustrates the effectiveness of delta hedging a caplet.

EXAMPLE 25.6: Delta Hedging a Caplet

- Consider the CFP data.
- Today is time 0, $T = 1$ year, $i(0,T) = i(0,1) = 0.0421$, $\delta = 0.4986$ year, $B(0,T+\delta) = B(0,1.4986) = \$0.95$, $k = 0.04$, and $v_T = 0.15$. Today's caplet price of \$172,842.45 is based on a notional principal $L_N = \$100$ million (see Example 25.3).
- As just discussed, a delta-neutral portfolio is obtained by hedging one long caplet position with a purchase of $n = N(d_1)[1 + i(0,T)\delta]$ shares of the zero-coupon bond. This creates a delta-neutral portfolio with initial value $V = c + nB(0,T+\delta)$.
- We compute the values of $\Delta V = \Delta c + n\Delta B(0,T+\delta)$ to see how the delta hedge works for different simple forward rate changes. The results are reported in Table 25.3. For simplicity, we assume that the simple forward rate can magically change without changing time.
- The first column reports the different simple forward rates $i(0,1)$ starting from 0.0421, given in the middle row. The rates differ from the starting value by 100, 10, or 1 basis points.
  - Column 2 lists the bond $B(0,T + \delta)$ prices corresponding to the different rates obtained from expression (25.21b).
  - Column 3 reports the caplet values corresponding to the different rates.
  - To see how the hedge performs, we first compute the number of shares of the zero-coupon bonds needed to hedge one caplet. This is given by expression (25.22e). Using $N(d_1)$ with our basic data, we get

$$
\begin{aligned}
n &= N(d_1)(1 + i\,[0,T] \times \delta)L_N \\
&= 0.6616 \times (1 + 0.0421 \times 0.4986) \times 100 \text{ million} \\
&= 67,553,564.09
\end{aligned}
\tag{25.24a}
$$

  - The final column reports the changes in the hedged portfolio's value for the different simple forward rates:

$$
\begin{aligned}
\Delta V &= \Delta c + n\Delta B(0,T+\delta) \\
&= [c(\Delta t) - c(0)] + n[B(\Delta t) - B(0)] \\
&= (\text{New call price} - 172,852.22) + 67,553,564.09 \times (\text{New bond price} - 0.950054)
\end{aligned}
\tag{25.24b}
$$

  - For example, in row 4, for $i(0,1) = 0.0420$, we get $\Delta V = (169,739 - 172,852.22) + 67,553,564.09 \times (0.950100 - 0.950054) = \$22.20$.

TABLE 25.3: Delta Hedging Errors for a Caplet

$i(0,1)$	$B(0,T+\delta)$	c	ΔV
0.0321	0.954716	8,088.79	150,212.61
0.0411	0.950518	142,989.05	1,495.93
0.0420	0.950100	169,739.89	22.20
0.0421	**0.950054**	**172,852.22**	**0**
0.0422	0.950007	175,991.68	5.23
0.0431	0.949590	205,424.69	1,244.00
0.0521	0.945436	575,720.16	90,953.48

■ The table shows that for small changes in forward rates, the delta-neutral portfolio's value changes are small (for example, when $i[0,1] = 0.0420$, $\Delta V = 22.20$), but for larger changes in forward rates, the hedging error increases significantly (for example, when $i[0,1] = 0.0521$, $\Delta V = 90,953.48$). Consistent with the underlying theory, this shows that *for small changes in simple forward rates, the hedge performs quite well.*

Gamma Hedging

When Δt is small, delta hedging works well because the change in the simple forward rates will be small. But if the hedging interval Δt is large, then the change in the simple forward rates will be large, and one needs to gamma hedge. *Gamma hedging* is hedging the changes in delta in addition to the changes in interest rates (akin to the approach in chapter 20).

Gamma hedging is a valid procedure because the risk of changes in interest rates is already priced into the valuation methodology. We note, however, that gamma hedging is less important for interest rate derivatives as compared to stocks because the changes in forward rates $i(t,T)$ are smaller over daily and weekly trading intervals than price changes are for a stock.

As discussed in chapter 20, adding a gamma hedge on top of a delta hedge requires an additional hedging security. Two choices seem natural here: another zero-coupon bond or another caplet. If we use another zero-coupon bond, then we need to know the impact of changing $i(0,T)$ on this other zero-coupon bond. This is a complex problem that is not easily handled in the HJM libor model. Alternatively, we can use another caplet on the same forward rate but with a different maturity. We take the second approach because this caplet's delta is available as an analytic expression. As with delta hedging, we set up a delta–gamma hedge at time 0, but we could have done this at any time t.

Let c_2 be another caplet on the same maturity forward rate but with a different strike rate. We form a portfolio consisting of the initial caplet c_1, n_1 number of shares of the zero-coupon bond $B(0, T + \delta) \equiv B$, and n_2 number of shares of the additional caplet with a different strike rate. Then, the change in the value of the resultant portfolio over the time interval $[t, t + \Delta t]$ is

$$\Delta V = \Delta c_1 + n_1 \Delta B + n_2 \Delta c_2 \qquad (25.25a)$$

Then, to be delta and gamma neutral, we need to choose both n_1 and n_2 such that

$$\Delta V = \left(\frac{\partial c_1}{\partial i} \Delta i + n_1 \frac{\partial B}{\partial i} \Delta i + n_2 \frac{\partial c_2}{\partial i} \Delta i \right)$$
$$+ \frac{1}{2} \left(\frac{\partial^2 c_1}{\partial i^2} \Delta i^2 + n_1 \frac{\partial^2 B}{\partial i^2} \Delta i^2 + n_2 \frac{\partial^2 c_2}{\partial i^2} \Delta i^2 \right) = 0. \qquad (25.25b)$$

Equating the terms in the first parentheses (which has the coefficients of Δi) and the second parentheses (which has the coefficients of Δi^2) to zero, we get two equations in two unknowns. Their solution is

$$n_2 = \left(\frac{\partial^2 c_1}{\partial i^2} \frac{\partial B}{\partial i} - \frac{\partial c_1}{\partial i} \frac{\partial^2 B}{\partial i^2} \right) \div \left(\frac{\partial c_2}{\partial i} \frac{\partial^2 B}{\partial i^2} - \frac{\partial^2 c_2}{\partial i^2} \frac{\partial B}{\partial i} \right) \qquad (25.25c)$$

$$n_1 = - \left(\frac{\partial c_1}{\partial i} + n_2 \frac{\partial c_2}{\partial i} \right) \div \frac{\partial B}{\partial i} \qquad (25.25d)$$

These give the prescribed holdings for setting up a delta-gamma-neutral portfolio. Because the computation is otherwise similar to that contained in chapter 20 we do not provide a numerical example to illustrate this procedure.

25.10 American Options, Futures, Swaptions, and Other Derivatives

How does one price and hedge American options, futures, and other interest rate derivatives? Unfortunately, the HJM libor model's formulas are of little help. To understand why, we have to explore some technical considerations. Note that in the specification of the HJM libor model (assumption A6), we did not need to specify the number of factors generating the evolution of the term structure of zero-coupon bond prices. This is because the pricing of a single caplet only requires the specification of the relevant simple forward rate and the $(T + \delta)$ maturity bond. However, for more complex interest rate derivatives, a specification of the factor structure and the evolution of the *entire term structure* of zero-coupon bond prices are required. This is similar to what we did in chapter 24 but extended to the continuous-time setting.

For pricing American options, just as in the BSM model, numerical procedures need to be employed. The discrete-time HJM model as presented in chapters 23 and 24 can be used in this regard. The parameters to input into the discrete-time

HJM model to obtain the HJM libor model as the time step goes to zero are given in the appendix to chapter 24.

Similarly, the pricing of futures, swaptions, and other interest rate derivatives requires the use of numerical methods.[6] This is because under the HJM libor model, the implied continuously compounded forward rates do not have a lognormal distribution. Consequently, the evolution of the term structure of continuously compounded forward rates is quite complex. The discrete-time HJM model as presented in chapters 23 and 24 can provide a numerical procedure for use in this regard. A presentation of the analogous continuous-time HJM model is left for more advanced courses (see, e.g., Jarrow [2002b] for an introduction to such models).

25.11 | Summary

1. Caplets and floorlets are European call and put options, respectively, on interest rates (as measured by simple forward rates). They trade as bundles: a cap is a collection of caplets with identical terms and conditions, except for their expiration dates, and a floor is a similar collection of floorlets.

2. Fischer Black (1976) developed a model that was later modified to price caplets. Black's original model was inconsistent with the no-arbitrage assumption.

3. Sandmann et al. (1995), Miltersen et al. (1997), and Brace et al. (1997) independently developed the HJM libor model, which assumes that simple forward rates are lognormally distributed in an HJM model. The simple forward rate is defined at time 0 and applies over the time interval $[T, T + \delta]$, that is,

$$i(0,T) = \left(\frac{B(0,T)}{B(0,T + \delta)} - 1 \right) \times \frac{1}{\delta}$$

4. The HJM libor model formula for caplet pricing is

$$c = B(0,T + \delta)\,[i(0,T)N(d_1) - kN(d_2)] \times \delta \times L_N$$

where $B(0,T + \delta)$ is today's price of a zero-coupon bond that matures at time $(T + \delta)$, T is the caplet's maturity date, δ is the time period that interest is earned, $i(0,T)$ is the simple forward rate per year effective over the interval $[T, T + \delta]$, $N(\,.\,)$ is the cumulative standard normal distribution function (with mean 0 and standard deviation 1), $d_1 = (\log\left[i(0,T)/k\right] + v_T^2 T/2)/v_T\sqrt{T}$ and $d_2 = d_1 - v_T\sqrt{T}$, k is the strike rate, v_T is the average forward rate volatility over the caplet's life, and L_N is the notional principal.

5. The easiest inputs to obtain are the strike rate k, expiration date T, and time period that interest is earned δ because they are written into the contract. Forward rates are the same as forward rate agreement rates, which are quoted in the OTC market. FRA rates or Eurodollar rates (for maturities up to one year) and swap rates (for maturities beyond one year) can be used to compute zero-coupon bond prices.

---

[6] If the simple forward rate is assumed to be lognormal, then the swap rate, being an average of forward rates, is not log normally distributed so that a simple Black-type model does not apply.

6. The average forward rate volatility is computed by the equation

$$\nu_T = \sqrt{\frac{\int_0^T \sigma_s^2 ds}{T}}$$

where σ_s is the time s — maturity simple forward rate $i(0,s)$'s volatility per year.

7. Just as for the BSM formula, one can use market prices of caps, as portfolios of caplets, to find that average forward rate volatility ν_T that best matches market prices. This is the implied volatility.

8. Caplet–floorlet parity is given by

$$c - p = B(0, T + \delta) \, [i(0,T) - k] \times \delta \times L_N$$

where c and p are today's (time 0) prices of caplets and floorlets that have strike rate k and expiration date T, respectively; $B(0, T + \delta)$ is today's price of a zero-coupon bond that pays \$1 at time $(T + \delta)$; $i(0,T)$ is the simple forward rate over the period $[T, T + \delta]$; and L_N is the notional principal.

9. The HJM libor model can be used for delta and gamma hedging interest rate risk. The delta hedge is obtained by buying $N(d_1)[1 + i(0,T) \times \delta]L_N$ shares of a zero-coupon bond worth $B(0, T + \delta)$. Gamma hedging takes a similar approach. However, these techniques do not extend to more complex interest rate derivatives like American options and futures contracts, which do not have closed-form solutions.

25.12 | Cases

Risk at Freddie Mac (Stanford Business School Case F270, European Case Clearing House Case). The case considers the interest rate risk management of Freddie Mac's mortgage portfolio.

Student Educational Loan Fund Inc. (Abridged) (Harvard Business School Case 201083-PDF-ENG). The case studies how an organization that makes student loans can use an interest rate derivative to change the loan terms from a variable-rate loan with semiannual payments to a fixed-rate loan with equal monthly payments.

Remy Cointreau: Debt Management and Yield Curves (Case 111-039-1, European Case Clearing House Case). The case examines interest rate risk management at a leading wines and spirits manufacturer, which keeps a large inventory and which has a significant amount of financial debt of different maturities.

25.13 | Questions and Problems

25.1. In the Heath–Jarrow–Morton libor model, what are the two assumptions that differ relative to the Black–Scholes–Merton model?

25.2. a. In the HJM libor model, is it a simple interest rate or a continuously compounded interest rate that follows a lognormal distribution?

    b. Why is this difference important (hint: relates to Black's formula)?

    c. In the HJM libor model, is the volatility of the simple forward rate of interest a constant, or does it depend on time?

25.3. Discuss the history of evolution of interest rate option pricing models that started from the BSM model and ended with the HJM libor model.

25.4. In pricing a caplet with maturity T and strike rate k, at what date is the payment received, and what is the payoff at time T?

25.5. Use the caplet valuation formula, expression (25.5), to answer the following question. Suppose two investors disagree on the expected percentage change in the simple forward rate over the caplet's life. Will the two investors still agree on the caplet's price?

25.6. Suppose that the time 0 simple forward rate $i(0,2)$ is 0.045 per year, the notional principal is L_N is \$40 million, the strike rate k is 0.04 per year, the time period for interest computation δ is three months, the caplet matures in $T = 2$ years, the average forward rate volatility is 0.15 per year, and a zero-coupon bond maturing after 2.25 years is worth $B(0, T + \delta) = \$0.89$ today. What is the value of the caplet?

25.7. In the HJM libor caplet value, because the volatility of the forward rate changes over the caplet's life, what volatility is input into the formula? How does this differ from the volatility input into the BSM model for an equity option?

25.8. There are two ways to estimate the forward rate's average volatility over the caplet's life. What are they? What are their advantages and disadvantages?

25.9. Given the following data, compute the historical volatility of the constant-maturity forward rates.

Weekly Forward Price Data						
	Constant Maturity Simple Forward Rate $i(n,s)$					
Week n	$s=0$	$s=0.25$	$s=0.5$	$s=0.75$	$s=1.00$	$s=1.25$
1	0.1020	0.1060	0.1120	0.1160	0.1230	0.1160
2	0.1050	0.1070	0.1140	0.1160	0.1260	0.1190
3	0.1080	0.1090	0.1150	0.1180	0.1270	0.1230
4	0.1090	0.1110	0.1150	0.1210	0.1280	0.1250
5	0.1100	0.1130	0.1180	0.1210	0.1290	0.1280
6	0.1100	0.1150	0.1190	0.1250	0.1300	0.1310
7	0.1110	0.1150	0.1200	0.1240	0.1340	0.1310
8	0.1120	0.1160	0.1210	0.1270	0.1340	0.1350
9	0.1120	0.1170	0.1210	0.1280	0.1350	0.1360
10	0.1110	0.1180	0.1210	0.1270	0.1360	0.1310
11	0.1090	0.1170	0.1200	0.1260	0.1350	0.1280
12	0.1070	0.1130	0.1180	0.1230	0.1290	0.1210

T is 1.25 years; δ is 0.5 years.

25.10. Given the market price of the caplet is $209,801.727, and using the following inputs for the caplet (notional $100 million, strike rate $k = 4$ percent, maturity 1 year, six-month bbalibor $i(0,1) = 0.421$ with $\delta = 0.4986$, $B(0,T + \delta) = \$0.95$) compute the implied average forward rate volatility over the caplet's life.

25.11. Is the forward rate an unbiased estimate of the future spot rate of interest? Explain your answer.

25.12. Why are the actual and pseudo-probabilities different? Do the actual probabilities influence the caplet's value? Explain your answer.

25.13. Is the caplet's value equal to the expected discounted value of its payoff at maturity using the actual probabilities? If not, provide and explain the correct answer.

25.14. Consider a floorlet that has the identical terms as the caplet in problem 25.6. Using caplet–floorlet parity, compute the floorlet's value.

25.15. If you want to hedge a caplet using a zero-coupon bond of maturity $(T + \delta)$, what is the hedge ratio that you should use?

25.16. Given the caplet solution in problem 25.6, compute the caplet's delta.

25.17. Why would one use gamma hedging with the HJM libor model? Why would one not use vega hedging with the HJM libor model?

25.18. What is caplet–floorlet parity? Explain your answer.

25.19. If one wants to price an American option using the HJM libor model, is there a closed-form solution? If not, how can one price such an option?

25.20. How would one price an interest rate futures in the HJM libor model?

26

Risk Management Models

26.1 | Introduction

Even in the rarefied world of global investment banking, Goldman Sachs Group Inc., whose star-studded list of former employees includes a prime minister of Italy, several US Treasury secretaries, a World Bank president, and some central bank governors, enjoys a pristine reputation. According to Nocera, in December 2006, Goldman Sachs discovered that various risk measures, including value-at-risk (VaR), indicated that something was wrong in the mortgage-backed securities market.[1] The company convened a meeting of risk managers and senior executives. They scrutinized every trading position, debated the results from their financial models, discussed the market, and decided to "get closer to home" (which means, in trader lingo, to reduce their mortgage-backed securities risk exposure). This move enabled Goldman Sachs to avert billions of dollars in losses when the housing market crashed in summer 2007 and to avoid the fate of many failed Wall Street firms like Bear Stearns and Lehman Brothers.

This story also highlights what Bernstein (1998) described as "a persistent tension between those who assert that the best decisions are based on *quantification and numbers, determined by the patterns of the past* [emphasis added], and those who base their decisions on *more subjective degrees of belief about the uncertain future* [emphasis added]."[2] What good are models that fail when they are most needed? This is an often-heard criticism coming from practitioners, prophets, and even some professors who experienced the financial crisis of 2007.

We disagree! Our reading of the crisis is very different. In the Goldman Sachs example, both "mind" and "model" worked exactly as they should. By identifying trouble brewing, the models did their job. A refined understanding of models—their benefits and limitations—saved the day. Alternatively stated, it is not the models being poor but the poor use of models that helped caused the financial crisis.

This chapter concludes our study of derivatives pricing models. The first twenty-five chapters have shown us how to price and hedge derivatives subject to market risk, which includes the risks generated by equity prices, commodity prices, foreign currencies, and interest rates. This chapter combines this knowledge and adds the remaining risks—credit, liquidity, and operational—to build a unified risk management framework, unique in its construction and presentation.

An outline for this chapter is as follows. First, we present the financial risk management framework using the firm's balance sheet as the focal point for analysis (see Figure 26.1). The firm's risk is characterized by the firm's equity loss distribution. Well-known risk management tools such as VaR and scenario analysis are easily understood from this perspective. Next, we study the four risks, market risk, credit risk (from which the concept of real options follows), liquidity risk, and operational risk, and discuss how to model each of these in a consistent fashion.

---

[1] "Risk Mismanagement," *New York Times*, January 4, 2009.

[2] See *Against the Gods: The Remarkable Story of Risk* by Peter L. Bernstein (1998, p. 6).

We conclude this chapter with our analysis of the credit crisis of 2007–9, and we comment on the future of models and traded derivatives.

The first four sections of this chapter on risk management are written at a higher level than the previous twenty-five chapters were. This is done because risk management and generalizing the assumptions underlying the Black–Scholes–Merton (BSM) and Heath–Jarrow–Morton (HJM) models are the next steps in derivatives pricing and hedging, and we wanted to give the reader a flavor of what's to come. As such, these four sections give a quick overview of the relevant topics and the mathematics involved, not an in-depth analysis. The last two sections, on the credit crisis and the future of derivatives and models, however, are written at an introductory level and require no new analytical techniques.

26.2 | A Framework for Financial Risk Management

From a society's point of view, the most important use of derivatives models is in their application to managing the risk of a firm's equity capital (corporation, financial institution) or an individual's wealth. By managing this equity risk, the key players in the economy hold assets and liabilities more aligned with their needs and preferences. These firms and individuals hedge risks they want to avoid and speculate on risks for which they have special knowledge. This risk management facilitates the optimal allocation of risk across the economy, increasing societal welfare and economic growth. The models presented in the first twenty-five chapters of this book can be used as the foundation for financial risk management.

Financial risk management is the management of the risk of a firm's (corporate or financial) equity capital. To understand the issues involved in managing a firm's equity risk, we need to visit the typical firm's balance sheet presented in Table 26.1. A *balance sheet* gives a snapshot of a firm's financial condition by summarizing its assets, liabilities, and ownership equity on a specific date.

On the left side of the balance sheet are the firm's *assets*, which provide economic benefits to the firm. We write the time t asset's value as A_t (see chapter 1 for the definitions of *assets*, *liabilities*, and other relevant terms). Depending on whether the assets are for the short term (one year or less) or the long term, assets (and liabilities) are further classified as current or noncurrent, respectively. *Current assets* include cash, accounts receivable, and inventory. *Long-term assets* consist of both financial and real assets—property and equipment.

On the right side of the balance sheet are the firm's liabilities and equity. The *liabilities* are a firm's obligations that require payment at some future date. We denote their time t value by L_t. *Equity* is the shareholder's wealth, analogous to an individual's wealth, its time t value denoted by E_t.

By definition, the difference between the firm's assets and liabilities is the shareholder's equity. Hence the familiar accounting identity holds:

$$A_t - L_t \equiv E_t \tag{26.1}$$

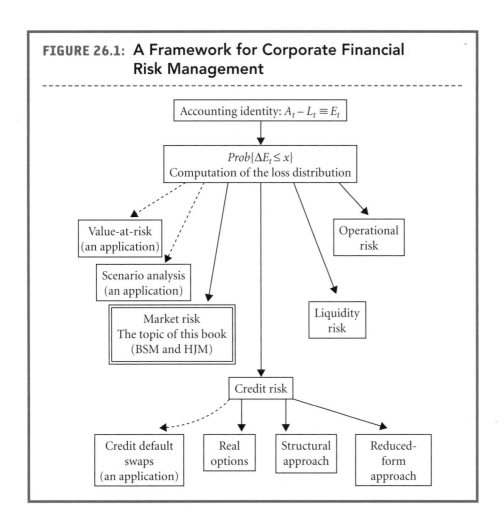

FIGURE 26.1: A Framework for Corporate Financial Risk Management

Accounting identity: $A_t - L_t \equiv E_t$

$Prob\{\Delta E_t \leq x\}$
Computation of the loss distribution

Value-at-risk (an application)

Scenario analysis (an application)

Market risk
The topic of this book
(BSM and HJM)

Operational risk

Liquidity risk

Credit risk

Credit default swaps (an application)

Real options

Structural approach

Reduced-form approach

Risk management can be understood by focusing on the various components of this basic accounting identity. The firm's management controls the purchase and sale of the firm's assets (called the *capital budgeting decision*), the accumulation of the firm's liabilities (the composition, term structure, and magnitude), and the magnitude of the equity (dividends, new issuance). These decisions are the domain of corporate finance (see Ross et al. 2004).

For risk management purposes, the equity holders are concerned with changes in the equity's value over some time interval $[t, t + \Delta t]$. For many decisions, Δt might be a day, a week, or a year. In symbols, the change in the equity value is defined as

$$\Delta E_t \equiv E_{t+\Delta t} - E_t \text{ over } [t, t + \Delta t] \tag{26.2}$$

Since this is for internal risk management, before bankruptcy and/or liquidation proceedings, it is possible that given a large enough loss, the value of the firm's equity could become strictly negative, $E_{t+\Delta t} < 0$, wiping out all of the firm's equity and even more.

TABLE 26.1: A Firm's Balance Sheet

Assets A_t	Liabilities L_t
Current assets	■ Accounts payable
■ Cash and cash equivalents	■ Financial liabilities
■ Accounts receivable	■ Pension fund obligations
■ Inventories	
Long-term assets	**Equity E_t**
■ Financial assets	■ Ownership shares
■ Property, plant, and equipment	

Of course, from expressions (26.1) and (26.2), the change in equity value is determined by the changes in the value of the assets and liabilities:

$$\Delta E_t \equiv \Delta A_t - \Delta L_t \tag{26.3}$$

where $\Delta A_t \equiv A_{t+\Delta t} - A_t$ and $\Delta L_t \equiv L_{t+\Delta t} - L_t$.

The primary tool to use for analyzing changes in the firm's equity is its probability distribution, that is,

$$\text{Prob}\{\Delta E_t \leq x\} = \text{Prob}\{\Delta A_t - \Delta L_t \leq x\} \tag{26.4a}$$

for all values x.

From this distribution, one can determine all risk management measures of interest to equity holders and regulators. For example, the probability that the firm will be insolvent over the time interval $[t, t + \Delta t]$ is given by

$$\text{Prob}\{\Delta A_t - \Delta L_t \leq -E_t\} \tag{26.4b}$$

The firm is **insolvent** if the change in the value of the equity (the left side of the inequality) is negative and greater than or equal to the existing value of equity. In terms of the balance sheet, this occurs if the change in the assets minus the change in the liabilities is negative and greater than the magnitude of the equity cushion at time t. For example, if assets increase by \$1 billion and liabilities increase by \$5 billion, and the value of shareholders' equity is \$3.5 billion, then

$$\Delta E_t \equiv \Delta A_t - \Delta L_t = 1 - 5 = -4 < -3.5 = -E_t$$

and the firm is insolvent.

Note that this condition implies that since the equity shares are of limited liability, after bankruptcy proceedings and/or liquidation, the value of the equity becomes zero, and the liability holders eventually suffer the extra losses that the equity holders do not.

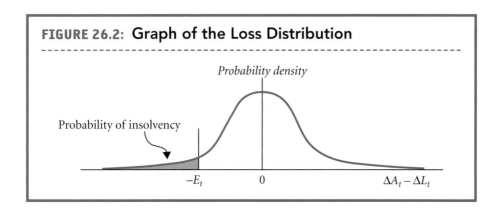

FIGURE 26.2: **Graph of the Loss Distribution**

Regulators are concerned with the ability of financial institutions and some large corporations, deemed too big to fail, to remain solvent, that is, to have enough equity capital to fulfill the obligations promised to its liabilities. For these capital determination decisions, one focuses on the lower tail of this distribution, where the change in equity value is negative (see Figure 26.2). The change in the value of equity is negative if the firm has losses. This occurs if the change in the value of the assets is less than the change in the value of the liabilities. Taking this regulatory perspective, the distribution for the changes in the value of the firm's equity is called the **loss distribution**. For these risk management decisions, we need to understand how to compute this loss distribution. This is the topic of the next section.

26.3 | Computing the Loss Distribution

Computing the loss distribution for changes in the firm's equity value is a difficult task. To facilitate this task, one can think of the value of the firm's assets and liabilities as functions of a vector of state variables, X_t, describing the state of the economy at time t, that is, $A_t(X_t)$ and $L_t(X_t)$. The state variables could be macroeconomic quantities like inflation, gross domestic product, and unemployment, or they could be the prices of the primary or basic securities themselves: zero-coupon bond prices, stock prices, commodity prices, or foreign currency exchange rates. When computing these asset and liability values, of course, one must first decompose these values into their component parts and model each component part separately.

It is important to recognize that the functions $A_t(X_t)$ and $L_t(X_t)$ are those formulas determined by the derivatives pricing theory studied in the previous chapters, for example, the BSM formula for stock options or the HJM formula for caps, where X_t corresponds to the price of a stock and the term structure of zero-coupon bond prices, respectively. When computing these formulas, four risks need to be included: market, credit, liquidity, and operational. These four risks were discussed briefly in chapter 1. Let us recall these descriptions.

Market risk is the risk from random movements in stock prices, interest rates, foreign currencies, and commodity prices. *Credit risk* corresponds to the risk that a contractual claim will not be executed as agreed, thereby leading to default. *Liquidity risk* is the risk that when trading large quantities of a financial security in a short time period, there will be a quantity impact on the price to the trader's disadvantage. Last, *operational risk* is the risk that the firm's operations may generate losses because of errors, mismanagement, fraud, accidents, or legal considerations.

The first twenty-five chapters of this book have concentrated on market risk. In these chapters, *by assumption*, we excluded credit, liquidity, and operational risk. The extension of our models to these other three risks is discussed later on in the chapter. For the moment, however, let us suppose that we know how to include all four risks in our valuation formulas.

Next, given an assumed probability distribution for ΔX_t that incorporates all four of these risks, one can then determine the probability distribution for the firm's assets, liabilities, and, finally, equity using the functions determined by derivatives pricing theory:

$$\text{Prob}\{\Delta E_t(X_t) \le x\} = \text{Prob}\{\Delta A_t(X_t) - \Delta L_t(X_t) \le x\} \text{ for all } x$$

Summarizing, a *method for computing the probability distribution for losses is*:

1. Choose the primary securities or state variables describing the state of the market or the economy.

2. Assume an arbitrage-free random evolution for the primary securities in a complete market setting or a random evolution for the state variables.

3. Value all of the firm's assets and liabilities as derivatives on the primary securities or state variables. This gives the functional forms for their values: $A_t(X_t)$ and $L_t(X_t)$.

4. Compute the distribution for the changes in the assets and liability values based on the functional forms and the assumed evolutions. This computation could be generated using Monte Carlo simulation methods or analytic formulas. If necessary, to simplify this computation, one can use linear and quadratic approximations for the values via the derivative's deltas and gammas.

Note that correlations across the changes in the collection of asset and liability values within the firm are generated by the dependence of the functional forms on the common primary securities or state variables vector X_t. This state variable dependence includes changes in equity value resulting from changes in the health of the economy as reflected in the business cycle. In turn, the dependence on the business cycle captures correlated defaults within the firm's asset and liability portfolio. In practice, the computation becomes complex and is often generated using Monte Carlo simulation techniques rather than analytic formulas. The details of these methods are left for future reading and can be found in more advanced books.

26.4 | Value-at-Risk and Scenario Analysis

The approach we have presented for computing the loss distribution underlies two common risk management statistics—VaR and scenario analysis—both of which are used extensively by corporations, policy makers, and regulators.

Value-at-Risk

Value-at-Risk (VaR) was originated in 1989 by Sir Dennis Weatherstone, then the chairman of J. P. Morgan & Co. Sir Dennis desired a one-page report that could measure the total risk faced by his global banking firm. He wanted it placed on his desk within fifteen minutes of the New York Stock Exchange's close. This 4:15 report summarized the risk of J. P. Morgan's balance sheet using VaR.

VaR is a summary measure of the loss distribution for the change in the firm's equity value over a fixed period of time $[t, t + \Delta t]$, where Δt could be a day, week, or a year. Using the accounting identity relating the firm's equity to the firm's assets and liabilities, **VaR (VaR_α) for an α loss probability** is that number such that

$$\text{Prob}\{\Delta E_t \leq - VaR_\alpha\} = \text{Prob}\{\Delta A_t - \Delta L_t \leq - VaR_\alpha\} = \alpha$$

In words, VaR_α is that dollar amount that the firm's losses will exceed with probability α (see Figure 26.3). In practice, α is often set to be 1 or 5 percent. A minus sign appears before VaR_α in this expression so that the computed $VaR_\alpha > 0$. Let us consider some VaR computations to help us understand its application and significance.

To understand how to use VaR_α in risk management decisions, let us suppose that $\alpha = 0.01$ is the insolvency probability that the firm and the regulators feel is appropriate. Given the VaR_α, the firm's management can consider if it is properly capitalized for its insolvency risk by comparing VaR_α to the firm's existing equity capital position E_t.

FIGURE 26.3: Value-at-Risk

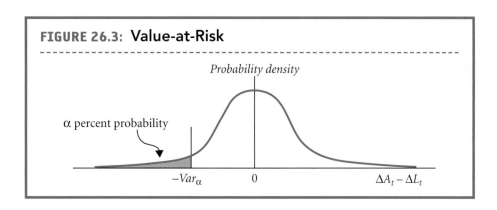

EXAMPLE 26.1: Computing Value-at-Risk

- To compute VaR, one views the firm as a portfolio of "securities," where the securities are the firm's assets and liabilities. The assets have a positive portfolio weight, while the liabilities have a negative weight. Of course, the portfolio weights must sum to one.

- Consider a firm which has an asset and liability portfolio consisting of three companies (fictitious names) Aztec, Inca, and Mayan corporations, with portfolio weights as given in Table 26.2A. Furthermore, let the daily returns on these three companies be normally distributed with means, volatilities, and correlations as given in Tables 26.2A and 26.2B. This characterizes the random evolution of the primary securities underlying the firm's assets and liability portfolio.

- To compute a daily VaR based on this normal distribution, we need to first compute the expected daily return and volatility of the firm's asset and liability portfolio. The daily expected return of this portfolio is

$$E(r_p) = \sum_{i=1}^{3} w_i E(r_i)$$
$$= (3/4) \times (0.001) + (3/4) \times (0.0005) - (1/2) \times (0.001)$$
$$= 0.000625$$

The daily return variance of this portfolio is

$$\sigma_p^2 = \sum_{i,j=1}^{3} w_{i,j}^2 \text{covariance}(r_i, r_j)$$
$$= (3/4)^2(0.0134164)^2 + (3/4)^2(0.0089443)^2 + (-1/2)^2(0.0178885)^2$$
$$+ 2(3/4)(3/4)(0.0134164)(0.0089443)(0.5)$$
$$+ 2(3/4)(-1/2)(0.0134164)(0.0178885)(0.9)$$
$$+ 2(3/4)(-1/2)(0.0089443)(0.0178885)(0.5)$$
$$= (0.0001012 + 0.000045 + 0.00008) + (0.0000675 - 0.000162 - 0.00006)$$
$$= 0.0002262 - 0.0001545$$
$$= 0.0000717$$

where we have used the well-known result that covariance$(r_i, r_j) = \sigma_i \times \sigma_j \times$ correlation(r_i, r_j), where i and j denote the companies, which are labeled 1, 2, and 3, respectively.

- The daily volatility is the square root of the variance:

$$\sigma_p = +\sqrt{0.0000717} = 0.0084676$$

TABLE 26.2A: Expected Return, Volatility, and Portfolio Weights

	Aztec Corp. (Company 1)	Inca Corp. (Company 2)	Mayan Corp. (Company 3)
Expected daily return	0.001	0.0005	0.001
Daily volatility of the returns	0.0134164	0.0089443	0.0178885
Portfolio weights	3/4	3/4	−1/2

TABLE 26.2B: Correlation of Daily Expected Returns

	Aztec Corp.	Inca Corp.	Mayan Corp.
Aztec Corp.	1	0.5	0.9
Inca Corp.	0.5	1	0.5
Mayan Corp.	0.9	0.5	1

- Third, we can now compute the daily VaR at the 5 and 1 percent levels. Recall from statistics that for a normal probability distribution, 95 percent of the values lie within 1.65 standard deviations of the mean.
  - The 5 percent left tail is $1.65 \times 0.0084676 = 0.0139715$ units away from the mean.
  - Hence the 95 percent confidence level or $-\text{VaR}_{0.05}$ is $0.000625 - 0.0139715 = -0.0133465$.
  - This means that there is only a 5 percent chance that the firm will lose more than 1.33 percent of its value on any given trading day.

- As 99 percent of the values lie within 2.33 standard deviations of the mean, we get the following:
  - The 1 percent left tail is $2.33(0.0084676) = 0.0197295$ units away from the mean.
  - The 99 percent confidence level or $-\text{VaR}_{0.01}$ is $0.000625 - 0.0197295 = -0.0191045$.
  - Thus there is only a 1 percent chance that the firm will lose more than 1.91 percent of its value on any given trading day.

- If $\text{VaR}_\alpha < E_t$, then the firm's insolvency probability is less than the desired α probability, and the firm is properly capitalized. Indeed, if a loss equal to VaR_α occurs, then there is enough equity capital to buffer this loss. The firm does not become insolvent.

- If $\text{VaR}_\alpha > E_t$, then the firm's insolvency probability is greater than α, because there is not enough equity capital to cover the VaR_α losses. The firm needs either to (1) add more equity capital to its balance sheet or (2) restructure the risk of its assets and liabilities to reduce the loss probability. For example, (1) the firm can issue new equity or cut dividend payments and (2) it could sell assets and use these funds to reduce its liabilities.

If it is used as the sole measure to quantify a firm's risk, VaR_α has a number of failings. First, it does not consider the magnitude of the losses beyond the α level. For example, if the VaR_α is $100 million, a 1 percent loss of an additional $150 million beyond the VaR_α is treated equally in the VaR_α computation as an additional $500 million loss beyond VaR_α. Clearly these different losses should not be treated as of equal risk to the firm. Second, in particular situations, VaR_α penalizes diversification. Traditional portfolio theory views diversification of an asset and liability portfolio as beneficial because it reduces risk. The fact that VaR_α can increase instead of decrease when a portfolio becomes more diversified is problematic. This possibility is illustrated in the next example.

EXAMPLE 26.2: VaR$_\alpha$ Penalizes Diversification

■ Strangely, VaR$_\alpha$ can increase when a portfolio becomes more diversified! This is counter to the intuition that you developed taking a modern investment course where diversification reduces risk. This implies, of course, that VaR$_\alpha$ is not always a good measure of a firm's risk.

■ Suppose that there are two loans A and B that can be used to constitute a firm's assets. Let A and B have the loss distributions given in Table 26.3. Loans A and B are similar in that both have no loss with probability 0.9991 and a $1 loss with probability 0.0009. We assume that the probabilities of default are statistically independent for loans A and B.

TABLE 26.3:

Loss	Prob(loss A)	Prob(loss B)	Prob(loss $[A+B]/2$)
$0	0.9991	0.9991	0.99820081
$0.5	0	0	0.00179838
$1	0.0009	0.0009	0.000000081

■ We compare two hypothetical firms. One firm invests a dollar in loan A. The second firm invests $0.50 equally in both loans A and B. The second firm, of course, has the more diversified loan portfolio because it is spreading its $1 investment across two loans whose losses are statistically independent.

■ The second firm's return is given in the third column. With probability $(0.0009)(0.0009) = 0.000000081$, both loans A and B will default, giving a $1 (= $0.5 + $0.5) loss to the second firm. With probability $2(0.0009)(0.9991)$, either loan A or loan B will default, but not both, giving a $0.50 (= $0.5 + $0) loss to the second firm. With probability $(0.9991)(0.9991)$, neither loan will default, giving a $0 loss to the second firm.

■ Let us choose $\alpha = 0.001$ for our VaR computation. The nondiversified firm consisting of only loan A has VaR$_{0.001}$(A) = $0 because no losses occur with probability greater than 0.001. But the diversified firm has VaR$_{0.001}$([A+B]/2) = $0.50 because with probability 0.00179838, a loss of $0.5 happens. The diversified firm's VaR is larger! Hence the diversified portfolio would require more capital based on this measure alone, which is an incorrect decision.

Because diversification reduces risk, this last failing is a serious flaw in using VaR$_\alpha$ as a risk measure. Used in isolation for the determination of equity capital, VaR$_\alpha$ is a dangerous statistic because of the two failings just discussed. However, used in conjunction with other risk measures, it is a useful tool in the risk manager's toolbox.

Scenario Analysis

During the financial crisis of 2007, the Federal Reserve Board required banks receiving funds under the Troubled Asset Relief Program to compute an alternative risk measure to decide if they could repay their TARP funds.[3] This alternative

[3] "Pay up! The U.S. Federal Reserve Asks Banks to Submit TARP Repayment Plans," *New York Daily News*, November 24, 2009.

measure is based on scenario analysis, another useful technique in one's risk management toolbox.

Scenario analysis (which also goes by the popular name *stress testing*) starts with a selection of a particular set of scenarios that the firm wants to protect against. These scenarios correspond to various states of the economy represented by paths of the state variables ΔX_t over the time period $[t, t + \Delta t]$. For example, if X_t represents a collection of macroeconomic variables (such as inflation, gross domestic product, unemployment, and interest rates), then a set of scenarios might be that interest rates increase by 1 percent, unemployment increases by 5 percent, inflation increases by 5 percent, and GDP falls by 2 percent. For these scenarios, the firm wants to compute the losses realized on its assets and liabilities to see if it has sufficient equity capital to avoid insolvency.

Using our notation, the firm picks a particular ΔX_t and computes

$$\Delta E_t(X_t) = \Delta A_t(X_t) - \Delta L_t(X_t)$$

Given the formulas for the values of the assets and liabilities as a function of the state variables, one then computes the change in the firm's equity capital, and if it is negative and exceeds the current equity capital position, one knows that this scenario would cause the firm to become insolvent.

EXTENSION 26.1: Risk Measures

Value-at-risk is a useful risk measure, but as noted in the text, it has some flaws. As might be expected, there are other risk measures that could be used either in conjunction with or instead of VaR_α.

The study of risk measures for use in the determination of equity capital began with the paper by Artzner et al. (1999). They defined *coherent risk measures*. To understand what these are, we need to step back and begin with the definition of a risk measure.

A **risk measure** is a positive real valued function that quantifies the "risk" to changes in a firm's equity capital—losses—over some time period. The loss to a firm's equity capital is, of course, a random variable. By this definition, there are an unlimited number of risk measures. For example, the maximum loss, the expected loss, the standard deviation of the loss, VaR_α for an arbitrary α, and the present value of the loss are all risk measures.

This leads to the question, how does one decide which risk measures are useful?

The answer is that to be of any use, a risk measure needs to possess some desirable properties or axioms that make it a "good" risk measure. Artzner et al. defined four such axioms. To state these axioms, we need some additional notation.

Let $\rho(\,.\,)$ be a risk measure and let ΔE be the change in a firm's equity over a fixed time period. Let r be the return on a riskless asset (a money market account) over this same time period.

Now we can state the four axioms:

(Translation invariance) $\rho(\Delta E + \alpha) = \rho(\Delta E) - \alpha$
(Subadditivity) $\rho(\Delta E_1 + \Delta E_2) \leq \rho(\Delta E_1) + \rho(\Delta E_2)$
(Positive homogeneity) For $\lambda \geq 0, \rho(\lambda \Delta E) = \lambda \rho(\Delta E)$
(Monotonicity) For $\Delta E_1 \leq \Delta E_2, \rho(\Delta E_2) \leq \rho(\Delta E_1)$

The translation invariance axiom states that if one adds α units of equity capital to the firm and invests it in a riskless asset, the risk measure declines by exactly α units. Subadditivity implies that a diversified portfolio (combining two firms' equity capital) is no more risky than the sum of each separate firm's capital positions. Positive homogeneity states that if you expand a firm's assets and liabilities proportionately, the risk increases proportionately as well. Last, monotonicity states that if changes in a firm's equity capital always exceed another firm's (both plus and minus), then the firm with the larger changes is more risky. Any risk measure that satisfies these four axioms is called a **coherent risk measure**.

As one might expect, there are many coherent risk measures and many risk measures are not coherent. For example, VaR_α is not a coherent risk measure because as shown in a previous example in the text, it violates the subadditivity axiom. Perhaps surprising the premium paid for an insurance policy to insure against the firm's default is not a coherent risk measure either because it violates the translation axiom.

An example of a coherent risk measure is the expected value of ΔE. A more sophisticated coherent risk measure is the expected shortfall, defined as $\widetilde{E}\{\Delta E | \Delta E \leq -\text{VaR}_\alpha\}$, where $\widetilde{E}\{.| \Delta E \leq -\text{VaR}_\alpha\}$ denotes a conditional expectation given that losses in equity values exceed VaR_α. The proof that expected shortfall is a coherent measure can be found in Follmer and Schied (2004).

Whether coherent risk measures are the proper risk measures depends on whether the four axioms are deemed reasonable, and there is considerable disagreement on this point. For example, Jarrow (2002a) does not like the translation invariance axiom precisely because it excludes the premium paid for an insurance policy to insure against the firm's default as a coherent risk measure. To rectify the situation, Jarrow proposes an alternative set of axioms that generates what he calls insurance risk measures. Other sets of axioms are also possible, and other risk measures can be characterized in this manner. The study of risk measures is an exciting area of current research (for a good summary of the different axiom selections, see Follmer and Schied 2004).

In this circumstance, if it is believed that this scenario is likely, the firm can either (1) add more equity capital to its balance sheet or (2) restructure the risk of its assets and liabilities to reduce the loss probability. Given that the loss is scenario specific, it might also be possible to hedge this loss using derivatives, as discussed in the previous chapters.

The problem with scenario analysis is that it does not assign probabilities to the various scenarios selected. Hence the firm's management does not know the probability that this scenario will occur. Of course, this failing can be overcome by selecting the scenarios to be considered in conjunction with the probability distribution for ΔX_t. Unfortunately, this procedure and related computations is left for more advanced courses.

26.5 | The Four Risks

The Basel Committee's *Risk Management Guidelines for Derivatives* (July 1994) identified the following risks in connection with an institution's derivative activities.[4] In contrast to the Basel Committee, we include legal risk in operational risk. Otherwise, the two sets of definitions are identical.

[4] See www.bis.org.

- *Market risk* is the risk to a firm resulting from adverse movements in market prices.

- *Credit risk* is the risk that a counterparty will default on an obligation.

- *Liquidity risk* is the risk that a firm may not be able to liquidate an asset or liability position without incurring losses due to a quantity impact on the market price.

- *Operational risk* is the risk that law suits, human error, operation failures, and inadequate controls will result in losses.

This section discusses each of these risks and how to model them using the derivatives pricing technology.

Market Risk

The pricing and hedging of market risk using derivatives has been the emphasis of this book. The market risks considered in chapters 1–25 included changes to stock prices, commodity prices, foreign currency exchange rates, and interest rates. Our models were generated under a set of assumptions that excluded credit risk (by assumption A2), liquidity risk (by assumptions A1 and A3), and operational risk (obviously!). To include these additional risks, we need to relax the assumptions and consider more general models. The remainder of this section discusses these generalizations.

Credit Risk

Credit risk is the risk that a counterparty will default on a contract. This is an important consideration in trading activity because all counterparties may default. An example serves to illustrate this risk. On June 26, 1974, the West German bank Bankhaus Herstatt, which had received Deutschemark payments, was forced into liquidation by West German regulators before it could make corresponding dollar payments in New York (which had a six-hour time difference), causing losses for its counterparties. This incident alerted the market about **cross-currency settlement risk**, also known as **Herstatt risk** (which Reuters Financial Glossary defines as "the risk that when dealing with an overseas client a bank may not be able to recover its funds if the counter party defaults on its payment obligation"[5]). This event led to the development of a continuously linked settlement system for foreign exchange payments.

There are two approaches to modeling credit risk: structural and reduced-form models. **Structural models** are sometimes called *contingent claims models*, as originated by Merton (1974). Jarrow and Turnbull (1992, 1995) originated **reduced-form models** to overcome a restrictive assumption contained in structural models. Structural models assume that all of the firm's assets trade in frictionless and competitive markets and, therefore, their prices are observable. This

[5] http://glossary.reuters.com/index.php/Herstatt_Risk.

assumption is usually violated in practice. Most firms' assets are very illiquid and often do not trade, for example, a firm's home office building or manufacturing plant, including the manufacturing equipment. In contrast, reduced-form models replace this assumption with a weaker restriction. Reduced-form models only assume that a subset of the firm's liabilities (debt) trade. The subset of the firm's liabilities that must trade is the one for which pricing and hedging is being considered. This small difference, however, leads to a big change in valuations and risk management.

From an economic perspective, structural models are best applied to internal management decision making, in which, even though the assets do not trade in frictionless and competitive markets, the management can "observe" their prices. In this context, structural models aid economic intuition. In contrast, reduced-form models are best applied to pricing, hedging, and risk management decisions that involve the trading of credit risky securities in financial markets. As such, they are the preferred modeling approach to risk management in our current market environment. They are easily estimated, and empirical studies show that they fit market prices well (for a review, see Jarrow 2009).

Structural Models

To understand the intuition behind the structural models, it is best to start with Merton's (1974) original formulation. We consider a simple firm with the liability structure given in Table 26.4. As before, this firm has assets with time t value A_t against which it has issued debt. The debt consists of a single zero-coupon bond with face value K and maturity date T. We let L_t be the time t value of the firm's debt and E_t be the time t value of the firm's equity. This is the simplest liability structure a firm can possess. This firm is too simple for this model to be used in practice, but it is just right for us to understand the economics.

Merton's structural model is a transformation of the BSM model of chapter 19. The structural model uses assumptions A1–A8 from the BSM model, with two modifications. First, assumption A2, no credit risk, is removed because the purpose of the structural model is to understand when the firm will default on its debt. Second, the firm's asset value replaces the stock price in assumptions A7 and A8. In particular, the structural model assumes that the firm's assets trade continuously in time and that the asset value process follows a lognormal distribution. Assumption A6, no interest rate uncertainty, is retained.

TABLE 26.4: A Firm's Time t Balance Sheet	
Assets A_t	**Liabilities L_t**
	Zero-coupon bond
	■ Maturity T
	■ Face value K
	Equity E_t

We let the continuously compounded riskless spot rate of interest per year be denoted r. Hence a default-free zero-coupon bond paying a dollar at time T has time t value

$$B(t,T) = e^{-r(T-t)}$$

In this firm, the time T value of the firm's debt and equity is completely determined by the debt's covenants. At the debt's maturity, the equity holders decide whether to pay off the debt. They will do so if and only if the value of the firm's assets exceeds the debt's face value. Otherwise, default occurs. Hence the time T value of the equity can be written as

$$E_T = \max[A_T - K, 0] \tag{26.5}$$

We see that the equity's value is equivalent to the payoff from a European call option on the firm's value, with maturity date T and strike price K.

In essence, the debt holders, and not the equity holders, own the firm. The equity holders have retained the option to buy the firm back from the debt holders at time T for K dollars. They will do so at time T if the value of the assets exceeds this purchase price. Hence we can write the value of the equity at time t to be equal to

$$E_t = c(A_t, K, T) \tag{26.6}$$

where $c(a,b,T)$ represents the value of a European call option at time t on an asset with current price a, strike price b, and maturity date T.

Using the accounting identity relating the value of the firm's equity to its assets and liabilities, we see that the debt's time T value is equal to the value of the assets less the value of the equity, that is,

$$L_T = A_T - E_T = A_T - \max[A_T - K, 0] \tag{26.7}$$

Simple algebra shows that we can rewrite the debt's time T value as

$$L_T = \min[K, A_T] = K - \max[K - A_T, 0] \tag{26.8}$$

The debt's value at maturity is seen to be equal to the smaller of the face value of the debt or the firm's asset value. Alternatively, the debt's time T payoff is equal to the face value of the debt less the payoff to a European put option on the firm's value, with maturity date T and strike price K. The time t value is therefore

$$L_t = Ke^{-r(T-t)} - p(A_t, K, T) \tag{26.9}$$

where $p(a,b,T)$ represents the value of a European put option at time t on an asset with current price a, strike price b, and maturity date T. This shows that the firm's risky debt is valued less than a similar maturity default-free zero-coupon bond ($Ke^{-r(T-t)}$). The decrease in value is equal to the put option's value in expression (26.9).

Using the lognormal distribution assumption, we can give an explicit formula for the debt's time t value:

$$L_t = A_t N(-d_1) + Ke^{-r(T-t)} N(d_2) \qquad (26.10)$$

where $N(\,.\,)$ is the cumulative standard normal distribution function which has mean 0 and standard deviation 1,

$$d_1 = \frac{\log\left(\dfrac{A_t}{K}\right) + \left(r + \dfrac{\sigma^2}{2}\right)(T - t)}{\sigma\sqrt{T - t}}$$

$d_2 = d_1 - \sigma\sqrt{T - t}$, and σ is the asset return's volatility per year.

This expression has a nice economic interpretation. The debt's value is equal to the risk-adjusted probability of default times the firm's value plus the risk-adjusted probability of no default times the discounted face value of the debt. The two terms represent the possible payoff scenarios for the firm's debt, depending on if the firm defaults (the first term) or does not (the second term).

It is easy to show that as the firm's asset volatility increases, the value of the firm's debt decreases. Since the firm's asset volatility σ is under the control of management, the decreasing value of the debt as σ increases leads to the *shareholder/debt holder conflict* (see Ross et al. 2004, p. 640). Understanding the shareholder/debt holder conflict is just one use of the structural model. Another is that it can be used to provide insights into the firm's investment/capital budgeting decisions. This is the theory of *real options* (see Extension 26.2).

The structural model can be extended to consider more complex liabilities issued by the firm. However, this extension becomes quite difficult to solve analytically because the entire liability structure of the firm needs to be specified and all of the liability values solved simultaneously. In this regard, numerical procedures need to be employed (for some of these extensions, see Jones et al. 1984; Leland 1994).

EXTENSION 26.2: Real Options

Option pricing theory can be used to understand how a firm should make its investment decisions. In the past, this field was called *capital budgeting*. Today it is called **real options**, the title of this extension. This is because embedded in most of the firm's investment decisions are options, which were often ignored in classical capital budgeting.

Real options theory usually proceeds under the same assumptions as the structural model. The model uses assumptions A1–A8 from the BSM model, with the same two modifications: first, assumption A2, no credit risk, is removed; second, the firm's asset value replaces the stock price in assumptions A7 and A8. In particular, it is assumed that a particular subset of the firm's assets trades continuously in time and that this asset's value process follows a lognormal distribution. Assumption A6, no interest rate uncertainty, is retained. We let the riskless spot rate of interest per year be denoted r. Of course, just as in the structural model, many of these assumptions can be relaxed, but with increasing analytical and computational complexity.

We explain real options theory using an example. Let us consider a gold mining company that is thinking about purchasing a new gold mine. The purchase price for the mine is P_0 dollars. The management has studied the cost of extracting the gold and believes it can extract one production unit (one hundred tons) for a cost of U_0 dollars. Gold trades, and it has a market price of A_t dollars per unit at time t. It takes T time units to extract the gold from the mine.

Last, the management also realizes that after the initial unit of gold is extracted from the mine at time T, it can invest an additional K dollars to extract another k units of gold, where $0 < k < 1$. For simplicity (although this is not necessary for the analysis), we assume that the additional k units have a present value of A_T at time T.

This extra opportunity to invest at time T is an embedded real option that the management wants to include in its decision. This embedded option is a European call option on gold with a strike price of K and a maturity date time T. Hence its payoff is

$$C_T = \max[kA_T - K, 0] \tag{1}$$

Under the no-arbitrage and complete market assumption, we know that we can use risk-neutral valuation to determine the present value of the gold within the gold mine. The present value is the sum of the initial unit of gold plus the embedded option, that is,

$$\text{Present value} = E^{\pi}(A_T)e^{-rT} - U_0 + E^{\pi}(\max[kA_T - K, 0])e^{-rT} \tag{2}$$

Using the fact the price of gold is a martingale under the risk-neutral probabilities, and using some simple algebra on the value of the embedded call option, we can rewrite this as

$$\text{Present value} = A_0 - U_0 + kc_0(A_0, K/k, T) \tag{3}$$

where $c_0(a,b,T)$ is the time 0 value of a European call option on an asset with price a, strike price b, and maturity date T.

Using the lognormal assumption for the evolution of the gold's price, we can determine the value of the call option to be

$$\text{Present value} = A_0 - U_0 + kA_0 N(d_1) - Ke^{-rT}N(d_2) \tag{4}$$

where $N(.)$ is the cumulative standard normal distribution function, which has mean 0 and standard deviation 1,

$$d_1 = \frac{\log\left(\dfrac{A_0}{K/k}\right) + \left(r + \dfrac{\sigma^2}{2}\right)T}{\sigma\sqrt{T}}$$

$d_2 = d_1 - \sigma\sqrt{T}$, and σ is the price of gold's return volatility per year. Given this present value, management should purchase the gold mine if the present value exceeds the purchase price P_0 dollars.

As illustrated by this example, real options theory applies derivatives pricing theory to any and all options embedded within a firm's investment decisions. A classic textbook on this topic is Dixit and Pindyck (1994).

Reduced-Form Models

The second class of credit risk models are called reduced-form models. To understand the intuition behind the reduced-form model, it is best to start with Jarrow and Turnbull's (1992, 1995) original formulation. The reduced-form model is an extension of the HJM model of chapters 23–25. The reduced-form model uses all of the assumptions A1–A7 from the HJM libor model, with two modifications. One, assumption A2, no credit risk, is removed because the purpose of the reduced-form model is to price and hedge risky debt. The second modification is that the simple (default free) forward rates need not follow a lognormal distribution. Other evolutions are possible, and for the purposes of this section, we keep the evolution completely arbitrary.

Note that unlike the structural model discussed in the previous section, reduced-form models consider an economy with random interest rates. This is of particular importance in the risk management of fixed-income securities where interest rate and credit risk are paramount.

We let r_t denote the random default-free spot rate of interest (continuously compounded), and $B(t,T)$ the time t value of a default-free zero-coupon bond paying a dollar at time T. In addition to assumptions A1–A7, the reduced-form model needs two more assumptions to characterize a firm's risky debt. For easy comparison to the structural model, we consider a firm that has as one of its liabilities a zero-coupon bond with face value K and maturity date T. This assumption is easily relaxed in a reduced-form model, unlike the complexity that arises when relaxing this same assumption in a structural model.

The first additional assumption is as follows.

A8. The firm's zero-coupon bond trades continuously in time.

Note that unlike the structural model, the reduced-form model only assumes that this particular debt issue trades. The firm's other liabilities need not trade. This overcomes the key limitation of the structural model discussed previously.

The second additional assumption characterizes the payoffs to the risky debt issue if the firm defaults. This characterization, therefore, must include two components: (1) an assumption about when default occurs (i.e., specifying a random default time) and (2) an assumption about the loss rate on the debt issue in the case of default.

A9. The firm's default time τ is the first jump time of a Poisson process with intensity $\lambda > 0$. In the event of default, the loss rate is $(1 - \delta)$, where $0 < \delta < 1$ is the debt's recovery rate.

The default intensity λ is the probability of default per unit time, given that the firm has not yet defaulted. The firm's default time is denoted by τ. The loss rate is given by the fraction $(1 - \delta)$, where δ is the recovery rate. All of these parameters are easily estimated using historical data, a topic we leave to more advanced courses.

The payoff to the debt can be written abstractly as

$$K1_{\{\tau > T\}} + \delta K1_{\{\tau \leq T\}} \tag{26.11}$$

where

$$1_{\{\tau > T\}} = \begin{cases} 1 & \text{if} \quad \tau > T \\ 0 & \text{if} \quad \tau \leq T \end{cases}$$

The symbol $1_{\{\tau > T\}}$ is called an *indicator function*. It takes the value 1 if default does not occur by time T and the value 0 otherwise. Using this indicator function, expression (26.11) shows that the debt's payoff is equal to K dollars if no default occurs prior to the debt's maturity and δK dollars otherwise. The payoff in default is only $\delta < 1$ percent of the original face value of the debt K.

Let L_t denote the time t value of this debt issue. Under the no arbitrage assumption, just as in the HJM model, it can be shown that there exists risk-neutral probabilities π such that all default-free zero-coupon bonds and the firm's debt are martingales, after normalization by the value of a money market account. This implies that

$$B(t,T) = E^{\pi}\left(e^{-\int_t^T r_s ds} \right) \tag{26.12a}$$

$$L_t = E^{\pi}\left(K1_{\{\tau > T\}} e^{-\int_t^T r_s ds} + \delta K1_{\{\tau \le T\}} e^{-\int_t^\tau r_s ds} \right) \tag{26.12b}$$

Expression (26.12a) is just the familiar risk-neutral valuation formula. The price of a default-free zero-coupon bond is just the expected discounted value of a dollar paid at time T, where one discounts using the spot rate of interest. Expectations are computed using the risk-neutral probabilities.

Expression (26.12b) also uses risk-neutral valuation. This expression shows that the debt's value is equal to its expected discounted payoff across the two possibilities regarding default: (1) the debt does not default before maturity, in which case it receives its face value K, and (2) default occurs prior to maturity, in which case the debt receives its recovery value. One discounts, as before, using the spot rate of interest, and expectations are computed using the risk-neutral probabilities.

Using properties of the Poisson process and expression (26.12a), one can show that (see Jarrow 2009)

$$L_t = e^{-\tilde{\lambda}(T-t)} KB(t,T) + \int_t^T \tilde{\lambda} e^{-\tilde{\lambda}(s-t)} \delta KB(t,s) ds \tag{26.13}$$

where $\tilde{\lambda}$ is the risk-neutral default probability per unit time.

We see here that the risky zero-coupon bond is worth less than the default-free zero-coupon bond $KB(t,T)$. The first term represents the expected discounted value of the promised payment conditioned on no default. Here $e^{-\tilde{\lambda}(T-t)}$ is the risk-neutral probability of no default. The second term represents the expected discounted value of the recovery value conditioned on default, where $\tilde{\lambda} e^{-\tilde{\lambda}(s-t)}$ is the risk-neutral probability of default at time s. One sums across all times s where default is possible, yielding the integral in the second term.

The risk-neutral probability of default $\tilde{\lambda}$ per unit time differs from the actual default probability λ by a risk premium. If default risk is idiosyncratic (firm specific), however, then the risk-neutral and actual default intensities are equal (see Jarrow 2009). After conditioning on the state of the economy, it is likely that what causes one firm to default versus another is idiosyncratic. It is an open research question as to whether this is true.

Unlike the structural model, it is very easy to extend the reduced-form model to have more complex default processes, to price other traded liabilities issued by the firm, and to price credit derivatives. Extension 26.3 shows how to apply reduced-form models to price credit default swaps that were introduced in chapter 7.

EXTENSION 26.3: Credit Default Swaps

Credit default swaps are term insurance contracts written on traded bonds with a maturity date, a notional value, and a premium. If the insured bond defaults during the life of the contract, then the CDS seller pays off the difference between the notional and market value of the bond. Of course, the market value declines due to default. For this coverage, the CDS buyer pays a regular premium payment.

The remainder of this extension shows how one can use the reduced-form model to price CDS. We use the same model as in the previous section and consider a CDS written on a bond issued by our firm with maturity date T^*, coupon payments, and a notional value of $1. We denote the time t price of this coupon bond by L_t.

We let τ be the firm's random default time, and if the firm defaults prior to the coupon bond's maturity date, we assume that the bond incurs a loss of $(1 - \delta)$ dollars, where δ is the recovery rate.

We can now value a CDS on this coupon bond. We let the CDS have a maturity date $T < T^*$ and a notional value equal to $1. In this CDS, the protection seller agrees to pay the protection buyer the loss on the debt if the firm defaults before the maturity date of the CDS. In return, the protection buyer pays a constant dollar spread c times the notional value at the fixed intermediate dates $1, 2, \ldots, T - 1$. These payments continue until the swap's maturity or the default date, whichever happens first.

Using the risk-neutral valuation procedure, the time t value of the CDS to the protection seller is therefore

$$\text{CDS}_t = E^\pi \left(\sum_{k=1}^{T-1} c 1_{\{\tau > k\}} e^{-\int_t^k r_s ds} - (1 - \delta) 1_{\{\tau \leq T\}} e^{-\int_t^\tau r_s ds} \right) \tag{1}$$

This is the present value of the premiums received (the summation term) less the losses paid if default occurs. It can be shown that this can be simplified to

$$\text{CDS}_t = c \sum_{k=1}^{T-1} e^{-\tilde{\lambda}(k-t)} B(t,k) - (1 - \delta) \tilde{\lambda} \int_t^T e^{-\tilde{\lambda}s} B(t,s) ds \tag{2}$$

where $\tilde{\lambda}$ is the risk-neutral default probability per unit time.

The market clearing CDS rate c is that spread that gives the CDS zero value, that is,

$$c = (1 - \delta) \tilde{\lambda} \frac{\int_t^T e^{-\tilde{\lambda}s} B(t,s) ds}{\sum_{k=1}^{T-1} e^{-\tilde{\lambda}(k-t)} B(t,k)} \approx (1 - \delta) \tilde{\lambda} \tag{3}$$

We see that the CDS rate is approximately equal to the risk-neutral expected loss (per year)—the risk-neutral default probability times the loss rate—on the firm's debt. The CDS price takes into account risk aversion through the use of the risk-neutral probabilities.

CDS trade on many firms' debt issues, and the market uses CDS spreads and expression (3) to infer the market's view of the risk of default as reflected in the implied risk-neutral default probability (for a given recovery rate).

The reduced-form methodology is also easily employed to understand and price even more complex credit derivatives like collateralized debt obligations (see Jarrow 2009).

Liquidity Risk

Liquidity risk corresponds to the relaxation of the competitive markets assumption. Recall that the competitive markets assumption implies that all traders act as price takers, that is, their trades have no impact on the buying or selling price. Liquidity risk occurs when there is a quantity impact of a trade on the price obtained. Quantity impact occurs in actual markets due to market power (size) or **asymmetric information** (which means the counterparties have differential information, e.g., a seller is likely to know more about a used car's quality than the buyer). Market power is easy to understand. Buying a large quantity of any security changes the price because the buyer needs to induce the seller to sell. Asymmetric information causes a quantity impact because if one believes that the seller is informed and selling because the security is worth less than its current price, clearly the selling price must decline. In conjunction, these two reasons imply that selling (buying) large quantities of a security usually decreases (increases) the price obtained. When markets are volatile and disrupted, the quantity impact is larger than when markets are quiet and stable.

The failure of Long-Term Capital Management (LTCM) in 1998 is perhaps the most infamous example of the importance of liquidity risk. LTCM was a hedged fund started by John Meriwether, ex–Salomon Brothers bond traders, and several finance academics in 1994. Using convergence arbitrage trading strategies in bond markets, they had phenomenal profit performance for the first four years of their life, providing returns in excess of 20 percent. A characteristic of their bond arbitrage trading strategies was that they required large leverage to transform small differences in bond spreads into large returns for their clients. This, of course, implies a small capital position.

LTCM's performance turned bad in May and June 1998, when mortgage-backed securities lost significant value. Then, Russia's defaulting on its debt in August 1998, and the resulting market reactions, caused significant losses in LTCM's asset value. This loss in asset value resulted in LTCM receiving margin calls for its futures positions and collateral calls for its swap positions. To obtain the additional capital, LTCM had to sell its assets. Selling assets when the market is spooked and declining is problematic. These asset sales resulted in increased value losses for LTCM as the process of selling large quantities of securities caused the market to drop further. A cascade of additional margin and collateral calls and market drops resulted, eventually leading to the failure of LTCM and the bailout of LTCM organized by the

New York Federal Reserve Bank to avoid a financial market collapse (for a detailed history, see Jorion 2000).

There are two approaches to modeling liquidity risk, which differ based on the permanence of the quantity impact of a trade on the price. If the quantity impact on the price is temporary, then liquidity risk is analogous to an endogenous transaction cost. By temporary, we mean that the quantity impact on the price only lasts for the trade under consideration, and after the trade, the price reverts back to its proper value. Çetin et al. (2004) were the first to study this approach in the context of derivatives pricing. Fortunately, the derivatives pricing methodology extends under this form of liquidity risk. Hence all of the results previously studied in chapters 1–25 apply directly, with few, if any, changes.

If the quantity impact on the price is permanent, however, then liquidity risk takes on a different characterization. In this case, traders can act strategically and manipulate the price to their advantage. Here liquidity risk needs to include the consideration of market manipulation. Jarrow (1992, 1994) was to first to study manipulation in the context of derivatives pricing. Unfortunately, the standard derivatives pricing methodology fails to hold under this form of liquidity risk. Pricing and hedging become context specific, depending on the traders, their strategies, and the market setting. Here all of the results previously studied in chapters 1–25 fail to apply, and new models are needed. The extensions in this case are the subject of current research.

Operational Risk

Operational (and legal) risk is the risk inherent in running a financial institution. These risks usually cause only small losses, but sometimes they have resulted in large blowouts. A stunning example of operational risk happened on December 8, 2005, when a broker at Japan's Mizuho Securities Company transposed the quantity and the selling price in the company's order processing system. He mistakenly typed an order to sell 610,000 shares of a small company J-Com at 1 yen instead of the other way round. The error was detected only a minute and a half later, but the Tokyo Stock Exchange's all-electronic trading system thwarted all cancellation efforts. The result was a loss of $335 million.[6] In February 7, 1991, traders at now-defunct Wall Street firm Salomon Brothers submitted an unauthorized customer bid in the amount of $1 billion as what Salomon termed a "practical joke" to tease an employee, but they failed to stop those bids on time, and an extra $1 billion worth of bonds got purchased. Eventually, the acquired securities were transferred to Salomon's account at no loss to the firm (see Chatterjea 1993).

Good management controls and procedures can minimize operational risk. Consequently, the control and minimization of this risk really falls under the heading of business management or organizational behavior and not finance. Nonetheless, for pricing and hedging this risk, finance is again useful.

[6] See "Mizuho Settles Trade Debacle; Japanese Minister Scolds Brokers for Taking Advantage of Error," *Wall Street Journal*, December 14, 2005.

Operational risk can be modeled using the same mathematics as used in the reduced-form credit risk models. Indeed, operational risk can be viewed as a negative event, which if it occurs, generates a loss to the firm. This is exactly how the reduced-form credit risk models view default. Consequently, the modeling techniques used in credit risk can be applied to operational risk (see Jarrow 2008; Jarrow et al. 2010a).

The only substantive difference between these two models is that there is more publicly available data on credit risk events (realizations and losses) then there are on operational risk events. However, these differences are narrowing as various industry groups are creating operational risk databases.

26.6 | The Credit Crisis of 2007

Given our increased understanding of the risks embedded in risk management models and decision making, it is instructive to study the credit crisis of 2007 using our accumulated knowledge. The genesis of the 2007 credit crisis was the residential housing price bubble and crash of the recent past (see Figure 26.4). The content of this presentation is based on Jarrow (2012). Figure 26.6 gives an overview of the players and economic considerations involved in the credit crisis.

Residential Housing Price Bubble

The residential housing market and related construction industries are a large and important sector in the economy. A home is one of the largest components of a typical household's wealth. The key cause of the recent expansion in the housing price boom (early 2000s to the crash) was a low interest rate environment and a shift toward lax mortgage lending standards and easy credit. The lax lending standards occurred in the mortgage loan origination process.

MORTGAGE LENDING The market for mortgage loans is characterized by asymmetric information between the borrowers, who know their ability to pay, and the mortgage lenders, who have only incomplete information on the borrowers. Because of this asymmetric information in issuing loans, the *loan origination process* involves significant fixed costs related to setting up the infrastructure necessary to evaluate loan applicants' creditworthiness, to issue loans, to service payments, and to handle the legal process if default occurs. Financial institutions, therefore, perform loan origination because they have the necessary resources and expertise.

The loan originators finance the loans they issue with debt and equity. This is called *direct lending*. To take advantage of the economies of scale in their infrastructure, however, the loan originators often sell mortgage loans to third parties. The third parties are (1) the government-sponsored enterprises Fannie Mae and Freddie Mac and (2) the entities that issue *asset-backed securities (ABS)*. This is called *indirect lending*. When mortgages are sold to third parties, the loan originators receive fees for originating and for servicing the loans.

There is an incentive problem with originating loans if mortgage originators do not hold the loans in their inventory. If the loans default, the costs are not borne by the mortgage originators but by the third party. When mortgages are sold to third parties, the mortgage originators are only responsible for fraudulently issued loans. Hence, under the right circumstances, indirect lending has the potential to generate lax lending standards, where loans are issued to borrowers who should not receive the loans.

That the lending standards became lax in the early 2000s is well documented in the financial press. Prior to the new millennium, mortgage loans were mainly issued to good-credit borrowers, requiring large down payments (20 percent was typical), with a requisite documentation of income. In contrast, in the mid-2000s, loans were issued to lower-credit-risk borrowers, called *subprime borrowers*, with little or no down payments and often without adequate documentation of income. **Subprime borrowers** are those with low credit scores and very little equity in their home purchases. Furthermore, to induce homeowners to borrow, teaser rates and/or no principal prepayments for a couple of years were common in new mortgages. When the teaser period ended, as long as home values kept rising, the mortgages could be refinanced at new teaser rates, keeping the mortgage payments low and affordable. Problems arose when home values stopped rising.

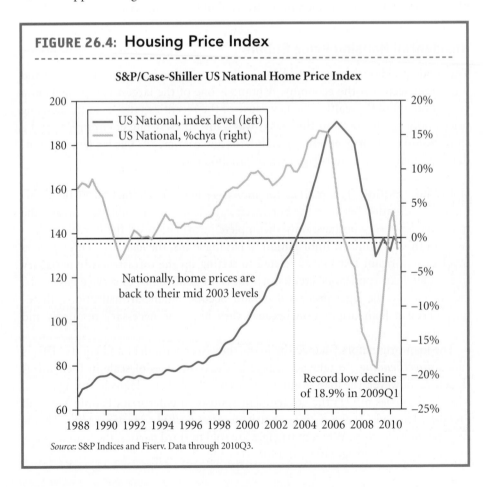

FIGURE 26.4: Housing Price Index

S&P/Case-Shiller US National Home Price Index

— US National, index level (left)
— US National, %chya (right)

Nationally, home prices are back to their mid 2003 levels

Record low decline of 18.9% in 2009Q1

Source: S&P Indices and Fiserv. Data through 2010Q3.

EXCESS SUPPLY OF FUNDS FOR SUBPRIME MORTGAGES The lax lending standards were caused by an unusually large excess supply of funds available for such mortgage loans in the 2000s. Two forces generated this excess supply of funds for subprime mortgage loans. First, US government policies were introduced that were designed to encourage home ownership by low-income families. This greatly increased the supply of cheap credit available from the government-sponsored enterprises Fannie Mae and Freddie Mac. Second, an unusual excess demand for subprime mortgage credit derivatives—ABS, **collateralized debt obligations (CDOs)**, and **collateralized debt obligations squared (CDO^2s)**—held by financial institutions and investment funds occurred. These credit derivatives are explained in a subsequent section. This excess demand generated, in turn, an increased supply of funds available for subprime mortgages through the creation of ABS.

Two root causes generated this excess demand for subprime mortgage–related credit derivatives by financial institutions and investment funds. One cause was the agency problems inherent in the compensation structures for the management of financial institutions and investment funds. The second cause was the incentive problems inherent in the way credit rating agencies are paid for their services. We discuss each of these in turn.

Agency Problems

Proprietary trading managers and investment fund managers at financial institutions receive a significant portion of their compensation through a yearly bonus based on their short-term trading performance. The yearly bonus is often multiples of a base salary. This bonus scheme drives a wedge between the interests of the shareholders and those of the management, called the **agency problem**. The shareholders desire long-term wealth maximization, but managers are motivated by short-term bonuses. These two objectives are in conflict. Because the managers act as agents for the firm's shareholders, an incentive conflict arises. This is the agency problem.

The managers in these financial institutions, often constrained to invest in *investment-grade bonds*, sought the highest yield to maximize short-term profits. Investment-grade bonds are those highly rated by the credit rating agencies. This includes bonds rated AAA, AA, A, and BBB by Standard and Poor's (S&P). The idea, of course, is that the credit ratings hold default risk constant. Prior to the crash, AAA-rated ABS, CDO, and CDO^2 bonds were paying significantly higher yields than equivalently rated US Treasuries. Consequently, AAA-rated ABS, CDO, and CDO^2 bonds were in great demand.

Investment fund management trusted the rating agencies' ratings. They did this, partly, because the CDO and CDO^2 bonds were based on complex payoff structures that were difficult to understand and model. Hence the investment funds, motivated by their short-term bonuses, did not do their own due diligence. Clearly, because the yields on AAA-rated ABS, CDO, and CDO^2 bonds exceeded those on US Treasuries, no one believed they were of equal risk. However, the market was not aware that the risks were as different as they really were owing to the credit agencies' misratings of the ABS bonds.

Although proprietary trading groups at large financial institutions had more expertise available to evaluate the securities, their incentive structures motivated their decisions as well, and they also invested heavily in the ABS and CDO bonds; examples include Merrill Lynch and Bear Stearns.

These investment strategies generated portfolios of bonds that were much riskier than portfolios of similarly rated maturity US Treasuries. When the housing boom crashed and the underlying mortgage pools started defaulting, these bond portfolios lost significant value. If the portfolios had been in the similarly rated maturity US Treasuries, no significant losses would have occurred.

Credit Rating Agencies

Credit rating agencies evaluate corporate and ABS, CDO, and CDO^2 (structured) debt issues, assigning them ratings as to their credit quality. Information on a borrower's creditworthiness is costly to obtain with economies of scale in its collection. As such, this asymmetric information market structure provides a natural setting for the existence of credit rating agencies.

GOVERNMENT REGULATIONS In the United States, credit rating agencies are those firms designated by the Securities and Exchange Commission (SEC) as "national statistical rating organizations," which include Moody's, S&P, and Fitch Investor Services, among others. Across time, various government regulators have introduced rules that include credit ratings. For example, SEC regulations require the use of ratings in the issuance of certain types of debt. Both the SEC and the Labor Department have "prudent man" rules that limit acceptable investments by money market funds and pension funds, respectively, to investment grade bonds. Banking regulators (see the Basel I and II capital requirements) determine capital requirements for debt issues based on their ratings, with prohibitions on holding speculative securities. The higher the credit rating on a debt issue is, the less capital is required to back an investment in the debt. Ratings are also used to determine the eligibility of securities used as collateral for margin lending. These regulations mandating the use of credit ratings accentuate the importance of credit ratings in market activity (for a more in-depth discussion of the credit rating industry, see Cantor and Packer 1994).

INCENTIVE CONFLICTS Rating agencies are paid by the entities that issue the debt. This payment is not a one-time fee but can be better characterized as a stream of future payments for continued updates on the credit evaluations. It is quite common, therefore, that borrowers choose among rating agencies based on the ratings obtained. To get their business, the credit rating agencies provide better ratings than are deserved. This payment fee structure obviously creates a conflict of interest for the rating agency between issuing accurate ratings and retaining business.

MISRATINGS It is a fact that the credit rating agencies misrated both corporate and structure debt prior to the credit crisis. Evidentiary of corporate debt misratings are the failures or near-failures (saved by government assistance) of the large investment and commercial banks Bear Stearns, Lehman Brothers, Merrill Lynch, Citigroup, the insurance company AIG, and the government-sponsored enterprises Fannie Mae and Freddie Mac, among others. The institutions were highly rated only months before they failed. Evidentiary of structured debt misratings were the massive downgrades of AAA-rated CDO and CDO^2 debt to junk status in a very short time span during the midst of the credit crisis. Much has been written on these misratings.

The misratings occurred both because of the conflict of interest and because the rating agencies used poor models to estimate default risk (see Jarrow 2011). In addition to the poor models, the parameters estimated in their structured debt models were based on historical data that did not include the changed and more lax lending standards discussed earlier.

Given the importance of accurate credit ratings in the industry, these misratings resulted in the excess demand for subprime mortgage credit derivatives. This in turn resulted in investment funds having riskier portfolios than the ratings of the bonds indicated and financial institutions having insufficient capital to cover the losses eventually realized in their loan portfolios. Insufficient capital and too much risk caused the failure of these financial institutions and the financial crisis.

Credit Derivatives

Three credit derivatives played a key role in the residential mortgage market and credit crisis: ABS, CDOs, and CDO^2s.

ABS This section discusses subprime ABS. An ABS is best understood as a liability issued by a firm or corporation, although the legal structure of the entity issuing an ABS is quite different from that of a typical corporation, usually a **special purpose vehicle** (**SPV**). A firm's balance sheet consists of assets and liabilities. The assets purchased by an SPV are called the **collateral pool**—the collateral underlying the SPV's liabilities. The collateral pool of the ABS involved in the credit crisis consisted primarily of subprime residential mortgage loans. (In this case, the ABS are sometimes called **residential mortgage–backed securities** [**RMBS**]; however, for consistency in the presentation, we will continue to call them ABS.)

To help finance the purchase of the collateral pool, the SPV issues debt. The debt is issued in various **bond tranches**, from the senior bond tranches to the mezzanine to the junior bond tranches. These bond tranches have different claims to both the cash flows from the collateral pool and any losses realized on the collateral pool, called the **waterfall**. The cash flows, consisting of interest and principal payments, are paid to the most senior bonds first, then to the mezzanine bonds, then the junior bonds, with the residual going to the equity (see Figure 26.5). The losses are realized in the reverse order, starting with the equity first, moving to the junior, the mezzanine, and then the senior bond tranches. As such, the senior bond tranches are the safest, with respect to default risk, while the equity comprises the riskiest securities in this regard.

With respect to the housing price boom and the financial crisis, the ABS creation process helped provide the funds that fueled the unprecedented issuance of subprime mortgage loans. The incentive problems in the mortgage origination process (discussed previously) led to the lax lending standards and easy credit that generated the excess demand for mortgage loans by homeowners. The demand for the ABS bonds was generated, indirectly, by the excess demand for CDOs and CDO^2 AAA-rated bonds (to be discussed later) by financial institutions and investment funds. The CDO and CDO^2 creation process required the ABS bonds.

FIGURE 26.5: ABS Bond Tranches

Assets	Liabilities	Waterfall	
	Senior bond tranches	Cash flows	
	Mezzanine bond tranches		
Collateral pool	Junior bond tranches		Losses
	Equity		

CDOs AND CDO^2s A CDO is a type of ABS. The key difference between an ABS and a CDO is in the composition of the collateral pool. A subprime ABS has a majority of subprime residential mortgage loans in its collateral pool. These loans do not actively trade in financial markets. In contrast, a subprime CDO has a majority of mezzanine subprime ABS bonds, rated below AAA, in its collateral pool. These ABS bonds are traded in financial markets. Another minor difference is that CDO waterfalls can be more complex, with various triggers that redirect cash flows to more senior tranches if certain collateralization or interest coverage ratios are violated.

Given the complexity of the collateral pool and waterfall rules, CDOs are complex and difficult to understand securities. An additional complication in understanding CDOs is that each SPV is different in terms of its waterfalls, making modeling a tedious SPV-by-SPV exercise. This complexity provided a convenient excuse for many financial institutions and investment funds not to do their own due diligence but to rely solely on the credit rating agencies in this regard. Consequently, the traditional safeguards that would mitigate the credit risk in a transaction were absent.

CDO^2s are CDOs but where the collateral pool mainly consists of mezzanine, junior, or even the equity tranche bonds from subprime CDOs. Hence a CDO—squared! This is hard to believe, perhaps, but they existed.

The costs of creating a CDO (and CDO^2) are quite large, including lawyer, rating, and investment banking fees, and the collateral pool's assets trade in the over-the-counter market, unlike the collateral pool of ABS home mortgages. Thus the CDO equity would have negative value, and the CDOs would not be created unless the ABS bonds in the collateral pool were undervalued and/or the CDO bonds issued were overvalued.

It is unlikely that the ABS bonds in the collateral pool were undervalued. In contrast, there is significant evidence that the CDO bonds were overvalued. CDOs were created in massive quantities before the crisis, and there is significant evidence that the AAA-rated CDO bonds were misrated. This implies that the creation of CDOs was to exploit a "rating arbitrage" because of the rating agencies' misratings of the bonds. CDOs existed to transform junk bonds into gold—AAA bonds with high yields. Alchemy finally worked! The same is true of CDO^2s.

With respect to the housing price boom and the financial crisis, CDOs and CDO^2s played a key role. These securities were held by investment funds at financial institutions, pension funds, and retirement funds operated by corporations and government agencies. First, these funds overpaid for the bonds purchased, although they were making healthy profits prior to the crisis. Second, when housing prices crashed and mortgages defaulted, these CDO and CDO^2 bonds lost significant value. This value loss created severe hardships and/or failures of corporations (e.g., General Motors), state governments (e.g., California, New York), sovereign nations (e.g., Iceland), and investment banks (e.g., Bear Stearns, Merrill Lynch). Rated AAA at the onset, the loss on these structured bonds was unprecedented by historical precedence of similar AAA-rated debt issues. The reason for this unprecedented loss, of course, is that the structured debt was misrated from the beginning, for reasons we have previously discussed.

The Housing Price Crash

The housing price bubble was too good to last. Housing prices crashed for three reasons. First, the supply of subprime home borrowers became exhausted, which removed the demand. Second, interest rates started to rise because of worries about inflation owing to increases in the budget deficit from the Iraq War. Third, rising oil prices because of the Iraq War caused an increase in gas prices that impacted the ability of many subprime borrowers to meet their mortgage payments.

In conjunction, these economic forces caused an increased incidence of subprime mortgage defaults. Mortgage defaults led to foreclosures, causing housing prices to fall. This, in turn, led to additional defaults as teaser rate periods ended and refinancing became impossible for many borrowers because their home values had dropped below their mortgage principals.

As mortgage defaults occurred, the subprime residential mortgage ABS, CDO, and CDO^2 bond tranches lost value. These credit derivative losses eroded the capital of financial institutions, and investment funds lost significant value. This loss in aggregate wealth and the correlated failures of financial institutions froze financial markets with severe negative consequences to the real economy, eventually causing unemployment and the Great Recession.

Regulatory Reforms

To correct the structural problems that created the credit crisis, regulatory reforms need to be implemented. This process is currently under way. First and most important, it was the credit agencies' misratings that created the environment in which the misincentives of the various market participants took hold. Indeed, if the credit agencies' ratings had been correct, then even given the various misincentives, the market forces generating the credit crisis would have been muted. This is because if the credit agencies had done their job, the following would have occurred:

- Financial institutions and investment funds would not have invested in credit derivatives because the securities would have been seen to be too risky.

- The demand for indirect lending to subprime mortgages would have disappeared, except for government-sponsored enterprise lending by Fannie Mae and Freddie Mac. This may have eliminated the mortgage originators' lax lending standards from taking hold.

- The equity capital held in financial institutions would have been more appropriate because the regulators themselves would have had proper information regarding the likelihood and cost of financial failure.

Consider some reasonable proposals for change, some of which have already been included in the Dodd-Frank Wall Street Reform and Consumer Protection Act. First, the payment structure of the credit rating agencies needs to change. The users of the ratings should pay for the rating agencies' services; the rating agencies should not be paid by those that are rated. This reform appears unlikely to happen, and it is not part of the Dodd-Frank reform package. Second, credit ratings should be removed from all government regulations, thereby removing artificially created demand for the use of ratings. This reform is part of the Dodd-Frank reform package.

Next, the misincentive structures of the market participants need to be reformed. The compensation schemes of financial management need to be changed to be consistent with maximizing long-run performance and not short-term bonuses. Vesting or delaying payment of yearly bonuses over a multiple-year period can help remedy this situation. Because of pressures from the banking regulators, many financial institutions are instituting these reforms.

Continuing, mortgage originators should be required to hold some percentage of their originated loans in inventory. A mechanism that avoids the mortgage originators' cherry-picking the best loans also needs to be included. This is also part of the Dodd-Frank reform.

Last, Fannie Mae's and Freddie Mac's business needs to be separated from government policy and government ownership. They should become private corporations, subject to market forces. Government policy regarding low-income housing should only be implemented through fiscal policy and tax incentives. This shift in government activity is outside the Dodd-Frank reform but is currently hotly debated due to the huge losses incurred by Fannie Mae and Freddie Mac.

FIGURE 26.6: **The 2007 Financial Crisis**

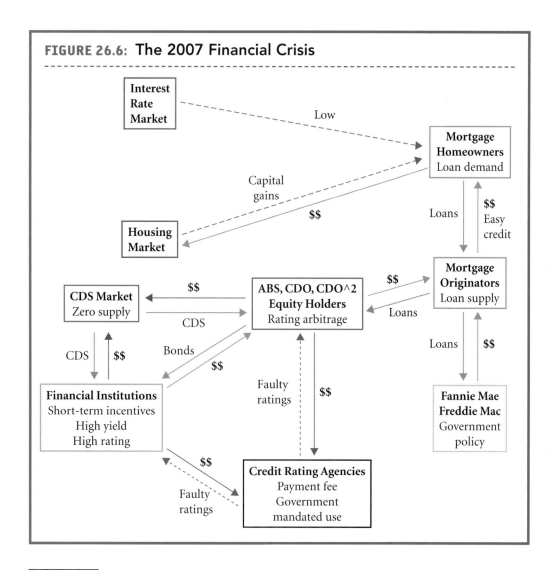

26.7 | The Future of Models and Traded Derivatives

The credit crisis of 2007 and its resulting aftermath created a discomfort with risk management models and derivatives. This discomfort raises the question as to the future of risk management models and derivatives. This section addresses this question, in light of what we have now studied in this book. The following discussion is based on Jarrow (2011).

Model Risk

When using financial risk management models, one must recognize that there is model risk. Model risk occurs because models are approximations—

smplifications—of a complex reality. Statisticians Box and Draper (1987, p. 74) said, "Remember that all models are wrong: the practical question is how wrong do they have to be to not be useful."

A model's usefulness—the quality of the approximation—needs to be judged relative to a purpose. Very crude models can be useful for decision making in some contexts, whereas more sophisticated models are needed in others. The usefulness of the model should be tested and continually validated to assure continued accuracy of the approximation.

To understand how to test a model, we first need to divide a model's assumptions into two types: robust and critical assumptions. A robust assumption is one in which the implications of the model only change slightly if the assumption is modified only slightly. In contrast, a critical assumption is one in which the implications of the model change discretely if the assumption is only changed slightly.

This distinction is important because since models are approximations of a complex reality, we may not get the assumptions exactly correct. With robust assumptions, we do not need to worry too much. For small errors in the robust assumptions, the implications only change by a small amount. We need to be careful, however, with the critical assumptions. If we get the critical assumptions wrong, by just a little, the implications completely change.

Now to test a model, one needs to test all the model's relevant implications and all the assumptions, if possible. Sometimes, however, not all the assumptions can be tested. In this case, one must test all the critical assumptions. If any of the implications or critical assumptions are rejected, the model should not be used. Why? Because using an incorrect model generates poor risk management decisions.

If a model is accepted for use, the implications and critical assumptions need to be continually monitored and validated because markets are dynamic and constantly changing. It is always possible that if the market's structure shifts because of regulatory or institutional changes, the underlying assumptions may no longer be reasonable approximations. If this happens, then pricing and hedging will no longer work.

The best way to understand models and their use is to consider an analogy. Models are analogous to medical prescription drugs. Prescription drugs have great medical benefits if used properly, with educated use. If used wrongly, however, prescription drugs can have negative consequences, even death. Because prescription drugs can cause death if used incorrectly, this does not mean that we should stop using them. It does mean, however, that we need educated and regulated use. In fact, prescription drugs should probably be used more because they save and prolong lives. The same is true of models.

Financial markets have become too complex to navigate without risk management models. Determining a price—fair value—is sometimes not an issue because in many cases, expert judgment may provide reasonable estimates. However, the following are true:

- There is no way to hedge a portfolio, that is, determine hedge ratios, without a model.

- There is no way to price a derivative in an illiquid market without a model.

These issues are at the heart of risk management. Hence financial risk management models are here to stay.

Derivatives

Derivatives have existed for thousands of years. They have continued to exist (trade) across different centuries, across different governments, and across different economic systems. Despite occasional uproars about their evil uses, derivatives have continued to trade because they help complete markets and, consequently, improve societal welfare. If history shows us nothing else, it shows us that derivatives are here to stay!

Given this insight, the best way to live with derivatives is through education and knowledge. We have started you on this journey to understanding with the content of this book, but this is just the beginning! There is much more to learn and master. We have just walked with you on only the first part of your journey to understanding derivatives, and it is now time for us to leave. However, we leave you knowing that you are well prepared for the obstacles ahead.

26.8 | Summary

1. A firm's risk management decisions can be understood using the firm's balance sheet and computing the firm's loss distribution defined as $\text{Prob}\{\Delta A_t - \Delta L_t \le x\}$, where the time t asset's value is A_t, the time t liability is L_t, and $\Delta A_t \equiv A_{t+\Delta t} - A_t$ and $\Delta L_t \equiv L_{t+\Delta t} - L_t$ correspond to the change in the value of the assets and liabilities, respectively, over the interval $[t, t + \Delta t]$.

2. Value-at-risk (VaR_α) for an α loss probability is that number such that $\text{Prob}\{\Delta A_t - \Delta L_t \le - \text{VaR}_\alpha\} = \alpha$. In some cases, VaR_α penalizes diversification, which is a failing in this risk management statistic.

3. Scenario analysis (which also goes by the popular name stress testing) starts with a selection of a particular set of scenarios (or states of the economy) that the firm wants to protect against. For these scenarios, the firm wants to compute the losses realized on its assets and liabilities to see if it has sufficient equity capital to avoid insolvency. Scenario analysis's major failing is that it does not assign probabilities to the various scenarios.

4. Credit risk is the risk that a counterparty will fail to execute on the terms of a contract. There are two models for quantifying credit risk: structural and reduced-form models. The structural model is useful for internal management decision making and understanding the economics of the firm's balance sheet, whereas the reduced-form model is useful for pricing and hedging credit-risky instruments trading in the financial markets.

5. Both liquidity and operational risk can be modeled using the techniques studied in this book. Operational risk uses the same models as credit risk.

6. The 2007 credit crisis was a result of a residential housing price bubble and crash. Lax mortgage lending and low interest rates generated the bubble. The

lax mortgage lending standards were caused by government policies encouraging low-income home ownership and the exponential growth of the subprime residential ABS, CDO, and CDO^2 markets.

7. The exponential growth of the subprime residential ABS, CDO, and CDO^2 markets was generated by high yields on misrated ABS, CDO, and CDO^2 bonds. The misratings were issued by the credit rating agencies, whose incentives were skewed because of their payment fee structure. Short-term bonus incentives of financial managers buying these securities also fueled the growth of these structured debt markets.

8. The bursting of the housing price bubble caused the financial crisis as financial institutions lost significant wealth because of their investments in the ABS, CDO, and CDO^2 bonds.

9. Models are needed for risk management in complex financial markets. To avoid model misuse, better education on models is needed.

26.9 | Cases

Amaranth Advisors: Burning Six Billion in Thirty Days (Richard Ivey School of Business Foundation Case 908N03-PDF-ENG, Harvard Business Publishing). This case studies the staggering losses encountered by a hedge fund and introduces concepts like liquidity risk, value-at-risk, spread trades, and the use of derivatives.

Delphi Corp. and the Credit Derivatives Market (A) (Harvard Business School Case 210002-PDF-ENG). This case considers the use of credit derivatives to hedge credit risk and/or to speculate on the price of corporate debt and also how credit derivatives affect the incentives of creditors to negotiate with a distressed company attempting to avoid bankruptcy.

CITIC Tower II: The Real Option (University of Hong Kong Case HKU199-PDF-ENG, Harvard Business Publishing). This case studies real options involved in the decision to purchase newly reclaimed land in Hong Kong for the purpose of building an office building at an appropriate time in the future.

26.10 | Questions and Problems

26.1. When using value at risk at the 5 percent level to determine equity capital, do the debt holders need to worry about the magnitude of the losses at the 1 percent level? Explain.

26.2. Consider a firm whose business is to purchase distressed debt, that is, bonds of firms that have defaulted, hoping to profit from the bankruptcy resolution process. Which of the four risks (market, credit, liquidity, and operational) does this distressed debt investment firm consider when evaluating the distressed debt? Explain.

26.3. Suppose you enter into a $5 bet with a friend on the winner of a soccer game. What risks do you face in this gamble?

26.4. In the structural credit risk model, it is claimed that the debt holders own the firm, and not the equity holders. Explain why.

26.5. Since the equity holder's position is equivalent to a call value on the firm's assets, and the equity holders manage the firm's assets, can they increase the value of their equity by increasing the firm's asset volatility? Explain your answer.

26.6. What are the three risks faced by a bond in the reduced-form credit risk model?

26.7. Which risks caused the hedge fund Long-Term Capital Management to fail?

26.8. Explain why operational risk and credit risk can be modeled using similar techniques.

26.9. What assumption makes the structural model not useful for actual pricing and hedging but makes the reduced-form model appropriate for these activities?

26.10. Your grandmother gives you an old silver flower vase as a birthday gift. You want to sell it to buy a new computer. What risks do you face with respect to this asset?

26.11. Internet markets—like eBay—decrease which risk of holding assets?

26.12. When homeowners borrow using a mortgage, they usually need to provide a down payment, usually somewhere between 5 percent and 20 percent of the house's value. What risk is the down payment reducing?

26.13. What is a credit default swap?

26.14. What is an ABS? What is a waterfall in an ABS?

26.15. What is a CDO? How does a CDO differ from an ABS?

26.16. What is a CDO^2?

26.17. Why are models analogous to prescription medical drugs? Are derivatives likely to discontinue trading? Explain.

The next two questions are based on the following data for three companies.

Expected Return, Volatility, and Portfolio Weights

	Ali Co. (Company 1)	Barb Co. (Company 2)	Cao Co. (Company 3)
Weekly expected return	0.0020	0.0025	0.0030
Weekly volatility of the returns	0.03	0.04	0.05
Portfolio weights	1/3	1/3	1/3

Correlation of Expected Returns

	Ali Co. (Company 1)	Barb Co. (Company 2)	Cao Co. (Company 3)
Ali Co.	1	0.4	0.8
Barb Co.	0.4	1	0.5
Cao Co.	0.8	0.5	1

26.18. Compute the weekly 95 percent and 99 percent value-at-risk for Ali Co.

26.19. Compute the weekly 95 percent and 99 percent value-at-risk for a portfolio consisting of the three stocks in equal proportions.

26.20. Now that you have completed the book and are on your way to mastering derivatives, briefly discuss your views as to whether derivatives are good or bad? Feel free to use the internet to get some quotes to support your answer.

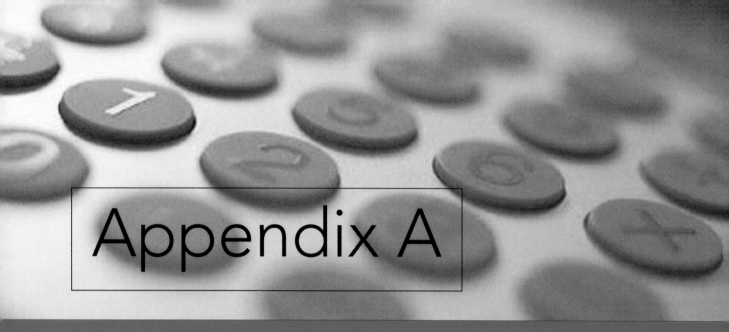

Appendix A

Mathematics and Statistics

A.1 | Exponents and Logarithms

Exponents and logarithms are useful for valuing cash flows across time and for computing continuously compounded returns.

Exponents

Arithmetic classes taught us that 2 times 2 is 4, and algebra classes showed us that we can write this as 2^2 (read "2 raised to the power of 2"). Here 2 is an **exponent** denoting the number of times 2 multiplies itself.

We can generalize this example and write "x multiplied by x" as x^2. We can generalize further to denote "n products of x" as

$$x^n \equiv x \times x \ldots n \text{ times} \tag{1.1}$$

The $\equiv$ sign denotes that "this is true by definition."

An exponent may also be a fraction that denotes a root or a radical. For example, $x^{1/2}$ means $x^{1/2} \times x^{1/2} = x$; we also write $x^{1/2}$ as $\sqrt{x}$ and read it as "square root of x." When generalized, $x^{1/n}$ is the "nth root of x," and it is also expressed as $\sqrt[n]{x}$, which means

$$x^{1/n} \times x^{1/n} \ldots n \text{ times} \equiv x \tag{1.2}$$

Negative exponents are used to create an inverse. For example, 2^{-1} is $1/2^1 = 1/2$. This is generalized to define

$$x^{-n} \equiv 1/(x \times x \ldots n \text{ times}) \equiv 1/x^n \tag{1.3}$$

Of course, the preceding expression is only defined when x is not equal to zero (in notations, $x \neq 0$); moreover, $x^0 = 1$, when $x \neq 0$. These puzzling results can be explained by the law of exponents. You can write x raised to the power 0 as

$$x^0 = x^{m-m} = x^m \times x^{-m} = x^m/x^m = 1$$

This holds true when x does not equal zero. When $x = 0$ and we raise it to the power 0, then we have zero in the denominator, and we are essentially dividing by 0, which is forbidden by mathematicians because it gives nonsensical results.

Next we write some useful properties of exponents (see Table A.1). We state the laws and give an example illustrating their use.

Logarithms

We only consider natural logarithms in this book (see Table A.2). The natural logarithm, written as **log(x)**, is defined by

$$\log(x) = y \text{ is equivalent to } e^y = x \tag{1.4}$$

where e is the **Euler number**, approximately 2.711828, defined as the limit

$$e = \lim_{n \to \infty} \left(1 + \frac{1}{n}\right)^n \tag{1.5}$$

when n goes to infinity or as the infinite series

$$e^x = 1 + \frac{x}{1} + \frac{x^2}{1 \times 2} + \frac{x^3}{1 \times 2 \times 3} + \cdots + \frac{x^n}{n!} + \cdots \qquad (1.6)$$

for any real number x. Notice that a representative term in expression (1.6) is given by the $(n+1)$th term $x^n/n!$, where $n!$ is read as **n-factorial** and is defined by $n! = n \times (n-1) \times \ldots \times 3 \times 2 \times 1$ and $0! = 1$.

Continuous Compounding

If X dollars is invested today at an interest rate r that is compounded m times per year, and m becomes infinitely large, then it has the time T value

$$X[(1 + r/m)^m]^T = X[(1 + r/m)^{m/r}]^{rT} \rightarrow Xe^{rT} \qquad (1.7)$$

because $(1 + r/m)^{(m/r)} \equiv [1 + 1/(m/r)]^{(m/r)} = (1 + 1/n)^n$ goes to e as $n = m/r$ goes to infinity.

This can be used to model dividend yields. Consider buying one unit of a stock that pays dividends at a continuous rate of δ per year. Assume that the dividends are reinvested back into the asset (see section 12.3).

To model this, we start by dividing the year into m periods of equal length and assume that a dividend of δ/m times the stock value is paid at the end of each interval. At each payment date, we use the dividend to buy more of the stock. Consequently, the value of the position in the stock grows just like compound interest. Here, δ/m is compounded m times per year, where m becomes infinitely large. Then, our one unit in the stock grows to

$$[(1 + \delta/m)^m]^T \equiv [(1 + \delta/m)^{(m/\delta)}]^{\delta T} = e^{\delta T} \quad \text{units after } T \text{ years} \qquad (1.8)$$

This happens because $(1 + \delta/m)^{(m/\delta)} \equiv [1 + 1/(m/\delta)]^{(m/\delta)} = (1 + 1/n)^n$ goes to e as $n = m/\delta$ goes to infinity.

TABLE A.1: Laws of Exponents

Laws of Exponents	Examples
1. $x^m x^n = x^{m+n}$	$x^2 x^3 = x^5$
2. $x^{-m} = \dfrac{1}{x^m}$	$x^{-2} = \dfrac{1}{x^2}$
3. $x^{m-n} = \dfrac{x^m}{x^n}$	$x^{5-3} = \dfrac{x^5}{x^3} = x^2$
4. $x^0 = x^{m-m} = x^m \dfrac{1}{x^m} = 1$, when $x \neq 0$	$x^0 = x^{5-5} = \dfrac{x^5}{x^5} = 1$
5. $\left(x^m\right)^n = x^{mn}$	$\left(x^2\right)^3 = \left(x^2\right)\left(x^2\right)\left(x^2\right) = x^6$
6. $x^m y^m = (xy)^m$ and $x^m/y^m = (x/y)^m$	$x^5 y^5 = (xy)^5$ and $x^4/y^4 = (x/y)^4$

TABLE A.2: Laws of Logarithms

Laws of Exponents	Examples
1. $\log(xy) = \log x + \log y$	$\log 50 = \log 5 + \log 10$
2. $\log(x/y) = \log x - \log y$	$\log(10/2) = \log 10 - \log 2 = \log 5 + \log 2 - \log 2 = \log 5$
3. $\log(x)^n = n \log x$	$\log 2^3 = \log 8 = \log(2 \times 2 \times 2) = 3 \log 2$ and $\log 2^{1/5} = (1/5) \log 2$
4. $\log 1 = 0$	$\log 1 = 0$ because $e^0 = 1$

A.2 | The Binomial Theorem

One of the first facts you learn in algebra is how to square the sum of two variables x and y:

$$(x + y)^2 = x^2 + y^2 + 2xy$$

The expression $(x + y)$ is called a **binomial** because it is the sum of two terms. Next comes the cubic expansion of a binomial:

$$(x + y)^3 = x^3 + 3x^2y + 3xy^2 + y^3$$

One can expand this binomial for an arbitrary integer n. The **binomial theorem** provides a method for doing this:

$$(x + y)^n = \binom{n}{0}x^n y^0 + \binom{n}{1}x^{n-1}y^1 \cdots + \binom{n}{j}x^{n-j}y^j \cdots + \binom{n}{n-1}x^1 y^{(n-1)}$$

$$+ \binom{n}{n}x^0 y^n = \sum_{j=0}^{n} \binom{n}{j}x^{n-j}y^j \tag{2.1}$$

where the **binomial coefficient** (which is the number of ways of selecting j things out of a possible number of n things) can be expressed as

$$\binom{n}{j} = \frac{n!}{j!(n-j)!} \tag{2.2}$$

Here the expression $n!$ is called n-factorial and is defined as

$$n! = n \times (n-1) \times (n-2) \times \ldots \times 2 \times 1 \tag{2.3}$$

For example, $4! = 4 \times 3 \times 2 \times 1 = 24$ and $1! = 1$, and by definition, $0! = 1$. Moreover, $n! = n(n-1)! = n(n-1)(n-2)!$, and so on.

A.3 | The Normal Distribution

A standard normal distribution function has a mean equal to 0 and a standard deviation equal to 1. The normal distribution function is denoted by $N(d)$. This gives the probability that the underlying normal random variable z will take a value less than or equal to d, that is, $N(d) = \text{Prob}(z \le d)$.

This probability can be obtained from a normal distribution table (see Table A.3) or using computer software (e.g., spreadsheets). Usually, normal distribution tables give probabilities for z greater than 0.

The normal density represents the mathematical derivative of the normal distribution function. The normal density function is symmetric around mean 0 (see Figure A.1) and is shaped like a bell. Because the normal density function is symmetric around 0, if you want to compute $N(-d)$ for some negative value, use $N(d) + N(-d) = 1$.

EXAMPLE 1: Cumulative Standard Normal Distribution

- From the cumulative standard normal distribution table (Table A.3),

$$N(0.75) = 0.7734$$

  This is the probability that a normal random variable will have a value of 0.75 or less.

- Likewise,

$$N(0.55) = 0.7088$$

- Or you can use spreadsheet programs like Excel or Lotus Notes to compute cumulative normal. Excel will use the command $= \text{NORMSDIST}(z)$, where z is the underlying normal random variable (in Lotus Notes, use the command @NORMAL(z,0,1,0)).

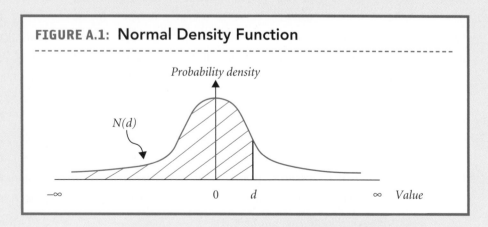

FIGURE A.1: Normal Density Function

TABLE A.3: Cumulative Normal Distribution Function

	0	0.01	0.02	0.03	0.04	0.05	0.06	0.07	0.08	0.09
0	0.5	0.504	0.508	0.512	0.516	0.5199	0.5239	0.5279	0.5319	0.5359
0.1	0.5398	0.5438	0.5478	0.5517	0.5557	0.5596	0.5636	0.5675	0.5714	0.5753
0.2	0.5793	0.5832	0.5871	0.591	0.5948	0.5987	0.6026	0.6064	0.6103	0.6141
0.3	0.6179	0.6217	0.6255	0.6293	0.6331	0.6368	0.6406	0.6443	0.648	0.6517
0.4	0.6554	0.6591	0.6628	0.6664	0.67	0.6736	0.6772	0.6808	0.6844	0.6879
0.5	0.6915	0.695	0.6985	0.7019	0.7054	0.7088	0.7123	0.7157	0.719	0.7224
0.6	0.7257	0.7291	0.7324	0.7357	0.7389	0.7422	0.7454	0.7486	0.7517	0.7549
0.7	0.758	0.7611	0.7642	0.7673	0.7704	0.7734	0.7764	0.7794	0.7823	0.7852
0.8	0.7881	0.791	0.7939	0.7967	0.7995	0.8023	0.8051	0.8078	0.8106	0.8133
0.9	0.8159	0.8186	0.8212	0.8238	0.8264	0.8289	0.8315	0.834	0.8365	0.8389
1	0.8413	0.8438	0.8461	0.8485	0.8508	0.8531	0.8554	0.8577	0.8599	0.8621
1.1	0.8643	0.8665	0.8686	0.8708	0.8729	0.8749	0.877	0.879	0.881	0.883
1.2	0.8849	0.8869	0.8888	0.8907	0.8925	0.8944	0.8962	0.898	0.8997	0.9015
1.3	0.9032	0.9049	0.9066	0.9082	0.9099	0.9115	0.9131	0.9147	0.9162	0.9177
1.4	0.9192	0.9207	0.9222	0.9236	0.9251	0.9265	0.9279	0.9292	0.9306	0.9319
1.5	0.9332	0.9345	0.9357	0.937	0.9382	0.9394	0.9406	0.9418	0.9429	0.9441
1.6	0.9452	0.9463	0.9474	0.9484	0.9495	0.9505	0.9515	0.9525	0.9535	0.9545
1.7	0.9554	0.9564	0.9573	0.9582	0.9591	0.9599	0.9608	0.9616	0.9625	0.9633
1.8	0.9641	0.9649	0.9656	0.9664	0.9671	0.9678	0.9686	0.9693	0.9699	0.9706
1.9	0.9713	0.9719	0.9726	0.9732	0.9738	0.9744	0.975	0.9756	0.9761	0.9767
2	0.9772	0.9778	0.9783	0.9788	0.9793	0.9798	0.9803	0.9808	0.9812	0.9817
2.1	0.9821	0.9826	0.983	0.9834	0.9838	0.9842	0.9846	0.985	0.9854	0.9857
2.2	0.9861	0.9864	0.9868	0.9871	0.9875	0.9878	0.9881	0.9884	0.9887	0.989
2.3	0.9893	0.9896	0.9898	0.9901	0.9904	0.9906	0.9909	0.9911	0.9913	0.9916
2.4	0.9918	0.992	0.9922	0.9925	0.9927	0.9929	0.9931	0.9932	0.9934	0.9936
2.5	0.9938	0.994	0.9941	0.9943	0.9945	0.9946	0.9948	0.9949	0.9951	0.9952
2.6	0.9953	0.9955	0.9956	0.9957	0.9959	0.996	0.9961	0.9962	0.9963	0.9964
2.7	0.9965	0.9966	0.9967	0.9968	0.9969	0.997	0.9971	0.9972	0.9973	0.9974
2.8	0.9974	0.9975	0.9976	0.9977	0.9977	0.9978	0.9979	0.9979	0.998	0.9981
2.9	0.9981	0.9982	0.9982	0.9983	0.9984	0.9984	0.9985	0.9985	0.9986	0.9986
3	0.9987	0.9987	0.9987	0.9988	0.9988	0.9989	0.9989	0.9989	0.999	0.999
3.1	0.999	0.9991	0.9991	0.9991	0.9992	0.9992	0.9992	0.9992	0.9993	0.9993
3.2	0.9993	0.9993	0.9994	0.9994	0.9994	0.9994	0.9994	0.9995	0.9995	0.9995
3.3	0.9995	0.9995	0.9995	0.9996	0.9996	0.9996	0.9996	0.9996	0.9996	0.9997
3.4	0.9997	0.9997	0.9997	0.9997	0.9997	0.9997	0.9997	0.9997	0.9997	0.9998

(continued)

TABLE A.3: (Continued)									
3.5	0.9998	0.9998	0.9998	0.9998	0.9998	0.9998	0.9998	0.9998	0.9998	0.9998
3.6	0.9998	0.9998	0.9999	0.9999	0.9999	0.9999	0.9999	0.9999	0.9999	0.9999
3.7	0.9999	0.9999	0.9999	0.9999	0.9999	0.9999	0.9999	0.9999	0.9999	0.9999
3.8	0.9999	0.9999	0.9999	0.9999	0.9999	0.9999	0.9999	0.9999	0.9999	0.9999
3.9	1	1	1	1	1	1	1	1	1	1
4	1	1	1	1	1	1	1	1	1	1

A.4 | A Taylor Series Expansion

Formally introduced by the English mathematician Brook Taylor in 1715, a **Taylor series** allows us to express special functions as an infinite sum of terms involving polynomials.

Single Variable

The Taylor series expansion of a single variable function $f(x)$ that is infinitely differentiable in a neighborhood of a number a is given by the power series

$$f(x) = f(a) + \frac{f^1(a)}{1!}(x - a) + \frac{f^2(a)}{2!}(x - a)^2 + \cdots \frac{f^{(n)}(a)}{n!}(x - a)^n + \cdots \quad (4.1)$$

where $n! = n \times (n - 1) \times \ldots \times 2 \times 1$ denotes the factorial of n and $f^{(n)}(a)$ denotes the nth derivative of f evaluated at the point a. Notice that f^0 is defined to be f itself and $(x - a)^0$ and 0! are both defined to be 1; f^1 and f^2 are customarily written as f' and f'', respectively.

Consider the function graphed in Figure A.2. A Taylor series approximation of this function at the point $x = a$ using just the first two terms is given by

$$f(x) \approx f(a) + f'(a)(x - a) \quad (4.2)$$

Algebra tells us that the right side of this expression is a straight line tangent to the function $f(x)$ at $x = a$. Expression (4.2) shows that this straight line (shown by a dashed line in the figure) is an approximation to the function $f(x)$ at $x = a$.

Such approximations work well for small changes in x around $x = a$. A better approximation for larger changes in the variable x is obtained by retaining the second derivative as given by

$$f(x) \approx f(a) + f'(a)(x - a) + \frac{1}{2}f''(a)(x - a)^2 \quad (4.3)$$

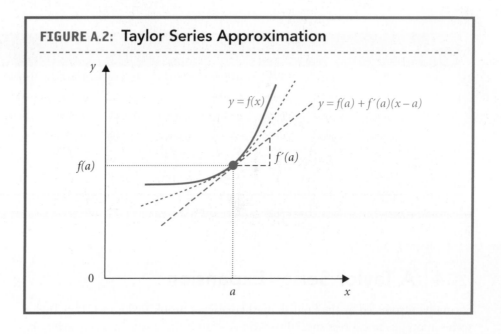

FIGURE A.2: Taylor Series Approximation

Multiple Variables

The Taylor series for a well-behaved function of multiple variables can be expressed as

$$f(x_1, \ldots, x_d) = \sum_{n_1=0}^{\infty} \cdots \sum_{n_d=0}^{\infty} \frac{(x_1 - a_1)^{n_1} \ldots (x_d - a_d)^{n_d}}{n_1! \ldots n_d!} \left(\frac{\partial^{n_1 + \cdots + n_d} f}{\partial x_1^{n_1} \cdots \partial x_d^{n_d}} \right)(a_1, \ldots, a_d)$$

(4.4)

To illustrate this general result, consider a function f of two variables x and y. The Taylor series expansion to the second order about the point (a, b), writing $(x - a)$ as Δx, and $(y - b)$ as Δy, is

$$f(x, y) \approx f(a, b) + \frac{\partial f(a, b)}{\partial x} \Delta x + \frac{\partial f(a, b)}{\partial y} \Delta y$$

$$+ \frac{1}{2!} \left[\frac{\partial^2 f(a, b)}{\partial x^2} \Delta x^2 + \frac{\partial^2 f(a, b)}{\partial y^2} \Delta y^2 + 2\Delta x \Delta y \frac{\partial^2 f(a, b)}{\partial x \partial y} \right]$$

(4.5a)

Writing $f(x, y) - f(a, b)$ as Δf, and moving the first term on the right side of this expression to the left side gives the simpler expression

$$\Delta f \approx \frac{\partial f}{\partial x} \Delta x + \frac{\partial f}{\partial y} \Delta y + \frac{1}{2!} \left[\frac{\partial^2 f}{\partial x^2} \Delta x^2 + \frac{\partial^2 f}{\partial y^2} \Delta y^2 + 2\Delta x \Delta y \frac{\partial^2 f}{\partial x \partial y} \right]$$

(4.5b)

These results are used in chapters 20 and 25.

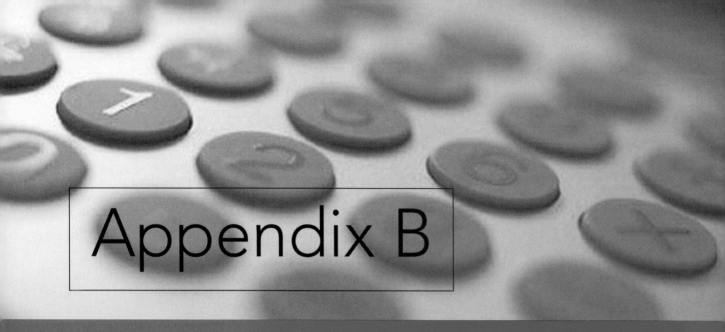

Appendix B

Spreadsheet Software

The latest version of this book and the present documentation can be downloaded from the book's website at wwnorton.com/studyspace. We suggest that you visit this website at regular intervals to get the latest releases of the software and to be informed about any other news related to the book. Despite our best efforts, there may be some mistakes. We would be grateful if you would bring them to our notice.

B.1 | Starting the Software[1]

Enabling Macros

When you open the workbook, please make sure that you authorize the macros therein to run. As the procedure to achieve this is slightly different for various versions of Excel, we suggest that you consult your software documentation and/ or ask for the advice of an experienced Excel user in the case you need help. It is possible for macros to be suppressed (to be prevented from running) silently if Excel has been set up that way, so you might not be warned explicitly that macros do not run. Generally, if you open the workbook and it does not work as described subsequently, you should assume that macros do not run normally.

The workbook should be compatible with all versions of Excel going back at least to Excel 2000, even though support will be provided only for versions of Excel after Excel 2007. Some versions of Excel running on Apple computers do not include Visual Basic for Applications (VBA)—on these, the workbook will not run.

Features

The workbook helps one to understand the models presented in this book. As this is a textbook, the models (especially Heath–Jarrow–Morton, HJM) have a relatively small number of time steps. This makes the models more comprehensible but limits the accuracy of the results when compared to actual market prices.

The aim of the software is not only to compute values but also to generate live models. Live models link the inputs and outputs by appropriate formulas so that changes in the inputs are immediately propagated through the model and are simultaneously reflected in all the outputs. For example, if one defines a thirty-two-step binomial model to value a call option, the value of the call changes immediately if the user modifies, say, the current stock price, the strike price, the volatility, the maturity of the call, or any other parameter that is an input to the binomial call valuation model.

Inputs

The user can input values in all cells marked with a light green color. In addition, the user can make various choices through the widgets (buttons, checkboxes,

---

[1] Tibor Jánosi, PhD (Cornell University), wrote the spreadsheet software and assisted with writing this appendix.

listboxes, and comboboxes). Actions are triggered either automatically or through the use of command buttons. We avoid using toolbars or defining ribbon elements to maximize the portability of the workbook across various versions of Excel.

The software imposes few, if any, restrictions on the inputs. It is thus possible to define models that are extreme or degenerate cases of the regular textbook cases or that are—in a strict sense—incorrect. For example, one can define stock prices whose evolution is characterized by a very large or very low volatility, including zero volatility and even negative volatility. Stock prices are not restricted to being positive. Besides understanding the behavior of the models in the regular realm of parameters, the reader is encouraged to examine such extreme or degenerate cases and to try to understand the results. Often such cases yield insights that are overlooked in a more conventional framework.

B.2 | Bin+BSM.Input

In this worksheet, the user enters the inputs for both the binomial and the Black–Scholes–Merton model (BSM). These inputs are the stock price, the strike price, the interest rate, the time to maturity, and the volatility. Note that although we use the term *stock*, our discussion applies to any generic asset that satisfies the requisite properties (see chapters 17–19). Under the inputs box is another box that enables the user to compute a dividend adjusted stock price by inputting the original stock price, the dividend yield, and the maturity. Computed is the dividend adjusted stock price, which must be manually copied into the box above as if it were the unadjusted stock price (see Chapter 19, section 10).

B.3 | BSM

This worksheet explores the BSM model and its relation with the binomial model.

Inputs

There are no inputs on this worksheet. Values for European calls and puts are computed automatically based on the user inputs from worksheets "Bin+BSM.Input" and "Binomial." The strike price is input on the "Binomial" worksheet, while all other inputs are on "Bin+BSM.Input." The input values are repeated on this worksheet for easy reference, but they can only be changed on worksheets "Bin+BSM. Input" and "Binomial."

Computing Greeks

The values of the option Greeks (delta, gamma, rho, theta, and vega) are also computed. Partial computations (results) are shown to make it easier for readers to check their work if computing by hand. Moreover, they give one a better sense of where the final result comes from. For example, one can see that for various parameter choices, some terms in the BSM formulas are highly significant, whereas others are not.

Convergence of Binomial to BSM

A panel titled "Testing the Binomial Model's Convergence to BSM Limit" allows one to compare computed BSM values with the results of the binomial model with the same inputs for various time steps. The binomial model is a discrete approximation to the BSM formula, and this panel allows the reader to explore this approximation. The user can specify the steps in a binomial model up to 1,024, but the computer will refuse to run models with more than 128 intervals if a user is using the old version of an Excel workbook (an xls file), which can have at most 256 columns. If you are using the modern Excel file format (an xlsm file) and run it on a post-2007 version of Excel, then the computer will run bigger models, but you will still get a warning for step numbers of 256 or greater. Results for the various binomial models are combined to predict the final result with a precision greater than that of any individual binomial step. This is done using Richardson's extrapolation, which is a standard approximation algorithm based here on using two or three of the previously obtained results.

Output Graphs

The dependence of call and put values on the inputs, as well as that of their Greeks, is shown in the leftmost graph visible on this page. The chart selection box enables the user to choose the graph to be shown by clicking on the green cell and then scrolling down to the selected choice. One can choose the instrument type (American or European), the independent variable (the five inputs), and the dependent variable (instrument value or Greek). Thus this chart selection box generates a total of $2 \times 5 \times 6 = 60$ graphs!

Implied Volatilities

Another panel on this worksheet enables the computation of implied volatilities using the user inputs for all parameters on worksheet "Bin+BSM.Input," except the volatility. The user needs to input prices for the puts and calls in this panel (the green cells). Note that the implied volatilities are computed for the same set of strike prices for both European puts and calls. The panel contains the values of the computed implied volatilities for the puts and calls. The implied volatilities are graphed immediately below the panel.

B.4 | Binomial

This worksheet illustrates the binomial model. Note that the screen is split into two and that the division is frozen.

Inputs

The panel labeled "Inputs" contains the inputs to the binomial model specified by the user on the "Bin+BSM.Input" worksheet. The only input the user can specify in this panel is the number of the time steps (the green cell).

Directly under the input box are some preliminary outputs computed after the time step is selected. These are the length of the time step in years, the interest rate per time step, the up and down factors, and the pseudo-probabilities. These quantities are completely determined by the inputs. Note, however, that there is one choice box hidden in the cell labeled "approx." By clicking on this cell and scrolling down, one can choose either the Jarrow–Rudd or Cox-Ross--Rubinstein binomial approximation to the BSM model (see chapter 18). The Jarrow–Rudd approximation is the default selection.

Payoff Function, Instrument Type

The option to be valued needs to be specified. This is done using the two boxes to the right of the input boxes labeled "Payoff function" and "Instrument type." The panel labeled "**Instrument type**" enables one to select European or American payoffs. This should be selected first.

The panel labeled "**Payoff function**" allows the user to define the option to be valued. Using the scroll-down button in the combobox, one can choose a call, put, digital call, digital put, or arbitrary payoff at maturity or at the time of early exercise (if applicable). The structure of this panel is designed so that a virtually infinite variety of instruments can be valued.

- Note the existence of two green input cells in this panel. The "**Underlying**" cell contains the value of the underlying's price for which the payoff is computed at maturity. This is *not* the current stock price (which is specified in the "Inputs" panel), nor is it necessarily the actual value of the underlying at some point in the evolution of its price—it is just a price parameter that will be referenced in the arbitrary payoff function defined by the user.

- The other green input in this panel is labeled "**Strike**," and it should be used as such when valuing (European/American, regular/digital) calls and puts. This strike price is for both the "Binomial" and the "BSM" worksheets.

- As mentioned earlier, the combobox allows the user to choose one of five payoff function alternatives; the first four correspond to regular and digital calls and puts. In this case, "Strike" should be interpreted as a true strike price. The fifth choice is labeled "Arbitrary."

- "**Arbitrary**" allows for the definition of an arbitrary payoff function that depends on the current price of the underlying and one additional fixed (given) parameter (the "Strike"). It is thus not possible to define payoffs that depend on the history of the underlying's price such as a payoff equal to the average past price (sampled discretely) of the underlying. However, it *is* possible to define payoffs equal, say, to the square of the difference between the current stock price and the "Strike."
  - When choosing the "Arbitrary" option, the cell labeled "Payoff" becomes red and contains the word "FORMULA" in bold white characters; this is to remind the user that the payoff formula must be defined explicitly. For example, to implement a payoff equal to the square of the difference between the current stock price and the "Strike," one proceeds as follows: (1) click in cell "Payoff" and enter "=("(do *not* enter the quotes); (2) click on cell "Underlying" (note

that the text "underlyingInFormula" appears in the formula bar!); (3) enter "-" in the formula bar; (4) click in the vicinity of cell "Strike" and use the arrow keys to select this cell (note that the text "strikeInFormula" appears in the formula bar!); (5) enter ")^2" in the formula bar; and (6) type "ENTER" to finish editing the formula. The final form of the formula should be "=(underlyingInFormula-strikeInFormula)^2."

- *Important*: The arbitrary payoff can be used to value, for example, zero-coupon bonds (a constant payoff function equal to 1), a portfolio of different options (define the different options' payoffs and sum), and compound options (options on options). The user is restricted only by her imagination.

■ Once the payoff function is chosen, the "**Instrument type**" panel allows the user to choose between European and American flavors of the instrument at hand. When the user is satisfied with the setup, the "**Calculate**" button triggers the setup of the model and its computations. The results are shown below the "Payoff function" and "Instrument type" panels.

■ Note that the detailed results are shown on the "Bin.Inst.Val" (instrument valuation), "Bin.Under.Evol" (underlying's evolution), "Bin.MMkt.Units" (number of money market units in the hedging portfolio), and "Bin.Under.Units" (number of the underlying's units in the hedging portfolio) worksheets. These worksheets also allow the user to examine the formulas that the binomial model specifies for the given situation.

The Matrix

The recombining nature of the (basic) binomial model allows for a compact representation of the lattice, thus allowing one to generate relatively large models with hundreds or even thousands of time steps, depending on the capacity of your worksheet (old-style xls files only admit 256 columns, whereas new-style worksheets allow for many more) and the resources of your computer such as processor power and internal memory. The smallest model accommodated by the worksheet contains only one time step.

■ The matrix displayed in the bottom right corner of the worksheet represents the binomial model. The matrix is surrounded by columns labeled $0, 1, 2, \ldots, N$ and rows labeled $0, 1, 2, \ldots, N$. This matrix is the binomial lattice. The root (origin) of the lattice is in the top left corner of the matrix (cell [0,0] relative to the lattice and not the excel worksheet coordinates). The values for the time steps are given diagonally, connecting the equal-numbered northeast column and southwest row. For example, starting at cell (0,0) at time 0, the time 1 up node is cell (0,1) and the time 1 down node is cell (1,0) in the matrix; starting from time 1 in the up node (cell [0,1]), the time 2 up node is cell (0,2) and the time 2 down node is cell (1,1); starting from time 1 in the down node (cell [1,0]), the time 2 up node is cell (1,1) and the time 2 down node is cell (2,0); and so forth. Note that the (up and down) node is equal to the (down and up) node because it is a lattice.

■ A cell labeled "**Quantity shown**" enables the user to change what is shown in the matrix. Clicking on the scroll-down button enables the user to show in the lattice either the underlying stock price, or the option valuation, or the hedge ratio m (the number of the underlying's units in the hedging portfolio), or n, which is the number of money market accounts in the hedged portfolio. Only one of these can be shown at any time.

- A group of cells to the left of the matrix, starting with the cell labeled "**Address**," allows the user to investigate the structure of the binomial lattice by examining in great detail the values associated with the active cell, as long as the active cell is within the then-current lattice. To understand this functionality, it helps to generate a moderate-sized lattice for an American instrument that will be exercised early on certain paths. Click inside the matrix while watching the group of cells described here. Then use the arrow keys (or the mouse, but the keyboard is better) to watch how the information listed on the left end of the screen reflects and details the information in the matrix.

- Note that when studying the convergence of the binomial model to the BSM limit on the "BSM" worksheet, the program modifies the "Binomial" worksheet's setup so that the respective calculations can be performed as needed. Do not be surprised if the setup of the "Binomial" worksheet changes after you have visited the "BSM" worksheet and run the computations in the panel labeled "Testing the Binomial Model's Convergence to Black–Scholes–Merton Limits."

B.5 | Bin.Print

This worksheet can be used to capture and print a snapshot of the first few (up to five) time steps of the binomial lattice set up using the "Binomial" worksheet. If the respective model has more than five time steps, then only a partial view of the model can be shown and printed.

- The user enters the number of desired steps in the green cell labeled "**Steps**"; this number should be between 1 and 5. The actual number of allowed steps can differ from this; it is the minimum of the user-entered value, 5, and the actual number of time steps in the current binomial model.

- There are eight comboboxes under the heading "**Shown in cells**"; the user can select the value of each independently of all the others. Most choices are self-explanatory; there is also a "Leave empty" choice.

- When the "**Generate lattice**" button is pressed, a recombining lattice is created using a traditional layout using the values from the "Binomial" worksheet and its subordinated pages. The actual values shown are those specified by the comboboxes. If the last few consecutive comboboxes are all set to "Leave empty," those cells will not be used (they will not occupy space) in the generated lattice. If there are "Leave empty" comboboxes in between other choices, the respective cells will be generated in the lattice, but they will be left empty. Such functionality can be useful, for example, to introduce spacing (distance) between the printed values but also to leave certain spaces that the user can fill in with his own (hand) calculations, to verify his understanding of the model's workings.

- If the user changes the number of time intervals in the binomial model on worksheet "Binomial" and this number thus becomes smaller than the number of the time intervals shown in the lattice on the "Bin.Print" worksheet, then this latter lattice will show nonsensical (often zero) values in the nodes that correspond to nonexistent nodes on the "Binomial" worksheet.

- Note that the print setup of "Bin.Print" is always adjusted so that this worksheet prints on one page only.

B.6 | Bin.xxx.xxx

Four additional worksheets are provided, as follows:

1. **Bin.Inst.Val** (instrument valuation)
2. **Bin.Under.Evol** (underlying's evolution)
3. **Bin.MMkt.Units** (number of money market units in the hedging portfolio)
4. **Bin.Under.Units** (number of the underlying's units in the hedging portfolio)

These worksheets are used (1) to hold the information that will be shown on worksheet "Binomial" and (2) to allow the user to examine in detail the formulas that govern the computation of all relevant quantities in a binomial model.

B.7 | HJM Tree

When one sees this spreadsheet for the first time, it appears blank, with the exception of a collection of panels on the far left side of the page. These panels enable the user to construct an HJM tree and, after construction, to save the constructed HJM tree to a library for future use, if desired.

Cleanup

The first button seen is labeled "**Cleanup**." The "Cleanup" button can be pushed at any time; it will remove all data from this sheet and return this page to its blank state. It will also remove all data from the "HJM Options" and "HJM Fwd+Fut" worksheets. This is because the data on these latter two worksheets depend on and are subordinated to the data on the "HJM Tree" worksheet. If the data on the "HJM Tree" worksheet are gone, the data on the subordinated sheets will be removed as well.

Draw Tree

In the "HJM Tree" box, the "**Draw Tree**" button draws an HJM tree of the size indicated by the user in the green cell labeled "Intervals." The size is the number of time intervals in the tree; sizes must be between 1 and 6, inclusive. No larger-sized trees will be generated owing to the space restrictions inherent in excel worksheets.

Building a Tree

After completing these two boxes, one needs to fill in the entries to the HJM tree. Three choices are possible: "Fill Tree," "Config Fill," or "Load library." We discuss each of these in turn:

- The "**Fill Tree**" button fills a tree with bond price evolution data based on the HJM model specification current in the workbook. Should the user wish to examine or change this specification, she should push the "**Config[ure] Fill**" button *before* the bond price evolution is generated. For details, please see the description of the "Configure" worksheet.

- Alternatively, it is possible to get data from the library of saved trees by hitting the "**Load library**" button. Only trees whose sizes are compatible with the size of the tree given in the "Intervals" cell are loaded; they are shown in the combobox above the "Load library" button. When (and if) a user chooses a tree name from this combobox, the appropriate bond price evolution is loaded into the already drawn tree.

- With **manual tree modification**, once a tree is created, it is possible to change any of the entries in the green cells in the tree. This is done simply by clicking on a green cell and changing the number. Hitting return saves the changed number. As such, this feature enables the user to experiment with defining bond price evolutions that admit arbitrage or with entering the HJM trees found in textbooks (as constructed by default, the HJM trees are arbitrage free). Note that a tree previously saved in the library could allow for arbitrage, as the user could have modified it after it was constructed. This flexibility is consistent with the authors' desire to let readers experiment with these models.

- After a tree is created, pushing the "**HJM Params./Fwd Rates**" button populates the bond price evolution with all the derived parameters discussed in the textbook. These include the value of the money market account, the spot rate, the up and down factors for all zero-coupon bonds, and all of the pseudo-probability pairs. An additional tree is generated; this contains the evolution of the forward rate curve corresponding to the specified bond price evolution.

- To save the current tree for future use, the user can specify a tree name, then push the "**Save Tree**" button. Duplicate names cannot be defined. One can review the sizes and names of trees in the library as well as delete unneeded trees by pressing the "**Manage Library**" button. For details, see the description of the "Configure" worksheet.

B.8 | HJM Options

This worksheet implements the valuation of caplets, floorlets, and swaptions. The maturity date of the caplet and floorlet corresponds to the date at which the spot rate is determined (which is one day before the "true" maturity). Without loss of generality, all options are valued for a notional of $1. To obtain larger notional values, one simply needs to multiply the answer by the notional value. Only one such instrument of each type can be valued at a time (but one can value one instrument of each of the three defined types, if one wishes). Valuation trees can be generated in any order.

Inputs

The inputs to the options are given in the boxes in the green cells. After specifying the inputs, one pushes the calculation button, and a tree appears with the derivative's values plus the hedged portfolio's holdings (m, n) at each node in the tree. The bond used to hedge the option under consideration is always the longest-maturity zero-coupon bond in the tree.

Valuation

Valuation is done for the HJM tree specified in the "HJM Tree" worksheet. Models remain live; that is, for example, changing the strike price of a caplet immediately changes the values in the corresponding valuation tree. Also, if one changes the bond price evolution (or part of it), this is immediately reflected in, say, the caplet's valuation tree.

Cleanup

The button "Cleanup" will remove all data from the "HJM Option" worksheet but will not delete anything from other worksheets (contrast this with the discussion of the "Cleanup" button on the "HJM Tree" worksheet).

B.9 HJM Fwd+Fut

This worksheet implements the valuation of the Eurodollar futures and forward rate agreements (FRAs), as discussed in the textbook. As with "HJM Option," without loss of generality, these contracts are valued for a notional of $1. To obtain larger notional values, one simply needs to multiply the answer by the notional value. Only one instrument of each type can be valued at a time (but one can value one instrument of each type, if one wishes). Valuation trees can be generated in any order.

Inputs

The inputs to the contracts are given in the boxes in the green cells. After specifying the inputs, one pushes the calculation button, and a tree appears with the derivative's values plus cash flows (if any) and the hedged portfolio's holdings (m, n) at each node in the tree. For the FRA, the bond used to hedge the option under consideration is always the longest-maturity zero-coupon bond in the tree. For the Eurodollar futures, the user can choose the maturity of the hedging bond in the green box labeled "Hedge mat." If the user chooses a bond for hedging purposes whose maturity is less than that of the Eurodollar futures contract, error values will occur. This is correct because after a (hedging) bond matures, it no longer exists and cannot be used to hedge the longer-dated Eurodollar futures. Again, these features are included in the workbook to help you better understand the model.

Valuation

Valuation is done for the HJM tree specified in the "HJM Tree" worksheet. Models remain live, as discussed previously.

Cleanup

The button "Cleanup" will remove all data from the "HJM Fwd+Fut" worksheet but will not delete anything from other worksheets (contrast this with the discussion of the "Cleanup" button on the "HJM Tree" worksheet, which deletes all information in the workbook).

Technical Considerations

If you examine the hedging formulas for Eurodollar futures (m and n), you will note Excel formulas that involve the OFFSET function. This function makes it possible to write formulas that calculate the region (cell) from which they take values (as opposed to taking values from fixed cells, as in a regular formula). However, such formulas are harder to understand because one has to evaluate the arguments of OFFSET first to establish what cells are actually referenced in the formulas, and only then can one compute the actual numerical value. The same observation applies to the use of OFFSET when computing the swap values in the swaption trees.

The reason we need OFFSET is flexibility—maintaining the live characteristics of formulas in complex situations (e.g., when changing the hedging instrument or when summing a variable number of discount factors such as in the valuation of a swap's fixed side). However, using OFFSET extensively would make formulas harder to read for the average user. Therefore we do it for Eurodollar futures and swaps to show we can do it to achieve flexibility and liveness, but otherwise, we hold back to favor simplicity.

B.10 | Libor

This worksheet computes the HJM libor model. Because this worksheet is very similar in structure and functionality to the "BSM" worksheet, which we described previously, we only point out the major differences.

Inputs

Because the libor model's inputs are used only on this worksheet, the user can specify the model's parameters directly. These are given in the panel labeled "Inputs"—the green cells.

Computing Greeks

Only two Greeks are computed on this worksheet, in line with the textbook's view that the libor model is not very suitable for hedging applications and that the HJM should be used instead in these contexts.

Output Graphs

The leftmost graph shows only the dependence of the selected instrument's value on the inputs that collectively determine its value. Thus the leftmost box contains within it, by scrolling down and selecting a choice, $2 \times 5 = 10$ charts!

Implied Volatilities

Implied volatilities are computed in a manner similar to that described for the "BSM" worksheet.

Convergence of Binomial to HJM

Note that no study of convergence to the HJM value is undertaken. This is because the size of HJM models needed for a good match is too great to fit the HJM model on a spreadsheet. This is not because we would need too many intervals to obtain good convergence but rather because the HJM model uses nonrecombining lattices, whose number of nodes increases very quickly with the number of time steps. Unfortunately, there is no easy way to arrange the nodes of bigger HJM lattices on an Excel spreadsheet so that the user can still easily perceive its structure, as it was done with the binomial model.

B.11 | Configure

On this worksheet, the user can specify the parameters that govern the creation of the HJM trees (the bond price evolution in the HJM model). The procedure followed is documented in Jarrow (2002b).

Randomly Generated Trees

The user can choose to allow random values for both the bond prices and the volatility structure of the forward rate curve (note that obvious restrictions are imposed on these values so that, for example, bond prices are positive and implied forward rates are all positive). While the user cannot specify the volatility structure in this case, it is possible to impose a volatility structure that is increasing, constant, or decreasing in time.

Input-Generated Trees

The user can fully specify the HJM structure using the green cells in the box labeled "HJM Configuration Parameters." Bond prices are specified either directly or by specifying corresponding forward rates. To avoid arbitrage, the bond prices must be strictly positive. The volatility structure must also be fully specified in this mode. The volatility structure specified here is the volatility structure used for all nodes in the tree. These volatilities correspond to absolute (and not proportional) changes to forward rates in each time step.

Library-Loaded Trees

A second panel on this page allows for the user to load the HJM tree data from the library of HJM trees that have been created and saved previously. When the "Load HJM tree data" button is pushed, a list of tree names is loaded. Each name is prefixed by the size of the corresponding tree, which is between 1 and 6. The list is sorted based on tree size. The user can click any tree names to select them and can scroll down to find trees that do not fit on the first page of the list box. Hitting "Delete selected trees" will delete all trees that are selected at that time. It is possible to delete all trees stored in the library at a given time (i.e., the library can be left empty).

B.12 | Technical Details

The implemented models allow great liberty in choosing the inputs; this includes erroneous inputs that will generate incorrect results. Should this happen, incorrect numerical results will be shown and/or Excel will produce its usual error messages, but any errors should disappear as soon as a correct combination of input parameters is used. This feature allows the reader to experiment with live formulas and to understand the models in depth, as opposed to just seeing sanitized and simple examples, which most other textbooks present.

- The authors allowed for model sizes that should run reasonably well on modern computers. Still, depending on your hardware and the installed operating system, as well as on the particular version of Excel that you run, a binomial model with, say, 1,024 steps might run slow or might exhaust some resources on your computer (such as memory). If you experience such behavior, close your workbook, reopen it, and use a smaller model. The issue should not arise for HJM trees, which are limited to at most six time intervals.

- One can always save the workbook after using it and filling it with data. This feature can be valuable, for example, after you have manually entered values in a large HJM tree and saved it in the library. If you wish to use the HJM later, it might make sense to save the workbook (and hence the HJM tree library). If you use a workbook for a long time, it is possible for the workbook to become unstable and to exhibit erratic behavior at times. In the past, this behavior was not unusual when using large, complex Excel workbooks for a long time, and it was due to the accumulation of internal errors over time because of the incorrect functioning of Excel proper. This problem has been alleviated with recent releases of Excel; should you experience it, however, you can always keep a pristine copy of the workbook or download a new (and possibly updated) one from the book's website at wwnorton.com/studyspace.

Glossary

Algorithmic trading or algo Trading using an algorithm (which is a set of rules or sequence of steps) to identify patterns in real-time market data and exploit potentially profitable trading opportunities.

American depository receipt A US exchange-traded security that has a fixed number of foreign stock shares as the underlying.

American option An option that can be exercised anytime during its life.

Annual Percentage Rate (APR) The restatement of an interest rate (e.g., continuously compounded) in terms of an annualized simple interest rate.

Arbitrage A trading strategy that has a chance to make riskless profits without requiring a net investment of funds.

Arbitrageur Trader who attempts to make arbitrage profits from price discrepancies.

Arbitration A system of mediating disputes before going to the courts.

Ask (or offer) price The price at which a dealer offers to sell securities to a customer.

Asset-backed security (ABS) Bond issued by a specialized purpose vehicle (SPV) that is backed by assets as collateral.

At-the-money (option) An option whose underlying asset's price is close to the exercise price.

Audit trail A detailed information record of a financial security transaction.

Backward induction A mathematical technique for solving a problem where one starts at the last date in a model and obtains the solution by working backward through time.

Backwardation A forward or futures market where the forward or futures price is lower than the spot price, respectively.

Banging (or marking) the close Manipulating prices by trading a large security position leading up to the market close followed by offsetting the position before the end of trading.

Banker's discount yield The rate used for quoting Treasury bills.

Basel Committee on Banking Supervision Established in 1974 by the Group of Ten countries' central-bank governors; formulates broad supervisory standards and recommends statements of best banking practice.

Basis The spot price minus the futures price.

Basis point (or bp) One-hundredth (1/100th) of 1 percent.

Bbalibor The daily rate determined by the British Bankers' Association by collecting libor quotes on Eurodollar deposits (or time deposits in nine other currencies) with maturities ranging from overnight to a year from a panel of major banks and computing a trimmed average.

Bearish trade A trade benefiting if security prices decrease in value.

Bid price The price at which a dealer offers to buy securities from a customer.

Binomial stock price evolution A model of a stock price evolution using a tree in which from any point in time onward, the stock price takes only one of two possible values.

Block trade Stock trade involving ten thousand shares or more.

Bond or fixed-income security The debt issued by a borrower who promises both to pay interest on the borrowing and to repay the principal borrowed at some future date (see consols for an exception).

Bond-equivalent yield The holding period return earned on a bond if held until maturity.

Bootstrap method The technique of creating a zero-coupon bond price term structure from market data (including computation of any missing prices by interpolation).

Broker A financial intermediary who matches buyers and sellers and earns commissions for this service.

Bullish trade A trade benefiting if security prices increase in value.

Butterfly spread An option trading strategy created by trading four options of the same type (all calls or all puts) with three different strike prices: two options with extreme strike prices are purchased (written) and two options are written (purchased) with middle strike prices.

Buying hedge (or long hedge) Taking a long position in a forward or a futures contract to hedge the price risk from a spot market purchase.

Buy–write (option) Simultaneously buying the underlying asset and selling the call.

Calibration A mathematical technique that estimates a derivative pricing model's parameters by equating the model's price to the market price.

Call option A financial security that gives the owner the right to buy a specified quantity of a financial or real asset on or before a fixed future date by paying an exercise price agreed on when the contract is written.

Callable bond A bond whose issuer has the option to repay the principal and terminate the bond before maturity.

Cap A portfolio of caplets.

Capital gain or loss (Gain) Realized by selling an asset at a price higher than the purchase price. (Loss) Realized by selling an asset at a lower price than the buying price.

Caplet A European call option on an interest rate.

Cash settlement Ending a derivatives contract by making a cash payment instead of exchanging physical securities.

Cash-and-carry argument An argument used to determine the forward price where one purchases the underlying commodity with borrowed cash and holds the commodity until the forward contract's maturity date.

Central limit theorem (CLT) A key theorem in probability that states that the distribution for the average of a collection of independent random variables, when "standardized" (by subtracting from the average the common mean and dividing the expression by the standard deviation of the average), approaches a standard normal distribution as the sample size increases.

Cheapest-to-deliver bond An embedded option available to the seller of a Treasury bond futures contract by which one can deliver any one of several Treasury bonds at expiration.

Clearing (a trade) When buy and sell orders are matched, the trade is officially recognized, and the trade is recorded by the exchange's clearinghouse.

Clearing member Exchange member (broker and dealer) who clears trades.

Clearinghouse An entity associated with or part of an exchange that clears trades.

Close (futures market) The end of a day's trading session.

Closed-end fund Investment company that takes cash for the issuance of shares at inception, but no additional shares are issued thereafter.

Closing transaction (or a reversing trade) A trade that cancels an outstanding open position.

Collar (Option) A portfolio that combines a long position in the underlying asset with a long put and short call (with different strike prices) so that the resultant portfolio has truncated payoffs on both the up and down sides. (Market regulation) A trading restriction that prohibits the buying or selling of stocks when the stock price moves by more than a certain number of points.

Collateralized debt obligation (CDO) An asset-backed security whose collateral pool consists of ABS bonds, as distinct from mortgage loans. CDO bonds are partitioned into seniority tranches that specify the interest and principal payments the bonds receive.

Collateralized debt obligation squared (CDO^2) An asset-backed security whose collateral pool consists of CDO bonds.

Combination strategy A portfolio of options of different types on the same underlying asset with the same expiration date where the options are either all purchased or written.

Commercial paper A promissory note, issued by a company, that matures in 270 days or less and that is sold as a zero-coupon bond.

Commercial trader (futures) Futures trader such as a farmer, manufacturer, or commodities dealer who has legitimate hedging needs because of her commercial activity with the underlying commodity.

Commitment of Traders (COT) A weekly report published by the Commodity Futures Trading Commission that shows aggregate commercial and noncommercial trader positions in certain futures and options markets.

Commodity (US futures contract) The CFTC Act of 1974 defines a commodity to include any "goods and articles . . . and all services, rights, and interests" on which contracts for future delivery can be written.

Commodity Futures Trading Commission (CFTC) The US federal government agency regulating futures and futures on option markets.

Commodity indexed note A derivative whose holder receives a payment tied to the return on a physical commodity or a commodity index.

Commodity pool (or commodity fund) Investment fund investing in commodity futures.

Commodity swap A swap in which one counterparty makes a floating payment that is tied to the changes in a commodity price or the return on a commodity price index.

Competitive market An idealized description of a market populated by a large number of traders who are too insignificant to influence prices.

Complete market A market where sufficient securities trade so that investors can obtain any desired future payoffs.

Condor spread An option portfolio created by trading four options of the same type (all calls or all puts) with four different strike prices: two options with extreme strike prices are purchased (written) and two options are written (purchased) with middle strike prices.

Consol A bond that never pays back the principal but pays interest at a promised rate forever.

Consumer Price Index (CPI) An index measuring the cost of a typical household's goods and purchased services.

Contango A forward or a futures market where the forward or futures price is higher than the spot price.

Convenience yield A benefit that accrues to the holder of a physical commodity.

Convertible bond A bond whose holder has the option to convert the bond into a fixed number of shares of the borrowing company's stock.

Cost-of-carry model A model that determines a forward price of a commodity under the assumption that buying and carrying the commodity to the future has interest as the only cost.

Counterparties The traders (buyer and seller) in a financial transaction.

Coupon A periodic interest payment made on a bond.

Coupon bond A bond that pays interest (coupons) periodically to the bondholder.

Covered (option trade) An option trade that is accompanied by a position in the underlying asset that reduces the overall risk; the special case of a cash-secured put (a short put trade in which the writer deposits an amount equal to the strike price with the broker) is also considered a covered trade.

Credit default swap A derivative security that provides insurance against the event that the issuer of a bond might default and the bond declines in value.

Credit swap A swap in which both payments are based on individual stock returns in the same industry but with different credit ratings.

Cross-hedge (imperfect hedge) A hedge in which the spot and futures positions do not exactly offset each other.

Cross-trade An offsetting or noncompetitive match of a buy and sell order; normally banned, but permitted in special cases.

Cum-dividend The price of a stock before it goes ex-dividend.

Currency swap A swap involving an exchange of payments in one currency for that in another. A plain vanilla currency swap (or a cross-currency swap) between two counterparties involves (1) an exchange of equivalent amounts in two different currencies on the start date, (2) an exchange of interest payments on two currency loans at intermediate dates, and (3) a repayment of the principal amounts on the loans at the ending date.

Current assets These are cash or cash-equivalent assets held for collection, sale, or consumption within the enterprise's normal twelve-month operating cycle; all other assets are noncurrent.

Current liabilities The liabilities settled within the enterprise's normal twelve-month operating cycle, or those held for trading, or those for which the entity does not have an unconditional right to defer payment beyond twelve months; other liabilities are noncurrent.

Daily settlement (futures) Crediting/debiting of the day's gains/losses to a futures contract's margin account.

Dark pool (or dark pool of liquidity) Secretive trade matching networks for institutional traders that do not send orders directly to an exchange or that are not displayed in a limit order book.

Day order A limit order that gets cancelled if it is not executed by the end of the trading day during which it is placed.

Day trader Trader who tries to profit from daily price movements, opening trading positions in the morning and closing them out at night.

Dealer A financial intermediary who posts prices at which she buys (wholesale or bid price) or sells (retail or ask price) securities.

Default A failure to pay a promised payment on a financial contract at the promised time.

Delivery date (or maturity date) A predetermined date on which a seller of a futures contract agrees to deliver the underlying commodity to the buyer in exchange for the futures price.

Delivery period (futures) Time period during which delivery of the underlying commodity, as stipulated in a futures contract, can occur.

Delta The sensitivity of an option price to changes in the underlying asset price.

Delta-neutral A portfolio whose delta is zero.

Derivative (or a derivative security) A financial contract that derives its value from an underlying variable such as a stock price, a commodity price, or even an interest rate.

Diagonal spread A portfolio obtained by buying an option with a particular expiration date and strike price and simultaneously selling an option with a different expiration date and different strike price, where the options (both calls or both puts) have the same underlying asset.

Discriminatory auction An auction where the successful bidders pay their bid prices to purchase the item being sold.

Diversifiable risk A risk that can be eliminated in a portfolio of securities via diversification.

Dividend Payment in the form of cash or stocks made to existing stockholders.

Dividend yield A stock's dividend payment expressed as a fraction of the stock price.

Dollar return The value of an invested dollar on a future date.

Dual trading Allowing a market participant to act as a broker and dealer on the same day, though not on the same transaction.

Duration The weighted average of time to payment of a bond's cash flows where the weights correspond to the present value of the cash flows received on the respective dates.

Dynamic hedging A hedge that is regularly adjusted over time to maintain a riskless position.

Efficient market A market in which security prices "fully and accurately" reflect all relevant information.

Electronic communications network (ECN) An electronic system that automatically matches publicly displayed buy and sell orders at specified limit order prices.

Employee stock options Call options on the stock that are granted by a company to employees as a form of non-cash compensation.

Equilibrium model Model that determines prices by requiring the equality of supply and demand.

Equity option Option that has common stock as the underlying.

Equity swap A swap in which one side makes a floating payment tied to the return on a stock or a stock index.

Equity-linked note (ELN) A combination of a zero-coupon (or a low-coupon) bond with a return based on the performance of a single stock, a basket of stocks, or a stock index.

Euribor (Euro Interbank Offered Rate) An interest rate index computed on Euro Interbank term deposits.

Eurobond An international bond that is denominated in a currency not native to the issuing country.

Eurocurrency Time deposits in a bank denominated in a currency outside the borders of the country where the bank is located.

Eurodollar Dollar-denominated time deposits held in a bank outside the United States.

European option An option that can be exercised only at the expiration date.

Exchange A physical or electronic location where buyers and sellers meet to trade a standardized commodity under a given set of rules.

Exchange of physicals (EFP) Terminating a futures contract with a spot trade in which the buyer and the seller privately negotiate the delivery of the commodity at a location different from those in the futures contract.

Exchange rate The price of one currency in terms of another.

Exchange-traded fund (ETF) Investment company that gives shareholders fractional ownership rights over a basket of securities.

Exchange-traded note (ETN) Bond issued by an underwriting bank, which promises to pay a return (minus any fees) based on the performance of a market benchmark (like a commodity price index) or some investment strategy.

Ex-dividend date The date after which the stock owner does not get the last announced dividend.

Execution A trade is executed when the counterparties agree on the terms, conditions, price, and quantity and commit to transact.

Exercise price (or strike price) The predetermined price that an option holder pays to exercise the option.

Exotic (derivative) Complex derivatives that are not ordinary call or put options.

Expectations hypothesis The hypothesis that zero-coupon bonds of different maturities are perfect substitutes.

Expense ratio (mutual fund) A mutual fund's annual operating expenses expressed as a percentage of average net assets.

Expiration date (option) The last day that an option holder gets to exercise the option.

Extendible bond A bond whose holder has the option to extend the bond's life.

Fail to deliver In a repurchase agreement, when a counterparty fails to deliver the securities, the loan is extended by a day at no extra interest.

Federal funds market A borrowing or lending market for cash among US banks.

Federal Reserve System (the Federal Reserve or simply "the Fed") The central bank of the United States.

Financial Accounting Standards Board (FASB) A private, not-for-profit organization whose primary purpose is to establish financial accounting standards that govern the preparation of financial reports by nongovernmental entities.

Financial assets Paper assets such as stocks, bonds, and currencies that represent claims to real assets.

Financial engineering The science of applying engineering tools to develop financial contracts to meet the needs of an enterprise.

Financial futures (or financials) Futures contracts based on financial assets (like foreign currencies) or financial variables (like interest rates).

Financial Industry Regulatory Authority (FINRA) A self-regulatory organization created by combining the self-regulatory functions of the New York Stock Exchange and the National Association of Securities Dealers.

Fixed price offering An offer to sell securities where the price, the interest rate, and the maturity are announced beforehand.

Floor A portfolio of floorlets.

Floor broker A broker working on an exchange floor.

Floorlet A European put option on an interest rate.

Forex swap (or FX swap) A swap in which (1) the contract starts with an exchange of one currency for another and (2) it ends with a reverse exchange of these cash payments, with interest, at a subsequent date.

Forward contract A binding agreement between a buyer and a seller to trade some commodity at a fixed price at a later date.

Forward price (or delivery price) The fixed price in a forward contract in which the counterparties agree to trade a commodity on a future delivery date.

Forward rate The rate one can contract today on riskless borrowing or lending over a future time period.

Forward rate agreement A derivatives contract that pays off based on the interest rate for borrowing (or lending) over some future time period.

Forward rate curve The graph of forward rates as a function of the time to maturity.

Front running Trading based on nonpublic information about an impending transaction by another person.

Fundamental analysis Security analysis that involves reading accounting and financial information about a company to determine whether the share is overvalued or undervalued.

Futures commission merchant (FCM) A futures trade facilitator who provides a one-stop service for all aspects of futures trading.

Futures contract A futures contract is an exchange-traded agreement between a buyer and a seller to trade some commodity at a fixed price at a later date.

Gamma The sensitivity of the delta to changes in the underlying asset price.

Gilt security Bond issued by the UK government.

Good-till-canceled (GTC) order A limit order that stays open indefinitely until it is executed or closed by the trader who placed the order.

Great Recession A commonly used term for 2007–9, when many countries suffered a decline in output and experienced large unemployment.

Gross domestic product The market value of all goods and services produced in a year in a country.

Hedge Protecting one's investment against loss by making balancing or compensating contracts or transactions.

Hedge fund A private actively managed investment fund that utilizes sophisticated strategies to generate returns for high-net-worth individuals.

Hedge ratio The number of shares of the stock to trade for each option to remove all of the price risk from the resulting portfolio.

Hedger Trader whose aim is to reduce preexisting risk by trading derivatives and other securities.

High-frequency trading A computerized trading strategy pursuing fleeting profit opportunities by trading at the blink of an eye.

Horizontal spread (time or calendar spread) A portfolio obtained by buying an option with a particular expiration date and simultaneously selling an option with a different maturity date, where the options (both calls or both puts) have the same underlying asset and the same strike price.

Hybrid debt (or structured note) A derivative security created by combining a bond and equity or a derivative (a forward, an option, or a swap).

Implied volatility An option's underlying asset's return volatility computed by equating the option's market price to the option's model price.

Index (stock market) A measure computed by taking the average of a portfolio of stock prices.

Index arbitrage An arbitrage trading strategy based on a discrepancy between a stock market index and a futures contract on the index.

Index mutual fund (or stock index fund) A mutual fund that holds a basket of securities in the same proportion as an index it tries to replicate.

Indexing A popular name for investing in index portfolios.

Indication schedule (swap) A list of the various rates at which a swap dealer bank is willing to trade against six-month bbalibor.

Inflation A rise in a general consumer price level.

Initial margin (or performance margin) Before initiating a trade, a trader must keep this amount (in the form of cash or high-quality, low-risk securities) as collateral with the broker.

Insurance A financial contract that requires the buyer to make periodic payments to an insurance company for protection against a loss event.

Intercommodity spread (futures) A spread established by simultaneously buying and selling futures contracts on different commodities with the same or different delivery months.

Interest rate The rate of return on cash borrowed or lent.

International Money Market A division of the Chicago Mercantile Exchange (now part of the CME Group), where futures on foreign currencies trade.

International Organization of Securities Commissions (IOSCO) An international cooperative body of securities regulators.

International Swaps and Derivatives Association (ISDA; previously International Swap Dealers Association) An industry body consisting of financial institutions, businesses, governmental entities, and other end users that trade over-the-counter derivatives.

In-the-money (option) An option having a positive value when immediately exercised.

Intracommodity spread (futures) A spread established by simultaneously buying and selling futures contracts on the same commodity but with different maturities.

Intrinsic value (Asset) The present value of future cash flows, also known as fundamental value. (Option) The larger of the cash flow obtained by immediately exercising an option or zero.

Law of one price The condition that the same future cash flows, no matter how they are created, have the same market price.

LEAPS (Long-Term Equity Anticipation Securities) Exchange-traded long maturity options that have maturities up to three years.

Leverage The borrowing used to purchase a security or portfolio of securities.

Liability A financial obligation that requires the holder to make payments at some future date.

Libor (London Interbank Offered Rate) and libid An annualized interest rate at which a bank offers to lend surplus funds to another bank for a fixed time period in the London market. Libid (London Interbank Bid Rate) is a similar rate at which a bank bids funds.

Limit order A trade given to a broker that must be filled at the stated or a better price or not traded at all.

Limit order book A dealer's book (or an electronic record system) that records orders waiting to be filled.

Listing requirements Criteria that a company must satisfy to trade its stock on an exchange.

Long The buyer of a security.

Maintenance margin The minimum amount that a trader must keep in a margin account to keep a trading position open.

Margin Collateral kept by a trader with a broker to cover the risk of losses on a transaction.

Margin call A directive by a broker to increase the cash in a margin account when a trade position loses value and declines below the maintenance margin.

Marked-to-market (futures) A futures position is marked-to-market at the end of each trading day when gains and losses incurred on the futures contract are added to the trader's margin account.

Market close (or the closing call) The last minute of trading during which a closing price or a closing range is established.

Market corner A market in which a manipulator has control over the deliverable supply of a security or commodity so that short sellers are forced to pay the manipulator a high price to fulfill their contract obligations.

Market imperfections (or market frictions) Impediments or costs to a trade such as transaction costs (brokerage commissions and bid–ask prices), trading restrictions, or taxes incurred when transacting in a security.

Market maker Specially designated dealer on many exchanges who posts ask and bid prices and stands ready to trade at those prices.

Market manipulation Trading securities using market power or other means to influence a securities price to one's own profit advantage.

Market order A trade that must be immediately transacted at the best available price.

Market portfolio A portfolio that holds all the risky assets in a market in the same proportions as they exist in the economy.

Market-value (or capitalization) weighted average A stock price index computed by multiplying each company's share price by a weight that is proportionate to its market value (or capitalization) and then computing their average.

Mark-to-model The valuation of assets and liabilities via the use of a model.

Married put A portfolio obtained by simultaneously buying a put and its underlying asset.

Martingale A stochastic process in which the expected value at a future date equals its current value.

Martingale pricing A method of derivatives pricing that involves computing the expected discounted payoffs to the derivative using the pseudo-probabilities and discounting them backward through time with the riskless rate.

Master Agreement (ISDA) A comprehensive document that consists of the legal conditions agreed to when trading over-the-counter derivatives.

Modified duration Duration divided by one plus the bond's yield.

Money market account An investment account that earns the risk-free rate each period.

Mortgage A loan that requires regular repayment of interest and principal where the loan is collateralized by a home or building.

Municipal bond (muni) Bonds issued by state, local, or municipal governments whose holders typically enjoy a variety of tax-exemption benefits on interest earned.

Municipal swap A financial swap that has a state, local, or municipal government as one of the counterparties.

Mutual fund Open-end investment company that takes new investments and allows investors to redeem their shares at any time.

Naked trading strategy Option trade involving a single option with no corresponding position in the underlying asset.

National Association of Securities Dealers (NASD) A self-regulatory organization that was created under the provisions of the US Securities Exchange Act of 1934 for regulating the US securities industry.

National Association of Securities Dealers Automated Quotations (NASDAQ) Initially a computer bulletin board system that listed stock price quotes; evolved to become the world's first electronic stock exchange.

National Futures Association (NFA) An industry organization that does a host of self-regulatory, training, promotional, and other activities for futures contracts.

Net asset value (NAV) A company's total assets minus its total liabilities.

Net present value Today's value of a set of future cash flows, subtracting the initial cost.

Noncommercial trader (futures) Trader other than a commercial trader; usually associated with speculation in futures contracts.

Nondiversifiable risk Risk that cannot be eliminated through diversification in a portfolio of securities.

Normal backwardation A forward or futures market in which the forward or futures price, respectively, is less than the expected future spot price.

Notional principal A principal amount that is used for computing cash flows in a derivatives transaction but never changes hands between the counterparties.

Notional variable Variable such as interest rate, inflation rate, and security index that exists as a notion rather than as a traded asset.

On-the-run issue vs. off-the-run issue Newly auctioned Treasury security vs. an issue that has been auctioned earlier.

Open interest The total number of outstanding derivatives contracts.

Open-end company Investment company that is open to additional investments.

Opening call (futures) The initial time period for trading a futures contract.

Open-outcry trading A traditional method of trading futures contracts in which the floor broker or dealer has to cry out the bids and asks in the trading pit so that others may participate.

Option class The set of all call options or put options with a particular underlying asset.

Options Clearing Corporation (OCC) A clearinghouse for most exchange-traded options in the United States.

Options on futures (or futures options) Options that have a futures contract as the underlying asset.

Options series A set of options with identical terms and conditions.

OTC Bulletin Board (OTCBB) A regulated quotation service that displays real-time quotes, last-sale prices, and volume information on over-the-counter equity securities.

Out trade A trade that cannot be cleared by a clearinghouse because of the recording of incorrect information.

Out-of-the-money (option) An option that generates a negative cash flow when immediately exercised.

Over-the-counter (OTC) market Anywhere trading takes place other than an organized exchange.

Overwrite (option) Selling a call option after purchasing the underlying stock.

Par bond A bond for which the coupon rate is the same as its yield so that the bond's price is the same as the bond's face value.

Par swap rate The swap rate initially set on a swap to give it zero initial value.

Payout ratio The ratio of dividends paid on a stock to earnings per share.

Physical delivery (forward and futures contracts) The process of closing out a forward or a futures contract by physically delivering the underlying asset or its ownership rights.

Pink quote An electronic system that displays quotes from broker dealers for small stocks trading in the over-the-counter markets.

Pit (ring) Polygonal area on an exchange floor where futures trading takes place.

Plain vanilla derivatives Market jargon for the simplest derivatives contracts.

Ponzi scheme An investment scheme that pays early investors' returns from the cash coming from later investors.

Portfolio insurance Synthetic put options created by trading the underlying stock and money market account using the option's delta.

Position limit The maximum number of futures (derivatives) contracts that a trader can hold on a particular side of the market.

Position trader (trend follower) Speculator who maintains trading positions for longer than a day.

Post (trading post) Specified places on an exchange's trading floor where traders meet to trade.

Premium (option) The price of an option.

Price bubble The difference between an asset's market price and its fundamental value.

Price discovery The process of discovering the price of a commodity through the interactions of buyers and sellers in a market.

Price limit (daily; or the maximum daily price fluctuation) Maximum price change allowed during a trading day.

Price-weighted average (stock index) A stock index computed by taking a simple average of the prices of the stocks composing the index.

Primary dealer Big securities firms that actively bid in Treasury auctions and with whom the Fed buys and sells Treasuries to conduct open-market operations.

Primary market The market in which a security is first sold to the public.

Principal Amount due on a bond at maturity.

Program trading Trading that takes place using a computer program.

Protective put A portfolio consisting of buying the put to protect the downside risk of the underlying asset that was previously purchased.

Pseudo-probability (martingale probability or risk-neutral probability) The risk-adjusted probability used in martingale pricing for computing derivatives prices.

Put option A financial security that gives the right to sell a specified quantity of an underlying asset on or before a fixed future date by paying an exercise price.

Putable bond A bond that gives the holder the option to end the bond at certain specific dates.

Put–call parity A mathematical relation linking prices of a call, a put, a stock, and a bond.

Random walk A stochastic process whose changes are independent and identically distributed random variables.

Ratio spread An option trading strategy where the number of calls (or puts) purchased is different from the number of calls (or puts) sold.

Real asset Asset including land, buildings, machines, or commodities, which have a physical form.

Reinsurance The practice of insurance companies buying insurance policies on the tail risks generated by the insurance policies they have issued.

Repurchase agreement ("does a repo") The borrowing of cash (and the loaning of securities) done by selling high-quality securities and then agreeing to purchase them back at a fixed date (often the next day) at a higher price.

Residential mortgage–backed security (RMBS) An asset-backed security whose collateral pool consists of residential mortgage loans.

Rho A measure of the change in an option value due to a change in the risk-free interest rate.

Risk premium The excess expected return per unit of risk on a security.

Risk-neutral valuation A method for computing a derivative's value by computing its expected payoffs using the pseudo-probabilities and discounting using the risk-free rate.

Round lot A trading unit of stocks, usually based on one hundred shares.

Round trip (commissions for trading futures) No commission charged when entering a position but full commission charged at the time of closing.

Savings and loans bank A special kind of bank in the United States that specializes in home mortgage lending.

Scalper Speculator who trades many times a day with the hope of picking up small profits from each transaction.

Scenario analysis (stress testing) A method for computing losses based on identifying possible future scenarios for the economy.

Seat (in the context of a securities exchange) Membership on an exchange.

Securities and Exchange Commission (SEC) The US federal government agency in charge of regulating equity and equity options markets.

Securitization The process of combining many individual loans and debts into a collateral pool and selling claims against them to third-party investors.

Security A financial contract (such as a stock, bond, or derivative) that gives its holder ownership rights over some future cash flows.

Self-financing trading strategy A trading strategy over multiple periods that requires no cash inflow or outflow at intermediate dates.

Self-regulatory organization (SRO) An organization made up of members of an industry or a profession that exercises regulatory authority over it.

Semiannual bond equivalent basis Computing interest over a half-year period under the assumption that the year has 365 days and the interest is computed over the actual number of days in the six-month period.

Separate trading of registered interests and principal of securities (STRIPS) Zero-coupon bonds that can be created by separating out different cash flows from a Treasury security.

Settlement The last step of a security transaction where the buyer pays cash and gets the ownership rights over the security.

Settlement date (forward rate agreement) The date on which a forward rate agreement's reference rate is determined.

Settlement price (futures) The last trading price or an appropriate price determined by an exchange's settlement committee, which is used for daily settlement of the futures contract.

Shareholder's equity (equity) The assets owned minus the liabilities incurred by a company.

Short Market jargon to mean the seller of a security.

Short selling Borrowing and selling a security one does not own.

Simple forward rate The forward rate expressed as an annualized simple interest rate.

Special purpose vehicle (SPV) A legal entity set up for the purpose of issuing liabilities that are backed by a collection of assets in a collateral pool.

Specialist A dealer-broker market maker whose job is to make an orderly market in securities assigned to him.

Speculation The taking of risky trades in the hope of obtaining positive returns.

Spin-off The creation of an independent company by selling shares or distributing as new shares an existing business or a division of a parent company.

Spot price (or cash price) The price for an immediate transaction of a commodity or security.

Spot rate The yield on the shortest-maturity default-free zero-coupon bond.

Spread trading Trading that involves buying one or more securities and selling similar securities with the aim of generating arbitrage profits as the price differences converge.

Stock A limited liability asset that gives the investor ownership rights over the residual value of a company.

Stock price evolution A model that describes how a stock price evolves randomly across time.

Stop-loss order A limit sell order that is placed below current market prices or a limit buy order that is placed above current prices.

Storage costs Costs that are incurred for storing a physical commodity in the context of the cost-of-carry model.

Straddle (called put-to-call strategy in London) An option trading strategy that involves simultaneously buying (or selling) a call and a put on the same underlying asset with the same strike price and expiration date.

Strangle An option trading strategy that involves simultaneously buying (or selling) a call and a put on the same underlying asset with the same expiration date but different strike prices.

Subprime lending (also known as B-paper, near-prime, or second chance lending) The practice of making loans to borrowers who do not qualify for the best market interest rates (the prime market) because of a poor credit history.

Swap (financial swap) An agreement between two counterparties to exchange a series of (usually) semiannual cash flows over the life of the contract.

Swap buyer Counterparty to a (plain vanilla) financial swap that pays fixed and receives the floating rate.

Swap facilitator (swap bank) Financial intermediary who acts as a broker or performs the role of a dealer in the swap market.

Swap issuer (initiator) A party that initiates a financial swap by seeking out counterparties to complete the transaction.

Swap rate The predetermined interest rate that a financial swap counterparty pays in exchange for a well-known reference rate such as the bbalibor. This rate gives the swap a zero value at initiation.

Swaption An option that has an interest rate swap as the underlying asset.

Synthetic index A portfolio created for the purpose of replicating the returns on an index.

Synthetic option A portfolio of traded securities that replicates an option's payoff and consequently must have the same price as the traded option to avoid arbitrage.

Tail risk The risk of occurrence of infrequent events that lie on the tail of a probability distribution.

Technical analysis A security analysis technique that involves looking at price patterns and related measures to predict whether a stock's price is overvalued or undervalued.

Tenor (maturity or term of a swap) Time duration of a financial swap.

Term structure of interest rates The graph of yields or forward rates versus the time to maturity.

Theta A measure of the change in an option's value given a decrease in the option's time to maturity.

Tick size (minimum price fluctuation) The minimum price move for an exchange-traded security.

Ticker (trading) symbol The abbreviation that identifies an exchange-traded security.

Ticker tape The running paper tape or electronic panel displaying a variety of prices, quotes, and relevant news to subscribers located both in and off the exchange.

Time spread (calendar spread) A spread established by simultaneously buying and selling futures contracts on commodities with different delivery months.

Time value (option) An option's premium (or price) minus its intrinsic value.

Total return index An index that assumes that all disbursements from the companies in the index get reinvested in a hypothetical index portfolio.

Total return swap A swap where one counterparty pays the total return on a price index in exchange for a fixed or floating interest rate payment.

Trading at settlement (or TAS) Special futures contracts in which the counterparties decide at the time of trading that the contract price will be the day's settlement price plus or minus an agreed differential.

Trading volume (or volume) The total number of contracts or securities traded during a trading day.

Treasury bill (T-bill) US government debt sold in the form of a zero-coupon bond that has a maximum maturity of one year.

Treasury inflation protected security (TIPS) Treasury security that adjusts for inflation and pays a guaranteed real rate of return to the investors.

Treasury note and bond (T-note and T-bond) Treasury securities that make semiannual coupon payments with original maturity of more than one year to up to ten years in the case of a Treasury note and more than ten years in the case of a Treasury bond.

Treasury security (Treasuries) Debt issued by the US federal government.

Treasury–Eurodollar (TED) spread The difference between the bbalibor rate for US dollars and Treasury rates of equivalent maturities.

Underlying (for a derivative) A reference asset or a notional variable whose price or value determines the derivative's payoff.

Uniform price auction An auction in which all successful bidders pay the same price (the highest losing bid or the lowest winning bid).

Upstairs market A market away from the trading floor in which large-sized trades are negotiated, with or without the help of brokers.

Value-at-risk (VaR) The dollar amount that the firm's losses will exceed with a given probability (such as 1 percent or 5 percent) over a prespecified time interval.

Variation margin An amount equal to the change in the futures settlement price from the previous trading day that is credited or debited to a trader's account.

Vega A measure of the change in an option's value given a change in the underlying asset's return volatility.

Vertical spread (money, perpendicular, or price spread) A portfolio consisting of buying an option with a particular strike price while simultaneously selling an option with a different strike price, where the options (both calls or both puts) have the same underlying asset and expire on the same date.

VIX (CBOE Volatility index) A measure of the market's near-term volatility as implied by the Standard and Poor's 500 stock index option prices.

Wall Street An expression for investment banking companies, many of which have offices near Wall Street in New York's financial district.

Warehousing swap A risk management technique used by swap providers in which they enter into different swaps on both the buy and sell side of the market and hedge the residual risk.

Wash sale A sell and buy transaction for the same commodity initiated without the intent to make a bona fide transaction.

When-issued market A specialized forward market for Treasury securities that opens before the actual securities are auctioned.

Wild card play (T-bond futures) An embedded option available to the seller of Treasury bond futures to issue the notice of intention to deliver for a few hours after the market closes.

Writer (option) Seller of an option.

Yield (yield to maturity or internal rate of return) The interest rate that discounts a bond's cash flows to equal its current price.

Yield curve A graph of bond yields as a function of maturity.

Zero-cost collar A portfolio that combines a long position in the underlying asset with a long put and a short call so that the resultant portfolio has truncated payoffs on both up and down sides.

Zero-coupon bond A bond that pays no interest but is sold at a discount from the principal.

Zero-sum game A game in which one trader's gain is the other's loss.

References

Allen and Overy, 2002. "An Introduction to the Documentation of OTC Derivatives." www.isda.org.

Alletzhauser, Albert J., 1990. *The House of Nomura: The Inside Story of the Legendary Japanese Financial Dynasty.* Harper Perennial, New York.

Amemiya, Takeshi, 1994. *Introduction to Statistics and Econometrics.* Harvard University Press, Cambridge, Mass.

Amin, Kaushik I., and Robert A. Jarrow, 1991. "Pricing Foreign Currency Options under Stochastic Interest Rates." *Journal of International Money and Finance* 10(3), 310–29.

Arrow, Kenneth J., 1953. "Le rôle des valeurs boursières pour la répartition la meilleure des risques." *Econometrie* 11, 41–48. (Trans. 1964, "The Role of Securities in the Optimal Allocation of Risk-Bearing." *Review of Economic Studies* 31(2), 91–96.)

Arrow, Kenneth J., and Gerard Debreu, 1954. "Existence of an Equilibrium for a Competitive Economy." *Econometrica* 22(3), 265–90

Artzner, Philippe, Freddy Delbaen, Jean-Marc Eber, and David C. Heath, 1999. "Coherent Measures of Risk." *Mathematical Finance* 9(3), 203–28.

Bachelier, Louis J.-B. A., 1900. *Théorie de la Spéculation.* Gauthier-Villars, Paris.

Bakshi, Gurdip, Charles Cao, and Zhiwu Chen, 1997. "Empirical Performance of Alternative Option Pricing Models." *Journal of Finance* 52(5), 2003–49.

Bank, Peter, and Dietmar Baum, 2004. "Hedging and Portfolio Optimization in Financial Markets with a Large Trader." *Mathematical Finance* 14(1), 1–18.

Bank for International Settlements, 2005. *OTC Derivative Market Activity in the First Half of 2005.* Monetary and Economic Department, Bank for International Settlements, Basel, Switzerland.

Baxter, Martin W., and Andrew J. O. Rennie, 1996. *Financial Calculus: An Introduction to Derivatives Pricing.* Cambridge University Press, Cambridge.

Bernstein, Peter L., 1992. *Capital Ideas: The Improbable Origins of Modern Wall Street.* John Wiley, Hoboken, N.J.

Bernstein, Peter L., 1998. *Against the Gods: The Remarkable Story of Risk.* John Wiley, New York.

Bhattacharya, Mihir, 1983. "Transactions Data Tests of Efficiency of the Chicago Board Options Exchange." *Journal of Financial Economics* 12(2), 161–85.

Bhattacharya, Utpal, and Hazem Daouk, 2002. "The World Price of Insider Trading." *Journal of Finance* 57, 75–108.

Billingsley, Patrick, 1995. *Probability and Measures.* 3rd ed. John Wiley, New York.

Black, Fischer S., 1976. "The Pricing of Commodity Contracts." *Journal of Financial Economics* 3(1–2), 167–79.

Black, Fischer S., and Myron S. Scholes, 1973. "The Pricing of Options and Corporate Liabilities." *Journal of Political Economy* 81, 637–59.

Black, Fischer S., Emmanuel Derman, and William W. Toy, 1990. "A One-Factor Model of Interest Rates and Its Application to Treasury Bond Options." *Financial Analysts Journal* 46, 33–39.

Box, George E. P., and Norman R. Draper, 1987. *Empirical Model-building and Response Surfaces.* John Wiley, New York.

Brace, Alan, Dariusz Gatarek, and Marek Musiela, 1997. "The Market Model of Interest Rate Dynamics." *Mathematical Finance* 7(2), 127–55.

Brealey, Richard A., and Stewart C. Myers, 2003. *Principles of Corporate Finance.* 7th ed. McGraw-Hill, New York.

Brennan, Michael J., and Eduardo S. Schwartz, 1979. "A Continuous Time Approach to the Pricing of Bonds." *Journal of Banking and Finance* 3(2), 133–55.

Brickley, James A., and John J. McConnell, 1987. "Dividend Policy." In *The New Palgrave: A Dictionary of Economics.* Edited by John Eatwell, Murray Milgate, and Peter Newman. W. W. Norton, New York. (Repr. 1989, *The New Palgrave: Finance.*)

Campbell, John Y., Andrew W. Lo, and A. Craig MacKinlay, 1996. *Econometrics of Financial Markets.* Princeton University Press, Princeton, N.J.

Cantor, Richard, and Frank Packer, 1994. "The Credit Rating Industry." *Federal Reserve Bank of New York Quarterly Review* 19(2), 1–26.

Castelli, Charles, 1877. *The Theory of "Options" in Stocks and Shares.* Fred C. Mathieson, London.

Çetin, Umut, Robert A. Jarrow, and Philip E. Protter, 2004. "Liquidity Risk and Arbitrage Pricing Theory." *Finance and Stochastics* 8(3), 311–41.

Chance, Don M., 2008. "A Synthesis of Binomial Option Pricing Models for Lognormally Distributed Assets." *Journal of Applied Finance* 18(1), 38–56.

Chang, Carolyn W., and Jack S. K. Chang, 1990. "Forward and Futures Prices: Evidence from Foreign Exchange Markets." *Journal of Finance* 45(4), 1333–36.

Chatterjea, Arkadev, 1993. *Market Manipulation and a Model of the United States Treasury Securities Market.* Unpublished PhD dissertation, Cornell University, Ithaca, N.Y.

Chatterjea, Arkadev, and Robert A. Jarrow, 1997. "Market Manipulation, Price Bubbles, and a Model of the U.S. Treasury Securities Auction Market." *Journal of Financial and Quantitative Analysis*, 33(2), 255–89.

Cornell, Bradford, and Marc R. Reinganum, 1981. "Forward and Futures Prices: Evidence from Foreign Exchange Markets." *Journal of Finance* 36(12), 1035–45.

Courtault, Jean-Michel, Yuri Kabanov, Bernard Bru, Pierre Crépel, Isabelle Lebon, and Arnaud L. Marchand, 2000. "Louis Bachelier on the Centenary of *Théorie de la Spéculation.*" *Mathematical Finance* 10(3), 341–53.

Cox, David R., and Hilton D. Miller, 1990. *The Theory of Stochastic Processes.* Chapman Hall, London.

Cox, John C., Stephen A. Ross, and Mark Rubinstein, 1979. "Option Pricing: A Simplified Approach." *Journal of Financial Economics* 7(3), 229–63.

Cox, John C., Jonathan E. Ingersoll, and Stephen A. Ross, 1981. "A Re-examination of Traditional Hypotheses about the Term Structure of Interest Rates." *Journal of Finance* 36(4), 769–99.

Cox, John C., Jonathan E. Ingersoll, and Stephen A. Ross, 1985. "A Theory of the Term Structure of Interest Rates." *Econometrica* 53(2), 385–407.

Culbertson, John M., 1957. "The Term Structure of Interest Rates." *Quarterly Journal of Economics* 71(4), 485–517.

Dash, Mike, 2001. *Tulipomania: The Story of the World's Most Coveted Flower and the Extraordinary Passions It Aroused.* Three Rivers Press, New York.

DeGroot, Morris H., and Mark J. Schervish, 2011. *Probability and Statistics.* 3rd ed. Pearson Addison Wesley, Boston.

Dezhbakhsh, Hashem, 1994. "Foreign Exchange Forward and Futures Prices: Are They Equal?" *Journal of Financial and Quantitative Analysis* 29(1), 75–87.

Dixit, Avinash K., and Robert S. Pindyck, 1994. *Investment under Uncertainty.* Princeton University Press, Princeton, N.J.

Duffie, Darrell, 1989. *Futures Markets.* 1st ed. Prentice Hall, Englewood Cliffs, N.J.

Duffie, Darrell, 2001. *Dynamic Asset Pricing Theory.* 3rd ed. Princeton University Press, Princeton, N.J.

Dunn, Kenneth B., and Kenneth J. Singleton, 1986. "Modeling the Term Structure of Interest Rates under Nonseparable Utility and Durability of Goods." *Journal of Financial Economics* 17(1), 27–55.

Easterbrook, Frank H., 1986. "Monopoly, Manipulation and the Regulation of Futures Markets." *Journal of Business* 59(2), 103–27.

Edwards, Franklin R., and Cindy W. Ma, 1992. *Futures and Options.* McGraw-Hill, New York.

Ehrlich, Paul R., 1968. *The Population Bomb.* Ballantine, New York.

Eisenberg, Larry, and Robert A. Jarrow, 1994. "Option Pricing with Random Volatilities in Complete Markets." *Review of Quantitative Finance and Accounting* 4(1), 5–17. (Repr. 1998, *Volatility: New Estimation Techniques for Pricing Derivatives*, Risk, London.)

Engle, Robert F., and Joshua V. Rosenberg, 2002. "Empirical Pricing Kernels." *Journal of Financial Economics* 64(3), 341–72.

Feynman, Richard P., 1998. *The Meaning of It All: Thoughts of a Citizen-Scientist.* Perseus Books, Reading, Mass.

Filer, Herbert J., 1959. *Understanding Put and Call Options.* Popular Library, New York.

Finucane, Thomas J., 1997. "An Empirical Analysis of Common Stock Call Exercise: A Note." *Journal of Banking and Finance* 21(4), 563–71.

Fischel, Daniel R., and David J. Ross, 1991. "Should the Law Prohibit 'Manipulation' in Financial Markets?" *Harvard Law Review* 105(2), 503–53.

Fisher, Irving M., 1930. *The Theory of Interest.* Macmillan, New York.

Follmer, Hans, and A. Schied, 2004. *Stochastic Finance: An Introduction in Discrete Time.* 2nd ed. Walter de Gruyter, Berlin.

French, Kenneth R., 1980. "Stock Returns and the Weekend Effect." *Journal of Financial Economics* 8(1), 55–69.

French, Kenneth R., and Richard Roll, 1986. "Stock Return Variances: The Arrival of Information and the Reaction of Traders." *Journal of Financial Economics* 17 (1), 5–26.

Froot, Kenneth A., David S. Scharfstein, and Jeremy C. Stein, 1994. "A Framework for Risk Management." *Harvard Business Review* 72(6), 91–102.

Gastineau, Gary L., and Mark P. Kritzman, 1996. *The Dictionary of Financial Risk Management.* Frank J. Fabozzi Associates, New York.

Gelderblom, Oscar, and Joost Jonker, 2005. "Amsterdam as the Cradle of Modern Futures and Options Trading, 1550–1650." In *The Origins of Value: The Financial Innovations That Created Modern Capital Markets.* Edited by William N. Goetzmann and K. Geert Rouwenhorst. Oxford University Press, New York.

Glasserman, Paul, 2003. *Monte Carlo Methods in Financial Engineering.* Springer Science + Business Media, New York.

Greenbaum, Stuart I., and Anjan V. Thakor, 2007. *Contemporary Financial Intermediation.* 6th ed. Academic, Burlington, Mass.

Grossman, Sanford J., and Joseph E. Stiglitz, 1980. "On the Impossibility of Informationally Efficient Markets." *American Economic Review* 70(3), 393–408.

Hao, Jia, Avner Kalay, and Stewart Mayhew, 2010. "Ex-Dividend Arbitrage in Option Markets." *Review of Financial Studies* 23(1), 271–303.

Harrison, J. Michael, and David M. Kreps, 1979. "Martingales and Arbitrage in Multiperiod Securities Markets." *Journal of Economic Theory* 20(3), 381–408.

Harrison, J. Michael, and Stanley R. Pliska, 1981. "Martingales and Stochastic Integrals in the Theory of Continuous Trading." *Stochastic Processes and Their Applications* 11(3), 215–60.

Heath, David C., and Robert A. Jarrow, 1988. "Ex-Dividend Stock Price Behavior and Arbitrage Opportunities." *Journal of Business* 61(1), 95–108.

Heath, David C., Robert A. Jarrow, and Andrew J. Morton, 1992. "Bond Pricing and the Term Structure of Interest Rates: A New Methodology for Contingent Claims Valuation." *Econometrica* 60(1), 77–105.

Hicks, John R., 1946. *Value and Capital.* 2nd ed. Clarendon Press, Oxford.

Higgins, Leonard R., 1902. *The Put-and-Call.* Elfingham Wilson, Royal Exchange, London.

Ho, Thomas S. Y., and Sang-Bin Lee, 1986. "Term Structure Movements and Pricing Interest Rate Contingent Claims." *Journal of Finance* 41(5), 1011–29.

Ho, Thomas S. Y., and Sang-Bin Lee, 2004. *The Oxford Guide to Financial Modeling: Applications for Capital Markets, Corporate Finance, Risk Management and Financial Institutions.* Oxford University Press, New York.

Hughston, Lane P., 1996. "The New Interest Rate Models." In *The New Interest Rate Models.* Risk Books, London.

Hull, John C., 2002. *Options, Futures, and Other Derivatives.* 5th ed. Prentice Hall, Upper Saddle River, N.J.

Jarrow, Robert A., 1981. "Liquidity Premiums and the Expectations Hypothesis." *Journal of Banking and Finance* 5(4), 539–46.

Jarrow, Robert A., 1992. "Market Manipulation, Bubbles, Corners, and Short Squeezes." *Journal of Financial and Quantitative Analysis* 27(3), 311–36.

Jarrow, Robert A., 1994. "Derivative Security Markets, Market Manipulation and Option Pricing Theory." *Journal of Financial and Quantitative Analysis* 29(2), 241–61.

Jarrow, Robert A., 1999. "In Honor of the Nobel Laureates Robert C. Merton and Myron S. Scholes: A Partial Differential Equation That Changed the World." *Journal of Economic Perspectives* 13(4), 229–48.

Jarrow, Robert A., 2002a. "Put Option Premiums and Coherent Risk Measures." *Mathematical Finance* 12(2), 135–42.

Jarrow, Robert A., 2002b. *Modeling Fixed Income Securities and Interest Rate Options.* 2nd ed. Stanford University Press, Palo Alto, Calif.

Jarrow, Robert A., 2008. "Operational Risk." *Journal of Banking and Finance* 32(5), 870–79.

Jarrow, Robert A., 2009a. "Credit Risk Models." *Annual Review of Financial Economics* 1, 37–68.

Jarrow, Robert A., 2009b. "The Term Structure of Interest Rates." *Annual Review of Financial Economics* 1, 1–28.

Jarrow, Robert A., 2011. "Risk Management Models: Construction, Testing, Usage." *Journal of Derivatives* 18(4), 89–98.

Jarrow, Robert A., 2012. "The Role of ABS, CDS and CDOs in the Credit Crisis and the Economy." In *Rethinking the Financial System.* Edited by Alan S. Blinder, Andrew W. Lo, and Robert M. Solow. Russell Sage Foundation, New York.

Jarrow, Robert A., and George S. Oldfield, 1981. "Forward Contracts and Futures Contracts." *Journal of Financial Economics* 9(4), 373–82.

Jarrow, Robert A., and Philip E. Protter, 2008. "An Introduction to Financial Asset Pricing." In *Handbook in OR & MS* 15. Edited by John R. Birge and Vadim Linetsky. Elsevier, The Netherlands.

Jarrow, Robert A., and Andrew Rudd, 1982. "Approximate Option Valuation for Arbitrary Stochastic Processes." *Journal of Financial Economics* 10(3), 347–69.

Jarrow, Robert A., and Stuart M. Turnbull, 1992. "Credit Risk: Drawing the Analogy." *Risk Magazine* 5(9).

Jarrow, Robert A., and Stuart M. Turnbull, 1995. "Pricing Derivatives on Financial Securities Subject to Credit Risk." *Journal of Finance* 50(1), 53–85.

Jarrow, Robert A., and Stuart M. Turnbull, 2000. *Derivative Securities*. 2nd ed. South-Western, Cincinnati, Ohio.

Jarrow, Robert A., Haitao Li, and Feng Zhao, 2007. "Interest Rate Caps 'Smile' Too! But Can the LIBOR Market Models Capture the Smile?" *Journal of Finance* 62(1), 345–82.

Jarrow, Robert A., Jeff Oxman, and Yildiray Yildirim, 2010. "The Cost of Operational Risk Loss Insurance." *Review of Derivatives Research* 13(3), 273–95.

Jarrow, Robert A., Philip E. Protter, and Kazuhiro Shimbo, 2010. "Asset Price Bubbles in Incomplete Markets." *Mathematical Finance* 20(2), 145–85.

Jegadeesh, Narasimhan, 1993. "Treasury Auction Bids and the Salomon Squeeze." *Journal of Finance* 48(4), 1403–19.

Johnson, R. Stafford, 2004. *Bond Evaluation, Selection, and Management*. Blackwell, Cambridge, Mass.

Johnston, Elizabeth T., and John J. McConnell, 1989. "Requiem for a Market: An Analysis of the Rise and Fall of a Financial Futures Contract." *Review of Financial Studies* 2(1), 1–23.

Johnston, Jack, and John DiNardo, 1997. *Econometric Methods*. 4th ed. McGraw-Hill, New York.

Jones, E. Philip, Scott P. Mason, and Eric Rosenfeld, 1984. "Contingent Claims Analysis of Corporate Capital Structures: An Empirical Investigation." *Journal of Finance* 39(3), 611–25.

Jordan, Bradford D., and Susan D. Jordan, 1996. "Salomon Brothers and the May (1991) Treasury Auction: Analysis of a Market Corner." *Journal of Banking and Finance* 20(1), 25–40.

Jorion, Philippe, 2000. "Risk Management Lessons from Long-Term Capital Management." *European Financial Management* 6(3), 277–300.

Jovanovic, Franck, and Philippe Le Gall, 2001. "Does God Practice a Random Walk? The 'Financial Physics' of a Nineteenth-Century Forerunner, Jules Regnault." *European Journal of the History of Economic Thought* 8(3), 332–62.

Knoll, Michael S., 2008. "The Ancient Roots of Modern Financial Innovation: The Early History of Regulatory Arbitrage." *Oregon Law Review* 87(1), 93–116.

Krugman, Paul R., Maurice Obstfeld, and Marc Melitz, 2011. *International Economics: Theory and Policy*, 9th ed., Prentice-Hall, Upper Saddle River, N.J.

Lamont, Owen A., and Richard H. Thaler, 2003. "Can the Market Add and Subtract? Mispricing in Tech Stock Carve-outs." *Journal of Political Economy* 111(2), 227–68.

Leland, Hayne, 1994. "Corporate Debt Value, Bond Covenants, and Optimal Capital Structure." *Journal of Finance* 49(4), 1213–52.

Lintner, John, 1956. "Distribution of Incomes of Corporations among Dividends, Retained Earnings, and Taxes." *American Economic Review, Papers and Proceedings* 46(2), 97–113.

Lintner, John, 1965. "The Valuation of Risk Assets and the Selection of Risky Investments in Stock Portfolios and Capital Budgets." *Review of Economics and Statistics* 47(1), 13–37.

Lutz, Friedrich A., 1940. "The Structure of Interest Rates." *Quarterly Journal of Economics* 55(1), 36–63.

Lynch, Peter (with John Rothchild), 1989. *One Up on Wall Street: How to Use What You Already Know to Make Money in the Market*. Simon and Schuster, New York.

Macaulay, Frederick R., 1938. *Some Theoretical Problems Suggested by the Movements of Interest Rates, Bond Yields and Stock Prices in the United States since 1856*. National Bureau of Economic Research, Cambridge, Mass.

MacKenzie, Donald, and Yuval Millo, 2003. "Constructing a Market, Performing Theory: The Historical Sociology of a Financial Derivatives Exchange." *American Journal of Sociology* 109(1), 107–45.

Malkiel, Burton G., 2003. *A Random Walk Down Wall Street*. 8th ed. W. W. Norton, New York.

Malkiel, Burton G., and Richard E. Quandt, 1969. *Strategies and Rational Decisions in the Securities Options Markets*. MIT Press, Cambridge, Mass.

Markowitz, Harry, 1952. "Portfolio Selection." *Journal of Finance* 7(1), 77–91.

Marshall, Alfred, 1920. *Principles of Economics*. Macmillan and Co., London.

Mehrling, Perry, 2005. *Fischer Black and the Revolutionary Idea of Finance*. John Wiley & Sons, Hoboken, N.J.

Merton, Robert C., 1973a. "Theory of Rational Option Pricing." *Bell Journal of Economics and Management Science* 4(1), 141–83.

Merton, Robert C., 1973b. "An Intertemporal Capital Asset Pricing Model." *Econometrica* 41(5), 867–87.

Merton, Robert C., 1974. "On the Pricing of Corporate Debt: The Risk Structure of Interest Rates." *Journal of Finance* 29(2), 449–70.

Merton, Robert C., 1977. "An Analytic Derivation of the Cost of Deposit Insurance and Loan Guarantees: An Application of Modern Option Pricing Theory." *Journal of Banking and Finance* 1(1), 3–11.

Merton, Robert C., and Myron S. Scholes, 1995. "Fischer Black." *Journal of Finance* 50(5), 1359–70.

Miller, Merton H., 1986. "Financial Innovation: The Last Twenty Years and the Next." *Journal of Financial and Quantitative Analysis* 21(4), 459–71.

Miller, Merton H., 1997. *Merton Miller on Derivatives*. John Wiley, New York.

Miller, Merton H., and Franco Modigliani, 1961. "Dividend Policy, Growth, and the Valuation of Shares." *Journal of Business* 34(4), 411–33.

Miltersen, Kristian R., Klaus Sandmann, and Dieter Sondermann, 1997. "Closed Form Solutions for Term Structure Derivatives with Log-Normal Interest Rates." *Journal of Finance* 52(1), 409–30.

Modigliani, Franco, and Merton H. Miller, 1958. "The Cost of Capital, Corporate Finance, and the Theory of Investment." *American Economic Review* 48(3), 261–97.

Modigliani, Franco, and Richard Sutch, 1966. "Innovations in Interest Rate Policy." *American Economic Review* 56(1/2), 178–97.

Mood, Alexander M., Franklin A. Graybill, and Duance C. Boes, 1974. *Introduction to the Theory of Statistics*. McGraw-Hill Higher Education, New York.

Mossin, Jan, 1966. "Equilibrium in a Capital Asset Market." *Econometrica* 35(4), 768–83.

Nelson, Samuel A., 1904. *The A B C of Options and Arbitrage*. S. A. Nelson, New York.

Ofek, Eli, Matthew Richardson, and Robert F. Whitelaw, 2004. "Limited Arbitrage and Short Sales Restrictions: Evidence from the Options Markets." *Journal of Financial Economics* 74(2), 305–42.

Overby, Brian, 2007. *The Options Playbook*. TradeKing.

Pan, Jun, 2002. "The Jump-Risk Premia Implicit in Options: Evidence from an Integrated Time-Series Study." *Journal of Financial Economics* 63(1), 3–50.

Park, Hun Y., and Andrew H. Chen, 1985. "Differences Between Futures and Forward Prices: A Further Investigation of Marking to Market Effects." *Journal of Futures Markets* 5(1), 77–88.

Park, James A. 1799. *A System of the Law of Marine Insurances*. Macmillan and Co., London.

Park, Yoon S. 1984. "Currency Swaps as a Long-Term International Financing Technique." *Journal of International Business Studies* 15(3), 47–54.

Paulson, Jr., Henry M., 2010. *On the Brink: Inside the Race to Stop the Collapse of the Global Financial System*. Business Plus, New York.

Qin, Wang X. and Nick Ronalds, 2005. "China: The Fall and Rise of Chinese Futures, 1990–2005." *Futures Industry Inside* May/June, www.futuresindustry.org/fi-magazine-home.asp?a=1038.

Rebonato, Riccardo, 2002. *Modern Pricing of Interest Rate Derivatives: The LIBOR Market Model and Beyond*. Princeton University Press, Princeton, N.J.

Rendleman, Richard J., and B. Bartter, 1979. "Two State Option Pricing." *Journal of Finance* 34(5), 1092–110.

Rendleman, Richard J., and Christopher E. Carabini, 1979. "The Efficiency of the Treasury Bill Futures Market." *Journal of Finance* 34(4), 895–914.

Ross, Stephen A., Randolph W. Westerfield, and Jeffrey Jaffe, 2004. *Corporate Finance*. 7th ed. McGraw-Hill/Irwin, New York.

Samuelson, Paul A., 1965a. "Rational Theory of Warrant Pricing." *Industrial Management Review* 6, 13–39.

Samuelson, Paul A., 1965b. "Proof That Properly Anticipated Prices Fluctuate Randomly." *Industrial Management Review* 6, 41–50.

Samuelson, Paul A., and Robert C. Merton, 1969. "A Complete Model of Warrant Pricing That Maximizes Utility." *Industrial Management Review* 10(2), 17–46.

Sandmann, Klaus, Dieter Sondermann, and Kristian R. Miltersen, 1995. "Closed Form Term Structure Derivatives in a Heath Jarrow Morton Model with LogNormal Annually Compounded Interest Rates." *Proceedings of the Seventh Annual European Research Symposium*, Bonn, September.

Sarnoff, Paul, 1965. *Russell Sage, the Money King.* Obolensky, New York.

Sawyer, Nick, 2007. "What's the Score." *Risk* Magazine, 20(7), 25–29.

Scholes, Myron S., 1998. "Derivatives in a Dynamic Environment." *American Economic Review* 88(3), 350–370.

Schwager, Jack, 1992. "Bill Lipschutz: The Sultan of Currencies." In *The New Market Wizards: Conversations with America's Top Traders.* Harper Collins, New York.

Sharpe, William F., 1964. "Capital Asset Prices: A Theory of Market Equilibrium under Conditions of Risk." *Journal of Finance* 19(3), 425–42.

Sharpe, William F., 1978. *Investments.* Prentice Hall, Englewood Cliffs, N.J.

Sharpe, William F., 1995. "My Evolution as an Economist." Address delivered at Trinity University, San Antonio, Texas. In *Lives of the Laureates: Thirteen Nobel Economists.* Edited by William Breit and Roger W. Spencer. MIT Press, Cambridge, Mass.

Sharpe, William F., Gordon J. Alexander, and Jeffery V. Bailey, 1999. *Investments.* Prentice Hall, Englewood Cliffs, N.J.

Shiller, Robert J., 1989. "The Term Structure of Interest Rates." In *Handbook of Monetary Economics.* Edited by Benjamin Friedman and Frank Hahn. North-Holland, Amsterdam.

Shreve, Steven E., 2004. *Stochastic Calculus for Finance II: Continuous Time Models.* Springer Science + Business Media, New York.

Simon, Julian L., 1981. *The Ultimate Resource.* Princeton University Press, Princeton, N.J.

Solow, Robert M., 1956. "A Contribution to the Theory of Economic Growth." *Quarterly Journal of Economics* 70(1), 65–94.

Sowell, Thomas, 1995. *The Vision of the Anointed: Self-Congratulation as a Basis for Social Policy*, Basic Books (a member of the Perseus Books Group), New York.

Sullivan, Joseph, 1988. *The Way It Was: An Oral History of Finance 1967–1987.* William Morrow & Company, Inc., New York.

Summers, Lawrence H., 1999. "Distinguished Lecture on Economics in Government: Reflections on Managing Global Integration." *Journal of Economic Perspectives* 13(2), 3–18.

Sundaresan, Suresh, 1984. "Consumption and Equilibrium Interest Rates in Stochastic Production Economies." *Journal of Finance* 39(1), 77–92.

Thorp, Edward O., and Sheen T. Kassouf, 1967. *Beat the Market: A Scientific Stock Market System.* Random House, New York.

Tumbridge and Co., 1875. *Secrets of Success in Wall Street.* New York.

Varian, Hal R., 1992. *Microeconomic Analysis.* 3rd ed. W. W. Norton, New York.

Varian, Hal R., 2003. *Intermediate Microeconomics: A Modern Approach.* 6th ed. W. W. Norton, New York.

Vasicek, Oldrich A., 1977. "An Equilibrium Characterization of the Term Structure." *Journal of Financial Economics* 5(2), 177–88.

Vega, Joseph Penso, de la, 1688. *Confusión de Confusiones (Confusions and Confusions).* Republished, Sonsbeek Publishers, 1970, Arnhem, Netherlands.

West, Mark D., 2000. "Private Ordering at the World's First Futures Exchange." *Michigan Law Review* 98(8), 2574–615.

Wilmott, Paul, 1998. *Derivatives: The Theory and Practice of Financial Engineering.* John Wiley, Chichester, England.

Notation

$A(t)$ Value of a money market account that starts with an investment of \$1 and earns the default-free spot rate each period (chapters 1–25) or the value of a firm's assets (chapter 26).

$b(t)$ Basis ($\equiv$ spot price minus futures price) at time t.

$B(t,T)$ The price at time t of a zero-coupon bond paying \$1 at time T (sometimes shortened as $B(t)$ or B).

B_E Zero-coupon bond price in a foreign country (in "European terms").

C Cash flow or a bond's coupon.

c European call price or caplet price (chapters 1–25) or the market clearing CDS rate (chapter 26).

c_A American call price.

$corr$ Correlation coefficient.

cov Covariance.

δ Dividend yield (chapters 1–24), or the time interval for computing a simple forward rate (chapter 25), or the recovery rate (chapter 26).

div Dollar dividend.

dur Duration of a bond.

dur_M Modified duration of a bond.

Δ (Delta) Change in a variable's value.

e Exponential function.

$E(t)$ A firm's equity value at time t.

$E(\,.\,)$ Computing expectation of the expression inside parentheses.

$E^\pi(\,.\,)$ Computing expectation of the expression inside parentheses using the pseudo-probabilities denoted by π.

f_{FRA} Forward rate agreement rate.

$f(t,T)$ Forward rate contracted at time t that is effective over the time period $[T,T+1]$.

$F(t,T)$ Forward price at time t for a contract maturing at time T (sometimes shortened as F).

F_A Forward price of a non-US currency in American or dollar terms.

F_E Forward price of a non-US currency in European terms or in terms of a currency other than the US dollar.

$\mathcal{F}(t)$ Futures price at time t.

g Storage cost (annual rate).

G Storage cost (lump sum).

h The minimum-variance futures hedge ratio.

i Simple ("domestic" or "dollar") interest rate per year; i_E is ("European" or "foreign") interest rate per year.

I Index.

i_{fut} Futures interest rate.

i_S Swap rate.

$i(t,T)$ Simple forward rate considered at time t, which becomes effective at time T.

$\log$ Natural logarithm.

L Principal or par value of a bond.

$L(t)$ Value of a debt issue at time t.

L_N Notional principal.

λ Probability of default per unit time (in reduced-form model). $\bar{\lambda}$ is the risk neutral default probability.

μ Expected return (chapters 1–24) or expected percentage change in the simple forward rate (chapter 25).

$N(x)$ Cumulative standard normal distribution function with mean 0 and standard deviation 1.

$N'(x)$ Standard normal density function.

p European put price (chapters 1–20) or floorlet price (chapters 21–26).

p_A American put price.

P Bond price.

$Prob$ Probability.

$Prob_\pi$ Probability that a random variable takes on certain values when π is the underlying probability.

ϕ Term for risk adjustment in pseudo-probability.

π Pseudo-probability that a stock price moves up.

$\pi(t,T)$ Pseudo-probability that a T-maturity zero-coupon bond moves up at time t.

PV   Present value.

q Actual probability that a stock price moves up.

$q(t)$ Actual probability that the term structure of zero-coupon bond prices moves up at time t.

r Continuously compounded interest rate per year. r_E Foreign interest rate (interest rate in "European" terms).

$R(0,T)$ Dollar return at time T from investing \$1 in risk-free bonds today (chapters 1–20).

$R(t)$ Default-free spot rate of interest declared at time t that applies to the time period $[t,t+1]$.

R_E "Dollar return" concept applied to investment in foreign currencies (in European terms or in terms of a currency other than the US dollar).

Ref   Reference rate (bbalibor or euribor in most cases) announced on some future date.

$S(t)$ Stock price or spot price of a commodity at time t.

S_A Spot exchange rate in American terms.

S_E Spot exchange rate in European terms.

S_{CDIV} Stock price cum-dividend.

S_{XDIV} Stock price ex-dividend.

sd Standard deviation.

σ Standard deviation (volatility) of stock return per year.

θ Stock's risk premium.

υ Average forward rate volatility.

U, D Up and down factor, respectively, in a single-period or multiperiod binomial option pricing model.

$u(t,T)$, $d(t,T)$ Up and down factor, respectively, in an HJM multiperiod binomial interest rate option pricing model.

var   Variance.

VaR_α Value-at-risk for an α percent loss probability.

y The convenience yield per year (chapter 12), or the yield on a coupon-bond (chapters 21 - 26).

Y Lump sum convenience yield.

Additional Sources and Websites

Journals

Academic journals are the best source for research on derivatives and risk management. They include the following.

General Finance Journals

- *Annual Review of Financial Economics*, www.annualreviews.org/journal/financial
- *Finance and Stochastics*, www.springer.com/mathematics/quantitative+finance/journal/780
- *Financial Analysts Journal*, www.cfapubs.org/loi/faj
- *Financial Management*, www.fma.org/Publications/FM/FMIndex.htm
- *Journal of Banking & Finance*, www.journals.elsevier.com/journal-of-banking-and-finance/
- *Journal of Finance*, www.afajof.org/details/landingpage/2866131/About-the-JF.html
- *Journal of Financial and Quantitative Analysis*, www.jfqa.org
- *Journal of Financial Economics*, http://jfe.rochester.edu
- *Mathematical Finance*, www.onlinelibrary.wiley.com/journal/10.1111/(ISSN)1467-9965
- *Review of Financial Studies*, http://rfs.oxfordjournals.org

Derivatives and Risk Management Journals

- *Journal of Derivatives*, www.iijournals.com/toc/jod/current
- *Journal of Fixed Income*, www.iijournals.com/toc/jfi/current
- *Journal of Futures Markets*, http://onlinelibrary.wiley.com/journal/10.1002/%28ISSN%291096-9934
- *Journal of Risk*, www.thejournalofrisk.com
- *Review of Derivatives Research*, www.springer.com/business+%26+management/finance/journal/11147
- *Risk Magazine* (publishes mathematical finance articles), www.risk.net/risk-magazine

Economics Journals with Occasional Articles on Derivatives and Risk Management

- *American Economic Review*, www.aeaweb.org/aer/index.php
- *American Journal of Agricultural Economics*, http://ajae.oxfordjournals.org/
- *Econometrica*, www.wiley.com/WileyCDA/WileyTitle/productCd-ECTA.html
- *Journal of Economic Perspectives*, www.aeaweb.org/jep/
- *Journal of Economic Surveys*, www.wiley.com/WileyCDA/WileyTitle/productCd-JOES.html
- *Journal of Political Economy*, www.press.uchicago.edu/ucp/journals/journal/jpe.html
- *Review of Economics and Statistics*, www.mitpressjournals.org/loi/rest

Mathematics, Statistics, and Management Journals with Occasional Articles on Derivatives and Risk Management

- *Annals of Applied Probability*, www.imstat.org/aap/
- *Journal of the American Statistical Association*, www.amstat.org/publications/jasa.cfm
- *Stochastic Processes and Their Applications*, www.journals.elsevier.com/stochastic-processes-and-their-applications/

Newspapers and Magazines

Business newspapers and magazines frequently write about derivatives and risk management.

- *Barron's*, http://online.barrons.com
- *Bloomberg*, www.bloomberg.com
- *The Economist*, www.economist.com
- *Financial Times*, www.ft.com
- *Futures and Options World*, www.fow.com
- *Harvard Business Review*, http://hbr.org/magazine
- *Investor's Business Daily*, www.investors.com
- *New York Times*, www.nytimes.com
- *Wall Street Journal*, http://online.wsj.com

Government Agencies

Nowadays, many government agencies have websites; examples follow.

- US Department of the Treasury, www.treasury.gov
- Bank for International Settlements, www.bis.org
- Board of Governors of the Federal Reserve System, www.federalreserve.gov
- Federal Reserve Bank of New York, www.newyorkfed.org
- International Monetary Fund (IMF), www.imf.org
- US Securities and Exchange Commission, www.sec.gov
- US Department of the Treasury, www.treasury.gov
- World Bank Group, www.worldbank.org

Industrial Associations and Bodies, Self-Regulatory Organizations

Many industry associations and bodies as well as self-regulatory organizations disseminate information through websites.

- CFA Institute, www.cfainstitute.org
- Financial Accounting Standards Board (FASB), www.fasb.org
- Financial Industry Regulatory Authority (FINRA), www.finra.org
- Global Association of Risk Professionals (GARP), www.garp.org
- International Association of Financial Engineers (IAFE), http://iafe.org
- International Swaps and Derivatives Association Inc. (ISDA), www2.isda.org
- National Futures Association (NFA), www.nfa.futures.org
- Securities Industry and Financial Markets Association (SIFMA), www.sifma.org

Exchanges

Most exchanges have websites that include a description of their business, a historic timeline, contract specifications, price and volume information, and educational and promotional material.

- BM&FBovespa, www.bmfbovespa.com.br/en-us/home.aspx?idioma=en-us
- Chicago Board Options Exchange (CBOE), www.cboe.com
- CME Group, www.cmegroup.com
- Eurex (includes ISE), www.eurexchange.com and www.ise.com

- Korea Exchanges (KRX), http://eng.krx.co.kr
- Multi Commodity Exchange of India (MCX), www.mcxindia.com
- NASDAQ OMX, www.nasdaqomx.com
- National Stock Exchange of India (NSE), www.nseindia.com
- NYSE Euronext, https://nyse.nyx.com and https://europeanequities.nyx.com/
- Russian Trading Systems Stock Exchange (RTS), www.rts.ru/en/

Financial Institutions

Predictions on market directions and economic conditions, advice on trading strategies, and risk management–related issues are found in bulletins, newsletters, and research reports from a wide variety of sources, including banks, brokerage firms, commodity trading advisors, credit rating agencies, finance companies (including mutual funds), and hedge fund managers. These can be found on their respective websites.

Books on Derivatives and Risk Management

Following is a representative list of books on derivatives and risk management. A comprehensive list can be found on the book's website.

Abu-Mostafa, Yaser S., Blake LeBaron, Andrew W. Lo, and Andreas S. Weigend (eds.), 2000, *Computational Finance 1999*.

Acharya, Viral V., Thomas F. Cooley, Matthew P. Richardson, and Ingo Walter (eds.), 2010, *Regulating Wall Street: The Dodd-Frank Act and the New Architecture of Global Finance*.

Andersen, Leif B. G., and Vladimir V. Piterbarg, 2010, *Interest Rate Modeling*, 3 volumes.

Augen, Jeffrey, 2011, *Microsoft Excel for Stock and Option Traders: Build Your Own Analytical Tools for Higher Returns*.

Back, Kerry, 2010, *A Course in Derivative Securities: Introduction to Theory and Computation*.

Barker, Philip, 2007, *Java Methods for Financial Engineering: Applications in Finance and Investment*.

Baxter, Martin, and Andrew Rennie, 1996, *Financial Calculus: An Introduction to Derivatives Pricing*.

Bielecki, Tomasz, Damiano Brigo, and Frederic Patras, 2011, *Credit Risk Frontiers: Subprime Crisis, Pricing and Hedging, CVA, MBS, Ratings, and Liquidity*.

Bouzoubaa, Mohamed, and Adel Osseiran, 2010, *Exotic Options and Hybrids: A Guide to Structuring, Pricing and Trading*.

Boyle, Phelim, and Feidhlim Boyle, 2001, *Derivatives: The Tools That Changed Finance*.

Brandimarte, Paolo, 2006, *Numerical Methods in Finance and Economics: A MATLAB-Based Introduction*, 2nd edition.

Brigo, Damiano, and Fabio Mercurio, 2006, *Interest Rate Models: Theory and Practice: With Smile, Inflation and Credit*.

Butler, Cormac, 2009, *Accounting for Financial Instruments*.

Chacko, George, Vincent Dessain, Peter Hecht, and Anders Sjoman, 2006, *Financial Instruments and Markets: A Casebook*.

Chacko, George, Anders Sjöman, Hideto Motohashi, and Vincent Dessain, 2006, *Credit Derivatives: A Primer on Credit Risk, Modeling, and Instruments*.

Chaplin, Geoff, 2010, *Credit Derivatives: Trading, Investing, and Risk Management*.

Choudhry, Moorad, 2010, *The Repo Handbook*, 2nd edition.

Chriss, Neil A., 1997, *Black–Scholes and Beyond: Option Pricing Models*.

Culp, Christopher L., 2006, *Structured Finance and Insurance: The ART of Managing Capital and Risk*, 2nd edition.

Das, Satyajit, 2005, *Credit Derivatives: CDOs and Structured Credit Products*, 3rd edition.

DeRosa, David F., 1998, *Currency Derivatives: Pricing Theory, Exotic Options, and Hedging Applications*.

Dixit, Avinash K., and Robert S. Pindyck, 1994, *Investment under Uncertainty*.

Duffie, Darrell, 1989, *Futures Markets*.

Duffie, Darrell, and Kenneth J. Singleton, 2003, *Credit Risk: Pricing, Measurement, and Management*.

Edwards, Franklin R., and Cindy W. Ma, 1992, *Futures and Options*.

Embrechts, Paul, Claudia Klüppelberg, and Thomas Mikosch, 1997, *Modelling Extremal Events for Insurance and Finance*.

Fabozzi, Frank J. (ed.), 2005, *The Handbook of Mortgage Backed Securities*, 6th edition.

Fabozzi, Frank J. (ed.), 2011, *The Handbook of Fixed Income Securities*, 8th edition.

Fabozzi, Frank J., Roland Fuss, and Dieter G. Kaiser, 2008, *The Handbook of Commodity Investing*.

Fabozzi, Frank J., and Vinod Kothari, 2008, *Introduction to Securitization*.

Figlewski, Stephen, William L. Silber, and Marti G. Subrahmanyan, 1990, *Financial Options: From Theory to Practice*.

Flavell, Richard, 2010, *Swaps and Other Derivatives.*

Fouque, Jean-P., George Papanicolaou, Ronnie Sircar, and Knut Sølna, 2011, *Multiscale Stochastic Volatility for Equity, Interest Rate, and Credit Derivatives.*

Froot, Kenneth A. (ed.), 1999, *The Financing of Catastrophe Risk.*

Geman, Hélyette, 2005, *Commodities and Commodity Derivatives: Modelling and Pricing for Agriculturals, Metals and Energy.*

Glasserman, Paul, 2003, *Monte Carlo Methods in Financial Engineering.*

Haug, Espen G., 2006, *The Complete Guide to Option Pricing Formulas,* 2nd edition.

Ho, Thomas S. Y., and Sang-Bin Lee, 2004, *The Oxford Guide to Financial Modeling: Applications for Capital Markets, Corporate Finance, Risk Management, and Financial Institutions.*

Hughston, Lane P. (ed.), 1997, *Vasicek and Beyond: Approaches to Building and Applying Interest Rate Models.*

Hughston, Lane P. (ed.), 2000, *The New Interest Rate Models: Recent Developments in the Theory and Application of Yield Curve Dynamics.*

Hull, John C., 2011, *Options, Futures, and Other Derivatives,* 8th edition.

Jarrow, Robert A. (ed.), 1998, *Volatility: New Estimation Techniques for Pricing Derivatives.*

Jarrow, Robert A., 2002, *Modeling Fixed Income Securities and Interest Rate Options,* 2nd edition.

Jarrow, Robert A., 2008, *Financial Derivatives Pricing: Selected Works of Robert Jarrow.*

Jarrow, Robert A., and Andrew Rudd, 1983, *Option Pricing.*

Jarrow, Robert A., and Stuart M. Turnbull, 2000, *Derivative Securities,* 2nd edition.

Jha, Siddhartha, 2011, *Interest Rate Markets: A Practical Approach to Fixed Income.*

Jorion, Philippe, 2006, *Value at Risk: The New Benchmark for Managing Financial Risk,* 3rd edition.

Kat, Harry M., 2001, *Structured Equity Derivatives: The Definitive Guide to Exotic Options and Structured Notes.*

Lindsey, Richard R., and Barry Schachter, 2009, *How I Became a Quant: Insights from 25 of Wall Street's Elite.*

Lipton, Alexander, and Andrew Rennie, 2011, *The Oxford Handbook of Credit Derivatives.*

Mason, Scott P., Robert C. Merton, Andre F. Perold, and Peter Tufano, 1995, *Cases in Financial Engineering: Applied Studies of Financial Innovation.*

McDonald, Robert L., 2009, *Derivatives Markets,* 3rd edition.

McLaughlin, Robert M., 1998, *Over-the-Counter Derivative Products: A Guide to Legal Risk Management and Documentation.*

McMillan, Lawrence G., 2012, *Options as a Strategic Investment,* 5th edition.

McNeil, Alexander J., Rüdiger Frey, and Paul Embrechts, 2005, *Quantitative Risk Management: Concepts, Techniques, and Tools.*

Miller, Merton H., 1997, *Merton Miller on Derivatives.*

Natenberg, Sheldon, 1995, *Option Volatility and Pricing: Advanced Trading Strategies and Techniques,* 2nd edition.

Pachamanova, Dessislava, and Frank J. Fabozzi, 2010, *Simulation and Optimization in Finance + Website: Modeling with MATLAB, @Risk, or VBA.*

Pearson, Neil D., 2002, *Risk Budgeting: Portfolio Problem Solving with Value-at-Risk.*

Rebonato, Riccardo, 1999, *Volatility and Correlation: In the Pricing of Equity, FX and Interest-Rate Options.*

Rebonato, Riccardo, 2002, *Modern Pricing of Interest-Rate Derivatives: The LIBOR Market Model and Beyond.*

Rendleman, Richard J., 2002, *Applied Derivatives: Options, Futures and Swaps.*

Ritchken, Peter, 1996, *Derivative Markets: Theory, Strategy, and Applications.*

Ronn, Ehud I., 2003, *Real Options and Energy Management: Using Options Methodology to Enhance Capital Budgeting Decisions.*

Saunders, Anthony, and Linda Allen, 2010, *Credit Risk Management In and Out of the Financial Crisis: New Approaches to Value at Risk and Other Paradigms,* 3rd edition.

Schönbucher, Philipp J., 2003, *Credit Derivatives Pricing Models: Model, Pricing and Implementation.*

Shiller, Robert J., 2004, *The New Financial Order: Risk in the 21st Century.*

Shimko, David C. (ed.), 2004, *Credit Risk: Models and Management,* 2nd edition.

Shreve, Steve E., 2005, *Stochastic Calculus for Finance I: The Binomial Asset Pricing Model; Stochastic Calculus for Finance II: Continuous-Time Models.*

Siegel, Daniel R., and Diane F. Siegel, 1990, *Futures Markets.*

Smithson, Charles W., 1998, *Managing Financial Risk: A Guide to Derivative Products, Financial Engineering, and Value Maximization,* 3rd edition.

Stigum, Marcia L., and Anthony Crescenzi, 2007, *Stigum's Money Market*, 4th edition.

Sundaresan, Suresh, 2013, *Fixed Income Markets and Their Derivatives*, 4th edition.

Tavakoli, Janet M., 2008, *Structured Finance and Collateralized Debt Obligations: New Developments in Cash and Synthetic Securitization*, 2nd edition.

Tuckman, Bruce, and Angel Serrat, 2011, *Fixed Income Securities: Tools for Today's Markets*, 3rd edition.

Van Deventer, Donald R., and Kenji Imai, 2013, *Financial Risk Analytics: A Term Structure Model Approach for Banking, Insurance and Investment Management*.

Van Deventer, Donald R., and Kenji Imai, 2003, *Credit Risk Models and the Basel Accords*.

Van Deventer, Donald R., Kenji Imai, and Mark Mesler, 2013, *Advanced Financial Risk Management: Tools and Techniques for Integrated Credit Risk and Interest Rate Risk Managements*, 2nd edition.

Veronesi, Pietro, 2010, *Fixed Income Securities: Valuation, Risk, and Risk Management*.

Name Index

Akerlof, George A., 283
Alexander, Gordon J., 79
Alletzhauser, Albert J., 185
Amemiya, Takeshi, 331n10
Amin, Kaushik I., 351
Arrow, Kenneth, 8, 433, 435
Artzner, Philippe, 751

Bachelier, Louis, 140, 431–34, 534
Bailey, Jeffery V., 79
Bank, Peter, 511
Barings, Francis, 311n1
Bartter, Brit J., 430, 433, 435, 476
Bakshi, Gurdip, 551
Baum, Dietmar, 511
Baxter, Martin W., 435n4, 647
Bergstresser, Charles, 145
Bernanke, Ben, 6
Bernstein, Peter L., 493, 741
Bhattacharya, Mihir, 422
Bhattacharya, Utpal, 61n6
Black, Fischer S., 8, 12–13, 368, 429, 434, 451, 491–94, 500, 648, 706–8, 736
Blanchard, Olivier, 21
Bolton, Anthony, 368
Born, Brooksley, 241
Box, George E. P., 772
Brace, Alan, 649, 708, 736
Braddock, John, 382n8
Brealey, Richard, 284, 581
Brickley, James A., 283
Buffett, Warren, 10, 11, 249, 368, 388, 416

Campbell, John Y., 140
Cantor, Richard, 766
Carabini, Christopher E., 95
Carey, Charles P., 348
Castelli, Charles, 534
Çetin, Umut, 762
Chang, Carolyn W., 95
Chang, Jack S. K., 95
Chatterjea, Arkadev, 41, 367, 762
Chen, Andrew H., 95
Coase, Ronald, 7–9
Cornell, Bradford, 95
Courtault, Jean-Michel, 433
Cox, David R., 523

Cox, John C., 94, 430, 433, 435, 476, 578
Culbertson, John M., 578

Daouk, Hazem, 61n6
Dash, Mike, 361
De la Vega, Joseph Penso, 343–44
Debreu, Gerard, 8, 433, 435
DeGroot, Morris H., 331n9
Deveshwar, Y. C., 104
Dezhbakhsh, Hashem, 95
DiNardo, John, 331n10
Dixit, Avinash K., 757
Dow, Charles, 145
Draper, Norman R., 772
Drew, Daniel, 372
Duffie, Darrell, 111, 191, 324, 518
Dunn, Kenneth B., 578

Easterbrook, Frank H., 248
Edelman, Asher B., 134
Edwards, Franklin R., 94
Ehrlich, Paul R., 202, 203
Eisenberg, Larry, 545
Emery, Henry Crosby, 341n1
Engle, Robert F., 368, 551
Evans, George W., 548

Fama, Eugene, 140, 493
Feynman, Richard, 429
Filer, Herbert J., 347
Finucane, Thomas J., 422
Fischel, Daniel R., 248
Fisher, Irving M., 578
Fisk, James, 245
Follmer, Holmer, 752
Friedman, Milton, 41, 190
Froot, Kenneth A., 310

Gabre-Madhin, Eleni Zaude, 103
Gastineau, Gary L., 163
Gelderblom, Oscar, 187, 341, 343
Glasserman, Paul, 111, 518
Goekjian, Chris, 620
Gould, Jay, 245
Graham, Benjamin, 11
Greenbaum, Stuart I., 616
Greenspan, Alan, 10, 11, 241, 352

Gross, David, 10
Grossman, Sanford, 141

Hao, Jia, 422
Harrison, J. Michael, 433, 435
Harte, John, 203
Heath, David C., 160n1, 420n3, 536, 648, 706
Hicks, John, 8, 578
Higgins, Leonard R., 397, 534
Ho, Thomas S. Y., 435, 648, 679, 706
Holden, Craig W., 563
Holdren, John, 203
Honkapohja, Seppo, 548
Hughston, Lane P., 648

Ingersoll, Jonathan E., 94
Ito, Kiyosi, 431, 433, 434

James, William, 367n2
Jarrow, Robert A., 41, 94, 160n1, 223, 261, 295n3, 324, 351, 367, 417n2, 420n3, 430, 433–35, 441, 476, 491, 496, 499, 511, 519, 536, 545, 578, 648–49, 669, 677, 691, 700, 701, 706, 725, 726, 735, 752–54, 758, 759, 762, 763, 767, 771, 796
Jegadeesh, Narasimhan, 249
Johnson, R. Stafford, 616
Johnston, Elizabeth T., 191
Johnston, Jack, 331n10
Jones, E. Philip, 756
Jones, Edward, 145
Jonker, Joost, 187, 341, 343
Jordan, Bradford D., 249
Jordan, Susan D., 249
Jovanovic, Franck, 431n2

Kassouf, Sheen T., 432
Kendall, Maurice, 140
Keynes, John Maynard, 8, 226, 433
Knoll, Michael, 402
Kolmogorov, Andrei, 433
Kosuga, Vincent W., 246, 247
Kreps, David M., 433, 435
Kritzman, Mark P., 163
Krugman, Paul R., 168n5

Subject Index